EDITORS

ENCYCLOPEDIA OF PSYCHOLOGY

Encyclopedia of Psychology

Alan E. Kazdin
Editor in Chief

VOLUME 6

American Psychological Association

OXFORD
UNIVERSITY PRESS

2000

AMERICAN
PSYCHOLOGICAL
ASSOCIATION
Washington, D.C.

OXFORD
UNIVERSITY PRESS

Oxford New York
Athens Auckland Bangkok Bogotá Buenos Aires Calcutta
Cape Town Chennai Dar es Salaam Delhi Florence Hong Kong Istanbul
Karachi Kuala Lumpur Madrid Melbourne Mexico City Mumbai
Nairobi Paris São Paulo Singapore Taipei Tokyo Toronto Warsaw

and associated companies in
Berlin Ibadan

Published by American Psychological Association
750 First Street, NE, Washington, D.C. 20002-4242
www.apa.org
and
Oxford University Press, Inc.
198 Madison Avenue, New York, New York 10016
www.oup.com

Library of Congress Cataloging-in-Publication Data
Encyclopedia of psychology / Alan E. Kazdin, editor in chief
p. cm.
Includes bibliographical references and index.
1. Psychology—Encyclopedias. I. Kazdin, Alan E.
BF31 .E52 2000 150'.3—dc21 99-055239
ISBN 1-55798-187-6 (set); ISBN 1-55798-655-X (vol. 6)

AMERICAN PSYCHOLOGICAL ASSOCIATION STAFF

Gary R. VandenBos, Ph.D., *Publisher*
Julia Frank-McNeil, *Commissioning Editor*
Theodore J. Baroody, *Senior Development Editor*
Adrian Harris Forman, *Project Editor*

OXFORD UNIVERSITY PRESS STAFF

Karen Casey, *Publisher*
Claude Conyers, *Commissioning Editor*
Marion Osmun, *Senior Development Editor*
Matthew Giarratano, *Managing Editor*
Peri Zeenkov and Norina Frabotta, *Project Editors*
Nancy Hoagland, *Production Manager*
Jessica Ryan and Will Moore, *Production Editors*
AEIOU, Inc., *Index Editor*
AEIOU, Inc., Linda Berman, Denise McIntyre,
Space Coast Indexers, Inc., Linda Webster, *Indexers*
Suzanne Holt, *Book Design*
Joan Greenfield, *Cover Design*

3 5 7 9 8 6 4 2

Printed in the United States of America
on acid-free paper

O CONTINUED

OPTIMISM AND PESSIMISM. Optimists are people who expect good things to happen to them; pessimists are those who expect bad things. Folk wisdom has long held that this difference matters, and contemporary research supports this assertion. Just as commonsense definitions of optimism and pessimism rest on expectations for the future, so do scientific theories. These theories thereby link optimism and pessimism to a long tradition of expectancy-value models of motivation. The result is that the optimism concept, although based in folk wisdom, is also firmly grounded in decades of work on motivation and behavior.

Expectancies are pivotal in contemporary theories of optimism, but there are two ways to think about expectancies and measure them, leading to two distinct literatures. One approach measures expectancies directly, asking people to indicate their extent of agreement with statements such as, "I'm always optimistic about my future." The other approach measures expectancies indirectly, examining how people explain events. If your explanation for a bad outcome implies that the cause will be present in the future and will apply to many kinds of events, you probably expect bad outcomes. If your explanation implies changeable causal forces that apply only narrowly, you are probably more optimistic about the future.

Motive Models and Optimism

As noted, defining optimism and pessimism in terms of expectancies creates a link to expectancy-value motive theories. That link is central to much of what follows. Expectancy-value models begin with the idea that behavior is aimed at attaining desired goals (*values*). Without a goal that's valued, there is no reason to act. The other critical element is expectancy: confidence or doubt about being able to attain the goal. If the person lacks confidence, again there will be no action. Only with sufficient confidence do people act and remain engaged in efforts.

These principles pertain to specific values and focused confidence, and they also apply to general optimism and pessimism. The "confidence" at issue is simply broader in scope. Indeed, these principles provide the basis for many predictions about optimists and pessimists: When confronting a challenge, optimists should take a posture of confidence and persistence, even if progress is difficult or slow; pessimists should be more doubtful and hesitant. This divergence should also be displayed—maybe even amplified—under adversity. Optimists are likely to believe that adversity can be handled successfully, pessimists are likely to anticipate disaster.

Behavioral Effects of Optimism

Research on optimism and pessimism has examined a wide variety of questions. Let us consider first studies that focus on behavioral tendencies (and the outcomes to which they lead). In a highly competitive field, such as sales, the work can be frustrating, because one often encounters failure. Potential customers sometimes decide not to buy the product or decide to buy from someone else. To be effective requires persistence in the face of adversity. Optimists (assessed by explanatory style) apparently exerted such effort, as reflected in sales levels over a 2-year period. Optimists were also less likely than pessimists to have quit their jobs during the first year.

Another example of persistence comes from work on maintenance of physical health. Optimists, confident about reaching the goal of good health, should be more likely than pessimists to pursue health promotion and less likely to engage in risky behaviors. One study of health promotion followed a group of heart patients in a cardiac rehabilitation program. Optimism related to success in lowering levels of body fat and overall coronary risk, and to increases in exercise across the rehabilitation period. Another study followed coronary artery bypass patients for 5 years after surgery, and investigated their lifestyles at that point. Optimists were more likely than pessimists to be taking vitamins, to be eating low-fat lunches, and to be enrolled in a cardiac rehabilitation program.

Heart disease certainly isn't the only aspect of health that is responsive to behavior. Another obvious health risk related to behavior is human immunodeficiency virus (HIV) infection. By avoiding certain sexual practices (e.g., sex with unknown partners), people reduce their risk of infection. One study of HIV-negative gay men revealed that optimists reported having fewer anonymous partners than pessimists. This suggests that optimists were making efforts to reduce their risk, thereby safeguarding their health.

This discussion concerns the idea that optimism leads to effort and pessimism leads to giving up. Thus far the focus has been on persistence. What about giving up? Several kinds of health-relevant behaviors seem to reflect this tendency. One such behavior is drinking alcohol. Excessive alcohol consumption is often seen as occurring in the service of an escape from one's problems. If so, pessimists should be more vulnerable than optimists to alcohol abuse.

At least two studies support this prediction. A study of women with a family history of alcoholism found that pessimists were more likely than optimists to report drinking problems. Another study examined people who had already been treated for alcoholism and were now entering an aftercare program. This study found that pessimists were more likely to drop out of the aftercare program and to return to drinking than optimists. These two studies converge in showing that pessimists display a form of disengagement—alcohol consumption—more than optimists.

People can give up in many ways. Alcohol dulls awareness of failures and problems. People can also turn their backs on their problems by distracting themselves. Even sleeping can help people escape from situations they don't want to face. Sometimes, though, giving up is more complete. Sometimes people give up not just on specific goals, but on all the goals that define their lives, by committing suicide. Pessimism has been found to be a key indicator of suicide risk (even stronger than depression).

Emotional Consequences

People's behavioral responses to adversity or difficulty are important, but behavior is not the only response in these situations; people also experience emotions. Difficulties elicit a mixture of feelings, and optimism influences the balance among the feelings. Again, predictions are easily derived from theory. Optimists expect to have positive outcomes, even when things are difficult. This confidence should yield a more positive mix of feelings. Pessimists expect negative outcomes. This should be related to more intense negative feelings—anxiety, sadness, or despair.

Many studies have examined relationships between optimism and distress in people facing adversity. The range of stressors in this research is enormous. Studies have examined students entering college, employees of businesses, and survivors of missile attacks and earthquakes. Other studies examined people caring for cancer patients, for patients with Alzheimer's disease, and patients with rheumatoid arthritis. Studies examined the experiences of people dealing with medical procedures such as abortions, attempts at *in vitro* fertilization, childbirth, bypass surgery, and bone marrow transplantation. Others have examined how people deal with the diagnosis of cancer, HIV infection, and progression of AIDS. Thus, many of the studies examine people who are undergoing serious life crises, rather than just the ordinary problems of daily life.

One early study examined the development of depressed feelings after childbirth, a moderately common occurrence. Women in this study completed measures of optimism and depression in their third trimester of pregnancy. They completed the depression scale again three weeks after giving birth. Optimism related to lower initial depressive symptoms; optimism also predicted lower postpartum depressive symptoms when controlling for initial levels of depression. Thus optimism predicted resistance to the *development* of depressive symptoms.

Another, more recent study examined reactions to the diagnosis of and treatment for early-stage breast cancer. Patients were interviewed at diagnosis, the day before surgery, 7 to 10 days after surgery, and 3, 6, and 12 months later. Optimism was assessed at the time of diagnosis and was used to predict distress levels later. Optimism related to lower distress over time, beyond the effect of medical variables and beyond the effects of earlier measures of distress. Thus, optimism predicted resilience to distress through the first year following diagnosis and surgery.

Origins

A final question to be addressed here concerns the origins of optimism and pessimism. Many aspects of personality are genetically influenced and evidence from twin studies suggests that this is so with optimism (assessed both as expectancies and as explanatory style). As is always true in considering heritability, there remains a question about whether optimism is *itself* heritable, or whether it shows heritability because it relates closely to some other aspect of temperament. Optimism relates to neuroticism and extraversion, both of which are known to be genetically influenced. Although it appears that optimism and pessimism are distinguishable from them, it may be that optimism's heritability is largely a product of these associations.

Another potential influence on an optimistic versus pessimistic outlook is early childhood experience. Many theories maintain that early childhood is an important time. Erikson's theory of personality development holds that infants who experience the social world as predictable develop a sense of "basic trust," whereas infants who experience the world as unpredictable develop a sense of "basic mistrust." These qualities resemble optimism and pessimism. Discussions of attachment similarly hold that some infants (and adults) are securely attached in their relationships, others are not. Adult attachment security correlates with optimism, suggesting that optimism may derive in part from the early childhood experience of secure attachment to a caregiver.

[*See also* Personality Traits.]

Acknowledgments. The author's work on this article was supported by the National Cancer Institute (CA64710).

Bibliography

Carver, C. S., Pozo, C., Harris, S. D., Noriega, V., Scheier, M. F., Robinson, D. S., Ketcham, A. S., Moffat, F. L., & Clark, K. C. (1993). How coping mediates the effect of optimism on distress: A study of women with early stage breast cancer. *Journal of Personality and Social Psychology, 65*, 375–390. Describes a study of the experiences of women being treated for early-stage breast cancer, and how optimism and pessimism influenced the ways in which the women coped and their success in doing so.

Carver, C. S., & Scheier, M. F. (1998). *On the self-regulation of behavior.* New York: Cambridge University Press. Includes a discussion of the expectancy-value models of motivation that underlie today's viewpoints on optimism.

Carver, C. S., & Scheier, M. F. (1999). Optimism. In C. R. Snyder (Ed.), *Coping: The psychology of what works.* New York: Oxford University Press. Reviews in greater detail the literature of how the traits of optimism and pessimism influence people's attempts to cope with adversity.

Peterson, C., & Seligman, M. E. P. (1984). Causal explanations as a risk factor for depression: Theory and evidence. *Psychological Review, 91*, 347–374. Describes the reasoning behind explanatory style as a way of thinking about pessimism.

Seligman, M. E. P. (1991). *Learned optimism.* New York: Knopf. Discusses the idea that people who are not now optimistic can become optimists.

Charles S. Carver

ORAL STAGE. *See* Psychosexual Stages.

ORGANIC MENTAL DISORDERS. *See* Alzheimer's Disease.

ORGANIZATIONAL MANAGEMENT. Various kinds of managers and organizations have been with us since time immemorial. However, the systematic study of organizational managers is a fairly recent phenomenon that encompasses numerous considerations, including what they do and how selection, education, training, and experience are used to provide a fit with their organization.

An organization is a collection of people working together in a division of labor to achieve a common purpose. Managers are organization members who are responsible for work that is accomplished through the performance contributions of one or more other persons. Managers carry out their responsibility by engaging in management, which involves achieving organizational goals through the four management process functions of planning (setting performance standards and deciding how to achieve them), organizing (arranging tasks, people, and other resources to accomplish the work), leading (inspiring people to work appropriately to achieve high performance), and controlling (measuring performance and taking action to ensure desired results). These management process functions are carried on within a fast-moving setting with many interruptions and fragmented activities, accompanied by an emphasis on short bursts of oral communications from and to many people. Thus managing is an ongoing process and involves knowing how to perform the major functions necessary to achieve the organization's goals or common purpose, typically referred to as organization performance.

In considering the similarities and differences between managers and leaders or between management and leadership, we can take any of three fundamental views of the relationship. One view treats management and leadership as mutually exclusive: Management stabilizes, leadership is change oriented. Another view treats the two as synonymous: Anyone occupying a managerial position is also a leader. Finally, the view we emphasize is that leadership and management (change and stability) are distinct but complementary.

An Organizational Management Framework

Given these preliminaries, we now present a framework designed to integrate the diverse and largely separate managerial literature. Essentially, the framework views the organizational manager as performing managerial roles to carry out the previously mentioned management process functions that are necessary to obtain satisfactory performance. The roles are composed of sets of related behaviors and are influenced by organization factors and by manager factors. Managerial performance is contingent upon the degree of fit between manager and organization factors. Fit is achieved through managerial selection and development and through training and experience, discussed later.

Organization Factors. Although managers of all types are viewed as performing the management process functions, the emphasis they place on various roles will be influenced by both organization and manager aspects. Such aspects define the limits of managerial discretion—the scope of action available to a manager. Rosemary Stewart, in *Choices for the Manager* (Englewood Cliffs, N.J., 1982), deals with discretion in terms of a framework consisting of demands, constraints, and choices. Demands compose an inner core of what anyone on the job must do. Constraints are an outer boundary that limits what managers can do. Choices, then, are the in-between area formed by the opportunities that exist for those in similar positions to do different work in different ways from other managers.

Besides the organizational demands, constraints, and choices that influence managers, organizational vertical hierarchy levels and horizontal responsibility areas are important. Vertically, managerial jobs fall into three broad hierarchical categories: bottom, middle, and top. Each of these categories, in turn, can have varying numbers of levels, depending upon the organization. At the bottom are those first-line managers who directly supervise employees. At the very top are those managers—often termed presidents or chief executive officers—ultimately responsible for the entire organization.

One conceptualization, stratified systems theory, has extended this notion by arguing that there are no more than two managerial levels at the bottom, two at the middle, and two at the top. Each level has systematically more complex requirements. These requirements can be measured by the length of time required to complete the manager's key tasks and the increasing complexity required of managers' cognitive processes at higher levels in the organization. Although it is not universally accepted, this framework is one way of systematizing hierarchical differences in managerial jobs.

In addition to vertical differences, managerial jobs differ horizontally according to the nature of the responsibility involved. Thus we find departments of research and development, engineering, production, human resources, marketing, finance, and the like. Responsibilities also can be divided into those of functional managers, general managers, and project managers. Functional managers handle given areas covering specialized functions such as production or engineering. General managers have responsibility for the entire organization or substantial parts of it. Project managers have responsibility for coordinating efforts involving people in different organizational units working on the same project.

Manager Factors. Besides the organizational factors shown in Figure 1, there are numerous managerial factors that affect a manager's roles carried out as part of the management process functions. The first of these are work agendas, discussed by John P. Kotter in *General Managers* (New York, 1982).

Work Agendas. These agendas are a loosely connected set of tentative goals and tasks that a manager is trying to get accomplished across time to reach a desired future state. Managers usually develop them shortly after assuming their specific position and change them as needed over time. The agendas tend to be relatively informal and involve anybody necessary to accomplish them. They focus on both goals and tasks, but goals tend to be emphasized more than tasks at higher levels of the organization.

Demands, constraints, and choices (such as organizational and unit plans, policies and procedures, unique tasks, and problems assigned by others) and the manager's knowledge base and attributes influence the manager's work agendas. Although demands, constraints, and choices help shape the managerial agendas, it is a reciprocal relationship. The manager's contacts with others help shape and influence these organizational factors. The managerial agendas can have an impact on the organizational and unit plans, policies, and procedures within which managers operate, and their agendas influence the tasks and problems assigned to them by others, especially across time.

Knowledge Base. In terms of the manager's knowledge base, Kotter emphasizes detailed knowledge of the industry and firm, including technical knowledge, knowledge of organizational policy and practice, culture, and personalities of key organizational members, and information about suppliers. Robert Sternberg (*Journal of Management*, 1997, *23*, pp. 475–493) further categorizes managerial knowledge as either tacit or explicit. Tacit knowledge is specific, procedural knowledge learned from experience on the job. Explicit knowledge is declarative knowledge learned from books or through training and education. The importance of tacit and explicit knowledge bases has been emphasized by the classic management writers such as Henri Fayol in *General and Industrial Management* (London, 1949), but has been underresearched by later scholars.

Traits and Cognitive Capacity Ability. Traits represent habitual ways of thinking that predispose one to certain behaviors. The literature suggests quite a bit of agreement on key managerial traits, but the traits tend to be utilized somewhat differently by different researchers. Traits may be predictor, mediating, or moderating variables in the management process. Here, we use two broad clusters in addition to the cognitive capacity/ability category so that the traits listed in Table

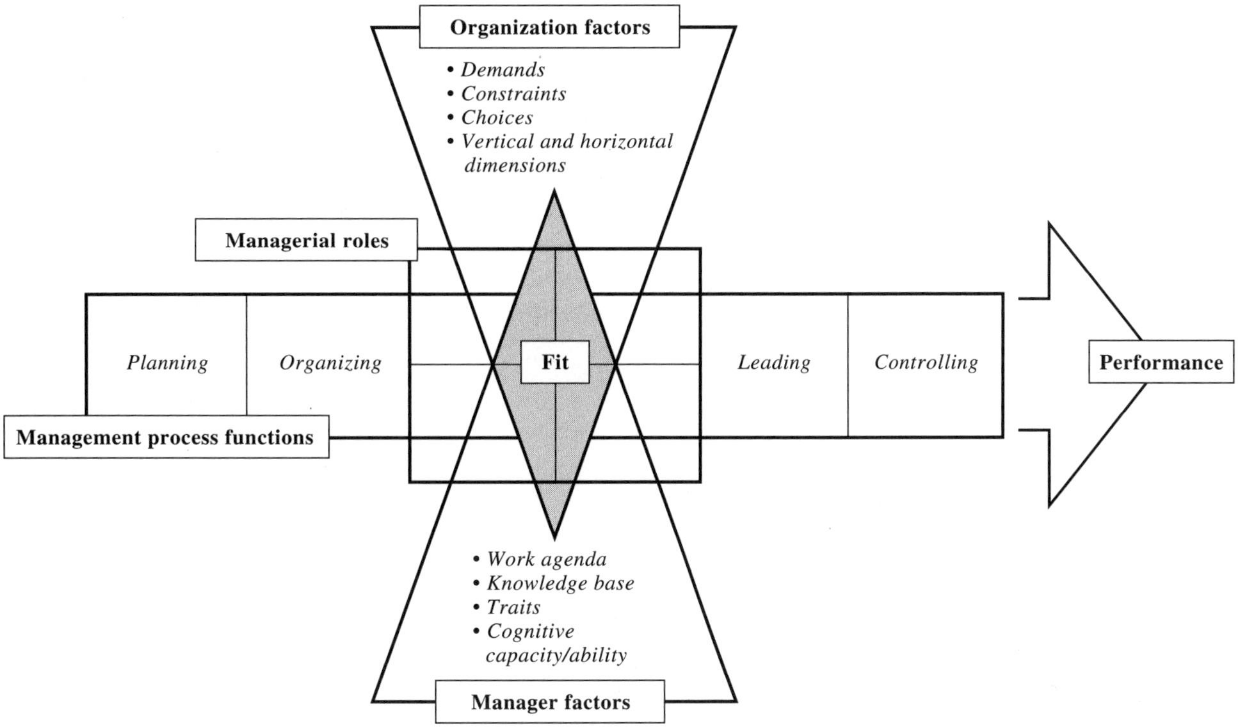

ORGANIZATIONAL MANAGEMENT. Figure 1. Organizational management framework

1 are both predictors and mediators of managerial outcomes.

The first cluster is concerned with a predisposition to manage and the confidence that one can manage. Given that the first cluster is activated, then the second cluster focuses on facilitating the manager's enactment of the roles indicated in Figure 1 and described shortly. Table 1 shows the facilitating cluster to consist of emotional maturity, integrity, originality/creativity, and flexibility/adaptability. Figure 1 also directly links both clusters to work agendas, to the management process functions, and to performance.

The third cluster is cognitive capacity/ability, which includes not only traditional IQ measures but also measures of cognitive complexity. Among other things, this attribute deals with analytical and synthesizing ability, judgment, strategic thinking capacity, multidimensional thinking, and long-term thinking capacity.

Managerial Roles. To carry out the management process functions necessary for organizational or unit performance, managers engage in roles—sets of related behaviors. Numerous taxonomies of managerial behavior exist. However, the language and terms used to describe what managers do are not consistent among researchers. Even so, despite the numerous taxonomies that have been used to analyze and classify managerial behavior, there is an approximate correspondence among the various categories of managerial behaviors described in each of these taxonomies (three of which are shown in Figure 2). Again, these roles are useful primarily in terms of the purpose they serve in performing the management process functions depicted in Figure 1.

Henry Mintzberg, in *The Nature of Managerial Work* (New York, 1973), discusses his development of a framework with ten managerial roles, as shown in Figure 2. His role framework has served as the basis for the work of numerous others, such as Gary Yukl and Robert Quinn, which include both broader sets of behaviors and more specific descriptors. Yukl, in *Leadership in Organizations* (Englewood Cliffs, N.J., 1994), discusses his integrating taxonomy of 14 "managerial practices," as shown in Figure 2.

Robert Quinn, in *Beyond Rational Management* (San Francisco, 1988), uses a framework with eight roles that covers much of the content of Yukl's taxonomy. Quinn's framework differs from others in that it is built around an underlying assumption that managerial work is paradoxical—managers must simultaneously address the natural conflict between a flexibility-versus-control focus and an internal-versus-external focus. Each of these four foci calls for differing managerial roles, two for each focus (see Figure 2). An assumption concerning those managerial roles is that the ones in

ORGANIZATIONAL MANAGEMENT. Table 1. Key manager factors of traits and cognitive capacity/ability*

Predisposition and Confidence to Manage	Facilitation of Role Behaviors
• Dominance (California Personality Inventory)	• Energy level and stress tolerance
• McClelland's achievement motivation	• Integrity
• McClelland's power motive	• Emotional maturity
• Motivation to manage	• Originality/creativity
• Self-confidence, self efficacy about being a successful manager	• Flexibility/adaptability
• Internal locus of control (feeling of being in control)	• Psychological types (Meyers-Briggs Type Indicator)
Cognitive Capacity/Ability	
• Intelligence	
• Ability to analyze and synthesize	
• Judgment	
• Strategic thinking capacity	
• Capacity to think multidimensionally	
• Long-term thinking capacity	

*The data are from House and Aditya (1997), Howard and Bray (1988), Hunt (1991), Jaques (1996), Locke et al. (1991), and Yukl (1998).

the same quadrants are similar in nature and those in opposite quadrants are opposite or competing in nature. Thus the mentor and facilitator roles are similar to each other but are very different from the producer and director roles.

Quinn argues, with some evidence, that the most productive managers are "behaviorally complex," as does the Leaderplex model discussed by Robert Hooijberg, J. G. Hunt, and George Dodge (*Journal of Management*, 1997, 23, 375–408). That is, productive managers have role profile scores (a measure of a manager's behavioral complexity) that tend to be high and balanced across the eight roles across time. Successful managers are capable of exhibiting appropriate behavior as required by their organizational surroundings. Managers would emphasize different roles to perform different management process functions appropriate for specific contingencies created by discrete organization and management factors at a given time (see Figure 1).

Manager Selection, Education, Training, and Experience

These areas offer ways to try to get a better fit between the previously described managerial job requirements and the managerial attributes needed to meet these requirements. Managerial selection is a way of choosing from a pool of candidates the people who are believed to best meet managerial job requirements either currently or in the future. Some organizations depend more heavily on selection than others in obtaining this job and person fit. Candidates are selected according to current fit and then reassigned or promoted based heavily on their initial selection characteristics. Other organizations rely more heavily on education, training, and experience to maintain the fit across time. Many organizations utilize a mix of both kinds of approaches.

To select the best candidates from the pool, of course, one first must have an idea of the managerial attributes needed and a way of measuring these attributes in the managerial job candidates. Figure 1 shows a way to start in terms of knowledge base, traits, and cognitive capacity/ability. A more specific way to determine the managerial attributes is by using various types of job analysis procedures to identify the requirements of various managerial positions within a particular organization. With a job analysis, information about role requirements and critical behaviors can be used to infer the managerial knowledge, traits, and cognitive capacity/ability required for job performance.

Once the above steps are carried out, candidate attributes must be assessed to determine how well they fit the job requirements. Interviews, tests, background checks, and references may be used. Some larger organizations utilize assessment centers. These centers typically use a wide range of tests and exercises designed to provide a rational and/or empirical linkage to desired attributes and behaviors. Well-trained assessors observe and analyze the candidates and prepare performance summaries. One commonly used assessment center work simulation is an in-basket exercise wherein participants are confronted with a realistic managerial in-basket of memoranda, daily reports, and the like and are asked to respond appropriately and realistically to each item. Assessors then evaluate such areas as de-

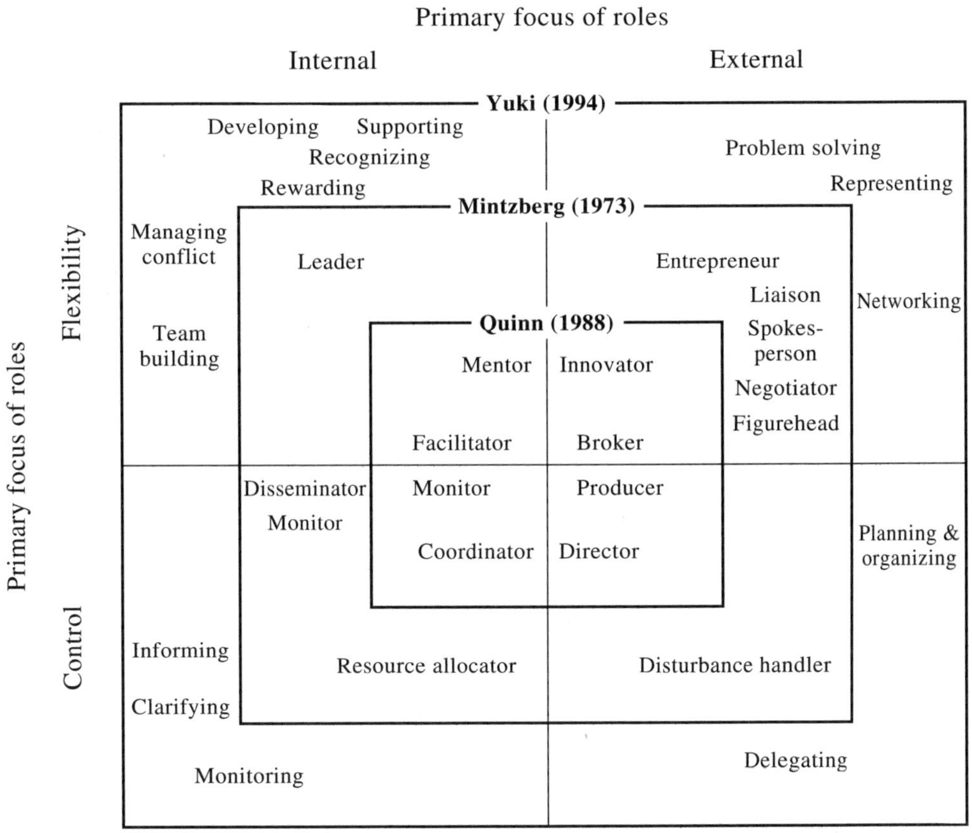

ORGANIZATIONAL MANAGEMENT. Figure 2. Managerial roles

cision making, output rate, and whether the candidate acts independently or seeks guidance from others.

AT&T is well known for its use of an assessment center and an in-basket exercise. Over more than 30 years, its experts were able to make reasonably accurate predictions about managerial job success.

Development through Education, Training, and Experience. A developmental framework discussed by William Heisler and Phillip Benham (*Journal of Management Development*, 1992, *11*, 16–31) categorizes managerial development activities through education (capacity to think critically about complex issues requiring judgment), training (capacity to apply job-related knowledge to job tasks as skills), and experiences (opportunities to perform assignments that enhance job performance and career advancement).

Education is designed to be long-term and cumulative and typically includes degree programs (e.g., BBA or MBA, nondegree short courses (e.g., management development courses or programs), and in-house seminars with an emphasis on specific organizations. The short courses or executive MBA programs continue to be the primary source of education for middle- and upper-level managers.

Two such short- and long-term development courses are those created by Robert Quinn, Sue Faerman, Michael Thompson, and Michael McGrath, discussed in *Becoming a Master Manager* (New York, 1996), and by David Whetten and Kim Cameron in *Developing Management Skills* (New York, 1994). Both emphasize roles, and each utilizes a well-developed process of preassessment, traditional reading, analysis, practice, and application of role-related activities.

The training component tends to be narrower in scope than education and to have immediate job-specific applications. Either internal trainers or external vendor/consultants can deliver employer-sponsored training programs. Most large organizations offer such training. A wide range of methods is used, depending on the specific kind of training involved. The previously mentioned education programs also can be tailored to provide training in these areas as a part of the emphasis on enhancing roles and behaviors. In addition to management training, there are numerous more specialized leadership training programs based on the applications of specific leadership theories.

Some organizations carefully track the development of their managers through sophisticated human resource planning systems. They combine education, training, and experience to provide the necessary candidates for various managerial positions. Among the developmental experiences used are rotation from one managerial job to another in a different functional area, assignments to special projects, understudy assignments, and assignments to mentors. There also are more general experiences outside the job that are often considered in various life-cycle and career-stage models.

The armed forces have systematically integrated experience with education and training for many years. Nonmilitary organizations have been less systematic about such integration. However, one recently developed integrative instrument, Benchmarks, is discussed by Cynthia McCauley and Michael Lombardo in Kenneth Clark and Miriam Clark, eds., *Measures of Leadership* (West Orange, N.J., 1990, pp. 535–545). Benchmarks taps the skills and perspectives that managers do *not* bring to the job but that can be developed. Related to Benchmarks and discussed by Marian Ruderman, Patricia Ohlott, and Cynthia McCauley (in *Measures of Leadership*, pp. 547–562) is the Job Challenge Profile, which measures various aspects of managerial job experiences perceived to be developmental. Together, these instruments tie together experience and development.

The above and other work, such as the aforementioned AT&T study, have shown the importance of job challenge in the early years of a manager's career. Key events, such as increase in job scope, special projects, and exposure to role models, tend to be particularly important. The use of job assignments for their management development potential provides a twist on the emphasis on fit that underlies candidate selection, since it recognizes that for important development to occur, managers must be assigned to challenging jobs, even where the fit may not be as good as in other jobs.

Use of the kinds of education, training, and experience discussed herein seems to be increasing in frequency. However, although there is some support for the usefulness of these activities, by and large, evidence of usefulness is not very systematic.

Psychologists and Organizational Managers

Most of the psychologists working with organizational managers are industrial/organizational, or I/O, psychologists. They function in both practice and research areas, with considerable overlap between the two—many I/O psychologists in research settings such as universities become involved in practice and vice versa. I/O psychologists are concerned with the development and application of scientific principles to the workplace.

There are two major divisions in I/O psychology: industrial (or personnel) and organizational. Both are relevant for organizational managers. The "I" side is represented by such concerns as managerial job design, selection, placement, education, experience, performance appraisal, and the like. The "O" side is primarily concerned with understanding organizational aspects and their impact on managers and employees and their behaviors, attitudes, stress, motivation, and the like. The I/O psychologists' emphasis on research and/or practice is particularly relevant to the issue of managerial attributes and roles and their linkage to the management process functions and to performance (the components of Figure 1). These psychologists are in a position to help design more systematic assessment programs for the various components in the organizational management framework, including selection, training, and experience.

[*See also* Leadership; Organizational Theories; *and* Organizations.]

Bibliography

Bartol, K. M., & Martin, D. C. (1991). *Management*. New York: McGraw-Hill. A representative textbook on principles of management that provides a suggestion for tying together the classical management process functions perspective with various other managerial approaches.

Barnard, C. (1938). *The functions of the executive*. Cambridge, MA.: Harvard University Press. A scholarly classic that describes managers within their organizational environments, anticipating many of the broad themes that have emerged in contemporary treatments of management and organizations.

Bass, B. M. (1990). *Handbook of leadership* (3rd ed.). New York: Free Press. Provides the most comprehensive treatment of leadership that we know of and also includes much work on what many would describe as management.

Carroll, S. J., & Gillen, D. A. (1987). Are the classical management functions useful in describing managerial work? *Academy of Management Review, 12*, 38–51. Evaluates the usefulness of the classical management functions perspective and compares some of the newer managerial conceptualizations with this perspective and with each other. We owe much to this article for the organizational management framework we use here.

Clark, K. E., & Clark, M. B. (Eds.). (1990). *Measures of leadership*. West Orange, NJ: Leadership Library of America. A comprehensive treatment of the theoretical and empirical work from many sources on leaders and managers, covering education and training, methods of selection, and analyses of organizational systems and processes. We owe much to this treatment in the writing of this article.

Drucker, P. F. (1974). *Management: Tasks, responsibilities, practices*. New York: Harper & Row. An insightful treatment of management and managers from one of the best known scholars in the field.

Gardner, W. J., & Marinko, M. J. (1996). Using Myers-Briggs

Type Indicator to study managers: A literature review and research agenda. *Journal of Management, 22*, 45–83. A review of the research into the relationships between psychological types as measured by the Myers-Briggs Type Indicator (MBTI) and managerial attributes, behaviors, and effectiveness.

House, R. J., & Aditya, R. (1997). The social scientific study of leadership: Quo vadis? *Journal of Management, 23*, 409–475. A comprehensive review of numerous perspectives, covering leadership and some aspects of management, with a rigorous conceptual and empirical focus.

Howard, A., & Bray, D. W. (1988). *Managerial lives in transition: Advancing age and changing times*. New York: Guilford Press. Describes the use by AT&T of an assessment center approach to selecting managers, spanning some 30 years.

Hunt, J. G. (1991). *Leadership: A new synthesis*. Newbury Park, CA: Sage. Treats leadership and management from a multiple-organizational-level perspective, with special emphasis on strategic managers or leaders, and extends Jaques' stratified systems theory.

Jaques, E. (1996). *Requisite organization* (Rev. ed.). Arlington, VA: Cason Hall. A treatment of the author's stratified systems theory, which concerns the linkage between increasing organizational complexity and managerial cognitive complexity or capacity as one moves up the hierarchy of the "requisitely structured organization."

Locke, E. A., Kirkpatrick, S., Wheeler, J. K., Schneider, J., Niles, K., Goldstein, J., Welsh, K., & Chah, D.-O. (1991). *The essence of leadership: The four keys to leading successfully*. New York: Lexington Books/Free Press. A succinct but comprehensive treatment of managerial leadership, emphasizing motives and traits, knowledge, skills and ability, and vision.

Phillips, R. L., & Hunt, J. G. (Eds.). (1992). *Strategic leadership: A multiorganizatonal-level perspective*. Westport, CT: Quorum. A number of cutting-edge aspects of strategic leadership/management emphasizing differing vertical organizational requirements are explored by experts using Jaques's stratified systems theory as a point of departure.

Quinn, R. E. (1988). *Beyond rational management: Mastering the paradoxes and competing demands of high performance*. San Francisco, CA: Jossey-Bass. Theoretical and empirical development of the Competing Values Model (CVM) of managerial and organizational performance.

Quinn, R. E., Faerman, S. R., Thompson, M. P., & McGrath, M. R. (1996). *Becoming a master manager* (2nd ed). New York: Wiley. Utilizes a step-by-step approach to developing behavioral complexity, utilizing Quinn's Competing Values framework.

Schermerhorn, J. R., Jr., Hunt, J. G., & Osborn, R. N. (2000). *Organizational behavior* (7th ed.). New York: Wiley. A representative treatment of human behavior in organizations that emphasizes the role and scope of organizational management and managers.

Spector, P. E. (1996). *Industrial and organizational psychology: Research and practice*. New York: Wiley. A comprehensive overview of I/O psychology, with emphasis on management and the impact of I/O psychology on management practice.

Yukl, G. (1994, 1998). *Leadership in organizations* (3rd and 4th eds.). Upper Saddle River, NJ: Prentice Hall. A comprehensive yet parsimonious review of existent leadership theory and research that provides a concise overview of the field of leadership.

James G. (Jerry) Hunt and George E. Dodge

ORGANIZATIONAL PSYCHOLOGY. *See* Industrial and Organizational Psychology.

ORGANIZATIONAL THEORIES. Organizational studies is a fragmented field. Its foundations are the disciplines of psychology, sociology, and economics, along with applied fields such as industrial psychology, labor relations, human resource management, organization development, and management. Each field of inquiry focuses on different phenomena, employs different research methods, and makes different assumptions about the nature of people and about organizations and their purpose in society. This diversity has prevented the emergence of a common language or theory of organizations (Pfeffer, 1997).

Diverse perspectives can be synthesized by adopting the following metaframework and assumptions about the nature of people and organizations (Katz & Kahn, 1978; Pfeffer, 1997; Schein, 1970, 1990):

- People are multifaceted and complex. They have needs to acquire—the dominant view of economists—but they also have needs to bond with others, to learn and grow, and to defend their self-esteem (Lawrence, 1998). People join organizations with a mix of these needs, and organizations are capable of reshaping their relative salience and strengths through selection and socialization.
- Organizations are complex open social systems that adapt and cope to survive and prosper. Successful adaptation requires an effective exchange with the environment. The value of the organization's outputs (satisfaction of members, customers, shareholders, and other stakeholders) must exceed the cost of resources utilized to produce those outputs. By "complex" is meant that many facets of the organization—its design, people, culture, leadership behavior, and human resource policies and practices, as well its various subunits, such as divisions, groups, and geographic entities—are interdependent and are continuously engaged in a process of mutual adaptation to achieve "fit" or congruence. By an "open system" we mean that the organization is subject to influence by

the external environment, largely through the influence of the society on its members.

- Over time, organizations develop a distinctive and persistent pattern of behavior or culture. Culture is defined as the assumptions, beliefs, and resultant behaviors that leaders invent or discover to solve problems in the external and internal environment and that they teach to new members as the correct way of perceiving, thinking, and acting to solve problems (Schein, 1990). The tendency of managers to attract, select, and release people based on how similar they are to those already in the organization increases the strength of the culture (Schneider, 1994). Organizations vary in the strength of their culture, however, and subcultures typically exist in their various parts and subunits.
- Organizational behavior is resistant to change because of human cognitive processes and defensive routines. People make sense of past behavior by forming beliefs that rationalize it and by escalating commitment to it. They also avoid embarrassment and threat to self and others. These human characteristics prevent managers from learning that their actual behavior—their theory in action—is inconsistent with their stated aspiration—their espoused theory. These human characteristics cause organizational policies and practices to persist in the face of new realities unless skills and norms of inquiry are developed (Argyris & Schon, 1996).

Organizational behavior appears to be a product of the confluence of several forces whose interaction and mutual adaptation governs the evolution of the organization over time. It has led to a number of so-called "fit" or "congruence" frameworks and theories (Beer, 1980).

Figure 1 suggests that organizational behavior is shaped by four forces: the organization's environment and the choice its leaders make about strategy, the organization's design, the people selected and promoted, and the behavior of leaders and their top team. Organizations naturally evolve toward alignment of these elements. Implicit in this formulation is a contingency perspective that holds that the best way to organize and manage people depends on the situation (Lawrence & Lorsch, 1967). Whereas contingency theory has dominated the field of organizational design, the field of organization development (OD) has had a normative perspective (Burke, 1982). Though concerned with improving organizational performance, its intervention theories and methods embrace values such as trust, collaboration, empowerment, participation, and open confrontation of conflict. Since OD practitioners are concerned with changing behavior through developing commitment to new norms, this normative stance is not surprising.

Both the contingent and normative perspectives are valid given the demands for high performance in the ever more turbulent environment most organizations face at the end of the twentieth century. Considerations of efficiency and effectiveness demand congruence between environment, people, leadership, and organization design. Intense competition demands continuous change and adaptability. Adaptability requires confrontation of conflict, collaboration, and commitment—the underlying values of organization development.

Organizational Culture and Behavior and Performance

Cross-sectional studies demonstrate that organizational behavior and culture are correlated with company performance. Collins and Porras (1994), for example, showed that firms with strong "cultlike" cultures, founded by chief executive officers (CEOs), who focused on building an institution as much as on making a profit, outperformed comparison companies that did not have these characteristics. The so-called built-to-last companies showed a return in 1990 of $6,356 per dollar invested in 1936, compared with a return of $955 for the comparison companies. These firms adapted strategically through experimentation rather than planning. Other studies have shown that organizations with intergroup cooperation, a strong culture, a multiple stakeholder orientation, and a reputation for having good leaders showed better financial performance than comparison organizations in the same industry. Employee-centered organizational climates have been found to be associated with high customer satisfaction. Action research studies have shown that interventions to change organization design and behavior result in improved productivity and faster product development. New manufacturing plants that involve and empower employees perform more effectively on a number of dimensions than their traditional more hierarchical counterparts (Beer & Walton, 1990; Pfeffer, 1998).

The relationship between organizational behavior and performance found in study after study begs the question of causality. The fact that organizational interventions to change organizational design and behavior lead to improved performance supports the view that behavior causes performance. Good performance could, however, also cause changes in behavior, given new lessons and resources. From the managerial point of view, planned change in organizational behavior is the essential first step to improving performance. Conversely, improving performance may reinforce management's planned change efforts and provide resources that enable further investment in organization development.

Environment and Strategy

Organizational environments can be formed by the certainty of information available to managers, the intensity of competitive rivalry, the industry, the operating

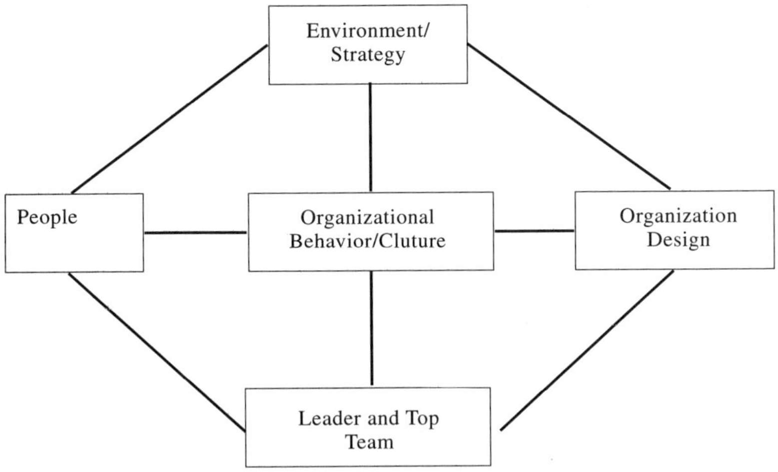

ORGANIZATIONAL THEORIES. Figure 1. Organizational alignment model.

technology employed, the labor markets from which the organization recruits, the societal culture in which the organization is located, and the institutional and political context in which top management is embedded. These facets of the environment affect behavior in the organizations through their influence on choices leaders make about strategy, organization design, people, human resource policies, and leadership style.

Lawrence and Lorsch (1967), for example, found that high-performing companies in uncertain environments differed from high-performing companies in certain environments in their structure and mode of conflict resolution. The former were characterized by horizontal team structures that facilitate coordination across functional departments and by an openness to constructive conflict. The strategy a firm chooses—how it will compete with its rivals—has also been found to be consistently associated with the type of organization structure adopted and with the leadership style employed (Miles & Snow, 1978). Thus managers appear to make choices about organization design and management process based on their functionality—that is, on how well organizational arrangements will enable the implementation of the organization's strategic task.

Another body of research and theory argues for the view that managers make choices based on cultural and political dimensions of their environment. National culture, for example, has been shown to be associated with employees' tolerance for uncertainty and their attitude toward and acceptance of hierarchical authority (Hofstede, 1980). These national characteristics in turn affect management's choices about how to organize and manage people. Institutional theorists argue that managers adopt new management practices to imitate what other firms are doing, particularly in their industry. Resource dependence theories argue that managers are influenced by constituencies in their environment on which they rely for resources (Pfeffer, 1997). In a competitive environment, however, managers must design organizations to function effectively even if that design deviates from norms imposed by national culture and the political context.

Organizational Design

The structure, systems, and human resource policies and practices of a firm shape organizational behavior. Decisions about structure and systems are key to implementing strategy (Galbraith, 1973). Decisions about human resource policies affect levels of employee commitment (Pfeffer, 1998).

All organizational design decisions must balance two opposing considerations—differentiation and integration. Differences between departments in the type of work performed, the time horizon of the work, and people's skills and interpersonal orientation are the source of creative energy needed for innovation. Integration across differentiated departments is required to respond to market needs speedily, efficiently, and effectively (Lawrence & Lorsch, 1967).

Functional structures—departments coordinated by a common boss—are most effective in implementing a low-cost strategy in a relatively stable environment. A decentralized divisional structure is most effective when the strategy is to innovate by moving into new markets and geographic regions. In this structure integration occurs primarily within decentralized units, though the larger corporation also strives to coordinate, albeit more loosely, the activities of its separate divisions. As the environment has become more dynamic and demanding, matrix or team-based structures have emerged as a means of obtaining both high differentiation and integration. "Integrators" lead cross-functional teams as program, product, business, or project managers. Team members are accountable to both the functional department manager and the coordinating business or program manager. In the 1990s, pressures for performance have led to the network organization (Nohria & Eccles, 1992). It enables independent organizations to integrate their efforts through informal relationships and contractual agreements called alliances and partnerships.

Companies with higher than average economic performance have been found to adopt a similar set of mutually reinforcing high-commitment human resource policies and practices. Pfeffer (1998) finds that seven policies characterize these companies:

- employment security
- selective hiring of new personnel
- high involvement in self-managed teams and decentralized decision making
- comparatively high compensation contingent on organizational performance
- extensive training
- reduced-status distinctions and barriers with respect to language, offices, wage differences, and dress
- extensive sharing of financial information throughout the organization

The key to an effective organization is to align the structure with strategy and at the same time to design high-commitment human resource policies and practices.

Leader and Top Team

There is little doubt that leader values and style influence organizational behavior through choices about organizational design and human resource policies. Traditional assumptions that the hierarchy must be used to control uncommitted employees cause managers to impose top-down control rather than exploring organizational designs that foster employee involvement and commitment (Walton, 1985). Leaders who have high needs for control are unlikely to be comfortable with matrix or team-based structures that delegate authority and rely on commitment as the source of control. Efforts to change organizations toward less traditional structures such as matrix or high-commitment human resource systems have often stalled because of inconsistency between the leader's assumptions, values, and skills, and the behavioral profile demanded by the organizational design to which the leader made a commitment in the design stage.

Leadership style also affects employee attitudes and motivation directly. Virtually all studies of leadership point to the importance of two concerns that effective managers must balance and integrate (Yukl, 1998). One has to do with people—how to involve, motivate, and even inspire them to achieve organizational goals. The other has to do with task accomplishment—how to structure work so that it is accomplished efficiently and effectively. Which of these dimensions leaders choose to emphasize and how they integrate them reflects their assumptions about people and the situation in which they manage. To the extent to which leaders assume that people are incapable and uncooperative, they control what people do and how they do it. To the extent that leaders assume people are responsible and capable, they rely on people to plan and structure work.

Situational factors, such as how routine the task is, the ability, needs, and commitment of subordinates, and the culture of the organization, also determine which leadership style will be most effective and will be chosen (Yukl, 1998). In general, the more defined the task and the less capable and committed people are, the more leaders will adopt a controlling style. For example, top-down leadership is most prevalent in businesses that are implementing cost-driven strategies and that are organized vertically by function. Collaborative styles are most prevalent in complex multiproduct organizations with horizontal team-based matrix structures. To the extent, however, that managers want to develop subordinates, they must delegate authority beyond the capability or readiness of subordinates to be self-controlling.

People

Without people who possess the capabilities and the personal predisposition needed to implement its strategy and structural design, an organization cannot be effective. Selective hiring is therefore critical for effectiveness. What this means differs from one organization to another depending on its strategy and values. Whatever the capabilities required, however, companies can help their cause by a favorable selection ratio. Many companies do not invest sufficient resources to do this (Pfeffer, 1998). It is also necessary for companies to assess the essential personal qualities (intelligence, judgment, cooperation, initiative, or ability to learn) that are not easily changed through training rather than selecting based on technical capabilities that can be taught. Equally important is careful assessment of candidates for promotion to ensure that their attitudes and capabilities fit the culture the organization wants to develop. Only in this manner can the culture be changed or maintained. Sophisticated methods for developing and validating assessment methods have been developed by industrial psychologists.

Organization Change and Development

Although organizational alignment is essential for harmony and efficiency, it also creates a persistent pattern of behavior that is not easily changed. Yet an increasingly turbulent and changing environment demands change.

Two overarching opposing theoretical perspectives about organizational change exist. Agency theory, propagated by economists, emphasizes the importance of linking top management's incentives to the creation of economic value for shareholders. Behavioral theories emphasize the importance of participative processes that develop commitment to the change. Embedded in these two theoretical perspectives are different levels of analysis and values. Economists are concerned about economic outcomes and do not typically concern themselves with organizational behavior inside the firm. Behavioral scientists studying behavior in the firm focus more on intermediate outcomes such as commitment and teamwork and less on economic returns. Though economists and behavioral scientists approach the question of organizational effectiveness from different perspectives, they are both concerned with how to overcome the tendency of managers to avoid hard truths about their effectiveness and that of their organization.

Agency theorists see capital markets as the means for regulating the behavior of managers. They argue for financial incentives to motivate managers. Failure is to be met with removal of top management. Their view is supported by research. Firms that survive a dramatic shift in the basis of competition seem to do so only after they undergo change in their top management team. Organization development theory and practice, on the other hand, stresses diagnosis of behavioral problems based on data collection and feedback to leaders (Beer, 1980; Beer & Walton, 1990; Burke, 1982). Both fields are concerned with improving performance, but their assumptions about how sustained commitment to high performance can be achieved are quite different. Economists emphasize extrinsic motivation and external control, whereas OD theorists and practitioners emphasize high-involvement processes that will develop internal commitment to organizational and personal change. These typically require process consultants to help the organization confront its own inadequacies and plan change.

Despite the fact that a comprehensive theory that resolves these different views does not exist, research in the field of organization development has yielded considerable insight into how corporate leaders motivated by environmental pressure can lead planned change effectively (Beer, Eisenstat, & Spector, 1990). Effective leaders mobilize energy for change by clarifying for organizational members why it is needed and by articulating a new vision of the future. They avoid imposing programs of change from the top, however. Instead, effective corporate leaders encourage, even demand, that leaders of various subunits manage performance improvement by involving their top teams in redefining goals, strategy, and values. This is followed by collecting data about the alignment of the organization and people with the new direction and the use of the data to stimulate personal and organizational change. Staffing changes must follow if and when individuals do not develop the commitment or skills demanded by the new organizational arrangements.

Organizational changes often stall, however, due to the inability of the leader to confront resistance to change and develop required commitment and skills. Only effective governance mechanisms advocated by economists, pressures from capital markets, and a responsive board of directors can influence corporate leaders to confront painful realities. Of course, within the larger firm, top management must play the same role with respect to leaders in lower level units.

In practice, many actors—top management, employees, or their union representatives, and external constituents such as shareholders and consultants—are involved in the drama of organizational change. No commonly accepted organization change and development theory or practice exists that specifies how these diverse actors and their disparate values and intervention methods might be integrated to achieve a speedy, efficient, and effective organizational transformation. An overarching theory would have to be able to predict the performance and human outcomes expected from alternative organization change and development strategies. To be able to be implemented, such a metatheory would also have to specify the means by which a variety of actors and stakeholders with different values might be brought together to craft a consensus about the process—sequence and speed—by which the organization will be changed. This is the challenge faced by the field of organizational behavior and development.

[*See also* Industrial and Organizational Psychology; Organizational Management; *and* Organizations.]

Bibliography

Argyris, C., & Schon, D. A. (1996). *Organizational learning: II. Theory, method and practice.* Reading, MA: Addison-Wesley.

Beer, M. (1980). *Organization change and development: A systems view.* Santa Monica, CA: Goodyear.

Beer, M., Eisenstat, R., & Spector, B. (1990). *The critical path to corporate renewal.* Boston: Harvard Business School Press.

Beer, M., & Walton, E. (1990). Developing the competitive organization: Interventions and strategies. *American Psychologist, 45*(22), 154–161.

Burke, W. W. (1982). *Organization development: Principles and practices.* Boston: Little, Brown.

Collins, J. C., & Porras, J. I. (1994). *Built to last.* New York: Harper Business.

Galbraith, J. R. (1973). *Designing complex organizations.* Reading, MA: Addison-Wesley.

Hofstede, G. (1980). *Culture's consequences: International differences in work-related values.* Beverly Hills, CA: Sage.

Katz & Kahn. (1978). *The social psychology of organizations.* New York: Wiley.

Lawrence, P. R. (1998). *Toward a unified theory of organizational life.* Boston: Harvard Business School Press.

Lawrence, P. R., & Lorsch, J. (1967). *Organization and environment*. Boston: Harvard Business School Press.
Miles, R. E., & Snow, C. C. (1978). *Organization strategy, structure and process*. New York: McGraw-Hill.
Nohria, N., & Eccles, R. G. (Eds.). (1992). *Networks and organizations: Structure, form, and action*. Boston: Harvard Business School Press.
Pfeffer, J. (1997). *New directions for organization theory*. New York: Oxford University Press.
Pfeffer, J. (1998). *The human equation*. Boston: Harvard Business School Press.
Schein, E. H. (1970). *Organizational psychology* (2nd ed.). Englewood Cliffs, NJ: Prentice Hall.
Schein, E. H. (1990). Organizational culture. *American Psychologist, 45*, 109–119.
Schneider, B. (1994). The people make the place. *Personnel Psychology, 40*, 437–454.
Walton, R. E. (1985). Toward a strategy for eliciting employee commitment based on policies of mutuality. In R. E. Walton & P. R. Lawrence (Eds.), *HRM trends and challenges* (pp. 35–65). Boston: Harvard Business School Press.
Yukl, G. (1998). *Leadership in organizations*. Upper Saddle River, NJ: Prentice Hall.

Michael Beer

ORGANIZATIONS are a pervasive part of everyday life. They provide membership and employment that deeply influence the quality of human existence. They are also sources of many of the norms and values that shape the social reality of the surrounding world.

Definition, Attributes, and Types of Organizations

In the pursuit of productive ends, people enact three different kinds of social arrangements. Sometimes they work alone, as individuals, to produce simple commodities, as in instances of subsistence farming wherein laborers work small plots of land to support themselves and their families. Alternatively, they join together in temporary relationships, in markets, to produce outcomes requiring only occasional interaction and cooperation, as in the hand-knitting industries of the northeastern United States. In other instances they form lasting relationships, in organizations, to produce things requiring joint effort and more permanent coordination. An organization is thus a type of social arrangement formed for productive purposes that is marked by enduring patterns of coordinated interdependence.

Fundamental Attributes

Coordinated interdependence in organizations arises out of two fundamental attributes, each possessed to some degree by every organization. One of these consists of differentiation among members and their work, and is traceable to the division of labor, or the splitting of complex tasks into smaller, specialized jobs. The broad task of manufacturing automobiles can be divided into narrower assembly-line jobs like those of the chassis welder, finish painter, interior specialist, and trim installer. Similarly, the general task of underwriting life insurance can be broken into specialized office jobs in such areas as actuarial projection, policy preparation, premium collection, and claims processing. Through differentiation, people working together in organizations have the potential to produce outcomes beyond the abilities of individuals working alone or in less lasting relationships. Few people possess the knowledge and skills to manufacture cars on their own or provide life insurance without ready support. In performing specialized jobs, however, people working together in organizations can produce complex outcomes without exceeding personal limitations.

The second fundamental attribute contributing to coordinated interdependence is the integration of purpose that occurs as work on the many jobs in an organization is consolidated into a meaningful whole. Whether the productive potential of the division of labor will actually be realized depends on the extent to which divided work is rechanneled toward the completion of the organization's larger task. Although it is not necessary for every individual in an organization to espouse the same organizational purpose, it is imperative that the various purposes pursued fit together in a way that keeps everyone working toward interlocking ends. Achieving integration of purpose, and, in addition, developing a balance between integration and differentiation, is essential to productive organizational existence.

Types of Organizations

Current approaches to differentiating and integrating work in organizations owe much to Max Weber's classic theory of bureaucracy (e.g., Gerth & Mills, 1946), wherein Weber indicated that productivity and efficiency are stimulated in organizations by: (1) dividing work into specialized jobs; (2) selecting and promoting individuals to perform these jobs on the basis of ability and expertise; and (3) managing relations among jobs and job performers through rules, regulations, and hierarchical supervision.

Key elements of contemporary organizational approaches are also traceable to Frederick W. Taylor's pioneering work on task management, in which Taylor advocated management centralization—the separation of the management of work and design of jobs from work performance and job incumbency—as well as: (1) selection and training procedures aimed at matching worker abilities to job requirements; (2) supervisory monitoring to ensure workforce adherence to specified work policies and procedures; and (3) work-flow planning to clarify worker responsibilities and eliminate work interruptions (1912).

Touched on in Weber's and Taylor's writings are many of the topical focuses of the modern-day fields of industrial/organizational psychology and human resource management, including staffing and selection, compensation administration, and employee training and development. Also highlighted are two characteristics—Weber's job specialization and Taylor's managerial centralization—that are especially useful in defining and describing different types of organizations. In fact, specialization and centralization together form the basis of the often-cited distinction between mechanistic and organic organizations, drawn initially by Burns and Stalker (1961). On the one hand, mechanistic organizations are centralized in the sense that prerogatives to make decisions and control productive resources are retained by an organizational elite of top managers. Jobs within such organizations are highly specialized, that is, simplified and restricted in scope. The organizations themselves are efficiency oriented and excel when their work requires an inflexible, machinelike approach to performance. On the other hand, organic organizations are decentralized, meaning that decision-making prerogatives are shifted downward from the managerial elite and shared among individuals of lesser organizational status. Work in organic organizations is lower in specialization, and the jobs performed within them require more in the way of generalist knowledge, skills, and abilities. Such organizations are oriented toward adaptability in the face of change, and perform best when their work requires learning, innovation, and flexibility.

Structural Types. By also considering differing approaches to departmentation, or the integration of work activities through the formation of subunit groups, the mechanistic-organic distinction can be further divided into a finer grained—and more pragmatically grounded—taxonomy of four types of organization structure. An organization's structure consists of the formally patterned work interactions, job demands, and coordination mechanisms that give shape and a sense of permanence to the organization. One type of structure, the functional structure, is a type in which work is highly specialized and integrated according to similarities in jobs performed and functions served, leading to the development of departments of marketing, accounting, human resources, and so forth. Decision making is highly centralized within such structures, with members of top management making most or all important decisions. In contrast, the divisional structure is a type in which work is highly specialized but integrated according to similarities in outputs produced, clients served, or geographic locations occupied, leading to the formation of such subunits as an avionics division or a military contracts division or a Western European division. Decision making is somewhat decentralized, with decisions about organization-wide strategy being made at the top but decisions about divisional operations being distributed between the organizational elite and lower-level divisional managers.

The multiunit structure is one in which work is less specialized, often being performed by teams of generalists and integrated into relatively autonomous business units according to similarities in output, client, or location. Decision making is decentralized due to the autonomy of the various units, with operational decision making resting within each unit—often involving nonmanagerial members of work teams in recurrent data-interpretation and problem-solving activities—and with every unit having managerial input into organization-wide strategic planning. Finally, the network structure is in some respects an organization of organizations, since what would be autonomous units in a multiunit structure become completely separable entities, connected by networks of information flows and work-flow interdependence. Work is generalized, with each unit having its own complement of internal departments and the ability to survive alone. Network integration occurs along divisional (product, client, location) lines, with each unit held accountable for a particular divisional responsibility. Decision-making is extremely decentralized, retained largely as the prerogative of each networked unit.

Of the four structural types just described, the functional type is the most mechanistic and the network type the most organic. The divisional and multiunit types are middle-range alternatives, being decreasingly mechanistic and increasingly organic in character. Due to these differences, each structural type has characteristic strengths and weaknesses that make it vulnerable to the influence of various contingency factors, considered later.

Cultural Types. Besides highlighting different structural patterns, Burns and Stalker's mechanistic-organic distinction also accentuates differences in the ways of thinking that emerge in different kinds of organizations, which results in important contrasts in organizational culture. An organization's culture consists of socially produced norms, values, and symbols that sanction members' behaviors and suggest situated meanings for their actions. Toward the mechanistic extreme is a type of culture best described as bureaucratic, emphasizing the importance of adherence to rules, regulations, and established ways of doing things. More consonant with the organic extreme is a type referred to in the literature on organizational culture by such labels as *Type Z*, *Intuition-thinking*, and *Work hard/Play hard*. In stressing innovation and flexibility, an adaptive culture of this type is geared toward the anticipation and acceleration of change in the organization's work and composition.

In most instances there is some degree of consistency, or "fit," between an organization's culture and its structure, as when a bureaucratic culture is paired with a functional structure or when an adaptive culture predominates in an organization also possessing a network structure. This consistency occurs because cultural symbols, norms, and values influence structural development, and structural constraints and opportunities shape cultural meanings. It also occurs because the same people, work, and contingency factors that shape an organization's structure similarly influence its culture. Nevertheless, instances sometimes arise when an organization's culture is at odds with its structure, as would be exemplified by a network structure coexisting with a culture stressing bureaucratic rule-following. Such inconsistency often reflects recent change, either in the organization's structure or culture, its work, or the contingency factors with which it must deal.

Contingency Factors. The fact that a variety of different types of organizations exist can be traced to the influence of factors that shape or constrain the task-related success of each particular organizational type. A structure and culture that work for one organization may not contribute to the acceptable performance of another, due to the effects of a number of variables commonly referred to as contingency factors.

Some contingency factors establish the macro framework within which an organization must operate. One of these, ecological drift, influences the mix of resources available for use by the organization in producing outcomes and sustaining coordinated interdependence. Entire populations of organizations may come into existence as ecological drift makes available new combinations of resources, as occurred when the invention of steam locomotion triggered the development of the railroad industry. Populations may also decline as ecological drift robs organizations of needed resources, as happened to the railroads upon the development of jet travel and truck transportation. Population ecology thus constrains the existence of broad types of organization at a given point in time (Hannan & Carroll, 1992).

In addition, another factor, the institutional milieu, shapes the macro framework by providing social legitimization for some mixes of organizational purpose and form, but not others (Scott, 1995). Patterning a new fast-food franchise after a successful chain already in existence increases the likelihood that the newcomer and its products will gain ready public acceptance. Organizing a hospital along the lines of a mass-production manufacturer, however, is unlikely to yield the social legitimacy needed to participate in the provision of health care.

Within the broad framework of ecological and institutional constrains, other contingency factors influence the relative suitability of different forms of organization. One of these is the core technology of equipment, processes, and knowledge used within an organization to produce its outputs. Generally speaking, technologies that are routine and well understood match the capabilities of mechanistic organizations, which tend to be efficient but inflexible due to their high specialization and centralization. In contrast, technologies that are nonroutine or poorly understood more closely align with organic organizations, which encourage innovation and flexibility due to their decentralization but lack efficiency due to their low specialization (Woodward, 1975). Consequently, in productive, successful organizations, extreme technological routine tends to be most often associated with the functional structure and bureaucratic culture, and least often with the network structure and adaptive culture.

Also influential is the task environment surrounding the organization, consisting of the industries, markets, and regulatory frameworks that shape organizational actions. Environments that are stable and unified fit best with the attributes of mechanistic organizations, while environments that are changing or differentiated more closely match the characteristic strengths of organic organizations (Lawrence & Lorsch, 1967). Organizations with functional structures and bureaucratic cultures are best equipped to respond to the demands of stable, unified environments, and divisional, multiunit, and network structures coupled with adaptive cultures enable organizations to be more responsive to the demands of environmental change or differentiation.

Finally, the social norms and values of the social culture surrounding an organization are a direct source of the norms and values in the organization's culture, and can also influence the suitability of a particular organizational structure. For example, social cultures supportive of high power distance, defined as social acceptance of and allowance for significant hierarchical differentiation in power and social status, promote norms within an organization's culture that justify the centralization of mechanistic organizations. In contrast, social cultures inclined toward lower power distance promote the development of organizational cultures with norms that are more supportive of the decentralization of organic organizations (Hofstede, 1984). So, Asian proclivities toward high power distance are supportive of functional and divisional structures, as well as those aspects of the bureaucratic type of organizational culture that favor power and status differentiation along hierarchical lines. Conversely, Israeli and Australian tendencies toward low power distance are more supportive of multiunit and network structures, as well as with those features of the adaptive type of organizational culture that promote equalization of power and status.

Organizations as Psychological Contexts

Through its division of labor and integration of purpose, every organization serves as a psychological context that influences the attitudes and behaviors of its members. At the same time, member attitudes and behaviors shape the features of this context, contributing to continuities and changes in differentiation and integration.

Effects of Organizations on Individuals and Groups. As indicated, the organizational context can be broken down into structural and cultural subcontexts. In addition, a third subcontextual element, that of organizational roles, is experienced as members form and receive social expectations concerning the activities and outcomes of individual job holders. This third aspect of the organizational context grows out of the other two, developing as structural job demands and patterns of interdependence interact with cultural norms and values in shaping member behaviors.

Structural Effects. An organization's structure exerts contextual effects primarily through the kinds of jobs it contains, the types of decision-making it permits, and the degree of interconnectivity it allows. For instance, the specialized, simplified jobs found in functional structures lack significant skill variety and task identity, where the former characteristic reflects the degree to which a job requires its holders to use varied abilities, and the latter refers to the extent to which doing a job results in an outcome that is complete enough to be readily identified. Research on job design has indicated that such jobs offer little opportunity for internal work motivation and tend to be associated with high absenteeism, turnover, and dissatisfaction, especially for individuals who are oriented toward gains in personal growth and development (Hackman & Oldham, 1980).

In contrast, generalist jobs in network structures afford far more skill variety and tend to have higher task identity, since a single job holder is often responsible for doing a sequence of tasks that draws on diverse abilities and results in a completed cycle of service provision or product manufacture. For individuals with high needs for growth and development, such work is experienced as internally motivating and contributes to reduced absenteeism and turnover, and heightened satisfaction. Lying between these extremes are the jobs and psychological outcomes most often experienced in divisional and multiunit forms of organization, with the reduced specialization of divisional forms affording enough skill variety and task identity to stimulate modest internal motivation and a moderate drop in absenteeism, turnover, and dissatisfaction, and the modest generalization of multiunit forms allowing the variety and identity needed to support somewhat more internal motivation and an even greater drop in negative psychological outcomes.

In constraining decision-making processes, an organization's structure also influences the amount of autonomy, or control over decision-making processes and outcomes, exercised by members and groups within the organization. For instance, the extreme centralization of a functional structure allows individuals and groups below the level of managerial elite little autonomy, undermining subordinates' acceptance of, satisfaction with, and willing enactment of decisions, even though decision-making processes may progress quite rapidly. Alternatively, the extreme decentralization of a network structure spreads involvement and autonomy among individuals and groups throughout the organization, thus enhancing everyone's commitment, satisfaction, and decision implementation. However, decision processes are slower due to the involvement of a larger number of participants. The mid-level amounts of decentralization in divisional and multiunit structures allow moderate autonomy, and therefore greater acceptance and satisfaction, and surer execution among lower-level members, than is likely in functional structures, but lesser amounts than in network structures. In both middle-range instances, decision making is moderate—between the two extremes—in speed.

By limiting the amount of interconnectivity among individuals, an organization's structure can also affect the productivity of subunits—groups or teams—within the organization. Structures toward the mechanistic extreme, particularly functional structures, whose high specialization and centralization support the least amount of interconnection, contribute to high subunit productivity when simple tasks are performed. Such tasks demand only minimal skills and abilities, and require little or no exchange of information, so subunit members are able to perform them without having to interact with anyone else. However, complex tasks, which demand higher skills and significant information exchange, require significant interpersonal interaction and tend to overwhelm forms of structure that fail to include high internal interconnection. Subunit performance suffers under such circumstances. In contrast, structures toward the organic extreme, especially network structures, whose low specialization and high decentralization stimulate rich interconnection, are likely to contribute to high subunit productivity when the task at hand is complex, since information can be readily shared and skills easily pooled. However, such structures tend to depress the level of subunit productivity on simple tasks, because otherwise productive resources must be channeled toward maintaining unnecessary interconnection.

Cultural Effects. In general, cultural norms, values, and symbols act as social information that members use when making sense of themselves and their organization (Trice & Beyer, 1993). For example, values stressing "quality is job one," can lead to interpretations of workplace activities and outcomes that differ from those framed by values emphasizing "satisfying cost-conscious consumers." Similarly, an organization symbolized by a predator such as a lion or hawk is likely to be interpreted in terms that differ from the image communicated by a symbol of shelter, like an umbrella or roof.

Besides these general tendencies, important contextual effects of an organization's culture also stem from the degree to which bureaucratic norms, values, and symbols influence thought, perception, and behavior within the organization. Although a bureaucratic culture can support efficient performance and high productivity, it can also have unintended negative effects. For instance, normative adherence to rules and regulations can sometimes contribute to behavioral rigidity that stultifies innovation and creativity. Under such circumstances, an organization's members tend to direct attention toward ensuring that personal behaviors are defensible within the organization's rules and regulations, irrespective of whether those behaviors appear "correct" in an objective sense. Members are also apt to devote substantially less effort to satisfying customers or producing at more than a minimal level.

In fact, within bureaucratic cultures, performance objectives developed initially as minimum performance expectations often come to be recast as maximum performance targets. Researchers discovered evidence of this shift and examined its consequences for individual and group productivity during the Hawthorne Studies, a famous series of workplace experiments conducted between the two world wars at a Western Electric plant near Chicago, Illinois. Employees expected to increase performance in response to various workplace improvements instead restricted output to original, minimal levels or below and went so far as to punish "rate busters" who failed to accede to restrictive norms (Roethlisberger & Dickson, 1939). Analysts later attributed the workers' restrictive activities to the bureaucratic cultural tendencies at the Hawthorne plant, coupled with cohesion among workers that had developed due to commonly held fears of possible layoffs in response to productivity improvements.

In contrast, the norms, values, and symbols of an adaptive culture can encourage openness, learning, creativity, and flexibility in member thoughts and organizational behaviors. However, they can also have unintended negative consequences. For example, the emphasis on change and innovation that permeates an adaptive culture may encourage process loss, that is, lost production due to excessive communication or ineffectual experimentation. Also associated with an adaptive culture may be problems with ambiguity or overload in the performance responsibilities communicated as role expectations.

Role Effects. Roles develop out of formal job expectations communicated through structural job descriptions, and emergent social expectations communicated through cultural norms. When an individual's role is clearly specified, internally consistent, and not overly demanding, the individual has the opportunity to perform effectively and satisfy formal and emergent expectations. However, when a role is ambiguous, includes conflicting expectations, or contributes to overload in job responsibilities and requirements, feelings of stress may develop, positive attitudes such as satisfaction and commitment may weaken or disappear, and the role holder's performance may suffer. Role ambiguity, role conflict, and role overload are thus unintended consequences of the process of role formation and communication that can have adverse psychological effects.

Situational Strength. Despite the fact that in most instances the organizational context is a powerful influence, there are situations when individual differences exert stronger effects. For example, stress symptoms exhibited on the job are sometimes more strongly predicted by the level of personal stress reported before job entry than by contextual role characteristics; individual or group habits formed in other circumstances can supersede contextual constraints in shaping day-to-day workplace activities; and individuals whose work involves significant danger and isolation, such as firefighters, often find themselves able to resist bureaucratic rules and ignore contextual controls over their work. The situational strength of the organizational context thus merits careful consideration in any analysis of contextual effects (Mowday & Sutton, 1993).

The Effects of Individuals and Groups on Organizations

Organizational contexts are products of numerous social and psychological processes, since people acting together are the ultimate source of the rules, jobs, norms, and so forth that constitute organizational structures, cultures, and roles. Especially noteworthy origins of contextual features include the aggregate thoughts, feelings, and behaviors of organizational members; the design interventions and symbol manipulation of organization leaders; and the systemic process of organization development.

Aggregate Thoughts, Feelings, and Behaviors. "People make the place," according to Schneider

(1987). In aggregate, the cognitions of individual members govern the structural and cultural possibilities that can be imagined, enacted, and reformed. Gross patterns in these cognitions also shape contexts, as when "slow" learners actually encourage more learning and innovation in organizations than do "fast" learners, because the latter learn quickly what the former acquire only through lengthy exploration and experimentation. Emotions also play a role, contributing to a general positive or negative affective tone that influences acceptance of the existing context or search for contextual alternatives. Finally, members' behaviors serve as a repository and reminder of the roles, rules, norms, and symbols that make up their organization's context—as the organization's memory, so to speak.

Leaders and Leadership. Due to their power and position, leaders are particularly active in the process of context-shaping in organizations. As a case in point, leaders are directly involved—whether as centralized decision makers or decentralized coparticipants—in managing the organization design processes that shape structures and the jobs within them. Therefore, the degree of job specialization, decision centralization, and so forth in an organization is traceable to leaders' actions. Reengineering interventions, which transform organizational subunits from functional groups into cross-functional teams, are another way in which leaders exercise influence over the structural context. By facilitating the development of cohesive relations across functional distinctions, reengineering strengthens structural integration and enhances interpersonal collaboration. Coincidentally, in successful reengineering interventions, structural and cultural characteristics move from generally mechanistic to organic in form.

In the process of providing an organization's membership with a sense of vision, direction, and purpose, leaders also invent, manipulate, and discredit cultural symbols (Pfeffer, 1981). Stories exchanged among members to convey an organization's cultural norms and values often originate in leader behaviors, as exemplified by sagas told about organization founders and their early successes. Moreover, rituals that reinforce cultural understandings often incorporate leaders or leadership myths, as in annual banquets in which corporate officials conduct awards ceremonies. In ways such as these, leaders are critical keepers and shapers of organizational culture.

Organization Development

Organization-wide attempts to shape the organizational context often fall within the realm of organization development, a domain of research and practice that focuses on stimulating and managing large-scale organizational change (French & Bell, 1995). Organization development interventions, which consist of various techniques intended to stimulate and manage change, focus on improving interpersonal relations, strengthening group performance, or increasing organizational effectiveness through such processes as role analysis, team building, and survey feedback. In all such interventions, organization members participate as decision makers and problem solvers in order to learn how to identify problems, structure solutions, and encourage implementation. Organization development is thus an effective way of introducing organic approaches to problem identification and solution into mechanistic organizations, and is also useful as a means of encouraging further organic learning and growth in organizations already organic in form.

Research Issues

As research has progressed on organizations and related psychological processes, several issues have emerged that will continue to require consideration in the future.

Quantitative Versus Qualitative Methods. Qualitative research is performed on data acquired in nonnumerical form and is reported most typically in case analyses or narrative accounts. Quantitative research, in contrast, is performed on data acquired in numerical form and almost always involves the application of statistical analyses. Quantitative methods have long dominated research in the area of organizational structure and in the fields of industrial-organizational psychology, organizational behavior, and human resource management. Research on organizational culture, however, has favored qualitative methods. Two problems have emerged as a consequence. First, the integration of structural and cultural research has grown tenuous, as increasing methodological noncomparability has precluded direct comparison. Second, methodological arguments between proponents of the two approaches have sometimes overwhelmed topical inquiry, leading many observers to question whether much organizational research is truly "organizational." Resolution of this issue would seem to require recasting both approaches as complementary methods of inquiry, and appears essential to the development of a consolidated body of knowledge about organizations and their members.

Institutional Versus Questionnaire Data Collection. Within quantitative organizational research, another recurring issue concerns the use of institutional or questionnaire data-collection procedures. Institutional procedures request expert informants to provide factual information about organizations or organizational processes, for instance, the number of members on a company's board of directors or the length of time between the inauguration and completion of a sales campaign. Questionnaire procedures request representative respondents to provide personal opinions about organizational characteristics or processes, for example, the degree to which organizational procedures seem to be written down or the extent to which workplace compensation is administered fairly. Analyses have indicated that the same multiple-respondent procedures likely to improve data reliability in questionnaire procedures may attenuate informant expertise in institutional procedures, and that the two approaches can yield widely differing characterizations of the same organizational features and processes. Each of these findings is troublesome, and both appear related to issues of interrater agreement.

Multilevel Research. Multilevel research crosses levels of analysis, for instance, associating individual-level outcomes like satisfaction with group or organization-level factors such as structure. A particularly knotty problem emerges when questionnaire data collected from individual respondents are aggregated to produce measures of higher-level phenomena, as is the case of measures of organizational climate and similar variables, but low agreement (consensus) is found among the answers of different respondents. Is the aggregate measure truly representative of conditions at the higher level of analysis? In general, observers suggest that the absence of agreement among raters undermines any claim to be measuring higher-level phenomena. At best, in the absence of interrater agreement, only the measurement of psychological perceptions or reactions can be claimed. To the degree that future research continues to delve into relationships between psychological and organizational variables, multilevel issues can be expected to remain problematic.

Performance Measurement. As suggested by Rousseau, comparisons of supposedly similar measures of group or organizational performance sometimes show evidence of substantial inconsistency, and performance improvements at the individual and subunit levels that should enhance performance at the organizational level often do not (1997). To some extent, the first discrepancy may be an accurate reflection of reality, since the finding that mature organizations are more likely than younger organizations to perform at the same levels on multiple measures of performance seems to suggest that time is required for organizations to learn how to do several things well. Nonetheless, calls for widespread use of multidimensional measures of group and organizational performance appear to merit further consideration.

Content Issues. Finally, a primary issue related to research on organizational-psychological relationships concerns the absence of enough research to support anything more than general conclusions. In particular, far greater attention needs to be directed to subunits as they function within organizational contexts. A considerable amount of knowledge has accumulated concerning the effects of individual, aggregate demographic, and group-level characteristics on group or team processes and outcomes. Little has been done, however, to examine how the structural and cultural features of the surrounding organization might impinge on those same group or team effects. In conclusion, the same statement is also fitting as a summary of the broader field of research on relationships between organizations and the psychological states of their members. Such research merits considerably more attention than it has received to date.

[*See also* Leadership; Organizational Management; *and* Organizational Theories. *Also, many associations, institutions, and organizations are the subjects of independent entries.*]

Bibliography

Burns, T., & Stalker, G. M. (1961). *The management of innovation*. London: Tavistock.

French, W. L., & Bell, C. H., Jr. (1995). *Organization development: Behavioral science interventions for organizational improvement*. Englewood Cliffs, NJ: Prentice Hall.

Gerth, H. H., & Mills, C. W. (1946). *From Max Weber: Essays in sociology*. New York: Oxford University Press.

Hackman, J. R., & Oldham, G. R. (1980). *Work redesign*. Reading, MA: Addison Wesley.

Hannan, M. T., & Carroll, G. R. (1992). *Dynamics of organizational populations*. New York: Oxford University Press.

Hofstede, G. (1984). *Culture's consequences: International differences in work-related values*. Beverly Hills, CA: Sage.

Lawrence, P. R., & Lorsch, J. W. (1967). *Organization and environment*. Homewood, IL: Irwin.

Mowday, R. T., & Sutton, R. I. (1993). Organizational behavior: Linking individuals and groups to organizational contexts. *Annual Review of Psychology, 44*, 195–229.

Pfeffer, J. (1981). Management as symbolic action: The creation and maintenance of organizational paradigms. In L. L. Cummings & B. M. Staw (Eds.), *Research in organizational behavior* (Vol. 3, pp. 1–52). Greenwich, CT: JAI Press.

Roethlisberger, F. J., & Dickson, W. J. (1939). *Management and the worker*. Cambridge, MA: Harvard University Press.

Rousseau, D. M. (1977). Organizational behavior in the new organizational era. *Annual Review of Psychology, 48*, 515–546.

Schneider, B. (1987). The people make the place. *Personnel Psychology, 40*, 437–453.

Scott, W. R. (1995). *Institutions and organizations*. Thousand Oaks, CA: Sage.

Taylor, F. W. (1912). *The principles of scientific management*. New York: Norton.

Trice, H. M., & Beyer, J. M. (1993). *The cultures of work organizations*. Englewood Cliffs, NJ: Prentice Hall.

Woodward, J. (1975). *Industrial organization: Theory and practice*. London: Oxford University Press.

John A. Wagner III

OSGOOD, CHARLES EGERTON (1916–1991), American psychologist. Osgood stands as a major figure in the field of psychology in general and psycholinguistics in particular. His contributions greatly influenced psycholinguistics, political and cross-cultural psychology, and experimental psychology.

Born in Somerville, Massachusetts, in 1916, Osgood's formative years were difficult. When he was 6 years old his parents were divorced, forcing him to be shuttled among family members until he was 18. In 1935, he entered Dartmouth College as an aspiring writer. Dreams of a literary career, however, were promptly dismissed on encountering Theodore Karwoski, a psychology professor, who became a mentor for Osgood and greatly influenced him through much of his professional career.

As a doctoral student at Yale University (1940–1946), Osgood taught undergraduate psychology courses, studied psycholinguistics, and came under the influence of Clark Hull's neobehaviorism. After Yale, he worked at the Smoky Hill Army Air Force Base in Salina, Kansas, where he conducted research for the Office of Scientific Research and Development. He continued his research at the University of Connecticut, where he taught graduate students and wrote one of his most important contributions, *Method and Theory in Experimental Psychology* (New York, 1953). Largely through the influence of O. Hobart Mowrer, Osgood was hired in 1950 at the University of Illinois, where he spent the rest of his academic career.

Theoretically, Osgood formulated a kind of neobehaviorism that was intended to make explicit what was only implicit in Hullian behaviorism. Osgood liked to refer to psycholinguistics as the "representational mediation process," and his orientation led to much research for many years. With Percy Tannenbaum and George Suci, his first research assistant, Osgood published *The Measurement of Meaning* (Urbana, Ill., 1957), a classic exposition of the semantic differential method for representing word meanings along various dimensions. In the article "Is a Boulder Sweet or Sour?" (*Contemporary Psychology*, 1958), the Harvard psycholinguist Roger Brown reviewed the book, attacking Osgood's definition of meaning (Osgood obviously thought it sweet while Brown thought it sour). Despite continuing attacks by Noam Chomsky and others during the 1960s, controversy over the semantic differential did not prevent its snowballing into decades of further research. Osgood's own work continued in the direction of cross-cultural studies of meaning, which led to an interest in international relations. His book *Graduated Reciprocation in Tension-Reduction* (Urbana, Ill., 1960) detailed the GRIT strategy for avoiding armed conflict and made him a recognized authority on foreign affairs. In 1966, he testified on psychological aspects of international relations before the U.S. Senate Committee on Foreign Affairs, in a session chaired by Senator William Fulbright.

With the book *Approaches to the Study of Aphasia* (Osgood & Miron, 1963), Osgood extended his psycholinguistic research beyond semantics to the field of language pathology. Although this work did not have a large impact, it was an important contribution in the area of neuropsychology of language.

In recognition of his prolific contributions, Osgood received the Distinguished Scientific Contribution Award in 1960 of the American Psychological Association and was elected its president three years later; in 1972, he was elected to the National Academy of Sciences. Although he remained highly productive for years after his major influential period, Osgood was plagued by problems with alcohol. Forced into retirement after contracting Korsakoff's syndrome, he spent most of his remaining years in a nursing home near Urbana, where he died on 15 September 1991.

[*Many of the people mentioned in this article are the subjects of independent biographical entries.*]

Bibliography

Works by Osgood

Osgood, C. E. (1980). Charles E. Osgood. In G. Lindzey (Ed.), *A history of psychology in autobiography* (Vol. 7, pp. 335–393). San Francisco: Freeman.

Osgood, C. E., May, W. F., & Miron, M. S. (1975). *Cross-cultural universals of affective meaning.* Urbana: University of Illinois Press.

Osgood, C. E., & Miron, M. S. (Eds.). (1963). *Approaches to the Study of Aphasia.* Urbana: University of Illinois Press.

Osgood, C. E., & Tzeng, O. C. S. (Eds.). (1990). *Language, meaning, and culture: The selected papers of C. E. Osgood.* New York: Praeger. Contains a comprehensive bibliography of Osgood's works.

Works about Osgood

Brewer, W. F. (1994). Charles Egerton Osgood: 1916–1991. *American Journal of Psychology, 107*, 582–597.

Brown, R. W. (1958). Is a boulder sweet or sour? *Contemporary Psychology, 3*, 113–115.

Robert W. Rieber

OUTPATIENT TREATMENT. *See* Day Treatment.

P

PAIN. [*This entry comprises two articles. The lead article discusses the physiological mechanisms of pain. The companion article defines and explains both chronic and acute pain and the means by which psychologists assist patients in the management of their pain. See also* Endorphins *for a discussion of their relation to pain.*]

Mechanisms

The complexity of pain is suggested by its official definition according to the International Association for the Study of Pain: "An unpleasant sensory and emotional experience associated with actual or potential tissue damage, or described in terms of such damage." Pain is simultaneously a sensation and an emotion, caused by ongoing or recent tissue damage, the possibility of tissue damage, or even nervous system dysfunction in the absence of tissue damage. Although pain is a completely subjective experience that resists verbal description, all agree on its aversive nature. Pain is by far the leading reason people seek health care. It not only accounts for much suffering, but may also contribute to mortality by adversely affecting the immune system. Nonetheless, pain serves important adaptive functions including warning of impending injury, encouraging recuperation after injury, and signaling of danger to conspecifics. Persons born with congenital insensitivity to pain have greatly shortened life spans. Complicating our understanding of pain is the unreliable relationship of the external stimulus to the internal perception; depending on the circumstances, mild (even absent) noxious stimuli can produce excruciating pain and intensely noxious stimuli can be perceived as innocuous.

The fundamental nature of pain was a subject of much controversy in the early part of the twentieth century. One view held that no specific system existed to mediate pain; instead, pain resulted from the overstimulation of other senses. Indeed, blinding light and deafening noise are both perceived as painful, as, of course, are extremes of heat, cold, or pressure. Opposing this "pattern theory" of pain was the "specificity theory," which suggested that specific pain receptors in the body project to a pain center in the brain. It is now quite clear that specialized receptors for pain, called "nociceptors," exist: they are free nerve endings in the skin and visceral organs, and can be activated by intense thermal or mechanical stimuli, as well as a variety of chemicals released by damaged cells (e.g., protons, adenosine triphosphate, serotonin, bradykinin, prostaglandins). Activated nociceptors generate impulses that travel via small, myelinated and even smaller, unmyelinated axon fibers to the dorsal horn of the spinal cord, where they release excitatory amino acid transmitters (e.g., glutamate) and peptides (e.g., substance P, calcitonin gene-related peptide, somatostatin).

A synthesis of pattern theory and specificity theory arrived in the form of Melzack and Wall's "gate control theory," which, although now disproved in its details, remains critically important for its conceptual and heuristic value. The theory proposed that all afferent fibers in the skin—large "touch" fibers and small "pain" fibers alike—are activated by noxious stimuli, and converge on and excite pain "transmission" neurons in the dorsal horn of the spinal cord. These fibers also synapse on neurons in the substantia gelatinosa (SG), the outermost layer of the dorsal horn; large fibers excite SG neurons and small fibers inhibit them. When SG neurons are active, the theory proposed, they inhibit the transmission neurons, effectively closing the "gate" and preventing a pain message from being passed to higher brain centers, now known to include the thalamus, insula, sensory cortex, and anterior cingulate gyrus. Importantly, these higher brain centers can also exert descending control on the spinal gate, in effect permitting or blocking their own input. Thus, pain perception, according to gate control theory, is a function of the relative amount of activity in large and small fibers, and is significantly influenced by psychological factors via descending central control.

The reality of descending modulation of pain information was proven by the striking demonstration that electrical stimulation of certain brain areas (e.g., the midbrain periaqueductal gray and the brain stem rostroventral medulla) could cause profound pain inhibition, or analgesia. Further study revealed that stimulation-produced analgesia and analgesia produced by various extracts of the opium poppy (e.g., morphine) had neuroanatomical and neurochemical similarities. Soon afterward, the opiate receptors and endogenous opioids (e.g., endorphins) mediating both phenomena were discovered. [*See* Endorphins.] The adaptive significance of an endogenous analgesic mechanism was appreciated by the demonstration of its activation by exposure to environmental stressors. In addition to systems responding to danger by producing stress-induced analgesia, antianalgesic systems responding to safety cues have been found.

A peculiar property of pain concerns changes (i.e., plasticity) that occur following injury. Instead of showing adaptation, like most sensory receptors, nociceptors display sensitization, becoming more easily and more strongly activated. Parts of the body quite distant from the site of injury may also exhibit hyperalgesia (i.e., increased sensitivity to pain) and allodynia (i.e., pain from innocuous stimuli), suggesting central nervous system involvement. It is currently thought that by a process analogous to hippocampal long-term potentiation, spinal cord pain transmission neurons may "wind up" to become more sensitive to subsequent input. [*See* Long-Term Potentiation.] In addition, previously "silent" touch fibers may alter their properties and become sensitive to pain signals. In perhaps the most striking example of nervous system plasticity following injury, many amputees experience "phantom limb pain" localized to regions of space where an amputated limb would otherwise be. In this and many other examples of chronic "neuropathic" pain related to nerve injury, the pain becomes independent of any noxious stimulation or afferent input and resides entirely in the brain.

A fuller understanding of pain is complicated by the increasing realization of its multifaceted nature. Mechanisms underlying different types of pain—transient/prolonged, somatic/visceral/musculoskeletal, thermal/mechanical/inflammatory/neuropathic—have been dissociated anatomically, neurochemically, and genetically. Similar dissociations have been made between different components of pain: sensory-discriminative, motivational-affective, and cognitive-evaluative. Although severe pain can be controlled effectively mostly by opiate therapy, an increasing appreciation of basic pain mechanisms may lead to more effective, safe, and tolerable analgesic strategies.

Bibliography

Bonica, J. J. (Ed.). (1990). *The management of pain* (2nd ed.). Philadelphia: Lea & Febiger.

Chapman, C. R., & Loeser, J. D. (Eds.). (1990). *Issues in pain measurement*. New York: Raven Press.

Fields, H. L. (1987). *Pain*. New York: McGraw-Hill.

Kelly, D. D. (Ed.). (1986). Stress-induced analgesia. *Annals of the New York Academy of Sciences, 467*. The proceedings of a major conference on the topic.

Melzack, R., & Wall, P. D. (1965). Pain mechanisms: A new theory. *Science, 150*, 971–979. The original article on the gate control theory.

Merskey, H., & Bogduk, N. (Eds.). (1994). *Classification of chronic pain: Descriptions of chronic pain syndromes and definitions of pain terms* (2nd ed.). Seattle: IASP Press. The product of the International Association for the Study of Pain's Taskforce on Taxonomy.

Wall, P. D., & Melzack, R. (Eds.). (1999). *Textbook of pain* (4th ed.). Edinburgh: Livingstone.

Willis, W. D. (Ed.). (1992). *Hyperalgesia and allodynia*. New York: Raven Press.

Jeffrey Mogil

Models and Management

Pain is a common experience in human lives. Although unpleasant, pain may be functional, signaling that there is a problem requiring attention. Much of the pain experienced is of no significant consequence, remitting spontaneously or with analgesic medication. On the other hand, pain may be persistent, and despite various attempts to improve, it may continue to compromise the quality of life.

Pain is classified along a temporal dimension into acute (e.g., postsurgery), recurrent (e.g., migraine), and chronic (e.g., back pain). For many forms of chronic or recurrent pain, there is no demonstrative physical pathology that can explain the presence and extent of pain, and there seems no functional reason for such pain syndromes.

Although pain is generally considered a physical phenomenon, it involves various cognitive, affective, and behavioral factors. According to the International Association for the Study of Pain (*Classification of Chronic Pain*, Seattle, 1994, p. 210), pain is "an unpleasant sensory and emotional experience associated with actual or potential tissue damage, or described in terms of such damage." Thus, pain is a perceptual event that must be distinguished from the activation of sensory transduction in nerves—nociception. All pain has both neurophysiological and psychosocial components, although the weight of the psychosocial factors may be greater as pain becomes chronic.

Conceptualizations of Pain

The concept of pain has undergone multiple transformations. Dichotomous views of pain as either a somatic or a psychological event have been most prevalent. In the past quarter century, however, a shift in thinking has been ushered in by the gate control theory posed by Ronald Melzack and Patrick D. Wall (*Science*, 1965, 150, 3699–3709).

Sensory Model. Historically, pain was viewed as a sensory experience dependent on the extent of noxious sensory stimuli impinging on the individual. From this perspective, there are two ends of a pain pathway where sensory stimulation at the periphery has a direct stimulatory effect at the other end, located in the brain. The core of the sensory model is that the amount of pain is a direct result of and proportional to the degree of sensory input impinging on nerve fibers. The sensory model has remained largely unchanged despite its inability to account for a number of observations. For example, patients with equivalent degrees and types of tissue pathology vary widely in their reports of pain severity and their responses to identical treatment. Surgical procedures designed to cut or block the nerves that convey information about tissue damage may fail to alleviate pain. Moreover, even with advanced technology, in many instances no physical basis for pain can be identified; conversely, many asymptomatic people may reveal significant pathology but report no pain.

Psychogenic Perspectives. When physical explanations prove to be inadequate to explain symptoms, psychological alternatives have been promoted. If the pain reported is disproportionate to the objectively determined physical pathology or if the complaint is recalcitrant to "appropriate" treatment, then pain is often assumed to be psychological in origin. Thus, dichotomous reasoning is invoked: when the report of pain occurs in the absence of or is "disproportionate" to objective physical pathology, *ipso facto*, the pain must be caused by personality factors or psychopathology. There are minimal data supporting the psychogenic perspective.

Motivational View. A variation of the dichotomous somatic-psychogenic perspective is the motivational model that assumes that, in the absence of objective pathology, the complaint of pain results from symptom exaggeration or malingering. This perspective further assumes that pain complaints are motivated by financial gain. There are, however, no data demonstrating a decrease in pain subsequent to receiving disability compensation.

Although psychological factors undoubtedly play an important role in pain perception and response, the above models view physical and psychological factors as largely independent. Before considering models that attempt to integrate psychological factors with somatic factors, it is useful to examine the nature of the psychological factors involved in detail.

Psychological Contributors to Pain

Psychologists have made important contributions to understanding pain by demonstrating the importance of psychosocial and behavioral factors in the etiology, severity, exacerbation, and maintenance of pain. Several effective treatments have been developed based on these factors.

Learning Mechanisms. People express pain in various ways (e.g., verbal complaints, motor behaviors, and help-seeking behaviors—"pain behaviors"). Such behaviors may be functional in the acute stage of pain. However, people may also acquire maladaptive behaviors through learning. Avoidance responses may result from the associative learning. Subsequently, through reinforcement, people may learn to exhibit the same behaviors in the absence of nociception. For example, many patients with chronic pain avoid physical activities and rely heavily on medications despite the absence of tissue pathology that can account for such behaviors. Such overt pain behaviors in the absence of pathology are considered maladaptive and central in the maintenance of chronic pain (Wilbert Fordyce, *Behavioral Methods for Chronic Pain and Illness*, St. Louis, 1976).

From the operant perspective, chronic pain is conceptualized as a set of behaviors that are observable, communicate about suffering, and are capable of eliciting a response from observers. Thus, the overt behaviors become the primary target of treatment because pain, per se, is not observable.

Social Learning Mechanisms. The social learning perspective proposes that acquisition of pain behaviors may result from observational learning. People can acquire responses that were not previously in their behavioral repertoire by observing these behaviors in others. In particular, people learn about symptoms and appropriate responses vicariously from their environments. Expectancies and behavioral responses to nociception are based on prior learning history. This may contribute to the marked variability observed in response to objectively similar degrees of physical pathology.

Cognitive Factors. Patients' cognitive processes have been demonstrated to influence the perception of and adaptation to nociception. Attentional factors are important in pain experience since pain is a conscious experience, and when attention is allocated to sensory processing, increased pain perception is reported. In addition, variable responses to experimentally induced pain are commonly observed when subjects' expectations are manipulated. Beliefs about pain interact with attention to and appraisal of sensory events. Thus, people who expect a noxious experience may devote greater attention and interpret sensory experience as more aversive than those who do not. Maladaptive thoughts also contribute to distress and exacerbate the perception of pain. Moreover, if people believe that their pain is uncontrollable, feelings of pessimism, helplessness, and hopelessness may escalate. On the other hand, if individuals believe that they are able to use coping skills effectively (self-efficacy beliefs), their tolerance of aversive situations will increase. These thoughts have a reciprocal influence on physiological, emotional, and behavioral aspects of pain.

Gate Control Model. Melzack and Wall were the first to integrate physical and psychological factors in pain perception, incorporating three dimensions: sensory-discriminative, motivational-affective, and cognitive-evaluative. The gate control theory proposes that a mechanism in the spinal cord acts as a "gatekeeper" that controls nociception. The gating mechanisms are considered to be supported by the inhibitory activity of large-diameter nerve fibers and the facilitating activity of small-diameter nerve fibers in the spinal cord. Additionally, the model postulates that the cortical variables, such as anxiety, memory, and attention, interact with the spinal gating system to determine the final product: pain perception.

Diathesis-Stress Model. The diathesis (predisposition)-stress model postulates that there are interactions among predisposing factors (e.g., low sensory threshold), aversive events (e.g., injury), and learning. Maladaptive physiological responses (e.g., muscle tension) may be learned by predisposed individuals who encounter an aversive event. Both associative and operant learning can facilitate the maintenance of pain and functional limitations. A series of psychophysiological studies have demonstrated the site-specific hyperreactivity of muscle tension in patients with chronic pain when facing psychologically challenging situations, suggesting that chronic pain may be explained by the interaction of a predisposition to selective muscle tension and a psychological stressor.

Cognitive-Behavioral Model. The cognitive-behavioral model postulates that individuals' subjective interpretations of their physical conditions and coping resources interact reciprocally with physiological, emotional, and behavioral aspects of pain. Patients' beliefs, appraisals, and expectations are postulated to have an effect on behavior leading to energy expenditure, perseverance, and avoidance, contributing to increased emotional distress and disability.

Assessment of Pain

There is no "pain thermometer" to objectify the experience of pain. The person is the primary source of information. The complexity of the multifactorial nature of pain requires the psychological evaluation of pain to involve the many areas of pain: sensory perceptive, affective, cognitive, and behavioral, as well as physical. Numerous self-report inventories and observational methods have been developed specifically for the assessment of pain (see Dennis Turk and Ronald Melzack, *Handbook of Pain Assessment*, New York, 1992). Additionally, various measures that were developed to assess other areas that are also relevant to pain (e.g., depression, anxiety) have been used. The interpretation of these results, however, must be cautious if the instruments are not validated in the pain populations. For example, scores on depression measures may be inflated in people with chronic pain due to common neurovegetative symptoms associated with both disorders.

For patients with chronic pain, psychological interviews are often conducted to determine the psychological factors contributing to pain and disability and to identify any behavior or affective disorders associated with the condition. Establishing the psychosocial history is helpful in determining relevant psychological factors that should be considered when planning treatment. Affective disorders, anxiety, and substance abuse are the problems most commonly observed. Since these conditions are not only problems themselves but also reduce the effectiveness of rehabilitation, treating the associated psychological disorders by integrating psychological and physical interventions is essential.

Treatment of Pain

Most acute pain resolves successfully over time with avoidance of activity or with analgesic medication. Treatment of chronic pain is more complicated since these patients have a substantially compromised quality of life, functional limitations, and psychological distress associated with multiple treatment failures. Pharmacological and surgical interventions seem to have only limited efficacy in patients with chronic pain. Operant-based treatments have been demonstrated to be successful in reducing overt pain behaviors in a subset of patients, although pain may persist. The most successful treatments have been those that incorporate psychological factors and methods with behavioral and physical ones.

A wide range of psychological interventions have been used successfully in treatment to help people deal with or control their pain. Biofeedback and relaxation have been used alone and in conjunction with other cognitive techniques to treat chronic headaches and facial pain. In a number of clinical reports, hypnosis has been used successfully with acute pain, pain associated with burns, and with patients with metastatic disease. Cognitive and behavioral coping skills, along with problem-solving, communication skills, and psychotherapeutic approaches, have been combined with physical modalities in the treatment of chronic pain syndromes. The application of these psychological interventions has been successfully modified for use with pain sufferers across the age span.

In addition to their physical benefits, all of the psychological modalities contribute to improvement of self-efficacy beliefs by providing patients with the opportunity to evaluate themselves positively. Patients are encouraged to become active pain managers rather than passive patients who believe that their pain can be "cured" only by physical intervention.

In summary, pain is not just a sensory event to which people react. Rather, it is a complex, multifactorial, perceptual phenomenon—a unique subjective experience that may be modulated by individuals' attitudes, beliefs, expectations, emotional state, and environmental responses. Regardless of the source, nature, or duration of pain, psychological factors influence the person's experience. As pain becomes chronic, the weight of psychological factors becomes greater because of the increasingly complex interaction among the cognitive, behavioral, affective, and physiological aspects of pain. Various behavioral and cognitive techniques can be incorporated in the treatment of chronic pain, with the purpose of modifying maladaptive thinking, increasing self-efficacy, and acquiring skills to manage pain and reduce disability.

Bibliography

Fields, J. L. (Ed.). (1989). *Core curriculum for professional education in pain.* Seattle: IASP Press. Provides an outline of the range of areas that should be familiar to all health-care professionals who evaluate and treat people with diverse pain states.

Flor, H., Birbaumer, N., & Turk, D. C. (1990). The psychobiology of chronic pain. *Advances in Behavior Research and Therapy, 12,* 47–84. Presents the basis for the diathesis-stress model of chronic pain based on biopsychosocial integration.

Gatchel, R. J., & Turk, D. C. (Eds.). (1996). *Psychological approaches to pain management: A practitioner's handbook.* New York: Guilford Press. Provides a detailed description of the most commonly used, psychologically based treatments for chronic pain with diverse populations across the life span.

Melzack, R., & Wall, P. D. (1983). *The challenge of pain.* New York: Basic Books. Provides a review of the history of pain and describes the details of the gate control theory.

Merskey, H., & Bogduk, N. (Eds.). (1994). *Classification of chronic pain. Descriptions of chronic pain syndromes and definitions of pain terms* (2nd ed.). Seattle: IASP Press. Defines all terminology associated with pain and provides a classification system for diagnosing all chronic pain states.

Dennis C. Turk and Akiko Okifuji

PAKISTAN. The end of British rule in India led to the independence of Pakistan in August 1947. The present geographical boundaries of the country date from December 1971, when East Pakistan became the independent state of Bangladesh. At the time of independence only two colleges taught psychology: the Government College, Lahore, where psychology, as was common practice until the 1960s, was taught as part of the philosophy syllabus, and Forman Christian College, Lahore. The first independent psychology department was founded at Karachi University with Qazi Muhammad Aslam, whose academic background was in philosophy, as chair. Psychology achieved independent status at the Government College, Lahore (University of the Punjab) in 1962, with Dr. Muhammad Ajmal as its first chair. The psychology department at the University of Sindh became independent in 1960, with Dr. Rafia Hasan as chair. Syed Muhammad Hafeez Zaidi observed in *Frontiers of Psychological Research in Pakistan* (Karachi, Pakistan, 1975) that the tradition was for philosophy teachers to become psychologists. This resulted in the adoption of traditional indigenous psychology that was also oriented toward philosophy. Hafeez Zaidi wrote two articles on the early days of Pakistani psychology (*American Psychologist,* 1959, *14,* 532–536; *Psychologia,* 1958, *1,* 187–190). Today, Pakistan has five major departments of psychology, two in Lahore (Punjab), two in Sindh (Karachi, Jamshoro), and one in Peshawar (NWFP). The former three departments offer master's of arts/science degrees, while the latter two departments also offer a 3-year bachelor of arts/science (Honors) program. All departments and institutes offer master's of philosophy or doctoral degree programs. There are also two institutes, the Muhammad Ajmal National Institute of Psychology (Islamabad) and the Institute of Clinical Psychology (Karachi). A total of 25 doctoral degrees have been given by these psychology departments and institutes.

Founders of Scientific Psychology

Syed Muhammad Hafeez Zaidi (1926–1986) was educated at the Muslim University of Aligarh (India) and received a doctoral degree from the University of London under the supervision of R. W. Russell. He began his career as a lecturer at Dacca University, and then worked as a social psychologist for several years at the Pakistan Academy for Village Development, East Pakistan. He moved to Karachi University where he made a major contribution to social and cross-cultural psychology through his original research and theoretical writings on Pakistan psychology. He was an editor of the first professional psychology journal in the country (*Pakistan Journal of Psychology*, abstracted in *Psychological Abstracts*) which was first published in June 1965. He made several visits to the United States as a visiting professor. Dr. Zaidi's continuing research interests and publications were in the area of social change. The basic assumption for studies of social change in developing countries is that the society is in transition and therefore under stress. His interest in erratic behavior resulting from stress began with his doctoral work on reactions to stress (*Genetic Psychology Monographs*, 1960, 62, 41–104). Much of his work on the impact of socioeconomic changes on rural sociocultural institutions in Pakistan up to 1968 has been incorporated in *Village Culture in Transition* (Honolulu, 1970). The book also explores the dynamics of change and conflict in East Pakistan (now Bangladesh). In another study on sociocultural change and value conflict (In Caudill & Lin, Eds., Honolulu, Hawaii, 1969), Zaidi analyzed Pakistani sociocultural conflicts in greater detail. The increasing influx of rural people to the towns and cities is a major source of disorganization of traditional behavior patterns. The enormous impact of rural migration to the cities of the Third World continues to create huge problems for both the cities they migrate to and the villages they leave behind. Zaidi has argued that for quite some time the migrant retains a village style of life and belief, thus remaining a "peasant in the city." Zaidi coauthored a cross-cultural study in the early 1970s with L. Sechrest and T. L. Fay as senior authors (*Journal of Cross-Cultural Psychology*, 1972, 3, 41–56). Zaidi contributed a chapter to *Cross-Cultural Perspectives on Learning* (R. W. Brislin, S. Bochner, & W. J. Lonner, Eds., New York, 1975) on the social and psychological adjustment of foreign Asian and African students in Pakistan.

Muhammad Ajmal (1920–1994) earned a doctoral degree from London University, and taught psychology as well as philosophy at the Government College, Lahore. Although trained in the Western intellectual tradition and a great proponent of Jung's analytical psychology, Ajmal laid the foundations of an indigenous psychotherapy. He developed a Sufi doctrine (divinely inspired humanism), as an indigenous approach to healing along scientific lines (*Muslim Contributions to Psychotherapy and Other Essays*, Islamabad, 1986). The Sufic psychotherapy inspired his students and gave rise to a subdiscipline of Muslim psychology at the Government College, Lahore. One of his students, Syed Azhar Ali Rizvi, took a leading role in the establishment of the Institute of Muslim Psychology, Lahore.

Shahabuddin Muhammad Moghni (1925–1990) earned a master's degree from Muslim University, Aligarh, and a doctoral degree in experimental psychology from London University under the supervision of R. W. Russell. He was the founding chair of the psychology department, University of Peshawer, which was established in 1964. He developed a well-equipped experimental laboratory there, and under his dynamic leadership the first 2-week seminar of senior psychologists from throughout Pakistan took place in October 1966 at Peshawar University to discuss academic and professional issues. The Pakistan Psychological Association was established at the meeting. The Peshawar psychology department published a research journal, *Pakistan Psychological Studies* beginning in 1969, with Dr. Moghni as editor. A doctoral degree program was established between 1973 and 1974. Under his leadership a number of doctoral degrees were awarded, and those psychologists are now faculty members. Dr. Moghni's original research involved studying motives. He developed attitude scales to differentiate the respondents on the strength of their achievement-oriented, power-oriented, and affiliation-oriented attitudes. In March 1968, the first Pakistan Psychological Association conference was held in Dacca, East Pakistan, where Dr. Moghni gave his presidential address on the role of achievement motivation in national development. During 1980 and 1981 he worked with David McClelland at Harvard University as a postdoctoral fellow. The second area of Moghni's research interest involved the development of objective-type tests for secondary school examinations. Most of his studies were published in *Pakistan Psychological Studies*. Later, Moghni became interested in the scientific study of the development of *millat*, Muslim nationalism, not only as it affected Pakistani Muslims, but Muslims in general. This was a move toward establishing an indigenous psychology in Pakistan.

Important Figures in Psychology

Farrukh Z. Ahmad, who earned his doctoral degree at Stanford University, joined the University of Karachi in 1962 as a lecturer. She was the founder-director of the Institute of Clinical Psychology, where post master's diploma/master's in philosophy/doctoral degree programs were established. Ahmad's long experience of teaching and practice in clinical psychology has led to two books (*Dependency in Psychotherapy*, University of Karachi, 1988; *Mental Health and Patterns of Child Rearing*, University of Karachi, 1993). Dr. Ahmad became editor of the *Pakistan Journal of Psychology* after Professor Zaidi moved to Nigeria, and in 1990 became a founding editor of *Pakistan Journal of Clinical Psychology*, remaining a regular contributor to both journals.

Nazre Khalique (University of Karachi) has a doctoral degree from Patna University, India. His work has centered around research on bureaucratic values, developed by Leonard Gordon (*Work Environment Preference Schedule*, Albany, NY, 1968). Khalique determined the validity of bureaucratic orientation measures at both adult and elementary-secondary school levels. His other work examines the relationship between bureaucratic norms and dehumanizing attitudes toward people of lower status. He has also worked on the concept of social facilitation. An important work on bureaucratic orientation made a cross-cultural comparison of Pakistani students with their American and Japanese counterparts (*Psychologia*, 1974, *17*, 71–74). His other contributions to important international journals include a longitudinal study of conflicting communications conducted with students of varying ages (Khalique & Haque, 1979).

Afzal Imam of the University of Karachi has a doctoral degree from the University of Wales. He suggests that neutral techniques of data collection are highly suitable for application in developing countries because they do not require expensive equipment. Imam has conducted several naturalistic studies on helping behavior (*Pakistan Journal of Psychology*). He has also researched field dependence measured by the Rod and Frame test, and carried out studies on incidental learning.

Abdul Haque (master's degree from Patna University, India), trained in cross-cultural psychology at the East-West Culture Learning Institute, Honolulu, has been a visiting professor at the psychology department, University of Sindh at Jamshoro. His research interest in the India-Pakistan conflict began with the September 1965 war between the two countries. The origins of the conflict lay in the history of Hindu-Muslim relations over many decades. There have been three wars with India since the creation of Pakistan. More recently, both India and Pakistan have demonstrated their nuclear capabilities. The conflict has deep psychocultural and historical roots. The mutual negative stereotyping (mirror image of the enemy) was investigated using the Katz–Braly technique, based on studies conducted in India and Pakistan, and was demonstrated by the present author (*Pakistan Journal of Psychology*, 1973, *6*, 13–22). The 1965 war study was first reported by the author as a cross-cultural note (*Journal of Social Psychology*, 1968, *74*, 285–286). Several war studies have been reported in the *Pakistan Journal of Psychology*. A discussion of the persistence of stereotyping during the 1971 war was also published in the same journal (1971, *4*, 31–41). Indian aggression toward East Pakistan in 1971 caused the breakup of Pakistan, and consequently conflict between the two countries has intensified. The Salal Accord in 1976 was the first major treaty between the two neighboring states when agreements on civil aviation, communications, resumption of diplomatic relations, and trade were made. In 1978, several cricket and hockey matches were played, with much public enthusiasm on both sides, between Pakistan and India. During the same year political leaders' visits and cultural exchanges took place. These cooperative efforts motivated the present author to measure expected future cooperation and conflict levels between Pakistan and India as measured by compassion-compulsion levels (Haque, 1979).

During the 1973 Arab-Israeli war Haque and Lawson (1980) studied (1) mirror-image concepts of Arabs and Israelis, and (2) whether the mirror-image concept could be broadened to include images in reciprocal stereotyping of the two groups during the war to include stereotyping of the allies on each side. The demonstration of the mirror-image phenomenon beyond the immediate enemy has been cited in Fisher (*Social Psychology: An Applied Approach*, New York, 1982). On 11 July 1979, the American Skylab satellite fell to earth in western Australia. For several days before its fall, those parts of the earth on its route were tense and apprehensive. Pakistan radio and television had reported that the Skylab might fall somewhere in the region. When emotional tension was at its height, data were collected from male and female Sindh University students. They completed semantic differential scales and were also asked to comment on the situation (Haque & Zaidi, *Political Psychology*, 1981–1982, *3*).

As a cooperating researcher in a 30-country project cited by Best and Williams (*Handbook of Cross-Cultural Psychology*, Boston, 1997), the present author published a paper on sex stereotypes and development of sex-trait stereotypes based on data collected from Muslim young adults and children (Rath, Asthana, Sinha, & Sinha, Eds., *Diversity and Unity in Cross-Cultural Psychology*, Amsterdam, 1982). The author argued that Pakistani girls and boys are trained early in life, via Muslim cultural traditions, for sex-differentiated roles. In a paper on "The Importance of Psychological Characteristics: A Seven-Country Study," Pakistan participated as a junior partner. The paper was published in the *International Journal of Psychology* (1995, *30*, 529–550). In that study, Pakistan's results showed that trait importance and favorability were closely related (i.e., good traits are important but not bad traits).

Other important researchers include Mah Nazir Riaz, chair of the department of psychology at the University of Peshawar, who has a doctoral degree from that university. Her major areas of research have been in creativity and child rearing, most of her papers appearing in *Pakistan Journal of Psychological Research* and *Psychological Studies*. The Urdu version of Child PARQ and Child PAQ were used in child rearing research. Alay Ahmad has a doctoral degree from the University of Peshawar. His specialty is mass media. His doctoral work was on the effects of television viewing on Pakistani children's reading of printed pages activity levels and it was published in Japan (1980). Other contributions by Alay Ahmad were published in *Psychological Studies* and *Pakistan Journal of Psychology*.

Najama Najm has a doctorate from an American university and is chair of the department of applied psychology at the University of the Panjab. Najm's main interests are in clinical psychology and social variables. Najm is an editor of the *Pakistan Journal of Behavioral Sciences* which was founded in 1990. Ruhi Khalid has a doctorate from a British university and has published papers on social identity and intergroup behavior in the *Pakistan Journal of Behavioral Sciences*. Azhar Ali Rizvi, founder-director of the Institute of Muslim Psychology, formerly chair of the psychology department, Lahore (University of the Punjab), is an editor of *Zehan* (Mind), the Urdu journal of Muslim psychology. Rizvi's book, *Muslim Traditions in Psychotherapy and Modern Trends* (Lahore, 1994) results from intensive research on Sufi scholars of the Indo-Pakistan subcontinent (particularly the works of Maulana Ashraf Ali Thanvi and Shah Waliullah) which have bearing on mental health. According to Rizvi, the concept of abnormality is synonymous with the distance one maintains from the creator, and therapy is geared to reduce the distance through cognitive understanding and strengthening faith in God.

The Muhammad Ajmal National Institute of Psychology

Established in 1976, the National Institute of Psychology was given the status of a Center of Excellence in Psychology, and eventually moved to Quaid-e-Azam University, Islamabad. Since 1984 it has offered M.Phil./Ph.D. degree programs. The institute regularly presents national seminars and workshops. Before it founded a M.Sc. degree program, the institute was much involved in psychological research on educational programs, adaptation and development of foreign tests for use in Pakistan, and social-psychological research, including crime and deviant behavior. The institute publishes monographs, books, and tests along with a biannual journal, *Pakistan Journal of Psychological Research* (PJPR), which was founded in 1986 under the editorship of Z. A. Ansari. The journal has an international board of consulting editors. The institute also publishes a quarterly *NIP Newsletter*. The institute library is quite rich, with hundreds of reference works and back issues of journals. Z. A. Ansari was the major force behind the overall development of the institute before moving to the International Islamic University of Malaysia in the early 1990s. One of the most prominent names associated with the institute is that of Dr. Ansari, whose main research interests have been in educational problems and the development and validation of educational tests. He has published in national and international journals. Ashiq Ali Shah, who has a doctorate from Berlin University has focused on social psychology. Before joining the International Islamic University of Malaysia, he published a number of articles on aspects of social psychology in the *Pakistan Journal of Psychological Research* and international journals. A number of doctoral candidates completed their doctorates under his guidance, including a dissertation on the development of an indigenous Salma-Shah Depression scale in 1990.

Naeem Tariq has a doctorate from the National Institute of Psychology. He is an editor of the *Pakistan Journal of Psychological Research*, where he has published a number of articles on crime and other deviant behavior. Drs. Seema Pervez and Ghazala Rehman have focused on child development and Rorschach technique, respectively. Dr. Ghazala has developed an indigenous measure of religiosity and has also developed a cultural adaptation of the Pickford Projective Pictures.

Psychology Journals in Pakistan

There are three journals today: the *Pakistan Journal of Psychological Research* (PJPR), the *Pakistan Journal of Psychology* (PJP), and the *Journal of Behavioral Sciences* (JBS). Both *Pakistan Psychological Studies* and *Psychology Quarterly* have ceased publication. In 1982, Z. A. Ansari analyzed a sample of the articles published in Pakistan journals between 1965 and 1980. He found that 50% were of purely theoretical nature, 7% were case studies, while 43% were empirical. The present author generated seven broad areas of research articles published in three Pakistan journals between 1986 and 1996 (see Table 1). As can be seen from the table, the trend has changed from a preference for theoretical articles. Clinical studies are now at the top of the list and social-psychological research occupies second place. Psychological testing and industrial-organizational studies have middle positions, and cross-cultural research occupies the lowest position. Between 1986 and 1996 there was major emphasis on clinical research, particularly in the *Pakistan Journal of Psychology*.

Indigenization of Psychology in Pakistan

Hafeez Zaidi (1979), in his paper on cross-cultural psychology, was the first Pakistani psychologist to make critical comments on Western ethnocentrism, particularly the views expressed by L. W. Doob in the early 1960s and Inkeles in the late 1970s. This response on the part of Zaidi and other cross-cultural psychologists gave rise to the subdiscipline of indigenous or cultural psychology within the discipline of cross-cultural psychology.

There are two broad categories of indigenous psy-

PAKISTAN. Table 1. Areas of research in Pakistani professional journals (1986–1996)

	PJPR (1986–1996)	PJP (1986–1996)	JBS (1990–1996)	Total	%
Clinical	13	26	08	47	27.33
Cross-cultural	04	02	00	06	03.49
Developmental	05	00	06	11	06.40
Educational	07	01	03	11	06.40
Industrial/organization	16	05	04	25	14.53
Social	21	08	14	43	25.00
Testing	22	03	04	29	16.86
Total	88	45	39	172	100.0

chology: (1) indigenous psychology (i.e., developing a psychology consistent with cultural traditions), and (2) indigenization (i.e., the transformation of imported elements of modern psychology to make them relevant to the particular sociocultural setting (D. Sinha, *Handbook of Cross-Cultural Psychology*, Vol. 1, Boston, 1997). Sinha lists four types of indigenization from the available literature, and here we will discuss two types: (1) substantive indigenization, which refers to making psychology problem oriented; (2) indigenization of methods relating to the process of transforming an instrument to make it appropriate for the target population.

In the framework outlined by D. Sinha (1997), the work of Ajmal (1969, 1986) and Rizvi (1994) belong in the category of indigenous psychology. Ajmal introduced Sufi doctrine (spiritual healing) and mental health practices consistent with Muslim cultural traditions. In his 1986 book Ajmal highlights the role the traditional *sufi* (mentor) had played in promoting mental health for the *saliks* (seekers of God). (See Sinha, 1997; Zaman, 1991.) Rizvi's (1980) work on Ashraf Ali Thanvi, a Sufi scholar of the Indo-Pakistan subcontinent on reading therapy, and on healthy and unhealthy personality (Rizvi, 1994) is important.

There was a call for Islamization of knowledge after Al-Faruqi (1921–1986) argued (1982) that social science disciplines are "at once humanistic and *ummatic* (i.e., the social nature of human activities) in character." He urged Muslim social scientists to analyze and solve human problems by following the Qur'an and teachings of the Prophet Muhammad. Dr. Moghni's work on national development and economic transformation is indigenization in the field of social psychology. It should be noted that while the works of Pakistani psychologists may legitimately appear under the heading of indigenous psychology, there has been little theoretical work in this area.

Zaidi, a leading social psychologist, has emphasized the need for social-psychological research in Pakistan. Although trained in experimental research, he has utilized his knowledge of psychology to make it socially relevant. Earlier, the three India-Pakistan armed conflicts since independence in 1947 were mentioned (Haque, 1979). The doctrine of *low intensity conflict* (a term borrowed from political science), and more recently, nuclear deterrence, has maintained an uneasy peace in the region. But to truly get beyond the state of conflict, both India and Pakistan need to recognize the importance of mutual security rather than national security alone. A healthier preoccupation for these states would be an emphasis on better education, better care for children, elimination of poverty and corruption, etc. It should be noted that in the West there is little questioning of the role of psychology in national development, while in Pakistan we are still at the stage of seeking recognition for psychology as a scientific discipline, presenting our case to planners and policy makers.

Ansari (1986), in an introductory editorial to the *Pakistan Journal of Psychological Research*, viewed the application of psychological knowledge to solve social problems as meaningful and relevant. Since then the journal has published empirical research in educational and social psychology, and research also related to psychological testing. Much work has been done on the adaptation of various tests originally published in the West, their translation into Urdu, the national language of Pakistan, in order to make them culturally relevant. The *Pakistan Journal of Psychological Research* has been particularly active in this area, publishing material on development of a questionnaire for assessing schoolchildren's study problems; a cognitive development task battery for elementary schoolchildren; translation and adaptation of vocational interest inventory; and a boredom proneness scale. The Anjum-Khalique Type-A scale was published in the *Journal of Behavioral Sciences* in 1992. Earlier, a version of MMPI adapted for use with schizophrenics was published in the *Pakistan Journal of Psychology*. It should be noted, however, that these tests, although they were developed to be appropriate to Pakistani culture, were based on tests that were originally developed in the West.

[*See also* India.]

Bibliography

Ajmal, M. (1969). Muslim traditions in psychotherapy. *Pakistan Psychological Studies, 1*, 57–68.

Ajmal, M. (1986). *Muslim contributions to psychotherapy and other essays.* Islamabad: National Institute of Psychology, Centre of Excellence.

Ansari, Z. A. (Ed.). (1986). Editorial. *Pakistan Journal of Psychological Research, 1*, 1–2.

Ansari, Z. A. (1992). *Quranic concepts of human psyche.* Islamabad: International Institute of Islamic Thought and Institute of Islamic Culture.

Haque, A. (1979). Cooperation and conflict between Pakistan and India as related to compassion-compulsion attitudes. *Peace Research, 11*, 133–140.

Haque, A., & Lawson, E. (1980). Mirror image hypothesis in the context of Arab-Israeli conflict. *International Journal of Intercultural Relations, 4*, 107–112.

Khalique, N., & Haque, M. (1979). Conflicting communications: A longitudinal study. *International Journal of Behavioral Development, 2*, 207–209.

Rizvi, A. A. (1980). Reading therapy of Ashraf Ali Thanvi. *Psychology Quarterly, 14*, 33–39.

Rizvi, A. A. (1994). *Muslim traditions in psychotherapy and modern trends.* Lahore: Institute of Islamic Culture.

Sinha, D. (1997). Indigenizing psychology. In J. W. Berry, Y. H. Poortinga, & J. Pandey (Eds.), *Handbook of cross-cultural psychology: Vol. 1. Theory and method* (pp. 131–169). Boston; Allyn & Bacon.

Thanvi A. A. (1971). *Tarbiat-ul-salik.* Lahore: Jamia Ashrafia.

Zaidi. S. M. H. (1979). Applied cross-cultural psychology: Submissions of a cross-cultural psychologist from the third world. In L. H. Eckenberger, W. Lonner, & Y. H. Poortinga (Eds.), *Cross-cultural contributions to psychology* (pp. 236–243). Amsterdam: Swets & Zeitlinger.

Zaman, R. M. (1991). Clinical psychology in Pakistan. *Psychology and Developing Societies, 3*, 221–233.

Abdul Haque

PAN, SHU (1897–1988), Chinese psychologist. Shu Pan was born 13 July 1897 in Yixing in Jiangsu Province, China, and died 26 March 1988 in Beijing. Shu Pan graduated from the department of philosophy of Beijing University in 1920, went to the United States in 1921, and was awarded a master's degree from Indiana University in 1923 and a doctoral degree from the University of Chicago in 1926. In 1927 he returned to China, where he was appointed professor and head of the Department of Psychology of Central University in Nanjing. After the founding of the People's Republic of China in 1949, Pan became president of Nanjing University. In 1956 Pan moved to Beijing to take the position of director of the Institute of Psychology of the Chinese Academy of Sciences. This position lasted from 1956 to 1983, when he became honorary director of the Institute of Psychology of the Chinese Academy of Sciences. He became a member of the Chinese Academy of Sciences in 1955. From 1955 to 1984 Pan served as president of the Chinese Psychological Society. During his long term of office, the Cultural Revolution took place between 1966 and 1976; during this time, psychology was denounced and the Society ceased to function.

In the early years of his academic career, Shu Pan did research in experimental psychology. He studied the perception of Chinese characters in the United States. His other research involved learning, memory, and aesthetic judgment. He also wrote papers on the study of consciousness. During the 1950s and 1960s he published papers on the subject matter, task, and methods of psychology. He maintained that psychology is a science midway between natural science and social science and possesses the attributes of both. Gradually shifting his interests to methodological issues in psychology, Pan discussed the relation between the mind and higher nervous activity, proposing that the body is the principal bearer of the mind and the mind is the action of the body (i.e., materialistic monism of the mind-body relationship). He divided psychological processes into cognitive activity and volitional activity to replace the traditional classification of mental activities into cognition, feeling, and the will.

Devoting his life to the development of Chinese psychology, Shu Pan published 10 books and approximately 120 papers. Even during the most trying years of the Cultural Revolution, when psychology was denounced as a pseudoscience and most psychologists were sent to labor on farms and in factories, Pan, himself under persecution, continued to write on psychological theory. After the Cultural Revolution these writings were published as a book entitled *Notes on Psychology* (1984).

In his late years, Shu Pan tried to establish a psychological system based on Marxist philosophy. He stressed the importance of basic methodological research in psychology and stated that the establishment of a correct basic theory in psychology may guide the course of research that directs the development of psychology. He pointed out that Chinese psychology should not consist merely of copying Western psychology. Psychology should serve China's socialist construction and contribute to the progress of society. Shu Pan believed that Chinese psychologists should strive to build a psychology with Chinese characteristics.

Bibliography

Pan, S. (1930). *Foundation of social psychology*. Shanghai: World Book Press.

Pan, S. (Ed.). (1980). *Educational psychology*. Beijing: People's Educational Press.

Pan, S. (Ed.). (1984). *Notes on psychology*. Beijing: People's Educational Press.

Pan, S., & Gao, J. (Eds.). (1983). *Research on ancient Chinese psychological thought*. Nanchang: Jiangxi People's Publishers.

Pan, S., & Jing, Q. (Eds.). (1991). *Chinese encyclopedia: Psychology*. Beijing: Chinese Encyclopedia Publishers.

Qicheng Jing

PANIC DISORDER is an anxiety disorder characterized by recurrent panic attacks, or discrete episodes of abrupt and intense fear or discomfort. Panic attacks are distinct from gradually building anxiety and are defined by a cluster of physical and cognitive symptoms (see Table 1). Autonomic nervous system activation, including accelerated heart rate, rapid or irregular breathing, and increased blood pressure is common during panic attacks. Although panic attacks occur in all anxiety disorders, panic disorder is distinguished by unexpected attacks that seem to occur "from out of the blue." More situationally triggered attacks may be present as well. Furthermore, panic disorder entails at least one month of persistent apprehension about the recurrence of panic or its consequences, or a significant behavioral change. In summary, panic disorder is characterized by unexpected panic attacks and anxiety about future attacks.

Panic disorder is sometimes accompanied by agoraphobia, or avoidance or endurance with dread of situations from which escape might be difficult or where help is unavailable in the event of a panic attack or panic-like symptoms, such as the loss of bowel control. Typical agoraphobic situations include shopping malls, waiting in lines, movie theaters, traveling by car or bus, crowded restaurants and stores, being far from home, and being alone.

Some theorists propose that agoraphobic fears are secondary to panic. In support of this, persons with agoraphobia who seek treatment almost always report a history of panic that preceded their agoraphobia. Others suggest they are co-occurring but distinct disorders. In support of their positions, epidemiological studies of the general population find higher prevalence rates for agoraphobia without a history of panic disorder than for panic disorder (Kessler et al., 1994). Possible reasons for this disparity between population-based and clinic samples include the misdiagnosis of agoraphobia due to the reliance on non-face-to-face interviews by lay interviewers in epidemiological studies. Also, individuals who panic may be more likely to seek help.

Agoraphobia ranges from mild fear of one or two situations to being severely housebound. It tends to increase as the history of panic lengthens; however, a significant proportion of people panic for many years without developing agoraphobic limitations. Nor is agoraphobia reliably related to the age of panic onset, frequency of panic, or the severity of panic attack symptoms. Those with agoraphobia may be more concerned with being judged negatively by others, but the strongest predictor is gender. Females increasingly predominate as the degree of agoraphobia worsens (e.g., Thyer, Himle, Curtis, Cameron, & Nesse, 1985).

Rarely does panic disorder occur in isolation. Commonly co-occurring conditions include specific phobias, social phobia, dysthymia (Sanderson, DiNardo, Rapee, & Barlow, 1990), and generalized anxiety disorder, major depressive disorder, and substance abuse (Goisman et al., 1994). Also, a large percentage are judged to have personality disorders, although these data tend to be unreliable.

Mean age of onset ranges from 23 to 29, although panic occurs in children and adolescents as well. Panic disorder, particularly when accompanied by agoraphobia, tends to be chronic. For example, the probability of achieving an 8-week remission over the course of one year is .42 for panic attacks and .15 for panic and agoraphobia (Goisman et al., 1994). Also, of those who remit, relapse rates are relatively high (.31 and .35, respectively; Keller et al., 1994).

Various biopsychosocial factors may contribute to panic disorder. Familial factors are involved, as first-degree relatives are at three to four times greater risk for developing panic disorder (e.g., Crowe, 1985). In addition, there is some evidence for a specific genetic contribution for panic attacks (e.g., Martin, Jardin, Andrews, & Heath, 1988), although genetic influences remain weaker than environmental influences overall.

PANIC DISORDER. Table 1. Panic Attack Symptoms

Shortness of breath or smothering
Heart palpitations or racing or pounding heart
Chest pain or discomfort
Trembling or shaking
Feeling of choking
Sweating
Feeling dizzy, unsteady, lightheaded or faint
Hot or cold flashes
Nausea or abdominal distress
Feelings of unreality or detachment
Numbness or tingling
Fears of dying
Fears of going crazy or losing control

The presence of behavioral inhibition in infants (i.e., withdrawal, seeking comfort from familiar others, and the suppression of ongoing behavior when confronted with unfamiliarity or novelty, as well as autonomic hyperarousal), may increase the risk of panic disorder as well as other anxiety and mood disorders (e.g., Hirshfeld et al., 1992). Psychosocial factors include stress. A large percentage of researchers report stressors around the time of the first panic attack, although it is unclear whether more stressors are actually experienced or life events are viewed as more stressful. Finally, beliefs that bodily sensations, such as a racing heart, are indicative of serious danger, such as heart attack, predict panic attacks and the chronicity of panic disorder (e.g., Ehlers, 1995).

Reliability and Validity

When diagnosing panic disorder, careful consideration is given to medical conditions that cause panic-like symptoms (e.g., thyroid conditions, caffeine or amphetamine intoxication, and drug withdrawal). Other medical conditions may exacerbate panic disorder, but panic would likely continue even when the medical condition was alleviated (e.g., mitral valve prolapse and asthma). Another source of diagnostic confusion arises from the ubiquitous nature of panic attacks, occurring across all anxiety disorders. Despite these diagnostic issues, panic disorder, as defined by the *Diagnostic and Statistical Manual of Mental Disorders* (American Psychiatric Association, 1994), is diagnosed very reliably when using structured or semistructured diagnostic instruments (e.g., DiNardo, Moras, Barlow, Rapee, & Brown, 1993). Although these data are based on earlier versions, current criteria for panic disorder are probably equally reliable.

The validity of the diagnostic classification is shown by features of panic disorder such as age of onset and patterns of comorbidity that are distinct from other anxiety disorders. In addition, the effectiveness of treatments that specifically target panic attacks and agoraphobia attest to diagnostic validity.

Prevalence

Prevalence estimates for adults are 2.3% in the last 12 months and 3.5% lifetime (Kessler et al., 1994). Conservative estimates suggest that an additional 3.3 to 4.6% experience nonclinical panic, or occasional panic attacks. Also, from 0.6 to 4.7% of adolescents are estimated to suffer from panic disorder.

Age, Racial, Ethnic, and Gender Differences

A substantial number of children and adolescents report panic attacks, although panic symptoms prior to adolescence are most often an associated feature of another anxiety disorder. It is hypothesized that most children do not possess the cognitive capacity to fear loss of control or going crazy, which is typical of "out of the blue" panic attacks.

Research on cross-cultural, ethnic, and racial differences is very limited. There are a variety of culture-related forms of anxiety that seem to overlap with panic disorder as conceptualized by Western societies. Examples include *koro* in South and East Asia, where panic-like symptoms are associated with intense, acute fear of the penis shrinking into the body, or the nipples retracting and breasts shrinking, and eventual death. Another example is *ataques de nervios*, found among Puerto Ricans and other Hispanic-Caribbean peoples. The symptoms resemble panic disorder but prominently feature uncontrollable shouting and attacks of crying.

Within North American culture, epidemiological studies find few racial differences with respect to panic disorder, although African Americans may be at higher risk for agoraphobia along with other phobias. Associated features of panic disorder are generally similar, although African Americans with panic disorder appear more prone to isolated sleep paralysis (Friedman et al., 1994). Finally, anxious African Americans are generally less likely to seek help from mental health professionals and may respond slightly less well to behavior therapy, although the data are contradictory and limited.

The level of agoraphobia relates to female gender and low masculinity traits (Chambless & Mason, 1986). Once agoraphobia is accounted for there are few gender differences, although women remain at slightly higher risk for panic disorder. Gender roles and expectations, fewer opportunities for females to repeatedly confront feared situations such as travel away from home, and stronger tendencies for women to worry and ruminate may contribute to gender differences (Craske & Glover, in press).

Social Impact

The costs of untreated panic disorder are extensive and include psychiatric conditions, such as depression, substance abuse, and suicidality. Medical costs include increased cardiac, respiratory, gastrointestinal, and neurological illnesses, and increased mortality (Zaubler & Katon, 1996). Financial burdens are also strong, such as increased health care utilization, increased use of welfare, and impaired work productivity and employment status. Furthermore, panic disorder impairs marital and social functioning and results in overall life dissatisfaction.

Treatment and Prevention

Unfortunately, as many as 60% of panic sufferers do not seek treatment, despite the availability of two highly effective treatment approaches. The first is a psychological approach, known as cognitive-behavioral therapy, tailored specifically to overcome fears of bodily sensations (such as a racing heart) and agoraphobic situations. This approach was developed by researchers such as David Barlow in the United States, David M. Clark in England, and Lars-Goran Ost in Sweden. Treatment involves education, modifying misperceptions and erroneous beliefs, corrective breathing or relaxation, and repeated, systematic confrontation with feared sensations and situations. This treatment is highly effective for panic attacks (e.g., 75 to 100% panic free) and panic disorder. It is very effective for agoraphobia also, and the results are generally long-lasting. Furthermore, the development of panic disorder is dramatically arrested by instituting exposure strategies immediately following initial panic attacks.

The second treatment is pharmacotherapy, originally spearheaded by Donald Klein in the United States, who first showed that tricyclic antidepressants were particularly effective for panic attacks. Subsequently, high potency benzodiazapines in the 1980s and selective serotonin reuptake inhibitors in the 1990s have proven very effective for panic attacks, although relapse upon medication withdrawal is sometimes problematic. Finally, the combination of psychological and pharmacological approaches may yield even more effective outcomes, although long-term effects from their combination remain under investigation.

Bibliography

American Psychiatric Association. (1994). *Diagnostic and statistical manual of mental disorders* (4th ed.). Washington, DC: Author.

Chambless, D. L., & Mason, J. (1986). Sex, sex-role stereotyping and agoraphobia. *Behaviour Research and Therapy, 24*, 231–235.

Craske, M. G., & Glover, D. A. (in press). Anxiety disorders. In E. M. Palace (Ed.), *Women's health: A behavioral medicine approach*. New York: Oxford University Press.

Crowe, R. R. (1985). The genetics of panic disorder and agoraphobia. *Psychiatric Developments, 2*, 171–186.

DiNardo, P. A., Moras, K., Barlow, D. H., Rapee, R. M., & Brown, T. A. (1993). Reliability of *DSM–III–R* anxiety disorder categories using the Anxiety Disorders Interview Schedule-Revised (ADIS-R). *Archives of General Psychiatry, 50*, 251–256.

Ehlers, A. (1995). A 1-year prospective study of panic attacks: Clinical course and factors associated with maintenance. *Journal of Abnormal Psychology, 104*, 164–172.

Friedman, S., Paradis, C. M., & Hatch, M. (1994). Characteristics of African American and White patients with panic disorder and agoraphobia. *Hospital and Community Psychiatry, 45*, 798–803.

Goisman, R. M., Warshaw, M. G., Peterson, L. G., Rogers, M. P., Cuneo, P., Hunt, M. F., Tomlin-Albanese, J. M., Kazim, A., Gollan, J. K., Epstein-Kaye, T., Reich, J. H., & Keller, M. B. (1994). Panic, agoraphobia, and panic disorder with agoraphobia: Data from a multicenter anxiety disorders study. *Journal of Nervous and Mental Disease, 182*, 72–79.

Hirshfeld, D. R., Rosenbaum, J. F., Biederman, J., Bolduc E. A., Faraone, S. V., Snidman, N., Reznick, J. S., & Kagan, J. (1992). Stable behavioral inhibition and its association with anxiety disorders. *Journal of the American Academy of Child and Adolescent Psychiatry, 31*, 103–111.

Keller, M. B., Yonkers, K. A., Warshaw, M. G., Pratt, L. A., Gollan, J. K., Massion, A. O., White, K., Swartz, A. R., Reich, J., & Lavori, P. W. (1994). Remission and relapse in subjects with panic disorder and panic with agoraphobia. *Journal of Nervous and Mental Disease, 182*, 290–296.

Kessler, R. C., McGonagle, K. A., Zhao, S., Nelson, C. B., Hughes, M., Eshleman, S., Wittchen, H. U., & Kendler, K. (1994). Lifetime and 12-month prevalence of *DSM–III–R* psychiatric disorders in the United States. *Archives of General Psychiatry, 51*, 8–19.

Martin, N. G., Jardine, R., Andrews, R., Andrews, G., & Heath, A. C. (1988). Anxiety disorders and neuroticism: Are there genetic factors specific to panic? *Acta Psychiatrica Scandinavica, 77*, 698–706.

Sanderson, W. C., DiNardo, P. A., Rapee, R. M., & Barlow, D. H. (1990). Syndrome comorbidity in patients diagnosed with a *DSM–III-R* anxiety disorder. *Journal of Abnormal Psychology, 99*, 308–312.

Thyer, B. A., Himle, J., Curtis, G. C., Cameron, O. G., & Nesse, R. M. (1985). A comparison of panic disorder and agoraphobia with panic attacks. *Comprehensive Psychiatry, 26*, 208–214.

Zaubler, T. S., & Katon, W. (1996). Panic disorder and medical comorbidity: A review of the medical and psychiatric literature. *Bulletin of the Menninger Clinic, 60* (Suppl. A), A12–A38.

Michelle G. Craske

PARALLEL DISTRIBUTED PROCESSING. *See* Connectionism.

PARANOIA OR DELUSIONAL DISORDER. Delusional disorder is a relatively uncommon, but not rare, psychiatric illness. Since the beginning of the twentieth century this disorder has been referred to by a variety of nosological terms, including *paranoia, paranoid psychosis*, the *paranoid state, paranoid condition, paranoid reaction, paraphrenia, paranoid disorder, paranoia vera, conjugal paranoia, delusional insanity*, and *delusional monomania.* Although the diagnostic criteria for delusional disorder have varied over time, the core defining feature of the disorder has remained the stable presence of nonbizarre delusions in the absence of a diagnosis of schizophrenia, schizoaffective disorder, or major affective disorder. Following onset, delusional disorder tends to be relatively stable over the individual's lifetime, and although some impairment in functioning may be present, it is frequently not prominent and does not require psychiatric hospitalization.

The criteria for delusional disorder, according to *DSM–IV* (American Psychiatric Association, 1994) include the following:

1. Nonbizzare delusions of at least one month's duration (that is, delusions that involve plausible, real-life situations such as having a disease, being infected, being followed or persecuted, being deceived by a mate, being loved at a distance; distinguished from bizarre delusions involving mechanisms not believed to exist, such as being controlled by a microchip implanted in the brain or believing others can hear one's thoughts).
2. The person has never met Criterion 1 for schizophrenia (bizarre delusions or two of the following: delusions, hallucinations, disorganized speech, grossly disorganized or catatonic behavior, or negative symptoms such as affective flattening, alogia, or avolition). Olfactory and tactile hallucinations may be present if they are consistent with the delusional theme.
3. Aside from the direct effects of the delusion(s), functioning is not clearly impaired and behavior is not strange or bizarre.
4. If mood episodes have been present with the delusion(s), they have been relatively brief in duration.
5. The delusions cannot be attributed to organic factors such as substance abuse or a medical condition.

Specific types of delusions are coded in *DSM–IV* based on their content, including "erotomanic" (another person, usually of higher status, is in love with the person); "grandiose" (the person has special powers, attributes, wealth, etc.); "jealous" (the person's sexual partner has been unfaithful); "persecutory" (the person is being treated malevolently); "somatic" (the person has an illness or another physical defect); "mixed" (more than one of the above delusions are present, with no one theme predominating); "unspecified."

History of the Concept

The word *paranoia* derives from the Greek words for "beside" and "self" and was used in ancient times to refer to insanity, madness, and delirium, as well as "thinking amiss," "going astray," or "folly" (Lewis, 1970). Although the term fell out of use over the following 2,000 years, it was revived by Karl Ludwig Kahlbaum in the nineteenth century to refer to psychiatric disorders that were characterized by persistent delusions (Lewis, 1970). Over the following years the term *paranoia* was used to describe various conditions, with little agreement except for the presence of delusions.

One of Emil Kraepelin's contributions to the description of delusional disorder was the clear distinctions he drew between dementia praecox (schizophrenia), manic-depressive insanity (bipolar disorder), and paranoia (delusional disorder). Over time Kraepelin's view of paranoia evolved significantly, including his view of the importance of stable, nonbizarre delusions and its relatively good prognosis. In 1918 Ernst Kretschmer theorized that "sensitive" personality types were prone to develop paranoia following key experiences that led to the formation of stable delusions (Tanna, 1974). He noted that these patients did not tend to develop schizophrenia. This work was important for two reasons. First, it stimulated other theories concerning the role of personality in the development of delusional disorders, which, despite minimal supporting evidence, continue to occur. Second, Kretschmer's hypothesis that personality factors predispose some individuals to develop delusions under certain circumstances led to Scandinavian theories of reactive psychosis (Tanna, 1974), such as that of Gabriel Langfeldt.

The basic definitions of delusional disorder in the *DSM* series retain much of the original concept of Kahlbaum and Kraepelin. As the word *paranoia* became increasingly common in the vernacular to refer to interpersonally malevolent or persecutory types of delusions, and ample evidence indicated that paranoid disorders frequently contained other themes as well (e.g., somatic, jealousy; Winokur, 1977), paranoid disorders were renamed *delusional disorders* to highlight the importance of delusions.

Successive editions of the *DSM* series have been aimed at sharpening the distinction between delusional disorder and schizophrenia and major affective disorder. One method has been to emphasize the nonbizarre nature of delusions in delusional disorder (that is, the beliefs refer to situations that are possible, however implausible), although there are difficulties in distinguishing reliably between bizarre and nonbizarre delusions. Another strategy for distinguishing delusional disorders from the other disorders has been to specify that when functional impairment occurs, it can be attributed directly to the delusions rather than to other symptoms (e.g., negative symptoms, hallucinations).

Validity of Delusional Disorder

A significant amount of evidence supports the validity of delusional disorder as a separate diagnostic entity. As Kendler (1980) noted, four types of information bear on the validity of delusional disorder: family psychopathology studies, longitudinal stability of the disorder, demographic differences from schizophrenia and major affective disorder, and the course and outcome compared to these other disorders.

Family psychopathology studies have compared the presence of psychiatric disorders in the relatives of persons with schizophrenia, delusional disorder, and major affective disorder. The extent to which a family history of mental illness in persons with delusional disorders resembles that of persons with either schizophrenia or major affective disorder would suggest that delusional disorder is a variant of one of these other disorders rather than a distinct psychiatric disorder. Ample research has shown that the rates of schizophrenia-spectrum disorders and major affective disorders are not increased in the families of patients with delusional disorder, suggesting that delusional disorder is not linked to either of these disorders. Limited research suggests that compared to other psychiatric disorders, relatives of patients with delusional disorder are more likely to be considered suspicious, jealous, secretive, or delusional. Thus, some of the characteristics of delusional disorder appear to be linked to familial traits.

Research also suggests that the diagnosis of delusional disorder is relatively stable over time, at least in the middle to later phases of the disorder. However, some recent research indicates that during the early course of the illness, delusional disorder may be unstable, suggesting that the diagnosis should be regarded as provisional until the disorder has been stable for several years. Because delusional disorder does not tend to evolve into another specific disorder over time, such as schizophrenia, as observed by Kraepelin and Kretschmer, more support is provided for its diagnostic uniqueness.

Kendler (1980) has summarized research comparing the demographic characteristics of persons with delusional disorders to the demographic characteristics of persons with schizophrenia and major affective disorders. Compared to patients with schizophrenia, those with delusional disorder are more likely to be female, tend to be admitted to a psychiatric hospital for the first time at a later age, and are more likely to be married. Compared to patients with major affective disorders, those with delusional disorder are more likely to be male and to come from a disadvantaged background. The demographic profile of persons with delusional disorder is clearly distinct from that of persons with schizophrenia and major affective disorders.

Finally, longitudinal follow-up studies of delusional disorder indicate that the long-term course of the disorder is better than that of schizophrenia but worse than that of major affective disorders (Opjordsmoen, 1988; Winokur, 1977). In summary, research on the family history of persons with psychiatric illness, stability of the condition, demographic characteristics, and course of the illness support the validity of delusional disorder as a separate diagnosis.

Prevalence, Demographics, and Course of the Illness

Delusional disorder is an uncommon psychiatric disorder. Based on data summarized across 17 large studies (including six studies with over one thousand cases of delusional disorder), Kendler (1982) reported that delusional disorder accounted for an average of 1.3% of all admissions to psychiatric hospitals and functional psychosis for 3.8% of all admissions. Two reports from Scandinavia indicate that the prevalence of delusional disorder is 24–30/100,000 (or about 0.03%) (Kendler, 1982) compared to about 1,000/100,000 (1%) for schizophrenia.

Kendler's (1982) review indicated that a slight majority of patients with delusional disorder were women, most had been married, and most came from disadvantaged backgrounds, including lower education and poorer financial conditions. Although the gender composition and marital status of persons with delusional disorder are markedly different from those of persons with schizophrenia, in which most persons are male and have never married, their socioeconomic backgrounds are similar. The most distinct sociodemographic feature of delusional disorder concerns patients' country of birth. Immigrants are significantly more likely to develop delusional disorder than people who remain in their country of origin, whereas immigrant status is not related to the development of schizophrenia or major affective disorder (Kendler, 1982).

Kendler's (1982) review also indicated that the period of first hospital admission for delusional disorder is middle age, with the largest number of patients admitted between the ages of 40 and 50. This age of first admission is substantially higher than for schizophrenia and somewhat higher than for the major affective disorders. It is also likely that many patients with delusional disorder are never admitted to a hospital, making it more difficult to determine the age of onset of the illness. Furthermore, the low prevalence of delusional disorder in the general population has made it difficult to assess its natural long-term course in the community, resulting in its omission from large community-based epidemiologic studies such as the Epidemiologic Catchment Area (ECA) study and the National Comorbidity Survey (NCS).

Similarly, the long-term course of delusional disorder is not easily characterized because patients with the most severe disorders are most likely to be hospitalized and receive treatment. However, research suggests that the course of delusional disorder is less severe than that of schizophrenia, although somewhat worse than that of the major affective disorders. In a long-term follow-up study of 71 patients with delusional disorder, Opjordsmoen (1988) reported that after 22 to 39 years, delusions had faded in 61% and 37% had demonstrated a full recovery. At a 3-year follow-up after admission, Winokur (1977) reported that 60% of patients with delusional disorder remained delusional, but 31% were considered "socially recovered." On long-term follow-up, Retterstöl (1970) found that 79% of patients with delusional disorder were self-supporting, 39% had been readmitted to a psychiatric hospital, and 27% were still psychotic. These outcomes were favorable compared to those of patients with schizophrenia, of whom only 31% were self-supporting, 90% had been readmitted to a hospital, and 87% were still psychotic.

Etiology

The etiology of delusional disorder is unknown. As previously discussed, delusional disorder does not appear to be related to either schizophrenia or major affective disorders (Kendler, 1984). The higher rates of jealousy, suspiciousness, or secretiveness found in the relatives of patients with delusional disorder provide indirect evidence that family transmission may play a role in the development of delusional disorder, although family factors could include both biological (genetic) and environmental contributions.

Cognitive theories have been advanced to account for the formation of delusions that are present across different disorders. According to the "anomalous experience hypothesis" (Maher, 1974), the cognitive processes involved in the development of delusional thinking are the same as those used in nondelusional or scientific reasoning. Individuals experience events (either environmentally or internally in the peripheral or central nervous system) that demand explanation and understanding. In an attempt to understand their anomalous experiences, they generate potential explanations that may be misunderstandings but that nevertheless produce relief from the confusion experienced. Then they attend selectively to evidence supporting their beliefs and ignore evidence contradicting it, thereby reinforcing their conviction in the beliefs.

There is some evidence consistent with the anomalous experience hypothesis of delusions, as reviewed by Manschreck (1995): (1) delusions are often present in individuals with no cognitive impairment; (2) delusions can be induced in normal persons under conditions in which they have anomalous experiences; and (3) delusions frequently co-occur in cases of undiagnosed sensory defect or in combination with hallucinations. However, these findings are not specific to delusional disorder; instead, they pertain more generally to the development of delusions.

Treatment

Relatively little has been firmly established regarding the treatment of delusional disorder. To evaluate the effects of antipsychotic medications, research has examined the course of delusional disorder in patients prior to the discovery and widespread use of antipsychotics in contrast to the course of the disorder after these drugs were in regular use. In contrast to schizophrenia, in which the introduction of antipsychotic medications resulted in a dramatic improvement in the course of the illness, there was no discernible improvement in outcome for patients with delusional disorder who used antipsychotic drugs. This finding is in agreement with the general consensus that most antipsychotic medications have little effect on delusional disorder (e.g., Winokur, 1977) and provides further support for the independence of delusional disorder from schizophrenia.

Some evidence does suggest that the antipsychotic drug pimozide is more effective than traditional antipsychotics in the treatment of delusional disorder. In a review of case reports, Munro and Mok (1995) reported that 65% of 143 patients with delusional disorder treated with pimozide recovered compared to only 23% of 53 patients treated with other antipsychotics. Recent case studies also suggest that delusional disorder may respond to atypical antipsychotic medications such as clozapine and risperidone, although more research on this is needed. Similarly, some reports indicate that antidepressant medications (e.g., selective serotonin reuptake inhibitors) may be useful in the treatment of delusional disorder, but no controlled research has been conducted.

Like pharmacological treatment, psychological treatment for delusional disorder has not been studied systematically because of its low prevalence. In recent years, cognitive-behavior therapy has been used for the treatment of psychosis, primarily in patients with schizophrenia, with some success. These approaches focus primarily on developing a collaborative relationship with the patient aimed at helping him or her evaluate the evidence supporting delusional beliefs and, when appropriate and possible, modifying these beliefs accordingly. Although cognitive-behavior therapy for delusional disorder has not been evaluated systematically, it appears to hold promise as a useful intervention for this disorder.

Summary

Delusional disorder is an uncommon, but not rare, psychiatric disorder characterized by the presence of delusions in the absence of other symptomatology found in schizophrenia-spectrum disorders and major affective disorders. Delusional disorder was first described over one hundred years ago, and modern conceptualizations of the disorder are quite similar to those in the earliest writings about it. Research on family history, stability of the disorder, demographic correlates, and course and outcome support the validity of delusional disorder as a separate diagnostic entity. The onset of delusional disorder usually occurs in middle age, later than that of schizophrenia. The disorder is more common in individuals with lower socioeconomic status and among immigrants. Delusional disorder is relatively stable over time, with a long-term outcome intermediate between that of schizophrenia and major affective disorders. Little has been established definitively in terms of treatment for delusional disorder, although traditional antipsychotic drugs do not appear to be useful. Some evidence indicates that pimozide is effective in the treatment of delusional disorder, but more research is needed on this question. Cognitive-behavior therapy for persons with delusions has been shown to be beneficial for schizophrenia and appears to have promise for the treatment of delusional disorder. However, controlled trials of cognitive-behavior therapy for delusional disorder have not yet been conducted.

Bibliography

American Psychiatric Association. (1994). *Diagnostic and statistical manual of mental disorders* (4th ed.). Washington, DC: Author.

Kendler, K. S. (1980). The nosological validity of paranoia (simple delusional disorder): A review. *Archives of General Psychiatry, 37*, 699–706.

Kendler, K. S. (1982). The demography of paranoid psychosis (delusional disorder): A review and comparison with schizophrenia and affective illness. *Archives of General Psychiatry, 39*, 890–902.

Kendler, K. S. (1984). Paranoia (delusional disorder): A valid psychiatric entity? *Trends in Neuroscience, 7*, 14–17.

Lewis, A. (1970). Paranoia and paranoid: A historical perspective. *Psychological Medicine, 1*, 2–12.

Maher, B. A. (1974). Delusional thinking and perceptual disorder. *Journal of Individual Psychology, 30*, 98–113.

Manschreck, T. C. (1995). Pathogenesis of delusions. *Psychiatric Clinics of North America, 18*, 213–229.

Munro, A., & Mok, H. (1995). An overview of treatment in paranoia/delusional disorder. *Canadian Journal of Psychiatry, 40*, 616–622.

Opjordsmoen, S. (1988). Long-term course and outcome in delusional disorder. *Acta Psychiatrica Scandinavica, 78*, 576–586.

Retterstöl, N. (1970). *Prognosis in paranoid psychoses*. Springfield, IL: Charles C. Thomas.

Tanna, V. L. (1974). Paranoid states: A selected review. *Comprehensive Psychiatry, 15*, 453–470.

Winokur, G. (1977). Delusional disorder (paranoia). *Comprehensive Psychiatry, 18*, 511–521.

Kim T. Mueser

PARANOID PERSONALITY DISORDER. As defined in *DSM–IV* (American Psychiatric Association, 1994), paranoid personality disorder (PPD) is characterized by maladaptive variants of six personality traits: mistrust/suspicion, antagonism, autonomy, hypersensitivity, hypervigilance, and rigidity. PPD differs from transitory suspicious states that we all may experience, as well as from systematized paranoid delusional states associated with certain Axis I disorders (e.g., schizophrenia, delusional disorder). PPD is considered to be among the more severe personality disorders both in terms of defensive style used (e.g., projection, denial) and in terms of the level of dysfunction commonly seen (Millon & Davis, 1996). Because of general mistrust, individuals with PPD rarely present for treatment, and they are unlikely to volunteer for psychological research studies. For this reason, most of the literature that focuses on PPD is based on clinical formulations and case studies. The small number of empirical PPD studies, however, do tend to support the validity of this diagnostic category (e.g., Turkat, Keane, & Thompson-Pope, 1990).

Descriptive Features

Individuals with PPD experience interpersonal problems because of their tendency to mistrust others and to react with hostility to perceived threats. They often look for "proof" of their suspicions in the actions of others and are reluctant to consider alternative explanations. Unfortunately, individuals with PPD are reluctant to check with others regarding these maladaptive beliefs. Therefore, they often act on their suspicions and assume malicious intent in others when none exists. The resulting antagonistic stance may provoke hostile reactions in others, which in turn only serves to confirm their maladaptive belief that the world is a malicious and threatening place. Additional features of PPD include rigid value systems, intolerance of ambiguity, social isolation, guardedness, emotional distance, pathological jealousy, aggressive outbursts, problems in initiating or maintaining romantic relationships, divorce, difficulty keeping a job, and recurrent litigation for perceived injustices (American Psychiatric Association, 1994; Benjamin, 1993; Meissner, 1978; Millon & Davis, 1996).

Emil Kraepelin often is cited as a major influence on establishing the diagnostic category of paranoid personality (American Psychiatric Association, 1952) or, more recently, paranoid personality disorder (PPD). Despite the long-standing clinical interest in paranoid states and paranoid personality, relatively little empirical research has been conducted on this personality disorder. Minor revisions to the PPD criteria set have been made since the publication of *DSM–III* (American Psychiatric Association, 1980), but these changes are based largely on committee decisions rather than empirical data. Nevertheless, most of the *DSM–III–R* PPD (American Psychiatric Association, 1987) criteria have satisfactory sensitivity and specificity (Bernstein, Useda, & Siever, 1993), and adequate interrater and test-retest reliability are observed for the diagnosis of PPD (Zimmerman, 1994). It was hoped that the *DSM–IV* revisions would increase the sensitivity and specificity of the PPD criteria, but this remains to be demonstrated.

Relation to Other Disorders

Historically, paranoid traits such as mistrust or hostility were thought to predispose one to develop paranoid psychoses later in life (e.g., late paraphrenia, dementia praecox). However, this proposition has not been tested adequately with a prospective research study. Implicit in many of the theories and observations regarding paranoia is that paranoia is a dimensional construct ranging from normal transitory suspicious states to paranoid delusions as well as delusional disorder (e.g., Meissner, 1978). Although individuals with PPD may experience transitory quasi-psychotic episodes when under stress, the deterioration of functioning commonly associated with the psychotic symptoms of schizophrenia is not seen in PPD.

Still, clinicians and researchers alike are faced with the often difficult task of attempting to differentiate between relatively transitory mistrustful beliefs, an overly valued belief, and delusions. Ascertaining the level of impairment and dysfunction associated with a suspicious and antagonistic interpersonal style is difficult as well. The therapeutic environment, with its emphasis on trust and disclosure, is often overwhelming to the client with PPD. The client may not be capable of distinguishing presenting problems (such as stress, depression, and anxiety) from a paranoid perspective on the world. Lack of insight into the nature of his or her problems and difficulty with self-disclosure may delay the gathering of pertinent information relevant to verifying a diagnosis of PPD.

Epidemiology

Paranoid features and PPD have been observed in a variety of clinical and nonclinical populations; higher rates are reported among men than among women (American Psychiatric Association, 1994). It is clear that the rate of PPD generally fluctuates according to the diagnostic scheme used, the type of assessment instrument used, and the samples investigated. PPD prevalence rates of 0.5 to 2.5% in the general population, 10 to 30% in psychiatric inpatient settings, and 2 to 10% in outpatient mental health clinic settings have been reported (American Psychiatric Association, 1994). Unfortunately, there are no recent studies that provide prevalence rates of PPD according to the *DSM–IV* criteria.

It is generally acknowledged that cultural differences as well as rural versus urban factors may influence the degree to which behaviors are labeled as paranoid and are considered dysfunctional. *DSM–IV* highlights the need to assess possible cultural determinants of behaviors suggesting PPD. However, studies on the influence of culture on the diagnosis of PPD have not been reported.

Etiology

In general, most theories of PPD focus on genetics and family environment. PPD (as well as schizotypal and schizoid personality disorders) is believed to be related genetically to schizophrenia and is, therefore, considered a "schizophrenia spectrum" disorder. Consistent with this purported link, studies have indicated an increased risk of PPD in the relatives of patients with schizophrenia (Nigg & Goldsmith, 1994) as well as in the relatives of those with delusional disorders (Webb & Levinson, 1993). Turning to the psychosocial realm, parental neglect or domination, abuse, isolation, exposure to violent adults, and the infliction of pain have also been cited as risk factors. There is some empirical evidence suggesting a relation between parental aggressiveness and later development of aggression and hypervigilance (two core traits of PPD) in offspring, but there are no data indicating that early home environmental factors are associated specifically with the development of PPD (Norden, Klein, Donaldson, Pepper, & Klein, 1995). Although the effects of punitive or traumatic experiences are believed to interact with a genetic predisposition toward a paranoid style or core features of PPD (Siever & Davis, 1991), specific environmental or genetic influences that may moderate or mediate the development of PPD traits have not been identified (Nigg & Goldsmith, 1994). Finally, some investigators believe that paranoia is etiologically related to depression and is a defense against anxiety. However, more research is needed to address these hypotheses before conclusions can be drawn.

Treatment

The treatment of PPD is challenging primarily because of the difficulty in establishing a therapeutic relationship with these individuals. Those with PPD typically do not seek treatment specifically for their paranoia, often drop out of therapy, resist self-disclosure, or resist following treatment regimens. Furthermore, they have been characterized as "difficult" patients, exhibiting more dysfunctional behavior relative to other clinical populations, with a poorer prognosis (Millon & Davis, 1996).

Although the psychodynamic literature offers many theoretical perspectives on both the etiology and treatment of paranoid states (e.g., Meissner, 1978), the cognitive-behavioral and interpersonal perspectives offer more specific treatment guidelines (e.g., Beck, Freeman, & Associates, 1990; Benjamin, 1993; Turkat & Maisto, 1985). Briefly, these prescriptions include increasing the PPD individual's sense of self-efficacy, reducing anxiety in response to perceived negative evaluation by others, improving certain interpersonal skills (e.g., trust, communication, perspective-taking), and helping the client adopt more realistic attributions of the motives of others. It should be noted, however, that there are no treatment studies assessing the relative effectiveness of any interventions for PPD.

In summary, this well-recognized and interesting clinical disorder unfortunately has received relatively little research attention over the years. For this reason, we know much less about PPD's etiology, course, and treatment than we do about most other *DSM–IV* conditions. Further, early studies of PPD (e.g., before the publication of *DSM–III*) were based on samples that are not representative of our current diagnostic conceptualization. Assessment of PPD using the most recent definition (i.e., in *DSM–IV*) will allow us to obtain more accurate estimates of the prevalence of PPD in both clinical and nonclinical samples. Additional family history and twin studies, as well as further investigation of biological correlates of PPD, should increase our understanding and help refine our description of PPD. Finally, prospective longitudinal studies of those at risk for developing PPD will help shed light on the purported causes of PPD.

[*See also* Personality Disorders.]

Bibliography

American Psychiatric Association. (1952). *Diagnostic and statistical manual of mental disorders.* Washington, DC: Author.

American Psychiatric Association. (1980). *Diagnostic and statistical manual of mental disorders.* (3rd ed.). Washington, DC: Author.

American Psychiatric Association. (1987). *Diagnostic and statistical manual of mental disorders* (3rd ed., rev.). Washington, DC: Author.

American Psychiatric Association. (1994). *Diagnostic and statistical manual of mental disorders* (4th ed.). Washington, DC: Author.

Beck, A. T., Freeman, A. T., & Associates (1990). *Cognitive therapy of personality disorders.* New York: Guilford Press.

Benjamin, L. S. (1993). *Interpersonal diagnosis and treatment of personality disorders.* New York: Guilford Press.

Bernstein, D. P., Useda, D., & Siever, L. J. (1993). Paranoid personality disorder: Review of the literature and recommendations for *DSM–IV. Journal of Personality Disorders, 7,* 53–62.

Meissner, W. W. (1978). *The paranoid process.* New York: Jason Aronson.

Millon, T., & Davis, R. (1996). *Disorders of personality: DSM-IV and beyond.* New York: Wiley.

Nigg, J. T., & Goldsmith, H. H. (1994). Genetics of personality disorders: Perspectives from personality and psychopathology research. *Psychological Bulletin, 115,* 346–380.

Norden, K. A., Klein, D. N., Donaldson, S. K., Pepper, C. M., & Klein, L. M. (1995). Reports of the early home environment in *DSM–III–R* personality disorders. *Journal of Personality Disorders, 9,* 213–223.

Siever, L. J., & Davis, K. (1991). A psychobiologic perspective on the personality disorders. *American Journal of Psychiatry, 148,* 1647–1658.

Turkat, I. D., & Maisto, S. A. (1985). Application of the experimental method to the formation and modification of personality disorders. In D. H. Barlow (Ed.), *Clinical handbook of psychological disorders* (pp. 157–184). New York: Guilford Press.

Turkat, I. D., Keane, S. P., & Thompson-Pope, S. K. (1990). Social processing errors among paranoid personalities. *Journal of Psychopathology and Behavioral Assessment, 12,* 263–269.

Webb, C. T., & Levinson, D. F. (1993). Schizotypal and paranoid personality disorder in the relatives of patients with schizophrenia and affective disorders: A review. *Schizophrenia Research, 11,* 81–92.

Zimmerman, M. (1994). Diagnosing personality disorders: A review of issues and research methods. *Archives of General Psychiatry, 51,* 225–245.

Timothy J. Trull and J. David Useda

PARAPLEGIA. *See* Rehabilitation Psychology.

PARAPROFESSIONALS. A mental health paraprofessional (formerly called a nonprofessional) is someone without postbaccalaureate education in one of the mental health professions such as psychology, psychiatry, social work, or psychiatric nursing, who functions in a formal helping role for others. Identifying the formal social status of a paraprofessional helps clarify who falls into this category. For example, although friends, relatives, and neighbors can be helpful in times of need, these individuals are not, strictly speaking, mental health paraprofessionals. Members of various self-help organizations such as Alcoholics Anonymous and Gamblers Anonymous are also not usually called paraprofessionals because people join these organizations to obtain help for their own problems, not to be therapists or helpers for others.

Paraprofessionals are a diverse group whose members include high school and college students, homemakers, retirees, or other members of the community. Most paraprofessionals are unpaid volunteers who work on a time-limited basis in special programs, but there are also full-time paid staff positions for paraprofessionals. Most of the latter positions are in the child welfare and child protective systems, in residential treatment and developmental disability centers, and in the psychiatric units of general hospitals.

Sometimes the term indigenous paraprofessional is

used to describe those who are similar in background, culture and/or social status to those they are helping. Indigenous paraprofessionals would include peer counselors in high school and college settings, or members of different racial, cultural, or socioeconomic groups.

History

Paraprofessionals have always been involved in some way in helping programs in the United States, beginning with the large mental health hospitals that were established in the 1800s (Greenblatt, York, & Brown, 1955). Paraprofessionals in these hospitals were an important part of the therapeutic milieu and played an instrumental role in treatment. Over the ensuing years, the use of paraprofessionals waxed and waned, but accelerated dramatically during the 1960s. Some have identified the widespread use of paraprofessionals during this time period as a revolution in mental health. For example, in the late 1960s projects funded by the National Institute of Mental Health used over 10,000 paraprofessionals in some therapeutic or preventive capacity (Sobey, 1970).

Effectiveness

There are more than 1,000 outcome studies attesting to the therapeutic effectiveness of paraprofessionals. Paraprofessionals have been used successfully as counselors or therapists for clients of all ages and with many different types of problems such as disruptive behavior, academic problems, depression, anxiety, and schizophrenia (Durlak, 1979; Gershon & Biller, 1977; Karlsruher, 1974). More recently, paraprofessionals have been used to conduct prevention programs targeting drug use, academic performance, and various behavioral and social problems (Durlak, 1997).

Paraprofessionals may be effective, but how do their outcomes compare to those obtained by professionals? In 1979, a systematic review of the literature comparing the effectiveness of paraprofessional and professional helpers offered a startling conclusion: in general, paraprofessionals achieved therapeutic results as good as those produced by professionals (Durlak, 1979). This finding created controversy when it appeared, but studies involving paraprofessionals have subsequently been dissected and reanalyzed several times with essentially the same results (Christensen & Jacobson, 1994). Now there is general acceptance of the notion that carefully selected, trained, and supervised paraprofessionals can offer high quality mental health services. A program relying on paraprofessionals should not be viewed as second-rate or inferior because of the characteristics of its staff. A professional mental health degree is not a requirement for an effective change agent.

At the same time, it is important not to misinterpret outcome studies involving paraprofessionals. Research does not support the position that paraprofessionals and professionals are interchangeable, or that state licensing and certification boards should do away with restrictions on service providers.

This is because research has studied paraprofessionals who function in carefully circumscribed roles. In research studies paraprofessionals are not asked to fulfill all the tasks that can be assumed by professionals such as assessment and diagnosis, the planning and organization of service programs, decisions about when to initiate or end interventions, or program evaluation. Moreover, paraprofessionals' activities are usually concentrated on delivering specific interventions. That is, paraprofessionals usually conduct only one type of treatment or deal almost exclusively with one type of problem or target population. In other words, the effectiveness of paraprofessionals has usually occurred in situations in which their activities have been limited, and they have been carefully selected, trained, and supervised by professionals. Therefore, there is no evidence that anyone can offer mental health care, and there remains a need to evaluate and monitor those wishing to offer mental health care to ensure their competency.

Training

If individuals such as college undergraduates and homemakers could be successful helpers, then many of the technical and theoretical components present in professional training programs are not essential in learning how to conduct a specific intervention. Those who worked with paraprofessionals began developing brief, practical training programs in which the elements of the helping process were simplified and operationalized. Many successful paraprofessional training programs followed social learning principles (Durlak, 1983). First, trainers identified the set of skills needed to conduct a particular intervention, and then clearly defined each skill. Using a step-by-step approach, trainers then selected one skill, modeled its effective use, asked the paraprofessionals to practice the skill, and then provided immediate feedback and support. This cycle continued until trainees had developed proficiency in each targeted skill. Several brief, structured training programs for different helping skills were developed using this approach, and training materials began appearing that were suitable for a variety of situations (e.g., Borck & Fawcett, 1983; Danish & Hauer, 1978).

Contemporary approaches to psychotherapy now emphasize the need for manuals as one requirement for empirically validated interventions (Task Force on Promotion and Dissemination of Psychological Procedures, 1995). Manuals describe the specific steps or elements of an intervention and are important for replication in other settings and in training personnel to conduct the intervention in a consistent and faithful manner. In other words, the current emphasis on detailed program manuals dovetails with earlier efforts to systematically train paraprofessionals in helping skills. These two developments are relevant for preparing professionals as well as paraprofessionals to implement different types of therapeutic and preventive interventions.

Summary

There is no question that the use of paraprofessionals has increased the quantity and range of services available to the general public. There never has been nor will there ever be a sufficient number of mental health professionals to meet the need and demand for service. Using paraprofessionals therefore increases the number of people who can be helped. In some cases, it would be impossible to offer programs without paraprofessionals. For instance, there are hundreds of suicide prevention and crisis hot lines and call-in centers throughout the country that could not exist without paraprofessional personnel. In addition, many prevention programs now follow a model in which professionals function in a consultative and collaborative relationship with local community residents (i.e., community gatekeepers and paraprofessionals) and it is the latter personnel who are usually responsible for conducting the intervention (Durlak, 1997). In summary, mental health care has been enhanced because paraprofessionals have been used in different ways to extend and expand the range of services customarily offered by professionals.

Bibliography

Borck, L. E., & Fawcett, S. B. (1983). *Learning counseling and problem-solving skills.* New York: Haworth Press.

Christensen, A., & Jacobson, N. S. (1994). Who (or what) can do psychotherapy: The status and challenge of nonprofessional therapies. *Psychological Science, 5,* 8–14. Reviews the controversy surrounding paraprofessionals and updates research findings.

Danish, S. J., & Hauer, A. L. (1978). *Helping skills: A basic training program.* New York: Human Sciences Press. An example of a structured training manual.

Durlak, J. A. (1979). Comparative effectiveness of paraprofessional and professional helpers. *Psychological Bulletin, 86,* 80–92. Offers the conclusion that paraprofessionals and professionals obtain comparable therapeutic outcomes.

Durlak, J. A. (1983). Training programs for paraprofessionals: Issues and guidelines. In A. M. Jeger & R. S. Slotnick (Eds.), *Community mental health: A behavioral-ecological perspective* (pp. 445–457). New York: Plenum Press. Discusses effective training approaches for paraprofessionals.

Durlak, J. A. (1997). *Successful prevention programs for children and adolescents.* New York: Plenum Press. Offers numerous examples of paraprofessionals in prevention programs.

Gershon, M., & Biller, H. B. (1977). *The other helpers: Paraprofessionals and nonprofessionals in mental health.* Lexington, MA: Heath. An extensive review of the use and effectiveness of paraprofessionals.

Greenblatt, M., York, R., & Brown, F. (1955). *From custodial to therapeutic patient care in mental hospitals.* New York: Russell Sage Foundation. Discusses the history of mental hospital care.

Karlsruher, A. E. (1974). The nonprofessional as a psychotherapeutic agent: A review of the empirical evidence pertaining to his effectiveness. *American Journal of Community Psychology, 2,* 61–77.

Sobey, F. (1970). *The nonprofessional revolution in mental health.* New York: Columbia University Press. Examines how over ten thousand paraprofessionals were used in federally funded research programs.

Task Force on Promotion and Dissemination of Psychological Procedures. (1995). *The Clinical Psychologist, 48,* 3–23.

Joseph A. Durlak

PARAPSYCHOLOGY is the branch of psychology that studies a group of phenomena collectively known as *psi,* a term referring to the transfer of information or energy that cannot be explained by known physical or biological mechanisms. Psi phenomena include *extrasensory perception* (ESP), the acquisition of information without mediation by the sensory system(s), and *psychokinesis* (PK), action with mediation by the motor system. ESP, in turn, is manifested by *telepathy* (thought transference), *clairvoyance* (perception of objects that are not present in the sensory field), *precognition* (perception of future events), and *postcognition* (the perception, as opposed to the memory, of past events).

Parapsychology is a branch of psychology because the phenomena it studies are mental (e.g., perceptual) or behavioral in nature. It should be understood at the outset that psi phenomena might well be explained in terms of normal processes. Thus, what appears to be clairvoyance might simply reflect an individual's high degree of sensory acuity; what appears to be telepathy might reflect cues inadvertently transmitted by one person and unconsciously picked up by another; what appears to be precognition might merely be coincidence; and what appears to be psychokinesis might be a product of simple fraud. Most psychologists incline toward these sorts of explanations for ostensibly paranormal phenomena.

Parapsychologists, however, argue that at the very least the phenomena of psi represent anomalies of experience, thought, and action: statistical deviations from chance that cannot be explained in terms of known processes or established theories. Whereas some parapsychologists believe that psi phenomena might be understood in terms of some hitherto unknown sensory modality or physical force, others believe that psi constitutes evidence for paranormal processes that lie outside the domain of normal science.

Parapsychology has its origins in nineteenth-century spiritualism, as represented by the work of F. W. H. Myers (1843–1901), an English writer. Although Descartes's dualism proposed that the mind is independent of the body, by the nineteenth century, virtually all scientists had adopted some version of materialism, which holds that brain processes constitute the biological substrate of mental life. Spiritualism revived dualism by postulating the existence of soul (or, in secular terms, mind) as a nonphysical entity that survived bodily death, and formed the basis for such fads as the Ouija board, mediums, and seances. In contemporary psychology, spiritualistic concerns with the soul, life after death, channeling, and reincarnation are represented by the field of transpersonal psychology and research on so-called near-death and out-of-body experiences.

In 1882, Myers founded the Society for Psychical Research in London; along with American psychologist William James and others, he also founded the American Society for Psychical Research in 1884. In this context, *psychical* refers to the dualistic notion of a disembodied mind to mental states, such as clairvoyance, which have no basis in physical reality. In the early twentieth century, Stanford, Harvard, and other universities administered funds specifically established to study spiritualistic and psychical phenomena, initiating an era of credulous and skeptical ghost hunting by professionals and amateurs alike.

At Harvard, J. B. Rhine (1895–1980) conducted psychical research with William MacDougall; in 1927, he and his wife, Louisa Rhine, moved with MacDougall to Duke University. The Rhines eventually established the Duke Parapsychology Laboratory and ushered in an era of controlled, quantitative research on psi. Their research on ESP employed a deck of 25 Zener cards, on which were printed one of five symbols: star, circle, cross, square, or wavy line: the volunteer's task was to guess which card was being viewed by the experimenter. When statistical analysis yielded a success rate greater than would be expected by chance, Rhine claimed to have demonstrated ESP. Unfortunately, other laboratories generally failed to replicate these positive results, and research on ESP and PK fell into a decline.

Interest in parapsychology was revived in the 1970s by media attention to Uri Geller, an Israeli magician who claimed to be able to bend spoons by mere thought (though, famously, not in the presence of Johnny Carson, a television talk-show host who was himself an accomplished stage magician). Additional centers for parapsychological research were established at the Stanford Research Institute (now known as SRI International), Princeton, and other institutions. At SRI, Russell Targ and Harold Putoff conducted a series of experiments on remote viewing, in which the "percipient" described his or her clairvoyant impressions of a randomly chosen geographical site being visited by a target team. Helmut Schmidt, at Boeing Scientific Research Laboratories, tested volunteers' ability to predict the output of a machine that generated random numbers according to emissions from a radioactive source. At Princeton, Robert Jahn examined volunteers' ability to influence the output of a different kind of random number generator based on electronically generated noise. All three researchers reported significant deviations from chance, and thus significant evidence for psi.

A great deal of contemporary parapsychological research employs the Ganzfeld technique, which resembles Rhine's experiments with Zener cards. Ganzfeld, a term derived from Gestalt psychology, refers to a homogeneous sensory field, without any imperfections or boundaries. In the Ganzfeld experiments, participants relax in a reclining chair, translucent shields are placed over their eyes, and white noise is played through earphones. The general idea is that the Ganzfeld should increase psi effects by reducing distraction from the sensory environment. And indeed, Ganzfeld experiments conducted in the late 1970s and early 1980s by the late Charles Honorton (then affiliated with the Psychophysical Research Laboratories in Princeton, New Jersey) and others did appear to yield above-chance levels of psi performance. However, a 1985 review by Ray Hyman, a psychologist and skeptic of paranormal claims, revealed a number of methodological problems with those studies. For example, many of the experiments suffered from inadequate randomization of trials or left open the possibility of contamination through sensory leakage. In 1986, Hyman and Honorton issued a joint communique setting out minimal methodological standards for future Ganzfeld research.

An obvious problem with evaluating research on psi is that most scientific journals prefer to publish studies that yield positive, statistically significant outcomes. Therefore, any review of the published research on psi is likely to exclude many negative studies that remain unpublished. In an attempt to rectify the "file drawer" problem, the *Journal of Parapsychological Research* actively solicits both positive and negative studies. Still, it is somewhat disconcerting that failures to replicate psi effects have sometimes been interpreted as positive evidence for psi: the argument being that the later experiments involved skeptics whose negative attitudes paranormally affected the experimental outcomes. Of course, such a "Heads I win, tails you lose" position renders parapsychological claims scientifically untestable. Interestingly, comprehensive reviews indicate that experiments conducted with participants who believe in psi are more likely to yield positive results than those with participants who are skeptical. However, it is not clear whether this "sheep versus goats" effect reflects individual differences in paranormal ability or merely individual difference in acuity to subtle sensory cues. Claims that psi abilities are enhanced while dreaming or during hypnosis or sensory deprivation are based on very weak evidence.

During the 1980s, U.S. intelligence and military analysts took a national security interest in claims for ESP and PK emanating from the Soviet Union. In 1988, a committee of the National Research Council (NRC), the operating arm of the National Academy of Sciences, examined the literature on psi at the request of the U.S. Army. The NRC committee determined that the remote viewing, random number generation, and Ganzfeld paradigms examined were beset by major methodological problems, particularly inadequate randomization, sensory leakage, and the use of multiple tests for psi that spuriously inflated the probability levels associated with experimental outcomes. As such, the committee concluded that there was no scientific justification for claims about ESP, PK, or their practical significance. This remains the firm view of the scientific establishment.

In response to the NRC committee, Daryl Bem, a psychologist and accomplished stage magician, wrote an article with Honorton defending the Ganzfeld experiments and reviewed a new set of experiments that apparently met most of the standards set out by Hyman and Honorton (Bem & Honorton, 1994, is one of the few instances where parapsychological research has been published in a mainstream psychology journal). In reply, Hyman found some persisting methodological difficulties. In his reanalysis, eliminating these problems reduced performance to chance levels. A rejoinder by Bem (Honorton had died since their joint project began) discounted Hyman's criticism, but the fact remains that there have been no independent replications of the Ganzfeld effect using the improved methodology outside Honorton's laboratory. This leaves open the possibility that, despite Honorton's efforts to the contrary, some subtle bias may have contaminated the studies conducted in his laboratory. In fact, Milton and Wiseman ("Does psi exist?" *Psychological Bulletin*, 1999) reviewed the results of 30 additional Ganzfeld experiments, which also apparently met the Hyman–Honorton standards. This database, which was more extensive than the one reviewed by Bem and Honorton (1994), yielded no evidence of psi.

Even if parapsychological research fails to reveal previously unrecognized sensory modalities, or to challenge established physical laws, the subjective experiences associated with psi are psychologically interesting. Many parapsychologists began their research careers because of some compelling subjective experience of clairvoyance, precognition, or the like, that seemed to escape mundane explanation. Indeed, this was the source of William James's fascination with spiritualism and psychic phenomena; it is interesting to note that James conducted an experimental test with his friend Myers, that whoever died first should attempt to communicate with the survivor. The test failed. James also arranged a replication with his wife, which, apparently, also failed. Nevertheless, James felt that the experience of the paranormal was psychologically interesting and should be studied for what it might reveal about normal mental life.

Psychometric surveys indicate wide individual differences in paranormal experiences. Almost by definition, these subjective experiences occur outside controlled laboratory settings. It seems likely that some of these experiences are artifacts of biases and shortcomings that infect human judgment generally. Thus, we may be more likely to notice, and remember, the rare experience in which we thought about someone just before they called on the telephone, than the many experiences in which this coincidence did not occur. Moreover, it is possible that individual differences in the experience of ESP may be related to a cognitive capacity for absorption in sensory or fantasy experience, a facet of openness to experience, a major dimension of personality. Similarly, individual differences in PK, as reflected in the Ouija board, may be related to a capacity for dissociation, which allows people to engage in behavioral activities outside conscious awareness. Absorption and dissociation probably lie at the heart of near-death and out-of-body experiences, as well. As William James argued a century ago, it is possible to take people's anomalous experiences seriously without necessarily embracing claims about the paranormal origins of these experiences.

But one does not have to be a parapsychologist to study anomalous experience. It is enough simply to be a cognitive, clinical, personality, or social psychologist. The central claim of parapsychology goes beyond experience and encompasses the claim that the anomalous phenomena of psi are not mediated by the sensory or motor systems normally associated with sensation and action. In this respect, parapsychology confronts the scientist with a difficult conundrum. Science will not progress unless the investigator is open to new observations that might challenge established (and cherished) theories. At the same time, however, scientists must approach any startling new claim with an attitude of skepticism; otherwise, society is left vulnerable to the ravages of junk and pathological science. Justice is done to both science and society when startling claims are evaluated according to the most stringent methodological standards. The evidence is not all in, and it is best to keep an open mind, but when one removes outright fraud, poor methodology, and capitalization on chance, there appears to be little or no psi left to explain.

Bibliography

Alcock, J. E. (1987). Parapsychology: Science of the anomalous or search for the soul? *Behavioral & Brain Sciences, 10*, 539–643. Skeptical review of modern evidence for psi accompanied by a more positive review of the same literature by Rao and Palmer (1987), critical commentary on both articles by more than four dozen writers on both sides of the dispute, and responses from the authors.

Bem, D. J., & Honorton, C. (1994). Does psi exist? Replicable evidence for an anomalous process of information transfer. *Psychological Bulletin, 115*, 4–18. Responds to the NRC's critique of the Ganzfeld (see Druckman & Swets, 1988) by reviewing positive results obtained from more recent experiments that were, apparently, methodologically more rigorous than their forebears. Followed by a critical commentary by Hyman (pp. 19–24) and a response by Bem (pp. 25–27), the entire package vividly represents the debate over contemporary parapsychological research. The follow-up study by J. Milton and R. Wiseman (1999) appeared in *Psychological Bulletin, 125*, 387–391.

Druckman, D., & Swets, J. A. (1988). *Enhancing human performance: Issues, theories, and techniques*. Washington, DC: National Academy Press. First report of the NRC's Committee on Techniques for the Enhancement of Human Performance. Chapter 9 presents the committee's detailed (and skeptical) methodological review of experiments on remote viewing, random number generation, and the Ganzfeld. It is essential reading for anyone who wishes to understand the debate over parapsychology.

James, W. (1902). *The varieties of religious experience*. London: Longmans, Green. James's influential attempt to approach the experience of the divine from the standpoint of pragmatic philosophy and experimental psychology. Republished by Harvard University Press in 1985 as part of *Collected works of William James*, now out of print; various editions are widely available in used bookstores. James's view of spiritualist and psychical phenomena is also represented in two books of James's lectures, reconstructed by historian Eugene Taylor in *William James on exceptional mental states: The 1986 Lowell lectures* (New York, Scribner, 1982); see also Taylor's book, *William James on consciousness beyond the margin* (Princeton University Press, 1996).

Myers, F. W. H. (1903). *Human personality and its survival after bodily death* (Vols. 1 & 2). London: Longmans, Green. The founding document of nineteenth-century spiritualism, forerunner to both modern parapsychology and to contemporary studies of the near-death experience.

Rao, K. R., & Palmer, J. (1987). The anomaly called psi: Recent research and criticism. *Behavioral & Brain Sciences, 10*, 539–643. Two proponents review modern evidence for psi (see Alcock, 1987).

Reed, G. (1972). *The psychology of anomalous experience*. New York: Houghton Mifflin. In the tradition of William James, Reed attempted to explain subjective experiences of the paranormal in terms of normal cognitive and personality processes. A similar effort was made by L. Zusne and W. H. Jones in their book, *Anomalistic psychology: A study of extraordinary phenomena of behavior and experience* (Hillsdale, NJ, Erlbaum, 1982).

Rhine, J. B. (1933). *Extrasensory perception*. Boston: Society for Psychical Research. The first sustained effort to study ESP through controlled scientific experiments. Reprinted, in a revised edition, in 1973; see also Rhine's *New frontiers of the mind* (New York, Farrar & Rinehart, 1937). Both the British and American societies for psychical research are still in existence, and both publish scientific periodicals, the *Journal for Psychical Research* and the *Journal of the American Society for Psychical Research*. They have their skeptical counterpart in the Committee for Scientific Investigation of Claims of the Paranormal, and its journal, *The Skeptical Inquirer*.

John Kihlstrom

PARASOMNIAS. *See* Enuresis; Nightmares; Night Terrors; Sleeptalking; *and* Sleepwalking.

PARENT-CHILD RELATIONSHIP. [*This entry provides a broad survey of the parent-child relationship. It is chronologically divided into three articles*: Childhood; Adolescence; *and* Adulthood.]

Childhood

The parent-child relationship and parenting practices have received considerable theoretical and empirical attention as important influences on children's development. Through the study of parenting in diverse cultures, Le Vine (1988) advanced the idea that parents around the world share three major goals for their children: (a) the survival goal (providing for the health and safety of their children); (b) the economic goal (ensuring that their children acquire the skills and resources needed to be economically productive adults); and (c) the cultural goal (ensuring that their children acquire the basic cultural values of the group).

The ways in which these goals are met are obvious—through parent-child interaction and the parent-child relationship. This relationship is a bidirectional one, with parents influencing their children as their children influence them (Bell, 1968; Lerner, 1994). Beginning in infancy, parents both socialize and meet the needs of their children through their daily interactions. The quality of these interactions is an important influence on the developing infant and child. The parent-child relationship is critical, therefore, for healthy development, and depends on the continuous interaction between the child and the adults in his or her context.

Initially, infants communicate their needs through crying, smiling, and motor activity, and parents interpret these signals and respond to their infant's needs; the infant, in turn, responds to the parents. The mutual responsiveness between caregiver and child is termed *synchrony*. Synchrony has been referred to by researchers as an emotional attunement (Stern, 1985). In other words, caregivers and infants coordinate their interactions, respond to each other, and modify their actions according to the other's response. The smiling, looking, and cooing of the infant are responded to by the caregiver, who changes the pace, timing, and level of stimulation according to the infant's responses. In order for the caregiver and the infant to be in "sync," the caregiver must be sensitive to the infant's needs, recognize when the infant is overstimulated, and modify his or her behavior accordingly. If infants receive appropriate stimulation and their needs are being met, they will begin to feel that the world is a trusting place, that they can count on others, and that they are able to explore the world because their other needs are met. The term *sensitive caregiving* has been used to describe the type of caregiving that is responsive to the infant's needs and that affects the development of a healthy relationship between infant and caregiver; researchers have called this relationship *attachment*.

Attachment is defined as "an affectional tie that one person or animal forms between himself and another specific one—a tie that binds them in space and endures over time" (Ainsworth, 1982). In addition to attachment with parents, infants form attachment relationships with many individuals including siblings, grandparents, and babysitters. Once attachment relationships form between infants and caregivers, they seek to be close to one another: the infant uses proximity-seeking behaviors such as climbing on the mother's lap or approaching and following the father. Infants also make attempts to stay in close physical contact with their attachment figure, called "contact-maintaining" behaviors, such as crying when being put down, or clinging (Ainsworth, 1982).

This notion is similar to the idea of sensitive caregiving: if the parent can identify and meet the infant's needs, the infant will develop a sense of trust, and the stage will be set for further healthy development. Surely there is great diversity in infants with respect to the quality of the attachment relationships they form with others. Many factors can affect the quality of the relationship between the infant and his or her parents. Parental stress, infant temperamental difficulty, and insensitive caregiving can all influence attachment. We should note here, however, that infants are resilient and can be exposed to brief periods of nonoptimal parenting without harm. Experts have noted that when there is insensitive parenting continuously or for long periods, the child can be affected negatively.

If forming healthy attachments to caregivers is important, then it follows that early attachment relationships should influence development. When an infant feels secure in his or her relationship with the mother or caregiver, he or she is free to explore the environment, thus affecting cognitive growth. Many studies have concluded that attachment relationships during infancy are correlated with later cognitive and social development. These studies are not entirely consistent or entirely clear in their results. Overall, Ainsworth (1982) maintained that if parents are inconsistent in responding to their infant's signals, they will also be inconsistent in how they socialize their child later on in development. Of course, parents can change their caregiving styles over time, but researchers have found that if family factors remain stable, parenting characteristics seem to be consistent.

Researchers have always been interested in the specific ways that parents influence their child's development. In the United States it has been found that child-rearing practices vary widely but share similar dimensions. Baumrind, a prominent researcher in the area of parenting, described three general types of parental caregiving practices (1971). Not only has the description of parenting behaviors from her studies been replicated in other research, but these practices have also been found to be related differently to child behavior. Whereas these relationships seem to be consistent in the majority of research studies, we must stress that there is no guaranteed formula for success in parenting. Some very loving and caring parents may have children who are severely maladjusted, and parental abuse and neglect will vary in the effect it has on the child. We will note the trends in what seems to be optimal parenting and call attention to cultural differences.

According to Baumrind (1971), parents seem to differ in their control, communication, and warmth, and in the maturity demands they impose upon the child. The following types of parenting exemplify these differences. One type of parent Baumrind identified is labeled the *authoritarian* parent. This type of parent tries to shape, control, and evaluate the behavior and attitudes of the child in accordance with a typically absolute standard of behavior. This parent stresses the value of obedience to his or her authority, and imposes high maturity demands on the child. He or she favors punitive, forceful measures to curb the child's behaviors. There is little parent-child communication and, thus, the parent does not encourage verbal give-and-take. Instead, he or she believes that a child should accept the word of the parent for what is correct conduct. These parents seem aloof from their children; they show little affection.

A second type of parent Baumrind identified is labeled the *permissive* parent. This type of parent behaves toward the child in a nonpunishing, accepting, and affirming manner. The parent consults with the child about family policy and offers rationales for rules imposed. The parent does not impose many maturity demands on the child, and the atmosphere that the parent provides is warm and accepting, with good communication. The parent is a resource for the child but does not view himself or herself as an active agent in the shaping of the child's behaviors. The parent largely allows the child to govern his or her own behavior, avoids exercising control over the child, and often does not encourage the child to obey external standards (Baumrind, 1971).

The third type of parent that Baumrind identified is labeled the *authoritative* parent. This type of parent tries to direct his or her child's activities through the use of reason and explanations. This parent sets limits and enforces rules for behavior, but does so in a warm and communicative atmosphere. Firm control is exercised over the child but not to the extent that the child is overburdened with restrictions. High maturity demands are imposed, but the parent takes into account the developmental needs, specific interests, and behavioral capabilities of the child when deciding how to treat the child. This type of parenting keeps the parents' rights in mind, combines power with warmth and reasoning, and sees the rights and duties of parents and children as complementary (Baumrind, 1971).

In addition to a follow-up of the original sample as they developed into adulthood, Baumrind's research has been extended to other samples (Baumrind, 1991). Baumrind's original findings about the consequences of these parenting styles for children's development have been supported. Although parents of differing styles desire their children to show similar socially competent behaviors (friendly, cooperative, achievement oriented, independent), these styles are not all related to social competence in the child.

Extremely authoritarian or permissive parenting has equally bad consequences for children's development, and neither is as effective in leading to desired child behavior as is authoritative parenting. Authoritarian parents tend to have children who are obedient but unhappy, permissive parents have children who lack self-control, and authoritative parents have children who are the most happy, successful, and socially competent.

Studies assessing parenting style in relation to academic achievement report that children with authoritative parents have higher grades and have more positive attitudes toward school compared to children with authoritarian or permissive parents (Baumrind, 1971). Authoritative parents also tend to be more involved in their children's education, for instance, through participation in activities and helping with homework. The more parents are involved in their children's education, the better children perform in school (Gottfried, 1991). These findings suggest a mediated effect of parenting style on academic performance through parental involvement.

In addition to the evidence that certain types of parenting behaviors are related to positive outcomes in children, research has also demonstrated the reciprocal nature of the parent-child relationship. When children are doing well, it has positive effects on parents, which in turn will affect their parenting. To illustrate, Maccoby and Martin (1983) found that parents report closer relationships with their children when their children display behavioral competence, high academic performance, high self-esteem, and a lack of negative characteristics such as depression, drug use, and deviant behaviors. Closeness in family relationships has predicted parental satisfaction and childrens' participation in family activities. Conversely, child conduct problems have been found to have a negative impact on parents.

As noted, Baumrind and others extended her original research, and found that several other types of parenting can be described. First, the permissive pattern can be divided into two distinct forms that differ in their warmth and responsiveness. In the *democratic-indulgent* form of permissive parenting, the parent does not exert control or restrictions but provides a warm and responsive atmosphere for the child. In the *rejecting-neglecting* form of permissive parenting, the parent is cold and unengaged, but not to an extreme; parents are uninvolved and let the child do anything he or she desires unless the child's health or safety is at risk.

Parenting and Family Change

Structural changes in families (e.g., divorce, single-parent families, maternal employment) have led to concerns over how these changes may influence parenting and the parent-child relationship. In the last two decades of the twentieth century, the United States has witnessed considerable variation in American families and, particularly, in the roles of mothers and fathers. A staggering divorce rate, escalating rates of both single-parent and blended-family homes, and dramatic increases in mothers entering the workforce have all contributed to a changing picture of family life in America. With a 50% divorce rate, it is estimated that more than half of all youth will spend some amount of time in a single-parent family before the age of 18. Moreover, the preponderant majority (approximately 90%) of single-family homes are homes without a father. In part, as a consequence of this trend, over 50%

of mothers of infants and up to 80% of mothers of teenagers are now employed either full- or part-time (U.S. Department of Labor, 1998).

Divorce

Research suggests that the first few years following a divorce are associated with more behavior problems in children. In general, divorce has been associated with problems in social development and with lowered academic achievement in children (Hetherington & Clingempeel, 1992). More specifically, children often react by displaying impulsive, aggressive, and noncompliant behaviors, especially boys. However, there are many variables that influence the way a child reacts to his or her parents' divorce, and consequently, there is a great deal of variation in both child and parent behaviors postdivorce (Buchanan, 1998). The child's age, sex, temperament, and the availability of social supports all play a role in how well he or she will adjust to the breakup of the marriage. Parents' psychological well-being and how they themselves react to the divorce are also crucial. For example, Wallerstein and Kelly (1980) suggested that the circumstances accompanying marital dissolution may lead to a disorganized family situation that they called "minimal parenting." Parents may be so involved with their grief, anger, and other problems surrounding the divorce that little time is left for the parenting role. In fact, research has suggested that the postdivorce mother's discipline tends to become even more harsh and she tends to make fewer demands and not communicate freely with her children, whereas fathers tend to show more indulgent and permissive behaviors after the breakup. Higher levels of family functioning following divorce have been associated with consistent and appropriate discipline practices. Moreover, it is important to realize that divorce is not a static event, but rather a series of transitions that may include changes in living arrangements, housing, family responsibilities, and income level, which may all impact both the quality of parenting and childrens' adjustment to the marital dissolution.

Maternal Employment

As to whether maternal employment affects parenting and the parent-child relationship, the findings are complex. Overall, it seems that maternal role satisfaction has a more powerful influence on mother-child interaction than employment status per se. That is, mothers who are satisfied with their role, employed or not, show more positive interactions with their children (Lerner, 1994). Several studies have suggested that higher role satisfaction leads to more positive outcomes for children. Early researchers reported that children of satisfied mothers perceived their mothers as showing more positive affect and less severe discipline practices. On the contrary, mothers who were dissatisfied perceived their children to be more argumentative. Similarly, children with unemployed mothers who desired to be working scored lower on school achievement and adjustment measures.

Other research has suggested that role satisfaction leads to self-fulfillment and to the enhancement of self-esteem in the mother and, as such, these qualities lead to more sensitive mothering and to more positive mother-child interactions. Thus, role satisfaction may influence the child through the quality of the mother-child relationship. Both mothers and fathers report more closeness with their seventh-grade children when mothers have high levels of satisfaction with their employment status. Thus, it seems that maternal role satisfaction is a key factor in whether or not the mother's employment outside the home will affect her parenting. In fact, both maternal role satisfaction and satisfaction with parenting are positively associated with more educational stimulation and higher achievement in children (Gottfried, 1991).

"Male Homemakers" and Single Fathers

A shift away from the traditional family structure has been taking place in the United States, influenced at least in part, by the increase in mothers' labor force participation. These increases have contributed to the sharp rise of the dual-income family and, to a lesser extent, to the idea of the male homemaker, defined by Kantorowski Davis and Chavez (1995) as a "male who spends the majority of his time and energies engaged in family life and household maintenance and who is economically dependent on an adult female with whom he has made a home" (p. 258). A recent qualitative study of 22 Hispanic male homemakers living in southern California revealed that only one stayed home voluntarily, 13 were employed, and all of the 9 who were unemployed were currently looking for work (Kantorowski Davis & Chavez, 1995). Although the majority of men in the study viewed their role as a temporary one, several reported closer relationships with both their spouse and their children. Because of the limited number of men in the male homemaker role, research is scant. More research has involved men who also play a dominant role as caregivers, the single, custodial father.

Since 1970, the number of single father–headed households has increased dramatically. To illustrate, there were fewer than 400,000 single male heads of households with at least one child under the age of 18 in 1970. By 1990, however, this number tripled to 1,351,000. Accordingly, the number of children being raised in single-father families has almost tripled to include 2,016,000 children in 1991. In terms of parenting and the father-child relationship, single fathers raising girls under the age of 13 had significantly fewer problems with their children and thus higher quality relationships than fathers raising any other sex-age combination. Kantorowski Davis and Chavez (1995) also stated that single fathers who were involved in child care while they were married, who fought for custody of their children in a court of law, and who were supported by others in their fight, reported higher quality relationships with their children.

Cross-Cultural Parenting

Parenting and child-rearing practices are strongly related to the attitudes, beliefs, traditions, and values of the particular culture or ethnic group within which the family belongs. Consequently, many differences in parenting, as well as similarities, exist among different cultural groups. For example, Chinese adults describe their own child-rearing practices as more controlling than Caucasian American parenting practices (Chao, 1982), whereas Chinese parents tend to be less emotionally expressive and stress the importance of family obligations. Some research suggests that African American mothers demand strict compliance from their children, especially those mothers who are less educated or who are raising their children alone. In Israel, parents value independence and self-confidence and expect their children to be adventurous and mischievous. On the contrary, parents living among the Kwoma in New Guinea and the Zinacantecans of Mexico believe that their children are in danger due to supernatural forces and thus tend to keep their children close, quiet, and calm.

Variations in discipline practices also differ among cultural groups. The Japanese, for example, rely on consequences and feelings of others, whereas Americans are more likely to use power assertion or rely on rules as a means of discipline. However, when American mothers are compared to German mothers, it is the German mothers who are more likely to employ power assertions to discipline their children. It is evident that much variation exists among parenting practices, but parents tend to rear their children in ways that encourage competencies and successful functioning within their culture and society (Ogbu, 1987).

Bibliography

Ainsworth, M. D. S. (1982). Attachment: Retrospects and prospects. In C. M. Parkes & J. Stevenson-Hinde (Eds.), *The place of attachment in human behavior* (pp. 44–67). New York: Basic Books.

Baumrind, D. (1971). Current patterns of parental authority. *Developmental Psychology Monographs, 4*(1, Pt. 2).

Baumrind, D. (1991). Parenting styles and adolescent development. In J. Brooks-Gunn, R. Lerner, & A. C. Petersen (Eds.), *The encyclopedia of adolescence* (pp. 746–758). New York: Garland.

Bell, R. Q. (1968). A reinterpretation of the direction of effects in studies of socialization. *Psychological Review, 71*, 81–95.

Buchanan, C. M. (1998, March). *The impact of divorce on adjustment during adolescence.* Paper presented at the national invitational conference on Resilience Across Contexts: Family, Work, Culture, Community, Philadelphia, PA.

Chao, P. (1982). *Chinese kinship.* London: Routledge, Chapman, & Hall.

Gottfried, A. E. (1991). Maternal employment in the family setting: Developmental and environmental issues. In J. V. Lerner & N. L. Galambos (Eds.), *Employed mothers and their children* (pp. 63–84) New York: Garland.

Hetherington, E. M., & Clingempeel, W. G. (1992). Coping with marital transitions: A family systems perspective. *Monographs of the Society for Research in Child Development, 57*(2–3, Serial No. 227).

Kantorowski Davis, S., & Chavez, V. (1995). Hispanic househusbands. In A. M. Padilla (Ed.), *Hispanic psychology: Critical issues in theory and research* (pp. 257–270). Thousand Oaks, CA: Sage.

Lerner, J. (1994). *Working women and their families.* Thousand Oaks, CA: Sage.

Le Vine, R. A. (1988). Human parental care: Universal goals, cultural strategies, individual behavior. In R. A. Le Vine, P. M. Miller, & M. M. West (Eds.), *Parental behavior in diverse societies. New directions for child development* (No. 40, pp. 3–12). San Francisco: Jossey-Bass.

Maccoby, E. E., & Martin, J. A. (1983). Socialization in the context of the family: Parent-child interaction. In P. H. Mussen (Series Ed.) & E. M. Hetherington (Vol. Ed.), *Handbook of child psychology: Vol. 4. Socialization, personality, and social behavior* (4th ed., pp. 1–102). New York: Wiley.

Ogbu, J. U. (1987). Variability in minority school performance: A problem in search of an explanation. *Anthropology and Education Quarterly, 18*, 312–334.

Stern, D. (1985). *The interpersonal world of the infant: A view from psychoanalysis and developmental psychology.* New York: Basic Books.

U.S. Department of Labor. (1998). *Current population survey.* Washington, DC: U.S. Bureau of Labor Statistics.

Wallerstein, J. S., & Kelly, J. B. (1980). *Surviving the breakup: How children and parents cope with divorce.* New York: Basic Books.

Jacqueline V. Lerner and Domini R. Castellino

Adolescence

Jean Jacques Rousseau (1712–1778) proposed an age-dependent strategy to educate children during their course from childhood to adulthood. He saw the period of adolescence as a specific period of transition with sensitive tasks to be accomplished by either educators or parents in order to resolve the contradiction between freedom and authority for one's own individuation.

Whereas reflections on parent-infant and parent-child relationships have a long history, the parent-adolescent relationship did not gain the same kind of attention for a long time. Discussions about the quality of mother-child relationships date to Erasmus Rotterdamus (1466/69–1536) and Leon Vives (1492–1540), who advised mothers to be very careful when talking to their children, and who attempted to spread the spirit of humanism within mother-infant dialogues. Prior to this time, the belief about predestination of a child's fate—in the tradition of Augustinus—was the customary way to think about a child's possible pathway in life.

Enthusiasm about the possibility of creating a new human through influences in his or her social world may be seen as a continuation of the tradition of humanism. In this tradition, Rousseau offered an age-specific approach to foster children's development until the period of early adolescence, a time where he thought that a child's ability for true reasoning started. He advised teachers and pedagogues to be careful with the adolescent child driven by an antagonism between reason and impulse. This antagonism between self-love and selfishness was one of Rousseau's most ardent topics: The passion for freedom and realization of self turns against the voices of others, parents and teachers, whom the child used to obey.

From the turn of the twentieth century until the 1950s, adolescence was conceptualized as a period of increased conflict with parents in terms of psychoanalytic concepts such as development of the ego, individuation and separation, attachment and detachment. For example, Anna Freud (1958) saw adolescence as a period of "second individuation," alluding to the first individuation process at the end of the second year. Blos (1941) discussed the developmental period of adolescence as a time in which children not only begin to detach from their parents emotionally, but also begin to criticize basic worldviews and become cognitively more independent from their parents' ways of thinking. It was the work of Erik Erikson (1959) that paved the way to understand adolescence as major transition in a sequence of the continuous developmental process during the life span. Individuation became a central concept, a process in which the antagonisms of separation and closeness, or autonomy and dependency in the parent-child relationship have to be resolved. In his epigenetic diagram, Erikson was the first to try to elaborate a developmental process from birth to death, including stages in adulthood. What much later became known as the transition paradigm was founded in Erikson's idea about the dialectics of development that demands, for example, a solution between two different pathways such as trust versus mistrust during the first year, or identity versus role diffusion during adolescence.

John Hill (1987) studied the occurrence of conflicts in the parent-adolescent relationship over different historical periods and found that conflicts were not about fundamental themes concerning life and death, society, and values, they were about everyday quarrels and bickering (e.g., monopolizing the telephone, not cleaning up, styles of dress, or coming home too late). In recent times, authors have described the period of adolescence as a phase where a new balance has to be established in an already existing relationship within the family context. Thus, during the last decades of the twentieth century, the focus on adolescents has turned from an end-of-childhood and start-of-rational-thinking orientation toward a more cultural and life-span perspective: from a storm-and-stress attitude in parent-child discussions to a more sobering view on the trivial everyday bickering in parent-child communications during this period; and last, but not least, from a dyadic parent-adolescent influence model to a larger triadic family model with the parent-parent relationship included in a wholistic family perspective, giving the child more privacy and autonomy.

Parent-Adolescent Relationships Within the Family Life Cycle

Critical periods in a family's life cycle are times when changes in extant relationships are necessary and a new balance for the developing family has to be found. Coping with these changes are considered "family tasks" (Duvall, 1977) in analogy with David Havighurst's concept of developmental tasks. During transition periods, all families face a series of tasks that often not only require rearrangements in everyday life, but also imply new approaches to dealing with the changing needs and skills of children. During the transition process from childhood to adolescence, major changes are expected. Both generations pass through a critical phase: Adolescents experience a metamorphosis of body shape and widen their cognitive and social horizon, and parents go through a phase in which they recognize the first signs of decay in their appearance and in which they begin to reflect on their own life. Parents have to maintain the relationship with the child who is about to detach from existing family bonds and develop new orientations toward peers and the outside world. By the same token, adolescents begin to affirm their own interests and increase their efforts to gain more autonomy and independence. Both parents and adolescents have to find a solution for reconciling two opposing tendencies and are at the crossroads to either let a child develop his or her own identity or to cut the extant relationship. As Smetana (1995), in a number of studies has shown, a step-by-step transfer of responsibility and autonomy from parents to adolescents has better developmental consequences than an all-or-nothing solution with permanent conflicts about this issue. When parents and adolescents agree about a step-by-step transfer, children become self-reliant, trusting, responsible, and warm persons, ready to engage in others' problems.

Parent-adolescent relationships do undergo some changes during the passage from childhood to adulthood that may produce a feeling of insecurity and ambivalence in both parents and adolescents. However, it is not just a new effort to gain independence that induces feelings of ambivalence and doubts about a long-lasting and well-established relationship, it is the demand to renegotiate this relationship. At earlier stages of development, transitions are managed by parents and children in a specific way. Thus, the entire family scenario is brought back to life and the traditions of handling developmental shifts reverberate through the current demand for change in an extant relationship.

Parental Styles in the Parent-Adolescent Relationship

Parent-adolescent relationships have been categorized according to either parenting styles, such as authoritarian or liberal attitudes toward child rearing, or communication behaviors, such as verbal support or destruction, interruptions or supplementary comments, or integrative or distancing communications during discussions. Baumrind (1991) found differences in adolescents' development between authoritative and democratic styles on the one hand, and authoritarian and disinterested styles on the other. Whereas adolescents from families with a democratic or authoritative style show more prosocial and socially competent behavior, take fewer drugs, and have less internalization or externalization symptoms, adolescents who have experienced authoritarian or disinterested parental styles show increased internalization or externalization symptoms, take drugs, display more antisocial behaviors, and have a low degree of individuation. Communication styles between parents and adolescents have been defined as being either enabling or constraining in light of different outcomes in adolescents' development, such as identity formation, self-esteem, perspective-taking skills, or social competence (Hauser, Powers, & Noam, 1991). For example, an enabling style is characterized by supportive statements, a positive and warm atmosphere of exchange, and a strong intention to find a common solution. In contrast, a constraining style is characterized by distortion, devaluation of the adolescents' statements, diffusion of meaning, and the absence of a perspective about a common solution.

Most of the studies about parental style have applied observational techniques (both video and audio recordings) and also questionnaires. Differences in the families' communication patterns provide valuable information about the production and handling of meaning inside the family. This information serves as useful clues about potentials children can develop. Family-specific communication contexts tend to remain essentially the same, not only when different situations are compared, but also when families are monitored through a major developmental period.

Mother-Adolescent and Father-Adolescent Relationships

Studies focusing on differences between mothers' and fathers' influence on adolescent development have revealed that fathers may have a greater impact compared to mothers. Parke and Buriel (1998) claimed that fathers provide the model for separateness, mothers the model for connectedness. Thus, fathers may convey to their adolescent children a sense of identity and autonomy by their more playful and egalitarian exchanges. Fathers more than mothers help their children to consolidate their striving for independence. Even though fathers' presence in the family is far less than that of mothers, fathers do make a unique contribution to the child's socialization, and to his or her development of both cognitive and social skills in early and middle childhood as well as in early and mid-adolescence. Moreover, the expression of emotions in a family or in a relationship appears to be one of the major pathways to the acquisition of social competence in children. The exchange between parents and children about emotions, both positive and negative, is another aspect that has emerged as a new access for understanding differences in the development of children: Fathers are the important partners in parent-child relationships, and can assist their sons to regulate anger and aggressive tendencies.

The Impact of the Parent-Parent Relationship on Adolescents' Development

Adolescence is the period where maladjustment and externalizing or internalizing symptoms become more obvious than during earlier periods. Aside from direct aspects that characterize parent-child relationships and outcomes that seem to be associated with symptomatic developments, a growing corpus of data shows that the quality of the relationship between the parents has an essential impact on an adolescent's developmental pathway.

During the last decade, the quality of parent-parent communication has been recognized as being a salient predictor for adolescents' symptom development. For example, exposure to marital conflict was found to be associated with both internalizing and externalizing behavior in children. When children experienced marital discord in the family, social competence and acceptance by peers was lower, compared to children who did not have such experiences with their parents' relationship. In addition, eating disorders or drug dependence were analyzed and found to be associated with the family's emotional climate and the amount of ambivalent messages exchanged among family members. Finally, marital satisfaction during the child's adolescence has been found to be an important predictor of subsequent emotional and physical health of children 6 years later.

In a meta-analysis, Erel and Burman (1995) found that marital communication in the family appears to be highly influential for a child's acquisition of social skills and the quality of well-being in the family. Even the degree of harmony and the kind of consensus-seeking or dissent-confirming behaviors found in parent-parent discussions affect the child's well-being. Thus, the quality of parent-parent relations exhibit a spillover effect for parent-child relationships. It can be assumed that a family's framework for interpretation, which is produced by the specific modes of communication between members, has an important impact on both individual well-being and personality development during the transition period from childhood to adolescence.

Gender Differences in Parent-Adolescent Relationship

Mixed results characterize the existence of gender differences in parent-adolescent relationships. A complex pattern was identified when identity strength and experienced communication patterns were examined for all four possible gender-specific family dyads. Adolescents who rated highest in both identity exploration and role-taking skills had at least one parent with whom they had an individuated relationship. When differences between mothers and fathers in their relationship with their adolescent children were considered, degrees of involvement and modeling of autonomy and independence were highly different.

Gender differences were also discovered when dyadic designs with mother-daughter or mother-son relationships as well as with father-daughter or father-son relationships were analyzed. During adolescence, fathers tend to accept their sons' striving for autonomy, if, and this is crucial, the sons' level of identity is high. Sons tend to introduce their disagreements directly, and fathers accept this difference. With daughters, fathers' communication behavior in discussions appears to be quite different. Fathers interrupt their daughters more often and less often accept their opinions.

Differences occur in the quality of the mother-son and father-daughter relationship. Most parent-adolescent distress is reported from mother-son and from father-daughter dyads, with mother-son distress occurring most during early adolescence, and distress between fathers and daughters occurring most during mid-adolescence. On the other hand, mothers tend to be more open with their adolescent children's point of view and, by the same token, adolescents feel more accepted by their mothers than by their fathers. However, when the influence of adolescent gender on outcome variables, such as school achievement, was investigated together with variables such as maternal warmth, monitoring, or autonomy giving, gender was only a weak moderator variable compared to the impact of differences in mothers' parenting style. In a meta-analysis in which Russell and Saebel (1997) studied investigations covering all ages of gender differences in the parent-child relationship, relatively few consistent gender differences remained statistically relevant.

Parent-Adolescent Relationships in Divorced Families

As conflictual parent-parent relationships have been shown to produce spillover effects for parent-child relationships, children and adolescents' behaviors after divorce cannot solely be attributed to the act of divorce alone. Rather, impairment in development can be seen as a product of children's experiences in their families long before parents separate or divorce, as they grow up in the context of a deteriorating parent-parent relationship. Thus, behavior problems, maladjustments, poor social skills, and—particularly during adolescence—disengagement from the family as well as an increased orientation toward peer groups is more prevalent in children from divorced than from nondivorced families. Moreover, academic achievement and antisocial behavior also appear to be strongly influenced by family status.

Different types of impacts have been discovered with regard to age, gender, and the larger social milieu. Children in middle childhood who live with their same-sex parent in a supporting social context do better after divorce than small children or adolescents who live with the opposite-sex parent in an aversive environment. Boys experience more aversive treatments from divorced mothers than do girls. As a more general pattern, children from divorced and stepparent families experience greater difficulties in their social relations, academic achievement, and adjustment. By the same token, children in stepfamilies experience stepfathers who are less engaged and give less guidance than do biological fathers. Moreover, in a longitudinal study, Hetherington et al. (1992) found that, particularly during early adolescence, remarriage does not improve adjustment problems of children. When school-age children from divorced and nondivorced families were compared, only slight differences were discovered; these slight differences, however, tended to increase in adolescence and early adulthood. Only few gender differences in boy's and girl's adaptation to remarriages have been found.

Working Mothers and Influences on the Quality of Relationships

Much of the research that deals with effects of maternal employment on child development is focused on working mothers versus nonworking mothers and their infants or preschool children. As a consequence, most investigations have analyzed day-care influences on children whose mothers have joined the workforce. As an overall result, it has been found that with adequate care, no detrimental effects occur during early development, even up to early adolescence. Moreover, up to the age of 12, no relationship between maternal employment and any developmental domain for either gender was discovered. In addition, there were no correlations between maternal employment and role arrangement in the family when gender-specific effects were studied. Only in case of an obviously inequitable division of parental working patterns and family roles (that is, in a dual-earner family with traditional roles) do children seem to exhibit poor socioemotional adjustment and low self-esteem and peer acceptance. Generally, mixed results occurred when child-rearing practices of working and nonworking mothers were directly compared. Employed mothers did encourage their children more than did nonemployed mothers to become independent and to take over responsibility for household tasks at an earlier age; however, maternal employment has also been linked to lack of monitoring and lower school performances (Crouter, MacDermid, McHale, & Perry-Jenkins, 1990).

Maternal working patterns in the family have an enormous impact on the adolescents' experience of their parents' approach to sharing child care and socialization tasks. In families where mothers enter the workforce when children are still very young (3½ years old), youth between 8 and 12 years old experience greater father involvement compared to single-earner families. It should be noted, however, that an overarching secular trend tends to blur all kinds of differences found for single- and dual-earner families. As more and more children grow up in dual-earner homes, other variables than just the fact of having a working mother apparently become more relevant. For example, the degree of general parental involvement, the quality of the home environment, and, last but not least, the quality of the parent-parent relationship appear to be of greater importance for children's and adolescents' developmental pathways. In general, maternal employment seems to facilitate changes in the mother-adolescent relationship during the transition period.

Ethnicity and Parent-Adolescent Relationships

It is a general question how macrocontexts and the fact of being a member of a minority and a specific ethnic group affect aspects of identity formation and contribute to the concrete formatting of interactions within the family. Research investigating formats of the parent-adolescent relationship can be partitioned into two groups: comparisons between a specific ethnic minority group such as African, Asian, or Mexican American, and European American groups, and research on a more differential level analyzing constancies and variations within such groups. One common criterion for the distinction among ethnic groups—the degree of individualism versus collectivism—has often been used as a general guideline for parents' socialization goals. However, this distinction has not been found to be as valid as had been believed (Parke & Buriel, 1998). Instead, the larger context of the individual's immigration history seems to be more important for the characterization of the parent-adolescent relationship in an immigrant group. Intergene-rational tensions might grow out of unequal degrees of acculturation in parents and their adolescent children.

The process of the adolescent's individuation tends to create increased conflicts in immigrant families because of frictions between cultures to concede independence to children within the family at certain developmental stages. It is within this larger cultural context that parents are able to accept their children's efforts for autonomy and separation and to support the common search for a new balance in the parent-adolescent relationship. A common solution in these families is biculturalism.

Moreover, adolescents may also function as cultural brokers for their families if their parents insist on preserving their native language as the major language in parent-adolescent communication; thus, parents may use language as a tool of authority. Children who grow up in two different cultural contexts also tend to develop optimal skills to switch repertoires of behaviors appropriate in the two different cultures. As mediators, children may maintain strong emotional bonds with their parents, as they have the possibility to view both sides of the acculturation issue: keeping a cultural context with a specific value system versus the cost of giving it up. Thus, an adolescent's efforts to gain autonomy in a parent-adolescent relationship in an immigrant family must be seen in a different light compared to the efforts of an adolescent who grows up in a single-culture family.

In regard to the analysis of parent-adolescent relationships in African American families, a necessary shift from a pathological-disorganizational to a strength-resiliency perspective has been emphasized. An elaboration of the positive aspects of the specific family structures is required when the quality of parent-child relationships in African American families is being assessed. Extended family structures with a strong sense for family obligations, fluidity of household boundaries, and frequent interaction with relatives are characteristics of socialization opportunities in this ethnic group. Parent-child relationships have been depicted as being more dominated by physical than by verbal cues. However, this behavior is not associated with love withdrawal or harshness. Parental authority and strict control have been found to be an adaptive way to socialize children in a minority group and in dangerous neighborhoods.

In general, when parent-adolescent relationships in minority or immigrant families are considered, special attention should be given to the separation-autonomy task and to the attempt to reconcile ethnicity within mainstream American culture. It seems that parental sensitivity to cultural diversity has positive outcomes for adolescents' ethnic identity. Warm, regulating, autonomy-promoting parenting behaviors leading to positive outcomes in children and adolescents are also predictive of ethnic pride.

Historical Influences on Parent-Adolescent Relationships

The parent-adolescent relationship is not only subject to cultural influences, but also to historical changes. Like the Great Depression during the late 1920s in the United States, or the fundamental cultural changes in Russia after the October Revolution, parent-adolescent relationships cannot be considered without taking into account major historical changes. Economic crises exert an age-specific impact on individual developmental pathways: An adolescent's early takeover of responsibility in the family may lead to high self-esteem in the adult, but a quite different, more detrimental, influence may occur for younger children, as parent-child relationships are changed and younger children develop low self-esteem patterns (Elder, 1974).

It should also be noted that after dramatic economic changes in Eastern Europe, family structures, particularly parent-adolescent relationships, have changed. For example, a 13-year-old adolescent child who today is washing car windshields in the streets of Moscow and acting as the main breadwinner in a large family, plays a different role in that family than during times of stable economic conditions. Thus, the parent-adolescent relationship cannot be evaluated alone by traditional norms in terms of the degree of autonomy granted by parents.

Future studies on the parent-adolescent relationship, therefore, should concentrate on the complexity of influences of the family and the larger cultural and historical context of individual development in an attempt to integrate macro- and microlevels:

> Perhaps, on reflection, the next essential step is to not just study adolescent behavior and development within context (using a person × situation design) but to delineate and investigate the social processes that create contextual influences, at the microlevel and macrolevel, on individual development. (Adams, 1996, p. 307)

Bibliography

Adams, G. R. (1996). Reflections: On the past and the future. In G. R. Adams, R. Montemayor, & T. S. Gullotta (Eds.), *Psychosocial development during adolescence* (pp. 300–307). Thousand Oaks, CA: Sage.

Baumrind, D. (1991). Effective parenting during the early adolescent transition. In P. A. Cowan & M. Hetherington (Eds.), *Family transitions* (pp. 111–163). Hillsdale, NJ: Erlbaum.

Blos, P. (1941). *The adolescent personality.* New York: Appleton-Century.

Crouter, A. C., MacDermid, S., McHale, S. M., & Perry-Jenkins, M. (1990). Parental monitoring and perceptions of children's school performance and conduct in dual- and single-earner families. *Developmental Psychology, 26,* 649–657.

Duvall, E. (1977). *Marriage and family development.* Philadelphia: Lippincott.

Elder, G. H. (1974). *Children of the great depression: Social change in life experiences.* Chicago: University of Chicago Press.

Erel, O., & Burman, B. (1995). Interrelatedness of marital and parent-child relations: A meta-analytic review. *Psychological Bulletin, 118,* 108–132.

Erikson, E. H. (1959). Identity and the life cycle. *Psychological Issues, 1.*

Freud, A. (1958). Adolescence. *Psychoanalytic Study of the Child, 13,* 255–278.

Hauser, S. T., Powers, S. I., & Noam, G. G. (1991). *Adolescents and their families.* New York: Free Press.

Hetherington, E. M., Clingempeel, W. G., Anderson, E. R., Deal, J. E., Hagan, M. S., Hollier, E. A., & Lindner, M. S. (1992). Coping with marital transitions: A family systems perspective. *Monographs of the Society for Research in Child Development, 57*(2–3, Serial No. 227).

Hill, J. P. (1987). Research on adolescents and their families: Past and prospect. In W. Damon (Ed.), *New directions for child development: Adolescent health and social behavior* (Vol. 37, pp. 13–32). San Francisco: Jossey-Bass.

Parke, R. D., & Buriel, R. (1998). Socialization in the family: Ethnic and ecological perspectives. In N. Eisenberg (Ed.), *Mussen's handbook of child psychology.* New York: Wiley.

Russell, A., & Saebel, J. (1997). Mother-son, mother-daughter, father-son, and father-daughter: Are they distinct relationships? *Developmental Review, 17,* 111–147.

Smetana, J. G. (1995). Parenting styles and conceptions of parental authority during adolescence. *Child Development, 66,* 299–316.

Kurt Kreppner

Adulthood

The examination of parent–adult child relationships is a complex undertaking, made increasingly so by the trend toward greater longevity and its attendant expansion of the portion of life spent in adulthood. This

PARENT-CHILD RELATIONSHIP: Adulthood. Table 1. Normative intergenerational family life: Concurrent transitions

Generation 1: Parents	Generation 2: Adult Children	Generation 3: Grandchildren
Empty nest	Launching employment	
Children-in-law relations Grandparenthood	Partner selection Childbearing or adoption	 Infancy
Retirement	Career investment Child rearing	Childhood education
Caregiving to frail peers Widowhood	Caregiving to elders Parental loss	Caregiving to elders Grandparental loss
	Empty nest	Launching employment
Grandchildren-in-law relations Great-grandparenthood	Children-in-law relations Grandparenthood	Partner selection Childbearing or adoption
. . .	Retirement . . .	Career investment Child rearing . . .

Note: Relationship designations in the table are indicated using traditional terminology but are intended to include both related and chosen family members; relatedness can occur through marriage, participation in marital-like liaisons, childbearing, adoption, and fictive kin choices.

demographic shift has resulted in great variation in the positions that parents and their offspring occupy along the adult life course; that is, the relationship may comprise parents who are at midlife, retirement, or old age, and children who are young adults newly launched from the family of origin, mature adults with children of their own, or who are themselves old with very old parents. Adequate understanding of the expectations and psychological effects of parent–adult child relationships must, therefore, include consideration of the age and life course position of members in the affiliation. Typically parallel family life transitions for parents and adult children appear in Table 1. The entries illustrate concomitant family events as experienced across generations, and imply that a given event can have relational implications up and down the generational lines.

Other significant influences on parent-child relations throughout adulthood include gender, marital and parental status of the offspring, health status of the parents, and the composition of the parental dyad (married or partnered, separated or divorced, involved in a fairly new romantic liaison, or bereft of a partner). Relationships between older parents and their adult progeny do not exist in isolation, but emerge from a shared history spanning many years during which the course of the relationship was being charted. They endure within a social context that is ever-changing in its introduction of various stressors and supports related to economic resources, mobility patterns, and technologies of communication and health care.

Major Areas of Study and Related Findings

Knowledge about elderly parent–adult child dyads has developed primarily through a collection of independent exploratory and descriptive studies focusing on various aspects of the relationship, usually based on variables of personal well-being or relationship satisfaction. The major findings rendered from this body of research fall within two domains: relationship dynamics and relationship consequences.

Dynamics of the Parent–Adult Child Relationship. Relationship dynamics are the processes by and through which aging parents and their adult children remain involved with one another. This line of research has challenged theories and stereotypes based implicitly on isolated nuclear families. Studies indicate that alienation of adult children from parents is rare; a vast majority of adults maintain enduring relationships with their parents and adult children throughout life. The prevailing dynamics described in the literature include affectional ties, mutual aid and instrumental exchange, social support and interaction, filial maturation, spatial proximity, and caregiving.

Affectional Ties. Emotional attachment is the single most salient construct for examining the dynamics of parent-child relationships across the entire life span. It is particularly important in the study of aged parents and their adult children, considering that continuation of the relationship is a matter of choice rather than physical and material dependence in most cases. Indeed, perceptions of closeness and positive sentiment appear to be the prevailing dynamic operating in the adult parent–child bond.

Also bearing on the relationship are dynamics related to family members' feelings of obligation, sense of duty, or perceptions of social responsibility. Although duty does not carry the same positive connotations as sentimental attachment, both concepts are grounded in an experience and acceptance of interpersonal caring among family members. Ties of affection might diminish and be replaced by bonds of duty when the health of the old parent deteriorates and the adult child is faced with caregiving decisions. Nevertheless, this affection-duty shift does not indicate a lack of caring, but rather, may represent a protective psychological process in which the members disengage prior to the death of the parent in preparation for loss of the relationship.

The experience of emotional closeness and positive sentiment between parents and their adult children is independent of direct contact or interaction with one another and remains intact over time and distance. This is the case particularly between mothers and daughters whose affectional ties are closest, followed, in descending order, by those in father-daughter, mother-son, and father-son dyads.

Mutual Aid and Instrumental Exchange. Another dynamic that serves to maintain the parent-child relationship throughout adulthood is exchange of money and services between the generations. The direction of exchange for money and gifts flows predominantly from parent to child, irrespective of their individual income levels, whereas the direction for exchange of services and assistance (e.g., chores, home repairs) is from child to parent. Direct helping exchanges are correlated with residential nearness, although transactions of money and goods are not. Some visits between older parents and adult children are scheduled for the purpose of task accomplishment and are characterized by a concentration of many instrumental exchanges during a discrete period of time. The nature and number of these exchanges vary across racial ethnic groups according to their available resources and filial expectations.

Offering assistance in times of ill health is usually an intragenerational exchange, with spouses or partners providing the greatest aid to one another. In cases where peers are unavailable or unable to serve in this capacity, health care assistance flows predominantly up the generations, from adult child to parent. Thus, care provision is mutual over the life span, with parental care to young children later reciprocated by adult children's assistance to frail elderly parents.

Social Support and Interaction. Counter to instrumental exchanges, which can be impeded by residential distance, expressive exchanges in the form of social support and interactions take place between parents and adult children regardless of distance through visits, phone calls, letters, and more recently through on-line computer technologies of e-mail and family chat rooms. The process of intergenerational support and interaction is important primarily for reasons of companionship and prevention of the older parent's isolation, but nonfamilial supports of the parent (e.g., friend and neighbor relationships, civic memberships) are equally salient, if not more so, for a sense of social connection and well-being. Even so, expressions of social support and interaction between parents and their adult children are valued because they serve as symbolic evidence of intact attachments and fulfilled responsibility.

The question of who assumes responsibility for initiating personal interactions in older parent–adult child relationships has not been adequately answered. Research suggests that parents and their adult offspring hold differing perceptions of the nature of the relationship and have varying expectations about the levels and types of interaction that are desired, expected, initiated, and received in the process of maintaining the relational bond.

Filial Maturation. Cultivation of parent–adult child relationships occurs as parents and adult children move through time, experiencing their individual processes of aging in concert with differing but concurrent progression through stages in the family life cycle, as illustrated in Table 1. When children move out of the parental home and establish their own residences and families of procreation, the parent-child relationship usually becomes more voluntary, peerlike, and friendly. Parents exert less control and are relieved of responsibility and decision making; meanwhile, adult children begin to identify with the values and experiential histories of their parents. The dynamic of filial maturation in the United States seems to oblige parents to refrain from giving advice regarding, and passing judgment on, the choices and behavior of adult children. Simultaneously, children are expected to adopt parental values and complete socially prescribed transitions in a timely fashion. Both sets of family members are obliged to demonstrate more tolerant and less reactive attitudes and behavior toward one another. Failure on the part of parents or adult children to meet the expectations associated with filial maturation render the process destructive, rather than constructive, for the relationship.

Geographic and Residential Propinquity. The parent–adult child relationship has been irrevocably altered by two demographic trends related to spatial proximity: unprecedented increase in geographic mobility and decline in intergenerational coresidence. Most adults, including those in parent–adult child dyads, state a preference for independent living arrangements and indeed maintain separate households. The most prevalent exception to this rule is a small percentage who share dwellings, most notably, widows residing with youngest daughters. Increasing numbers of old parents and adult offspring live at great distances from one another, but report that lack of propinquity does not significantly impinge upon the affectional ties and expressions of social support and interaction, which are maintained through visits, mail, and electronic communication. Even so, as parents grow older, they tend to migrate toward at least one of their adult children.

Caregiving. The study of parental caregiving has exploded in the past decade, generating a vast literature on the relational issues, benefits, and burdens associated with this family dynamic. A parent's experience of ill health, which may precipitate care provision by an adult child, is itself a correlate of diminished well-being. Likewise, one's inability to engage in reciprocal exchanges of aid and instrumental help, often concomitant with illness and the need for family care provision, is associated with a decline in relationship satisfaction. From the perspective of the adult care provider, attending to the needs of an ill parent often is marked by a shift from attachments of affection to attachments of duty. Daughters and daughters-in-law typically perform the hands-on caregiving tasks, whereas sons are more likely to assume financial and other managerial responsibilities. Recent research shows that parental caregiving affects adult children's relationships not only with their parents, but also with their partners and offspring. Partners and offspring often get involved, at least to some extent, in caregiving tasks.

Consequences of the Parent–Adult Child Relationship. A discussion of the short- and long-term consequences of parent–adult child relationships necessarily begins with a question: Consequences for whom and regarding what? The primary focus of research on parent–adult child relationships has been on the elderly members of the dyads, centering on questions related to their perceptions of well-being and life satisfaction. A few ancillary reports have addressed the effect of the relationship on both members' sense of biographical continuity and belonging. Studies about how the relationship affects the adult children tend to be framed around caregiving issues, and also tend to emphasize their negative aspects.

Well-Being and Life Satisfaction. Whereas adult children and their later-life parents choose to maintain enduring relationships and engage in exchanges of goods, services, and regular social interaction, having children does not necessarily increase the happiness of old people. The connection depends upon both the parents' physical health and their assessment of how their children are faring in adulthood. To the extent that adult children do affect parental well-being, the most important influences include children's level of success, adoption of and adherence to parental values, and movement through socially accepted life stages of achieving independence, employment, marriage, place making, childbearing, and child rearing. These are far more salient indicators of parents' well-being and satisfaction than the virtually inconsequential factors of geographic closeness to, frequency of contact with, or exchange of mutual aid with, offspring. One may infer that parents place greater value on measures that reflect their successful performance as socialization agents who prepared their children for competent independence than on those that might suggest a more dependent adjustment of their children to adult life.

The emphasis placed on filial obligations, and hence the tie between parent-child relations and parental well-being, varies across cultural groups, however. For example, elders who value the traditional as opposed to the nuclear family structure, such as recent immigrants from Asia or parents of Eastern European heritage, hold explicit expectations for filial piety in a context of patriarchal hierarchy. Well-being among members of this population is influenced by the extent to which their adult children fulfill traditional norms of obligation. In contrast, African Americans tend to hold more implicit norms of filial responsibility and to place more emphasis on egalitarian values and collateral relationships. Their well-being depends on having needs met within a loose-knit, flexible network of relatives and fictive kin.

Biographical Continuity. An important consequence of parent–adult child ties is provision of biographical continuity for the members of the dyad. Parent-child bonds are characterized by a long, shared history of which several decades may be lived out in adulthood. This relationship constitutes the rubric from which all past and future family experiences gain meaning and potency. The effects of relationship maintenance can be, on the positive side, the realization of family solidarity, an enduring sense and expression of belongingness, identity, shared values, and positive sentiment. Contrarily, on the negative side, the effects can be embroilment in ongoing family conflict or disengagement rather than solidarity over the same issues of belongingness, identity, values, and experiences of sentiment. In either case, such effects are unique to the parent–adult child bond, as other human relationships do not cover the same powerful history in which the participants are dually engaged in the ongoing construction of identity, meaning, and character.

Stress, Burden, and Coping. The experiences of caring for a frail or ill parent are sharply different depending on the gender of the adult child. Sons typically report limited stress and burden, related to the peripheral nature of their involvement, which is focused on provision of specific, narrowly defined services. Daughters, however, expend considerable time and energy in caregiving that results in strained coping ability and psychological and relational stress, both between parent and child and within the daughter's marital or marital-like relationship, if one exists.

Stress and burden also result from other aspects of the parent–adult child relationship, namely children's stress related to the interference of parents in childrearing practices with the third-generation progeny and parents' stress related to disappointment in adult children's nonnormative life choices or failure to achieve economic or residential independence. In all cases of stress-provoking relations—caregiving, interference, and unrealized parental expectations—families protect their lifelong attachments by using coping strategies such as shifting from affectional to obligatory ties, to allow the continuation of the parent–adult child relationship.

Theories

Knowledge about the parent-child bond in adulthood has emerged through a series of independent, sometimes atheoretical, exploratory, and descriptive studies related to particular aspects of the relationship or perceived problems being faced by aging parents and their adult children. Indeed, commentaries on the state of the field have repeatedly charged scholars to concentrate efforts on theoretically grounded investigations. Although progress is being made in this area as evidenced by explication and recommendation of various frameworks in more recent studies, the state of this science relative to theoretical infusion and sophistication lags behind knowledge of parent-child relations at earlier junctures in the life course. Major theories informing the study of parent-child bonding in adulthood include social exchange, stress and coping, attachment, symbolic interactionism, and family solidarity.

Social Exchange Theory. This theory is the prevailing paradigm used in the study of parent–adult child dyads. It offers predictions and explanations of human relationships based on reciprocal, balanced exchanges of extrinsic and intrinsic benefits and costs of interaction. Social exchange describes a process by which interpersonal trust and commitment develop over time, increasing the likelihood that people will continue their investment even when certain exchanges are reduced, as in the case of geographic distance, or become unbalanced, as in the case of caregiving for an elderly parent.

Stress and Coping. These theories focus on factors that cause tension and anxiety, on methods of contending with stressors, and on positive and negative outcomes of stressful situations. This theoretical approach has made important contributions to knowledge about the experience of family responsibility and burden and how to support families in handling their caregiving roles. Reliance on stress models has been challenged recently, however, particularly by feminist scholars who suggest that stress frameworks limit the understanding of complexities inherent in intergenerational care provision by failing to consider the meaning that caregiving has for adult children, the relational attachments that prompt persons to provide care, and the processes by which caregiving decisions are made.

Attachment Theory. This theory, originating in the field of child development to explicate parent-infant bonding, has been extended to studies of intergenerational ties throughout the life span. Applied to adulthood, the theory examines the effects of predispositions to feel and act in prosocial ways. Concepts drawn from attachment theory have been useful in examining major relationship dynamics between old parents and adult children, including the development and demonstration of affectional ties, the maintenance of social interaction across great spans of time and distance, and motivations for caregiving.

Symbolic Interactionism. This theory emphasizes the process by which individuals develop personal meanings, perceptions, and expectations through involvement with others in a symbolic environment. Given the fact that parent–adult child relationships are voluntary and highly salient, emerging from mutually informed biographies, application of symbolic interactionism to the study of this relational dyad offers promise of increased understanding not simply of what happens between parents and adult children, but also why and how interactions take place and what they mean for each individual.

Family Solidarity. According to this theory, cohesion among family members is reflected in six forms of solidarity: associational, the frequency and patterns of interaction; affectual, demonstrating the type and degree of positive sentiments; consensual, signifying agreement on values, beliefs, and attitudes; functional, referring to exchange of resources and assistance; normative, implying commitment to family roles and obligations; and structural, opportunities for interaction provided by the number and type of family relationships. Examination of these dimensions of solidarity leads to greater understanding of the ties that link individuals to the family group and to one another or keep them separate.

The overarching theoretical assumptions directing the study of parent-child relationships in adulthood constitute an unwieldy intersection between the orientations of individual and family development. Rather than achieving a genuine integration of these two realms, the result has been a trade-off in which individual measures of well-being, satisfaction, or stress have been applied to and extracted from family data; likewise, family phenomena of concurrent life staging and filial maturity have been disassembled and constrained by individual orientations. Complicating this theoretical difficulty are the additional questions of how societal, demographic, historical, and other environmental influences affect the dynamics and consequences of parent-child relationships in adulthood. Perhaps ecosystemic theoretical frameworks, with their focus on family interaction within larger contexts, could help inform the future study of this relationship.

Research Strategies

Investigators have studied parent-child relationships in adulthood primarily through the use of cross-sectional designs utilizing quantitative methods to measure established variables by traditional indicators. Scholars recognize the limitations of this approach and are increasingly calling for innovative designs. These include longitudinal studies to track the development of the relationship throughout and across the parallel life trajectories of parents and children, enabling the discovery of antecedents and predictors of different relationship dynamics and consequences; qualitative studies to ask and answer questions of relationship meaning and process; replicated studies to substantiate or amend scattered findings; studies of racially and ethnically diverse families and of those that migrate; and research designs that include comparison groups of childless adults and adult children with deceased parents. Investigators must ask new questions or examine familiar topics in new ways, such as focusing on the benefits of coresidence or caregiving and care receipt. Incorporation of fresh approaches into the parent–adult child research literature will enhance the depth and breadth of understanding about this crucial and long-standing relationship.

Bibliography

Allen, K. R., Blieszner, R., & Roberto, K. A. (2000). Families in the middle and later years: A review and critique of research in the 1990s. *Journal of Marriage and the Family, 62.* Fourth of a series of decade review articles; summarizes conceptual, theoretical, methodological, and substantive advances, including a section on complexities in parent–adult child relationships.

Bengtson, V. L., & Achenbaum, W. A. (Eds.). (1993). *The changing contract across generations.* New York: Aldine de Gruyter. Multidisciplinary perspectives on issues of generational and age-group relationships including historical and social contexts of the generational contract, discussions of family issues and generational conflict, and analyses of policy implications.

Bengtson, V. L., Rosenthal, C., & Burton, L. (1995). Paradoxes of families and aging. In R. H. Binstock & L. K. George (Eds.), *Handbook of aging and the social sciences* (4th ed., pp. 253–282). San Diego: Academic Press. Reviews research on five issues about family gerontology research findings that do not necessarily correspond with everyday opinions; paradoxes concern the decline of the American family, caregiving role conflicts and rewards, the place of elders in minority families, the place of men in aging families, and intergenerational solidarity and conflict.

Bengtson, V. L., Schaie, K. W., & Burton, L. M. (Eds.). (1995). *Adult intergenerational relations: Effects of societal change.* New York: Springer. Each chapter is followed by commentaries from two other scholars; the afterword ties the book together in an examination of six controversies surrounding adult intergenerational relationships.

Blieszner, R., & Bedford, V. H. (Eds.). (1995). *Handbook of aging and the family.* Westport, CT: Greenwood Press. Many chapters are relevant to the study of parent–adult child relationships, including those on the family context of aging, demographic trends, theoretical frameworks and research methods, parent-child and grandparent-grandchild relations, policy and legal issues, cultural diversity and rurality, and a section on turning points and interventions.

Brubaker, T. H. (1990). Families in later life: A burgeoning research area. *Journal of Marriage and the Family, 52,* 959–981. Third of a series of decade review articles; assesses progress in family gerontology research in the 1980s and provides a summary of research findings, including those related to parent–adult child relationships.

Burton, L. (Ed.). (1992). A new look at families and aging [special issue]. *Generations, 16*(3).

Hareven, T. J. (Ed.). (1996). *Aging and generational relations over the life course.* New York: de Gruyter. Historical and cross-cultural perspectives on parent–adult child and other family relationships.

Mancini, J. A. (Ed.). (1989). *Aging parents and adult children.* Lexington, MA: Lexington Books.

Mancini, J. A., & Blieszner, R. (1989). Aging parents and adult children: Research themes in intergenerational relations. *Journal of Marriage and the Family, 51,* 275–290. Analysis of research methods and findings related to parent–adult child roles and responsibilities, parent–adult child interaction patterns, and the influence of this relationship on well-being. Concludes with suggestions for research and theory development.

Mangen, D. J., Bengtson, V. L., & Landry, P. H., Jr. (Eds.). (1988). *Measurement of intergenerational relations.* Newbury Park, CA: Sage. Presents the origins and development of family solidarity theory, measures of solidarity dimensions, and results of empirical studies of the theory.

Norris, J. E., & Tindale, J. A. (1994). *Among generations: The cycle of adult relationships*. New York: Freeman. This slim textbook includes a chapter specifically on parent–adult child relations; other chapters highlight the implications of other family relationships for the parent-child bond.

Pillemer, K., & McCartney, K. (Eds.). (1991). *Parent-child relations across the life span*. Hillsdale NJ: Erlbaum. Chapters relevant to adult parent–child relationships cover attachment theory, filial maturity, distressed and conflictual relationships, normative obligations to help each other, and generational equity and inequity.

Rossi, A. S., & Rossi, P. H. (1990). *Of human bonding: Parent-child relations across the life course*. New York: de Gruyter. Report of an in-depth study of relationships among three generations in Boston area families; the research, grounded in family solidarity theory, emphasizes the influence of gender and the history of the relationship on adult parent–child interactions.

Ryff, C. D., & Seltzer, M. M. (Eds.). (1996). *The parental experience in midlife*. Chicago: University of Chicago Press. The sections on parents and children as adults and on parent-child relations in midlife, including a chapter on midlife relations as antecedent to parent-child relations in old age, are especially relevant.

Streib, G. F., & Beck, R. W. (1980). Older families: A decade review. *Journal of Marriage and the Family, 42*, 937–956. Second of a series of decade review articles; assesses progress in family gerontology research in the 1970s and provides a summary of research findings, including those related to parent–adult child relationships.

Troll, L. E. (1971). The family of later life: A decade review. *Journal of Marriage and the Family, 33*, 263–290. First of a series of decade review articles; assesses progress in family gerontology research in the 1960s and provides a summary of research findings, including those related to parent–adult child relationships.

Rosemary Blieszner and Nancy Poe Wingfield

PARENTING. *See* Parent-Child Relationship.

PARENT MANAGEMENT TRAINING (PMT) refers to treatment procedures in which parents are trained to alter their child's behavior at home. The goals of PMT are to develop positive prosocial behaviors and to decrease deviant behaviors. PMT has been applied widely to many problem domains (e.g., child compliance, tantrums, enuresis, tics, eating disorders, hyperactivity, adherence to medical regimens) and populations (e.g., preschool children through adolescents and youths with a diagnosis of autism, mental retardation, learning disability, conduct disorder, attention-deficit/hyperactivity disorder).

Background

Although the development of PMT can be traced to several influences, two are particularly noteworthy. First, operant conditioning, elaborated by B. F. Skinner (*The Behavior of Organisms: An Experimental Analysis*, New York, 1938), describes and explains how behavior can be acquired and influenced by a variety of stimuli and consequences. Operant conditioning encompasses basic (e.g., in animal laboratory) and applied (e.g., extensions to diverse populations, including clinical samples) research and serves as a foundation for the techniques that make up PMT.

Second, research has demonstrated that individuals in everyday life can greatly influence responses of other people based on specific ways in which they interact. A well-researched area of study in which this has been elaborated has focused on parent discipline practices and the development of aggressive behavior in children (G. R. Patterson, *Coercive Family Process*, Eugene, OR, 1982). Parental attention to deviant behavior, inattention to prosocial behavior, coercive punishment, poor monitoring of child activities, and failure to set limits unwittingly develop and exacerbate aggressive child behavior. Several studies have shown that parenting practices play a significant role in the development of such behavior and that changing these practices reduces noncompliant, aggressive, and antisocial child behavior.

Key Principles and Techniques

Antecedents, behaviors, and consequences, sometimes referred to as the ABCs, are key ingredients of PMT and are used to alter behaviors of the parents and the child. Antecedents consist of setting events and stimuli that occur prior to behavior and that can be used to promote and directly facilitate behavior. Examples include verbal and physical aids (prompts), instructions, and modeling. Behaviors are the positive prosocial behaviors that are to be developed. Even when the primary goal is to eliminate behaviors (e.g., fighting, stealing, arguing), the focus is on developing prosocial or positive behaviors that reduce the likelihood of the undesired behaviors. Consequences are the events that follow behavior and that can be used to alter the likelihood of such behavior in the future. Positive reinforcement is the key concept and consists of providing social (attention, praise) and sometimes token (points or stars with backup value) reinforcers for behavior. Mild punishment is also used as a consequence (e.g., brief time-out, loss of tokens or privileges), although for several reasons, such as the deleterious side effects of punishment, these play a subservient role to positive reinforcement.

Many procedures can be derived from the general principles (e.g., reinforcement, punishment, extinction;

Kazdin, 1994). These include diverse types of prompts, ways of scheduling consequences, types of consequences, and ways of involving the child and others, such as siblings and peers, in the program. How the procedures are implemented is critical. For example, positive reinforcement at the beginning of a behavior-change program is optimally effective when it is administered contingently (only when the behavior occurs), frequently, immediately, and usually for small increments of behavior. These and related parameters influence the magnitude and durability of behavior change and are relevant in the treatment sessions, as the therapist develops the skills of the parents, and at home, as the parents develop the behaviors of the child.

Characteristics of Treatment

Treatment is conducted primarily with the parent(s), who implement several procedures at home. The parents meet with a therapist who teaches them to use specific procedures to alter interactions with their child, to promote prosocial behavior, and to decrease deviant behavior. Parents are trained to identify, define, and observe problem behaviors in new ways. Careful specification of the problem is essential for the delivery of reinforcing or punishing consequences and for evaluating whether the program is achieving the desired goals. The treatment sessions provide concrete opportunities for parents to see how the techniques are implemented, to practice and refine use of the techniques (e.g., through extensive role playing), and to review the behavior-change programs used at home. Parent-managed reinforcement programs for child deportment and performance at school, completion of homework, and activities on the playground are routinely included, with the assistance of teachers, as available.

Duration of treatment has varied depending on the severity and type of child dysfunction. The most frequent applications are for oppositional and aggressive children. Programs for young, mildly oppositional children usually last from 6 to 8 weeks. With clinically referred aggressive children, the programs usually last from 12 to 25 weeks. PMT is a way of changing how parents interact with their children. Hence, the length of the program refers to the training period. Ideally, the parenting behaviors developed in treatment continue in everyday life.

In most applications, PMT has been administered to families individually in clinic settings. Group administration has been facilitated greatly by the development of videotaped materials that present themes, principles, and procedures to the parents of children with conduct problems. Randomized controlled trials have shown that video-based treatment, particularly in group format and when supplemented with therapist-led discussions, leads to clinically significant changes that are maintained at follow-up one and three years later. The opportunity to disseminate research findings to clinical practice, based on empirically tested videotapes, is unique within child and adolescent therapy research. PMT has also been extended to community settings, and it is effective when provided in small parent groups in neighborhoods in which the families reside. Community applications may permit dissemination of treatment to families that otherwise might not attend the usual mental health service facilities.

Current Evidence

PMT has been evaluated in scores of randomized controlled clinical trials with youths varying in age from 2 to 17 years old. Studies have compared PMT to no-treatment or waiting-list control conditions and to other treatments (e.g., community-based treatment, family therapy, individual therapy). The outcome studies support several conclusions:

- PMT has improved child and adolescent behavior at home, at school, and in the community, as measured by parent and teacher reports, direct observation of behavior, and institutional records (e.g., school truancy, police contacts, arrest rates).
- The magnitude of change has brought conduct-problem behaviors to nonclinical levels of functioning at home and at school, based on normative data from same-age peers.
- Treatment gains have been maintained one to three years after treatment.
- Improvements have also been documented in child behaviors not focused on directly in treatment, in behaviors of siblings in the home, and in maternal psychopathology, particularly depression.

Considerable attention has been devoted to identifying parent and family characteristics that contribute to outcome. Family socioeconomic disadvantage, marital discord, high parental stress and low social support, single-parent families, harsh punishment practices, and parent history of antisocial behavior predict who remains in treatment, the magnitude of change among those who complete treatment, and the extent to which changes are maintained at follow-up. Those families at greatest risk often respond to treatment, but the magnitude of effects is attenuated as a function of the extent to which these factors are present. Among child characteristics, more severe and chronic symptoms predict reduced responsiveness to treatment.

Overall Evaluation

Perhaps the most important point to underscore is that no other technique for children and adolescents with behavioral problems has been studied as thoroughly as has PMT. The procedures and practices that are used in PMT (e.g., various forms of reinforcement and punishment practices) have been widely and effectively applied outside the context of child problems. For example, the techniques have been applied in diverse settings (psychiatric hospitals, rehabilitation facilities, nursing homes, special education and regular classrooms, the military, business and industry) for purposes of treatment, rehabilitation, and education. A great deal is known about the procedures and parameters of delivery that influence the effectiveness of reinforcement and punishment. Consequently, very concrete recommendations can be provided to change behavior and to alter programs when behavior change has not occurred.

Several resources are available to facilitate use of PMT in clinical settings and in research. In addition to the videotapes already mentioned, treatment manuals are available for clinicians that convey the structure and focus of treatment sessions. Books and pamphlets for parents are also available that convey basic concepts and show how to apply various techniques. In short, several training materials are available for professionals, as well as their clients.

PMT makes several demands on the parents, such as mastering educational materials that explain major principles underlying the program, systematically observing deviant child behavior and implementing specific procedures at home, attending weekly sessions, and responding to frequent telephone contacts made by the therapist. The demands on some families may be too great for them to participate in treatment. PMT also makes demands of the therapist. PMT requires mastery of several principles and of procedures that derive from these principles. Antecedents and consequences for behavior have to be administered in quite special ways to ensure their effectiveness. The requisite skills in administering these within the treatment sessions can be readily taught, but they are not trivial. Unfortunately, few training programs in child psychiatry, clinical psychology, and social work are available that expose individuals to PMT.

Bibliography

Forehand, R., & Long, N. (1996). *Parenting the strong-willed child.* Chicago: Contemporary Books. This is a popular book for parents that conveys key procedures that can be used to alter child behavior.

Kazdin, A. E. (1994). *Behavior modification in applied settings* (5th ed.). Pacific Grove, CA: Brooks/Cole. This book reviews the principles of operant conditioning on which parent training is based, how these principles are implemented, and applications for many different settings well beyond interventions in the home.

Kazdin, A. E. (1997). Parent management training: Evidence, outcomes, and issues. *Journal of the American Academy of Child & Adolescent Psychiatry, 36,* 1349–1356. This article reviews current evidence on the effectiveness of parent management training and current strengths and limitations of the approach.

Serketich, W. J., & Dumas, J. E. (1996). The effectiveness of behavioral parent training to modify antisocial behavior in children: A meta-analysis. *Behavior Therapy, 27,* 171–186. This article reviews evidence for PMT for a specific clinical problem and serves as a useful resource for further reading of primary sources.

Webster-Stratton, C. (1996). Early intervention with videotape modeling: Programs for families of children with oppositional defiant disorder or conduct disorder. In E. D. Hibbs & P. Jensen (Eds.), *Psychosocial treatment research of child and adolescent disorders: Empirically based strategies for clinical practice* (pp. 435–474). Washington, DC: American Psychological Association. This chapter presents a series of studies on the effectiveness of parent training and illustrates some of the excellent research on this treatment.

Alan E. Kazdin

PARSONS, FRANK (1854–1908), founder of vocational guidance. With the founding of the Vocation Bureau in Boston and the posthumous publication of Parsons's book *Choosing a Vocation* (Boston, 1909), the foundation was in place for modern career intervention theory. In this seminal book, Parson suggested three essential components to the career counseling process: (1) accurate self-knowledge, (2) information about occupations and the principles of success, and (3) true reasoning on the relations of these two groups of knowledge.

Born and reared in Mount Holly, New Jersey, Parson enrolled at Cornell University at the age of 16, graduating 3 years later as a civil engineer. After initial employment with a railroad, he was caught up in a national economic panic resulting in his working as a laborer in an iron company. With this first-hand knowledge of employment conditions in industry and his readings in economic theory, Parsons began to shape his philosophy as a social reformer. He then turned to a career in public education in Southbridge, Massachusetts. During his stint as a teacher, he studied law, passing the bar exam with exceptionally high scores. Subsequently, he worked as an editor, college professor, writer and lecturer on political economy, social reformer, and as a counselor.

The historical period of Parsons's contributions was one of confusion and optimism. The industrial revolution resulted in a work force concentrated in cities, a demand for a skilled workforce, and uncertainty in the labor market. Parsons espoused a philosophy—mutualism—that shared many ideas with the Populist party.

Mutualism advocated public ownership of utilities, education of the public about their civic duty and rights, improvement of public education, women's suffrage, and the awakening of the moral conscience of people to remedy the evils of an unjust society. His views led to his dismissal from a faculty position at what is now Kansas State University, but they also exerted influence on many people, including Theodore Roosevelt, who read his extensive correspondence, articles, and books. He also advocated some social Darwinist notions that, when examined by today's standards, appear elitist.

Parsons never married, never sought riches as an end, and died nearly destitute following a long illness. Instead, he dedicated his life to serving others and addressing social ills. One of the problems he confronted was the difficulty adolescents had in dealing with the complex conditions and demands of modern life, indicating a need for assisting people in making career choices and plans. His visionary idealism resulted in an organized plan that was translated into practice; practice that continues today in schools and other career counseling settings.

Bibliography

Brewer, J. M. (1942). *History of vocational guidance*. New York: Harper.

Davis, H. V. (1969). *Frank Parsons: Prophet, innovator, counselor*. Carbondale, IL: Southern Illinois University Press.

Dixon, D. N. (1987). From Parsons to profession: The history of guidance and counseling psychology. In J. A. Glover, & R. R. Ronning (Eds.), *Historical foundations of educational psychology* (pp. 107–119). New York: Plenum.

McDaniels, C., & Watts, G. (Eds.). (1994). A thematic issue on the life and work of Frank Parsons. *Journal of Career Development, 20*, 261–332.

David N. Dixon

PASTORAL COUNSELING. Pastoral counseling is as old as religious tradition, and as new as the birth of psychoanalysis. The religious counselor was an integral part of the early Israelite courts, and in the Christian Bible, the notion of *counselor* was even used to characterize the activities of the Holy Spirit. There has never been a time in the history of the Judeo-Christian religion when religious leaders have not had, as one of their functions, the counseling and spiritual direction of their congregants. At the same time, this ancient notion of counseling has taken on a far more complex and expansive reality with the modern development of the human sciences, particularly psychology and psychiatry. Indeed, the contemporary pastoral counseling movement may be seen as one of the many attempts to graft to a traditional activity the theories, research, and praxis of much of contemporary psychology, particularly psychology's expression in the various forms of counseling and psychotherapy.

The Definitional Dilemma

From its inception as a self-conscious movement within the theological community, modern pastoral counseling has been faced with myriad problems of definition. In its *1998 Directory* (Fairfax, Va., 1998), the American Association of Pastoral Counselors defined pastoral counseling as "a process in which a pastoral counselor utilizes insights and principles derived from the disciplines of theology and the behavioral sciences in working with individuals, couples, families, groups, and social systems toward the achievement of wholeness and health" (p. xi), and the pastoral counselor as "a minister who practices pastoral counseling at an advanced level which integrates religious resources and insights from the behavioral sciences" (p. xi). Imbedded in these formal definitions are the signs of how difficult it has been for pastoral counselors, particularly pastoral counseling specialists (those not serving primarily in congregations), to obtain unambiguous status in both the behavioral science community and in the religious/theological community. In one sense, the beginning of contemporary pastoral counseling may be traced to the cultural and intellectual concerns contained in the continuous dialogue between science and religion. That dialogue has had sundry implications, some of them brought into focus in the development of pastoral counseling and in its modern expression within a culture wider than the religious contexts in which it evolved.

This definitional battle has spawned a variety of attempts to arrive at an accurate and acceptable terminology, including the introduction of the term *pastoral psychotherapist*, frequently used interchangeably with *pastoral counselor*. This issue of nomenclature is partly an expression of identity factors, which have perennially characterized the pastoral counseling movement. Because both internal self-understandings, as well as a variety of external forces, always generate professional identity, achieving an authentic identity is an ongoing project for most professions. This has been particularly true for pastoral counselors because in both theory and praxis, two rich conceptual worlds are constantly at interface: the religious/theological and the behavioral/social sciences

History

The modern pastoral counseling movement has its roots in a variety of contemporary developments in which religion and science, spirituality and health, and spiritual direction and psychotherapy, interact. Intellectually, William James's classical work, *The Varieties of Religious Experience: A Study of Human Nature* (Cambridge, Mass., 1902/1985), provided one of the bases for the subject of the psychological study of religion to gain acceptance into theological schools' curricula, particularly in American Protestant seminaries. This intellectual introduction interfaced with a variety of developments attempting to relate religion and health, particularly the Emmanuel movement, an organization formed in 1904 with the purpose of bringing together medicine and religion under the conviction that the healings reported in the Christian Bible continue in the contemporary world.

Much of this renewed interest in the religion/health relationship found expression in what has come to be known as the clinical pastoral education (CPE) movement. That movement was an attempt to bring theological students, ordained clergy, members of religious orders, and specially trained laypersons into closely supervised encounters with persons in crisis. The early contexts for clinical pastoral education were general and mental hospitals and correctional institutions, agencies in which ministerial students came into close contact not only with suffering patients, but with physicians, nurses, social workers, psychologists, and psychiatrists.

It is impossible to understand the development and spread of pastoral counseling without a grasp of clinical pastoral education. Indeed, modern pastoral counseling—no matter how specialized and how closely identified with current human sciences it has become—is deeply colored by the long and rich history of pastoral care. In a very real sense, pastoral counseling is part of the wider history of pastoral care.

Throughout this history of attempts to interface modern psychological science with religious and theological systems, a cadre of writers and researchers have endeavored to articulate the issues and problems implicit in any interdisciplinary project: Anton Boisen, often considered the father of clinical pastoral education and the man who coined the phrase "the living human document" as a focus of study and care, was one of the first to attempt to introduce a psychosocial perspective into theological education and to challenge the strictly classical type of education found in most seminaries at the turn of the century. Seward Hiltner, frequently considered the father of contemporary pastoral theology, was a strong critic of pastoral counseling whenever it appeared to overidentify with the psychological and psychiatric theories and practices of the day. Other significant pioneers in the development of pastoral counseling were Wayne Oates, Paul E. Johnson, Carroll Wise, Howard Clinebell, and John Patton.

Despite vigorous attempts to build theory and produce literature, there has been no single and systematic theoretical system and undergirding pastoral counseling. For the most part, its literature has been characterized by a tendency to borrow from a variety of secular systems, particularly in the early days from Rogerian person-centered psychotherapy and from developments in psychodynamic psychotherapy. Relating and integrating these theories into theological systems of thought, particularly those theological frameworks developed by liberal theologians such as Paul Tillich and Neibuhr, occupied a great deal of the pastoral counseling's literature for nearly a century.

Although empirical research (empirical in the sense of American psychology's meaning of that term, that is, quantifiable) has been light, pastoral counseling has generated a significant body of knowledge and professional procedures. Its scholarly and professional journals include the *Journal of Pastoral Care, Pastoral Psychology, Abstracts of Research in Pastoral Care and Counseling*, the *Journal of Supervision and Training in Ministry*, the *Journal of Pastoral Counseling, Pilgrimage: Psychotherapy and Personal Exploration*, the *Journal of Psychology and Judaism*, and the *Journal of Psychology and Theology*, as well as several foreign journals. It has also produced a major dictionary, Rodney Hunter's *Dictionary of Pastoral Care and Counseling* (Nashville, Tenn., 1990) and numerous reference resources.

Professional Status

Regarding its professional status, pastoral counseling as a speciality has had difficulty becoming part of the wider psychological and psychotherapeutic communities. Pastoral psychology and the psychology of religion—two of its intellectual foundations—have not found a secure place in the typical university academic divisions. Instead, they frequently have found a home in theological schools and seminaries, particularly of the liberal variety. This reality, coupled with a host of political and turf propensities both in psychology and theology, has required pastoral counselors to legitimize their profession by identifying with more established disciplines and professions. One of the implications of this is that in the areas of licensing and certification, pastoral counselors have been forced to secure credentials under other rubrics. Although several states do have licensing laws specifically for pastoral counselors, more likely than not pastoral counselors tend to secure their secular status by fulfilling requirement as psychologists, professional counselors, social workers, or marriage and family therapists.

Much of pastoral counseling literature deals with issues inevitably raised by any radical interdisciplinary and radically systemic approach to viewing the whole human condition (physical, psychological, social, ethical, and spiritual). Several perennial controversies have tended to surface and remain unresolved:

1. The identity of the pastoral counselor; for example, in what way is he or she *different* from the secular counselor or psychotherapist?
2. What are the most creative and authentic ways to integrate the human sciences into the theological/faith paradigms?
3. What is needed to make pastoral counseling an integral part of the wider health/therapy cultures without loosing its unique identity rooted in faith and spirituality?
4. Is it possible for the pastoral counselor to be radically *inclusive* (gender, faiths, ethnicity, etc.) in building theory and practice, and at the same time gain a proper place in the wider therapeutic projects?

Future of the Profession

There is a current surge of interest in spirituality on the part of psychology and psychotherapy, characterized by such works as E. P. Shafranske's *Religion and the Clinical Practice of Psychology* (Washington, D.C., 1996) and P. S. Richards and A. E. Bergin's *A Spiritual Strategy for Counseling and Psychotherapy* (Washington, D.C., 1997). Equally evident and relevant is the fact that the health communities are finally recognizing the relationships between health and religion. As a result, the pastoral counseling movement's history and propensities are beginning to be sought out by many secular caregivers, particularly those theoreticians and practitioners who wish to be more holistic than previous generations. Because pastoral counseling has demonstrated a degree of effectiveness in the art of integrating religious, spiritual, and ethical factors into the physical/psychological/social matrix, part of its future may be to provide a resource in both the evolution of psychology as a science and a profession and in the revamping of theory and practice in counseling and psychotherapy.

Bibliography

Boisen, A. T. (1993). *The exploration of the inner world.* New York: Harper & Brothers. A partly autobiographical account of the author's battle with mental illness, which led to his notion of the "living human document," and his stress on the importance of theological education including a clinical dimension.

Clinebell, H. (1984). *Basic types of pastoral care and counseling.* Nashville, TN: Abingdon. Covers the typical topics of an introduction to modern pastoral counseling with a particularly strong emphasis on the systemic and interdisciplinary nature of pastoral counseling.

Hiltner, S. (1976). *Pastoral counseling.* Nashville, TN: Abingdon. Critiques the origin and direction of pastoral counseling as a specialized expression of ministry and defines many of the perennial issues of the movement.

Holifield, E. B. (1983). *A history of pastoral care in America: From salvation to self-realization.* Nashville, TN: Abingdon. Includes a scholarly elaboration on ways in which pastoral counseling reflected much of what was happening in the secular developments of American psychology in the twentieth century.

Kemp, C. F. (1947). *Physicians of the soul: A history of pastoral counseling.* New York: Macmillan. Outlines the development of pastoral care and counseling from the early Christian church to modern times.

Patton, J. (1983). *Pastoral counseling: A ministry of the church.* Nashville, TN: Abingdon. Stresses the importance of pastoral counseling to identify more with its religious and theological roots and less with secular counseling and psychotherapy.

Strunk, O., Jr. (Ed.). (1973). *Dynamic interpersonalism for ministry: Essays in honor of Paul E. Johnson.* Nashville, TN: Abingdon. A Festschrift illustrating the attempt to integrate philosophical, theological, sociological, social ethics, psychological, and psychiatric notions into a pastoral counseling paradigm.

Thornton, E. E. (1970). *Professional education for ministry: A history of clinical pastoral education.* Nashville, TN: Abingdon. Traces the early developments of clinical pastoral education and how it changed theological education in the twentieth century.

Wise, C. (1983). *Pastoral psychotherapy: Theory and practice.* Northvale, NJ: Jason Aronson. Makes a claim for a notion of pastoral psychotherapy that includes a strong psychoanalytic orientation that would be equally available for congregational pastors as well as pastoral counseling specialists.

Orlo C. Strunk, Jr.

PATTERN RECOGNITION. Perceiving the visual world around us is one of the most basic acts of everyday experience. Although pattern recognition may seem effortless, it is actually a complex problem: so much so, that the visual areas responsible for this process occupy up to one-half of our cerebral cortex. Fundamental to perception is the transformation of the light array that falls on the retinas into coherent surfaces and objects. How this is done is still a matter of some debate, but results from psychophysical, neuropsychological, and physiological studies point toward a remarkably adaptive system that supports a wide range of recognition tasks.

The Flexibility of Human Recognition

One of the hallmarks of the human pattern recognition system is its extreme flexibility. As observers, we are able to identify objects under a wide array of conditions that confound even the most powerful computer vision systems. For example, we can recognize objects at many different categorical levels (e.g., Snoopy, beagle, dog, animal). Often, however, it is assumed that objects are first identified at the *entry level* (Jolicoeur, Gluck, & Kosslyn, 1984), defined as the name generated or matched most rapidly to a given object, for example, "apple" or "bird" (although less typical instances may be first identified at a more specific level, for example, "penguins").

Whereas entry-level recognition is certainly an important element of everyday recognition, it is not the only level at which objects are recognized. We often identify objects at a more specific level, sometimes referred to as the *subordinate level*, for example, a "McIntosh apple" or a "white-breasted nuthatch." Such finer discriminations require additional perceptual analysis and thus typically take longer than entry-level judgments. Beyond subordinate level recognition, we also recognize objects at the *individual* or *exemplar* level, for example, "the MacIntosh apple I brought for lunch." Making such judgments requires specific information about a given individual object and consequently even greater perceptual analysis.

The fact that we are capable of performing any of these tasks with remarkable precision indicates that visual recognition is best thought of as a continuum ranging from rather coarse to incredibly fine perceptual discriminations (Tarr & Bülthoff, 1995). As pointed out by Marr and Nishihara (1978), there is a trade-off between the information that captures the more general and less variable properties of objects, and the information that captures the finer and more variable details of objects. Thus, we may need more than one visual recognition system to support categorization at many different levels.

Pattern Perception

Before objects can be identified at any level, the contours and surfaces defining them must be grouped into coherent wholes or patterns. Remember that what arrives at our eyes is just an array of light intensities, but what we perceive are surfaces and objects. At the most elementary level it is clear that our visual system performs a *feature analysis* at every location in the scene. What this means is that the optic array is transformed into a description of local visual properties, for example, the orientation of edges or the color of restricted regions. This recoding provides important information about what is happening in the scene in terms of visual properties that we "care" about, but does not tell us how to put such features together to form more complex percepts. Thus, it is typically assumed that, following feature detection, principles of *perceptual organization* are used to combine local features into more global structures, for example, extended contours or textured three-dimensional surfaces. Principles such as *similarity* (similar features are grouped together) or *good continuation* (features that form a straight line or a smooth curve are grouped together) were originally elucidated by the Gestalt school of psychology during the early 1900s and, remarkably, they are still considered fundamental today.

Beyond such simple principles, there are many other processes that appear to contribute to the perception of complex patterns (for a good overview of many aspects of pattern perception, see Rock, 1990). Two of the best known are *structure-from-motion* and *shape-from-shading*. In the former case, three-dimensional surfaces can be perceived because local two-dimensional motions can be integrated according to the principle that they must all arise from a single moving rigid object whose surface orientations only change gradually. Likewise, by attending to the change in shading (or texture for that matter) over a surface, and again assuming only gradual shifts in orientation, we can perceive the three-dimensional shape of an object. Even these principles, however, are insufficient to specify completely the complex nature of a typical scene. What is ultimately necessary is that we separate each object from both other objects and the background, a process known as *figure-ground* segregation. Presumably, we rely on cues such as discontinuities in color, texture, or shape, but the precise mechanisms for segregating figure from ground are still poorly understood: Indeed, this is one of the reasons why computer vision systems are so bad at object recognition.

Recognizing Objects in a Changing World

Compounding the already difficult task of segmenting individual objects from a complex scene is the variability we encounter in viewing conditions at different moments in time. The recognition system must contend with images of objects that vary with changes in almost any viewing parameter, including occlusion, illumination, orientation, three-dimensional viewpoint, position, size, or configuration (see Figure 1). Almost any source of variability may affect recognition performance with recent evidence suggesting that the degree to which a change impairs recognition depends on the categorical level of the recognition judgment. For example, increasing the visual similarity between the actual target object and other potential target objects typically increases recognition costs across changes in viewpoint (Tarr, 1995). As discussed in the following section, the bulk of object recognition research has focused on variability due to changes in viewpoint, presumably because rotating an object in depth produces such dramatic changes in the image.

Current Theories of Object Recognition

How the visual system compensates for variation in the image forms the core of almost all current theories of object recognition. As a starting point, most theories assume either relatively *image-invariant* or relatively *image-dependent* representations. Viewpoint is often

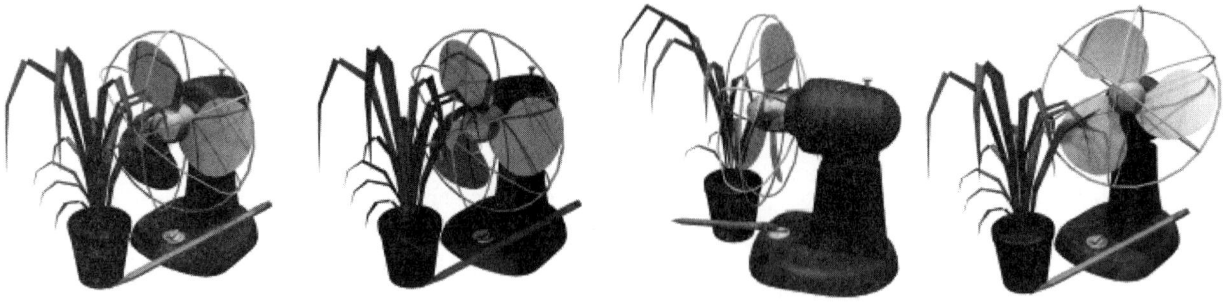

PATTERN RECOGNITION. Figure 1. Examples of some of the variability the visual recognition system must overcome. From left to right we can still recognize the fan despite partial occlusion, a change in illumination, a change in viewpoint, and a change in configuration.

taken to be the diagnostic case, and theories typically predict either small and discrete performance costs across changes in viewpoint (Biederman, 1987) or large and continuous performance costs across changes in viewpoint (Tarr, 1995). One might think that because we are able to recognize known objects quite well from almost any viewing position that object representations must be viewpoint invariant. In fact, since we are already familiar with real-world objects from many different viewpoints, it is just as likely that we have learned multiple viewpoint-specific representations for each known object or class.

One method for investigating these alternatives involves teaching observers to name novel objects from a single orientation and then testing observers' generalization to new picture-plane orientations (Tarr & Pinker, 1989). Observers were fastest at the familiar orientation and progressively slower at unfamiliar orientations farther and farther from the trained orientation. With practice, however, observers became equally fast at all known orientations. Such learning may be analogous to the apparent viewpoint independence exhibited for known objects: invariance obtained by virtue of already knowing what an object looks like from multiple vantage points. This conjecture can be tested by introducing additional new orientations for the now-familiar objects. In this condition observers continued to show equivalent performance for all familiar orientations, but they took longer to recognize the objects in unfamiliar orientations—now, however, with performance dependent on the *nearest familiar* orientation. Similar results have also been obtained for novel three-dimensional objects rotated in depth (Tarr, 1995).

Other evidence for multiple image-dependent representations, often referred to as *view-based models*, comes from physiological research. For example, Logothetis, Pauls, and Poggio (1995) trained monkeys to recognize novel objects from several different three-dimensional viewpoints. With practice the monkeys, like humans, became equally good at recognizing the objects from any of the training viewpoints. When Logothetis et al. recorded the electrical responses of neurons in the inferior temporal cortex of the trained monkeys, they found that many cells responded selectively to a previously novel object and, crucially, maximally to a single viewpoint that had been shown during training. As with recognition performance in humans, there was a gradual decrease in a given cell's response as the preferred object was rotated away from the familiar viewpoint. Thus, a collection of neurons, with subsets of these neurons tuned to different views, may represent a three-dimensional object. There are, however, some problems with this explanation. For instance, there is as yet no clear definition of what object properties are included in each view.

The best known alternative to view-based models are *structural-description* models that typically assume image-invariant representations (Biederman, 1987; Marr & Nishihara, 1978). Such models make two fundamental assumptions: (a) objects are remembered through features that are stable over changes in the appearance of the object; and (b) configurations of such features are described relative to one another rather than relative to the observer or the world. In one version of a structural-description model, Marr and Nishihara proposed that observers could use the major axes of an object to recover the three-dimensional parts of an object. They further suggested that the parts were three-dimensional volumes described in a viewpoint-independent manner; therefore, once an object's parts were determined, its description in memory would be identical regardless of the observer's vantage point. Biederman proposed a similar model in which there is only a limited set (approximately thirty) of qualitatively defined three-dimensional volumes, for example, "brick" or "cone." (The term *qualitative* refers to the fact that many slightly different representations all count as instances of the same type of thing; for example, a variety of boxes of different heights and widths might all be considered to be "bricks.") The positive aspect of restricting the kinds of parts used in the representation is that it is easier to determine the description of an object; the negative aspect is that only a limited set of objects can be described. A second problem with models that use three-dimensional parts is that they must develop ways to consistently determine three-dimensional information from two-dimensional input.

One element that appears to be missing from both view-based and structural-description models is how to account for the flexibility of recognition across different categorical levels. It has often been claimed that structural descriptions are best suited to distinguishing between visually dissimilar objects (typically, entry-level categories), whereas view-based models are best suited to distinguishing between visually similar objects (typically, subordinate level categories or individuals). Such a claim is not entirely satisfactory if visual recognition is to be thought of as continuum. Where does one draw the boundary between one process and the other? Moreover, although it is known that damage to parts of the visual system can result in *object agnosia* (an inability to visually identify certain types of objects), there is little evidence to suggest that agnosic individuals simply lose the ability to recognize objects at either the entry level or the subordinate level (the pattern expected if one of the two systems is removed). Rather, agnosic individuals seem to show a more complex pattern of sparing and loss. Thus, in contrast to earlier conclusions, the recent neuropsychological literature does not support separable recognition systems for different levels of analysis. One possibility is that we have only a single visual recognition system that can be fine-tuned in response to perceptual experience, thereby mediating recognition at multiple categorical levels/degrees of visual similarity. Indeed, both view-based and structural-description theorists have begun to consider the possibility of a single recognition system that can support both coarse categorical judgments and finer discriminations, adaptively selecting the most appropriate features according to the task at hand.

Face Recognition

Although the notion of a unified recognition system is appealing, there are certain phenomena that point toward at least some specialization in recognition mechanisms. One of the most notable examples is the case of face recognition, where brain-injured patients, brain-imaging studies, and behavioral results all appear to indicate a face-specific recognition system. Perhaps the most compelling piece of evidence is the phenomenon of *prosopagnosia*, a syndrome in which brain injury to visual cortex results in a profound inability to recognize individual faces (see Farah, 1992). Although it has been argued that prosopagnosic individuals are more impaired at recognizing faces relative to other objects, it is possible that face recognition occurs at a more subordinate level as compared to common object recognition. Indeed, almost all prosopagnosic individuals have some difficulties recognizing nonface objects.

More evidence for face-specific processing was found by using PET (positron emission tomography) imaging and fMRI (functional magnetic resonance imaging), which showed that certain areas of the inferior temporal cortex are more active for face recognition as compared to common object recognition (Sergent, Ohta, & MacDonald, 1992). As mentioned, faces and common objects, however, are generally recognized at different categorical levels: faces at the individual level and common objects at the class level. What happens when common objects are also recognized at a more specific level? Using fMRI, Gauthier, Anderson, Tarr, Skudlarski, and Gore (1997) observed that the same areas of the inferior temporal cortex found to be more active for face recognition are also more active for subordinate level recognition of common objects as compared to entry-level recognition of the same objects. Therefore, this area of the inferior temporal cortex is more plausibly involved in finer levels of recognition, regardless of stimulus class, rather than in face recognition per se.

Finally, there are many studies that have reported face-specific behavioral effects. One of the most interesting is that of "holistic" processing for faces. Tanaka and Farah (cited in Farah, 1992) found that observers were poorer at recognizing part of a trained face, for example, "Bob's nose," if other parts of the face, for example, the eyes, were transformed from the original configuration. This configural sensitivity is surprising in that the recognition of an individual part would seem to be independent of other features. In contrast, identifying individual parts of trained houses did not produce this effect, suggesting face specificity. On the other hand, observers are almost always perceptual experts at individual face recognition, but rarely so for other classes of objects (exceptions being birdwatchers and the like). To test whether perceptual expertise rather than the stimulus class produces configural sensitivity, Gauthier and Tarr (1997) created a novel class of objects, "Greebles" (see Figure 2). Observers unfamiliar with Greebles did not show configural sensitivity. Greeble experts (created through 10 hours of training), however, showed configural sensitivity in identifying individual Greeble parts. Thus, factors such as the degree of perceptual expertise, rather than the stimulus class,

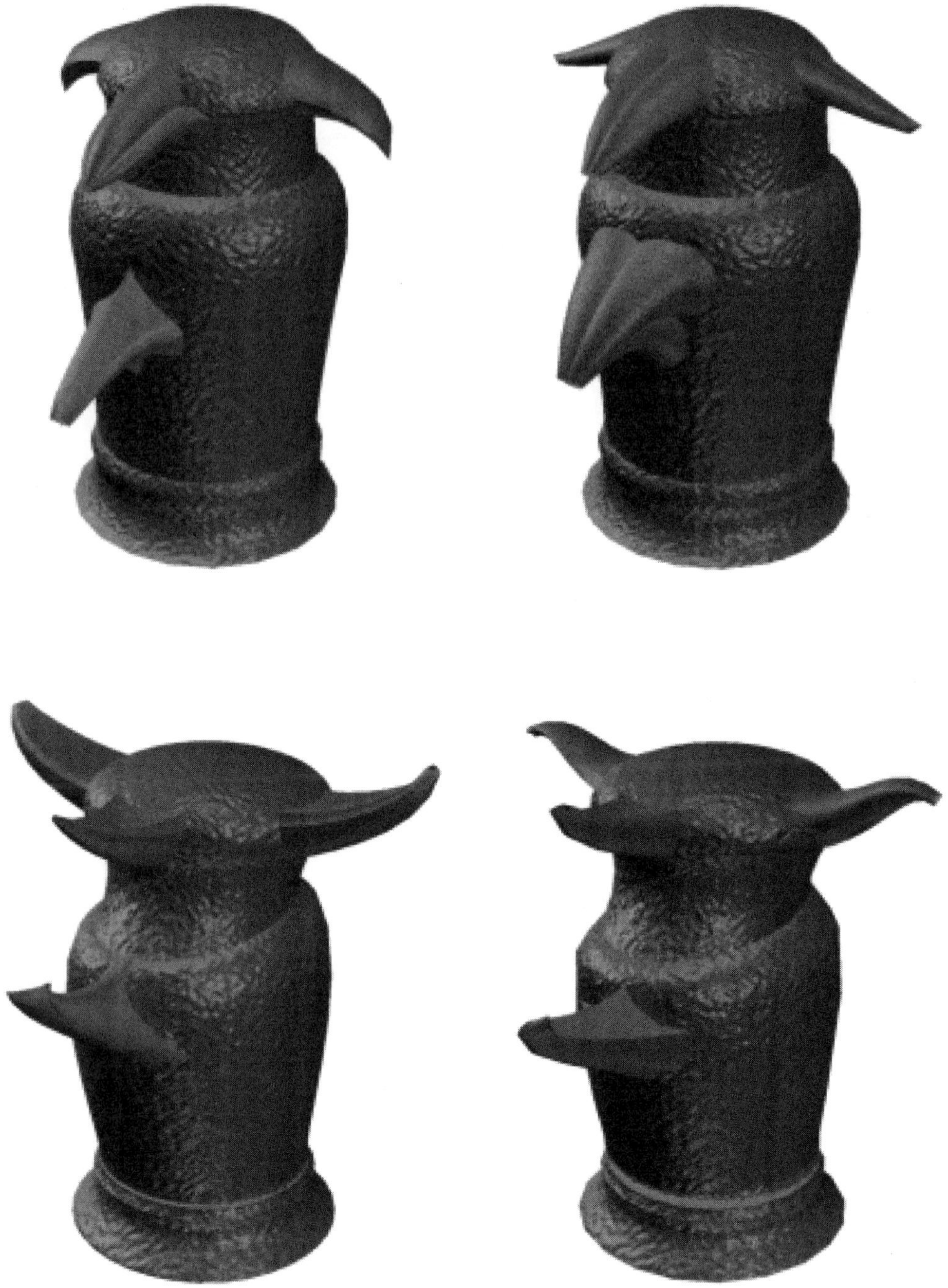

PATTERN RECOGNITION. Figure 2. Figures of Greeble objects used to study perceptual expertise. As with faces, Greebles are organized hierarchically into different categorical levels (gender, family, and individual); four Greebles from one family are shown, the top two being of one gender and the bottom two being of the other gender.

are apparently responsible for what was previously thought to be face-specific processing.

Bibliography

Biederman, I. (1987). Recognition-by-components: A theory of human image understanding. *Psychological Review, 94*, 115–147.

Farah, M. J. (1992). Is an object an object an object? Cognitive and neuropsychological investigations of domain-specificity in visual object recognition. *Current Directions in Psychological Science, 1*, 164–169.

Gauthier, I., Anderson, A. W., Tarr, M. J., Skudlarski, P., & Gore, J. C. (1997). Levels of categorization in visual object studied with functional MRI. *Current Biology, 7*, 645–651.

Gauthier, I., & Tarr, M. J. (1997). Becoming a "Greeble" expert: Exploring the face recognition mechanism. *Vision Research, 37*, 1673–1682.

Jolicoeur, P., Gluck, M., & Kosslyn, S. M. (1984). Pictures and names: Making the connection. *Cognitive Psychology, 16*, 243–275.

Logothetis, N. K., Pauls, J., & Poggio, T. (1995). Shape representation in the inferior temporal cortex of monkeys. *Current Biology, 5*, 552–563.

Marr, D., & Nishihara, H. K. (1978). Representation and recognition of the spatial organization of three-dimensional shapes. *Proceedings of the Royal Society of London B, 200*, 269–294.

Rock, I. (Ed.). (1990). *The perceptual world.* New York: Freeman.

Sergent, J., Ohta, S., & MacDonald, B. (1992). Functional neuroanatomy of face and object processing: A positron emission tomography study. *Brain, 115*, 15–36.

Tarr, M. J. (1995). Rotating objects to recognize them: A case study of the role of viewpoint dependency in the recognition of three-dimensional objects. *Psychonomic Bulletin and Review, 2*, 55–82.

Tarr, M. J., & Bülthoff, H. H. (1995). Is human object recognition better described by geon-structural-descriptions or by multiple-views? *Journal of Experimental Psychology: Human Perception and Performance, 21*, 1494–1505.

Tarr, M. J., & Pinker, S. (1989). Mental rotation and orientation-dependence in shape recognition. *Cognitive Psychology, 21*, 233–282.

Michael J. Tarr

PAVLOV, IVAN PETROVICH (1849–1936), Russian physiologist and functionalist psychologist. Pavlov was born in Ryazan, a small, historic town located about 100 miles from Moscow. Pavlov's father, Pyotr, a well-educated and respected Russian Orthodox priest, encouraged his children's intellectual pursuits. Pavlov's mother, Varvara, a priest's daughter, though illiterate, was a woman of intelligence. After the death of her third child she suffered a nervous disorder, a condition that may explain Pavlov's subsequent interest in abnormal psychology and psychiatry.

Traditionally, priests' sons were destined for the priesthood, and therefore, in the 1860s, Pavlov attended the Ryazan Ecclesiastical Seminary. Seminary education emphasized classics and theology, but in the 1860s Western scientific works became available in the Russian language. In the Ryazan public library, Pavlov read renditions of Darwin's theory of evolution by the Russian popularizer Dimitry I. Pisarev and the German zoologist Carl Vogt, a physiology book by the English philosopher George H. Lewes, as well as Ivan M. Sechenov's *Reflexes of the Brain.*

Impressed by such works, Pavlov rejected a career in the church and in 1870 entered the natural sciences section of the Faculty of the Physical-Mathematical Sciences of the Imperial University of Saint Petersburg. In 1883, having submitted a dissertation on certain functions of the heart, Pavlov was awarded the doctor of medicine degree by the Military-Medical Academy of Saint Petersburg. Intermittently from 1884 to 1886, Pavlov worked abroad in the laboratories of the leading German physiologists Rudolph Heidenhain and Carl Ludwig.

In 1890, Pavlov was appointed professor of pharmacology and, in 1895, professor of physiology at the Military-Medical Academy. Beginning in the early 1890s, he explored the processes of digestion by using surgical procedures that allowed him to observe the working of the stomach and its various glands in normal animals. This research was deemed so valuable that he was awarded the 1904 Nobel Prize in physiology or medicine. However, in the early 1900s, Pavlov shifted his research from the digestive processes to the investigation of the functions of the brain by the Pavlovian conditioning method.

Pavlovian Conditioning

Influenced by Darwin's concept of the struggle for existence and within the scope of his current research interests, Pavlov, in the late 1890s, hypothesized that the upper tract of animals' digestive system responded differently to diverse foods, namely, with a small salivary secretion to moist foods, such as meat, and a larger salivary secretion to dry foods, such as bread powder. In 1898 Pavlov's student, the physician S. G. Vul'fson, working on his doctoral dissertation at Pavlov's physiological laboratory of the Institute of Experimental Medicine in Saint Petersburg, found experimental support for Pavlov's hypothesis. Serendipitously, Vul'fson discovered that after eating moist and dry foods, dogs "teased" from afar by these foods responded with proportional but diminished salivary secretion. Pavlov was, of course, aware that dogs' salivation in response to stimuli directly impinging upon their senses was an innately established reflex. Salivation at the mere smell and sight of food, however, was acquired activity, established by neural connections within the animals' cerebral cortex. Salivary secretion reflected cortical processes; the salivary flow was a sensitive, precise, easily accessible and objective indicator of neural processes. Acquired salivary responses to stimuli were, therefore, primarily of methodological importance, useful in the study of physically healthy animals' cortical processes. The Pavlovian approach was of revolutionary significance because other contemporary methods explored cortical processes by surgical extirpation performed on an already traumatized animal.

Vul'fson's original method was subsequently modified when the Pavlovian V. N. Boldyrev found that any originally indifferent stimulus from virtually any sensory modality, such as sound or light, became an acquired, or conditioned stimulus (CS) that evoked the conditioned salivary response (CR) provided that this originally indifferent stimulus was closely followed, that is, reinforced by the unconditioned stimulus (UCS) such as food. Therefore, from 1906 on, Pavlov and his disciples used Boldyrev's experimental design—the Pavlovian salivary conditioning method—in exploring an animal's cortical processes.

From 1897 to 1936, at least 146 Pavlovians—physicians, graduate students and a few permanent coworkers—investigated, usually at Pavlov's request, animals' brain functions. They produced at least 532 papers involving salivary reflex conditioning. On the basis of these findings, Pavlov formulated the theory of higher nervous activity, which described the function of the brain of complex organisms in interaction with the ever-changing, external, mainly social, environment.

Pavlov insisted that his theory was purely physiological, but actually it was a psychological theory conceptualized on three levels: (a) the behavioral level, which considered the organism's overt interaction with the external environment; (b) the physiological level, involving a complex interaction of the brain's neural excitatory and inhibitory processes, which irradiated and then concentrated in the foci of original irradiation; and (c) the conscious level, which was identical with physiological processes, but experienced subjectively.

Conceptualization of Normal Behavior

Observing the normal behavior of dogs in the laboratory, Pavlov noted stable individual differences in their responses to the environment. He considered such differences to be innately determined characteristics of the nervous system—temperaments. He proposed that temperaments were determined by three neural parameters: (a) the strength level of excitation and inhibition, (b) the interrelation between excitation and inhibition, and (c) the rapidity of the spread of these processes. Pavlov observed four temperament types, which corresponded to Hippocrates' humors: choleric, melancholic, sanguine, and phlegmatic. Pavlov was especially interested in the "weak" temperament, that is, of animals and humans having low levels of excitation and inhibition because such organisms could not withstand taxing environmental conditions and were, therefore, prone to become neurotic and psychotic.

Pavlov held that the complex organism's survival, or adjustment, in a continuously changing environment depends upon its innately determined mechanisms—the *unconditioned reflexes*, which, when complex, Pavlov called instincts. He identified many instincts, of which the most important were: the sexual instinct that enabled the phylogenetic continuity of the species; and two instincts crucial to individuals' ontogenetic survival, namely, the defensive instinct aimed at avoiding noxious or harmful stimuli, and the alimentary instinct prompting the organism's food seeking and eating behavior.

Animal and human adjustment to the environment was much enhanced by the *conditioned reflexes* (CRs). Conditioned reflexes were acquired when the occurrence of any stimulus that was followed by an unconditioned stimulus (UCS) became a conditioned stimulus (CS). This meant that, on the neural level, excitation brought forth by any stimulus spread from its cortical locus to another locus of excitation brought on by the UCS. On the psychological level, an association was established between CS and UCS. The acquisition of a CS allowed the organism to react to signals coming from afar so that it did not have to come into immediate contact with that part of the environment. Thus, for example, a hungry dog that was previously conditioned to find food in a specific place, can see from afar whether food is or is not presently there instead of wasting its energy by going there.

As the environment was continuously changing, however, a previously acquired CS may no longer help the organism's adjustment in the environment. Yet, the CR could be relatively easily extinguished whenever the occurrence of a CS was no longer followed by the UCS.

In Pavlov's theory, the CRs established in the cortical regions of the brain were evoked by signals emanating from the external environment and, therefore, constituted the first signaling system. As the human environment was mostly social, however, adjustment was further enhanced by the second signaling system, or language consisting of words that were either pronounced, heard, or seen. The second signaling system signified an abstraction of the encountered environment.

The relationship between the two signaling systems affected both normal and abnormal individuals' general orientation. In normal individuals, the domination of the first signal system over the second characterized the visualizing, artistic type, whereas the domination of the second signal system over the first characterized the verbal, thoughtful type. In addition, each type was susceptible to a different neurosis.

According to Pavlov, the human environment was very complex so that successful adjustment required the acquisition and extinction of complex behavior. In the 1930s, Pavlov held that complex behavior was formed by numerous conditioned stimuli that were received by the analyzers, that is, sensory mechanisms, and then impinged on the cerebral cortex either simultaneously or in a temporal order. In the cerebral cortex, the CSs were integrated to form a dynamic stereotype, that was a well-organized Gestalt-like entity. Pavlov provided experimental evidence for the dynamic stereotype. When a series of stimuli of various modalities, such as sounds, lights, or touch, were presented in a set order and each was reinforced by UCs, then any presented constituent stimulus of that dynamic stereotype evoked all the other responses belonging to that dynamic stereotype. In Pavlov's view, a well-established dynamic stereotype was a habit. Such a dynamic stereotype could generalize from one environmental situation to another; could differentiate between several environmental situations; and could be extinguished if its occurrence was no longer reinforced by environmental contingencies.

Pavlov distinguished between adjustment and knowledge. Both processes involved the establishment of association, but whereas adjustment was acquired or extinguished through conditioning, the acquisition of knowledge about the relationships among intrinsically connected natural phenomena was obtained through trial and error. Pavlov reached this conclusion in the 1930s, after having received a gift of two chimpanzees that in Pavlov's laboratory were given problems involving manual manipulation, such as fitting sticks of different shapes into appropriate openings, or building a tower consisting of piled up boxes of different sizes to reach a suspended bait. In opposition to Wolfgang Köhler's insight explanation of problem solving, Pavlov maintained that such solutions occurred through the chaotic method, a term synonymous with trial and error.

Whereas the irradiation of cortical excitation instigated and maintained active behavior, irradiation of cortical inhibition slowed down, or restrained, behavior. Daily behavior was based upon the intricate interplay of irradiated cortical excitation and inhibition, but normal sleep was the result of extensive irradiation of inhibition over large parts of the central nervous system.

Conceptualization of Abnormal Behavior

In the 1930s, Pavlov studied the etiology and treatment of abnormal behavior. Already in the 1920s, the Pavlovian M. K. Petrova had systematically explored in the laboratory the formation of experimental neuroses, that is, behaviors that deviated from the normal higher nervous activity. Then, in the 1930s, Pavlov, guided by psychiatrists, observed patients' behavior at the Neurotic and Psychiatric Clinics in Leningrad. Pavlov merged the experimental and clinical approaches to conclude that the theory of higher nervous activity could properly explain the causes of neuroses and psychoses and suggest appropriate therapy.

In Pavlov's conceptualization, neurosis was a chronic disturbance of the higher nervous activity. Animal experiments showed that neuroses occurred when the organism's behavior was disturbed by powerful CSs, when environmental demands overwhelmed the inhibitory processes, or when a conflict occurred between irradiated neural excitation and inhibition. These difficult conditions disturbed and exhausted the neural processes so that behavior became ineffective and less adjustive. The "weak" temperament type was especially prone to neuroses because its neural processes were not strong enough to be conditioned sufficiently. Specifically, psychasthenic neuroses occurred in "weak" individuals of the thoughtful type, whereas hysterical neuroses were found in "weak" individuals of the artistic type.

In the 1930s, Pavlov attempted to elucidate the causes of schizophrenia. It occurred in people of the "weak" temperament type who developed improperly during their childhood and were subjected to severe traumatic experiences during their youth. The inhibitory processes during this period failed to defend them from powerful overexertion so that the highest regions of their central nervous system were physiologically damaged. As therapy for schizophrenia, Pavlov recommended rest and prolonged sleep induced by soporific pharmaceuticals.

Pavlov's Defense of Human Rights

Pavlov considered himself to be a Russian patriot, but not an ally of the Bolshevik regime despite its generous support of his research. Denied permission to emigrate in the early 1920s by Lenin, Pavlov, in university lectures attacked the Soviet regime's destructive policies. Devoted to scientific truth, Pavlov defended human rights and academic freedom, and, although not devout, advocated toleration of religious expression.

Bibliography

Works by Pavlov

Pavlov, I. P. (1927). *Conditioned reflexes: An investigation of the physiological activity of the cerebral cortex* (G. V. Anrep, Trans. and Ed.). London: Oxford University Press/Humphrey Milford.

Pavlov, I. P. (1932). The reply of a physiologist to psychologists. *Psychological Review, 39*, 91–127.

Pavlov, I. P. (1955). *Selected works* (J. Gibbons, Ed. and S. Belsky, Trans.). Moscow: Foreign Languages Pub. House.

Pavlov, I. P. (1957). *Experimental psychology and other essays*. New York: Philosophical Library.

Pavlov, I. P. (1994). *Psychopathology and psychiatry* (Intro. by G. Windholz). New Brunswick, NJ: Transaction.

Works about Pavlov

Frolov, Y. P. (1937). *Pavlov and his school: The theory of conditioned reflexes* (C. P. Dutt, Trans.). New York: Oxford University Press.

Todes, D. P. (1995). Pavlov and the Bolsheviks. *History and Philosophy of the Life Sciences, 17*, 379–418.

Windholz, G. (1986). A comparative analysis of the conditional reflex discoveries of Pavlov and Twitmyer, and the birth of a paradigm. *Pavlovian Journal of Biological Science, 21*, 141–147.

Windholz, G. (1987). Pavlov as a psychologist: A reappraisal. *Pavlovian Journal of Biological Science, 22*, 103–112.

Windholz, G. (1990). The second signal system as conceived by Pavlov and his disciples. *Pavlovian Journal of Biological Science, 25*, 163–173.

Windholz, G. (1991). I. P. Pavlov as a youth. *Integrative Physiological and Behavioral Science, 26*, 51–67.

Windholz, G. (1996). Pavlov's conceptualization of the dynamic stereotype in the theory of higher nervous activity. *American Journal of Psychology, 109*, 287–295.

George Windholz

PAVLOVIAN CONDITIONING. *See* Classical Conditioning.

PEABODY PICTURE VOCABULARY TEST. Now in its third edition (PPVT–III), the Peabody Picture Vocabulary Test (PPVT) measures a child's knowledge of words without requiring oral expression. The PPVT–III manual describes the test as a measure of "achievement in receptive vocabulary attainment for standard English" and as "a screening test of verbal ability" (Dunn & Dunn, 1997, p. x) for persons 2½ through 90 years of age. The test is administered by showing the examinee a page containing four numbered black-and-white line drawings. The examiner says a word and the subject points to or indicates the number of the picture that best defines the word. For example, for the word *island*, four geographic bodies (a mountain, cliff, hills, and an island) might be pictured. There are approximately two hundred items, including categories of words such as actions, animals, tools, adjectives, buildings, geographical scenes, household objects, shapes, and people. Start-and-stop rules are applied so that only those questions appropriate for the examinee's age or ability are given.

The PPVT–III is comprised of two parallel forms of similar difficulty. The test was standardized on a large, representative sample of U.S. children, adolescents, and adults. The sample was matched to the proportions in the U.S. population by gender, geographic region, parents' or examinee's educational level, and race-ethnicity. The PPVT–III yields a standardized IQ-type total score set at a mean of 100 and standard deviation of 15 (identical to major intelligence tests) called a Standard Score Equivalent rather than an IQ. This score has very good reliability and evidence for the test's validity is mainly provided on the basis of the relationships between the PPVT–III and several intelligence tests.

What Does the PPVT Measure?

The PPVT–III manual provides various explanations of what the test measures. The authors call the PPVT–III

1. a measure of standard English vocabulary;
2. a screening test for verbal ability;
3. a test of verbal ability (not the same thing as a "screening test of . . ."):
4. a screening test for scholastic aptitude; and
5. a hearing vocabulary measure.

The similarities and differences among the various definitions are not provided. However, a considerable amount of validity research involves the relationships between the PPVT–III and intelligence tests such as the Wechsler and Stanford–Binet. In fact, the PPVT–III related significantly and highly with the total test scores these instruments yield as well as with the vocabulary subtests included in these measures. This suggests that the PPVT is probably best viewed as a verbal measure of general ability like the verbal scales included in the Wechsler and Stanford–Binet tests, but one that uses a limited method (picture vocabulary) rather than a variety of methods (as is the case for the major intelligence tests). Although the use of verbal knowledge to measure intelligence has been questioned (Kaufman & Kaufman, 1983; Naglieri & Das, 1997), the PPVT approach is consistent with ability as it has been traditionally defined.

[*See also* Testing.]

Bibliography

Dunn, L. M., & Dunn, L. M. (1997). *Peabody picture vocabulary test third edition.* Circle Pines, MN: American Guidance Service. This includes the PPVT–III manual, technical references, stimulus manual, and related administration materials.

Kaufman, A. S., & Kaufman, N. L. (1983). *Kaufman assessment battery for children.* Circle Pines, MN: American Guidance Service. This test was among the first to separate verbal knowledge from the measurement of ability and provide evidence of its effectiveness.

Naglieri, J. A., & Das, J. P. (1997). *Das Naglieri cognitive assessment system interpretive handbook.* Chicago: Riverside. This book describes a modern theory of intelligence defined from a cognitive perspective that excludes measures of verbal knowledge.

Jack A. Naglieri

PEACE is an environment, a state in which individuals, families, and, collectively, societies and countries move along naturally from birth, through the stages of development, to death, repeating the cycle of life. Using Erik Erikson's eight ages of man from *Childhood and Society* (New York, 1950), individual peace can be said to begin with the establishment of basic trust in the infant, which evolves ultimately to the eighth age of ego integrity—the final state of peace—in which the individual feels assured of the meaning and achievement of his or her life and enjoys a sense of spiritual fulfillment.

It is far easier to imagine individuals experiencing peace in their lifetime than to identify such orderly continuity in the history of societies and states. Yet there may be no better measure of peace than the state of the individual and the family. It is again with these units of humanity that one tracks the breakdown of peace at any given time in history. When one considers Abraham Maslow's hierarchy of human needs, it is the denial of that most basic of physiological needs—for food—that generates the most predictable individual and group violence, at least in urban settings. Political scientists see violence as a sign of institutional failure and systemic breakdown. Weak political institutions in a society and malfunctioning systems that fail to provide food, water, shelter, and, less physiologically, education and employment are often associated with violence and repression. Sudden shocks, like the collapse of markets in single-commodity economies, or more insidious ecological assaults such as sustained drought are also examples of systemic breakdown that create conditions for political violence either within the state or through wars of aggression beyond state borders.

Whatever the circumstances of systemic breakdown, once one group or nation physically attacks and causes traumatic losses in another, a psychological relationship of aggressor and victim is created that can endure for centuries. The violence is seen and felt as an assault on the identity and collective self-worth of the victimized group and a potential precursor to its subjugation or even annihilation. The psychology of victimhood is, in fact, a psychophysiological permanent state of alertness on the part of victimized groups or nations. They are not susceptible to rational acts or peace processes. In these cases, episodic peace agreements rarely signify peace, but more frequently truces ornamented by documents that delude the victor and vanquished alike. Thus England's first military forays into Ireland in the eleventh century CE have a linear connection to the Protestant Loyalist terrorist attacks and Irish Republican Army bombs today. Jewish religious extremists who today plot the destruction of the Dome of the Rock and Al-Aqsa mosque in historic Jerusalem are driven both by the outrage of the Holocaust and by the memory of the Second Temple's destruction by the Romans in 70 BCE.

Serbs murdering Bosnian Muslims shouted revenge for their defeat at Kosovo by the Ottoman Turks in 1389. The newly emergent national consciousness of Germany was stunned by Napoleon's invasion of Prussia in 1805. It was experienced as a disaster by the intelligentsia. Germans were to remember not only the humiliation of occupation but also the enduring futility of their attempts to win the respect and esteem of the French. In their resultant chronic, if periodically suppressed, narcissistic rage, the German nation took revenge with three invasions of France in 1871, 1914, and 1939. It was, in fact, the Franco-German experience of the horrors of war that inspired these two nations to build a peace between them that became an extraordinary model for psychologically based strategies of peacemaking.

At the end of World War II, the most devastating, civilian-murdering conflict in human history, surviving democratic leaders looked at the rubble and ashes and vowed never to repeat the insanity. While the Cold War's nuclear balance of terror in one dramatic way promised to undermine this vow, it also reinforced the sense of the insanity of international relationships. Perhaps the most important leaders determined to change dramatically the way nations relate to each other were those of France and Germany, represented by Robert Shuman, Jean Monnet, and Konrad Adenauer. These men took on the structural, systemic factors in the genesis of war and changed them forever. The first major step was the establishment of the European Coal and Steel Community, designed to destroy the ability of any state to build tanks and other heavy weapons of war. In other words, the Coal and Steel Community was a structural mechanism to make war in Western Europe impossible in the future. This logic evolved to produce the common market concept, the European Community and, today, the European Union, where functional relationships across fast-disappearing borders provide material incentives that reinforce the peace. But the Franco-German partnership also dealt comprehensively with the psychological tasks of making and sustaining peace in a model with worldwide applicability.

The Europeans did not have *The Need to Have Ene-*

mies and Allies (Northvale, N.J., 1988) or *Bloodlines* (New York, 1997), seminal works of psychiatrist and political psychologist Vamik Volkan, that explain the roles played by historic wounds to the group self or nation and the phenomenon of group regression in the face of systemic stress that creates a fertile ground for the destructive, narcissistic, charismatic leader inclined to organize mass aggression and violence. But the French and German partners did know intuitively that they had to treat the pathology of their relationship if they were to survive the twentieth century. Thus French men and women, led, significantly, by victims of Gestapo brutality, took the lead in extending the hand of reconciliation to their German counterparts. Germans responded with acknowledgement and contrition for the crimes of the Nazi era. Through their positive gesture in cooperation, the French implied a willingness to forgive. Joint teams of historians reviewed and purged textbooks of negative stereotypes and wrote true accounts, regardless of the shameful truth dealt to either side, but especially to the Germans. Students, workers, businesspeople, journalists, academics, and artists built cross-border alliances.

Political psychologists have studied the accounts of this master reconciliation and adapted its methods to conflicts in the Middle East, Northern Ireland, South Africa, the Balkans, China-Japan, and endless other ethnic and sectarian conflicts. The most effective third parties are increasingly cognizant of the power of memory and the burdens of history on a peace process. They use their skills as facilitators in small group dialogues to expand the knowledge of the adversaries and to promote subtly, in its natural rhythm, the acknowledgment, contrition, forgiveness transaction as the core of reconciliation. The Truth and Reconciliation Commission in South Africa fulfilled this function. Prime Minister Tony Blair is slowly leading Britain to acknowledge its moral responsibilities to the Irish people, as in his apologetic acknowledgement of England's role in the potato famine of 1846–1848. Healing themes have been regular subjects of the American Psychological Association's Division 48, peace studies. Division 39, psychoanalytic psychology, which published "Psychoanalytic Perspectives on War" in 1991, noted the critical psychological importance of integrity in international relationships if war is to be averted.

[*See also* International Relations; *and* War and Conflict.]

Bibliography

Erikson, E. H. (1950, 1985). *Childhood and society*. New York: Norton.

Maslow, A. H. (1954). *Motivation and personality*. New York: Harper.

Montville, J. V. (1989). Psychoanalytic enlightenment and the greening of diplomacy. *Journal of the American Psychoanalytic Association, 37*, 297–318.

Montville, J. V. (1991). The arrow and the olive branch: A case for track two diplomacy. In V. Volkan, J. V. Montville, & Julius (Eds.), *The psychodynamics of international relationships* (Vol. 2, pp. 161–175). Boston: Lexington Books.

Montville, J. V. (1993). The healing function in political conflict resolution. In Sandole, & van der Merwe (Eds.), *Conflict resolution theory and practice* (pp. 112–128). Manchester and New York: Manchester.

Spiro, M. (1986). *Culture and human nature: Theoretical papers of Melford Spiro* (Kilborne & Langness, Eds.). Chicago: University of Chicago Press.

Volkan, V. (1988). *The need to have enemies and allies: From clinical practice to international relationships.* Northvale, NJ: Jason Aronson.

Volkan, V. (1997). *Blood lines.* New York: Farrar, Straus and Giroux.

Joseph V. Montville

PEAK EXPERIENCES. The peak experience is a state of consciousness, consisting of intense awareness, unusual insight, and extreme positive affect (e.g., supreme peacefulness or ecstasy). It is often argued that individuals cannot create or will this subjective state: a peak experience happens to the person; the person does not initiate it. During the peak experience, individuals often feel that they have lost a sense of time and space and that they are transcending the bounds of mundane reality. In addition to positive affect, individuals describe feelings of wonder, awe, and reverence, both during and after the peak experience.

Though peak experiences can be produced by a wide range of human endeavors and interactions, some of the most common catalysts are childbirth, parenting, love relationships, experiences in nature, aesthetic encounters, moments of intellectual insight, mystical experiences, and athletic accomplishments. Individuals emerge from a peak experience with the conviction that they have gained unique knowledge about themselves and the world and that they have been transformed by this experience. Once the peak experience has passed, individuals retain a vivid memory of it, though they may struggle to articulate its exact nature to others. The aftereffects of a peak experience, as reported by individuals who have undergone one, is a more positive view of oneself and one's role in the world, a surge of creativity and increased spontaneity, a conviction about the inherent value of life, and a wish to return to this heightened subjective state.

History of the Concept

The concept of a peak experience was introduced by Abraham H. Maslow, one of the founders of humanistic psychology (Maslow, 1970), during his original study of the psychological characteristics of self-actualizing people. Many of the self-actualizing individuals, whom Maslow saw as having achieved the highest levels of human potential in both personal accomplishment and dedication to the service of others, reported moments of unique insight and transcendent ecstasy that had transformed their lives. To characterize these quasi-mystical experiences, Maslow drew upon William James's (1902/1985) criteria for a mystical experience: (1) ineffability; (2) noetic quality (providing unique knowledge or insight); (3) transiency; and (4) passivity.

At first Maslow believed that access to a peak experience differentiated self-actualizing people from other individuals. He subsequently revised this position to suggest that all individuals have the potential to undergo a peak experience (self-actualized individuals may simply have more of them) and that peak experiences may vary in intensity from mild to more extreme (Maslow, 1968). He also proposed that not all self-actualized individuals have peak experiences. Self-actualized "peakers" were more likely to engage in a nonjudgmental, egoless, present oriented form of cognition ("Being-cognition" or "B-cognition"), whereas self-actualized nonpeakers were more oriented to practicality, goal setting, and ego-based achievement ("Deficiency-cognition" or "D-cognition").

Research

Though Maslow surveyed college students to collect examples of their peak experiences, he did not conduct any formal or quantitative analysis of the data drawn from this sample or from his original self-actualizing individuals. Maslow himself questioned how one might determine the external validity of such a private and nearly ineffable experience. Though individuals often claimed a life-transformative effect, Maslow pointed out the difficulty of linking major life changes to a single moment of heightened awareness.

Subsequent descriptive research has examined peak religious experiences (M. Laski, *Ecstasy: A Study of Some Secular and Religious Experiences*; Bloomington, Ind., 1962), peak athletic experiences (K. Ravizza, "Peak experiences in sport," *Journal of Humanistic Psychology*, 1977, *21*, 57–67), and peak experiences of meditators (Y. Sakairi, "Peak experience: Its features and mental health of peak experienced meditators," *Japanese Journal of Hypnosis*, 1991–1992, *36*, 95–103). Other research has sought to identify the fundamental dimensions and meanings of peak experiences (J. H. Hallaq, "Scaling and factor analyzing peak experiences," *Journal of Clinical Psychology*, 1977, *33*, 77–82; S. Wilson & R. C. Spencer, "Intense personal experiences: Subjective effects, interpretations, and after-effects," 1990, *Journal of Clinical Psychology*, *46*, 565–573). Dan McAdams, a personality researcher (McAdams, Hoffman, Mansfield, & Day, 1996), has collected memories of peak experiences in order to demonstrate that individuals with a strong motive for relationship and intimacy or a strong motive for power, self-mastery, and prominence will recall peak experiences that highlight these respective concerns.

Related Terms

Gayle Privette (1983) provided a useful taxonomy of peak experience and the overlapping concepts of peak performance (Privette & Landsman, 1983, "Factor analysis of peak performance: The full use of potential," *Journal of Personality and Social Psychology*, 1983, *44*, 195–200) and flow (Csiksentmihalyi, 1990). Although all three experiences involve intense absorption, positive affect, loss of time and space, and an enhanced valuing of the world and/or self, they differ in the following ways. Peak experiences are encountered passively rather than actively; they do not necessarily involve a behavioral transaction; and awareness of the self and its desires diminishes. Peak performances are exceptional instances of behavior that are intentionally sought. Awareness of self and the activity is heightened, and motivation is at its zenith. Flow experiences are intrinsically enjoyable activities that diminish consciousness of the self and reflect an optimal match between the skills of the individual and the challenges of the activity. Neither the transcendent insight of the peak experience nor the exceptional achievement of the peak performance are requisites for the flow experience.

[*See also* Mysticism.]

Bibliography

Csiksentmihalyi, M. (1990). *Flow: The psychology of optimal experience*. New York: Harper & Row. This carefully researched but highly readable work is a contemporary extension of Maslow's concepts of peak experiences and self-actualization. It examines the pleasure and satisfaction that craftspeople, athletes, artists, and professionals find through absorption in their life activities. The author emphasizes the value of "autotelic" activities in which the doing of the activity is its own reward, regardless of its other meanings or purposes. The resulting "flow" experiences are similar to Maslow's "being-cognition," or "B-cognition," in which individuals are present oriented and aware of a benign connection to their surroundings and the larger universe.

James, W. (1985). *The varieties of religious experience*. Cambridge, MA: Harvard University Press. (Original work published 1902.) James's eloquent writings on mystical experiences served as the inspiration for Maslow in developing the concept of peak experience. James attempts to define the essential features of mystical experiences and then presents a series of first-person accounts demonstrating their diverse origins, ranging from religious ecstasy to drug and alcohol use to artistic and natural encounters. James's overarching theme is that the existence of an altered state cannot be denied, but its claim to superior insight or authority remains an empirical question for those who have not participated in the mystical encounter.

Joyce, J. (1928). *A portrait of the artist as a young man*. New York: Modern Library. (Original work published 1916.) Before Maslow created the psychological term *peak experience*, the writer James Joyce had employed the term *epiphany* to describe moments of creative insight and personal revelation. In a well-known example, Stephen Dedalus, the young artist of this book's title, hearing his name called out over and over by his friends, has a peak experience by the ocean waters in which he realizes his artistic calling and the full significance of his heroic name:

Maslow, A. H. (1970). *Farther reaches of human nature*. New York: Viking Press. All of Maslow's books are compilations of articles, chapters, and lectures that he published or presented previously. In chapter 12, "Education and Peak Experiences," Maslow reprints an article based on a lecture he gave to a group of music educators. His theme is that the teaching of the arts should be less analytic and objective and more focused on creativity and imagination, thereby maximizing opportunities for peak experiences and transcendent personal growth.

Maslow, A. H. (1968). *Toward a psychology of being* (2nd ed.). New York: Van Nostrand Reinhold. Collects some of Maslow's most thoughtful and systematic articles and lectures, including a chapter that focuses on changes in consciousness and values brought on by peak experiences and one that describes how peak experiences alter self-understanding and the nature of one's relationship to others and the external world.

Maslow, A. H. (1970). *Motivation and personality* (2nd ed.). New York: Harper & Row. Contains Maslow's earliest published papers on his theory of motivation, his conception of a hierarchy of needs, and his initial inquiry into the nature of self-actualizing people.

McAdams, D. P., Hoffman, B. J., Mansfield, E. D., & Day, R. (1996). Themes of agency and communion in significant autobiographical scenes. *Journal of Personality, 64*, 339–377. Demonstrates the utility of peak experiences as a research tool for collecting meaningful autobiographical memories from individuals. These memories can then be studied for what they reveal about persisting and dominant themes in individual personality.

Privette, G. (1983). Peak experience, peak performance, and flow: A comparative analysis of positive human experiences. *Journal of Personality and Social Psychology, 45*, 1361–1368. Provides a clearer definition of peak experience in relation to other constructs of self-actualization—flow and peak performance. Its analysis provides both conceptual and graphical depictions of their shared and distinctive features.

Jefferson A. Singer

PEAK PERFORMANCE. *See* Sport Performance Interventions.

PEARSON, KARL (1857–1936), British statistician and biometrician. Pearson founded and led the English biometric school that created the modern field of statistics. His own papers for about two decades after 1894 defined many of the basic methods and tools of statistical analysis, methods that helped to reshape large parts of the biological, medical, social, and behavioral sciences. He developed his mathematical ideas with specific reference to scientific problems, focusing especially on biological evolution and eugenics but extending also to astronomy, psychology, medicine, and social questions. Through his technical papers, his vast correspondence, his philosophical and historical writing, and his personal instruction of young scientists in his laboratories at University College, London, Pearson diffused his statistical methods to a wide audience. He had strong convictions about biology and statistics, and his career was marked by many bitter controversies.

Pearson was the son of a London barrister, William Pearson, and his wife Fanny Smith and was descended from Yorkshire Quakers on both sides. At about the time of his marriage to Maria Sharpe, in 1890, he assessed his own character as divided between his energetic, domineering, egocentric father and his gentle, selfless mother, emotional almost to the point of hysteria. He was educated mainly at University College School, London, and then at King's College, Cambridge. At Cambridge, he finished "third wrangler" in the all-important mathematical tripos in 1879. He spent the next year in Heidelberg and Berlin, studying philosophy, physics, and law. Back in London, he completed his legal study and was called to the bar in 1881. His, however, was an extraordinarily restless intellect. He wrote a romantic epistolary novel, *The New Werther*, in 1880, and then a "nineteenth-century passion play" in 1882. He gave lectures on socialism and undertook the study of German religious history. In the late 1880s, he was founding member of a "men and women's club" and a leading feminist. Meanwhile, he was appointed to a chair in applied mathematics at University College, London, in 1884, where for about a decade his scientific research was devoted mainly to the theory of elasticity.

From 1891 to 1894, Pearson also held an appointment as lecturer in geometry at Gresham College, London. His first year of lectures formed the basis for a highly influential philosophical work, *The Grammar of Science* (1892). This was a moral philosophy of science, espousing positivism derived from romanticism. He identified science with socialism, urging that a proper scientific education was the way to discipline the unruly intellect and to guard it against selfish prejudice.

Citizenship implies a subordination of self to rules of method, rules that are not restricted to any particular subject matter, but apply as well to social inquiry as to physics.

In 1892, Pearson was just beginning to work seriously in statistics. His inspiration had come partly from Francis Galton's eugenic and biometric writings, but above all from his London colleague, the biologist Walter Frank Raphael Weldon. Weldon asked Pearson for mathematical help with problems raised by his statistical studies in biology. Pearson and Weldon remained close friends and allies until Weldon's death in 1906 and worked together on problems of biometry and evolution. Pearson was also strongly committed to eugenics. The broad field of quantitative studies of heredity formed the main subject matter of his statistical researches. He came to see statistics, however, as the core of scientific method, and his mathematics was allied to the philosophical perspective of *The Grammar of Science*.

Pearson's statistical achievement cannot be reduced to any particular tools, but Pearsonian statistics were identified most closely with two methods of analysis. One was correlation, a tool for associating quantitative variables such as height of parents and height of offspring, or achievement in mathematics and achievement in literature. The other was the chi-squared test, used to decide whether a line or curve provided a sufficiently good fit to empirical data. Correlation became the most important statistical tool in psychology until it was largely replaced by Ronald A. Fisher's "analysis of variance" in the 1930s and 1940s. Fisher believed that statistical inference should be linked to experimental design. Although this kind of statistics had been pioneered in Pearson's laboratory by William Sealy Gosset, ("Student") Pearson was dubious. His skepticism provided one of the main reasons for his long and unpleasant disagreement with Fisher.

Pearson directed several laboratories at University College, dedicated to statistics and eugenics. Many noted biometricians and statisticians, including Udny Yule, Major Greenwood, Raymond Pearl, and Gosset, came to study with him. His son Egon also became a noted statistician and succeeded him in the chair of statistics when Karl retired. At the same time, his eugenics chair went to Fisher.

[*Many of the people mentioned in this article are the subjects of independent biographical entries.*]

Bibliography

Eisenhart, C. (1970). Karl Pearson. *Dictionary of scientific biography* (Vol. 10, pp. 447–473). New York: Scribner's.

Kevles, D. (1985). *In the name of eugenics: Genetics and the uses of human heredity*. New York: Knopf.

MacKenzie, D. (1981). *Statistics in Britain 1865–1930: The social construction of scientific knowledge*. Edinburgh: Edinburgh University Press.

Magnello, Eileen (1998). Karl Pearson. In P. Armitage and T. Colton (Eds.), *Encyclopedia of biostatistics*. New York: Wiley.

Norton, B. J. (1978). Karl Pearson and statistics: The social origin of scientific innovation. *Social Studies of Science, 8*, 3–34.

Pearson, E. S. (1938). *Karl Pearson: An appreciation of some aspects of his life and work*. Cambridge: Cambridge University Press.

Porter, T. M. (1986). *The rise of statistical thinking 1820–1900*. Princeton: Princeton University Press.

Stigler, S. M. (1986). *The history of statistics: The measurement of uncertainty before 1900*. Cambridge, MA: Harvard University Press.

Theodore M. Porter

PEDIATRIC PSYCHOLOGY is an interdisciplinary field addressing the interaction of physical, behavioral, and emotional development with health and illness issues affecting children, adolescents, and families. Related to the larger field of health psychology, pediatric psychology differs not only in the focus on children and adolescents, but also in its emphasis on the contexts of the child within a family, and in schools and medical settings. Furthermore, the child is viewed as an organism in continual development with reciprocal influence with the environment including parents, siblings, peers, and others. Pediatric psychology tends to take a normative developmental view of adaptation to stress resulting from physical conditions, medical treatments, and psychosocial interactions with family and peers, rather than a psychopathological view of children's adjustment to disease.

Pediatric psychology has ties to many aspects of child-related psychology and medical specialties. Clinical, clinical child, and developmental psychology are associated fields; related terms include *developmental and behavioral pediatrics, child health psychology*, and *pediatric behavioral medicine*. This field has both basic and applied aspects in research and practice. Research is aimed at enhancing an understanding of the psychosocial implications of medical conditions, whereas clinical practice focuses on the implementation of effective interventions for medical-psychological problems in children and families.

Types of problems encountered by pediatric psychologists include those seen in traditional mental health settings for children such as psychopathology, noncompliance with parents, and academic difficulties. Frequently seen in pediatric settings are developmental issues and problems related to illness, disease, and health, which often interact with psychosocial concomitants of stress, coping, and adaptation. Children must adjust to the diagnosis of a disease, to pain associated with the disease, medical treatments, disruption of daily life, and the reactions of family and peers. Pediatric psychologists assist in these situations.

The specialty of pediatric psychology developed as pediatric and psychological practitioners found that they could not meet the challenge of critical childhood problems from within the frameworks of either traditional pediatrics or traditional mental health. As a result, the field has been largely pragmatic in its applications and research, and is multitheoretical in approach by selecting parts of psychological theories most useful to the problems at hand. Psychologists have been practical in trying to solve the referral problems uniquely presented in pediatric settings. Early work required attention to development and validating the treatment interventions. Evidence is increasing that pediatric psychological interventions are effective in eliminating or managing pediatric behavioral problems in time-efficient and economical ways. Additionally, studies have shown that these interventions decrease the necessity for, and costs of, medical treatments. These lines of research help position pediatric health psychology as a scientifically applied field, not just an intuitive and well-intentioned one.

Theory-driven research has increased for conceptualizing children's adjustment to chronic disease, for example, utilizing models of coping and adjustment and family systems approaches. Although the field was founded on practical needs, much research today does not address immediate service needs; instead, it focuses on psychological characteristics of the child, family, or medical personnel that may be related to adjustment to disease and disability. Such research investigates the connections or associations between medical and psychological phenomena. This work will assist in a better understanding of the elements and process of various pediatric and psychological phenomena. This better understanding can translate into methods and techniques useful in making more effective interventions.

The work of scientist clinicians in pediatric psychology may be categorized into three overlapping types. First, pediatric psychologists make interventions for the successful treatment or management of medical-psychological disorders. These include treatments for problems such as encopresis (inappropriate bowel movements) and enuresis (bed wetting). Interventions have also been made for weaning a child from reliance on a respirator or on a tracheotomy cannula for breathing. Operant conditioning techniques may be employed for infant rumination or chronic vomiting, food refusal, or recurrent abdominal pain. Pediatric psychologists may apply behavioral techniques to increase the caloric intake of child with cystic fibrosis, an infant with failure-to-thrive (an infant who has not grown in weight and height), or an adolescent with anorexia. Early infant stimulation and parent training may be involved in working with failure-to-thrive infants and premature infants. Cognitive-behavioral interventions for attention-deficit hyperactivity disorder are often conducted. Behavioral interventions have demonstrated effectiveness in managing these problems, sometimes in conjunction with medication. Thus, interventions can include cognitive-behavioral, behavioral, psychoeducational, family therapy, and other techniques that meld multiple theoretical approaches.

Second, pediatric psychologists apply psychological principles to understanding and intervening with the psychological-behavioral concomitants of disease, disabilities, and medical procedures. These concomitants are the related issues of the pediatric conditions. This work has included preparation programs to reduce medical fears in children undergoing hospitalization and surgery, to increase a child's coping abilities with aversive medical procedures such as bone marrow aspirations or burn debridement by reducing pain and distress through relaxation and distraction, and to help adjustment to a chronic illness such as diabetes or cystic fibrosis. Psychologists are frequently called in to help increase a child's adherence with medical treatments, such as for eating and exercise regimens for diabetes or chest physiotherapy for cystic fibrosis.

Third, pediatric psychology has, since its beginning, focused on the healthy development of children and adolescents. This focus has emphasized the prevention of disease and injury and promotion of health in childhood. Prevention and promotion are important for health in childhood as well as in later adulthood. Preventive interventions for injuries might include, for example, information dissemination and behavioral incentives to increase children's use of car seat belts and bicycle helmets. Developmentally appropriate preventive curricula have been designed for the prevention of adolescent pregnancy and sexually transmitted disease. Helping children with chronic illnesses reintegrate into their families and schools may prevent long-term adjustment problems by informing siblings and peers about the disease and its treatment. Health promotion activities conducted by child health psychologists often teach skills to refrain from smoking and substance abuse or to promote healthy eating and exercise habits.

Pediatric psychologists work in a variety of medical settings and community programs. Inpatient units might be hematology/oncology for treatment of cancer, leukemia, or AIDS, endocrinology for treatment of diabetes, pulmonary medicine for asthma and cystic fibrosis, or rehabilitation medicine for head and spinal cord injuries. In outpatient units, such as primary care offices or pediatric psychology units of hospitals, referrals may be made for the treatment of behavioral/emotional problems (often presenting first in a pediatrician's office), follow-up to the child's inpatient care for medical problems, or psychological management of biopsychosocial adjustment associated with a disease or injury.

Pediatric psychologists frequently consult with pediatricians and other medical specialists, nurses, social workers, and child life specialists in children's medical units. Given the differences in professional training and culture, skill in interdisciplinary consultation must be developed. Additionally, psychologists need skills in interacting with children, their parents, and extended family in stressful circumstances. Pediatric psychologists often explain that, although physical/medical treatments for pediatric problems may have been sought, psychological interventions may be more appropriate and effective. The remedy for some physical problems may be behavioral or psychological in nature.

The origin of the term *pediatric psychology* is credited to one of the founders, Logan Wright, who, in a germinal article published in the *American Psychologist* in 1967, described a role model of a psychologist working in a children's hospital in the pediatrics department. Early contributors included Dorothea Ross with her work on hyperactivity, Lee Salk, whose popular books translated psychology to a lay public, and Marvin Ack for his work in improving the psychological environment of children in hospitals. Later prominent contributions have been made by Dennis Drotar on the professional transactions between psychologists and pediatricians, Gerald P. Koocher in psychological aspects of life-threatening disease for children, Annette M. La Greca on adherence to medical regimens for chronic illness, Barbara G. Melamed for empirically supported preparation of children for hospitalization and surgery, Carolyn S. Schroeder in establishing model service delivery in primary care settings, Donald K. Routh for work in mental retardation and developmental disabilities, and Lizette Peterson on the prevention of problems in childhood.

Training for pediatric psychology is generally within clinical child psychology or applied developmental psychology at the predoctoral level. Specialization typically occurs at the internship and postdoctoral levels. The field is represented by scientific and professional articles published in the *Journal of Pediatric Psychology* sponsored by the Society of Pediatric Psychology, the organizational home for the field (Division 54 of the American Psychological Association). Other journals in health and clinical psychology frequently publish material related to this field. Pediatric psychologists practice in children's hospitals, health maintenance organizations, and tertiary care medical centers as well as in primary care settings such as pediatricians' outpatient offices. Increasingly, training and research are being conducted at universities in addition to medical centers and developmental disabilities units. As a result of the need for better understanding and effective interventions, this field has become a vibrant one for clinical practice and scientific research at the interface of psychology and pediatrics.

Bibliography

Drotar, D. (1995). *Consulting with pediatricians: Psychological perspectives.* New York: Plenum Press. Outlines the problems and benefits of consulting relationships between professionals with a goal to improving psychological and medical services for children, adolescents, and families in pediatric settings.

Gross, A. M., & Drabman, R. S. (Eds.). (1990). *Handbook of clinical behavioral pediatrics.* New York: Plenum Press. Reflects an orientation to an interdisciplinary integration between behavioral psychology and pediatric medicine, and describes assessment and intervention for clinical disorders and issues of professional collaboration.

Magrab, P. R. (Ed.). (1978). *Psychological management of pediatric problems* (Vols. 1 & 2). Baltimore, MD: University Park Press. Among the first books to describe in detail the available research and clinical lore for the developing field of pediatric psychology. Recent books may have more updated information; however, this work influenced the developmental course of the field in both empirical research and clinical applications. Chapters were written by the major contributors to the field.

Melamed, B. G., & Siegel, L. J. (1980). *Behavioral medicine: Practical applications in health care.* New York: Springer. Authors apply a behavioral perspective to the problems of physical illnesses and to the psychological problems resulting from medical illnesses. Behavioral medicine is a broader-based concept than pediatric psychology, but this book applies behavioral principles to many pediatric situations.

Olson, R. A., Mullins, L. L., Gillman, J. B., & Chaney, J. M. (Eds.). (1994). *The sourcebook of pediatric psychology.* Boston: Allyn & Bacon. Provides a practical source information on pediatric psychological interventions for a range of medical problems; each topic is discussed by both physicians and psychologists with clinical case examples.

Roberts, M. C. (Ed.). (1995). *Handbook of pediatric psychology* (2nd ed.). New York: Guilford Press. Sponsored by the Society of Pediatric Psychology, with peer-reviewed contributions from leading researchers and clinicians of the field, 40 chapters comprehensively cover professional issues, cross-cutting issues, prevention and promotion, physical conditions, developmental, behavioral, and emotional problems, and special topics in pediatric psychology.

Roberts, M. C., Koocher, G. K., Routh, D. K., & Willis, D. J. (Eds.). (1993). *Readings in pediatric psychology.* New York: Plenum Press. Sponsored by the Society of Pediatric Psychology, this text highlights articles exemplifying various aspects of research and practice in pediatric psychology. Carefully selected articles published in the *Journal of Pediatric Psychology* detail the early development of the field, as well as studies of

chronic and life-threatening conditions, children's perceptions of pediatrics, pain and distress in children, and professional issues.
Routh, D. K. (Ed.). (1988). *Handbook of pediatric psychology*. New York: Guilford Press. Sponsored by the Society of Pediatric Psychology (with a second edition published in 1995), chapters cover life-threatening conditions and chronic diseases, medically related behaviors, management of pain and discomfort, and professional, ethical, and legal issues.
Schroeder, C. S., & Gordon, B. N. (1991). *Assessment and treatment of childhood problems: A clinician's guide*. New York: Guilford Press. Describes techniques of assessment and interventions for developmentally appropriate and behaviorally based practice of pediatric psychology. Founded on empirical work, the clinician authors apply the comprehensive assessment-to-intervention system to numerous problems occurring in childhood and adolescence with a focus on outpatient and community applications.
Tuma, J. M. (Ed.). (1982). *Handbook for the practice of pediatric psychology*. New York: Wiley. Contributed to the early conceptualization and development of the field by examining assessment, intervention, consultation, research, and training regarding the psychological concomitants to illness in children.
Wright, L., Schaefer, A. B., & Solomons, G. (1979). *Encyclopedia of pediatric psychology*. Baltimore, MD: University Park Press. An ambitious work encapsulating the state of knowledge at the time, this encyclopedia covers 114 pediatric problems synthesizing research for assisting in diagnosis and treatment; Logan Wright, the lead author, is a founder of the field.

Michael C. Roberts

PEDOPHILIA involves recurrent, intense sexual fantasies or behavior over at least 6 months between a person who is at least 16 years old and a prepubescent child who is at least 5 years younger. Fantasies or behavior may range from undressing the child, genital exposure and masturbation, and sexual fondling, to fellatio, cunnilingus, or vaginal or anal penetration with the penis or other objects. Sexual attraction may be to male children, female children, or both, and it may be exclusive to children or nonexclusive, in which a person is sexually attracted to children as well as adults. Estimates of the proportion of pedophiles who molest female versus male children range from 2:1 to 11:1. The existence of pedophilia in females is questionable.

Many pedophiles establish a relationship with a potential victim by playing games with them, or teaching them a sport or how to play a musical instrument. Other relatively common methods of recruiting victims include baby-sitting, giving bribes, taking the child for an outing, and giving them a ride home. Pedophiles may have distorted beliefs that the child is willingly engaging in sex and may be benefitting from it. Men who sexually molest children may use their position of authority or power over the child to prevent disclosure of the sexual abuse.

Familial and nonfamilial pedophilic behavior may covary with victim gender. In a study of 222 child molesters in a forensic setting, 84% of incest offenders victimized girls, whereas 47% of extrafamilial offenders did so (Pawlak, Boulet, & Bradford, 1991). Five percent of incest offenders molested both sexes, and 18% of extrafamilial offenders did so. The age of the youngest victims was 10 years for the incest offenders and 9 years for nonfamilial offenders. Extrafamilial child molesters are more likely to admit to sexual attraction to children than incestuous men are.

Retrospective studies suggest higher rates of being sexually victimized during childhood among pedophiles than other nonsexual offenders or nonoffenders (Dhawan & Marshall, 1996; Freund & Kuban, 1994). In a prospective study, children under the age of 12 who were sexually abused were at greater risk to engage in a variety of sexual behaviors involving other children, including rubbing against them, undressing them, and touching their genitals (Friedrich et al., 1992).

Classification

Child molesters are "specialists" insofar as they tend not to be involved in antisocial behaviors other than child molestation. Less than 10% of child molesters may be formally diagnosable as psychopathic. A minority of pedophiles perpetrate physical violence against the children they sexually victimize. Only 11% of a forensic sample of 263 men determined to be pedophiles by criteria of the *Diagnostic and Statistical Manual of Mental Disorders* of the American Psychiatric Association (4th ed.) were rated as having used physical force against victims (Greenberg, Bradford, & Curry, 1996).

Men's sexual arousal in response to stimuli involving children has been used to assess pedophilic interests. The reliability and internal consistency of penile measures of sexual arousal range from .73 to .95. These reliabilities approximate what would be considered an acceptable range from a psychometric perspective.

For most pedophiles, stimuli involving physical force (e.g., rape) are less sexually arousing than stimuli involving consenting sex (e.g., with adults or with children). Although measures of penile tumescence to pedophilic stimuli successfully discriminate between child molesters and men who have not molested children, they generally do not discriminate between child molesters and other sexually deviant individuals, such as rapists. The measures are not valid in assessing men who have been accused of child molestation but who have not admitted to molesting children. Faking can also be problematic. Fifty to eighty percent of sexual offenders and nonoffenders have been found to be able to inhibit their penile tumescence during assessments.

Prevalence and Incidence

The sexual abuse of children is a serious social problem. Estimates of prevalence rates of child sexual abuse range from 5 to 45% among females and from 7 to 22% among males, with lower rates in general samples and higher rates in selected samples (e.g., clinical samples). However, only 3 to 4% of men admit to engaging in sexual contact with children, although not all men who engage in this contact fit the diagnostic criteria for pedophilia. Given higher victim-prevalence rates, it is likely that the rates from studies of men who admit to engaging in sexual contact with children are underestimates of the actual prevalence of pedophilia.

Many male children may develop sexual interest in other children. In a retrospective study of 78 heterosexual college men, 55% reported that while they were children they were curious about seeing other nude children (Freund & Kuban, 1993). However, this sexual interest decreased or ceased for most of these men by age 12 and persisted into adulthood for only 14% of the sample. Nevertheless, studies of adult men suggest that 12 to 32% who have not engaged in sexual contact with children self-report sexual arousal or exhibit penile tumescence to pedophilic stimuli.

Treatment and Prevention

At least one in four child molesters who do not receive treatment interventions molest additional children (Hall, 1995). Cognitive-behavioral and antiandrogen treatments are more effective than either behavioral treatments, comparison treatments, or no treatment. Both cognitive-behavioral and antiandrogen treatments yield recidivism rates of 13%, versus 41% for behavioral treatments and 27% for other treatments or no treatment (Hall, 1995). Cognitive-behavioral programs typically target sexual arousal to children, cognitive distortions about paraphilias, and social-skills deficits. Antiandrogen treatments reduce the production of hormones associated with sexual arousal and behavior; behavioral treatments focus on reducing sexual arousal to children.

Because pedophilia involves illegal behavior (child molestation), most pedophiles do not voluntarily seek treatment, so treatments provided in clinical settings do not reach undetected pedophiles who have not been adjudicated. Thus, preventive interventions that reach a broader range of men are necessary. Whereas most efforts to prevent child sexual abuse have been oriented toward potential victims, a much greater emphasis on males as potential perpetrators is warranted (Hall, 1996).

[*See also* Sexual Disorders.]

Bibliography

Dhawan, S., & Marshall, W. L. (1996). Sexual abuse histories of sexual offenders. *Sexual Abuse: A Journal of Research and Treatment, 8,* 7–15.

Freund, K., & Kuban, M. (1993). Toward a testable developmental model of pedophilia: The development of erotic age preference. *Child Abuse and Neglect, 17,* 315–324.

Freund, K., & Kuban, M. (1994). The basis of the abused abuser theory of pedophilia: A further elaboration on an earlier study. *Archives of Sexual Behavior, 23,* 553–563.

Friedrich, W. N., Grambsch, P., Damon, L., Hewitt, S. K., Koverola, C., Lang, R. A., Wolfe, V., & Broughton, D. (1992). Child sexual behavior inventory: Normative and clinical comparisons. *Psychological Assessment, 4,* 303–311.

Greenberg, D. M., Bradford, J. M. W., & Curry, S. (1996). Are pedophiles with aggressive tendencies more sexually violent? *Bulletin of the Academy of Psychiatry and Law, 24,* 225–235.

Hall, G. C. N. (1995). Sexual offender recidivism revisited: A meta-analysis of recent treatment studies. *Journal of Consulting and Clinical Psychology, 63,* 802–809.

Hall, G. C. N. (1996). *Theory-based assessment, treatment, and prevention of sexual aggression.* New York: Oxford University Press.

Pawlak, A. E., Boulet, J. R., & Bradford, J. M. W. (1991). Discriminant analysis of a sexual-functioning inventory with intrafamilial and extrafamilial child molesters. *Archives of Sexual Behavior, 20,* 27–34.

Gordon C. Nagayama Hall

PEER COUNSELING. The exact origin of peer counseling is difficult to pinpoint, since it is such a generic concept. Gray and Tindall (1980) defined peer counseling "as a variety of inter-personal helping behaviors assumed by nonprofessionals who undertake a helping role with others" (p. 5). As Varenhorst (1992) noted, peer counseling is an umbrella term covering a variety of helping behaviors conceptualized as counseling, tutoring, helping, facilitating, or supporting. Myrick, Highland, and Sabella (1995) noted that peer counselors are referred to as peer facilitators, helpers, leaders, mentors, pals, tutors, and counselors, and as big brothers and big sisters.

When one mentions peer counseling, school settings typically come to mind; however, peer counselors are also found in religious and community settings, the business world, and government settings. With 90% of the American population professing a belief in God, many people turn to their church when experiencing life problems. To meet this increasing need for help and support, church leaders are enlisting the aid of church members to offer counseling and to lead groups focusing on topics such as premarital counseling, marital enrichment, coping with loss, and spiritual growth. Peer counselors enhance the services that churches provide to members.

Similarly, use of peer counselors within community settings significantly increases outreach possibilities. For example, peers commonly man hot lines, facilitate self-help and support groups, and help bridge the gap between the limited numbers of professional helpers and the increasing numbers who need mental health services. Gray and Tindall (1980) noted that underserved populations are particularly found among those who are poor or in rural areas. In a book on health counseling, Roth-Roemer, Robinson Kurpius, and Carmen (1998) pointed out that individuals undergoing some type of life crisis, such as being diagnosed with a terminal illness, coping with a loved one who has Alzheimer's disease, or making life changes after a heart attack, often turn to peers for help. Community agencies are finding that training someone who has had similar experiences to lead self-help, support, or psychoeducational groups is an effective way to meet these evolving community needs.

Within the world of work, the use of peer counselors is also expanding. At Bell Atlantic, selected employees have been trained to assist coworkers in planning their career development within the company. Mountain Bell trained employees to help those whose positions were being cut when the company experienced downsizing after divestiture. Even the federal government has recognized that the personal and interpersonal needs of its employees can be met by peer helpers and leaders. This evolving use of peer counselors leads to the questions: Who can be a peer counselor, and what type of training is needed?

To answer these questions, it is best to turn to the school setting where the formalized use of peer counselors has been reported in the literature. Peer counseling benefits not only the helpee but also the helper. This is partially explained by Loevinger's (1976) theory of stages of ego development and Kohlberg's (1975) stages of moral development. Theoretically, in role-playing (serving as a peer helper), the developmental stage of the participant is enhanced. This hypothesis was supported by research on high school and middle school students who, during the peer counseling training, spent considerable time talking about themselves and their concerns, which resulted in their own personal growth and enhanced self-esteem, communication, and problem-solving skills. Other research has reported that peer counselors increased their ability to use active listening and problem-solving skills after training.

The National Peer Helpers Association has provided guidelines for training peer helpers, and detailed training programs have been developed by Akita and Mooney (1982) and Tindall (1994). Peer counselors can be self- or other-nominated. One project polled an entire student body to arrive at a list of students, teachers, and staff viewed as natural helpers. Frequently nominated individuals are interviewed by a selection committee to determine their readiness to serve as a peer counselor. Peer counselors within a school setting can participate on a voluntary or course credit basis, as long as they meet regularly with a mental health professional for supervision. Peer counselors in religious, community, business, and government settings also need to be closely supervised. Peer counselors are nonprofessionals and sometimes encounter individuals with problems beyond their skill level. Supervision protects the helpee and ensures the best possible intervention by the peer counselor. Regardless of setting, training needs to include increased self and other awareness, active listening skills, problem identification and solving skills, and referral skills. Ongoing supervision allows for continued training and skill development.

Although the efficacy and effectiveness of peer counseling are increasingly being demonstrated, some believe only mental health professionals should provide counseling services. Nonetheless, as more people are needing mental health care or support, peer counseling is a viable complement to traditional mental health care.

Bibliography

Akita, J., & Mooney, C. (1982). *Natural helpers*. Seattle, WA: Comprehensive Health Education Foundation.

Gray, H. D., & Tindall, J. A. (1980). *Peer counseling*. Muncie, IN: Accelerated Development, Inc.

Kim, S., McLeod, J. H., Rader, D., & Johnston, G. (1992). An evaluation of prototype school-based peer counseling program. *Journal of Drug Education, 22,* 37–53.

Kohlberg, L. (1975). Counseling and counselor education: A developmental approach. *Counselor Education and Supervision,* 14, 250–256.

Loevinger, J. (1976). *Ego development*. San Francisco: Jossey-Bass.

Morey, R. E., Miller, C. D., Rosen, L. A., & Fulton, R. (1993). High school peer counseling: The relationship between student satisfaction and peer counselors' style of helping. *School Counselor, 40,* 293–300.

Myrick, R. D., Highland, W. H., & Sabella, R. A. (1995). Peer helpers and perceived effectiveness. *Elementary School Guidance and Counseling, 29,* 278–288.

Robinson, S. E., Morrow, S., Kigin, T., & Lindeman, M. (1991). Peer counselors in a high school setting: Evaluation of training and impact on helpees. *School Counselor, 39,* 35–40.

Roth-Roemer, S. L., Robinson Kurpius, S. E., & Carmen, C.

(1998). *The emerging role of counseling psychology in healthcare.* Chicago: Norton.

Sprinthall, N. A., Hall, J. S., & Gerler, E. R. (1992). Peer counseling for middle school students experiencing family divorce: A deliberate psychological education model. *Elementary School Guidance and Counseling, 25,* 279–294.

Stuart, C. (1994). Resilient adolescents and peer counseling: Issues and opportunities. *Journal of Emotional and Behavioral Problems, 3,* 48–49.

Tindall, J. A. (1994). *Peer power.* Muncie, IN: Accelerated Development, Inc.

Varenhorst, B. B. (1992). Developing youth as resources to their peers. *Journal of Emotions and Behavioral Problems, 3,* 10–14.

Sharon E. Robinson Kurpius

PEIRCE, CHARLES S. (1839–1914), scientist and philosopher. Born in Cambridge, Massachusetts, the son of Harvard mathematician Benjamin Peirce and Sarah Hunt Mills Peirce, Peirce began his career as a working scientist. Although he had shown reflective interests from his youth, his work gradually evolved toward philosophical writings. His career parallels the professionalization of psychology in his day because Peirce imported the methods and the authority of science as well as particular examples of experimental work into his theories. His scientific philosophy was an inspiration for psychologists eager to wean the new field away from association with introspective philosophy.

Peirce's family, and especially his father, who was instrumental in national scientific organizing, encouraged his early mathematical and scientific interests. Peirce was a child prodigy, at first with elaborate puzzles and scientific experimentation, and then with youthful reading of philosophy and logic. Perhaps because of his much fostered genius, or because of his painful facial neuralgia, he was arrogant and aloof from most people. He clinched his social alienation when he divorced his wife, Harriet Melusina Fay, and soon married Juliette Pourtalai. Despite his privileged family background, he found it difficult to get permanent work. With a small inheritance, he and his wife moved to Milford, Pennsylvania, in 1887, where he lived, happily married but socially ostracized, in poverty but in constant intellectual production for the rest of his life. He never completed a book of his philosophy, but he wrote large numbers of reviews, encyclopedia entries, and unpublished notes and essays.

The main goal of Peirce's thought was to overturn the rationalist tradition of René Descartes. Against Descartes's starting point in universal doubt, Peirce maintained that all thought begins subjectively. Critiquing Descartes's belief in the ability of human consciousness to grasp truth intuitively, accurately, and unmediated by prior knowledge or patterns, Peirce proposed that knowledge will always be comprehended in signs, external to the mind, which assist the development of thought. These indirect and mediated cognitions suggest an epistemology of uncertainty, but Peirce was at bottom a realist. While no one can be sure of such permanent truth at any one time, the constant road of inquiry, guided by the inquisitiveness of scientific research, will achieve real truth in the long run, through repeated self-correction. Peirce's picture of self-correcting science, uncannily similar to Karl Popper's theory of falsification, allows both for fallibility in any particular investigation and for an intense faith in scientific reasoning in general.

Much of Peirce's thinking contributed to the methodology of many working scientists in the twentieth century, including experimental psychologists. Peirce was a pioneer in the mathematics of probabilities and statistics, which have become so crucial in the handling of data. In much of his own early scientific research, he used probabilities to gain accurate measures of gravity and astronomical distances and to measure errors in scientific research with great precision.

Peirce also contributed directly to the emerging profession of psychology during the early, scientific phase of his career. His astronomical work in the 1870s led to his only book published in his lifetime, *Photometric Researches* (Leipzig, 1878). Related to his analysis of the size and age of stars, Peirce did extensive evaluations of the appearance of light in human visual perception. He conducted research on the way the eye detects increasing brightness of any one color, and he observed that "all colors are yellower when brighter" ("Note on the Sensation of Color," in *Writings,* 1986, Vol. 3, pp. 211–216).

Further consideration of Peirce's role in the history of psychology invites comparison with William James. Peirce influenced James deeply in his youth while they were both members of the Metaphysical Club in the 1860s and 1870s, where Peirce developed the rudiments of pragmatism, which James popularized. A key to their differences is that James regarded pragmatism in psychological terms as a theory of knowledge, while Peirce defined it logically as a theory of meaning. While James is often credited with being the founder of American psychology, Peirce's wide-ranging scientific work included activity in psychology that precedes James's. Peirce was aware of Wilhelm Wundt's laboratory work and many of his early theoretical papers include psychological issues years before James became established in the field. Peirce reviewed James's *Principles of Psychology* with a characteristic criticism of his friend, whose work he said is "averse to the logical explanation" (*Nation,* 1891, p. 33).

Even as Peirce distanced himself from James's psychology, so too did the psychological profession as a whole. The discipline of psychology, like the philosopher Peirce, maintained faith in the truth-gathering capacity of experimental science.

[*See also* Vision and Sight, *article on* Behavioral and Functional Aspects; *and the biographies of Descartes and James.*]

Bibliography

Works by Peirce

Peirce, C. S. (1931–1934, 1958). *Collected papers of Charles Sanders Peirce* (8 vols.). (C. Hartshorne, P. Weiss, & A. W. Burks, Eds.). Cambridge: Harvard University Press.

Peirce, C. S. (1955). *Philosophical writings of Peirce.* (J. Buchler, Ed.). New York: Dover.

Peirce, C. S. (1966). *Charles S. Peirce* (P. P. Wiener, Ed.). New York: Dover.

Peirce, C. S. (1982–1992). *Writings of Charles Sanders Peirce* (M. H. Fisch et al., Eds.). Bloomington: Indiana University Press.

Peirce, C. S. (1991). *Peirce on signs* (James Hoopes, Ed.). Chapel Hill: University of North Carolina Press.

Works about Peirce

Apel, K. O. (1981). *Charles S. Peirce.* Amherst: University of Massachusetts Press.

Brent, J. (1993). *Charles Sanders Peirce.* Bloomington: Indiana University Press.

Colapietro, V. (1989). *Peirce's approach to the self.* Albany: State University of New York Press.

Esposito, J. (1980). *Evolutionary metaphysics.* Athens: Ohio University Press.

Feibleman, J. K. (1969). *An introduction to the philosophy of Charles S. Peirce.* Cambridge: MIT Press.

Goudge, T. (1950). *The thought of C. S. Peirce.* Toronto: University of Toronto Press.

Murphey, M. G. (1961). *The development of Peirce's philosophy.* Cambridge: Harvard University Press.

Orange, D. (1984). *Peirce's conception of God.* Lubbock, TX: Institute for Studies in Pragmatism.

Potter, V. (1996). *Peirce's philosophical perspectives.* New York: Fordham University Press.

Raposa, M. (1989). *Peirce's philosophy of religion.* Bloomington: Indiana University Press.

Skagestad, P. (1981). *The road of inquiry.* New York: Columbia University Press.

Paul Croce

PERCEPTION AND ACTION. One function of vision is to construct an internal representation of the external world: a model of the real thing that can serve as a perceptual foundation for cognitive operations. This perceptual or "reconstructive" function of the visual system is the one that has been studied the most by psychologists and other scientists. But vision does more than provide us with a percept of the world of objects beyond our bodies; it also guides our actions with respect to those objects.

The visual control of action requires computations that are quite different from those leading to the conscious perception of objects and their relations. Control of a motor act—from picking up a morsel of food to throwing a spear at a fleeing antelope—requires precise information about the actual size and location of the target in the metrics of the real world. Our experiential perception of the target object is of little use here. This is because we tend to perceive the size and location of an object primarily in relation to other objects and surfaces in the scene. The metrics of perception are relative, not absolute: a fact that explains why we have no difficulty watching television, a medium in which there are no absolute metrics at all. But television does provide the most important source of metrical information that we use in the real world: the relative size and distance of objects in the scene. But this kind of information is of only limited use in the control of actions. To pick up your coffee cup, it is not enough to know that it is farther away from you than the bowl of cornflakes and closer to you than the jar of marmalade. The neural systems programming and controlling your grasping movement must have access to accurate metrical information about the location of the cup. Furthermore, that information must be computed in egocentric frames of reference; in other words, frames of reference that take into account the instantaneous position of your arm, hand, and fingers. Several things follow from this line of argument. First, since the computations leading to action must be metrically accurate (and highly reliable), they must depend on visual mechanisms that at some stage are quite separate from those mediating our perception of the world. Second, because different kinds of actions (e.g., manual grasping movements versus saccadic eye movements) require that the computations be performed within different egocentric frames of reference, there are likely to be several different visual mechanisms for the control of action, each specialized for the control of different effector systems.

For most of us, it might seem counterintuitive that the visual control of our actions is mediated by mechanisms that are separate from those mediating our experiential perception of the world. Nevertheless, there is plenty of evidence that such a division of labor is exactly what occurs. One important piece of evidence is the organization of the projections from the eye to the brain. The most prominent of these is the one going from the retina to the dorsal lateral geniculate nucleus of the thalamus and from there to primary visual cortex, the so-called geniculostriate pathway, which has been shown to be essential for conscious sight. But there are many other projections as well, projections that go directly from the retina to structures in the brain that are quite separate from the geniculostriate pathway. One of these is a projection that runs from the retina to the superior colliculus, a phylogenetically ancient structure in the midbrain. The superior colliculus appears to play a critical role in the elicitation of reflexive eye and head movements to visual events that suddenly occur in the peripheral visual field. On many occasions, we make these orienting movements before we are actually aware of any visual stimulus at all. Another retinal projection goes directly to the hypothalamus where it helps entrain our circadian rhythm to the local night-day cycle. Another goes to the pretectum (a complex of nuclei between the midbrain and the thalamus) that, among other things, plays an important role in controlling the size of our pupils in response to light (the pupillary light reflex). Still other projections form a collection of pathways that terminate in three separate nuclei deep in the midbrain, the so-called accessory optic system. These three nuclei (whose cells show sensitivity to movement of almost the entire visual field across the retina) work together with the vestibular system in controlling our posture and regulating the position of our eyes as we move about. The visually driven outputs controlled by these structures—orienting movements, synchronization of the circadian rhythm, the pupillary light reflex, posture, and a number of other movements—are controlled by visual inputs that lie quite outside visual perception. We do not perceive the stimuli controlling these behaviors for the simple reason that they are processed by neural structures that are separate from the set of retinal projections that subserves our visual perception: the geniculostriate pathway.

But the story does not end here. A multiplicity of different visual areas in the cerebral cortex are served by the geniculostriate pathway, and not all of them are involved in mediating conscious sight. Some of them appear to have more to do with the on-line control of action than they do with perception per se. In fact, two separate "streams" of projections emanating from the primary visual cortex have been identified: a ventral stream projecting eventually to the visual areas in the temporal cortex and a dorsal stream projecting to visual areas in the posterior parietal cortex. Early on, it was suggested that the ventral stream plays a critical role in the identification and recognition of objects, whereas the dorsal stream mediates the localization of those same objects. Some have referred to this distinction in visual processing as one between *what* versus *where*. Recent findings from a broad range of studies in both humans and monkeys, however, have forced a reinterpretation of the division of labor between the two streams.

Evidence from neuropsychological studies suggests that the dorsal stream is a visual action pathway and that it contributes little to our perception of the world. It has been known for a long time that individuals with damage to the dorsal stream, particularly the superior parts of the posterior parietal cortex, have difficulty reaching in the correct direction to objects (even though they have no difficulty reaching out and grasping different parts of their own body indicated by the experimenter). Some individuals with damage to this region show an inability to rotate their hand or open their fingers properly to grasp an object placed in front of them, even when it is always placed in the same location. But not all individuals with posterior parietal damage show the same kind of visuomotor deficits. Some have difficulty with hand postures, some with controlling the direction of their grasp, and some with foveating the target. Indeed, depending upon the size and locus of the lesion, an individual can demonstrate any combination of these visuomotor deficits. Different subregions of the dorsal stream, it appears, support the visual control of different kinds of motor acts. Nevertheless, despite their problems in visuomotor control, individuals with damage to the dorsal stream are usually able to describe the orientation, size, shape, and even the relative spatial location of the very objects that they are unable to reach toward, grasp correctly, or move their eyes toward.

The ventral stream projecting to the temporal lobe has been more closely linked with visual perception than with the visual control of action. Individuals with brain damage in this region show the complementary pattern of deficits and spared visual abilities to individuals with damage in the posterior parietal cortex. Thus, individuals with ventral stream damage have great difficulty recognizing common objects on the basis of their visual appearance, but have no problem grasping objects placed in front of them or moving through the world without bumping into things. Consider, for example, a young woman (D. F.) who suffered damage to her ventral stream as a result of anoxia from carbon monoxide poisoning. Even though D. F.'s low-level visual abilities are reasonably intact, she can no longer recognize everyday objects or the faces of her friends and relatives, nor can she identify even the simplest of geometric shapes. (If an object is placed in her hand, of course, she has no trouble identifying it by touch.) Remarkably, however, D. F. shows strikingly accurate guidance of her hand and finger movements when she attempts to pick up the very objects she cannot identify. Thus, when she reaches out to grasp objects of different sizes, her hand opens wider midflight for larger objects than it does for smaller ones, just like it does in people with normal vision. Similarly, she rotates her hand and wrist quite normally when she reaches out to grasp objects in different orientations, and she places her fingers correctly on the boundaries of objects of different shapes. At the same time, she is quite unable to describe or distinguish among any of these objects when they are presented to her in simple discrimination tests. In other words, D. F.'s visual system is no longer able to deliver any perceptual information about the size, shape, and orientation of objects in the world. Yet at the same time, the visuomotor systems in D. F.'s brain that control the programming and execution of visually guided actions remain quite sensitive to these same object features.

These neurological observations fit well with what is known about the anatomy and electrophysiology of the dorsal and ventral streams in the monkey. For example, the ventral stream in the monkey receives its input largely from the central portion of the visual field, whereas the dorsal stream receives input from the entire visual field, including the far periphery. Not surprisingly, the receptive fields of cells in the higher areas of the ventral stream almost always include the fovea. Cells in this region of the ventral stream are tuned to the features of objects, and many of them show remarkable categorical specificity; some of these category-specific cells maintain their selectivity irrespective of viewpoint, retinal image size, and even color. They are little affected by the concurrent motor behavior of the monkey, but are modulated by how often the visual stimulus has been presented and whether or not it has been associated with reward. Such observations are consistent with the suggestion that networks of cells in the ventral stream are more concerned with the enduring characteristics of objects than they are with moment-to-moment changes in the visual array. The object-based description that the ventral stream delivers would appear to form the basic raw material for recognition memory and other long-term representations of the visual world.

In sharp contrast to the cells in ventral stream areas, cells in the posterior parietal cortex are greatly dependent on the concurrent motor behavior of the animal with respect to the visual stimulus. Indeed, separate subsets of visually sensitive cells in this region have been shown to be implicated in visual fixation, pursuit and saccadic eye movements, visually guided reaching, and the manipulation of objects. In short, cells in the dorsal stream show both sensory-related and motor-related activity: just the sort of activity one would expect to see in a system dedicated to the visual control of action. The dorsal stream is also intimately connected with subcortical visual structures such as the superior colliculus, which has a long evolutionary history of visuomotor control.

Evidence from anatomical and electrophysiological studies in the monkey and neuropsychological studies in brain-damaged individuals supports the idea of separate visual systems for perception and action. What about studies of vision in normal observers? Is there any evidence for dissociations between vision for perception and vision for action in them? In fact, there are a number of clear demonstrations of such phenomena. For example, it has long been known that our perception of the position of a small dot is affected, to a large degree, by the position of the frame surrounding the dot. Thus, when the frame is moved unexpectedly to the left, we typically see the frame as stationary and the dot as moving to the right. Nevertheless, our visuomotor systems are rarely fooled, and when we are asked to point to the dot, our pointing movements are not influenced by changes in the position of the frame, and we typically continue to point in the correct direction. Similar dissociations have been observed with respect to object size. Thus, the scaling of grasping movements are unaffected by typical size-contrast illusions that have a profound affect on perceptual judgments of size. Such paradoxes show that what we think we "see" is not always what guides our actions, which provides powerful evidence for the parallel operation within everyday life of two types of visual processing, each apparently designed to serve quite different purposes, and each characterized by quite different properties.

[*See also* Cognitive Psychology.]

Bibliography

Goodale, M. A. (1996). Visuomotor modules in the vertebrate brain. *Canadian Journal of Physiology and Pharmacology, 74*, 390–400. Provides a concise review of work on visuomotor control in mammalian and nonmammalian vertebrates, relating the findings to what is known about the organization of the human visual system.

Haffenden, A., & Goodale, M. A. (1998). The effect of pictorial illusion on prehension and perception. *Journal of Cognitive Neuroscience, 10*, 122–136. Presents experimental evidence to show that familiar illusions affecting perceptual judgments of object size have no effect on the scaling of the grasp.

Jeannerod, M. (1997). *The cognitive neuroscience of action.* Oxford, UK: Blackwell. An excellent review of work on the neural substrates of skilled movements, including a discussion of motor imagery and its relation to intention.

Kowler, E. (1995). Eye movements. In S. M. Kosslyn & D. N. Osherson (Eds.), *Visual cognition* (Vol. 2, pp. 215–265). Cambridge, MA: MIT Press. Presents a concise account of the control of eye movements from a cognitive perspective.

Milner, A. D., & Goodale, M. A. (1995). *The visual brain in action.* New York: Oxford University Press. Provides a comprehensive review of the evidence for separate visual pathways for perception and action.

Warren, W. H. (1995). Self-motion: Visual perception and visual control. In W. Epstein & S. Rogers (Eds.), *Handbook of perception and cognition: Vol. 5. Perception of space and motion* (pp. 263–325). San Diego, CA: Academic Press. Reviews the literature on the visual control of locomotion and its relation to the visual perception of space.

Zeki, S. (1993). *A vision of the brain*. Oxford, UK: Blackwell. A comprehensive, if idiosyncratic, account of the organization of the human visual system that brings an historical approach to the subject.

Melvyn A. Goodale

PERCEPTUAL CONSTANCIES refer to the organism's immediate awareness of the permanent properties of objects and surfaces in the surrounding environment, such as size, shape, lightness, and color. It is obviously very important that an organism be able to respond to these enduring properties of objects in order to recognize them and interact with them by reaching, avoiding, and so on. But how can this be accomplished given the great variety of distances, viewpoints, and conditions of illumination under which objects are viewed? These produce large but transient and accidental changes in the retinal image that do not reflect the intrinsic properties of objects and surfaces. For example, the angular size projected by an object diminishes in proportion to its distance (see Figure 1). We do not correspondingly see objects shrink as they increase their distance from us. Similarly, the luminance of an object (defined as the amount of light reflected off it) increases enormously as the object goes from a dim room to bright sunlight, yet we continue to see white objects as white and black objects as black, somehow picking up that property of the surface that does not change as illumination changes: the *proportion* of incident light reflected back. How do we compute the real size of an object or the intrinsic reflectance properties of a surface in the face of huge changes in retinal size and retinal luminance? These questions are typical of the constancy problem, whose solution is one of the brain's greatest achievements. More cortex is probably devoted to solving it than to any other task of the human mind.

The term *constancy* has traditionally been used for the detection of permanent qualities of objects or surfaces. This article will deal with these traditional constancies. Broadly speaking, however, almost all of perception could be regarded as concerned with the constancy problem. (Its other main concern is with the location and motion of the observer.) It is increasingly realized, for example, that the perception of direction, motion, and stereoscopic depth are also based on complex processing that somehow takes into account the effects of viewing conditions like distance, eye movements, and head position; terms like *direction constancy* or *stereo depth constancy* are used to describe these achievements.

Early ideas about constancy were based on the sensation-perception distinction, in which the perception of the real properties of objects are considered to be judgments, which take sensations or experiences of the basic image properties and associate them with other information, such as distance in the case of size, or ambient illumination in the case of lightness, to form perceptions. The implication of this view is that perception is a cognitive act based on the sensory experiences of image properties. This view is no longer considered valid for reasons that will be considered in the following.

First, this view is undermined by the finding that people are much more accurate in reporting the real sizes, shapes, and lightnesses/color of objects in a scene than in reporting the corresponding image or "projective" properties, even when an effort is made to do so. (Leonardo da Vinci suggested interposing a sheet of glass between the scene and the eye to assist artists in achieving projective accuracy.) Although, for example, people can match objects at different distances for angular size when they are presented monocularly in the

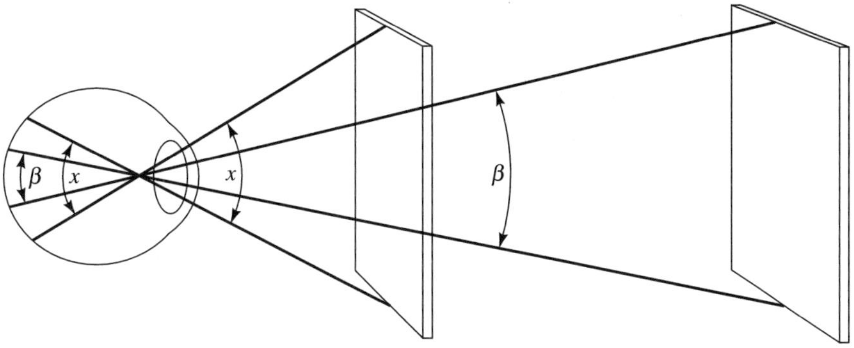

PERCEPTUAL CONSTANCIES. Figure 1. The angular size projected by an object at the eye diminishes in proportion to its distance. From Rock, I. (1984). *Perception*, p. 24. Scientific American Library. WH Freeman. New York.

dark, they are quite unable to do so when the objects are part of a scene. Judgments tend to "regress to the real object" (Thouless, 1931). Sedgwick (1986) provided a good summary of this literature. Some idea of the difficulty in sensing image properties is illustrated in Figure 2a. At first sight, it may seem obvious that the projective sizes of the men are different (sensation) and their real sizes are the same (perception). It comes as a surprise (see Figure 2b) to realize how much regression to the real object there is in evaluating the projective sizes in Figure 2a. In viewing a real scene, the difficulty in seeing image properties and relationships and the ease in perceiving real properties is even greater than in a picture.

A second problem applies to any version of the idea that perception of a property is based on the sensory registration of that property with other information "taken into account." The most popular theory of size perception is the size-distance invariance hypothesis that states that perceived size is directly proportional to both angular size and to perceived distance. Perceived distance is said to be based on distance "cues." The difficulty with this theory is that people are better at reporting the intrinsic properties of objects, such as their real size, than at reporting the information on which this is said to depend, such as distance. Many attempts have failed to support the size-distance invariance hypothesis (for reviews, see Gillam, 1995; Sedgwick, 1986). In fact, in many cases perceived size has more influence on perceived distance than the reverse: a phenomenon known as the size-distance paradox. For example, the zenith moon looks larger than the horizon moon (the moon illusion) and accordingly looks nearer. This makes it logically incoherent to use the greater apparent distance of the horizon moon as an explanation of the moon illusion. Similar difficulties have been found with respect to using perceived slant to account for shape constancy or perceived illumination to account for lightness constancy.

If perception of the intrinsic properties of objects and surfaces in a scene are not based on sensations, and they are not based on perceived distance, slant, and illumination, what are they based upon? In trying to answer this question, I shall deal with each of the major constancies in turn, beginning with size constancy. There is no question that the perception of size becomes more accurate as cues to distance are added. The question is whether the effect these cues have on size perception is indirect, that is, mediated by distance or is a direct effect on size itself. The failure of the size-distance invariance hypothesis supports the view that the effect must be a direct one. Gibson (1966) is the best-known proponent of this position. He pioneered analysis of the complex information about the properties of the world available in the *optic array* (the structured light projected from the

(a)

(b)

PERCEPTUAL CONSTANCIES. Figure 2a–b. Illustrating the difficulty of perceiving relative projective size correctly when viewing objects at different distances, the 2 men are the same size in both pictures. From Rock, I. (1975). *An introduction to perception.* New York: Macmillan, pp. 48, 49.

PERCEPTUAL CONSTANCIES. Figure 3. The projection in the optic array of a ground plane on which textured elements (bricks) form a size gradient. The two objects reveal their identical size by each resting on one ground element. From Gillam, B. (1981). False perspectives. *Perception, 10*, 313–318, p. 316.

PERCEPTUAL CONSTANCIES. Figure 4. According to the horizon ratio principle, the horizon line intersects objects standing on the ground at a height equal to the viewer's eye level. Since a greater proportion of the tree is above the horizon we perceive it as taller than the telegraph poles, which all have the same horizon ratio. From Goldstein, E. B. (1987). *Sensation and perception* (3rd ed.). Belmont, CA: Wadsworth, p. 268.

surfaces of the environment to a station point such as the eye). Figure 3 shows the projection in the optic array of a ground plane on which are texture elements (bricks) forming a size gradient. Given the constraint that these ground plane elements are actually of equal size (a constraint that arises from reliable properties of the terrestrial environment), the relative sizes of objects placed on the ground plane can be judged according to the number of texture elements they cover where they meet the ground. The relative sizes of the two objects shown can immediately be seen, according to Gibson, because it is given by the relative amount of texture they cover. Distance estimates are not required. Other direct methods of perceiving real size include the relationship between an object and its surrounding framework in the optic array and the horizon ratio relation (Sedgwick, 1986). The horizon of the ground on which a person is standing is always at eye height. Objects standing on the ground are taller than the observer's eye height in the same proportion as their height exceeds that of the horizon (measured from the bottom of the object in the optic array). Similarly, objects are shorter than the observer's eye height in the same proportion as their height is less than that of the horizon (see Figure 4). The horizon ratio relation is particularly interesting in that it shows how information in the optic array can specify size without distance information. Supporters of the taking-distance-into-account theory, such as Rock (1984), often concede the possibility of direct perception in the case of "pictorial" information such as I have considered so far, but argue that direct perception cannot account for the known influence on size of factors such as stereopsis and convergence. These, it is argued, can only have an influence through an effect on perceived distance. This is not so. Binocular vision effectively provides two different

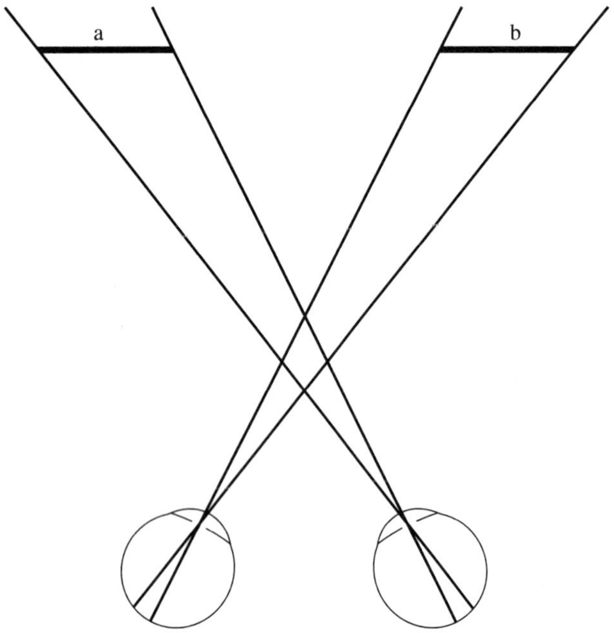

PERCEPTUAL CONSTANCIES. Figure 5. The images a and b are polarized so that the left eye sees only b and the right eye sees only a. These images taken together geometrically specify an object which is both close and small. From Gillam, B. (1995). The perception of spatial layout. In W. Epstein & S. Rogers (Eds.), *Perception of space and motion.* San Diego, CA: Academic Press.

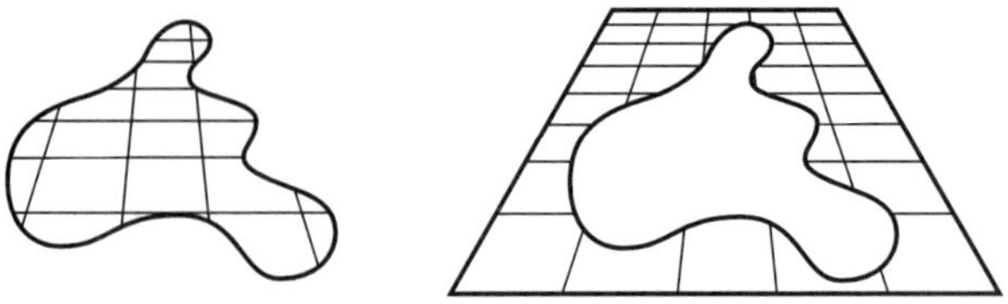

PERCEPTUAL CONSTANCIES. Figure 6. Shape specified by texture scale. The shape of a slanted object can be specified by either (a) the texture covering it or (b) the texture that it covers. From Sedgwick, H. (1986). Space and motion perception. In K. R. Boff, I. Kaufman, & J. Thomas (Eds.), *Handbook of perception and human performance.* Vol. 1: *Sensory processes and perception.* New York: Wiley, p. 21–26.

perspective views of a scene in which the vertical and horizontal locations of points in the environment are specified just as well as the depth (see Figure 5). Similarly, the evidence points very strongly toward a direct scaling of size by convergence because size is so much more reliably scaled by convergence than is distance (convergence micropsia); for a fuller discussion of these issues, see Gillam (1995).

Shape constancy similarly can be based on information in the optic array, which directly specifies shape. In Figure 6 it can be seen that if an area is lying on a background, its shape can be specified by the texture within it if this is regular, or by the texture it overlays. Similarly, shape for any random polygon lying on a surface can be specified by linear perspective (converging lines in the optic array) if the horizon of the surface and the relative lengths of the sides are known (Sedgwick, 1986). Incidentally, it should be noted in considering the information about three-dimensional layout given by perspective that vanishing points and horizons need only be implicit to have an effect. As would be expected, data indicate that shape constancy for monocularly viewed polygons is good when they are seen lying on a receding surface, but poor when they are viewed in isolation.

For isolated shapes, constancy is much better in binocular vision. As in the case of size constancy, this has been taken to mean that shape must be mediated by perceived slant. Again, this is not necessarily the case. The two different perspective views available in binocular vision specify shape just as adequately as they specify slant (Gillam, 1995). Given the poor relationship found empirically between perceived shape and perceived slant, it seems increasingly likely that shape is given directly by information in the optic array(s).

It is generally agreed that lightness constancy is based on contextual information of various kinds, rather than on perceived illumination level for which there are few known cues. In fact, the perception of lightness, of levels and variations in illumination and of transparency, all seem to result from a parsing process in which many aspects of the visual input play a part. The most important finding with respect to context is Wallach's (1948) ratio principle. He showed that perceived lightness is a function not of luminance, but of the *ratio* of the luminance of a surface and the luminance of the surround. For planar surfaces this would automatically compensate for the level of illumination because an increase in illumination would not only increase the luminance of the surface, but also the luminance of the surround, keeping the ratio constant and the perceived lightness constant. A simple ratio principle would not work, however, unless the object and surround were receiving the same illumination. It has become clear that exactly what context is used for computing luminance ratios depends on an analysis of three-dimensional spatial structure and also on grouping. Surrounds that are remote in depth or at a different orientation from the test surface, and are therefore likely to be differently illuminated, will be weighted less heavily. A ratio analysis would also be inadequate if local context were all that counted, because every time an object is moved to a new background, the ratio would change and constancy would fail. Mechanisms have been proposed by which more remote contexts can influence perceived lightness (e.g., Land, 1977; for a summary of many of these factors, see Gilchrist, 1994). Many aspects of color constancy can be subsumed under the same principles as lightness constancy. *Color* refers to the intrinsic reflectance property of a surface with respect to wavelength, and *color constancy* refers to the ability to perceive this correctly despite changes in the wavelength of the illuminant. Land's retinex theory bases color constancy on a comparison of the lightness responses of the different color channels. Others, such as Brainard, Wandell, and Chichilnisky (1993), have proposed models incorporating constraints present in natural images in order to tease out properties of the illuminant from the intrinsic reflecting properties of a surface.

Constancy, or the ability to respond to the stable properties of the physical world, is perception's principal task. Its achievement uses a wealth of information in the visual input and a great deal of brain power. Although the visual system tends to resolve certain properties of the surrounding world such as size-distance or lightness-illumination in an interdependent way, there is no reason to believe that one of these has primacy over the other.

Bibliography

Brainard, D. H., Wandell, B. A., & Chichilnisky, E. J. (1993). Color constancy: From physics to appearance. *Current Directions in Psychological Science, 2*(5), 165–170.

Gibson, J. J. (1966). The senses considered as perceptual systems. Boston: Houghton Mifflin.

Gilchrist, A. L. (Ed.). (1994). *Lightness, brightness, and transparency.* Mahwah, NJ: Erlbaum.

Gillam, B. (1995). The static perception of spatial layout. In W. Epstein & S. Rogers (Eds.). *Perception of space and motion.* San Diego, CA: Academic Press.

Holway, A. H., & Boring, E. G. (1941). Determinants of apparent visual size with distance variant. *American Journal of Psychology, 54,* 21–37.

Kilpatrick, F. P., & Ittleson, W. H. (1953). The size-distance invariance hypothesis. *Psychological Review, 60,* 223–231.

Land, E. H. (1977). Retinex theory of color vision. *Scientific American, 237,* 108–128.

Rock, I. (1984). *Perception.* New York: Freeman.

Sedgwick, H. A. (1986). Space perception. In K. Boff, L. Kaufman, & J. Thomas (Eds.), *Handbook of perception and human performance* (Vol. 1, chap. 21). New York: Wiley.

Thouless, R. H. (1931). Phenomenal regression to the real object. *British Journal of Psychology, 21,* 339–359.

Wallach, H. (1948). Brightness constancy and the nature of achromatic colors. *Journal of Experimental Psychology, 38,* 310–324.

Barbara Gillam

PERCEPTUAL ORGANIZATION refers to the way in which perceptual experience is structured and how that perceived structure arises from sensory stimulation. It is most often concerned with hierarchical part-whole relations among perceived entities, such as object parts, whole objects, and groups of objects, but has applications to many other phenomena in which more global context strongly influences local perceptions.

The study of perceptual organization was pioneered in the early 1900s by members of the Gestalt school of psychology, whose demonstrations revolutionized the field of perception. Previously, perceptual theory was dominated by the structuralist school, which claimed that complex perceptions consisted of atoms of elementary color sensations that were assembled simply by learned associations due to spatial and temporal contiguity. Gestalt theorists rejected both assumptions, arguing instead that perception was holistic and intrinsically organized because of interactions between stimulus structure and underlying brain processes.

Grouping

Max Wertheimer (1923/1950), one of the founding fathers of the Gestalt movement, initially posed the problem of perceptual organization by asking how people manage to perceive organized scenes consisting of meaningful objects coherently arranged in space, rather than the chaotic, dynamic juxtaposition of millions of different colors registered by individual retinal receptors. He attempted to answer this question by identifying stimulus factors that caused simple arrays of visual elements to be perceived as organized into distinct groups. The factors he identified are usually called the laws (or, more accurately, principles) of grouping, several of which are illustrated in Figures 1a–f: proximity, similarity of color, similarity of size, common fate due to similarity of motion, good continuation, and closure. More recently, other principles have been identified (e.g., Palmer & Rock, 1994), including common region (Figure 1g), element connectedness (Figure 1h), and synchrony (not illustrated). In each case, elements that have a stronger relation in terms of the specified property (i.e., those that are closer, more similarly colored, etc.) tend to be grouped together. These so-called laws are actually *ceteris paribus* rules: all else being equal, the elements most closely related by the specified factor will be grouped together. They cannot predict the result when two or more factors vary in opposition (e.g., Figure 1i, where proximity

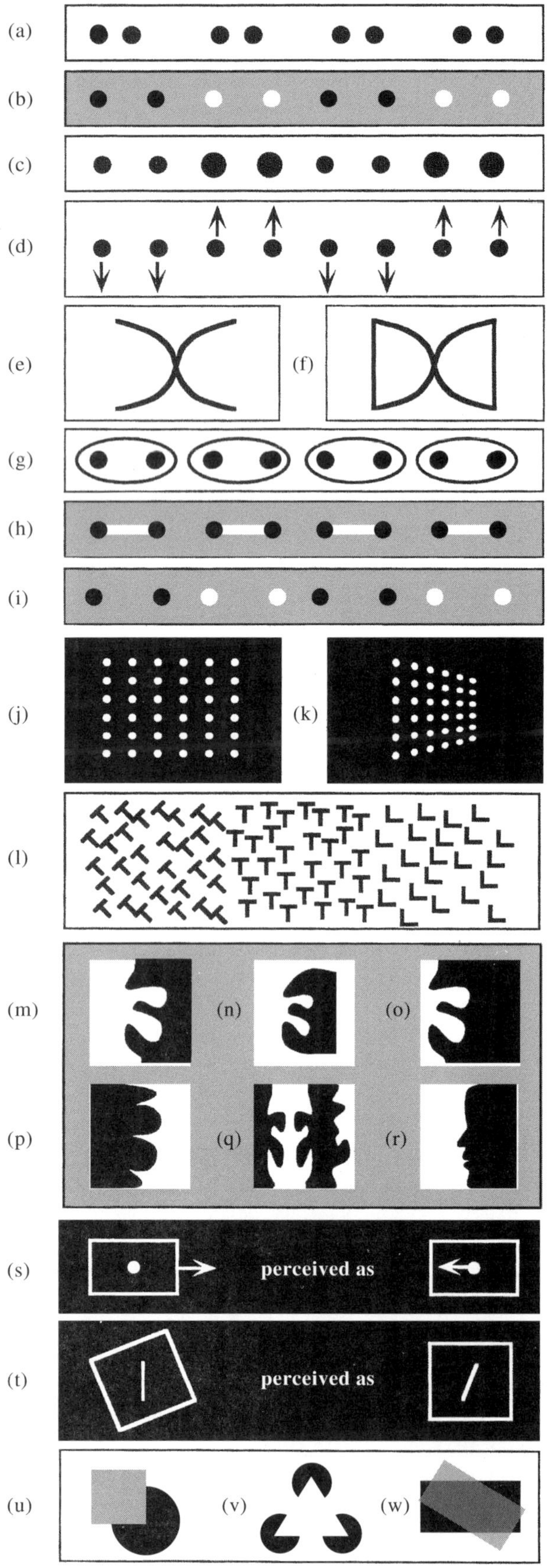

PERCEPTUAL ORGANIZATION. Figure 1. The laws (or principles) of grouping: (a) proximity; (b) similarity of color; (c) similarity of size; (d) common fate due to similarity of motion; (e) good continuation; (f) closure; (g) common region; (h) element connectedness; (i) proximity competing with color similarity; (j) array of beads; (k) array of beads slanted in depth; and (l) texture segregation. Figure-ground organization in perceptual organization: (m) ambiguity; (n) surroundedness; (o) size; (p) convexity; (q) symmetry; and (r) meaningfulness. Frame of reference in perceptual organization: (s) induced motion; and (t) rod-and-frame effect. Figural interpolation in perceptual organization: (u) amodal completion; (v) illusory contours; and (w) color scission. (Adapted from Palmer, 1999.)

competes with color similarity) because the rules fail to specify how multiple factors are integrated. No general theory has yet been formulated that overcomes this problem, although researchers have begun to turn their attention in this direction.

Gestalt theorists implied that grouping is an early phenomenon in vision, but more recent evidence has shown that perceived grouping can be strongly influenced by processes that occur later than one might expect, including depth perception, lightness constancy, completion of partly occluded figures, and illusory contours (Palmer & Rock, 1994). For example, when an array of luminous beads like that shown in Figure 1j was presented to observers in the frontal plane, they saw it grouped into columns rather than rows because of the greater vertical proximity of the beads. When the same array was slanted in depth, as illustrated in Figure 1k, so that the images of the beads were closer together horizontally on the retina, observers still reported grouping by columns while viewing the array with full binocular depth information. This result is consistent with grouping being governed by the perceived proximity of the beads in three-dimensional space rather than by their projected proximity on the two-dimensional retina.

A phenomenon related to grouping that has been studied more recently by perceptual psychologists is texture segregation: the division of images into regions based on texture. Figure 1l shows an example in which three regions of texture have been created by filling them with large numbers of closely spaced elements. Most observers perceive the left (tilted Ts) and central (upright Ts) regions to be more distinct than the central (upright Ts) and right (upright Ls) regions, even though most people find that, as individual figures, upright and tilted Ts look more alike than an upright T and an upright L. This difference results from the fact that line orientation is a particularly salient feature for texture processing, whereas the configuration of lines of the same orientation is not. Although texture segregation is influenced by many of the same factors as perceptual grouping, the relation between these two phenomena is not yet clear.

Figure-Ground Organization

Another important phenomenon of perceptual organization is figure-ground organization (Rubin, 1921). In Figure 1m, for instance, one can perceive either a white object on a black background or a black object on a white background with nearly equal ease. The crucial feature of figure-ground organization is that the boundary between two regions is perceived as belonging to the figure and not to the ground. As a result, the figure seems "thinglike," has definite shape, and appears closer, whereas the ground appears farther and to extend behind the figure. Psychologists have identified many factors that affect figure-ground organization (Figure 1n–r), including surroundedness, size, convexity, symmetry, and meaningfulness. These principles are also properly viewed as *ceteris paribus* rules: all else being equal, the surrounded, smaller, more convex, symmetrical, or meaningful region tends to be seen as figure. As a result, they suffer from the same problem as the principles of grouping: they cannot predict the result when two or more factors conflict. No satisfactory theory has yet been proposed that integrates multiple factors.

Figure-ground organization is clearly related to depth perception in the sense that the figural region is perceived as closer, but the connection goes deeper than this. The factors that influence figure-ground assignment are generally compatible with the hypothesis that its goal is to distinguish image regions corresponding to objects from those corresponding to spaces between objects (Palmer, 1999). Objects tend to be convex, symmetrical, meaningful, and both smaller than, and surrounded by, the surfaces against which they are seen.

Frames of Reference

A third important phenomenon of perceptual organization is that certain properties of objects are perceived relative to a frame of reference determined by more global sensory structure. Motion and orientation provide two compelling examples. In induced motion (Figure 1s), a slowly moving, larger object surrounds a smaller, stationary object in an otherwise dark environment. Surprisingly, observers perceive the frame as still and the dot as moving in the opposite direction (Duncker, 1929/1950). An analogous illusion occurs when the moon appears to move through a cloud that appears stationary. In the rod-and-frame effect (Figure 1t), observers perceive an upright rod as tilted when it is presented inside a tilted room or (less effectively) inside a large luminous rectangle in an otherwise dark environment (Asch & Witkin, 1948). This orientation illusion occurs most profoundly when one perceives a vertical chandelier as hanging obliquely inside a tilted room in an amusement park's fun house. Larger, surrounding objects or surfaces thus tend to be taken as the frame of reference for the smaller objects they enclose.

Figural Interpolation

Several other phenomena concerned with the interpolation of unseen portions of figures are generally viewed as also falling within the domain of perceptual organization. Amodal completion refers to the perception of partly visible figures as completed behind an occluding object. Figure 1u, for example, is invariably perceived as a complete circle behind a square even though only three fourths of it is actually showing. Illusory contours refer to the perception of a figure defined by edges that are not physically present in the image. As Figure 1v illustrates, an illusory figure is perceived when aligned contours in the inducing elements cause them to be seen as partly occluded by a figure that has the same color as the background (Kanizsa, 1979). Color scission (Figure 1w) refers to the splitting of perceived color into one component due to an opaque figure and another component due to a translucent figure through which the farther figure is seen (Metelli, 1974).

Although these examples hardly exhaust the phenomena of perceptual organization, they are among the most important examples in the visual domain. Gestalt psychologists also investigated the perceptual organization of sounds, a topic that has been extended significantly by modern researchers (e.g., Bregman, 1990).

Ambiguity and Multistability

Many demonstrations of perceptual organization depend on ambiguity: the possibility of seeing the same stimulus as having two or more different organizations. In figure-ground organization, for example, Figure 1m illustrates a case in which sometimes one region is perceived as figure and sometimes the other is. Once both possibilities have been perceived by an observer, perception of ambiguous figures is usually multistable: It flips spontaneously back and forth among the alternatives. Gestalt psychologists believed that this phenomenon resulted from neural fatigue as different sets of neurons got tired of firing after doing so for a long time (Köhler, 1940). Similar ideas have been pursued by modern theorists through neural network simulations of ambiguity and multistability in which assemblies of mutually excitatory units compete with each other by mutual inhibition in dynamic interaction (e.g., Grossberg & Mingolla, 1985)

Attention and Organization

Recent research has suggested intimate links between organizational processes and perceptual attention going in both directions (e.g., Prinzmetal, 1995). One relation is that attention is deployed to objects formed by lower-level organizational processes such as grouping or texture segregation. Figure 1l shows that one can more easily attend to the left third of the array (the tilted Ts) than to the left half (the tilted Ts and half of the upright Ts) because bottom-up organizational processes define the left third as a unified perceptual object, but not the left half. Another relation between attention and organization is that attending to different parts or aspects of an image can affect how it is perceived to be organized. Figure 1i shows that one can see the dots as grouped either by proximity or color by attending selectively to one or the other of these properties.

Development

Modern investigations of perceptual development demonstrate that, contrary to the nativistic beliefs of gestalt theorists, most principles of organization are not present at birth, but develop at different times during the first year of life. By clever use of habituation techniques with infants, researchers have been able to discover the earliest ages at which various grouping factors affect perception (Spelke, 1990). By 4 months of age, for example, infants spontaneously group spatially separated elements by common fate when they move together. Static grouping factors, like various forms of similarity and good continuation, do not emerge until several months later. It is not yet clear what, if any, grouping mechanisms are present at birth, however.

Theories of Perceptual Organization

Gestalt psychologists proposed that phenomena of perceptual organization support the doctrine of holism, the claim that the whole is different from the sum of its parts. They attempted to explain such holistic effects in terms of the principle of Prägnanz (also known as the minimum principle), the claim that the percept will be as "good" as the stimulus conditions allow. This means that the preferred organization should be the simplest, most regular possibility compatible with the constraints imposed by the stimulus image. Unfortunately, the gestaltists did not provide an adequate definition of goodness, simplicity, or regularity, so their central claim was untestable in any rigorous way. Later theorists have attempted to ground these concepts in objective analyses, suggesting that simple perceptions correspond to low information content and/or economy of symbolic representation. Nongestalt theorists typically appeal instead to Helmholtz's likelihood principle that the perceptual system chooses the most likely (rather than the simplest) interpretation. The difficulty in discriminating between these two alternatives arises in part from the fact that the most likely interpretation is usually the simplest, in some plausible sense (see Pomerantz & Kubovy, 1986, for a review of this issue).

Many phenomena of perceptual organization have resisted explanation since their discovery. Gestalt theorists favored physiological accounts because of their belief in psychophysiological isomorphism: the hypothesis that conscious experience (psycho-) and its underlying brain mechanisms (physiology) have the same abstract structure (isomorphism). Gestaltists, therefore, appealed to the brain's inherent self-organizational properties in explaining the structure of conscious perception. The most notable attempt along these lines was Köhler's (1940) famous speculation that the brain achieved an optimal organization for perception by the activity of electromagnetic fields in the cerebral cortex that settled into states of minimum energy, much as soap bubbles stabilize into perfect spheres, which are minimal both in energy and in complexity. Although subsequent physiological results discredited the brain-field conjecture, the more abstract idea of a physical Gestalt, a dynamical physical system that reaches equilibrium in minimum energy configurations, is compatible with modern investigations of recurrent neural networks (e.g., Grossberg & Mingolla, 1985). These networks of neuronlike units are able to converge on an optimal solution to complex problems by settling into a minimum defined by an energylike function. Such ideas suggest new theoretical approaches to the many important organizational phenomena Gestalt psychologists discovered more than a half century ago.

Bibliography

Asch, S. E., & Witkin, H. A. (1948). Studies in space orientation: I. Perception of the upright with displaced visual fields. *Journal of Experimental Psychology, 38*, 325–337.

Beck, J. (1966). Effects of orientation and shape similarity on perceptual grouping. *Perception and Psychophysics, 1*, 300–302.

Bregman, A. S. (1990). *Auditory scene analysis: The perceptual organization of sound.* Cambridge, MA: MIT Press. Contains the most comprehensive modern treatment of organization in auditory perception.

Duncker, K. (1937). Induced motion. In W. D. Ellis (Ed.), *A sourcebook of Gestalt psychology* (pp. 161–172). London: Routledge & Kegan Paul. (Original work published 1929)

Grossberg, S., & Mingolla, E. (1985). Neural dynamics of form perception: Boundary completion, illusory figures, and neon color spreading. *Psychological Review, 92*(2),

173–211. An example of how phenomena of perceptual organization can be modelled using dynamic neural networks.

Kanizsa, G. (1979). *Organization in vision: Essays on gestalt perception.* New York: Praeger. A compilation of the most important works by this highly regarded modern Italian Gestalt psychologist, with many fascinating demonstrations of visual phenomena.

Kellman, P. J., & Shipley, T. F. (1991). A theory of visual interpolation in object perception. *Cognitive Psychology, 23,* 141–221.

Koffka, K. (1935). *Principles of gestalt psychology.* New York: Harcourt, Brace. One of the most comprehensive statements of Gestalt psychology; covers not only perceptual organization, but topics concerning memory, problem solving, and social psychology.

Köhler, W. (1940). *Dynamics in psychology.* New York: Liveright. Köhler's book represents a milestone in the development of gestalt theory, especially in making connections to brain function.

Metelli, F. (1974). The perception of transparency. *Scientific American, 230*(4), 90–98.

Palmer, S. E. (1999). Gestalt perception. In R. A. Wilson & F. C. Keil (Eds.), *The MIT encyclopedia of the cognitive sciences* (pp. 344–346). Cambridge, MA: MIT Press.

Palmer, S. E. (1999). *Vision science: Photons to phenomenology.* Cambridge, MA: MIT Press. Chapter 6 contains an up-to-date and comprehensive overview of the field of perceptual organization in vision, including all of the topics mentioned here.

Palmer, S. E., & Rock, I. (1994). Rethinking perceptual organization: The role of uniform connectedness. *Psychonomic Bulletin & Review, 1*(1), 29–55. Reinterprets many topics in perceptual organization within a modern computational framework.

Pomerantz, J. R., & Kubovy, M. (1986). Theoretical approaches to perceptual organization: Simplicity and likelihood principles. In L. K. Kenneth, R. Boff, & J. P. Thomas (Eds.), *Handbook of perception and human performance, Vol. 2: Cognitive processes and performance* (pp. 1–46). New York: Wiley. A comprehensive review and commentary on the relative merits of different theoretical approaches to perceptual organization, especially Prägnanz versus likelihood principles.

Prinzmetal, W. P. (1995). Visual feature integration in a world of objects. *Current Directions in Psychological Science, 4,* 90–94. A succinct review of modern findings concerning the relation between attention and organization.

Rubin, E. (1921). *Visuell Wahrgenommene Figuren* [Visual perceptions of figures]. Copenhagen: Glydenalske.

Spelke, E. S. (1990). Principles of object perception. *Cognitive Science, 14*(1), 29–56. Reviews the experimental evidence on the development of perceptual organization in infants (part of a special issue of this journal on perceptual and cognitive development).

Wertheimer, M. (1950). Laws of organization in perceptual forms. In W. D. Ellis (Ed.), *A sourcebook of Gestalt psychology* (pp. 71–88). London: Routledge & Kegan Paul. Classic article on perceptual grouping that helped to define the gestalt movement in psychology. (Original work published 1923 as Untersuchungen zur Lehre von der Gestalt, *Psychology Forschung, 4,* 301–350.)

Stephen E. Palmer

PERFORMANCE ASSESSMENT. *See* Work Performance.

PERFORMING ARTS. Psychological perspectives on the performing arts are somewhat diverse. They need to be because the performing arts are themselves varied. The domains receiving the most attention in the psychological literature and research are literature and drama, dance, acting, and music. Each of these must be described in behavioral terms (e.g., writing rather than literature, or acting rather than theater) because most of the empirical work in this area focuses on the artists and their personalities, backgrounds, and talents. Much less research has been directed to the domains as field and as independent of behavior. This emphasis on the individual no doubt reflects psychology's emphasis on human behavior.

Even with the diversity among the performing arts a few commonalities have been uncovered in the psychological and interdisciplinary studies of the performance arts. These are reviewed below. Analyses within specific performing arts are first reviewed.

Music, Writing, and Acting

In one report from the 1989 *Creativity Research Journal,* Judith Alter tested the hypothesis that there would be personality differences among various groups of music students (e.g., those studying at a university vs. at a conservatory). Alter administered the Adjective Check List to define personality profiles and found numerous differences between the music students and a normative sample. The music students had higher mean scale scores on self-confidence, personal adjustment, ability, defensiveness, autonomy, and exhibitionism, just to name some clear examples. The music students also had higher Action Preferences. Alter concluded that a profile must be used to characterize the personalities of music students, and that there are differences between music students studying at a university and those in a conservatory.

Cognitive approaches to music are available. Berliner, for example, reported (1997) that, in addition to mastering the harmonies and melodies of particular pieces of music, that, in order to improvise, jazz musicians also master methods for the transformation of harmonies and melodies. In the same volume Keith Sawyer identified rules used when jazz performers collaborate and improvise. Note, then, that there are social and cognitive bases for jazz improvisation. The rules identified in the research are especially interesting in that the concept of rules implies a structure and routine that can seem antithetical to the idea of improvisation.

Certain forms of writing require social interaction. Steven Pritkzer, who was himself once a writer and producer of TV situation comedies, and I found dynamic hierarchies among the teams who write sitcoms. Experience and personality were influential, including the "need for control" on the part of the person in charge (the so-called Show Runner). Pritzker and Runco identified several decision-making styles that are used by individuals who write TV scripts. These decision-making styles suggest that writing performances, like musical performances, reflect social and cognitive processes.

Some research on artists utilizes case study and biographical methods. Doris Wallace, for example, reported a biographical analysis of the novelist, Dorothy Richardson. Perhaps most important was Wallace's support for the idea that creative work tends to be protracted. Even sudden insights—such as Richardson's recognition of the need for a stream of consciousness perspective within a novel—may actually have long histories. They are often based on a multitude of experiences, though the writer or creator may not be aware of the actual breadth of the relevant experience. Admittedly, novelists' work is less performance-oriented than that of the writers of TV sitcoms. Still, it could be argued that novels are performance, albeit with a long interval between the creative activity and the presentation to the audience.

Jill Nemiro (1998) described her qualitative analysis of actors. Nemiro distinguished between *originating* artists and *interpretive artists*. Actors are primarily interpretive; they read a script that was composed by some other (originating) artist.

Nemiro's investigation was largely qualitative, as are many studies of creativity and performing artists. The strengths and weaknesses of qualitative research are reviewed by Michael Moore (*Creativity Research Handbooks*). There are, however, more objective approaches. Dean Simonton, for example, has applied historiometric techniques directly to the arts. Historiometry uses data from eminent (historical) figures, including both productivity counts, objective indices of the originality of particular works (e.g., melodic originality), and information about family background (e.g., birth order) and personality. It thus uses data about the artist him- or herself as well as data about the creative product. In one series of studies Simonton used the frequency of performance as an index of eminence. Perhaps his most intriguing findings are those indicating that eminence can be predicted from melodic originality. Indeed, only a handful of notes—the first notes in a musical score—can be used to very accurately predict fame. In his Arnheim Award paper presented to the American Psychological Association (*Creativity Research Journal*, 1998,) Simonton describes historimetric analyses of opera.

Some bidirectionality is apparent in psychological studies of the arts. A writer may, for example, draw from his or her experience when working, thus demonstrating how the individual creator or performer can influence the artwork; but the artwork may in some ways also influence the creator or performer. The influence is in that sense bidirectional. As an extreme example, consider Kaun's conclusion (*Journal of Economic Psychology*, 1991,) that "writers die young." Kaun found that the lifespan of writers was the shortest of any group of professionals. Kaun explored a number of explanations for this, including the lifestyle expected of writers (which may include alcohol), the delayed gratification, and the isolation that may be necessary during some phases of the work. Delayed gratification was implied earlier, when I mentioned the interval between the writing of a novel and the appearance in print (and presentation to an audience). The fact that there is often isolation when writing a novel suggests something about asocial activity, which would be avoided in most performing arts and are immediately presented to the audience.

Arnold Ludwig presented data on the mental disorders of various groups of artists. Mental disorders were defined as manifested in alcoholism, substance abuse, depression, mania, and anxiety. The overall figure for theater artists was quite high (74% incidence), as was the lifetime incident rate for music/singing/dance (68%). For comparison, the rate for writers was 78%, for composers 60%, and for architecture 52%.

There is some controversy about which domains are performing arts and which are not. As suggested above, we might ask whether writing is a performing art if the creative act occurs when the individual is alone and isolated. To the extent that the eventual product is shared, at least *it* has the opportunity to perform. It is, however, static, and it is not the individual who is performing live.

Issues in the Performing Arts

Several other issues deserve to be mentioned. Sawyer (1997) uncovered six critical questions in his studies of performance. They were:

1. Methodology. Many psychological techniques have been used to study the performance arts. Interviews are often conducted with artists, for example, some of which are qualitative, others quantitative. Bio-

graphical studies are plentiful, and occasionally observational techniques are employed. As is true throughout empirical psychology, each method has its strengths and weaknesses. Some of the difficulties are especially acute in this area, however, because interpretations of the arts are by nature subjective, and this can conflict with efforts toward objective research.

2. Performances tend to be social, but creativity need not be social (Runco, 1995). Consider the personal motivations and self-expression that can lead to art and insight. Consider also scientific creativity—though science has its performance aspects (Crease, 1997; Kasof, 1995).
3. Why is performance studied less often than productivity? Granted, psychology aspires to the scientific method; but in a sense creative work and art are not amenable to entirely objective analyses. Moreover, an emphasis on products can too easily ignore the individual involved and overlook the actual mechanisms that led to the creative work. Studies of products are useful and objective but offer limited information about people and the creative processes used by performing artists.
4. What aspects of everyday life are performances? Sawyer included studies of conversation and education in his collection; however, his concern was performance creativity and not the performance arts.
5. Why is watching a performance different from admiring static artwork? What qualities are distinctive?
6. How is the creative process related to actual creative performance; that is, to actual manifest creative action and behavior?

Discussion

Some of the most useful studies of the performing arts and artists recognize both personal processes (personality and cognition) as well as social processes. A blending of psychological and social perspectives was implied in the research on collaborations and decision styles of jazz musicians and the writers of scripts for TV. This blend may be best articulated by the recent *systems theories* of creativity. Mihalyi Csikszentmihalyi, for example, argued that creativity can only be understood by recognizing how the *field* and the *domain* interact with the *individual*. In Csikszentmihalyi's view it can be cyclical, with creative individuals influencing the field and eventually the domain, which in turn influence individuals working within that domain. This theory is very applicable to studies of the performance arts because performances are typically social, and they are most influential when there is a change in the field, the domain, or both.

Clearly, nonpsychological perspectives on the performance arts can inform psychological analyses. A reading of history, for example, shows that the performance arts were once not considered "art." Of course, the concept of art has changed significantly through the ages (e.g., from functional to an end in itself), but of most relevance may be what Daniel Boorstin (1992) referred to as a change "from ritual to drama" (p. 206). In his words:

> In drama man found ways to create unique events for delight, reflection, and dismay, and so make experience outlast the actor. But the idea of drama did not come quickly nor easily. The role of *spectator*, the person who stood outside the actor, was not obvious, for the shared communal experience was overwhelming. The chorus came before the solo. In ancient Greece, from the 7th century B.C. we see the slow stages by which man discovered that he need not always be a participant. In a new kind of immortality man could now outlive time, relive earlier times, foreshadow later times by witnessing actors on a stage. . . . To achieve this demanded courageous acts of imagination. (pp. 206–207)

Poets used drama to experiment, which suggests that new arts splintered from existing forms; what may be most significant, however, is the separation of the actor from the spectator. This was necessary for the concept of *performance*.

Just as it is useful to look back and consider how the concept of performance has evolved in the past, so too can we consider what is to come. A hint of what is in store was given by Sawyer (1997) in his edited volume, *Performance Creativity*. This volume contains chapters covering various domains of performance, including those mentioned above, but also domains that are not typically recognized as arts. Included here are education, scientific performance, and interactions in everyday life, such as everyday conversation. Each of these may be social performances, and each may involve creative efforts. It appears that the concept of performance is continuing to evolve.

[*See also* Arts Therapy; *and* Creativity.]

Bibliography

Boorstin, D. J. (1992). *The creators.* New York: Random House.

Hamilton, L. (1998). *The person behind the mask: A guide to performing arts psychology.* Norwood, NJ: Ablex. This volume describes the author's own experiences and clinical work with performers. She covers the entire career span.

Lindauer, M. (Ed.). (1998). Interdisciplinarity, the psychology of art, and creativity. *Creativity Research Journal, 11* (Special Issue). This volume contains articles on writers, as well as discussion about the need to integrate psychological approaches to the study of the arts with other disciplines.

Runco, M. A. (1999). Creativity need not be social. In A. Montuori (Ed.), *Social creativity.* Cresskill, NJ: Hampton

Press. This chapter describes problems with a social view of creative work. It concludes that process views are the most useful for the study of creativity.

Sawyer, R. K. (1997). *Creativity in performance*. Norwood, NJ: Ablex. This volume contains chapters on jazz, comedy writing, improvisational theater, and poetry, as well as chapters on everyday performances, such as education. It has two chapters presenting cross-cultural views of creative performances.

Mark A. Runco

PERSONALITY. There are two major components to the field of personality psychology, which involve the systematic study of individual differences in characteristic patterns of thinking, feeling, and behaving. Each component is emphasized to a greater or lesser extent by various personality psychologists. The first involves an emphasis on defining and understanding individual differences, in particular personality characteristics (for example, individual differences in sociability or irritability). The second involves an emphasis on ways in which the various parts of the person are organized, what is called a "holistic" or "organismic" emphasis. Through the combination of these points of emphasis, personality psychologists seek to understand both principles of functioning that are common to all people and also that which makes persons unique in their characteristic pattern of functioning.

In the past, personality psychology was dominated by grand theories often derived from the clinical setting. Currently three major theoretical perspectives—psychoanalytic, trait, and social-cognitive—are influential. Each of these perspectives is associated with distinctive concepts and points of research emphasis. The psychoanalytic perspective is associated with an emphasis on unconscious processes, the interplay among motives, and the effects of early experiences on personality development. The trait perspective is associated with an emphasis on basic structural units, temperament, and cross-situational consistencies in behavior. The social-cognitive perspective is associated with an emphasis on cognitive processes, expectancies and beliefs, and situational-domain specificity of personality functioning. The history of the field and specifics of the major theories are covered elsewhere. This article focuses on the methods and content of personality research.

Research Methods and Conceptual Foundations

In addition to its subject of inquiry, the field of personality psychology is defined by its research methods and conceptual foundations. There are three distinct research traditions in the field—clinical, correlational, and experimental—each of which is associated with different areas of inquiry and theoretical conceptualizations. Clinical research involves the systematic, in-depth study of individuals, often in the clinical or psychotherapeutic setting. Most of the grand theories of personality, ranging from Freud's psychoanalytic theory and later developments in object relations theory, to the phenomenological-humanistic theory of Carl Rogers, to the personal construct theory of George Kelly, have emanated from the psychotherapeutic setting. Although the primary conceptual emphasis in these theories differs, focusing on the unconscious and motivation in psychoanalysis, on the concept of the self in Rogerian theory, and on constructs or ways of construing the world in Kelly's theory, they have a common source of observation in the clinical setting and an organismic emphasis.

Correlational research involves the use of self-report questionnaires and the method of factor analysis to determine the basic dimensions of personality—the field's equivalent of the periodic table of the elements. The major conceptual unit associated with such research is the "trait," defined as a disposition to think, feel, and behave in a characteristic way over a range of situations. Typically, large numbers of subjects respond to questionnaire items, and the data are factor analyzed to determine those responses that tend to go together, forming thereby the basic dimensions of personality.

The experimental approach in personality psychology emphasizes the development of general laws of psychological functioning that apply to all individuals. During the 1940s and 1950s, many personality psychologists within the experimental tradition applied principles of stimulus-response (S-R) learning theory to the formulation of principles of personality functioning. Noteworthy here was the social learning theory of Neal Miller and John Dollard. Currently social-cognitive theory, which emphasizes cognitive processes and the contextualization or domain specificity of behavior, represented by the works of Albert Bandura and Walter Mischel, as well as more generally information processing approaches to personality, are expressive of this research tradition. Research within this tradition often bridges the field of personality with the fields of cognitive psychology and social psychology.

In emphasizing the existence of these distinct research traditions and the associated differing conceptualizations, a few points are noteworthy. First, the existence of multiple research traditions is characteristic of many fields within psychology. Second, theoretical differences exist within each tradition of research. Third, hypotheses generated by a theory associated with one tradition often are investigated through other research procedures as well (e.g., psychoanalytic hypotheses investigated through correlational or experimental research). Thus, progress in the field reflects the contributions of all three traditions of research.

Research Topics

Current personality research is diverse and tends to focus on specific problems or content domains rather than broad theoretical issues. The following categories are illustrative of research in the field.

Units of Personality—Traits, Motives, and Cognitions. Historically, personality psychologists have emphasized three conceptual units—traits, motives, and cognitions. The trait was emphasized by Gordon W. Allport in his book *Personality: A Psychological Interpretation* (1937), to which many contemporary personality psychologists date the beginnings of the field. Trait theory developed as a major approach to personality theory during the 1940s and 1950s, mainly through the efforts of Raymond B. Cattell and Hans J. Eysenck, both of whom used factor analyses of questionnaire data, as well as other data, to determine the basic dimensions of personality. During the 1960s and 1970s, many personality psychologists questioned the extent to which people display broad consistencies or regularities in behavior and, instead, suggested that people vary in their behavior in response to situational variation. Criticism of the trait view, and associated methods of personality assessment, became crystallized in Walter Mischel's book *Personality and Assessment* (1968), leading to what was called the "person-situation controversy." Subsequent research, notably the work of Seymour Epstein, focused on dispositional regularities that could be observed if behavior was aggregated over situations. Thus, although recognizing the importance of situational influences, trait psychologists suggest that there is sufficient evidence of individual consistency of functioning across situations to speak in terms of basic dimensions of personality along which individuals differ.

Over the past decade, a broad consensus has emerged among trait psychologists concerning the basic dimensions of personality. Known as the "Big Five" (Lewis Goldberg) or the "Five-Factor Model" (Paul T. Costa, Jr., and Robert R. McCrae), the following five dimensions are viewed as the major individual difference variables: Neuroticism, Extraversion, Openness to Experience, Agreeableness, and Conscientiousness. Validating evidence in support of the model comes from data indicating a genetic contribution to the traits, data reflecting agreement between self-ratings and ratings by peers and partners, cross-cultural agreement concerning the basic dimensions, evidence of considerable stability of trait scores once individuals reach adulthood, and the predictive utility of trait measures in occupational settings. Relationships have been found between trait measures and measures of motivation, the tendency to experience particular affects, individual differences in ways of coping with stress, and types of psychopathology. In addition, Jerry Wiggins has found relationships between individual differences in traits and differences in interpersonal functioning on the dimensions of agency (e.g. dominance) and communion (e.g., nurturance).

The motive concept is used to explain what activates and directs behavior, the why of human behavior. Four theories of motivation have dominated the field: drive or tension-reduction theories, incentive theories, cognitive theories, and growth or self-actualization theories of motivation. Early motivation research in personality was influenced by the drive theory, tension-reduction views of Freud, and Hullian S-R theory. In his classic work *Explorations in Personality*, (1938), Henry Murray emphasized the concept of need, which he used in the same sense that others used the concept of drive. In what stands as a monumental effort in the field, David McClelland and his colleagues developed a fantasy measure of one of Murray's needs, the need for achievement, and related variation in this need both to individual performance in situations of moderate risk and to periods of societal economic rise and decline. Subsequent attention was given by his students, David Winter and Dan McAdams, to the power and intimacy motives. Here, too, fantasy measures were used to assess individual differences on the relevant motives. Individuals high on power motivation have been found to seek leadership roles and offices, to be assertive and controlling in interaction with others, and to have problems in love relationships. Individuals high on intimacy motivation have been found to spend more time involved with others, to seek closer physical proximity to others, and to make more "we" and "us" references than is characteristic of those scoring low on intimacy motivation. An important element of this research is the demonstration that fantasy and self-report measures of motivation result in different scores and have different relationships with other variables of interest.

For many years there was a loss of interest in the concept of motivation, largely because of the demise of the drive concept near the end of the 1950s and the force of the cognitive revolution. However, over the past two decades there has been a resurgence of interest in this area, particularly in terms of incentive theories of motivation, that is, theories that emphasize the purposive, goal-directed nature of behavior. Incentive theories of motivation go back to William McDougall and Edward Chase Tolman. These views were rejected by psychologists who viewed them as teleological and mentalistic. Developments in cybernetics and the cognitive revolution, however, gave support to approaches to motivation that emphasized the goal concept and related personality concepts such as life tasks (Nancy Cantor), personal strivings (Robert Emmons), personal projects (Brian Little), and current concerns (Eric Klinger). What is common to these concepts is an emphasis on purposive, goal-directed behavior, that is, the view that the person's behavior is organized around the pursuit of desired endpoints or goals. The goal concept involves cognition, both in terms of a mental representation of an endpoint toward which behavior is directed and in terms of representations of plans or paths for attaining the goal. However, the goal concept also involves affect, and it is affect that gives the goal a motivational component. From the standpoint of goals, personality is defined by the nature of the person's goal system, including the relations among goals (i.e., the complexity of organization and the degree of integration or conflict among goals) and the plans for achieving them. Research has focused on individual differences in goals and the effects of goals on information processing and health. Cognitive processes have been demonstrated to be affected by goals; progress toward goals has been demonstrated to be associated with positive affect and movement away from them to be associated with negative affect; and individuals with specific, obtainable, integrated goals have been found to have better emotional and physical health than individuals without goals, with vague or unattainable goals, or with goals that conflict with each another.

Like incentive theories, cognitive theories of motivation emphasize cognitive processes. Instead of a hedonic emphasis, as in goal attainment, there is an emphasis on motivation in terms of prediction of events and cognitive consistency. Considerable research indicates that people are motivated to reduce uncertainty and cognitive conflict or inconsistency. What remains to be determined is whether uncertainty and inconsistency per se are motivating or whether they are motivating because of the tension or threat that can be associated with them.

Self-actualization theories of motivation were popular during the 1960s, most specifically associated with the writings of Carl Rogers and Abraham Maslow, and were part of the philosophy of the Human Potential Movement. Robert W. White's 1959 critique of traditional (i.e., drive or tension reduction) theories of motivation and his formulation of the concept of competence motivation (i.e., the motivation to deal competently or effectively with the environment) also lent support to this point of view. This theoretical perspective has been associated with research by Edward Deci and Richard Ryan demonstrating the difference between intrinsic motivation, or the motive to engage in a task because of an interest in the task itself, and extrinsic motivation, or the motive to engage in a task because of the rewards that follow successful completion. In contrast with the principles of reinforcement theory, there is evidence that rewards are not necessary for learning to occur and may actually interfere with task performance and the motivation for future learning.

Turning to cognitive units, during the 1950s and 1960s there was considerable interest in the concept of cognitive style, that is, individual differences in characteristic ways of thinking or processing information. For example, Herman Witkin explored the implications of individual differences in the ability to perceive part of the field independently of its surroundings, a dimension called "field independence–field dependence." Compared to field-dependent people, field-independent people were found to be more active in their coping efforts, more able to control their impulses in a flexible manner, and less bothered by feelings of inferiority. Other dimensions of cognitive style related the degree to which the person views phenomena in abstract as opposed to concrete terms and the degree to which the person represses as opposed to remaining sensitive to feelings.

More recent research efforts have focused on individual differences in causal attributions made for events (i.e., explanatory style) and expectancies concerning the future (e.g., optimism-pessimism). Most influential has been the work of Martin Seligman that focuses on three dimensions of causal attribution: internal-external, stable-unstable, and global-specific. Individual differences in attributions are associated with a wide range of consequences. For example, the tendency to make internal, stable, and global attributions for negative events has been found to be associated with depression and poorer recovery from cancer. Such a pessimistic explanatory style has also been found to be associated with less motivation, poorer performance, and generally more negative emotion than an optimistic explanatory style.

Although some personality psychologists continue to emphasize the importance of such stylistic variables, and see them as a useful interface between personality and cognition, other personality psychologists question the cross-situational generality suggested by the style concept and focus instead on the implications of specific ways of processing information for other aspects of personality functioning. Such research is associated, in the main, with social cognitive theory and the information processing approach to personality. Within this context there is research on individual differences in specific expectancies, attributions, schemas or constructs, and beliefs, and the implications of such differences for many areas of functioning. Specific causal attributions have been related to various emotions and varying degrees of motivation, as have specific beliefs concerning the self and the world. For example, Bernard Weiner has demonstrated that attributions of controllability for personal failure are associated with emotions such as guilt, shame, and humiliation, whereas attributions associated with uncontrollability for personal failure do not lead to such self-criticism. Similarly, attributions of controllability for failure in others are associated with anger, blame, and stigmatization, whereas attributions of uncontrollability for failure are associated with sympathy, compassion, and offers of assistance. In other research conducted within a social cognitive, attributional framework, Carol Dweck has demonstrated that attributions of poor performance to a fixed aspect of the self (e.g., ability) have deleterious effects on future motivation and performance relative to attributions to more malleable aspects of the self (e.g., effort). For example, children who view intelligence as a fixed entity tend to face relevant challenges feeling anxious and vulnerable, whereas children who view intelligence as incremental or malleable tend to face such challenges with effort and enthusiasm.

Although often treated as separate lines of research, the three defined units generally are seen as having implications for one another. For example, individual differences in traits are viewed as associated with differences in motives and cognitive aspects of functioning, and motives and cognitions (e.g., attributions) are viewed as having causal implications for one another.

Personality Development. Two aspects of personality development are of particular interest to personality psychologists. The first involves the question of determinants of personality, the second the question of stability and change in personality over time. In relation to determinants, at various points the field has shifted between an emphasis on environmental determinants and an emphasis on genetic determinants, the nature/nurture issue (although all psychologists recognize that genes and environments always have an impact on one another). Of late there have been major contributions by behavior geneticists to understanding the importance of genes in personality development. There is evidence that genes play a role in shaping virtually every aspect of personality functioning, greater for aspects of functioning such as temperament and lesser for aspects of functioning such as values. The current heritability estimate for personality overall is 40%. Genes exert their influence directly through their effects on the biological functioning of the organism and indirectly through their influence on the environment; that is, genes affect how the person responds to the environment, the responses elicited from the environment, and the selection of environments with which to interact. Thus, current behavioral geneticists suggest that one of the major contributions of their efforts is, and will be, a greater understanding of which aspects of the environment are key for personality development. The key point made to date, in particular by Robert Plomin, is the extent to which siblings from the same family are different as a result of nonshared family environments; that is, siblings growing up in the same family experience very different family environments, in part because of the genetic differences among the siblings and the consequent effects on the environment.

As noted, personality psychologists also have been interested in the question of stability and change over time. Interestingly enough, both psychoanalytic and trait theorists suggest considerable personality stability over time, the former because of the influence of early experiences on character development, the latter because of the influence of genetic factors. However, other than evidence of stability of trait scores after the age of 25, the evidence for change probably is as good as that for stability. This area of research is challenging, given the difficulty of applying comparable personality measures across different age groups, the possible different phenotypic manifestations of the same underlying or genotypic personality characteristic, and the likelihood of different degrees of stability for different characteristics and for different degrees of environmental impact.

One of the ways in which personality psychologists have studied stability and change in personality development, as well as the processes involved in such development, is through longitudinal research, that is, through the study of the same individuals over extended periods of time, with repeated measurements at various time intervals. Two major studies are noteworthy: the Berkeley Institute of Human Development's longitudinal study, known mainly through the works of Jack Block, and the Swedish Study of Individual Development and Adjustment, known mainly through the works of David Magnusson. Both studies indicate considerable evidence for the continuity of personality development over time and for the antecedents in childhood of such important developments as depression and antisocial behavior. At the same time, these and other longitudinal studies indicate that personality development is a complex process reflecting the interplay between biological and environmental (familial, societal) variables. A holistic systems approach to personality development is emphasized.

The Unconscious. The concept of the unconscious is important to personality psychologists for both theoretical and methodological reasons. From a theoretical standpoint, there are widely differing views concerning the importance of unconscious processes in personality functioning. From a methodological standpoint, an emphasis on unconscious processes, as in mechanisms of defense, calls into question the utility of many kinds of self-report data. During the period of domination by the behaviorist perspective, interest in unconscious processes was looked on with skepticism. With the cognitive revolution, however, there has been a surge of research interest in unconscious processes, both from a psychoanalytic perspective and from an information processing perspective. Considerable evidence has been obtained of information processing that goes on outside of awareness and of the influence of such processing on memory, perception, affect, attitudes, and motivation. At the same time, a distinction has been made by

John Kihlstrom between the dynamic unconscious of psychoanalytic theory and the cognitive unconscious of cognitive psychology. Whereas the former emphasizes motives and wishes, defensive functions, and irrational thought, the latter makes no major distinction between conscious and unconscious processes in terms of content, form, or function.

The Self. Historically, interest in the concept of the self has waxed and waned. It was a major focus of theory and research during the 1940s and 1950s, but interest declined thereafter because of lack of agreement concerning definition and measurement among investigators. Since 1980 research has burgeoned, in particular with the treatment of the self as a schema or construct from a social cognitive, information processing standpoint, as in the works of Hazel Markus, E. Tory Higgins, and William Swann. A number of features are noteworthy in relation to this approach to the self. First, rather than a focus on the individual's global self-concept, the focus is on contextualized selves, what is called a "family of selves." Second, there is interest in how the concept of the self influences other cognitive processes. For example, there is evidence that we attend to and learn self-relevant information more quickly than information that is not relevant to the self and that we recall self-relevant information better than nonrelevant information. Third, research on the self as a cognitive structure has been tied to research on motivation and emotion. For example, aspects of the self, called "possible selves" and "self-guides," represent goals for the individual to attain. Discrepancies between standards for the self and actual performance are associated with emotions such as anxiety, guilt, and shame. In addition, it has been demonstrated that relevant constructs concerning the self can be activated on a conscious or unconscious basis. Fourth, there is evidence that we seek not only self-enhancement but also self-verification; that is, we seek information that enhances our sense of self but also information that verifies our current self-concept, even if this interferes with the self-enhancement bias. In other words, there is a self-confirming bias that may operate in concert or in conflict with the self-enhancement bias. Fifth, Bandura has emphasized the role of self-efficacy beliefs, defined as the perceived ability to cope with specific tasks or situations, in influencing our motivation in a situation, as well as our emotional reactions while anticipating a situation or being involved in it. Finally, there has been a growth of interest in cultural variations in the self. In particular, research has focused on differences between the self in individualist and collectivist societies.

In addition to the social-cognitive interest in the self, psychoanalytic followers of object relations theory (i.e., an emphasis on relationship-seeking rather than on instinctual gratification) have been interested in the early development of conscious and unconscious mental representations of the self, as well as in the development of problems of self-definition and vulnerability to blows to self-esteem. A concept of particular theoretical and clinical interest is of narcissism, or preoccupation with the self and preservation of self-esteem. The important clinical observations of narcissistic functioning have led to the development of associated personality measures, and to empirical exploration of the relation between narcissistic functioning and other aspects of personality functioning. For example, individuals scoring high on narcissism have been found to make more self-references; to be more exhibitionistic, controlling, and critical of others; and to show more of a self-enhancement bias than individuals scoring low on measures of this personality characteristic.

Emotion, Adaptation, and Health. Personality research has focused on the areas of emotion, adaptation, and health separately, as well as on their interrelations. In terms of emotion or affect, there has been an effort, led by Paul Ekman and Carroll Izard and influenced by the thinking of Silvan Tomkins, to define the primary, basic emotions that are universal. In relation to this, it is suggested that part of personality is the extent to which individuals tend to experience specific affects and combinations of affects. In terms of adaptation, research has been stimulated by the work of Richard Lazarus on appraisal processes in relation to stress and coping with stress. According to this view, in conditions of stress, a primary appraisal is made of whether a threat or danger is present, followed by a secondary appraisal of the potential for overcoming the threat; that is, the degree of stress experienced is a result of two appraisal processes, one evaluating the degree of potential harm or threat and the other the potential for coping successfully with the threat. Research by Lazarus and others has explored the diverse means used by subjects to cope with stress, in particular focusing on the difference between efforts to alter the situation and efforts to alter the emotional response to the situation. There is evidence of both stability and variability in methods individuals use to cope with stressful situations; that is, from a transactional view, any single coping effort involves both personality characteristics of the individual and affordances in the situation or context. According to Lazarus and others, the emotions experienced and the coping methods used have important implications for health.

There have been many efforts to tie other personality characteristics to measures of physical health including, from a social-cognitive view, the relation between self-efficacy beliefs and health and, from a trait view, the relation between scores on trait dimensions and measures of health. Another area of interest, as in the research of Charles Carver and Michael Scheier, is the relation between individual differences in optimism and consequences for health. Optimism, defined as the belief that good, as opposed to bad, things will generally occur in one's life, has been related to subjective well-being and more successful outcomes of medical treatments. Currently, research is directed both to establishing the boundaries of influence of such psychological processes and to the biological processes forming the link between personality variables and health.

Personality and Biology. Over the past decade, there has been increased interest in establishing linkages between personality variables and biological processes. One aspect of this has already been noted: the effort to form links between personality variables and health outcomes. A second aspect is an effort to tie individual differences in traits to individual differences in biological functioning. Research in this area is directed to discovering specific genes associated with major personality traits and to discovering the hormonal and neural correlates of personality functioning. Finally, a major development in the field has been the effort to relate evolutionary theory to principles of personality functioning, most notably in the works of David Buss and Robert Hogan. According to this view, basic psychological mechanisms and dimensions of personality are the result of evolution and have endured because they are adaptive for survival and reproductive success. Related research has focused on male-female mate preferences.

Issues in the Field and Challenges for the Future

A number of issues have historically been present in the personality field, some of which are implicit or explicit in the research areas discussed above. Perhaps the overriding issue in the field concerns the structure and organization of personality. Although personality psychologists continue to emphasize and do research on traits, motives, and cognitions, there is no agreement concerning the basic units of personality or the relations among the units. In addition, there is a need to develop concepts that focus on the system aspects of personality functioning (e.g., conflict, coherence). A related issue concerns the relative emphasis on discrete units as opposed to a more holistic, organismic perspective. A second issue involves the relative merits of different research strategies, for example, the relative merits of clinical observations, the use of correlational data, and the use of experimental investigations. Of particular importance here is the development of personality measures that show correspondence across data sources and methods of observation. A third issue involves the relative importance of conscious and unconscious processes and the implications of unconscious processes for the use of self-report measures; that is, if unconscious processes are significant, whether motivated or otherwise, then under which conditions can we make use of self-report data? This is a major question since much of current personality research remains based on such data. Much of what is included in these three issues is covered by the concept of construct validity in terms of the development of concepts that are part of a theory and measures of the concepts that are associated with predicted empirical findings.

A fourth issue for the field is the conceptualization of the dynamic interaction between personal dispositions and situational contingencies. The person-situation controversy contrasted the trait emphasis on broad consistencies in individual behavior with the social-cognitive emphasis on the contextualization of behavior. However, all personality psychologists recognize that dispositions exist in individuals and that individuals are responsive to situational contingencies. Thus, the task is one of developing a model of personality functioning that reflects the ongoing interactions, or transactions, between individuals and environments.

Finally, there is the issue of the kinds of laws of personality functioning that are possible given the variation in cultures and the idiosyncratic meanings individuals give to events; that is, is it possible to develop laws of personality functioning that are universal?

A major challenge for personality psychologists in the future will be to integrate the findings from biology and neuroscience without becoming reductionistic; that is, while building on findings in the biological sciences and making sure that their concepts are in accord with them, personality psychologists must continue to emphasize a different level of analysis and focus on the integrated functioning of the organism as a whole. Personality psychologists have made enormous gains in methodological sophistication and empirical findings. It is these issues and challenges that remain part of the field.

[*See also* Personality Disorders; Personality Psychology; Personality Traits; *and* Temperament.]

Bibliography

Allport, G. W. (1937). *Personality: A psychological interpretation.* New York: Henry Holt. A classic personality text to which many date the beginnings of contemporary personality psychology.

Bandura, A. (1986). *Social foundations of thought and action: A social cognitive theory.* Englewood Cliffs, NJ: Prentice Hall. A comprehensive statement about a social-cognitive conceptualization of personality.

Goldberg, L. R. (1993). The structure of phenotypic personality traits. *American Psychologist, 48,* 26–34. A statement of the current consensus among trait psychologists concerning the basic personality traits.

Greenberg, J. R., & Mitchell, S. A. (1983). *Object relations in psychoanalytic theory*. A comprehensive presentation of current object relations theory.

Hall, C. S., & Lindzey, G. (1957). *Theories of personality*. New York: Wiley. A classic personality text that covers the grand theories of personality up to that time.

Hogan, R. R., Johnson, J. A., & Briggs, S. R. (Eds.). (1997). *Handbook of personality psychology*. Orlando, FL: Academic Press. A recent edited volume covering much of the current field.

McCrae, R. R., & Costa, P. T., Jr. (1990). *Personality in adulthood*. New York: Guilford Press. A presentation of current trait theory and evidence of longitudinal stability of personality.

Mischel, W., & Shoda, Y. (1995). A cognitive-affective system theory of personality: Reconceptualizing the invariances in personality and the role of situations. *Psychological Review, 102*, 246–286. A recent formulation of social-cognitive theory.

Murray, H. A. (1938). *Explorations in personality*. New York: Oxford University Press. A classic presentation of a theory of personality and related research involving the intensive study of individuals.

Pervin, L. A. (Ed.). (1990). *Handbook of personality: Theory and research*. New York: Guilford Press. A recent edited volume covering much of the current field.

Pervin, L. A. (1996). *The science of personality*. New York: Wiley. A recent text that covers in depth the research noted in this article.

Lawrence A. Pervin

PERSONALITY AND INTELLIGENCE. Despite frequent (and ongoing) debates throughout the history of psychology, "personality" and "intelligence" continue to be two of the most popular and important concepts both in the formal scientific literature and in popular discussions of psychological phenomena. That is because both concepts refer to broad, powerful attributes of humans that are believed to underlie cognition, motivation, and behavior in many different settings. To the extent that such beliefs can be verified, psychology's goals of understanding, predicting, and improving significant aspects of human behavior and development can be greatly facilitated through the use of these concepts.

Although personality and intelligence both provide useful ways of summarizing consequential individual differences in human functioning, they are not designed to answer the same kinds of questions. Personality focuses on "content" questions addressing the substance, organization, or meaning of a person's thoughts, feelings, perceptions, and actions. Intelligence focuses on "effectiveness" questions that seek to determine how well people are functioning with respect to some internally or externally defined criterion.

The links between personality and intelligence are important for three reasons. First, there is considerable interest in determining whether certain personality dimensions, types, or patterns are associated with effective (intelligent) behavior in significant life contexts. Conversely, there is widespread concern about nonnormative personality characteristics that may impair or inhibit the capacity for intelligent behavior. Finally, there appears to be a growing realization that assessments of intelligence may be of little value if they do not take into account the goals and contexts organizing an individual's personality.

The psychological literature is filled with studies addressing these issues. Most of these studies have been guided by a "nomothetic" approach in which all individuals are described using the same dimensions or categories (e.g., personality traits, primary abilities, diagnostic categories). Recently, however, a more complex way of conceptualizing the relationship between personality and intelligence has developed. This view suggests that the criteria for evaluating intelligence should vary from one person to the next, depending on each individual's personality. This "idiographic" approach to understanding the relationship between personality and intelligence is manifested most prominently in conceptual frameworks emphasizing the importance of personal and social goals in defining the appropriate criteria for intelligence assessments (e.g., Cantor & Harlow, 1994; Ford, 1994). These frameworks, many of which point to the selective impact of life contexts and cultural settings in shaping personal and social goals, are on the cutting edge of theory and research on topics such as motivation, creativity, wisdom, and social and practical intelligence (Ford, 1992; Maciel, Heckhausen, & Baltes, 1994; Sternberg, 1985).

Psychometric Approaches to Personality and Intelligence: Dimensional Linkages

The most widely used but probably the least productive vehicle for understanding the relationship between personality and intelligence has been the traditional psychometric approach. This nomothetic conceptualization assumes that there are a relatively small number of trait or ability dimensions underlying most aspects of intellectual and social behavior. Once these qualities have been identified, multivariate correlational studies can be designed to identify areas of overlap between personality and ability profiles. Many such studies have been conducted both within and across the domains of personality and intelligence.

One problem with this approach is that it is not clear if consensus can be reached about the fundamental dimensions to be used for describing and assessing personality and intelligence. Prominent trait frameworks within the personality literature range from the "Big Three" (Eysenck, 1991) and "Big Five" (McCrae & Costa, 1997) models of personality to Cattell's Sixteen

Personality Factor taxonomy (Cattell, 1971). Although there is substantial overlap in these frameworks, there are also significant remaining disagreements about which traits should be regarded as truly fundamental (Eysenck, 1991). Similarly, psychometric theories of intelligence range from frameworks with one or two factors ("g" or general intelligence; fluid and crystallized intelligence) to models with anywhere from a half dozen to over 100 primary abilities (e.g., multiple intelligences; Guilford's Structure of Intellect) (Sternberg, 1982). Given the lengthy but still uncertain history of theory and research flowing from efforts to identify underlying trait and ability dimensions, settling on a particular "best" way of describing personality and intelligence for all humans does not seem to be a likely outcome. It is also not clear that such a consensus would be desirable given the diversity of attributes, capabilities, and challenges faced by people in different settings and cultures.

Moreover, regardless of the number of categories used, most efforts to link psychometrically derived indices of personality and intelligence have yielded few correlations of statistical and theoretical significance (Zeidner, 1995). Consistent with this result, psychometric theorists' typical answer to the challenge of trying to capture the variance associated with both domains simultaneously has been simply to add or incorporate intelligence into their preferred personality taxonomy. In short, describing people on generalized trait or ability dimensions has not yet proven to be a productive way of understanding the relationship between personality and intelligence.

Psychoeducational and Psychopathology Approaches to Personality and Intelligence: Categorical Linkages

Personality scholars and professionals in applied fields such as special and remedial education and clinical, counseling, and school psychology have also tended to adopt a nomothetic approach to understanding the relationship between personality and intelligence. However, in doing so, they have focused less on universal dimensions and more on recurring cognitive-emotional-behavioral (personality) "types" or diagnostic categories that describe particular subsets of people with shared characteristics. This approach has been vastly more useful than the psychometric approach in terms of practical applications, although it too has been limited by the fact that the classification schemes generally do not vary from one individual to the next.

School-based professionals, for example, typically work with standardized diagnostic categories that describe broad, prototypical patterns of social, emotional, and intellectual functioning that cut across the domains of personality and intelligence (Braden, 1995). Such categories typically describe, either implicitly or explicitly, ways in which intellectual deficits may impact personality functioning or ways in which personality deficits may inhibit intelligent functioning. For example, students classified as mentally retarded or learning disabled may be seen as having limitations or vulnerabilities that are manifested not only in academic or vocational tasks, but also in settings likely to influence personality development in fundamental ways (e.g., through opportunities for social learning with peers or through the impact of stereotypic beliefs about individuals with particular kinds of disabilities). The cumulative impact of these experiences may, in turn, facilitate or constrain intellectual development and the use of existing intellectual capabilities. Conversely, students with emotional or attentional disorders may be regarded as having the potential to function well in academic settings, but only if high-amplitude arousal processes (e.g., anger, anxiety, depression) or the thought patterns underlying such arousal can be properly regulated (e.g., through medication or behavioral interventions).

Clinical and counseling psychologists have also been concerned with various forms of psychopathology that can impair or interfere with capabilities for effective functioning. In this approach, psychopathology is most often defined in terms of symptom clusters (syndromes) that are associated with agreed-on diagnostic labels. These syndromes reflect broad patterns of thought, emotion, perception, and action (i.e., personality patterns) that frequently lead to unintelligent behavior or that serve as powerful obstacles to the development of more effective behavior patterns (Endler & Summerfeldt, 1995). Such categories include paranoid, schizoid, antisocial, histrionic, narcissistic, avoidant, dependent, obsessive-compulsive, and passive-aggressive personality disorders, as well as mood disorders of various kinds.

Goal-Based Approaches to Personality and Intelligence: Motivational Linkages

In this more idiographic conceptualization, personality and intelligence are linked primarily by an individual's "personal goals" (i.e., thoughts about desired or undesired futures) and the choices and investments that follow from efforts to accomplish those goals (Cantor & Harlow, 1994; Ford, 1992, 1994; Sternberg & Spear-Swerling, 1998). Scholars adopting this approach have generally focused more on competence development and personal growth than on personality or intellectual dysfunction, although this approach is also highly applicable to the latter set of phenomena (e.g., Ford, 1995).

A central premise of this approach is that it makes sense to assess effective functioning (intelligence) in some domain only if an individual is pursuing significant goals in that domain. Goal choices may be self-directed (based on personal interests and priorities) or contextually directed (based on contextual or cultural opportunities and demands), but in either case, intelligence reflects the attainment of personally meaningful goals within important life contexts.

Personality becomes a significant part of this way of understanding human intelligence when it is defined primarily in terms of a person's repertoire of core goals or life pursuits. From this perspective, the core of an individual's personality is represented by the goals he or she pursues on a recurring basis in everyday life and the ways in which the individual goes about trying to accomplish those goals. The thoughts, feelings, perceptions, and actions associated with the pursuit of meaningful goals are assumed to be represented in stable cognitive constructions known as "schemas" (Cantor & Harlow, 1994; Ford, 1992). Authentic assessments of intelligence can be designed by focusing on the effectiveness of these schemas in guiding thought and action over time and across contexts.

Although goal-based analyses of personality and intelligence are appropriate for all age groups, the potential utility of conceptualizing personality and intelligence in this manner is especially compelling for adolescents and adults (Ford, 1994; Maciel et al., 1994). As life paths diverge, there is an increasing need to understand what it is that people are trying to accomplish before drawing conclusions about how intelligent they are or how intelligent they might be in a particular setting. Ford (1994) has introduced the concept of "personal intelligence" to explain how one might go about conducting an idiographic assessment of intelligence based on this view. In his Assessment of Personal Intelligence template, progress within all of an individual's major goal domains is assessed on seven different aspects of effective functioning (i.e., breadth of general goal-relevant knowledge, depth of specialized knowledge, performance accomplishments, automaticity or ease of functioning, skilled performance under challenge, generative flexibility, and speed of learning or behavior change).

Sternberg and Spear-Swerling's (1998) concept of "personal navigation," with its emphasis on self-direction, flexibility, and overcoming obstacles, also provides a useful vehicle for advancing goal-based models of personality and intelligence. Unlike most concepts in psychology, personal navigation simultaneously emphasizes the contributions of both the person and the environment to the content and effectiveness of a person's functioning. Moreover, rather than focusing on the stable, enduring aspects of personality and intelligence (e.g., mental abilities and personality traits or syndromes), the concept of personal navigation emphasizes the potential for significant change in what people do and how well they do it. Analogous to a game of Scrabble, personal navigation reflects the need to adapt to changing circumstances and to make the most out of one's current and potential future opportunities. With the right combination of motivation, skill, and luck, it is always possible to build new capabilities and accomplishments on the foundation of personality and intelligence that has developed throughout one's life.

[*See also* Five-Factor Model of Personality; Intelligence; *and* Sixteen Personality Factor Questionnaire.]

Bibliography

Braden, J. P. (1995). Intelligence and personality in school and educational psychology. In D. H. Saklofske, & M. Zeidner (Eds.), *International handbook of personality and intelligence* (pp. 621–650). New York: Plenum Press. Exemplifies the category-based psychoeducational approach to personality and intelligence.

Cantor, N., & Harlow, R. (1994). Social intelligence and personality: Flexible life-task pursuit. In R. J. Sternberg, & P. Ruzgis (Eds.), *Personality and intelligence* (pp. 188–217). New York: Cambridge University Press. Summarizes a goal-based, contextual view of personality and intelligence that is on the cutting edge of theory and research in this field.

Cattell, R. B. (1971). *Abilities: Their structure, growth, and action.* Boston: Houghton Mifflin. Describes Cattell's 16 Personality Factor model and its implications for human behavior and development.

Endler, N. S., & Summerfeldt, L. J. (1995). Intelligence, personality, psychopathology, and adjustment. In D. H. Saklofske & M. Zeidner (Eds.), *International handbook of personality and intelligence* (pp. 249–284). New York: Plenum Press. Exemplifies the category-based psychopathology approach to personality and intelligence.

Eysenck, H. J. (1991). Dimensions of personality: 16, 5, or 3? Criteria for a taxonomic paradigm. *Personality and Individual Differences, 12,* 773–790.

Ford, M. E. (1992). *Motivating humans.* Newbury Park, CA: Sage. Presents an integrative theory of motivation, Motivational Systems Theory (MST), which defines motivation as the organized patterning of an individual's personal goals, emotions, and personal agency beliefs. Based on Donald Ford's Living Systems Framework, MST provides a strong theoretical foundation for a goal-based conceptualization of personality and intelligence.

Ford, M. E. (1994). A living systems approach to the integration of personality and intelligence. In R. J. Sternberg, & P. Ruzgis (Eds.), *Personality and intelligence* (pp. 188–217). New York: Cambridge University Press. Outlines how the Living Systems Framework can be used to integrate personality and intelligence both conceptually and operationally through the use of an assessment of "personal intelligence."

Ford, M. E. (1995). Advances in motivation theory and research: Implications for special and remedial education. *Intervention in School and Clinic, 31,* 70–83. Outlines how MST can be applied to help facilitate the social and intellectual development of students with mild disabilities.

Maciel, A. G., Heckhausen, J., & Baltes, P. B. (1994). A life-span perspective on the interface between personality and intelligence. In R. J. Sternberg, & P. Ruzgis (Eds.), *Personality and intelligence* (pp. 61–103). New York: Cambridge University Press. Outlines the life-span developmental view of personality and intelligence, with wisdom as a sample application. Provides a goal-based approach for understanding successful aging in terms of selective optimization with compensation.

McCrae, R. R., & Costa, P. T., Jr., (1997). Personality trait structure as a human universal. *American Psychologist*, 52, 509–516. Data from a variety of cultures (German, Portuguese, Hebrew, Chinese, Korean, and Japanese; $N = 7134$) are compared to the American factor structure for the Five-Factor (Big Five) model of personality. The authors conclude that there is support for their view that personality trait structure is universal.

Sternberg, R. J. (Ed.). (1982). *Handbook of human intelligence*. New York: Cambridge University Press.

Sternberg, R. J. (1985). *Beyond IQ: A triarchic theory of human intelligence*. New York: Cambridge University Press. Presents an organized set of three intelligence theories, including a contextual theory that provides a strong foundation for conceptualizing links between intelligence and personality functioning.

Sternberg, R. J., & Spear-Swerling, L. (1998). Personal navigation. In M. Ferrari, & R. J. Sternberg (Eds.), *Self-awareness: Its nature and development* (pp. 219–245). New York: Guilford Press. A new concept (personal navigation) is introduced in an effort to capture more effectively the meaning and significance of broad patterns of self-directed behavior over time in challenging life contexts.

Zeidner, M. (1995). Personality trait correlates of intelligence. In D. H. Saklofske & M. Zeidner (Eds.), *International handbook of personality and intelligence* (pp. 299–319). New York: Plenum Press. Critical review of empirical work linking personality and intelligence, primarily from a psychometric perspective.

Martin E. Ford

PERSONALITY DEVELOPMENT. [*This entry provides a broad survey of personality development. It is chronologically divided into three articles*: Infancy and Early Childhood; Middle Childhood and Adolescence; *and* Adulthood and Aging. *For a general discussion on personality, see* Personality. *See also* Personality Disorders; Personality Psychology; *and* Personality Traits.]

Infancy and Early Childhood

Early childhood development is normally split into major periods marked by qualitative changes in child behavior, at 2 to 3 months, at 7 to 9 months, and at around 18 months. The first 2 months of life were traditionally regarded as marked by disorganization and passive withdrawal. More recent research on infant behavior (Stern, 1985) has revealed that infants come into the world with cognitive, emotional, and social capacities that enable them to seek stimulation actively and regulate their own behavior through environmental interactions. They have prewired knowledge of the world. So, for example, they are able to integrate information across the senses, as well as detect and remember aspects of the environment that are unchanging. Thus they are able to recognize their mother, imitate facial expressions, and manifest at least three affect states: distress, contentment, and interest (Meltzoff, 1990).

At 2 to 3 months a range of developments occur, all of which serve to enhance infants' appeal to others. For example, their cooing becomes responsive, and they develop the ability to engage adults in synchronous, reciprocal social interchanges (Beebe, Lachmann, & Jaffe, 1997). The nature of the caregiver's responsiveness in these interchanges has far-reaching implications for child development. At 7 to 9 months children develop focused attachment, that is, they act as if they understand that their thoughts, feelings, and actions can be understood by another person (Stern, 1985). They thus signal for parental intervention at night, show preferred attachment to a small number of caregiving adults, and adjust their reaction to unfamiliar stimuli on the basis of the responses of their primary caregiver. At around 18 months, the acquisition of language and other indicators of enhancing body capacity (e.g., symbolic play) enables the child to have complex negotiations with the caregiver, develop true interactive play with peers, and develop moral emotions such as embarrassment and empathy and, a few months later, guilt, pride, and shame (Emde, Kubicek, & Oppenheim, 1997).

Throughout this period, individual differences arise as a consequence of a complex interplay of constitutional and environmental factors. Genetic and environmental regulators of behavior transact continually, mutually influencing one another, with genes acting as biological regulators and cultural, familial, and parental characteristics acting as social regulators (Sameroff, 1992). The interaction of these factors is evident. For example, so-called difficult infants (irritable, hard to soothe, fearful of novelty) are likely to be responded to negatively by most caretakers, however sensitive and positively disposed, which is likely to compound their constitutional problems.

Infant temperament has been a consistent focus of investigations since the time of Thomas and Chess's classic studies going back to the 1950s. Temperament is now considered a heritable biological predisposition to respond to the environment in consistent ways. Research on behavioral inhibition is perhaps the most fully explored example of such temperamental predisposition. Harvard psychologist Jerome Kagan has defined this pattern of responses as manifested in wariness and avoidance or fear in response to unfamiliar people or events; it is present in 15% of middle-class samples and is evident by 18 months (Kagan, Reznick, & Snidman, 1988). This pattern appears to be related to physiological markers such as the reactivity of the hypothalamic-pituitary-adrenal (HPA) axis. The transactional processes present in normal development are well illustrated in a recent study. Behaviorally inhibited toddlers who had insecure attachment to their parent showed elevated cortisol responses. Inhibited toddlers who were securely attached did not show such responses (Nachmias, Gunnar, Mangelsdorf, Parritz, & Buss, 1996). Behavioral inhibition also relates to the level of input of the sympathetic nervous system on the heart (vagal tone). Behaviorally inhibited children may show signs of avoidance because their more intense sympathetic input amplifies their responses to unfamiliar situations.

The MacArthur longitudinal twin study indicated that an inhibited pattern of behavior was highly heritable. Even though behavioral inhibition changed considerably between 14 and 24 months, this study of fraternal and identical twins revealed that the change was due primarily to genetic rather than environmental factors (Plomin, et al., 1993). This and other studies suggest that the genes determining personality may "turn off" or "turn on" at different ages. Genes are also context dependent. The MacArthur twin study also revealed that the extent of empathic response shown by a child in response to distress of another is highly heritable at 24 and 36 months. Monozygotic (identical) twins were far more similar in the level of empathy they showed to strangers who acted as if they were hurt than dizygotic (nonidentical) twins. However, this difference between identical and nonidentical twins disappeared when it was the mother who feigned being hurt. In relation to the mother, twin pairs showed similar levels of empathy regardless of their genetic similarity. It seems that socialization influences shared by the twins in their interactions with the parents were a major influence on mothers, but not on the tester, and in this latter context, genetic influences could manifest more readily.

Thus no simple model of genetic versus environmental contributions to development is likely to be satisfactory. Genetic influences are powerful determinants of personality development but are not environmentally immutable. Behavioral inhibition as a temperament in infancy is likely to be linked to the development of anxiety and other psychiatric disorders later in childhood. Behavioral inhibition is more common in children of parents with anxiety-related psychiatric disorders, and behaviorally inhibited infants are more likely to develop psychiatric problems including anxiety at school age (Biederman et al., 1993).

Early personality development is shaped by a range of environmental factors. Family structure is obviously a key variable. Parental separation or divorce has for some time been known to undermine the child's social and intellectual development. It is now generally accepted that it is marital conflict, particularly the young child's exposure to interparental anger, the expression of physical hostility, disagreements over child rearing, and lack of adequate conflict resolution that carry the most serious consequences for the child's self-esteem, emotion regulation, and cognitive development (Easterbrooks, Cummings, & Emde, 1994). Maltreatment of young children has a profound effect on personality development. Physically, psychologically, or sexually abused youngsters show a range of social and emotional problems including indiscriminate sociability, poor affect regulation, heightened aggression, social withdrawal, inconsistent and unpredictable social signals, and major dysfunctions of self-development, particularly lowered self-esteem (Cicchetti & Toth, 1995). At least some of these adverse consequences may be due to the neurodevelopmental impact of severe deprivation. Extreme deprivation, such as that suffered by children in Romanian orphanages, has been shown in brain imaging studies to cause permanent frontotemporal dysfunction in late- (after eight months) as opposed to early-adopted babies. Maternal depression during the first year of life has measurable impact on social development, as well as on a range of neurophysiological abnormalities (Field, Fox, Pickens, & Nawrocki, 1995).

Less extreme variation in the quality of parenting also has important influences on the development of personality. In particular, parenting that is based on coercion and power assertion rather than supportive guidance fosters the development of noncompliant, aggressive oppositional behaviors. Interestingly, it is not just the overall amount of harsh, aggressive, explosive, and inconsistent parenting of a young child that predicts problems of personality development. It seems rather that it is the amount of conflict or negativity directed against a specific child in that family (in other words, the difference between the treatment of that child and of other children—the environment that it does not share with siblings) is most relevant to the child's development (Reiss et al., 1995).

An important mediator of many early environmental influences on child development is the quality of attachment that the infant develops with the primary caregiver. The influential work of John Bowlby inspired developmental researchers to operationalize the amount of security that the infant feels when facing environmental challenges in the presence of the caregiver. A reliable laboratory procedure exists that differentiates one-year-old infants whose bond to the caregiver is secure. These infants turn to the caregiver after a distressing period of separation and are reassured and readily comforted. Some infants suppress attachment behaviors and appear to avoid the caregiver, showing physiological but not behavioral signs of distress. Other infants intensify signals of distress and other attachment behaviors yet reject attempts at soothing. These insecure patterns are labeled "anxious-avoidant" and "anxious-resistant," respectively. A fourth pattern manifested in bizarre or odd behaviors in relation to the caregiver (e.g., hitting the caregiver or head banging) is particularly common in maltreated youngsters. The quality of the early infant-caregiver relationship appears to have an impact on the development of emotion regulation. Secure attachment to the caregiver is associated with an expectation, based on past experience of interaction, that the caregiver will be effective in restoring homeostasis. This expectation gradually permits the normal development of the internal regulation of affect. Insecure patterns of attachment mark less successful early interactional experiences that force the child to develop precocious internal affect regulation strategies. Avoidant children habitually downregulate at least the behavioral aspects of affect, whereas resistant children develop the opposite strategy, hoping to elicit assistance in a context where it is not reliably available (Sroufe, 1996). A disorganized pattern perhaps indicates the absence of assistance and the experience of being overwhelmed by emotion.

Attachment classifications have substantial stability across the life span. Recent studies have been able to assess attachment in adulthood. The narrative coherence of adults when recounting their childhood history of attachment relationships appears to be a good indicator of attachment security. The avoidant pattern is signaled by a dismissing style in which recollections of early relationships are sparse, denigration of attachment relationships is common, and individuals make unusually powerful claims for self-sufficiency. The resistant pattern corresponds to a narrative style in which persistent dissatisfaction is indicated by the speaker's continued preoccupation with childhood hurts and slights from parents and the presence of often considerable anger about such experiences. Disorganized attachment in infancy also has a parallel in adult narratives. The speaker, when discussing the loss of an attachment figure or an experience of trauma or abuse, indicates the disorganization of the attachment representation by lapses in concentration, leading to slips of the tongue, unrealistic magical thinking, or other indicators of an underlying irrationality in relation to these events (Main & Hesse, 1995). The challenging discovery from longitudinal studies is that the infant's behavior at 18 months predicts, in 70 to 80% of cases, how these same individuals recount their childhood narratives in early adulthood. It seems that early attachment patterns are relatively enduring, or at least the patterns of relationship between child and caregiver manifested in the first year of life sets the pattern for the rest of childhood. Although substantial differences exist among studies, it may be legitimately claimed on the basis of longitudinal studies that securely attached infants tend to grow up healthier in terms of capacity to express emotion, more adaptive social relationships, greater competence in terms of language skills, and a more positive self-image. Disorganized infants are more likely to develop substantial social problems at school, to exhibit aggression, and to develop a variety of psychiatric difficulties (Lyons-Ruth, 1996).

An important aspect of attachment research concerns intergenerational consistencies of attachment classification. A number of laboratory studies have reported that the infant's attachment classification to the parent is predicted by the attachment classification of that parent obtained in some studies before the birth of the child (Fonagy, Steele, & Steele, 1991). Some of the most powerful influences of early experience that show continuities to later experience have been demonstrated across generations in terms of parenting behavior. The most likely mediator of these intergenerational associations is to be found in parenting behavior—namely, greater sensitivity to the infant's needs. Caregivers who are secure in relation to their own past are more aware of the infant's needs; consequently, the infant is likely to develop a firmer expectation that its distress will be met by comforting from that caregiver. This intergenerational association has important policy implications. Sensitive parenting, to some degree at least, may be taught or trained; thus, well-focused strategies for prevention could enhance the number of securely attached infants in a population. As the old adage goes: "Treat your child the way you would like your grandchildren to be."

A major controversy concerning early development concerns the impact of nonmaternal care on personality development in early childhood (e.g, day care). Some attachment theorists have argued that daily separations from the mother might undermine the child's confidence in her availability or the mother's ability to react in a sensitive manner to the child. Several studies in the 1980s confirmed that insecure attachment was more common in infants who were in child care for over 20 hours per week during the first year of their lives. Interestingly, more recent studies no longer report this association. A definitive, major multisite U.S. study of 1,153 mother-infant dyads found no significant differences in attachment security related to child care participation (NICHD Early Child Care Research Network, 1997). It seems that as a consequence of either generally improved levels of parenting or improved quality of child care, child care in the first year of life no longer has direct effects on attachment security. However, children who have the double jeopardy of less sensitive and responsive caregiving in child care and in the infant-mother relationship are far more likely to be insecure. It seems that maternal sensitivity is the more critical variable. Relatively less sensitive mothers who place their child in child care are more likely to have insecure relationships with these children than equally insensitive mothers who spend more time with their infants.

Day care has also been linked to an increased likelihood of behavioral problems at 3 and 4 years of age. The earlier the initiation of nonmaternal care, the greater the observed behavioral problems have been, and these effects were still observable at school age. A number of studies have, however, failed to replicate the association between quantity of early nonmaternal child care experience and noncompliance, aggression, and problem behaviors. The above-mentioned NICHD study, for example, found little evidence of short-term effects of nonmaternal care and no evidence of impact at 3 years. The quality of nonmaternal care is undoubtedly an important predictor, with unstable patterns of care carrying the highest risk. The disadvantages associated with nonmaternal care are most likely to be linked to the limitations the latter imposes on the mother's opportunity to get to know her child. Time away from the child may undermine a parent's ability to get to know the child well, which in turn may compromise the parent's capacity to manage the child's behavior effectively and skillfully. It should also be noted that parents face a substantial challenge in managing the demands of work and child care, and thus may simply lack the patience and energy required for adequate parenting.

In conclusion, it seems that notwithstanding the importance of genetic factors, child-caregiver relationships are critical in early childhood in providing youngsters with support, encouragement, continuity, and emotional nourishment, which constitute the essentials of normal personality development. These relationships are essential for the evolution of social skills such as turn-taking, reciprocity, and cooperation, as well as a sense of initiative and self-directiveness. Empathy for others and a wish to care and help develop during toddlerhood, and the acquisition of these capacities depends on a responsive caregiver-child relationship.

Bibliography

Beebe, B., Lachmann, F., & Jaffe, J. (1997). Mother-infant interaction structures and presymbolic self and object representations. *Psychoanalytic Dialogues, 7*, 113–182.

Biederman, J., Rosenbaum, J. F., Bolduc-Murphy, E. A., Faraone, S. V., Chaloff, J., Hirshfeld, D. R., & Kagan, J. (1993). A 3-year follow-up of children with and without behavioral inhibition. *Journal of the American Academy of Child and Adolescent Psychiatry, 32*, 814–821.

Cicchetti, D., & Toth, S. L. (1995). A developmental psychopathology perspective on child abuse and neglect. *Journal of the American Academy of Child and Adolescent Psychiatry, 34*, 541–565.

Easterbrooks, M. A., Cummings, E. M., & Emde, R. N. (1994). Young children's responses to constructive marital disputes. *Journal of Family Psychology, 8*, 160–169.

Emde, R., Kubicek, L., & Oppenheim, D. (1997). Imaginative reality observed during early language development. *International Journal of Psycho-Analysis, 78*(1), 115–133.

Field, T., Fox, N., Pickens, J., & Nawrocki, T. (1995). Relative right frontal EEG activation in 3- to 6-month-old infants of depressed mothers. *Developmental Psychology, 31*, 358–363.

Fonagy, P., Steele, H., & Steele, M. (1991). Maternal representations of attachment during pregnancy predict the organization of infant-mother attachment at one year of age. *Child Development, 62*, 891–905.

Kagan, J., Reznick, J. S., & Snidman, N. (1988). Biological bases of childhood shyness. *Science, 240*, 167–173.

Lyons-Ruth, K. (1996). Attachment relationships among children with aggressive behavior problems: The role of disorganized early attachment patterns. *Journal of Consulting and Clinical Psychology, 64*, 32–40.

Main, M., & Hesse, E. (1990). Parents' unresolved traumatic experiences are related to infant disorganized attachment: Is frightened and/or frightening parental behaviors the linking mechanism? In M. T. Greenberg & D. Cicchetti (Eds.), *Attachment in the preschool years: Theory, research, and intervention* (pp. 161–182). Chicago: University of Chicago Press.

Meltzoff, A. N. (1990). Towards a developmental cognitive science. The implications of cross-modal matching and imitation for the development of representation and memory in infancy. *Annals of the New York Academy of Science, 608*, 1–37.

Nachmias, M., Gunnar, M. R., Mangelsdorf, S., Parritz, R. H., & Buss, K. (1996). Behavioral inhibition and stress reactivity: Moderating role of attachment security. *Child Development, 67*, 508–522.

NICHD Early Child Care Research Network. (1997). The effects of infant child care on infant-mother attachment security: Results of the NICHD study of early child care. *Child Development, 68*, 860–879.

Plomin, R., Emde, R. N., Braungart, J. M., Campos, J., Corley, R., Fulker, D. W., Kagan, J., Reznick, J. S., Robinson, J., & Zahn-Waxler, C. (1993). Genetic change and continuity from fourteen to twenty months: The MacArthur Longitudinal Twin Study. *Child Development, 64*, 1354–1376.

Reiss, D., Hetherington, E. M., Plomin, R., Howe, G. W., Simmens, S. J., Henderson, S. H., O'Connor, T. J., Bussell, D., Anderson, E. R., & Law, T. (1995). Genetic questions for environmental studies: Differential parenting and psychopathology in adolescence. *Archives of General Psychiatry, 52*, 925–936.

Sameroff, A. J. (1992). Principles of development and psychopathology. In A. J. Sameroff & R. N. Emde (Eds.), *Relationship disturbances in early childhood: A developmental approach* (pp. 17–32). New York: Basic Books.
Sroufe. L. A. (1996). *Emotional development: The organization of emotional life in the early years.* New York: Cambridge University Press.
Stern, D. N. (1985). *The interpersonal world of the infant: A view from psychoanalysis and developmental psychology.* New York: Basic Books.

Peter Fonagy

Middle Childhood and Adolescence

Personality refers to the characteristic tendencies of an individual to behave, think, and feel in certain ways that are not shared by all members of the culture. These individual tendencies are described by personality traits such as "aggressive," "distractible," or "fearful." In contrast to narrative personality descriptions in everyday conversation and in literature, personality traits are explicitly measured in today's personality psychology by studying the variation of trait scores across the members of a particular population (e.g., aggressiveness scores in 11-year-old Canadian children). The trait score of a particular child receives psychological meaning when it is contrasted with the distribution of trait scores in the reference population. For example, instead of describing a child as "aggressive," more specific statements can be made such as "This child is more aggressive than 84% of same-age Canadian children."

The personality of a child is described by a pattern of many different traits. Again, the pattern of a particular child receives psychological meaning by contrast with the other patterns in the population. For example, similar patterns can be grouped together, resulting in a personality type that is represented by a prototypical pattern. For example, undercontrolled children are characterized by high scores in the traits impulsivity, restlessness, and distractibility.

Description of Personality

Analyses of free descriptions of older children by their parents and teachers showed that approximately 80% of the descriptions refer to one of the Big Five factors of personality: extraversion, neuroticism, agreeableness, conscientiousness, and culture. These factors have also been identified in Q-sort descriptions when parents characterize a child by rank-ordering many trait terms and in teacher ratings of their students. Thus, there is increasing evidence that adults describe older children and adolescents on the same dimensions that they use to characterize the personalities of adults. In addition to the Big Five, Q-sort studies have provided evidence for two additional temperamental factors that seem specific to childhood and adolescence: activity and irritability.

Analyses of personality patterns repeatedly confirmed three main personality types for childhood and adolescence: resilient (cognitively, emotionally, and socially competent), overcontrolled (shy, emotionally unexpressive, lacking some interpersonal skills), and undercontrolled (impulsive, restless, distractable). In late childhood and adolescence, highly overcontrolled subjects display internalizing problems such as low social self-esteem, loneliness, and depression, whereas highly undercontrolled subjects are characterized by externalizing problems such as school absence, drug use, dropping out of school, and delinquency.

In addition to these major trait factors and types, numerous more specific traits have been studied. For example, a trait of particular relevance to adolescence is the tendency to be self-conscious about one's appearance to others (public self-consciousness) and to fantasize about an imaginary audience watching one's accomplishments as well as one's failures. This tendency peaks in mid-adolescence.

Short-Term Stability of Personality

The concept of personality assumes that personality is a stable property of individuals at each point in time; it may change, but only infrequently or slowly. By contrast, one's daily mood is not a personality trait because it frequently changes from day to day. This common assumption about personality traits (and thus personality patterns) becomes a testable hypothesis in personality psychology. In order to qualify as a personality trait, the rank order of individuals on a trait is required to be highly stable over short periods of time such as 2 weeks. The stability of a trait can be quantified by correlating the rank order of many individuals on the trait at two points in time; the conventional criterion for a stable trait is a correlation coefficient of .80.

Trait judgments by parents, teachers, and the subjects themselves reach that level of stability in late childhood. Behavioral observations and physiological measures (e.g., heart rate) reach that criterion too if they are sufficiently aggregated over time. For example, the observed aggressiveness of fourth graders during school breaks is not sufficiently stable from day to day, but if children's aggressiveness is averaged over 3 weeks of observation, this measure of aggressiveness will satisfy the .80 criterion. This observation illustrates the important conceptual point that traits cannot be equated with individual instances of behavior: they are regularities of behavior.

Long-Term Change of Personality

High short-term stability does not preclude long-term personality change for two reasons. First, long-term change may occur continuously in many children but may be too slow to affect short-term stability seriously. Second, even if long-term change comes about by a sudden jump from one level of competence to another or by a spurt of development, such strong change will occur only in a minority of individuals for any brief observation period because developmental change typically occurs at different points in time in different subjects of the same age. Thus, short-term stability of personality is compatible with long-term personality change.

The stability of a trait is a measure of the predictability of the trait over development: high stability means that each individual's future position in the population can be predicted from her or his past position. A general principle of personality development is that stability declines as the prediction interval increases. For example, the stability of aggressiveness, corrected for measurement error, is approximately .76 over 1 year and .60 over 5 years during childhood and adolescence. However, as long-term stability varies from trait to trait, general estimates of stability are not possible.

Nevertheless, three generalizations can be made from the many existing longitudinal studies of personality development. First, from middle childhood through adolescence, most personality traits can be predicted on a better than chance basis for any prediction interval, but they show lower stability than the intelligence quotient (IQ)—probably the most stable individual characteristic, with a stability above .90 over 5 years, corrected for measurement error. Second, the stability of traits increases with the age at the first trait assessment. For example, 5-year stability for aggressiveness is lower from ages 6 to 11 than from ages 11 to 16.

Third, if one of the assessments is made in early adolescence (i.e., 12 to 15 years of age), stability can be lower, and sometimes, paradoxically, long predictions from late childhood to early adulthood are better than shorter predictions from late childhood to early adolescence. This pattern seems to be due to two different factors. First, in early adolescence, a strong spurt in development occurs for some traits, such as pitch discrimination or awareness of one's public appearance. Because children differ widely with regard to the onset of such spurts, their personality is determined to some extent by the timing of the onset. For example, a girl with a poor ability to discriminate pitch who matures early may suddenly be better than average relative to her age group. Pubertal timing effects mask stable differences in pitch discrimination ability.

Second, adolescence-limited differences obscure other stable differences. One example is antisocial tendencies in Western cultures. In addition to early-developing antisocial tendencies that are highly stable (see below), males experience a sharp increase in the frequency of antisocial behavior with the onset of puberty and a later decline. The increase is due mainly to antisocial acts committed by a large proportion of males who do not show antisocial behavior in midchildhood or midadulthood. Thus, adolescence-limited antisocial behavior overlays a persistent antisocial trait. This example also illustrates the case of personality characteristics that are specific to a particular developmental phase.

Continuity of Personality Traits

Antisocial behavior is also a good topic for a discussion of the continuity of traits. Kagan (1980) distinguished between homotypic continuity (a trait is expressed in the same behavior at different ages) and heterotypic continuity (the same trait is expressed in different behaviors as different ages). Huesmann and colleagues (1984) found strong evidence for the heterotypic continuity of antisocial behavior between the ages of 8 and 30: classmates' judgments of aggressiveness with peers predicted strongly the number of criminal convictions at 30 years of age. Furthermore, 22 years after the subjects' childhood aggressiveness was assessed, the aggressiveness of the subjects' children was better predicted by the subjects' childhood aggressiveness than by their own adult aggressiveness. Thus, the prediction was stronger for the subjects' children than for the subjects themselves—probably because aggressiveness displays homotypic continuity across generations but not across age.

Thus, the low stability of a trait over a long developmental period may indicate (1) that different individuals develop differently in the same homotypic trait or (2) no homotypic continuity of the trait. Because of the latter possibility, heterotypic continuity cannot be excluded. Asendorpf (1992) suggested a method to evaluate the homotypic continuity of traits empirically. Traits are judged in different samples at different ages, and behavioral correlates of the trait judgments are studied empirically. The traits show homotypic continuity to the extent that their behavioral correlates are similar. Asendorpf showed that shyness had highly similar correlates in childhood and adulthood, suggesting high homotypic continuity for this trait. Instability of shyness between childhood and adulthood can thus be attributed to true changes in shyness.

Explanation of Personality

There is now converging evidence from many large-scale studies that personality differences in late childhood and adolescence are due substantially to genetic differences; depending on the specific trait, age, and culture, 30 to 50% of the observed differences in a trait seem to be due to genetic differences. These are estimates based on indirect evidence from adoption and twin studies; research on the direct identification of genes or gene patterns that cause personality differences is still in its infancy.

The remaining differences in personality traits are due to environmental differences. An important insight of behavior genetic researchers is that, contrary to assumptions of traditional socialization theories, environmental differences that are shared by siblings (e.g., the parenting style of their parents or the socioeconomic status of the family) explain almost nothing about the personality of children and adolescents. Instead, nonshared environmental differences such as a different prenatal environment, different treatment by the same parents, different experiences with teachers and peers, and asymmetries in the sibling relationship may explain why children who grow up in the same family often develop very different personalities.

In addition, more recent research on socialization emphasizes the active role that not only adolescents but also children play in their own socialization. Correlations between parenting and children's personality that were traditionally interpreted as reflecting influences of parenting on children's personality are now open to additional interpretations, such as the shared genes of parents and children and the influence of children on their parents' parenting style. For example, the well-established correlation between boys' aggressiveness and their parents' restrictive parenting may be due partly to the fact that aggressive boys force their parents to become restrictive. Thus, linear-causal theories such as "parenting causes personality" theories have given way to more complex theories that assume continuous, reciprocal influences between children and their environment or that stress the importance of a fit between personality and the environment. With increasing independence from their family of origin, children and adolescents select, modify, and construct environments that fit their already existing personalities. For example, one of the major problems with adolescents' antisocial tendencies is that such youngsters tend to develop friendships with, or join cliques of, similarly disposed individuals who reinforce their antisocial tendencies, resulting in an unfortunate personality-environment fit that may be the major reason why antisocial tendencies are so difficult to change.

Explanation of the Stability of Personality

From this more dynamic view of the transaction between personality and environment, the observable stabilization of personality differences during childhood and adolescence is an active achievement of the developing person. Stability is due not only to (1) the constancy of genome differences, but also to (2) the stability of the environment (e.g., social risk factors are often as stable as IQ), (3) the increasing ability to control one's environment according to one's personality, and (4) the increasing stability of the self-concept about one's personality because of the tendency to feel and act consistent with one's self-concept.

Explanation of Personality Change

Recent developmental genetic research has pointed out that genes can have a destabilizing influence on personality. For example, identical twins are more similar with regard to sudden spurts or delays in IQ development than fraternal twins, and some pathological genetic effects begin to operate only in later childhood or adolescence. The widely held belief that genetic influences on personality show up early and stabilize personality is incorrect. It is grounded in the false assumption that genetic effects can be equated with one's genome. However, it is not the platonic existence of genes in one's genome that is crucial for genetic effects on personality but rather gene activity, and gene activity may change considerably over the period of development. Thus, personality change can be due to genetic effects.

More obviously, drastic changes in one's environment can also induce personality change. Many studies have found that traits are less stable for children and adolescents experiencing parental divorce or unemployment than for those experiencing more stable family environments. Less clear is the impact of specific critical life events on children's personalities, such as the death of a parent or the family's movement to a new town, with accompanying loss of the peer network. It seems that it is not the event itself but how children cope with it that determines its consequences. Because how they cope is a function of their personalities, reciprocal influences between personality and the consequences of life events (and in some instances even their occurrence) are likely to be at work. For example, children's personalities to some extent predict their proneness to accidents.

Wanted: A Theory of Personality Development

Presently there is no theory that accounts for a major portion of what we know about personality development from middle childhood through adolescence. Personality in this age period is not determined by early experiences in the family of origin, as Freud believed, nor is it simply a product of environmental reinforcement, as the behaviorists believed, and Piaget was basically silent about personality differences. Stage theories such as Erikson's are to some extent useful for the description of universal trends of development, but personality differences in the social-emotional domain cannot be reduced to spurts or delays in universal developmental processes. Current cognitive theories of development are therefore not very useful for explaining personality development. Developmental behavioral genetics provides a bird's-eye view of the relative importance of various genetic and environmental factors that contribute to personality differences, but this branch of population genetics does not specify developmental mechanisms (except for metaphors such as "genes are switched on/off during development") or explain the existence of such mechanisms as a result of genetic or cultural evolution.

Fragmentary theorizing about mechanisms of personality development abounds (e.g., the concepts of genotype-environment covariation, transactions between persons and their environment, and the person-environment fit), but lacking is a common, integrative framework that would embrace these and other mechanisms.

Bibliography

Asendorpf, J. B. (1992). A Brunswikean approach to trait continuity: Application to shyness. *Journal of Personality, 60*, 53–77.

Caspi, A. (1998). Personality development across the life course. In N. Eisenberg (Ed.), *Handbook of child psychology: Vol. 3. Social, emotional, and personality development* (5th ed., pp. 311–388). New York: Wiley.

Digman, J. M. (1989). Five robust trait dimensions: Development, stability, and utility. *Journal of Personality, 57*, 195–214.

Elkind, D., & Bowen, R. (1979). Imaginary audience behavior in children and adolescence. *Developmental Psychology, 15*, 38–44.

Erikson, E. H. (1950). *Childhood and society*. New York: Norton.

Halverson, C. F., Jr., Kohnstamm, G. A., & Martin, R. P. (Eds.). (1994). *The developing structure of temperament and personality from infancy to adulthood.* Hillsdale, NJ: Erlbaum.

Huesmann, L. R., Eron, L. D., Lefkowitz, M. M., & Walder, L. O. (1984). Stability of aggression over time and generations. *Developmental Psychology, 20*, 1120–1154.

Kagan, J. (1980). Perspectives on continuity. In O. G. Brim, Jr., & J. Kagan (Eds.), *Constancy and change in human development* (pp. 26–74). Cambridge, MA: Harvard University Press.

Lytton, H. (1990). Child and parent effects in child conduct disorder: A reinterpretation. *Developmental Psychology, 26*, 683–697.

Moffitt, T. E. (1993). Adolescence-limited and life-course-persistent antisocial behavior: A developmental taxonomy. *Psychological Review, 100*, 674–701.

Plomin, R. (1986). *Development, genetics, and psychology.* Hillsdale, NJ: Erlbaum.

Scarr, S., & McCartney, K. (1983). How people make their own environments: A theory of genotype → environment effects. *Child Development, 54*, 424–435.

Jens B. Asendorpf

Adulthood and Aging

Personality development in adulthood often refers to change in a direction that is in some sense desirable or important for humanistic understanding. Do human beings increase in maturity, become wiser, or perhaps actualize themselves? If some do, what are their characteristics? A number of theorists have conceptualized master traits indicative of ideal development. For example, Allport (1961) offered five criteria of maturity: emotional security and regulation of behavior by rules for reducing friction and obtaining rewards in social life (adjustment); the capacity for investing in significant endeavors, as opposed to egoistic preoccupation or focus on bodily needs; capacity for compassionate and intimate relations with others; reality orientation and perceptiveness in appraisal of self and others; and a personally derived philosophy of life.

Theories of Development

Jung (1960) and Erikson (1963) offered theories of desirable development that included the idea of distinctive changes over particular parts of the life span. Jung conceptualized the waxing of the ego in the first half of life and its waning in the second half. He was particularly interested in inner life during this second phase. He described the process of individuation, beginning at ages 35 to 40, which involved awareness of and relation to previously semiconscious aspects of personality, such as one's shadow, animus or anima, and the totality that he called the self. Erikson paid more attention to young adulthood and to social life. In his theory, young adults developed a sense of their place and purposes in society (identity), then the ability to share their life closely with another (intimacy), then the ability to care about the development of human beings generally (generativity), and finally to see their life in perspective and accept it (integrity). Jung's focus on intrapsychic development and Erikson's on psychosocial development illustrate a difference in point of view that continues.

Erikson's conceptualization is an example of a stage theory. In stage theories, development means the acquisition of a new structure or the change from an old structure to a new one. Development proceeds through a series of interrelated phases, each with a different quality or organization. Progress or the lack of it at one stage affects progress at later stages. Thus identity and intimacy in young adulthood are seen as providing the basis for generativity in middle age.

Other stage theorists have used Werner's general concept of development as a process of increasing differentiation and integration (see *Comparative Psychology of Mental Development*, Chicago, 1948). As applied to adult personality, differentiation emphasizes the cognitive, such as the ability to analyze a whole into parts and to respond flexibly and appropriately to changing situations, and integration includes coordinating and accepting different aspects of one's personality. Stage theorists have also elaborated or extended Piaget's concepts of cognitive structures, stages, and processes. (See J. Piaget, *Biology and Knowledge*, Chicago, 1971.) Drawing on these and other sources, Loevinger (1976) conceptualized and measured stages in the development of the ego as the master trait of personality. At the higher stages, autonomy and conscious awareness become key features of the personality.

Some theorists conceptualize development as involving both progression and retrogression. For Baltes (1997), development is any gain or loss in the adaptive capacity of the organism. Gains are always accompanied by losses. What characterizes adult development in humans is the changing ratio of expected gains and losses with age or, in Baltes's very broad conceptualization, the operation of declining evolutionary selection benefits with age (after the reproductive years), along with increases in the use of cultural advantages, such as education, and the decreasing efficacy of these advantages in the later years. The mature personality is one that maintains resiliency and well-being in the aging self.

Other theorists have avoided the concepts of progression and retrogression, preferring to study merely the sequence of environments or situations that adults encounter as they age or the characteristics of individuals at particular periods of life. For example, Levinson and colleagues (1978) held the view that there are seasons of life, each with its own opportunities and constraints. They understood the life structure at any age as a system that needs to be changed repeatedly as the environment and the individual change. However, they believed that the life structure and transitions between life structures have characteristic features at different periods of adulthood.

Neugarten (1968) called attention to the importance for adult development of age norms, that is, social expectations that are different for people of different ages and are internalized by them. Whereas Levinson believed that the stages of adult life were universal, Neugarten described class and cultural differences in how stages were differentiated and experienced. For example, noting that lives in the Western world were becoming longer and vigorous until later in life, she advocated a distinction between the "young-old" and the "old-old" that has come to be adopted.

Challenges in the Study of Adult Personality Development

Conceptualizations of adult development are often so complex or unspecific that it is not clear what to measure or how to measure it. Thus, the refinement of concepts and the development of tools are important. The notion of development implies change, but there are many kinds of change, and the measurement of change remains a controversial area. Most researchers believe that the social environment plays an important role in development, but it is not easy to evaluate cultural and historical influences. One needs different studies of the same individuals over time (longitudinal samples) conducted over different periods of history. The fact that there are now a number of such studies, begun at various times during the twentieth century, provides an important opportunity for the study of personality development in adulthood. However, different studies have seldom used the same measures at the same ages. Cross-sectional studies (using adults of different ages studied at the same time) can often be designed to provide the same measures at the same ages, but the influence of age is confounded with that of birth cohort: for example, much of the decline in intelligence that had been attributed to age on the basis of cross-sectional studies was shown to be a function of cohort differences in education. There are also period effects to be taken into account. In a given social climate, adults of different ages may all respond in a more individualistic or optimistic manner than they did at a different time of testing. Or one social climate may favor an attitude such as optimism in young people, whereas a later social climate may favor it in older people. A variety of techniques may be used to analyze or reduce these effects.

Normative Personality Change with Age

Normative personality change is change that most people show. Several cross-sectional studies using personality inventories indicate that across cultures or ethnic groups, males and females tend to increase in self-control and pleasantness and to decrease in social vitality from adolescence to old age. Several longitudinal studies in the United States report similar findings (Itelson & Kwan, in press). Some studies support Vaillant's (1977) thesis that coping techniques become more flexible with age. It is an important first statement that adults tend to improve on Allport's (1961) first criterion of maturity (adjustment) as they age, but data are insufficient to support conclusions about his other criteria or about many tenets of other developmental theorists. Even in the case of adjustment, change does not occur evenly throughout adulthood, and not all individuals become better adjusted with age.

Factors Conducive to Normative Development

There are at least three factors that tend to produce normative change in adulthood.

Biological and Systemic Changes. Physical and cognitive capabilities change over the course of adulthood. Awareness of decline is a major component of the feeling of aging, and both this awareness and the changes themselves affect how people behave. For example, they cause older adults to regulate their behavior more carefully than do young adults. Some theorists emphasize maturational or systemic changes with age. Labouvie-Vief (in *Human Development*, 1982) offered a model in which the cognitive and emotional systems become more interconnected over the course of adulthood through maturation and general experience.

The Age-Graded Social World. All societies assign roles and statuses to individuals in part on the basis of age, although the strictness of age norms varies with time and place. People appraise themselves and others in terms of these age norms. For example, young adults make commitments and settle down, in part because they feel they should and others expect them to do so. They become more dependable.

Period of Life. In each period of life characteristic physical and cognitive features, interpersonal patterns, and life concerns shape personality. Young adults seek to find and make their place, the middle-aged to enhance and maintain it, and older adults to cope with decreasing abilities and centrality in the social world. Of course, the same period of life is experienced differently by different individuals in different cultural settings. It is not to be expected that exactly the same changes will be found across studies; one looks instead for patterns and trends.

Young adults are thought to be more malleable than older adults, and studies bear out this expectation. Young adulthood is said to be a difficult period because there is much to learn and many adjustments to be made. It is a period when one's identity in the adult world is tested, found wanting, or consolidated. Here again, several longitudinal studies show more negative emotion or lower self-esteem at this time of life than in middle age.

Some theorists have seen middle age as the critical period of adult development. Levinson and colleagues (1978) described what they termed the "age-40" transition as a time of beginning to reconcile opposites in one's personality (an idea taken from Jung). On the basis of interviews, Neugarten (1968) described the competence of the middle-aged, their responsibilities for both younger and older people, and their range of empathy and reflectiveness. In middle age, she observed, there is a major shift in the sense of time: One's life becomes structured in terms of time left to live rather than time since birth. Research confirms that many individuals, especially women, increase in confidence, competence, intellectuality, and social skills between young adulthood and middle age.

Several studies of personality change from middle age to later periods report a decline in assertiveness and concern with individual achievement. Control of behavior continues to increase. In their social contacts, older individuals look less than young people do for stimulation or information; rather, they choose the company of people who provide warmth and security. Marriages are more pleasant. The older individual becomes less confrontational, less complex in self-representation, more self-accepting, and more adaptable in setting personal goals and in dealing with others.

Individual Differences in Development

Although adults change in some of the same ways as they age, some develop sooner or more than others, and people develop along different tracks.

Factors Affecting the Amount or Timing of Development. Some aspects of adult development depend on opportunities to develop independence, competence, confidence, and perspective. Social class structures these opportunities. Lower-class people tend to work at simple jobs, but doing complex work increases one's cognitive flexibility and breadth of interest. Education and status of work shape lifestyles that affect self-esteem, choice of mate, and the resources one has to contribute to the welfare of others. In a large sample of adults, college-educated respondents reported substantially more generative feelings and behavior than those with less education. Occupations and roles offer particular restrictions or opportunities for development. For example, clinical psychologists show more gain in wisdom than other people. Social events affect adult development in diverse ways. According to Stewart and Healy (1989), those that an individual experiences in late adolescence or young adulthood are more likely to influence the formation of adult identity. Thus, the Women's Movement had more influence on women who were in college during the middle to late 1960s than on women who were older and already committed to a life as homemaker at this time. Individual differences in personality affect the amount and timing of development. Men who had been shy as children married, became fathers, and established careers 3 to 4 years later than other men.

The various factors that have been mentioned interact in important ways. For example, many veterans of World War II and the Korean War were enabled to go to college by the GI Bill of Rights, with a marked boost to their career success and self-esteem. These social events affected the opportunity structure for personality development. However, some men were affected more than others: personality change was most pronounced in boys who had been young children in deprived families during the Great Depression, had poor relationships with their fathers, and had been passive and low in morale before they entered military service.

Factors Associated with Developmental Track. People may differ in the order of areas in which they show development. Gender affects opportunities for development, just as social class does, but it can also be regarded as providing different tracks. The most important personality changes in adulthood, according to Gutmann (1987), are associated with the assumption of gender roles in young adulthood and the later relaxation of these roles. Young men are described as assertive and self-disciplined, young women as nurturant and compliant. With age, men become more self-indulgent and relational, and women become more assertive. In some theories, the integration of masculine and feminine traits (androgyny) is a developmental achievement, one that is more needed and more possible after young adulthood. In D. P. McAdams's version (*Power, Intimacy, and the Life Story*, New York, 1985), power and intimacy are major life themes but are not necessarily associated with gender.

Individual differences in personality can set different tracks. Kohut (*The Restoration of the Self*, New York, 1977) distinguished self-oriented and other-oriented individuals. The self-oriented seldom attain the relational sensitivity and ease of the other-oriented, nor are they likely to feel as caring about people. However, some of them can proceed along another line of development, becoming creative and attaining self-insight and wisdom. For people on different tracks, different experiences may be important for development. Career effort and success were found to be related to the development of identity and generativity in women who had creative potential (openness, complexity, and unconventionality), although not in other women.

Processes in Adult Development

Through what processes do we become more mature, better adapted, or more individuated? Some psychologists have used the concepts of assimilation and accommodation to understand personality development. According to Block (*Developmental Psychology*, 1982), when people assimilate their experience, there is no change or elaboration of personality schemas. People generally assimilate when they can. However, when experience challenges their adaptive strategies, they may accommodate, that is, make changes in their existing adaptive structures. Developmentally, adaptation to such challenges requires a move from egocentricity to a wider and more flexible perspective. A study of midlife women found that those high in ego development, as compared with those low on this characteristic, had gained greater tolerance and achievement via independence. They tended to have chosen challenging life paths and reported difficult times in their adult lives that required the construction of new schemas.

Other psychologists look to identity or self processes as the dynamism of adult development. For example, Cross and Markus (*Human Development*, 1991) conceptualized possible selves, or elements of the self-concept that represent what a person could become, as agents in life-span change. Possible selves provide incentives for behavior, either to be approached or avoided. Recalibrations to increase or protect self-esteem can lead to changes in self-concept and behavior.

According to Baltes (1997), successful aging involves the processes of selection, optimization, and compensation. Selection is used in choosing one's goals or how one spends one's time; optimization is used in behavior-enhancing factors such as goal commitment and practice; and compensation is used in repatterning of goals and behavior-enhancing factors to counteract new limitations.

These and other ideas about processes of development should repay much further investigation. Adult development consists of many kinds of change, subject to many kinds of influence. The topic is complex, and as the life span lengthens, there are new challenges to aging well.

Bibliography

Theoretical and Classic Works

Allport, G. W. (1961). *Pattern and growth in personality*. New York: Holt, Rinehart, & Winston.

Baltes, P. B. (1997). On the incomplete architecture of human ontogeny. *American Psychologist, 52*, 366–380.

Erikson, E. (1963). *Childhood and society* (2nd ed.). New York: Norton.

Gutmann, D. L. (1987). *Reclaimed powers: Toward a new psychology of men and women in later life*. New York: Basic Books.

Jung, C. G. (1960). The stages of life. In H. Reed, M. Fordham, & G. Adler (Eds.), *Collected works* (Vol. 8, pp. 387–403). Princeton, NJ: Princeton University Press. Much of Jung's writing concerns adult development; this chapter is directly related to that subject and is broad in scope.

Levinson, D., Darrow, C. M., Klein, E. B., Levinson, M. H., & McKee, B. (1978). *The seasons of a man's life*. New York: Knopf.

Loevinger, J. (1976). *Ego development*. San Francisco: Jossey-Bass.

Neugarten, B. L. (Ed.). (1968). *Middle age and aging*. Chicago: University of Chicago Press. This excellent collection includes several of Neugarten's own best essays.

Stewart, A. J., & Healy, J. M., Jr. (1989). Linking individual development and social changes. *American Psychologist, 4*, 30–42.

Vaillant, G. E. (1977). *Adaptation to life: How the best and brightest came of age*. Boston: Little, Brown.

Current Scholarly Overviews and Methodological Discussion

Caspi, A., & Roberts, B. W. (1999). Personality continuity and change across the life course. In L. A. Pervin & O. P.

John (Eds.), *Handbook of personality: Theory and research* (2nd ed., pp. 300–326). New York: Guilford Press.

Heatherton, T. F., & Weinberger, J. L. (Eds.). (1994). *Can personality change?* (pp. 201–225). Washington, DC: American Psychological Association. This volume includes chapters presenting different views on personality change in adulthood and discussions of techniques for measuring change.

Helson, R., & Kwan, V. (in press). Personality change in adulthood: The broad picture and processes in one longitudinal sample. In S. Hampson (Ed.), *Advances in personality psychology* (Vol. 1). London: Routledge.

McAdams, D. P., & Aubin, E. de St. (Eds.). (1998). *Generativity and adult development: How and why we care for the next generation.* Washington, DC: American Psychological Association.

Ravenna Helson

PERSONALITY DISORDERS. Each person has a personality, or a characteristic manner of thinking, feeling, behaving, and relating to others. A personality disorder occurs when there is a constellation of personality traits that results in a clinically significant impairment in social or occupational functioning or personal distress. Disorders of personality have been recognized throughout the history of medicine and the science of psychopathology (Millon et al., 1996), from the four temperaments of the fourth-century Greek physician Hippocrates (phlegmatic, sanguine, choleric, and melancholic) to the present-day classification of mental disorders provided by the fourth edition of the American Psychiatric Association's *Diagnostic and Statistical Manual (DSM–IV)*.

Description

Personality disorders are chronic and pervasive behavior patterns that are evident from young adulthood, characterize everyday functioning, and remain throughout most of one's life, although most disorders of personality will decrease in severity as one ages, due to biological changes and a gradual adaptation to environmental pressures. There will be indications of a personality disorder during childhood, and one can technically diagnose a personality disorder in someone younger than eighteen. Personality disorders are not usually diagnosed, however, until a person is an adult, as most personality traits, whether adaptive or maladaptive, may not be fully developed or stabilized until adulthood.

Personality disorders are among the most prevalent and problematic of mental disorders. Personality disorders have substantial public health costs, as persons with a personality disorder appear to be particularly heavy users of clinical, forensic, and other social agencies. Personality disorders are the most commonly diagnosed conditions within clinical settings, and they may also be among the most common within nonclinical, community populations. However, it is difficult to estimate their prevalence within the community as there has not been a systematic study of the epidemiology of all of the personality disorders within a representative sample of the population.

DSM–IV includes 10 personality disorders: (1) paranoid (distrust and suspiciousness, as suggested in part by suspecting that others are exploiting, harming, or deceiving oneself); (2) schizoid (anhedonic detachment, as suggested in part by neither desiring nor enjoying close relationships); (3) schizotypal (peculiar eccentricities, odd thinking, and interpersonal deficits, such as odd beliefs, magical thinking, and aberrant perceptual experiences); (4) antisocial (disregard for and exploitation of others, such as repeatedly performing exploitative acts that are grounds for arrest); (5) borderline (marked instability in relationships, identity, behavior, and affect, such as intense, volatile interpersonal relationships); (6) histrionic (attention-seeking emotionality, such as theatrical, dramatic displays to draw attention to oneself); (7) narcissistic (insecure grandiosity, such as excessive and inappropriate arrogance); (8) avoidant (social inhibition, such as being unwilling to get involved with others unless certain of being liked or accepted); (9) dependent (intense emotional and needy dependency on others, such as urgently and indiscriminately seeking another relationship when a close relationship ends); and (10) obsessive-compulsive (preoccupation with orderliness, perfectionism, and control, such as being preoccupied with details, rules, lists, order, organization, or scheduling that the major point of an activity is lost).

These 10, however, do not exhaust all possibilities of clinically significant maladaptive personality traits. The most common personality disorder diagnosis within clinical settings is personality disorder, not otherwise specified. This diagnosis is used by clinicians when they conclude that the patient does have a personality disorder but he or she fails to meet the diagnostic criteria for any one of the ten disorders included within *DSM-IV*. Many other variants of personality disorder have indeed been identified and are currently being researched, including, but not limited to, the (1) negativistic (passive-aggressive and negativistic attitudes, as suggested in part by being repeatedly sullen, argumentative, and critical of others); (2) depressive (characteristically pessimistic, gloomy, and cheerless); (3) self-defeating (repeatedly engaging in self-defeating and self-denigrating behaviors); and (4) sadistic (characteristically cruel and demeaning toward others).

Diagnosis

Reliable diagnosis of personality disorders is very important for clinical research and practice, as many studies have indicated a substantial impact of personality disorders on the presentation, course, and treatment of other mental disorders. For example, a depressive mood disorder will be experienced and manifested differently for persons with a dependent, narcissistic, or antisocial personality disorder. Whereas the dependent person will experience feelings of deprivation, loss, loneliness, and unlikeability and the narcissistic person will experience feelings of defeat, failure, and self-blame, the antisocial person may turn to alcohol and drugs to self-medicate.

Personality disorders, however, are difficult to diagnose reliably. One reason is that many persons fail to recognize the maladaptivity of their personality traits. Some personality disorders are in this sense described as being ego syntonic. Friends, colleagues, employers, and spouses will often be more aware of the maladaptive behavior pattern than the person with the personality disorder. Personality disorders may even include a fundamental distortion in how one views oneself and other persons. Some personality disorders involve a maladaptively inflated, arrogant view of oneself (e.g., narcissistic), whereas others involve a maladaptively devalued, derogatory view of oneself (e.g., avoidant). Some personality disorders involve an excessively mistrustful, suspicious perception of others (e.g., paranoid), whereas others involve an excessively trusting view of others (e.g., dependent).

Personality disorders are also difficult to diagnose reliably because of the breadth of the behavior pattern that is involved. It is difficult to reduce a constellation of personality traits that are expressed across a wide array of situations (e.g., lack of empathy, arrogant attitudes, and sense of entitlement for the diagnosis of narcissistic personality disorder) to simply eight to ten specific behaviors that can be readily assessed without the need of much professional judgment. Only one of the personality disorders within *DSM–IV* (i.e., antisocial) appears to be diagnosed reliably by mental health professionals in general clinical practice. However, all of the personality disorders can be diagnosed reliably with the aid of semistructured interviews that facilitate a comprehensive, systematic, and replicable assessment of each of the diagnostic criteria.

An additional complication in the diagnosis of personality disorders is their differentiation from one another. If a person meets the *DSM–IV* diagnostic criteria for one personality disorder, it is likely that he or she will meet the criteria for another. In fact, many patients meet the criteria for three, four, five, and even more personality disorder diagnoses. Clinicians, however, justifiably prefer to provide just one diagnosis to each patient, because it is not clinically or theoretically meaningful to say that someone has multiple personality disorders, each with its own distinct etiology and pathology, interacting within one another in a manner comparable to having more than one physical disorder. On the other hand, it is equally difficult to determine which single diagnosis should be given when the patient meets the criteria for more than one disorder.

Many researchers suggest that the problem is due to the failure of the traditional medical approach to diagnosis in which a single diagnostic category is provided to describe the underlying syndrome. One word is rarely adequate in fully describing the personality of another person, as individuals are characterized by a constellation of personality traits. People with personality disorders may likewise be characterized by a constellation of maladaptive (and adaptive) personality traits, all of which are on a continuum with one another and with normal personality functioning. Personality disorders may be simply maladaptive, extreme variants of traits that are present within all persons to varying degrees. It is normal and desirable to be confident, but not to be arrogant (a symptom of the narcissistic personality disorder). It is adaptive to be agreeable but not to be submissive (a symptom of the dependent personality disorder). It is adaptive to be conscientious but not to be perfectionistic (a symptom of the obsessive-compulsive).

Another controversy in the diagnosis of personality disorders is whether some of them represent sex-biased characterizations of gender-related traits (Widiger, 1998). This issue has been discussed most extensively with respect to the *DSM–IV* histrionic and dependent personality disorders. These two personality disorders are diagnosed in women more often than in men, and they do appear to involve, at least in part, symptomatology that is closely related to stereotypic feminine traits (e.g., emotionality, attention-seeking, and seductiveness in the diagnosis of the histrionic personality disorder, and submissiveness, neediness, and self-sacrifice in the diagnosis of the dependent). Studies have also indicated that clinicians will at times overdiagnose the histrionic and dependent personality disorders in females.

However, to the extent that personality disorders represent maladaptive variants of commonly occurring personality traits, one might expect to find differential sex prevalence rates of personality disorders consistent with the average differences in personality between men and women. Women might, on average, be relatively more emotional, compliant, altruistic, modest, and agreeable than men. One might therefore expect more women than men to have personality disorders characterized, in part, by maladaptive, extreme variants of these traits. Other personality disorders are diagnosed more frequently in males (e.g., antisocial and obsessive-compulsive) because they involve, at least in part, maladaptive variants of stereotypic masculine behaviors (e.g., normal tough-mindedness that is more evident in males has a more extreme, maladaptive variant of callousness that is present within the antisocial personality disorder).

A comparable issue is a potential cultural bias. Personality disorders are present across all societies and cultures. However, cultures may also vary, at least to some extent, in the personality traits that are valued (or devalued). It is unclear whether the personality disorders within the *DSM–IV*, and the diagnostic criteria for them, are equally valid across all cultures. One of the definitional criteria for a personality disorder in *DSM–IV* is that the behavior pattern deviates markedly from the expectations of a person's culture. However, one should not infer from this requirement that a personality disorder is simply a deviation from a cultural norm. Deviation from a cultural norm is not necessarily maladaptive or suggestive of the presence of psychopathology. Similarly, conforming to a cultural norm is not necessarily healthy. Many of the personality disorders do appear to represent, at least in part, excessive, extreme variants of behavior patterns that are encouraged within the society in which the person was raised. For example, as noted above, the dependent and histrionic personality disorders do appear to involve extreme variants of traits that are encouraged, valued, or socialized (whether appropriately or inappropriately) in females. In this respect, the dependent personality disorder does not represent a deviation from a cultural norm, but rather an exaggerated conformity to a norm that is in some respects maladaptive to ideal functioning.

The purpose of the requirement of a cultural deviation within the definition of a personality disorder is to emphasize that a behavior pattern that appears to a clinician to be excessive, aberrant, or deviant from the cultural norms of the clinician, may be quite normative and adaptive from the perspective of the patient's culture. Clinicians interviewing or treating persons from different cultural backgrounds should be sensitive to the variations in norms and expectations across different cultures. What might appear to be an excessive emotionality within a male patient or an excessive submissiveness in a female patient, from the perspective of a clinician with only a limited experience of cultural diversity, may in fact be quite normal and adaptive for the patients within the social, cultural background in which they must function.

Treatment

The presence of a personality disorder will have a significant impact on the treatment of other mental disorders. Personality disorders are given special recognition within *DSM–IV* by being placed on a separate axis of diagnosis to ensure that all clinicians assess for their presence. This emphasis is in recognition of their prevalence and potential impact upon the treatment of other mental disorders. The presence of a *DSM–IV* personality disorder will complicate substantially the treatment of an anxiety, mood, substance, or other mental disorder. For example, the presence of a dependent personality disorder will increase the likelihood that the person will become inordinately attached to or dependent upon the clinician for emotional support, whereas the presence of a borderline personality disorder will increase the likelihood of intense, disruptive, and at times manipulative emotional reactions (Benjamin, 1993; Stone, 1993). The presence of some personality disorders (e.g., antisocial) may even constitute a reason for excluding or dismissing a person from a treatment program.

Personality disorders may themselves be the focus of treatment, and there are in fact many clinics nationwide devoted to the treatment of these disorders. However, personality disorders are among the most difficult of mental disorders to treat, largely because personality traits are so chronic, pervasive, and ego syntonic. However, it is not the case that the personality is unable to change or that personality disorders are unresponsive to treatment. There are no treatment programs that can reliably effect a fundamental and permanent change to personality, but there are many effective treatment programs that can reduce significantly the most maladaptive and troublesome aspects of a personality disorder. For example, pharmacologic interventions are helpful in reducing the affective instability of borderline personality disorder, the cognitive-perceptual aberrations of the schizotypal personality disorder, and the feelings of anxiety of the avoidant personality disorder (Stone, 1992). Cognitive-behavioral techniques are helpful in addressing the false and debilitating assumptions, irrational reasoning, distorted perceptions, habitual misunderstandings, and other faulty cognitive schemas that are fundamental to all of the personality disorders (Beck & Freeman, 1990). Interpersonal therapies address the repetitive patterns of intense and harmful relationships that are often central to the pain and suffering of the person with the personality disorder and his or her significant others (Benjamin, 1993; Kiesler, 1996). Psychodynamically oriented therapies are helpful in increasing self-reflection and in appreciating the historical development of the maladaptive personality traits within the context of conflicted, neglectful, abusive, or otherwise pathologic relationships (Benjamin, 1993; Stone, 1992, 1993). Many clinicians, however, will be eclectic in their approach to the treatment of personality disorders, drawing upon all of these theoretical orientations in an effort to provide a treatment program that is optimal to the individual patient (Stone, 1993).

Etiology

The eclectic nature of the treatment of personality disorders is perhaps consistent with the multifactorial nature of their etiology. There does not appear to be a specific etiology for any one of the *DSM–IV* personality disorders. Personality traits and personality disorders appear to be the result of both biogenetic and environmental variables interacting with one another over the course of fetal, childhood, and adolescent development (Widiger & Sanderson, 1997).

Heredity appears to be important for the development of most personality traits, and the same does appear to be true for maladaptive personality traits and personality disorders (Nigg & Goldsmith, 1994). Twin and family history studies also suggest that many of the personality disorders have a genetic linkage to other mental disorders. For example, the avoidant personality disorder appears to be related to the anxiety disorder of social phobia, schizotypal personality disorder with schizophrenia, and borderline personality disorder with mood and impulse dyscontrol. An alternative conceptualization of the personality disorders is to consider them to be characterological variants of these disorders and qualitatively distinct from normal personality functioning. This may be particularly true for schizotypal personality disorder which involves the presence of cognitive and interpersonal deficits and eccentricities (e.g., magical thinking, aberrant perceptual experiences, odd speech, peculiar behaviors, social anxiety, suspiciousness, and lack of close friends) that were originally identified in the biological relatives of persons diagnosed with schizophrenia.

The genetic dispositions, however, are unlikely to involve specific genes for specific personality disorders. Persons appear instead to inherit a variety of cognitive and affective dispositions or deficits that interact over time with social, familial, and other environmental experiences to develop a particular maladaptive behavior pattern. For example, the dependent personality disorder that involves excessive submissiveness, clinging, and intense fears of separation, may be due in some cases to the interaction of an anxious-fearful temperament with a parental infantilization during a developmental period in which individuation and separation normally occur (Bornstein, 1993; Widiger & Sanderson, 1997). Dependent persons may turn to a parental figure to provide reassurance, security, and confidence that they have substantial difficulty generating for themselves due to an anxious-fearful temperament. However, the development of a more healthy self-confidence and assertiveness may be discouraged by a clinging protectiveness and sustained attachment by the parents, perhaps encouraging in dependent persons a fundamental belief that their sense of self-worth is contingent on the support from and importance they have to another person. Comparable interactions of temperamental dispositions with social, familial experiences may provide the explanation for the etiology of other personality disorders (Widiger & Sanderson, 1997).

[*See also* Antisocial Personality Disorder; Borderline Personality Disorder; Narcissistic Personality Disorder; Obsessive-Compulsive Personality Disorder; Paranoid Personality Disorder; Personality; Personality Psychology; Personality Traits; *and* Schizophrenia.]

Bibliography

American Psychiatric Association. (1994). *Diagnostic and statistical manual of mental disorders* (4th ed.). Washington, DC: Author. Provides brief description and official diagnostic criteria for personality disorders.

Beck, A. T., & Freeman, A. (1990). *Cognitive therapy of personality disorders.* New York: Guilford Press. Cognitive model for the etiology and treatment of personality disorders.

Benjamin, L. S. (1993). *Interpersonal diagnosis and treatment of personality disorders.* New York: Guilford Press. Object-relational (psychodynamic and interpersonal) model for the description and treatment of personality disorders.

Bornstein, R. F. (1993). *The dependent personality.* New York: Guilford. Scientific and clinical review of the dependent personality disorder.

Kiesler, D. J. (1996). *Contemporary interpersonal theory and research. Personality, psychopathology, and psychotherapy.* New York: Wiley. Interpersonal model for the diagnosis, etiology, and treatment of personality disorders.

Millon, T., Davis, R. D., Millon, C. M., Wenger, A. W., van Zuilen, M. H., Fuchs, M., & Millon, R. B. (1996). *Disorders of personality: DSM-IV and beyond.* New York: Wiley. Current and historical overview of personality disorders.

Nigg, J. T., & Goldsmith, H. H. (1994). Genetics of personality disorders: Perspectives from psychology and psychopathology research. *Psychological Bulletin, 115,* 346–380. Scientific review of research on heritability of personality disorders.

Stone, M. (1992). Treatment of severe personality disorders. In A. Tasman & M. B. Riba (Eds.), *Review of psychiatry* (Vol. 11, pp. 98–115). Washington, DC: American Psychiatric Press. Scientific review of treatment for personality disorders.

Stone, M. (1993). *Abnormalities of personality: Within and beyond the realm of treatment.* New York: Norton. Psychodynamic and pragmatic overview of treatment of personality disorders.

Widiger, T. A. (1993). The DSM-III-R categorical personality disorder diagnoses: A critique and an alternative. *Psychological Inquiry, 4,* 75–90. Scientific critique of medical, categorical model of personality disorder diagnosis.

Widiger, T. A. (1998). Sex biases in the diagnosis of personality disorders. *Journal of Personality Disorders, 12,* 1–24. Comprehensive overview of controversies concerning sex and gender bias.

Widiger, T. A., & Sanderson, C. J. (1995). Assessing personality disorders. In J. N. Butcher (Ed.), *Clinical personality assessment: Practical approaches* (pp. 380–394). New

York: Oxford University Press. Clinical and scientific overview of assessment of personality disorders.

Widiger, T. A., & Sanderson, C. J. (1997). Personality disorders In A. Tasman, J. Kay, & J. A. Lieberman (Eds.), *Psychiatry* (Vol., 2, pp. 1291–1317). Philadelphia, PA: W. B. Saunders. Clinical and scientific overview of diagnosis, etiology, and treatment of personality disorders.

Thomas A. Widiger

PERSONALITY INVENTORIES. *See* Personality Psychology, *article on* Methods of Study.

PERSONALITY PSYCHOLOGY. [*This entry comprises three articles: an overview of the broad history of the field from its inception to the present; a survey of the principal theories that have determined the course of development of the field; and a historical review of the methods (including personality inventories) that have been employed in this field. For a general discussion on personality, see* Personality. *See also* Personality Disorders; *and* Personality Traits.]

History of the Field

Personality psychology is the scientific study of the whole person. The central aim of the field of personality psychology is to provide a scientific account of human individuality. Personality psychology shares much in common with social and clinical psychology, but important differences may also be discerned. Although both personality and social psychology examine the behavior and experience of individual persons in social situations, social psychologists tend to put human sociality in the foreground of their inquiries, paying somewhat closer attention to situational and contextual determinants of behavior, while personality psychologists have traditionally emphasized internal behavioral determinants such as traits, needs, motives, and the self.

Going back to the nineteenth century, a strong clinical tradition has had a major impact on the development of personality psychology, but clinical and personality psychology still differ in their respective emphases on abnormal and normal human functioning. Personality psychologists tend to study more-or-less enduring and stable individual differences in relatively normal adults. Moreover, they have traditionally assigned a central role to human motivation and the internal dynamics of human behavior, including both conscious and unconscious motivational forces, factors, and conflicts. Personality theories have aimed to synthesize cognitive, emotional, motivational, developmental, and social aspects of human individuality into integrative frameworks for making sense of the individual human life.

Personality psychology became an identifiable discipline in the social and behavioral sciences in the 1930s. During that decade a number of separate lines of inquiry came together, culminating in the highly integrative programs for the field developed by Gordon Allport, Henry Murray, and Kurt Lewin, and in the publication of the field's first authoritative textbook, Allport's *Personality: A Psychological Interpretation* (1937). Allport defined personality as "the dynamic organization within the individual of those psychophysical systems that determine his [or her] unique adjustments to his [or her] environment" (p. 48). The first issue of the journal *Character and Personality* appeared in 1932. It aimed to join German studies of character with British and American studies of individual differences in persons, incorporating case studies, correlational surveys, experiments, and theoretical discussions. Furthermore, from the beginning, personality psychology was strongly influenced by the psychoanalytic tradition. Derived from case studies in therapeutic settings, the theories of Sigmund Freud, Carl Jung, Alfred Adler, and other psychoanalysts had a significant impact on early research and writing in personality psychology.

Historical Roots: Ancient and Modern

Although personality psychology may be viewed as a relatively young science, it is surely a very old source of human wonderment, for in the Western traditions the desire to understand the whole person can be traced back at least as far as the ancient Greeks. The most enduring conceptualization of individual differences in personality was initially proposed by Hippocrates (c. 400 CE), who distinguished among sanguine (cheerful, enthusiastic), choleric (angry, irritable), phlegmatic (stolid, apathetic), and melancholic (depressive) types of persons, each temperament type linked to a particular bodily humor. The ancient idea that personality is rooted in bodily differences can be traced forward to nineteenth-century phrenology and Kretschmer and Sheldon's morphological theory of personality. Although humors, head bumps, and body shape are no longer viewed as the biological determinants of personality types, contemporary inquiries focus on brain activity and neurophysiological determinants.

Another ancient source of modern personality psychology is Theophrastus (c. 300 CE), a pupil of Aristotle. Theophrastus composed literary sketches of common personality types, such as "the flatterer" and "the penurious man." These character sketches foreshadow a literary tradition in personality that can be traced through the medieval hagiographies of Christian saints, the development of biography and autobiography as self-elucidating art forms, and the portrayal of the personality and life course of fictional characters in modern drama, short stories, and novels. In that each sketch focuses on a single behavioral disposition, the writings of Theophrastus also presage the empirical identification and measurement of dispositional personality traits.

It was not until the nineteenth century, however, that scientists developed methods for assessing individual differences in traits. Of particular importance in this regard were the pioneering studies of Francis Galton on mental testing and Alfred Binet on intelligence, the invention of the correlation coefficient and factor analysis, and the emergence of formal test theory as a conceptual framework for personality assessment. Spurred by the mobilization of large military forces in World War I, psychologists began to invent self-report, multi-item tests to assess individual differences in personality functioning. Woodworth's Personal Data Sheet was used to screen out men who were unfit for military service because of personality maladjustment. Woodworth's measure was a forerunner of the Minnesota Multiphasic Personality Inventory (MMPI)—the most well-known standardized inventory for assessing personality. While the MMPI assesses dimensions linked to psychopathology, personality psychologists have developed a number of inventories for measuring individual differences in normal traits, such as the California Psychological Inventory and the Personality Research Form.

While traits may be viewed as different pieces of the personality, the idea that a person is a uniquely patterned and unified whole is a major theme of late-nineteenth-century scholarship associated with the *Geisteswissenschaften* tradition in social science and the writings of Comte, Dilthey, and Stern. This tradition had a major impact on Allport's vision for the field of personality and is reflected in the subsequent humanistic theories of personality offered by Carl Rogers and Abraham Maslow. Freud and the psychoanalysts, too, approached personality as an integrated whole, seeking to understand the dynamic origins of human behavior and experience. Freud argued that biologically anchored drives concerning sexuality and aggression provide the energy and the direction for human behavior, though their manifestations are disguised through the defensive machinations of the ego and the generally antagonistic demands of the social world. Behavior is determined by (mostly internal) forces (often rooted in childhood experience) over which the individual has little control; these forces are in constant conflict with each other, resulting in perpetual anxiety; the forces and conflicts themselves are typically unconscious; and only through the laborious work of psychoanalytic interpretation, often starting with the interpretation of dreams, may the individual bring the unconscious material to conscious light.

After Freud, psychoanalytic theories have tended to deemphasize the working of biological drives and highlight instead the adaptive powers of the ego (e.g., Hartmann, Erikson), the cultural and social determinants of personality (e.g., Horney, Fromm), and the intrapsychic representations of emotionally charged interpersonal relationships (e.g., Fairbairn, Winnicott, Kohut). Furthermore, the psychoanalytic tradition has tended to eschew the experimental and statistical conventions of quantitative science for the intensive examination of the individual case. As such, psychoanalysts have approached personality from what Allport called an *idiographic* perspective. The idiographic perspective on personality focuses on the unique patterning of the individual person, whereas the contrasting *nomothetic* perspective looks for general laws that apply to many or all persons. The intellectual tension between idiographic and nomothetic perspectives is a defining feature of the history of personality psychology.

The Formation of Systems: 1930–1950

In 1937, Allport's vision for personality psychology was a humanistic alternative to the prevailing mechanistic paradigms of stimulus-response psychology. In addition, it was an optimistic antidote to Freudian determinism and the growing emphasis in clinical writings on human pathology. Beginning with the proposition that every individual is a unique whole, Allport articulated a theoretical system that emphasized the rational and forward-looking aspects of human functioning and the individual's striving for inward unity. In Allport's system, human motivation and individual differences are accounted for by traits. A personality trait is "a neuropsychic structure having the capacity to render many stimuli functionally equivalent, and to initiate and guide equivalent [meaningfully consistent] forms of adaptive and expressive behavior" (1961, p. 347).

Allport's was one of a host of grand systems for personality proposed in the 1930s, 1940s, and early 1950s. In *Explorations in Personality* (1938) Henry Murray and his colleagues at the Harvard Psychological Clinic blended insights from Freud and Jung, themes from literature and medicine, and their own quantitative and qualitative research on autobiography, imagination, and human behavior to articulate a new "personological" system. Whereas Allport viewed the mind as rational and orderly, Murray focused attention on the irrational, unconscious, and conflictual aspects of human life. Murray's personology emphasized the workings of approximately 20 psychological needs, such as the needs for achievement and affiliation, and the interaction of needs with environmental opportunities and constraints. Neal Miller and John Dollard attempted to integrate psychoanalytic and learning theory by translating a number of classic Freudian concepts into the more objective and operational language of drive, cue, response, and reinforcement. Relying on factor analysis of self-report questionnaires, Raymond B. Cattell developed a comprehensive system of personality that brought together traits, states, and roles into a specification equation designed to predict precisely what a person will do in a given situation. Other factor-analytic theories were proposed by J. P. Guilford and Hans Eysenck.

By the early 1950s, the many grand theories of personality could be divided into psychoanalytic and psychosocial theories, temperament and trait models, approaches emphasizing needs and motives, humanistic self theories, organismic theories, and social-learning theories drawn from behaviorism. In a very influential textbook entitled *Theories of Personality*, Hall and Lindzey (1957) described and organized these grand systems in great detail and compared their agendas for personality research. Amidst the rich diversity of the grand theories, four relatively consistent conceptual trends may be discerned. First, most personality systems created in the 1930s and 1940s were based on the assumption that personality contains many different constructs organized on a number of different levels. Second, despite the plethora of variables, many systems maintained that the person could still be viewed as a unified and organized totality. Third, motivation was typically understood in tension-reduction terms. Following Freud and Hull, theorists typically argued that human organisms seek some sort of equilibrium, drives or needs increase tension, and the organism is motivated to act upon drives or needs in order to reduce tension, which is ultimately satisfying or reinforcing. Fourth, many systems conceived of personality development in terms of learning in society. The individual begins life as an assumedly self-centered creature, but over time he or she becomes socialized. Development is continuous and relatively gradual, a product of basic principles of learning that remain pretty much the same across the entire life-span.

The Elaboration of Constructs: 1950–1970

With the tremendous expansion of higher education after World War II, university psychology departments grew and became more specialized, spawning professional specializations in such personality-related areas as clinical, counseling, and industrial-organizational psychology. In the United States, increased federal funding supported personality research in laboratories and field settings. Personality psychologists focused their efforts on the examination and elaboration of particular personality constructs such as extraversion, anxiety, the need for achievement, field independence, and other internal variables that could be reliably and validly measured and whose impact on behavior could be directly observed. Overall, personality psychology turned away from the grand theories of the 1930s and 1940s and came to focus instead on problems and controversies concerning the measurement of constructs. Guiding questions of the day included these: What constitutes a valid measure of a personality construct? Are objective measurements of personality superior to clinical intuitions? Do personality scales measure what they say they measure or do they simply assess a person's style of responding to tests?

Postwar personality psychologists borrowed liberally from the grand theories of the previous decades to identify important individual-difference variables for hypothesis-testing research. But with few exceptions, they abandoned the integrative spirit that is so apparent in the writings of Allport and Murray. By the end of the 1960s, the quest to understand the whole person was seen by many as anachronistic in an era of no-nonsense factor analysis and tough experimental design. Furthermore, sociologists like Erving Goffman argued that much of life is mere role-playing and impression management in response to situational demands and that no unifying or unified core of the person needs to be considered in understanding what people do and think. Similarly, many social psychologists and social-learning theorists were beginning to suggest that the nature of the situation, not the person, is the primary determinant of how a person will behave. By the end of the 1960s, the stage was set for an ideological battle between the "trait psychologists" and the "situationists."

One of the unifying themes of the grand theories from the 1930s and 1940s was the central role of tension reduction in human motivation. Beginning in the 1950s, however, this idea came under attack from a number of different directions. Research on animals began to suggest that organisms are often motivated to increase tension and seek out greater levels of stimulation. In a devastating critique of the concept of tension reduction in human behavior, Robert White argued for a reconceptualization of motivation along the lines of mastery and competence. In the 1950s and 1960s, psychology as a whole was beginning to experience the cognitive revolution. The gradual erosion of the doctrine of tension reduction was part of a larger transformation in psychology from a mechanistic, drive-oriented, stimulus-response viewpoint to a more cognitive model of human behavior and experience emphasizing information processing, image making, and the subjective construction of meaning. George Kelly's personal construct theory of personality was a harbinger of cognitive things to come. According to Kelly, a person functions like a quasi-scientist seeking to predict and control his or her world through the use of cognitive categories, or personal constructs. In the 1960s, some personality psychologists began to couch their explanations for behavior in strikingly cognitive and social-cognitive terms, suggesting that human action is rather more guided by rational plans and goals than driven by blind instinct and need.

Crisis and Renewal: 1970–The Present

The 1970s witnessed a crisis of confidence in personality psychology. Some critics argued that because personality psychologists had abandoned grand theory in favor of tight experimental research, personality psychology had lost its center—its commitment to studying the whole person. Others contended that personality constructs themselves were scientifically useless and may indeed exist nowhere but in the minds of personality psychologists. Beginning with his book *Personality and Assessment* (1968), Walter Mischel argued forcefully against the efficacy of trait concepts and in favor of a cognitive-social-learning approach that viewed the situation as the prime determinant of behavior. Mischel launched a decade-long debate in the field over the relative efficacy of internal dispositional and external situational variables in the prediction of behavior.

In an effort to improve the predictive power of traditional trait measures, some personality psychologists championed the judicious use of (a) moderator variables—variables that moderate the relation between a trait and corresponding behavior—and (b) aggregation. By aggregating particular instances of behavior across situations and over time, personality psychologists could obtain more reliable indices of the behavioral trends that trait measures are designed to predict. By the time the dust from the trait versus situation debate settled in the early 1980s, personality psychologists seemed to have strengthened their commitment to a general interactionist position—that behavior is a function of a complex interaction of internal personal factors and external forces in the environment.

The strong renewal of confidence and vigor in personality studies since the early 1980s is evident in many different areas. With respect to individual differences, personality traits have enjoyed a strong comeback, fueled by (a) improvements in research designed to show linkages between trait scores and behavioral indices, (b) longitudinal data suggesting considerable consistency in relative personality trait scores over time, (c) behavior genetic studies indicating that most traits are at least moderately heritable, and (d) the emergence of some consensus concerning a taxonomy of traits.

With respect to the last point, many personality psychologists have rallied around the five-factor model of personality traits, or the "Big Five." Factor analytic studies suggest that the vast universe of trait terms can usually be mapped nicely into five general galaxies. One popular version of the Big Five labels the factors as extraversion, neuroticism, agreeableness, conscientiousness, and openness to experience. Others have adopted Eysenck's three-factor solution of extraversion, neuroticism, and psychoticism. Beyond the realm of traits, personality psychologists have expressed considerable enthusiasm for cognitive-motivational constructs that capture, in more specific detail than is typically possible with general traits, the dynamic and self-regulating aspects of human behavior and experience. Such constructs as life tasks, personal strivings, goals, self-schemas, defensive strategies, personal scripts, and relational modes all tap into what persons desire and fear, and how they seek to obtain what they desire and avoid what they fear in particular contexts.

Recent years have also witnessed resurgent interest in integrative theorizing in personality studies and a renewed commitment to studying the whole person. Jack Block and colleagues at the Institute for Personality and Social Research have continued classic longitudinal studies examining continuity and change in patterns of personality characteristics, focusing especially on the constructs of ego control and ego resilience. Robert Hogan has synthesized evolutionary, sociological, and psychodynamic sources to create a socioanalytic theory of personality. Jane Loevinger has borrowed frameworks from cognitive-developmental psychology to articulate her influential stage-theory of ego development. Silvan Tomkins has formulated an ambitious script theory for personality, viewing discrete affects such as joy and fear to be the prime motivators of behavior and comprehending personality structure and function in terms of self-defining affective scenes and scripts. Tomkins's dramaturgical approach anticipates a new generation of "narrative" theories in personality psychology, such as Hubert Hermans's dialogical theory of self and Dan McAdams's life-story model of identity. Narrative approaches suggest that persons experience unity and purpose in their lives by fashioning and internalizing life stories, and integrating the reconstructed past, perceived present, and anticipated future into a self-defining narrative or personal myth.

Bibliography

Allport, G. W. (1937). *Personality: A psychological interpretation.* New York: Henry Holt. In this first authoritative textbook in the field of personality psychology, Allport lays out a full agenda for the scientific study of the whole person.

Allport, G. W. (1961). *Pattern and growth in personality.* New York: Holt, Rinehart, & Winston.

Block, J. (1971). *Lives through time.* Berkeley, CA: Bancroft Books. Block blends idiographic and nomothetic approaches in this classic study of adult lives from the

Institute for Personality and Social Research (formerly the Institute for Personality Assessment and Research, or IPAR) at the University of California, Berkeley.

Carlson, R. (1971). Where is the person in personality research? *Psychological Bulletin, 75,* 203–219. In this major critique, Carlson calls for a return to grand theory and the study of the whole person during a time when personality psychologists were narrowly focused on measurement issues and single constructs.

Craik, K. H., Hogan, R., & Wolfe, R. N. (Eds.). (1993). *Fifty years of personality psychology.* New York: Plenum Press. In this collection, eminent personality psychologists provide historical perspectives on the field and look to the future.

Cronbach, L. J., & Meehl, P. E. (1955). Construct validity in psychological tests. *Psychological Bulletin, 52,* 281–302. In this classic statement in personality assessment, the authors set forth principles for constructing and interpreting measures of personality constructs.

Dollard, J., & Miller, N. E. (1950). *Personality and psychotherapy.* New York: McGraw-Hill. In a grand effort to synthesize divergent traditions, the authors seek to reconcile Hullian behaviorism and Freudian psychoanalysis.

Freud, S. (1916/1961). *Introductory lectures on psychoanalysis.* In J. Strachey (Ed.), *The standard edition of the complete psychological works of Sigmund Freud* (Vols. 15–16). London: Hogarth Press. These lectures provide a good overview of Freud's psychoanalysis, which was a seminal influence in the history of personality psychology.

Hall, & Lindzey, (1957). *Theories of personality.* New York: Wiley. A highly influential textbook that summarizes and systematizes the grand personality theories proposed in the first half of the twentieth century.

John, O. P. (1990). The "Big Five" factor taxonomy: Dimensions of personality in the natural language and in questionnaires. In L. Pervin (Ed.), *Handbook of personality theory and research* (pp. 66–100). New York: Guilford Press. John provides a detailed historical overview of the development of the five-factor model for personality traits.

Kelly, G. (1955). *The psychology of personal constructs.* New York: W. W. Norton. One of the first cognitive approaches to personality was Kelly's personal-construct theory, presented in full in this book.

McAdams, D. P. (1997). A conceptual history of personality psychology. In R. Hogan, S. Briggs, and J. Johnson (Eds.), *Handbook of personality psychology* (pp. 3–39). San Diego, CA: Academic Press. This chapter presents a full history of the field of personality, focusing mainly on conceptual developments in the twentieth century.

McClelland, D. C. (1961). *The achieving society.* New York: D. Van Nostrand. In what is perhaps the quintessential example of the elaboration of a single personality construct, McClelland applies the need for achievement to the study of the economic rise and decline of entire societies.

Mischel, W. (1968). *Personality and assessment.* New York: Wiley. Mischel launched the person-versus-situation debate in this highly critical text that seeks to replace trait concepts with a social-learning perspective in personality.

Murray, H. A. (1938). *Explorations in personality.* New York: Oxford University Press. With his colleagues at the Harvard Psychological Clinic, Murray presents his full personological system, defines and describes a vast array of new personality constructs, presents new methods of assessment emphasizing thematic and biographical approaches, and illustrates the application of personology in a lengthy case study.

Sanford, R. N. (1963). Personality: Its place in psychology. In S. Koch (Ed.), *Psychology: A study of a science* (Vol. 5, pp. 488–592). New York: McGraw-Hill. Sanford situates personality psychology in the constellation of social sciences and discusses historical roots and traditions of the field.

White, R. W. (1959). Motivation reconsidered: The concept of competence. *Psychological Review, 66,* 297–333. White offers a broad and devastating critique of tension-reduction models of human motivation, signaling a critical historical shift in personality theorizing.

Dan P. McAdams

Theories

Personality theories are systematic accounts of human nature. The classical theories were grand psychological cosmologies aspiring to explain the entire universe of human behavior. Targeting the "big potatoes" ideas of the human enterprise, the grand theories sought to explain not only normal and abnormal behavior but also the enduring puzzles of human existence, such as love and hate, freedom and dignity, life and death.

Families of Personality Theory

One widely accepted way to classify theories of personality places them into the historically primary families of psychodynamic, behavioral, and humanistic theories. Each family spawned at least one significant offspring that attempts to update or revise the parent tradition from which it originated. Figure 1 provides a concise map of the founding families and their progeny.

Psychology has also embraced the seemingly more commonsense approach of trait and type theories of personality. In the main, trait and type models are created independently of the founding families of theory and stand apart from that classification scheme. Gordon Allport (1897–1967), a psychologist who merits the title "father of personality psychology," created one of the first modern trait theories that organized personality around cardinal (e.g., "Machiavellian"), central (i.e., major, e.g., "gregarious"), and secondary, or minor, trait labels. Such traits were thought to be descriptors of enduring dispositions to action that gave per-

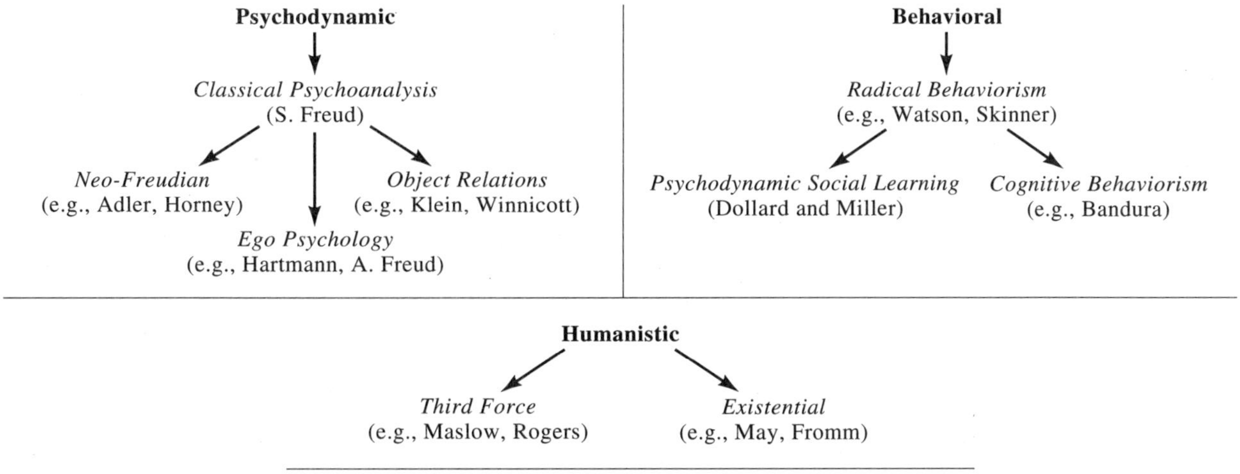

PERSONALITY PSYCHOLOGY: Theories. Figure 1. The main families of personality theory and their offspring.

sonality its consistency and uniqueness. British psychologist Hans Eysenck's (1916–1997) introversion-extroverion and stability-neuroticism (anxiety) dimensions exemplify the statistical approach by grouping correlated traits into bipolar dimensions, with opposites anchoring each extreme. A contemporary, widely accepted set of five such dimensions includes Eysenck's introversion and neuroticism dimensions, along with the bipolar dimensions of openness to experience, conscientiousness, and agreeableness. The "Big Five," as these traits are often called, are supported by a wide array of empirical measurements that might make it possible to describe any personality by assessing the person's unique profile of positions on each of the trait dimensions.

Psychodynamic Theories

The grand theories were constructed by acutely introspective people. Attentive to their own needs and conflicts, the authors of "big potatoes" theories created models of human personality that may have been partly derived from the anxieties, conflicts, and humiliations they found disquieting in themselves. The "creator-reflective" character of the grand theories is especially evident in Freud's psychoanalysis, the grand patriarch of all personality theories.

Classical Psychoanalysis. Drawing on his own family experiences and a daily half hour of introspection that he called his self-analysis, Sigmund Freud (1857–1939) devoted nearly 50 years to devising and revising his account of human conduct. For this Viennese neurologist-psychiatrist, the dynamic unconscious, an inchoate and energetic part of the mind, was the core of human character. Seething with the energy of Darwinian survival furies such as hunger, aggression, and sexual and procreative urges, only the recently acquired and very thin veneers of civilization—what Freud called simply the "I," or social intelligence of the ego, and its moral counterweight, the superego—constrain these passions of the unconscious to barely manageable limits. But, Freud argued, in the blink of an evolutionary eye, passion overpowers reason and self-interest overwhelms ethics. Thus, in Freudian theory, humans are unmasked as voracious, lustful, aggressive creatures competing with others of like mind. Not a pretty picture, but one which Freud nevertheless elaborated into an explanation of neurotic symptoms, humor, dreams, and interpersonal conflicts. For a substantial segment of the twentieth century, Freud's model was the prototypical canvas on which other theorists painted added detail or against which they reacted by overpainting the original with a radically different portrait. For better or worse, his ideas were pivotal and seminal in the field of personality theory.

Sigmund Freud's master work is *The Interpretation of Dreams*, which he published in 1899 even though the publisher chose the turn-of-the-century date as its copyright. This book sets forth Freud's thesis that dreams are unconsciously disguised fulfillments of unacceptable wishes. *The Interpretation of Dreams* also contains Freud's first complete account of the Oedipus complex in which, extending the metaphor of the Sophoclean tragedy, he described the conflicted loving, hateful, and fearful urges that children of four or five years experience in the relationship with their parents.

Psychodynamic Ego Psychology. By the time of Freud's death in 1939, scholars both inside and outside orthodox psychoanalysis were voicing the need for changes to the classical Freudian model. One wind of change, called ego psychology, was inadvertently given its start by Freud's daughter Anna (1895–1982). Her 1936 monograph *The Ego and the Mechanisms of Defense* focused new attention on the intelligence of self-protective strategies in a way that suggested the possibility of an expanded role in psychoanalysis for reasoned conduct rather than the narrow focus on irrational unconscious forces that had prevailed under her father's leadership. With the tacit permission of Anna Freud, ego psychology blossomed in the works of her close associate, Viennese psychiatrist Heinz Hartmann (1894–1970). Hartmann theorized about a "conflict-free" role of the ego, thereby making the ego relatively independent of the id's unconscious strivings. Hartmann also brought interpersonal relations and healthy problem solving out of the wings and onto center stage. From its inception, however, the goal of ego psychology was to update orthodox psychoanalysis and bring it into line with ongoing research in the wider field of developmental psychology, without demolishing the house Freud built.

Erik Erikson (1902–1994), a child psychoanalyst who studied with and completed his training analysis with Anna Freud before emigrating to America, constructed a psychosocial model of the ego's development from cradle to grave. By widening his theoretical focus to include interpersonal issues of trust, independence, identity, and competence throughout the life cycle, Erikson greatly expanded psychoanalysis beyond its self-imposed confinement to the arena of sexual and aggressive drive satisfaction and conflict. He retained much of the orthodox formulation, but did so while subordinating these motives to his own conceptions of significant cultural developmental milestones. Thus, Erikson's ideas achieved a far wider acceptance than classical psychoanalysis had ever enjoyed both inside and outside of psychology and psychiatry.

Psychodynamic Object-Relations Theory. Two other revisionist traditions had more radical aims. Object relations theory, initially associated with the work of Melanie Klein (1882–1960), a child psychoanalyst, mounted a direct assault on orthodox psychoanalysis. Object relations theorists all but abandoned id-ego-superego warfare in favor of assorted models of interpersonal transactions during personality development. With the so-called British object relations school, including D. W. Winnicott (1896–1971), a pediatrician turned psychoanalyst, and W. R. D. Fairbairn and Harry Guntrip, as well as the more contemporary object-relationship theorists in America, such as Margaret Mahler (1897–1985), Heinz Kohut (1913–1981), and Otto Kernberg, psychoanalytic theory addressed earlier and earlier phases of life. The classical war of id passion against ego reason was gone; transactions with "love objects" took the place of drive theory. Parental love, empathy, altruism, trust, and the formation of personal identity became the poles of the psychoanalytic compass and served as the main descriptors of human conduct.

Psychodynamic Neo-Freudian Theory. At about the same time that object relations theory was gaining ground on the interpersonal front, a diverse assortment of thinkers loosely identified as neo-Freudians were also introducing drastic changes into psychoanalysis. Carl G. Jung (1875–1961), the Swiss psychiatrist and, for a brief time, Sigmund Freud's own choice to succeed to the leadership of psychoanalysis, was one of the first "orthodox" analysts to break with the orthodoxy by introducing radically revised conceptions of Freud's ideas. Jung quite literally became a "new" Freudian by supplementing Freud's concept of a personal unconscious with the proposal of a collective unconscious, or storehouse of universal human memories and emotional images, called archetypes. Jung also abandoned Freud's concept of sexual and aggressive drives as central human motivators in favor of a more interpersonal (some would say "transpersonal" or even existential) model of the human self striving toward actualization of its inner destiny.

Other neo-Freudians emerged, each emphasizing some "new" aspect of human personality that Freud had allegedly ignored or underemphasized. Karen Horney (1885–1952) focused psychoanalytic method on fundamental interpersonal issues, such as the basic anxiety of feeling powerless or small, and on neurotic needs, including unsatisfiable strivings for dominance, prestige, and power, or intensely driven dependency desires to have a partner in life take over one's responsibilities. Alfred Adler (1870–1937), the inventor of the "inferiority complex," also left Freudian sexual and aggressive theory behind, preferring to understand people as compensating for their perceived inferiorities by striving for superiority in a lifelong struggle to turn weakness into strength.

By the late 1960s in America, classical psychoanalysis as a theory of personality and as a method of treatment for psychological disorders in the form created by Freud existed only in the history books. The ego psychologists had diminished the role of unconscious conflict as the motor of personality; the object-relations theorists had replaced the cardinal motives of sex and aggression with the interpersonal processes of empathy and identification; and the neo-Freudians had turned the spotlight away from individual unconscious strivings toward cultural and interpersonal transactions. Equally important, empirical research in psychotherapy seemingly demonstrated that psychoanalysis as a treatment for neurosis had been oversold. Behavior therapy emerged from the school of behaviorism to challenge psychoanalysis successfully on the two fronts it had dominated: the theoretical understanding of human nature and the treatment of psychological dysfunction.

The Behaviorisms

Psychodynamic theorists did not doubt that human conduct *had* to be explained in terms of "inner," often unobservable, personality events and states. In contrast, thinkers from the behavioral tradition limit their explanations and inferences to the behavior itself. The laboratory rather than the consulting room became the source of ideas for understanding personality and treating its disorders.

Radical Behaviorism. John Broadus Watson (1878–1958) articulated the first coherent form of radical behaviorism in his 1913 groundbreaking paper published in the journal *Psychological Review*. An admirer of Charles Darwin's theory of evolution, Watson wanted the young discipline of psychology to be scientific and biological rather than literary or philosophic. Watson's influential ideas, typically stated in the most attention-getting and extreme form he could muster, included three assumptions:

1. *Radical empiricism*: Only observable variables that are susceptible to measurement are legitimate for psychological science. Therefore, unobservable, nonempirical entities such as mind, thought, and self-awareness are mere illusions.
2. *Evolutionary continuity*: Watson asserted that there is "no dividing line between man and brute," evolutionarily speaking—a statement which would almost certainly have made Darwin choke. But Watson felt justified in arguing that experimentation with simpler organisms such as rats was the royal scientific road to a systematic understanding of more complex human behavior.
3. *Radical reductionism*: Watson believed that to be scientific, psychology would ultimately have to explain behavior in increasingly reductionistic terms at lower and lower levels of analysis. Thus, he believed that Pavlovian conditioned reflexes were a fundamental unit that explained complex behaviors. With continued research, reflexes would be understood at the level of brain and spinal cord cells, then at the level of the molecules constituting these tissues, then at the level of the atoms constituting the molecules, and so on. One side effect, however, was that personality theory as such ceased to be relevant under radical behaviorism. Personality now was equivalent and limited to observable behavior.

However, it was not until the late 1930s, with B. F. Skinner's (1904–1990) pioneering work in instrumental learning by reinforcement, that radical behaviorism became a dominant force in American psychology and, ironically for a discipline that had dismissed traditional personality phenomena as mere mentalisms, the "new" Skinnerian radical behaviorism gradually increased its impact on personality theory. To his credit, Skinner was less quick than Watson to dismiss Freud's contribution to understanding human affairs and less radical in jettisoning the classical issues of human nature that had engaged philosopher-psychologists throughout the centuries. Instead, Skinner embarked on a program to translate important psychodynamic concepts, such as motivated forgetting (repression) of anxiety-triggering ideas, sexual and aggressive conflicts, and "neurotic" symptoms (e.g., phobia) into scientifically testable hypotheses rooted in the language of instrumental learning taken from the animal laboratory.

Although Skinner himself did not use this term, personality was now understood as the organism's behavioral repertoire in interaction with environmental contingencies of reinforcement. Understand the pattern of rewards and punishments that maintain or suppress behavior and you understand "personality." At core, therefore, Skinner was true to his Watsonian intellectual heritage, and he insisted that a scientific psychology limit its subject matter to observable behavior.

Cognitive Behaviorism and Social Learning. By the mid-1960s, however, a new behaviorism was emerging. Earlier, at Yale University in the 1950s, psychologists Neal Miller and John Dollard had attempted a systematic translation of psychodynamic theory into a reinforcement learning model, but their excellent work received little support from the wider community of psychology. Dollard and Miller had called their effort a *social learning theory* to emphasize their conviction that a full theory of personality had to draw on psychology, anthropology, psychoanalysis, and social psychology. But psychodynamic thinkers felt that the theory trivialized important personality dynamics by resorting to animal experimentation. Scientifically minded psychologists felt that that the theory relied too heavily on untestable psychoanalytic concepts. No one was happy with the result. Consequently, by the mid-1960s the time was right for a "social learning" theory to fill the void if it could boast of no debt to psychodynamic traditions and lay claim to a scientifically respectable heritage in laboratory experimentation. Such a theory could position itself simultaneously to break new ground in personality psychology by exploring cognitive (i.e., mental) phenomena as long as it did so within the context of precise and well-controlled experimentation.

Albert Bandura and Richard H. Walters precisely assembled this combination of ingredients with the publication of their small but influential 1963 monograph *Social Learning and Personality Development*. Behaviorism was growing increasingly cognitive, and mental phenomena which would have given Watson and Skinner apoplectic fits were now deemed suitable psychological fare. Bandura insisted that human behavior was a multidimensional and interactive phenomenon that could be understood only by taking account of multiple and simultaneous determinants, including the organism's expectations and interpretations. This view, called reciprocal determinism, assumes that human behavior can be made scientifically sensible only when a person's private meanings are taken into account. A person's subjective understandings, the environment, and the person's behavior in that environment reciprocally influence and mutually regulate each other.

Bandura's sophisticated interactionist perspective and restoration of psychological variables had wide appeal. Traditional concepts that even classical psychodynamic theorists would find congenial were now central in the new cognitive behavioristic personality theory. Impulse control, identification with models, feelings of helplessness and mastery, personal and interpersonal conflict and defense, consistency of conduct over time and across situations, and many more traditional personality phenomena became the focus of social learning research. Personality, in its full and rich variety, had returned to psychology.

Humanistic and Existential Theory

Orthodox psychoanalysis and radical behaviorism shared at least one significant assumption about human nature. In their most extreme initial statements, both theories pictured people as relatively passive objects who are provoked to react by internal and external stimulation. This passive-agent view of human nature rests on the assumption that behavior is largely or completely determined by powerful forces stemming from the biological constitution of the person and its dependence on the environment. It is true that cognitive behaviorism and contemporary psychodynamic models such as ego psychology and object relations theory were designed in part to circumvent this simplistic viewpoint of their parent theories. It is equally true, however, that an opposing, third point of view emerged in reaction to the more narrowly conceived classical formulations.

"Third Force" Humanistic Theory. Called third-force psychology by Abraham Maslow (1908–1970), one of its pioneering founders, the humanistic viewpoint is an optimistic philosophical statement about the complexity of human nature and an elucidation of human strengths and vulnerabilities more than it is a coherent theory of personality. Maslow's "third-force" theory focused not on the pathology of personality but on the best and brightest self-actualized human beings that Maslow could find in life and in history. For Maslow, who ironically began his career as a behaviorist but became disenchanted with what he perceived to be behaviorism's sterility, the self-actualized person is an exceptional human being who is essentially culturally independent, reality-oriented, and motivated by needs for achievements "higher" than mere survival, including what he called the meta-needs of truth-seeking, beauty-seeking, and order. In a similar vein, but from a clinical-counseling perspective, Carl R. Rogers (1902–1987) constructed a humanistic theory of personality that stressed the developmental importance of parental unconditional positive regard for the child during its critical formative years. Without this unqualified loving acceptance, Rogers argued, the developing person cannot achieve status as a fully functioning person (comparable to Maslow's self-actualized person) with a coherent self capable of independent thought, self-acceptance, and empathy for others.

Humanistic Existential Theory. Humanistic-existential theories can trace at least their most immediate roots to the twentieth century's pre– and post–World War II existential philosophers, who raised questions about humanity's place in the universe, the purpose or aimless absurdity reflected in the choices of an individual life, and the consequences of the unique human ability to anticipate death and worry anxiously about fate. Variants of the humanistic tradition amalgamate psychodynamic principles with existential philosophy. Rollo May (1909–1994), a psychologist who popularized European existentialism in American psychology, created an existential psychoanalysis (or psychoanalytic existentialism) that stressed issues drawn from both camps. May argued that personality was a "process of being" (*Dasein* is the German technical term), a journey rather than a destination, launched in a world fraught with anxiety-triggering chaos and the potentially unpredictable interventions of destiny and fate. As with the European existentialists from whom he borrowed freely, May believed that the unique human capacity to anticipate one's own end could have a powerful shaping influence on the way a person chooses to live. Other notable theorists who adopted the existential viewpoint in their efforts to create a psychodynamic humanism include R. D. Laing (1927–1989) and Erich Fromm (1900–1980), both of whom believed that normal personality functioning always rests on a foundation of personal meaning created with great effort in the face of an otherwise absurd, sometimes petty, and sometimes mean, world.

The most recent psychological trend is toward the construction of narrower, more empirically based and less philosophical models of personality. However, it is unlikely that the grand theories will entirely lose their place in the spotlight. Drawn from psychoanalysis, behaviorism, and humanism, the grand theories address the enduring issues of human existence and often embody the essence of psychology as science and art. They are the psychological constructions of human thinkers reflecting on the psychology of human beings in the search for some common ground between the self and the other.

Bibliography

General and Historical Works on Personality Theories

Allport, G. (1937). *Personality: A psychological interpretation.* New York: Henry Holt. The classic presentation of the historical, philosophical, and psychological roots of the concept of personality that helped establish this field as a subdiscipline of psychology.

Costa, Paul T., & Widiger, Thomas A. (Eds.). (1994). *Personality disorders and the five-factor model of personality.* Washington, DC: American Psychological Association. Survey of research and opinion on a very influential contemporary trait model of personality and its relevance to disorders of personality.

Ellenberger, H. (1970). *The discovery of the unconscious.* New York: Basic Books. A very complete historical account of the development of the psychodynamic tradition in psychology and psychiatry.

Monte, C. F. (1995). *Beneath the mask: An introduction to theories of personality* (5th ed.). New York: Harcourt Brace Jovanovich. Comprehensive and developmental presentation of the main theories of personality, with significant attention to the influence of each theorist's life history on his or her theory. The book is updated regularly.

Stolorow, R. D., & Atwood, G. E. (1979). *Faces in a cloud: Subjectivity in personality theory.* New York: Jason Aronson. An analysis of the contribution of the life experiences of several important theorists to each of their theories.

Works on Classical Psychoanalysis

Freud, S. (1900). *The interpretation of dreams.* In J. Strachey (Ed. and Trans.), *The standard edition of the complete psychological works of Sigmund Freud* (Vols. 4–5). London: Hogarth, 1953. Freud's masterpiece, in which he recounts not only his theories about the nature of dreams, but also his concepts of the structure of the mind and the Oedipus complex.

Freud, S. (1933). *New introductory lectures on psychoanalysis.* In J. Strachey (Ed. and Trans.), *The standard edition of the complete psychological works of Sigmund Freud* (Vol. 22). London: Hogarth, 1964. The best, most concise, and most readable introduction by Freud himself to his theory during the latter part of his career.

Works on Ego Psychology and Object Relations Theory

Freud, A. (1936). *The ego and the mechanisms of defense.* In *The Writings of Anna Freud* (Vol. 2).

Greenberg, J. R., & Mitchell, S. A. (1983). *Object relations in psychoanalytic theory.* Cambridge, MA: Harvard University Press. A scholarly account of the origins, cultural history, and impact of several object relations theories on orthodox psychoanalysis.

Hartmann, H. (1939, 1958). *Ego psychology and the problem of adaptation.* New York: International Universities Press. The classic monograph by the "father of ego psychology" describing the justification for strengthening and widening the classical conception of the ego to include "conflict-free" functioning and adaptation to the interpersonal world.

Works on Radical Behaviorism

Buckley, K. W. (1989). *Mechanical man: John Broadus Watson and the beginnings of behaviorism.* New York: Guilford Press. A thoughtful biography and cultural history of the man who put radical behaviorism on the map, along with a concise introduction to the philosophy of this school.

Skinner, B. F. (1953). *Science and human behavior.* New York: Free Press. Radical behaviorist Skinner translates Freud into learning theory and behavioristic language and analyzes the significance of psychodynamic theory for "scientific" psychology.

Works on Cognitive Behaviorism (Social Learning Theory)

Bandura, A. (1986). *Social foundations of thought and action. A social-cognitive theory.* Englewood Cliffs, NJ: Prentice Hall. The most complete account of the data and theory of contemporary cognitive social learning theory by its founder.

Bandura, A., & Walters, R. (1963). *Social learning and personality development.*

Dollard, J., & N. Miller. (1950). *Personality and psychotherapy: An analysis in terms of learning, thinking and culture.* New York: McGraw-Hill. The first, and still excellent, social learning theory that attempted to translate some psychodynamic ideas into behavioral ones.

Works on Humanistic and Existential Theories

Fromm, E. (1976). *To have or to be?* New York: Harper & Row. A sound introduction to the central issues of existential humanism by a theorist who began his career as a psychoanalyst.

May, Rollo. (1958). The origins and significance of the existential movement in psychology. In R. May, E. Angel, and H. F. Ellenberger (Eds.), *Existence: A new dimension in psychiatry and psychology.* New York: Basic Books. Although old, this book, and the article above, remain the best one-stop source for an introduction to existentialism in psychology.

May, R. (1983). *The discovery of being: Writings in existential psychology.* New York: Norton. A good sampler of the ideas of one of the pioneers in humanistic existential psychodynamic theory.

Christopher F. Monte

Methods of Study

The emergence of personality psychology in the 1930s as a distinct field of scientific inquiry was signaled by the pioneering textbooks of G. W. Allport (*Personality:*

A Psychological Interpretation, 1937) and R. Stagner (*The Psychology of Personality*, 1937). From its very beginnings, personality psychology has had available a wide array of methods of study. These methods seek to capture specific kinds of information essential in the description and understanding of persons.

In its most generic sense, our knowledge of persons derives from a rich variety of sources of information about them, including their everyday conduct; the impressions they make upon others; their self-characterizations; their behavior in standardized test situations; their imaginative and interpretive productions; their life histories and fate in society; and their general reputation in their community.

Methods of study have been devised within personality psychology to examine each of these seven types of information. Historical trends reveal that the scientific attention granted to these methods has fluctuated. Some have shown continued, sustained development and others arrested or interrupted development. Nevertheless, this discipline has been guided by the recognition that scientific investigation of personality requires multiple and diverse forms of inquiry.

Field Studies of Everyday Conduct and Experience

Persons are known by the characteristics of their everyday conduct. For example, one meaning of a personality trait concept such as dominance is that a person so described tends, over a period of observation, to display a relatively high frequency of prototypically dominant acts, such as taking charge of a situation after an accident. Thus, one way in which personality is revealed is through the situated, daily actions of individuals.

Historically, field studies of personality have experienced an interrupted form of development, following important initial attention. For example, in 1929, T. M. Newcomb published his analysis of daily records made by counselors monitoring the extraverted behaviors of boys at a summer camp. In their *One Boy's Day* (1951), R. G. Barker and H. F. Wright required 422 pages to present a comprehensive descriptive record of the ongoing behavior of one lad on 26 April 1949, in Oskaloosa, Kansas. Subsequently, these intensive and promising approaches to field studies of everyday conduct were relatively neglected as a method of personality inquiry.

During the past two decades, however, field studies of personality have gained renewed interest. One concern has dealt with the flow of experience in naturally occurring situations and its implications for the subjective well-being of the person. A second focus has been on the manifestation of personality dispositions in everyday life, as monitored by the frequency of an individual's trait-prototypic acts.

The methodological challenge of field studies of conduct and experience is to move investigations out of personality assessment centers and laboratories and into the everyday settings in which persons live their lives. Recent technical developments are facilitating this endeavor. In studies using experience sampling, small, portable, freely programmable microcomputers can be attached to a person's belt and serve as both report prompter and recorder. Programmed for a time-sampling design, the computer sounds a beeper and the research participant enters coded information about setting, emotion, intentions, and behavior at the time of the beep. For analyses of an individual's entire day's activities, monitoring teams tracking persons within their daily environments can supplement their written descriptions by continuous video recordings made with miniaturized, battery-powered video cameras and wireless clip-on microphones. Finally, miniaturized physiological monitors can provide continuous indicators for stress and emotional state.

The goal of field methods is to achieve greater ecological validity for personality research. Studying the ongoing experience and everyday conduct of persons in their ordinary settings requires attention to a number of methodological issues. First, the extent to which participants in field studies react to being observed and monitored places some limitation on the naturalness of the results. Thus, reactivity must be systematically studied. Second, the flow of experience and conduct must ultimately be coded into one or more categorization systems. These conceptual and procedural options must then be systematically examined. Finally, the selection of research topics may reveal a cumulative selection bias, either toward the typical, humdrum, and quotidian facets of a person's life on the one hand, or the unusual but consequential and revealing episodes on the other. How to strike a scientifically useful balance requires consideration in its own right.

Observer-Based Assessments

Persons are known through the impressions they make on others. Thus, the human observer is an important instrument for monitoring and interpreting information about the personality of individuals. Furthermore, ordinary language is rich in terms to describe persons.

Historically, observer-based assessments of personality have enjoyed continuous attention and a steady form of development. For example, in his *Judging Human Character* (1922), H. L. Hollingworth had summarized research on the use of trait ratings and similar instruments and had identified many of the issues entailed in their use. Four decades later, in *The Q-sort Method in Personality Assessment and Psychiatric Research* (1961), J. Block offered an explicit rationale for using observer impressions in personality assessment, emphasizing the aggregation of independently rendered judgments by multiple observers for achieving and documenting the reliability of these measures. More recently, D. A. Kenny, in *Interpersonal Perception: A Social Relations Analysis* (1994), gave an overview of basic questions that must be addressed by research investigating perception of persons and, thus, the processes by which observers describe other individuals.

The goal of observer-based assessment of personality is to make full use of the integrative interpretive skills that human observers possess for monitoring and depicting the personality of other individuals. The tools available in everyday life for conveying these impressions of others include the rendering of narrative accounts of their typical and salient acts and deeds, and the use of trait-descriptive adjectives.

A series of studies beginning in the 1920s has been devoted to compiling the full domain of ordinary language trait-descriptors and examining the structure revealed by their co-occurrent usage by observers in describing persons. This extended research program has identified at least five major bipolar personality dimensions (i.e., the "Big Five" factors): extraversion (e.g., outgoing versus reserved); agreeableness (e.g., sympathetic versus fault-finding), conscientiousness (e.g., organized action versus careless); emotional stability (e.g., calm versus anxious); and openness (e.g., imaginative versus the commonplace).

The bipolar-trait rating format has long provided a flexible method for gathering observer judgments of personality. For comparative purposes, the selection of trait descriptors can be guided by the Big Five factor dimensions. In contrast to rating scales, the adjective checklist (ACL) format allows observers to move quickly through a larger array of trait descriptors in depicting a person (for a standard version widely used in research, see the *Adjective Check List Manual*, Palo Alto, CA, 1983, by H. G. Gough and A. B. Heilbrun, Jr.). Another widely used observational assessment instrument is the California Q-set, introduced by J. Block in 1961. This procedure entails a standard set of descriptive phrases (e.g., "has insight into own motives and behaviors," "is critical, skeptical, not easily impressed") that are sorted by the observer according to their relative value in characterizing the person being depicted. Finally, in contrast to these structured formats, observers can be encouraged to generate a free description of the person, as in the form of character sketches, letters of recommendation, obituaries, and eulogies.

An informed use of observer-based assessments of personality entails a recognition that reliable findings must be empirically demonstrated and require an aggregation of judgments recorded independently by a panel of observers. Furthermore, some persons are described with greater consensus than others, and some facets of personality are judged with greater agreement than others. Finally, in interpreting findings, the context of the observational assessment must be taken into account, for example, the type of acquaintance between the observer and the target person, the amount of overlap in observation among assessors, and the nature of any prior communication among them.

Personality Scales and Inventories

Persons are known through their own self-reflective assertions and claims about themselves. Thus, the self-descriptions of individuals about their own actions, beliefs, emotions, habits, interests, and other characteristics offer an important form of information about their personality.

Historically, personality scales and inventories have experienced a continuous form of scientific development and emerged between 1945 and 1980 as the predominant method of study in personality psychology. Early landmarks included the 1917 Woodworth Personal Data Sheet, a multi-item scale for psychoneurotic tendencies, and a series of multiscale inventories assessing interest patterns, personal values, traits, and psychopathological tendencies: the Strong Vocational Interest Blank (1927), the Vernon and Allport Study of Values (1931), the Bernreuter Personality Inventory (1932), and the Minnesota Multiphasic Personality Inventory (1943), respectively.

A major purpose of personality scales and inventories has been the prediction of important interpersonal and life outcomes. An overview of this research tradition was provided by J. S. Wiggins in his *Personality and Prediction: Principles of Personality Assessment* (1973). These methods of study have contributed to research on how personality characteristics interact with contextual factors in an understanding of such topics as creative accomplishment, managerial effectiveness, marital satisfaction, and subjective well-being. The applied aspiration has been to facilitate personal decision-making regarding important life choices and self-development, as well as institutional decision-making regarding the selection and assignments of newcomers in organizations and institutions.

At least three broad strategies of personality scale development have been employed. In the deductive approach, the constructs to be assessed are derived from theoretical orientations. For example, the Myers-Briggs Type Indicator was inspired by C. G. Jung's formulation of psychological types, while both the Personality Research Form and Gough and Heilbrun's ACL scales were guided by H. A. Murray's taxonomy of needs.

In the inductive approach, scale constructs emerge from factor analysis of the structure of relevant domains of items or terms. Such instruments include the Eysenck Personality Inventory and the Sixteen Personality Factor Questionnaire. In addition, the NEO Personality Inventory builds upon the Big Five factor structure of trait descriptors.

The external approach anchors constructs in real-world designations. This strategy is represented by three inventories initially based on indicators of folk concepts (the California Psychological Inventory) psychodiagnostic categories (the Minnesota Multiphasic Personality Inventory), and occupational categories (the Strong-Campbell Interest Inventory). Although emphasis on one strategy or another has fluctuated over time, it is evident from these examples that each approach is capable of generating inventories useful in research and practice.

A major challenge for this method of study is to demonstrate that personality scales provide information above and beyond the self-reported endorsements of their item content. In response, this tradition of research has achieved an impressive array of self-critical strengths and standards, with the role of aggregation being recognized in achieving adequate levels of reliability. For some inventories, special scales and other techniques have been employed to identify and take into account test-taking intentions, for example, to create a favorable impression ("faking good") or negative impression ("faking bad"). Construct validation, conceptual analysis, and heterotrait-heteromethod matrices have yielded empirically based, cumulative evidence for many scales regarding the psychological meaning and implications of their scores. Obviously, these achievements also hold relevance for the critical analysis of measures generated by other methods of personality study.

Standard Test Situations

Persons are known by how they react to specific kinds of challenges and tasks. Thus, how persons perform in standard test situations provides an important source of information about their personality. In addition, systematic examination of sources of influence on behavior in such controlled situations can generate knowledge about the dynamics of person-situation transactions.

Historically, this method of study has experienced a continuous form of scientific prominence in personality psychology. In their *Studies in the Nature of Character (Volumes 1–3*, 1928–1930), H. Harthshorne, M. A. May, and F. K. Shuttleworth reported on the use of an ingenious set of standard situations to examine differences among children in their honesty and dishonesty (for example, receiving more than the correct change, having the opportunity to cheat at a party game and on an examination). In *A Dynamic Theory of Personality* (1935), K. Lewin summarized his research team's laboratory investigations of such topics as level of aspiration and selective memory for interrupted tasks. The use of standard situations was an important feature of pioneering personality assessment center programs, such as that for the U.S. Office of Strategic Services (*Assessment of Men*, 1949). Standard elicitors, such as films of industrial accidents, continue to play an important role in psychophysiological studies of stress and emotion.

Standard test situations have been used in personality psychology for two purposes; first, to examine the parameters of the situated behavior and sources of influence in systematic fashion, and second, to identify the implications of variations among persons in their conduct within a situation. Thus, this method of study is valuable in the analysis of personality dynamics and in the assessment of individual differences in personality. For example, standard situations have tested the extent to which children voluntarily delay use or consumption of rewards (e.g., toys and candies). They have been used to examine factors influencing the delay of gratification, such as the direction of attention away from the reward, or participation in distracting activities.

In addition, individual differences among children in their delay of gratification within such test situations have been related to concurrent observer descriptions of being planful and reflective, and to later ratings on self-control in adolescence. Similarly, a procedure devised by S. Asch for gauging an individual's resistance to group pressure has been used both to identify situational factors influencing conformity behavior and to assess individual differences in independence of judgment. Finally, two noteworthy situational procedures have been widely used in assessment centers to measure individual differences in interpersonal and strategic styles. The Leaderless Group Discussion brings together six unacquainted persons to analyze and resolve a problem. The In-Basket Test engages a person to role-play a decision-maker dealing with the varied issues typically found in a manager's in-basket.

As in instances of multiple observers and multiple scale items for other methods, the informed use of standard test situations entails the recognition that aggregation of multiple measures is required to achieve reliability. An important distinction must be drawn between the use of standard situations for assessing individual differences and their use in gauging the relative influence of a person's characteristics versus situational factors in explaining variations in the situated conduct. For the latter purpose, this method is constrained in certain respects because the personalities of individuals are manifested as much in the situations they select and shape in their everyday lives as in their conduct within any specific situations established by the researcher.

Imaginative and Constructive Techniques

Persons are known through expressions of their imaginative life and the ways they construe their life experiences. Thus, the distinctive products that persons generate through their perceptions and interpretations, fantasies, stories, and other imaginative and constructive formats yield information about their personalities.

Historically, imaginative and constructive techniques have experienced a continuous development, with a period of particularly strong prominence during the 1940s through the 1960s. Projective techniques made an early appearance: in 1910, C. G. Jung published his pioneering applications of the word association method, and in 1921 H. Rorschach reported on his inkblot test in *Psychodiagnostics: A Diagnostic Test Based on Perception*. Subsequently, C. D. Morgan and H. A. Murray gave the first account of their Thematic Apperception Test (TAT) in 1935, and G. A. Kelly introduced his Role Construct Repertory Test (Rep Test) in 1955 in *The Psychology of Personal Constructs*.

The aim of imaginative and constructive techniques is to provide stimulus materials and tasks that evoke the apperceptive and interpretive capacities and styles of individuals. Thus, for example, they ask persons to indicate what they perceive as the possibilities in the form, color, and shading of symmetric inkblots (Rorschach inkblots), what story line might surround a particular picture (TAT), and what psychological attributes they construe as differentiating among significant individuals in their lives (Rep Test).

Imaginative and constructive techniques continue to be found among current methods in the study of personality. J. Loevinger's Sentence Completion Test of Ego Development (SCT) adapts a format first introduced in the 1920s, in which a person is presented with a set of sentence beginnings and asked to complete them. An SCT manual provides a scoring system for six sequential stages of ego development: impulsive, self-protective, conformist, conscientious, autonomous, and integrated.

The research tradition inspired by analyzing the narratives elicited from the TAT has generated scoring systems for coding stories on such motives as achievement, affiliation, intimacy, and power. The coding systems have also been adapted for more general use by D. C. McClelland, D. G. Winter, and others to score motive patterns in children's readers, political documents and speeches, literary texts, and other imaginative verbal productions. In a further extension of this approach, D. P. McAdams's life-story method employs a standard interview elicitation schedule to explore an individual's personal identity (see his *Stories We Live By: Personal Myths and the Making of the Self*, 1993). The analysis examines the individual's life story through consideration of the narrative's affective tone, imagery, motive patterns, core episodes, key characters, and ideological setting.

One challenge for imaginative-constructive methods of study has been to achieve a shift from the use of the techniques by individual interpreters in clinical professional practice to their application in scientific research, with its standards of reproducibility and validity. Contemporary research techniques for this method of study are typically accompanied by coding systems and training manuals aimed at affording adequate levels of interscorer reliability. Research use is expected to address such potentially distorting influences as individual differences in verbal productivity. Furthermore, the techniques are employed within empirical research programs that can yield cumulative evidence for gauging their construct validity and predictive utility as measures of personality (see C. Smith [Ed.], *Motivation and Personality: Handbook of Thematic Content Analysis*, 1992).

Life History Analysis

Persons are known by the kinds of lives they have lived. In this sense, much of our knowledge concerning the personality of individuals can be considered to be historical in nature. Although the amount of information available about their pasts may vary among persons, nevertheless, such information offers an important source for understanding their personality.

Historically, within personality psychology, the method of individual life history analysis has experienced interrupted development. Attention to psychological biography was prominent within the field in the 1920s and 1930s. As a guide for researchers in psychology and other social sciences, J. Dollard published his *Criteria for Life History Analysis* in 1935, and in 1942 G. W. Allport examined the value of such sources as autobiographical accounts, diaries, and letters in his *Use of Personal Documents in Psychological Science*. Erik Erikson's *Childhood and Society* (1950) included analyses of the early lives of Maxim Gorky and Adolf Hitler, which was followed by his studies of Martin Luther and Mohandas K. Gandhi. However, the field's interest in the analysis of individual life histories declined from the mid-1940s through the 1960s. Subsequent revival of attention to this method of study was signaled by W. M. Runyan's integrative 1982 volume *Life Histories and Psychobiography: Explorations in Theory and Method*.

The aim of life history analysis is to achieve an objective account of the events and experiences of a person's life from birth until death. As a method of study of personality, the analysis of individual life histories must be informed by explicit use of psychological knowledge, organized within the framework of life-span personality development, situated within the person's socio-cultural context, and compiled, conducted, and interpreted using the methods of historical research. Life histories of this kind draw upon both personal life stories rendered by the individuals themselves and community-generated life stories about them offered by their life-long circle of acquaintances. However, a life history analysis integrates them with other sources of information in aspiring to achieve an overarching and objective account of the person's life.

Approaches to life history marshall the investigative resources of personality psychology and several other fields of inquiry. The cumulative craft wisdom of biographical studies is drawn upon by A. C. Elms in his *Uncovering Lives: The Uneasy Alliance of Biography and Psychology* (1994). The methods of historical inquiry are pertinent to treating an individual life as history in their sensitivity to the fragmentary survival of evidence, commitment to chronological and causal accounts, textual skepticism, and attention to corroboration, sourcing, and context. The relevance of these endeavors is reviewed in W. M. Runyan's *Psychology and Historical Interpretation* (1988). Longitudinal research programs that monitor persons over many years of their lives are providing pertinent empirical generalizations and conceptual frameworks for analyzing individuals and their personalities over the course of their lives. The application of specific statistical techniques, such as time series analysis, has been advanced by D. K. Simonton (see his *Genius and Creativity: Selected Papers*, 1997).

A number of challenges face the development of individual life history analysis as a method of study in personality psychology. The strengths and limitations of the case study as a mode of inquiry are appraised by D. P. Bromley in *The Case Study Method in Psychology and Related Disciplines* (1986). More specifically, many key events in the life of a person are open to an abundance of possible interpretations; analyses are required for critically evaluating alternatives with regard to their explanatory value. From a broader perspective, criteria must be established for gauging progress in the overall understanding of any particular individual's life history. As in any area of sustained inquiry, progress in life history analysis will require a substantial community of mutually critical scholars and scientists in order to advance an open, consensually shared, and evolving area of knowledge.

Reputational Analysis

Persons are known through their reputations in society at large. How they have become collectively represented throughout their social networks is a product of ongoing community observation and communication. Thus, a person's prevailing reputation is an inescapable part of social reality for the individual as well as a source of information about their personality.

Historically, reputational analysis has experienced an arrested form of scientific development within personality psychology. M. A. May's dual conception of personality viewed the person not only as a self-reflexive agent of action but also as an entity whose "social stimulus value" is perceived by others (see his "The foundations of personality" in P. S. Achilles's *Psychology at Work*, 1933). However, in his influential *Personality: A Psychological Interpretation* (1937), G. W. Allport rejected reputational analysis as a focus for the study of personality, and development of the method thereafter has lagged. Recent efforts finally to initiate programmatic research using this method of study are reviewed in D. P. Bromley's *Reputation, Image and Impression Management* (1993).

The goal of reputational analysis is to make use of the ways in which persons are collectively represented in their own communities as a source of information about their personalities. In doing so, this method of study draws upon the ongoing and pervasive opportunities of community members to learn about an individual's conduct, and their capacity to interpret and communicate direct observations and secondhand information in forming their beliefs and opinions about a person.

To assess reputation, the size and boundaries of a person's social network must be gauged and its membership specified. Means of representative sampling from this community of potential informants must be employed. Studies reported in such journals as *Social Networks* are examining these procedural issues. Recording techniques encompass those used in observer-based assessment, such as free descriptions, trait ratings, adjective checklists, Q-sortings, and others. Analysis of the structure of these descriptive portrayals of the reputation of a person, derived from representative community members, may reveal that a strongly consensual portrait exists, or that a set of multiple depictions prevails, or that generally low levels of agreement among informants is found.

Reputations evolve during a person's lifetime and, to a varying extent, posthumously. Reputational depictions are typically retrospective and may lag behind changes in an individual's conduct and life circumstances. Periods of challenge and crisis, such as job change or severe illness, may evoke a fresh new look by community members and a revision of the person's reputation. Reputation holds consequences for persons regarding decision-making about them by other individuals and institutions, and can be viewed as an asset or liability. Thus, to varying degrees, persons exert efforts to achieve an accurate awareness of their prevailing reputations and to influence the reputational process and product. Legal systems typically seek a degree of fairness in the reputational process by affording recourse to remedies for libel and slander that circulate falsely to third parties, and by property laws for protecting any commercial value of a person's name, image, and associated reputation.

Employing reputational analysis as a method of personality study requires an understanding of the social processes that generate reputation. Reputation derives from transactions between the conduct of a person and that individual's social network, and emerges from the flow of communication via such modes as gossip, chat, and confidences. Greater knowledge is required of factors influencing the spread, density, and durability of information about persons. Although community members share an interest in maintaining the predictive validity of the collective representations of individuals, more tendentious aims of bolstering or denigrating reputations of others must also be understood and taken into account in the use of this method of study.

Conclusion

Historical trends reveal an uneven distribution of scientific attention and investment among different kinds of information about personality and the methods associated with them. Observer-based assessment methods, personality scales and inventories, standard test situations, and imaginative-constructive techniques have enjoyed steady attention and use. In contrast, field studies of everyday conduct, life history analyses, and reputational analyses have suffered from relative neglect during certain periods in the scientific development of personality psychology. The present situation resembles the founding era of the field. Broad-based commitment to all methods of inquiry is evident, although the challenge to achieve greater integration among them remains.

Personality psychologists employ their methods separately or in combination, depending on the purpose of the scientific investigation or applied program. A challenge to personality psychology is to integrate all of these forms of information into an overall sense of the person as a whole. This task constitutes both a conceptual challenge that must be addressed by personality theorists and a methodological challenge to personality assessors, to organize and examine the interrelationships among varied forms of information about persons. Thus, from its outset in the 1930s, personality psychology has featured multimethod personality assessment programs, in which diverse methods are employed to assess the same sample of persons (see, for example, H. A. Murray's classic *Explorations in Personality*, 1938).

Finally, a distinction is useful between these methods of study as sources of personality data on the one hand, and research design and analysis on the other. The methods of study we have reviewed can be employed within many types of research design, including the naturalistic, quasi-experimental, and experimental modes. Furthermore, personality data generated in this fashion can be interpreted by various analytic approaches, including narrative case studies, behavioral genetic analysis, generational cohort analysis, social relations analysis, and cross-cultural comparison. These approaches, in turn, are often used in conjunction with statistical techniques such as correlational and factor analysis, analysis of variance, structural equation techniques, and other forms of multivariate statistical analysis. However, the methods of study in personality psychology deal with the heart of the matter, yielding that array of information holding distinctive importance for describing and understanding individual persons as they live and experience their lives within their communities.

Bibliography

Angleitner, A., & Wiggins, J. S. (Eds.). (1986). *Personality assessment via questionnaires: Current issues in theory and measurement*. New York: Springer-Verlag. An overview of issues in the construction and interpretation of personality scales and inventories.

Craik, K. H. (1986). Personality research methods: An historical perspective. *Journal of Personality, 54*, 18–51. A treatment of comparative patterns of historical development among methods of study and the implications of methodological pluralism.

Emler, N. (1990). A social psychology of reputation. In W. Stroebe, & M. Hewstone (Eds.), *European review of social psychology* (Vol. 1, pp. 171–193). New York: Wiley. An analysis of the social dynamics of the reputational process.

Funder, D. C., & West, S. G. (Eds.). (1993). Viewpoints on personality: Consensus, self-other agreement, and accuracy in personality judgment. Special issue. *Journal of Personality, 61*, 457–807. An overview of research issues concerning observer-based assessments of personality.

Goldberg, L. R. (1971). A historical survey of personality scales and inventories. In P. McReynolds (Ed.), *Advances in personality assessment* (Vol. 2, pp. 293–336). Palo Alto, CA: Consulting Psychologists Press. Thorough coverage of the early historical development of personality scales and inventories.

Gough, H. G., & Bradley, P. (1996). *CPI manual* (3rd ed.). Palo Alto, CA: Consulting Psychologists Press. An illustration of the empirical and interpretive information provided by comprehensive contemporary manuals for multiscale personality inventories, in this case, the California Psychological Inventory (CPI).

John, O. P. (1990). The "Big Five" factor taxonomy: Dimensions of personality in the natural language and in questionnaires. In L. A. Pervin (Ed.), *Handbook of personality: Theory and research* (pp. 66–100). New York: Guilford Press. An historical overview of the emergence and implications of the "Big Five" dimensions of personality identified in observer-based trait descriptions of other persons.

Loevinger, J. (1979). Construct validity of the sentence completion test of ego development. *Applied Psychological Measurement, 3*, 281–311. An illustration of the kinds of empirical evidence that can be gathered for gauging the validity of research-oriented imaginative-constructive methods of personality study.

McAdams, D. P., & Ochberg, R. L. (Eds.). (1988). Psychobiography and life narratives. Special issue. *Journal of Personality, 56*, 1–326. A sampling of developments emerging from the revival of life history analysis as a method of personality study.

Shoda, Y., Mischel, W., & Peake, P. K. (1990). Predicting adolescent cognitive and self-regulatory competencies from preschool delay of gratification: Identifying diagnostic conditions. *Developmental Psychology, 26*, 978–986. Illustrates the use of standard test situations for investigating dynamic processes, conditions, and long-term implications of individual differences with regard to delay of gratification.

Tennen, H., Suls, J., & Affleck, G. (Eds.). (1991). Personality and daily experience. Special issue. *Journal of Personality, 59* 313–662. Illustrative research in the use of field studies for investigating daily events and experiences.

Walsh, W. B., & Betz, N. E. (1995). *Tests and assessments* (3rd ed.). Englewood Cliffs, NJ: Prentice Hall. An introduction to assessment methods and their applications.

West, S. G. (Ed.). (1986). Methodological developments in personality research. Special issue. *Journal of Personality, 54*, 1–331. A survey of methodological approaches and issues in the study of personality.

Kenneth H. Craik

PERSONALITY TRAITS. People love to talk about personality. We can spend hours discussing the characteristics of individuals, such as the grumpiness of our boss, the cheerfulness of the plumber, and even the loyalty of our dog. When people talk about personality, they often use traits. For example, when asked to write a personality description of a friend, many students produce a list of personality trait descriptors. (The 10 most frequently generated traits are friendly, caring, intelligent, happy, lazy, moody, shy, outgoing, selfish, and kind; John, 1990, p. 92). Apparently, laypeople think that traits are central to personality.

Likewise, some personality researchers consider traits as the major units of personality. For example, Hofstee (1984) stated plainly that "personality psychology is about traits" (p. 75), and Buss (1989) entitled an article "Personality as Traits." Obviously, there is more to personality than traits, but traits have clearly loomed large throughout the history of personality psychology.

What Is a Trait?

Broadly speaking, personality traits are consistent patterns in the way individuals behave, feel, and think. For example, when we describe an individual as "kind," we mean that this individual tends to act in a kind manner over time (both last week and this week) and across situations (both with the elderly neighbor and with the lame dog). This broad definition implies that traits can serve three major functions: They may be used to summarize, to predict, and to explain a person's conduct.

Traits provide economical ways to summarize how one person differs from another; attributing the trait "kind" to a person summarizes a history of many different acts of kindness. Traits allow us to make predictions about the person's future behavior; the bride expects the kind bridegroom to become a kind husband. Finally, traits suggest that the explanation for the person's behavior will be found in the individual rather than in the situation; a kind person will act kindly even when there is no situational pressure or external reward for doing so, thus suggesting some internal process or mechanism that is producing the behavior. This analysis of the trait concept is consistent with causal attribution theory, which views traits as stable and internal and thus as distinct from states that are temporary and externally caused. According to many psychologists, furthermore, traits are also conceptually and empirically distinct from motives (e.g., the need for affiliation) measured with projective techniques, such as the Thematic Apperception Test.

This broad characterization generally captures how traits are conceptualized in the current literature on personality. However, it is also somewhat vague and glosses over a number difficult and unresolved issues. Part of the problem is the conceptual pluralism and diversity that characterize the field of trait psychology. It is difficult, if not impossible, to generate a generally accepted definition of the trait concept in part because "traits are many things to many theorists" (Wiggins, 1997, p. 98). Indeed, a recent issue of the journal *Psychological Inquiry* was devoted to an extensive critique of the trait concept (Pervin, 1994), followed by a debate about its definition, conceptual status, and empirical foundation. This debate shows considerable disagreement on various issues, even among trait advocates, and the reader is advised to consult this excellent source for further background and detail. In this article, we focus on the major issues that have concerned trait researchers and review the contributions they have made.

What Are the Major Personality Traits?

Like any field of scientific study, research on personality traits needs a descriptive model, or taxonomy, of its subject matter. Such a taxonomy would permit researchers to study specified domains of traits rather than examining separately the thousands of particular traits that might make human beings individual and unique. Over the past 40 years, the number of personality concepts, and of scales designed to measure them, has escalated, and there is no end in sight. Researchers as well as applied personality assessors are faced with a bewildering array of trait measures from which to choose. In the English language alone, there are more than five thousand words describing personality traits. As Cattell (1965) put it, "The trouble with measuring traits is that there are too many of them!" (p. 55). Finding a way to organize all these different traits into a coherent structure has been a major concern of trait researchers.

Numerous proposals for such an overarching structure have been made. Some models were derived on a purely theoretical basis, such as Block's constructs of ego resilience and ego control and Jung's personality types operationalized in the popular Myers-Briggs Type Indicator. Most empirical models have been based on factor analysis, a statistical technique that can identify groups of related traits. For example, the traits talkative, gregarious, and outgoing form a correlated cluster, suggesting an underlying factor of sociability. One of the pioneers of the factor-analytic approach was Cattell (1965), who concluded that as many as 16 personality factors were needed to account for individual differences in personality traits. Cattell's model was not generally accepted, in part because the 16 "primary" factors measured by his 16PF questionnaire were not independent but intercorrelated.

At about the same time, Eysenck, Guilford, and others developed and promoted their own models of personality structure (and associated personality inventories). These models differed not only from Cattell's but also from each other. Eysenck (1967) argued against overlapping primary factors, instead favoring a smaller number of unrelated secondary or "super-factors." Eysenck's P-E-N model postulates three broad super-factors: Psychoticism includes traits typically related to delinquency, such as aggression, antisocial behavior, and impulsivity. Extraversion implies an energetic approach to the social and material world and includes traits such as sociability, activity, and assertiveness. Neuroticism contrasts emotional stability and even-temperedness with negative emotionality, such as feeling anxious, nervous, sad, and tense.

For years, debates raged among the proponents of these and many other models regarding the number and nature of the basic dimensions of personality traits, and the field remained fragmented and in disarray. Since the 1980s, a gradual improvement in the quality and sophistication of methods, especially factor analysis, has led to the beginning of a consensus. Many researchers now agree that traits can be usefully organized in terms of five broad bipolar dimensions (John, 1990; Costa & McCrae, 1992); they are widely known as the "Big Five," not because they are so great but because of their extraordinary breadth and level of abstraction. Extraversion (vs. Introversion) and Neuroticism (vs. Emotional Stability) are essentially the same as in Eysenck's model. Agreeableness (vs. Antagonism) and Conscientiousness (vs. Lack of Direction) are independent dimensions that importantly differentiate the low end of what Eysenck conceptualized as a unitary dimension of Psychoticism. Finally, Openness to Experience (vs. Closed-mindedness) describes the breadth, depth, and complexity of an individual's mental and experiential life and has its roots in several of Cattell's primary factors (e.g., imaginative, experimenting).

A frequent objection to structural models like the Big Five is that a few broad dimensions cannot possibly capture all of the variance in personality traits. This objection overlooks the fact that personality traits need to be conceptualized within a hierarchical structure. In Costa and McCrae's (1992) NEO Personality Inventory-Revised, a questionnaire commonly used to measure the Big Five, each of the five super-factors is defined in terms of six more specific facets or primary traits, each of which is defined by eight even more specific items. From this hierarchical perspective, the debate between Eysenck and Cattell about the correct number of factors really reflects different preferences: for a few very broad constructs or for a larger number of more narrowly defined constructs.

With its hierarchical underpinnings, the Big Five structure can help bring order to the vast number of trait concepts and allow researchers to identify and articulate similarities and differences among the many alternative models of personality structure. For example, the Negative Emotionality and Constraint dimensions from Tellegen's Multidimensional Personality Questionnaire can be mapped onto the Big Five dimensions of Neuroticism and Conscientiousness, respectively. However, the Big Five structure is not the last word in trait taxonomies; research continues to determine how best to interpret and label the factors, which specific facets constitute the factors, and whether there are other basic dimensions yet to be discovered. Some researchers have argued that the Big Five structure ignores evaluative aspects of personality and that two additional, highly evaluative dimensions are needed in addition to the Big Five.

How Are Traits Measured?

Another long-standing concern is how traits should be assessed. Traits are individual difference dimensions, like physical height or weight, along which individuals can be ordered. However, unlike physical characteristics, personality traits are hypothetical constructs that can never be observed directly. Instead, they must be inferred. Moreover, there is no single perfect measure of a trait; trait assessment must therefore rely on multiple measurements. Thus, the demonstration of converging evidence across methods has been an important goal of trait assessment and has led to an approach to measurement known as *construct validation* (Cronbach & Meehl, 1955).

Because each data source has unique strengths and limitations, the construct validation approach emphasizes that we should collect data from *lots* of different sources (Cattell, 1965) and so the acronym LOTS has particular appeal.

L data refer to life event data that can be obtained fairly objectively from the individual's life history or life record, such as graduating from college, getting married or divorced, and joining organizations. For example, police records of arrests and convictions have been used as a measure of Psychoticism.

O data refer to judgments by observers, ranging from observations of specific aspects of behavior to more global ratings. Examples are systematic observations, behavior rated from videotapes, and reports from knowledgeable informants such as peers and spouses. *O* data obtained through unobtrusive observations can be particularly useful to make trait inferences, such as using the individual's seating position relative to a stranger as a measure of extraversion.

T data refer to information from test situations that provide standardized measures of motivation, performance, or achievement and from experimental procedures that have clear and objective rules for scoring performance. Examples include the length of time an individual persists in working on a puzzle or delays gratification in a standardized situation.

Last, but not least, there are *S* data that refer to self-reports. Self-reports have been the staple diet in trait assessment, and hundreds of personality questionnaires have been developed. Compared to the other methods, asking the person directly is a very efficient way of collecting information about traits. In general, individuals are in a good position to report on their own traits because they have access to their private thoughts and feelings and can observe themselves over time and across situations. However, some theorists have argued that self-reports are not the best way to measure personality traits because self-reports may be biased by socially desirable response tendencies. Two kinds of biases have been studied extensively. *Impression management* refers to deliberate attempts to misrepresent one's personality (e.g., "faking good"), and *self-deceptive enhancement* refers to honestly held but unrealistic self-views. Impression management appears to have little effect in research contexts where individuals participate anonymously and are not motivated to present themselves in a positive light; self-deception is not simply a response style but is related to substantive personality traits, such as disagreeableness and narcissism.

What Do Traits Predict?

Measures based on *L*, *O*, and *T* data can help evaluate the validity of the more easily obtained self-report measures. Such multimethod designs are needed to establish empirically how much trait assessments converge across methods. This is a topic of much current research activity; for an excellent overview, see the special issue of the *Journal of Personality* (Funder & West, 1993). When reliable measures are used, *S* and *O* data show substantial convergent validity; self-peer and self-spouse validity correlations for the Big Five exceed .50 (Costa & McCrae, 1992).

There have been fewer studies examining whether self-report trait measures can predict *T* and *L* data, but findings are beginning to accumulate. Self-report measures have been shown to predict diverse behaviors, such as arrival times at meetings, smiling and laughter, and performance on creativity tests, as well as important life outcomes, such as performance at school and at work, delinquency, heart disease, and mortality. Whether a person does well in school, shoplifts, or dies early are complex and multiply determined variables, which themselves are difficult to measure reliably and validly and include a good portion of chance (e.g., being struck by lightning). As one would expect, therefore, the validity correlations in these studies range from the .20s to the .50s. These effect sizes do not indicate that traits are unimportant but rather that other factors also play a role. Validity correlations of .30 have sometimes been criticized as "explaining only 10% of the variance," seemingly suggesting that these effects are small and of little value. However, the meaning of correlational effect sizes is now better understood; we know that even correlations of .30 represent substantial and important effects, enhancing the ability to predict outcomes from 50:50 chance levels to 65:35, that is, an improvement of 30% in the accuracy of prediction. Because personality traits predict job performance, they are frequently used in personnel selection.

What Are the Origins of Traits?

A third theme in research on personality traits is the origin of the stable individual differences we see in adulthood. Much research has focused on the "nature-nurture" issue: whether adult personality traits reflect inheritance, environmental experiences, or both. For a long time, some psychologists were reluctant to accept the view that personality has a genetic basis, emphasizing instead the importance of the family environment, such as the effects of parenting. However, at this point, a fair amount of data indicate that both genetic and environmental factors play an important role.

Research designed to determine the genetic and environmental contributions to personality traits has mostly relied on twin designs. Researchers have compared the similarity of the personality traits of identical twins (who share 100% of their genes) with the similarity of fraternal twins (who share about 50% of their genes). By comparing twins reared together in the same family with twins reared apart, researchers have estimated the effects of genes, shared family environment, and unique environment (i.e., experiences not shared with the other twin). The conclusions are remarkably consistent. Genetic factors account for about half of the reliable variance. The other half is explained by factors related to the unique environment, whereas the shared family environment seems to have few if any systematic effect. These effects were demonstrated initially for the temperamentally based Extraversion and Neuroticism factors (Eysenck, 1967), but they seem to hold equally for all of the Big Five dimensions (Loehlin, McCrae, Costa, & John, 1998).

These findings were surprising, less for showing that genetic factors are important than for emphasizing the effects of the unique environment. Much current research focuses on the processes that make the children growing up in the same family experience the family environment so differently. Sulloway (1996) marshaled evidence for the importance of birth order, arguing that children compete with their siblings and create unique niches within the family. Harris (1995) emphasized that the peer group and other experiences outside the family create a unique environment for the child. In short, the "nurture hypothesis" is no longer viewed as the single or even the dominant influence on personality; it is now undisputed that biological factors also influence what the individual learns and how personality develops. Somewhat ironically, the research initially aimed to demonstrate the importance of genes has led to new discoveries about the kinds of environmental experiences that may impact the developing individual.

The finding that all of the Big Five dimensions have a genetic basis has encouraged a renewed search for the biological processes underlying personality traits. Some (although not all) trait researchers have long believed that traits refer to "neuropsychic entities" that would one day be discovered (Allport, 1968). Early research on temperament traits (i.e., those that emerge early in life) provided indirect evidence: some individual differences are present at birth, stable across the life span, and pervasive in their influence. Eysenck (1967) was one of the first to propose specific biological mechanisms of sensitivity to arousal and punishment to account for individual differences in Extraversion and Neuroticism.

Spurred by the rapid advances in neuroscience, the 1990s witnessed new enthusiasm for studying the biological structures and processes presumably underlying traits, such as specific gene loci, brain regions (e.g., the amygdala), neurotransmitters (e.g., dopamine), hormones (e.g., testosterone), and so on. Many of the initial findings are exciting, although preliminary, and must await confirmation and replication before we can draw strong conclusions.

Are Traits Causal Concepts?

Researchers who conceptualize traits as neuropsychic structures take a "causal" view of traits, but not all trait researchers agree with that view. The "summary" view conceptualizes traits as descriptive summaries of an individual's past behavioral conduct and refrains from invoking traits as causal or explanatory concepts. Accordingly, if Gordon has exhibited a certain frequency of fastidious acts, we can appropriately summarize his conduct with the trait fastidious. These two views differ with regard to the ontological status they accord the trait concept: The summary view does not regard traits as real entities, whereas the causal view regards traits as entities that exist "in our skins" (Allport, 1968, p. 49). Thus, according to the summary view, it is impossible for individuals to have a trait without having previously expressed it, even if they never had an opportunity to do so. For example, even if Robinson Crusoe was biologically extraverted, the summary view would consider him introverted until Friday arrived on his deserted island, providing frequent opportunities for social interactions.

A third view conceptualizes traits as "dispositions," defined as tendencies to behave in certain ways in certain kinds of situations. Ryle (1949) used the analogy of the brittleness of glass: Brittleness can be thought of as the tendency to shatter when struck, but a glass is considered brittle even if it has never been struck or shattered. Thus the dispositional view defines traits in terms of "if-then" propositions that some personality theorists regard as a promising direction for trait psychology. Whether or not dispositions are causal concepts remains a matter of debate.

Summary and Conclusions

In our initial definition of the trait concept, we emphasized that traits can serve three potential functions: to summarize, predict, and explain individuals' conduct. Regarding the first function, traits can indeed provide efficient summaries, but it is important not to overstate the consistency of behavior, thinking, and feeling across different situations and contexts. Second, traits are useful for predicting important personal and social outcomes, but traits are not the only important predictor. Third, although traits alone are not sufficient explanations, they provide at least the beginning of an explanation. Because traits do not explain the proximal causes of behavior or provide a developmental account, they need to be supplemented by dynamic and processing concepts, such as motives, schemas, plans, projects, and life stories (McAdams, 1995). Nevertheless, as knowledge about trait structure, measurement, and origins accumulates, the trait concept will serve increasingly important functions for describing and understanding individuals.

[*See also* Extraversion and Introversion; Five-Factor Model of Personality; NEO Personality Inventory; Optimism and Pessimism; Personality; Personality Development; Personality Disorders; Personality Psychology; *and* Resilience.]

Bibliography

Allport, G. W. (1968). Traits revisited. In *The person in psychology: Selected essays by Gordon W. Allport* (pp. 43–66). Boston: Beacon Press.

Buss, A. H. (1989). Personality as traits. *American Psychologist, 44,* 1378–1388.

Cattell, R. B. (1965). *The scientific analysis of personality.* Baltimore: Penguin Books.

Costa, P. T., Jr., & McCrae, R. R. (1992). *NEO-PI-R: Professional manual.* Odessa, FL: Psychological Assessment Resources.

Cronbach, L. J., & Meehl, P. E. (1955). Construct validity in psychological tests. *Psychological Bulletin, 52,* 281–302.

Eysenck, H. J. (1967). *The biological basis of personality.* Springfield, IL: Charles C. Thomas.

Funder, D. C., & West, S. G. (1993). Consensus, self-other agreement, and accuracy in personality judgment: An introduction. *Journal of Personality, 61,* 457–476.

Harris, J. R. (1995). Where is the child's environment? A group socialization theory of development. *Psychological Review, 102,* 458–489.

Hofstee, W. K. B. (1984). What's in a trait: Reflections about the inevitability of traits, their measurement, and taxonomy. *Personality Psychology in Europe, 1,* 75–81.

John, O. P. (1990). The "Big Five" factor taxonomy: Dimensions of personality in the natural language and in questionnaires. In L. A. Pervin (Ed.), *Handbook of personality: Theory and research* (pp. 66–100). New York: Guilford Press.

Loehlin, J. C., McCrae, R. R., Costa, P. T., Jr., & John, O. P. (1998). Heritabilities of common and measure-specific components of the Big Five personality factors. *Journal of Research in Personality, 32,* 431–453.

McAdams, D. P. (1995). What do we know when we know a person? *Journal of Personality, 63,* 365–396.

Pervin, L. A. (1994). A critical analysis of current trait theory. *Psychological Inquiry, 5,* 103–113.

Ryle, G. (1949). *The concept of mind.* New York: Barnes and Noble.

Sulloway, F. J. (1996). *Born to rebel: Birth order, family dynamics, and creative lives.* New York: Pantheon Books.

Wiggins, J. S. (1997). In defense of traits. In R. Hogan, J. Johnson, & S. R. Briggs (Eds.), *Handbook of personality psychology* (pp. 97–115). New York: Academic Press.

Oliver P. John and Samuel D. Gosling

PERSONAL SPACE. *See* Privacy.

PERSON-CENTERED COUNSELING. *See* Client-Centered Therapy.

PERSON-MACHINE SYSTEMS. The design and evaluation of person-machine systems is an area of applied psychology that deals with the impact of technology on humans. People use a variety of technology-based systems in their lives. These systems range from performing a simple task such as using a lawn mower, to operating a computer, driving an automobile, monitoring a power plant, flying a spacecraft, or managing an air traffic control system. The influence of technology in modern life is pervasive, and demand for improvements in the interaction between humans and technology is almost limitless.

Human factors, or ergonomics, is concerned with ways of designing jobs, machines, operations, and work environments so that they are compatible with people. This area of expertise is multidisciplinary and involves expertise primarily in psychology, industrial engineering, and computer science. The human factors practitioner applies existing human performance knowledge to the design or modification of equipment, and also generates new experimental data required for equipment design. Simultaneous consideration of the human, the task, and the environment is needed to provide usable person-machine systems.

The overall approach is user-centered design in which the end user is considered throughout the entire system design process. The growing importance of this approach has resulted in general strategies for designing person-machine systems. For example, MANPRINT (MANpower, PeRsonnel INTegration) has become a general design philosophy for designing military equipment and systems for soldiers in the U. S. Army (Booher, 1990). The MANPRINT philosophy integrates several areas of user concerns: human factors engineering, personnel selection, training, health hazards, and safety throughout system development. The MANPRINT approach stresses continually trading off system design with training in order to reduce total system cost and improve user performance. Likewise, usability engineering (Wixon & Wilson, 1997) is an accepted design approach for computer companies to use when developing software applications such as text editors, drawing packages, and spreadsheets. This approach to human-computer systems involves setting usability goals, testing for usability, and communicating usability concerns for effective system redesign.

System Design Approaches

Because of the complexity of most person-machine design problems, the expertise of several disciplines besides psychology is required. Consequently, most system design projects involve multidisciplinary teams representing a variety of technical skills. Psychologists often work with engineers, computer scientists, physiologists, industrial designers, and subject matter experts in design teams. In fact, the area of human factors and ergonomics has developed into a specialty area of graduate training in both engineering and psychology

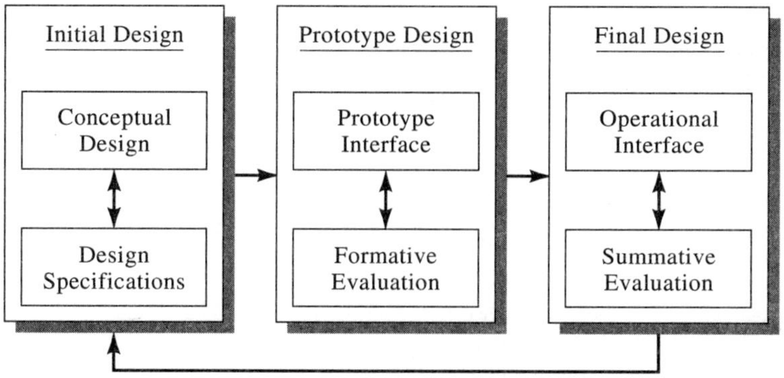

PERSON-MACHINE SYSTEMS. Figure 1. Stages in the iterative design of person-machine systems. (Adapted from Kies, Williges & Rosson, 1998, 776–791. Copyright 1998 by Wiley.)

where the practitioner learns interdisciplinary skills in order to work effectively. Multidisciplinary teams use two general approaches to develop person-machine systems.

Life Cycle Design. Traditionally, large-scale person-machine systems, such as weapons systems, have been designed from a life cycle point of view. A typical systems engineering approach includes phases of a system life cycle, such as needs and requirements analysis, conceptual design, preliminary design, detailed design and development, system integration and testing, production and/or construction, utilization and maintenance support, and phaseout or disposal (Blanchard & Fabrycky, 1998).

The philosophy of MANPRINT (Booher, 1990) stresses the importance of human-centered design throughout all phases of a system life cycle. Typically, human factors information required in life cycle design includes activities such as functional analysis, system use scenarios, activity and task analyses, human-machine task allocations, user interface design, training requirements, and user performance tests and evaluations.

Iterative Design. Although there is an implied sequence of steps in the life cycle approach to systems design, most complex systems cannot be designed in a simple linear fashion. In fact, the accepted design approach for developing software interfaces involving human-computer interaction is an iterative design that involves usability evaluations throughout. Kies, Rosson, and Williges (1998) described a general approach to iterative design with three major phases: initial design, prototype design, and final design. The major components involved in these three phases, as well as the iterative relationships among them, are depicted as a closed-loop system shown in Figure 1; all three phases rely heavily on user inputs and evaluation.

Initial Design. Design specifications based on user, task, and function analyses, as well as user scenarios and conceptual design, are considered in an iterative fashion during initial design. As design specifications are refined through cognitive evaluations, the overall initial design becomes more detailed and concrete.

Prototype Design. Once the initial design is sufficiently specified, this concept is instantiated in a prototype. The prototype is a simulation that provides a concrete "look and feel" of the person-machine system but is not completely operational in terms of total functionality. Formative evaluation using usability methods is conducted on the prototype, and the prototype is modified based on the results of the usability evaluation. The prototype interface and formative evaluation of it are revised in an iterative fashion until the specified usability goals are met, and the prototype evolves into the final design.

Final Design. The end result of the prototype design phase is an operational interface that provides full system functionality. Summative evaluation using controlled testing methods involving actual end users is conducted on the operational interface to ensure that the overall person-machine system design goals as specified in the final version of the conceptual design are met. The results of summative evaluation can be fed back to the initial design stage to be used in the next revision of the system.

System Design and Analysis Methods

Although many of the methods used by psychologists in other specialties are appropriate for the design of person-machine systems, several techniques have been developed specifically for this area of applied psychology. Table 1 lists some of these major methods.

Handbooks and Standards. Design information and guidance for person-machine systems exist in the form of handbooks and standards. This information is based on both empirical research results and expert experience that provide "best-use" recommendations. Much of the research in human factors and ergonomics is directed toward providing data to support design implications.

Integrated summaries of research areas, as well as design guidelines, checklists, and recommendations,

PERSON-MACHINE SYSTEMS. Table 1. Summary of useful person-machine system design methods

Handbooks	*Computer-Based Ergonomic Tools*
Perception and human performance	MicroSaint
Human factors and ergonomics	CAD
Human–computer interaction	COMBIMAN
	SAMMIE
Standards	Transom JACK
ISO standrds	
ANSI standards	*Ethnographic Methods*
OSHA standards	Study of work
MIL-STD standards	Contextual inquiry
NASA-STD-3000	Participatory design
	Scenario-based design
Human Factors Methods	Interaction analysis
Operational analysis	
Activity analysis	*Experimental Designs*
Functional flow	Multivariate analyses
Decision/action analysis	Factorial designs
Information requirements analysis	Efficient experimental designs
Functional allocation	Sequential experimentation
Task analysis	Empirical model building
Fault tree analysis	
Failure modes and effects analysis	*Usability Evaluation Methods*
Timeline analysis	Rapid prototyping
Link analysis	Critical incidents analysis
Simulation	Verbal protocols
Operational sequence analysis	Usability heuristics

are presented in handbooks. Both general and specific topic area handbooks are available. General person-machine systems handbooks such as Boff, Kaufman, and Thomas (1986) and Salvendy (1997) provide information on sensory processes and perception, cognitive processes and performance, job design, equipment/workplace/environmental design, design for health and safety, performance modeling, evaluation, human-computer interface, and applications of human factors. Alternatively, Helander, Landauer, and Prabhu (1997) compiled a handbook specifically related to human-computer interactions (HCI). Their handbook includes 62 topics organized around nine major sections: issues, theories, models, and methods of HCI; design and development of software systems; user interface design; evaluation of HCI; individual differences and training; multimedia, video, and voice; programming, intelligent interface design, and knowledge-based design; input devices and design of workstations; and computer-supported cooperative work and organizational issues in HCI.

Design guidance can also be codified into specific design requirements or standards, rather than just recommendations and guidelines. Chapanis (1996) provided a listing of the common standards developed by the International Organization for Standardization (ISO), American National Standards Institute (ANSI), Occupational Safety and Health Administration (OSHA), and military standards (MIL-STD) that relate to human-machine systems. The most comprehensive set of human factors standards appears in the six-volume NASA-STD-3000. Although this standard was developed for space missions, NASA-STD-3000 also serves as a general set of human factors and ergonomics standards covering areas such as anthropometry and biomechanics, human performance capabilities, natural and induced environments, crew safety, health management, architecture, workstations, activity centers, hardware and equipment, design for maintainability, facility management, and extravehicular activities.

Human Factors Methods. Chapanis (1996) described the vast amount of information that must be generated in a user-centered system design and provided a sequenced listing and description of human factors methods: operational analysis, analysis of similar systems, activity analysis, critical incident study, functional flow, decision-action analysis, action/information requirements analysis, functional allocation, task analysis, fault tree analysis, failure modes and effects analysis, time line analysis, link analysis, simulation, controlled experimentation, operational sequence analysis, and workload assessment. For example, link analysis might be quite useful in designing the arrangements of physical components as well as describing the interpersonal aspects of the workplace.

Human factors methods can be used to develop various types of documentation needed in person-systems design to summarize the information concerning human use. Specifically, Chapanis (1996) described operational needs documents, operational concept documents, specifications, requirements rationale reports, design descriptions, design rationale reports, and reviews. In large, complex procurements, such as military systems, a set of formalized review documents might include operational readiness review (ORR), systems requirements review (SRR), system design review (SDR), software specification review (SSR), preliminary design review (PDR), critical design review (CDR), and test readiness review (TRR).

Computer-Based Ergonomic Tools. Computer-aided design (CAD) tools are available for general systems design. Most CAD software packages provide flexible graphics tools to visualize various components of the system being designed. When CAD procedures are used in person-machine systems, these tools are tailored to aid in design by including the human component of the system. For example, task network models such as MicroSaint can represent a flow diagram of the task involving people and equipment in order to estimate workload analysis. Other CAD tools include anthropometric and ergonomic data in order to incorporate considerations of human physical capabilities directly into the design; COMBIMAN, SAMMIE, and Transom JACK are examples of this type of ergonomic CAD tool.

Ethnographic Methods. Ethnography incorporates a variety of techniques used to characterize how people interact with others and with the artifacts of technology in realistic work settings. Either passive observations or direct interviews and discussions can be used for collecting data. In most cases experts must be trained to collect data and interpret results obtained from ethnographic studies. Kies, Williges, and Rosson (1998) described studies of work, contextual inquiry, participatory design, scenario-based design, and interaction analysis as useful ethnographic methods that can be employed in the formative stages of person-machine system design. Studies of work and contextual inquiry provide background by analyzing currently existing systems, whereas participatory and scenario-based design procedures are focused more explicitly on managing the initial and formative stages of a new system design. Interaction analysis of conversations is an approach to organizing, interpreting, sharing, and controlling group work settings. Usually, these techniques are combined into one cohesive analysis. Consequently, the resulting data collected from ethnographic methods form the basis of a rich, interpretive description of human-machine systems drawn from naturalistic environments. Although these descriptions are usually quite detailed, they are limited by the skill and bias of the interpreter and may lack precision.

Experimental Design. Methods involving controlled testing during system design and analysis usually incorporate some form of experimental design and subsequent statistical analysis of the resulting data. Williges (1995) provided an overview of stages and considerations in the experimental design process used in human factors. Both the dependent variables (i.e., measures of human performance) and the independent variables (i.e., system parameters investigated in an experiment) need to be considered carefully in the design of an experiment. The complexity of human factors experiments requires consideration of data-reduction techniques including hierarchical, blocking, fractional-factorial, and central-composite designs that allows the investigator to evaluate several independent variables simultaneously. Often, multivariate analyses are needed to analyze the simultaneous effects of several dependent variables.

Kies, Williges, and Rosson (1998) described factorial experimental designs, efficient experimental designs, sequential experimentation, and empirical model building as important controlled testing procedures to use during the initial and summative evaluation stages of system design. Experimental designs provide both descriptive and predictive data for system design and evaluation, but care must be taken to collect data on a representative sample of actual users and include all the critical design parameters in the experiment in order for the results to generalize to the realistic work environment.

Usability Evaluation Methods. Usability has become an accepted criterion for the evaluation of HCI software interfaces. Hix and Hartson (1993) described the usability development process in detail and reviewed a number of formative evaluation methods and tools: rapid prototyping tools for developing interfaces during iterative design; the use of critical incidents recorded by both expert evaluators and end users that lead to either exceptionally good or poor performance; the use of both concurrent and retrospective verbal protocols whereby users describe their actions; heuristic evaluations where experts use a checklist of HCI design principles; and computer-based evaluation tools such as the interface design environment and analysis lattice (IDEAL) for collecting, summarizing, and analyzing audio and video usability data. All of these methods are part of their iterative approach to HCI design.

Human Consideration in Systems

Human capabilities and limitations need to be considered in person-machine systems. Various aspects determine the compatibility of the tools, equipment, and workplaces that people use. Table 2 lists some of the major human considerations that must be made in human-machine system design.

Human Physical Capabilities. Many parameters relating to human physical capabilities must be evalu-

PERSON-MACHINE SYSTEMS. Table 2. List of human considerations in person-machine system design

PHYSICAL CAPABILITIES
Skeletal system
Muscular system
Neuromuscular system
Respiratory system
Circulatory system
Metabolic system
Biomechanics
Biorhythms
Anthropometry

Workplace Design
Working posture
Workplace seating
Standing workplace
Strength requirements
Design of heavy work
Manual materials handling
Fatigue
Occupational stress
Boredom
Working and eating habits
Shift work

Environmental Factors
Visibility
Luminance ratios
Reflectance
Glare
Thermal comfort
Heat and cold stress
Sound measurement
Hearing loss
Hearing protection
Noise exposure limits
Annoyance noise
Vibration
Acceleration
Motion sickness

Individual Differences
Special needs of users
Design sizes
Universal design
Adjustable design

SENSORY CAPABILITIES
Vision
Accommodation
Visual acuity
Contrast sensitivity
Adaptation
Color discrimination
Text design
Graphics
Symbols
Codes
Quantitative displays
Qualitative displays
Warning lights
Representational displays
Heads-up displays

Audition
Sound thresholds
Relative discrimination
Absolute identification
Localization
Alarms

COGNITIVE ABILITIES
Signal detection theory
Information theory

Spatial Perception
Depth perception
Visual momentum
Visualization
Navigation
Virtual reality

Attention Sharing
Selective attention
Focused attention
Divided attention
Single resource theory
Multiple resource theory

Memory
Encoding
Storage
Retrieval
Short-term memory
Long-term memory
Chunking

Error Analysis
Mistakes
Slips
Lapses
Reliability analysis
Error monitoring
Error tolerant design
Help systems

Decision Making
Hypotheses
Choice of actions
Payoffs
Uncertainty
Decision aiding

Workload Analysis
Pupil dilation
Heart rate variability
Primary task
Secondary task
SWAT
NASA TLX

Process Control
Monitoring
Vigilance
Control
Fault diagnosis
Information feedback
Automation
Situation awareness

MOTOR ABILITIES
Manual Control
Hick's law
Fitt's law
Schmidt's law
S–R compatibility
Crossover model
Optimal control model
Predictor displays

Speech Communication
Articulation index
Preferred-octave level
Preferred noise level
Digitized speech
Synthesized speech
ASR
Content analysis

ORGANIZATIONAL CONCERNS
Macroergonomic analysis
Sociotechnical theory
Team performance
Consensus building
Group decision making
Interpersonal communication

ated in human-machine systems. For example, Kroemer, Kroemer, and Kroemer-Elbert (1997) discussed physiological parameters related to the skeletal, muscular, neuromuscular, respiratory, circulatory, and metabolic systems. In addition, biomechanics, thermal environments, biorhythms, and anthropometry are important. For example, measurements of the human body in terms of both static and dynamic anthropometry must be considered in systems designed for human use. Various tables of anthropometric data exist that provide body dimensions and reach envelopes of different populations of users (e.g., men, women, wheelchair users, and so on) that the ergonomist can use in systems design.

Workplace Design. The physical work space must be the appropriate size to accommodate the user. This raises difficult design issues when the real estate available for workstations is severely limited, as in automobile, aircraft, and space station environments. Kroemer and Grandjean (1997) discussed other physical factors that must be considered in occupational ergonomics. Design of heavy work, manual materials handling, and fatigue depend upon the physical capabilities of the person. Optimizing working posture, workplace seating, standing workplaces, and strength requirements is necessary to minimize fatigue and avoid injury. Other issues, such as occupational stress, boredom, working and eating habits, and work schedules, also need to be considered in the design of work.

Environmental Factors. Proper design also includes protection from environmental stressors related to illumination, climate, noise, and motion (Sanders & McCormick, 1993). Visibility, luminance ratios, reflectance, and glare are factors to consider in designing lighting environments. Climate considerations include parameters of thermal comfort, heat and cold stress, and heat exchange. Sound measurement, loss of hearing, hearing protection devices, exposure limits, and annoyance are problems and issues associated with noisy environments. Since humans are often exposed to motion in the workplace, the effects of vibration, acceleration, disorientation, and motion sickness must also be considered.

Individual Differences. To account for varying physical capabilities of users, attention must be given to appropriate dimensions of individual differences, such as gender and race. Likewise, physical, sensory, and cognitive disabilities of the user must be accommodated in the overall system design. Various computer-based augmentations may provide accommodations for users with physical or mental limitations that result in special needs.

Three alternate design approaches are used to accommodate individual differences instead of merely designing for the average user. First, the system can be designed using standard sizes for the individual while also allowing for various sizes of protective clothing. Second, a universal design approach can be used in an attempt to accommodate all users within a certain range; for example, data from the fifth to ninety-fifth percentile of the driver population can be used to design an automobile seat. Third, an adjustable design approach can be used that can be tailored to a particular user based on special needs or requirements; for example, wheelchairs should be designed with flexible adjustments to accommodate the idiosyncratic characteristics of a variety of physical disabilities.

Human Sensory Capabilities. Information input to the human occurs through human sensory channels. An understanding of sensory psychology, including the human haptic, olfactory, kinesthetic, visual, and auditory modalities is essential for effective system design. Although all human senses need to be considered, the visual and auditory channels are the primary input channels in most system applications. Boff et al. (1986) presented a detailed discussion of various human visual and auditory sensory capabilities relevant to person-machine systems.

Vision. Sanders and McCormick (1993) pointed out that accommodation, visual acuity, contrast sensitivity, adaptation, and color discrimination are central visual capabilities to consider in designing text, graphics, symbols, codes, quantitative and qualitative visual displays, signal and warning lights, representational displays, and heads-up displays used in person-machine systems. Within each of these visual display categories they described a subset of parameters to consider. For example, when computer screens are used for reading text, they recommended that the designer consider the following factors: display resolution, polarity, and color; text typography and size; screen design density, grouping, complexity, and highlighting; and reading distance.

Audition. Understanding the measurement of sound and human hearing perception is essential because auditory inputs are often used in human-machine systems. Sanders and McCormick (1993) suggested that sound detection thresholds, relative discrimination, absolute identification, and localization capabilities are critical to the design of auditory displays such as warning and alarm signals.

Human Cognitive Abilities. Given the presence of the ubiquitous computer in our lives, many modern person-machine systems require information processing on the part of the user. Cognitive psychologists and applied experimental psychologists have developed theories of human information processing that need to be considered in systems design. Several theories are based on models borrowed from signal detection theory and information theory that originally were developed in other disciplines. These theories have been used as both normative and descriptive models of various aspects of human information processing. Wickens (1992) provided a detailed discussion of various cognitive abilities that impact the design of human-machine systems: spatial perception, attention sharing, human memory, error analysis, decision making, workload analysis, and process control.

Spatial Perception. Human perception of space and spatial relationships is important in the design of information displays that depict orientation and navigation information, such as attitude and area navigation displays in aircraft cockpits. Applying concepts of depth perception, visual momentum, and visualization of information can improve map navigation as well as navigation in complex data spaces involving three dimensions. An understanding of the concepts of human spatial perception is necessary to instill a sense of presence and minimize disorientation in training simulators and virtual reality environments.

Attention Sharing. Human attention can be selective, focused, or divided. In many system applications, such as driving an automobile in heavy traffic while changing radio stations and talking on a cellular telephone, the human is required to time-share attention across several information sources. Single resource theory and multiple resource theory are alternative models used to describe time-sharing skills and abilities under varying attention demand levels. The single resource theory assumes a single resource pool for attention demand. Alternatively, a multiple resource theory assumes three dimensions that include stages (encoding versus responding), modality (auditory versus visual), and processing (spatial versus verbal) of attention resources. Attention selection and demands have implications for the degree of mental workload required of users in person-machine systems.

Human Memory. Three stages of memory include encoding, storage, and retrieval. Within memory storage, both short-term (or working memory) and long-term memory need to be considered. For example, short-term memory can be considered in terms of either verbal or spatial memory capabilities. Long-term memory, on the other hand, is concerned with procedural information, declarative organization, and mental models. Memory capacity has implications for the choice of information modality, the chunking of information in systems, and the training, transfer, and retention of human skills when using these systems.

Error Analysis. Human performance is not always completely accurate. A study of human error can often suggest improvements in system design and training. Errors can be classified as mistakes, slips, and lapses. Mistakes are errors of interpretation and understanding of the situation that subsequently result in incorrect actions. Slips are wrong actions that are accidentally taken when the situation is understood correctly. Lapses represent failures to carry out the correct action when known. Human reliability analysis, error monitoring, error tolerant design, and help systems are approaches and concepts resulting from error analysis of person-machine systems.

Decision Making. Hypotheses (i.e., diagnosis and prediction) and choice of actions are considered in human decision making. Both payoffs and uncertainty affect human decision making. Bayes theorem is a useful normative model of human decision making and has been used to document the primacy effect and conservative tendency of human decision making under uncertainty. In general, humans tend to persist in seeking support for original hypotheses and adopt subjective probabilities that are not as extreme as objective probabilities. In designing human-machine systems for optimal decision making, other considerations besides understanding individual decision-making capabilities need to be made, for example, decision aiding and team decisions may also be important.

Workload Analysis. A major issue in the design of person-machine systems is the amount of mental workload required by the individual using the technology in the system. Physiological metrics such as pupil dilation and heart rate variability, primary and secondary task performance, and rating scales such as SWAT and NASA TLX have been used to assess mental workload. Probably the most widely used metric of mental workload, due to ease of use, is a rating scale. For example, the NASA TLX scale considers the dimensions of mental demand, temporal demand, physical demand, performance, effort, and frustration level.

Process Control. Many systems involving people require the human to monitor and control complex, interrelated processes over a period of time. Industrial manufacturing processes and nuclear power plants are examples of process systems. Both the normal operation of these systems and the handling of emergency situations must be considered. Issues of monitoring, vigilance, control, fault diagnosis, information feedback, automation, and situation awareness are all dependent on the information-processing and cognitive abilities of the human working in process control systems.

Human Motor Abilities. In most person-machine systems, the human output is some type of motor response. Sanders and McCormick (1993) and Wickens (1992) summarized motor response considerations in system design. Actual manual control such as driving an automobile, or spoken output such as verbal discourse during a videoconference, are the two most common types of motor control outputs made by humans in systems.

Manual Control. Human movement, whether discrete in the form of using a keyboard on a computer workstation or continuous when using a control yoke and rudder to fly an airplane, is probably the most common form of motor output in a person-machine system. Research on human movement has resulted in formulations such as Hick's law for choice reaction time, Fitt's law for movement time, and Schmidt's law for movement accuracy. Principles of stimulus-response compatibility have been developed to determine the direction of control movement. Manual control theory can be used to describe and model continuous tracking tasks performed by humans (e.g., the crossover model and the optimal control model). These models are instrumental in developing innovative displays for continuous tracking; for example, predictor displays help humans to control systems with long response lags, such as in the control of super tankers that respond slowly because of their tremendous mass.

Speech Communication. From a system design point of view, speech intelligibility, or the ability to recognize a message correctly, is critical. Intelligibility depends upon several components of the communication system: speaker characteristics, message content, distortions in the transmission system, and noise environment. For example, standard metrics such as the articulation index, preferred-octave speech interference level, and preferred noise level can be used to evaluate speech intelligibility. Both digitized and synthesized speech are used in computer-generated speech output systems. Intelligibility of machine-based speech is a major consideration in usability. Likewise, automated speech recognition (ASR) technology allows computer recognition of speech. An ASR system, however, is still somewhat limited in terms of speech recognition accuracy and works best when it is speaker dependent, uses a limited vocabulary, and only discrete word recognition is required. Finally, the relative role of human speech as compared to other channels of communication in person-machine systems is often considered. Speech content analysis metrics are used for these assessments.

Organizational Considerations. Macroergonomics underscores the importance of considering the influence of the organization in sociotechnical systems used by people. Sociotechnical system theory and analysis of both the work system structure and process add another important dimension to user-centered design. Issues related to the influence of technology such as computer-augmented video conferencing on the improvement of team performance, consensus building, group decision making, and interpersonal communication are addressed in macroergonomic design procedures.

Personnel Training

Not every person can operate every system. Consequently, selection is often used to test for prerequisite skills and abilities of a safe and proficient user. System users often require some type of training in order to use a system successfully. Both motor and cognitive skills need to be trained. People need to be trained to fly airplanes, drive highway vehicles, and navigate ships. Often a synthetic training device or simulator is used to train these skills. Human factors specialists are concerned with understanding skill development and maximizing the amount of positive transfer from simulator training to actual job performance.

Goldstein (1993) described an overall systems approach to training operators. His approach involves three major phases: specification of training requirements, development of the training program, and evaluation of training effectiveness. As shown in Figure 2, his approach can be considered a closed-loop system involving a variety of steps. The training system involves trainees who complete training and graduate upon completion. Subsequent evaluation of the graduates can provide information for training redesign and improvement, thereby making the training system a closed loop.

Training Requirements. A training needs analysis must be conducted to determine training requirements. This analysis can use a variety of data collection techniques and sources of information obtained at the organization, task, and trainee level of observation. Usually the results of the training needs analysis are summarized in terms of behavioral or performance objectives for the subsequent development of the training program. Training objectives can also be used to determine criteria and metrics for evaluating training in terms of original learning, transfer of training to actual job performance, and retention of training skills.

Training Program. Two major activities occur during training development. First, the actual training content is developed based on behavioral objectives. Second, the appropriate methods, techniques, and media

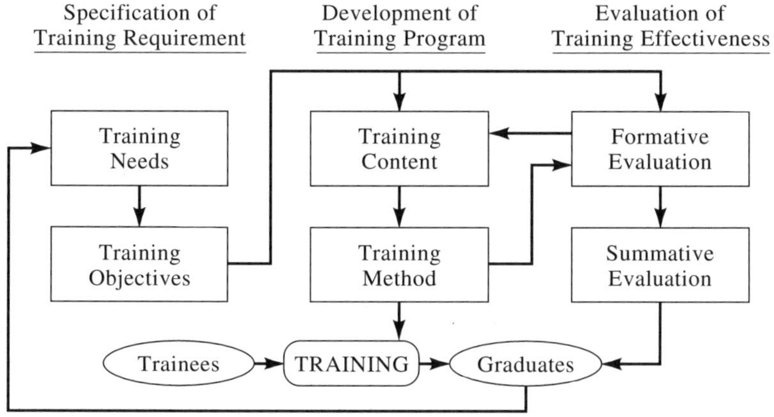

PERSON-MACHINE SYSTEMS. Figure 2. Stages in a systems approach to designing training systems. (Adapted from Goldstein, 1993.)

are chosen for implementation. A variety of methods including lectures, synthetic training devices, computer-assisted instruction, multimedia, and textbooks need to be considered in a trade-off analysis in order to determine the best combination of methods for a particular training requirement. The final training program results from combining the training contents with the delivery methods.

Training Evaluation. Evaluation of training effectiveness is conducted throughout the training system. Formative evaluation occurs in an iterative fashion during the development of the training program as shown in Figure 2. This evaluation uses subject matter experts and actual trainees as a way of finalizing and optimizing the training program. Once the training program is completed, summative evaluation is conducted on the graduates to determine if they have accomplished the training objectives; summative evaluation results can also be used to revise the entire training program.

Goal of User-Centered Design

Person-machine systems must be designed from the human's point of view in order to be effective. The overriding goal of this approach is to develop a usable system. To accomplish this goal, human factors and ergonomic considerations must be incorporated early and continuously throughout the design process. Usability as measured by time, errors, and satisfaction is rapidly being accepted as the major criterion for evaluating tools, workplaces, and systems. The ultimate test of their effectiveness is whether or not people accept and use these systems. Technology is constantly providing new challenges for user-centered designs of person-machine systems. As innovations such as advanced medical equipment, digital libraries, and intelligent transportation systems become more prevalent in our society, the demand for human-centered design will only increase.

Bibliography

Blanchard, B. S., & Fabrycky, W. J. (1998). *Systems engineering and analysis* (3rd ed). Englewood Cliffs, NJ: Prentice Hall.

Boff, K. R., Kaufman, L., & Thomas, J. P. (Eds.). (1986). *Handbook of perception and human performance* (Vols. 1 & 2). New York: Wiley.

Booher, H. R. (Ed.). (1990). *MANPRINT an approach to systems integration.* New York: Van Nostrand Reinhold.

Chapanis, A. (1996). *Human factors in system engineering.* New York: Wiley.

Goldstein, I. L. (1993). *Training in organizations* (3rd ed.). Pacific Grove, CA: Brooks/Cole.

Helander, M. G., Landauer, T. K., & Prabhu, P. V. (Eds.). (1997). *Handbook of human-computer interaction* (2nd ed.). Amsterdam: Elsevier.

Hix, D., & Hartson, H. R. (1993). *Developing user interfaces.* New York: Wiley.

Kies, J. K., Williges, R. C., & Rosson, M. B. (1998). Coordinating computer-supported cooperative work: A review of research issues and strategies. *Journal of the American Society for Information Science, 49*(9), 776–791.

Kroemer, K. H. E., & Grandjean, E. (1997). *Fitting the task to the human* (5th ed.). London: Taylor & Francis.

Kroemer, K. H. E., Kroemer, H. J., & Kroemer-Elbert, K. E. (1997). *Engineering physiology* (3rd ed.). New York: Van Nostrand Reinhold.

Salvendy, G. (Ed.). (1997). *Handbook of human factors and ergonomics* (2nd ed.). New York: Wiley.

Sanders, M. S., & McCormick, E. J. (1993). *Human factors in engineering and design* (7th ed.). New York: McGraw-Hill.

Wickens, C. D. (1992). *Engineering psychology and human performance* (2nd ed.). New York: HarperCollins.

Williges, R. C. (1995). Review of experimental design. In J. Weimer (Ed.), *Research techniques in human engineering* (pp. 49–71). Englewood Cliffs, NJ: Prentice Hall.

Wixon, D., & Wilson, C. (1997). The usability engineering framework for product design and evaluation. In M. Helander, T. K. Landauer, & P. Prabhu (Eds.), *Handbook of human-computer interaction* (2nd ed., pp. 653–688). Amsterdam: Elsevier.

Robert C. Williges

PERSONNEL SELECTION. [*This entry comprises two articles*: Techniques and Instruments *and* Selection and the Law. *The lead article provides a broad typology of various techniques and instruments used by psychologists (and others) in personnel selection. The companion article examines the legal dimensions of personnel selection and the involvement of psychologists.*]

Techniques and Instruments

Organizations of all types—profit and nonprofit, volunteer and nonvolunteer, military and civilian, public and private—face decisions about the processes by which individuals join the organization. In some settings, such as employment, the organization has a relatively fixed number of positions. When the number of applicants exceeds the number of positions available, some selection technique is needed to determine which individuals will be offered employment. Although random or quasi-random selection is possible (e.g., hiring on a first-come, first-served basis), most organizations accept the premise that there are individual characteristics that are related to job success, and view the surplus of applicants to openings as an opportunity to identify those individuals most likely to meet the criteria of job success most highly valued by the organization.

A wide array of techniques are used by employers as input to selection decisions. These include tests, interviews, evaluations of past performance, and job simulations, among others. Some, such as tests, are closely identified with the field of psychology. Others, such as interviews, developed outside the field of psychology but have been the focus of considerable effort on the part of psychologists who have attempted to improve their effectiveness. For still others, such as astrology or graphology, the role of psychologists has focused on the critical and scientific evaluation of claims made by proponents of the techniques.

The initial identification of potential selection devices is commonly based on the use of job analysis to identify, generally via expert judgment, individual characteristics linked to successful performance of important job behaviors. In some cases, potential measures are assembled for tryout without clear *a priori* notions as to which ones are most strongly job related. In either instance, the predictor measures initially selected can be viewed as hypotheses to be tested through the use of validation processes. Empirical or judgmental validation processes confirm or fail to confirm links between predictor measures and subsequent job behaviors. The use of selection techniques for which job relatedness has not been established through appropriate validation techniques runs contrary to sound professional practice (*Standards for Educational and Psychological Tests*, Washington, D.C., 1985, and *Principles for the Validation and Use of Personnel Selection Procedures*, Bowling Green, Ohio, 1987).

Discussions of different selection techniques are complicated by the common confounding of the construct or characteristic measured and the measurement methods used. Consider, for example, the interview. Some interviews are essentially orally administered job knowledge tests, whereas others seek insight into personality characteristics, vocational interests, work values, work habits, or some combination of these factors. This makes questions such as "Is the interview a useful selection technique?" or "Is the interview a better selection technique than a test?" generally unanswerable. A sound course of action begins by specifying the work behaviors of interest to the organization. For example, one organization may be trying to identify employees who will do the fastest and most efficient work, whereas another may focus on identifying employees with strong interpersonal skills in providing service to the customer. This may lead the first organization to focus on assessing the knowledge and skill of prospective employees and the second to focus on their personality characteristics. The question then becomes one of determining which measurement methods are most effective in shedding light on the characteristics of interest to the organization.

A variety of criteria may be considered in choosing among different selection techniques. The first is the validity of the technique in predicting the behaviors of interest for the job in question. This is the preeminent concern, as a selection technique that does not predict performance is of no value, regardless of its standing on the criteria to follow. But when multiple selection techniques that predict performance to some degree are available, employers may face the choice between maximizing validity and maximizing some of the other criteria to follow. A second criterion is the cost of developing, administering, and scoring the selection device. A third is feasibility and ease of administration. Concerns about test security, for example, may require an organization to use a selection tool that can be administered simultaneously to all candidates, thus precluding the use of techniques requiring individualized administration over an extended period of time. A fourth criterion is the acceptability, or "face validity," of the selection procedure to the candidates. A fifth involves the effects of the procedure on the employment opportunities of various minority groups protected by civil rights laws. Selection techniques on which members of one gender or race score, on average, lower than members of another are subject to careful scrutiny. It is generally accepted that if two selection procedures are essentially equivalent in validity but differ in their impact on protected groups, the procedure with less impact should be chosen. A subject of continued contention, though, is whether organizations should be permitted or required to choose less valid selection techniques in the interests of increasing minority group hiring.

There is no commonly accepted taxonomic structure for classifying selection techniques. They vary on a variety of dimensions. One is whether they focus on a sample of current behavior (e.g., tests, job simulations) or on an evaluation of past behavior (e.g., letters of recommendation). A second is the degree to which the evaluation process is standardized. At one extreme is the use of standardized tests, whereby test content, testing conditions, and scoring rubrics are identical for all candidates; at the other is an informal interview process, whereby interview content and evaluation standards are unspecified and vary widely across interviews. A third is the distinction between "samples" and "signs." This reflects a continuum anchored at one end by methods that reflect samples of job-relevant behavior (e.g., asking candidates for a lifeguard position to retrieve a dummy from the bottom of a pool), and anchored at the other end by methods that may have no logical or intuitive link to job performance but that may prove useful if supported by empirical evidence linking scores on the selection device to job performance. Extreme examples would be claims that astrological sign or color preference predict job performance. Empirical evidence would be needed to show that a candidate's standing on variables such as these is a useful signal of the likelihood of effective job performance.

Selection Tools That Sample Current Behavior

A variety of procedures used to assess potential employees will now be discussed.

Cognitive Ability Tests. Standardized tests of cognitive abilities are among the most extensively researched methods used in selection. Although paper-and-pencil administration and the multiple-choice format are commonly used, other modes of administration (e.g., computer) and other response formats (e.g., free response) are possible. A key characteristic of these tests is that they are not specific to a particular job, but rather tap basic characteristics relevant in many settings (e.g., verbal, numerical, and reasoning abilities). As such, they are of greatest use in settings where applicants do not come to the job with prior experience or training and thus cannot be evaluated for their job-specific knowledge and skill. An extensive body of research shows that cognitive ability tests consistently predict both success in training and level of task performance on the job across the entire job spectrum, with the strength of the test-performance relationship increasing with the complexity of the job.

Psychomotor, Sensory, and Physical Ability Tests. Like cognitive ability tests, standardized psychomotor, sensory, and physical ability tests tap basic characteristics relevant in many settings rather than attempting to replicate a specific job. Research has identified a large number of these abilities, with psychomotor abilities including domains such as dexterity, coordination, steadiness, precision, and speed of movement; sensory abilities including the domains of vision and hearing; and physical abilities including domains such as strength, flexibility, and coordination. Within each of these domains, finer distinctions can be made (e.g., finger vs. hand dexterity; static vs. dynamic strength). Careful job analysis is required to identify the specific abilities involved in the performance of a given job.

Job Knowledge Tests. Job performance commonly requires a body of both declarative knowledge (facts, terms, concepts) and procedural knowledge (knowing how to apply this declarative knowledge to the job). For areas of knowledge not learned subsequent to hiring, knowledge tests are commonly used as part of selection systems. In contrast to the ability tests discussed above, knowledge tests are specific to a particular job, and care must be taken in the test development process to ensure a close match between test content and areas of knowledge that are important for job performance and that are needed prior to job entry. Although a paper-and-pencil multiple-choice format is common, other formats are also used. Oral or video administration may be used to avoid confounding knowledge with reading comprehension, and oral or written free-response formats may be used.

Skill Tests, Work Sample Tests, and Simulations. Skill may be viewed as knowledge and ability applied to a specific content domain. Tests in this category involve asking candidates to demonstrate their performance in the content domain of interest. The label "skill test" is commonly used when the test content is applicable to a variety of jobs (e.g., a test of keyboard skills); the label "work sample" is commonly used when the test content is designed to sample directly or simulate closely the content of a specific job (e.g., asking candidates for a computer programming job to debug a program). Like knowledge tests, tests in this category are useful for testing skills that are expected prior to hiring. As many jobs are complex and involve a multitude of tasks, testing typically focuses on sampling or simulating the performance of critical tasks rather than the entire job. The close link between test content and job content makes this type of test appealing to both job applicants and organizations, and research finds this type of test the best predictor of task performance in settings where skills are needed prior to hiring.

Trainability Tests. The tests discussed above involve measuring skills that candidates bring to the workplace. In settings where skill development takes place after hiring and where training is lengthy and/or expensive, the work sample concept can be modified to sample not job content but rather training program content. This procedure is sometimes called *miniature job training*. Candidates go through a sample or simulation of the training for the job in question and are then tested on the knowledge and skills taught in the training session, using knowledge or skill tests as discussed above.

Personality Inventories. Two very different types of personality measures are encountered in selection contexts: measures of normal-range personality and measures of psychopathology. Normal-range measures are used to measure characteristics hypothesized as predictive of success on important dimensions of job performance, and measures of psychopathology (e.g., the Minnesota Multiphasic Personality Inventory) are used in the limited set of jobs where there is high risk to the public should an individual with severe pathology be hired (e.g., jobs where weapons are involved, such as police work). Although it is common to use personality inventories to measure a variety of personality characteristics, measures of a single characteristic are also sometimes used. The prototypical measure is a self-report, fixed-response test in which candidates are asked to indicate the degree to which various statements describe them or to choose which of a number of statements is most descriptive of them. Interest in using personality measures for selection has grown rapidly in recent years because of advances in developing a common language for describing personality characteristics. Although there are many examples of effective use of personality measures in selection settings, a personality measure should not be used without evidence of its effectiveness in predicting the job behaviors of interest to the organization. Sometimes listed as a separate category, "integrity tests" are a type of personality measure commonly used in settings where employers are concerned about counterproductive behavior such as theft.

Measures of Interests and Values. Measures of interests and values are commonly used in helping students and adults to make decisions regarding occupational and career choices. They are predictive of satisfaction with one's chosen occupation, but research generally does not support links with job performance among individuals who have chosen a given occupation. Therefore, these measures are not commonly used in selection settings. Any such use should be accompanied by research showing the value of such measures for the setting in question.

Interviews. The use of interviews in hiring decisions is nearly universal. It is virtually unheard of for an individual to be hired without an interview. Psychological research has been very critical of informal, unstructured interviews, finding low levels of interinterviewer agreement and evidence that interviewer judgments may be influenced by irrelevant factors, such as first-impression bias. Much more success has been found with structured interviews, including factors such as standardization of interview content, development of guidelines for evaluating responses, interviewer training to avoid potential biases, and the use of multiple interviewers. Approaches that use job analysis to develop interview questions probing for prior experiences reflecting important job skills or questions that seek candidate responses to job-based scenarios have met with considerable success.

In-Depth Assessments. Various combinations of selection techniques such as those described above may be used in conjunction, with the results integrated judgmentally to form an overall evaluation of a candidate. "Individual psychological assessment" typically involves a psychologist's use of a battery of tests and inventories in conjunction with a lengthy interview. The information elicited is commonly integrated into a narrative report describing the candidate's strengths and weaknesses, usually accompanied by a recommendation about the candidate's fit to the job in question. "Assessment centers" focus strongly on job simulations, most commonly for managerial jobs, and may also include tests and interviews in addition to multiple simulation exercises. A hallmark of assessment centers is the use of simulation exercises in which multiple candidates participate simultaneously (e.g., working as a group to solve a problem), with their performance observed and evaluated by several trained assessors.

Selection Tools That Evaluate Past Behavior

A variety of background criteria are also used to evaluate potential employees.

Education. Although educational requirements for jobs are common, psychological research suggests that they are not strong predictors of job performance. Employers commonly set such requirements as a proxy for a direct measure of some skill or ability (e.g., requiring a high school degree because of literacy demands on the job). In the absence of a close link between educational attainment and the skill or ability of interest, the inference that educational attainment ensures that candidates possess the needed skills is questionable. Direct measurement of the needed skill or ability is likely to be a better predictor of performance.

Experience/Seniority. As with education, psychological research does not find length of experience to be a strong predictor of performance. Different individuals develop as a result of job experience in different ways and at different rates. Thus a direct measure of the skill or ability of interest is likely to be a better predictor of performance.

Licensure and Certification. A variety of professions and occupations require a demonstration that a body of knowledge or an area of skill has been acquired, either as a requirement before initial entry into the field or to certify a more advanced level of knowledge or skill. Licensure and certification commonly involves job knowledge and/or work sample testing, often in conjunction with other requirements, such as completion of an educational curriculum. As licensure examinations certify whether an individual has achieved a threshold level of knowledge or skill, employers may do additional screening to differentiate among multiple candidates who have met this requirement.

Biographical Data. Information about a candidate's background, most commonly obtained via a resumé or application blank, is routinely used in the initial screening of job applicants. Psychologists have investigated ways of systematizing the evaluation of biographical data. One method is to develop formal scoring systems to permit more standardized evaluation of application blanks and resumés. Information is sometimes collected in multiple-choice format, whereas other approaches require written narratives describing relevant experiences. A hallmark of psychological investigation of biographical data is empirical research linking candidates' responses to subsequent job performance. Systematically collected and scored biodata have a strong record of success in predicting job performance.

Judgmental Evaluations of Past Performance. Judgments about past performance are obtained via letters of recommendation, reference checks, and performance appraisals from previous jobs. The value of such information is often quite limited because of factors such as a tendency for recommendation letters to be strongly positive and fear on the part of prior employers of legal liability if a negative evaluation is provided. Although this approach is commonly used, its limitations are a key reason for the use of direct assessment of candidate characteristics.

Selection Devices with No Direct Link to Current or Past Work Behavior

There is a long history of movements arising that propose that insight into human character and behavior can be derived from seemingly innocuous behaviors, events, or indicators. Claims have been made that insight into future job performance can be obtained from astrological signs, handwriting analysis, body type, head size and shape, color preference, blood type, and a variety of other indicators. Handwriting analysis (graphology) is perhaps the most commonly advocated and most used technique of those listed here. To date there is no consistent pattern of results that supports the use of any of these methods. For techniques such as these, the research paradigm employed in the evaluation of all proposed selection devices applies: obtain large samples of individuals (to prevent chance findings from small samples), obtain scores on the proposed selection device from these individuals, obtain subsequent measures of the job behaviors of interest, and carefully evaluate the relationship between scores on the selection device and scores on the performance measure.

Bibliography

Arvey, R. D., & Faley, R. H. (1988). *Fairness in selecting employees* (2nd ed.). Reading, MA: Addison-Wesley.

Ash, R. A., Johnson, J. C., Levine, E. L., & McDaniel, M. A. (1989). Job applicant training and work experience evaluation in personnel selection. In K. Rowland, & G. Ferris (Eds.), *Research in Personnel and Human Resource Management, 7*, 183–226.

Barrick, M., R., & Mount, M. K. (1991). The big five personality dimensions and job performance: A meta-analysis. *Personnel Psychology, 44*, 1–26.

Dunnette, M. D., & Hough, L. M. (Eds.). (1990). *Handbook of industrial and organizational psychology* (2nd ed., Vol. 1). Palo Alto, CA: Consulting Psychologists Press.

Dunnette, M. D., & Hough, L. M. (Eds.). (1991). *Handbook of industrial and organizational psychology* (2nd ed., Vol. 2). Palo Alto, CA: Consulting Psychologists Press.

Eder, R. W., & Ferris, G. R. (Eds.). (1989). *The employment interview: Theory, research, and practice.* Newbury Park, CA: Sage.

Guion, R. M (1998). *Assessment, measurement, and prediction for personnel decisions.* Mahwah, NJ: Erlbaum.

Hunter, J. E., & Hunter, R. F. (1984). Validity and utility of alternative predictors of job performance. *Psychological Bulletin, 96*, 72–98.

Jeanneret, R., & Silzer, R. (Eds.). (1998). *Individual psychological assessment.* San Francisco: Jossey-Bass.

Sackett, P. R., & Wanek, J. E. (1996). New developments in the use of measures of honesty, integrity, conscientiousness, dependability, trustworthiness, and reliability for personnel selection. *Personnel Psychology 47*, 787–829.

Schmitt, N., & Borman, W. (Eds.). (1993). *Personnel selection in organizations.* San Francisco: Jossey-Bass.

Stokes, G. S., Mumford, M. D., & Owens, W. A. (Eds.). (1994). *Biodata handbook.* Palo Alto, CA: Consulting Psychologists Press.

Thornton, G. C., III, & Byham, W. C. (1982). *Assessment centers and managerial performance.* New York: Academic Press.

Paul R. Sackett

Selection and the Law

Title VII of the Civil Rights Act of 1964 brought a new dimension to the professional responsibilities of psychologists engaged in personnel selection. The professional responsibility to meet legal guidelines was emphasized in 1971 in the Supreme Court's decision in *Griggs v. Duke Power* (1971). In that case, two standardized tests (the Wonderlic Personnel Test and the Bennett Mechanical Comprehension Test) were used to select workers for a power plant. It is undisputed that no test validation had been conducted by the company. Buying tests from test publishers and relying on their representation that the tests were useful was standard practice at that time. In addition, the company relied on test publishers' interpretation of Title VII that professionally developed tests were, per se, not discriminatory.

Disparate Impact

In the *Griggs* case, the Supreme Court introduced the concept of "disparate impact," which was not contemplated by Congress when Title VII was enacted. Basically, as the concept has evolved, the plaintiff has the burden of proving disparate impact. There are complex statistical and other issues that are still being debated in the courts. Simply stated, a significant difference in the selection rate of the minority group compared to the nonminority group is usually considered disparate impact. As a simpler rule of thumb, the Uniform Guidelines (1978) find disparate impact if the selection rate of one group is less than 80% of that of another group. Once disparate impact has been demonstrated, the burden then shifts to the defendant to prove that the tests are job relevant.

Guidelines, Standards, and Principles for Validation

Under the Uniform Guidelines, American Psychological Association *Standards* (1985), and SIOP *Principles* (1987), there are three established validation techniques: construct, criterion-related, and content validity approaches. Construct validity depends on empirical studies. No court has accepted construct validity evidence as the sole justification for the job relevance of a test. Although construct validity is now seen as the basis for all validation approaches (Binning & Barrett, 1989), it has limited importance in court decisions.

Criterion-related validity is either concurrent or predictive. Earlier, some courts believed that predictive validity should be the preferred validation approach. However, since the Supreme Court decision in *Washington v. Davis* (1976), construct, criterion-related, and content validation approaches have all been viewed as equal.

A criterion-related validation study is usually criticized by the plaintiff's expert because the validity coefficient (the correlation between the test and the measure of job performance) is either not statistically significant or too low. As a predicate to the requirement for a validation study, there must be evidence of disparate impact. For example, in *Melendez v. Illinois Bell* (1996), the parties stipulated that there had been disparate impact against Hispanics based on the use of a standardized cognitive ability test to measure learning potential for management positions. The test was designed to measure mathematics, grammar, reading comprehension, and the ability to follow directions. The court concluded that the test was not valid. The court noted that although there was no difference in job performance between Hispanics and Whites, there was a significant difference in test scores.

It should be noted that concepts such as "differential prediction" and "differential validity" are seldom if ever an issue in reported court decisions. It appears to be well accepted by plaintiffs' experts that tests make the same predictions for all groups and that there is no statistically significant difference between validity coefficients.

In *Albemarle Paper Co. v. Moody* (1975), the Supreme Court carefully examined a concurrent validation study by comparison with the professional standards and the Uniform Guidelines. The Court found the validation study materially defective, with an "odd patchwork of results" (p. 431). The Court was particularly critical of the subjective supervisory rankings, with their confusing instructions to "determine which ones [employees] they felt irrespective of the job that they were actually doing, but in their respective jobs, did a better job than the person they were rating against" (p. 431).

The courts examine performance appraisals to determine if they are job related on a logical basis. Even when employee performance appraisals are part of a selection process, the courts have not required a formal validation process (Barrett & Kernan, 1987).

The courts follow the same logical, job-related procedure when interviews are used for selection. The courts do not require formal validation. Although judgmental procedures can have disparate impact, a formal validation study is not required (*Watson v. Fort Worth Bank & Trust*, 1988). The EEOC (1983) stresses that every question in an interview should contribute to judging the qualifications of the individual for the job in question. It should be noted that each state may have restrictions on the types of questions that may be asked during an interview.

Content Validity

Because of the difficulty of conducting criterion-related studies, content validity evidence has become more important in demonstrating that tests are job relevant. In South Carolina, the National Teachers Examinations were used to certify teachers and to determine their pay levels. The Supreme Court accepted a *post hoc* content validity study (*National Education Assoc. v. South Carolina*, 1978).

The critiques of content validation studies often involve issues such as the adequacy of the job analysis, the breadth of coverage of the tests, and whether or not content-valid tests can be used to rank examinees. Simply stated, courts have usually upheld even minimal job analysis procedures. Courts have also accepted tests that measure job knowledge but no other construct (*Nash v. Consolidated City of Jacksonville*, 1996). Job knowledge is probably the most common construct measured by content-oriented tests.

There is less uniform opinion on the issue of ranking examinees. In general, tests have been used to rank applicants if the tests have been found to be content valid and have acceptable psychometric qualities such as adequate reliability and differentiation between examinees (e.g., *Nash v. Consolidated City of Jacksonville*, 1996).

Banding

Banding has usually been discussed in the industrial organizational literature as a new concept. "Banding" refers to a variety of techniques designed to place applicants in broad "score bands." For example, all scores between 90 and 100 are considered the same because of measurement error. The idea is that there is no statistical difference between test scores within the band. The applicants are then selected at random or by some other means from within that band (Cascio, Outtz, Zedeck, & Goldstein, 1991).

In fact, the concept of banding is not new. In civil service testing, it is quite common for the top three scorers or sometimes the top ten scorers to be considered by the appointing authority. The final selection might be based on an interview or seniority, for example.

Banding is also not unusual in the private sector. In *Detroit Edison v. National Labor Relations Board* (1979), the Supreme Court noted that the test battery used to select instrument maintenance personnel had a minimum cutoff score and that persons who scored above that level were then selected based on seniority.

More recent issues have involved the use of minority status. This factor has been introduced in the remedial phase of court cases. During the liability phase of the cases, some courts have found disparate impact and have ruled that the tests were not valid. Subsequently, some form of banding has been introduced as a remedy (e.g., *Sims v. Montgomery County Commission, 1997*).

The future of banding is doubtful unless there has been an *a priori* finding of discrimination. Any type of minority preference banding would have to be based on a court finding that there had been prior discrimination, and banding would be a remedy ordered by the court or approved by the court in a consent decree (*Sims v. Montgomery County Commission, 1997*). Giving preference to women or minorities was made unlawful by Section 106 of the Civil Rights Act of 1991. This section states that it is unlawful "to adjust the scores of, use different cutoff scores for, or otherwise alter the results of, employment related tests on the basis of race, color, religion, sex or national origin." Organizations that had standardized test scores or utilized out-of-rank-order hiring or promotion voluntarily changed their procedures after the passage of the Civil Rights Act of 1991 (e.g., *Billish v. City of Chicago*, 1992).

Another possibility is random selection from a band of test scores. There are at least four arguments against this approach. First, it introduces random error into the selection process. Second, random selection within a band may not increase the proportion of minority group members that would be selected or promoted (*Brown v. City of Chicago*, 1998). Third, most of the litigation involving testing and alternative selection procedures has been in the public sector. Most public organizations are governed by civil service rules that mandate a competitive exam when the scores are rank ordered to eliminate political and personal favoritism (e.g., *Pahaham v. Danbury Police Dept.*, 1997). Civil service rules may forbid random selection from a band (*City of Philadelphia v. Fraternal Order of Police*, 1990). Fourth, many public and private organizations have their personnel testing practices constrained by a collective bargaining agreement between the union representing the employees and the organization. These agreements often specify the types of tests and how test scores will be used (e.g., *Suppan v. City of Allentown*, 1997). The courts have routinely upheld these agreements where there is no evidence of discrimination, even if there is disparate impact.

Attempts to introduce banding have been met with opposition. In general, state and municipal civil service laws would have to be changed before banding of any type would be accepted by the courts. The concept of a competitive exam and merit-based hiring does not fit with the idea of selecting candidates at random from a wide test score band.

Validity Generalization

Research on the generalizability of the validity of tests has provided substantial evidence that cognitive ability is a valid predictor of job performance across all jobs (Schmidt & Hunter, 1981). However, although this may be a good scientific generalization, the concept of validity generalization has never been accepted by the courts. If the concept was accepted, an organization could merely purchase an off-the-shelf cognitive ability test and use it for any job. No job analysis study or any other validation approach would be required. Both district and appeals courts have rejected this concept (e.g., *EEOC v. Atlas Paper Box Co.*, 1989).

Personality Testing

Personality testing has been used routinely in the private sector for more than 50 years. Only recently has its use in personnel selection become a legal issue. Four areas of concern that arise when using personality tests in selection are privacy, political attitudes, civil service testing, and the dictates of the Americans with Disabilities Act of 1990.

Many states, such as California, have laws that protect the privacy of examinees. Many personality tests have items that reveal political attitudes or can be considered an invasion of privacy. An item-by-item examination has revealed some items that many test takers would regard as offensive (*Soroka v. Dayton Hudson Corp*, 1991). Other tests have been found to reveal political attitudes in areas such as the legalization of drugs (*Thompson v. Borg-Warner*, 1996).

In the public sector, personality tests have been used to both increase prediction of job performance and reduce disparate impact (Sackett & Ellingson, 1997).

In civil service testing, a number of issues surface when personality tests are used as competitive exams. These include perceptions that the tests are biased against minorities, that the items do not appear job relevant, that there appear to be no right answers, and that personality tests can be faked.

One drawback in using personality tests for selection is the issue of faking. There is considerable debate within the literature as to whether faking occurs and, if it does occur, what the effects are. There is some evidence that although faking may affect individual scores, it does not affect the predictive validity of the measurements (Barrick & Mount, 1996). By contrast, there is evidence that the validity of an instrument is lost if an individual is faking. Incorporating warning and lie scales into personality inventories are two ways in which faking can be reduced and/or detected. However, Hogan, Hogan, and Roberts (1996) claimed that although people can fake when told to do so, most people do not fake on personality measures.

Americans with Disabilities Act

The Americans with Disabilities Act (ADA, 1990) created the possibility that certain personality tests could often be considered medical examinations. Psychological examinations are considered medical if their results can lead to the identification of a mental disorder or impairment (EEOC, 1995). However, psychological examinations or personality inventories designed to measure constructs such as honesty, tastes, and/or habits are not considered medical (EEOC, 1995). If a personality test is considered a medical exam, it cannot be given before a provisional job offer.

The ADA requires the organization to make a reasonable accommodation if the test taker states that an accommodation is required. The case law in this area is relatively new, so this discussion will rely heavily on the EEOC's interpretation of the ADA and the rules of federal agencies. The tester may request documentation supporting the existence of a disability. The tester can then interact with the examinee to determine the appropriate accommodation. For example, the job being applied for may require rapid reading of complex material. If a reading comprehension test is the basic selection tool, then giving the examinee a reader would be a reasonable accommodation because reading comprehension is a requirement of the job. A specific case-by-case analysis is required to determine what is a reasonable accommodation in the testing situation. Much of the litigation involves the accommodation required for legal, medical, and teaching certification. There is often wide disagreement between opposing experts as to whether there is a disability and what is the appropriate accommodation. Typical reasonable accommodations for a learning disability include more time to take the test, use of a computer, allowing test takers to circle multiple-choice answers, and the use of large print (*Bartlett v. New York State Board of Law Examiners*, 1997).

Age Discrimination in Employment Act

There are some cases involving individuals over age 40 alleging discrimination because of testing. One persistent issue is rejection of an older applicant because he or she is overqualified. When the term *overqualified* is not defined, at least one court has found this to be a euphemism for "too old" (*Miller v. Cigna*, 1995). Most courts have taken the position that being labeled overqualified because of having more experience or education is not age discrimination (e.g., *Senner v. Northcentral Technical College*, 1997). Although experience is correlated with age, the Supreme Court ruled that it is not age discrimination (*Hazen Paper v. Biggins*, 1993). In fact, factors such as high salary, ample retirement benefits, and proximity to retirement do not violate the Age Discrimination in Employment Act in selection and termination decisions despite their obvious correlation with age (*Sperling v. Hoffmann-La Roche*, 1996).

Bibliography

Albemarle Paper Co. v. Moody, 422 U.S. 405 (1975).

American Educational Research Association, American Psychological Association, & National Council on Measurement in Education. (1985). *Standards for educational and psychological testing*. Washington, DC: Author.

Barrett, G. V., & Kernan, M. C. (1987). Performance appraisal and terminations: A review of court decisions since *Brito v. Zia* with implications for personnel practice. *Personnel Psychology, 40*, 489–503.

Barrick, M. R., & Mount, M. K. (1996). Effects of impression management and self-deception on the predictive validity of personality constructs. *Journal of Applied Psychology, 81*, 261–272.

Bartlett v. New York State Board of Law Examiners, 970 F. Supp. 1094 (S.D. N.Y. 1997).

Billish v. City of Chicago, 962 F. 2d 1269 (7th Cir. 1992).

Binning, J. F., & Barrett, G. V. (1989). Validity of personnel decisions: A conceptual analysis of the inferential and evidential bases. *Journal of Applied Psychology, 74*, 478–494.

Brown v. City of Chicago, U.S. Dist. LEXIS 10721 (N.D. Ill. 1998).

Cascio, W. F., Outtz, J., Zedeck, S., & Goldstein, I. L. (1991). Statistical implications of six methods of test score use in personnel selection. *Human Performance, 4*, 233–264.

City of Philadelphia v. Fraternal Order of Police, 132 Pa. Comm. 631 (Commonwealth Court of PA, 1990).

Detroit Edison v. National Labor Relations Board, 440 U.S. 301 (1979).

EEOC v. Atlas Paper Box Co., 868 F. 2d 1487 (6th Cir. 1989).

Equal Employment Opportunity Commission et al. (1978). Uniform guidelines on employee selection procedures. *Federal Register, 43*(166), 38290–38315.
Equal Employment Opportunity Commission et al. (1979). Adoption of questions and answers to clarify and provide a common interpretation of the uniform guidelines on employee selection procedures. *Federal Register, 44* (43), 11996–12009.
Equal Employment Opportunity Commission et al. (1980). Adoption of additional questions and answers to clarify and provide a common interpretation of the uniform guidelines on employee selection procedures. *Federal Register, 45*(87), 29530–29531.
Equal Employment Opportunity Commission. (1983, February). *Pre-employment inquiries and equal employment opportunity law.* Washington, DC: EEOC Office of Public Affairs.
Equal Employment Opportunity Commission. (1995). *ADA enforcement guidance: Preemployment disability-related questions and medical examinations.* Washington, DC: Bureau of National Affairs.
Griggs v. Duke Power, 401 U.S. 424 (1971).
Hazen Paper v. Biggins, 507 U.S. 604 (1993).
Hogan, R., Hogan, J., & Roberts, B. W. (1996). Personality measurement and employment decisions: Questions and answers. *American Psychologist, 51,* 469–477.
Melendez v. Illinois Bell Telephone Co., 79 F. 3d 661 (7th Cir. 1996).
Miller v. Cigna, 47 F. 3d 586 (3rd Cir. 1995).
Nash v. Consolidated City of Jacksonville, 85 F. 3d 643 (11th Cir. 1996).
National Education Assoc. v. South Carolina, 434 U.S. 1026 (1978).
Pahaham v. Danbury Police Dept., 981 F. Supp. 74 (D. Conn. 1997).
Sackett, P. R., & Ellingson, J. E. (1997). The effects of forming multi-predictor composites on group differences and adverse impact. *Personnel Psychology, 50,* 707–721.
Schmidt, F. L., & Hunter, J. E. (1990). The validity and utility of selection methods in personnel psychology: Practical and theoretical implications of 85 years of research findings. *Psychological Bulletin, 124,* 262–274.
Senner v. Northcentral Technical College, 113 F. 3d 750 (7th Cir. 1997).
Sims v. Montgomery County Commission, 119 F. 3d 9 (11th Cir. 1997).
Society for Industrial and Organizational Psychology. (1987). *Principles for the validation and use of personnel selection procedures* (3rd ed.). College Park, MD: Author.
Soroka v. Dayton Hudson Corp., 18 Cal. App. 4th 1200 (Cal. Ct. App. 1991).
Sperling v. Hoffman-La Roche, 924 F. Supp. 1396 (D. N.J. 1996).
Suppan v. City of Allentown, 1997 U.S. Dist. LEXIS 12790 (E.D. Pa. 1997).
Thompson v. Borg-Warner, 1996 U.S. Dist. LEXIS 4781 (N.D. Calif. 1996).
Washington v. Davis, 426 U.S. 229 (1976).
Watson v. Fort Worth Bank & Trust, 487 U.S. 977 (1988).

Gerald V. Barrett

PERSUASION. *See* Attitudes, *article on* Attitude Change.

PERU was the birthplace of one of the most advanced pre-Colombian civilizations of America, the Inca. The different cultures that preceded and contributed to the development of the Inca empire had created a cultural environment without equal in America before the arrival of the Europeans. During the time of the Spanish colonization, Peru was a very important country because of its central location, with a considerable cultural, philosophical, and artistic development; it also had an important education center, the Universidad de San Marcos, and a cultural elite that was always in contact with Europe.

Peruvian philosophy was phenomenological, and until very recently was opposed to approaches that had a quantitative or scientific basis, or were considered technological. This had a very negative effect on the development of psychology, and despite the efforts of pioneers such as Walter Blumenfeld (1882–1967), Peruvian psychology was heavily influenced by the holistic and intuitive, rather than the experimental and objective approaches. The first true psychological researches were in the field of educational psychology in the areas of learning, child development, and intellectual performance (see Alarcón, 1980). However, the medical psychiatrists were interested in the psychological characteristics of the Peruvians and measured cognitive and personality variables in order to assist clinical diagnoses. The philosophers were interested in the philosophy of the mind and their writings were concerned with this area. These three influences—education, medicine and philosophy—molded the first stages of Peruvian psychology, a situation similar to several other Latin American countries.

In 1912, J. McKnight from the Teachers College of Columbia University presented the results of his research into the physical and mental characteristics of Peruvian children. This is the first investigative work ever regarded as scientific in the history of Peruvian psychology. It led to many other studies in the areas of psychometry, child development, academic performance, learning, attention, memory, retention, reading comprehension, and similar themes.

Another influential researcher was the German psychologist Walter Blumenfeld (1882–1967), who arrived in Lima in 1935 to direct the Institute of Psychology and Psychotechniques (Instituto de Psicología y Psicotecnia), and teach courses in experimental psychology. In Germany he was recognized for his work in the areas of perception and cognitive psychology. His principal responsibility in the institute was to develop psychotechnical tests for use in education and industry, as well as teach courses on experimental psychology. The Institute was equipped with modern laboratory equipment imported from Germany. Blumenfeld initiated experimental psychology in Peru as well as writing books in both German and Spanish. He was concerned with the creation of a solid base for experimental psychology and the development of a scientific approach for its application to the social situation in Peru.

The work of Blumenfeld is a marked contrast to his contemporary Honorio Delgado (1892–1969), a psychiatrist, humanist, and philosopher who was also extremely influential in the development of Peruvian psychology. He insisted that psychology must be based on intuition and began to work in psychoanalysis, and was able to obtain Freud's recognition. His work *El Psicoanálisis* [Psychoanalysis] was published in 1919 and is one of the first works on this topic to be published in Spanish. He also published a biography of Freud entitled *Sigmund Freud*, in 1926. Later he left this approach, arguing that it was mechanistic and pansexual. He dedicated himself to developing a line of humanistic psychology based on the work of Husserl, and proposed a spiritual psychopathology.

His followers, including psychologists, psychiatrists and philosophers, developed a line of spiritual and speculative psychology. They considered it a discipline related to philosophy and their objective was the discovery of psychological phenomena: mental life or the conscience. The methodology of this speculative psychology included the spiritual sciences that had been in vogue in Germany.

Another influential force in Peruvian psychology was the National Psychopedagogical Institute, founded in 1941. Its objective was "the holistic study of the Peruvian child and adolescent." One of its most important researchers was Walter Blumenfeld, and his team included pedagogues and psychiatrists. Annexed to the Institute was a School of Experimental Application and for many years it published the *Boletín del Instituto Psicopedagógico Nacional* [Bulletin of the National Psychopedagogical Institute]. The institute was operational in two periods, the first between 1941 and 1950, and the second from 1956 to 1964. In 1965 it was transferred to the Universidad de San Marcos and became incorporated within the university. The most significant contribution of the institute to psychology in Peru was that it rationalized and institutionalized research. Before the institute, there had been sporadic, nonsystematic research. Its work resulted in the development of psychopedagogy in secondary schools and in the Faculties of Education and Philosophy and Literature in Peruvian universities. There were research programs in psychology, many of them directed by Blumenfeld.

There are a number of medical psychiatrics who were influential in the development of psychology in Peru. They include Hermilio Valdizán, considered the father of Peruvian psychiatry, and Carlos Alberto Seguín, an important researcher into indigenous psychiatry and psychology. It was these psychiatrists who introduced the Rorshach Test, the TAT and other projective tests to Peru and also taught future generations of psychologists.

The academic university course of psychology was created in 1963 in the Universidad de San Marcos with the formation of a Department of Psychology within the Faculty of Literature. Its origin can be traced back to 1955 when the Section of Psychology was created in the Institute of Philosophy and Psychology. Later the department became the Faculty of Psychology, an independent Faculty of the University. Other universities followed and created their own faculties. The structure of the undergraduate course follows that of most Latin American countries, with a 5- or 6-year duration (see Ardila, 1978, 1986). At the end of the theoretical course there is a supervised internship whose purpose is to develop the practical skills necessary for the profession. The main areas of internship are clinical, educational, social, and industrial psychology. The student must also present a thesis to obtain the degree title of "Psychologist," a certificate that entitles him or her to work in any of these areas. The majority of the theses are based on empirical research using correlational techniques.

The scientific research programs are mainly in the fields of clinical and educational psychology and are commonly carried out by the universities. The results are published both nationally and internationally, mainly in Latin American journals. Much of this work is directed toward psychometrics, the standardization intelligence tests, personality, and vocational guidance. There is also an increasing amount of research into the experimental analysis of behavior led by the psychologist José Anicama. Other important researchers are Reynaldo Alarcón, Rafael Navarro, and Ramón León. The area of social and community psychology has also reached a certain degree of development, including a number of studies concerned with the psychology of poverty.

Bibliography

Alarcón, R., et al. (Eds.). (1976). *La investigación psicológica en el Perú* [Psychological research in Peru]. Lima: Sociedad Peruana de Psicología, Memorias del Primer Congreso Peruano de Psicología.

Alarcón, R. (Ed.). (1980). *Psicología en el Perú* [Psychology in Peru]. Special issue: *Revista Latinoamericana de Psicología, 12* (2).

Ardila, R. (1978). *La profesión del psicólogo* [The profession of psychologist]. Mexico: Trillas.

Ardila, R. (1993). *La psicología en América Latina, pasado, presente y futuro* [Psychology in Latin America: Past, present, and future]. Mexico: Siglo XXI Editores.

Rubén Ardila

PESSIMISM. *See* Optimism and Pessimism.

PESTALOZZI, JOHANN HEINRICH (1746–1827), Swiss educator. Pestalozzi wrote extensively on educational and social reform and put his educational ideas into practice in several experimental schools. His first school, for poor children, was founded in 1775 at Neuhof; it closed in 1780, in large part because of Pestalozzi's financial ineptitude. He did not run a school or teach again until 1799. In the interim, he wrote on a wide variety of social and educational issues. His only popular success was the romantic novel *Leonard and Gertrude*, published in 1781, which was intended as an exposition of his educational ideas. In 1798 Pestalozzi set up another school for poor children, which closed after only a few months. Almost immediately Pestalozzi began a series of teaching posts in Burgdorf. Positive evaluations of his efforts by the town school commission led, in 1800, to the use of the castle at Burgdorf for his own school. In 1804 this school was also forced to close for political and financial reasons. In 1801, Pestalozzi had published *How Gertrude Teaches her Children*, a more systematic presentation of his educational ideas than *Leonard and Gertrude*. It was this book that established Pestalozzi's reputation throughout Europe. Pestalozzi went to Yverdon in 1804 and started yet another school, which lasted until 1825, when financial problems, as well as disagreements among the staff, led to its closure. Pestalozzi died 2 years later.

Pestalozzi's ideas were immensely popular in Europe and were spread not only in his writings, including teaching manuals for particular content areas, but also through the schools themselves. Prominent and influential visitors included Johann Gottleib Fichte, Johann Friedrich Herbart, and Friedrich Froebl, the founder of the kindergarten movement, who spent more than a year at Yverdon. After Pestalozzi's death, Horace Mann visited German and Swiss schools and worked to incorporate Pestalozzi's ideas into the school system of Massachusetts.

Pestalozzi's ideas about the education of young children were in marked contrast to the educational practice of the time. Almost anyone could open a school, regardless of educational or psychological qualifications. Rote memorizing of the catechism was a major goal of early education; severe physical punishment was common. Pestalozzi proposed a number of changes. First, he emphasized direct observation of the physical world: he rejected the heavy use of books as the sole source of knowledge, at least during the early years, and rote memorization at any age. Children were to learn through their own senses, often outside the classroom; only then were children to read about general and abstract ideas. Second, the first qualification of a teacher was affection for children; teachers needed to provide the love and security of a family. Pestalozzi disapproved of corporal punishment and rarely viewed it as necessary. Finally, Pestalozzi proposed that teachers themselves needed to be taught about the nature of children and the best methods for teaching them. His schools served not only as demonstrations of his ideas, but also as schools for teachers. Pestalozzi's ideas revolutionized and humanized the treatment of young children in schools; he also revolutionized, if not created, teaching as a professional discipline.

Bibliography

Downs, R. B. (1975). *Heinrich Pestalozzi.* Boston: Twayne.

Pestalozzi, J. H. (1977). *"How Gertrude teaches her children."* In D. A. Robinson (Ed.), *Significant contributions to the history of psychology, 1750–1920* (Series B, Vol. 2, pp. 17–391). Washington, DC: University Publications of America. (Original work published 1801)

Silber, K. (1976). *Pestalozzi: The man and his work* (4th ed., rev.). London: Routledge & Kegan Paul.

Emily S. Davidson

PET. *See* Brain Imaging Techniques.

PHALLIC STAGE. *See* Psychosexual Stages.

PHARMACOTHERAPY. *See* Psychopharmacology, *article on* Pharmacotherapy.

PH.D. *See* Doctoral Degree.

PHENOMENOLOGICAL PSYCHOLOGY. The term *phenomenological* is often used by psychologists to refer simply to the subjective point of view, as well as to the world as seen through the perspective of a particular person. The term has, however, a long history in the field of psychiatry, beginning with Karl Jaspers and continuing with the work of Eugene Minkowski, Ludwig Binswanger, Viktor von Gebsattel, Medard Boss, Frederik Buytendijk, Jan van den Berg, Kurt Goldstein, Viktor Frankl, and others. In contemporary psychiatry, the term tends to be used superficially to refer to the symptomatology pertaining to various diagnostic entities. The aforementioned European psychiatrists, however, used this term in a much more systematic way to refer to the entire existential structure of a person's lived world. The roots of all the phenomenological psychopathogists can be traced to Edmund Husserl; many of them were influenced by Martin Heidegger as well.

The phenomenological movement in American psychology was bolstered in the late 1950s by the publication of Rollo May's landmark volume, *Existence: A New Dimension in Psychiatry and Psychology* (1958), and by the establishment in 1959 of an innovative graduate program in psychology at Duquesne University. The intellectual roots of this program, as well as of May's volume, were European in origin, including philosophers, psychiatrists, and philosopher-psychiatrists whose texts, mostly untranslated, had begun to be communicated within both academic and clinical circles in Europe and America. Not only were there two distinct circles of existential psychologists already developing in America (grouped respectively around Rollo May and Viktor Frankl), but also a humanistic movement, all of which were to have their influence on the emerging field of phenomenological psychology. Throughout the 1960s and into the early 1970s, the term *existential psychology and psychiatry* was used much more frequently than in the last quarter of the twentieth century to refer to this movement (although at the time it was considered less a movement per se, and more an attitude). In fact, the term *existential psychology* originally embraced a more overarching vision, wherein phenomenology was understood as the first stage of development within a larger professional and academic discipline (see May, 1969).

As in the case with existentialism, existential psychology is not a true system, but rather a term used to refer to what appears in retrospect as a movement consisting of like-minded individuals who had familiarized themselves with the thought of such thinkers as Kierkegaard, Nietzsche, Marx, Freud, Buber, Heidegger, and Sartre (as well as with the writings of literary artists like Kafka and Dostoevsky) and found in their writings a basis for understanding what was being discovered in personality research and confronted in consulting rooms. Psychologists like Rollo May, Gordon Allport, Carl Rogers, R. D. Laing, Viktor Frankl, Erich Fromm, and James Bugental were less concerned with methodological issues and more concerned with the themes that were the upshot of existential thinking. Freedom, alienation, the facticity of death, estrangement of self from other, the falling into "inauthenticity," the possibility of becoming an "authentic self," ontological guilt, and the experience of nothingness all served as a basis for understanding the plights of humanity in the twentieth century.

Existential psychology was, at the outset, associated more with an optimistic approach to psychotherapy than with formal research. Its representatives devoted themselves to healing the lost souls, the "hollow" men and women of our time, who have lost touch with themselves, their fellow humanity, and their sense of wonder in the face of the transcendent. Thus, Rollo May wrote *The Cry for Myth* (1990) and *Man's Search for Himself* (1953) based on his therapeutic contact with modern-day people whose central complaint can be described as a loss of meaning. Viktor Frankl's reflections as a survivor of Nazi death camps took this one step further in his similarly titled book (*Man's Search for Meaning*, 1963). Erich Fromm, on the other hand, wrote a commentary on modern humanity's refusal to take responsibility for itself in his books ironically titled *The Sane Society* (1955) and *Escape from Freedom* (1941). Thomas Szasz turned our attention to "the manufacture madness" and "the myth of mental illness," and R. D. Laing founded a residential clinic where he attempted to live with and understand people labeled as psychotic. His work with schizophrenics lent itself especially well to a dialogue with Sartre's thinking, particularly his writings on concrete relations with others and his existential psychoanalyses; the outcome was Laing's own classic texts *The Divided Self* (1965) *The Politics of Experience* (1967), and *Sanity, Madness, and the Family* (1964).

Eventually, Adrian Van Kaam (1966) would write a book that articulated not simply the foundations of existential psychology, but rather the existential foundations of all psychology, expressing the hope that by the next century existential psychology would not be necessary any more, because, hopefully, by then all psychology would be truly existential (in the sense of having escaped the pitfalls of positivism and embraced the holistic perspective of existential-phenomenology). By the end of the 1960s, Duquesne University's program was using the term *existential-phenomenological* to refer to its paradigm, with the intent of acknowledging its indebtedness both to existential thinking for providing a new philosophical anthropology, and to phenomenology for providing a new approach and methodology for research. From that time forward, it has been the rule rather than the exception to see the full term *existential-phenomenology* used in book titles and conference papers. The term *existential* seemed to carry more weight in the earlier days of the movement, perhaps because it triggered associations to both philosophical and literary writings on freedom, angst, authenticity, death, and so on. Eventually, through conventional usage, it became understood that the shorter term, *phenomenological psychology*, implied existential influences, even if only tacitly.

Although there are many individuals and institutions throughout North America, Europe, and South Africa contributing to the development of this new paradigm, phenomenological psychology has been developed in a systematic way in America primarily at Duquesne University and at the many schools to which its graduates have migrated. From the early 1960s into the 1980s, the Duquesne school consisted of both a research paradigm for qualitative research that was phenomenologically based, and an application of existential-phenomenological principles to clinical assessment and psychotherapy. Inspired originally by the thought of Husserl, Heidegger, Sartre, and Merleau-Ponty, psychologists at Duquesne developed an empirical-phenomenological procedure with the aim of using it to clarify the essence of various kinds of psychological phenomena through an investigation of specific experiences in which these phenomena are revealed.

The key to this method is not simply that its data consist of verbal testimonies of various types of experience; this alone merely qualifies it more generally as a type of qualitative research. The hallmark of the phenomenological method in psychology is its *thematization of how an individual co-constitutes the world of experience* that has been described in self-report data, therapy transcripts, or other forms of expression. Data analysis consists of the identification of constitutive "horizons" or "modes of presence" that make possible the experience of the situations described. There is a turning, then, from given facts (the data as presented) to intended meanings (the data as understood by the researcher)—from the simple *givenness* of the situation in the individual's experience to a reflective apprehension of that situation's meaning as having been co-constituted ("intended") by the individual's consciousness, or existential presence. This is by no means a return to introspectionism: As Sartre dramatically observed, if one could ever get "inside" a consciousness, one would be seized upon by a whirlwind and thrown back out into the world! Phenomenological psychology is, emphatically, the study of persons in situations.

The psychological work of empirical-phenomenological research consists of the researcher entering into dialogue with the data. The researcher's involvement in co-constituting the findings is often attacked as a form of subjectivism; however, from within the phenomenological understanding of the interpretive process, such an involvement of the knower with the known is inevitable. Indeed, it expresses the implication of the principle of intentionality for the research process itself. This does not mean, however, that the procedure involves some kind of introspection that is inaccessible to someone wishing to verify the reliability of the findings; nor does it imply some kind of relativism or privatism in the understanding of data. This is, first, because what is being known here is not some inner realm to which there exists only private access; rather, what is being known here is precisely the relationship of the individual to the world, and this relationship is not accessible by turning inward (wherever that might lead). Merleau-Ponty argued that whenever we do succeed in having something worthwhile to say about our own experience, it is because we are looking at it the way another person would, that is, from a third-person point of view. Furthermore, the researcher, upon entering into a dialogue with the data, is not attempting to look inside his or her own consciousness of the data, but is, rather, engaged in a narrative act of understanding a life situation. The interpretive process here is circumscribed, of course, by the researcher's perspective on the data. But this perspective is made explicit to anyone reading the analysis, in the form of a set of research questions and guiding principles. This leads not to *relativism*, but to a simple acknowledgment of the *relativity of understanding*.

Following Heidegger, existential-phenomenological psychologists acknowledge the impossibility of presuppositionless knowledge, and hence have accepted the notion that all description is already interpretation. This means that no claims of universality (as was the case in Husserl's "pure" phenomenology) are to be made in empirical-phenomenological research; rather, research results are presented as tentative statements opening upon a limitless field of possible interpretations. Although phenomenological psychologists follow hermeneutic principles first articulated by Dilthey, they stop short at the kind of relativism associated with emerging postmodernist traditions. Evidence for this is to be found in the insistence that research results be adequate to a body of facts or data (a modified version of the correspondence criterion for truth) rather than merely being required to "hang together" in a clear and cogent manner (a coherence criterion for truth favored by narrative psychologists). The emphasis of this research paradigm can be described as a fidelity toward the phenomenon. A psychological phenomenon is understood here not as an event "in itself," but rather as something that occurs "for someone." The situations in which I experience anger, jealousy, joy, futility, intimacy, courage, self-esteem, self-deception, clinical insight, being victimized, and so on, are not approached by the phenomenological psychologist as though there were some objective reference point from which to observe and describe the events taking place. Rather, there is an acknowledgment of an always already existing perspective through which the individual experiences his or her world, and, in turn, through which the researcher takes up the experience of the research participant.

The key principle for verifying the findings of this research is for the reader to look at the data from the perspective of the research questions posed to the data, and to assess if the findings presented ring true as possibilities of meaning. This is where the hermeneutic principle of *Wiederholung* ("repetition," better translated as "retrieval") enters into empirical-phenomenological research in psychology. One does not expect to be able to repeat someone else's analysis and get the same results; rather, one looks to see if one can retrieve similar meanings from the data, when looking through the filter of the research questions that were posed to the data by the researcher. Phenomenological psychologists do indeed filter their research data, not through formulas or statistics, but through frameworks of understanding and questions born from their own involvement with the data. Just as the dialectical relationship between person and world is accessible to critical reflection on the part of the researcher, so also is the dialectical relationship between researcher and research findings accessible to critical reflection on the part of other researchers. As colleagues and co-researchers, we coexist within a hermeneutic circle of interpretation and understanding.

Another hermeneutic principle at work in empirical-phenomenological research is the acknowledgment and utilization of a set of guiding principles derived from the investigations of philosophical phenomenologists. Among the foundational ideas that guide the reflective work of phenomenological psychologists are concepts such as intentionality, worldhood, embodiment, existence, freedom, and temporality. Such concepts serve as a medium, or lens, through which we understand the phenomenal world before us. This approach to the use of concepts in psychological research is consistent with the original Greek meaning of *eidos* (from which we derive the English word "idea"), which meant both something that is seen and something by means of which one sees. In this sense, fundamental concepts are ways of seeing that enable something to be seen.

Doing psychology phenomenologically is ultimately predicated upon a *sensitivity to meanings* that is the cumulative result of a disciplined apprenticeship in human science methodology. This approach draws heavily upon empathy as an investigatory posture. In empathy, I participate in the other's positioning himself or herself from a unique perspective within a situation. In reading self-report data empathically, attention is directed to the subtleties contained in language, through which worlds of experience are revealed (and also concealed). In particular, the phenomenological psychologist attends to ways in which an individual's participation in the co-creation of experience is revealed. The operative principle here is Husserl's notion of intentionality, a teleological construct that refers to our psychological involvement in the world of experience: a concept that replaces the natural scientific principle of causality as the defining principle of psychological inquiry.

Husserl originally outlined the possibility for phenomenological psychology as an eidetic discipline, that is, a strictly philosophical enterprise aimed at laying the foundations for an empirical psychology. In agreement with Dilthey, Husserl believed that description, rather than explanation, was to be the means for identifying the essential constituents of psychological phenomena. His unique, and problematic, idea was that an a priori, or propaedeutic, understanding of one's subject matter must be accomplished before engaging in empirical investigations. (This idea was subsequently rejected by Sartre and Merleau-Ponty.) Husserl's original aim for his phenomenological psychology was an epistemological one: he wanted to establish a set of principles that would preclude the various species of "psychologism" (e.g., the reduction of an idea to the cognitive acts that produce it) prevalent in his day. It is also significant that for Husserl, the term *empirical psychology* meant, specifically, the scientific investigation of consciousness; the study of bodily events concomitant to specific conscious experiences belonged properly to the field of psychology. Thus, for Husserl, the term *physiological psychology* would be an oxymoron.

If the interest of Husserl's "pure" phenomenology was to articulate the intentionality of consciousness in such a way as to ground all assertions, philosophical or otherwise, in the relationship of consciousness to its objects (all consciousness is consciousness *of* something), Husserl's followers expanded and deepened this interest to embrace the full relationship between subject and world. By applying hyphens to Husserl's (1913/1982) expression, Heidegger (1927/1962) introduced "Being-in-the-world" as the indissoluble intentional unity that can be further articulated in terms of its existential characteristics. These *existentialia* are the ontological conditions of possibility for human existence; as such, they express the ways that we *have to be*, in whatever ways we may *happen to be*. Among the *existentialia* described by Heidegger are language, understanding, speech, moodedness, spatiality, temporality, care, and Being-toward-death: all equiprimordial in their constitutive function with respect to human existence. This means that no one existential characteristic has priority over the others, but rather each is mutually implicated by the other. Thus, one cannot talk about the spatiality of a particular person's world without invoking the ways in which this person understands the world, which in turn will be based upon the ways in which this person anticipates death, how this then finds expression in the person's attunement to others, and is at the same time a function of the disclosive power of language and expression.

Influenced by Hegel, Husserl, and Heidegger, Sartre

wrote extensively about consciousness, concrete relations with others, freedom, and responsibility. He viewed each life as a unique event in which a given moment or segment of experience finds its place within a totality of involvements, where each moment is comprehensible on the basis of past experiences (although being irreducible to them). His existential psychoanalysis, which is a form of inquiry aimed at the individual life history, attempts to understand how we live ourselves in time, facing the conditions within which we find ourselves, and finding our way to our "ownmost" possibilities of selfhood and fulfillment in a world we inhabit with others. Merleau-Ponty's phenomenology was also centered on existential issues, with an emphasis on the nature of human embodiment and the relation of language to existence. Drawing upon his study of Gestalt psychology as well as of classical physiology, Merleau-Ponty provided an original synthesis of his philosophical and psychological predecessors in *Structure of Behavior* (1942/1963), and *Phenomenology of Perception* (1945/1962), which together are among the most psychologically oriented of the philosophical texts in phenomenology. Taking as his point of departure Sartre's (1943/1956) notion of the body as one's point of view on the world, Merleau-Ponty developed an ontology of the body as the perceptual and expressive vehicle of subjectivity. With Merleau-Ponty, the philosophical investigation of human experience itself becomes an activity of the "body-subject," and philosophy turns from shadows on the wall to the "prose of the world."

Although contemporary existential-phenomenological psychologists respect Husserl's original aim, they have developed a method that incorporates hermeneutic and dialectical principles, which has taken them far beyond the bounds of an eidetic science. Merleau-Ponty critiqued the idea that an eidetic science should necessarily precede an empirical science; and, following Heidegger (who stated that our essence *lies in* our existence), he claimed that eidetic investigation could only proceed in dialectical relation with its empirical foundations. The very intuition of essences, of which Husserl spoke, itself presupposes a consciousness engaged with concrete reality. Thus, the post-Husserlian project for an existential-phenomenological psychology recasts this discipline from a propaedeutic, purely eidetic, and thus philosophical one, to a heuristic process in which the tensions between the eidetic and empirical are resolved as we enter into the hermeneutic circle of interpretation.

Existential phenomenology has helped to establish a new paradigm for psychological research as well as for clinical interventions, insofar as no one psychological function or experience can be viewed any longer in isolation from another. It makes little sense to the phenomenologist to separate the discussion of perception and personality (as they always are in introductory psychology textbooks), for there is no personality that exists in isolation from the perceived world, and there is no human perception that is not already the expression of a particular personality. The same goes for motivation, cognition, emotion, development, intelligence, social psychology, and so on: Following the principle of Gestalt, no constituent within a structure can be considered apart from the structure as a whole. Likewise, each moment of our lives is treated in relation to our life as a whole: The part is viewed from the perspective of the whole. Finally, with its emphasis on human freedom in the co-constitution of meaning, existential-phenomenological psychology opens the door for a more hopeful approach to psychotherapy, one based on the possibility that disturbed people can choose to constitute their lives in less disturbing ways. We are neither trapped by our situation nor trapped by our past. This is not to deny that there are limiting conditions to our freedom, but rather to acknowledge that the paramount feature of psychological life is our existential aptitude for grasping and adapting to our situations in new ways.

[*See also* Existential Psychology; Gestalt Psychology; Phenomenology; *and* Psychology, *article on* Post World War II.]

Bibliography

Binswanger, L. (1963). *Being-in-the-world* (J. Needleman, Ed.). New York: Basic Books. Essential reading for anyone interested in a psychiatric application of Heidegger's phenomenological anthropology; one of the seminal texts in Daseinsanalysis.

Boss, M. (1979). *Existential foundations of medicine and psychology* (S. Conway & A. Cleaves, Trans.). Northvale, NJ: Jason Aronson. (Original work published 1971.) Boss's magnum opus based on Heidegger's ontology of existence, this work has the distinction of representing the only psychological application of Heidegger's thought that was endorsed by Heidegger himself.

Casey, E. S. (1976). *Imagining: A phenomenological study*. Bloomington: Indiana University Press.

Casey, E. S. (1987). *Remembering: A phenomenological study*. Bloomington: Indiana University Press. Both Casey volumes are meticulous applications of Husserl's method of intentional (*noetic–neomatic*) analysis. They are perhaps the best demonstrations of Husserl's project for a phenomenological psychology.

Colaizzi, P. F. (1973). *Reflection and research in psychology: A phenomenological study of learning*. Dubuque, IA: Kendall/Hunt. A cogent demonstration of the empirical-phenomenological research paradigm developed at Duquesne University, this text compares individual intuition to empirically based phenomenological analyses, and proposes a procedure that consists of a synthesis of empirical and intuitive phenomenological methods. The text includes demonstrations of this procedure as applied to the phenomenon of learning, and concludes with an uncompromising critique of traditional empirical psychology.

Fuller, A. (1990). *Insight into value: An exploration of the premises of a phenomenological psychology.* Early chapters offer a clear and compelling introduction to phenomenology and existential phenomenology. The remainder of the text consists of a dialogue between existential phenomenology and Gestalt psychology in an effort to formulate a concrete understanding of the interpretive process.

Giorgi, A. (1970). *Psychology as a human science: A phenomenologically based approach.* New York: Harper & Row. The paradigmatic text for phenomenological psychology that clarifies the importance of the methodological concept of approach, based on Dilthey's distinction between the natural sciences and the human sciences. This text also articulates a new vision for psychological theory and research, influenced strongly by Merleau-Ponty's notion of structure.

Giorgi, A. et al. (1971–1983). *Duquesne studies in phenomenological psychology* (Vols. 1–4). Pittsburgh: Duquesne University Press. Four volumes of articles in the theory and application of a human science psychology grounded in the existential phenomenological tradition.

Giorgi, A. (Ed.). (1985). *Phenomenology and psychological research.* Pittsburgh: Duquesne University Press. A statement by the editor of research principles well grounded in the works of Merleau-Ponty, followed by four applications. Wertz's chapter on "Being Criminally Victimized" is without question the most empirically extensive, reflectively impressive, and best-written application of the Duquesne paradigm in print.

Heidegger, M. (1982). *Being and time.* (J. Macguame & E. Robinson, Trans.). New York: Harper & Row. (Original work published 1927.) This is the book without which there would not be an existential phenomenological psychology today. It marks the most radical break with the tradition of Western thought of Derrida and others. But most important, it serves as the ontological foundation for the psychological (as well as ontological) work of thinkers like Sartre, Merleau-Ponty, Levinas, Boss, and others.

Husserl, E. (1978). *Phenomenological psychology* (J. Scanlon, Trans.). Boston: Martinus Nijhoff. (Original lecture course given 1925.) Husserl's application of constitutive phenomenology to the psychology of perception is developed in this series of lectures demonstrating that phenomenology can be carried out in a mundane as well as transcendental attitude; a general conceptualization, or eidetics, of perception is established with the intent of guiding future empirical research. (It is here that Husserl most explicitly acknowledged his indebtedness to Dilthey.)

Husserl, E. (1982). *Ideas pertaining to a pure phenomenology and phenomenological philosophy—First Book: General introduction to a pure phenomenology* (F. Kersten, Trans.). Boston: Martinus Nijhoff. (Original work published 1913.) Husserl's critique of the naturalistic prejudice is here followed by his presentation of the fundamental phenomenological outlook, the procedure of a phenomenological method, and a sketch of the general structures of "pure consciousness."

Keen, E., (1970). *Three faces of being: Toward an existential clinical psychology.* New York: Appeton-Century-Crofts. A clear introduction to existential psychology and Daseinsanalysis that includes the author's own synthesis of ideas, as well as summaries of Freud's case studies on the rat man and the psychotic Dr. Schreber, and a reprint of Binswanger's "Case of Ellen West," a classic paper in the Daseinsanalytic tradition.

May, R., Angel, E., & Ellenberger, H. F. (Eds.). (1958). *Existence: A new dimension in psychiatry and psychology.* New York: Simon & Schuster. The landmark text that first introduced existential psychiatry to the American reader; contains an excellent introduction by the editors, as well as classic writings by Ludwig Binswanger, Von Gebsattel, and others.

May, R. (Ed.). (1960). *Existential psychology* (2nd ed.). New York: Random House. An anthology with contributions from humanistic and existential psychologists (Maslow, Rogers, Allport, and May) on the Continental intellectual foundations for American humanistic psychology. Includes an annotated bibliography on existential and phenomenological psychology.

Merleau-Ponty, M. (1962). *Phenomenology of perception* (C. Smith, Trans.). London: Routledge & Kegan Paul. (Original work published 1945.) One of the three most important foundational tests for an existential phenomenological psychology (along with Heidegger's *Being and Time* and Sartre's *Being and Nothingness*).

Merleau-Ponty, M. (1962). *The primacy of perception* (J. Edie, Ed.). Evanston IL: Northwestern University Press. This text is a collection of essays on psychology, art, and history. Of particular interest is the author's summary and defense of the central thesis of his *Phenomenology of Perception.* In addition, this volume includes a translation of his lecture course at the Sorbonne on "The Child's Relations with Others," which is the only existing excursion into a phenomenological approach to developmental psychology. Merleau-Ponty's important theoretical essay on "Phenomenology and the Sciences of Man" should be of interest to philosophers of science as well as those concerned with the dialectics of interrogation and similar methodological issues. The essay "Eye and Mind" on Descartes, Monet, and Cezanne, was the last piece Merleau-Ponty saw published in his lifetime.

Merleau-Ponty, M. (1963). *The structure of behavior* (A. Fisher, Trans.). Pittsburgh: Duquesne University Press. (Original work written 1938 and published 1942.) This is Merleau-Ponty's first book. Its first half is an unusual dialogue between the empirical physiological psychology of behavior (e.g., reflexology) on the one hand, and phenomenology on the other; the second half develops Merleau-Ponty's own vision of the structures of behavior in a radically gestalt interpretation.

Pollio, H. R. Henley, T., & Thompson, C. B. (1998). *The phenomenology of everyday life*. Cambridge, UK: Cambridge University Press. Half of this text is devoted to foundational issues in existential-phenomenological psychology, including theoretical and methodological issues, influenced to a large extent by Heidegger and Merleau-Ponty, as well as by Buber, James, and Sartre. The second half consists of research demonstrations of the phenomenological paradigm as applied to topics drawn from everyday life, including interpersonal relations, feeling lonely, and the meanings of death in the context of life.

Sartre, J. P. (1948). *The emotions: Outline for a theory* (B. Frechtman, Trans.). New York: Philosophical Library. (Original work published 1939.) This is a small work that brings Sartre's "freedom-ism" to bear on the concrete psychological problem of emotions; in this work, Sartre first critiqued a variety of psychological approaches to emotion, such as the James–Lange and psychoanalytic theories, and then he developed his own theory, maintaining that emotions are chosen by people in order to avoid personal responsibility.

Sartre, J. P. (1956). *Being and nothingness: A phenomenological essay on ontology* (H. Barnes, Trans.). New York: Philosophical Library. (Original work published 1943.) This test develops the principles upon which Sartre founded his "existential psychoanalysis." His concrete illustrations of complex dialectical and ontological formulations of our nature as embodied consciousnesses help psychologists to appreciate the philosophical underpinnings of the work of existential psychologists such as Rollo May and R. D. Laing.

Spiegelberg, H. (1972). *Phenomenology in psychology and psychiatry*. Evanston, IL: Northwestern University Press. A virtual encyclopedia of all the figures who made important contributions to the phenomenological approach to psychology and psychiatry.

Valle, R. (Ed.). (1998). *Phenomenological inquiry: Existential and transpersonal dimensions*. New York: Plenum Press. A sequel and companion to the previous text, which incorporates both existential and transpersonal research approaches to research. The early chapters by Rolf von Eckartsberg (excerpted from his 1986 monograph, "Life-World Experience: Existential-Phenomenological Research Approaches in Psychology") provide an incisive overview of the entire field of existential phenomenological psychology. Other chapters explore methodological issues (such as the reliability of interpretive psychological research) and provide demonstrations of various research paradigms inspired by phenomenological philosophy.

Valle, R. S. & King, M. (Eds.). (1978). *Existential-phenomenological alternatives for psychology*. New York: Oxford University Press. This volume includes methodological contributions as well as research applications in the areas of learning, body image, perception, memory, person perception, anxiety, and cognitive development. There are also clinical applications in the areas of assessment, psychopathology, psychotherapy, and counseling.

Van den Berg, J. (1972). *A different existence: Principles of phenomenological psychopathology*. Pittsburgh: Duquesne University Press. A classic text introducing the reader in a clear and straightforward fashion to the phenomenological way of understanding our relationship to the world of things, to others, to our bodies, and to time.

Van Kaam, A. (1966). *Existential foundations of psychology*. Pittsburgh: Duquesne University Press. This text, which came out of Van Kaam's early work in the psychology departments at both Case Western Reserve and Duquesne Universities, articulates the foundations of traditional scientific psychology in contrast to a human science psychology, each as seen from the perspective of existential philosophy. The text also proposes a methodology for an anthropological psychology, that is, a psychology founded upon the principles of existential and phenomenological thought.

Scott D. Churchill

PHENOMENOLOGY as a systematic approach to philosophy and psychology was instituted by Edmund Husserl's numerous writings on the nature of subjectivity. Interestingly, the time during which Husserl wrote on the primacy and nature of consciousness almost exactly corresponds to the time in which Freud wrote about the primacy and nature of the unconscious. Both were students of Franz Brentano, who taught that the proper object of psychology was the sense, or meaning, or intent, of experience, rather than its mechanisms. To speak of the psyche as intentional is to acknowledge that it is always *directed toward* something. Husserl developed his "pure" phenomenology as a rigorous science that would explore the *intentional* foundations of knowledge (whereas Freud developed his psychoanalysis as a scientific psychology aimed at uncovering *unconscious* intentions). Husserl's interest can be described as a transcendental inquiry aimed toward the *a priori* structures of consciousness: the conditions of possibility for human experience, as well as for the knowledge systems based upon that experience. Husserl's aim was to overcome the pitfalls of relativism by founding knowledge on the appearance of self-evident matters to consciousness.

The term *phenomenology* derives from two Greek words, *phainomenon* and *logos*, which when put together mean "the letting appear of what shows itself from itself." Heidegger suggested that this means, in effect, the turning of one's regard toward the multiplicity of experiences wherein everything to which we relate shows itself. In simpler terms, phenomenology is the disclosure of things or events as they occur *for someone*, with the ultimate aim of uncovering and articulating the modes of presence that co-constitute, and thus make possible, the perception of all things and events. Phenomenology is also a philosophical position that asserts that objectivity is an unreachable ideal, and that what heretofore has passed for objectivity is, more accurately, the result of intersubjective agreement. Thus, the phenomenologist smiles and winks when hearing someone talk about "objective facts" or "the event as it really happened" or even "absolute Truth," for it is precisely one's perspective (on facts, events, truths) that cannot be disassociated from whatever it is one is talking about. Perspectivity is thus the central theme of all phenomenological explications.

Philosophical Precursors

Husserl's work can be seen both as a continuation of the work of certain continental philosophers, such as Kant and Hegel, and also as a response to the empiricism that had come to command the philosophical foundation of psychology. Hegel had used the term *phenomenology* in 1807 to delineate a field of investigation of stages in the evolution of the mind's absolute knowledge of itself. Although Hegel carried out a kind of transcendental analysis of subjectivity, his interest was in characterizing the "Divine Mind" or Spirit (*Geist*) that would make possible the world as we know it. Husserl's own thought was, however, hardly influenced by Hegel's version of transcendental idealism. The radicality of his phenomenology lies in his overcoming Descartes's mutually exclusive categories of mind and body, subject and world, toward a mutually reciprocal "intentionality" of consciousness and life world.

The priority of conscious experience as the concrete foundation for intentionality reverses the usual priority of the objective over the subjective that positivism promotes. Nowhere can this reversal of priority better be seen than in the method of the phenomenological reduction, which requires us to set aside or bracket our natural belief in mundane reality, because that belief obscures the intentional experience that makes possible our taken-for-granted sense of the world. What gets bracketed in the reduction is the world as thematized from the natural standpoint, namely, the belief that the world exists independently of subjectivity (i.e., a belief that the world *actually is* the way it appears to the perceiver). The setting aside of this belief is not a denial of the existence of the real world, but only a methodological device that allows us to concentrate on something else. In its place, a different belief comes into play: a belief that experienced meanings are the correlates of particular attitudes assumed by consciousness. There is a turning, then, from "given facts" (*data*) to "grasped meanings" (*noemata*). Indeed, when one hears phenomenology defined as a study of appearances, this means precisely that it focuses on the individual's experience or co-constitution of what is given, rather than on the object itself that is given. Because attending to natural reality is our everyday attitude, we need the special method of the reduction to turn our attention back to consciousness, as well as to bracket the naturalistic prejudice by which the world of experience has typically been reduced to objective facts.

This priority given to consciousness over and above the objects of consciousness is prefigured in Kant's *transcendentalism*, a term that Husserl borrowed and used extensively to describe his own philosophy. Kant had attempted to discover the logical prerequisites (or necessary conditions) for human experience of the world, calling these *a priori* conditions "transcendental," since they make possible the experience of the world and thus cannot be contained in the world. Husserl wanted to turn to the lived acts of consciousness that make possible, or constitute, our experience of mundane reality. Kant had distinguished *phenomena* (the way things appear to consciousness) from *noumena* (the actual independently existing things themselves). Having established the transcendental ego as the ultimate knowing agency, Kant denied in principle the possibility of attaining knowledge of the world as it exists apart from the agency that seeks to know it. Where Husserl departed from Kant was in his insistence that the affairs to which consciousness returns be self-evident, that is, based upon an immediate self-showing, and thus not reducible simply to the transcendental schemas that enable such evidence to come into view. Husserl thereby sought to escape the pitfalls of rationalism and empiricism, realism, and idealism, by locating truth in "Being in the world" (Husserl, 1913/1982).

Of all authors considered to be precursors to Husserl's formulation of phenomenology, Brentano is the most immediate, since Husserl studied with him and explicitly recognized an indebtedness to Brentano's act theory of consciousness. In his *Psychology from an Empirical Standpoint* (New York, 1874/1973), Brentano established an epistemological basis for the division of scientific disciplines into those that study what is accessible to external perception (i.e., the senses) and those that study what is accessible only through inner perception (i.e., intuition). Following Brentano, Husserl saw that the field of lived experience is given to an inner perception (not to be confused with *introspection*), and thus delineates a field of knowledge that can be adequately intuited. Before encountering Brentano, Husserl had studied mathematics, asking more and more foundational questions concerning the possibility of knowing mathematical entities. These epistemological questions began to consume Husserl, and he found in Brentano's work an opening to the phenomenology of mathematics, asking, what acts of consciousness allow one to know mathematical entities? This question was soon widened to ask, what acts of consciousness allow one to know the entire variety of theoretical as well as worldly entities that we encounter in life? This relationship of conscious act (*noesis*) to intended meaning (*noema*) is what would eventually be expressed by the term *intentionality*.

The Notion of Intentionality

Husserl's central insight, which would become the fundamental tenet of phenomenology, is that consciousness is always and essentially intentional, that is, oriented toward a world of emergent meaning: "Consciousness is always consciousness-of-something." Moreover, if there is no subject or consciousness without a world toward which it is aimed, there is also no objective world without a consciousness for which it exists. This is why, phenomenologically speaking, we do not describe an object (the *noumenon*, or the thing "in-itself"), but rather the object *as it exists for consciousness* (the *phenomenon*, or the thing "in-itself-for-someone"). Intentionality thus refers to this fundamental relationship of consciousness to world.

Brentano had used the adjective *intentional* to describe simply the directionality of consciousness, that is, its orientation toward a meaningful world. With Husserl, this term became a noun (*intentionality*), describing the fundamental characteristic of all perceptions, ideas, intuitions, and memories, namely, the irreducible relationship between knower and known. The concept of intentionality enables philosophy to advance beyond the limiting horizons of both subjectivism and objectivism, first of all by making clear that every statement is a description neither reducible to the object of perception (as in scientific realism with its empiricist epistemology), nor to the subject of perception (as in idealism with its mentalist epistemology). Rather, every statement is always already a description that bears reference to, and expresses, the structural relationship between consciousness and world; thus, every statement that we make expresses our intentional relationship to what we are speaking about.

Although it was originally developed in an analysis of perceptual objects, the concept of intentionality has been expanded by later phenomenologists to be applied to the whole array of human experience. It indeed serves as the essential foundational principle for phenomenological psychology. It is also the one concept in which phenomenology's stress on an orientation toward the future is most evident. It provides a clear contrast with empiricist philosophers' emphasis on the role of past experiences in determining the experienced present. This stress on future orientation was eventually taken in a purposive sense by existential phenomenologists. Husserl proposed that it is only because of our capacity to anticipate, or *intend*, future possible experiences that we can have a sense of present perceptual reality. Because at any one time we can experience only one perspectival view of an object, the possibility of our experiencing the object as a whole is called into question. Husserl thus developed his "horizonal" theory of perception, in which he proposed that in and through any presently experienced perspective we anticipate an entire system of future possible views (the perceptual horizon): we anticipate being able to perceive the backside of an object even if we cannot experience it directly at the moment. Were it not for this kind of anticipatory intentionality, we could not have a perceptual sense of an object beyond its own immediate mode of self-givenness.

As is apparent from the discussion up to this point, Husserl's phenomenology was a distinctively philosophical discipline. It was further divided into psychological and transcendental counterparts, both of which nonetheless retained the distinctive flavor of a philosophical endeavor. For Husserl, eidetic psychology must precede and serve as a propaedeutic basis for empirical psychology. Indeed, what he would later refer to as the "crisis" of European sciences is the fact that the sciences have proceeded to investigate their subject matters without first pausing to reflect upon the proper nature of, and requisite methodology for, these matters. Ideas pertaining to the nature of psychological phenomena, discovered through eidetic intuition, would properly guide empirical research, and therefore should occupy the psychologist's attention prior to engaging in empirical research.

Husserl's Contemporaries

Alexander Pfänder and Karl Jaspers deserve special mention, insofar as these thinkers were contemporaries of Husserl who engaged in phenomenological investigations of psychological phenomena. Pfänder's most comprehensive work on "the nature of the psyche" was never translated into English and thus has not had the impact on American psychology that it otherwise might have had. His studies of motivation and volition first appeared in 1900 and are among the most important (though often neglected) contributions to phenomenological psychology. Jaspers is well known in psychological and psychiatric circles not only for the tremendous scope of his description and analysis of psychopathologies, but also for being a pioneer in the interface between philosophy and psychiatry. His *General Psychopathology* (Chicago, 1913/1963) is phenomenological both in the sense of its being descriptive (though not yet eidetic) and insofar as his methodology employs an application of Wilhelm Dilthey's principle of *Verstehen* (understanding the part from the point of view of the whole, rather than the other way around, as in Cartesian analysis).

Alfred Schutz, like Jaspers, was interested in the affairs of consciousness within the sphere of mundane life, and thus described his own work as a phenomenology of and within the natural attitude. Taking Husserl's transcendental insights as a point of departure, Schutz focused on the constitution of the social world. His research was primarily concerned with the commonsense structures of consciousness by which individuals are able to comprehend and co-constitute the nature of social reality. He also provided psychology with a useful paradigm for the description of perceptual and cognitive styles. Schutz's writings on social relations constitute part of the foundation of social constructionism.

Max Scheler was interested in emotional life, and wrote extensively on the essence of feelings, values, and love. His books on sympathy and *resentiment* are of particular interest to psychologists. He developed a philosophical anthropology that would serve as the basis for a sociology of knowledge and thus, like Schutz, Scheler became a precursor for the development of social constructionism.

Husserl's Legacy: Existential Phenomenology

In the wake of Husserl's pure, or transcendental, phenomenology, there developed a strain that is commonly referred to as *existential phenomenology*. Beginning with Heidegger's fundamental analysis of existence in *Being and Time* (1927/1962), there soon followed Jean-Paul Sartre's effort to synthesize his understanding of Hegel, Husserl, and Heidegger into a statement of phenomenological ontology in his well-known but often misunderstood work, *Being and Nothingness* (1943/1956). Both Heidegger and Sartre were indebted to Kierkegaard for his focus on the individual situated subject (rather than some universal subject), as well as for his emphasis that truth exists most profoundly at the individual level. In particular, Kierkegaard's psychologically poignant analyses of fear, anguish, and despair served as points of departure for both Heidegger's and Sartre's thinking on these subjects. With regard to the predecessors of the existential phenomenologists, it is worth noting that Heidegger was also indebted to Dilthey as the source of inspiration for his own inquiries into human temporality. Moreover, it was Dilthey who first emphasized the importance of *Verstehen* ("understanding") as opposed to explanation in the approach to psychological life and human history. Dilthey proposed a radical distinction between the sciences of nature (*Naturwissenschaften*) and the sciences of culture (or human studies; *Geisteswissenschaften*). The former were characterized by explanation and the latter by understanding. *Verstehen* consists of a synthesis of all the powers of the psyche: thinking as well as sensing, feeling, intuiting, imagining, remembering, and so on. More importantly, understanding is what gives us access to the meaning of human events—to the purposes or goals embodied in individual acts. Heidegger would later employ this "understanding" in his own existential-hermeneutical method, and also included understanding among the essential existential characteristics of human existence.

Borrowing from existential thought that predated Husserl's phenomenology, existential phenomenologists attempted to infuse phenomenology's descriptive field of immediate experience and intentionality with the concept of freedom. To say that human subjects are intentional is to say that we are purposive, Sartre insisted. To be intentional is to be aimed, and we are free to choose how we are aimed toward our future. If, as Husserl proposed, our orientation toward the future establishes our sense of the world, then we are free to intend our sense of the world as we will: the world is never given to us as a brute reality. Not only our world, but also our past, is constituted by acts of consciousness that are fundamentally future oriented. Just as there is no brute reality assigned to the world independent of meaning-giving acts of consciousness, there is no brute reality to people's past. We can at any time reconstitute the meaning that the past holds for us, and in that sense we can reconstitute the past itself; as always for phenomenology, experienced meanings have priority over, and in fact determine, our sense of reality, whether it is the reality of the world or the reality of the past.

The greatest import of Husserl for psychology is probably to be found in his later thinking, which bears the influence of Heidegger, and which in turn served as a point of departure for Merleau-Ponty's phenomenological and psychological inquiries. In Husserl's *The Crisis of European Sciences and Transcendental Phenomenology* (1939/1970), we see at once a phenomenology still grounded in a transcendental standpoint, but also aimed at a radicalization of the relationship among philosophy, science, and society. For science to be not only relevant to the more mundane tasks of human life, but also to be free from distorting (ideological, theoretical) interests that can alienate the scientist from the interests of humanity (and even do violence to our essential nature), scientific inquiry must be grounded in a philosophy that is capable of (a) avoiding relativistic standpoints, while (b) directing the scientist toward an understanding of human affairs that is both faithful to human nature and serves humanity's best interests. For psychology, this means the development of a paradigm that avoids the biases of both mentalism and materialism, in order to formulate an understanding of human life that embraces the structure, or Gestalt, wherein consciousness and body are integral to each other, and relative to which psychological interventions would be addressed.

[*See also* Hermeneutics; Phenomenological Psychology; *and* Psychology, *articles on* Nineteenth Century through Freud *and* Renaissance through Enlightenment.]

Bibliography

Dilthey, W. (1977). *Descriptive psychology and historical understanding* (R. M. Zaner & K. L. Heiges, Trans.). The Hague: Martinus Nijhoff. (Original works published 1924 and 1927.) This text introduces the reader to the spirit of a phenomenological approach to psychology without requiring the reader to first master the philosophical foundations of transcendental phenomenology, as in the case of reading Husserl. This edited volume contains two critical essays. The first ("Ideas Concerning a Descriptive and Analytical Psychology") clarifies the project for a descriptive rather than an explanatory psychology (which later became the basis for Karl Jaspers's *General Psychopathology*). The second ("The Understanding of Other Persons and Their Expressions of Life") is a brief and very clear introduction to the the meaning of *Verstehen* ("understanding") as the defining methodological criterion for knowledge about the psyche. The text also serves as an introduction to hermeneutics.

Embree, L. Behnke, E., Carr, D., Evans, J., Huertas-Jourda, J., Kockelmans, J., McKenna, W., Mickunas, A., Mohanty, J., Seebohm, T., and Zaner, R. (Eds.). (1997). *Encyclopedia of phenomenology*. Boston: Kluwer. This contemporary source draws on multiple authors to explain the main concepts of phenomenology in great detail. In addition, the encyclopedia includes expansive sections on relations between phenomenology and other approaches to philosophy and the human sciences.

Gurwitsch, A. (1964). *The field of consciousness*. Pittsburgh: Duquesne University Press. (Original work published 1957.) Beginning with a discussion of William James, Jean Piaget, and the Gestalt theories of Koehler and Kafka, this book presents a thoroughgoing phenomenological analysis of the organization of consciousness and the perception field. One of the most impressive applications of Husserl's method ever published.

Gurwitsch, A. (1974). *Phenomenology and the theory of science* (L. Embree, Ed. & Trans.). Evanston, IL: Northwestern University Press. A collection of essays that presents the more difficult aspects of Husserl's philosophy of science, in a way that makes his import for psychology more apparent.

Heidegger, M. (1962). *Being and time* (J. Macquarrie & E. Robinson, Trans.). New York: Harper & Row. (Original work published 1927.) This is the phenomenological work that makes the most radical break with modern philosophy and its immanent Cartesianism. After studying with Husserl, Heidegger developed this phenomenological ontology, which is both more existential and more hermeneutic than Husserl's work. The central concept of *Dasein*, through which the essence of human being is defined as "being-in-the-world," departs from Husserl's more subjectivist constitutive phenomenology; but, in other regards, the book continues themes, such as the centrality of time consciousness, that were first introduced by Husserl. Its main contribution to psychology is the philosophical anthropology that was not, in fact, the ultimate aim of the book, but that was nonetheless taken up by a new breed of psychiatrists as an alternative to the more constricting models of the human person afforded by psychoanalysis and medicine.

Husserl, E. (1970). *The crisis of European sciences and transcendental phenomenology* (D. Carr, Trans.). Evanston, IL: Northwestern University Press. (Original work published 1939.) Husserl's last published book takes a more cultural and historical approach to phenomenology than did his earlier works, discussing phenomenology in the context of the historical development of Western natural scientific thinking; this work is considered a bridge from the main body of Husserl's pure phenomenology to the existential phenomenology that was espoused by many of his followers, such as Sartre and Merleau-Ponty.

Husserl, E. (1982). *Ideas pertaining to a pure phenomenology and a phenomenological philosophy—First book: General introduction to a pure phenomenology* (F. Kersten, Trans.). Boston: Martinus Nijhoff. (Original work published 1913.) This is Husserl's most complete and programmatic statement concerning the methods and findings of "pure" phenomenology, in which the being of all entities is understood as constituted in, and through, acts of consciousness; thus, Husserl's pure phenomenology is also known as "constitutive" phenomenology.

Levinas, E. (1973). *The theory of intuition in Husserl's phenomenology* (A. Orianne, Trans.). Evanston, IL: Northwestern University Press. (Original work published 1963.) A clear introduction to the philosophical method of phenomenology by an important figure within the movement.

Merleau-Ponty, M. (1962). *Phenomenology of perception* (C. Smith, Trans.). London: Routledge & Kegan Paul. (Original work published 1945.) This is an extremely synthetic book, incorporating phenomenology with many of the insights of Gestalt psychology regarding perception and behavior; like his earlier text, *The Structure of Behavior*, it exhibits an unusual mastery of empirical psychology for a philosophical book. (These two books served, in fact, as Merleau-Ponty's doctoral dissertation.)

Natanson, M. (1973). *Edmund Husserl: Philosopher of infinite tasks*. Evanston, IL: Northwestern University Press. Perhaps the single clearest introduction to the entire scope of Husserl's work, this is also one of the most engaging texts ever written in the field of phenomenology.

Pfänder, A. (1967). *Phenomenology of willing and motivation* (H. Spiegelberg, Ed. & Trans.). Evanston, IL: Northwestern University Press. (Original works published 1900–1963.) This volume contains the only translated texts of this important contemporary of Husserl. It is of historical significance because it contains the earliest published work in phenomenological psychology, pertaining to the phenomenon of motivation and volition.

Ricoeur, P. (1967). *Husserl: An analysis of his phenomenology* (E. G. Ballard & L. E. Embree, Trans.). Evanston, IL: Northwestern University Press. A more advanced introduction to the various aspects of Husserl's phenomenology, including summaries of his important studies on empathy and intersubjectivity during the 1920s that often are neglected.

Sartre, J. P. (1956). *Being and nothingness: A phenomenological essay on ontology* (H. Barnes, Trans.). New York: Philosophical Library. (Original work published 1943.) Sartre's extraordinarily expansive and systematic investigation on the place of freedom in human existence. He defined any denial of personal freedom in establishing the meaning of one's life as "bad faith" (or self-deception). It is in this book that Sartre developed the idea of an existential psychoanalysis that can replace the deterministic Freudian psychoanalysis that, in Sartre's opinion, amounts to a formal system of self-deception. Indeed, for Sartre, all empirical psychologies provide us with systems of excuse, insofar as they preclude the possibility of taking responsibility for one's actions.

Scheler, M. (1954). *The nature of sympathy* (P. Heath, Trans.). New Haven: Yale. (Original work published 1923.) Scheler was influenced by Husserl, but took off in his own direction by developing a philosophical anthropology, based on his analyses of various affective states. This text is a very accessible treatment of sympathy and "fellow feeling."

Schutz, A. (1967). *The phenomenology of the social world* (G. Walsh & F. Lehnert, Trans.). Evanston, IL: Northwestern University Press. (Original work published 1932.) The legacy of Husserl lives on in this application of the fundamental principles of phenomenology to social psychology and sociology. A programmatic statement for a methodological approach to all aspects of intersubjective life.

Spiegelberg, H. (1982). *The phenomenological movement* (3rd ed.). Boston: Kluwer. Spiegelberg's comprehensive survey of all major and minor figures in philosophical phenomenology has almost become a primary source in its own right because of the thorough and deep portrayals of the array of movements that make up phenomenology.

Scott D. Churchill and Paul Richer

PHILOSOPHICAL PSYCHOLOGY. *See* Theoretical and Philosophical Psychology.

PHILOSOPHY. [*This entry comprises three articles:*

An Overview
Philosophy of Mind
Philosophy of Science

The first article discusses the discipline of philosophy, its fundamental questions, historical development, major theories and approaches. The second article examines how the categories of "the mental" and "the physical" are to be understood in relation to one another and the dilemmas of the mind-body problem. The third article provides a broad profile of the nature of theory and explanation in psychology. *See also* Epistemology; *and* Metaphysics.]

An Overview

Philosophy (from the Greek word for "love of wisdom") arose in ancient Greece, where it was understood as including any pure intellectual inquiry conducted for its own sake. Plato (427–347 BCE) maintained that philosophy replaced the unquestioning acceptance of myths with rationally justified belief. In this tradition, modern philosophy still defines itself as critical and rational inquiry into fundamental questions. In modern times, much of the traditional subject matter of philosophy has been delegated to the special sciences. Ever since the eighteenth century, *natural philosophy* (the study of nature) has been the provenance of physics and chemistry; by the mid-nineteenth century, *moral philosophy* (the study of humans) was turned over to such newly formed sciences as psychology and sociology. Even though much of the content of philosophy is now handled by the special sciences, colleges and universities continue to have philosophy departments, and philosophy remains central to most liberal arts programs. There are outstanding graduate programs in philosophy at Harvard, Princeton, and New York University, and philosophers participate in such major cognitive science programs as that at Rutgers University. The American Philosophical Association numbers over 8,000 members, and there are scores of journals printing philosophy articles, most notably the *Journal of Philosophy, Philosophical Review*, and *Noûs*.

Most philosophers would agree that there are at least five main areas of philosophy: (a) *metaphysics*, the study of the ultimate nature of reality (e.g., the nature and existence of mind and matter, the question of the existence of God, the soul, and free will); (b) *epistemology*, or the theory of knowledge, which asks about the source, extent, and justification of knowledge; (c) *ethics*, the inquiry into right action and living a good life; (d) *aesthetics*, the study of the beautiful, with special emphasis on art; and (e) *logic*, the formulation and justification of the principles of right reasoning. In addition, the field of philosophy includes a variety of second-order inquiries (e.g., philosophy of religion, philosophy of art, political philosophy, and philosophy of law), which focus on the concepts, presuppositions and methods of other fields. Philosophy departments also provide courses in the history of philosophy, feminist philosophy, and non-Western philosophies.

As a rule, philosophers eschew empirical research and concern themselves with formulating general truths about certain "big questions," solely on the basis of rational reflection. In the past, philosophy has been characterized as a priori knowledge, independent of any particular experiences, in contrast to the a posteriori knowledge derived from experience. Alternatively, philosophy has been described as *analytic*, the result of analyzing concepts, rather than *synthetic*, making substantive claims about reality. But in recent years this vocabulary has been called in question. Most philosophers today concern themselves with articulating the insights embodied in our educated common sense by reflecting on our intuitions about what things are or ought to be, and then arguing for or against those commonsense views. Philosophical discourse is dialectical: It involves presenting arguments for a view, considering criticisms and objections, and then reformulating the view with the goal of arriving at the truth, or at least at a reflective equilibrium, about the topic.

Although this characterization of mainstream philosophy describes a great deal of philosophical discourse, the actual practice of many philosophers is different. Among philosophers, a distinction is usually made between *analytic* (primarily Anglo-American) and *continental* (e.g., French and German) approaches, and even within these approaches there are differences in method. One extremely influential movement within current analytic philosophy, the approach called *naturalism*, regards philosophy as an extension of science, and tries to integrate philosophical questions into scientific inquiry. In contrast, the continental school called *phenomenology* calls for bracketing, or setting aside all scientific assumptions in order to describe our ordinary sense of reality prior to reflection and theorizing. Whereas most mainstream philosophers seek a correct account of reality, pragmatists often describe their goal as discovering what "works" for our lives. A number of philosophical schools (e.g., Marxism, feminist philosophy, postmodern theory) dedicate themselves to criticizing rather than defending so-called common sense. And philosophy's commitment to rationality is side-stepped to some extent by existentialists, who make fundamental emotional experiences, like dread or anxiety, their starting points.

Many of the concepts and concerns central to psychology originally came from philosophy. At the beginning of Western philosophical thought, Plato drew a sharp distinction between the mind and the body, and distinguished three components of the soul: reason, passion, and spirit. *De Anima*, by Aristotle (384–322 BCE), contains a faculty psychology, which characterizes the faculties in terms of what they do. Reflections on the inner life in the writings of Stoics and medieval religious philosophers expanded Western thought about the soul or mind. But it was the work of René Descartes (1596–1650), the "father of modern philosophy," that brought reflection on psychological issues to the highest level of articulation. In Descartes's view, known as *Cartesian dualism*, the mind and body are distinct substances, known through introspection and sensory perception, respectively. Although these two substances causally interact so long as one is alive, they are capable of existing independently of each another. One crucial function of the mind, as Descartes conceived it, is to represent material objects by means of ideas.

The thought of Descartes paved the way to what came to be known as "the new way of ideas," the philosophical approach that focuses not on objects in the world, but rather on the representations we have of those objects in our minds. The British empiricists, especially John Locke (1632–1704) and David Hume (1711–1776), tried to formulate a science of the mind on an equal footing with the physical sciences. Such a science would explain all mental phenomena as arising from sensory impressions and undergoing changes according to lawlike associationist principles. Most philosophers on the European continent, in contrast, were rationalists who believed that some ideas are innate and so are known directly to reason. One of the most sophisticated accounts of the mind formulated in the late eighteenth century, that of Immanuel Kant (1724–1804), tried to show how the mind starts with empirical data and then processes the data according to innate forms of perception and synthesizing principles.

With the advent of experimental psychology in the mid-nineteenth century, psychologists tried to distinguish their form of inquiry from the speculative methods of philosophers. Nevertheless, philosophy has continued to be tightly bound up with developments in psychology, both stimulating new lines of inquiry and building on psychological discoveries and theories. For example, the conception of the unconscious, formulated by philosophers from Gottfried Leibniz (1646–1716) to Friedrich Nietzsche (1844–1900), had an impact on Freud's depth psychology. In the United States, the reflections of philosopher psychologists like Williams James (1842–1910) and John Dewey (1859–1952) led to the formulation of extremely influential psychological concepts. And the theories of the mind developed by philosophers like Franz Brentano (1838–1917), Edmund Husserl (1859–1938), and Maurice Merleau-Ponty (1908–1961) have influenced Gestalt and phenomenological approaches, whereas the existentialism of Martin Heidegger (1889–1976) and Jean-Paul Sartre (1905–1980) has had a strong impact on existentialist and humanistic movements in psychology.

A number of directions of current philosophical inquiry have a bearing on psychology. The field of *philosophical psychology* studies folk psychology, the commonsense view of the mental, which is embodied in our everyday ways of talking about mental phenomena. The attempt to get clear about the assumptions and views implicit in our ordinary discourse about the mental might prove helpful in trying to bridge the gaps between psychological theories, brain science, and everyday life. The *philosophy of mind* deals with such issues as personal identity, the "mind-body problem," and the issue of mental causation. Concerning the question of the relation between mind and body, most contemporary Anglo-American philosophers are materialists, which means that they deny that the mind is anything other than the brain and central nervous system. In addition, the philosophy of science has contributed important ideas about theory formation and confirmation, and ethics explores the basis of values, the meaning and implications of moral discourse, and principles of proper conduct in professional life.

The cognitive revolution in the 1950s led to a number of research programs in which philosophers and psychologists worked closely together. Noam Chomsky's views about universal grammar supported the idea of innate capacities in the mind. *Cognitive science* is an interdisciplinary research program that tries to explain cognition in terms of rule-governed symbol manipulation as modeled by computers (Haugeland, 1997) and attempts to account for the intentional or representational capacities of the mind in terms of, for example, a "language of thought" (Fodor, 1983). Philosophers have also been influential in developing the theory of connectionism, which attempts to explain the mental in terms of networks of units similar to the networks of neurons in the brain.

Among those who question the possibility of achieving a final explanation of the mental in scientific terms are philosophers like Thomas Nagel and John Searle (1994). These philosophers, sometimes known as mysterians, argue that scientific approaches to the mind cannot account for such basic phenomena as the qualitative feel ("qualia") of sensations or the nature of consciousness itself. Drawing on an old tradition in continental philosophy, hermeneutic philosophers like Charles Taylor (1985) and Paul Ricoeur argue that understanding human phenomena is more like textual interpretation (a matter of interpreting meanings) than it is like scientific explanation. Finally, postmodern figures like Jacques Lacan, Jacques Derrida, Michel Foucault, and Julia Kristeva emphasize the social construction of mental phenomena and attempt to deconstruct the assumed dichotomies that are central to mainstream thought about the mind.

[*See also* Moral Discourse.]

Bibliography

Block, N. (Ed.). (1980). *Readings in philosophy of psychology* (Vols. 1 & 2). Cambridge, MA: Harvard University Press.

Chomsky, N. (1972). *Language and the mind.* (Enl. ed.). New York: Harcourt Brace Jovanovich. Proposes a way of understanding the large-scale structure of mind by way of an understanding of the structure of language.

Churchland, P. M. (1989). *A neurocomputational perspective: The nature of mind and the structure of science.* Cambridge, MA: MIT Press. Shows the importance of neuroscience for philosophy of mind.

Dennett, D. C. (1987). *The intentional stance.* Cambridge, MA: MIT Press. Shows the importance of central concepts in cognitive science for philosophy of mind.

Fodor, J. A. (1983). *The modularity of mind.* Cambridge, MA: MIT Press.

Goldman, A. I. (Ed.). (1993). *Readings in philosophy and cognitive science.* Cambridge, MA: MIT Press. Excellent collection of articles by philosophers and psychologists working in this area.

Haugeland, J. (1997). *Mind design: Philosophy, psychology, artificial intelligence* (Rev. & enl. ed.). Cambridge, MA: MIT Press. Valuable, though challenging, overview of key issues in philosophical psychology.

Melchert, N. (1991). *The great conversation: A historical introduction to philosophy.* Mountain View, CA: Mayfield. Clear historical overview of the main schools of philosophy.

Merleau-Ponty, M. (1962). *Phenomenology of perception* (C. Smith, Trans.). New York: Humanities Press.

Pinker, S. (1997). *How the mind works.* New York: Norton. Best work showing the current state of philosophical thought about the mind.

Searle, J. R. (1994). *The rediscovery of the mind.* Cambridge, MA: MIT Press. Plea for the recognition of the importance of consciousness.

Taylor, C. (1985). *Human agency and language.* Cambridge, UK: Cambridge University Press. Employs existentialist, phenomenological, and hermeneutic approaches in understanding humans.

Charles Guignon

Philosophy of Mind

The 1990s saw a resurgence of a radical reductionist program to eliminate mind as it is understood in "folk psychology." The program was spearheaded by a group of philosophers and scientists who called themselves eliminative materialists (Churchland, 1984). This posture harks back to the radical behaviorism of the earlier part of the century. But in *Plans and the Structure of Behavior*, the book often cited as initiating the cognitive revolution in psychology, Miller, Galanter, and Pribram (1960) declared themselves subjective behaviorists. They showed how one could "do science" on the expressions of verbal behavior (folk psychology) by experimental analysis and by "enactment," that is, by simulations of such expressions in computer programs in order to understand thought processes. Several further publications (Pribram 1971a, 1971b, 1979, 1986) made a plea for a comprehensive holistic psychology, a science of mind, that would embrace the contributions of behavioral, cognitive, and existential approaches.

Neuropsychology, along with other branches of neuroscience, has made great technical and conceptual strides since these publications. These advances make it most worthwhile to reflect, once more, on whether we are better able to frame an encompassing science of mind that addresses the issues that sages have been pondering throughout the ages.

There are two dualities that have plagued thoughtful philosophers, dramatists, mystics, and scientists over at least the past two millennia. One of these is the mind/brain duality itself. The other is a duality within mind, two ways in which the experiencing subject experiences the self: as a body-centered *me* and as an episode-centered, narrative *I* (Pribram & Bradley, 1998).

A caveat: Thinking in terms of dualities is a primitive analytical tool. To deconstruct any issue in terms of dualities can only serve as a first step. Dualities can serve dialectically to provide a synthesis and from there a hierarchically organized tree of systems, subsystems, and supersystems. There are other forms of organization less amenable to dichotomizing, for instance, the distributed/enfolded order characteristic of holography and the multivariate phase spaces used in nonlinear dynamics. I will use these tools where appropriate to characterize one or another of the dualities under discussion; however, doing so tends to blur the boundaries between the dualities.

A Synoptic History of the Mind/Brain Duality

Today we usually attribute the sharp distinction between mind and matter to Descartes. However, René Descartes articulated a duality that goes back to the origins of propositional utterances: a subject, an object, and a verb that ascribes to the subject an aspect partaken of, or an "intention" taken toward an object. Holophrases, words such as *om* in Sanskrit and *yaveh* in Hebrew, which mean "being," enfold, or rather fail to unfold, propositional meanings. Holophrases are said to have preceded propositional utterances in the development of languages, just as holophrases precede the development of language in children. The process of being becomes *a* being, a subject with a beard who hands commandments to Moses, an object.

For Descartes, the thinker is subject; all else is object. Immanuel Kant, however, pointed out that the objects of thought are ideas, and ideas have two sources: sensory-initiated phenomenal experience (images of objects) and noumena, the thinker's reasoned contributions. Thus, the thinker and the contents of thought all became subjective, and knowledge of the objective, "material" aspect of the world became "iffy."

Arthur Schopenhauer, bothered by this indeterminacy (our inability to "really" know the world because of our entanglement in it), came to emphasize the role of the thinker, of energy and "will," of intentions, in unraveling the iffiness of the images. He noted that the unraveling of the world knot, made up as it is of entanglements of phenomena and noumena, is up to us. This provides us with the freedom to explore and with the opportunities to shape the world we inhabit. Today we often hear that the solution to certain of our social problems is not just money but political will. This insight is very much in line with that of Schopenhauer.

In a sense, Schopenhauer returned to the wholeness that the holophrase encompasses and indicated that humans, by virtue of operating in a proposition-like mode, by their intentions, have the opportunity to mold the images or representations they experience and therefore their interpretation of the world.

Enter Brain Science

Descartes, Kant, and Schopenhauer knew that, among other determinants, the organization of psychological experience owed something to the way the brain works. A wealth of detail has been added in the past two centuries so that even B. F. Skinner, a pioneer radical behaviorist who led a lifelong crusade against folk psychology and toward a behavioral science of the "empty organism," in 1989 ended his career a year before his death with the following revised insight:

> There are two unavoidable gaps in any behavioral account: one between the stimulating action of the environment and the response of the organism and one between consequences and the resulting change in behavior. Only brain science can fill those gaps. In so doing it completes the account; it does not give a different account of the same thing. (p. 13)

Initially, certain psychological "faculties" were shown to be dependent on the normal functioning of systems that could be more or less localized within the brain. The anatomical connectivity of these systems and their electrophysiological response to sensory input have now been described.

Over the decades, early crude findings were sharpened as better techniques became available. Studies that aim to localize relationships between types of psychological experience and brain systems have attained vigor from revolutionary procedures such as computerized tomography and nuclear resonance imaging.

On the brain's convexity, we can roughly make out a three-tiered arrangement for these systems. Each major sensory apparatus has a fairly direct input to areas in the cortex. Immediately surrounding these areas are others that, when electrically stimulated, originate movements of the musculature associated with each of the sense organs (e.g., eye muscles for vision, ear muscles for hearing, and body muscles for somatic sensations). These areas are extrinsically connected, that is, connected to organs in the periphery of the body and therefore provide perspectives relating the body to the world beyond.

Surrounding these extrinsic areas are sensory-specific areas that are primarily connected intrinsically, that is, to other brain structures. These areas provide perspectives that are intrinsic to the entities perceived, perspectives such as those provided by color and object constancy. Finally, there are areas that operate on inputs from a variety of senses that relate their perspectives to each other. All of these areas and the brain systems that they represent are involved in organizing our phenomenal perceptions. In today's terminology we call them *sensory-driven aspects of perception* (see Pribram, 1991). Another set of systems, more noumenal in their function, is located frontally and on the limbic medial border of the brain's hemispheres. These systems and their functions in organizing our experience will be dealt with in the last part of this article.

However, there are types of psychological experience that cannot be so readily divided up with regard to the brain systems that organize them: aspects of conscious awareness, memory storage and retrieval (remembering), and the ability to transfer what has been learned in one situation to another situation, or, what has been learned in one way to another way (for instance, with one hand to another hand). These types of interpretations of the world knot have been found to depend, in part, on processes that are distributed in the brain. Once again, new techniques are invigorating investigation: this time it is the development of massively parallel computational architectures and the use of multiple recordings with microelectrodes.

"The Hard Problem"

Great interest has developed in trying to come to grips with the mind/brain duality. In part this is due to the outstanding successes in the psychological and neurosciences. The apparent gap between mind and matter is being filled with a plethora of data that firmly establish, in great detail, the way in which our experience can be related to brain organization. This success recalls the recent successes in Darwinian theory, where the evolutionary gap between human and nonhuman primates is being filled with new discoveries almost daily.

But some philosophers are still not satisfied. They divide the issue into hard and easy: What we are accomplishing, they claim, is the easy part. They point out that to some considerable extent the cognitive revolution in experimental psychology and its influence on neuropsychology is not only successfully formulating a true psychological science that takes subjective experience seriously, but at the same time is filling the mind/brain gap. But they note that it is much harder to bridge the gap between our personal experience and the experience of others, which we validate through communication by way of verbal and instrumental behaviors.

The philosophers who are not satisfied do have a point, and the point harks back to Descartes, Kant, and Schopenhauer. There is a duality between my subjective experience and that of others. Nonetheless, I believe the current philosophers are in error in restricting the hard problem to conscious awareness of our experience. Descartes's duality was corrected by Kant; *all* our experience involves phenomenal representation and noumena. Neither our senses nor our cognitions readily provide us with unadulterated replicas of what is "out there." That is why we must apply ourselves to understand, not only conscious awareness, but the origins of all our experience. In short, the hard problem applies to all knowledge and all science, not only to the study of consciousness.

The hard problem is the problem of *knowing*, the ontological problem of epistemology. It is the problem of unraveling the world knot, almost harking back to the Cartesian problem of cogito versus all else. However, the new way that Kant and Schopenhauer sensed the all-else, indeed adds to our sophistication, in that the all-else is to be included in the hard problem: to resolve this problem on the plane that they established does require active involvement, intent, and will. Neuropsychological and neuroscientific research is the current expression of this intent.

A final point. While psychologists and neuroscientists are resolving the mind/matter duality from one perspective, quantum physicists have been tackling the issue from another. Niels Bohr, Werner Heisenberg, Wolfgang Dirac, and Eugene Wigner, each in his own way, noted that how we approach an observation determines it to a large extent. As Wigner described it to me personally some years ago, we no longer have observables in quantum physics, we have only observations. Bohr's complimentarity and Heisenberg's indeterminacy principles make the same Kantian point (see Stapp, 1972, a superb summary of their thinking). All of science, not just psychological science, is beholden to the hard problem.

Where does that leave us? In other essays, I have noted that our intense interest in the mind/matter duality was fostered by the industrial revolution. Most scientists are materialists and have begotten mentalists (e.g., Searle, 1983; Sperry, 1980) who perceive flaws in the materialist position. But materialism and mentalism bear the same relationship to each other as *down* and *up*: one would not exist without the other. Which comes first, our experience of the material world or the material brain that makes the experience possible? Is the chicken an egg's way of reproducing itself—or is it the other way around?

The information revolution is beginning to shift the ground from an intense interest in a mental/material duality to the issue that occupied Plato and Aristotle: the ideal versus the real. Already, some mathematicians (e.g., Roger Penrose) have, not unexpectedly, declared themselves on the side of Plato. Dualities such as these are extremely helpful in exposing issues, but they are relatively primitive tools. Pre-Socratic holistic pragmatisms such as that practiced by Pythagoras in dividing a vibrating string in half to discover the principle of the octave or, for that matter, the American pragmaticism of Charles Peirce, help to place such dualities in proper perspective.

A Duality Within Subjective Experience

As noted, within Descartes's cogito itself, several different conceptions (different dualities) have caught the attention of philosophers. One, most clearly enunciated by Brentano (1973), is the duality between the perceiver and the perceived. This also reflects the Cartesian duality; the perceiver is minding; all else is that which is being perceived and minded. But contrary to Descartes, Brentano was less interested in that which is being perceived but with the perceiver. Shades of Schopenhauer emerge as the perceiver "intends" his perceptions: he can even intend inexistent percepts such as unicorns.

Brain research has shown (see Pribram & Bradley, 1998) that systems occupying the posterior convexity of the cerebral hemispheres are involved in organizing Brentano's (1973) duality. When the parietal lobe systems are injured, the individual may no longer feel the arm on the side opposite the brain injury to be his or her own. (One of my students who suffered such an injury dubbed her arm Alice and stated that "Alice doesn't live here anymore.") Despite this loss of belongingness, the arm routinely performs many tasks, such as bringing a cup of coffee to the person's mouth, much to the surprise of the person when he or she becomes aware of what has happened.

Damage farther back in the convexity produces "blindsight." Here again, the person can perform many routine tasks that demand an optical input from the blind side, but is unaware of (is blind to) that input. With an intact brain, we are aware both of ourselves as "see-ers" and of what is being seen.

In these and similar instances, awareness of one's bodily self and the environment are impaired: Alice isn't any longer part of me; the blindsighted, optically guided behavior isn't mine. From such observations one can infer that ordinarily these brain systems operate to allow awareness of a corporeal *me* to occur. When impairment takes place, the distinction in awareness between perceiver and perceived no longer exists, much as a person with color-blindness cannot differentiate between red and green. In the absence of differentiation, neither color exists for that person. In the absence of awareness of the difference between perceiver and perceived, neither exists.

There is another totally different duality that has concerned philosophers. In addition to a self, a *me*, the concern has been with a transcendental awareness of one's unity with a larger, more universal order. Jung's (1933) archetypes address this aspect of experience. Paradoxically, this experience is as intensely personal as it is holistic. The experience cannot be analyzed into "in here" versus "out there" as in Brentano's intentionality. Rather, it partakes of a holy, healthy awareness that lacks boundaries.

Psychological and brain science have recently made great strides in understanding this type of awareness. First, Endel Tulving (see Pribram & Bradley, 1998) differentiated two types of human memory: a dictionary or semantic type and another that deals with episodes of one's experience. At the same time, research with nonhuman primates has distinguished a difference between brain systems that deal with reference memory and those that deal with trial-by-trial types of processing.

There is good evidence from human neuropsychological research that allows identification between the processes responsible for semantic memory and those of reference memory. These processes are impaired when the posterior convexity of the brain is damaged. Referencing is what is entailed in the Brentano duality, the ability to be aware of the distinction between perceiver and perceived.

There is also good evidence obtained with animals that trial-by-trial processing leads to remembering unique instances and therefore to the processing of episodes. Episodic processing is impaired by damage to the limbic systems that lie on the inner border (thus the term *limbic*) of the hemispheres of the brain.

Impairment of episodic processing leads to a surprising difficulty. Individuals with such impairment are personable and able to interact socially on a moment-by-moment basis by virtue of their intact semantic/referential processing. An interruption or distraction will, however, totally erase the episode from further awareness as if that unique instance had never taken place. Therefore, over time, over successive episodes, no personal hermeneutic, narrative *I* becomes established.

The episodic processing that leads to experiencing a narrative *I* is separate from that leading to a corporeal *me*. Children who have bilateral damage to the limbic systems from birth can learn to read and have other aspects of semantic processing that are unimpaired. A case history dramatically demonstrates the deficiency in constructing a narrative *I*. This child was born with large cysts involving the limbic and frontal part of his brain. He underwent two surgeries before the age of 6 months. He has never given any evidence of episodic memory; however, he was capable of learning verbal language to age-appropriate levels. At age 8 he was able to give his name, age, birthday, and names of family members. He reported his favorite game, television program, and favorite color across trials. Expressive language capabilities were age appropriate, and there were no obvious weaknesses in grammar. Despite this, he was unable to recall what he had eaten for breakfast a few hours earlier. He was unable to correctly identify an examiner with whom he had worked that morning from among a group of four people. He was unable to say what he had eaten for lunch after returning from a restaurant.

Obviously, episodic processing is not necessary for the establishment of normal semantic processing. The converse is also true: children who suffer injury to the systems that process the corporeal *me* for instance, those who are spastic from birth, have no difficulty with episodic processing and develop a normal narrative *I*.

Such children also develop normal semantic processing, indicating that the *me* has two distinct aspects: one related to sensory input and another to motor output. This separation of motor skills from body awareness is due to the increased importance of these somatic motor systems. The distance senses depend on their motor components primarily to enhance sensory processing. By contrast, the somatic motor system has the ability to skillfully and dramatically change the environmental input. As a result, the motor systems in primates, including those of humans, become more distinctly separated from the somatic sensory input systems, whereas there is more overlap between input and output in the distance senses.

The brain systems that organize episodic processing also have inputs and outputs and these also overlap considerably. A mediobasal motor system covers the anterior portions of the limbic cortex and centers on the amygdala, a basal ganglion. Electrical stimulation of this cortex produces marked changes in heart and respiratory rate, blood pressure, and gastrointestinal contractions. In contrast to the results of electrical stimulation of the somatic motor cortex, only gross turning of the body and eyes away from the side of stimulation were produced (Pribram, 1961).

Also, the input from the body comes mainly from tracts concerned with visceral, autonomic, pain, and temperature stimuli. Together these inputs can be classified as mediating hedonic (pleasant/unpleasant) emotional aspects of awareness. There is, therefore, not surprisingly, an anatomical-physiological relationship between hedonic and episodic processing. After all, the narrative *I* experiences the episodes, and research has shown that rewards and deterrents are critical in "stamping in" an episode so that it becomes a remembered part of the personal narrative (Pribram, 1970).

Schopenhauer emphasized the importance of the body in the organization of intention, of will, although he failed to distinguish between the body as a skilled *me* and the body as a hedonic *I*. *Plans and the Structure of Behavior* (Miller et al., 1960) separated these aspects of will by distinguishing between motivations (hedonic) as predispositions and intentions as dispositions. Intentions, in turn, are divided into strategies (prior intentions) and tactics (intentions in action, as Searle (1983) called them).

There is a relationship between emotion, motivation, strategy, and tactics. As William James pointed out, emotions stop at the skin, motivations (termed *instincts* in the literature of that time) reach beyond. To implement motivations we develop intentions, both strategic and tactical. Separate brain systems are related to each of these behavioral categories: amygdala to emotion; caudate putamen to motivation; anterior frontal cortex to strategies; and the more posterior frontal, the precentral cortex to tactics.

Schopenhauer, though well read in the Upanishads, failed to follow them in their emphasis on the hedonic aspects of wholeness, as exemplified in gardening or in lovemaking, and he therefore failed to understand fully the holistic transcendental aspect of the *I*. Despite his attempts to ground the will in the body, Schopenhauer's development of body involvement in untangling the world knot results in a corporeal *me*, not a holistic *I*. The consequences of this failure led both Nazi (idealistic) and communist (materialist) philosophies to neglect individual incentive, and paradoxically, to an unhealthy, unholistic, unholy society.

If we follow the lead of the eliminative materialists, our society might end similarly. As a judge pointed out at a recent meeting devoted to consciousness studies, reducing psychology to neurons is a category error that would destroy our entire moral structure; we cannot hold neurons accountable for our behavior. One of the eliminatists (Francis Crick) has noted that categories are human inventions and that we often change categories as our knowledge increases. But this misses the point: the category error deals not with how we categorize per se, but with the level or scale with which the category deals. Thus, the sections here detailing the role of brain systems in organizing the *me* and the *I* deal with one level of inquiry only. At a more encompassing level, ego- and allocentric organization of the *me* depend, of course, on environmental input to the senses. In the same fashion, the organization of the *I* depends on input from a caretaking person and all further social transactions experienced by and processed by a person. It is only the processing medium provided by the brain that is the focus of neuropsychological research.

The category error is not just a trivial philosophical contrivance: making this error has serious personal and social consequences. Kant (who was trained in the law), Schopenhauer, and even earlier, the Upanishads, illuminated this healthier alternative to eliminatism: the humble realization that the way to knowing is all of a piece, that the hard problem encompasses all of knowing, and that it takes personal involvement and dedicated work to unravel the world knot.

[*See also* Agency.]

Bibliography

Brentano, F. W. (1973). *Psychology from an empirical standpoint*. London: Routledge & Kegan Paul.

Churchland, P. (1984). *Matter and consciousness*. Cambridge, MA: MIT Press.

Jung, C. G. (1933). *Modern man in search of a soul*. Harvest Books.

Miller, G. A., Galanter, E., & Pribram, K. H. (1960). *Plans and the structure of behavior*. New York: Holt.

Peirce, C. S. (1934). Pragmatism and pragmaticism. *Collected Papers* (Vol. 5, pp. 34–131). Cambridge, MA: Harvard University Press.

Pribram, K. H. (1961). Limbic system. In D. E. Sheer (Ed.), *Electrical stimulation of the brain* (pp. 311–320). Austin: University of Texas Press.

Pribram, K. H. (1970). Feelings as monitors. In M. B. Arnold (Ed.), *Feelings and emotions* (pp. 41–53). New York: Academic Press.

Pribram, K. H. (1971a). The realization of mind. *Synthese, 22*, 313–322.

Pribram, K. H. (1971b). *Languages of the brain: Experimental paradoxes and principles in neuropsychology*. Englewood Cliffs, NJ: Prentice Hall.

Pribram, K. H. (1979). Behaviorism, phenomenology and holism in psychology: A scientific analysis. *Journal of Social and Biological Structure, 2*, 65–72.

Pribram, K. H. (1986). The cognitive revolution and mind/brain issues. *American Psychologist, 41*, 507–520.

Pribram, K. H. (1991). *Brain and perception: Holonomy and structure in figural processing*. Mahwah, NJ: Erlbaum.

Pribram, K. H., & Bradley, R. (1998). The brain, the me and the I. In M. Ferrarri & R. Sternberg (Eds.). *Self-awareness: Its nature and development* (pp. 273–307). New York: Guilford Press.

Searle, J. R. (1983). *Intentionality: An essay on the philosophy of mind*. Cambridge, UK: Cambridge University Press.

Skinner, B. F. (1989). The origins of cognitive thought. *American Psychologist, 44*(1), 13–18.

Sperry, R. W. (1980). Mind/brain interaction—mentalism, yes—dualism, no. *Neuroscience, 2*, 195–206.

Stapp, H. (1972). The Copenhagen interpretation. *American Journal of Physics, 40*(8), 1098–1116.

Karl H. Pribram

Philosophy of Science

Advances in formal logic made during the late nineteenth and early twentieth centuries encouraged the search for a universal character of science, or as Rudolf Carnap hoped, a logical syntax of the language of science." Combining Ernst Mach's views on science (i.e., sensationalism, Humean causality) with Ludwig Wittgenstein's and Bertrand Russell's theories of logical atomism, members of the Vienna circle (e.g., Moritz Schlick, Otto von Neurath, Philipp Frank, Rudolph Carnap) recommended a verificationist view wherein atomistic propositions in the language of science were thought to be proven true through empirical investigation.

Positivists relied heavily on Newtonian mechanics as an example of the type of scientific program that might emerge from adherence to their prescriptive rules of scientific conduct. In psychology, several productive research programs modeled themselves upon positivist visions of science. Psychologists, such as Clark Hull and Kenneth Spence, accepted notions such as Bridgman's (1928) operationism, believing that the meaning of a concept was synonymous with the corresponding set of operations used to measure that construct. Some positivists were too quick to condemn the nonpositivist approaches to research in psychology because these programs failed to conform to orthodox positivist methodology. When several of these nonpositivist research programs subsequently flourished, psychology concluded that positivist proscriptions were overly narrow and potentially injurious to research in psychology.

Several developments in philosophy of science around the mid-twentieth century were also responsible for the decline in logical positivism. Positivists, following Mach's sensationalism, believed science could produce atomic facts: the momentary sensations in the sensory fields of individual persons. Science, then, would discover regularities among these facts, which could be described in an entirely clear and unambiguous formal language (as suggested by Russell). Science was to be a net of propositions that were thrown over reality to ascertain the regularities present in the world. For members of the Vienna circle, a proposition was empirically meaningful (i.e., worthy of consideration by scientists) if and only if a method for verifying (confirming or testing) it could be described. This verifiability principle was first subverted by Karl Popper (1959), who offered his own principle: Empirical propositions should be known by their potential falsifiability. Popper attempted to extend his falsification principle to the domain of scientific theories where, unfortunately, it also did not work well.

On Popper's view, no amount of evidence could ever prove a particular theory true, since there were always many theories consistent with a particular set of evidence. However, evidence might be used to falsify theories. Thus, Popper saw scientists as offering theoretical accounts in their domain of interest and then conducting experiments designed to disprove these theories. A theory that consistently weathered serious attempts at falsification could then be accepted by the scientific community as the best available account of the phenomenon at that time. [*See* Epistemology.]

Imre L. Lakatos found Popper's notion of falsification too simple to describe scientific practice appropriately. Falsifying a theory would imply disproving a central tenet of that theory (part of theory's "hard core") and this was, according to Lakatos, supposed to be the part of the theory that was beyond empirical challenge. However, the hard core of every theory is surrounded by a "protective belt" of auxiliary questions/hypotheses. Any experiment's ability to falsify is dependent upon definitions, calculation procedures, instrumentation, and the like in the theory's protective belt. Thus, disconfirming evidence may reflect a problem in the theory's protective belt, rather than implicating problems in the hard core. Instead of a strict falsificationist strategy, Lakatos's methodology of scientific research programmes urges scientists to consider whether early studies lead to fruitful exploration of other aspects of the theory's resources (called a progressive problem shift in research programs) or whether early research disappointments require subsequent, ad hoc adjustments to the theory's protective belt to deflect the force of the disappointing findings (called degenerative problem shifts in research programs). Although an improvement on Popper's strict falsificationist approach, Lakatos's system seemed to reflect an idealization of scientific practice, rather than a careful analysis of episodes in the history of science itself.

Kuhn (1962) observed that science was not a straightforward process whereby theories gradually improved over time. Rather, he viewed science as going through periods of normal science (wherein steady progress within a particular paradigm might occur) that was occasionally interrupted by periods of revolutionary science (where a different and sometimes incommensurate paradigm replaced the old paradigm). Kuhn's work appealed heavily to the history of science to produce its image of scientific practice.

On the role of epistemic values in scientific progress, both Kuhn (1977) and McMullin (1983) held that theories are neither confirmed as true nor completely falsified. Rather, truth becomes an ideal, or a "horizon concept," of the scientific enterprise, even though we may never be able to assert the truth in a definitive manner of any component of science along the way. Thus, reliance upon the epistemic values typically leads to a moderate realist position and could be distinguished from a strict realist account (such as Rom Harre's or Roy Bhaskar's critical realism, that is, that science discovers truths about the world) and an antirealist (or instrumentalist) account (where even considering the truth value of scientific propositions represents a fundamental misunderstanding of the scientific enterprise). [*See* Metaphysics; *and* Postmodern Psychology.]

The basic aim or goal of science is understanding, and this understanding is achieved through theoretical knowledge. Because (a) empirical "facts" can support a multitude of incompatible theoretical positions (the underdetermination thesis), and (b) as Norwood Hanson noted, observations in science are theory dependent, the link between theory and observation must be tentative. That is, one can never choose between competing theories by simply looking toward the "brute facts" and "allowing the facts to speak for themselves," as the standard positivist view had held. McMullin held that the appraisal of theory is, in important respects, closer in structure to value judgment than it is to the rule-governed inference that the classic tradition in philosophy of science took for granted.

What are the criteria whereby choices among theories are made? Kuhn and McMullin recommended such epistemic values as predictive accuracy, fertility, internal coherence, external consistency, and unifying power as criteria that will move theoretical explanations closer to the ideal or horizon concept of truth. The warrant for such belief lies in the history of science, as theoretical explanations possessing these epistemic values have tended to represent superior scientific endeavors.

Within psychology, our positivist leanings led researchers to emphasize the hypothetico-deductive model to understand the relationship between theories and facts. First exploited by Galileo, the hypothetico-deductive model combines both the inductive and deductive moments captured in earlier philosophies of science into an interactive process wherein a theory prompts empirical studies, the results of which might then produce changes in theory, which in turn suggest additional experiments, and so forth.

Over time, psychology's positivist antirealism has gradually shifted toward a more moderate realist stance. After initially believing that any theoretical construct ought to contain no more meaning than the operations used to specify that construct, Kenneth MacCorquodale and Paul Meehl expanded psychology's focus beyond definitional operationalism by distinguishing intervening variables (concepts with no surplus meaning) from hypothetical constructs (theoretical entities that offer rich conceptual resources far beyond their initial operational specifications). Since 1960, psychological research has demonstrated the superiority of theories that eschew positivist prohibitions not to stray past simple definitional operationalism. For example, Campbell and Fiske's (1959) approach to construct validity emphasizes convergent and discriminant validity ascertained through the multitrait-multimethod matrix approach (ideally analyzed by structural equation modeling). This modest realist approach is best understood philosophically from Cook's (1985) postpositivist critical multiplist perspective. Methodologically, hypothetical constructs (terms in a theory) and multiple operational definitions of the various theoretical terms take part in an iterative process wherein several definitions of several constructs are initially employed to specify (i.e., triangulate upon) the constructs of interest. The resulting theoretical model then can be employed to actually improve the measurements that initially were employed to define the theoretical constructs. The scientific model that energizes these methodological strategies postulates a world populated by real psychological properties (e.g., intelligence, achievement, frustration, aggression, ego strength, peer pressures) that of necessity are measured imperfectly. However, careful study and modification of our initial operational definitions can improve our measurement strategies and move them toward the never-achievable horizon concept of perfect measurement of our theoretical entities. As Donald Campbell suggested, psychologists ought to be ontological realists and epistemological fallibilists.

Whereas accurate measurement (as seen in the preceding construct validation issues and strategies) is an important scientific function, from the Kuhn and McMullin perspectives, it represents a penultimate task to the central task of science, namely, the selection, from among several competing theories, of the theory in closest agreement with the epistemic values.

Science's Role in Philosophy of Science

A distinction must be made between the academic discipline called philosophy of science and each scientist's personal, implicit (and explicit) philosophy of science. The former is typically explored by historians and philosophers (and on occasion by scientists) who are intrigued by the historical development of science and the study of epistemology. That is, they seek to understand the social, political, and intellectual contexts that fueled or inspired the maturation of various scientific disciplines. These scholars have constructed elegant theories to help shed light on how and when various disciplines made advances, or even experienced revolutions. However, the progress of science itself is not dependent on the insights of these scholars. Although there may be advantages to understanding these arguments, strict adherence to teachings in philosophy of science might actually be detrimental to the advance of science.

It can be argued that the step from technician to scientist is made when one frees his or her practice of research from blind obedience to convention, and develops an explicit understanding of the complex interaction between the methods of a discipline and the assumptions of the discipline's scientists. Such an understanding can decrease the likelihood that an individual scientist would allow the discipline's methodological tail to wag his or her theoretical dog (as was the case for logical positivism and psychology).

Kuhn's view of the progress of science can serve as a useful orienting mechanism for this discussion. In his model, science proceeds through a series of stages of normal and revolutionary science. In times of normal science a particular paradigm dominates, and the majority of the scientific advances take place within that paradigm's frame (or view of the world, notion of science, etc.). An oft-cited example is that of Newtonian physics. Revolutionary science is exemplified by a radical paradigm shift. In physics, Einstein's introduction of relativity and the advent of quantum theory presumably occasioned a paradigm shift. The shift to a relativistic physics was revolutionary because basic concepts of time, space, matter, and causality were drastically altered. One might claim that similar changes have occurred in psychology.

New paradigms, for example, Freudian psychodynamics, during the first half of the twentieth century, offered researchers a complete package of ontological and epistemological commitments (e.g., id, ego, superego, unconscious motives, transference), favored methodologies (e.g., dream analysis, hypnosis, projective techniques, free association), along with an established research literature (e.g., established empirical relationships, clinical demonstrations, case studies). Together, these assumptions, techniques, and empirical findings melded to form a more or less coherent picture of the world of human action—from a psychodynamic perspective. If one is inclined to see psychodynamic construals of human motivation as a paradigmatic step in the science of human action, then Freud was clearly involved in creating a scientific revolution. Freud's correspondence and published works reveal that he was convinced that he was bringing about a scientific revolution in our thinking about human action; similarly, B. F. Skinner promoted a behavioral revolution; Carl Rogers, Gordon Allport, and Henry Murray engineered a humanistic revolution; Ludwig von Bertalanfy and Gregory Bateson fathered a cybernetic or systemic revolution; George Kelly produced a constructivist revolution; and so forth.

Although it is open to argument which conceptual breakthroughs are to be accorded revolutionary status, it is clear that each perspective on human action affords a radically different conception of human nature. For revolutionary thinkers, the issues of philosophy of science are critically important, as their critics frequently press them to justify their conceptual systems in light of the prevailing philosophy of science. But by their own admission, many of psychology's theoretical innovators knew very little about philosophy of science. Rather, they knew something important about their subject matter: human nature.

Revolutionary, scientific thinkers need not care what philosophers of science think about their proposed reconceptualizations of their subject matter. This is because the relevant jury for such ideas is the community of *scientists* in their own field. The success of scientific revolutions is determined by the acceptance of the new paradigm by scientists in that domain, not by philosophers of science. "Good science is what good scientists do," might serve as an appropriate rule of thumb in this regard. If (over the long haul) research psychologists find it scientifically productive (vis-à-vis the epistemic values) to think of human beings as reinforcement maximizers, or as active construers, or as self-determining active agents, or unconsciously motivated, then psychologists should push forward with these newer paradigms, in spite of the fact that such construals might not square well with prevailing philosophies of science.

History and philosophy of science might be helpful to researchers when they are prescriptive. That is, history can point out numerous ways that scientific insights have been achieved, demonstrated, and expressed throughout the history of science. In doing so it might afford scientists alternative routes to solutions of research problems. However, it falls to the working scientist (not the historian or philosopher of science) to convert a fertile idea from the history of science into a demonstration that the research community will find compelling.

The raw data for improving philosophies of science must come from science. Scientists must first conduct programs of science (some later determined to have been "good" science and other efforts deemed "bad") before philosophers of science can reflect upon which characteristics of the good science made it good. The major task of philosophers of science is to reconstruct rationally temporary theories of what produced progress within science. However, the next successful scientific revolution might furnish evidence suggesting that these temporary theories of science are inadequate. The hope is that (in the long run) amendments will lead to a better understanding of the nature of good science. Just as current theories in science do not tell the Truth about the world, current construals of science within philosophy of science also do not speak the Truth. But there is ample justification for believing that our current theories of human nature are closer to the truth about human nature than were the theories of psychologists from a century ago. Similarly, current beliefs about the nature of science in philosophy of science are likely to be closer to the Truth about science than were their predecessors.

One can now see why philosophy of science might be ill advised to channel scientific practice into the accepted modes of inquiry within the current view of science (i.e., to be proscriptive, to tell scientists what they must *not* do). In being proscriptive, the philosopher of science might cut off the stream of revolutionary scientific innovations: innovations that later could have been the source of successful scientific revolutions. Because it is this evolving corpus of successful scientific paradigms that serves as the raw data necessary to improve our evolving notions of what constitutes good science (within philosophy of science), it is an essential component for future development. To constrain scientific rationality to only one approach (by considering all other forms as unscientific) would be to move toward a self-fulfilling prophecy where scientific rationality is decreed to be what a certain view of science says it should be. Such a constrained view would produce science consistent with the regnant philosophy of science, which might, in turn, appear to verify the validity of the model.

This last point is important when addressing psychologists, because it helps to clarify why many research psychologists have found their experiences with philosophy of science unsatisfactory. Logical positivism was a philosophy of science of considerable importance to psychology in the twentieth century. The advocates of positivism all too often exhibited autocratic styles and authoritarian positions regarding what constituted good science. Committed to operationalism and championing the deductive-nomological view of hypothesis testing, positivists frequently disparaged alternative views of scientific rationality. Thus, for many research psychologists, their experience with philosophy of science consisted of a brush with positivist orthodoxy.

Evolutionary Change in Science

Laudan's (1984) reticulational model of scientific change, proposes that changes in any of the three levels of scientific activity (the axiological, or the aims and goals of science; the methodological; or the factual, which includes both theories and evidence) are possible at any point in time. Such changes are usually not accompanied by suggested modifications at other levels, as Kuhn's revolutionary analysis would suggest. Kuhn spoke of quick, radical reconceptualizations (using terms like *conversion experience, gestalt shifts, incommensurable worldviews*) when paradigm shifts occur at moments of revolutionary science. For Laudan, several scientists, working over an extended period of time, make piecemeal amendments to the regnant paradigm. These minor changes gradually coalesce and result in a substantial shift in paradigmatic characteristics. On Laudan's view, small changes on one level, if they prove successful, might actually produce changes at other levels also, which could, in time, lead to the massive conceptual changes associated (in retrospect) with paradigm shifts. However, whereas many such minor changes are suggested, few are successful, and fewer still lead to changes at other levels. But it is precisely this trial and error, piecemeal approach that constitutes the fuel for scientific change and the backbone of scientific rationality.

Seeing paradigmatic changes in science as part of an evolutionary process, allows for a slightly revised conception of the role of working scientists in the process of change. Rather than seeing ourselves as something like worker bees conducting the simple puzzle-solving tasks of normal science (as Kuhn's revolutionary view implies), many of us are instead contributing small theoretical and methodological innovations that will cumulatively represent the seeds for scientific revolutions. The increasing evidence of multiple, simultaneous discoveries in science suggests that an army of scientists prepares the conceptual ground so that a great new insight is possible (perhaps even inevitable). This vision is quite different from the position that a few great geniuses are responsible for great ideas.

[*See also* Postmodern Psychology.]

Bibliography

Bridgman, P. W. (1928). *The logic of modern physics.* New York: Macmillan.

Campbell, D. T., & Fiske, D. W. (1959). Convergent and discriminant validation by the multitrait-multimethod matrix. *Psychological Bulletin, 56,* 81–105.

Cook, T. D. (1985). Postpositivist critical multiplism. In R. L. Shotlandff & M. M. Mark (Eds.), *Social science and social policy* (pp. 21–62). Thousand Oaks, CA: Sage.

Howard, G. S. (1985). The role of values in the science of psychology. *American Psychologist, 40,* 255–265.

Kourany, J. (Ed.). (1987). *Scientific knowledge: Basic issues in the philosophy of science.* Belmont, CA: Wadsworth.

Kuhn, T. S. (1962). *The structure of scientific revolutions.* Chicago: University of Chicago Press.

Kuhn, T. S. (1977). *The essential tension.* Chicago: University of Chicago Press.

Laudan, L. (1984). *Science and values: The aims of science and their role in scientific debate.* Berkeley: University of California Press.

Marx, M. H., & Goodson, F. E. (1976). *Theories in contemporary psychology* (2nd ed.). New York: Macmillan.

McMullin, E. (1970). The history and philosophy of science: A taxonomy. In R. Stuewer (Ed.), *Historical and philosophical perspectives of science: Vol. 5. Minnesota studies in the philosophy of science* (pp. 12–67). Minneapolis: University of Minnesota Press.

McMullin, E. (1983). Values in science. In P. D. Asquith & T. Nickles (Eds.), *Proceedings of the 1982 Philosophy of Science Association* (Vol. 2, pp. 3–23). East Lansing, MI: Philosophy of Science Association.

Popper, K. (1959). *The logic of scientific discovery.* New York: Basic Books.

George S. Howard

PHOBIA. *See* Social Phobia; *and* Specific Phobia.

PHONEMES. *See* Phonology; *and* Speech Production.

PHONETICS (or the phonetic sciences) studies the mechanisms of human vocal communication. It attempts to discover and explain what happens at any of several stages in the speech chain: (a) converting the stored instructions for pronunciation in the mental lexicon into a motor program to control the movements of the speech organs; (b) implementing that program to cause the coordinated movement of the speech articulators (lungs, larynx, jaw, tongue, soft palate, lips); (c) realizing the aerodynamic consequences of the articulatory movements; (d) generating sound; (e) transforming sound waves into sensory neural signals by the ear; and (f) the hearer's decoding of the neural signals in order to recover the distinctive phonetic elements of speech and thus words and syntactic structures intended by the speaker. Additionally, phonetics studies: (g) how nonlinguistic information, for instance, emotion and attitude, may be conveyed by the voice (e.g., by prosodic parameters such as voice pitch, loudness, and voice quality); and (h) the phenomenon of sound symbolism, where certain speech sounds are hypothesized to have nonarbitrary correlations with meaning. Psychology is one of the phonetic sciences and has been actively involved especially in areas (a), (e), (f), (g), (h) and, in general, with the evolutionary origins and the learning of speech. Psychology has also contributed to the study and amelioration of aspects of pathological speech.

Phonetics is one of the oldest of the behavioral sciences, beginning with the achievement of a reliable and objective method of describing speech sounds' articulation by the Hindu grammarian Panini in approximately the sixth century BCE. Progress on the more directly observable articulatory and acoustic stages of speech has steadily accelerated from the late eighteenth century to the present. Studies of the more inaccessible aspects, in which psychologists have been active, are still in their infancy.

Questions typically raised about the assembly of the motor program for speech include:

- How is pronunciation represented mentally (articulatory or acoustic-auditory targets or, if both, which is primary)?
- How are the scores of speech muscles coordinated (e.g., is there a metacommand structure governing all the muscles involved in a single gesture like raising the tongue body for a /k/, and are the oral gestures tightly synchronized with laryngeal gestures, or is there a certain temporal latitude)?
- What are the units (phonemes, that is, distinctive speech sounds like /p/ as in 'pin', /s/ as in 'sin', /θ/ as in 'thin', or syllables or parts of syllables or even whole words)?
- Is there any structure imposed on this string of units, for example, a hierarchical arrangement or a grouping of some elements (candidates include the foot (= stressed syllables plus adjacent unstressed syllables), the phrase (= a grouping of sounds involved in shaping the intonation of utterances)?
- What is the role of various forms of feedback in ongoing speech production (e.g., tactile, proprioceptive, auditory)?

Questions about the role of phonetics in speech perception include: What acoustic details help to differentiate the linguistic units as well as the nonlinguistic emotional and attitudinal messages in speech? This has been one of the most productive areas of phonetic research in the last half of the twentieth century, and is responsible in large part for the success of much of speech technology (automatic text-to-speech synthesis and automatic speech recognition). The overriding and still largely unsolved problem in speech perception is how the hearer manages to extract the "same" linguistic unit from a signal that varies because of differences in speakers' vocal tract dimensions, rates of speaking, degrees of emphasis placed on individual words, degrees of loudness, degree of formality, and types of ambient noise. This problem is part of the general problem of perceptual constancy studied in experimental psychology: how an invariable percept is extracted from variable sensory input.

Studies of how the auditory system transforms the acoustic speech signal follows the tradition of some of the pioneers of sensory psychological research, including Hermann von Helmholtz (1821–1894), the German polymath. The problem in this area is figuring out how cues necessary for speech perception can be derived from what is known from physiological research about how the ear transforms the acoustic input. There is some data reduction that goes on, for example, in lumping closely spaced resonances, but there is also some enhancement of the signal, for example, sharpening the onsets of sounds. It is hoped that applying auditory transforms to the acoustic speech signal may improve efforts at automatic speech recognition by, among other things, normalizing the speaker- and style-dependent variations mentioned previously.

Studies of how the speaker's attitude or emotional state may be coded in speech starts with the anecdotal observation that hearers can often detect whether speakers are angry, depressed, or excited, and possibly whether they are being deceptive or not. Research in this area ranges from perceptual studies to determine what emotions listeners can reliably detect, as well as acoustic analysis of speech to find the parameters correlated with identifiable emotions. It is believed that some emotional states produce physiological conditions in the speech organs that have detectable consequences in the voice signal, for example, nervous tension can produce a tremor in the vocal cords, which in turn produces the familiar "quaver" in the voice.

In the acquisition of the sounds of a language, the questions are different depending on whether it is the sounds of the first language or a subsequent language. The uniformity and age-linked acquisition of the sounds (as well as the syntax) of the first language is cited as the primary evidence that a capacity for speech must be genetic (nature), although obviously learning the sounds of one language as opposed to another requires learning through experience (nurture). The sound system of the first language invariably interferes with the learning of the sounds of a second (or subsequent) language by anyone past what is believed to be a "critical age," variously estimated as age five to the onset of puberty. Although fluency may be attained in virtually every other part of language (lexicon, syntax), a foreign accent frequently remains.

The origin of speech and language has been a topic for conjecture from ancient times. Shortly after Darwin's *The Origin of Species* (1859), much speculation centered around trying to identify a sound-producing activity that early man might have engaged in that could have evolved into speech and language, for example, vocalizations to coordinate group work. Today it is generally recognized that it is the psychological capacity to associate meanings with arbitrary strings of signal elements that is of primary importance in the evolution of language, and thus this symbolizing ability might be separated from the origin of speech, that is, vocal communication, *per se*. There is no consensus on any of these matters, but there are active debates among psychologists, neurophysiologists, and evolutionary biologists on whether vocalized mouth gestures (e.g., pointing with the tongue and lips) or chewing might be the precursors to speech, and whether the human vocal tract shows any special anatomical adaptations for speech.

Normally, it is held that meaning is assigned arbitrarily to the sound sequences constituting words: it is the arbitrary combination and permutation of the finite inventory of sounds in a given language that permits the conveyance of an essentially unlimited number of meanings. Sound symbolism (also *phonosymbolism* or *phonetic iconism*), however, posits the existence of a few cases where meaning is conveyed directly by sounds. Naturally, the range of meanings so conveyed must be limited, for example, size, speed, or smooth versus jagged outline. Sound symbolism is studied within psychology for what it may reveal about the association of meaning and sign, the origin of speech, and synesthesia (associations of symbols across different sense modalities).

Communication disorders due to phonetic difficulties are of various sorts: (a) abnormalities of the speech articulators, for example, cleft palate, absence of all or part of the tongue, surgical removal of the larynx; (b) abnormalities of the speech perception system, for example, varying degrees of deafness; (c) injury to the speech centers of the brain (due to stroke or injury), resulting in, for example, aphasia or dysarthria; and (d) etiologies that are not known precisely, such as stuttering and autism, but which apparently have both psychological and genetic components. All speech disorders may have psychosocial consequences. Psychologists study these in order to aid diagnosis, to understand them, and, possibly, to suggest therapeutic measures. Studies of speech disorders caused by brain injury provide a kind of window to the brain on the principle that one can often understand how an inaccessible system works by observing its behavior when it is broken.

Some parts of the speech production system occasionally break down even in nonpathological speakers. Systematic study of speech errors or spoonerisms of the sort "teep a cape" for "keep a tape" provide evidence on the structure of the speech program before it is transformed into motor commands. Word retrieval errors, called tip-of-the-tongue phenomena, where a speaker fails to recall a target word or name but can retrieve some of its phonetic features, such as its initial sound or its number of syllables, help to reveal some aspects of how pronunciation is represented in the mental lexicon.

[*See also* Speech Production.]

Bibliography

Asher, R. E., & Simpson, J.M.Y. (Eds.) (1994). *The encyclopedia of language and linguistics*. Elmsford, NY: Pergamon Press. Several entries cover topics in phonetics: articulatory phonetics, history of phonetics, speech perception, communication disorders, and so on.

Brown, W. S. (1991). A review of the tip-of-the-tongue experience. *Psychological Bulletin, 109*, 209–223.

Fromkin, V. (1973). *Speech errors as linguistic evidence*. The Hague, Netherlands: Mouton.

Hardcastle, W. J., & Laver, J. (Eds.). (1997). *The handbook of phonetic sciences*. Oxford, UK: Blackwell. The most recent definitive survey of all areas of phonetics.

Hinton, L., Nichols, J., & Ohala, J. J. (Eds.). (1994). *Sound symbolism*. Cambridge, UK: Cambridge University Press.

Hurford, J. R., Studdert-Kennedy, M., & Knight, C. (Eds.). (1998). *Approaches to the evolution of language: Social and cognitive bases*. Cambridge, UK: Cambridge University Press.

Jenkins, J. J., Strange, W., & Polka, L. (1995). Not everyone can tell a 'rock' from a 'lock': Assessing individual differences in speech perception. In D. J. Lubinski & R. V. Davis (Eds.), *Assessing individual differences in human behavior: New concepts, methods, and findings* (pp. 297–325). Palo Alto, CA: Davies-Black. Review of evidence that second-language learners may be unable to hear some differences in the speech sounds of the target language.

Miller, J. L., & Eimas, P. D. (Eds.). (1995). *Speech, language, and communication*. San Diego, CA: Academic Press.

Roy, N., & Bless, D. M. (1999). Toward a theory of the dispositional bases of functional dysphonia and vocal nodules: Exploring the role of personality and emotional adjustment. In R. D. Kent & M. J. Ball (Eds.), *The handbook of voice quality measurement*. San Diego, CA: Singular Press.

Scherer, K. (1989). Vocal correlates of emotional arousal and affective disorders. In H. Wagner & A. Manstead (Eds.), *Handbook of social psychobiology* (pp. 165–197). New York: Wiley.

John J. Ohala

PHONOLOGY is the subdiscipline of linguistics that deals with the sound structure of words and sentences. [*See* Psycholinguistics.] The basic assumption is that each word of a language is a sequence of sounds. The sound segments that serve to differentiate words are called phonemes; each language has an inventory of phonemes. For instance, English has the phonemes /p/ and /b/ (the slashes indicate the phonemic status of these sounds) because *pat* and *bat* are two different words. The difference between [p] and [p^h] as in *pot* [p^hət] versus *spot* [spət] (the brackets are a convention of phonetic transcription) is not a phonemic difference because a lexical contrast between [pət] and [p^hət] is impossible in English; aspiration of consonants is a predictable subphonemic phenomenon in English.

Each language has restrictions on the possible combinations of phonemes into morphemes (the minimal meaningful units of a language from which words are constructed; these restrictions are called the phonotactics of that language. For example, whereas *prot* is a possible (though nonexisting) word in English, *mpot* is not. In addition, morphemes exhibit alternations. For instance, the Dutch morpheme *naad*, "seam," is pronounced as [nat], whereas in the plural form *naden* [nadən], the morpheme *naad* is pronounced as [nad]. This alternation follows from the restriction that voiced obstruent consonants like /b/ cannot occur in word-final position and are therefore pronounced as their voiceless counterparts. Phonology aims at characterizing the linguistic knowledge involved in phonotactics and in alternations (the variation in the phonological shape of morphemes within words and larger units such as phrases) and investigates to what extent the principles involved apply to all languages and which of them are language specific.

The sound structure of a word is not just as a linear string of segments. There are also suprasegmental properties; each word exhibits a hierarchical organization of its sounds. A word consists of one or more syllables, and there are principles, partially language universal, for the division of a word into syllables. The syllables are the bearers of suprasegmental properties such as stress and tone.

Phonological knowledge is usually represented in terms of symbolic representations and manipulations thereof. The phonological forms of morphemes and words are listed in the lexicon of a language as sequences of phonemes, the so-called underlying forms. These underlying forms are the inputs of phonological rules or constraints, which then determine the phonetic forms of words. These phonetic forms are still abstract, symbolic representations and are interpreted as instructions for the human articulatory apparatus, which then turns these phonetic forms into directly observable physical events.

The existence of such underlying forms which differ from phonetic forms, has been the subject of a theoretical controversy called the abstractness controversy: To what extent can abstract underlying forms be assumed to have psychological reality? For instance, is it justified to assume an underlying form /sign/ for *sign* [sain] because of its relation to *sɪgnal* [sɪgnəl], and can the phonetic form [sain] be derived by means of phonological rules? Is such an account just a descriptive trick that recapitulates the history of the form of these words, or is it really the way in which speakers of English store their knowledge about *sign*? This abstractness debate thus reflects the more general psychological issue of the balance between storage and computation. The fact that a particular phonetic form of a morpheme can be computed by rule on the basis of a more abstract underlying form does not necessarily imply that the speaker, when using that morpheme, computes its phonetic form from an underlying form; it is also possible to store the different phonetic forms of a morpheme with a specification of the contexts in which they have to be used, because storage might be much faster in actual speech processing than computation.

Phonology is thus relevant to general debates in psychology about theoretical models of human knowledge. In addition to the issue of storage versus computation, the question of whether we should conceive of human knowledge in terms of symbolic representations or connectionist networks is also informed by the study of phonology. Connectionist models represent knowledge as a network of relations between pieces of information, the strength of which is described in probabilistic terms.

These issues relate to the types of evidence used in phonological research. Traditionally, phonologists' data comprise observations of how native speakers pronounce words, intuitions of native speakers about possible pronunciations of words, and possible and impossible sound sequences. Sometimes, the psychological reality of rules is assumed if the rule expresses a correct generalization about the phonology of the language involved. Other phonologists claim psychological reality for a phonological rule only if native speakers appear to apply the postulated rule to new cases that they have not come across before. For instance, the rule in Dutch, mentioned previously, that obstruents are voiceless in word-final position is spontaneously applied to borrowed words and interferes with second-language acquisition. Initially, a native speaker of Dutch learning English will pronounce *red* as [rɛt] instead of [rɛːd]. Psycholinguists have also used the spontaneous application of a certain rule to new cases as positive evidence for the psychological reality of a phonological rule.

Additional evidence for the psychological status of an underlying form or a rule can be provided by patterns of language change. For instance, Middle Dutch was subject to a process of lengthening of vowels in open syllables, as in *pad* [pat], "path,"–*paden* [paːdən], "paths." After this rule disappeared from Dutch, some of the alternations between short and long forms of the relevant morphemes were kept. This proves that this vowel length distinction had been lexically encoded; that is, both phonetic forms of the morpheme were listed (and not computed by rule), because otherwise this alternation could not have survived the loss of the rule of lengthening. Kiparsky (1982) has stressed the point that language change functions as a window on linguistic competence.

The methodological problem involved is that data that bear directly on the general psychological issues mentioned above are not always available. Additional evidence can be provided by experiments of nature, namely, speech errors, and by experiments to create errors. For instance, the fact that, in spoonerisms, such as *the bean is dizzy* for *the dean is busy*, the /b/ and /d/ that are interchanged are in the same syllable-initial position suggests that the organization of sounds into syllables has psychological reality and is not just a convenient descriptive invention of linguists. The psychological reality of relatively abstract underlying phonological forms has also been investigated by means of psycholinguistic experimentation (see Lahiri & Marslen-Wilson, 1991).

The main psychological issues related to phonology are the acquisition of phonological competence, speech perception, and speech production. In the study of phonological acquisition the main issue is whether the phonological system can be acquired on the basis of general learning principles or by making use of genetically encoded principles and parameters. In models of speech perception, in particular that of word recognition, the basic issue is how use is made of phonological knowledge such as phonotactic constraints in processing and recognizing words. Models of speech production make up a model of phonological encoding that specifies how the speaker computes the correct phonetic forms of his or her messages. Phonological skills, in particular the segmentation of speech into discrete sounds, are a prerequisite for reading and writing, and lack of this kind of phonological awareness has been proposed to be a main cause of dyslexia.

The relation between phonology and psychology can also be investigated by taking the human speaker as our point of departure. We then investigate to what extent the phonological system is shaped by the often opposing requirements of perception and production of speech. That is, we can also look for psychological explanations of the nature of the phonological system. Ease of perception requires a careful and meticulous rendering of the underlying forms of morphemes, whereas ease of production requires the speaker to be as sloppy as possible in the pronunciation of concatenations of morphemes in order to get a smooth articulation of the sequence of sounds. A recent form of phonological theory, optimality theory, provides a formal model of how to rank the impact of such opposing constraints on the phonetic forms of words.

There is evidence that the phonological system, although it will reflect these contradictory demands of perception and production, nevertheless possesses a certain autonomy. This evidence concerns sign languages, which do not make use of sounds but of body movements. Although such sign languages do not make use of perception by ear and of production by means of the human vocal apparatus, they nevertheless have a formal system regulating the forms of signs that strongly resembles that of phonology. [*See* Hearing.] This suggests a certain degree of cognitive autonomy for phonology, independent of the substance of realization of its forms.

[*See also* Dyslexia; Language, *article on* Language Acquisition; Reading; Speech Production; Sign Languages; *and* Writing.]

Bibliography

Chomsky, N., & Halle, M. (1968). *The sound pattern of English.* New York: Harper & Row. Seminal study of phonology in the theoretical framework of generative grammar.

Fromkin, V. (Ed.). (1980). *Errors in linguistic performance: Slips of the tongue, ear, pen, and hand.* New York: Academic Press. With catalogue of types of speech errors.

Goldsmith, J. (1995). *The handbook of phonological theory.* Cambridge, MA: Blackwell. Survey of recent theoretical issues in phonology.

Kehoe, M., & Stoel-Gammon, C. (1997). The acquisition of prosodic structure: An investigation of current accounts of children's prosodic development. *Language, 73,* 113–144. Review of current studies of phonological acquisition.

Kenstowicz, M. (1994). *Phonology in generative grammar.* Cambridge, MA: Blackwell. Handbook of present-day phonological theory.

Kiparsky, P. (1982). *Explanation in phonology.* Dordrecht, Netherlands: Foris. Language change as a window on the nature of linguistic competence.

Lahiri, A., & Marslen-Wilson, M. (1991). The mental representation of lexical form: A phonological approach to the recognition lexicon. *Cognition, 38,* 245–294. Psycholinguistic evidence for the (degree of) abstractness of underlying phonological forms.

Levelt, W. J. M. (1989). *Speaking: From intention to articulation.* Cambridge, MA: MIT Press. Survey of psychological research on speech production.

Marslen-Wilson, W., & Komisarjevsky-Tyler, L. (1980). The temporal structure of spoken language understanding. *Cognition, 8,* 1–71. The role of phonology in word recognition.

McCarthy, J. J., & Prince, A. (1994). Generalized alignment. In G. E. Booij & J. van Marle (Eds.), *Yearbook of morphology 1993* (pp. 79–151). Dordrecht, Netherlands: Kluwer. One of the few published expositions of optimality theory.

Sandler, W. (1993). Sign language phonology. *Phonology, 10(2),* 165–308. Collection of articles on sign language phonology.

G. E. Booij

PHOTOGRAPHIC MEMORY. *See* Eidetic Imagery.

PHRENOLOGY has been praised, taught in medical schools, researched, and popularized for 200 years. It has also been ridiculed, vilified, satirized, experimentally refuted, and considered heretical for virtually the same length of time. With the hindsight of two centuries, one can easily recognize a confluence of eighteenth-century ideas that naturally lead to phrenological doctrine: the faculty psychology of Thomas Reid, the physiognomy of Johann Lavater, the materialistic physiology of the *idéologues* ("sensationalists") such as Julien de la Mettrie, Etienne Condillac, Claude Helvétius, and Cabanis, and the renewed interest in functional neuroanatomy and neuropathology seen in Morgagni, Swedenborg, Prochaska, and Unzer.

Mainstream phrenology, that which was linked to psychology and medicine, was a prominent issue in medical society meetings and in research publications until the 1860s, after which time its empirically supported components were largely absorbed into commonly accepted views of the brain and brain function. In the meantime, popularized phrenology had become the staple of itinerant quacks and charlatans; phrenological guides to character and personality, elaborate machines for measuring the bumps on the head and sideshow readings and demonstrations occupied a measurable proportion of popular culture well into the twentieth century. In what must be one of history's most delectable ironies, both the science and the quackery trace their origins to the same two individuals, Franz Joseph Gall (1758–1828) and Johann Gaspar Spurzheim (1776–1832).

Biographical Sketches of Gall and Spurzheim

Gall was born in Tiefenbronn near Pforzheim in the Grand Duchy of Baden in 1758; his parents were Roman Catholic of Italian descent (family name, Gallo). He began medical studies in Strasbourg, France, in 1777 and completed his medical degree at the University of Vienna in 1785. He published a book on practical medicine in 1791. By 1794 his medical practice was sufficiently established in Vienna that he was offered a position as the emperor's physician, which he turned down. Gall was giving public lectures on his theory of the functions of the brain as early as 1796 in Vienna; his first published statement on organology appeared 2 years later as a letter in a German periodical. At the end of 1801, Austrian Emperor Francis I wrote to Gall decreeing that he discontinue teaching his doctrine concerning the head because it was materialistic and opposed to morals and religion (Ackerknecht & Vallois, 1956).

Spurzheim was born in Longvich near Treves on the Moselle in the Rhine region in 1776; his parents were Lutheran of German descent. He matriculated from the University of Treves in 1791 and moved to Vienna in 1792 to study medicine. By 1799 he had heard of Gall and began auditing his lectures. In 1804 he became Gall's assistant, doing the anatomical dissections for Gall's presentations. In 1805 Gall and Spurzheim left Vienna to lecture in various cities across Northern Europe, eventually settling in Paris in 1807. They presented a memoir on the anatomy of the brain to the French Institute in 1808, and in 1810 published the first volume of the major work that defined *craniology* (Gall's term) or *phrenology* (Spurzheim's term). Halfway through the completion of volume two of the anatomy and physiology of the nervous system, Spurzheim left for Vienna, where he completed his doctorate in medicine in 1813. Gall finished the remaining volumes by himself and then reissued the work (Gall, 1822–1825) minus the anatomical plates and with the addition of rebuttals against various critics; he died in Paris in 1828. Between 1815 and 1832, Spurzheim published several works on phrenology, on the anatomy of the brain, and on education (Spurzheim, 1818, 1821/1847, 1826, 1832). He made his first visit to England in 1814, traveled to Scotland in 1815, returned briefly to London and then to Paris in 1817, remaining there until 1824 when the French government passed a decree against "unapproved" public lectures. In 1825 he returned to England and Scotland and then traveled to the United States in 1832, where he died the same year in Boston.

Principles of Phrenology

Although Gall launched phrenology before Spurzheim joined him, and although they worked independently after 1813, their contributions to the phrenological theory of brain function were generally coherent and complementary. Gall remained more interested in developing his theory, whereas Spurzheim, after they separated, seemed more willing to export phrenological ideas into applied domains. They nominally disagreed on how many faculties there should be, and Spurzheim tended to emphasize the brighter, more uplifting side of human nature. Otherwise, they both accepted the fundamental principles that Gall early laid down: the faculties are innate, each person may have more or less of a faculty, they have their seat in the brain, and they are essentially distinct and independent from each other and therefore have their seat in distinct and independent parts of the brain. As for the majority of the faculties, Gall (who had proposed 27) and Spurzheim (who had variously proposed 31, 35, and 37) agreed on them as well; for example, amativeness (physical love), acquisitiveness (desire to own), adhesiveness (affection), calculation, language, and others were common to both.

For those faculties that they agreed on, they also agreed on their brain localization; for example, amativeness was situated in the cerebellum and language was situated in the ventrolateral frontal lobe. Finally, Gall and Spurzheim appear to have agreed on the "methods" of phrenological research: observation of individual cases of people with exceptional or unusual degrees of one or another faculty, for example, criminals, to be studied for their large organ of destructiveness; mentally deficient people, to be studied for their smaller organs of language, calculation, and causality; or parents, to be studied for the size of their organ of philoprogenitiveness (love of one's offspring). Observations, which became the "data" of phrenological science, typically involved "discovering" that an over- or underdeveloped faculty was manifested by an enlarged or diminished overlying skull (Ackerknecht, 1958; Combe, 1835; Hollander, 1920; Whitaker, 1996b; Williams, 1894; Young, 1970).

Phrenology as Science

If one agreed with the fundamental principles and also accepted the list of faculties, phrenological studies were perfectly acceptable clinical science for the nineteenth century. Consider, for example, the study published in *Phrenological Journal and Miscellany*, by Alexander Hood, of several patients with disturbances of language from strokes (Hood, 1824; Whitaker, 1998; Whitaker & Grou, 1991). Hood's analysis of the location of lesions causing aphasia permitted him to establish the individuality of the organ of language and to confirm the accuracy of its place in the brain (above and behind the socket of the eye). By comparing several different aphasic cases, Hood fractionated the organ of language into one part directly controlling the articulatory muscles, another controlling verbal expression, and a third controlling the memory or ideas for words. This was a remarkably prescient clinical-experimental conclusion, employing the theoretically coherent, albeit to us implausible, clinical-pathological correlation method derived from phrenology. Hood concluded with the homily, as Gall had stressed for years, that one must have good theory before studying the brain so that the evidence of impaired function may be properly related to the elements of the theory. In Hood's case, the theory was the map of the phrenological organs neatly painted on a plaster bust, but the method was good science.

Impact of Gall's and Spurzheim's Ideas

Beginning in 1802, dozens of "auditors" of Gall's lectures published treatises of the new physiology of the brain, some critical and some laudatory, in French, German, Italian, Dutch, and English (Clarke & Jacyna, 1987). Between 1810 and 1832, in addition to the numerous publications by Gall and Spurzheim, there were press releases, publications of lectures in medical journals such as the *Lancet*, critical reviews in various academy and society publications by eminent scientists, the founding of phrenological societies complete with their own journals and a sufficiently large clientele willing to pay admission to phrenological lectures and demonstrations as to leave Gall, Spurzheim, Combe, and others in quite satisfactory economic conditions (Ackerknecht, 1958). What may have been *une lubie* ("a fad") to Parisian society in the early 1800s was a feature of Western culture by the end of the nineteenth century. Consider that Combe's (1835) phrenological manifesto had sold 80,500 copies by 1847 and over 300,000 copies by 1860; it was one of the four best-selling books of the nineteenth century, the others being the *Bible*, *Pilgrim's Progress*, and *Robinson Crusoe*.

The parallel between phrenological principles and those of contemporary neurology, neuropsychology, and cognitive neuroscience is regularly noted (Whitaker, 1996a). To temper that observation, remember that Gall, Spurzheim, Combe, and their followers did not always adhere to their own scientific methods. Pierre Flourens conducted experiments in 1824 in which he extirpated the cerebellum of several animals; he observed that the lesioned animals exhibited no decrease in sexual activity, data that directly refuted the phrenological claim that the organ of amativeness (physical love) was the cerebellum. Gall rejected Flourens's experimental data, and most other phrenologists, with the notable exception of Bouillaud, tacitly followed Gall's lead. To what extent this damaged the scientific credibility of phrenology is difficult to determine. It is also the case that after the 1830s, much of phrenological practice had taken a turn toward the type of quackery and charlatanism found in mesmerism, patent medicines, and electric corsets, hats, and trusses. On the other hand, France's leading physician of the early nineteenth century, François Joseph Victor Broussais, known as the emperor of medicine to modern historians, taught phrenology to medical students at the University of Paris in 1836.

From the scientific perspective, the question of the localization of brain functions, particularly language, remained a major point of debate in medical societies and academies from the 1820s to the 1860s; in virtually every medical publication in Europe during this time there was an autopsy report, identifying the location of the brain lesion and the impairment sustained by the patient before death, with a comment on whether this case did or did not support the ideas of Gall and Spurzheim regarding localization of brain functions. Eventually, the weight of establishment science turned toward (a greatly modified) phrenological doctrine after the publication of Paul Broca's celebrated cases in the early 1860s. And of course, the term *phrenology* was no longer used in mainstream psychology and medicine. Given that the impact of phrenology on the development of neuroscience is still being discussed and evaluated, one must conclude that phrenology was indeed an historical milestone.

Bibliography

Ackerknecht, E. H. (1958). Contributions of Gall and the phrenologists to knowledge of brain function. In F. N. L. Poynter (Ed.), *The history and philosophy of knowledge of the brain and its functions* (pp. 149–153). Oxford, UK: Blackwell.

Ackerknecht, E. H., & Vallois, H. V. (1956). *Franz Joseph Gall, inventor of phrenology and his collection* (Wisconsin Studies in Medical History No. 1). Madison: University of Wisconsin Medical School, Department of History of Medicine.

Aubert, D., & Whitaker, H. A. (1996). The third decade of 19th-century brain localization in Paris: How basic ideological assumptions constrained experimental studies of the cerebral lobes. *Brain & Cognition, 32*, 104–000.

Clarke, E., & Jacyna, L. S. (1987). *Nineteenth-century origins of neuroscientific concepts*. Berkeley: University of California Press.

Combe, G. (1835). *The constitution of man considered in relation to external objects* (5th American ed.). Boston: Chase, Nichols & Hill.

Gall, F. J. (1822–1825). *Sur les fonctions du cerveau et sur celle de chacune de ses parties* [On the functions of the brain and each of its parts]. (Vols. 1–6). Paris: F. Schoell.

Hollander, B. (1920). *In search of the soul and the mechanism of thought, emotion and conduct* (Vols. 1 & 2). London: Kegan Paul, Trench, & Trubner.

Hood, A. (1824). Case 4th–July 28, 1824 (Mr. Hood's cases of injuries of the brain). *Phrenological Journal and Miscellany, 2*, 82–94.

Spurzheim, G. (1818). *Observations sur la phrénologie, ou la naissance de l'homme* [Observations about phrenology, or the birth of man]. Paris: Treuttel & Weurtz.

Spurzheim, G. (1826). *The anatomy of the brain with a general view of the nervous system*. (Translated from unpublished French manuscript by R. Willis.) London: S. Highley.

Spurzheim, G. (1832). *Outlines of phrenology*. Boston: March, Capen & Lyon.

Spurzheim, G. (1847). *Education: Its elementary principles founded on the nature of man* (9th American ed.). New York: Fowlers & Wells. (Original work published 1821 under the title *Elementary principles of education founded on the study of the nature of man*.)

Whitaker, H. A., & Grou, C. (1991). Spurzheim's legacy: The case of Adam M'Conochie (1824). *Neurology, 41*, 239.

Whitaker, H. A. (1996a). Historical antecedents to Geschwind. In S. C. Schachter & O. Devinsky (Eds.), *Behavioral neurology and the legacy of Norman Geschwind* (pp. 63–69). New York: Lippincott-Raven.

Whitaker, H. A. (1996b). [Review of the book *Reader in the history of aphasia: From Franz Gall to Norman Geschwind*, Paul Eling (Ed.).] *Historiographia Linguistica, 23* (1/2), 182–187.

Whitaker, H. A. (1998). The history of neurolinguistics: From the beginnings to the 1970s. In B. Stemmer & H. A. Whitaker (Eds.), *The handbook of neurolinguistics*. San Diego, CA: Academic Press.

Williams, W. M. (1894). *A vindication of phrenology*. London: Chatto & Windus.

Harry A. Whitaker

PHYSICAL DISABILITIES. Physical disability is a common experience of everyday life and of the professional domain of practicing psychologists. A population-based survey of disability found that 13.5% of the adult population living in private households had disabilities. The most common disabilities were locomotion and hearing, but the most common severe disabilities were locomotion and personal care (e.g., dressing, toileting). The causal conditions were largely those having increasing incidence with greater age, such as arthritis and deafness. Approximately 70% of disabled adults living in private accommodation are over 60 years old.

Many conditions have a gender, ethnicity, and social class bias in distribution. For example, rheumatoid arthritis is more common in women. Because women live longer, disabled women are, on average, older than disabled men. For some conditions, such as accidental injury, the gender difference is due to behavioral factors: Men engage in more risky activities. Martin, Meltzer, and Elliot (1988) found no evidence of ethnic differences in prevalence of disability. Virtually all diseases are more common in more deprived social groups, reflecting the widely recognized susceptibility to ill health of poorer people.

Disabling diseases vary in their effects on life expectancy, and this has important implications for considering incidence and prevalence data. Thus a relatively uncommon condition with onset in childhood but low associated mortality can have a higher prevalence than a condition with high incidence that appears in older people and has a short survival time. For example, the incidence of amyotrophic lateral sclerosis (ALS)/motor neurone disease (MND) is about 1 in 75,000, but given its average onset in 50- to 60-year-old people and the fact that most patients die within 5 years, it is a disease with relatively low prevalence.

Definition and Assessment

Disability is defined in a variety of ways, with resulting problems in measurement and communication of results. In 1980, the World Health Organization (WHO) defined disability in terms of a person's activities as "Any restriction or lack (resulting from impairment) of ability to perform an activity in the manner or within the range considered normal for a human being" (WHO, 1980, p. 28). This contrasted with impairment, which was defined at the level of structure and function of the body, and handicap, defined in terms of social roles and disadvantage. These definitions were widely criticized, and WHO has recently proposed that these three dimensions be redefined and renamed impairment, activity, and participation (WHO, 1997). Other authors use the word *disability* differently, sometimes using the term to refer to the WHO concepts of impairment or of handicap.

Disability is usually measured by assessing performance of everyday activities, commonly referred to as "activities of daily living" or ADL. The selection of items, the method of assessing performance, and the scaling of items to give an overall score show immense diversity, and existing scales clearly measure a variety of different but overlapping concepts. Assessments include self-care items, such as washing, dressing, feeding, and toileting, and mobility items, such as standing, using stairs, and walking for a specified distance. Some measures assess the "normality" of performance and may require observation of the performance of the activity. Others pay little heed to the mode of performance and concentrate on whether the activity, for example, washing oneself, was achieved. Items are scored in diverse ways, and the method of combining items reflects a wide variety of scaling techniques, including (weighted) additive, Thurstone, and Guttman scaling. Thus the methods of assessment reflect different underlying models of the nature of disability.

Explanatory Models

The WHO (1980) model proposed that disability is the result of physical impairment, which in turn results from disease or disorder, and that impairment can result in handicap either directly or through disability. So, for example, an individual experiencing a stroke (disorder) might have impaired leg functioning (impairment), resulting in limitations in mobility (disability), and therefore be unable to continue to work (handicap). By contrast, facial scarring due to burn injuries may not result in any limitations of activity but might lead to difficulties in appearing in public places and thus to social handicap.

This is primarily a medical or biological model, attributing disability to failure of physiological systems. By contrast, the social model of disability proposes that the limitations placed on the individual are due to constraints in the social and physical environment and that functional limitations are determined as much socially as biologically. Because disability is defined in behavioral terms, a variety of psychological models that predict behavior can readily be applied. These models would suggest that disability is determined by the individual's beliefs and emotions, by antecedents and consequences, by skills and habits, and so forth. Medical, social, and psychological models need not be in conflict, as many social factors are likely to operate by psychological mechanisms to alter the relationship between the components of the WHO model.

The WHO model has rarely been tested or evaluated, but it is clear that neither disease nor impairment accounts for all the variance observed in disability. At the same time, it has been demonstrated that psychological factors, for example, perceptions of control, predict and may determine level of disability when disease or disorder and impairment have been accounted for. Many treatment interventions that successfully reduce disability also enhance mood and feelings of self-efficacy, and it is plausible that these emotional states and control cognitions determine disability levels. Thus a combined medical and psychological model would appear to be needed.

Social and Emotional Impact

As proposed in the WHO model, disability results in various limitations in social functioning. These limitations will be influenced by physical constraints in the environment, by stigmatizing reactions from others, by overprotection by immediate family members or caretakers, and by the level of formal and informal practical and emotional support available. For example, behavioral programs in which social attention is contingent on successful performance rather than on limitations have been shown to enhance activity levels. Much recent research has examined the impact of disability on caretakers, as well as on the disabled persons.

Psychologists have frequently noted the association between disability and low mood or emotional disorder, but many studies are cross-sectional and observational in design, and it is therefore often difficult to disentangle cause and effect. It seems likely that both effects occur. That is, disability results in depression, and depressed individuals are likely to be more disabled given comparable levels of impairment.

Psychological Treatment

Psychological treatments are directed to reducing the disability or the impact of the disability or both. Those directed to reducing impact are similar to other cognitive behavioral programs that aim to reduce emotional and social consequences of life events and difficulties; they concentrate on cognitive reframing and stress management skills. Programs directed to reducing disability per se are more akin to other programs that aim to achieve behavioral change. Although they may include stress management techniques, they also include elements designed to increase motivation by enhancing self-efficacy or altering contingencies and to develop (for example, by physical therapy) skills and habits required to achieve the performance of activities.

Bibliography

Johnson, R. J., & Wolinsky, F. D. (1993). The structure of health status among older adults: Disease, disability, functional limitation, and perceived health. *Journal of Health and Social Behaviour, 34*, 105–121.

Johnston, M. (1997). Representations of disability. In K. Petrie & J. A. Weinman (Eds.), *Perceptions of health and illness* (pp. 189–212). Amsterdam: Harwood.

Kaplan, R. M., Atkins, C. J., & Reinsch, S. (1984). Specific efficacy expectations mediate exercise compliance in patients with COPD. *Health Psychology, 3*, 223–242.

Lorig, K., Seleznick, M., Lubeck, D., Ung, E., Chastain, R. L., & Holman, H. R. (1989). The beneficial outcomes of the arthritis self-management course are not ade-

quately explained by behavior change. *Arthritis and Rheumatism*, 32, 91–95.
Martin, J., Meltzer, H., & Elliot, D. (1988). *The prevalence of disability among adults*. London: HMSO.
World Health Organization (1980). *International classification of impairments, disabilities and handicaps*. Geneva, Switzerland: Author.
World Health Organization (1997). *Towards a common language for disablements: ICIDH*. Geneva, Switzerland: Author.

Marie Johnston

PHYSICAL FITNESS. *See* Exercise and Physical Activity; *and* Sport Psychology.

PIAGET, JEAN (1896–1980), Swiss child psychologist and epistemologist. Piaget is universally known for his studies of the development of intelligence in children. Although he played a crucial role in shaping twentieth-century child psychology, he considered psychology to be a tool of epistemology (which was for him essentially the theory of scientific knowledge) and identified his domain as "genetic [i.e., developmental] epistemology." Piaget thus studied the growth of *intelligence*, by which term he meant chiefly the capacities, structures, and notions that make scientific thought possible. He described development as a sequence of stages from birth through adolescence. The stages appear at variable ages in different cultures and settings, but their order is invariable. A prolific author, Piaget wrote over 50 books and hundreds of articles.

Piaget was born in 1896 in the French-speaking Swiss city of Neuchâtel to an agnostic medievalist and a religious mother with socialist leanings. He precociously became a professional in mollusk classification and was published in specialized journals. After a doctoral thesis on the taxonomy of Alpine mollusks (1918) and studies in psychology and philosophy in Zurich and Paris, he joined, in 1921, the Jean-Jacques Rousseau Institute of Geneva, founded by Édouard Claparède (1873–1940) as a center for research on child development and education. He later taught experimental and developmental psychology, sociology, and history and philosophy of science, mostly at the University of Geneva. From 1929 to 1967, Piaget directed the International Bureau of Education, originally established to coordinate educational information and research, and to promote peace and international understanding through education. In 1955, with support from the Rockefeller Foundation, he created the interdisciplinary International Center for Genetic Epistemology (which closed in 1984). The Archives Jean Piaget in Geneva collect Piaget's publications and related secondary literature.

After his discovery in 1912 of *Creative Evolution*, by the French philosopher Henri Bergson (1859–1941), Piaget became interested in the nature of life and evolution, rejected the Darwinian theory of natural selection (to which he would always prefer a form of Lamarckism), and adopted the basic postulate of his later thought: the idea that the theory of knowledge and the theory of life are inseparable. During World War I, while active in socialist and Christian youth groups, Piaget went through deep crises where issues of personal identity combined with religious and political questions, revolt against bourgeois conservatism and official churches, the discovery of God's fraternity with humanity, and the aspiration to work for the "new birth of Christianity." These crises can be traced through Piaget's youthful writings (*The Mission of the Idea*, 1915; "The Mysteries of Divine Suffering," 1916) and were described by him in *Recherche* (1918), an autobiographical novel and philosophical essay.

In *Recherche*, Piaget sketched a theory of organic, psychological, and social phenomena based on the idea of equilibrium between parts and wholes. Real-life disequilibria (within a society, for example, between individual and collective interests) tend toward an ideal equilibrum that preserves the integrity of parts and wholes alike. Disequilibria, however, can turn into such events as the then-raging world war. Piaget wished his theory to help make possible the new birth of Christianity and the postwar reconstruction of humanity. Much of his later thinking built directly on his youthful speculations and values, but its empirical impetus derived from his own reaction against the metaphysical and mystical inclinations of his adolescence.

Upon leaving for Paris in 1919, Piaget was recommended to Théodore Simon (1873–1961), a former collaborator with Alfred Binet (1857–1911), by Pierre Bovet (1878–1965), a friend of his family and director of the Rousseau Institute. Simon asked him to standardize Cyril Burt's intelligence tests on Parisian children. Soon, the study of children's reasoning became the empirical field where Piaget would pursue his intellectual projects.

In the early 1920s, Piaget devised a "clinical method" that combined the use of items from intelligence tests, new problem-solving situations, and open-ended conversations with school-age children. In his first five books (1923–1932), he studied the child's language, reasoning, conceptions of the world, theories of causality, and moral judgment. He found that children are at first "egocentric" (i.e., experienced difficulty to take another person's point of view) and attached to concrete appearances but that they gradually move away from egocentrism and become capable of thinking abstractly and logically. Earlier child-study examined mainly the contents of the child's mind and inventoried age-related behaviors. The novelty of Piaget's research was that it concentrated on the main features of the child's "mentality"; in so doing, it drew inspiration from work by the French ethnologist Lucien Lévy-Bruhl (1857–1939), who described "primitive mentality" as prelogical and mystical.

The young Piaget was involved with psychoanalytic theory and practice. His first psychological article dealt with the relations of psychoanalysis and child psychology, a Swiss specialty with which he became familiar in Zurich. In Geneva, he was psychoanalyzed by the Russian Sabina Spielrein (1885–1941/42). His first books bear the traces of his psychoanalytic interests and reveal several major influences: that of the Zurich psychiatrist Eugen Bleuler (1857–1939), who coined the term *schizophrenia* and described "autistic thinking" (to which Piaget compared the child's egocentrism); that of two of his Paris teachers, the psychiatrist Pierre Janet (1859–1947) and the philosopher Léon Brunschvicg (1869–1944); and that of James Mark Baldwin (1861–1934), an American pioneer of "genetic" psychology and epistemology.

In his first books, Piaget considered the development of intelligence as a process of socialization of thought, and he attributed great developmental import to social interactions among peers and between children and adults. His writings rapidly won him an international reputation; within the progressive education movement, they were seen as providing scientific support for pedagogical methods based on "self-government" and the child's activity. In the 1920s, Piaget also investigated the adaptation of mollusks, and he wrote about epistemological, sociological, and religious topics. In all domains, development went from egocentrism (largely manifested as children's dependence on perceptual appearances and acceptance of external authority) toward logical thinking and cognitive and moral autonomy. Piaget saw such development as a progress from the child and the primitive to the adult and the modern, from authoritarian regimes to parliamentary democracy, and from dogmatic religions to liberal Protestantism.

Starting in the mid-1920s, Piaget studied his three children (born in 1925, 1927, and 1931) and recorded his observations in three great classics. *The Origins of Intelligence* (1936, a splendid introduction to Piaget's work) and *The Construction of Reality* (1937) describe how basic forms of intentionality and of the categories of object, space, causality, and time evolve, during the "sensorimotor" period, between the newborn's reflex activities and the emergence of language at about 18 months. *Play, Dreams, and Imitation* (published in 1945 but largely composed earlier) deals with the development of mental representation up to the age of 6. Later authors criticized Piaget for drawing general conclusions from the detailed observation of a very small number of subjects, who happened to be his children. At the time, however, studying one's children was current and legitimate within psychology.

Particularly in *The Origins of Intelligence*, Piaget elaborated links between biological, epistemological, and psychological theories. He defined human intelligence as a form of adaptation that prolongs organic adaptation and functions according to the same mechanisms, "assimilation" and "accommodation." Piaget asserted the primary role of activity and sought to avoid both nativism and empiricism. He later termed his approach constructivist because it assumes that the concepts and structures of intelligence are successively constructed and reconstructed by means of the physical and mental activities whereby the organism adapts to the external world.

In the 1930s, Piaget and his former student Bärbel Inhelder (1913–1997) started collaborating. Their 1941 book on the child's understanding of quantity conservation was the first of many others. While Inhelder inspired much of the concrete psychological research, Piaget focused on his epistemological goals, and elaborated logical models for describing mental "structures" and "operations." Together, they wrote books on the development of the conceptions of movement, speed, time, space, geometry, chance, and probability. Their work on inductive reasoning led to the definition of the final developmental stage of "formal operations," characterized by the capacity for hypothetico-deductive thinking, and resulted in two influential books, *The Growth of Logical Thinking from Childhood to Adolescence* (1953) and *The Early Growth of Logic in the Child* (1959).

Piaget remained active until the end of his life. In addition to the aforementioned works, Piaget, Inhelder, and their research team wrote on the mechanisms of perception, the relations between memory and intelligence, mental image, causal and physical explanations, the grasp of consciousness, contradiction, generalization, possibility, and necessity. Thirty-seven volumes of the collaborative *Études d'épistémologie génétique* appeared between 1957 and 1980. In his later work, Piaget conceptualized mental development and the history of science as a process of "equilibration" toward an increasingly larger capacity for assimilating the world.

Piaget also published a number of theoretical books, such as *Insights and Illusions of Philosophy* (1965), *Biology and Knowledge* (1967), *Structuralism* (1968), *Genetic Epistemology* (1970), *Adaptation and Intelligence* (1974), *The Equilibration of Cognitive Structures* (1975), *Behavior and Evolution* (1976), and *Psychogenesis and the History of Science* (1986). Piaget's three-volume *Introduction à l'épistémologie génétique* (1950) has not been translated into English.

Piaget and his collaborators created many original and ingenious problem-solving situations that became paradigms for research all over the world. In one famous instance, children face a scale model of three mountains and are asked to choose from a series of pictures the one that represents the mountains as seen by a doll sitting at other positions. Younger subjects systematically identify the doll's viewpoint with their own. The studies of "conservation" provide further examples: the child is presented with two identical balls of clay; the shape of one is modified, and the experimenter tries to find out whether the child thinks the amount, weight, or volume of clay has changed or not. Other situations involve manipulating blocks or pouring identical quantities of liquid in differently shaped containers. In one study of inductive reasoning, subjects were asked to discover the factors (length, thickness, etc.) that make metal rods more or less flexible. The study of the "object concept" by observing infants's reactions after an object disappears from their view has given rise to countless variations.

After the 1960s, Piaget's work inspired huge amounts of empirical research throughout the world. His 1932 book on the child's moral judgment was crucial for Lawrence Kohlberg (1927–1987), the American student of moral development. Most "Piagetian" research is disconnected from the theoretical goals of genetic epistemology. Indeed, it was Piaget's investigative techniques, his formulation of new problems, insightful observations, and emphasis on the development of cognitive capacities that contributed in fundamental ways to shape contemporary child and cognitive psychology. Piaget has been criticized for underestimating children's cognitive competencies, considering that the structure of intelligence is homogeneous (rather than domain specific), being insensitive to cultural variability, and particularly for neglecting the interpersonal and affective dimensions of development. In the 1980s and 1990s, it was fashionable to contrast his viewpoint to the cultural-historical approach of the Soviet developmentalist Lev Vygotsky (1896–1934). Piaget, however, remains a major reference in developmental psychology, and Piagetian research is carried out in many countries, especially in educational psychology.

Piaget's work encouraged the belief that instruction must adapt to the child's developmental level, had direct impact on moral and science education, and inspired remedial procedures. It also stimulated philosophical discussions about psychology and the human sciences. Piaget attributed to psychology a preeminent place among the sciences, since, he said, only psychology studies the development of the logico-mathematical operations that make science possible. But he insisted he was not primarily a psychologist, and he explained that he studied the "epistemic" rather than the "psychological" subject. A balanced assessment of Piaget's contribution must take these claims seriously. In addition, his work spans about 70 years and includes not only psychology but also sociology, philosophy of science and religion, theory of knowledge, education, and biology. This diversity must be taken into account and placed in biographical and historical perspectives if one is to reach a full understanding of Piaget's place in modern thought.

Bibliography

Works by Piaget

Bibliographie Jean Piaget. Geneva: Fondation Archives Jean Piaget, 1989. An indispensable tool; almost exhaustive; supersedes previous bibliographies.

Conversations with Jean Piaget (1989). By Jean-Claude Bringuier. (B. Miller-Gulati, Trans.). Chicago, IL: University of Chicago Press, 1989. Useful (particularly Bringuier) introductions to the man and his ideas. Bringuier's original is *Conversations libres avec Jean Piaget*. Paris: Laffont, 1977.

The following are collections of articles from the 1940s through the 1960s. Useful to grasp the diversity of Piaget's research interests.

Gruber, H., and Vonèche, J. (Eds.). (1996). *The essential Piaget: An interpretive reference and guide*. Northvale, NJ: Jason Aronson. A useful anthology.

Jean Piaget: The man and his ideas. Conversations with Richard I. Evans. New York: Dutton, 1973.

Piaget, J. (1952). Autobiography. In E. G. Boring et al. (Eds.), *A history of psychology in autobiography* (Vol. 4, pp. 237–256). Worcester, MA: Clark University Press. The most widely used source of biographical sketches. Particularly lacunary in the narrative of Piaget's youth.

Piaget, J. (1968). *Six psychological studies* (A. Tenzer, Trans. and Intro. by D. Elkind.) New York: Vintage. Original: *Six études de psychologie*. Paris: Denoël Gonthier, 1964.

Piaget, J. (1971). *Science of education and the psychology of the child* (D. Coltman, Trans.) New York: Viking Press. Original: *Psychologie et pédagogie*. Paris: Denoël, 1969.

Piaget, J. (1972). *Psychology and epistemology: Towards a theory of knowledge* (P. A. Wells, Trans.) Harmondsworth: Penguin. Original: *Psychologie et épistémologie*. Paris: Gonthier/Denoël, 1970.

Piaget, J. (1973). *The child and reality: Problems of genetic psychology* (A. Rosin, Trans.) New York: Grossman. Original: *Problèmes de psychologie génétique*. Paris: Denoël/Gonthier, 1972.

Piaget, J. (1973). *To understand is to invent. The future of education* (G.-A. Roberts, Trans.) New York: Grossman. Original: *Où va l'éducation*. Paris: Denoël/Gonthier, 1972.

Piaget, J. (1995). *Sociological studies* (T. Brown et al., Trans.; Intro. by L. Smith). London / New York: Blackwell. Translates the second, expanded edition of *Études sociologiques*. Geneva: Droz, 1977. First edition: Geneva, Droz, 1965.

Works about Piaget

Catalogue annuel. Geneva: Fondation Archives Jean Piaget, since 1975. Annual bibliographies of Piaget-related publications, with a valuable key-word index.

Boden, M. (1979). *Jean Piaget.* Harmondsworth: Penguin. A remarkable short introduction.

Chapman, M. (1988). *Constructive evolution: Origins and development of Piaget's thought.* New York: Cambridge University Press. An ambitious and penetrating analysis of Piaget's work. Not for beginners.

Smith, L. (Ed.). (1992). *Jean Piaget: Critical assessments* (4 vols.) London/New York: Routledge.

Vidal, F. (1994). *Piaget before Piaget.* Cambridge, MA: Harvard University Press. A historical and contextual biography that tries to correct the biases of Piaget's autobiography.

Fernando Vidal

PIÉRON, HENRI (1881–1962), French psychologist. Born in Paris and son of the inspector-in-chief of Public Education, Piéron was acquainted with most of the luminaries of French science from an early age. He was probably the most influential academic French psychologist of the first half of the twentieth century. Successor to Alfred Binet as director of the Sorbonne's Laboratory of Physiological Psychology in 1912, Piéron was a prime mover in establishing psychology as a scientific and professional discipline over the next 50 years.

Piéron's influence took many forms. He spoke out against metaphysical and spiritualistic views of psychology and biology from a behavioristic stance, attacked scientific fakery, and aggressively advanced psychology as a research science. His scientific influence was based on lectures, editorial work, and over five hundred research papers, monographs, and books on the neurophysiological bases of action and behavior in sleep and dreaming, memory, brain and thought, comparative psychology, professional topics, and the psychology of work. He shaped the character, legal standing, and many details of French psychological education, research, and service as an editor and as the founder or administrator of psychological, social, biological, educational, and general scientific research organizations and institutes. Among his positions and activities were secretary-general of the *Revue Scientifique* (1904), editorial secretary of the *Revue de Psychiatrie* (1907), editor of the seven-volume *Treatise of Applied Psychology* and author of its first volume, *Differential Psychology* (1949), and the longtime director and owner of *L'Année Psychologique*.

He was one of the founders of the French Institute of Anthropology (1910), and in 1920 he organized the Institute of Psychology at the University of Paris. In 1923 he was elected to the Collège de France to a newly created Chair of Physiology and Sensation. In 1925, he joined the supervising committee of some 75 laboratories of the École des Hautes Études and in 1937 became head of that group. His interest in the application of psychology culminated in 1938 with the founding of the Institute for the Study of Work and Vocational Guidance, which profoundly affected the academic and professional development of post–World War II French psychology.

Piéron was internationally prominent and in 1937 was president of the eleventh International Congress of Psychology, which met that year in Paris. He was also a major figure in French science and in 1940 became president of the French Association for the Advancement of Science. During World War II he remained in Paris, save for a brief prewar period in Bordeaux, when he headed an Air Force program in psychophysiology and personnel selection. When the war was over, he directed France's celebratory Congrès de la Victoire of 1945. Honors continued, and he was elected for 1951–1954 as the first president of the International Union of Scientific Psychology.

He was a totally engaged person: From his early career as a Dreyfusard to his World War II efforts to protect Jewish and activist colleagues and students, through his interwar-year efforts to improve the scientific status of psychology and its development as an applied discipline, to learning how to fly to do better research on training pilots, Piéron was always ready to take up intellectual, academic, and social challenges. Although he confessed that he was not a theoretician and accepted that he had made no world-shaking discoveries, as an activist in matters scientific and societal, Piéron expressed contentment in the belief that French psychology was different and better because of his efforts.

Bibliography

Piéron, H. (1927). *Thought and brain* (C. K. Ogden, Trans.). London: Kegan Paul.

Piéron, H. (1928). Emotion in animals and man. In M. R. Reymert (Ed.), *Feelings and emotions: The Wittenberg symposium* (pp. 284–294). Worcester, MA: Clark University Press.

Piéron, H. (1929). *Principles of experimental psychology* (J. B. Miner, Trans.). New York: Harcourt, Brace.

Piéron, H. (1952). Henri Piéron (D. MacQueen, Trans.). In E. G. Boring, H. S. Langfeld, H. Werner, & R. M. Yerkes (Eds.), *A history of psychology in autobiography* (Vol. 4, pp. 257–278). New York: Russell & Russell.

Piéron, H. (1956). *The sensations: Their functions, processes and mechanisms* (M. H. Pirenne & B. C. Abbott, Trans.). London: Garnett Miller.

Reuchlin, M. (1995). *Totalités, éléments, et structures en psychologie* [Totalities, components, and structures in psychology]. Paris: Presses Universitaires de France. A concise account of Piéron's views on science, research methods, psychological theory, and the nature of psychology's subject matter.

Richard A. Littman

PILLSBURY, WALTER B. (1872–1960), American psychologist. Pillsbury was born in Burlington, Iowa. He attended Penn College in Oskaloosa, Iowa, for two years and then transferred to the University of Nebraska. At Nebraska, Pillsbury met the psychologist H. K. Wolfe, who had received his doctorate from Wilhelm Wundt at Leipzig. Wolfe would influence Pillsbury toward both psychology and Cornell University.

Pillsbury graduated from Nebraska in 1892 and, after teaching briefly at Grand Island College in Nebraska, he went to Cornell in 1893 on a Sage Scholarship. There he became Edward B. Titchener's second doctoral student. Titchener had only come to Cornell from Leipzig the year before.

While at Cornell, Pillsbury translated, with Titchener, Oswald Külpe's *Einleitung in die Philosophie* (Külpe, 1897). He also threw himself into research and produced several publications while still a student, one of which was a landmark study on attention, called in those days apperception (Pillsbury, 1897). Pillsbury received his doctorate from Cornell in 1897, but Titchener kept him on for an additional postdoctoral year. After that year, Pillsbury accepted a position at the University of Michigan, even though Cornell matched the offer. Pillsbury wished to establish his own laboratory. Titchener made Pillsbury a cooperating editor of *The American Journal of Psychology* in 1897, a position he held until his death in 1960.

Psychology at Michigan was still within the department of philosophy. Pillsbury had informal control of the laboratory on his arrival and was made director of the laboratory formally in 1905. When the department of psychology separated from philosophy at Michigan in 1929, Pillsbury became its first chair. He held that position until his retirement in 1942.

The study of attention had begun in Titchener's laboratory at Cornell and continued to be a major thrust of Pillsbury's research program. In 1903, he wrote his classic book on attention, published initially in French as *L'Attention* (Paris, 1906). He rewrote and expanded the French work into *Attention* (New York, 1908) 2 years later. He published *The Psychology of Reasoning* (New York) in 1910, the same year he received his full professorship and the year he was appointed as advisory editor of the *Psychological Review* and elected president of the American Psychological Association.

Though Pillsbury was trained at Titchener's Cornell, he was there before the polarization of structuralism and functionalism took place and so was never devoted to one approach to psychology over another. His very successful introductory textbook, *The Essentials of Psychology* (1916), took an eclectic approach, drawing from the orthodox schools as well as the new behavioral approach. The book went to three editions by 1934.

Pillsbury was a prolific writer, producing a new book or new edition just about every 3 years throughout his career. One of these was his *The History of Psychology* (New York, 1929), though it had the misfortune to appear the same year as Edward G. Boring's monumental work. In all, Pillsbury published 11 books, several going through multiple editions, and 69 articles (McGrade & Dallenbach, 1961). He was also active in editorial work, being on the editorial boards of the *Psychological Review, The American Journal of Psychology*, and *The Journal of Social Psychology*.

Besides being president of the American Psychological Association, he was also president of the Western Psychological Association in 1907, and of the AAAS in 1913. He was elected to the National Academy of Science in 1925.

[*Many of the people mentioned in this article are the subjects of independent biographical entries.*]

Bibliography

Dallenbach, K. M. (1961). Walter Bowers Pillsbury: 1872–1960. *American Journal of Psychology, 74*, 165–173.

Külpe, O. (1897). *Introduction to philosophy* (W. B. Pillsbury and E. B. Titchener, Trans.).

McGrade, M. C., and Dallenbach, K. M. (1961). A bibliography of Walter Bowers Pillsbury. *American Journal of Psychology, 74*, 174–176.

Pillsbury, W. B. (1897). A study in apperception. *American Journal of Psychology, 8*, 405–413.

Rand Evans

PINEL, PHILIPPE (1745–1826), French physician and reformer. Pinel, physician in chief of Salpêtrière Hospice in Paris for the last 30 years of his life, is famous for bringing the study, treatment, and care of the mentally ill into the field of medicine. He is the author of three important books, *Nosographie philosophique* (Paris, 1798), *Traité médico-philosophique sur l'aliénation mentale ou la manie* (Paris, 1800), and *La médecine clinique* (Paris,

1802). He taught at the Paris Health School (the Revolutionary medical faculty) from 1795 on, as professor of "medical physics," and then as professor of internal medicine, was elected to the Academy of Sciences in 1803, decorated with the Legion of Honor by Napoleon Bonaparte and with the Cross of Saint Michael by King Louis XVIII.

His worldwide fame has long been based on the myth that he was the first doctor to liberate the insane from their chains at Bicêtre Hospice, at the height of the Revolution. Pinel "the chain-breaker" appears in every textbook of psychiatry, and in many textbooks of medicine. In fact, beginning in the late eighteenth century medical reformers in all western countries substituted humane restraints such as the straitjacket for chains in order to secure dangerous mental patients. Gladys Swain in her book, *Le sujet de la folie* (Toulouse, 1977), shows that the Pinel story was the work of his envious son, Dr. Scipion Pinel, who wished to obscure his father's real contributions.

The second half of the twentieth century saw Pinel's reputation distorted in another way. Michel Foucault and like-minded promoters of "antipsychiatry," considered Pinel as the first in a long line of dictatorial asylum-keepers who dominated and demeaned mental patients. The director of the asylum thus appears in Foucault's *The Birth of the Clinic* (1971/1975) as the "medical personage" who imposes silence, guilt, and total submission. Only now, owing to recent scholarship, is Pinel beginning to reemerge as the great doctor that his contemporaries honored.

Pinel was born in Roques (now department of the Tarn) into a family of country doctors and grew up in nearby Saint Paul Cap-de-Joux. Educated by the Fathers of the Christian Doctrine, a humanistic, Jansenist teaching order, he earned a master of arts degree in the humanities at their college in Toulouse. He then studied for a doctorate in theology but, on his twenty-fifth birthday, opted for the family profession, medicine. Having earned the medical degree in Toulouse in 1773, he journeyed to Montpellier, seat of France's oldest, famed medical school. Here he found a fabulous library and permission to follow the rounds of the doctors at the municipal hospital. He developed a method of taking individual patient histories over time; this method became an important diagnostic tool. Here began his emphasis on a trusting doctor-patient relationship. He adopted the doctrine of vitalism and became interested in nosology. He also learned English, thus gaining access to British, especially Scottish, psychology. He walked to Paris in 1778, in quest of a career.

For 15 years, Pinel lived on the fringes of the Paris medical world. He edited a newspaper, *Gazette de santé* (1784–1789), translated William Cullen's *First Lines in the Practice of Physick* (1785), reedited Giorgio Baglivi's *Opera Omnia* (1788), and helped edit a 12-volume French abridgment of the *Transactions of the Royal Society of London*. He also engaged in research in the natural sciences at the Paris Botanical Gardens and contributed significant papers in comparative anatomy. The Revolution at first changed little in his daily life.

Appointed "physician of the infirmaries" at Bicêtre, the large Parisian public hospice with 4,000 male inmates, in 1793, he met the experienced administrator, Jean Baptiste Pussin, and his wife and helpmate, Marguerite Jubline; when he encountered 200 mentally ill men, he found his calling. He speaks of "an undefinable thoughtful tenderness" that overcame him at the sight of these unfortunates. He decided to help them, declaring that they were not incurable outcasts, but patients whom physicians might be able to cure. Transferred to the Salpêtrière, the Parisian hospice for about 8,000 women, as physician in chief in 1795, he embarked on modernization and research, but mainly he prepared for his great experiment, the "general treatment" of the curable mentally ill, in 1802–1805. His management and procedures have been called "moral treatment" because no medication or physical intervention occurred, whereas close individual supervision and encouragement prodded the inmates in their progress toward recovery.

Pinel's *Nosographie philosophique* was hailed by the government as a long-awaited "elementary" text and crowned by the Academy of Sciences. Its six editions over 20 years (1798–1818) provided a generation of Paris medical students with their textbook in medicine. Critics, however, soon attacked Pinel's categories, especially fevers viewed as "essential diseases." Eventually, a brutal attack by Pinel's student François Broussais in 1816 dethroned the master.

Pinel's *Traité médico-philosophique* had a less obvious, though more lasting and deeper effect. It dignified "madness" as mental illness and thus brought it into the purview of physicians. He identified "periodic mania," studying the timing and frequency of relapses. He focused on the periods of sanity as moments when a skilled therapist can establish a relationship of trust with the patient. He identified the dangerous "reasoning mania," where the rational faculty remains intact, but a delusional premise may lead the madman to pursue outrageous thoughts and behaviors. The personal respect with which this prominent physician approached and discussed individual patients—all of them paupers—left a deep impression with the reading public. Nevertheless, most of the young doctors in the early nineteenth century veered toward the physicalist approach to mental illness, and it was not until the end of the century, with Jean Martin Charcot, that the psychologic approach resurfaced in France.

In his third book, *Clinical Medicine* (1802), Pinel recorded 256 histories of his patients in the general infirmary of the Salpêtrière where most of the patients were aged women. They became the subject matter of his crowded bedside lessons.

Pinel also left an important legacy for nineteenth-century psychiatry in the form of 30 articles he contributed to the *Dictionnaire des sciences médicales* and the *Encyclopédie méthodique médecine* between 1812 and 1821. His magisterial essays on alienation, mania, and melancholia helped define psychiatry, while his essays on asthenia and experience helped lay the foundation for geriatric medicine. He created the public asylum as part of a well-run general public hospital.

Pinel died at the Salpêtrière on 25 October 1826 and was buried in the Père Lachaise cemetery. His statue stands in front of the hospital where he lived and worked for 30 years.

Bibliography

Carlson, E. T., & Dain, N. (1960). The psychotherapy that was moral treatment. *American Journal of Psychiatry 11*, 519–524.

Grange, K. A. (1961). Pinel and eighteenth-century psychiatry. *Bulletin of the History of Medicine. 35*, 442–453.

Pinel, P. (1806). *A treatise on insanity* (D. D. Davis, Trans.) London: Cadell & Davies. (Original work published 1800)

Pinel, P. (1802, 1804, 1815). *La médecine clinique rendue plus précise et plus exacte par l'application de l'analyse ou Recueil et résultat d'observations sur les maladies aigües, faites à la Salpêtrière*. Paris: Brosson, Gabon, et Cie.

Riese, W. (1951). Philippe Pinel, his views on human nature and disease, his medical thought. *Journal of Nervous and Mental Disease, 114*, 313–123.

Riese, W. (1969). *The legacy of Philippe Pinel: An inquiry into his thought on mental alienation*. New York: Springer.

Weiner, D. B. (1979). The apprenticeship of Philippe Pinel, A new document: "Observations of citizen Pussin on the insane." *American Journal of Psychiatry 136*, 1128–1134.

Weiner, D. B. (Ed. & Trans.). (1980). *The clinical training of doctors: An essay of 1793*. Baltimore, MD: The Johns Hopkins University Press.

Weiner, D. B. (1992). Philippe Pinel's "Memoir on Madness" of 11 December 1794: A fundamental text of modern psychiatry. *American Journal of Psychiatry, 149*, 725–732.

Weiner, D. B. (1993). Le geste de Pinel: History of a psychiatric myth. In M. S. Micale & R. Porter (Eds.), *Discovering the history of psychiatry* (pp. 232–247). New York: Oxford University Press.

Woods, E., & Carlson, E. T. (1961). The psychiatry of Philippe Pinel. *Bulletin of the History of Medicine, 35*, 14–25.

Dora B. Weiner

PINTNER, RUDOLF (1884–1942), American psychologist. Rudolf Pintner was born in Lytham, England, educated in Scotland at the University of Edinburgh, and earned his Ph.D. from the University of Leipzig in 1913, during which time he also studied and worked under Wilhelm Wundt. He came to the United States in 1923 and taught at the University of Toledo and Ohio State University before settling in 1921 as professor of education at Teachers College, Columbia University, where he remained for the rest of his career.

Pintner was a prolific writer during his career. While enrolled in a graduate course at Columbia in the summer of 1912 with Harry Hollingworth, he published the English translation of Wundt's *Introduction to Psychology*. In addition to translating two other German books, he published much-cited and used textbooks on intelligence testing (1923), educational psychology (1929), and the psychology of the physically handicapped (1941). His most substantial work was in the area of mental testing. He published an annual review of research on intelligence testing in the *Psychological Bulletin* between 1926 and 1935, and with Donald Paterson in 1917 contributed *A Scale of Performance Tests*, which has had a lasting impact on the field of intelligence testing.

Pintner was one of the first to conduct research on the Binet Scale of Intelligence and was one of its most vocal critics. He found fault with its use as a test of general intelligence given its primarily verbal content and argued that many groups were thus significantly disadvantaged including immigrants, the deaf and hard of hearing, people with other handicaps/disabilities, and even the bilingual. In spite of the wide popularity of verbal intelligence tests of the time, Pintner's empirical and behavioral approach to mental testing gave voice to his concerns. He provided data showing that verbal tests were indeed biased against such groups and that nonverbal performance tests often nullified differences that had been found between American and foreign-born children on common verbal intelligence tests.

Pintner did not believe there was good evidence for a specific "faculty" of intelligence, and defined intelligence behaviorally as "an evaluation of the efficiency of a reaction or group of reactions under specific circumstances." In line with the times, he thought that mental traits were hereditary and that well-designed psychological tests were ultimately useful. He was concerned about test fairness and that test administration and scoring be objective. By the time of the 1931 edition of his 1923 book on intelligence testing, Pintner was doubtful about qualitative differences between Blacks and Whites on the traits measured by intelligence tests, found there were no such general differences between the genders in spite of a slight verbal superiority among girls, and was highly critical of research done on the intelligence of immigrants.

Eugenics was on the wane in America in the 1930s. Pintner was concerned about Henry Goddard's work on Ellis Island with the mental testing of immigrants, whereby Goddard had claimed that low intelligence/feeblemindedness could be detected "as the immigrants walk past" the examiner. Yet, like many others during this time, Pintner was worried about admitting "mentally inferior" immigrants whose so-called excessive breeding would add to the decline of intelligence in America and called for "increased vigilance."

Pintner's contributions to intelligence testing have a continuing legacy. Items from his performance scale still make up some of the content of the Weschler Scales, the most widely used tests of intelligence that measure both verbal and nonverbal intelligence, and his argument for the importance of nonverbal and spatial thinking has contributed to the field of neuropsychology. His influence is still strong in the area of learning disabilities through his work on concepts including underachievement, discrepancy, and test fairness.

Bibliography

Pintner, R. (1923). *Intelligence testing: Methods and results.* New York: Holt.

Pintner, R. (1929). *Educational psychology.* New York: Holt.

Pintner, R., Eisenson, J., & Stanton, M. (1941). *The psychology of the physically handicapped.* New York: Appleton-Century-Crofts.

Pintner, R., & Paterson, D. G. (1917). *A scale of performance tests.* New York: Appleton-Century.

Michael J. Kral

PIOTROWSKI, ZYGMUNT A. (1904–1985), Polish American psychologist. Piotrowski was born in Poznan, Poland, and received his formal education there, completing his doctorate at the University of Poznan in 1927. His dissertation on the perception of time reflected his fields of study, which included psychology, history of philosophy, and symbolic logic. Piotrowski accepted a fellowship for postdoctoral study at Teacher's College, Columbia University, in New York City in 1928. In 1932, he accepted a position at the New York Psychiatric Institute, where he remained until 1954. His work at the institute included both practical clinical work and psychopathological research under the direction of the psychologist, Carney Landis. From 1954 to 1957, Piotrowski performed similar services at the New Jersey Neuropsychiatric Institute under the direction of the psychiatrist, Nolan D. C. Lewis. From 1957 until his retirement in 1970, Piotrowski was professor of psychiatry and psychology at Thomas Jefferson University Medical College in Philadelphia, Pennsylvania. Following his retirement from academia, Piotrowski engaged in research on executive skills and success for a private consulting firm. Piotrowski frequently lectured on psychodiagnostics at many major universities in the United States and abroad.

Piotrowski's major contributions to psychology lay in the field of psychodiagnostics, particularly in the use of projective techniques. His 1957/1965 book, *Perceptanalysis* (Philadelphia), has been widely used, both in the United States and internationally. *Perceptanalysis* is a guide to the use of projective techniques, especially the Rorschach Projective Technique, in the assessment, diagnosis, and prognosis of personality and its disorders. When Piotrowski first began working at the New York Psychiatric Institute in the early 1930s, psychologists were typically limited to the administration of intelligence and vocational tests. Piotrowski soon saw the need for an instrument that would better screen for psychotics. He found the Rorschach Technique to be the most sensitive in revealing the whole personality of the individual, especially since it reflects performance on a task whose demands are not obvious and thus holds the potential for provoking nonconventional responses from the clinical population. Piotrowski found the Rorschach to be useful in revealing the peculiarities of thought and mood of psychotic individuals.

Piotrowski was the first to employ successfully the Rorschach in the accurate detection of organic pathology, specifically intracranial pathology in the absence of neurological signs (1937). His work in this area held application for neurology and psychosomatic medicine. Piotrowski also developed indices of schizophrenia that facilitated accurate diagnosis and prognosis of the disorder (1966). He also made significant contributions to the use of the Thematic Apperception Test in behavior disorders and dream analysis. His work on predicting executive success or failure based on projective assessments was widely respected (*The Frontiers of Management Psychology*, New York, 1964). Near the end of his career, Piotrowski successfully devised a computerized method of interpreting Rorschach results (1980).

Piotrowski was a person of great intellectual abilities, both analytical and synthetic. He was a remarkable teacher with an intense love of truth and great respect for his students. Honors that reflected his accomplishments were many and included the Distinguished Contribution Award from the Society for Personality Assessment (1971), the Distinguished Service Award from the Pennsylvania Psychological Association (1976), and a Distinguished Professional Contributions Award from the American Psychological Association (1980).

Bibliography

Piotrowski, Z. (1937). The Rorschach inkblot method in organic disturbances of the central nervous system. *Journal of Nervous and Mental Disease, 86*, 525–537.

Piotrowski, Z. (1964). Consistently successful and failing top business executives: An inkblot test study. In G. Fisk (Ed.), *The frontiers of management psychology*. New York: Harper & Row.

Piotrowski, Z. (1980). Computerized perceptanalytic Rorschach: The psychological X-ray in mental disorders. In J. Sidowski, J. Johnson, & T. Williams (Eds.), *Technology in mental health care delivery systems*. Norwood, NJ: Ablex.

Piotrowski, Z., & Efron, H. Y. (1966). "Evaluation of outcome in schizophrenia: The long-term prognostic test Index." In P. Hoch & J. Zubin (Eds.), *Psychopathology of schizophrenia*. New York: Grune & Stratton.

Wade Pickren

PITCH PERCEPTION. Communication of music and speech relies on human ability to hear the vibration rates of sounds as steady pitch percepts. Because of this major role, pitch perception has been studied by many scientists during the nineteenth and twentieth centuries in the context of developing knowledge of the mathematical representation of periodic sounds, inner-ear sound analysis, and the statistical representation of communicated information. Human performance in three different modes of inner-ear response for measuring pitch has been quantified through psychophysical experiments that use statistical measures. These measures reveal a clear relationship between two of the three modes and allow comparisons of the effectiveness of each mode in communicating musical notes.

Basic Facts of Pitch of Music and Speech Sounds

The psychophysical relationships between pitch and musical sounds are implicit in a millennia of musical development, as seen in the musical scale. Table 1 shows the equal-temperament standard scale for the fundamental frequencies of musical notes, its nominal pitch, for three octaves: the lowest, middle, and highest (Backus, 1977). The frequencies are the number of repetitions per second of the basic sound pattern, designated by units of hertz, in honor of the nineteenth-century discoverer of radio waves. The three columns for each octave show, respectively, the letter symbols for the major notes (white piano keys), the frequencies of the major notes, and the frequencies of the minor notes (black piano keys). The dashed lines indicate the range of piano notes, from A_0 to C_8. Each octave is composed of 12 notes with frequencies that increase by the twelfth root of two ($2^{1/12} = 1.0594631$), known as the equal-temperament semitone. Concert A (A_4) is defined as the standard (440 hertz), from which the frequencies of all other notes can be calculated. Musical science defines a convenient logarithmic measure of frequency ratio, the cents scale, as $1{,}200 . \log_2(f_2/f_1)$, for which the semitone is exactly 100 cents.

PITCH PERCEPTION. Table 1. Fundamental frequencies (f_0, in hertz) of musical notes in the tempered scale (U.S. standard)

C_0	16.352		C_4	261.63		C_8	4,186.0	
		17.324			277.18			4,434.9
D_0	18.354		D_4	293.66		D_8	4,698.6	
		19.445			311.13			4,978.0
E_0	20.602		E_4	329.63		E_8	5,274.0	
F_0	21.827		F_4	349.23		F_8	5,587.7	
		23.125			369.99			5,919.9
G_0	24.500		G_4	392.00		G_8	6,271.9	
		25.957			415.30			6,644.9
A_0	27.500		A_4	440.00		A_8	7,040.0	
		29.135			466.16			7,458.6
B_0	30.868		B_4	493.88		B_8	7,902.1	

Source: adapted from Backus (1977).

The scale implies that musical notes are communicated by physical sounds that vibrate at a uniform rate, defined as the fundamental frequency (f_0). Second, the scale implies the existence of a prominent pitch percept correlated with f_0. Sounds that vibrate uniformly have unique fundamental frequencies and are defined as periodic. The musical scale, which is governed by periodicity, is the alphabet of Western music. Some sounds in music, such as those produced by drums and bells, are not periodic and do not communicate a unique pitch. Periodicity serves a significant but less central role in communicating the phonetic alphabet of speech. The presence or absence of periodic vocal-cord vibrations distinguishes "voiced" from "unvoiced" consonants: *g* versus *k*, *d* versus *t*, *z* versus *s*, and *b* versus *p* (Miller & Nicely, 1955). All vowels are voiced, but vocal-tract control of the waveform of the sound, rather than its periodicity, is the main basis for vowel distinctions (Peterson & Barney, 1952). Pitch of speech also communicates prosodic distinctions. For example, a rising pitch at the end of an English sentence indicates a question. In singing, of course, the human voice functions as a musical instrument following the rules of music. Thus, the singing scale "do-re-mi-fa-sol-la-ti-do" corresponds to the major notes of an octave (e.g., C_3, D_3, E_3, F_3, G_3, A_3, B_3, C_4). That second "do" has the same name as the first because these notes, separated by an octave, are perceived as musically similar but not identical (Helmholtz, 1863).

A note one octave higher than another note has a fundamental frequency that is twice that of the lower

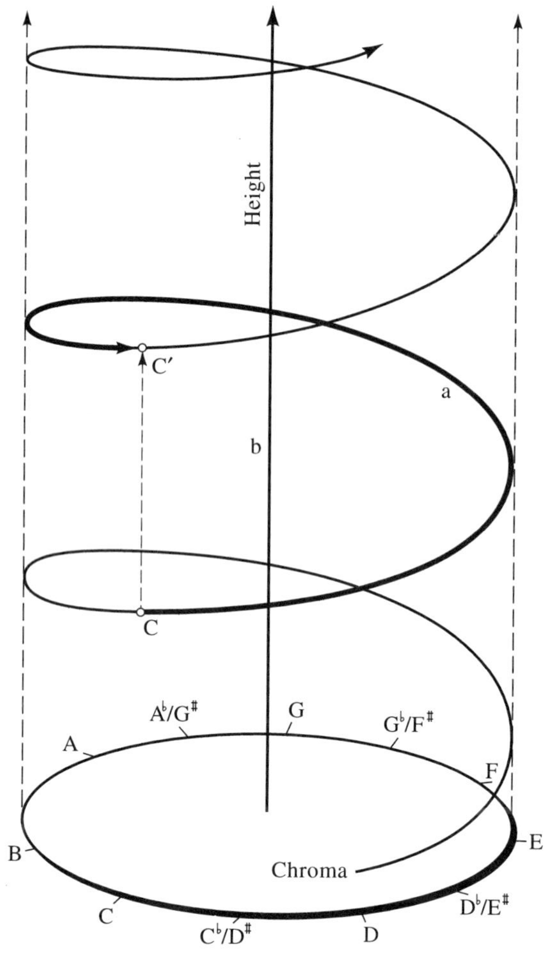

PITCH PERCEPTION. Figure 1. Classical helical representation of tone perception with dual dimensions of tone chroma and tone height. (From Shepard, 1982.)

note. Typically, the sequence of notes in a melody is restricted to an octave range. Music theorists have proposed that perceived similarities and differences in tones can be geometrically visualized as a helix, as shown in Figure 1 (Revesz, 1913; Shepard, 1964; 1982). Revesz proposed the helix on the basis of music theory, while Shepard derived the helix mathematically from the psychophysical judgments of similarities. This representation captures two perceptual dimensions of a simple tone: its chroma and height. The cyclical musical scale is represented by tone chroma, while the monotonic tone height scale has been identified with timbre and the mel pitch scale (Revesz, 1913; Ward & Burns, 1982). Notes separated by octaves have the same chroma. Each octave is represented by one rotation (360°) of the tone chroma scale, with 30° between successive notes in the standard tempered scale (Table 1). Though the chroma and height of simple sinusoidal tones are unambiguous, the musical notes produced by different musical instruments can produce complex tones with the same f_0 and tone chroma, but different waveforms and tone height (Backus, 1977).

The frequency spacing of the notes of the musical scale is logarithmic. This implies that melodies are communicated by the frequency ratios of the notes, relative to a reference note. In the equally tempered scale (Table 1), each of the 12 semitone notes in an octave increases in frequency from its lower neighbor by nearly 6%. Shifting the reference note of the melody (termed the key, tonic, or root) up or down the scale leaves the melody unchanged. The importance of frequency ratios was already observed by the Greek mathematician Pythagoras and his school (circa 540 BCE). They found that musical sounds produced by vibrating strings whose lengths are in the ratio of small integers (2:1, 3:2, 4:3) are pleasing and similar. For several hundred years, Western music has exploited the fact that the major triad, composed three notes in frequency ratio 4:5:6 (e.g., C, E, G = tonic, third, and fifth major notes), is very pleasing, or consonant, when the notes are played together or in succession (Backus, 1977). The perception of frequency ratios as pitch differences, known as musical intervals, is not a skill requiring rigorous musical training, because infants can recognize melodies despite shifts in key (Dowling, 1982). However, extreme changes in key that place notes above 4,000 hertz destroy melody perception (Rayleigh, 1896). The practice of music requires precise skills in the recognition and production of intervals. Some musicians possess absolute (perfect) pitch skills and can reliably name and play individual notes on the musical scale. All other musicians possess relative pitch skills and depend on their memory of frequent repetitions of the reference note to play in key.

Auditory Sound Analysis in Theories of Pitch

During the nineteenth and twentieth centuries, psychophysical research to quantify pitch perception and understand its mechanisms led to the growing knowledge that the inner ear (cochlea) operates approximately as a Fourier frequency analyzer of sounds. In 1822, Jean Baptiste Joseph Fourier mathematically proved that a periodic sound can in general be represented as a sum of simple sinusoidal tones, with frequencies that are integer multiples (harmonics) of its fundamental frequency, and with amplitudes and phases that are uniquely determined by the waveform. The relevance of Fourier's theorem for hearing was recognized by Georg Simon Ohm (1843), who proposed, in what is known as Ohm's law of hearing, that perception of a periodic sound is the sum of the elementary pitch percepts evoked by each harmonic tone, as defined by Fourier's mathematical law. Ohm claimed that each elementary pitch percept is determined by the amplitude

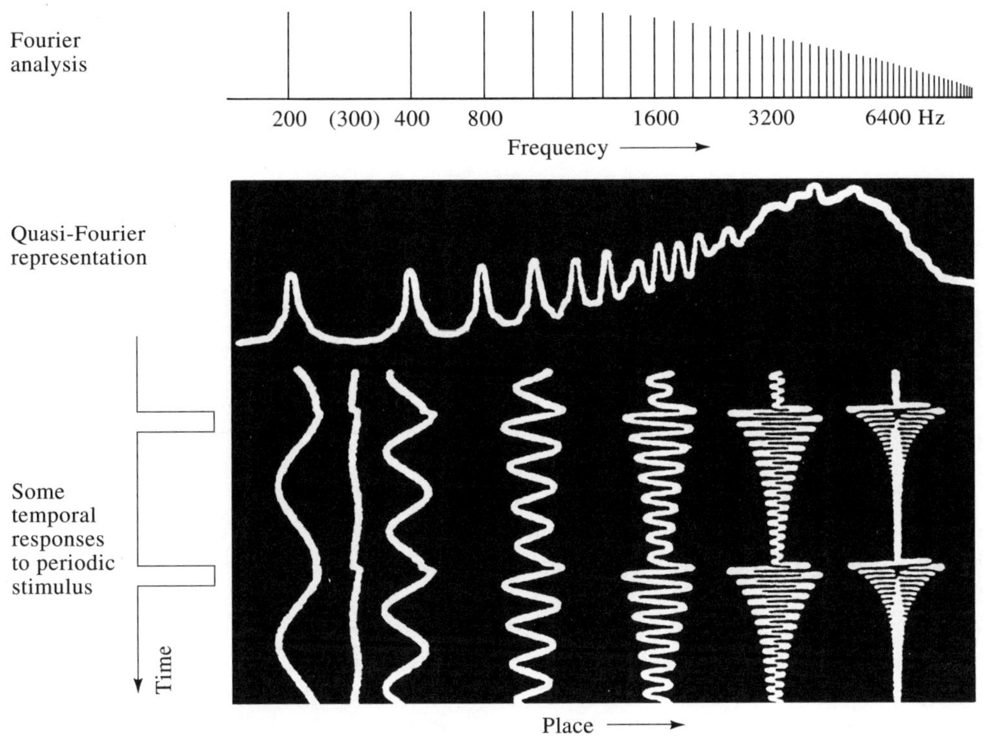

PITCH PERCEPTION. Figure 2. Schematic representation of frequency analysis by the inner ear. (From Schouten, 1970.)

and frequency of the harmonic, but not its phase. Hermann von Helmholtz, the nineteenth-century scientific giant and founder of modern auditory research, refined Ohm's law with his systematic research on musical phenomena and his proposals of underlying physiological mechanisms. [*See the biography of Helmholtz.*]

Key features and issues in Helmholtz's research are highlighted in Figure 2 by Schouten's schematic representation of the ear's frequency analysis (1970). In the figure, the periodic sound is a uniform sequence of short pressure pulses with a rate of 200 per second (= f_0). Fourier frequency analysis provides the distribution of harmonic amplitudes shown in the top line. Inner-ear analysis yields the quasi-Fourier amplitude distribution shown in the second line. The frequency axis represents the place of maximum response for each harmonic frequency within the inner ear, known as the frequency-place map (Helmholtz, 1863; Bekesy, 1960; Greenwood, 1990). Harmonic frequencies beyond the tenth or eleventh multiple of f_0 are not defined by distinct maxima in the inner ear, because the nearly constant relative bandwidth of the analyzing filters prevents the resolution of harmonics separated in frequency by less than about 10%.

Because of its limited frequency resolution, the inner ear produces temporal responses that preserve the fundamental periodicity of the stimulus with a waveform that is sensitive to the phases of the stimulus harmonics. The central auditory system reads the inner-ear's analysis via neurons arrayed along the frequency-place axis. Three modes of inner-ear response can communicate the stimulus period: (1) the temporal period of the unresolved upper harmonics; (2) the frequency of the resolved fundamental tone; and (3) the frequency pattern of the resolved harmonics (f_0 being the largest common factor). Helmholtz's place-pitch hypothesis emphasized the second of these, and held that the pitch of a musical note was communicated by the inner-ear place of f_0—the lowest peak in the quasi-Fourier spectrum. He demonstrated that, with training and special cues, the pitches of the resolved upper harmonics also can be perceived, in agreement with Ohm's law. On the other hand, perception of the unresolved higher harmonics is phase sensitive and, in his view, unrelated to pitch (see Plomp & Levelt, 1965). John William Strutt, a Nobel laureate in physical acoustics, known better by his honorary title Lord Rayleigh, reviewed auditory science at the close of the nineteenth century. He described how Helmholtz's research shifted scientific theory on mechanisms of pitch. Earlier, it was natural to favor temporal mechanisms because of the correlation between musical notes and stimulus periodicity. Helmholtz's frequency-place and place-pitch hypotheses made temporal central processing unnecessary, and auditory frequency measurement became identified with place.

Interest in temporal processing was revived by the Dutch communications scientist Schouten (1940), who demonstrated that the pitch of a note can be heard even when Fourier analysis provides no tone at the fundamental frequency. In his "residue theory," he proposed that the solution to this "problem of the missing fundamental" is provided by the periodic inner-ear response from unresolved stimulus harmonics. Schouten accepted Helmholtz's frequency-place hypothesis, which was confirmed by the Nobel laureate Georg von Békésy. [*See the biography of Békésy.*] However, he rejected Helmholtz's place-pitch hypothesis in favor of a temporal measurement. Since inner-ear responses for resolved harmonics are also periodic (see Figure 2), a single mechanism, based on temporal periodicity, could be responsible for the pitch of the fundamental period and its harmonic frequencies.

In 1949, Ernest Glen Wever proposed a "volley theory" in his theory of hearing, wherein groups of neurons acting in concert can preserve the periodic temporal structure of signals even when the frequency is too high to permit an accurate temporal response by a single neuron. A synthesis of place and time theories was proposed by Licklider (1951). His "duplex theory" describes a neural autocorrelation mechanism that maps residue pitch to place-pitch. [*See the biography of Wever.*]

Systematic studies of residue perception (mode 1) by Schouten and his colleagues demonstrated that low harmonics are more dominant than high harmonics in evoking pitch (Schouten, Ritsma, & Cardozo, 1962; Ritsma, 1967; Plomp, 1967). At the same time, studies of aural combination tones caused by inner-ear nonlinear distortion accounted for a strange anomaly discovered by Schouten and colleagues, in which harmonics lower than those in the stimulus can dominate its pitch (Goldstein, 1967; Goldstein & Kiang, 1968; Smoorenburg, 1970; Goldstein, 1973). While experiments confirm the existence of residue pitch (Miller & Taylor, 1948; Burns & Viemeister, 1976; Houtsma & Smurzynski, 1990), the dominance of low harmonics suggested that the harmonics that can be resolved by the inner ear are primarily responsible for pitch. This stimulated research on harmonic frequency pattern recognition, the third pitch mode, which brought new understanding of pitch psychophysics and the underlying mechanisms of all three modes (Goldstein, 1973; Wightman, 1973; Terhardt, 1974).

Pitch Memory

Bachem (1954) studied the precision of pitch memory for highly skilled musicians using simple-tone stimuli. The subjects listened to a series of eight different tones and, after a controlled time had elapsed, matched the

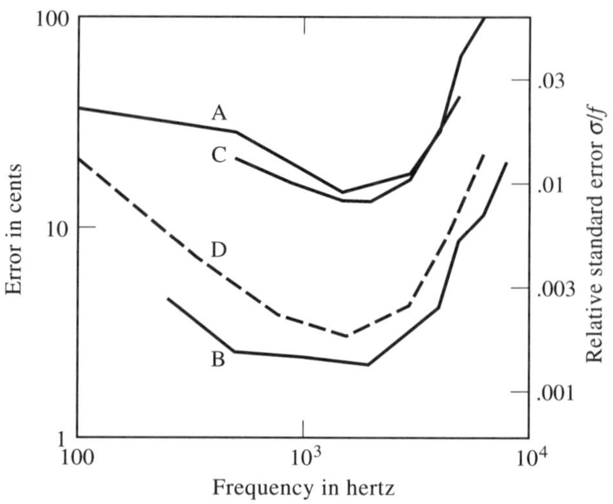

PITCH PERCEPTION. Figure 3. Precision of auditory measurement of the frequency of a single tone. Curve A: absolute pitch memory measured psychophysically for simple tones (Bachem, 1954). Curve B: frequency difference limen measured psychophysically for short pulses of simple tones (Moore, 1973). Curve C: precision of auditory representation of the frequencies of resolved harmonics in complex tone stimuli, calculated from psychophysical experiments on pitch recognition (Goldstein, 1973; Houtsma & Goldstein, 1972). Curve D: precision predicted from a statistical model of phase-locked auditory nerve responses (Goldstein & Srulovicz, 1977).

pitch of each tone by adjusting a tone generator. Bachem measured the relative standard error of the matching frequency (standard deviation divided by mean) from repeated matches of each of the eight tones as a function of the elapsed time. He reported his four best subjects, two with absolute pitch skills and two with relative pitch skills. For increases in elapsed time up to one minute, all subjects reported a similar loss of precision. At and beyond one minute (up to one week) subjects with absolute pitch reported a stable precision, while it continued to deteriorate with elapsed time for the others. Curve A in Figure 3 shows the mean precision for the two subjects with absolute pitch at one minute elapsed time. The measured precision shown by the right ordinate is also given in equivalent cents at the left. The latter is the value in cents of the frequency ratio ($1 + \sigma/_f$). Bachem's data provided the first clear quantification of Rayleigh's comment (1896) that musical tone perception ceases beyond about 4 kilohertz (C_8 in Table 1 is the highest piano note). However, tone perception does not cease above 4 kilohertz. Consistent with reports of other music theorists, Bachem recognized the dual percepts of tone chroma and tone height (see Figure 1). He identified the preci-

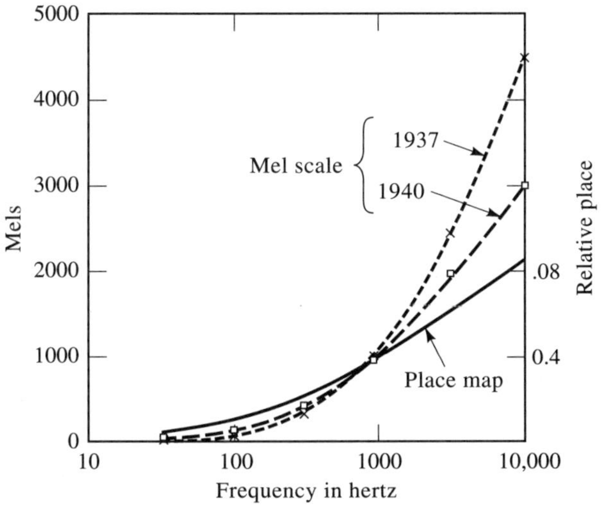

PITCH PERCEPTION. Figure 4. Psychophysical mel scale and cochlear frequency-place map. The two scales are simply related by a power law. (Adapted from Stevens et al., 1937, 1940; Greenwood, 1990.)

sion of pitch memory, which he measured with tone chroma. Ward and Burns (1982) suggest that the mel scale of pitch (Figure 4) measured by Stevens and his colleagues is a psychophysical scale of tone height. The original mel function was obtained by having subjects adjust the frequency of a tone until its pitch was half as high as that of a reference tone (Stevens, Volkmann, & Newman, 1937). The revised mel function was obtained by division of the mel scale into four subjectively equal parts (Stevens & Volkman, 1940). The mel scale defines a 1,000-hertz tone at a 40-decibels sound pressure level as 1,000 mels. No information is available on the precision of this scale in musical behavior.

Frequency Difference Limen

Moore (1973) studied the minimal detectable frequency difference (the "difference limen") for tone pulses of short duration (6.5–200 milliseconds). Two tone pulses that differ in frequency by Δf were presented in quick succession to the subject, who reported which tone was higher in pitch. The experiment estimated the standard error (standard deviation) of the measurement (Green, 1960). At all durations, similar deterioration in high-frequency precision as first reported by Bachem was found. Measurements for 200 ms (curve B in Figure 3) are representative of the frequency difference limen found with 500 ms durations (Wier, Jesteadt, & Green, 1977). Surprisingly, classical measurements of the frequency difference limen based on the detection of frequency modulation (Shower & Biddulph, 1931) show little high-frequency deterioration, suggesting that a different auditory mechanism detects modulation (Moore & Glasberg, 1989). In this experiment, no explicit distinction was made between frequency discrimination based on tone chroma or tone height. Curve B provides a lower bound that is consistent with Bachem's findings for precision of pitch memory with decreasing elapsed time, which he identified with tone chroma.

Harmonic Frequency Pattern Recognition

Experiments by Houtsma and Goldstein were conducted to clarify the role of harmonic frequency patterns (mode 3) in pitch perception (1972). Musically experienced subjects identified two-note sequences as one of eight possible musical intervals (Figure 5a). In their basic experiments, each note was communicated with a periodic sound comprising two successive harmonics above the fundamental. The harmonic numbers used for each note were randomly chosen (Figure 5c) to prevent successful interval perception on the basis of the frequencies of a single harmonic in the two notes. This manipulation of the stimulus effectively preserved the psychophysical correlate of stimulus periodicity, while randomizing the psychophysical correlate of place in inner-ear frequency analysis. Subjects' performance (Figure 6) was clearly best for low harmonics and reference notes (tonic) near 200 hertz. Most remarkably, the intervals could be identified equally well at low sound pressure levels when the two harmonics were presented monotically (to the same ear) or dichotically (one to each ear). This equivalence eliminated the possibility that the pitch of the missing fundamental was directly represented in the inner ear by temporal interaction of unresolved harmonics (mode 1) or by difference-frequency distortion (mode 2). At higher sound levels, monotic performance was generally better, because inner-ear nonlinearity introduces additional harmonics (Goldstein, 1967, 1973; Goldstein & Kiang, 1968; Robles et al., 1997). These experiments proved and quantified the effectiveness of the frequency spectrum of aurally resolved harmonics (mode 3) in communicating pitch.

Theories of Harmonic-Pattern Recognition

The foregoing experiments provided basic data for the theoretical understanding of the relationship between the elementary pitches derived from auditory Fourier analysis, and the fundamental pitch (f_0) perceived from harmonic frequency patterns in the absence of a fundamental tone. Proposed theories were guided by experiments with inharmonic stimuli by Schouten and his colleagues (Schouten, 1940; De Boer, 1956; Schouten et al., 1962; Smoorenburg, 1970), which implied algorithms predicated on harmonic frequency relations (Goldstein, 1973). Thus, Wightman's (1973) pattern transformation

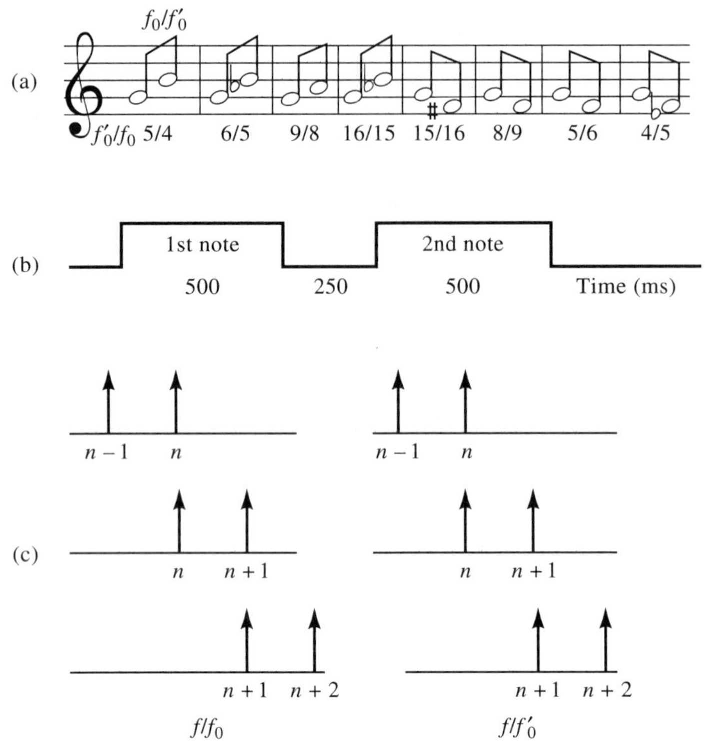

PITCH PERCEPTION. Figure 5. Experimental paradigm for musical interval identification: (a) a musical interval to be identified; (b) a time envelope of the two-note stimulus; and (c) three possible two-note stimuli for each of the two notes. For each note presentation, a random choice was made from three possible harmonic pairs. (From Houtsma & Goldstein, 1972.)

theory hypothesized a central auditory transformation of the quasi-Fourier response (Figure 2), with an algorithm similar to Fourier's theorem that explicitly reveals the temporal period of the original sound in close analogy with residue theory but without its phase sensitivity. Terhardt's virtual pitch theory hypothesized the central auditory measurement of pitch as the most common pitch generated by dividing each of the resolved stimulus frequencies by the integers 1 to 10 (1974). Goldstein's optimum processor theory extended optimum statistical processing for harmonic stimuli to complex tones in general, by hypothesizing the central estimation of fundamental frequency that best matched a fixed template of integer multiples of that frequency to those resolved by the inner ear (1973; Gerson & Goldstein, 1978). These theories can all be used to explain the experiments of Houtsma and Goldstein as the consequence of small random errors in the auditory representation of resolved stimulus frequencies.

Consider the computations that the central auditory system could use to find the fundamental frequency from measurements of the frequencies of the two successive harmonics in Houtsma and Goldstein's experiments. From the pitch experiments with simple tones by Bachem and Moore, one can expect limited precision in the auditory representation of the frequencies of the two resolved harmonics. One could propose that the central auditory system estimates f_0 as the difference of the two measured successive harmonic frequencies. However, two objections against this proposal have been raised. First, Schouten demonstrated that the pitch (f_0) of an harmonic stimulus lawfully changes when the frequencies of all the harmonics are shifted uniformly in one direction or the other (1940; Schouten et al., 1962). Thus, pitch does not depend upon difference frequency, which was maintained constant in these experiments. Secondly, Goldstein mathematically

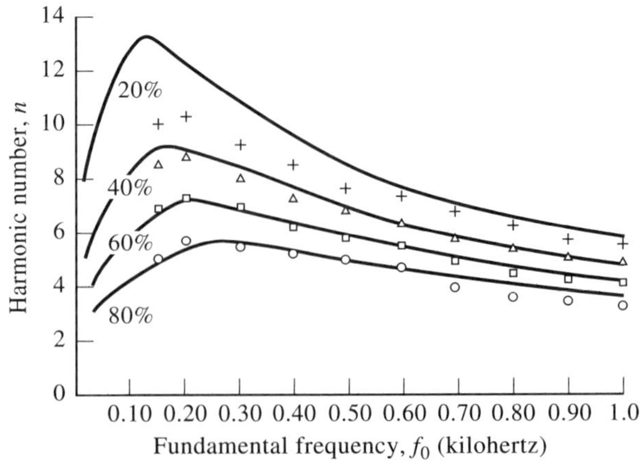

PITCH PERCEPTION. Figure 6. Contours of percent correct in musical interval identification. (From Goldstein, 1973; Houtsma & Goldstein, 1972.)

proved that any computation that minimizes the average errors in estimating f_0 from imprecise measurements of the two harmonic frequencies must utilize the fact that the actual frequencies are harmonically related (1973). For example, a stimulus comprising the fifth and sixth harmonics of 200 hertz ($= f_0$) should provide a measured frequency ratio near 6/5, and f_0 could then be estimated as the average of the lower frequency divided by 5 plus the higher divided by 6. However, because of the limited precision of the frequency measurements, the measured ratio will occasionally be closer to 5/4 or 7/6. Large errors in estimating f_0 would then occur. These considerations apply to all three theories described above.

A complete mathematical solution to the optimum estimation problem for two successive harmonics was given by Goldstein (1973). He showed that the incorrect responses in Houtsma and Goldstein's interval identification experiments can be accounted for by errors in measuring harmonic numbers. The precision in frequency measurement that best accounts for the data is shown in Figure 3 (curve C is the average for three subjects). (These statistical findings were later extended with computer simulations to tones with more than two harmonics [Goldstein et al., 1978; Gerson & Goldstein, 1978; Moore et al., 1984; Faulkner, 1985; Beerends, 1989].) The remarkable similarity to Bachem's precision for pitch (curve A) establishes a clear relationship between pitch perception for simple and complex tones. Recall that Bachem's data is representative of long-term memory for perfect pitch, while Moore's data (curve B) is representative of short-term memory for all trained subjects. This suggests the existence of a common mechanism of long-term memory for absolute pitch and relative pitch. Absolute pitch reflects voluntary access to this memory, which is otherwise limited to automatic access for interval perception. In memory research, voluntary access is associated with explicit memory, and inferred access with implicit memory. It is also clear that the higher precision of short-term memory is not accessed in the auditory measurement of harmonic relations.

Pitch Precision and Musical Scales

The precision of auditory frequency representation limits the number of notes in an octave that can be reliably communicated with tones. Psychophysical experiments on the identification of musical notes in a nonstandard quarter-tone scale by skilled musicians with and without absolute pitch skills were conducted by Ward and Burns (1982), and Burns and Campbell (1994). Quarter-tone scales, comprising 24 notes per octave, produced significant confusion between notes (typically 20% errors), while semitone scales, with 12 notes per octave, allowed near perfect identification. Limited precision of pitch can be thought of as causing a bell-shaped normal distribution of pitch percepts centered on true pitch, with the width of the distribution specified by the error in cents (Figure 3). Based on this model, Figure 7 shows the expected probability for the correct identification of notes in an equally tempered scale as a function of the density of notes. The top three curves, which were calculated for precisions representative of curves A and C in Figure 3, show the compatibility of the standard twelve-tone scale with the precision of long-term memory. In contrast, the bottom curve shows that the precision of 50 cents found by Houtsma and Smurzynski for residue pitch (mode 1) is incompatible with musical practice, as they indicated (1990). However, experiments by Klatt suggest that mode-1 precision may be adequate for speech (1973). The choice of 12 tones, rather than 10 or 11, in the standard equally tempered scale (Table 1) meets the requirement for accurate approximations (Backus, 1977) of the Pythagorean intervals (3/2, 4/3). At the other extreme, if the precision of short-term memory (curve B in Figure 3) were relevant for music, then a 48-tone scale would be practical. Other musical scales in relation to the standard equal temperament scale are discussed by Backus (1977) and Ward and Martin (1961).

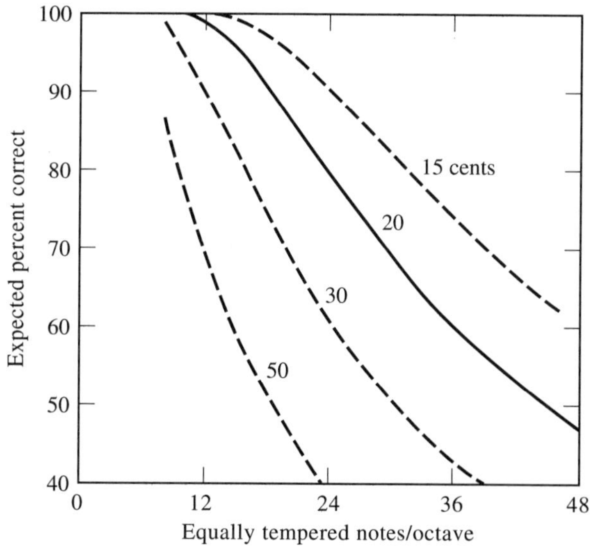

PITCH PERCEPTION. Figure 7. Note identification. Probability of correct note identification in modes one and two, expected from precisions found in psychophysical experiments as a function of the number of notes per octave (Calculated by author.)

Physiological Correlates of Pitch

The similarities among the errors in auditory frequency measurement, as shown by curves A, B, and C in Figure 3, suggest common auditory mechanisms. The limitation of musical pitch (tone chroma) to frequencies

(< 4–5 kilohertz) well below the audible limit for tone height (< 10–20 kilohertz), suggests pitch mechanisms based on temporal processing (Wever, 1949; Schouten, Ritsma, & Cardozo, 1962). Neurophysiological studies of action-potential responses in primary auditory neurons reveal neural phase locking to stimulus tones up to 4–5 kilohertz (Kiang, 1965; Johnson, 1980). Using models developed by Siebert for optimum estimation of the frequency of a simple-tone stimulus from phase-locked auditory nerve responses (1970), Goldstein and Srulovicz (1977) showed that frequency measurement based on time intervals between successive neural pulses accounts for the precision of psychophysical frequency judgments (curve D in Figure 3). The possibility that this form of neural measurement is used for mode 3 as well (Goldstein, 1978) is supported by successful applications of harmonic-pattern theories to frequency patterns defined by phase-locked auditory-nerve responses (Srulovicz & Goldstein, 1983; Miller & Sachs, 1984; Miller, Barta, & Sachs, 1987; Hartmann & Doty, 1996). Central mechanisms consistent with mode-3 operation have been discovered (Zatorre, 1988; Pantev, Hoke, Leutenhoener, & Lehnertz, 1989), and evidence for mechanisms based on neural phase locking is accumulating (Ohgushi, 1983; McKinney & Delgutte, 1999). A second physiological correlate of psychophysical frequency measurement is provided in the inner ear by the frequency-place map. It is shown in Figure 4 for humans (0.205. ln $(1 + f/_{165})$ by the solid line (Greenwood, 1990). The psychophysical mel scale for tone height is consistent with the hypothesis that it is a power-law function of mapped place. The original and revised mel scales are shown in Figure 4 to agree with place raised to the powers of 2 (dotted curve) and 3/2 (dashed curve), respectively. Thus, complementary physiological mechanisms based on the timing and place of neural activity may code the psychophysical dimensions of tone chroma and tone height (Figure 1).

The Status of Developing Theories of Pitch

Major scientific progress has been made in understanding the helix of tone perception. Physiological correlates of the dual percepts of tone chroma and tone height support elaboration of Wever's volley theory as the basis for pitch perception, and Helmholtz's place theory as the basis for tone height (see Figures 1, 3, and 4). Thus, Helmholtz's place-pitch hypothesis, which has long dominated pitch theory, is not supported (Goldstein, 1978; Hartmann & Doty, 1996; McKinney & Delgutte, 1999). New understanding of the cyclical nature of tone chroma is being developed from theories of pitch based on harmonic-frequency patterns. Although the period of a physical sound can be uniquely defined as the largest common denominator (f_0) of its harmonic frequencies, the pitch of such sounds can correspond to a submultiple of f_0 when it is in range of the key note (Houtgast, 1976; Gerson & Goldstein, 1978). Understanding of this multivalued relationship between pitch and f_0 and similarities among notes is extended in the other direction above f_0 by the concept that pitch is centrally represented by a template of harmonically related frequencies. Thus, two notes differing by less than four octaves are represented by templates that can share common harmonic frequencies (Goldstein et al., 1978) and be perceived as similar (Shepard, 1982). In further research, the concept of a central template, which except for fundamental frequency is independent of the stimulus has suggested new cognitive approaches for developing pitch theory (Hall & Peters, 1981; Duifhuis et al., 1982; Assman & Summerfield, 1990; Hartmann et al., 1990; de Cheveigne, 1997; Lin & Hartmann, 1998; Ciocca & Darwin, 1999). The new challenges focusing on central function and mechanisms vigorously sustain the scientific heritage of research to understand pitch perception in music and speech.

Bibliography

Bachem, A. (1954). Time factors in relative and absolute pitch determination. *Journal of the Acoustical Society of America, 26,* 751–753. Fundamental data on auditory memory for musical pitch of simple tones.

Backus, J. (1977). *The acoustical foundations of music* (2nd ed.). New York: Norton. A basic introductory text on musical and acoustical science.

Bekesy, G. V. (1960). *Experiments in hearing.* New York: McGraw-Hill (Reprinted by the Acoustical Society of America). Pioneering Nobel-award experiments on cochlear mechanics proving the existence of a cochlear frequency-place map.

DeBoer, E. (1956). *On the residue in hearing.* Ph.D. dissertation, Amsterdam University. Clarified controversies in confirming the existence of residue pitch.

Dowling, W. J. (1982). Melodic information processing and its development. In D. Deutsch (Ed.), *The psychology of music* (pp. 413–429). London: Academic. Describes invariance with changes in key for melody recognition by human infants.

Fourier, J. B. J. (1955). *The analytical theory of heat* (Trans. from French by A. Freeman). New York: Dover. (Original work published 1822.) Classical treatise provided the fundamental mathematical tool for frequency representation of sounds, and stimulated recognition of the analogous representation by the auditory system.

Gerson, A., & Goldstein, J. L. (1978). Evidence for a central template in central optimal processing for pitch of complex tones. *Journal of the Acoustical Society of America, 63,* 498–510. New experiments to support the extension of optimum processor theory to include the listener's expectation for the pitch range.

Goldstein, J. L. (1967). Auditory nonlinearity. *Journal of the*

Acoustical Society of America, 41, 676–689. Psychophysical experiments on aural combination tones suggesting their influence on pitch of complex tones.

Goldstein, J. L. (1973). An optimum processor theory for the central formation of the pitch of complex tones. *Journal of the Acoustical Society of America, 54*, 1496–1516. Pitch theory quantifies fundamental relations between errors in pitch of complex tones and auditory precision for single frequencies.

Goldstein, J. L. (1978). Mechanisms of signal analysis and pattern recognition in periodicity pitch. *Audiology, 17*, 421–445. An early review provides an easy entry into the details of optimum processor theory of pitch, and known physiological mechanisms.

Goldstein, J. L., & Kiang, N. Y. S. (1968). Neural correlates of the aural combination tone 2f1-f2. *Proceedings of the IEEE, 56*, 981–992. First physical evidence from the auditory nerve consistent with the existence of cochlear distortion tones, and with their influence on pitch of complex tones.

Goldstein, J. L., & Srulovicz, P. (1977). Auditory nerve spike intervals as an adequate basis for aural frequency measurement. In E. F. Evans, & J. P. Wilson (Eds.), *Psychophysics and physiology of hearing* (pp. 337–346). London: Academic. First theoretical evidence for a correlation between neural time processing and the psychophysics of frequency measurement.

Green, D. M. (1988). Audition: psychophysics and perception. In R. C. Atkinson, R. J. Herrnstein, G. Lindzey, & R. D. Luce (Eds.), *Stevens' handbook of experimental psychology* (2nd ed.), vol. 1 (pp. 327–376). New York: Wiley. Reviews pitch research in the broad context of psychophysics.

Greenwood, D. D. (1990). A cochlear frequency-position function for several species—25 years later. *Journal of the Acoustical Society of America, 87*, 2592–2605. Summary and unification of information on cochlear frequency-place maps.

Hall, J. W., & Peters, R. W. (1981). Pitch for nonsimultaneous successive harmonics in quiet and noise. *Journal of the Acoustical Society of America, 69*, 509–513. Defines an important constraint on physiological mechanisms for harmonic frequency pattern processing.

Helmholtz, H. L. F. (1954). *Sensations of tone* (Trans. from German by A. J. Ellis). New York: Dover. (Original work published 1863.) This treatise is the foundation of modern auditory science. A short introduction to this work was presented in an 1857 public lecture "On the physiological causes of harmony in music," in M. Kline (Ed.), 1962, *Helmholtz's popular scientific lectures* (pp. 22–58). New York: Dover.

Houtsma, A. J. M. (1995). Pitch perception. In B. C. J. Moore (Ed.), *Hearing* (pp. 267–295). San Diego: Academic. Reviews a wide range of pitch phenomena.

Houtsma, A. J. M., & Goldstein, J. L. (1972). The central origin of pitch of complex tones: evidence from musical interval recognition. *Journal of the Acoustical Society of America, 51*, 520–529. Provides fundamental psychophysical evidence for central auditory processing of harmonic frequency patterns for pitch.

Houtsma, A. J. M., & Smurzynski, J. (1990). Pitch identification and discrimination for complex tones with many harmonics. *Journal of the Acoustical Society of America, 87*, 304–310. Definitive data on auditory precision for residue pitch.

Johnson, D. H. (1980). The relationship between spike rate and synchrony in responses of auditory-nerve fibers to single tones. *Journal of the Acoustical Society of America, 68*, 1115–1122. Definitive data relevant for auditory frequency measurement from neural timing.

Kiang, N. Y. S., Watanabe, T., Thomas, E. C., & Clark, L. F. (1965). *Discharge patterns of single fibers in the cat's auditory nerve* (MIT Research Monograph 35). Cambridge: MIT Press. First reliable account of cochlear sound analysis, provides fundamental data for modeling.

Licklider, J. C. R. (1951). A duplex theory of pitch perception. *Experientia, 7*, 128–134. Influential proposal for neural mechanisms that combine place and time cues in pitch.

McKinney, M. F., & Delgutte, B. (1999). A possible neurophysiological basis of the octave enlargement effect. *Journal of the Acoustical Society of America, 106*, 2679–2692. Important experimental support for proposal by Ohgushi (1983).

Miller, M. I., & Sachs, M. B. (1984). Representation of voice pitch in discharge patterns of auditory nerve fibers. *Hearing Research, 14*, 257–279. First auditory-nerve experiment confirming the superiority of neural timing codes over place codes for pitch of complex tones.

Moore, B. C. J. (1973). Frequency difference limens for short duration tones. *Journal of the Acoustical Society of America, 54*, 610–619. Definitive experiments on effect of frequency.

Ohgushi, K. (1983). The origin of tonality and a possible explanation of the octave enlargement phenomenon. *Journal of the Acoustical Society of America, 73*, 1694–1700. Proposed that auditory neural-interval processing is responsible for the psychophysics of octave judgements.

Ohm, G. S. (1843). Ueber die Definition des Tones. *Annalen der Physik und Chemie, 59*, 513–565. Proposed relation of auditory and Fourier sound analysis was key to Helmholtz's research.

Pantev, C., Hoke, M., Luetenhoener, B., & Lehnertz, K. (1989). Tonotopic organization of the auditory cortex: Pitch versus frequency representation. *Science, 246*, 486–488. First evidence for a central place code for stimulus periodicity defined by harmonic frequency patterns.

Rayleigh, J. W. S. (1896). *Theory of sound* (2nd ed.). Reprinted 1945, New York: Dover. A critical review of hearing research is given in the final chapter of this classic treatise on physical acoustics. Study of pitch is prominent.

Revesz, G. (1913). *Introduction to the psychology of music* (Trans. from German by G. I. C. de Courcy). Published 1954, Norman: Univ. of Oklahoma Press. Discusses the helical model of pitch.

Ritsma, R. J. (1967). Frequencies dominant in the perception of pitch of complex tones. *Journal of the Acoustical*

Society of America, 42, 191–198. Important evidence for auditory processing of frequency patterns.

Robles, L., Ruggero, M. A., & Rich, N. (1997). Two-tone distortion on the basilar membrane of the chinchilla cochlea. *Journal of Neurophysiology*, 77, 2385–2399. First systematic report of cochlear mechanical distortion correlated with the psychophysics of aural combination tones.

Schouten, J. F. (1940). The residue and the mechanism of hearing. *Proc. Kon. Ned. Akad. Wetenscap.* (Royal Dutch Academy of Science), 43, 991–999. Schouten's research and scientific leadership revived investigation of pitch of complex tones based on temporal cues.

Schouten, J. F. (1970). The residue revisited. In R. Plomp and G. F. Smoorenburg (Eds.), *Frequency analysis and periodicity detection in hearing* (pp. 41–58). Leiden: Sijthoff. Reviews progress in residue research.

Schouten, J. F., Ritsma, R. J., & Cardozo, B. L. (1962). Pitch of the residue. *Journal of the Acoustical Society of America*, 34, 1418–1424. Presents new data and defines a two-component theory of pitch shift that stimulated the evolution of pitch theory.

Shepard, R. N. (1982). Structural representation of musical pitch. In D. Deutsch (Ed.), *The psychology of music* (pp. 344–390). London: Academic. Reviews research on pitch as a multidimensional percept.

Siebert, W. M. (1970). Frequency discrimination in the auditory system: place or periodicity mechanisms? *Proceedings of the IEEE*, 58, 723–730. Pioneered statistical modeling of auditory-nerve responses to quantify communication limits imposed by place and timing cues.

Smoorenburg, G. F. (1970). Pitch of two-frequency stimuli. *Journal of the Acoustical Society of America*, 48, 924–942. Definitive psychophysical experiments on the influence of aural combination tones on pitch of complex tones.

Srulovicz, P., & Goldstein, J. L. (1983). The central spectrum: A synthesis of auditory-nerve timing and place cues in monaural communication of frequency spectrum. *Journal of the Acoustical Society of America*, 73, 1266–1276. A neurally constrained optimum processor theory synthesizes research by Siebert and by Goldstein.

Stevens, S. S., & Volkmann, J. (1940). The relation of pitch to frequency: A revised scale. *The American Journal of Psychology*, 53, 329–353. Revision of the mel scale, which contemporary scientists identify with tone height.

Stevens, S. S., Volkmann, J., & Newman, E. B. (1937). A scale for the measurement of the psychophysical magnitude of pitch. *Journal of the Acoustical Society of America*, 8, 185–190. The original mel-scale proposal.

Terhardt, E. (1974). Pitch, consonance, and harmony. *Journal of the Acoustical Society of America*, 55, 1061–1069. A pitch theory based on harmonic frequency pattern recognition.

Ward, W. D., & Burns, E. M. (1982). Absolute pitch. In D. Deutsch (Ed.), *The psychology of music* (pp. 431–451). London: Academic. Identifies the dimension of tone height of the pitch helix with the mel scale. Reviews note identification experiments with quartertone scales.

Wever, E. G. (1949). *Theory of hearing*. New York: Wiley. A classical text of historical interest by the author of the "volley theory" for the mechanism of pitch.

Wightman, F. L. (1973). The pattern transformation model of pitch. *Journal of the Acoustical Society of America*, 54, 406–416. A pitch theory based on harmonic frequency pattern recognition.

Other articles cited in the text but not included in the bibliography are readily found in the *Journal of the Acoustical Society of America*, by the year of publication. These articles report additional supporting data and current research of interest for further study. This scientific journal, ranging over the broad interdisciplinary field of acoustics, continues since its inception in 1929 to be a major forum for research reports on pitch perception.

Julius L. Goldstein

PLACEBO EFFECT IN RESEARCH DESIGN. The term *placebo* originates from the Latin phrase "I shall please." This very early definition carried into modern usage with the frequent application of inert ingredients to accommodate individuals when their need for symptomatic relief was otherwise unmet. The placebo effect refers to the observation that the administration of inert substances or nonspecific treatments shows indications of producing "healing" results under some conditions. The ubiquity of the placebo effect is evident in the multiple physiological systems and disorders that have been demonstrably and significantly affected: a partial list includes angina, blood pressure, the common cold, cough, fever, panic disorder and psychiatric conditions, headache, psoriasis, insomnia, pain, rheumatoid arthritis, the effects of vaccines, and warts. Recent evidence summarized by H. Benson and R. Friedman (1996) also suggests that placebo effects may extend to "psychological well-being" and self-esteem, as, for example, in the effects of aerobic exercise. I. Wickram (1989) further suggested that the potential for the occurrence of a placebo response is predictable whenever there is an active ingredient present in a research design.

In research settings, placebo responses have been considered to be irritating phenomena or experimental artifacts. [*See* Artifact, *article on* Artifact in Research.] Many are the research trials in which the placebo response has been almost indistinguishable from the substance or agent under consideration. In research involving pharmacological interventions for panic disorder, for example, as many as one third of the participants have responded to a placebo, as reported in a recent review by R. Hirchfield (1996). Not only have placebo effects been frequently observed, but such effects have been found to be quite orderly. Where placebos have been explicitly studied in research designs:

- Such effects parallel the direction of the active substance under consideration.
- The strength of the placebo is proportional to the strength of the active substance.
- The side effects of the placebo are often similar to those of the active substance.
- The time course of the placebo effect is similar to that of the active substance.
- Dose-effect relationships are similar (more placebo produces more "benefit").

The antithesis of the placebo effect is the "nocebo," in which inert or nonspecific procedures cause harm. In the nineteenth century, for example, J. MacKenzie (1886) reported that an asthmatic individual who was allergic to roses experienced an allergic attack when exposed to an artificial rose.

Mechanisms of the Placebo Effect

The placebo effect has been variously attributed to suggestion, anxiety reduction, expectancy, and conditioning processes. Regardless of the behavioral, cognitive, or psychological processes invoked, if placebos have real and measurable effects (and there is little disagreement that they do, although some have argued that the effects are far less than claimed), the biobehavioral mechanisms by which they do so remain to be explained. As noted by White, Tursky, and Schwartz (1985) what does seem clear is that the mechanisms by which placebos exert their effects depend significantly on the context in which they are used or administered. In research design studies of placebo analgesia, for example, there is strong support for the involvement of endogenous opiate mechanisms and neurotransmitters, since pain inhibition by placebo both in animal studies using classical conditioning and in human studies can be blocked by the opiate antagonist naloxone.

In research design studies of immunoenhancement, the relevant biobehavioral mechanisms may involve, for example, interactions of the central nervous system (CNS) with organ systems that control the immune system, such as the spleen, lymphoid tissue, bone marrow, and the thymus. The involvement of the CNS fits well with the not uncommon conceptualization of placebo effects as classically conditioned, learned responses. As discussed by J. Turkkan (1989), the placebo effect may, in fact, be viewed as a prototypical case of such classical conditioning, with the inert sugar pill and Pavlov's bell sharing the functional role of "conditional stimuli." Research designs with animal subjects, for example, have successfully demonstrated classical conditioning of immune response indices such as histamine release, natural killer-cell activity, and adjuvant arthritis.

Motivation and Expectancy

Just as with active substances, instructions strongly modulate the placebo response. If individuals are told that they are receiving a placebo, there is less of a placebo effect; similarly, when placebos are given blindly and also accompanied by motivational and optimistic messages, the placebo effect is markedly enhanced. A dramatic example was a study by C. Butler and A. Steptoe (1986), in which individuals who were told that they were inhaling a "chest-constricting chemical" experienced bronchial spasm; when the same individuals were told they were testing the effectiveness of a bronchodilator, they did not experience bronchospasm. In each case, the inhaled substance was distilled water.

In an effort to tease apart such powerful instructional effects, the "balanced placebo research design" has been adopted in experimental studies. This is a two-by-two randomized design in which research participants are either "told placebo" or "told active ingredient" and are either "given placebo" or "given active ingredient." [*See* Randomized Experiments.] While this research design has allowed for some sophisticated parsing of the placebo effect, for many substances there is no simple way of blinding individuals to the placebo manipulation. Consider the difficulty, for example, of fashioning a placebo marijuana or tobacco cigarette that would mislead a research subject. In alcohol research, J. Mendelson and his colleagues (1984) have attempted to solve this problem by "floating" a small amount of ethanol on top of a placebo drink. If, however, research subjects are experienced users or are otherwise familiar with the interoceptive effects of a substance (e.g., the marijuana-induced heart rate acceleration), they can often guess whether or not they received an active ingredient and respond accordingly.

Further analyses of the drug versus placebo response have involved asking participants after completion of a research trial whether they believe that they received a placebo. Not surprisingly, individuals who expressed the belief that they had received a placebo showed less treatment effect than those who believed they had received the active drug, whether they had or not. W. Fordyce, for example, has explored the idea that, given sufficient rigorous research defining the drug-placebo ratio, dose, route of administration, as well as frequency and duration of medication, placebo might be programmed to partially replace active ingredients in selected therapeutic regimens. This is not exactly a new approach, since "pain cocktails" with multiple analgesic drugs gradually replaced by a placebo, have long been used in the treatment of chronic pain. The empirical basis for such interventions have been hitherto lacking, however, and questionable ethical issues remain unresolved, as reflected in a thorough review by G. Elander (1991).

Over 1,700 years ago, Galen wrote of the purveyors of therapeutic interventions that "he cures most in whom most are confident." We might paraphrase this today for the placebo effect in research design that "it affects most in which most are confident."

Bibliography

Benson, H., & Friedman, R. (1996). Harnessing the power of the placebo effect and renaming it "remembered wellness." *Annual Review of Medicine, 47*, 193–199.

Butler, C., & Steptoe, A. (1986). Placebo responses: An experimental study of psychophysiological processes in asthmatic volunteers. *British Journal of Clinical Psychology, 25*, 73–83.

Elander, G. (1991). Ethical conflicts in placebo treatment. *Journal of Advances in Nursing, 16*, 947–951.

Fordyce, W. (1976). *Behavioral methods for chronic pain and illness*. St. Louis: Mosby.

Hirchfield, R. (1996). Placebo response in the treatment of panic disorder. *Bulletin of the Menninger Clinic, 60*(Suppl. A), 76A–86A.

Kienle, G. S., & Kiene, H. (1996). Placebo effect and placebo concept: A critical methodological and conceptual analysis of reports on the magnitude of the placebo effect. *Alternative Therapeutic Health and Medicine, 2*(6), 39–54. This paper describes "gross exaggerations" of the placebo effect.

MacKenzie, J. (1886). The production of the so-called "rose cold" by means of an artificial rose. *American Journal of Medical Science, 91*, 45–57.

Marlatt, G. A., & Rohsenow, D. J. (1980). Cognitive processes in alcohol use: Expectancy and the balanced budget placebo design. In N. K. Mello (Ed.), *Advances in substance abuse: Behavioral and biological research*. Greenwich, CT: JAI Press. An explication of the balanced placebo design.

Mendelson, J. H., McGuire, M., & Mello, N. K. (1984). A new device for administering placebo alcohol. *Alcohol, 1*, 417–419.

Turkkan, J. S. (1989). Classical conditioning: The new hegemony. *Behavioral and Brain Sciences, 12*, 121–137.

Turner, J. A., Deyo, R. A., Loeser, J. D., Von Korff, M., & Fordyce, W. E. (1994). The importance of placebo effects in pain treatment and research. *Journal of the American Medical Association, 271*(20), 1609–1614. A recent review of placebo effects in pain patients.

White, L., Tursky, B., & Schwartz, G. (Eds.). (1985). *Placebo: Clinical phenomena and new insight*. New York: Guilford Press. A definitive edited volume with many chapters discussing the behavioral aspects of placebo effect.

Wickram, I. (1989). Classical conditioning and the placebo effect. *Behavioral and Brain Sciences, 12*, 160–161.

Jaylan S. Turkkan and Joseph V. Brady

PLATO (c. 428–347 BCE), Greek philosopher. Born and raised in Athens during the Peloponnesian War, Plato came from a wealthy aristocratic family active in the political life of Athens. Little is known about Plato's early life other than that he was well educated and associated with the philosopher Socrates. His family expected him to have a political career, but Plato developed an antipathy to politics in his early 20s. His uncle Critias was the leader of the council appointed to rule Athens after its defeat by Sparta. Although a supporter of their antidemocratic stance, Plato became disillusioned when the Thirty Tyrants adopted terrorist tactics and was relieved when democracy was restored. When the new democratic government sentenced Socrates to death, Plato abandoned politics for philosophy. He left Athens after Socrates' death, taking the first of several journeys to Italy and Sicily. On one such journey, Plato became acquainted with the Pythagorean school at Tarentum and became convinced of the significance of mathematics for philosophy.

Plato settled back in Athens and founded the Academy, the first institution of higher learning, in order to provide Athenian youth with a many-sided academic education that included lectures on geometry, arithmetic, astronomy, and music. Plato spent most of his life at the Academy, teaching and writing the dialogues that present the teachings of Socrates. In 367 BCE Plato's most famous student, Aristotle, came to join the Academy. Plato never married and died at the age of 80.

Most scholars distinguish between the historical Socrates of the early ethical dialogues (e.g., *Apology, Protagoras, Gorgias*) and the Platonic Socrates of the middle to late dialogues (e.g., *Meno, Phaedo, Republic, Timaeus, Phaedrus, Laws*). In these later dialogues, Plato shifted from the ethical discussions and dialectical method attributed to Socrates and developed a more differentiated view of the *psyche*, the theory of forms, and a theory of the state.

Because Plato initiated the investigation of psyche in his Socratic dialogues, he might be credited with the founding of psychology. In the early dialogues, Plato's character Socrates described a new concept of *psyche*: an active striving *psyche* that shapes our actions and thoughts. Socrates claimed that the care of the *psyche*, not the feeding or adornment of the body, is life's highest purpose. It is by nurturing the soul in its striving for the good, the true, and the beautiful that humans realize their essential nature.

In the later dialogues, Plato developed this new notion of the *psyche*. The immortality of the soul, only hinted at as a possibility by Socrates, became the cornerstone of Plato's theory of knowledge. As Plato shifted his focus from ethics to epistemology, he increasingly emphasized the intellectual functions of *psyche*, an emphasis that remains central to Western philosophy and psychology.

Plato's early dialogues challenged the relativistic

views of the Sophists expressed in Protagoras's claim that "Man is the measure of all things." In these dialogues Socrates employed the dialectical method to expose inconsistencies in traditional accounts of moral concepts like virtue or piety. Although Socrates' discussions undermined accepted beliefs, the Socratic method was not purely negative; Socrates believed that through patient search, commonly agreed upon definitions of moral concepts would be discovered.

Plato's later dialogues examined the sources of such common knowledge. In allegories presented in the *Republic* (the divided line, the allegory of the cave), Plato rejected the view that our senses provide such knowledge. His Pythagorean view of a mathematical reality underlying the physical world led him to posit a realm of Forms of knowledge, which provide templates for our conceptual understanding. First introduced in *Phaedo* (although implied in *Meno*), the theory of Forms provided the underpinning for all human knowledge.

To bridge the gap between the world of Forms and individual knowledge, Plato articulated a theory of innate ideas and a reminiscence theory of knowledge. According to Plato, the soul is immortal and carries within it memories from prior apprehension of the Forms. A careful exercise of reason can uncover these buried memories in any of us, as Plato's slave boy demonstration in the *Meno* shows, although some individuals are naturally more adept at this exercise.

Plato's more differentiated concept of the soul incorporated a model of intrapsychic conflict and a prescription for mental health. In the *Republic* and the *Phaedrus*, Plato described the tripartite soul, composed of reason (*logistikon*), courage or spirit (*thumos*), and appetite (*epithumetikon*). Plato's myth of the charioteer (*Phaedrus*) depicts the struggle among these parts of the soul, a struggle resolved only when reason and courage form an alliance to control the appetites. Plato's view of mental health as balance or harmony among discordant parts of the self has been enormously influential.

In the *Republic*, the tripartite account of the soul provided a model for the ideal form of society. Mirroring the three parts of the soul (reason, courage, and appetite) are three types of character (gold, bronze, and iron) and three sociopolitical classes (rulers, guardians or soldiers, and workers). According to Plato, the political health of the state, like the mental health of the individual, depends on the harmonious, orderly, and hierarchical relationship among the three classes, with workers being governed by the rulers and soldiers. In assuming that an understanding of human nature is the soundest foundation for social theory, Plato inspired a long tradition of thinkers who drew on psychology for their political thinking.

Plato's writings provided a fertile source of ideas for future generations. In developing and elaborating the concept of the *psyche*, he laid the groundwork for the discipline of psychology. He formulated a model of intrapsychic conflict that was echoed by Freud, and argued that harmony or balance was the fundamental principle of mental health. In emphasizing the intellectual functions of the mind over its moral and affective functions, he laid the groundwork for cognitive psychology. Plato's belief that social theory must be rooted in a theory of human nature and his account of character types continue to influence modern social and political psychology. Plato's work, along with the many reactions to it, strongly shaped the Western intellectual tradition that gave rise to psychology.

Bibliography

Crombie, I. M. (1962–1963). *An examination of Plato's doctrines* (Vols. 1 & 2). New York: Humanities Press.

Guthrie, W. K. C. (1962–1981). *A history of Greek philosophy* (Vols. 1–6). Cambridge, UK: Cambridge University Press. Both Crombie and Guthrie provide solid introductions to Plato's work and his influence on philosophy.

Hamilton, E., & Cairns, H. (Eds.). (1961). *The collected dialogues of Plato, including the letters.* New York: Pantheon.

Lovibond, S. (1991). Plato's theory of mind. In S. Everson (Ed.), *Companions to ancient thought: Vol. 2. Psychology* (pp. 35–55). Cambridge, UK: Cambridge University Press.

Popper, K. R. (1950). *The open society and its enemies: Vol. 1. The spell of Plato.* Princeton, NJ: Princeton University Press. This classic critique of the psychologically based social structure in Plato's *Republic* focuses on the antidemocratic character of Plato's ideal state.

Robinson, T. M. (1995). *Plato's psychology* (2nd ed.). Toronto: University of Toronto Press.

Taylor, A. E. (1936). *Plato, the man and his work.* New York: Dial Press. (Original work published 1926)

Tourney, G. (1965). Freud and the Greeks: A study of the influence of classical Greek mythology and philosophy upon the development of Freudian thought. *Journal of the History of the Behavioral Sciences, 1,* 67–85.

Tuana, N. (Ed.). (1994). *Feminist interpretations of Plato.* University Park: Pennsylvania State University Press. A collection of recent critiques leveled by feminists against Plato.

Deborah F. Johnson

PLAY. When studying play, there are several important factors to consider. First, one may study the antecedents of play, such as biological inheritance, historical and cultural influences, and the effects on play of differences in child rearing, family, peers, status, gender, and individual differences. Second, one can focus on play and games as systems of behavior and thought in their own right as play structures. Third, the consequences of play can be considered in terms of its effects on mental health and on various associated psychological processes, in particular classroom scholarship.

Antecedents

Play is an ambiguous phenomenon within twentieth-century intellectual life. Although appearing to be universal in some form in all humans and higher animals, its character is much affected by the requirements of the culture within which it takes place. In some societies adults prohibit children's play because of its interference with the need for children's labor in the repetitive agricultural cycle that marks the struggle for survival. This negativity toward play, however, does not seem to have been a characteristic of prior nomadic societies. The restriction or censure of play occurs in many cultures of low production throughout Africa and the Americas. In European history there was also a rejection of play during the several hundred years associated with the arrival of industrial work hours and puritanical negative attitudes toward the carnival-like nature of some earlier forms of play. The result of these several centuries of antagonism toward play as a useless activity has meant that most twentieth-century theories of play have been focused on showing how useful play actually is. Developmental psychology in particular has been much affected by the theory of evolution, which convinced many scientists that play had to be a form of species adaptation because it was found throughout evolutionary history and because, as one ascended through the species, its increasing use paralleled the increase in the complexity of the brain. As the most influential of all early play theorists, Karl Groos, said in his book *The Play of Man* (New York, 1899) that children do not play because they are young; they are young so that they can play. What every child play theorist since that time has sought to show, accordingly, is how play, in one way or another, is a preparation for child growth and socialization. Since the end of the nineteenth century, researchers have been striving to explain to an originally doubting civilization why play is worthwhile. The story of play in psychology, therefore, is the story of this striving and of the research that it has engendered. It should be pointed out, however, that the increasing twentieth-century belief that play is a useful phenomenon probably owes as much to practical successes in controlling children's play through school playgrounds, play therapy, organized sports, the vast expansion of consumer toys, and the ever-increasing availability of media entertainment.

Moving beyond these larger biological, cultural, and historical antecedents of play, parents, peers, social status, gender, and individual differences have more immediate influence on a child's play. For example, a very large literature has developed for parents on how to play with infants and preschoolers. This represents an enormous historical shift by modern generations of parents toward positive attitudes about play. The research literature does, in general, find positive correlations between infants' security, parental stimulation, and childrens' own exploratory behavior, fantasy play, and sociability levels. However, it is uncertain whether this is a direct effect of specific child-rearing variables or of the generally play-oriented traits or character of some families. Inversely, family conflict, particularly divorce, has been shown to correlate with children's regression to less complex play levels. There are a variety of other findings that also indirectly support the view that play can be stimulated in one way or another by family phenomena. Thus, fathers differ from mothers in playing more with their infants and indulging in more physical and rough-and-tumble play. In interviews about childhood play, however, parents say they prefer to play sports with their school-age children, but the children indicate they would prefer fantasy play with their parents. When they are allowed to play with adults, however, they may desire to completely dominate them, as Diana Kelly-Byrne shows in *A Child's Play Life* (New York, 1989). In general, social-class differences are evident in that physical play of various kinds is more characteristic of children of lower socioeconomic status, and imaginative play forms are relatively more typical of those of higher socioeconomic status. But as indicated above, this is probably an outcome of cultural expectations rather than an inevitable difference between children. What is neglected in much of the laboratory- and school-based research is that higher levels of play are usually only achieved by children playing with their best friends in familiar circumstances, so judgments about children's play responses in these situations may not reflect genuine play differences. There is also scattered research on the effects of different kinds of toys, games, and playgrounds on the behavior of children. The richer and more novel the stimuli, the more complex and imaginative the levels of play.

The differences that seem both the most obvious and the most stable in children's play are gender differences. It has been expected that these differences would decrease with increasing opportunity for active play and sports for girls; however, older gender-play traditions continue in most school playgrounds. Boys still engage more in forceful body contact, motor activity, and fantasied conflict; they occupy larger spaces and intrude on each other during the play; and their outcomes are well defined, with winners and losers. Girls, on the other hand, engage in more coordinated choral activity with rhymes and songs, part-body usage, and audiences; they use smaller spaces and engage in indirect competition with much turn-taking and more rules. Indeed, the gender differences are still sufficiently strong that it has been suggested that playgrounds may be the major cultural locations in which these differences are learned and can be freely expressed. Here peer socialization is at a maximum.

There has been some research, although not a great deal, on individual differences in play styles, some children being more playful, some more imaginative, some liking drama, some object construction. It might be suggested that what is needed is more research into all of the different possible types of play styles; those, for example, represented by comedians, explorers, athletes, gamesters, storytellers, and artists. Now that some of these have moved to the center of modern celebrity culture, and now that their play cultures are among the most central unifying forces in modern society, there is warrant for investigating the etiology of their play development rather than only what their play contributes to their own more "serious" educational activities.

Play Structures

The initial question to be asked is, What indeed are the basic forms or structures of play? It was first suggested that children's play, songs, rhymes, and games were a recapitulation of earlier phases of animal and human evolution, but this view achieved little credence in the twentieth century. These phenomena still persist in children's playground play but have been largely neglected subsequently by child development psychologists. Their structure is reviewed by Brian Sutton-Smith, Jay Mechling, Thomas W. Johnson, and Felicia R. McMahon and colleagues in *Children's Folklore: A Source Book* (Logan, Utah, 1995). It is clear not only that there is an alphabet of traditional play patterns available to most children but also that there are systematic hierarchical play patterns of admission and leadership that are a part of what children are learning while they are at play and without which the play simply cannot occur. Play is determined, that is, both by ludic forms (play motifs) and by child play politics. It may be this focus on child power relationships that makes most investigators unwilling to tackle childhood games.

Freud attributed the first genuinely psychological structures to play. Children, he said, need play because they do not have more sophisticated and logical ways of dealing with anxiety-producing events. Children repeat everything in play that they cannot deal with in life, and in so doing they change from being passive victims of their situation to becoming active masters. These conflictive actions, Freud said, take on such patterns in play as wish fulfillment and compensation. The psychodynamic play theorist who became most accepted, however, was Erik Erikson, who combined his knowledge of children with scholarship in anthropology. His book *Childhood and Society* (New York, 1950) was read by millions of American students in child development partly because it presented his more positive view of play sequences as a kind of integration through which the child creates model situations in which aspects of the past are relived, the present represented, and the future anticipated. It was an amazingly optimistic claim for an activity that had been typically derided during the prior centuries.

In the earlier part of this century discussions about play largely depended on speculations about history, culture, or play as therapy. From about the 1930s onward, however, the development of the quantitative data-gathering tradition for studying play became more central to developmental psychologists. For example, one of the earliest systematic data-collecting works on play was by Susan Parten of the Institute of Child Welfare at the University of Minnesota in 1932. What she discovered was that younger children in their preschool social groups went through a series of stages, from unoccupied behavior to onlooker behavior to solitary play to parallel play to associative play with others and, finally, at about 4 years of age, to cooperative play. Part of the reason her findings are important is that some 30 years later they were taken up by a number of other researchers and tested on other child samples. Briefly, the new research showed that what occurred in the original sample was not always replicated in later ones. Not all children proceed automatically through this series. Solitary play is not just the first step in social development; it is often a characteristic also of children at later stages and also of those who are otherwise socially quite mature. More important, and conversely, even infants engage in kinds of social and cooperative play with their parents. Thus each of these supposed social stages seems to actually require a discussion of competencies that occur diversely at different age levels.

The results of these studies indicate that Parten's global stages cannot predict the real complexities of social development and therefore have a limited usefulness for understanding the value of play. Still, this was one of the first approaches to analyzing some "structures" of play that was based on empirical studies. Further, Parten's concentration on the kinds of "integration" served by play still has considerable importance in evolutionary terms, because increases in population numbers have been related to more success in survival throughout human cultural evolution. It is not hard to believe that a major function of social play, both biologically and culturally, has been the reinforcement of the integration of the players into complex group relationships.

The biggest single breakthrough in the understanding of children's play structures and in increasing scholarly interest in them resulted from the appearance some 20 years later of Jean Piaget's book, *Play, Dreams and Imitation in Childhood* (New York, 1951). Its excellence lay first in the sheer copiousness and minuteness of Piaget's observed examples of the characteristics of the play of his own three children. Beyond that, he framed his observations in terms of a brilliant cognitive structural theory that he advanced to explain the meaning of the play that he observed. In brief, he declared that there were four major stages of cognitive development that could be illustrated through children's play. The stages proceeded from various types of sensorimotor or practice play in the first 18 months to various kinds of imaginary symbolic play over the next few years. These were followed in the early childhood years, ages 4 to 7, by more systematic concrete thinking involving role reversibility and reciprocity. This is when children begin to play games with rules and to bring a ritual orderliness to their symbolic play. Finally, by the end of childhood they could participate in relatively abstract forms of play, as in board games of strategy. For Piaget the function of these play structures was to assimilate the matters of everyday life into play, the structures of the play itself followed the same lines as indicated in his theory of cognitive structures. Just as Parten was impressed with what play could tell about the development of social behavior, so Piaget was impressed with what play could tell about the development of cognitive behavior. They believed that play was a very useful childhood activity promoting sociability on the one hand and thought on the other. Both in their individual ways were reversing the historical attitudes that play was a matter of relative triviality.

Another influential psychologist whose interest in play was also fairly exclusively cognitive was Daniel Berlyne (*Conflict, Arousal and Curiosity*, New York, 1969). His work led to many studies that attempted to distinguish the relative roles of exploration and play in cognitive development. Corinne Hutt was perhaps the leader in this work with children. She showed that, although exploratory behavior is largely controlled by the novel stimulus, play transcends the stimulus with its own interests (*Play: Exploration and Learning*, New York, 1989).

A major criticism of both Piaget's and Berlyne's work that has arisen over the past 30 years, however, has been that it overemphasizes the role of cognition and underestimates the role of social factors in play. This is one of the reasons why the work of the Russian researcher Lev Vygotsky has received increasing attention since the 1980s even though, like Piaget, he is otherwise centrally concerned with the function of symbolization in play. In *Mind and Society* (Cambridge, Mass., 1978), he places the origins of play within the social context and interactions of parents and children. He argues that the society organizes the cognitive structures that determine the symbolic processes that the child acquires. He presents his notion of the "zone of proximal development" to account for the way in which adults, by participating with children, lift the level of complexity in the child's play performances. This concept has had very strong influence on research into caretaker effects on child play. The results show that children do play at more complex levels when participating with caretakers, though they also show that the adults comment, suggest, and observe more than they actually participate in the child's play. Indeed, Vygotsky's orientation to play is best illustrated by the 70% of societies in the world whose social fabric is one of interdependence, in which the parents, when interacting with a child, imaginatively guide the use of symbols in a way that illustrates and supports the larger adult social fabric. Thus a play object that might be perceived as a cup is symbolized by the parent for the child as, for example, the cup of the father or the grandfather; while playing with the pretend object, the child is expected to act toward it as he or she would act toward that person in real life. This kind of heavy emphasis on imitative play is characteristic of most examples of children's play to be found in earlier cultures. A child in a more modern Western toy-laden home, on the other hand, is more often expected to play by him- or herself, or, alternatively, is stimulated to make up his or her own meanings for the ambiguous play objects. The adult provokes the child to act on his or her own. Both situations are social contexts but of quite different types. What may be important about Piaget is that his theory is an unwitting description of the way modern parents have come to look at their ludic responsibilities toward their children. They urge them on to autonomous activity with objects, granting those objects themselves a key function in the child's technical development, whereas, in older and more interpersonal ways of life such objects have a function subservient to the social context. Patricia Greenfield and Rodney Cocking give cross-cultural examples of this difference between the play of the modern individualistic and technology oriented family and the older, more collectively oriented family (*Cross-Cultural Roots of Minority Development*, Hillsdale, N.J., 1994).

The most original theory to break away from the Freudian, Piagetian, Berlynian, and Vygotskyan models of pretense, however, is that recently presented by R. Keith Sawyer, who in *Pretend Play as Improvisation* (Mahwah, N.J., 1997) uses models for play's structure drawn from the nature of conversational discourse and from the nature of improvisation in the realms of acting, music, literature, and jazz. He maintains that children's social imaginative play is a kind of improvisational performance in which the players interact with each other somewhat like adults do in a jazz ensemble.

By focusing on rule games, he says, both Vygotsky and Piaget miss out on this kind of collective improvisational play of 3- to 5-year-olds. Sawyer suggests that children first learn to converse with their parents. By about age 3 they can converse with other children, and increasingly thereafter they are helped by pretend play, which allows them to adopt dramatic play voices. It also lets them use their own voices to talk to others about what they are doing and sometimes even use yet another voice to tell the story that they are enacting. Their multiplicity of voices interacts with the multiplicity of the peers' voices, and what emerges are improvised performances that by about 6 years of age are carried out very competently. Instead of attributing the constancies across childhood simply to "tradition" or "rules," as others have done, Sawyer shows how children improvise such constancies by melding the rituals already inherent in the congeries of their voices, their play motifs, their politics, their language, their cognition, and so on. To him, collective play is an emergence of disparate and flexible voices. Not surprisingly, Sawyer, not unlike the earlier theorists, is once again most interested in the way in which this emerging improvisational competence contributes to the subsequent realistic role capacities of the children involved. Play is now a contribution to social competence, just as Piaget saw it as a contribution to cognitive competence and Vygotsky to symbolic competence. What they all neglect is the contribution that play makes to being a player and, as such, to the sense that play forms are their own reason for being. Presumably, the most basic question about children's play, one still not answered, is why they care so much about these ludic collectivities. Why must monsters, nonsense, and other quirky fabrications most excite and entertain them as human beings?

Play Consequences

Despite over 100 years of interest, we have not established very clearly what the function of play is in animal or human lives. In general, it is supposed that play is very important because it is found more in creatures of higher than those of lower cerebral complexity. More specifically, the absence of play in human adult lives is typically associated with aberration and breakdown, with psychosis, maladjustment, obsessiveness, and some forms of criminality. Further, those children who cannot succeed in playing with others during their school years are much more susceptible to school failure and withdrawal. Those who are low players as contrasted with high (more complex and more imaginative) players are similarly more isolated and anxiety ridden. In many cases play therapy has permitted some of these maladjusted to recover and assume more normal lives. Hospital play therapy is now also widely accepted as a successful treatment to alleviate the suffering and anxiety of hospitalized children. In one long-range research program into the functions of make-believe, described in *The House of Make-Believe* by Dorothy and Jerome Singer (Cambridge, Mass., 1992), it was shown that children who are more imaginative players in school are more able to tolerate frustration, are less aggressive, and do much better with school requirements than children who do not have this particular play potential.

Perhaps more important, it is has been shown that the adoption of "play"-oriented methods in schooling (compared with traditional academic methods) at both preschool and elementary school levels leads to greater happiness in school, less depression, more motivation for school subjects, and more long-term interest in school subject matters. Whether these changes that occur with school play pedagogy result from teachers' participation or from the effects of the play program is, however, not at present clear. Whatever the case, the use of play techniques in classroom teaching promises a more optimistic outlook on the part of both children and teachers, whether or not it makes much difference to academic scores.

For some time it has been a controversial issue whether some children of lower socioeconomic status or who are culturally deprived and who come to school without much capacity for imaginative school-centered activities should be helped by programs that teach them how to dramatize their feelings through stories and enactments. The issue was first raised by Sarah Smilansky in her book *The Effects of Sociodramatic Play on Disadvantaged Preschool Children* (New York, 1968). But others have suggested subsequently that these children are not actually deficient in fantasy but that, as mentioned earlier, in some cultures and subcultures children's play is treated negatively and in others children's play is locked into religious or ethnic attempts to maintain familial solidarity by repetitive and limited fantasy enactments. It needs to be remembered that the private and individualistic fantasies that we cherish in modern children are a relatively new occurrence in the world. We might say that their importance to us was forecast by the origins of the novel during the Renaissance a few centuries ago. Those who do not read fictional stories or live in a culture that does are not likely to encourage their children in such idiosyncratic behavior. It seems probable that the enormous emphasis given to the imagination of preschool children in most of the developmental psychology research on play and the corresponding neglect of the physical play and games that are also enjoyments of childhood arises from the key role that the individualized imagination now has in modern civilization. In this sense the orientation of scholarship toward the importance of pretend play is similar to that of Piaget, as well as most modern parents. Their primary attention is given to what they most value about the play of children, which is not games but the role their imaginations will play in the society in which they live.

In recent years there have been attempts to define play not only in terms of its developmental value but also in terms of its intrinsic motivation (play for play's sake) and of its self-actualizing properties (play as self-transcending). But although these are interesting concepts, as is play as a form of development, they are also mainly an expression of modern ethnocentric cultural values. They are values that derive from our positive cultural emphases on progress, on freedom, and on individuality, all commendable enough in themselves but insufficiently responsive to the wide varieties of play as we know them throughout culture and history. They are, for example, hardly of much relevance to the kinds of obligatory and collective play that have existed throughout most of history and that still occur in the modern world. As I have concluded elsewhere (*The Ambiguity of Play*, Cambridge, Mass., 1997), the meanings and functions of play have not yet been defined satisfactorily with any degree of scientific consensus.

[*See also* Play Therapy.]

Bibliography

Avedon, E. M., & Sutton-Smith, B. (1971). *The study of games*. New York: Wiley. This is a useful introduction to the concept of games as found in history, anthropology, folklore, recreation, the military, education, therapy, and social science.

Eisen, G. (1988). *Children and play in the Holocaust*. Amherst: University of Massachusetts Press. This startling account is a challenge to most modern, rather idealized, theories of children's play.

Ellis, M. J. (1973). *Why people play*. New York: Prentice Hall. This is a most useful brief overview of psychological theories of play.

Garvey, C. (1977). *Play*. Cambridge, MA: Harvard University Press. This book is an excellent introduction for students. Garvey is noted for her own original research on the way in which children's language is transformed during play.

Goldstein, J. H. (1994). *Toys, play and child development*. New York: Cambridge University Press. This is the best update on psychological research on toy play. Succeeds the work by B. Sutton-Smith, *Toys as culture* (New York: Gardner Press, 1986).

Fagen, R. (1981). *Animal play behavior*. New York: Oxford University Press. This is the best general overview of the copious research that has been done on animal play behavior. The author uses most interesting theoretical models to embrace the complexities of the behaviors that are reviewed.

Herron, R. E., & Sutton-Smith, B. (1971). *Child's play*. New York: Wiley. This contains many of the major articles published up to that date. It is complemented by the subsequent work of Jerome S. Bruner, Alison Jolly, and Kathy Sylva, *Play*. (New York: Basic Books, 1972).

Huizinga, J. (1955). *Homo ludens: A study of the play element in culture*. Boston, MA: Beacon Press. This was the first modern comprehensive history of the universal cultural nature of play. It offers a rich collection of historical material and a positive interpretation of the role of play in history, but the evaluation of the data is controversial.

Macdonald, K. (Ed.). (1993). *Parent-child play: Descriptions and implications*. New York: SUNY Press. This is a valuable update of the state of the research in this field, covering U.S. and cross-cultural data. See also J. L. Roopnarine, J. E. Johnson, and F. H. Hooper (Eds.), *Children's play in diverse cultures* (New York: SUNY Press, 1994).

Rubin, K. H., Fein, G. G. & Vandenberg, B. (1983). Play. In P. H. Mussen (Series Ed.) & E. M. Hetherington (Vol. Ed.), *Handbook of child psychology*: Vol. 4. *Socialization, personality, and social development* (4th ed., pp. 693–774). This is the most complete and scholarly review of psychological thought and research about children's play in the modern era. The authors have each made many important contributions to child play research.

Schwartzman, H. B. (1978). *Transformations: The anthropology of children's play*. New York: Plenum. This is a remarkable review of what is available in widely scattered anthropological and psychological sources, illuminated by the application of Batesonian metacommunication theory of play; see G. Bateson, *Steps to an ecology of mind*. (New York: Ballantine, 1872). Schwartzman's is probably the best single introduction in book form to the investigation of play in this century.

Spariosu, M. (1989). *Dionysus reborn*. Ithaca, NY: Cornell University Press. The author presents a brilliant rhetorical analysis of references in classical and modern literature to play in rational or irrational terms. His thesis is that play has been overrationalized in the literature and that it is more anarchic than is generally indicated.

Thorne, B. (1993). *Gender play, girls and boys in school*. New Brunswick, NJ: Rutgers University Press. This gives a startling account of the way in which school playgrounds are dominated by boys. It needs to be contrasted with Iona Opie, *The people in the playground* (New York: Oxford University Press, 1993), and both need to be seen against the more systematic research oriented focus of C. H. Hart, (Ed.), *Children on playgrounds* (New York: SUNY Press, 1993), and A. D. Pellegrini, *School recess and playground behavior* (New York: SUNY Press, 1995).

Brian Sutton-Smith

PLAY THERAPY. Originally conceptualized in strictly psychoanalytic terms, play therapy has evolved over the years to include a wide array of therapeutic approaches and techniques. Nevertheless, most of these divergent models of play therapy share some basic assumptions regarding the defining elements of play therapy. Here we define play therapy as a therapeutic approach characterized by: (1) an ongoing relationship between a trained therapist and a child client who exhibits behavioral and/or emotional difficulties; and (2) the use of a variety of play-based activities designed to induce therapeutic change in the client. Beyond such a basic definition, however, therapists adopting different models of play therapy often pursue significantly different therapeutic objectives and utilize widely divergent clinical techniques and tactics.

Sigmund Freud is generally credited with first recognizing the value of child analysis. His work with Little Hans, a 5-year-old neurotic boy, involved the direct observation of the child's developmental course and a recognition that children can communicate their thoughts and feelings in meaningful ways. During the 1920s, therapists began systematically to adapt the techniques of psychoanalysis for use with children. For example, Hermine von Hug-Hellmuth conducted therapy in the child's home and observed that children's play with their own toys often produced meaningful analytic material.

Two figures stand out as major contributors to the early development of play therapy as a viable therapeutic technique with children: Melanie Klein and Anna Freud. Melanie Klein was guided by the earlier work of Hermine von Hug-Hellmuth, and she also initially worked with children in their homes. Eventually, however, she saw children in her office and borrowed toys from her own children to use in play therapy. Klein was the first therapist to use a carefully planned playroom. She utilized a large number and variety of miniature figures, art materials, and kinesthetically stimulating toys (i.e., sand and water tables) to encourage children to generate meaningful play themes. Klein believed that children's play was the equivalent of free associations in adult psychoanalysis and that such play behavior could be "interpreted" by the therapist.

From the 1920s until her death in 1982, Anna Freud also contributed to the acceptance of play therapy as an important method for child treatment. A major contribution of Anna Freud's work was the recognition that a positive treatment alliance is an essential element in the therapeutic process with children. She noted that most children do not come to therapy voluntarily, so before starting analysis, Anna Freud bonded with a child so that the child liked and needed her.

Initially, the field of play therapy was divided between the interpretive approach of Melanie Klein and the more supportive approach of Anna Freud. As the literature on play therapy expanded rapidly in the 1930s, however, rigid adherence to either approach decreased significantly. Between the 1930s and 1950s, new play therapy techniques and models grew rapidly to treat children with social problems that were not appropriate for traditional psychoanalytic play therapy. David Levy, for example, developed "release therapy" to treat children who experienced a specific traumatic event. In this approach, toys and materials related to their trauma were made available to a child, and the child was encouraged to repeatedly reenact the traumatic event through play. The use of play therapy for the treatment of children who have experienced severe trauma or stress (e.g., natural disaster, family death, abuse) remains widespread today. By having the child reenact the traumatic event, the therapist helps the child overcome his or her sense of helplessness, and the therapist can correct misperceptions the child may have about themselves and the event. In the 1940s, Virginia Axline modified Carl Rogers's client-centered model of therapy with adults into a play therapy approach suitable for children. Her writings on the client-centered approach to play therapy remain highly influential today.

During the next four decades, the related but distinct concepts of play and play therapy have evolved as critical components of child development and child treatment. As greater understanding of children's play behavior has developed, this knowledge has been increasingly incorporated into play therapy approaches. Also, with the increased emphasis on cognitive and behavioral models of adult therapy, child therapists have adapted these approaches for use in their work with children.

Process and Approaches

The term *play therapy* encompasses a wide variety of clinical techniques and therapeutic approaches. A therapist using a nondirective approach to play therapy, for example, will pursue quite different treatment objectives and emphasize different play therapy techniques than a therapist adopting a cognitive-behavioral perspective. Nevertheless, most approaches to play therapy share a number of process elements.

Regardless of the particular approach adopted, most play therapists assume that the ability to engage in play is a major resource for children that can be used for a variety of therapeutic purposes. From this perspective, play represents a major form of communication for the child and a venue in which the child can grapple with problems and develop new cognitive, affective, and behavioral skills. Virtually all play therapy comprises both play and verbal interactions between the therapist and child. Play therapy typically is conducted in a playroom that is stocked with a variety of age- and gender-typical play materials that are consistent with the therapeutic orientation of the play therapist. Most often, these will include such items as an extensive set of arts and craft supplies, a family doll house and other miniature figures, puppets, and a variety of toys and games.

Despite the commonalities among many approaches to play therapy, significant differences in both goals and techniques exist. For example, the degree to which the therapist directs play and the type of verbal exchanges between the child and therapist will vary substantially depending on the therapist's clinical orientation. There are four major approaches to play therapy: psychodynamic, humanistic, developmental, and directive.

Psychodynamic Approach. The psychodynamic approach to child play therapy represents the earliest conceptual model for how to conduct psychotherapy with young children, and it has served as a foundation for many subsequent approaches to play therapy. Indeed, many of the basic principles and techniques associated with the dynamic approach have been incorporated into more recent models of play therapy.

One of the central assumptions of the dynamic approach is that children's play is an important form of communication, roughly equivalent to free association in adult clients. One of the therapist's primary jobs within this approach is to offer interpretations about such behavior to the child. Interpretations are therapist's comments designed to communicate to the child previously unrecognized (i.e., unconscious) relationships between thoughts, feelings, and behaviors or to increase a child's understanding of the causes of such behaviors and feelings. The objective of interpretations is to increase the child's understanding (i.e., insight), thereby increasing his or her control of behavior, emotions, and thoughts.

Within this approach, children are given extensive freedom to choose how they will spend the therapy session (e.g., drawing, playing games, talking, using puppets). During the early phases of therapy, the clinician becomes a compliant player in the child's activities and begins to comment on the metaphors that emerge during the child's play. As such metaphors of past and present concerns of the child are "played out" in the child's activities, the therapist's acceptance and interpretations of the play allow the child to construct and try new solutions to his or her conflicts.

Early on in the development of the dynamic approach to child play therapy, it was noted that children pose some unique challenges to the successful implementation of dynamic oriented techniques. For example, children often are less motivated to engage in therapy than adults, and they are less able to tolerate the anxiety and frustration that may accompany therapy activities. The creation of a strong "therapeutic alliance," therefore, is especially important and problematic in child play therapy. Additionally, children may find it difficult to engage in the self-observation implied in the therapist's interpretations, and they may find it difficult to understand and accept interpretations.

Because of these and other limitations associated with childhood, dynamic play therapists must continually monitor their relationship with the child and carefully plan interpretive interventions. Typically, a therapist will engage in an extensive period of preparation with the child before offering an interpretive statement. For example, the therapist will make observations about repeated behaviors and verbally reflect the feelings of the child as he or she engages in play. Each of these interventions focuses the child's attention on his or her behavior, thoughts, or feelings and lays the groundwork for the acceptance of a future interpretation. When working with children, the timing of such interpretations is critical. Also, an extensive period of "working through" such interpretations is required with children. Interpretations often will need to be repeated to the child in different play contexts and over an extended period of time.

The dynamic approach to play therapy has been extraordinarily influential in child therapy, and it remains a widely used approach today. However, because of increased controversy regarding many of its underlying assumptions and its therapeutic efficacy and efficiency, the dynamic approach has been modified significantly or replaced altogether by other approaches. Nevertheless, many of its basic techniques can be found in alternative models of play therapy.

Humanistic Approach: Client-Centered Play Therapy. The client-centered approach to play therapy is characterized by the extensive freedom given to the child client to direct play activities and child-therapist interactions. Within this approach, the therapist believes that the child is his or her own best source of positive growth and that, given the opportunity to explore his or her own feelings in a safe, nurturing environment, the child will learn to meet biological, intrapersonal, and interpersonal needs in adaptive, self-realizing ways.

Carl Rogers developed the humanistic model based on his belief that the primary motivation for human beings is to grow toward self-direction and self-actualization. He viewed psychopathology as a maladaptive response to environmental demands that stifle and distort such personal growth. According to Rogers, the goal of therapy should be to assist the client in moving away from patterns of thinking, feeling, and behaving that are governed by the judgments and expectations of others and in moving toward increased reliance on his or her own experiences in developing values and standards. Rogers's humanistic, client-centered theory was adapted by Virginia Axline for her work with children.

The goal of client-centered play therapy is to promote self-actualization by creating an optimal environment in which the therapist provides unconditional acceptance of the child and thereby reduces the conflict the child feels with the environment. The therapist works toward this goal first by establishing a warm and friendly relationship with the child and communicating acceptance of the child as he or she is; second, by establishing a feeling of permissiveness within simple limits so that children feel free to express all feelings they are experiencing; third, by verbally reflecting the children's feelings so that they gain increased insight into their thoughts, feelings, and actions; fourth, by letting the child direct the conversation and play; and fifth, by recognizing the gradual process of therapy and not attempting to rush the child-guided process. Humanistic play therapy is conducted by regularly exposing the child to the warm, accepting nature of the therapist within the trust-promoting environment of the playroom.

The nondirective approach to play therapy has been extended to the training of nonprofessionals as play therapists. For example, parents have been trained to facilitate behavioral changes within the home setting. The goal of such training is that parents will generalize their play therapy experiences to other parent-child interactions, thus moving closer to the optimal environment that humanistic therapists believe will most greatly facilitate child growth.

Developmental Approach: Theraplay. Several different types of play therapies can be clustered under the heading of developmental play therapy. Theraplay, developed by Ann Jernberg, is perhaps the most well-known of the developmentally oriented approaches to play therapy. Theraplay was developed for use with a wide range of child clients who experience difficulty in establishing and maintaining positive interpersonal relationships. The model is based on the assumption that healthy caretaker-child interactions in the first few years of life are critical for later mental health. Therapists working within the Theraplay approach believe that providing good caretaker-child interactions even later in life can have a positive impact on a child's ability to experience satisfying personal relationships.

The goal of Theraplay is to encourage a relationship between the therapist and the child that mimics positive early caretaker-child relationships. The therapist attempts to present activities that address four different types of early caretaker-child interactions: structuring, challenging, intruding, and nurturing. Structuring interactions are designed to allow the therapist to set limits and provide an orderly environment for the child. Challenge activities stimulate the child's development and enhance achievement. Intrusive interactions discourage the child from withdrawing from the real world and retreating into a fantasy life. And finally, nurturing interactions are designed to meet a child's need to be nourished, consoled, and comforted.

Throughout Theraplay sessions, therapists maintain a positive and playful attitude. They model for the child client the enjoyment derived from normal childhood fun. They attempt to convey to the child that social interactions can be positive and pleasurable experiences. Frequently, therapists use touch as an important method for connecting and communicating with children. The act of touching is viewed as an important part of early caretaker-child interactions, and it is used frequently throughout all Theraplay activities. Within this approach it is hoped that through such play activities the child will experience meaningful interpersonal interactions that will transfer to other significant relationships in the child's life.

Directive Approach: Cognitive-Behavioral Play Therapy. In recent years, more directive approaches to play therapy have gained in popularity, and emerging research supports the promise of these approaches. Cognitive-behavioral play therapy combines more traditional play therapy techniques with behavioral and cognitive techniques. Such an approach has proven useful in developing children's problem-solving and social skills and other cognitive and behavioral coping strategies.

In cognitive-behavioral play therapy, the therapist is more active than in traditional approaches to play therapy. For example, the therapist will identify specific goals for therapy, such as teaching new skills and behaviors, and will actively use a variety of cognitive and behavioral techniques to achieve these goals. Common behavioral techniques used in this approach include modeling, systematic reinforcement, shaping, and practice procedures. For example, a therapist might use tokens (later to be exchanged for backup prizes) and praise to gradually increase a shy child's verbal interactions. Additionally, the therapist (or other child) may actively model a target behavior and then reinforce the child for attempting the behavior. Reinforcement would continue as the child gradually increased his or her proficiency through practice and feedback.

Whereas behavioral procedures tend to focus on the development and maintenance of appropriate behaviors (as well as on decreasing unwanted behaviors), cognitive procedures are more likely to focus on children's thoughts, feelings, and problem solving. The therapist, for example, may assist the child in thinking of alternative solutions to a problem or may help the child consider alternative explanations for an event. Children may be taught to use coping self-statements to help them deal more effectively with stressful situations. Children may also be encouraged to monitor their thoughts and feelings and engage in self-reinforcement for appropriate behavior. As with learning new behavioral skills, these cognitive skills are developed through extensive modeling, shaping, practice, and reinforcement.

Many researchers have noted that one of the major advantages of cognitive-behavioral play therapy is the specificity of treatment goals and methods. Such an approach allows clear treatment objectives to be identified and specific procedures developed for achieving those objectives. This approach also lends itself to the conduct of well-designed treatment-outcome studies and research investigating the most important elements of play therapy.

Play Therapy Research

Despite the fact that play therapy remains one of the most often used psychological intervention strategies for young children, there is a striking absence of empirical research on the process and outcome of play therapy techniques. Instead, the interested reader will find an immense body of literature that is descriptive or theoretical in nature. The relatively few meta-analyses of child therapy outcome research that do exist either do not include play therapy as an independent category of analysis or lump all play therapies together into a single category. Such strategies make progress in identifying the most effective approaches to play therapy difficult at best.

Whereas systematic research into the processes and outcome of play therapy has been lacking, scientific interest in the nature of children's play has increased. Researchers in developmental, educational, and child psychology have begun to delineate the ways that children engage in play and the function that such play serves. This research on children's play provides important but indirect evidence for the potential positive impact of play therapy interventions. For example, play research has indicated that children's play promotes the development of various cognitive skills such as vocabulary and problem solving. Researchers have also reported that play promotes the expression and control of affect in children. Many researchers in the area of play therapy have suggested that such analyses of the play process can serve as the conceptual basis for a systematic investigation into play therapy.

It will be important for future researchers to examine the specific intervention components that represent the various schools of play therapy and identify which components are responsible for what types of change. For example, what is the impact of such nondirective and dynamic play therapy techniques as verbal following (i.e., verbally reflecting a child's behavior) and interpretation? What impact do more directive strategies such as token reinforcement and modeling have on behavior change? An emerging, but still small, body of research indicates that more directive play therapy techniques, such as those used in cognitive-behavioral play therapy, may be most effective in achieving specific communicative and behavioral goals.

In addition to a more detailed analysis of the play therapy process, researchers will also need to examine treatment-by-child interactions. For example, some research has found that puppet play has reduced preoperative anxiety about upcoming surgery in young children. But many questions remain unanswered: What types of problems are most likely to be ameliorated by a nondirective approach versus a cognitive-behavioral approach? What types of problems are most effectively dealt with in the contexts of school versus family versus individual therapy? These questions and many others relating to the process and outcome of play therapy remain largely unanswered. Unfortunately, the selection of play therapy techniques by both researchers and practitioners is often guided by unsubstantiated theory and anecdotal reports. Such an approach has resulted in a plethora of empirically undocumented play therapy strategies and inconsistent treatment outcome findings.

Conclusions

Play therapy has evolved from a strictly psychoanalytic treatment approach into a large family of therapy techniques that all recognize the value and therapeutic potential of a child's play. Unfortunately, systematic empirical research into the process and efficacy of these divergent approaches has not kept pace with the rapid growth of play therapy theory and practice. It will be important for future researchers to examine both those elements that differentiate these approaches and the commonalities that unite them. Such investigation is necessary to ensure continued progress in this rich area of treatment intervention for children.

[*See also* Play.]

Bibliography

Axline, V. M. (1969). *Play therapy* (Rev. ed.). New York: Ballantine Books.

Chethik, M. (1989). *Techniques of child therapy: Psychodynamic strategies.* New York: Guilford Press.

Freedheim, D. K. (Ed.). (1992). *History of psychotherapy.* Washington, DC: American Psychological Association.

Jernberg, A. M. (1979). *Theraplay: A new treatment using structured play for problem children and their families.* San Francisco: Jossey-Bass.

Knell, S. (1993). *Cognitive-behavioral play therapy.* Northvale, NJ: Aronson.

Kottman, T., & Schaefer, C. (1993). *Play therapy in action.* Northvale, NJ: Jason Aronson.

Kratochwill, T. R., & Morris, R. J. (Eds.). (1993). *Handbook of psychotherapy with children and adolescents.* Boston: Allyn & Bacon.

O'Connor, K., & Schaefer, C. E. (1994). *Handbook of play therapy: Advances and innovations.* New York: Wiley.

Sandler, J., Kennedy, H., & Tyson, R. L. (1980). *The technique of child psychoanalysis: Discussions with Anna Freud.* Cambridge, MA: Harvard University Press.

Schaefer, C. E., & Cangelosi, D. M. (1993). *Play therapy techniques.* Northvale, NJ: Jason Aronson.

Webb, N. B. (Ed.). (1991). *Play therapy with children in crisis: A casebook for practitioners.* New York: Guilford Press.

Gregory A. Waas and Diane M. Kleckler

POLICE PSYCHOLOGY involves the application of psychological knowledge to questions and problems encountered in law enforcement. One of several subspecializations within the area of legal psychology, police psychology should be distinguished from other law-and-psychology fields, such as forensic psychology, correctional psychology, and the psychology of litigation. The primary activities of police psychology are concentrated in five areas:

1. Assessing and consulting on the selection of candidates for law enforcement positions.
2. Training police officers in crisis intervention skills.
3. Providing interventions for police officers who suffer psychological distress as a result of their law enforcement duties.
4. Assisting and advising police officers with special forms of criminal investigation.
5. Developing interventions aimed at crime prevention and strengthening community relations.

Assessment and Selection of Police Officers

An early application of psychology to law enforcement occurred in 1916, when Lewis Terman, the Stanford University psychologist who revised Alfred Binet's intelligence scales to produce the Stanford–Binet intelligence test, measured the intelligence of 30 applicants for police and firefighter jobs in San Jose, California. A few years later, another testing pioneer, Louis L. Thurstone, assessed the intelligence of police candidates in Detroit. Throughout the years, psychologists continued to assess police candidates, and by the 1960s and 1970s, the period when police psychology became an established specialty, several national commissions, including the 1967 President's Commission on Law Enforcement and the Administration of Justice, recommended that all departments conduct formal psychological assessments of police candidates. These assessments typically include both measures of intelligence and some type of objective personality testing. By the 1990s, assessments of police candidates had become routine, partly because city governments were attempting to prevent or defeat lawsuits claiming that they were liable for dangerous or improper conduct by their police employees.

In theory, the assessment of candidates can focus on selecting those individuals who are most psychologically fit, or on eliminating those who appear least suited for police work. In practice, most assessments concentrate on screening out disturbed candidates because it is difficult to agree on what constitutes an ideal police profile. Screening relies on three tools: personal interviews, observations of candidates performing in special situations contrived to capture real-world police work, and psychological tests. Standardized tests of intelligence such as the Wechsler Adult Intelligence Scale and objective personality tests such as the Minnesota Multiphasic Personality Inventory-2 (MMPI-2) are the most commonly used instruments. In recent years, the Inwald Personality Inventory, a personality test designed specifically to identify psychologically unsuitable police candidates, has been used more frequently. Although the Inwald contains scales aimed at law enforcement characteristics (e.g., undue suspiciousness, trouble with law and society), its predictive validity is not significantly better than the MMPI-2.

The validity of psychological screening of police candidates is difficult to judge. Studies using police performance in the field as the criterion are so expensive and time-consuming that few departments conduct them. Instead, they examine the relationship between assessment results and supervisor ratings and/or the scores earned by recruits during training. The results are modestly positive, suggesting that the assessments afford at least enough predictive accuracy to justify their continued use and to withstand legal challenges that they have a disparate impact on certain groups of people.

Finally, most large-scale studies of police officers suggest that, as a group, they have average to above-average intelligence, do not score at the extremes on the major dimensions of personality, and are fairly conventional in their psychological adjustment. Most evidence also suggests that what has been described as a "police personality" arises more from shared occupational demands and experiences than from preexisting differences in temperament. Police officers tend to be politically conservative and loyal to one another, sometimes to the point of feeling isolated from, and cynical of, others. They are concerned with maintaining the status quo and typically pay considerable respect to authority. They report a strong motivation for serving others and for performing a job that allows them to exercise independence.

Training Police in Crisis Intervention Skills

The police are expected to resolve highly volatile disputes involving citizens who are mentally ill, intoxicated, angry, or motivated by political extremism. These situations pose significant risks to officers as well as to bystanders, so they are the subject of considerable psychological research. Special attention has been given to training the police in crisis intervention skills for the following three situations:

Interactions with the Mentally Ill. One result of the deinstitutionalization movement of the past 30 years has been that large numbers of citizens with severe mental illness find themselves without either reliable institutional or community-based care. Increasingly, the police have inherited the responsibility for supervising these individuals and deciding whether to arrest them, have them hospitalized, refer them for treatment, or offer on-the-spot counseling themselves. Historically, the police have been reluctant to arrest or hospitalize mentally ill individuals unless their behavior presents an obvious threat of danger. However, recently, it appears that arrest has become more frequent. Researchers who study this phenomenon report that the rate of severe mental illness is alarmingly high in local jail populations, almost as if the criminal justice system has become the default option for many former patients. At the same time that police are becoming more sophisticated in recognizing and managing mentally ill persons, the availability of public treatment services—other than through arrest—has been reduced. The tendency to "criminalize" the mentally ill is the unfortunate result.

Family Violence and Domestic Disturbances. About 25% of police deaths and assaults on officers take place when they respond to reports of family violence, and it is estimated that the police devote more time to domestic disturbances than they do to investigating murder, rape, and aggravated assaults combined. A major question about these incidents is whether it is better to arrest and criminally prosecute perpetrators of family violence or to provide crisis intervention and counseling as alternatives to arrest. The first project for training police to use crisis intervention rather than arrest in domestic disputes was developed in the late 1960s by psychologist Morton Bard in New York City. Since then, similar programs have been used in many other cities with mixed results. In the 1980s the pendulum swung back toward arrest as the preferred intervention for deterring repeated domestic violence. It is not clear which intervention is better for reducing recidivism, although the general climate favors arrest and criminal prosecution.

Hostage Negotiation. The massacre of 11 Israeli athletes taken hostage at the 1972 Olympic Games by Palestinian terrorists is generally regarded as the event that spurred the creation of new techniques for resolving hostage incidents. Developed over many years through extensive collaboration among behavioral science experts, military intelligence, and law enforcement officials, hostage negotiation involves the manipulation of the dynamics of hostage situations in order to end them with a minimum of violence. For example, one of the best-known dynamics is the Stockholm syndrome, which involves the mutually positive feelings that gradually develop between kidnappers and their hostages. Negotiators often try to take advantage of this dynamic and even become part of it themselves in order to steer the group toward a peaceful resolution.

Providing Psychological Services to Distressed Officers

Because police work is so stressful, a major role for police psychologists includes providing assessment and therapy services to officers who experience psychological problems related to their work. These services are often delivered following a violent incident in which the officer, a criminal suspect, and/or innocent bystanders are injured or killed. Many departments require officers who have been involved in these deadly force incidents to undergo a fitness-for-duty evaluation, designed to assess whether they have suffered psychological impairments that should prevent or delay a return to duty.

Stress management programs are now routinely available to police officers who, because of chronic stress or exposure to deadly force incidents, suffer psychological impairments. Another approach is to attempt to change those aspects of police work that officers find the most stressful. An example of this change is team policing, which is intended to increase officers' feelings of responsibility and satisfaction with decision making. If counseling is ultimately required for an officer, some departments encourage peer counseling where police officers share personal problems and discuss ways of coping with stress in order to reassure one another that their emotional reactions are normal. Other departments refer officers either to in-house individual counseling with psychologists who are department employees or to outside psychologists who consult with the department on a contractual basis.

Assisting and Consulting with Special Forms of Criminal Investigation

Because of their expertise in perception and memory, psychologists have conducted a large body of research on the factors that limit the accuracy of eyewitness identifications and the testimony that eyewitness provide during legal proceedings. As early as 1901, William Stern studied the accuracy of eyewitness memory by presenting pictures to students for 45 seconds of observation and then asking them to recall the pictures at various intervals. Based on hundreds of studies in this area, psychologists have recommended several reforms in the way police lineups and photo spreads are conducted. Police departments differ greatly in the extent to which they consider these results when conducting their lineups.

The police are eager to use techniques that increase the detail and usefulness of recollections by witnesses. Hypnotizing witnesses to facilitate their memory is one investigatory technique that has been credited with helping solve some notorious crimes such as the Boston Strangler and Chowchilla School Bus cases. Although hypnosis increases the amount of information that witnesses report remembering, it increases erroneous memories at the same time. U.S. courts have reached different conclusions about whether hypnotically refreshed testimony is admissible at trial, but the most commonly approved approach is to evaluate how the hypnotic sessions were conducted and make a case-by-case determination about admissibility. Courts look more favorably on memory-enhancement sessions that are conducted by specially trained psychologists or psychiatrists who are not employed by the prosecution, police, or defense attorney (e.g., see the 1980 New Jersey case of *State v. Hurd*). Admissibility of requested testimony is also more likely when the hypnotic sessions are tape recorded and attended only by the witness and the hypnotist.

Psychologists have studied or helped to develop three other special techniques used by police detectives. First, criminal profiling is a set of techniques used by the police to narrow an investigation to suspects who possess certain behavioral and personality features that are revealed by the way a crime was committed. Criminal profiling has been practiced at least since the late 1800s case of Jack the Ripper. Much of the research and training on profiling has been coordinated through the FBI Academy's National Center for the Analysis of Violent Crime. Profilers sketch a biographical description of the most likely type of suspect so that the police can better focus their investigation. Preliminary research suggests that profiling has some validity in helping the police concentrate in the right directions (see Pinizzotto & Finkel, 1990).

Second, the polygraph was introduced in 1917 by William Marston, an experimental psychologist who coined the term *lie detector*. Its use is based on the theory that lying will be accompanied by distinctive physiological reactions that suspects cannot control, thereby reliably distinguishing their truths from falsehoods. Considerable psychological research has been conducted on polygraphy, and the best estimate is that the technique has an overall accuracy rate of 65% or better. However, the meaning of this figure depends on the base rate (how often something happens) of liars and truth tellers among the tested population. As the frequency of lying increases, the polygraph will result in more liars being seen as truthful; as the base rate of lying drops, truth tellers are more likely to be seen as liars. Because of the controversies that surround the polygraph, most courts do not allow testimony about it in trials. However, it is widely used in the initial stages of criminal investigations, often to convince suspects that they should confess because they will be unable to "beat" the polygraph in the long run.

Third, psychologists have investigated the effects of various procedures that police use in eliciting confessions from suspects. Because confessions are recanted in about 20% of all criminal cases, it is important to understand the factors that might contribute to false confessions and to make sure that jurors use the appropriate amount of caution in evaluating confessions.

Interventions for Crime Prevention and Improved Community Relations

Psychologists often consult with police departments about managerial and organizational changes that would improve the agencies' overall functioning and reduce internal conflicts. In most cases, the consultation involves the principles of industrial/organizational psychology tailored to the unique demands of the law enforcement agency. In other instances, the consultation is directed to external problems, for example, when psychologists help departments design and evaluate interventions to prevent crime and improve community relations. Frequently, these two goals go hand in hand. A primary example is community-based policing, a policy that increases the number of direct contacts by police officers with citizens in a given neighborhood. The main assumptions of community-based policy are that the concentrated presence of the same police officers in a given neighborhood will promote a closer identification between the officers and the residents of the neighborhood, will increase the officers' knowledge of the hot spots for crime, and will "harden the target" for crimes by aggressively taking away the criminal opportunities afforded by abandoned houses, broken windows in buildings, and unsupervised spaces. As with most social reforms, the results of community-based policing are mixed: some cities report large reductions in rates of serious crimes along with improved public attitudes toward the police, whereas others indicate little change in crime rates or community relations.

The Future of Police Psychology

The recent history of law enforcement has seen increasing reliance on the application of science and technology to police work. The relevance of research discoveries in the behavioral sciences to police activities can therefore be anticipated to grow along with opportunities for psychologists to be employed and consulted by police departments. Although specialized degree programs in police psychology may emerge, the long-term advances in the field will most likely depend on new knowledge accumulating in traditional subdisciplines such as clinical psychology, social psychology, industrial/organizational psychology, and experimental psychology.

[*See also* Criminality; Forensic Psychology; *and* Law and Psychology.]

Bibliography

Ainsworth, P. B. (1995). *Psychology and policing in a changing world.* New York: Wiley.

Bartol, C. R., & Bartol, A. (1994). *Psychology and law: Research and applications.* Pacific Grove, CA: Brooks/Cole.

Blau, T. H. (1994). *Psychological services for law enforcement.* New York: Wiley.

Kurke, M. I., & Scrivner, E. M. (Eds.). (1995). *Police psychology into the 21st century.* Mahwah, NJ: Erlbaum.

Pinizzotto, X., & Finkel, X. (1990). *Law and Human Behavior, 14,* 215–234.

Wrightsman, L. S., Nietzel, M. T., & Fortune, W. H. (1998). *Psychology and the legal system.* Pacific Grove, CA: Brooks/Cole.

Michael T. Nietzel

POLITICAL BEHAVIOR. [*This entry describes the political processes and behavior at the level of the individual.*]

A great deal of research during the twentieth century explored psychological aspects of individual political behavior. Most of this research was driven by an underlying concern about the viability of democratic government. If democracies are to be effective, some political theorists say, then citizens must be well informed and thoughtful about their nation's political past, present, and future, and they must send messages to government in ways that direct its actions according to their desires. Consequently, much research has explored how people's political beliefs and attitudes are formed and changed, as well as the forces that inspire them to perform particular types of political behavior.

Political Attitude and Belief Formation and Change

A great deal of political psychology research has examined the origins and consequences of people's political attitudes and beliefs. We will describe a series of literatures on these topics, addressing the agents of attitude and belief change, the psychological ingredients of attitudes and beliefs, and the process by which attitudes and beliefs are integrated when people select from among competing candidates running for public office.

Agents of Change. News media coverage of politics shapes public attitudes in a number of ways. One effect is agenda setting, whereby the more coverage the media devote to an issue, the more nationally important people perceive the issue to be (Iyengar & Kinder, 1987). Another media effect is priming, whereby people judge the performance of government officials based mostly on issues heavily covered by the media (Krosnick & Kinder, 1990). News media coverage can also frame an issue by drawing people's attention to some aspects of the issue and ignoring others (Iyengar, 1991). The news media also make government especially salient as a force influencing social life, so people who are highly exposed to the media tend to credit or blame government more for the country's fortunes and misfortunes (Abramowitz, Lanoue, & Ramesh, 1988).

Political events and debates among political figures provoke public attitude change (Zaller, 1992). Commentaries by news reporters can cause sizable opinion change. Also, news stories reporting the opinions of experts on a topic or the findings of research studies tend to sway public opinion, as do speeches by presidents and other prominent political figures. Surprisingly, when interest groups strongly advocate a position, the public tends to move in the opposite direction. Wars, other international crises, and shifts in the state of the national economy provoke changes in public preferences regarding government policy. People are also sometimes persuaded to adopt certain attitudes toward specific government policies because the policies are endorsed by their preferred candidates during debates.

Ingredients of Beliefs and Attitudes. Ingredients of beliefs and attitudes include self-interest, ideology, and attributions.

Self-Interest. Many observers believe that a person's attitude toward a government policy is determined partly by his or her self-interest, which is "the short to medium-term impact on the material well-being of the individual's own personal life" (Sears & Funk, 1991). However, self-interest predicts attitude direction only when the potential gains or losses are substantial and people are well informed about those gains and losses (Sears & Funk, 1991). As such, self-interest has influenced voting on tax reform propositions and attitudes toward smoking restrictions. When people's self-interest is at stake in an issue, they manifest greater consistency among their attitudes on the issue and greater consistency between their attitudes and behaviors. The more self-interest is at stake in an issue, the more importance the person is likely to attach to his or her attitude on the issue (Boninger, Krosnick, & Berent, 1995).

Ideology. Politicians tend to be either liberals or conservatives, with each group generally having a different vision of what government should do. Therefore, citizens would presumably have an easy time choosing politicians to represent them in government if they themselves are also either consistently liberal or consistently conservative. However, most people are not and instead hold a mix of liberal positions on some issues and conservative positions on other issues.

Rather than simply reflecting liberal or conservative principles, people base their opinions on general values such as individualism (the belief that people should get ahead in life based on their own hard work) and egalitarianism (the belief that everyone should have an equal opportunity for advancement). Different people endorse these principles to differing degrees, and a particular person's views on policy issues often reflect these sorts of values and the person's perceptions of the relevance of these values to particular issues (Judd & Krosnick, 1991).

Attributions. In order to decide what they would like government to do, people must make sense of the political events that unfold around them. A principal aspect of making sense of events involves understanding what causes them. People appear to be systematic analysts of causality in politics, and the conclusions they draw from such analyses play important roles in their political reasoning.

One illustration of this process emerged when scholars discovered that the political party controlling the U.S. presidency tends to be reelected when the nation's economy is perceived to be good and tends not to be reelected when the economy is perceived to be deteriorating. Scholars initially presumed that this was so because people vote according to their pocketbooks; people who are doing well economically vote for the incumbent party, and the better the economy, the more such voters exist. However, it turns out that people do not attribute their own economic status to government action, so they don't vote their pocketbooks. Rather, people usually hold government responsible only for the entire country's economic situation and vote according to whether it seems to be good or bad (Feldman, 1984). Interestingly, women and liberals are especially likely to hold government responsible for the nation's economic condition (Iyengar, 1991).

Political attributions also influence people's attitudes on policy issues. For example, people who believe that generations of slavery and discrimination have prevented African Americans from having equal opportunities for success in contemporary society are especially likely to favor government programs to remedy this situation (Kinder & Sanders, 1996). Likewise, blaming government for poverty leads people to favor government programs to ameliorate poverty (Kluegel & Smith, 1986).

Attributions also play important roles in people's reasoning about political scandals. When a politician is found to have committed a misdeed of some kind, he or she often offers excuses (denying responsibility) and/or justifications (denying offensiveness) for the action. Politicians are viewed negatively when they claim ignorance as an excuse or when they blame their subordinates for committing the act. But when politicians convincingly explain the benefits of their action or explain past mitigating circumstances that justify it, people evaluate them more positively (McGraw, 1991).

Voter Decision Making. Research has explored processes of perceiving politicians and forming preferences among them.

Perceptions of Politicians' Attitudes. Some political theorists believe that for democracy to function, citizens must elect candidates with whom they agree on policy issues. In order to vote for candidates according to this criterion, citizens must decide what candidates' attitudes are toward various policies. Since the 1970s, political psychologists have been interested in the notion that people may project their own attitudes onto candidates they like and project disagreeable attitudes onto candidates they dislike. In this sense, people may rationalize their candidate preferences by distorting their sense of candidates' stands on policy issues.

Although many studies have reported results consistent with this hypothesis, there are shortcomings inherent in the methods used in these investigations. Recent research using improved methods has found no such distortions of candidates' attitudes to rationalize voters' likes and dislikes of candidates (Krosnick, 1990). Furthermore, people seem remarkably accurate in their perceptions of candidates' positions on issues, especially in light of the fact that candidates rarely state clearly where they stand (Page, 1978). Thus, the criterion that voters accurately perceive candidates' stands on issues is often met.

Candidate Preferences. How do voters decide which candidate to vote for in an election? Research on elections in the 1940s and 1950s showed that voters' choices were shaped partly by basic dispositions: demographic characteristics such as social class, religion, and place of residence (Lazarsfeld, Berelson, & Gaudet, 1944) and identification with a political party (Campbell, Converse, Miller, & Stokes, 1960). More recently, party identification has not been as powerful a determinant of votes, in part because identification with political parties has weakened (Wattenberg, 1991).

People are now more likely to vote for the candidate (1) with whom they most agree on policy issues they care most about (Krosnick, 1988a); (2) who most closely shares their ideology (Knight, 1985); (3) of the incumbent party if they believe that the incumbent has performed well in handling national problems (Fiorina, 1981); (4) who is perceived to possess more competence, integrity, leadership strength, and empathy (Kinder, 1986); and (5) who evokes more positive emotions from voters (Abelson, Kinder, Peters, & Fiske, 1982). People who are more knowledgeable about politics place more weight on policy issue and ideological agreement, whereas less knowledgeable people are more likely to vote based on the parties of the candidates, their perceived personalities, and the performance of the incumbent party in handling national problems (Knight, 1985).

Although some voters approach the candidate evaluation task in a memory-based fashion, most do so online (Lodge, McGraw, & Stroh, 1989). Less politically knowledgeable people tend to use a memory-based approach, entering the voting booth and making choices based on the considerations they can bring to mind (e.g., Kelley, 1983). More politically knowledgeable people tend to use an on-line approach, constructing evaluations of each candidate throughout the campaign and simply retrieving and comparing those evaluations in the voting booth.

Political Behavior

Citizens in a democracy communicate their preferences to elected officials through behavior: by helping organized lobbying efforts, by expressing attitudes publicly, by contacting legislators directly, by turning out to vote in elections, by participating in social protests, and more. Summaries of some research on each of these topics follow.

Issue Publics. The American electorate can be divided into "issue publics," small groups of people who are deeply concerned about a particular government policy issue (e.g., the abortion issue public, the gun control issue public). Issue public members are most likely to express their views on an issue to government officials, to contribute money to lobbying organizations, and to write letters to the editor that are published in newspapers and magazines (Schuman & Presser, 1981). Therefore, government policy on an issue is especially likely to correspond to the desires of the majority of the issue public (Krosnick & Telhami, 1995). Issue public members also vote for candidates who share their views on the issues they care about most, thus shaping government actions by selecting elected representatives as well (Krosnick, 1988a). People become members of an issue public because the issue is relevant to their material self-interest, to the interests or identities of individuals or groups with which they identify, or to their cherished values (Boninger, Krosnick, & Berent, 1995).

If issue public members are emotionally overwrought zealots, then one might imagine that they represent threats to rational and effective politics. But in fact, issue public members tend to have beliefs and attitudes that reflect systematic and informed perceptions of the political world. People who care deeply about an issue selectively expose themselves to information about that issue, think deeply about that information, and accumulate large stores of highly accurate knowledge in memory (Boninger, Krosnick, Berent, & Fabrigar, 1995). As a result, issue public members are especially likely to have firmly crystallized attitudes that are resistant to change (Krosnick, 1988b) and that reflect their core values (Krosnick, 1990).

Voter Turnout. Voting is one of the most common political activities in which citizens engage (Verba, Schlozman, & Brady, 1995). In order to vote in the United States, people must first be registered. People with greater cognitive resources (e.g., more education, more political experience, more political knowledge) and with strong ties to their communities are more likely to know how to register and are therefore more likely to do so (Rosenstone & Hansen, 1993).

Once registered, people must have the resources necessary to vote. Individuals with greater cognitive abilities are more likely to vote, in part because they are better able to process information relevant to the election (Rosenstone & Hansen, 1993). People with ties to the community care more about what others think of them and are therefore more likely to vote (a socially positive behavior) for self-presentational reasons (Rosenstone & Hansen, 1993). In addition, even a simple act like voting demands transportation and time, both of which are more likely to be had by those with economic resources (Rosenstone & Hansen, 1993). Racial minorities are less likely to vote, partly because they sometimes have fewer necessary resources (Verba & Nie, 1972).

Even registered and able respondents may not vote unless they are motivated to do so. Citizens may vote because they care about the outcome of an election or because they believe that their votes will affect the outcome (Verba & Nie, 1972). In addition, voter turnout is increased by having more positive attitudes toward the candidates in a race and preferring one candidate far more than the other (Rosenstone & Hansen, 1993).

Other Forms of Political Participation. Citizens' political participation can also include other activities. For example, many people engage in campaign-related behaviors, such as working on behalf of candidates or contributing money to campaigns (Verba et al., 1995). These types of activities can be done with relatively few resources and are performed by people with particular attitudes and demographic characteristics (e.g., Verba et al., 1995).

A smaller percentage of people engage in more costly, effortful types of participation, such as contacting a politician (Verba et al., 1995). Individuals often perform such activities when their interests or the interests of groups with which they identify are at stake (Verba et al., 1995). Parents play an important role in influencing the extent to which their children participate in politics, and citizens are especially likely to become active if they are asked to do so (Verba et al., 1995). Because more educated, wealthier people are more likely to be asked to perform effortful activities, they are more likely to do so (Verba et al., 1995).

A social movement occurs when a large group of people organize to pursue particular political goals. Participation in these movements results from a number of causal factors: (1) widespread dissatisfaction with public policy, which a social movement hopes to alter (Barnes, Farah, & Heunks, 1971); (2) psychological stress from a major social or economic event (such as an economic depression), which can inspire the hardest-hit individuals to express their frustration and solve it (Smelser, 1962); (3) people's desire to pursue their self-interests (Ferree, 1992), to express their values, or to protect social groups they care about (Johnson, Larana, & Gusfield, 1994); and (4) the availability of financial and other resources to support collective action (e.g., McCarthy & Zald, 1973).

People may also join social movements to express their social values or because of their identity in a group (Johnson et al., 1994). In fact, people sometimes engage in social protest to express a value even if they believe that they will gain nothing from the movement (e.g., Oliver, 1983).

Obedience to Authority. When and why citizens choose to obey political authorities has been the subject of much social psychological research (Tyler, 1990). The more people feel that the judgments, decisions, and procedures of the government are fair, the more obedient they are. Perceptions of fairness increase compliance with water restrictions (Tyler & Degoey, 1995), waste management laws (Ebreo, Linn, & Vining, 1996), and many other sorts of regulations. Unfortunately, authorities perceived to be legitimate can also elicit immoral or illegal behaviors from people (Kelman & Hamilton, 1989).

Authoritarians are people who are especially disposed to obey authority figures (Altemeyer, 1988). The trait of authoritarianism is composed of three attitudinal clusters: authoritarian submission (the degree to which a person feels that submission to governmental authority is legitimate), authoritarian aggression (the degree to which a person will be aggressive toward others in accordance with perceived governmental policy), and conventionalism (the degree to which a person complies with perceived governmental and societal norms).

Authoritarians tend to hold negative attitudes toward homosexuals (Haddock, Zanna, & Esses, 1993), African Americans (Duckitt & Farre, 1994), and environmentalism (Schultz & Stone, 1994) and positive attitudes toward harsh solutions to social problems (Peterson, Doty, & Winter, 1993). Authoritarians are also especially likely to vote for a bill to reduce benefits to immigrants (California Proposition 187; Quinton, Cowan, & Watson, 1996) and are especially likely to perform orthodox religious behavior (Leak & Randall, 1995).

Conclusion

As we hope this review makes clear, much fascinating research has illuminated the workings of the human mind in the context of politics. We have reviewed only a small portion of the research on the political psychology of the individual, and we encourage readers to consult books (e.g., Hermann, 1986) and review articles (e.g., Kinder, 1998) describing more of this work.

As a whole, this work suggests that people are generally well informed about many aspects of politics, and that they use systematic decision making in forming and changing their political beliefs and attitudes. Furthermore, political behavior appears to be instigated by considerations and forces that seem both reasonable and consonant with democratic political philosophy. Therefore, when taken together, these research findings suggest that the psychological conditions necessary for effective democracy often seem to exist.

[*See also* Political Decision Making; *and* Political Leadership.]

Bibliography

Abelson, R. P., Kinder, D. R., Peters, M. D., & Fiske, S. T. (1982). Affective and semantic components in political person perception. *Journal of Personality and Social Psychology, 42*, 619–630.

Abramowitz, A. I., Lanoue, D. J., & Ramesh, S. (1988). Economic conditions, causal attributions, and political evaluations in the 1984 presidential election. *Journal of Politics, 50*, 848–863.

Altemeyer, B. (1988). *Enemies of freedom: Understanding right-wing authoritarianism*. San Francisco: Jossey-Bass.

Barnes, S. H., Farah, B. G., & Heunks, F. (1971). Personal dissatisfaction. In S. H. Barnes & M. Kaase (Eds.), *Political action: Mass participation in five western democracies* (pp. 381–407). Beverly Hills, CA: Sage.

Boninger, D. S., Krosnick, J. A., & Berent, M. K. (1995). Origins of attitude importance: Self-interest, social identification, and value relevance. *Journal of Personality and Social Psychology, 68*, 61–80.

Boninger, D. S., Krosnick, J. A., Berent, M. K., & Fabrigar, L. R. (1995). The causes and consequences of attitude importance. In R. E. Petty & J. A. Krosnick (Eds.), *Attitude strength: Antecedents and consequences* (pp. 159–189). Hillsdale, NJ: Erlbaum.

Campbell, A., Converse, P. E., Miller, W. E., & Stokes, D. E. (1960). *The American voter*. New York: Wiley.

Duckitt, J., & Farre, B. (1994). Right-wing authoritarianism and political intolerance among Whites in the future majority-rule South Africa. *Journal of Social Psychology, 134*, 735–741.

Ebreo, A., Linn, N., & Vining, J. (1996). The impact of procedural justice on opinions of public policy: Solid waste management as an example. *Journal of Applied Social Psychology, 26*, 1259–1285.

Feldman, S. (1984). Economic self-interest and the vote: Evidence and meaning. *Political Behavior, 6*, 229–251.

Ferree, M. M. (1992). The political context of rationality: Rational choice theory and resource mobilization. In A. D. Morris & C. M. Mueller (Eds.), *Frontiers in social movement theory* (pp. 29–52). New Haven, CT: Yale University Press.

Fiorina, M. P. (1981). *Retrospective voting in American national elections.* New Haven, CT: Yale University Press.

Haddock, G., Zanna, M. P., & Esses, V. M. (1993). Assessing the structure of prejudicial attitudes: The case of attitudes toward homosexuals. *Journal of Personality and Social Psychology, 65,* 1105–1118.

Iyengar, S. (1991). *Is anyone responsible?* Chicago: University of Chicago Press.

Iyengar, S., & Kinder, D. R. (1987). *News that matters.* Chicago: University of Chicago Press.

Johnson, H., Larana, E., & Gusfield, J. R. (1994). Identities, grievances, and new social movements. In E. Larana, H. Johnson, & J. R. Gusfield (Eds.), *New social movements: From ideology to identity* (pp. 3–35). Philadelphia: Temple University Press.

Judd, C. M., & Krosnick, J. A. (1989). The structural bases of consistency among political attitudes: The effects of political expertise and attitude importance. In A. R. Pratkanis, S. J. Breckler, & A. G. Greenwald (Eds.), *Attitude structure and function* (pp. 99–128). Hillsdale, NJ: Erlbaum.

Kelley, S. (1983). *Interpreting elections.* Princeton, NJ: Princeton University Press.

Kelman, H. C., & Hamilton, L. (1989). *Crimes of obedience: Toward a social psychology of authority and responsibility.* New Haven, CT: Yale University Press.

Kinder, D. R. (1986). Presidential character revisited. In R. R. Lau & D. O. Sears (Eds.), *Political cognition* (pp. 233–255). Hillsdale, NJ: Erlbaum.

Kinder, D. R., & Sanders, L. M. (1996). *Divided by color: Racial politics and democratic ideals.* Chicago: University of Chicago Press.

Kluegel, J. R., & Smith, E. R. (1986). *Beliefs about inequality.* New York: Aldine.

Knight, K. (1985). Ideology in the 1985 election: Ideological sophistication does matter. *Journal of Politics, 47,* 828–853.

Krosnick, J. A. (1988a). The role of importance in social evaluations: A study of policy references, presidential candidate evaluations and voting behavior. *Journal of Personality and Social Psychology, 55,* 196–210.

Krosnick, J. A. (1988b). Attitude importance and attitude change. *Journal of Experimental Social Psychology, 24,* 240–255.

Krosnick, J. A. (1990). Americans' perceptions of presidential candidates: A test of the projection hypothesis. *Journal of Social Issues, 46,* 159–182.

Krosnick, J. A., & Kinder, D. R. (1990). Altering the foundations of support for the President through priming. *American Political Science Review, 84,* 497–512.

Krosnick, J. A., & Telhami, S. (1995). Public attitudes toward Israel: A study of attentive and issue publics. *International Studies Quarterly, 39,* 535–554.

Lazarsfeld, P. F., Berelson, B., & Gaudet, H. (1944). *The people's choice.* New York: Columbia University Press.

Leak, G. K., & Randall, B. A. (1995). Clarification of the link between right-wing authoritarianism and religiousness: The role of religious maturity. *Journal for the Scientific Study of Religion, 34,* 245–252.

Lodge, M., McGraw, K. M., & Stroh, P. (1989). An impression-driven model of candidate evaluation. *American Political Science Review, 83,* 399–419.

McCarthy, J. D., & Zald, M. N. (1973). *The trend of social movements in America: Professionalism and resource mobilization.* Morristown, NJ: General Learning Press.

McGraw, K. M. (1991). Managing blame: An experimental test of the effects of political accounts. *American Political Science Review, 85,* 1133–1157.

Oliver, P. (1983). The mobilization of paid volunteer activists in the neighborhood movement. *Research in Social Movements: Conflict and Change, 5,* 133–170.

Page, B. I. (1978). *Choices and echoes in presidential elections.* Chicago: University of Chicago Press.

Peterson, B. E., Doty, R. M., & Winter, D. G. (1993). Authoritarianism and attitudes toward contemporary social issues. *Personality and Social Psychology Bulletin, 19,* 174–184.

Quinton, W. J., Cowan, G., & Watson, B. D. (1996). Personality and attitudinal predictors of support of proposition 187—California's anti-illegal immigrant initiative. *Journal of Applied Social Psychology, 26,* 2204–2223.

Rosenstone, S. J., & Hansen, J. M. (1993). *Mobilization, participation, and democracy in America.* New York: Macmillan.

Schultz, P. W., & Stone, W. F. (1994). Authoritarianism and attitudes toward the environment. *Environment and Behavior, 26,* 25–37.

Schuman, H., & Presser, S. (1981). *Questions and answers in attitude surveys.* New York: Academic Press.

Sears, D. O., & Funk, C. L. (1991). The role of self-interest in social and political attitudes. In M. Zanna (Ed.), *Advances in experimental social psychology* (Vol. 24, pp. 1–91). Orlando, FL: Academic Press.

Smelser, N. J. (1962). *Theory of collective behavior.* New York: Free Press.

Tyler, T. R. (1990). *Why people obey the law.* New Haven, CT: Yale University Press.

Tyler, T. R., & Degoey, P. (1995). Collective restraint in social dilemmas: Procedural justice and social identification effects on support for authorities. *Journal of Personality and Social Psychology, 69,* 482–497.

Verba, S., & Nie, N. H. (1972). *Participation in America: Political democracy and social equality.* New York: Harper & Row.

Verba, S., Schlozman, K. L., & Brady, H. E. (1995). *Voice and equality: Civic voluntarism in American politics.* Cambridge, MA: Harvard University Press.

Wattenberg, M. P. (1991). *The rise of candidate-centered politics: Presidential elections of the 1980's.* Cambridge, MA: Harvard University Press.

Zaller, J. (1992). *The nature and origins of mass opinion.* New York: Cambridge University Press.

Allyson L. Holbrook, George Y. Bizer, and Jon A. Krosnick

POLITICAL DECISION MAKING. The decisions of a country's top-level political leaders are often profoundly consequential; they can have implications for social order and justice, economic prosperity and growth, and war and peace. What do the decision processes of these leaders look like? How are problems identified? How are choices made? To address these questions is to confront a problem: analysts have only limited access to those they seek to analyze. Elite decision makers rarely submit to in-depth interviewing by researchers. What information they do communicate may be distorted by the inaccuracies of memory, imperfect insight into their own thought processes and motives, and, not least, the desire to create a favorable impression. Memoirs and archival materials (memoranda, reports, and minutes of meetings) are not only subject to similar distortions, but also are never so complete as to fully identify who says what to whom with what intention and with what effect. Finally, even when the historical record is richly informative about particular episodes of elite decision making, one may wonder whether these episodes are representative of less well-documented ones.

Rational-Choice Approaches

Some approaches to the study of elite decision making require less access to elite decision makers than others. Notably undemanding in this respect are those that rely on rational-choice theory. The theory asserts that elites possess stable and ordered goals, assess the likely costs and benefits of available policy options in light of these goals, and rank the options accordingly. At least in principle, application of the theory is straightforward. Who are the relevant elites? These can be taken to be defined by the decision problem itself. What are their basic goals? These can be discovered in the public statements of elites or inferred from the bureaucratic roles they occupy. What options are available to elites and what are the costs and benefits of each option? Again, an analysis of the decision problem itself can reveal the likely answers. In short, rational-choice theory promises accounts of elite decision making that rely relatively little on information about the psychological processes of the people involved and much on the analyst's construction of the circumstances they face. In the rational-choice view, elite decision makers tend to respond to these circumstances in a highly rational fashion.

Can this view of elite rationality be defended? One supporting argument stresses the consequential nature of elite decisions: the high stakes involved in the issues are said to induce high levels of rationality in the decision makers. A second argument stresses the complexity of the political process: institutional checks and balances are said to prevent the translation of personal foibles into public policy. A third argument is perhaps most compelling: models consistent with the tenets of rational-choice theory have been used to predict elite policy choices successfully in a wide variety of contexts. Focusing on the Council of Ministers of the European Community, for example, political scientist Bruce Bueno de Mesquita has demonstrated the ability of an "expected-utility" model to predict council decisions regarding automobile regulations, air transport, bank policy, and regulation of radioactive emissions. Bueno de Mesquita's model requires estimates of each member's preferred policy position on an issue, the salience of the issue for each member, and the potential influence that each member could bring to bear on the others. The model itself consists of an algorithm, a mathematical recipe, that translates this information into a prediction of the council's final decision.

However, none of these arguments in support of rational-choice theory has escaped criticism. First, although the importance of the stakes and the arrangement of institutions might plausibly channel elite attention in a seemingly desirable direction, these same factors might just as plausibly produce the contrary effect by arousing multiple constituencies, concerns, and definitions of the situation. Second, although some rational-choice-inspired models do, indeed, predict elite behavior quite well, prediction is not the same as explanation. To show that elites make decisions *as if* they conformed to the theory is not to demonstrate that they do so in fact. Finally, considerable evidence suggests that, for all but the simplest decision problems, the degree of rationality described in rational-choice theory may not even be humanly possible. According to Herbert Simon, a Nobel laureate in economics, human rationality is best conceived as "bounded rationality"; because decision makers have limited cognitive capacities, they must resort to simplifying strategies when confronted with complicated choices. Examples of simplifying strategies include relying on a reduced representation of the problem, selectively attending to information, truncating the search for alternatives, or estimating consequences in an unsystematic manner.

Psychological Approaches

Most psychological approaches to the study of elite decision making rest on two assumptions. First, elites tend to be rational, but bounded in their rationality. Second, the issues they face tend to be characterized by complexity, uncertainty, and ambiguity. Elites must grapple with the need to reconcile multiple and competing values and interests; they frequently lack the information needed to assess the outcomes associated with various alternatives; and they may even find it difficult to determine their preferences in a given situation in the first place. To understand elite choices, then, requires more than a knowledge of the external circumstances they face. It requires a knowledge of how elites perceive and interpret their circumstances.

The process of elite decision making can be divided

into two phases: a representation phase, in which the problem is defined, and a solution phase, in which the solution is presented. The first phase can be said to begin with the perception of anomalous events. To make sense of these events, elites must develop a definition of the situation, a mental representation of the problem that will allow them to decide what to do. Arriving at this representation is likely to involve a (not necessarily thorough) consideration of past experience, present goals, and possible constraints in which their own knowledge and beliefs play a major role.

A principal method by which analysts have sought to identify elite beliefs is content analysis, the systematic examination of written or verbal records. Through content analysis, particular attention has been devoted to the "operational codes" of elites, their "cognitive maps," and their "cognitive complexity." The notion of an operational code was first introduced by the political scientist Nathan Leites in a 1951 study of the Soviet Politburo. Two other political scientists, Alexander George and Ole Holsti, refined the concept, and a third, Stephen Walker, developed systematic measurement procedures. Analyzing a leader's operational code involves answering a series of questions about his or her diagnostic propensities, choice propensities, and attitudes toward risk. For example: Does the leader regard politics as essentially cooperative or conflictful? Does the leader regard the political actions of others as generally predictable or unpredictable? Is the leader inclined to cooperative or competitive strategies? Is the leader generally risk averse or risk acceptant? Most operational code studies focus on heads of government or foreign ministers. Walker, for example, derived Henry Kissinger's operational code from writings and speeches and concluded that it affected Kissinger's behavior in the negotiations ending the Vietnam War.

A second approach to identifying elite beliefs is cognitive mapping. Developed in the early 1970s by political scientists Robert Axelrod, G. Matthew Bonham, and Michael Shapiro, cognitive mapping involves constructing a graph of nodes and arrows in which the nodes represent the concepts that elites employ in the discussion of an issue and the arrows represent the alleged causal relations among these concepts, either positive, negative, or neutral. The result is a picture of how concepts are perceived to relate to each other and the overall structure of these relationships. For example, Bonham and his associates constructed cognitive maps from early exchanges between President Kennedy and Premier Khrushchev on the topic of nuclear weapons testing and discovered apparent cultural differences between the two men in the basic knowledge structures they used to represent political reality. Examining later exchanges, however, the authors found that the cognitive maps of the men had grown more similar, a precondition, the authors hypothesized, for a test-ban agreement. Michael Young, a political scientist, has recently developed a much more elaborate, computer-based system for cognitive mapping, called "WorldView." "WorldView" distinguishes among six different kinds of causal assertions; identifies non-causal assertions about truth, falsity, possibility, and impossibility; and provides a variety of measures for describing the structure of cognitive maps and for comparing one map with another. A map's "size," for example, can be expected to indicate a policy maker's relative expertise.

A third approach, developed in the late 1970s by social psychologists Peter Suedfeld and Philip Tetlock, seeks to identify not the content of elite beliefs, but the cognitive complexity of belief structures. In this approach, cognitive complexity is defined and measured in terms of degrees of differentiation and integration. Differentiation refers to the number of dimensions and perspectives that a leader considers in the discussion of an issue, and integration refers to the number and nature of connections among the differentiated dimensions and perspectives. Elites high in cognitive complexity appear more sensitive to new information and better able to see policy options and opportunities for compromise. At the same time, they appear more likely to give undue weight to irrelevant information and more able to dismiss troublesome, inconsistent information. The level of cognitive complexity among elites may also affect their susceptibility to the influence of public opinion and interest groups: cognitive complexity appears to be enhanced by feelings of responsibility and accountability to others.

A different source of insight into the influence of problem representation on elite choices is "prospect theory," introduced in 1979 by psychologists Daniel Kahneman and Amos Tversky. Based on experimental evidence, prospect theory asserts that people tend to assess alternatives in relation to a reference point defining an acceptable outcome. Further, they tend to treat prospective deviations from this reference point as either "gains" or "losses," regarding losses as more painful than gains are pleasurable. Finally, people tend to be risk-acceptant in attempting to avoid losses and risk-averse in attempting to pursue gains. These results are significant because they suggest that, in the representation of a problem, the selection of a reference point and the labeling of alternatives (whether as "gains" or "losses") can have a profound effect on the willingness of elites to take risks. Prospect theory suggests, for example, that leaders will accommodate more slowly to losses than to gains and take more risks to maintain their international positions, reputations, and domestic political support than they will to enhance them.

The line between the problem representation and solution phases of a decision process is often difficult to draw. In some instances, a problem's representation will readily suggest its solution, with little need on the part of elites to generate alternatives. In other instances, the representation and solution phases will repeat themselves, with objections to a proposal for action leading to a new representation, a new proposal, a new objection, and so on, until an acceptable proposal is found. Studies of decision processes associated with foreign-policy crises in a variety of countries suggest that the first scenario is more likely where the policy group is small and homogeneous, or dominated by a leader who is insensitive to advice from others. The latter scenario appears more likely in large and heterogeneous groups. Each scenario can be seen to be associated with a particular decision-making malady, "groupthink" in the first case, and "bureaucratic politics" in the second.

Introduced by psychologist Irving Janis in a 1972 study centering on several U.S. foreign-policy fiascos, "groupthink" refers to a decision process in which participants let their desire for group unanimity override and cut short their critical appraisal of alternative courses of action. In Janis's theory, the antecedent conditions of groupthink are to be sought in feelings of stress among group members, group cohesiveness, a group's insulation from the judgments of qualified outsiders, an absence of systematic methods for gathering and appraising information, and in group leaders who assertively promote their own opinions. Subsequent research, both in the laboratory and in government archives, has tended to confirm the effects of only the last three of these conditions.

If "groupthink" describes a decision process with too much emphasis on achieving unity and not enough on generating debate, "bureaucratic politics" describes the opposite vice: a process with too much debate and not enough unity. Bureaucratic politics is said to occur when members of a decision-making group represent various government ministries, departments, agencies, or bureaus and seek to advance and protect the interests of their organization against challenges from competing organizations with little concern for government policy as a whole. One possible consequence of bureaucratic politics is policy stagnation, where the bargaining among decision makers results in deadlock, in the inability of decision makers to take collective action. A second possible consequence is policy incoherence, where the bargaining among decision makers results in compromises such that the policies pursued are either mutually contradictory or bear little relation to the problems they were meant to address.

Is either groupthink or bureaucratic politics a common feature of elite decision processes? What can be said about the quality of elite decision making in general? The available evidence is best suited to judgments that are limited, tentative, and comparative. Given the structural complexity of most governments today, bureaucratic politics would seem to be a more common problem than groupthink. Certainly, studies of cabinet decision making in European democracies lend support to this conclusion. But groupthink and bureaucratic politics are broad syndromes. Focusing on foreign-policy decision making in the American White House and working from a list originally developed by Janis, a number of researchers have sought to identify the presence or absence of a more narrowly defined set of defects. Janis's list includes gross omissions in surveying both alternatives and objectives, failure to reexamine the costs and risks of the preferred choice, poor information search, biased processing of available information, failure to reconsider originally rejected alternatives, and failure to work out implementation, monitoring, and contingency plans. Three generalizations emerge. First, elites appear to consider policy options one at a time on a yes-or-no basis more often than they weigh alternative policies against one another. Second, the biased use of available information appears to be a more common problem than the inadequate search for new information. Finally, the overall quality of decision making appears to vary considerably, not only between presidential administrations but sometimes within them. In a study of 19 international crises from 1945 to 1975, Janis, along with psychologist Gregory Herek and political scientist Paul Huth, concluded that White House decision processes were of high quality in eight crises and of low quality in seven. Perhaps these are the results to be expected of elites who tend to be rational, but bounded in their rationality.

[*See also* Decision Making; Political Behavior; Political Leadership; *and* Thinking, *article on* Problem Solving.]

Bibliography

Beach, L. R. (1997). *The psychology of decision making: People in organizations.* Thousand Oaks, CA: Sage Publications. Not specifically about political elites, but a clear, well-organized, and insightful survey.

Bonham, M. G., Sergeev, V. M., & Parshin, P. B. (1997). The limited test-ban agreement: Emergence of new knowledge structures in international negotiation. *International Studies Quarterly, 41,* 215–240. Illustrates basic techniques of cognitive mapping and discusses recent advances.

Bueno de Mesquita, B., & Stokman, F. N. (Eds.). (1994). *European Community decision making: Models, applications, and comparisons.* New Haven, CT: Yale University Press. Compares the predictive performance of two quite different rational-choice-inspired models.

George, A. L. (1980). *Presidential decisionmaking in foreign policy: The effective use of information and advice.* Boulder, CO: Westview Press. A classic. Integrates individual, small group, and organizational levels of analysis.

Herek, G. M., Janis, I. L., & Huth, P. (1987). Decision making during international crises: Is quality of process related to outcome? *Journal of Conflict Resolution, 31*, 203–226. Unusually ambitious and systematic attempt to assess the quality of elite decision processes.

Janis, I. L. (1982). *Groupthink: Psychological studies of policy decisions and fiascos* (2nd ed.). Boston: Houghton Mifflin.

Levy, J. S. (1997). Prospect theory, rational choice, and international relations. *International Studies Quarterly, 41*, 87–112. Discusses prospect theory, the challenges it poses for rational-choice theory, and its possible implications for foreign-policy decision making.

Simon, H. A. (1985). Human nature in politics: The dialogue of psychology with political science. *American Political Science Review, 79*, 293–304. Compares two conceptions of rationality in a critique of rational-choice theory.

Sylvan, D. A., & Voss, J. F. (Eds.). (1998). *Problem representation in foreign policy decision making*. Cambridge: Cambridge University Press.

Tetlock, P. E. (1998). Social psychology and world politics. In D. T. Gilbert, S. T. Fiske, & G. Lindzey (Eds.), *The handbook of social psychology: Vol. 2*. (4th ed., pp. 868–912). A masterful survey of an extensive literature.

't Hart, P., Stern, E. K., & Sundelius, B. (Eds.). (1997). *Beyond groupthink: Political group dynamics and foreign policy-making*. Ann Arbor: University of Michigan Press.

Vertzberger, Y. (1998). *Risk taking and decisionmaking: Foreign military intervention decisions*. Stanford, CA: Stanford University Press.

Walker, S. G., Shafer, M., & Young, M. D. (1998). Systematic procedures for operational code analysis: Measuring and modeling Jimmy Carter's operational code. *International Studies Quarterly, 42*, 175–190.

Fritz Gaenslen

POLITICAL LEADERSHIP. Any exploration of the psychological aspects of political leadership must first consider two fundamental questions: (1) Do individual leaders (as opposed to institutions, historical forces, and structural dynamics) make a difference in outcomes, and if so, under what circumstances? (2) Do specifically psychological characteristics of individual leaders (as opposed to rational self-interest or role requirements) make a difference, and if so, under what circumstances? While these questions recall the ancient philosophical debate about whether history is primarily shaped by "great" persons versus impersonal forces, Greenstein (1969/1987, pp. 33–62) has suggested a more nuanced set of answers. He argues that the effects of psychological characteristics of individual leaders will be greatest: (1) in new, unprecedented, or ambiguous situations, when the environment is unstable and open to restructuring; (2) in situations arousing strongly held beliefs or intense emotions that resonate with deep (unconscious or implicit) layers of personality; and (3) in situations that are especially demanding and require especially intense effort.

Issues of Method

The psychological study of political leadership also presents special problems of method. Although some leaders can be tested directly—for example, city officials, state legislators, and national parliamentary deputies—most of the really significant national and international leaders (and all historical figures) are not available for direct interviews, testing, or systematic laboratory experimentation. As a result, many of the concepts and methods used in laboratory and field studies of leadership cannot be directly and confidently applied to the psychological analysis of political leaders.

In consequence, much of our psychological knowledge about political leadership is built upon biographical studies of the characteristics and leadership style of particular leaders—ranging from Machiavelli's comparative study of Italian Renaissance rulers, published in 1513 as *The Prince*, to modern accounts of the lives and leadership of such figures as Mahatma Gandhi, Adolf Hitler, Franklin Roosevelt, and even Jesus Christ. Psychobiography involves the speculative interpretation of such known biographical facts in the light of personality theory (often psychoanalysis). The varying interpretations of Woodrow Wilson by Alexander and Juliette George, by Sigmund Freud and William Bullitt, and by Edward Weinstein, are early landmarks of this genre (Winter, 1992b; see also the studies reviewed by Glad, 1973). Although the method is not without its accomplishments, problems of validation and objectivity are obvious and severe (see Greenstein, 1969/1987, pp. 63–93; Runyan, 1984). Different interpretations of the same leader often cannot easily be reconciled, as in the case of the psychodynamic versus neurological interpretations of Wilson.

In recent decades, however, psychological researchers have developed a variety of methods for studying psychological characteristics of leaders indirectly, or "at a distance." One of the most widely used at-a-distance techniques is *content analysis of verbal or written materials* (see Winter, 1992a). Measures of achievement, affiliation, and power motivation, as well as other psychological characteristics, have been developed or adapted for use in this way (Winter, 1992a). Hermann (1984) also developed measures for nationalism, distrust, internal control, self-esteem, and task-versus-interpersonal orientation, and has aggregated these separate measures into a series of overall leader personality orientations. Other widely used content analysis measures include integrative complexity and explanatory style (see Winter, 1992a).

Researchers have also studied leaders' psychological characteristics by using standard personality instruments such as the Adjective Check List or trait-related phrases (Simonton, 1987), as well as rating scales and more elaborate Q-sorts, all completed by raters who have studied standard biographical materials. Other techniques that have been employed include analysis of nonverbal behavior, voice stress analysis (see Hermann, 1977), systematic specification of the leader's "operational code" or philosophical and instrumental beliefs (Hermann, 1977; Winter, 1996, pp. 287–288), and analysis of family constellation and birth order. Sometimes researchers have tried to study political leadership through laboratory simulation, using the familiar source of research participants, college undergraduates.

Examples of specific leaders studied by these systematic at-a-distance techniques include the following (see Winter, 1992a, 1992b; Post, in press): U.S. presidents Lyndon Johnson, Richard Nixon, George Bush, Ronald Reagan, and Bill Clinton (Renshon, 1995), as well as international leaders such as Saddam Hussein (see references in Winter, 1996, *passim*). Groups of leaders studied by these techniques include American, Soviet, and Chinese revolutionary leaders; nineteenth-century U.S. leaders on all sides of the slavery issue (Tetlock, Armor, & Peterson, 1994); U.S. presidents (Simonton, 1987; Winter, 1987); members of Congress and Supreme Court justices; British Members of Parliament; southern Africa political leaders; various world leaders (Hermann, 1984), Communist party secretaries general; and Politburo members in the former Soviet Union.

Dimensions of Political Leadership

Political leadership is surely not a unitary phenomenon. Depending on the situation, leaders may engage in a variety of different activities that demand a variety of psychological characteristics and resources. Consider, for example, the array of tasks confronting a political leader: picking advisors, seeking information, coming to a decision, articulating and aggregating interests, delegating tasks, extracting resources, handling conflict, monitoring results, and ensuring the loyalty of significant groups.

Hermann (1986) has suggested several contrasting conceptions or images of leaders that may help to illuminate different facets of political leadership: the *Pied Piper*, whose seeming magical qualities irresistibly draw followers away from their ordinary lives; the *puppet*, who is only able to do what followers want and lead them where they want to go; the *firefighter*, who meets crises by adapting resources to varying needs and monitoring varying results (every fire is different); and the *salesperson*, who promotes particular versions of reality and visions of the political task. These conceptions are not mutually exclusive: at different times and in different circumstances, each may be appropriate because it reflects an essential aspect of political leadership. For a full understanding of leadership, therefore, Hermann argues that researchers need to attend to several factors: the leader's *personality* (motivation, beliefs, style, ways of handling stress), skills, background, previous experience, stage of life, and health; the mechanisms of *recruitment* to leadership; the *characteristics of the followers*; the *relationship*(s) between leader(s) and led, or bases of power; and the institutional, legal, resources, cultural, and historical *context*. The collections of studies of the first few years of Bill Clinton's presidency, assembled by Renshon (1995), illustrates the value of focusing on these different factors.

It is thus not surprising that researchers have identified a wide variety of different dependent variables having to do with political leadership. Even the most basic question of what constitutes a "successful" political leader, can be answered in many ways. For example, "successful" American presidents could be defined as those who were elected by a wide margin of votes (sociometric success) or those who are rated as "great" by historians, but these two outcome variables are essentially uncorrelated (see Winter, 1987, p. 199). Simonton (1987) has further differentiated presidential success into five separate variables: electoral success, poll ratings, performance of the president's administration, ratings by historians, and overall political leadership.

Some researchers focus on predicting specific leader or administration *outcomes*, such as war and peace, effective political performance, and scandal (Simonton, 1987, pp. 97–165, Winter, 1987). Others attempt to translate general leadership concepts into measurable behaviors. For example, Max Weber's classic concept of *charisma* is the focus of much recent theorizing and research about "transformational" versus "administrative" leadership. House, Spangler, and Woycke (1991) have translated Weber's concept into a series of specific leader and follower behaviors that can be measured in the writings of subordinates. Thus, charismatic leader behaviors include self-confidence, strong ideological conviction, and high expectations of followers. Charismatic effects in the followers include expression of affect, sense of involvement, giving extra effort in one's "mission," and having a feeling of "backup."

Psychological Aspects of Successful Political Leadership

With these restrictions and cautions, some tentative generalizations can be drawn from the existing body of psychological research on political leadership. Successful or "great" political leaders (at least in the retrospective judgment of historians) tend to be comfortable seeking and using power (high power motive scores, high trait ratings of dominance and extraversion, and the impression of strength and activity; see Simonton, 1987; Winter, 1987). Such a concern with power, however, must be tempered with some sense of self-control or responsibility, lest it degenerate into the fantasies of omnipotence and limitless impact, as in the case of the Roman emperor Caligula or dictators such as Hitler in Germany and Pol Pot in Cambodia, who may be said to suffer from "malignant narcissism" (Post, 1993). Nevertheless, even "responsible" power concerns and motivation are also associated with war outcomes—suggesting that political greatness (at least retrospectively or in the minds of historians) is linked to successful aggression.

In contrast, the achievement and affiliation motives are not associated with success in political leadership positions. Achievement motivation predicts entrepreneurial success in business, but in politics it often leads to restless impatience and frustration (Renshon, 1995, pp. 127–129; Winter, 1996, pp. 138–143). And affiliation-motivated leaders may be seen as insufficiently universalistic ("nice," to their friends, but not "fair"), which may corrode the morale of their followers.

Judged in terms of electoral results, however, successful political leaders tend to show not so much a unique psychological pattern as simple congruence with their society, both in terms of motive profile (Winter, 1987) and in terms of opinion on major issues (Simonton, 1987, pp. 11–74). Of course opinion congruence could result from either simple concordance or Machiavellian manipulation. In times of social stress, voters—especially the more authoritarian ones—prefer "strong" presidents who score higher in power motivation (McCann, 1997). These results are consistent with models of leader-follower "contingency" derived from numerous laboratory and observational studies, as well as Erik Erikson's theory that many great leaders and religious or ideological innovators somehow implicitly display (or deliberately construct) personality characteristics and identity themes that are analogous or congruent to those of their contemporaries and followers.

Turning to more specific outcomes, we find some researchers focusing on abstract components of the leadership process: for example, overall involvement in and control of the policy-making process, tolerance for conflict, motivation for leading, preferred strategies for managing information, degree of coordination of advisors, and preferred strategies for resolving conflict.

Other researchers focus on outcomes described in everyday or historical terms. For example, war and aggression are often related positively to leaders' power motivation (Winter, 1987) and negatively to their integrative complexity (Suedfeld & Tetlock, 1977). Integrative complexity, in other words, makes it possible for leaders to envision alternatives, reconstrue interests, and so compromise in order to avoid conflict escalation. This is consistent with many other results linking integrative complexity to effective performance (Winter, 1996, pp. 201–206; Renshon, 1995). Thus, low integrative complexity seems to be one of the causes of the groupthink phenomenon, in which pressures toward in-group loyalty and uniformity interfere with good judgment. On the other hand, Tetlock, Armor, and Peterson (1994) showed that nineteenth-century U.S. leaders who were integratively complex tended to be caught in the middle on the slavery issue. This suggests that integrative complexity can get in the way of making clear-cut decisions, standing fast on important moral principles, and taking decisive action. The study of revolutionary leaders suggests that successful leaders can adapt their level of integrative complexity to the circumstances, a result echoed in U.S. presidents before and after inauguration (see Suedfeld, 1994).

Predicting Political Leadership

In studying political leaders, it is important to be clear—and modest—about the kinds of predictions to outcomes that are possible. Many factors are beyond the control of the leader (and even beyond the imagination of the researcher). For example, Winter, Hermann, Weintraub, and Walker (1991), had earlier suggested that because George Bush showed high levels of affiliation motivation and only moderate levels of power motivation, he would be a peacemaker, not prone to seek political ends through violence and war. However, the Iraqi invasion of Kuwait—scarcely predictable from Bush's personality—transformed the situation. A follow-up analysis discussed the congruence between Bush's motives and his behavior, given the stimulus of that invasion. The authors went on to suggest that the psychological study of political leaders can inevitably yield only conditional ("if/then") rather than unconditional predictions.

Future Directions in the Psychological Study of Political Leadership

In recent decades, leadership researchers have devoted more attention to issues of gender and leadership. As more and more women become political leaders, this same trend will no doubt emerge in the psychological analysis of political leadership. At the same time, there may also be a deeper theoretical link between gender and leadership. If, as many feminist theorists propose, "gender" is both the social organization of the relationship between the sexes *and* a primary way of signifying relationships of power, then it may indeed constitute a *primary model for all power*, on the part of both leaders and followers. That is, to "gender" something is to *introduce a force-field of power*, so that the relation of leader to follower is that of male to female (and vice versa). From this analysis, it therefore follows that political leadership and sexuality (the other connotation of "gender") may have many and deep symbolic linkages.

From a sociological perspective, if political leaders are the (often implicit) servants of elite groups and ruling classes, then their recruitment, socialization, scope for action, and goals can best be understood in the context of ruling class interests.

Finally, traditional "Western" models of psychology and politics can no longer be assumed to prevail (or apply to all people in all societies) in an increasingly diverse world. Even if the forces of globalization are at work on diverse styles of political leadership, the results will likely differ in important respects from familiar western models. To understand these processes, as well as psychological aspects of political leadership in Japan, China, and other countries of southeast and south Asia, researchers may find it useful to consider "Asian" conceptions of power and authority (Pye, 1985). More broadly and abstractly, *each* of the four dimensions of cultural difference conceptualized by Hofstede (1984) —individualism/collectivism, uncertainty avoidance, power distance, and gender differentiation—may play important roles, both in the styles and mechanisms of political leadership, on the one hand, and in the individual psychological factors associated with leadership, on the other.

[*See also* Political Behavior; *and* Political Decision Making.]

Bibliography

Glad, B. (1973). Contributions of psychobiography. In J. N. Knutson (Ed.), *Handbook of political psychology* (pp. 296–321). San Francisco: Jossey-Bass. Classic review of the origins, problems, and good and bad examples of psychobiographical studies (mostly of political leaders).

Greenstein, F. I. (1987). *Personality and politics: Problems of evidence, inference, and conceptualization.* Princeton, NJ: Princeton University Press. (Original work published 1969.) Thorough discussion of the circumstances under which individual psychological factors may make a political difference (chapter 2), and of the criteria for effective psychological studies of individual leaders (chapter 3).

Hermann, M. G. (1977). *A psychological examination of political leaders.* New York: Free Press. Discussion and illustrations of methods of studying leaders at a distance.

Hermann, M. G. (1984). Personality and foreign policy decision making: A study of 53 heads of government. In D. A. Sylvan & S. Chan (Eds.), *Foreign policy decision-making: Perceptions, cognition, and artificial intelligence* (pp. 53–80). New York: Praeger. Employs a series of personality and biographical variables, grouped into "orientations," to compare world leaders and their foreign policies.

Hermann, M. G. (1986). Ingredients of leadership. In M. G. Hermann (Ed.), *Political psychology: Contemporary issues and problems* (pp. 167–192). San Francisco: Jossey-Bass. Discussion of the major issues, perspectives, and frameworks for studying political leadership.

Hofstede, G. (1984). *Culture's consequences* (abridged ed.). Newbury Park, CA: Sage. Systematically presents four dimensions, which are relevant to political leadership, for comparing nations and cultures.

House, R. J., Spangler, W. D., & Woycke, J. (1991). Personality and charisma in the U.S. presidency: A psychological theory of leader effectiveness. *Administrative Science Quarterly, 36,* 364–396. Translates Weber's classic concept of charisma into variables that can be measured at a distance and in the memoirs of followers.

McCann, S. J. H. (1997). Threatening times, "strong" presidential popular vote winners, and the victory margin, 1824–1964. *Journal of Personality and Social Psychology, 73,* 160–170. Relates measures of the historical context, U.S. presidents' personalities, and election outcomes.

Post, J. M. (1993). Current concepts of the narcissistic personality: Implications for political psychology. *Political Psychology, 14,* 99–121. Elucidates a modern psychoanalytic concept applicable to many political leaders.

Post, J. M. (Ed.). (in press). *The psychological assessment of political leaders: Theory, method, and application.* n.p. A variety of modern at-a-distance personality assessment methods described and illustrated in application to U.S. President Bill Clinton and Iraqi President Saddam Hussein.

Pye, L. W. (1985). *Asia power and politics: The cultural dimensions of authority.* Cambridge, MA: Harvard University Press. Suggests the importance of cultural context and values in understanding political leadership.

Renshon, S. A. (Ed.). (1995). *The Clinton presidency: Campaigning, governing and the psychology of leadership.* Boulder, CO: Westview Press. The U.S. presidential election of 1992 and the early years of the Clinton presidency are examined from a variety of leadership and political psychology perspectives.

Runyan, W. M. (1984). *Life histories and psychobiography.* New York: Oxford University Press. Discusses issues, methods, and cautions in doing psychobiographies.

Simonton, D. K. (1987). *Why presidents succeed: A political psychology of leadership.* New Haven, CT: Yale University Press. Reviews the literature on assessing dimensions of greatness of U.S. presidents, and relates them to personality, biographical, and situational variables.

Suedfeld, P. (1994). President Clinton's policy dilemmas: A cognitive analysis. *Political Psychology, 15,* 337–349.

Suedfeld, P., & Tetlock, P. (1977). Integrative complexity of communications in international crises. *Journal of Conflict Resolution, 21,* 169–184.

Tetlock, P. E., Armor, D., & Peterson, R. S. (1994). The slavery debate in antebellum America: Cognitive style, value conflict, and the limits of compromise. *Journal of Personality and Social Psychology, 66,* 115–126. Reviews the literature on integrative complexity and suggests some of its hazards in political contexts.

Winter, D. G. (1987). Leader appeal, leader performance, and the motive profiles of leaders and followers: A study of American presidents and elections. *Journal of Personality and Social Psychology, 52,* 196–202. Relates the motive profiles of U.S. presidents, and concordance with the profiles of U.S. society, to electoral success and other measures of presidential outcomes.

Winter, D. G. (1992a). Content analysis of archival data, personal documents, and everyday verbal productions. In C. P. Smith (Ed.), *Motivation and personality: Handbook of thematic content analysis* (pp. 110–125). New York: Cambridge University Press. Survey of methods and results using content analysis to study individual leaders and collective elites.

Winter, D. G. (1992b). Personality and foreign policy: Historical overview of research. In E. Singer & V. Harper (Eds.), *Political psychology and foreign policy* (pp. 79–101). Boulder, CO: Westview Press. Suggests how objective measures can resolve conflicting psychobiographical interpretations, and surveys psychological factors associated with war and aggression.

Winter, D. G. (1996). *Personality: Analysis and interpretation of lives.* New York: McGraw-Hill. Presents methods and findings for many personality variables measured at a distance.

Winter, D. G., Hermann, M. G., Weintraub, W., & Walker, S. G. (1991). The personalities of Bush and Gorbachev measured at a distance: Follow-up on predictions. *Political Psychology, 12,* 457–464. Suggests that adequate predictions about leaders' behavior from psychological factors can only be made in probabilistic, if/then terms.

David G. Winter

PORNOGRAPHY. The term *pornography* was originally used to refer to various descriptions of the lives of prostitutes and is derived from the Greek *porngraphos* ("writing of harlots"). Within and outside the legal community, the terms *pornography* and *obscenity* have often been confused. *Obscenity* has mainly referred to filthy and disgusting acts or depictions that offend people's sense of decency. *Pornography* was traditionally not viewed as obscene in the sense of shame and filth. Catholic canon law initiated a confusion of the two terms, and Victorian morality reinforced the confusion. It seems unlikely that the two terms will become untangled, even in the work of psychologists.

The term *pornography* has been loosely applied to many forms of explicit (and even nonexplicit) depictions of sexual behavior. What depictions are considered pornographic depends, to a large extent, on the political and religious orientation of those who use these descriptions. For some, pornography is defined as depictions that elicit, or are intended to elicit, sexual arousal. Others have suggested that the label should apply only to materials that include degrading and dehumanizing images of women, not simply materials that are sexually arousing. And for still others, *pornography* refers only to those sexual depictions that are violent in nature. Many individuals have stressed the idea that the dehumanizing aspect of pornography distinguishes it from material that may be termed erotic.

These definitional problems have also surfaced when psychologists have studied the effects of pornography upon the viewer. As an aid in understanding the large amount of research in this area, researchers have grouped the variety of materials used in their research into a number of different categories. Rather than employing the term *pornography* directly, researchers tend to distinguish among several types of materials.

Types of Materials and Research

First, there is nonviolent, low-degradation, sexually explicit stimuli. This material is most consistent with the definition of *erotica* (e.g., nonviolent, noncoercive, and nondegrading, but sexually explicit). Research by social psychologists, as well as reports by national commissions both in Great Britain and the United States, have concluded that exposure to this type of material has no antisocial impact, such as increased aggression on the viewer.

A second category is nonviolent, high-degradation, sexually explicit stimuli. These materials are considered demeaning and degrading to women. Psychological research investigation this type of material has generally concluded that there are limited effects from exposure. After examining all the laboratory and correlational studies conducted with this type of material, researchers have generally concluded that individuals exposed to this form of pornography do not show any changes in antisocial attitudes or behavior. Other researchers, however, find evidence indicating some increase in negative attitudes toward women. The research in this area has tended to follow one of two particular methodologies. Studies of short-term exposure (less than 1 hour) have yielded mixed results. When effects do exist for this material, they are both fewer and weaker than antisocial effects from sexually violent material. Experimental studies using neutral exposure control groups compared with groups of participants exposed to either violent or nonviolent materials are rife with conflicting results. Studies of the effects of long-term exposure to nonviolent pornography have also yielded mixed results: some have found increases in negative attitudes about rape, whereas others have shown no effects.

An experiment by James Check (1985) was intended as a step toward disentangling the effects of prolonged exposure to sexually explicit images that were nondegrading (or neutral) from the effects of exposure to sexual portrayals that are dehumanizing or degrading. The results indicated that for some men (those with relatively high scores on a measure of psychoticism), exposure to both sexually degrading but nonviolent pornography and sexually violent pornography resulted in a tendency to say they would rape if assured of not being caught. Other studies, however, have failed to find effects for long-term exposure to nonviolent pornography. A study by Malamuth (1989) reported nonsignificant effects for participants' "likelihood of raping if assured of not being caught" (a measure on which Check had found effects) after substantial exposure to common forms of pornography. This remains an area where continued psychological research, as well as theoretical processes to account for any findings, is needed.

The final category is violent pornography, material that depicts sexual coercion in a sexually explicit context. For nearly two decades, researchers have been studying the effects of sexually violent material on male viewers. In one line of research the effects of depictions of rape have been examined. In another line the effects of exposure to films that depict graphic violence against women, often juxtaposed with mildly sexual scenes (slasher films), have been studied. Several types of negative effects occur after exposure to sexual violence. For example, certain men are sexually aroused from viewing violent images. Sexual arousal from aggression against women is also associated with a set of beliefs in which male dominance and female submissiveness are perceived as natural and justified, with the view that male-female relationships are fundamentally adversarial. Additional research indicates that men are likely to become desensitized to violence against women after viewing this material, and later report calloused attitudes about rape. Men also show increased aggression against women. A series of studies by Donnerstein, Linz, and Penrod (1987) examined the effects of violent pornography on aggression against women in the laboratory. As with other mass media depictions of rape, a common theme in violent pornography is that women derive pleasure from sexual aggression. In violent pornography, however, the effects might be accentuated by the explicit portrayals of sex and violence. It has been hypothesized that viewing an act of aggression in which the victim responds in a positive manner by showing pleasure might reduce aggressive inhibitions and justify aggressive behavior. Research supports this assumption.

Additional research suggests a link between self-reports of sexually violent behavior outside the laboratory and rape depictions in the media, but this link is indirect. In accounting for these complicated effects, Malamuth (1989) suggested that sexually violent media may affect men's attitudes, which, if combined with several other factors, may affect aggressive behavior in naturalistic settings. This implies that exposure to sex and violence in the mass media is not the most or even one of the most powerful influences on sexually violent behavior. Rather, it may be only one of the many factors that interact to affect responses. The nature of the effect and the degree of influence of sexually violent media will often depend, among other things, on the psychological background of the person exposed to the media stimuli and the sociocultural context in which exposure takes place.

In summary, research consistently indicates that exposure to depictions of violence against women either juxtaposed with mildly erotic scenes (slasher films) or in the form of sexually explicit or nonexplicit rape scenes results in callousness toward female victims of violence, especially rape victims, and other antisocial attitudinal, perception, and behavioral effects. Two important caveats need to be reiterated. First, these effects can occur without explicit sexual content. Many of the rape-related depictions used in the research described here would not be considered pornographic. In the lines of research cited here it appears to be the *message* about violence against women that is important in producing antisocial effects. The mere presentation of consenting sex, no matter how explicit, does not facilitate antisocial outcomes. Second, the effects in these studies are strongest for men who *already* possess certain attitudes or who are predisposed to sexual violence in some way. Specifically, the behavioral effects occur most consistently for those who already possess calloused attitudes about rape. These distinctions are crucial for the legal and educational solutions we might consider.

Finally, we would speculate that stronger effects might be expected for younger viewers because they lack the critical viewing skills and the experience necessary to discount the myths about women and sexual violence. To a young adolescent who is searching for information about sexual relationships, sexual violence in popular films (and on the Internet) may be a potent formative influence on attitudes toward sexuality. A young teenager's first exposure to sex may come in the form of a mildly erotic but violent movie, such as a slasher film. These films are not restricted because they do not carry an X rating. They can easily be rented at a video outlet or found on a late-night cable station.

The categories discussed here do not completely classify the materials into mutually exclusive categories. They have, however, allowed researchers to understand better the influence that pornography has upon the viewer. In many research studies, materials depicting similar themes and messages have also been employed. For example, research with graphically violent scenes of aggression against women, which are not sexually explicit, have been used in many studies. This research has shown that individuals exposed to this form of mass media can become desensitized to real violence against women. Although some consider these materials to fall under the heading of pornography, this has only led to further interpretation problems in the literature.

Future Research

With increased Internet usage, it is obvious that children and adults will have more opportunity to access pornographic images. For this reason, it is important to continue investigations in this area, and a number of possibilities can be suggested. First, further laboratory research should be undertaken to replicate and extend the existing lines of investigation about the effects that pornography and mass media depictions of sexual violence have on perceptions, attitudes, and behaviors in order to clarify past results and to generalize from results already obtained. Research on the effects of sexually violent media should include participants from segments of the population that have not traditionally been included in laboratory studies. The duration of behavioral and attitudinal changes seen in the laboratory must be more clearly determined, and the effects of nonviolent sexually explicit pornography should continue to be investigated. Further investigation into nonviolent pornography could contribute to the development of theories about which aspects of the pornographic presentation or viewing context interact to produce changes in attitudes and behavior.

Second, researchers should capitalize on naturally occurring changes in viewing patterns or the availability of sexually violent materials to assess simultaneous changes in potentially linked phenomena, such as sexual assault. For example, studies should be designed to examine changes in the frequency of violent events in a geographical region over a time period during which the availability of sexually violent portrayals clearly increased at a particular point.

Third, longitudinal investigations regarding the effects of exposure to pornography and sexual violence in the mass media on attitudes and behavior should be undertaken. These studies would provide solid, rather than circumstantial, evidence about the effects of pornography and sexual violence on the development of attitudes toward sexuality and aggression.

Finally, we need to develop strategies for limiting the harmful effects of these materials on adolescents, and increase the capacity of adolescents to withstand any possible negative effects of exposure to these materials. We can suggest that a systematic program of research whose goal is the development of a formal, easily administered educational program concerning media sexual violence be undertaken. The program should be suitable for high school educators. In order to create such a program, research is needed to examine what types of information would be most powerful in changing adolescents' attitudes about mass media sexual violence, the optimal format for adolescents to learn and incorporate these messages into their repertoire of values, the most effective communication source for conveying this educational information, and whether social psychological factors, such as a critical viewing companion, facilitate immediate and long-term changes in beliefs and attitudes about sexual violence. We believe that educational interventions will be effective to the extent that they are formed and administered on the basis of systematic research into each of these questions.

Bibliography

Check, J. (1985). *The effects of violent and nonviolent pornography*. Ottawa: Canadian Department of Justice.

Donnerstein, E., Linz, D., & Penrod, S. (1987). *The question of pornography: Research findings and policy implications*. New York: Free Press.

Linz, D. (1989). Exposure to sexuality explicit materials and attitudes toward rape: A comparison of study results. *Journal of Sex Research, 26*, 50–84.

Linz, D., & Malamuth, N. M. (1993). Communication concepts 5: Pornography. In S. Chaffee (Ed.) *Communication concepts series*. Thousand Oaks, CA: Sage.

Malamuth, N. M. (1986). Predictors of naturalistic sexual aggression. *Journal of Personality and Social Psychology, 50*, 953–962.

Malamuth, N. (1989). Sexually violent media, thought patterns, and antisocial behavior. *Public Communication and Behavior, 2*, 159–204.

Malamuth, N. M., & Donnerstein, E. (Eds.). (1984). *Pornography and sexual aggression*. San Diego, CA: Academic Press.

Ministerial Committee of Inquiry. (1990). *Report of the Ministerial Committee of Inquiry into pornography*. Wellington, New Zealand: Author.

Mulvey, E. P., & Haugaard, J. L. (1986). *Report of the Surgeon General's workshop on pornography and public health*. Washington, DC: U.S. Department of Health and Human Services.

U.S. Department of Justice. (1986). *Attorney General's Commission on Pornography: Final report*. Washington, DC: Government Printing Office.

Zillmann, D., & Bryant, J. (Eds.). (1989). *Pornography: Research advances and policy considerations*. Mahwah, NJ: Erlbaum.

Edward Donnerstein

PORTER, NOAH (1811–1892), American mental philosopher. Porter was born in Farmington, Connecticut, and graduated from Yale College in 1831. He was master of the Hopkins Grammar School in New Haven from 1831 until 1833 when he entered the Yale Divinity School. He studied with Nathaniel Taylor, a moderate Calvinist, and was ordained in 1836. He served congregations as pastor in New Milford, Connecticut

(1836–1843) and Springfield, Massachusetts (1843–1846). In 1846, he joined Yale College as Clark Professor of Moral Philosophy and Metaphysics, a position he held until his death. In 1853–1854, he studied philosophy with Adolf Trendelenburg at the University of Berlin. He was president of Yale College from 1871 until 1886, when he returned to teaching. His administration was marked by the expansion of the student body, a building program, and a spirited defense of the old required curriculum in opposition to the new elective system at Harvard. Porter's teaching to seniors included courses in mental and moral philosophy, the history of philosophy, evidences of Christianity, and natural theology.

Porter contributed to the history of psychology through his textbooks, *The Human Intellect* (New York, 1868) and his abridgement of that work, *The Elements of Intellectual Science* (New York, 1871). He defined psychology as the study of the human soul as revealed in sense perception and consciousness. Psychology was, for Porter, an inductive and empirical science whose subject was the facts of conscious experience as revealed through introspection, the only means by which the processes and activities of the soul could be known and examined. Understanding the processes of knowing and the knower was the primary task of Porter's psychology. His text acknowledged but paid little attention to the coordinate components of the soul, considered under the rubrics of feeling (sensibilities) and the will. Porter's psychology was a cognitive psychology emphasizing the nature of knowledge and the activities of knowing, thinking, and judging. Porter's soul was not the passive mind of associationistic psychology but an "active power"; in this, and in other positions, Porter stood in the tradition of the Scottish philosophy that dominated American philosophy in the nineteenth century.

The scientific (empirical and inductive) study of the human intellect was Porter's path to the principles and laws of all knowledge, including that of the natural world and the soul itself. Psychology constituted the necessary prerequisite for philosophical truth. As Porter expressed it, anyone

> who seeks to enter the temple of philosophy by any other approach than the vestibule of psychology, can never penetrate into its inner sanctuary; for psychology leads to and evolves philosophical truth, even though it is itself subordinate to philosophy. (*The Human Intellect*, p. 60)

The theistic philosophical cast to Porter's text, in which he presupposed and argued for the existence of God, placed it among the last of the texts of the old psychology, rejected by the advocates of the new laboratory psychology and eclipsed by their texts that embodied the results of the new experimental psychology.

Bibliography

Blau, J. L. (1952). *Men and movements in American philosophy*. New York: Prentice Hall. See pages 102–107 for a discussion of Porter's philosophy and the tradition of which he was a part.

Evans, R. B. (1984). The origins of American academic psychology. In J. Brozek (Ed.), *Explorations in the history of psychology in the United States* (pp. 17–60). Lewisburg, PA: Bucknell University Press. Porter is placed in the context of the early development of psychology within mental and moral philosophy.

Fay, J. W. (1939). *American psychology before William James*. New Brunswick, NJ: Rutgers University Press. The classic study of psychology in America from the colonial period to the advent of experimental psychology; for Porter, see pages 147–150.

Roback, A. A. (1952). *History of American psychology*. New York: Library Publishers. For a brief and critical analysis of Porter's psychology, see pages 88–91.

Alfred H. Fuchs

PORTUGAL. Until now there has been no study of the development of psychology in Portugal. There are only some useful, but limited contributions of a historical nature (Abreu, 1990; Borges, 1983; Gomes, 1990, 1994; Lima, 1949). As pointed out by Silva and Marques (1994), the development of psychology in Portugal has been strongly conditioned by the nature of the political and ideological regime that governed Portugal for most of the twentieth century.

Historical Background

Three broad periods can be distinguished in the historical development of scientific psychology in Portugal: (a) the nineteenth century with only a few forerunners and pioneers; (b) the first half of the twentieth century when psychology entered academic institutions, usually with an emphasis on applied fields; and (c) the present period, which begin in 1976, when full and diversified curricula were created, distinct faculties were established, and research expanded. Concerning the history of psychology in Portugal from the second half of the nineteenth century until the end of World War II, the obligatory reference is Lima (1949). Lima showed how the idea of psychology as a science gradually emerged from philosophy, theology, and metaphysics. In Portugal, the contributions of medical science have been especially important.

The teaching of psychology began in 1911. The first psychology courses, which still formed part of the philosophy curriculum, were given at the universities of Coimbra and Lisbon (Gomes, 1994). Several figures made fundamental contributions to scientific psychology at that time. In 1913, Alves dos Santos, who was strongly influenced by the ideas of Claparède and Flournoy (Geneva), and Toulouse and Pieron (Paris), founded the Laboratório de Psicologia in Coimbra. In 1915, Costa Ferreira organized the Instituto Médico-Pedagógico in Lisbon (Casa Pia). In 1925, Faria de Vasconcelos founded the Instituto de Orientação Profissional. In 1930, Matos Romão organized the Laboratório de Psicologia of the university of Lisbon (see Gomes, 1990, and Abreu, 1990, for more information about the circumstances surrounding these developments). Before the establishment of these laboratories, several psychological studies, mainly on abnormal behavior, had already been conducted in medical schools.

Regarding the teaching of psychology in universities, in 1957 after a curriculum reform, a new course, Introduction to Psychology, was introduced. Students could take the Introduction to Psychology courses in their first and fourth years, do some experimental work, enroll in a final psychology seminar, and prepare a dissertation in psychology (see Carneiro, 1997, for more information about the psychology dissertations presented at that time). Two years before, a medical psychology course was introduced in the medical schools.

In 1962, an association of Catholic congregations founded the Instituto Superior de Psicologia Aplicada (ISPA) in Lisbon, the first true school of psychology in Portugal. The aim of the ISPA was to provide training for the numerous teachers in private religious schools all over the country. In 1964, the ISPA admitted laypersons and underwent several curricula changes until, in 1973, its curricula was recognized by the Ministry of Education. Its diploma has been officially recognized since 1986.

In 1965, the Portuguese Psychological Society was founded by the few psychologists working in the Departments of Arts and the Departments of Medicine in the universities and by some secondary school teachers in charge of career counseling in high schools. Their objectives were (a) to promote scientific contacts among university-trained psychologists in Portugal, (b) to coordinate their activities, and (c) to promote their professional interests. A number of discipline-based working groups was created. In 1967, the *Revista Portuguesa de Psicologia* was launched, inaugurating the first psychology journal in Portugal. Since 1992, the Portuguese Psychological Society has been a member of the International Union of Psychological Science. In 1966, a study group separated from the Luso-Spanish Psychoanalytic Society and later formed the Portuguese Psychoanalytic Society, which in 1981 integrated the International Psychoanalytic Society.

In 1974, a major change occurred in Portuguese society after the fall of the authoritarian regime that had directed Portugal for more than 40 years. The conservative and repressive spirit of that regime had directly affected the intellectual and scientific life in Portugal, and had considerably slowed the development of social sciences. The third phase in the history of Portuguese psychology began in 1976. The changes that have taken place as Portuguese society has moved toward democracy over the last few years have produced extraordinary developments in psychology. In 1977 the High Studies of Psychology in the Universities of Coimbra, Lisbon, and Oporto were created, and later were elevated to the rank of Faculties (1980). More recently (1990) a degree in psychology was established at Minho University. In recent years several private institutions have established training departments in several areas of psychology (mainly organizational and health psychology).

Training in Psychology

The basic professional degree in Portugal is the 5-year undergraduate *licenciatura*, which is normally begun upon graduating from the Portuguese equivalent of high school at the age of 18, and is subsequently finished at the age of 23. Only selected students are allowed to enter the psychology curriculum. A nationwide selection committee is organized each year by the Ministry of Education to examine all academic curricula. Recent statistics show that psychology is one of the most demanding curricula. Students graduating with *licenciatura* can enroll in the master's degree program and then in the doctoral program. Starting in 1985, universities began offering 2-year master's degrees and 3- to 5-year doctorates. If there are master's degree programs in the university, there are usually no doctoral programs. The main requirement for the Ph.D. in psychology requires completing and defending a doctoral dissertation based on original research. The doctorate is not required to practice psychology, but it is obligatory for university teaching appointments. Because the graduate degree is not required to practice professionally, the majority of psychologists finish their academic preparation with the completion of the undergraduate *licenciatura*. Finally, some specialized training is available solely through professional associations (i.e., psychoanalysis, behavior therapy, cognitive therapy, and family counseling).

Main Research Topics

Research is done mostly within universities, mainly by academic staff or by students during the preparation of their master's or doctoral degrees under the supervision of a lecturer or professor. There are no strictly psychology researchers in Portugal yet. Although some good studies have already been published in international journals, the great majority of scientific works are still published in Portuguese in national reviews. As a consequence, the international scientific community has only a limited access to Portuguese psychology. The continuation of existing journals often depends on the dedication, as well as the financial resources, of their editors and/or publishers. The following psychology journals are currently printed in Portugal: *Análise Psicológica, Cadernos de Consulta Psicológica, European Journal of Psychology of Education* (the only one in English), *Psicologia, Psicologia, Educação e Cultura, Psicologia: Teoria, investigação e prática, Psychologica, Revista Portuguesa de Psicanálise, Revista Portuguesa de Psicologia, Revista de Psicologia Militar*. Identifying the main figures in scientific psychology is not an easy task. A blind search through the data bases offered by PsycLIT (1974–1996) showed that four Portuguese psychologists have published more than five papers in international journals: Fontaine, Gonçalves, Lourenço, and Neto. (The value of information of this kind is not known.)

Clinical Psychology. O. Gonçalves (1990) reviewed the literature about research and intervention in clinical psychology in Portugal. Four central themes of contemporary psychology are described: cognitive revolution, systemic perspectives, development theories, and attachment and object relations theory. Each of these themes is illustrated with research and intervention programs from Portuguese clinical psychology.

Cognitive Psychology. Experimental psychology has a long tradition in Portugal (since the foundation of the first laboratory in 1913). During the 1990s, the development of cognitive psychology and consequently the transformation of the science has taken place; studies of attention, perception, memory, and language have been undertaken (Pinto, 1991), as well as research on learning.

Developmental Psychology. A complete review can be found in Lourenço (1994). During the 1970s Portuguese developmental psychology was strongly influenced by the Piagetian tradition, and this of course means that cognitive development in childhood and early adolescence was the main topic of research. During the 1980s and 1990s, interest expanded to include other research topics, for instance, social development during childhood and adolescence, but also in all phases of adulthood, has drawn the attention of several research teams. Several investigators have also studied moral development in the tradition of Lawrence Kohlberg and the development of control beliefs.

Organizational Psychology. Organizational psychology is a very active field: organizational culture, leadership, job satisfaction, and effects linked to the introduction of new information and communication technologies and work situations are the focus of several research teams.

Psychological Assessment. An overview of the development that Portuguese experts in psychological assessment have brought to testing materials used with children and youth in the last three decades can be found in Montenegro (1992). This analysis concerns intelligence scales, spatial abilities tests, clinical and behavioral inventories, questionnaires, and projective techniques. Silva and Marques (1994) presented an overview of the teaching, study, and research on projective methods, which have found a respected place in psychological practice and research.

Social Psychology and Personality. A review in this area can be found in Neto (1996). Research conducted in Portugal can be categorized into 10 themes: social cognition, attitudes and values, prejudice and discrimination, social representations, social emotions and stress, personal control, intergroup relationships, group process, environmental influences, and cross-cultural relations. The consequence of such a diversity is that research is generally more data driven than theory driven. Empiricism and heterogeneity are dominant aspects of Portuguese social psychology.

Spheres of Activity

Psychology in Portugal is a very young profession. Today in Portugal there are almost 5,000 licensed psychologists (one psychologist for every 2,000 inhabitants). Women are in the majority, and psychology is becoming an increasingly feminized and saturated profession; graduates are having difficulty finding jobs. The majority of positions in psychology are in the areas of school, organizational/managerial, clinical, or forensic psychology.

Professional psychologists are not yet very well organized, and are divided among three associations: the Sociedade Portuguesa de Psicologia, the Associação Portuguesa de Psicologia, and the Associação dos Psicólogos Portugueses. There is one trade union, the Sindicato Nacional de Psicólogos. In the future, one useful goal of these associations and unions would be to collaborate with the Ministry of Work to define a legal status for the psychological profession.

Clinical Psychology. In the hospital, the clinical psychologist provides counseling during illness, which can contribute to the improvement of the patient's quality of life, and assists in the treatment of functional complaints. In geriatric and pediatric centers, the clinical psychologist performs typical tasks of assessment, counseling, therapy, and management. Clinical and health psychologists participate in the development of health-promoting campaigns on such problems as smoking, alcohol abuse, drugs, eating habits, and stress management. Psychiatric centers, mental health services, rehabilitation centers, family therapy centers, and psychiatric wards in general hospitals are also settings where psychologists exercise their competencies.

Forensic Psychology. It was only in the mid-1980s that Portuguese psychologists started to work in legal and forensic settings, namely, as probation officers or as educators in prisons. Although the number of professionals working in the Portuguese legal and penal system is considerable, psychological research is scant, mainly because scientific and academic preparation continues to be inadequate (R. Gonçalves, 1996).

Organizational Psychology. As in every developed country, Portuguese psychologists are in charge of recruitment, selection, outplacement, and training of professionals, and also provide managerial consulting. They work within industry itself as well as in independent centers. Recent technological innovations have created a demand for experts in occupational resettlement and in-service training. Psychologists are becoming involved in human resources management.

School Psychology. School psychology is the oldest and perhaps the best known branch of psychology in Portugal. The original emphasis on vocational counseling has been broadened to other relevant aspects of school psychology: determination of basic needs in education, the initial and continuous training of teachers, and instruction of the mentally handicapped. One of the consequences of the changes in the country as a whole has been reflected in the increasing demand for education from the family. School psychologists are trying to adapt traditional schools to the needs of a public that is increasingly heterogeneous.

The Future

It seems fair to say that psychology in Portugal is in a transitional state. The changes to date have been very positive. The notable growth of the discipline in the 1980s and 1990s suggests that psychology as a science and as a profession in Portugal will experience still further change in the form of continued growth and maturity.

For the harmonious development of psychology in Portugal, it seems essential that the legal status for university-trained psychologists be defined. Official status will help the public, the managers, and the political authorities to know better what they can expect (and not expect, for example, divination, spiritism) from trained psychologists. Until recently, the development of psychology in Portugal has proceeded by extension. The priorities now are training to strengthen and complement existing programs, and research to conduct a global reflection about what could be the specificity of Portuguese psychology research. Although improvements in the educational training of Portuguese psychologists have been substantial in the recent past, deficiencies in academic preparation must continue to be addressed. It would appear essential, if Portugal is to ensure adequate preparation of academic (and research-oriented) psychologists, that university curricula with doctoral programs in basic and applied psychology be developed in addition to existing professional training areas.

With respect to research, areas in which Portuguese psychologists could carry out original investigations are not very difficult to detect. The total number of Portuguese people living outside Portugal is about 4.5 million (for comparison, the number of Portuguese people living in Portugal is about 10 million.) Migration is thus a significant phenomenon in Portuguese society. For this reason it is evident that important specific contributions could be made by Portuguese psychologists on the psychological aspects of migration, as well as the psychological problems and the psychological opportunities, originated by contact with different languages and cultures. As stated by Neto (1997, p. 67), Portugal is a "natural social laboratory for psychology." Such contributions could be the work of international teams composed of psychologists from Angola, Brazil, Cape Verde, Guiné Bissau, Macao, Mozambique, São Tomé e Príncipe, as well as Western (host) countries. These contributions could, for example, be immediately useful for all people interested in (or in charge of) the construction of the European Union. Although there remains much work to be done to sustain and nurture the advancement of the discipline of psychology within Portugal, much has already been accomplished under the catalytic influence of the new democracy, and the future appears promising.

[*See also* Spain.]

Bibliography

Abreu, M. V. (1990). Os primeiros laboratórios de Psicologia em Portugal: Contexto e sentido da sua criação. *Jornal de Psicologia, 9*(1), 3–7.

Borges, I. (1983). A Psicologia em Portugal: Uma hipótese de abordagem histórica. *Jornal de Psicologia, 2*(2) 3, 10.

Carneiro, F. (1997). *A psicologia em Portugal*. Porto: Edição do autor.

Gomes, J. F. (1990). As origens do laboratório de psicologia experimental da Universidade de Coimbra. *Revista Portuguesa de Pedagogia, 24*, 3–38.

Gomes, J. F. (1994). O ensino da psicologia e da pedagogia nas universidades portuguesas de 1991 a 1973. *Revista Portuguesa de Pedagogia, 28*, 337–370.

Gonçalves, O. (1990). Psicologia clínica: Estado actual e perspectivas de futuro. *Jornal de Psicologia, 9*(1), 8–13.

Gonçalves, R. (1996). Psicologia da justiça: Um longo passado para uma designação recente. *Psicologia: Teoria, Investigação e Prática, 1*, 207–218.

Lima, S. (1949). A psicologia em Portugal. *Biblos, 25*, 277–285.

Lourenço, O. (1994). Psicologia do desenvolvimento em Portugal e Espanha: Temas de pesquisa, orientações teóricas, tendências emergentes. *Análise Psicológica, 4*(12), 547–565.

Montenegro, A. (1992). Foreign tests standardized in Portugal in the last three decades: An overview. *Psychologica, 8*, 185–193.

Neto, F. (1992, November). *A investigação em psicologia social em Portugal.* Paper presented at the first meeting of the Portuguese Psychological Society, Coimbra, Portugal.

Neto, F. (1997). *Estudos de psicologia intercultural: Nós e outros.* Lisboa: Fundação Calouste Gulbenkian.

Pinto, A. (1991). Reading rates and digit span in bilinguals: The superiority of mother tongue. *International Journal of Psychology, 26*, 471–483.

Silva, D., & Marques, M. E. (1994). The Rorschach and other projective methods in Portugal. In I. B. Weiner (Ed.), *Rorschariana 19: Yearbook of the International Rorschach Society* (pp. 24–46). Gottingen, Germany: Hogrefe & Huber.

Félix Neto

POSTMAN, LEO JOSEPH (1918–), American psychologist. Postman was born in St. Petersburg, Russia, and was naturalized as a citizen of the United States in 1944. He received his bachelor's degree from the College of the City of New York in 1943 and his master's degree (1944) and doctorate (1946) from Harvard University. He married Dorothy Lerman in 1945. He served as assistant professor at Indiana University from 1947 to 1948 and at Harvard from 1948 to 1950 before joining the faculty at the University of California, Berkeley, where he became professor of psychology in 1957 and professor emeritus in 1987.

He was editor (1961–1968) of the *Journal of Verbal Learning and Verbal Behavior*, which he cofounded with Benton Underwood, and associate editor (1968–1974) of the *Journal of Experimental Psychology*. As a member of the American Psychological Association, he served as president of both Division 1 (General Psychology) and Division 3 (Experimental Psychology). He was elected to the Society of Experimental Psychologists in 1959 and was awarded their Warren Medal in 1974 for his outstanding contributions to experimental psychology. He was vice-president of the American Association for the Advancement of Science and is a member of the National Academy of Sciences.

Postman published *Psychology of Rumor* (New York, 1947) with Gordon Allport. Their laboratory investigations of distortions in memory for pictures led to the postulation that rumors varied with situational ambiguity and thematic importance; their work helped to shape the conceptualization of research on the psychology of rumor in the ensuing decades. Postman also conducted a number of experimental studies with Jerome Bruner on perceptual defense and the influence of motivation on perception that contributed to the "new look" in perception in the 1950s.

Postman's early experimental studies of verbal learning and memory examined the effects of reward and punishment. E. L. Thorndike had begun the study of the effects of reward and punishment on human and animal behavior in formulating his law of effect. Postman assessed the literature that followed Thorndike's research and conducted his own studies to extend the understanding of the phenomena.

Postman also contributed to the literature on the "learning to learn" phenomenon. "Learning to learn" designated research on the improvement in learning from one learning situation to another. Postman explored such effects in human verbal learning experiments to examine the development of skills specific to a particular learning task and those skills that generalize to other tasks.

Postman's primary research contributions were his studies of variables influencing verbal learning and memory in the tradition of serial and paired associate learning that began with Hermann Ebbinghaus. Postman's systematic research efforts examined proactive and retroactive interference effects (i.e., the effects of prior and later learning) in the learning and subsequent recall and recognition of verbal associates to address theoretical questions in the interpretation of forgetting. His experimental investigations explored such variables as encoding of material to be remembered, the organization of memory, and extraexperimental interference effects on learning and memory.

Bibliography

Bruner, J. (1992). Another look at New Look 1. *American Psychologist, 47*, 780–783. Bruner comments on the "new look" in perception and some subsequent interpretations.

Postman, L. (1962). Rewards and punishments in human learning. In L. Postman (Ed.), *Psychology in the making* (pp. 331–401). New York: Knopf. This essay summarizes the research and cites some of Postman's studies on this issue.

Postman, L. (1969). Experimental analysis of learning to learn. In G. Bower & J. T. Spence (Eds.), *The psychology of learning and motivation* (Vol. 3, pp. 241–299), New York: Academic Press. Postman's essay describes the problem and the experiments that make up this research area, including some of his own laboratory studies.

Postman, L. & Underwood, B. J. (1973). Critical issues in interference theory. *Memory and Cognition, 1*, 19–40. This paper describes some of the theoretical issues of Postman's concern.

Rosnow, R. L. (1991). Inside rumor. *American Psychologist, 46*, 484–496. Rosnow describes the impact of the Allport–Postman studies of rumor on subsequent research in the field.

Alfred H. Fuchs

POSTMODERN PSYCHOLOGY refers to a number of approaches that radically challenge central assumptions inherent in a wide variety of psychological theories and practices. Drawing on recent writings by philosophers, literary critics, and social theorists, postmodern psychologists have called into question conventional understandings of the subject matter of psychology and of the functions of psychology in society. Their work is both critical and constructive: In addition to attempting to debunk or undermine many taken-for-granted theories and methods utilized by psychologists, most postmodernists working within psychology have also proposed alternative directions for the study of human phenomena and social life. Ultimately, such theorists endeavor to dramatically reenvision our conception of the potentials and limitations of psychological knowledge. Prominent movements or trends within psychology that can properly be termed postmodern include social constructionism, discourse analysis, dialogism, and the work of some feminist psychologists, critical psychologists, and historians of psychology. Among the most influential postmodern psychologists are Kenneth Gergen, Edward Sampson, John Shotter, Jill Morawski, Valerie Walkerdine, Jeanne Marecek, Rachel Hare-Mustin, and Kurt Danziger.

The term *postmodern* is a somewhat amorphous, elastic, and even contentious one. As far back as the 1940s and 1950s, but particularly since the 1970s, the words *postmodernism* and *postmodernity* have been used by various theorists in the humanities and social sciences for a variety of intellectual purposes. In aesthetics and cultural criticism, *postmodernism* has been used to refer to certain post–World War II movements in architecture and the arts. The term *postmodern* is also applied to some recent trends in philosophy, literary criticism, and social theory—including poststructuralism, deconstructionism, and neopragmatism—which are related to, but not identical with, postmodernist artistic trends. Finally, *postmodernity* is used to denote the particular historical period that generated all these cultural and intellectual developments. In such sociological accounts, the transition to global capitalism and rapid advances in computer and communication technology are seen to have engendered a set of social and psychological effects to which postmodern cultural and intellectual movements are a response. These three meanings of *postmodern* are overlapping and intertwined, but by no means identical. In the case of all three usages, postmodern forms, whether artistic, theoretical, or socioeconomic, are generally defined in terms of their being radically different from "modern" forms and from "modernity." Different commentators have delineated the nature and chronology of modernity and modernism in somewhat different ways (as is also the case with postmodernity), although these terms are often broadly identified with post-Cartesian philosophy, Enlightenment thought, and the scientific and industrial revolutions. A further point of contention is whether the postmodern turn in art and theory represents a radical rupture with the modern or is primarily a continuation or intensification of core modernist tendencies.

Postmodern psychology evinces all three meanings of the postmodern. However, postmodern psychologists have been particularly influenced by the writings of poststructuralist and postmodernist theorists, most notably Jacques Derrida, Michel Foucault, Jean-François Lyotard, and Richard Rorty. Influential postmodern psychologists such as Kenneth Gergen and Edward Sampson have drawn on the work of these theorists in order to challenge the underpinnings of psychological knowledge and practices in several far-reaching ways. In order to appreciate the nature of these postmodern critiques, it is necessary to recognize that, although psychology is an extraordinarily diversified field, most of its theories and research rest upon at least some, and usually most, of the following assumptions. First, the unit of analysis for psychologists is the individual human being (although of course psychologists study humans at a variety of different levels). Second, psychology is a science in the sense that it aims to discover, through the use of the scientific method, universal and ahistorical laws of human behavior. Third, psychological concepts correspond to empirical realities, mirroring natural forms; most psychological inquiry thus rests on an objectivist theory of knowledge. A corollary of this assumption is that psychological knowledge is value neutral, rather than being a function of particular groups' or individuals' interests and perspectives. Fourth, psychology—both pure and applied—functions in society mainly to improve the quality of life for individuals and groups, and in particular, to help foster greater individual freedom and self-mastery. Fifth, humans possess psychic "interiority": Mental processes, including cognition, motivation, and emotion, are located within the individual mind. Sixth, the individual self is a cohesive entity that is stable across time and situations.

Postmodern psychologists are by no means the only psychologists who have been critical of these assumptions. As discussed later in this article, Marxists, critical theorists, phenomenological and hermeneutic psychologists, and others have also challenged at least some of the assumptions listed here, but they have come to conclusions that are somewhat different from those of postmodernists. The latter can be distinguished from other nonobjectivist and critical psychologists largely by virtue of the extent to which they have drawn on ideas exemplified in the writings of Derrida and Foucault.

Jacques Derrida (1930–), the Algerian-born French literary theorist and originator of deconstructionism, has challenged prevailing philosophical understandings of truth, knowledge, language, and the mind. Most fundamentally, he contested the "metaphysics of presence" that underlies the entire Western cultural and philosophical tradition. The metaphysics of presence entails several core beliefs: First, language is a transparent medium that straightforwardly mirrors reality; second, reality is constituted of relatively stable, sharply demarcated natural kinds that can be clearly identified and represented linguistically; and third, all positive statements of meaning originate in individual minds—in the thoughts, motives, and intentions of individual subjects or authors. In his rebuttal of these assumptions, Derrida extended the work of structuralist and semiotic theorists to demonstrate that all words derive their meaning only in terms of their difference from other meanings within the general system of language. Every positive meaning—every "presence"—is thus infused with absent meanings or "traces" in terms of which it is formed. Since all identity is thus founded on difference, absent and unarticulated "others" always lurk, usually suppressed and concealed, in any positive meaning.

Michel Foucault (1926–1984), a French poststructuralist social theorist, introduced several ideas that have been used by postmodern psychologists to complement and extend Derridean analyses. Like Derrida, Foucault did not conceive of language as corresponding to a world of natural objects. He documented how, over the past 500 years, there have been several radical shifts in the linguistic and conceptual grids through which the world has been construed. He contended that the concepts of "man" and the "human being" are modern inventions and that psychology and psychiatry, which are founded on these constructs, originated in order to facilitate the legitimacy of modern democratic society. In premodern societies, Foucault argued, physical coercion was used to maintain social control. However, in modern liberal democratic societies, state governance is maintained largely by ensuring that the will of the people coincides with the social order. Beginning in the nineteenth century, the human sciences and helping professions arose to subject individuals' inner "souls" to surveillance and discipline. The intrusion of such modern social control into the inner recesses of the self was seen by Foucault to have been effected by means of a process he called normalization. In order to ensure that subjects will not only act in accord with, but will also experience themselves as endorsing, the social order, psychological theories and practices identify "others." These others exist both inside the self, as undesirable forms of experience and behavior, and outside the self, embodied in types such as the madman, child, invert, and pervert. Such internal and external others are then excluded or "rehabilitated" so that the self comes to experience itself and to be perceived as more closely harmonized with the "normal" order. Psychologists and psychiatrists tend to view themselves as working to extend human freedom, but Foucault and his followers argued that these professions ultimately promote increasingly effective, comprehensive, and insidious policing of the self.

Postmodern psychologists have drawn several implications from the work of Derrida and Foucault, and from related ideas found in the writings of the French postmodernist Jean-François Lyotard, the American neopragmatist Richard Rorty, and other postempiricist, hermeneutic, and ordinary language philosophers. The first implication they drew is that the objects studied by psychologists—from traits to neurotransmitters, operants to superegos, schemas to developmental stages—are not natural essences "out there" in the world. Rather, they are artifacts of the system of differences that is language, as it is deployed in particular social and cultural contexts. This has led to analyses of the metaphors and rhetorical structures in terms of which psychologists and others delineate the observational world. Such investigations demonstrate the socially constructed nature of psychological discourse, its historical and cultural contingency, the internal contradictions inevitably contained in such discourse, and the social effects of particular systems of psychological explanation.

A second direction taken by postmodern psychologists has been to focus on the suppression and marginalization of "otherness" that is entailed in the construction of psychological and psychiatric knowledge. According to Derridean analysis, all positive meanings are constituted through the (usually implicit) exclusion of differences and the imposition onto reality of a coherence and orderliness that it does not actually possess. Foucault made a related point when he asserted that modern categories of psychopathology and normality are constituted in relation to each other, and serve the function of sharply delineating the normal for the purposes of suppressing otherness so that the social order can be strengthened and legitimized. Postmodern psychologists take such analyses as cues to deconstruct psychological and psychiatric categories and norms in order to unmask the inevitable reification, domination, and exclusion that such meanings entail. They highlight how psychologists' depictions and appraisals of marginalized or devalued groups—including women, homosexuals, African Americans, non-Western cultural groups, and the "mentally ill"—have served to reinforce inequality in society through the portrayal of "different" types of experience and behavior as deviant or inferior. Postmodern psychologists suggest that the current degree of homogenization and exclusion of difference is not necessary for social order to be maintained and, in fact, runs counter to some of the core values of democracy.

A third tendency in postmodern psychology has

been to redirect the focus of inquiry from the individual mind to the relational or discursive field. As a corollary of this reenvisioning of psychology's unit of analysis, postmodernists also contend that autonomy is overemphasized as a psychological and moral ideal and should be replaced by a vision of human nature as interdependent and relational. In advocating such a shift, Sampson, Shotter, Gergen, and other psychologists drew not only on explicitly postmodern writings, but also on the ideas of Ludwig Wittgenstein, Gregory Bateson, George Herbert Mead, Lev Vygotsky, Mikhail Bakhtin, and many feminist thinkers. Such theorists depict human existence as fundamentally social or dialogical and consider all facets of the "mind" and "self" to be socially engendered, both in their origins and in their ongoing expressions. Postmodern psychologists attempt to demonstrate that psychological processes, including memory, emotion, cognition, identity, and personality are constituted contextually and relationally and need to be investigated in those terms. For example, rather than conceiving of memory as a trace in an individual's brain, they emphasize investigations of the social dynamics and situational contingencies involved in the elicitation of particular memories. Similarly, many postmodernists follow the Russian literary theorist Bakhtin in reconceptualizing cognition in social terms, as an "inner conversation" in which various types of others are invariably being addressed and answered. Gergen, in a particularly radical move, advocated that psychologists stop trying to scrutinize or understand psychic interiority altogether, and instead focus exclusively on how gestures and utterances take on meaning only in the context of particular relational interchanges. In pursuing these investigations, postmodern psychologists tend to use ethnographic and qualitative methods of social inquiry, including narrative and discourse analysis.

It is hardly surprising that an intellectual movement that strikes so directly at the central tenets of modern psychology has provoked controversy. But it is not only psychologists committed to an objectivist model of knowledge who take issue with the postmodern turn. Many of the most outspoken critics of postmodernism have been philosophers and psychologists—including Marxists, feminists, critical theorists, and hermeneuticists—who agree with much of the postmodern critique but disagree with some of the implications postmodern psychologists have drawn from it. Like postmodernists, Marxist and feminist psychologists explore how psychological theories and norms reinforce inequalities (specifically those of class and gender), concealing their ideological dimensions in ostensibly neutral and "objective" language. However, unlike postmodernists, psychologists influenced by Marxism believe that the critique of ideology should be framed in terms of a universalistic interpretive language of class struggle and emancipation. Critical theorists, most notably Jurgen Habermas, blend such Marxist themes with liberal, rationalist, hermeneutic, and psychoanalytic ideas to criticize what they view as the antirationalist and politically conservative implications of postmodernism: Habermasians believe that it is possible to arrive rationally at universal normative standards and procedures for enabling human freedom and autonomy, and that psychology can and should be linked to this project. Feminism is not a unified body of thought: There are radical, Marxist, Habermasian, liberal, and postmodernist versions of feminist theory and psychology. However, like Marxists and critical theorists, many feminist psychologists are concerned that postmodernist approaches furnish no basis for critique, agency, and resistance. Finally, hermeneutic psychologists, influenced by the philosophers Martin Heidegger, Hans Georg Gadamer, and Paul Ricoeur, agree with postmodernists that the historical and cultural dimensions of existence must be more fully integrated into psychological inquiry. However, they disagree with the claim of many postmodernists that there is no viable way to judge some interpretations and moral evaluations as being more adequate than others. The conversations between postmodernists and other critical psychologists are ongoing, and the question of how the discourse of critical and nonobjectivist psychology will be transformed as a result of such dialogical interchange is not yet settled.

Postmodern psychologists have made important contributions: They have promoted greater critical awareness of the ways in which psychological "truths" are embedded in social, cultural, and political frames, and they have helped to open up new horizons of inquiry into human nature and social life. However, it remains to be seen whether this field will be accommodated within mainstream psychology, completely transform the discipline as we know it, or settle into an independent disciplinary space.

[*See also* Feminism, *article on* Feminism and Philosophy; *and* Hermeneutics.]

Bibliography

Derrida, J. (1976). *Of grammatology* (G. Spivak, Trans.). Baltimore: Johns Hopkins University Press.

Flax, J. (1990). *Thinking fragments: Psychoanalysis, postmodernism and feminism in the contemporary West.* Berkeley: University of California Press. A lucid overview of the strengths and weaknesses of postmodern approaches, written from the perspective of a political theorist who is also a feminist and psychoanalyst.

Foucault, M. (1977). *Discipline and punish: The birth of the prison* (A. Sheridan, Trans.). New York: Random House.

Foucault, M. (1980). *The history of sexuality: Vol. 1. An introduction* (R. Hurley, Trans.). New York: Vintage Press.

Gergen, K. J. (1994). *Realities and relationships: Soundings in social construction*. Cambridge, MA: Harvard University Press.

Gergen, K. J., & Shotter, J. (Eds.). (1994). *Texts of identity*. Thousand Oaks, CA: Sage.

Henriques, J., Hollway, W., Urwin, C., Venn, C., & Walkerdine, V. (1984). *Changing the subject: Psychology, social regulation and subjectivity*. New York: Methuen. An important early attempt to apply poststructuralist and postmodern theories to psychological inquiry.

Jameson, F. (1991). The cultural logic of late capitalism. In *Postmodernism: Or the cultural logic of late capitalism* (pp. 1–154). Durham, NC: Duke University Press. Relates the rise of postmodern cultural movements to the globalization of late capitalism.

Kvale, S. (Ed.). (1994). *Psychology and postmodernism*. Thousand Oaks, CA: Sage.

Leary, D. E. (Ed.). (1990). *Metaphors in the history of psychology*. Cambridge, UK: Cambridge University Press. Studies by postmodernists and others of how metaphors have shaped psychological knowledge.

Lyotard, J.-F. (1984). *The postmodern condition: A report on knowledge* (G. Bennington & B. Massouri, Trans.). Minneapolis: University of Minnesota Press.

Potter, J., & Wetherell, M. (1987).*Discourse and social psychology*. Thousand Oaks, CA: Sage.

Sampson, E. E. (1993). *Celebrating the other: A dialogical account of human nature*. New York: Harvester Wheatsheaf.

Suzanne R. Kirschner

POSTSECONDARY EDUCATION. *See* College Teaching and Learning; *and* Technical and Professional Education.

POSTTRAUMATIC STRESS DISORDER. Although symptoms of posttraumatic stress disorder (PTSD) have long been recognized, it was not until 1980 that PTSD was formally defined and classified by the *Diagnostic and Statistical Manual of Mental Disorders* (American Psychiatric Association, 1994). PTSD is classified as an anxiety disorder that develops in some individuals after exposure to an extremely traumatic event(s). For an individual to be diagnosed with PTSD, the traumatic event(s) experienced or witnessed must involve actual or threatened death or serious injury, or a threat to the physical integrity of self or others. A response of intense fear, helplessness, or horror at the time of the event(s) must also be involved, although in children the response may be expressed instead by disorganized or agitated behavior. The disorder may occur in individuals who have experienced a broad range of traumatic events. Common examples include combat veterans, crime victims (e.g., rape, assault, robbery, or sexual abuse), prisoners of war, accident victims, survivors of major natural disasters, and those diagnosed with life-threatening illnesses. Lifetime exposure to such traumatic events appears to be common in community-based samples (36–86%), and the likelihood of developing PTSD increases as the intensity of the traumatic stressor increases.

Three symptom clusters (reexperiencing, avoidance/numbing, and hyperarousal) describe the clinical features of PTSD. First, the traumatic event is persistently reexperienced. Intrusive and disruptive memories of the trauma are common, as are frightening dreams or nightmares. Some individuals experience dissociative states (flashbacks) that last from a few seconds to a few hours, during which the traumatic event is relived. In rare cases, the individual may even behave as though experiencing the traumatic event again at that moment. Exposure to environmental stimuli that resemble an aspect of the traumatic event often evokes intense psychological distress and/or physiological reactivity. For example, combat veterans often become highly upset when they hear fireworks that remind them of gunfire, and they may notice their heart racing as if they were back in combat. Young children with PTSD may not necessarily have the sense that they are reliving their traumatic past, but rather may reexperience their trauma in symbolic ways. For example, they may exhibit general nightmares (e.g., frightening monsters), repetitive play (e.g., reenacting the trauma with toy figures), or somatic symptoms (e.g., headaches and stomachaches).

Second, such reexperiencing and reactivity leads to persistent avoidance of cues associated with the traumatic event. This includes efforts to avoid thoughts, feelings, or conversations about the trauma, as well as efforts to avoid activities or situations that arouse recollections of the trauma. On rare occasions, this avoidance may include amnesia for significant aspects of the trauma. Reduced emotional responsiveness to the external world is also common, with many individuals reporting decreased interest in activities they previously enjoyed, feeling detached or cut off from other people, or having reduced ability to feel emotions (especially those associated with love, happiness, joy, and sexuality). They may also experience a sense of a foreshortened future, as if they do not expect to have a career, marriage, or normal life span.

Third, persistent symptoms of increased arousal or anxiety that were not present before the trauma also cause disruption in the lives of those with PTSD. These symptoms include difficulty falling or staying asleep, irritability or outbursts of anger, difficulty concentrating, hypervigilance, and exaggerated startle response.

Finally, for a diagnosis of PTSD, the disturbance must last for at least 1 month and it must cause significant distress or impairment in social, occupational, or other important areas of functioning. It merits comment that many PTSD symptoms, such as impaired concentration, sleep disturbance, irritability, social avoidance, and sense of a foreshortened future are also found in other disorders (e.g., depression and anxiety). What seems to distinguish PTSD from other mood or anxiety disorders are the reexperiencing of symptoms (nightmares, flashbacks), physiological reactivity to trauma cues, and avoidance of trauma cues. There is also a distinct set of neurobiological markers that differentiates PTSD from other affective and anxiety disorders in laboratory studies, notably, changes on the hypothalamic-pituitary-adrenal axis.

Associated Disorders and Features

A distinct set of secondary symptoms, associated features, and concurrent psychiatric disorders are commonly found among those with PTSD. These individuals may experience strong feelings of guilt and shame, often related to having survived when others did not, to the things they did in order to survive, or to the belief that they allowed themselves to be victimized. In addition, a broad range of interpersonal problems are typically associated with PTSD. Many individuals with PTSD often feel misunderstood, alienated, and detached from others. Therefore, they may feel lonely and isolated from friends, family members, and society as a whole. Complicating matters is the finding that irritability, anger control deficits, interpersonal communication skill deficits, social anxiety, and social avoidance are commonplace. Thus, PTSD symptoms and the phobic avoidance of activities or situations that represent the trauma may interfere with interpersonal relationships and occupational functioning.

Studies examining physiological reactivity in trauma victims with PTSD have consistently found heightened reactivity to trauma-related cues as compared to trauma victims without PTSD. In these studies, trauma-related audio visual cues (sounds or pictures) or individually tailored script-driven imagery are presented while physiological responses such as blood pressure (BP), heart rate (HR), galvanic skin response (GSR), or forehead electromyogram (EMG) are measured. Trauma victims diagnosed with PTSD produce significantly larger BP and HR responses during cue exposure than do trauma victims without PTSD, although EMG and GSR have been less reliable in differentiating these groups. There is evidence that measurement of physiological reactivity may provide relatively good discrimination even when individuals are attempting to fake their responses. Interestingly, no differences have been found in general autonomic reactivity to nontraumatic cues between those with and without PTSD. Thus, the reactivity in those with PTSD appears to be elicited only in response to specific trauma-related cues.

Finally, there is typically a high prevalence of other psychiatric disorders in both civilians and combat veterans with PTSD. Acute concomitant disorders often include substance abuse, major depression, dysthymia, sexual dysfunction, and other anxiety disorders. Although rates for these disorders vary depending on the trauma population examined and the evaluation procedures used, studies have reported rates of concurrent mental disorders ranging as high as 80 to 100%. Personality disorders are also frequently diagnosed in PTSD populations, including borderline, schizoid, avoidant, and antisocial personality disorders. At present, the extent and nature of personality disorders in individuals diagnosed with PTSD is not well understood, and it is not clear whether trauma changes personality or if certain personality patterns predispose some towards traumatic experiences and/or PTSD. There is some evidence to provide partial support for both possibilities.

Prevalence and Course of PTSD

Epidemiological estimates of PTSD vary somewhat, depending on the method of evaluation and the population sampled, although most community-based studies indicate a lifetime prevalence ranging from 1 to 14%. Among traumatized populations, the percentage with PTSD is higher. It has been estimated that 9 to 31% of combat veterans have a lifetime history of PTSD, with current rates of the disorder ranging from 6 to 26%, depending on the particular war. African American, Hispanic, and Native American veterans have been shown to have higher absolute rates of PTSD than Caucasian veterans, although this difference disappears when factors such as premilitary trauma and degree of combat exposure are taken into consideration. For civilian crime victims, lifetime rates range from 18 to 28%, with current rates ranging from 5 to 11%.

Symptoms of PTSD can occur at any age, including early childhood, following the experience of trauma. Although symptoms are usually apparent within several weeks or months of the traumatic experience, there may be delayed onset of months or years before the symptoms appear. Duration of this disorder varies greatly, although approximately half of those developing it achieve full recovery without treatment within 3 months of symptom onset. However, in some cases symptoms are long lasting. For example, many veterans are still suffering severe and debilitating symptoms from wars fought more than 50 years ago (e.g., World War II). There is some evidence that social support, family history, childhood experiences, and personality variables may influence the development of the disorder, although it appears that PTSD can develop in anyone if the traumatic stress is severe enough.

Treatment of PTSD

At this point, PTSD treatment is still in the early stages of development, which is not surprising, given that formal recognition of the disorder is relatively recent (1980). A wide range of psychosocial and pharmacological treatments have been used with PTSD. However, there is surprisingly little research to indicate which treatments are most effective, and there is little general consensus among clinicians about which treatments should be used. Cognitive-behavioral treatments have been the most widely studied psychosocial interventions and include strategies such as exposure therapy (e.g., flooding and systematic desensitization), stress inoculation, cognitive processing therapy, anger management, social skills training, and relaxation training. The clinical efficacy of these interventions has been partially demonstrated, although the manner in which they can be most effectively implemented and combined with other treatments is still under investigation. Other common psychosocial treatments include psychodynamic, family, and marital therapy, peer-counseling groups (e.g., "rap" groups), and psychiatric inpatient settings. Pharmacological treatments have focused on the use of psychotropic medications (e.g., antidepressants and antianxiety agents) to reduce symptoms of depression, anxiety, and hyperarousal, as well as to help regulate the sleep cycle. However, there are few empirical data to guide psychiatrists in the prescription of these medications with PTSD patients, and no medication has been designed specifically for PTSD. In short, although some extant treatments have demonstrated clinical efficacy, we currently do not have a "cure" for the disorder, but rather view treatment strategies as ways to help manage the symptoms and improve quality of life.

[*See also* Combat; *and* Rape.]

Bibliography

American Psychiatric Association. (1994). *Diagnostic and statistical manual of mental disorders* (4th ed.). Washington, DC: Author.

Davidson, J. R. T., & Foa, E. B. (Eds.). (1993). *Posttraumatic stress disorder: DSM–IV and beyond.* Washington, DC: American Psychiatric Press.

Foa, E. B., & Riggs, D. S. (1995). Posttraumatic stress disorder following assault: Theoretical considerations and empirical findings. *Current Directions in Psychological Science, 4,* 61–65.

Foy, D. W. (Ed.). (1992). *Treating PTSD: Cognitive-behavioral strategies.* New York: Guilford Press.

Freedy, J. R., & Hobfall, S. E. (Eds.). (1995). *Traumatic stress: From theory to practice.* New York: Plenum Press.

Friedman, M. J., Charney, D. S., & Deutch, A. Y. (Eds.). (1995). *Neurobiological and clinical consequences of stress: From normal adaptation to PTSD.* Philadelphia: Lippincott-Raven.

Frueh, B. C., Turner, S. M., & Beidel, D. C. (1995). Exposure therapy for combat-related PTSD: A critical review. *Clinical Psychology Review, 15,* 799–817.

Giller, E. L. (Ed.). (1990). *Biological assessment and treatment of posttraumatic stress disorder.* Washington, DC: American Psychiatric Press.

Keane, T. M., & Wolfe, J. (1990). Comorbidity in posttraumatic stress disorder: An analysis of community and clinical studies. *Journal of Applied Social Psychology, 20,* 1776–1788.

Kulka, R., Schlenger, W., Fairbank, J., Hough, R., Jordon, B., Marmar, C., & Weiss, D. (1990). *Trauma and the Vietnam war generation.* New York: Brunnel/Mazel.

Shalev, A. Y., Bonne, O., & Eth, S. (1996). Treatment of posttraumatic stress disorder: A review. *Psychosomatic Medicine, 58,* 165–182.

B. Christopher Frueh

POVERTY. [*This entry provides a broad survey of poverty. It is chronologically divided into two articles:* Childhood Poverty *and* Adulthood Poverty.]

Childhood Poverty

The term *poverty* typically is used to refer to economic deprivation that results when income is insufficient to meet basic needs. It is commonly defined by cash income using the official federal poverty threshold as a marker. Developed in 1965 by Mollie Orshansky, an economist employed by the Social Security Administration, the poverty threshold was officially adopted by the government in 1969 to highlight the existence of poverty, to establish the need for antipoverty policies, and to provide an indicator of progress in the fight against poverty. It was originally based on the estimated cost of food (a very basic diet) multiplied by three, a formula adopted on the basis of a household budget study conducted in 1955 indicating that families typically spent about one third of their post-tax household income on food. The poverty threshold is adjusted annually for family size and inflation, but not for geographic region or noncash benefits (e.g., food stamps).

Although the validity of this index has been questioned on many grounds, it is widely used in both research and policy. Two points are important: First, it is an absolute dollar amount, not a percentage of the median income or a percentile. Therefore, it is theoretically possible for everyone to be above the poverty threshold. Second, it does not reflect how far below (or above) the threshold people fall (i.e., the poverty gap). Increasingly, researchers studying the effects of childhood poverty measure the poverty gap by computing an income-to-need ratio (calculated as household income/official poverty threshold for a child's household). An income-to-need ratio of 1.0 indicates that a household's income is equal to the poverty threshold. Smaller or larger ratios represent more or less severe poverty (or greater affluence), respectively.

In the 1960s, poverty was discovered by the media and political leaders, and a war was launched against it. As a result, the poverty rate for children declined from 27% in 1960 to 14% in 1969. However, it rose slightly throughout the 1970s and increased sharply during the recession of the early 1980s. Since that time, it has remained stubbornly high (around 20%). As of 1996, 21.8% of American children lived in families with cash incomes below the poverty threshold. Childhood poverty rates in America are about twice as high as those for most other Western industrialized nations. Unlike the United States, many Western industrialized countries have social insurance in the form of universal child allowances, universal health care, and free or inexpensive child care that reduce poverty while permitting parents to work.

Although the majority of poor children in the United States are of European ancestry, rates of childhood poverty among African American, Native American, and certain groups of Latino children typically are two to three times higher than that of non-Latino White children. Moreover, African American and Puerto Rican children are much more likely than non-Latino White children to experience long-term poverty and, if they are poor, to live in communities with high rates of poverty.

Theories About the Causes of Poverty

The question of what causes adult poverty and therefore poverty among children has evoked protracted and heated debate. Two schools of thought have dominated this debate. Structuralists argue that poverty is fundamentally an economic condition stemming from blocked opportunities. Although not disavowing that individual abilities and traits contribute to adult economic and occupational statuses, structuralists contend that institutional barriers and structural factors external to the individual are major determinants of poverty (e.g., historic and contemporary racism in the labor market, lending institutions, housing; poor quality schools; low wages paid by traditionally "female" jobs). For example, they point out that because of long-standing racial discrimination in education, employment, and housing, African American adults as compared with their White counterparts have lower levels of education, hold jobs with higher rates of displacement and lower rates of reemployment following layoffs, and are less likely to reside in suburbs and nonmetropolitan areas where most growth in entry-level jobs is occurring. Consequently, African Americans have higher rates of family and child poverty than do Whites. Likewise, given that children living in female-headed households are at much higher risk of being poor than those living in two-parent families, structuralists argue that historic and contemporary racism fosters high rates of poverty among African American children by undermining African American men's economic status and, hence, their "marriagability" (i.e., employed or earning wages above the poverty threshold; Wilson, 1987). It is well documented that entry into marriage is less likely and marital dissolution more likely if the husband is unemployed or poor than if the husband is employed or nonpoor.

In contrast to structuralists, culture of poverty theorists argue that poverty is the product of cultural and interpersonal processes that nurture individual traits incompatible with upward economic mobility. Specifically, they assert that (a) the poor have distinct values, aspirations, and psychological characteristics that (b) inhibit their achievement and produce behavioral deviances likely to keep them poor, and (c) persist across generations through the socialization of the young (Corcoran, Duncan, Gurin, & Gurin, 1985). Oscar Lewis (1966) coined the culture of poverty concept on the basis of his studies of poor people living in the ghettos of Latin America. Maintaining that poverty is more than a mere lack of economic resources, Lewis identified an array of psychological orientations and behaviors that he believed characterized the poor and rendered poverty self-perpetuating (e.g., lack of impulse control, strong present-time orientation, minimal ability to defer gratification and to plan for the future).

The debate between structuralists and culture of poverty theorists reached a feverish pitch during the 1960s and resurfaced in the 1980s and 1990s in discussions about the "underclass." Although the debate is far from resolved, several kinds of empirical evidence from nationally representative samples of individuals studied over a long period of time (i.e., longitudinal data), unavailable during the 1960s, pose serious challenges to the culture of poverty argument: (a) only a small subset of individuals who are ever poor remain poor for an extended period of time, although the bulk of those poor at a given time are accounted for by the long-term poor (Bane & Ellwood, 1986); (b) motivational differences between individuals (e.g., need for achievement, personal efficacy, orientation toward future) have been found to be largely the result of changes in economic status, not the cause of subsequent improvement or deterioration in economic status (Corcoran et al., 1985); (c) young adults from poor families show substantial upward mobility, with some research finding that only 20% of individuals who were at or near the poverty line as children are at or near the poverty line after leaving home (Corcoran et al.,

1985); (d) the majority of daughters from families highly dependent on welfare do not themselves (as adults) become dependent on welfare, although they have a greater likelihood of sharing this fate than daughters from nonrecipient families (Duncan, Hill, & Hoffman, 1988). Collectively, these findings suggest that the culture of poverty arguments are an inappropriate model for viewing the majority of people who are ever poor. They may have more validity for the subset of individuals who are persistently poor, but this remains to be demonstrated.

A third, less dominant school of thought emphasizes heritable (genetically transmitted) abilities and traits as critical factors that consign individuals to poverty status (Herrnstein & Murray, 1994). Proponents of this view, typically behavioral geneticists, mention numerous traits as possible influences on adult socioeconomic outcomes, but their argument rests primarily on IQ. Evidence exists that childhood IQ predicts adult occupational status, but it is also the case that father's educational level has been found to be a better predictor of occupational status than the individual's own childhood IQ score. School achievement and educational progress (particularly graduating from high school or college) are the clearest predictors of adult income and occupational status. Estimates of heritability for school achievement are consistently much lower than those for IQ (typically less than half).

Critics of the genetic explanation of poverty have made several compelling points. They note that few behavioral genetic studies include the full range of environments experienced by rich and poor children in the United States. This is pertinent, critics assert, because children living in poverty are exposed to more extreme environmental conditions than those in more comfortable circumstances, and such extreme conditions may exert a stronger influence, relative to genetic makeup, than is the case for children in relatively affluent families in the United States. They believe that if the full range of environments was represented in the behavioral genetic studies, even smaller estimates of heritability and larger estimates of environmental influences on occupational status would probably result. This argument finds some support in research with twins, indicating that estimates of heritability of performance on school achievement tests are considerably lower for children living in poor neighborhoods than for children from more affluent areas (Scarr, 1981).

Detractors of the genetic explanation also argue that the extant economic and social system is not based on a "natural" or universal set of criteria for sorting people by income groups. Rather, societal values, public policy, and economic forces are seen as major determinants of the number of people in poverty, as well as the rank ordering of people by income. For example, they point out that women's earnings are considerably lower than those of men, even when education, years of experience, and other indicators of individual attributes are taken into account. In many states, the average salary of high school coaches is much higher than the average salary of high school teachers in other subject areas, which in turn is markedly higher than that of child-care workers. Such data lead them to conclude that although skills in athletic coaching, teaching high school academic courses, and caring for children may have some genetic basis, the relative status and economic benefit accruing to people with these skills are a result of social values and structural conditions, not individual talents or behaviors (Huston, McLoyd, & Garcia Coll, 1997).

Notwithstanding the legitimacy of these arguments, behavioral geneticists are correct in their assertion that conventional research (i.e., research that does not use behavioral genetic methods) investigating relations among poverty, children's environment, and child outcomes within biologically related families confounds genetic and environmental influences and, hence, that these relations cannot be attributed solely to environmental influences (a point applicable to much of the research reviewed in the following section). It is beyond the scope of this article to describe and critique the methods used in behavioral genetic studies. Suffice it to say that these methods do provide information about heritability but they have several weaknesses for understanding environmental influences, and therefore cannot stand alone as the sole strategy for understanding either the causes or consequences of poverty. Converging evidence from multiple methods is more scientifically sound than that from any one method.

Investigations using a variety of methods provide strong evidence that poverty and related experiences influence children's development through environmental processes that go well beyond genetically transmitted attributes. These include longitudinal studies that attempt to distinguish the contribution of environmental factors versus genetic factors to the outcome being studied (e.g., analyses of effects of poverty on children's IQ that control for maternal IQ, maternal education, or both), studies that control for enduring family characteristics (and hence, any stable genetically based family attributes) by comparing siblings, and experimental studies of the effects of income, home environment, and preschool intervention.

Most scholars agree that individual abilities and traits, as well as many factors external to the individual, contribute to adult socioeconomic outcomes. Nonetheless, there is still considerable distance to travel toward truly integrative research that incorporates strong assessment of genetic and biological constructs with a sophisticated view of the environment at both the individual and social structural levels (for an extensive discussion of these issues and relevant research studies, see Huston et al., 1997; Rowe & Rodgers, 1997).

Effects of Poverty on Children's Development

Research on the effects of poverty on children's development focuses on three broad categories of outcomes, namely, cognitive functioning, school achievement, and socioemotional well-being. Poverty and income generally are found to be more powerful in accounting for differences in children's cognitive development and school achievement than differences in their socioemotional functioning.

Cognitive Functioning During Early Childhood. Family income and poverty status predict IQ scores in 5-year-olds, even after accounting for maternal education, family structure, ethnicity, and other differences between low- and high-income families. Moreover, poverty status at age 3 predicts children's IQ at age 5 even with age-3-IQ controlled. Several other important findings have emerged recently about the cognitive significance of various dimensions of poverty and income, among them: (a) income effects on IQ scores and other indicators of cognitive development are nonlinear, and specifically, are larger among children in families with incomes below or near the poverty line than among children in middle-class and affluent families; (b) persistent poverty has more adverse effects than short-term poverty, with children experiencing both types of poverty scoring lower than never-poor children; and (c) having a larger proportion of affluent neighbors is associated with higher IQ scores among 5-year-olds (but proportion of poor neighbors is unrelated to age-5 IQ scores), a relation that may reflect a salutary influence of neighborhood resources such as higher-quality kindergartens and increased presence of youth organizations and positive role models (Duncan & Brooks-Gunn, 1997).

Impairment of children's physical health status is a major pathway by which poverty hinders children's cognitive development. Because of inadequate nutrition, substandard, delayed, or total lack of prenatal care, and because of higher rates of exposure to legal and illegal drugs (e.g., nicotine, alcohol, cocaine), poor infants are more likely than nonpoor children to be born prematurely (gestational age of 36 weeks or less and birthweight of less than 2,500 grams) and to suffer a variety of perinatal illnesses. Prematurity, especially extremely low birth weight, increases risk for a series of respiratory, neurological, and learning disabilities, and increased severity of illness during the perinatal period predicts lower performance on IQ tests and tests of verbal skills. Equally as important, prematurity and perinatal complications are more likely to lead to longer-term cognitive problems if the child is poor than if the child is middle-class. Economically disadvantaged children are afforded fewer social, educational, and material resources that buffer the negative effects of prematurity and perinatal complications (McLoyd, 1998).

Lead poisoning also is a factor that contributes to the disparity in cognitive functioning between poor and nonpoor children. Elevated blood lead levels are associated with cognitive deficits, lower school achievement, and long-term impairment of neurological function. Poor children, especially those living in inner-city areas, have higher rates of elevated blood lead levels than nonpoor children. This is due to higher rates of residence in older housing that contains lead paint and lead-soldered pipes, and to increased exposure to industrial and automobile air pollution. Lead poisoning is more prevalent among African American children than in White children, a disparity traceable to long-standing housing discrimination that relegated African Americans in disproportionate numbers to poor, urban neighborhoods where inadequate housing units and local-level industrialization are concentrated (Crooks, 1995).

The effects of poverty on early cognitive functioning also are mediated through differences in the level of learning, academic, and language stimulation children receive in their home environment (as indicated, for example, by presence of toys that teach color, size, shape). Especially compelling are longitudinal data indicating that within-family decreases in income-to-need ratios and increases in the duration of poverty predict both deterioration in the quality of children's home environment and declines in child IQ scores (for an extensive review of these issues, see McLoyd, 1998).

Academic Achievement. Poor and low SES children, on average, perform significantly less well than nonpoor and middle-class children on numerous indicators of academic achievement (e.g., achievement test scores, grade retentions, placement in special education, high school graduation rate, high school dropout rate, completed years of schooling). In an analysis that provides some control for genetically based family characteristics, Duncan, Yeung, Brooks-Gunn, and Smith (1998) found that differences in family income experienced by siblings during the period between birth and age 15 predicted sibling differences in adult educational attainment, with income disparities between birth and age 5 being especially strong predictors.

School achievement, like cognitive functioning during the preschool years, typically declines with increases in the duration of poverty (Duncan & Brooks-Gunn, 1997). The preschool years appear to be a period of elevated vulnerability to the impact of poverty, at least in terms of years of schooling. Analysis of longitudinal data across the entire childhood period indicate that poverty during the first 5 years of life is far more detrimental to years of completed schooling than poverty during middle childhood and adolescence, an effect that is especially strong for African Americans compared to Whites (Duncan et al., 1998). This timing effect may reflect the influence of school readiness, and in turn, teachers' affective responses and achievement expectancies, both of which predict later school achievement. Because of labeling and low teacher expectations, poor children may experience considerable difficulty overcoming weak academic skills upon entry to public school. This difficulty may be even greater for poor African American children because they often labor under the added burden of negative racial stereotypes about cognitive ability.

The socioeconomic mix of children's neighborhoods has an impact on achievement, though considerably less than family characteristics. Adolescents who grow up in affluent neighborhoods complete more years of school and have lower school dropout rates than adolescents from similar families who grow up in poorer neighborhoods. The percentage of affluent neighbors has greater predictive power than the percentage of low-income neighbors, a finding that appears to endorse the notion that neighborhoods affect children's development through positive collective socialization (e.g., role models who enforce societal norms) and institutional resources. Interestingly, the impact of neighborhood resources on children's achievement is reported to be negligible, or inverse, during winter when schools are in session, but substantial during summer when schools are closed. In addition, summer gains are reportedly higher among children living in neighborhoods where the poverty rate is lower. When children are not in school, higher SES neighborhoods apparently are better able than poor neighborhoods to supplant cognition-enhancing resources furnished by the school during the academic year (Entwisle, Alexander, & Olson, 1997).

Research has documented several pathways by which poverty reduces school achievement, including less cognitive stimulation and fewer literacy resources in the child's home environment, and lower achievement expectations and emotional support by parents. Lower achievement expectations by teachers and negative perceptions of poor children by teachers (e.g., maturity, self-regulatory skills) also are important. Teachers who harbor such affectations provide children less positive attention, fewer learning opportunities, and less reinforcement of instances of good performance. As a consequence of differential expectations and treatment, objectively determined differences between the achievement of poor and nonpoor children may emerge or become exacerbated (e.g., test scores, grades) and, in turn, further buttress differences in teachers' achievement expectations.

Schools also contribute to the achievement gap between poor and affluent children through differences in instructional practices and educational resources. Schools that stratify classes by ability levels, compared to those that do not, typically produce greater social class differences in achievement between students in the same schools. Within the general range of financial and material resources usually available to schools, the precise level of these resources appears to be of little consequence for achievement outcomes. However, this does not mean that resources are not important. Many schools serving poor children are stunningly inadequate and lack even basic financial and material resources. Deficits in instructional tools, teacher morale, school climate, and other factors of the severity seen in these schools undoubtedly dampen educational outcomes (Kozol, 1991).

Not until the 1960s was reduction of poverty and its adverse effects formally articulated as federal policy. The arsenal of antipoverty programs initiated during this period included educationally oriented early childhood intervention, specifically Head Start, which continues to this day. It was based on two core assumptions buttressed by considerable empirical research available at the time, namely, that variation in environmental stimulation produced differences in children's intelligence (Hunt, 1961), and that the effect of the environment on intelligence and other human characteristics is greatest during the early and most rapid periods of development of characteristics (Bloom, 1964). Proponents essentially called for reducing poverty by equipping poor children with academically relevant cognitive skills during early life, which in turn was expected to prevent school failure, and ultimately, low employability and poverty.

The positive effects of cognitive stimulation afforded by educationally oriented early childhood intervention have been documented by a plethora of studies. Poor children who attend large-scale (e.g., Head Start) and small, model preschool intervention programs have superior academic readiness skills or show greater gains in these skills than their nonenrolled counterparts. These programs also lower rates of grade retention and/or assignment to special education, and enhance children's performance on standardized achievement tests. Unfortunately, cognitive and achievement gains produced by preschool education programs typically are lost by the third or fourth grade, if not before, although gains produced by model programs and programs of longer duration (i.e., more than 2 years) and greater intensity tend to persist longer. This diminution of effects appears to be partly due to low-quality schooling subsequent to the intervention. Moreover, despite gains, poor children who participate in large-scale preschool education perform markedly below national norms and below the performance of nonpoor children on standardized achievement tests at posttest and follow-up. In sum, although preschool intervention offers some protection from the negative effects of poverty, over the long run it does not bestow levels of cognitive and academic competence comparable to those seen among nonpoor children in the general population (for a review of relevant studies, see McLoyd, 1997).

Socioemotional Functioning. Poor children tend to experience more emotional and behavioral problems than their nonpoor counterparts, with differences generally being more pronounced for externalizing problems (e.g., delinquency, disobedience, fighting) than internalizing problems (e.g., anxiety, sadness/depression). Both types of problems become more prevalent the longer children have been living in poverty (McLoyd, 1990, 1998). Many theories assume that because there is generally more crime in poor neighborhoods than affluent neighborhoods, living in a poor neighborhood itself increases adolescents' chances of committing antisocial and delinquent acts (through peer influences, negative adult role models outside the family, etc.). Data on this point are contradictory, but also surprisingly thin.

Evidence from several empirical studies suggests that poverty elevates socioemotional problems in children partly by increasing parents' tendency to discipline children in a punitive and inconsistent manner and to ignore children's dependency needs. There also is an abundance of indirect evidence that poor children experience more socioemotional problems because of exposure to myriad negative life events (e.g., parental death, witnessing and being victimized by community violence) and adverse conditions (e.g., overcrowding) that exact demands exceeding their coping resources (McLoyd, 1998).

Several educationally oriented preschool interventions targeted at poor children have produced reductions in aggression, acting out, and antisocial behavior, and gains in self-esteem and social competence. Moreover, some have proved effective in reducing the number of probation cases, number of months on probation or parole, number of lifetime criminal arrests, and number of frequent offenders. Interventions that produce such effects typically are family focused, whereby preschool education is accompanied by various core services to parents and other family members (e.g., parenting education, assistance with housing, and legal problems). They appear to attenuate aggressive and delinquent behavior by reducing multiple risk factors associated with these outcomes (e.g., cognitive deficits; impaired socioemotional functioning in early life; low parental involvement with children; hostile or rejecting parenting; low levels of schooling and earnings during late adolescence). These hypothesized pathways have rarely been directly tested, but they are consistent with an extensive body of research on the precursors of delinquent and externalizing behaviors (for an extensive discussion of these interventions and studies of their efficacy, see McLoyd, 1997).

Bibliography

Bane, M. J., & Ellwood, D. (1986). Slipping into and out of poverty: The dynamics of spells. *Journal of Human Resources, 21*, 1–23.

Bloom, B. S. (1964). *Stability and change in human characteristics.* New York: Wiley.

Corcoran, M., Duncan, G., Gurin, G., & Gurin, P. (1985). Myth and reality: The causes and persistence of poverty. *Journal of Policy Analysis and Management, 4*, 516–536.

Crooks, D. (1995). American children at risk: Poverty and its consequences for children's health, growth, and school achievement. *Yearbook of Physical Anthropology, 38*, 57–86.

Duncan, G., & Brooks-Gunn, J. (Eds.). (1997). *Consequences of growing up poor.* New York: Russell Sage Foundation.

Duncan, G., Hill, M., & Hoffman, S. D. (1988). Welfare dependence within and across generations. *Science, 239*, 467–471.

Duncan, G., Yeung, W., Brooks-Gunn, J., & Smith, J. (1998). How much does childhood poverty affect the life chances of children? *American Sociological Review, 63*, 406–423.

Entwisle, D., Alexander, K., & Olson, L. (1997). *Children, schools, and inequality.* Boulder, CO: Westview Press.

Herrnstein, R., & Murray, C. (1994). *The bell curve: Intelligence and class structure in American life.* New York: Free Press.

Hunt, J. M. (1961). *Intelligence and experience.* New York: Ronald Press.

Huston, A., McLoyd, V. C., & Garcia Coll, C. (1997). Poverty and behavior: The case for multiple methods and levels of analysis. *Developmental Review, 17*, 376–393.

Kozol, J. (1991). *Savage inequalities: Children in America's schools.* New York: Crown.

Lewis, O. (1966). The culture of poverty. *Scientific American, 215*, 19–25.

McLoyd, V. C. (1990). The impact of economic hardship on Black families and children: Psychological distress, parenting, and socioemotional development. *Child Development, 61*, 311–346.

McLoyd, V. (1997). Children in poverty: Development, public policy, and practice. In I. Sigel & A. Renninger (Vol. Eds.), *Handbook of child psychology: Vol. 4. Child psychology in practice* (5th ed., pp. 135–208). New York: Wiley.

McLoyd, V. C. (1998). Socioeconomic disadvantage and child development. *American Psychologist, 53*, 185–204.

Rowe, D., & Rodgers, J. (1997). Poverty and behavior: Are environmental measures nature and nurture? *Developmental Review, 17*, 358–375.

Scarr, S. (1981). *Race, social class, and individual differences in IQ.* Hillsdale, NJ: Erlbaum.

Wilson, W. J. (1987). *The truly disadvantaged: The inner city, the underclass, and public policy*. Chicago: University of Chicago Press.

Vonnie C. McLoyd

Adulthood Poverty

The official U.S. poverty measure, developed by Mollie Orshansky in the early 1960s, provides a set of income thresholds for different family types based on family size and composition. Thresholds were computed by multiplying the cost of a minimum adequate diet (based on 1955 food budgets) for a given family type times three to allow for other expenses, because at that time, the typical family spent one third of its income on food. Thresholds are updated every year to account for inflation. Whenever a family's before-tax money income from all sources and all family members is less than the threshold, that family is defined as *poor*.

The poverty measure has not changed since the 1960s except for updating thresholds annually to account for inflation. In 1995, a National Research Council panel of experts reviewed the official measure and concluded that the measure, which compares poverty thresholds to before-tax money income, should be revised to adjust for work-related expenses (e.g., child care and transportation), taxes paid, in-kind benefits (e.g., food stamps), and out-of-pocket medical expenses (Citro & Michael, 1995). If the measure were adjusted in these ways, more working families would be counted as poor and some poor single-parent families would be classified as nonpoor.

Poverty rates very considerably across demographic groups. Dangizer and Gottschalk (1995, p. 67) reported:

> In any given year, non-Hispanic whites are better off (that is, they have a higher standard of living and a lower poverty rate) than blacks, Hispanics and other minorities; non-elderly adults are better off than children and the elderly; married-couple families are better off than female-headed families; workers with more education are better off than those with less education.

In 1996, 11% of Whites, 28% of Blacks and 29% of Hispanics were poor; 21% of children and 11% of the elderly were poor; 7% of individuals in two-parent families and 36% of individuals in mother-only families were poor.

Although the incidence of poverty is higher among particular demographic groups, the poverty population is heterogeneous. In 1993, 48% of the poor were non-Hispanic Whites, 21% were Hispanic, and 27% were Blacks. Children have higher rates of poverty than adults, but children made up only 41% of the poverty population in 1993. Whereas high school dropouts are disproportionately poor, 55% of the poor in 1993 had at least 12 years of schooling. Although single-parent families have very high rates of poverty, only 43% of the poor in 1993 lived in single-parent families.

The official poverty line is defined over a one-year period, but annual figures only provide a snapshot of the poor. Key questions are: What is the percentage of people trapped in long-term poverty? What is the percentage who are poor only temporarily? Blank (1997) tracked the poverty experiences of individuals over the 13-year period of 1979 to 1991 and reported that one in three people experienced at least 1 year of poverty over that period, and almost 1 in 20 were poor 10 or more years. Poverty is a widespread risk, but most people who become poor are not in long-term poverty. The incidence of long-term poverty is higher among Blacks, high school dropouts, individuals with health problems, and individuals living in single-mother families. Race differences in risks of long-term poverty are striking: fewer than 1 in 50 Whites were poor 10 or more years (1979–1991), but 1 in 6 Blacks were poor for that many years. There are no statistics on the incidence of long-term poverty among Hispanics because no study has tracked a national sample of Hispanic families over time. Given that annual poverty rates are almost identical for Blacks and Hispanics, a substantial minority of Hispanics may be stuck in long-term poverty.

What Causes Poverty: Explanations

Arguments over the "culture of poverty" in the 1950s and 1960s assumed considerable persistence of poverty but differed over whether this was due to cultural inadequacies of the poor or to structural barriers and discrimination faced by the poor (Patterson, 1986). Advocates of the culture of poverty argument asserted that the poor lived in a different culture than did the rest of society, that this culture was characterized by deviant values and behaviors, and that this culture was both "familial and intergenerational" (Patterson, 1986, p. 119). Critics of the culture of poverty, such as Eliot Liebow, argued that poverty was not due to the transmission of cultural deficiencies from parents to children but "stemmed from racial discrimination and lack of opportunities that affected individuals in each new generation" (Liebow, cited in Patterson, 1986, p. 123).

Debate between proponents of the cultural model and structuralists ended by the 1970s as researchers reported that little evidence supported the culture of poverty argument. In the 1980s, the issue of poverty reemerged as research on new longitudinal data sets showed that poverty persisted both within and across generations, and as public dissatisfaction with continuing high poverty rates and expanding welfare rolls increased. The issue of long-term poverty took center stage, and attention was focused on the emergence of an underclass and on intragenerational and intergenerational welfare dependency. Four theoretical perspectives were developed to explain persistent poverty: (a) the resources/skills model, (b) the family structure model, (c) the welfare trap model, and (d) Wilson's (1996) social isolation model. Whereas terminology differs somewhat (i.e., *underclass* replaced *culture of poverty* as the key term), the focus of these newer models is similar to the earlier ones in that resources, culture, community, and economic structure all play important roles.

Resources/Skills Model. The first explanation emphasizes the lack of material resources and investments in skills. Poor families must devote most of their resources to consumption, and have little time or money left over to devote to improving their own and/or their children's education and skills. As a result, poor children grow up to become poor adults.

If few material resources and a lack of skills are the reasons poverty persists within and across generations, then the new time limits on welfare could worsen many children's futures. One prediction is that this legislation will push 1.1 million additional children into poverty, and that over 8 million low-income families with children will lose income under the new legislation.

Family Structure Model. The second explanation holds that teen births, unwed births, and single parents are major causes of poverty, that is, teen childbearing and out-of-wedlock childbearing consign mothers and children to lives of poverty and dependency. According to this model, children raised by single mothers will grow up to be idle, unproductive, and poor adults.

The policy implications of the family structure model depend on why family structure is associated with poverty and why children raised in single-parent homes fare poorly. In the recent welfare reform debate, teen childbearing and out-of-wedlock parenting were cited as major causes of poverty and welfare dependency for women and their children. To the extent that these assertions are correct, policies that encourage girls to delay pregnancy until they are married and in their twenties may be appropriate.

Others argue that teen births and unwed births are a response to poor marriage and work opportunities and that most teen mothers and unwed mothers would be poor as adults even if they had avoided a teen birth and/or waited until they were married to bear children. In this case, policies that expand disadvantaged girls' economic opportunities might be more effective at preventing poverty.

Finally, family structure effects on children's attainments may be due to the psychological distress from losing a parent or to reduced parental supervision or to the absence of good role models for work and marriage (McLanahan & Sandefur, 1994). In this case, policies that try to strengthen families or address the distress and lack of role models in single-parent families may be useful.

Welfare Trap Model. According to the third model, welfare traps recipients and their children in poverty. This model has both cultural and incentive components. First, when individuals use welfare heavily and work rarely or intermittently, the stigma associated with welfare is diminished; a welfare culture develops, and individuals develop self-defeating work attitudes and poor work ethics that are passed on to their children. Second, welfare availability encourages individuals to bear children out of wedlock and avoid work. These choices, in turn, lead to long-term poverty: Welfare offers individuals an economic alternative to marriage and work.

If the welfare trap model were correct, then the new time limits on welfare make sense. Sharply reducing the amount of time individuals can receive welfare makes welfare a less attractive alternative to work and marriage (the incentive model) and reduces the exposure of children to nonworking welfare recipients (the cultural model). Since the problem arises from welfare itself, not from a lack of jobs, time limits alone should suffice. Studies of the effectiveness of state welfare reforms should provide useful evidence about the welfare trap model.

Wilson's (1996) Social Isolation Model. The fourth model focuses on the disappearance of work from poor, inner-city, minority communities. Wilson emphasized that economic structural changes, demographic changes, and changes in federal aid to cities have isolated inner-city communities in ways that reduce inner-city residents' and their children's chances of escaping poverty. First, and most important, globalization, technological upgrading, the decline of unions, and the shift of manufacturing employment from the cities to the suburbs means that the number of well-paid manufacturing jobs compatible with ghetto residents' skills and their access to them has dropped. This increases male unemployment, reduces the pool of employed men eligible for marriage, reduces marriage rates in the inner city, and increases the number of children raised in single-parent families. At the same time, the migration of middle-class Blacks from the inner city leaves the poor inner-city residents behind, weakens important socializing institutions such as churches, political machines, and community organizations (which in the past monitored behavior in inner-city neighborhoods and exposed poverty area residents to mainstream values and norms), reduces job-finding networks, and reduces the number of work role models. One result is that ghettos become increasingly disorganized and residents increasingly engage in activity in the underground economy. This type of activity bears high risks, including substance abuse, incarceration, and death. These risky behaviors, in turn, inhibit residents' employment prospects.

Although Wilson (1996, p. xix) identified a number

of structural conditions that have isolated the urban poor, he emphasized that "the disappearance of work and the consequences of that disappearance for both social and cultural life are the central problems in the inner-city ghetto." Wilson's model requires both economic and social service strategies to reverse the factors that have generated an urban underclass. If macroeconomic policies can provide jobs, and social services policies can combat the effects of social isolation, then reductions in negative attitudes and behaviors will result. Wilson's model also implies that time limits on welfare recipiency will be counterproductive unless accompanied by programs that provide jobs to poor women and provide the social services (e.g., day care, transportation) that will enable them to keep those jobs.

These models identify many factors that may cause poverty to persist within and across generations: lack of economic resources; inadequate education and skills; teen parenthood, nonmarital childbearing, growing up in a female-headed family; a welfare culture and perverse welfare incentives; underclass neighborhoods; and risky behaviors such as crime. The following summarizes the research evidence on how these factors affect poverty.

Lack of Economic Resources

Do children from poor families escape poverty as adults? *Inter*generational poverty looks much like *intra*generational poverty. There is considerable mobility: More than half of all Black children raised in long-term poor families (defined as poor during 50% of the years the child lived at home) and more than three fourths of White children raised in long-term poor families escape poverty in their 20s and 30s. But children raised in long-term poverty are more likely to be poor as adults than are nonpoor children. Almost half of all Black children (46.3%) raised in long-term poverty are poor as adults; this compares to 26.2% for nonpoor Black children. Almost one fourth of all White children (24.1%) raised in long-term poverty are poor as adults; this compares to 10.2% for nonpoor White children.

Even in a multivariate context, growing up poor is associated with large reductions in men's incomes. Men who grow up in middle-income families have incomes that are 40 to 60% higher than those of men raised in poor families, even after controlling for family structure, parental work hours, parental disability, parents' and neighbors' welfare use, mother's schooling, growing up in a poor neighborhood, level of state welfare benefits, labor market unemployment rates, and men's own schooling.

Skills: Schooling and Test Scores

Schooling is the strongest single predictor of earnings for both men and women, and returns to schooling have increased over time. In 1979, college-educated men earned about 33% more than men who stopped schooling after high school graduation; by 1989, college graduates earned 53% more than high school graduates. Test scores also matter. Cognitive test scores are strongly associated with earnings, even after controlling for years of schooling. Programs focused on increasing completed schooling and skills are an important part of any antipoverty strategy.

Growing up in a Female-Headed Family

Being raised in a nonintact family doubles the risk that a child will drop out of high school, more than doubles the risk that a child will have a teenage out-of-wedlock birth, and raises children's risks of being idle in their young adult years by 40% (McLanahan & Sandefur, 1994). A major cause of these increased risks is that children in nonintact families have fewer resources than do children in intact families: lower incomes, fewer parental noneconomic resources (measured by time spent with fathers, time spent with mothers, parental help with schoolwork, parental supervision, and parental aspirations), and fewer community resources (measured by census tract characteristics, school characteristics, and residential mobility) than do children in married-couple families. These resource differences account for much, but not all, of the risks of dropping out of high school, teenage premarital births, and idleness. Controlling for parental noneconomic resources alone reduces negative effects of family structure on the risk of dropping out of high school by 40%, the risk of a teenage out-of-wedlock birth by 40%, and the risk of being idle by over 67%. Controlling for both parental income and residential mobility (a proxy for change in community resources) lowers these risks by 76%, 75%, and over 90%, respectively.

Adults raised as children in nonintact families show diminished adult outcomes primarily because as children, they had less access to parental economic resources, parental noneconomic resources, and community resources. This is consistent with the resources/skills argument. But being raised in nonintact families significantly affects high school graduation and teenage fertility even after resources are controlled, suggesting support for sociological or psychological theories related to distress, socialization effects, role models, and so on.

Teen Parenthood

Despite the negative publicity about teen birth rates, the teen birth rate (i.e., the number of births per 1,000 females aged 15–19) declined steadily from 89.1 in 1960 to 50.2 in 1986. Between 1986 and 1991, the teen birth rate rose to 62.1 and then slowly declined to 54.7 in 1996. Until the 1990s, academics and policy makers agreed that teenage births damaged the future economic prospects of young women. This consensus was based on cross-sectional studies showing that women who had their first child as a teenager earned less, had lower family incomes, were more likely to be poor, and were more likely to receive welfare than women who avoided teen births, even after controlling for differences in measures of background characteristics such as parental schooling and family income.

Geronimus and Korenman (1992) challenged this consensus. They contended that past analyses did not control for all possible background differences between teen mothers and women who avoided a teen birth, such as parental values, school quality, or neighborhood resources, and that ignoring unmeasured background differences led previous researchers to overstate the negative consequences of teenage parenthood for women's economic futures.

In the 1990s, researchers exploited natural experiments to control for unmeasured background differences between teens who did and did not have a birth. First, analysts compared economic outcomes for samples of sister pairs from the same family where one sister had a teen birth and one did not. The logic behind sister comparisons runs as follows: Sisters are typically reared in the same families, grow up in the same neighborhoods, and attend the same schools. When researchers compare a woman with her own sister, they "hold constant" background factors (e.g., parental resources, school quality, neighborhood safety) that sisters have in common. Thus, sister comparisons provide more precise estimates of the effects of teen parenthood, independent of background, than do studies that control only measured background. Hotz, McElroy, and Sanders (1996) used a different technique to control for unmeasured differences between teen mothers and nonteen mothers. They compared adult economic outcomes of pregnant teenagers who miscarried to the outcomes of teens who gave birth. This allowed them to control for girls' propensities to become pregnant as teens.

These studies found that effects of teen parenting on women's earnings, labor force participation, and incomes are smaller than indicated by the cross-sectional research. The sisters studies typically found that effects of teen parenthood on adult incomes are much smaller than those found in analyses that only controlled for measured background. The size of the remaining effect of a teen birth on income varied from very small to large across these sisters studies. The modal finding was that a teen birth reduces girls' adult incomes by about 20%. Hotz et al. (1996) found no effects of teen parenting on girls' earnings or labor force participation in their late twenties. These studies do suggest that teen parenting lowers the probability of graduating from high school, increases the number of children a woman has, and increases the amount of time she spends as a single parent.

Out-of-Wedlock Childbearing

Increasing numbers of children are being born to unwed mothers. In 1993, 38% of all births were to unmarried women. Public discussions of unwed births often assume that most unwed mothers are teenagers, but about 70% of all unwed births in 1993 were to women aged 20 or older. Policy analyst Charles Murray (1993, p. 21) suggested that unwed births are a major source of societal problems: "Illegitimacy is the single most important social problem of our time—more important than drugs, poverty, crime, welfare, or homelessness because it drives everything else."

Given the prominence of unwed births in policy discussions, surprisingly few researchers have directly examined the consequences of nonmarital births for women's incomes and earnings. A notable exception is Kunz (1997), who used sister samples to estimate the effects of nonmarital births on women's adult incomes. He reported that nonmarital births substantially lower women's future incomes, even controlling for age at first birth and unmeasured background shared by sisters.

Virtually no published research has examined fathers of illegitimate children. The conventional wisdom is that many absent fathers pay minimal support, are often not employed, and live unstable lives, but more systematic research is needed on the skills, employment, earnings, and behavior of these fathers, and on the relationships of these fathers to their children.

The Welfare Culture and Welfare Incentives

The welfare culture model predicts that welfare traps recipients and their children in poverty by perversely affecting their work ethics, values, and behaviors. Opponents of this view claim that the alleged welfare trap is really a poverty trap: Both generations behave in similar ways because both face the same lack of resources and opportunities. This argument recalls Liebow's (cited in Patterson, 1986) critique of the culture of poverty.

Daughters raised in welfare homes are more likely to have teen out-of-wedlock births, to go on welfare, and to drop out of high school than are girls raised in nonwelfare homes. These parental welfare effects drop by as much as half, but often remain significant after adjusting for family background and neighborhood disadvantages. One shortcoming of this research is that unmeasured maternal or community characteristics associated with mother's welfare use may be causing children's low outcomes.

The key prediction of the welfare incentives model is that state welfare benefits encourage out-of-wedlock childbearing and family breakup. Analysts have investigated this by estimating nonmarital childbearing rates, teen childbearing rates, and divorce/separation rates as a function of state welfare benefits. Analysts have typically found that effects of state welfare benefits on childbearing behavior exist, but effects are modest (Moffitt, 1998).

Neighborhood Effects

Wilson (1996) claimed that poverty was increasing in inner-city neighborhoods; the evidence supports this claim. The number of people living in extremely poor (defined as neighborhoods in which 40% or more of residents are poor) neighborhoods almost doubled between 1970 and 1990. By 1990, almost 8 million people lived in extremely poor, inner-city neighborhoods. Blacks constituted about half of all residents in extremely poor neighborhoods; non-Hispanic Whites and Hispanics each constituted slightly less than one fourth of all residents.

Although the number of high-poverty neighborhoods grew rapidly in the 1970s and 1980s, the majority of the poor do not live in high-poverty neighborhoods. In 1990, only 12% of poor people lived in high-poverty neighborhoods, and only 25% of poor Blacks lived in high-poverty neighborhoods (Jargowsky, 1997).

Wilson (1996) also asserted that neighborhoods play an important role in perpetuating poverty and dependency. Evaluations of Chicago's Gautreaux experiment, which relocated Black public housing residents into subsidized city and suburban private apartments, support Wilson's assertion that neighborhoods matter. When analysts compared outcomes of children relocated to the city apartments to those of children relocated to suburban apartments, the children relocated to the suburbs were much less likely to drop out of high school, were considerably more likely to attend college, were more likely to be employed, and had higher earnings.

Several authors have estimated effects of childhood neighborhoods on children's schooling, behavior, fertility, and earnings using survey data (Brooks-Gunn, Duncan, & Aber, 1997). A major problem is that these studies typically defined *neighborhood* as the census tract or zip code in which the respondent resides, and aggregate measures of residents' characteristics (i.e., unemployment rates, poverty rates, etc.) serve as imperfect proxies for complex neighborhood processes such as school resources, community norms, social isolation, social control, peer group pressure, and the like. Many of these studies have found that some neighborhood characteristics have significant associations with a given outcome, but the size of childhood neighborhood effects, although significant, are smaller than are the effects of family characteristics, and neighborhood characteristics that "matter" vary across studies.

Crime

In 1993, 2.9% of men aged 25 to 34 were incarcerated (Freeman, 1996). The vast majority of these men were high school dropouts: a group that has been increasingly left behind in the economic restructuring of the 1980s and 1990s. Freeman estimated that one fourth of all young, male, high school dropouts, and half of all young, male, Black high school dropouts came under the supervision of the criminal justice system (i.e., were on probation, in jail, or paroled) in the 1980s. Freeman explored the extent to which jail or probation affected young men's later employment and earnings. Jail time reduced men's expected long-term employment by 25 to 30% and expected annual earnings by 45%. Probation reduced employment 10 to 15%, but had small effects on earnings.

Unanswered Questions

The research reviewed here raises five unanswered questions that need to be addressed:

1. How can schools and communities be changed to improve the educational and earnings outcomes of poor children?
2. What is it about bad neighborhoods that inhibits economic mobility?
3. Why and how much do unwed births lower women's future incomes?
4. Who are the fathers of the children born to teen mothers and unwed mothers? What roles do these fathers play in their children's lives? Can these roles be expanded?
5. How do welfare-to-work programs affect family self-sufficiency and children's adult outcomes?

Bibliography

Blank, R. (1997). *It takes a nation.* Princeton, NJ: Princeton University Press.

Brooks-Gunn, J., Duncan, G. J., & Aber, J. L. (1997). *Neighborhood poverty: Content and consequences for children.* New York: Russell Sage Foundation.

Citro, C. F., & Michael, R. J. (1995). *Measuring poverty: A new approach.* Washington, DC: National Academy Press.

Corcoran, M. (1995). Rags to riches. *Annual Review of Sociology, 21,* 237–267.

Danziger, S., & Gottschalk, P. (1995). *America unequal.* Cambridge, MA: Harvard University Press.

Freeman, R. B. (1996). *Crime and the economic status of disadvantaged young men.* Cambridge, MA: Harvard University, Department of Economics.

Geronimus, A. (1997). Teenage childbearing and personal responsibility: An alternative view. *Political Science Quarterly, 112* (3), 405–430.

Geronimus, A., & Korenman, S. (1992). The socioeconomic consequences of teen childbearing reconsidered. *Quarterly Journal of Economics, 107,* 1187–1214.

Hotz, J., McElroy, S., & Sanders, S. (1996). The costs and consequences of teenage childbearing for mothers. *Chicago Policy Review, Fall*, 54–94.

Jargowsky, P. (1997). *Poverty and place*. New York: Russell Sage Foundation.

Kunz, J. (1997). *Welfare and poverty: Pathways to adult economic outcomes*. Unpublished doctoral dissertation, School of Social Work, University of Michigan, Ann Arbor.

McLanahan, S., & Sandefur, G. (1994). *Growing up with a single parent: What hurts, what helps?* Cambridge, MA: Harvard University Press.

Moffitt, R. (1998). *The effects of welfare on marriage and fertility: What do we know and what do we need to know?* Baltimore: Johns Hopkins University, Department of Economics.

Murray, C. (1993, October 23). The coming white underclass. *Wall Street Journal*, p. 21.

Patterson, J. (1986). *America's struggle against poverty, 1900–1985*. Cambridge, MA: Harvard University Press.

Wilson, W. (1996). *When work disappears*. New York: Alfred A. Knopf.

Mary Corcoran

POWER. Although concern with social power undoubtedly dates to prehistory, the modern analysis of power can be credited to Machiavelli in the closing years of the fifteenth century. Machiavelli combined practical political experience with a desire to understand the workings of political systems. He began a line of inquiry into political power that was elaborated by political philosophers (Hobbes, Nietzsche) and became identified with the field of political science. Social power, however, was not long restricted to explicating the relationship between rulers and the ruled. It was soon seen as relevant to a large number of phenomena spanning all of the social sciences. In psychology this was especially true for psychologists interested in the study of interpersonal, intragroup, or intergroup relationships.

Because of the broad spectrum of interdisciplinary focus on social power issues, it is not surprising that there is considerable diversity concerning the proper definition of the concept. One can, however, make a rough tripartite taxonomy of the various definitions. Although the definitions are not strictly mutually exclusive, they do have sufficiently different points of emphasis that it may be instructive to treat them as separate categories. In ascending order of abstractness these can be termed: the personal, the relationship, and the social systems frameworks. Within each of these frameworks research has been concerned with how possessing high or low social power impacts upon the individuals' perceptions, cognitions, and behavior.

Personal Framework

The personal frameworks define social power as a trait, a personal attribute, of particular agents. People whose standings are high on this trait are able to induce the changes they desire in most, or all, of the individuals with whom they interact. The occurrence of high social power is typically studied in an asymmetric context. That is, the persons who have high power, or are dominant, assertive, or forceful, are contrasted to others who are low in power, those who are characterized as being submissive, nonassertive, or not forceful. An individual's amount of power is typically measured by questionnaire items requiring self-descriptions (see, e.g., Winter, 1973). Much of the research can be viewed as validating research, that is, research that shows high-power individuals are more influential or persuasive than their low-power counterparts.

There have, of course, been a number of substantive hypotheses tested. For example, it has been demonstrated that people high in possessing the power motive, compared to people low in the power motive, will perceive more social power in others. It is as if both highs and lows project their own power motive onto others. Although the power motive is not one of the five consistent personality traits found by factoring test responses, the trait of agreeableness is such a trait. High standing on agreeableness, which suggests willingness to be influenced and, thus, low power, has been shown to prevent conflicts with opposite-sex peers (Asendorpf & Wilpers, 1998).

Relationship Framework

In distinction to the personal framework, relationship frameworks treat social power as arising from, and restricted to, specific relationships. Three kinds of power formulations can be distinguished. These are formulations stemming from field theory, from decision-making concepts, and from interdependence concepts. Although each formulation comes from different traditions and lends itself to somewhat different experimental observations, there is usually no difficulty in stating one formulation in the terminology of the others.

Field theory conceptions have their roots in Kurt Lewin's field theory and have been comprehensively reviewed in Cartwright (1959). The basic conceptual tool for these formulations consists of specifying relationships among various types of psychological forces. Power is defined as the maximum resultant force person A (the agent) can bring to bear on person B (the target) with respect to some aspect of B's psychological environment. The resultant force consists of the force to comply minus the strength of the force to resist. In other words, A is said to have power over B if A enacts, or is potentially capable of enacting, behaviors that induce a compliance force on B to change in a given direction that is greater than the accompanying resistance force. For Cartwright, any disparity in the two forces, whether or not it produces change that is in the direction intended by A, is sufficient to define power. Most other authors who use a field theory conception define A's power by the magnitude of the intended changes induced in person B.

The strength of the inducing forces are not solely a function of A's ability to influence others. Their magnitude is also a function of how the compliance forces mesh with B's motives and goals. The magnitude of the compliance force on B is a joint function of the strength of A's act and the motive base to which it is relevant. For example, if roommate A wishes to be accompanied to a movie, even though roommate B is studying for a final examination, A will activate greater compliance forces by suggesting they go to a movie B wants to see compared to one to which B is indifferent.

Because compliance forces may stem from various resources controlled by the agent, it is possible to inquire whether different bases of power mediate different consequences for one or both members of the relationship. In order to answer this question French and Raven (1959) differentiated five bases of power: reward, coercive, referent, expert, and legitimate.

The use of reward power depends upon A's possessing some resource valued by B, which B believes can be obtained by complying with the meaning of A's intervention. Furthermore, because getting a reward is contingent on compliance, use of reward power depends upon A's ability to monitor B. Its use is also expected to increase B's attraction for A and, over time, to shade into referent power. The changes induced by reward power, however, are expected to endure only to the extent to which A remains salient to B. Coercive power is based on B's belief that A can mediate punishments, such as physical pain or withdrawal of desirable resources. It shares some features with reward power, that is, its use requires A to monitor B, who is expected to maintain changes only to the extent to which A remains salient. It is also expected to create different effects; the use of coercive power is expected to decrease B's attraction for A, who may be required to set up restraints to prevent B from withdrawing.

Referent power occurs when B identifies with, or is attracted to, Person A. Referent power can be effective without A's intention to influence and does not require A to monitor B. Expert power exists when B perceives A as possessing knowledge or skills. Legitimate power depends upon prior socialization such that the role or position occupied by A is perceived by B as having a "right" to influence B, who is "obligated" to accept the influence. Although an important base in its own right, legitimacy has significant implications when combined with reward and coercion. Money earned for exceeding a base rate of sales is legitimate and termed a *bonus.* Money spent to buy a juror's vote is illegitimate and is termed a *bribe.* Maintenance of changes induced by each of these three bases is thought to occur even in A's absence.

Soon after the identification of the five bases, an information base was added. Changes brought about from an information base, such as persuasion, were thought to be maintained independent of the surveillance or presence of A. Further refinements to the typology have also been made by identifying other variables that can mediate the impact of particular bases (see Raven, 1992). For example, it is recognized that reward and coercion can have personal or impersonal forms; that expert and referent power can be positive or negative; that legitimate power may be based on various normative obligations; and that the mode by which a base is implemented (strong or weak) can be critical to predicting its effectiveness.

Decision-making conceptions of power have sought to overcome the difficulties involved in attempting to make power comparisons among individuals who are in different relationships, such as comparing the power of various senators. These authors have accepted the general characteristics of power outlined by Simon (1953), who identified the causal role of the agent in affecting changes in the policies of others. These conceptions typically point to identifying power with respect to the probabilities that interventions have of implementing change (see, e.g., Dahl, 1957).

Interdependence formulations, in general, consist of comprehensive analyses of interpersonal processes. Thibaut and Kelley's analysis (1959; Kelley & Thibaut, 1978) views interactions as consisting of successive pairings of behaviors that produce a series of separate outcomes for each person. Each outcome has a subjective value to the individual on a goodness-poorness scale. Any given relationship can be summarized by a frequency count of the outcomes experienced by each participant. Power is defined in terms of the outcome effects created during the course of interaction. According to Thibaut and Kelley, person A's amount of power over B is defined by the range of outcomes through which A can potentially move B. The larger the range, the greater the power.

Given the outcome range definition, it becomes important to specify the general limits that bound a particular range. The upper limit of the range is set by the best available outcome, whereas the lower limit is set by the worst outcome B will endure without leaving the relationship. This lower limit is determined by the value B places on the next best relationship that is an alternative to the present one. As the value of the next best alternative relationship decreases, the range of outcomes B will endure increases and so will A's amount of power. This can be seen in the stages of heterosexual relationships. Access to alternatives to the present relationship is made progressively more difficult as a couple moves from casual dating to a formal engagement to exchanging marriage vows. This example illustrates not only how A's power increases as the availability of B's alternatives worsen, but also that the amount of power can be symmetrical. The progression increases both individuals' power over the other.

Social System Frameworks

Finally, there are those definitions that locate social power in social systems. They are typically dissatisfied with relationship frameworks whose conceptions of power, they argue, suffer from being too broad and ubiquitous. This viewpoint has been forcefully expressed by Hawley (1963), who wrote: "Every social act is an exercise of power, every social relationship is a power equation and every social group or system is an organization of power" (p. 422).

These frameworks typically focus on the decision-making roles in particular social structures. Hawley suggested measuring the way power is distributed by looking at the ratio of managerial roles to all other roles. The lower this ratio, the greater the concentration of power and the greater likelihood that such communities will be able to organize successfully to meet emergencies. Other, more complex, category schemes have also been suggested. As Michael Aiken (1970) noted: "What is common to these classificatory schemes is that each implies a scale that runs from concentration of community power and resources (elitist model) to dispersion of community power and resources (pluralist model)" (p. 488). Using this kind of scale, these studies have shown such associations as southern cities having more concentrated power than northern cities or that older cities have slightly more diffused power structures than younger cities.

Final Note

With the exception of the interdependence frameworks, power is basically defined by the amount of changes in B that can be attributed to the intervention, or presence, of A. Thus, they focus on asymmetrical power relationships. Interdependence frameworks can encompass both unequal, and equal, power relationships. For instance, in unequal relationships the powerful person has been shown to engage in quick and careless processing of relationship-relevant information and to enhance distancing from the other. Interdependence frameworks alone can investigate the impact of power equalities. It has been shown, for example, that in romantic relationships, the greater the mutuality of power, the better the couple adjustment.

Bibliography

Aiken, M. (1970). The distribution of community power: Structural bases and social consequences. In M. Aiken & P. E. Mott (Eds.), *The structure of community power* (pp. 487–525). New York: Random House.

Asendorpf, J. B., & Wilpers, S. (1998). Personality effects on social relationships. *Journal of Personality and Social Psychology, 74*, 1531–1544.

Cartwright, D. (1959). A field theoretical conception of power. In D. Cartwright (Ed.), *Studies in social power* (pp. 183–220). Ann Arbor, MI: Institute for Social Research.

Dahl, R. A. (1957). The concept of power. *Behavioral Science, 2*, 201–218.

French, J., & Raven, B. (1959). The bases of social power. In D. Cartwright (Ed.), *Studies in social power* (pp. 150–167). Ann Arbor, MI: Institute for Social Research.

Hawley, A. H. (1963). Community power and urban renewal success. *American Journal of Sociology, 48*, 422–431.

Henderson, A. H. (1981). *Social power: Social psychological models and theories*. New York: Praeger.

Kelley, H. H., & Thibaut, J. W. (1978). *Interpersonal relations: A theory of interdependence*. New York: Wiley.

Kramer, R. M., & Messick, D. M. (Eds.). (1995). *Negotiation as a social process*. Thousand Oaks, CA: Sage.

Pruitt, D. G., & Carnevale, P. J. (1993). *Negotiation in social conflict*. Pacific Grove, CA: Brooks/Cole. Power is relevant to negotiations; contains negotiation bibliography.

Raven, B. (1992). A power/interaction model of interpersonal influence: French and Raven thirty years later. *Journal of Social Behavior and Personality, 7*, 217–244.

Rusbult, C. E., & Van Lange, P. A. M. (1996). Interdependence processes. In E. T. Higgins & A. W. Kruglanski (Eds.), *Social psychology: Handbook of basic mechanisms and processes* (pp. 564–596). New York: Guilford Press. An excellent presentation of interdependence concepts and a section on power.

Schopler, J. (1965). Social power. In L. Berkowitz (Ed.), *Advances in experimental social psychology* (Vol. 2, pp. 177–218). San Diego, CA: Academic Press.

Simon, H. (1953). Notes on the observation and measurement of political power. *Journal of Politics, 15*, 500–516.

Thibaut, J. W., & Kelley, H. H. (1959). *The social psychology of groups*. New York: Wiley.

Winter, D. (1973). *The power motive*. New York: Free Press.

John Schopler

POWER ANALYSIS. *See* Data Analysis.

POWER MOTIVATION. Power is a concept fundamental to human social life. Hence the idea of a power motive (or striving to attain power) has a long history in philosophy and psychology—from the ancient Greek idea of strife (Empedocles), to more modern conceptions of a will to power (Nietzsche, later Adler), aggressive instinct (Freud), need for dominance (Murray), or agency (Bakan). In modern psychology, however, the most familiar form of this concept is the *power motive*. The power motive is measured through content analysis of thematic apperception (stories made up to dramatize pictures) or other verbal material, using a scoring system (like those for the achievement, affiliation, and intimacy motives) that is empirically derived from considering the categories of verbal imagery that actually increase as a result of experimental manipulation of power motivation. Winter (1973) modified and extended earlier thematic apperception measures (see also Smith, 1992, chaps. 19, 21), incorporating the results of many different power motive arousal experiments.

The content analysis measure of power motivation is often linked to similar measures of the achievement, affiliation, and intimacy motives. The key element of the scoring system is the desire to have impact on the behavior or emotions of another person, or to enhance one's prestige or reputation. The desire to experience such impact may be taken as the core of power motivation. Since people have many reasons for being defensive about exercising power, such a desire often registers only in implicit or unconscious forms.

Power as a *motive*, measured through content analysis of verbal behavior, should be distinguished from other power-related psychological concepts with which it is empirically uncorrelated. For example, power motivation measured in thematic apperception is not correlated with power as a goal that is directly accessible to consciousness and measured by self-report questionnaires. Nor is it related to self-report measures of other power-related variables such as traits (e.g., dominance, surgency, or extraversion), beliefs about power (e.g., authoritarianism or Machiavellianism), the sense of having power (internal control of reinforcements), occupying positions of power, or having skill in getting or using power.

People express their power motivation through a variety of different channels, sometimes depending on moderator variables such as social class, responsibility, or traits such as extraversion (see Winter, 1996, chap. 5 and pp. 666–669; also Winter, John, Stewart, Klohnen, & Duncan, 1998). Those with strong motivation are drawn to careers that permit direct and legitimate interpersonal power, for example, directing the behavior of others and using positive and negative sanctions, all within a "legitimate" institutional structure: business executive, teacher, psychologist or mental health worker, journalist, and the clergy. They are also active in organizations as members and officers.

To reach such goals, power-motivated people often employ strategies of becoming visible and well known, taking extreme risks, and acquiring and using prestige (or "self-display"). In contrast to achievement-motivated people, who might "build a better mousetrap so that the world would beat a path to their door," they might seek a more direct way of getting the world to come to their door, without building the better mousetrap. They are adept at building alliances, especially with lower-status or less well-known others who, with nothing to lose, may constitute a loyal base of support. In small groups, they tend to define the situation, encourage others to participate, and influence others; but they are not especially well liked and do not work hard or offer the best ideas. They are generative, especially in ways that fit with traditional sex-role conceptions. Overall, as leaders they are able to create high morale among their subordinates and tend to be viewed by their associates as charismatic and by historians as great (Winter, 1996, pp. 161–164). Thus, in times of social stress voters turn to leaders high in power motivation.

Several studies suggest a negative side to the power motive—perhaps supporting Lord Acton's famous dictum that "power tends to corrupt and absolute power corrupts absolutely." In experimental studies, small-group leader-managers high in power motivation are vulnerable to flattery and ingratiation by subordinates. While their groups are more cohesive and higher in morale, they are also less effective in gathering and using information and pay less attention to moral concerns. In negotiation or bargaining, people scoring high in power motivation tend to break agreements and demand better terms. When unconstrained by a sense of responsibility, they engage in a variety of "profligate impulsive" behaviors: verbal and physical aggression, excessive drinking and multiple drug use, gambling, and exploitative sex (Winter, 1996). Finally, they are vulnerable to boredom and anhedonia (Woike, 1994).

Most of these action correlates of the power motive are true for women as well as men (Winter, 1988; Winter & Barenbaum, 1985). In addition, men high in power motivation tend to inflict physical abuse on their partners and discourage them from having independent careers.

Research by McClelland and his colleagues, summarized in McClelland (1989), suggests that power motivation is associated with greater sympathetic nervous system arousal in response to threat and stress, lowered immune system efficiency, and more infectious diseases; also with higher blood pressure and a variety of cardiovascular problems.

High levels of power motivation are associated with aggression and war, both at the level of individual political leaders and at the level of governing elites and societies, especially in times of crisis (Winter, 1993).

Not much research has been done on the developmental antecedents of power motivation, but some longitudinal evidence suggests that it is fostered by early parental permissiveness (rather than restriction), especially with respect to sex and aggression.

Several investigators have explored ways in which power motivation might be "partitioned" or directed into prosocial (versus antisocial) channels: for example, through moderating effects of affiliation motivation in promoting generativity (Peterson & Stewart, 1993), responsibility (Winter & Barenbaum, 1985), or activity inhibition (McClelland, 1975), as well as other variables (Winter, 1973, chap. 5).

Bibliography

McClelland, D. C. (1975). *Power: The inner experience.* New York: Irvington. Combines power motivation with measures of maturity, and elaborates earlier laboratory research into analyses of history and religious belief.

McClelland, D. C. (1989). Motivational factors in health and disease. *American Psychologist, 44*, 675–683. Comprehensive review of links between power motivation, immune system functioning, and vulnerability to cardiovascular problems and disease.

Peterson, B. E., & Stewart, A. J. (1993). Generativity and social motives in young adults. *Journal of Personality and Social Psychology, 65*, 186–198. Links power motivation to generativity.

Smith, C. P. (Ed.). (1992). *Motivation and personality: Handbook of thematic content analysis.* New York: Cambridge University Press. Contains power motivation scoring systems, psychometric and validity data, and recommended methodological procedures.

Winter, D. G. (1973). *The power motive.* New York: Free Press. Chronicles development and validation of the modified measure of power motivation.

Winter, D. G. (1988). The power motive in women—and men. *Journal of Personality and Social Psychology, 54*, 510–519. Demonstrates lack of sex differences in arousal, internal structure, and action correlates of power motive scoring system.

Winter, D. G. (1993). Power, affiliation and war: Three tests of a motivational model. *Journal of Personality and Social Psychology, 65*, 532–545. Reviews previous political psychology research with individuals, and demonstrates link between high power motivation, measured at the level of the collectivity, and war.

Winter, D. G. (1996). *Personality: Analysis and interpretation of lives.* New York: McGraw-Hill. Chapter 2 discusses concept of motive, and chapter 5 reviews research on power motivation.

Winter, D. G., & Barenbaum, N. B. (1985). Responsibility and the power motive in women and men. *Journal of Personality, 53*, 335–355. Introduces measure of responsibility and shows that it (not gender) moderates relation of power motivation to prosocial versus "profligate" and impulsive behaviors.

Winter, D. G., John, O. P., Stewart, A. J., Klohnen, E., & Duncan, L. E. (1998). Traits and motives: Toward an integration of two traditions in personality research. *Psychological Review, 105*, 230–250. Demonstrates the theoretical and empirical independence of traits and motives, and shows how they jointly predict behavior over the life course.

Woike, B. A. (1994). Vivid recollection as a technique to arouse implicit motive-related affect. *Motivation and Emotion, 18*, 335–349. Presents recent research on the cognitive and affective processes underlying power motivation.

David G. Winter

PRACTICAL INTELLIGENCE. With surprising regularity, the best students in high school or college often have unremarkable success in their subsequent careers. Conversely, biographies of the most successful individuals in a wide variety of career domains describe unremarkable academic records. In medical school, a shake-up in class rank is commonly observed between the first 2 years of mostly academic lectures and the final 2 years of more clinical judgment and practice.

A number of factors probably account for these kinds of disparities between success in academic settings and success beyond the classroom. For example, chance in the form of events that one has little or no control over plays a role in career success. However, it also is the case that the transition from school to career involves a change in the mix of intellectual competencies that is required. Success in school requires the kind of academic intelligence that is assessed by the ubiquitous IQ test. Successful handling of the problems and tasks found in the everyday world require a more practical kind of intelligence.

One of the most exciting developments in the field of intelligence over the last decade has been an emergent interest in practical intelligence. As is the case for just about any topic on intelligence, defininitional issues remain problematic. And due to the relative recency of interest in practical intelligence, measures are in the primative stage relative to the ubiquitous IQ test.

Defining Practical Intelligence

Perhaps the most consistent theme over nearly a century of intelligence research is a marked inconsistency in how intelligence in defined. For example, when the editors of the *Journal of Educational Psychology* convened a symposium of 17 leading researchers in 1921 to have them describe their conception of intelligence, the result was 14 different answers and 3 nonreplies. When Sternberg and Detterman (1986) posed a similar question to contemporary researchers 65 years later, 25 different attributes of intelligence were mentioned (Sternberg & Berg, 1986), with no more consensus than in the 1921 symposium.

Despite the considerable variability in historical and current conceptions of intelligence, a common thread is the inclusion of intellectual competencies required for handling worldly as opposed to just classroom type problems. For example, Binet considered intelligence to be the collective faculties of "... judgment, otherwise called good sense, practical sense, initiative, the faculty of adapting one's self to circumstances" (Binet & Simon, 1916, pp. 42–43). Wechsler's definition of intelligence was similarly broad, namely, "The aggregate or global capacity of the individual to act purposefully, to think rationally and to deal effectively with his environment" (Wechsler, 1958, p. 7). Although little consensus exists about a definition of practical intelligence, four working definitions have been influential.

Exclusionary Definitions. Working definitions of practical intelligence based on exclusion focus on what practical intelligence is *not*. For example, Frederiksen (1986) considers practical intelligence to be displayed in one's cognitive responses to most of what happens outside the classroom. Support for a working definition based on exclusion is provided by reports of differences between the kinds of problems found in the classroom and on IQ tests—academic problems—and the kinds of problems found in the everyday world—practical problems (Neisser, 1976; Wagner & Sternberg, 1985). A sampling of these apparent differences is presented in Table 1. Academic problems are well defined and are formulated by others (e.g., a teacher or a textbook author). When teachers give problems to their students, the students may not always be sure of the answers but they usually will be sure about what the problems are. And for most academic problems, additional information is not required. In contrast, practical problems appear unformulated, and usually have a number of possible solutions, each associated with liabilities as well as assets. Additional information typically must be acquired to formulate and solve practical problems. Based on this analysis of academic and practical problems, a working definition of practical intelligence is the ability to solve the ill-defined problems that arise in daily life, for which there may be no clear-cut answers.

PRACTICAL INTELLIGENCE. Table 1. Characteristics that differentiate academic and practical problems

Academic Problems	Practical Problems
1. Well-defined	1. Ill-defined
2. Formulated by others	2. Requiring formulation
3. Complete	3. Incomplete
4. One correct answer	4. Multiple answers
5. One method of solution	5. Multiple methods of solution

Practical Know-How. An alternative working definition defines practical intelligence in terms of practical know-how or common sense. A number of expressions that refer to practical know-how are common in everyday parlance, such as being "street smart" and "knowing the ropes." An example of practical intelligence as practical know-how is provided by Berry and Irvine's (1986) cross-cultural study. They describe the *bricoleur*, a jack-of-all-trades who accomplishes repairs and odd jobs by employing whatever resources and materials are at hand, as opposed to modern service technicians who rely on specialized tests and tools, and replacement parts.

Wagner and Sternberg define practical intelligence in terms of a facility for acquiring *tacit knowledge*, practical know-how that is required to succeed in daily life including most career pursuits yet is rarely taught directly (Sternberg, Wagner, Williams, & Horvath, 1995; Wagner, 1987, in press; Wagner & Sternberg, 1985; 1990). Tacit knowledge typically is acquired from one's own experience or from that of a mentor. In a series of studies, measures of tacit knowledge distinguished between groups of individuals that varied in amounts of experience and training in fields such as academic psychology and business management. Performance on measures of tacit knowledge was related to criterion measures of performance in the careers examined, but largely was unrelated to traditional measures of academic aptitude.

Social Competence. Several approaches to the study of practical intelligence have focused on the concept of social competence. Ford (1986) suggests that practical intelligence involves the pursuit of transactional goals, that is, goals involve things outside the body, such as establishing a friendship with a potential playmate, as opposed to things that are thought to remain inside the body, such as mastering a new concept. Mercer (1979) developed a measure of social competence called the Adaptive Behavior Inventory for Children (ABIC). The measure involves a structured interview with a child's primary caretaker and yields scores for six kinds of social-role performance: family roles, community roles, peer roles, nonacademic school roles, earner/consumer roles, and self-maintenance roles. Use of the ABIC and similar measures has helped to distinguish children who learn slowly in school but perform adequately outside the school setting from other children who perform poorly in and out of the school setting.

Prototypes of Practical Intelligence. Neisser (1976) describes the practical intelligence of an individual by comparing the individual to the *prototypically intelligent person*. The prototypically intelligent person is the composite person that emerges when individuals are asked to describe the most intelligent person that they can imagine. Prototypes are expected to vary across cultures and across time periods within cultures. For example, verbatim memory was a prized intellectual asset in Western cultures before the advent of print, despite the fact that it is not as highly valued today in literate cultures (Olson, 1986). Sternberg, Conway, Ketron, and Bernstein (1981) asked lay persons and experts to rate how characteristic 250 descriptions were of an "ideally" (1) intelligent person, (2) academically intelligent person, and (3) everyday intelligent person. The results concerning the everyday intelligent person are of most interest here. The prototypical everyday intelligent person is characterized by practical problem-solving ability, social competence, character, and interest in learning and culture. Ford (1986) describes using similar methods to examine people's implicit conceptions of social competence. The prototypical socially competent individual is characterized by prosocial skills (i.e., responding to the needs of others), social-instrumental skills (i.e., knowing how to get things done), social ease (i.e., enjoying social activities and involvement), and self-efficacy (i.e., having a good self-concept).

Empirical Support for the Construct of Practical Intelligence

One source of empirical evidence that supports the construct of practical intelligence comes from life-span developmental studies. Although performance on measures of academic intelligence, and particularly fluid ability measures in which individuals solve abstract reasoning problems under time pressure, peaks in the late teens and then begins a slow decline thereafter, the ability to handle worldly affairs does not appear to show the same developmental function. Across many cultures, leaders in business and commerce, such as directors and chief operating officers of corporations, tend to be in their 50s and 60s. Automobile insurance rates, which are based on actuarial data, are highest for young drivers who are at the peak of academic intelligence.

Denney and Palmer (1981) gave 84 adults between the ages of 20 and 79 an academic reasoning task called the Twenty Questions Task (Mosher & Hornsby, 1966), and a practical reasoning task that asked for responses to situations such as the following: "Now let's assume that you lived in an apartment that didn't have any windows on the same side as the front door. Let's say that at 2 a.m. you heard a loud knock on the door and someone yelled, 'Open up. It's the police!' What would you do?" Performance on the academic reasoning task declined linearly from age 20 on. However, performance on the practical reasoning task increased to a peak in the 40- and 50-year-old groups, with some decline thereafter. Cornelius and Caspi (1987) carried out a similar study of 126 adults between the ages of 20 and 78 using different academic and practical tasks. The pattern of results was identical, with performance on the practical task at high levels for older adults even though performance on the academic task had declined.

Another approach to differentiating the constructs of academic and practical intelligence is to give a group of individuals both academic and practical tasks and then to examine the correlation between performance on the two kinds of tasks. Scribner (1984, 1986) found that "unskilled" milk-processing plant workers used sophisticated strategies for combining varied quantities (e.g., pints, quarts, gallons) of varied products (e.g., skim milk, 2% milk, whole milk, buttermilk) when filling orders. This amounts to doing arithmetic in one's head using differently based number systems because there are 2 pints in a quart, 4 quarts in a gallon, and so on. Skill at assembling orders was unrelated to the workers' levels of previous school performance, arithmetic test scores, or intelligence test scores. Ceci and Liker (1986, 1988) found that expert horserace handicappers used a complex and effective algorithm for predicting posttime odds (and thus which horse to bet upon) that included interactions among seven sources of information. Individual differences in the degree to which handicappers used this effective strategy were unrelated to the handicappers' IQ scores. Lave, Murtaugh, and de la Roche (1984) studied the everyday mathematics used by grocery store shoppers to determine the best buy when the same product comes in different quantities for different prices. Accuracy in picking the best size was unrelated to the shopper's scores on the MIT mental arithmetic test.

In a different domain, Wagner and Sternberg (1990) studied business managers who were participating in a leadership development program. The effectiveness of managers' problem-solving abilities was assessed by having them perform in simulated work environments, and then having panels of specially trained raters evaluate their performance. The managers also were given an IQ test and a measure of business tacit knowledge or practical know-how. The best predictor of problem-solving performance in the simulated work environments was tacit knowledge, with IQ also being predictive of problem-solving performance, although to a lesser degree. In keeping with results of the studies just described, the correlation between tacit knowledge and IQ did not depart significantly from zero. Finally, Mercer, Gomez-Palacio, and Padilla (1986) reported an ambitious study of nearly two thousand Anglo, Chicano, and Mexican children who were given the Adaptive Behavior Inventory for Children (ABIC), which is the measure of social role performance described previously, and the Wechsler Intelligence Scale for Children–Revised (WISC–R), a common IQ test. Virtually no relations were found between scores on the ABIC and IQ.

Conclusions

The phenomenal growth in activity and interest in the topic of practical intelligence represents one of the most exciting and promising developments in the field of intelligence. Despite the practical nature of most conceptions of intelligence, even the conceptions held by the developers of the early IQ tests, much of what we know about intelligence is limited to the subset of intellectual competencies that are of primary importance to performance in the classroom. The developing field of practical intelligence promises to expand our knowledge base to be more consistent with the range of intellectual competencies that characterize the conceptions of intelligence held by lay persons and experts alike. For further information, the interested reader is encouraged to consult one or more of the following references: Ceci (1990); Rogoff and Lave (1984); Scribner and Cole (1981); Sternberg and Wagner (1986, 1994); Sternberg, Wagner, Williams, & Horvath (1995); Wagner (1987, in press); and Voss, Perkins, and Segal (1991).

Bibliography

Berry, J. W., & Irvine, S. H. (1986). Bricolage: Savages do it daily. In Sternberg, R. J., & Wagner, R. K. (Eds.), *Practical intelligence: Nature and origins of competence in the everyday world* (pp. 271–306). New York: Cambridge University Press.

Binet, A., & Simon, T. (1916). *The development of intelligence in children* (E. S. Kit, Trans.). Baltimore: Williams & Wilkins.

Ceci, S. J. (1990). *On intelligence . . . more or less: A bioecological treatise on intellectual development.* Englewood Cliffs, NJ: Prentice Hall.

Ceci, S. J., & Liker, J. (1986). Academic and nonacademic intelligence: an experimental separation. In R. J. Sternberg & R. K. Wagner (Eds.), *Practical intelligence: Nature and origins of competence in the everyday world* (pp. 119–142). New York: Cambridge University Press.

Ceci, S. J., & Liker, J. (1988). Stalking the IQ-expertise relationship: When the critics go fishing. *Journal of Experimental Psychology: General, 117,* 96–100.

Cornelius, S. W., & Caspi, A. (1987). Everyday problem solving in adulthood and old age. *Psychology and Aging, 2,* 144–153.

Denney, N. W., & Palmer, A. M. (1981). Adult age differences on traditional and practical problem-solving measures. *Journal of Gerontology, 36,* 323–328.

Ford, M. E. (1986). For all practical purposes: Criteria for defining and evaluating practical intelligence. In Sternberg, R. J., & Wagner, R. K. (Eds.), *Practical intelligence: Nature and origins of competence in the everyday world* (pp. 183–200). New York: Cambridge University Press.

Frederiksen, N. (1986). Toward a broader conception of human intelligence. In Sternberg, R. J., & Wagner, R. K. (Eds.), *Practical intelligence: Nature and origins of competence in the everyday world* (pp. 84–116). New York: Cambridge University Press.

Lave, J., Murtaugh, M., & de la Roche, O. (1984). The dialectic of arithmetic in grocery shopping. In B. Rogoff & J. Lave (Eds.), *Everyday cognition: Its development in social context* (pp. 67–94). Cambridge, MA: Harvard University Press.

Mercer, J. R. (1979). *System of multicultural pluralistic assessment: Technical manual.* New York: Psychological Corporation.

Mercer, J. R., Gomez-Palacio, M., & Padilla, E. (1986). The development of practical intelligence in cross-cultural perspective. In Sternberg, R. J., & Wagner, R. K. (Eds.), *Practical intelligence: Nature and origins of competence in the everyday world* (pp. 307–337). New York: Cambridge University Press.

Mosher, F. A., & Hornsby, J. R. (1966). On asking questions. In J. S. Bruner, R. R. Oliver, & P. M. Greenfield (Eds.), *Studies in cognitive growth.* New York: Wiley.

Neisser, U. (1976). General, academic, and artificial intelligence. In L. Resnick (Ed.), *Human intelligence: Perspectives on its theory and measurement* (pp. 179–189). Norwood, NJ: Ablex.

Olson, D. R. (1986). Intelligence and literacy: The relationships between intelligence and the technologies of representation and communication. In Sternberg, R. J., & Wagner, R. K. (Eds.), *Practical intelligence: Nature and origins of competence in the everyday world* (pp. 338–360). New York: Cambridge University Press.

Rogoff, B., & Lave, J. (Eds.). (1984). *Everyday cognition: Its developmental and social context.* Cambridge, MA: Cambridge University Press.

Scribner, S. (1984). Studying working intelligence. In B. Rogoff & J. Lave (Eds.), *Everyday cognition: Its development in social context* (pp. 9–40). Cambridge, MA: Harvard University Press.

Scribner, S. (1986). Thinking in action: Some characteristics of practical thought. In R. J. Sternberg & R. K. Wagner (Eds.), *Practical intelligence: Nature and origins of competence in the everyday world* (pp. 13–30). New York: Cambridge University Press.

Scribner, S., & Cole, M. (1981). *The psychology of literacy.* Cambridge, MA: Harvard University Press.

Sternberg, R. J., & Berg, C. A. (1986). Quantitative integration: Definitions of intelligence: A comparison of the 1921 and 1986 symposia. In R. J. Sternberg & D. K. Detterman (Eds.), *What is intelligence? Contemporary viewpoints on its nature and definition* (pp. 155–162). Norwood, NJ: Ablex.

Sternberg, R. J., Conway, B. E., Ketron, J. L., & Bernstein, M. (1981). People's conceptions of intelligence. *Journal of Personality and Social Psychology, 41,* 37–55.

Sternberg, R. J., & Detterman, D. K. (Eds.). (1986). *What is intelligence: Contemporary viewpoints on its nature and definition.* Norwood, NJ: Ablex.

Sternberg, R. J., & Wagner, R. K. (Eds.). (1986). *Practical intelligence: Nature and origins of competence in the everyday world.* New York: Cambridge University Press.

Sternberg, R. J., & Wagner, R. K. (Eds.) (1994). *The mind in context.* New York: Cambridge University Press.

Sternberg, R. J., & Wagner, R. K., Williams, W. M., & Horvath, J. A. (1995). Testing common sense. *American Psychologist, 50,* 912–927.

Voss, J. F., Perkins, D. N., & Segal, J. W. (Eds.). (1991). *Informal reasoning and education.* Hillsdale, NJ: Erlbaum.

Wagner, R. K. (1987). Tacit knowledge in everyday intelligent behavior. *Journal of Personality and Social Psychology*, 52, 1236–1247.

Wagner, R. K. (in press). Practical intelligence. In R. J. Sternberg (Ed.), *Handbook of human intelligence*. New York: Cambridge University Press.

Wagner, R. K., & Sternberg, R. J. (1985). Practical intelligence in real-world pursuits: the role of tacit knowledge. *Journal of Personality and Social Psychology*, 48, 436–458.

Wagner, R. K., & Sternberg, R. J. (1990). Street smarts. In K. Clark & M. Clark (Eds.), *Measures of leadership* (pp. 493–504). Greensboro, NC: Center for Creative Leadership.

Wechsler, D. (1958). *The measurement and appraisal of adult intelligence* (4th ed.). Baltimore: Williams & Wilkins.

Williams, S. A., Denney, N. W., & Schadler, M. (1983). Elderly adults' perception of their own cognitive development during the adult years. *International Journal of Aging and Human Development*, 16, 147–158.

Richard K. Wagner

PRACTITIONER MODEL. The practitioner model of education and training is designed to prepare students for careers in the practice of psychology. Above all, professional psychologists need to develop the knowledge, skills, and attitudes required for effective professional service. Accordingly, the theories, methods, and substantive facts of scientific psychology are integrated throughout graduate study with extensive supervised experience in assessment, intervention, management, and other activities that occupy the daily work lives and constitute the main responsibilities of professional psychologists. Beyond emphasis on practical experience, the practitioner model is marked by a cluster of epistemological assumptions, role definitions, and specifications of content that define the model and distinguish it from others. Some form of practitioner model is taken for granted in other professions, but direct professional education was long delayed in psychology. Although applications of psychology began before the turn of the twentieth century, proposals for a practitioner model of training were not seriously considered until the 1960s, and detailed educational standards were not fully articulated until the final decade of the twentieth century.

Historical Development

Professional applications of psychology began almost as soon as psychology was established as a science, but training for professional work was severely limited in the years the field was forming. As the discipline grew, more and more psychologists found employment as practitioners in clinics, hospitals, counseling centers, and schools, and as consultants in business and industry. Educators gradually introduced some training for practice, but organized psychology adamantly sustained its official identity as a science, and opportunities for supervised professional experience were scanty and scattered. For more than the first half-century of psychology's existence, the prevailing practical aim of doctoral education in psychology was to prepare students for careers in teaching and scholarly research in the colleges and universities of the time.

This condition changed fundamentally after World War II. During the war, psychologists had offered impressive contributions in the selection and training of personnel, the design of military equipment, and the treatment of psychiatric battle casualties. After the war, federal funds were provided for the training of clinical and counseling psychologists to assist veterans in their return to civilian life. This led to rapid increase in the number of clinical and counseling programs in American universities, and required a redefinition of education and training that met demands for the preparation of competent practitioners, but also recognized the need for research to improve the limited, largely untested procedures then available to professional psychologists. A solution was found in the scientist-practitioner model of education, designed to prepare psychologists for careers of practice *and* research.

In Boulder, Colorado, in 1949, a conference of leaders in American psychology endorsed the scientist-practitioner concept. Standards for program accreditation subsequently incorporated the basic philosophy and structural features of the Boulder model, as it came to be called, and for a time all doctoral clinical and counseling programs in American psychology conformed to that pattern. In many ways, the model was successful. It continues as the guiding concept in the majority of programs in clinical, counseling, and school psychology. Within a decade, however, some limitations became apparent to critics. In many academic settings, research was valued more than professional service, and training for practice was often neglected or disparaged. Despite the emphasis on research in doctoral education, most graduates of scientist-practitioner programs did not publish any research following receipt of the scholarly Ph.D. By 1964, the number of psychologists employed in various forms of practice exceeded those employed in academic settings. Educational programs centered on research seemed ill-suited to the needs of psychologists entering careers of practice.

In 1964, a committee on the scientific and professional aims of psychology recommended the development of programs expressly designed to prepare students for careers of professional service. In 1965, a proposal to create practitioner programs leading to the doctor of psychology degree (Psy.D.) was debated at a national conference on the professional preparation of clinical psychologists. The proposal was not endorsed by conference participants, but some "recognition" was expressed, and the first Psy.D. program in the United

States was subsequently established at the University of Illinois. The Illinois program accepted its first class of students in 1968. The following year, the California School of Professional Psychology, a free-standing institution organized to train practitioners, established campuses in San Francisco and Los Angeles.

Slow growth of practitioner programs followed until 1973, when another national conference was convened in Vail, Colorado, to address issues in levels and patterns of training in professional psychology. The Vail conference resolved that psychology had matured sufficiently to justify programs explicitly designed to prepare students for practice, as well as programs primarily devoted to research. Over the following years, the number of professional schools and programs in the United States increased substantially. In 1976, the National Council of Schools of Professional Psychology (NCSPP) was founded to coordinate activities in developing programs. By 1997, the NCSPP roster listed 45 institutions whose programs followed the practitioner model of education, and more were forming outside the council.

The NCSPP, now renamed the National Council of Schools and Programs of Professional Psychology, conducts annual conferences to examine the basic issues and specific details of education and training for the practice of psychology. The following summary is based largely on resolutions developed in the 11 NCSPP conferences that took place before 1997.

Commitment to Education for Practice

Practitioner programs declare their purpose, publicly and unambiguously, to be preparation for the practice of psychology. Most signify their identity as professional programs by awarding the Psy.D. degree.

The Practitioner as Local Scientist

The core of effective practice is disciplined inquiry. The role of the practitioner in providing assistance to clients is that of local investigator bringing the most powerful available conceptions, the most illuminating methods of inquiry, and the most effective methods of change to the benefit of the case at hand. For many reasons, the simplifications and controls that are necessary and feasible in formal scientific research can rarely be exercised in practice. Still, the practitioner is cognizant of pertinent research, and professional studies themselves are designed to provide the carefully collected, critically examined data on which informed decisions and constructive actions can be based. Throughout training, every case becomes an exercise in disciplined inquiry.

Multiple Ways of Knowing

The varieties of clients and complexities of the issues that professional psychologists encounter require many ways of examining and understanding human conditions. The inquiries of the practitioner are grounded in psychological science, but are also enriched by a broad range of interdisciplinary perspectives. Many methods—qualitative as well as quantitative, subjective as well as objective—are flexibly employed to reach an understanding of maximum benefit to each client.

Core Competencies

Specific skills are required for the practice of psychology. Seven core competencies have been explicitly identified. Basic to all the others are the skills and attitudes of *relationship*, defined as the capacity to develop and maintain constructive working alliances with clients and the ability to work in collaboration with peers, members of other disciplines, consumers of services, and community organizations.

The assessment competency is also interwoven with all other aspects of professional practice. Assessment goes beyond narrow emphasis on tests, individuals, and disabilities to a multimethod approach that takes into account the sociocultural context of individual behavior, allows systematic study of groups and organizations, and focuses not only on limitations and dysfunctions but also on strengths and competencies.

Intervention includes psychotherapy, but is more broadly conceived as a class of activities that restore, sustain, or enhance effective functioning in clients through preventive, developmental, or remedial services. *Consultation* is a form of intervention in which the professional psychologist has no direct control over the change process, but brings the principles and procedures of psychology to bear on a problem through planned collaboration with clients or colleagues who are in a position to effect change.

Skills in research and evaluation are essential for all practitioners, but are seen as elements of practice rather than as ends in themselves. Practitioners engage the challenges of human conditions directly, starting with the needs of each client and employing appropriate methods, including those of research and evaluation, to study and improve the condition of the client.

As practitioners advance in their careers, many take responsibility for the management of programs and the supervision of less experienced practitioners. Competence in management requires knowledge of organizational behavior and the business aspects, laws, and regulations that affect practice. Competence in supervision is enhanced by providing advanced students opportunities to supervise the work of other students in the program, with the entire process under the supervision of faculty.

Core Curriculum

The broad range of professional psychology, embracing psychological functions of individuals, groups, and organizations among people of all ages, at all levels of effectiveness, in all the settings that human beings can enter and in which psychological services can be offered, requires equally comprehensive preparation. Specialization of services and educational programs can and does occur, not only among the commonly recognized specialties of clinical, counseling, school, and industrial/organizational psychology, but within specialties and among more recently emerging areas of practice, such as health psychology, forensic psychology, and sports psychology. Through all of these programs, however, a generic core of knowledge is preserved. All professional programs include content on the biological, cognitive-affective, social, and cultural bases of behavior, life-span development, dysfunctional behavior and psychopathology, quantitative and qualitative methods of inquiry, philosophical and historical foundations of psychology, and professional ethics and standards. In practitioner programs, special emphasis is placed on issues related to gender differences and cultural diversity.

Most distinctively, practitioner programs emphasize the actual performance of professional activities and the development of competencies through supervised experience in practicum settings. All programs require one year's experience in a predoctoral internship, and nearly all require a dissertation in which some form of disciplined inquiry is pursued in depth. Dissertations address the kinds of issues that practitioners encounter throughout their careers and employ methods that provide the most useful attainable knowledge about those issues. Types of dissertations include case studies, theoretical analyses, needs analyses, and program evaluations, as well as the group-based experiments and field studies that are the norm in research-oriented programs.

Integrative Pedagogy

Much of the material in the core curriculum is taught in didactic courses comparable with those of undergraduate study. To every possible extent, however, the seminars, practica, and supervisory sessions in which most professional training takes place are designed to integrate abstract knowledge with the practical realities of professional work. For example, a course in a particular form of treatment may begin with coverage of pertinent theory and research, proceed with examples of the treatment by the instructor and students, and end with questions about the merits and limitations of the method, which may lead to dissertation research and ultimate improvement of the method itself. Issues related to gender and cultural diversity are suffused throughout the curriculum and are common topics of dissertation research. Ethical issues are addressed in the context of questions that arise in the course of professional work.

Comparison With Scientist-Practitioner Programs

Most practitioner programs are located in professional schools or programs devoted to education for the practice of psychology. Graduate study emphasizes supervised experience and typically leads to the Psy.D. degree. Most scientist-practitioner programs are located in the academic departments of research universities devoted to the aims of research and education. Graduate study emphasizes the conduct of research and leads to the Ph.D. degree. Many scientist-practitioner programs discourage students who are interested in careers emphasizing practice from applying for admission. Others, however, offer preparation for practice and research and describe their programs as balanced. Differences between the latter programs and practitioner programs that define the central function of professional psychology as disciplined inquiry may be slight. In both cases, the aims of education are to instill a strong sense of social responsibility, to develop effectiveness in the skills of practice as well as the inquiries through which the profession advances, and to encourage a critical, inquiring attitude that inspires lifelong learning.

[*See also* Scientist-Practitioner Model.]

Bibliography

Peterson, D. R. (1997). *Educating professional psychologists: History and guiding conception.* Washington, DC: American Psychological Association. Conceptual statements and historical accounts by the founder of the first doctor of psychology program in the United States.

Peterson, R. L., Peterson, D. R., Abrams, J. C., & Stricker, G. (1997). The National Council of Schools and Programs of Professional Psychology educational model. *Professional Psychology: Research and Practice, 28,* 373–386. An easily accessible description of the practitioner model.

Peterson, R. L., Peterson, D. R., & Abrams, J. C. (in press). *Standards for the education of professional psychologists.* Washington, DC: American Psychological Association. A comprehensive statement of training standards as endorsed by the National Council of Schools and Programs of Professional Psychology.

Donald R. Peterson

PRAGMATICS. How do we make sense of language? Is it our knowledge of the meanings (semantics) of words and their grammatical structuring (syntax) that determines utterances' meaningfulness? Obviously these are necessary, but they alone will not allow the interpretation of "Do you know the time?" as a request for information rather than a yes-or-no question;

they alone will not allow comprehenders to go beyond the description of the state of affairs in "It's so hot in here" so as to interpret that utterance as a request to turn on the air conditioner or open the window. This is one area where pragmatics reigns. Pragmatics is speakers' knowledge of the principles that govern language use.

Pragmatics is commonly taken to be the field that analyzes language by reference to extralinguistic notions, such as information status (e.g., already known, in focus). Pragmatic meaning is assumed to rely heavily on the context of the speech situation, and so much so that it can even be canceled by the context (as in "It's hot in here, but don't open the window"). It is often taken as an optional inference that the addressee is to draw, based on indirect cues from the speaker. The field has been growing rapidly since the 1970s, rejecting, in varying degrees, the Chomskyan monopoly over linguistic analysis, since the large gap between the narrow meaning that the grammarian's semantics is able to supply and the richness of meaning that speakers intend and addressees generate in natural communicative encounters needed to be accounted for.

However, it is widely acknowledged that pragmatics, defined as involving reference to extralinguistic factors, is at most a perspective on language rather than a coherent field (Levinson, 1983). It has recently been proposed that the linguistic-extralinguistic division of labor should replace the previous grammatical-pragmatic distinction, relegating some so-called pragmatic phenomena to grammar—"linguistic pragmatics"—and some to extralinguistic, central-system cognitive processes—"central-system pragmatics" (Ariel, 1999; Kasher, 1982; Sperber & Wilson, 1986/1995). Linguistic pragmatics constitutes direct form-function correlations, where the functions are extralinguistic (functional grammar). Central-system pragmatics (Fodor, 1983) offers a general-purpose cognitive account for inferential processes used, although not exclusively, in utterance interpretation.

Linguistic pragmatic research focuses on conventional meanings attached to specific linguistic forms, which are extralinguistic in nature and do not affect the truth value of the proposition. Such meanings refer to notions like "discourse topic," "new," "old," or "accessible" information, and are argued to form part of the speaker's competence in her language (rather than her use-practices only). Some functional syntacticians merely argue that language does not tolerate identical paraphrases (Kuno, 1972; Prince, 1978). Hence, they suggest that semantic paraphrases are pragmatically different in that they impose different constraints on the use of a construction. Functional syntacticians seek to characterize those contexts in which one construction is appropriate where another is not. They then attach an extralinguistic meaning to marked (nonbasic) constructions. For example, *it*-clefts (as in "It was Mary who left") are contrasted with the canonical forms ("Mary left") and are argued to mark a piece of information (that someone left) as old (Prince, 1978); pronouns signal that the representation in memory of the entities being referred to is highly accessible, but definite descriptions mark a low degree of mental accessibility (Ariel, 1990). These functions restrict the use of linguistic forms to those contexts meeting their conditions.

Another, more radical branch of linguistic pragmatics assigns discoursal communicative functions a more significant role in language analysis. Typological functionalists, such as Chafe (1994), Du Bois (1987), Givón (1979), and Hopper and Thompson (1984), see grammar as a more or less frozen set of pragmatic-discoursal patterns. Pragmatic meanings do not merely form an additional layer of meaning; rather, they motivate the grammatical forms themselves. For example, these theorists propose that the universal noun/verb category distinction is a discourse-imposed distinction between discourse participants and discourse events. The concepts communicated do have a propensity for "nouniness" and "verbhood" (concrete objects and actions, respectively), but it is the discourse function that determines what concepts are coded by which part of speech. It is argued that all formal linguistic universals must be accounted for by pragmatic, discourse patterns.

Linguistic pragmatics is linguistic in that it accounts for linguistic units, be they morphemes, words, or whole constructions. Pragmatics, however, is more commonly associated with nonliteral, inferred meanings, namely, with what we term here central-system theories. Such analyses do not refer to specific linguistic forms and are not even restricted to linguistic products. According to Grice (1975), language use requires the cooperation of the parties involved. Speakers should cue their addressees to their communicative intention. To be cooperative, speakers should conform to four requirements (maxims):

1. They should provide sufficient (new) information that will not be too little or too much in a given situation.
2. Their information must be true and verifiable.
3. The information must be relevant to the topic discussed.
4. The information must be clear and unambiguous.

Following these requirements results in a coherent and straightforward discourse. On the assumption that speakers do not opt out of cooperation, however, they may deliberately and overtly violate one or more of these norms to achieve special goals. For instance, "It's hot in here" violates the informativeness requirement (1) since, by stating the obvious, it fails to provide new information. The overt violation is a signal to the addressee to go beyond the sentence meaning and generate the speaker's intended contextual meaning (termed conversational implicature). In contrast, a covert violation such as telling a lie, a violation of (2), does not prompt the addressee to go beyond the linguistic meaning and results in communication failure. According to Grice, then, making sense of an utterance involves recovering the speaker's intention, which often involves a pragmatic (central) meaning above the semantic meaning conveyed. Note that for Grice, linguistic or semantic meaning is equated with literal meaning. Though the Gricean model has been elaborated and improved on (Giora, 1988; Horn, 1984; Kasher, 1982; Levinson, 1983), the basic assumptions have remained the same.

An alternative theory to Grice's cooperation-oriented model is Sperber's and Wilson's relevance theory (1986/1995). According to this theory, human cognition tends to be geared to the maximization of relevance (the cognitive principle of relevance): it attends only to information that affects the cognitive environment, that is, enriches its set of assumptions, at a reasonably small processing cost. Every act of communication communicates a presumption of its own optimal relevance (the communicative principle of relevance). Hearers are equipped with a very general criterion for evaluating interpretations, which excludes all but a single interpretation. However, unlike the cooperative principle, the principle of relevance need not be "followed": it applies automatically without exception and cannot be violated.

The distinction between linguistic (including linguistic pragmatic) meanings and (inferred) extralinguistic (central pragmatic) meanings is assumed to have a psychological reality, that is, to involve different interpretative processes. Indeed, according to Grice, comprehenders compute the literal meaning first. If it is compatible with the situation or context it is accepted as the intended meaning and the search is stopped. If it is incompatible with the context it is rejected and replaced by an appropriate, contextually induced (implicated) nonliteral meaning. According to Grice and Searle (1979), literal (linguistic) meanings have a privileged status—they are always activated and always first. Using central-system pragmatics to interpret nonliteral utterances (e.g., metaphor, irony, or indirect requests) should, therefore, involve a sequential process.

The Grice-dubbed standard pragmatic model is consistent with the view that linguistic, in this case, lexical processes are autonomous and exhaustive. Context does not affect the initial access of a word's lexical meanings. Rather, it selects the appropriate meaning after the word's meanings have been retrieved (Gernsbacher, 1990; Swinney, 1979). However, some relevance theorists argue that comprehenders need not compute the literal (linguistic) meaning first. Instead, it is the meaning that achieves optimal relevance that enjoys a privileged status, be it literal (linguistic) or nonliteral (pragmatic). The assumption is that contexts are not given but searched for: Comprehenders access only contextual assumptions that render a newly stated assumption relevant. The possibility of a sequential process is thus rejected in favor of a direct-access model, which posits equivalent processes for literal (linguistic) and nonliteral (pragmatically inferred) interpretations. This processing model is consistent with a selective account of lexical access, according to which context directs access completely so that only the appropriate meaning is made available for comprehension (Glucksberg, Kreuz, & Rho, 1986).

Empirical evidence obtained in the last two decades has been contradictory. On the one hand, literal and nonliteral utterances have been shown to involve similar interpretive processes (see Gibbs, 1994, for a review). On the other hand, on-line measures showed that even when embedded in a rich context, metaphoric phrases required longer processing times than the same phrases used literally (Janus & Bever, 1985). Also, figurative referring expressions were found to take longer to read than their literal equivalents (Gibbs, 1994). Utterances used ironically were found to be processed literally initially and therefore to take longer to read than when used literally (Giora, Fein, & Schwartz, 1998).

How can these conflicting findings be reconciled? Rather than distinguishing between literal and nonliteral meanings, the relevant distinction should be between linguistic (including linguistic pragmatic meanings, which are conventional) and extralinguistic pragmatic meanings (which are inferred and nonconventional). Such a distinction is not identical with the literal-nonliteral distinction, because some nonliteral meanings get conventionalized in time (Traugott & König, 1991). Indeed, literal and nonliteral language use may be viewed as governed by a general principle of salience, according to which conventional meanings are always processed first. Thus, when, for example, *die*—the nonliteral meaning of the conventional idiom "kick the bucket"—is intended, it is accessed directly because it is a linguistic (conventional) meaning, (Gibbs, 1994); originally a conversational implicature, it has undergone semanticization. However, when a nonconventional meaning is intended (e.g., the meaning of ironies and novel metaphors), comprehension involves a sequential process, upon which the conventional (linguistic) meaning is processed initially, before the intended (nonliteral, extralinguistic) meaning is derived (Blasko & Connine, 1993; Giora, Fein, & Schwartz, 1998, but see Gibbs, 1994, for a different view). This is in line with the gradual process of grammaticizing central pragmatic meanings into linguistic ones (experiments with linguistic pragmatic meanings have hardly been conducted).

In conclusion, pragmatics, as it is commonly conceived of by linguists, is not a coherent field. Although all pragmatic research relies on language use in context, the role played by context is quite different for each branch of pragmatics. Only for central pragmatic interpretations is the specific context crucial, and only for central pragmatic interpretations is the intended meaning computed rather than accessed from the lexicon. Therefore, the current tendency is to distinguish between two types of pragmatic research. Linguistic pragmatic phenomena (information status markers and construction meanings) are conventional to a large extent and should pattern with grammatical phenomena processing-wise. Central-system pragmatic phenomena (conversational implicatures, novel metaphors, and ironies) are inferred meanings, generated by addressees taking into account the linguistic meaning of the utterance, but most importantly, on the basis of a set of general-purpose cognitive norms and the specific context of the utterance. Such pragmatic meanings require a sequential process for their derivation.

Bibliography

Ariel, M. (1990). *Accessing NP antecedents.* London: Routledge.

Ariel, M. (1999). Mapping so-called "pragmatic" phenomena according to a "linguistic-extralinguistic" distinction: The case of propositions marked "accessible." In M. Darnell, E. Moravcsik, F. Newmeyer, M. Noonan, & K. Wheatley (Eds.), *Functionalism and formalism in linguistics* (Vol. 2, pp. 11–38). Amsterdam: Benjamins.

Blasko, G. D., & Connine, C. (1993). Effects of familiarity and aptness on meta-processing. *Journal of Experimental Psychology: Learning, Memory, and Cognition, 19,* 295–308.

Chafe, W. L. (1994). *Discourse, consciousness, and time.* Chicago: University of Chicago Press.

Du Bois, J. (1987). The discourse basis of ergativity. *Language, 63,* 805–855.

Fodor, J. (1983). *The modularity of mind.* Cambridge, MA: MIT Press.

Gernsbacher, M. A. (1990). *Language comprehension as structure building.* Hillsdale NJ: Erlbaum.

Gibbs, R. W., Jr. (1994). *The poetics of mind.* Cambridge, UK: Cambridge University Press.

Giora, R. (1988). On the informativeness requirement. *Journal of Pragmatics 12,* 547–565.

Giora, R., Fein O., & Schwartz, T. (1998). Irony: Graded salience and indirect negation. *Metaphor and Symbol, 13,* 83–101.

Givón, T. (1979). *On understanding grammar.* New York: Academic Press.

Glucksberg, S., Kreuz, R., & Rho, S. H. (1986). Context can constrain lexical access: Implications for models of language comprehension. *Journal of Experimental Psychology: Learning, Memory, and Cognition, 12,* 323–335.

Grice, P. H. (1975). Logic and conversation. In P. Cole & J. Morgan (Eds.), *Speech acts: Syntax and semantics* (Vol. 3, pp. 41–58). New York: Academic Press.

Hopper, P., & Thompson, S. A. (1984). The discourse basis for lexical categories in universal grammar. *Language, 60,* 703–752.

Horn, L. (1984). Toward a new taxonomy for pragmatic inference: Q-based and R-based implicature. In D. Schiffrin (Ed.), *Meaning, form, and use in context: Linguistic applications* (pp. 11–42). Washington, DC: Georgetown University Press.

Janus, R. A., & Bever, T. G. (1985). Processing of metaphoric language: An investigation of the three-stage model of metaphor comprehension. *Journal of Psycholinguistic Research, 14,* 473–487.

Kasher, A. (1982). Gricean inference reconsidered. *Philoshopica (Gent) 29,* 24–44.

Levinson, S. C. (1983). *Pragmatics.* Cambridge, UK: Cambridge University Press.

Kuno, S. (1972). Functional sentence perspective. *Linguistic Inquiry, 3(31),* 269–320.

Prince, E. (1978). A comparison of WH-clefts and IT-clefts in discourse. *Language, 54,* 883–906.

Searle, J. (1979). *Expression and meaning.* Cambridge, UK: Cambridge University Press.

Sperber, D., & Wilson, D. (1995). *Relevance: Communication and cognition.* Oxford, UK: Blackwell.

Swinney, D. A. (1979). Lexical access during sentence comprehension: (Re)consideration of context effects. *Journal of Verbal Learning and Verbal Behavior, 18,* 645–659.

Traugott, E. C., & König, E. (1991). The semantics-pragmatics of grammaticalization revisited. In E. C. Traugott & B. Heine (Eds.), *Approaches to grammaticalization* (Vol. 1, pp. 189–219). Amsterdam: Benjamins.

Mira Ariel and Rachel Giora

PREGNANCY at its most elemental level can be viewed as a biological process necessary for the propagation of the human species. Of course, it is a complex amalgam of biological, social, and psychological factors that encompass the period before the pregnancy, the actual course of the pregnancy itself, and the postpartum period. These factors interact in a dynamic fashion, a process that includes acceptance of the pregnancy, physical and emotional changes, the changing relationship with mother and partner, cognitive changes associated with the role transition, actual labor and delivery, and the possibility of mental illness, particularly in the postpartum period.

Acceptance of Pregnancy

Although contraceptive and reproductive technology allows women a greater degree of control than ever over their fertility, the confirmation of a pregnancy is almost always a time for reflection and consideration of a potential new identity for the woman. At the extremes, some women deny their pregnancy, carry the fetus without attracting much notice, deliver an infant with no one in attendance, and sometimes dispose of the infant. These women often are young adolescents who have little understanding of their circumstance, feel they have little control over their lives, and see few if any sources of support in their social environment. At the other extreme, some nonpregnant women will act and look as if they are pregnant, a condition known as pseudocyesis. For most women the process of accepting a pregnancy occurs over time and reflects the degree to which she desired the pregnancy, her emotional and physical comfort, and her view of herself as a mother-to-be. The extent to which these responses are in a positive direction will reflect the degree to which a woman accepts her pregnancy.

Physical Problems

Physically and emotionally, women typically experience a wide range of symptoms in pregnancy that range from almost unnoticeable to severe and disabling in their severity. Although conceptually distinct, physical and emotional symptoms often covary and probably reflect overall adjustment to the pregnancy. Common physical symptoms during pregnancy include nausea, fatigue, backache, urinary urgency, cramps, and swelling in the extremities. It is common, for example, for nausea to be prominent early in pregnancy and disappear by the second trimester. Other symptoms, such as fatigue, may develop and continue at a relatively mild level throughout pregnancy. In other cases, severe physical symptoms may plague the entire course of pregnancy. Interestingly, many complaints that are attributed to pregnancy may be related to more practical issues such as concurrent demands of caring for a young child or aging parents or a demanding job. Although it is not always the case, persisting and painful physical symptoms may be a sign that a woman is not adjusting well to her pregnancy. Emotional symptoms such as depression, irritability, and anxiety are likely to be prominent, possibly as a cause, consequence, or as an expression of an underlying physical or psychiatric disorder. Significant and prolonged physical discomfort during pregnancy usually signals the need for medical and psychological evaluation.

Emotional Adjustment

Emotional adjustment is not independent of physical adjustment during pregnancy. Although it once was widely believed that emotional distress associated with physical symptoms in the first trimester of pregnancy gave way to enhanced psychological functioning in the second trimester, numerous research studies have found that although emotional symptoms are not disturbing for most women, many women are afflicted by minor emotional disturbance that continues throughout pregnancy and sometimes into the postpartum period. Comparisons between matched groups of pregnant and nonpregnant women have revealed that although somatic symptoms such as fatigue, sleep, and appetite disturbance and concern about health are clearly elevated in pregnant women, cognitive-affective symptoms such as sadness, discouragement, guilt, and pessimism are not elevated in pregnant women. Finally, although negative moods are at higher levels in pregnant than nonpregnant women late in pregnancy, positive moods are at essentially equivalent levels.

Relationship with Mother

An important element of adaptation to pregnancy is the woman's relationship with her mother. She serves as a principal role model for motherhood for her pregnant daughter, particularly in the case of the primiparous woman. The relationship of a woman and her mother during pregnancy is largely determined by their past history together. Women who have had a conflicted relationship with their mother will often try to repair it during pregnancy.

The mother-daughter relationship is important for several reasons. With respect to adult development, the first pregnancy is often the context in which a woman assumes a peer relationship with her mother and becomes more autonomous. Because of the support, both emotional and informational, that a mother can provide to her pregnant daughter, pregnancy also affords an opportunity for renewed closeness between mother and daughter. It is also the case that a positive mother-daughter relationship is associated with more positive attitudes toward pregnancy, better adaptation to the maternal role, better maternal health, and fewer perinatal complications.

Marital Relationship

The marital relationship will often be most satisfying during pregnancy, particularly a first pregnancy. In these cases, the couple is bonded together by planning for their child, and the quality of the relationship will be highly salient to both partners. Marital satisfaction tends to be highest early in marital relationships before the first child is born and late in an enduring relationship after the children have achieved independence. As a consequence, couples often experience a decline in their marital satisfaction after the first child is born.

There are several issues with which couples frequently contend during pregnancy, including the partner's acceptance of the pregnancy, the ability of the partner to provide support, particularly emotional support, the partner's commitment to the marriage, and sexual adjustment, particularly late in pregnancy and early in the postpartum period. Significant ambivalence about the impending birth of a child on the part of the father may increase or lengthen the period of ambivalence of the woman regarding her pregnancy. Partners have a large role to play in buffering, through their support, both emotional and physical difficulties experienced by their pregnant partner. Failure or inability to provide needed support often is associated with poorer adjustment on the part of women and sometimes with less optimal pregnancy outcomes. The partner's commitment to the marriage affects a woman's adjustment during pregnancy and has been found to be an important predictor of depression after childbirth. Finally, most couples must adjust to diminished interest in, and comfort with, sexual intercourse late in pregnancy and early in the postpartum period. Conflicts associated with different expectations can be a significant source of marital distress.

Motherhood Role

Taking on the maternal role is one of the most fundamental tasks of pregnancy and the postpartum period. In the first pregnancy the woman begins the gradual shift in identification from woman-without-child to woman-with-child, or mother as described by Lederman (1996). This process accelerates throughout pregnancy and continues into the postpartum period. At a conscious level, women talk to their mothers and friends with children. They read books on pregnancy, childbirth, and mothering. Pregnant women will buy clothes and furniture and create a nursery for the child. Each of these acts serves to prepare the woman for the maternal role (e.g., reading) or is a rehearsal for actual maternal behavior (e.g., buying infant clothes). Preparation for the maternal role also occurs at a less conscious level in the form of dreams and fantasies. In some cases, dream and fantasy material reflects ambivalence about the new role (dreams or fantasies that highlight lost independence and freedom).

Barriers to successful adaptation to the mother role include lack of positive experience with children. Women with positive past experiences with children are much better able to envision themselves as mothers and imagine deriving pleasure from the mother role than women who have been deprived of those experiences. Women who have been exposed to poor maternal role models, particularly their own mothers, will feel less prepared and able to make the transition. Conflict between the maternal role and other roles, especially the role of the working woman, is detrimental to the acceptance of the maternal role. This difficulty is especially acute when the woman believes that multiple roles cannot be enacted at the same time (e.g., working mother). This state of affairs can occur when women set very high standards for their role performance. Psychological and personality problems can slow the transition to the maternal role. Problems like anxiety and depression decrease the pleasure associated with anticipating the maternal role and sometimes interfere with practical activities associated with enacting the maternal role. Examples would include the woman who is too depressed to prepare for the arrival of the baby. Personality problems may leave some women so self-absorbed that they have difficulty imagining a role in which they must provide total care for another person. Unexpectedly difficult and painful deliveries can interfere with the development of the maternal role, as can a conflicted marital relationship.

Childbirth

Often in the third trimester of pregnancy, women and their partners attend childbirth preparation classes. These classes educate couples about the physical events of labor and delivery in order to reduce their uncertainty and fear about the process, and give the woman (with her partner) strategies, such as controlled breathing and relaxation, to increase her sense of control and her ability to self-manage pain during labor and delivery. Although childbirth preparation classes are almost universally accepted and assumed to be beneficial, there has been relatively little controlled research that documents their benefits.

There is little question that health behavior affects labor, delivery, and infant outcomes. Poor nutrition, lack of prenatal care, and abuse of tobacco, alcohol, and other drugs are associated with poor infant outcomes, such as prematurity, low birth weight, and a host of neurobehavioral problems for the infant. The impact of psychological factors such as negative events, stress, and psychological distress during pregnancy is less certain. Psychological distress, particularly in the third trimester, may be associated with preterm delivery.

Postpartum Adjustment

The normal course of adjustment in the postpartum period is for women to experience a period of very positive mood for the first few days, followed by a dip in mood around the third to the fifth day. This low mood has come to be known as the postpartum blues. It lasts anywhere from a few hours to several days and may affect between 40 and 80% of postpartum women. The causes of the blues are not well understood; however, they may be a combination of hormonal readjustment after delivery and general vulnerability to psychological distress. For example, mood during pregnancy and history of psychiatric disorder are risk factors for the blues. There appear to be few negative consequences of this blue period.

Approximately 10% of women experience a period of depression following childbirth that may be severe enough to require psychological or medical treatment. These postpartum depressions are characterized by symptoms such as low mood, appetite and sleep problems, fatigue, pessimism, difficulty concentrating and making decisions, and suicidal thoughts. Interestingly, depression is not more common in postpartum than nonpostpartum women. However, postpartum depressions can negatively affect a woman's relationship with her child and partner. Women who have experienced a postpartum depressions are at increased risk for future depressions, and the child born at the time of the postpartum depression is at increased risk for problems in social and cognitive development.

Prominent risk factors for postpartum depression include personal history of depression (before or during pregnancy), stressful life events during pregnancy or the early postpartum period, and poor marital relationship. Women who have been depressed in the past and who experience stressful life events are especially vulnerable to a postpartum depression. Hormonal factors (e.g., estrogen withdrawal) also may play a role in the development of postpartum depression; however, the evidence here is quite mixed.

Postpartum depression can be treated with conventional medical and psychological treatments that have been adapted for postpartum women. Although large-scale clinical trials have only been underway since the early 1990s, there is good evidence that medications such as nortriptyline and fluoxetine and psychotherapies such as cognitive-behavioral therapy and interpersonal psychotherapy are effective interventions for postpartum depression. The demonstrated efficacy of medical and psychological treatments for postpartum depression and the serious consequences of untreated depression for mother and child underscore the importance of early referral for treatment of the postpartum depressed woman.

[*See also* Women's Health Issues.]

Bibliography

Brockington, I. (1996). *Motherhood and mental health.* New York: Oxford University Press. A summation of the field of postpartum mental illness by an eminent British psychiatrist.

DiMatteo, M. R., Morton, S. C., Lepper, H. S., Damush, T. M., Carney, M. F., Pearson, M., & Kahn, K. L. (1996). Cesarean childbirth and psychosocial outcomes: A meta-analysis. *Health Psychology, 15,* 303–314.

Hedegaard, M., Henriksen, T. B., Sabroe, S., & Secher, N. J. (1993). Psychological distress in pregnancy and preterm delivery. *British Medical Journal, 307,* 234–239.

Istvan, J. (1986). Stress, anxiety, and birth outcomes: A critical review of the evidence. *Psychological Bulletin, 100,* 331–348.

Lederman, R. P. (1996). *Psychosocial adaptation in pregnancy: Assessment of seven dimensions of maternal development* (2nd ed.). New York: Springer. Explains adaptive challenges faced by women during pregnancy.

Mercer, R. T. (1995). *Becoming a mother.* New York: Springer. This work is a comprehensive review of the psychology of pregnancy using Reva Rubin's *Maternal Identity and Experience* (New York, 1984) as a starting point.

O'Hara, M. W. (1994). *Postpartum depression: Causes and consequences.* New York: Springer-Verlag. Presents the results of a prospective study of postpartum depression testing psychological and biological hypotheses; a unique feature of this work is that a matched control sample of nonpregnant/postpartum women were also included in the study.

Raphael-Leff, J. (1991). *Psychological processes of childbearing.* London: Chapman & Hall. The psychology of pregnancy presented from a psychodynamic perspective by a practicing psychoanalyst.

Shereshefsky, P. M., & Yarrow, L. J. (Eds.). (1973). *Psychological aspects of a first pregnancy and early postnatal adaptation.* New York: Raven Press.

Wideman, M. V., & Singer, J. E. (1984). The role of psychological mechanisms in preparation for childbirth. *American Psychologist, 39,* 1357–1371.

Wolkind, S., & Zajicek, E. (Eds.). (1981). *Pregnancy: A psychological and social study.* New York: Grune & Stratton.

Michael W. O'Hara

PREJUDICE is typically defined as a negative attitude toward individuals who are members of a particular group or toward a group as a whole. Like all attitudes, prejudice has a cognitive component (e.g., beliefs or stereotypes), an affective component (e.g., dislike), and a conative component (e.g., a predisposition to behave in hostile ways toward members of a group). Many psychologists maintain that, by definition, prejudice is irrational, faulty, and not grounded in reality. Current evidence suggests that prejudice can be implicit (i.e., unconscious) or explicit (i.e., conscious).

Origins of Prejudice

Psychological research has revealed that there are various origins of prejudice. First, personality can play a role, as American social psychologist Theodor Adorno argued (*The Authoritarian Personality*, New York, 1950). Adorno described the authoritarian personality as characterized by strict adherence to conventional ways of behaving, aggression toward people who violate conventional norms, rigid thinking, and exaggerated submission to authority. According to Adorno, individuals with such a personality profile are especially prone to being prejudiced. American social psychologist Bob Altmeyer (*Enemies of Freedom: Understanding Right-Wing Authoritarianism*, San Fancisco, 1988) provided a more contemporary approach to understanding the role of personality in prejudice.

However, clearly, not all individuals who harbor prejudice fit the authoritarian personality profile. A second origin of prejudice is competition between groups over scarce resources (i.e., realistic conflict theory). As American social psychologists Muzafer Sherif and Carolyn Sherif demonstrated in their classic experiment at a summer camp (*Groups in Harmony and Tension*, New York, 1953), competition engenders feelings of hostility and prejudice. Given historical distributions of resources, power and status within a given society, particular groups may be in enduring competition and thus develop strong prejudices toward each other.

Third, prejudice can stem from the motivation to enhance one's self-esteem, as emphasized in social identity theory. Pioneered by European social psychologist Henri Tajfel (*Human Groups and Social Categories: Studies in Social Psychology*, Cambridge, England, 1981), this theory states that biases and prejudice between groups arise from basic social categorization processes in which people see themselves as belonging to one group rather than to another. Specifically, individuals derive a sense of self-esteem through their identification as members of a particular group and, to the extent that their own group is viewed more favorably than other groups, their self-esteem will be further enhanced. This sets the stage for prejudice toward others in that derogating the other group and favoring one's own group may help to establish a positive social identity. Use of the minimal group paradigm has demonstrated the very fundamental nature of social identity processes. With this paradigm, individuals are categorized into groups based on entirely arbitrary characteristics. Even so, once categorization occurs, evidence of favoritism for one's own group and discrimination against the other group emerges.

A fourth origin of prejudice is related to basic cognitive processes that contribute to a tendency to categorize and stereotype others. As Gordon Allport, an American psychologist, so eloquently underscored in his seminal writings concerning the cognitive functions of stereotypes (*The Nature of Prejudice*, Reading, Mass., 1954), human beings are limited in their capacity for careful and thorough thought. The social environment is so complex and makes so many demands on our limited cognitive resources that a rather natural, albeit unfortunate, consequence is that simplification of the social environment often occurs through categorization and stereotyping. Once stereotypes (the cognitive component of prejudice) are in place, prejudice may follow.

A final origin of prejudice is cultural learning. Parents, friends, family, traditional social norms, and institutionalized patterns of discrimination provide ample opportunities for individuals to be exposed to the prejudiced attitudes and behaviors of others. Others' views, then, may be incorporated into an individual's own belief systems. Indeed, children often adopt the prejudiced attitudes of others before they even have the cognitive abilities or social opportunities to develop their own attitudes.

Although five distinct origins of prejudice have been identified, theorists would not contend that these origins operate independently. They may often co-occur, as when the cognitive efficiency that makes stereotyping adaptive is coupled with a social environment through which stereotypic beliefs can be readily learned. Prejudice is multifaceted, and a complete understanding of it is possible only when its potentially multiple determinants are considered.

Influence of Social and Historical Circumstances

The scientific study of prejudice as a social problem began in psychology around the 1930s, in the context of White racism in the United States. Since then, different origins of prejudice have been more or less emphasized during different periods of time. As John Duckitt, a South African social psychologist, has argued (*The Social Psychology of Prejudice*, New York, 1992), social and historical circumstances at particular times have caused attention to be focused on different origins and manifestations of prejudice. For example, the Nazi racist ideology evident during the 1950s spurred psychologists to search for the type of personality that would enable individuals to mobilize as a collective force with the goal of genocide. How could people commit such atrocities as those evident during World War II? The answer to the search was the authoritarian personality. However, because the widespread prejudiced attitudes in, for example, the U.S. South during the 1960s and 1970s could not be explained by personality alone, the emphasis shifted to sociocultural factors (i.e., cultural learning and realistic conflict). With the persistence of prejudice even after the civil rights movement and into the 1980s and 1990s, the emphasis shifted again, this time to studying the psychologically universal cognitive and motivational processes that contribute to prejudice. In general, social and historical circumstances occurring in North America have been most influential in terms of shaping research on prejudice, because research on prejudice traditionally has been undertaken mostly in North America. However, the influence of European scholars has recently grown.

Expressions of Prejudice

As emphasized by Gunnar Myrdal, an American psychologist (*The American Dilemma*, New York, 1944), being prejudiced is fundamentally inconsistent with thinking of oneself as a fair and decent person. Social norms suggesting that expressions of prejudice are unacceptable can heighten the salience of this inconsistency. Thus, the ways in which prejudice is expressed may undergo transformations with changes in the social climate concerning what is considered to be socially acceptable. Such transformations have been especially apparent in the U.S. context, and therefore many American psychologists have sought to understand the changing nature of expressions of prejudice. For example, lynching African Americans was at one time acceptable in the United States if they were perceived as "stepping out of line." Expressing open support for segregation was socially acceptable prior to the U.S. civil rights movement. Largely because of the civil rights movement and its consequences, subsequent expressions of prejudice frequently took on more subtle forms. The goal of many contemporary psychologists, therefore, is to understand the nature of these more subtle forms of prejudice. These efforts have given rise to theories to explain the various forms of subtle and often conflicting responses (i.e., involving both positive and negative tendencies) commonly observed from the 1970s to the present. Although the underlying prejudice typically is assumed to originate from the same sorts of factors described previously (especially the motivational, cognitive, and cultural origins), the ways in which prejudice is expressed depends on individuals' reactions to a social climate in which prejudice is generally considered to be unacceptable.

For example, American social psychologists Samuel Gaertner and John Dovidio (1986) advanced the theory of aversive racism to explain subtle expressions of prejudice. This theory maintains that many White Americans desire to view themselves as egalitarian and nonprejudiced but nonetheless possess unacknowledged prejudice toward African Americans. In an effort to maintain their egalitarian self-image, White Americans express their prejudice only in situations with ambiguous guidelines with respect to what would constitute evidence of prejudice or in situations that permit a nonracial explanation for differential treatment of African Americans.

Another explanation for contemporary expressions of prejudice is found in the theory of symbolic or modern racism, which was advanced by American political scientists and social psychologists such as John McConahay (1986). This theory posits that many White Americans harbor antiegalitarian sentiments and support the current racial status quo. At the same time, they adhere to abstract principles of fairness and justice. Consequently, their prejudice is expressed in abstract or symbolic ways that modern racists believe can be justified with nonracial explanations. For example, modern racists may claim that African Americans get more economically than they deserve and justify this claim with reference to affirmative action policies that supposedly provide unmerited advantages.

Another set of American social psychologists, Irwin Katz and Glen Hass (1988), argued that many White Americans are conflicted in their reactions to African Americans because of the American socialization process, which emphasizes commitment to both egalitarianism and individualism. Whereas the egalitarian value orientation leads White Americans to feel sympathetic toward African Americans' plight for equality, the individualistic value orientation encourages White Americans to view African Americans' disadvantaged status in terms of individual failings (e.g., failure to work hard enough). The attitudinal ambivalence that results from simultaneously endorsing positive and negative attitudes toward African Americans results sometimes in positive, and sometimes in negative, reactions to African Americans that often are polarized or extreme.

A final model that explains a form of subtle, contemporary prejudice was advanced by Patricia Devine (1989), an American social psychologist. Devine's dissociation model explains how many people who truly endorse low-prejudice and egalitarian attitudes nonetheless may continue to have prejudiced responses under certain circumstances. According to the model, cultural stereotypes (e.g., gays are promiscuous or African Americans are lazy) frequently are so well learned and often reinforced (e.g., through the media) that they can be activated with little attention, awareness, or intention. In contrast, people's low-prejudice beliefs often are developed only after they have already learned cultural stereotypes and, consequently, they require greater attention, awareness, and intention to be activated. The result is that stereotypes may spring to mind, rather automatically, before low-prejudice individuals have the opportunity to engage the more elaborate thought processes required for bringing their low-prejudice attitudes to mind. Prejudiced responses, thus, are likely when careful thought processes cannot be initiated so as to override the rather automatic effects of stereotype activation and use.

Measurement Issues

When blatant expressions of prejudice were more socially acceptable, researchers could obtain quite accurate measures of people's prejudiced attitudes simply by relying on standard attitudinal instruments. Given the increasing subtlety of expressions of prejudice, there is growing controversy over how prejudice can be adequately measured. Some researchers maintain that direct attitudinal measures that include questions relevant to people's attitudes can accurately assess prejudice (or at least consciously endorsed prejudice). Other researchers maintain that the press to provide socially acceptable, nonprejudiced responses to attitudinal questionnaires renders the results of direct attitudinal questionnaires rather meaningless. Still other researchers argue that direct measures of prejudice are useful in some contexts, but that indirect measures that assess implicit prejudice are useful in other contexts.

[*See also* Ageism; Discrimination; Racism; *and* Sexism.]

Bibliography

Banaji, M. R., & Greenwald, A. G. (1994). Implicit stereotyping and unconscious prejudice. In M. P. Zanna &

J. M. Olson (Eds.), *The psychology of prejudice: The Ontario Symposium* (Vol. 7, pp. 55–76). Hillsdale, NJ: Erlbaum.

Devine, P. G. (1989). Stereotypes and prejudice: Their automatic and controlled components. *Journal of Personality and Social Psychology, 56*, 5–18.

Devine, P. G. (1995). Prejudice and out-group perception. In A. Tesser (Ed.), *Advanced social psychology* (pp. 467–524). New York: McGraw-Hill.

Dovidio, J. F., & Fazio, R. H. (1992). New technologies for the direct and indirect assessment of attitudes. In J. Tanur (Ed.), *Questions about questions: Inquiries into the cognitive bases of surveys* (pp. 204–237). New York: Russell Sage Foundation.

Gaertner, S. L., & Dovidio, J. F. (1986). The aversive form of racism. In J. F. Dovidio & S. L. Gaertner (Eds.), *Prejudice, discrimination, and racism* (pp. 315–332). San Diego, CA: Academic Press.

Katz, I., & Hass, G. (1988). Racial ambivalence and American value conflict: Correlational and priming studies of dual cognitive structures. *Journal of Personality and Social Psychology, 55*, 893–905.

Katz, P. A., & Taylor, D. A. (1988). *Eliminating racism: Profiles in controversy*. New York: Plenum Press.

Macrae, C. N., Milne, A. B., & Bodenhausen, G. V. (1994). Stereotypes as energy-saving devices: A peek inside the cognitive toolbox. *Journal of Personality and Social Psychology, 66*, 37–47.

McConahay, J. B. (1986). Modern racism, ambivalence, and the modern racism scale. In J. F. Dovidio & S. L. Gaertner (Eds.), *Prejudice, discrimination, and racism* (pp. 91–126). San Diego, CA: Academic Press.

Monteith, M. J. (1996). Contemporary forms of prejudice-related conflict: In search of a nutshell. *Personality and Social Psychology Bulletin, 22*, 461–473.

Proshansky, H. M. (1966). The development of intergroup attitudes. In L. W. Hoffman & M. L. Hoffman (Eds.), *Review of child development research* (pp. 311–371). New York: Russell Sage Foundation.

Schuman, H., Steeh, C., & Bobo, L. (1985). *Racial attitudes in America: Trends and interpretations*. Cambridge, MA: Harvard University Press.

Stephan, W. G., & Stephan, C. W. (1996). *Intergroup relations*. Dubuque, IA: Brown & Benchmark.

Margo J. Monteith

PREMENSTRUAL SYNDROME. *See* Menstruation.

PRENATAL DEVELOPMENT. *See* Human Origins.

PRESCHOOL EDUCATION, generally described as programs for children under the age of compulsory schooling, is a vital part of the lives of many young children in the United States today. But the experiences they offer vary, depending on the purpose and nature of the preschool.

Historical Roots of Preschool Education

Historically, preschool education in the United States has taken various forms, including kindergartens, nursery schools, and day care centers. In most cases these forms are no longer distinct, even though each has its own historical set of purposes and goals.

Today, almost all children who are 5 years old have the opportunity to attend a public kindergarten that is run by elementary schools. Kindergartens are descended historically from the Froebel kindergarten movement, which began in Germany in the mid-1800s. While Friedrich Froebel's intentions were to redesign schooling for all children to allow the unification of "man with God," he started with children of preschool age. His pedagogy centered on "gifts" and "occupations" that children could explore through play. The "gifts" were manipulable objects, such as six colored balls to be presented in an ordered sequence so as to develop a sense of ordered reality. The "gifts" were intended to stimulate observation and allow self-expression. The "occupations" were art or craft activities, such as drawing, coloring, sewing, and modeling of clay, to train the hand, eye, and mind. Play was regarded as a spiritual activity, and classrooms for children were viewed as "gardens" where instruction occurred through pleasure.

The first kindergarten in the United States was opened in 1855 by a student of Froebel's. During the next decade, Froebel's influence spread and led to the opening of the first public kindergarten, in St. Louis in 1873. These "free kindergartens" were school-based programs, but they sometimes included home visits and mothers' groups, the aim of which was to extend the philosophical beliefs implemented in the kindergarten to child-rearing practices at home.

John Dewey, a philosopher at the University of Chicago, both lauded Froebel and departed from him significantly. He endorsed the view of the child as an "instrument" rather than a passive recipient of knowledge, but criticized Froebel's emphasis on direct imitation and a well-developed curriculum of specifically timed lessons. Instead, Dewey advanced the view that children come to understand the social world through free play. Dewey's influence is still present today. Many programs emphasize the kindergarten as a social community and the key role of play as a vehicle of learning.

The nursery school movement in the United States was rooted in social reform efforts. Margaret and Rachel McMillan, social activists in England who took on the cause of improving the health conditions of children, are often credited with the development of nursery schools. Their focus was on child health, as opposed to Froebel's concern for spirituality. The McMillan sisters founded an "open-air school"—built so that one side could be opened to let in sunshine and fresh air. Outside play was encouraged, and children were given baths, clean clothing, healthy meals, and medical and dental care. While a cognitive focus on sensory training was included, greater emphasis was placed on children's emotional development. Americans who visited the open-air schools took the focus on health with them to the United States. Such schools were first opened to children living in poverty but soon were desired by middle-class parents as well. Nursery schools rapidly increased in number in the 1920s; about half of those schools were affiliated with universities or colleges (Braun & Edwards, 1972), where nursery education intersected with scholarship in psychology and education.

The development of day nurseries comprised a third form of early education in the United States. These centers were developed largely by philanthropic groups during the late nineteenth century to serve working mothers and to prevent young children from being left unattended. Day nurseries were focused on the prevention of pauperism, not the enhancement of children's development. They emphasized children's basic health and hygiene needs. Whereas regular attendance was emphasized in kindergartens or nursery schools, children attended day nurseries only on the days their mothers worked. Activities with mothers focused on employment skills and etiquette rather than on child-rearing practices (O'Connor, 1995).

Psychology's Influence on Preschool Education

Psychology has exerted critical influences on preschool education throughout the twentieth century. G. Stanley Hall, often credited as the founder of the child study movement, advocated the scientific study of children. He championed the systematic collection of data and encouraged psychologists to study education and teaching. Hall held that the findings from psychological research should be disseminated to the public and translated into practice for raising and educating young children.

Hall's 1880 report, "The Contents of Children's Minds upon Entering School," concluded that children who had attended kindergarten demonstrated advantages over their peers in terms of power of observation, conduct, and school-readiness skills. He applied Darwinian theory to the study of mental development and asserted that each child recreates the stages of civilization. Hall came into conflict with Froebel's followers by arguing that the concentration on fine motor activity stressed in the Froebel kindergarten violated a principle of development (i.e., that fundamentals are developed before accessories) and thus could be harmful to the child.

Hall's call for a systematic study of children had a lasting influence. Arnold Gesell, a student of Hall, studied developmental sequences and emphasized the importance of "readiness" in the education of young children. Gesell's studies of normative developmental sequences served as a fundamental basis for preschool teachers' understanding of child development during the 1930s and beyond.

The theories of Sigmund Freud and John B. Watson represented conflicting views of the emotional development of young children, but both influenced public thinking about beneficial practices in child rearing and early childhood education. Freud's theory suggested to parents and teachers that the child has biologically programmed emotional needs and that self-expression and a strong self-concept (i.e., ego) were important for young children's mental health. In contrast, Watson emphasized the conditionality of emotional responses. He warned of the dangers of too much "mother love" and the need for preschool teachers to be professionals, not "sentimentalists."

Edward Thorndike, another psychologist who had been influenced by Hall's emphasis on systematic inquiry, stressed the importance of the "effects" of an individual's behavior on learning adaptive behaviors in the environment, and focused on the influence of repetition on the formation of habits. The importance of social habit formation became a critical part of *The Conduct Curriculum* (1923), developed for preschool and kindergarten programs in the 1920s. From that perspective, the goal of early education was to focus on training desirable behaviors, rather than centering on children's needs or impulses.

During the 1960s, the behavioral techniques of B. F. Skinner were incorporated into a number of preschool and kindergarten programs, especially those that serve young children who are disadvantaged or have disabilities. A few programs adopted Skinner's ideas about "direct instruction" or the "programmed learning" of content. More often, however, the programs were identified by their selective use of specific reinforcement for specific behaviors, the extinction of unwanted behaviors, and shaping techniques.

The partnership of psychology and preschool education—while sometimes collegial, sometimes contentious—has continued throughout the last three decades. The work of the Swiss psychologist Jean Piaget became well known in the United States in the 1960s and 1970s, and had an enormous theoretical effect on the pedagogical philosophy of a large range of preschool programs. Piaget's studies on children's cognitive structures and the way in which children construct knowledge and internal representations have influenced both the curriculum and philosophy of early education. Constructivist principles derived from Piagetian theory have been used to emphasize the importance of providing children with opportunities to construct knowledge through activities such as water, sand, and block play, as well as to encourage teachers to be guides rather than didactic instructors in their interaction with children (Goffin, 1994).

Although Lev Vygotsky's writings date from the 1920s, his work has become known in the United States only recently. His influence on early education is ever growing, with certain aspects of his work having important implications for instructional approaches in early education. His notion of learning as occurring within a "zone of proximal development" suggests that adults or more advanced peers can guide a child's instruction on a task too challenging for a child to achieve alone (Rogoff, 1990). Furthermore, his emphasis on the sociocultural foundation of development and learning has been instrumental in shaping early education's responses to the growing cultural diversity of preschoolers in the United States today (Mallory & New, 1994).

The work of psychologists J. McVicker Hunt and Benjamin Bloom also had important effects on the field of early childhood education. Historically, educators had believed that intelligence was fixed at birth and could not be altered. In the early 1960s Hunt demonstrated that intelligence is responsive to experience (Hunt, 1961), and Bloom showed that much of what is measured as intelligence (IQ) is developed in the first 3 to 5 years of life (Bloom, 1964). These findings gave added support to the early-childhood education movement, especially to the development of early intervention programs such as Head Start, which is aimed at improving the educational chances of children living in poverty by providing them with a preschool experience (Zigler & Valentine, 1979).

Current Issues in Preschool Education

Public interest in preschool education continues to be bolstered by psychological research. For example, recent studies on early development have stressed the importance of early experience on social interaction (Elicker, Englund, & Sroufe, 1992), the development of cognitive and language skills (Wachs, & Gruen, 1982), and the development of the brain (Shore, 1997). These studies have had a substantial impact on what is considered "developmentally appropriate practice," as suggested by the National Association for the Education of Young Children, that is, practices derived from developmental theory and that address the needs of the "whole child," not just academic skills, and are congruent with the needs of the family as well as the child (Bredekamp & Copple, 1997). The emphasis on the importance of early experience has also influenced policy makers interested in the prevention and amelioration of social inequities by early intervention, as well as parents and educators interested in promoting optimal development in children.

In addition to the focus on early experience, ecological models of development (Bronfenbrenner, 1989) have shifted the focus of study from interindividual aspects of the child to the child's development in a range of settings. Additionally, in developmental contextual models (Lerner, 1991), the relationship among levels of organization is emphasized. The child is now conceptualized as developing in mutually interacting and interdependent systems, including the family, school, neighborhood or community, the family's cultural and economic reference group(s), and the larger political and economic systems of the city, state, and nation. From this perspective, development is construed as a sociocultural as well as an individual phenomenon, and the preschool itself is viewed as one of several interacting systems that support the child.

The context of child rearing and preschool education in the United States has also changed considerably over the last 30 years, with families becoming more diverse both structurally and culturally, and people or institutions outside of the family assuming more responsibility for the care and education of young children. Preschool programs have had to respond to an increase in the proportion of mothers in the workforce and an increase in the number of one-parent families due to divorce, teen parenthood, and women choosing to have children outside of marriage.

Changes in the risk factors to which young children are exposed in U.S. society have also exerted pressures on early-education programs. Young children are threatened by prenatal and postnatal exposure to substance abuse, AIDS, crime and violence, and neglect and other forms of child abuse, and children growing up in poverty are those most likely to experience these threats. They are also most likely to drop out of school, become teen parents, spend time in prisons, and require public financial assistance (Children's Defense Fund, 1997).

In keeping with the historical development of nursery schools and day nurseries as avenues of social change, a number of psychologists and educators have proposed that comprehensive preschool and parent education programs be designed to improve the lives of young children by providing education and emotional support for them and their families, including a range of services. Early-education programs that integrate services, such as preschool, mental health, physical health, and family support are garnering public interest. Head Start has been singled out as a particularly valuable program of preschool and related services for children of low-income families, and expansion of its programs is growing nationally (Washington & Oyemade, 1995).

In response to social needs, public schools are also becoming increasingly involved in implementing programs for children younger than kindergarten age, although there is no consensus over whether preschools should become part of the public school system. Disagreement centers on whether public preschools should provide the nurturing and play-oriented experiences of quality nursery schools and day-care centers or should develop an academically focused curriculum (Hauser-Cram, Pierson, Walker, & Tivnan, 1991).

Another recent development in preschool education, as in education for older children, has been the movement to include children with special needs in classrooms with typically developing children. In response to the implementation of the Individuals with Disabilities Act (PL 102–119), and its mandate to include children with special needs in the "least restrictive" setting consonant with their needs, increasing numbers of children with disabilities are now being educated in classrooms with typically developing children. Evidence of the benefits of inclusionary practices in preschool for children with disabilities as well as their typically developing peers continues to mount, although debate exists over the extent to which preschool educators need to modify their typical classroom practices to include children with disabilities (Wolery & Bredekamp, 1994).

Conclusion

Preschool education has grown considerably from its early roots. It has been greatly influenced by research on the psychological functioning of the child, which has expanded to include an understanding of the child as developing in multiple intersecting settings. Preschool education has also been affected by the needs of families, and thus has been influenced by social issues that extend beyond the child alone. Both historically and currently, preschool education has often been called on to serve the dual roles of supporting the development of the young child and acting as an agent of social reform in improving the young child's life opportunities.

[*See also* Day Care. *Also, many of the people mentioned in this article are the subjects of independent biographical entries.*]

Bibliography

Bloch, M. N. (1987). Becoming scientific and professional: An historical perspective on the aims and effects of early education. In T. S. Popkewitz (Ed.), *The formation of school subjects: The struggle for creating an American institution* (pp. 25–62). New York: Falmer Press. A sociohistorical review that analyzes ways in which preschool education became professionalized.

Bloom, B. S. (1964). *Stability and change in human characteristics.* New York: Wiley.

Braun, S. J., & Edwards, E. P. (1972). *History and theory of early childhood education.* Belmont, CA: Wadsworth. A history of preschool education that includes reprints of primary sources.

Bredekamp, S., & Copple, C. (1997). *Developmentally appropriate practice in early childhood programs.* Washington, DC: National Association for the Education of Young Children. A revised and expanded statement of the NAEYC's position on appropriate practice in education and care for children ages 0 through 8 years. States principles underlying DAP and guidelines for making decisions in the classroom and other settings for young children.

Bronfenbrenner, U. (1989). Ecological systems theory. In R. Vasta (Ed.), *Annals of child development* (Vol. 6, pp. 187–251). Greenwich, CT: JAI Press.

Burke, A. (1923). *The conduct curriculum.* New York: Teachers College Press.

Children's Defense Fund (1997). *The state of America's children, yearbook 1997.* Washington, DC: Author.

Dunn, L., & Kontos, S. (1997). What have we learned about developmentally appropriate practice? *Young Children, 52*(5), 4–13. A review article outlining the extent to which DAP is incorporated into practice in early childhood education, and evidence of its effectiveness.

Elicker, J., Englund, M., & Sroufe, A. (1992). Predicting peer competence and peer relationship in childhood from early parent-child relationships. In R. D. Parke & G. W. Ladd (Eds.), *Family-peer relationships: Modes of linkage* (pp. 77–106). Hillsdale, NJ: Erlbaum.

Essa, E. (1995). *A practical guide to solving preschool behavior problems.* Albany, NY: Delmar. Recommendations for teachers coping with young children's behavior problems. Includes a variety of methods, including behavior modification techniques.

Goffin, S. G. (1994). *Curriculum models and early childhood education: Appraising the relationship.* New York: Merrill. Outlines the major curriculum models used in early childhood education today. Describes the historical context for the development of the different models.

Hall, G. S. (1980). The contents of children's minds upon entering school.

Hauser-Cram, P., Pierson, D. E., Walker, D. K., & Tivnan, T. (1991). *Early education in the public schools: Lessons from a birth-to-kindergarten program.* San Francisco: Jossey-Bass.

Hunt, J. M. (1961). *Intelligence and experience.* New York: Ronald Press.

Lerner, R. (1991). Changing organism-context relations as the basic process of development: A developmental contextual perspective. *Developmental Psychology, 27,* 27–32.

Mallory, B. L., & New, R. S. (1994). *Diversity and developmentally appropriate practice.* New York: Teachers College Press.

O'Connor, S. M. (1995). Mothering in public: The division

of organized child care in the kindergarten and day nursery, St. Louis, 1886–1920. *Early Childhood and Research Quarterly, 10,* 63–80.

Rogoff, B. (1990). *Apprenticeship in thinking: Cognitive development in social context.* New York: Oxford University Press.

Ross, E. D. (1976). *The kindergarten crusade: The establishment of preschool education in the United States.* Athens, OH: Ohio University Press. Describes the history of kindergarten in the United States as an agent of social reform and charity.

Shapiro, M. S. (1983). *Child's garden: The kindergarten movement from Froebel to Dewey.* University Park: Pennsylvania State University Press. Describes the history of the kindergarten movement as a reflection of social and intellectual history in the United States.

Shore, R. (1997). *Rethinking the brain: New insights into early development.* New York: Families and Work Institute.

Wachs, T., & Gruen, G. (1982). *Early experience and human development.* New York: Plenum Press.

Washington, V., & Oyemade, U. J. (1995). *Project Head Start: Models, strategies, and issues for the twenty-first century.* New York: Garland. Reviews the accomplishments of Head Start and outlines goals and strategies for the continuing development of this national intervention program.

Wolery, M., & Bredekamp, S. (1994). Developmentally appropriate practices and young children with disabilities: Contextual issues in the discussion. *Journal of Early Intervention, 18,* 331–341.

Zigler, E., & Valentine, J. (Eds.). (1979). *Project Head Start: A legacy of the war on poverty.* New York: Free Press.

Penny Hauser-Cram and Martha B. Bronson

PRESCRIPTION PRIVILEGES. One of the most controversial issues facing professional psychology during the 1990s was whether the profession should seek prescriptive authority. Supporters of prescription privileges view this as the next logical step in expanding the clinical scope of practice of psychologists. They argue that the ability to prescribe psychotropic drugs is a logical extension of other scope-of-practice battles that the profession has won, such as the right to independently bill third-party insurers and the acquisition of hospital practice privileges in numerous states. Just as psychologists have become more intimately and independently involved in the health care of the nation, other nonphysician health-care professions have also made extraordinary gains in expanding the scope of their practices. Thus, it is appropriate to view psychology's efforts to achieve prescriptive authority in the context of advances made by other health-care professions.

Early on in the history of the prescription-privileges movement, psychologists made the crucial decision to seek independent prescriptive authority. By virtue of the medical degree, physicians possess broad prescriptive authority, and, broadly speaking, can prescribe any legal agent for any condition.

Dentists, optometrists, and podiatrists are generally deemed limited-practice prescribers with independent status. This allows them to prescribe without physician involvement, but they are restricted in practice to specific body parts or conditions affecting those body parts. In contrast, physician assistants, nurse practitioners, and pharmacists are usually classified as "physician extenders" (although nursing is gradually transitioning into independent status). With certain exceptions, these professionals can prescribe only under some form of physician oversight.

Optometrists first obtained independent prescriptive authority to prescribe certain agents in the State of Indiana in 1935. Forty years later (in 1975) nurses obtained similar authority in North Carolina. Today dentists, optometrists, and podiatrists have the authority to prescribe, from varying forms of limited formularies, in all 50 states.

By 1997, nurses holding several different advanced-practice degrees had obtained the authority to prescribe from limited formularies in all but one state, and without physician oversight in 26 states. Physician's assistants possess the authority to prescribe under a physician's supervision in 40 states. Doctors of pharmacy have begun a similar legislative quest for independent prescribing authority.

The increased autonomy of nonphysician health-care professionals to prescribe is seen by many observers as an index of their maturation. Psychologists seeking prescription rights assert that the rapid inroads made by these groups toward controlling the prescription pad are harbingers of fundamental changes in the way health care is delivered in the United States and abroad, where nonphysician prescribing is already a relatively commonplace practice. They hold that prescriptive authority is a fundamental skill for psychologists who wish to remain competitive as health-care providers of the future.

A number of arguments have been promulgated in support of these assumptions. Those in favor point out that psychologists have more education and training in the assessment and psychosocial treatment of mental and emotional distress than any other profession. Thus, psychologists are seen as the logical providers of psychotropics and are well equipped to effectively combine pharmacological and nonpharmacological interventions. The vast majority of psychotropic drugs in this country are currently prescribed by nonpsychiatric physicians, with minimal training in the detection and management of mental illness. Such patterns of practice perpetuate a system in which psychotropic drugs are overprescribed, at the expense of behavioral interventions, although the latter are often more effective and have far fewer side effects. Proponents also note that currently, clients of psychologists needing psychotropics must also be seen by a physician solely for the purpose of obtaining medication. This involves unnecessary inconvenience and expense to the client, and increases the chance of miscommunication or adverse outcome. Those in favor of prescriptive authority also argue that this ability will expand psychologists' capability of working with the seriously mentally ill and other special populations. In sum, proponents believe that all classes of clients will be better served by psychologists who can prescribe psychotropics. Psychologists will be more likely to use drugs as adjuncts to well-designed psychotherapeutic regimens, rather than as the primary mode of intervention. Prescriptive authority will result in cost efficiencies and improve outcome, as psychologists will be able to independently manage both medications and psychotherapy throughout the episode of care.

Opposition to prescriptive authority comes both from within and outside psychology. Within the profession, those opposed fear that psychologists' core identity as behavioral scientists would be lost, and this would profoundly affect the importance attributed to basic science in graduate education. They also believe that the clinical practice of psychology has prospered, in part because it has focused on nonphysical interventions. Adding this component would cause the practice of psychology to lose its unique expertise in psychotherapy and behavioral assessment. Prescribing psychologists risk becoming medication dispensers, or "junior psychiatrists" who lack a medical education. Opponents predict a profound, negative impact on psychology's relationship with organized psychiatry, destroying collaborative relationships built over several decades. They fear that even psychologists who are not interested in prescribing medication will have to do so in order to compete with their peers and that malpractice premiums for all practicing psychologists, not just those prescribing, will rise sharply.

From outside the profession, opposition to psychologists prescribing comes generally from the medical profession, and specifically from organized psychiatry. Psychiatrists opposed to the notion assert that to prescribe psychotropics competently a medical education, including a psychiatric residency, is required. They predict that psychologists lacking such education will be public health hazards who will do harm to their clients.

Historical Perspective

In November 1984, U.S. Senator Daniel K. Inouye urged psychologists at the annual meeting of the Hawaii Psychological Association (HPA) to seek prescriptive authority in order to improve the availability of comprehensive, quality mental health care. The following year, Richard Samuels, as president of the American Psychology Association (APA) Division of Independent Practice, issued a similar call for action. Over the next several years, elected leaders of professional psychological associations began urging their colleagues to seek legislative authority to expand the boundaries of professional practice to include prescriptive authority.

In 1989, the APA Board of Professional Affairs (BPA) strongly endorsed immediate research and study regarding the feasibility of psychologists prescribing and the appropriate curricula in psychopharmacology so that psychologists might provide broader service to the public and more effectively meet the psychological and mental health needs of society. Further, BPA recommended, as APA's highest priority, that the profession prepare itself to meet the needs of the public for psychologically managed psychopharmacological interventions.

Actions Taken by the APA Governance

At the APA Council of Representatives meeting in Boston in 1990, a motion to establish an ad hoc Task Force on Psychopharmacology was approved by a vote of 118 to 2. The 1992 report to the Council concluded that practitioners, with combined training in psychopharmacology and psychosocial treatments, could be viewed as a new form of health-care professional, expected to bring to health-care delivery the best of both psychological and pharmacological knowledge. Further, the proposed new providers had the potential to dramatically improve client care and make important new advances in treatment.

The Task Force recommended training at three distinct levels: Basic Psychopharmacology Education for all graduate students in health-care provider programs; Collaborative Practice to enable psychologists to work more closely with medical prescribers; and Education for Independent Prescription Privileges.

Meanwhile, in some states psychologists introduced enabling legislation granting prescriptive privileges to psychologists with appropriate training. The first psychology prescription bill was introduced in the Hawaii State Legislature in 1985. After extensive hearings, the House of Representatives enacted a Resolution in 1990 calling for a series of roundtable discussions conducted by the State's Center for Alternative Dispute Resolution followed by a formal report and recommendations.

By 1995, prescribing bills had been introduced in five different states. Interestingly, in 1993 the Indiana legislature enacted into public law a provision expressly authorizing psychologists participating in a federal government–sponsored training or treatment program to prescribe, although this provision has never been implemented. The California Psychological Association (CPA), in collaboration with the California School of Professional Psychology, convened a special Blue Ribbon Panel of nationally renowned health professionals in May 1994, chaired by then APA president Ronald Fox, to identify a model curriculum for prescribing psychologists. At its August 1995 meeting in New York, the APA Council of Representatives endorsed prescriptive privileges for appropriately trained psychologists and called for the development of model legislation and a model training curriculum.

At the 1996 APA Toronto meeting, the Council adopted both a model prescription bill and a training curriculum. By this time the Committee for the Advancement of Professional Practice (CAPP) had assumed primary responsibility within the governance for legislative efforts to implement the new policy. The APA's model bill proposed postlicensure certification by state psychology licensing boards, which would determine the conditions under which practitioners would be authorized to prescribe independently. The model training curriculum for licensed psychologists called for a minimum of three hundred didactic contact hours in five core content areas, plus supervised, "hands-on" medication treatment of at least one hundred patients in both inpatient and outpatient settings.

At its 1997 convention in Chicago, the Council authorized its College of Professional Psychology to develop an examination in psychopharmacology suitable for use by state and provincial licensing boards once their legislatures have granted prescriptive authority to psychologists. Once again, when the Council voted on the proposal, after extensive deliberation, only two hands were raised in opposition.

The proactive stands taken by the Council had a major beneficial effect on the prescription movement at the state association level. By the beginning of 1998, prescription privileges legislation was either pending or about to be introduced in seven states—California, Florida, Georgia, Hawaii, Louisiana, Missouri, and Tennessee—with five others actively planning for the near future. Over 25 other associations had established task forces to coordinate activities for their states. Perhaps most impressively, innovative training modules, meeting the APA criteria, had been developed by several schools of professional psychology, the Georgia and Louisiana Psychological Associations, and the Prescribing Psychologists' Register (an independent organization). These training modules were specifically planned to meet the needs and employment constraints of licensed practitioners already in the field. Collaborative efforts with nursing schools to train psychologists to prescribe as advanced-practice nurses were also evolving. Surveys reported that nearly 75% of state associations' membership favored obtaining prescriptive authority, a very significant increase from the approximately 33% favorable ratings of surveys conducted only a decade before.

The Federal Government as a Model

During the Congressional deliberations on the fiscal year 1989 DoD Appropriations bill (P.L. 100–463), the Department was directed to institute a pilot training program to train military psychologists to prescribe. This project, which became the center of a controversial legislative battle in the U.S. Congress, eventually graduated 10 Fellows, each of whom received at least 1 year of didactic training and 1 year of clinical experience. These Fellows were assigned to military facilities across the country where they have amassed substantial caseloads and have demonstrated a history of safe and effective use of psychotropics by psychologists.

[*See also* Licensure.]

Acknowledgments. Note: The opinions of these authors represent their personal views and are not the official position of the U.S. Navy or Department of Defense.

Bibliography

Burns, S. M., DeLeon, P. H., Chemtob, C. M., Welch, B. L., & Samuels, R. M. (1988). Psychotropic medication: A new technique for psychology? *Psychotherapy, 25*, 508–515.

DeLeon, P. H., Fox, R. E., & Graham, S. R. (1991). Prescription privileges: Psychology's next frontier? *American Psychologist, 46*, 384–393.

DeLeon, P. H., & Wiggins, J. G. (1996). Prescription privileges for psychologists. *American Psychologist, 51*(3), 225–229.

Fox, R. E. (1988). Prescription privileges: Their implication for the practice of psychotherapy. *Psychotherapy, 25*, 501–507.

Sammons, M. T. (1994). Prescription privileges and psychology: A reply to Adams and Bieliauskas. *Journal of Clinical Psychology in Medical Settings, 1*(3), 199–207.

Sammons, M. T., Sexton, J. L., & Meredith, J. M. (1996). Basic Science Training in Psychopharmacology: How much is enough? *American Psychologist, 51*(3), 230–234.

Patrick H. DeLeon, Morgan T. Sammons, and Ronald E. Fox

PRESSEY, SIDNEY LEAVITT (1888–1979), American psychologist. A prodigious advocate of applied psychology, Pressey's influence touched a number of areas in the field of psychology. Fittingly for a psychologist who constantly emphasized the application of psychological principles to "real world" problems (particularly education), Pressey is most famous for his invention of the teaching machine, a device to assist teachers in the classroom. The fact that teaching machines would not gain popularity until the 1960s, nearly 40 years after his first machine was created, shows another aspect of Pressey's career: his ideas were far ahead of their time.

Pressey's interest in improving education was rooted in his youth. As he recalled in his autobiography (1967), he found school somewhat boring, seeing time and resources wasted and an educational system that could be made much better, more useful, and more efficient.

Pressey first became interested in psychology while an undergraduate at Williams College, eventually pursuing graduate study at Harvard University. There he was influenced by Robert M. Yerkes, who further fostered Pressey's interest in the application of psychology to "real world" problems (Pressey, 1967; Hobbs, 1980).

After doctoral study, Pressey became a research assistant at Indiana University, where he focused primarily on testing in schools (Pressey, 1967). In 1921, Pressey accepted a position at The Ohio State University, where he remained until retirement. After retirement, he continued to make significant contributions, especially in the area of geropsychology, up to his death in 1979.

Pressey's first book, coauthored with his first wife Luella Cole Pressey, was *Introduction to the Use of Standard Tests* (Yonkers, NY, 1922), which described the then current state of the art in testing. A second book, *Mental Abnormality and Deficiency: An Introduction to the Study of Problems of Mental Health* (New York, 1926), discussed psychopathology in plain terms, without jargon.

Pressey's major focus was on improving education. His textbook on educational psychology, *Psychology and the New Education* (New York, 1933), focused on applying psychological knowledge to the classroom, rather than describing theory. Another book, *Educational Acceleration* (Columbus, OH, 1949), advocated making education more efficient, especially for more advanced students.

Pressey's interests also extended into developmental psychology. His work *Life: A Psychological Survey* (New York, 1939) was one of the first human development texts written from a psychological, developmental, and educational rather than a biological perspective.

In 1924, Pressey created his first teaching machine (Benjamin, 1988). He developed many teaching machines, which he hoped would bring about a revolution in education. Specifically, Pressey wanted to build machines that would allow students quicker feedback and also reduce teacher workload. His first machine would show a multiple-choice question, with a key next to each option. A student would select a key, and, if correct, would move on to the next question. If a key corresponding to a wrong answer was selected, the student would have to try again until correct. Student performance was recorded by the machine and immediately available after all the questions were given (Pressey, 1967). Later versions of Pressey's teaching machines indicated what subject areas needed remedial work and could give a reward for good performance (a piece of candy).

As Benjamin (1988) points out, however, the teaching machine "appeared during the Great Depression when there was a great surplus of teachers and no public pressure to increase the pace of education" (p. 708). These devices were about 30 years ahead of their time, becoming popular in the 1960s (Benjamin, 1988). Pressey was outraged at the commercialization of these newer learning machines, which were being sold by the hundreds of thousands, partly because they were based on a Skinnerian approach to learning that Pressey, whose view of learning was cognitively oriented, did not agree with (Hobbs, 1980).

Pressey devoted a tremendous amount of time toward various professional organizations. He was a major force in the development of the American Psychological Association's Division on Maturity and Old Age (Division 20, now named Adult Development and Aging). Toward the end of his life, Pressey became interested in geropsychology, a topic that he wrote on a great deal, using his own personal experience as an older adult as inspiration.

Pressey was driven by the "conviction that psychology has major contributions to make to human welfare" (Hobbs, 1980, p. 671). His contributions to psychology were many, particularly in the fields of educational psychology and geropsychology, and were driven by his strong desire to apply psychological knowledge to improve the quality of life.

Bibliography

Benjamin, L. T., Jr. (1988). A history of teaching machines. *American Psychologist, 43*, 703–712. Discusses the history and development of teaching machines, including Pressey's contributions to their development and the controversy surrounding their popularization in the 1950s and 1960s.

Hobbs, N. (1980). Obituary: Sidney Leavitt Pressey (1888–1979). *American Psychologist, 35*, 669–671.

Pressey, S. L. (1948). The new division on maturity and old age: Its history and potential service. *American Psychologist, 3*, 107–109.

Pressey, S. L. (1967). Autobiography. In E. G. Boring & G. Lindzey (Eds.), *A history of psychology in autobiography* (Vol. 5, pp. 313–339). New York: Appleton-Century-Crofts. Pressey discusses his life and work, including his development of the teaching machine. This autobiography also conveys to the reader a brief sense of what Pressey was like as a person and his philosophy.

Frederick J. Kier

PREVENTION. [*This entry provides a broad survey of prevention. It comprises four articles:*

An Overview
For Infants and Young Children
For School-Aged Children and Adolescents
For Adults

The lead article provides a broad overview of prevention as a form of intervention in psychology. The three companion articles are organized chronologically from prevention for infants to prevention for adults. For a general discussion on intervention, see Intervention. *See also* Community Prevention and Intervention.]

An Overview

Psychologists use the term *prevention* to refer to behavioral, biological, or social interventions intended to reduce the risk of disorders, diseases, or social problems for both individuals and entire populations. Prevention efforts differ from treatment because they are directed at addressing problems before they occur. Rather than trying to undo entrenched pathology, the goal of prevention is to develop initiatives to forestall problems for people at risk, and to build strengths and competencies to enhance resilience and well-being. Unlike treatment interventions that occur primarily in clinical settings, prevention efforts can be found in a wide range of community settings including schools, neighborhoods, homes, workplaces, or hospitals and clinics. Prevention efforts tend to be proactive, and are often designed to reach out to entire populations facing similar risks and challenges, rather than waiting for people to develop problems and seek help from professionals.

Preventive interventions are targeted to reduce the risk of a specific problem, and therefore differ from more general promotion efforts that are directed at enhancing the overall health or development of individuals or populations. Psychologists have been most involved in prevention in the areas of community psychology and community mental health, health psychology, pediatric psychology, developmental psychology, and educational psychology. More recently, psychologists have helped to develop behavioral interventions to teach practices to reduce the risk of Human Immunodeficiency Virus (HIV) and Acquired Immune Deficiency Syndrome (AIDS). Prevention is emerging as a national priority. Over the last 20 years a number of commissions and task forces have recommended changes in national research priorities and services to increase their preventive emphasis. Successful prevention programs provide people and communities with new skills to cope more effectively, and provide social support in the face of life transitions. Beyond that, successful programs strengthen the natural supports available from family, community, or school settings.

The history of prevention has its roots in public health, where the prevention of infectious disease often involved measures such as water purification or inoculation. Today, prevention efforts in the community cover a much wider spectrum of activities. In most instances, psychologists form a collaborative relationship with other community members as they develop and test new preventive approaches. For example, psychologists are engaged in designing community programs to increase exercise, to help people stop smoking, and to help people control their diet. Psychologists who work in the schools may develop programs aimed at teaching primary and secondary school students methods to resist peer pressures to use drugs. At the same time, psychologists work with preschool teachers to create high quality preschool experiences to prevent later school failure. Still others may be helping to reorganize schools to ease the transition from elementary to secondary school. Psychologists concerned with mental health are developing programs that enhance coping skills to deal with various stresses. Psychologists have also worked with public health nurses to develop prenatal care programs and parent training to prevent problems in early childhood development. Finally, other prevention efforts developed by psychologists are aimed at helping individuals and families cope with life crises such as divorce, job loss, or serious illness in the family.

Generally speaking, prevention efforts cluster around several broad strategies. For example, some prevention programs are called milestone programs. They are directed at helping individuals and populations deal with the stresses and difficulties in transitions that occur at a particular stage in life, such as the child's transition from home to school. Other programs are aimed at promotion of healthy development or new skills because they assume that by strengthening skills and coping capacity, resistance to disease and disorder is also enhanced. Finally, system-oriented approaches are aimed at changing the settings, organizations, and communities in which we work and live, rather than at changing human behavior directly. The assumptions underlying this approach are that environmental change will reduce individual and group exposure to challenges and stresses that may place vulnerable populations at risk, and can be sustained by the community over time. Preventive strategies are also classified according to the benefits they provide relative to the risk they might produce. For example, universal prevention efforts are those regarded as safe for the entire population and that provide a nearly universal benefit, such as efforts to improve sanitation or water purification. On the other hand, a selective strategy may be aimed at a population at higher risk for disease or disorder, such as heavy smokers. Finally, indicated preventive strategies are much more intensive, and are aimed at individuals who show the beginning signs of disease or disorder, such as problem drinkers.

While the majority of prevention efforts have been directed at individuals early in their life course, focusing on children of preschool and school age, prevention efforts are needed over the entire life course. While the nature of risks change from infancy to school age to adulthood, the general principle that risks can be reduced for individuals and populations at any stage in the life course still holds. We can expect as the population ages in the United States that more and more prevention efforts will be directed at reducing the risk of disease and disorder in older populations. Psychologists also conduct research aimed at evaluating the effectiveness of prevention efforts. Surveys by the American Psychological Association and the Institute of Medicine, which summarize the results of large numbers of individual prevention research studies, indicate that prevention programs are effective for a wide range of populations across the age range, from conception to old age. Effective prevention efforts can now be a reality in all our communities, with the prospect of enhanced resilience and well-being over the entire life course.

Bibliography

Albee, G. W., & Gullotta, T. P. (Eds.). (1977). *Primary prevention works* (Vol. 6). Thousand Oaks, CA: Sage. A collection of effective prevention programs.

Durlak, J. A., & Wells, A. M. (1997). Primary prevention mental health programs for children and adolescents: A meta-analytic review. *American Journal of Community Psychology, 25(2),* 115–152. A detailed review summarizing the cumulative results of prevention programs for children and adolescents.

Heller, K. (1996). Coming of age of prevention science: Comments on the 1994 National Institute of Mental Health–Institute of Medicine prevention papers. *American Psychologist, 51,* 1123–1128. Historical and policy analysis of the IOM and NIMH reports.

Mrazek, P. J., & Haggerty, R. J. (Eds.). (1994). *Reducing risks for mental disorders: Frontiers for preventive intervention research.* Washington, DC: National Academy Press. A comprehensive review of conceptual, research, and policy issues on prevention compiled by the Institute of Medicine, National Academy of Sciences.

Price, R. H., Cowen, E., Lorion, R., & Ramos-McKay, J. (Eds.). (1988). *Fourteen ounces of prevention.* Washington, DC: American Psychological Association. A collection of model prevention programs spanning the life course.

Richard H. Price

For Infants and Young Children

Early intervention has attracted much national attention as scientists, health providers, educators, and policy makers have discovered what parents have known for centuries—that the first 3 years of life are a time of rapid change and opportunity in human growth and development. Infants triple their birth weight in the first year of life, and by the age of 3 years, they have mastered a wide range of skills and are able to walk, talk, solve basic problems, and form close relationships. The evidence of these developmental milestones can be gleaned from longitudinal research on infants and toddlers that has demonstrated the importance of the first three years of life for the formation of cognitive, language, motor, and emotional skills that guide later development.

Although species-specific maturation and self-righting tendencies may minimize the threat of negative environmental challenges during early development, many infants do not achieve the expected goals in growth or development. Prevention and early intervention programs are designed to ensure that disruptions to the developmental process are minimized and that families are supported in their mission of providing protection and nurturance to their young children. Prevention programs can be categorized into two broad categories based on the two primary challenges to children's development: environmental and biological risk.

Environmental Risk

Many of the environmental risks to young children are associated with poverty. The National Commission on Children indicates that over 20% of the children in the United States live in poverty (*Beyond Rhetoric: A New American Agenda for Children and Families*, Washington, DC, 1991). When children's age and ethnic status are considered, the poverty rates increase to 25% for infants and toddlers, 45% for African American children, and over 50% for African American children under age three. A similar trend is observed in other minority populations.

The negative influence of poverty on children's health and development has been well documented. Not only are children exposed to a variety of illnesses associated with crowding and unsanitary conditions, but they may have limited access to appropriate developmental challenges and stimulation. By entry to elementary school, deficits associated with poverty are well established. Poverty can affect children directly through lack of materials and services, and indirectly through increased family stress, which may interfere with parents' ability to be nurturant in their caregiving. Extreme forms of parental dysfunction, including abuse and neglect, are associated with poverty.

Biological Risk

Biological risks include chronic health or disabling conditions that undermine infants' development or place them at risk for developmental delays. In addition to problems associated with specific handicapping conditions, prematurity, low birth weight, and postnatal growth deficiency are relatively common concerns that may result in long-term academic and behavioral problems.

All too often, environmental and biological risks co-occur because children in low-income families are more vulnerable to biological challenges, such as growth deficiency. This double jeopardy poses challenges to categorical intervention programs that are directed toward only one problem area. Currently, integrated prevention and intervention programs have emerged that target both environmental and biological risks.

Prevention Programs

Mrazek and Haggerty (*Reducing Risks for Mental Disorders: Frontiers for Preventive Intervention Research*, Washington, DC, 1994) have categorized prevention programs along three dimensions: universal, selected, and indicated. Universal or population-based interventions are designed to prevent developmental problems and promote optimal health and development among all infants. Examples include mass media campaigns, public service announcements, or child protection policies designed to prevent abuse and neglect. Universal interventions can be very effective, particularly when they carry social and legal sanctions, but they often lack the specificity to reach families at highest risk.

Selective interventions are directed toward families of infants who are at risk of experiencing a negative outcome, such as infants growing up in low-income families or those with growth deficiencies. National programs for children in low-income families, such as Supplemental Food Program to Women, Infants, and Children (WIC) and Head Start are examples of selective interventions that are designed to promote healthy growth and development among at-risk children.

Indicated interventions are directed toward infants who are experiencing developmental delays or disabilities. The nation's commitment to promoting the development of children through indicated interventions is exemplified by passage of the Education for all Handicapped Children Act (PL 94-142), followed by passage of the amendments (PL 99-457), and the resulting services for children with special needs. In a meta-analysis of early intervention programs for children under age three years with developmental disabilities, Shonkoff and Hauser (*Pediatrics*, 1987, *80*, 650–658) found that although the degree of benefit varies by the children's disability, the most effective programs included a heterogeneous group of children, a structured curriculum, and a family orientation.

Evaluation of Prevention and Early Intervention

Early intervention has been dominated by transactional theories that view the central components of children's development to be the quality of the interaction between the infant and parent, the child-centered opportunities provided by the family, and guarantees of the child's health and safety. Given the complexity of early development and a theoretical understanding that interventions are unlikely to have uniform effects across children and families, there is a need for evaluations that go beyond efficacy to address the many questions regarding how early interventions work, for whom they are effective, under what conditions, and how much they cost. The long-term follow-up of early intervention programs have begun to address these questions.

Programs Assessing Environmental Risk. Although the early evaluations of the Head Start Program showed no gains in intellectual or affective domains during school-age years, long-term evaluations have demonstrated impressive effects. Berrueta-Clement and colleagues (*Changed Lives: The Effects of the Perry Preschool Program on Youths Through Age 19*, Ypsilanti, MI, 1984) reported that at age 19 years, children who had participated in the Perry Preschool Project had better academic performance, and lower rates of school dropout, delinquency, and teenage pregnancy than the control group youth. These findings illustrate that not only is it important to focus on outcome measures beyond IQ, but the effects of intervention may have a delayed impact.

Burchinal and colleagues (*Child Development*, 1997, *68*, 935–954) reported on the long-term effects of two early intervention programs (Abecedarian Project and Project CARE) designed to promote development among infants and young children from low-income families. Both projects were randomized clinical trials initiated within 3 months of birth and extending through the first 3 years of elementary school. During infancy and preschool years the Abecedarian Project examined center-based child care versus no treatment and Project CARE compared home visiting with and without center-based child care versus no treatment. The children who received early child care consistently achieved higher IQ scores than those who received home visiting only or those in no-treatment groups. Although there was an overall decline in cognitive performance over the 8-year study period, optimal performance was associated with early child care, a responsive home environment, and higher maternal IQ. It is this type of analysis that addresses the need for studies that move beyond efficacy to examine how early intervention enhances development and under what conditions.

Programs Assessing Biological Risk. The Infant Health and Development Project was an eight-site randomized clinical trial to evaluate early intervention among 985 infants born prematurely with a birth weight below 2,500 grams and no severe medical or neurological impairments (*Journal of American Medical Association*, 1990, *263*, 3035–3042). Children in the

3-year intervention program received home visits, an intensive center-based child development program, and parent-group meetings. All children received systematic evaluations when the intervention ended at 3 years of age, and follow-up evaluations at 5 and 8 years of age. When the children were age 3, those in the intervention group demonstrated better cognitive, receptive language, and behavioral development than children in the control group. Differences were accentuated among children in the heavier birth weight group (2,001–2,500 grams). By 5 years of age, the differences in development and behavior scores had attenuated and Brooks-Gunn and colleagues reported no overall differences by intervention history (*Journal of the American Medical Association*, 1994, *272*, 1257–1262). Similarly, at 8 years of age, McCarton and colleagues found no overall differences in performance by intervention history (*Journal of the American Medical Association*, 1997, *277*, 126–132). Within the heavier birth weight group, children who received intervention obtained higher scores in full-scale IQ, verbal IQ, performance IQ, mathematics, and receptive language than did control children. However, the differences were relatively modest (less than 0.5 standard deviations), suggesting the need to consider alternative strategies for early intervention among premature, low-birth-weight infants.

Home intervention is often regarded as a promising prevention strategy for children from at-risk families, but there have been few evaluations of home visiting programs that have focused on changes in children's development. Black and colleagues (*Pediatrics*, 1995, *95*, 807–814) conducted a one-year, randomized clinical trial of home intervention among full-term infants who had been healthy at birth, but whose weight-for-age dropped to below the fifth percentile prior to age 2. Most children were raised by single, African American mothers in low-income families. The infants who received the home intervention showed less decline in cognitive development, better receptive language, and a more child-centered home environment than those in the comparison group. At age 4, almost 2 years after the intervention ended, there were beneficial effects of the home intervention on motor development among all children and on cognitive development and behavior during play among children of mothers who reported low levels of depression, hostility, or anxiety (*Journal of Pediatric Psychology*, 1997, *22*, 597–616). Thus, the home intervention was not effective among mothers who reported signs of psychological distress, suggesting that a more intensive or mental health-oriented intervention may have been necessary.

Grantham-McGregor and colleagues (*American Journal of Clinical Nutrition*, 1997, *66*, 247–253) evaluated early home intervention involving nutrition and developmental stimulation among stunted children in Jamaica. Stunting is an indicator of chronic undernutrition and a common problem in developing countries. In the Jamaican study, stunted children ages 9 to 24 months were randomized into one of four groups: nutritional supplementation, developmental stimulation, both, or neither. At the end of a 2-year intervention there were beneficial effects of both interventions on children's development and the effects were additive. When follow-up was conducted at 7 or 8 years of age, there were no differences in cognitive or long-term semantic memory tasks, but children who received developmental stimulation had higher scores on perceptual-motor tasks than those who did not, and children who received either developmental stimulation or nutritional supplementation had higher scores on more of the assessments than would be expected by chance. These findings argue that disruptions to development can be prevented in very low-income communities by providing early developmental stimulation and nutritional supplementation.

The importance of conceptualizing programs to include both environmental and biological risks in prevention programs is illustrated by the home intervention program evaluated by Olds and colleagues (*Journal of American Medical Association*, 1997, *278*, 637–643). The intervention was designed to prevent low birth weight and to promote the development of infants born to women who were from low-income, rural families, many of whom were single or adolescent caregivers. Initial evaluation demonstrated reductions in reports of child abuse and neglect among the highest risk group of families. The durability of these findings is demonstrated by 15-year follow-up data demonstrating reductions in subsequent pregnancies, use of welfare, child abuse and neglect, and criminal behavior on the part of the mother, and points to the need to include assessment of families as a means of improving infant and child health.

Conclusion

Taken together, these findings offer cautious optimism regarding the long-term effects of prevention programs initiated during infancy. However, they highlight the complexity of early intervention, the importance of including families in the conceptualization of early intervention, and the need for additional research to determine how interventions work and when they are most effective. In many cases, the impact of the intervention varies by child (e.g., birth weight) or by family characteristics (e.g., maternal psychological functioning). Although much of the focus has been on the relationship between early intervention and cognitive functioning, long-term evaluations have found that early intervention can be linked to improvements in aspects of child and adolescent social competence and adjustment. Thus, outcome measures are needed that extend beyond typical indices of child development to incorporate social competence and family functioning.

Bibliography

Belsky, J. (1984). The determinants of parenting: A process model. *Child Development, 55,* 83–96.

Bronfenbrenner, U. (1993). Ecological systems theory. In R. Wozniak & K. Fisher (Eds.), *Specific environments: Thinking in contexts* (pp. 3–44). Hillsdale, NJ: Erlbaum.

Coie, J. D., Watt, N. F., West, S. G., Hawkins, J. D., Asarnow, J. R., Markman, H. J., Ramey, S. L., Shure, M. B., & Long, B. (1993). The science of prevention: A conceptual framework and some directions for a national research program. *American Psychologist, 48,* 1013–1022.

Guralnick, M. J. (Ed.). (1996). *The effectiveness of early intervention.* Baltimore, MD: Brookes.

Meisels, S. J., & Shonkoff, J. P. (Eds.). (1990). *Handbook of early childhood intervention.* Cambridge, England: Cambridge University Press.

Maureen M. Black

For School-Aged Children and Adolescents

Psychologists have long been involved in preventive school-based programs either directly or working in collaboration with educators, social workers, and other professionals. The roots of school-based prevention began during the Progressive era in the United States, a social-political movement starting around 1890. Concerned about the plight of poor immigrants, many policies were enacted that subsequently led to such developments as health education training for teachers, special classes for handicapped and sick children, counseling programs for youth and their families, and the first subsidized or free breakfast and school lunch programs (Tyack, 1992). In the 1920s specially trained visiting teachers, who were the historical forerunners of school social workers, conducted programs to promote positive personal and interpersonal qualities in young children—what would now be identified as social skills. Visiting teachers also worked with needy families and sought to modify the school environment to promote students' personal and academic growth. Some form of sex education has occurred in schools for over a century, and health education programs began in the early 1900s. Although some early attempts at school-based prevention were popular, the interventions were not carefully evaluated.

It was not until the late 1950s that several pioneering research projects conducted by psychologists began demonstrating the success of school-based prevention programs (e.g., see Cowen, Hightower, Pedro-Carroll, Work, & Wyman, 1996; Ojemann, Levitt, Lyle, & Whiteside, 1955; Glidewell, Gildea, & Kaufman, 1973). Prevention has become a very popular intervention in schools over the past few years. Each year millions of school children are exposed to one type of preventive program or another and during their entire school career most children participate in many such programs. For instance, the percentage of school districts reporting prevention programs on different topics (Collins et al., 1995) is as follows: alcohol or other drugs (90%), smoking (86%), acquired immune deficiency sydrome (AIDS)/human immunodeficiency virus (HIV) (86%), diet and nutrition (84%), sex education programs targeting sexually transmitted diseases or sexuality in general (84% and 80% respectively), emotional or mental health (74%), pregnancy prevention (69%), injury prevention and personal safety (66%), conflict resolution or violence (58%), and suicide (58%). These prevention programs vary widely in duration and scope. Some are very brief didactic programs that last only a class period or two while others are multiyear, multilevel efforts that involve parents.

Need for Prevention

There is a clear need for preventive programs for school children. Approximately one of every five children will eventually develop at least one clinical disorder, and, for a variety of reasons, less than one third of all children who need psychological treatment ever receive any formal care (Kazdin, 1990). Other estimates suggest that half of all 10- to 17-year-olds are at some level of risk for later problems related to delinquency, poor academic achievement, unprotected sexual intercourse, or drug use (Dryfoos, 1990). Finally, young people are increasingly becoming both the perpetrators and victims of various forms of interpersonal violence. Each year 3 million crimes occur near or in schools, which translates into one crime every 6 seconds. Because mental health and social service systems cannot begin to help all those with existing problems, effective prevention programs can play an important role in protecting the welfare of young people.

Terminology Regarding Prevention

Historically, three general types of prevention have been identified. Primary prevention is offered to nonclinical populations and refers to programs designed to prevent the development of new problems. Secondary prevention refers to intervention for those demonstrating early difficulties (i.e., subclinical level problems) and is intended to prevent the development of more serious dysfunction. Finally, tertiary prevention refers to interventions for those with established problems; these programs attempt to reduce the duration and negative consequences of existing disorders. The Institute of Medicine (1994) recommended dropping the term tertiary prevention because it is often confused with treatment and is not really designed to prevent the occurrence of new disorders. The institute also suggested that primary prevention be identified as universal preventive intervention or selective preventive intervention depending on population selection, and that secondary prevention be called indicated preventive intervention.

Another important distinction in primary prevention refers to the two ways populations are chosen for intervention. In a universal preventive intervention all members of the target group receive the intervention. For instance, the program would be offered to all first graders in a school, to all junior high school students, and so on. In selective preventive intervention, groups considered at risk for problems, but not yet demonstrating any difficulties, are targeted for intervention. The rationale behind this approach is that intervention can be most helpful for those at greater risk. For example, children from low-income households are at greater risk for academic problems, so a program might be specifically developed for this group of students. One variation of selective primary prevention is the milestone or transition approach. In this strategy children experiencing a potentially stressful transition or life event are targeted. The rationale here is that, unless children receive some help in mastering or negotiating a difficult life transition, they might develop adjustment difficulties. The most common transition for children is entry into a new school. Children experiencing parental separation and divorce are also at risk, and many programs for children of divorce have been school-based.

In summary, in primary prevention a program might be developed for all children (universal preventive intervention), or only for those considered to be at later risk for problems (selective preventive intervention). In indicated prevention (formerly, secondary prevention), only those who are displaying early forms of dysfunction receive attention. The choice of a preventive strategy depends on several factors including an effective method of identification of children at risk for different types of problems and the adequacy of resources for a universal intervention.

Major Themes in Prevention

In order for prevention to be successful it is important to know what factors produce problems and how these factors can be eliminated or modified. In other words, something negative cannot be prevented from happening unless its causes are known. There has been a substantial change over time in the theory and practice of school-based prevention as knowledge about child and adolescent development has expanded. Many early programs were based on the belief that there were singular causes for most problems and that these causes could be found within individuals. For example, many programs operated on the assumption that lack of knowledge was the source of many difficulties and that programs offering clear and accurate information would be successful. In other words, if children knew about the dangers of drugs, early pregnancy, sexually transmitted diseases, AIDS, and so on, they would act accordingly, that is, preventively. Some programs also emphasized the negative consequences of drugs or sexual activity. These early preventive programs were founded on faulty assumptions. One clear finding in prevention has been that information programs (that is, programs that try to influence youth primarily through didactic instruction and knowledge alone) do not significantly change behavior. Neither do programs that attempt to scare children and adolescents from engaging in risky behaviors. Information programs have not been effective in any area of prevention in which they have been tried. Children do need accurate information to guide their behavior, but knowledge alone is insufficient to produce significant behavioral change.

Although early findings from didactic programs were discouraging, these setbacks prompted preventionists to begin searching for more effective programs and useful theories. Over time, the thrust of school-based prevention has changed in several important ways with a substantial corresponding change in the success of intervention. New research and theories in prevention, in clinical and developmental psychology, and in epidemiology converged to set a new course for preventive trials.

Four main themes characterize many successful contemporary prevention programs: the principle of multiple determinism, a risk and protective factor paradigm, the importance of health promotion strategies, and the need for systematic skill training to teach school children new behaviors. Each of these themes is discussed below.

Most social scientists accept the principle of multiple determinism. Instead of one single influence or cause of behavior, theory and research indicate there are multiple influences that interact with each other to produce or to protect against negative outcomes. These influences are often described as risk or protective factors, that is, variables that increase or decrease the likelihood of future problems, respectively. Risk and protective factors exist at five interacting levels of influence for most outcomes. These levels are the individual, family, peer group, school (or other important social institution), and, finally, community, or society at large. For example, some risk factors for drug use include poor individual decision-making and refusal skills, family conflict and poor communication at home, peers who use drugs or otherwise act out, school curricula and policies that do not effectively discourage drug use, easy accessibility to drugs in the community, and media influences that portray drug-taking in a favorable light. Additional risk factors include being a man (men take more drugs than women), and coming from a low-income household.

Some of the risks for drugs are obviously more amenable to change than others. Protective factors that lessen the likelihood of drug use would include a heightened sense of self-efficacy and assertiveness in resisting social pressure, a close parent-child relationship, social support from peers, teachers, or others for not using drugs, and social policies that limit the availability of drugs. In other words, environmental and individual factors interact to influence drug use. An important finding in risk research is that risks tend to have multiplicative rather than merely additive effects. When risks multiply for a target population, so does the eventual likelihood of a negative outcome such as drug use.

As a result, the general intent of many school-based programs is to modify as many risk and protective factors as possible. To do so, preventionists have mounted multilevel interventions because risk and protective factors for different outcomes exist at multiple levels. This means that, in addition to offering a program for school children, the intervention may be extended to include parents, peers, school personnel, and the local community.

Another current theme in prevention is the creation of health promotion programs that attempt to enhance positive physical, social, psychological, or academic health. Health promotion is important because positive health is not merely the absence of problems. To say that a child is not anxious or depressed does not mean the child is self-confident, optimistic, or happy, which are all possible manifestations of positive mental health, psychological well-being, or wellness (Cowen, 1994). Decidedly positive characteristics of individuals and environments need to be developed and nurtured, not merely assumed to be present in the absence of maladjustment. Health promotion programs assume that as individuals become more capable and competent they should be better able to deal with future events or factors that lead to maladjustment. Empirical evidence indicates that health promotion programs have significant preventive impact (Durlak, 1997; Durlak & Wells, 1997).

Finally, there have also been changes in what individual characteristics are important. Preventionists now recognize that if children are expected to engage in new behaviors (e.g., refusing drugs, coping with stress more effectively) somebody must carefully and systematically teach them how to perform these new activities. Systematic skill training has become a prominent feature in many effective programs. This training employs a combination of modeling, behavioral rehearsal, and reinforcement techniques. Complex skills are broken down into smaller steps; adults or peers model the effective use of these skills; and then children have the opportunity to practice new behaviors until mastery is achieved. In many programs, the social environment is also modified by teaching parents or teachers how to sustain behavioral change by supporting and reinforcing children's newly acquired skills. Several personal skills have been improved through skill training depending on the specific goals of the program. These skills include communication and assertiveness, friendship making, safe sexual practices, interpersonal problem solving, decision making, and relaxation.

Outcomes in Prevention

There is now considerable evidence in support of these newer school-based prevention programs. Approximately 600 controlled-outcome studies appeared by the end of 1994 (Durlak, 1995) and many programs have been able to achieve positive results in both the short- and longer-term. Not every program has been successful, and there is still much to be learned about effective interventions. Nevertheless, there is a core group of findings suggesting that prevention is possible in the areas of mental health, delinquency, drug use, learning problems, and physical health. Outcome evaluations have indicated significant changes among program participants compared to control groups in the following areas following intervention: psychological difficulties involving depression and anxiety, antisocial problems such as aggression and school vandalism, various academic problems, drug use, pregnancy rates, and better physical health (Durlak, 1997; Durlak & Wells, 1997).

Furthermore, several studies have documented the practical benefits of school-based prevention. For instance, interventions have been able to reduce future drug use by up to 45%, adolescent pregnancy rates by 41%, mood disorders among adolescents by 56%, rates of aggression by 66%, and rates of peer bullying by 50% or more. (Peer bullying is physical or verbal aggression directed against peers.) Such findings clearly indicate that prevention can yield substantial practical benefits for program participants and society in general. Prevention seems well worth the effort. Finally, data are now appearing to indicate that prevention can be very cost effective and return $8.00, $13.00, or up to $45.00 in benefits for every dollar spent, depending on the target area and method of intervention. Reviews of prevention programs are available in several sources (Cowen, Hightower, Pedro-Carroll, Work, & Wyman, 1996; Durlak, 1995, 1997; Kirby et al., 1994; Slavin, Karweit, & Wasik, 1994, Tobler & Stratton, 1997).

In fact, all areas of school-based prevention have been characterized by several notable successes, except for suicide prevention (Mazza, 1997) and the prevention of sexual abuse (Rispens, Aleman, & Goudena, 1997). Although changes in attitudes and knowledge are frequently achieved in these two areas, it has been difficult to demonstrate that the future incidence of suicide or sexual victimization has been significantly affected as a result of intervention.

Summary

School-based prevention can clearly be an effective form of intervention that reduces the future rate of problems in school children. Future directions for research and practice include identifying how programs can be made more efficient and effective for different target groups, how the most successful programs can be disseminated into different school settings, and how to establish a secure administrative and financial base for prevention so that worthwhile programs reach as many young people as possible.

Bibliography

Collins, J. L., Small, M. L., Kann, L., Pateman, B. C., Gold, R. S., & Kolbe, L. J. (1995). School health education. *Journal of School Health, 65*, 302–311.

Cowen, E. L. (1994). The enhancement of psychological wellness: Challenges and opportunities. *American Journal of Community Psychology, 22*, 149–180.

Cowen, E. L., Hightower, A. D., Pedro-Carroll, J. P., Work, W. C., & Wyman, P. A. (1996). *School based prevention for children at-risk: The Primary Mental Health Project.* Washington, DC: American Psychological Association. Reviews the history and accomplishments of a project that has influenced many other programs.

Dryfoos, J. G. (1990). *Adolescents at risk: Prevalence and prevention.* New York: Oxford University Press. Reviews factors that place adolescents at risk and several successful preventive interventions.

Durlak, J. A. (1995). *School-based prevention programs for children and adolescents.* Thousand Oaks, CA: Sage. Describes many successful school-based interventions.

Durlak, J. A. (1997). *Successful prevention programs for children and adolescents.* New York: Plenum Press. Describes effective interventions in schools and other community settings.

Durlak, J. A., & Wells, A. M. (1997). Primary prevention mental health programs for children and adolescents: A meta-analytic review. *American Journal of Community Psychology, 25*, 115–152.

Glidewell, J. G., Gildea, M. C. L., & Kaufman, M. K. (1973). The preventive and therapeutic effects of two school mental health programs. *American Journal of Community Psychology, 1*, 295–329.

Institute of Medicine. (1994). *Reducing risks for mental disorders: Frontiers for preventive intervention research.* Washington, DC: National Academy Press. Overview of theories of prevention and representative programs.

Kazdin, A. E. (1990). Psychotherapy for children and adolescents. *Annual Review of Psychology, 41*, 21–54.

Kirby, D., Short, L., Collins, J., Rugg, D., Kolbe, L., Howard, L., Miller, B., Sonenstein, F., & Zabin, L. S. (1994) School-based programs to reduce sexual risk behaviors: A review of effectiveness. *Public Health Reports, 109*, 339–360.

Mazza, J. J. (1997). School-based suicide prevention programs: Are they effective? *School Psychology Review, 26*, 382–396.

Ojemann, R. H., Levitt, E. E., Lyle, Jr., W. H., & Whiteside, M. F. (1955). The effects of a "causal" teacher-training program and certain curricular changes on grade school children. *Journal of Experimental Education, 24*, 95–114.

Rispens, J., Aleman, A., & Goudena, P. P. (1997). Prevention of child sexual abuse victimizations: A meta-analysis of school programs. *Child Abuse and Neglect, 21*, 975–988.

Slavin, R. E., Karweit, N. L., & Wasik, B. A. (1994). *Preventing early school failure.* Needham Heights, MA: Allyn & Bacon. Review of the most effective academic interventions.

Tobler, N. S., & Stratton, H. H. (1997). Effectiveness of school-based drug prevention programs: A meta-analysis of the research. *Journal of Drug Education, 18*, 71–128.

Tyack, D. (1992). Health and social services in public schools: Historical perspectives. *The Future of Children, 2*, 19–31.

Joseph A. Durlak

For Adults

Advances over the past three decades have extended significantly the potential for the mental health disciplines to respond to the emotional and behavioral needs of individuals. An emerging portion of that expansion involves the application of psychological knowledge and principles to avoid or minimize the development of disorders. This contribution overviews the theory, methods, science, and politics of interventions designed to prevent emotional and behavioral disorders and promote mental health. Preventive interventions focused heavily on youth during the initial stages of the field's development (Price, Cowen, Lorion, & Ramos-McKay, 1988; Kessler & Goldston, 1986). This early emphasis reflected, in our view, the combined influences of the interests of prevention's early proponents (e.g., Cowen, 1973) and the assumption that some social systems (e.g., schools) were more receptive of such interventions than others (e.g., industry). Recent advances in the field, however, make evident both the need for and capacity to apply preventive and promotive interventions across the lifespan and across the variety of systems relevant to adulthood.

Initial forays by the mental health sciences and professions into preventive efforts were led by Caplan (1964), who recognized that the mental health disciplines had to move beyond sole reliance on treatment if they were to serve public needs. To organize initial efforts in this direction, Caplan urged mental health to adopt the goals of and the classification system for prevention extant in public health at the time (Commission on Chronic Illness, 1957). This system was centered around the epidemiological concept of caseness, i.e., confirmation that the diagnostic criteria defining a syndrome were met. Intervention categories were differentiated within this system in terms of their proximity to the fulfilment of diagnostic criteria.

Within this framework, *primary* prevention interventions are implemented prior to caseness. Successful interventions reduce prevalence (i.e., overall presence of cases of a target disorder in the population) by reducing incidence (i.e., the occurrence of new cases). Potential targets for such interventions range from the population at large, to asymptomatic subgroups targeted on the basis of epidemiologically defined risk, to subgroups presenting prodromal signs antecedent to diagnostic status. By contrast, *secondary* interventions seek to lower prevalence by reducing the duration of caseness (i.e., through the application of effective treatment). Combinations of sensitive screening procedures, which identify cases early and involve them in treatment, exemplify this category. Secondary approaches seek both a return to premorbid status and avoidance of subsequent episodes. Finally, *tertiary* interventions reduce the long-term disabilities and sequelae consequent to caseness. Rehabilitation strategies and support services exemplify tertiary approaches. If recurrence of disabling symptoms is avoided, secondary goals are achieved.

As noted earlier (Lorion, 1983), this organizational framework reflected the disorders (e.g., infectious diseases) and etiological processes of primary concern to public health practitioners at the time (e.g., the classic public health triad of host [the infected organism], agent [the cause of the infection (e.g., a virus)], and environment [the situational conditions under which pathogenesis is initiated]). The applicability of its underlying causal assumptions, however, to emotional and behavioral disorders has been challenged from the outset (e.g., Albee, 1982; Lamb & Zusman, 1979). As reflected in the work of Brofenbrenner (1979), Rutter (1989), and Sameroff and Fiese (1989), there is an emerging appreciation of the etiological complexity of emotional and behavioral problems involving biological, psychological, social, and environmental parameters. This complexity obscures determination of the onset of pathogenic processes, the presence of disorder, and thereby the designation of caseness (Lorion, Price, & Eaton, 1989). Unresolved, these challenges produce disagreements in the categorization of primary and secondary interventions and obstacles to the empirical verification of their efficacy.

Confronting similar challenges in some physical disorders, Gordon (1983, 1987) proposed an alternative conceptual schema for organizing preventive efforts. Weighting expected intervention risks with target selection, Gordon (1983) proposed that "universal," "selective," and "indicated" interventions should be designed for and targeted to "persons not motivated by current suffering" (p. 108) and, presumably not currently seeking nor in need of treatment. *Universal* interventions are applied to the population at large and combine low costs per contact with limited risk. Examples include public service announcements that advocate seat-belt use or discourage tobacco use. In the mental health realm, universal interventions include the "Friends can be good medicine" program implemented in California to enhance use of social support resources.

Selective interventions are targeted to segments of the population for which there is an epidemiologically established risk. Selection may be based on identified links among gender, ethnicity, economic status, or family history, for example, and the presence of emotional or behavioral disorders. Targeted subgroups have a higher likelihood of disorder and hence a more focused (and potentially more iatrogenic) intervention can be justified. Examples include programs targeted to families considering marital separation or divorce (Wolchik et al., 1993) or the recently widowed (Silverman, 1988). *Indicated* interventions target individuals (rather than subgroups) who present risk factors or prodromal signs indicating substantial individual risk for subsequent disorder. Examples of these approaches include programs for women presenting early indices of depression (e.g., Vega & Murphy, 1990).

Gordon's proposal was intended to stimulate development of preventive efforts and to make explicit how they were clearly distinct from treatment of symptoms and syndromes. In an important sense, Gordon's (1983) proposal offers a conceptual expansion of the original primary prevention category. His approach highlights the breadth of opportunity available to influence prevalence by intervening along that functional continuum ranging from health through various prodromal stages prior to meeting diagnostic criteria. The richness of this alternative system (see Mrazek & Haggerty, 1994) lies in its clarification of concepts of risk and vulnerability as applied to individuals, situations, and their combinations. It also lies in its clear distinction between the end-state conditions to be avoided (e.g., substance abuse or depression) and susceptible individuals. Sameroff (1977) made a similar plea in his early warning to preventionists that their efforts must not compromise respect for the humanity of the recipients of those efforts. In his advocacy for health promotion efforts, Cowen (1996) similarly urged program developers to recognize that removal or reduction of risks and vulnerabilities would leave individuals both empowered and likely to reach their potential. In their meta-analytic study of primary prevention programs, Durlak and Wells (1997) report clear evidence on the value of skill-building and competency enhancement as means of avoiding dysfunction, as well as improving quality-of-life, for at-risk youth.

Independent of the classificatory scheme adopted, epidemiology and developmental psychopathology provide the scientific foundations for meaningful advances in prevention. Application of case-control methodology, for example, enables epidemiologists to discern potential risks and protective factors associated with symptomatic and syndromal expression. Developmental psychopathology's longitudinal methods uncover the pathogenic processes defining vulnerability and modeling the evolution from health to pathology. Such methods have highlighted multifinality (i.e., documentation that common pathways are linked to diverse outcomes) and equifinality (i.e., documentation that diverse pathways are seemingly linked to common outcomes) as obstacles to simple causal models of emotional dysfunction (Cicchetti & Rogosh, 1996). Combined with revelations of the transactional exchanges between individual and ecological characteristics (e.g., Sameroff & Fiese, 1989) and the transitory nature of some risk factors whose influence changes across time and circumstance (Bell, 1986), the challenges confronting prevention designs seem formidable.

Absent a single identifiable cause or even unique pathway involving a finite set of causes for a specific emotional impairment, the task of prevention seems insurmountable. This is true until one appreciates that negative mental health outcomes result from complex causal chains whose links represent avenues for the simultaneous interruption of multiple chains. This opportunity to influence multiple causal chains simultaneously reflects the aforementioned multifinality and equifinality characteristic of pathogenesis. Thus, interventions that effect common risks should have measurable impacts across multiple outcomes. Although no particular intervention is likely to influence all pathways contributing to the occurrence of depression or violence, for example, it is possible that limited evidence of effectiveness reported to date (Mrazec & Haggerty, 1994) reflects the consequences of measuring single rather than multiple outcomes. From a practical perspective, the success of interventions designed to prevent multidetermined but common syndromes may be found in their cumulative reductions across related outcomes.

Thus, recent advances in conceptualizing pathogenic processes and in categorizing preventive interventions open a range of opportunities for reducing emotional disorders in the population generally and adult segments specifically. Space permits merely a sampling of strategies to reduce the prevalence of disorder through risk reduction or the enhancement of individual capacity to resist such risks.

Prevention of Adult Disorders

Epidemiological studies confirm the toll on the nation's adults of alcohol, drug abuse, and mental health (ADM) disorders. Rouse's *Substance Abuse and Mental Health Statistics Source Book* (1995) reports that in 1991, approximately 30% of the adult (15–54) population, in excess of 52 million people, suffered from some form of ADM disorder. In 1991, lifetime prevalence for any affective disorder approached 20% of the population; a major depressive episode was experienced in the lifetime of nearly 17% of respondents. Research findings to date, summarized in Mrazek and Haggerty (1994) reveal opportunities for reductions in these numbers.

Muñoz (1993) describes a randomized controlled study to prevent depression associated with poverty in Hispanic adults. The San Francisco Depression Prevention Research Project used cognitive behavioral techniques to increase program participants' capacity to handle negative mood states. Although the sample size was insufficient to document reductions in diagnosed depression, program participants were found to be significantly less pessimistic and to have fewer depressive signs and symptoms than their control counterparts. The intervention focused on thoughts and behaviors theoretically linked to the onset of depression. Vega and Murphy (1990) documented the value of indigenous support groups in reducing moderate levels of depressive symptoms in low-income Hispanic women. In this intervention, thoughts and behaviors placing one at risk for subsequent depression were reduced within a socially supportive peer group.

Silverman's (1988) "Widow-to-widow: A mutual help program for the widowed," exemplifies the capacity of a preventive intervention to accelerate the healing process following loss of a loved one. Involvement in a self-help support group enabled the recently widowed to experience fewer and less intense depressive symptoms, to cope with the practical demands of widowhood, and to resume social contact more than controls. Independent verification of the program's effects were reported by Vachon et al. (1982).

Price, van Ryn, and Vinokur (1992) designed Jobs Project for the Unemployed as a means of reducing risk for emotional problems following job loss. Recently unemployed individuals were randomly assigned to either a training group focusing on job-seeking skills and handling the emotional consequences of unemployment or a control condition. In addition to increasing the level of reemployment, the intervention significantly reduced depressive symptoms in participants.

With regard to violence in our communities, a problem the first author has labeled a community toxin, several interesting prevention programs seem to be yielding significant results. One involves sexual and physical violence education and prevention for NCAA athletic departments. Of the several thousand collegiate athletes exposed to a program highlighting predatory journalism, violence prevention tips, and education regarding the ramifications of the public's fascination with the fall from grace of athletes and celebrities, not one athlete has been subsequently formally charged with sexual or physical assault over the last ten years. Over a dozen athletes at these colleges who missed the program have been subsequently criminally charged, lending at least anecdotal evidence to the effectiveness of prevention programs with highly structured, captive audiences (Jackson, McDonald, & Davis, in press).

Other violence prevention programs of note include some of the newer acquaintance rape and violence prevention programming involving long-term follow-up and seem to be demonstrating a reduction in violence as well as increases in self-protective and safe-dating skills (Jackson, 1996). Hanson and Gidycz (1993) implemented an empirical college sexual assault prevention program with follow-up that demonstrated lasting changes in information and attitudes. There were, however, significant differences on some measures with regard to previous victimization history. Overall, nonvictims were much less likely to report victimization during the nine-week quarter than were victims of previous sexual assault, again, lending credence to Gordon's (1983) concern with differential risk and vulnerability.

Evaluating the Effects of Preventive Interventions

The defining goal of preventive interventions is self-evident (i.e., the reduction of the documented prevalence of a disorder through reductions in incidence or duration). As reflected in the examples described above, consistently achieving that goal across a range of adult emotional and behavioral disorders remains a significant challenge for prevention science. As argued by Kessler and Goldston (1986), Cowen (1996), and, most convincingly, by Mrazek and Haggerty (1994), clear progress is being made in meeting the theoretical, methodological, programmatic, and political aspects of this challenge. Undeniable advances have occurred in our understanding of etiology and the causal complexity of pathogenesis since Caplan's (1964) initial call for the mental health professions to adopt preventive strategies. Merging the techniques of epidemiology and developmental psychopathology has revealed the multiplicity of pathways antecedent to negative outcomes and simultaneously the multiplicity of opportunities for attacking the conditions leading to those outcomes.

Currently, although evidence of substantial and consistent program effects is rare (Mrazek & Haggerty, 1994), signs and symptoms appear much easier to reduce than rates of diagnostic conditions. Healing processes may be accelerated through program involvement, but natural processes appear to reduce negative outcomes in a substantial portion of those not participating in the preventive intervention. In other cases, negative conditions may only be delayed rather than avoided entirely. In addition, hoped for protective factors and resistance to further pathology either do not appear or already weakened states are further compromised by unforeseen or unavoidable stressful events (Dohrenwend, 1986).

Such is the nature of the difficulties we are confronting, and the design of evaluation studies must reflect its realities. As noted earlier, multifinality, if real, requires that consideration be given to the impact of an intervention across the range of disorders associated with the risk factor(s) addressed by the intervention. Important evidence of success may be lost when only depressive symptoms or only substance abuse is measured rather than both. If the intervention has measurable effects on each, then its cumulative value may justify further investigation with larger samples over a sufficiently long period to document potential preventive effects. In the conclusion of the Institute of Medicine's comprehensive examination of preventive science, the need for policy and funding practices to reflect the demands confronting prevention science is very explicit (Mrazek & Haggerty, 1994).

It is clear that proponents should be optimistic and realistic. Their efforts, if sustained and expanded, will ultimately achieve sought-for evidence of prevention's power to reduce the nation's burden of emotional and behavioral disorders. Reality, however, suggests that these gains will be made slowly, incrementally, and painfully rather than through quick-fixes. The previous brief survey of prevention-oriented studies argues for the critical importance of continued funding of, and focus on, preventive strategies and goals across the broadest possible range of emotional and behavioral disorders of adulthood.

Bibliography

Albee, G. W. (1982). Preventing psychopathology and promoting human potential. *American Psychologist, 37* (9), 1043–1050.

Bell, R. Q. (1986, August). *Changing psychological risk: Implications for mass-targeted mental health intervention and promotion.* Invited address presented at the annual meeting of the American Psychological Association, Washington, DC.

Bronfenbrenner, U. (1979). *The ecology of human development.* Cambridge, MA: Harvard University Press.

Caplan, G. (1964). *Principles of preventive psychiatry.* New York: Basic Books.

Cicchetti, D., & Rogosch, F. A. (1996). Equifinality and multifinality in development psychopathology. *Development and Psychopathology, 8 (4)*, 597–600.

Commission on Chronic Illness. (1957). *Chronic illness in the United States* (Vol. 1). Published for the Commonwealth Fund. Cambridge, MA: Harvard University Press.

Cowen, E. L. (1973). Social and community intervention. *Annual Review of Psychology, 24*, 423–472.

Cowen, E. L. (1996). The ontogenesis of primary prevention: Lengthy studies and stubbed toes. *American Journal of Community Psychology, 24 (2)*, 235–250.

Dohrenwend, B. P. (1986). Social stress and psychopathology. In M. Kessler and S. E. Goldston (Eds.), *A decade of progress in primary prevention* (pp. 87–114). Hanover, NH: University Press of New England.

Durlak, J. A., & Wells, A. M. (1997). Primary prevention mental health programs for children and adolescents: A metaanalytic review. *American Journal of Community Psychology, 25 (2)*, 115–152.

Gordon, R. (1983). An operational classification of disease prevention. *Public Health Reports, 98*, 107–109.

Gordon, R. (1987). An operational classification of disease prevention. In J. A. Steinberg & M. M. Silverman (Eds.), *Preventing mental disorders: A research perspective* (pp. 20–26). Rockville, MD: Department of Health and Human Services.

Hanson, K. A.,& Gidycz, C. A. (1993). An evaluation of a sexual assault prevention program. *Journal of Consulting and Clinical Psychology, 61*, 1046–1052.

Jackson, T. (Ed.). (1996). *Acquaintance rape: Assessment, treatment, and prevention.* Sarasota, FL: Professional Resource Press.

Jackson, T., McDonald, J., & Davis, J. (in press). *Violence prevention programs for athletes, Athletic Departments, and sports franchises.* Sarasota, FL: Professional Resource Press.

Kessler, M., & Goldston, S. E. (Eds.). (1986). *A decade of progress in primary prevention.* Hanover, NH: University Press of New England.

Lamb, H. R., & Zusman, J. (1979). Primary prevention in perspective. *American Journal of Psychiatry, 136 (1)*, 12–17.

Lorion, R. P. (1983). Evaluating preventive interventions: Guideline for the serious social change agent. In R. D. Felner, L. Jason, J. Moritsugu, and S. S. Farber (Eds.), *Preventive psychology: Theory, research, and practice* (pp. 251–272). New York: Pergamon Press.

Lorion, R. P., Price, R. H., & Eaton, W. W. (1989). The prevention of child and adolescent disorders: From theory to research. In D. Schaffer, I. Phillips, and N. B. Enzer (Eds.), *Prevention of mental disorders alcohol, and other drug use in children and adolescents* (pp. 55–96). Rockville, MD: Office for Substance Abuse Prevention.

Mrazek, P. J., & Haggerty, R. J. (Eds.). (1994). *Reducing risks for mental disorders: Frontiers for preventive intervention research.* Washington, DC: Institute of Medicine/National Academy Press.

Muñoz, R. F. (1993). The prevention of depression: Current research and practice. *Applied and Preventive Psychology, 2*, 21–33.

Price, R. H., Cowen, E. L., Lorion, R. P., & Ramos-McKay, (Eds.). (1988). *Fourteen ounces of prevention: A casebook for practitioners.* Washington, DC: American Psychological Association.

Price, R. H., van Ryn, M. F., & Vinokur, A. (1992). Impact of preventive job search intervention on the likelihood of depression among the unemployed. *Journal of Health and Social Behavior, 33*, 158–167.

Rouse, B. A. (1995). *Substance abuse and mental health statistics source book.* Rockville, MD: Substance Abuse and Mental Health Services Administration.

Rutter, M. (1989). Pathway from childhood to adult life. *Journal of Child Psychology and Psychiatry, 30*, 23–51.

Sameroff, A. J., & Fiese, B. H. (1989). Conceptual issues in prevention. In D. Shafffer, I. Phillips, & N. B. Enzer (Eds.), *Prevention of mental disorder, alcohol, and other drug use in children and adolescents* (pp. 23–54). Rockville, MD: Office for Substance Abuse Prevention.

Silverman, P. R. (1988). Widow-to-widow: A mutual help program for the widowed. In R. H. Price, E. L. Cowen, R. P. Lorion, & J. Ramos-McKay (Eds.), *Fourteen ounces of prevention: A casebook for practitioners* (pp. 175–186). Washington, DC: American Psychological Association.

Vachon, M. L. S., Sheldon, A. R., Lancee, W. J., Lyall, W. A., Roger, J., & Freeman, S. J. J. (1982). Correlated of enduring distress patterns following bereavement: Social network life situations and personality. *Psychological Medicine, 12*, 783–788.

Vega, W. A., & Murphy, J. (1990). Projecto Bienestar: An example of a community based intervention. In *Culture and the restructuring of community mental health: Contributions in psychology.* Series No. 16. (pp. 103–122). Westport, CT: Greenwood Press.

Wolchik, S. A., West, S. G., Westover, S., Sandler, I. N., Martin, A., Lustig, J., Tien, J.-Y., & Fisher, J. (1993). The children of divorce parenting intervention: Outcome evaluation of an empirically based program. *American Journal of Community Psychology, 21*, 293–331.

Raymond P. Lorion and Thomas L. Jackson

PREYER, WILHELM (1841–1897) Anglo-German developmental psychophysiologist. Born in England and christened William Terry Preyer, Preyer pursued his career in Germany as Wilhelm Preyer. He is best known to psychologists for his books on child psychology. As a Darwinian, he regarded all physiogenetic and psychogenetic developments as the adaptive expression of their evolutionary history. His books and monographs on child and embryological development led to his being called the father of child psychology and of behavioral embryology.

Preyer is most noted in psychology for *Die Seele des Kindes*, the first child psychology book, and the inspiration for the many that followed. Published in 1882, it was quickly translated into English and published in two volumes as *The Mind of the Child* in 1888–1889. In 1893, a popular book, *Mental Development in the Child*, was published for mothers about understanding their children by carefully observing and recording their development as Preyer himself had done; much of the *The Mind of the Child* consisted of detailed reports of his personal observations of his son at different ages in the areas of sensory development, speech, motor control, temperament, intention, self-recognition, and so on. Reviews of the work and findings on animals and humans by himself and others were included as a basis for a comparative psychology.

These three books alone would have assured Preyer a place in history, but they reflected only partially his great ability, energy, fecundity, and ambition. Before earning his medical degree in 1866, he studied in Claude Bernard's laboratory at the Sorbonne and wrote extensively on kidney, blood, respiration, and muscle physiology. A founding editor of *Zeitschrift fur Psychologie* (Journal of Psychology), he published research on vision, the localization of sound (for which he invented the sound helmet), motor activity and handwriting, sleep, and hypnotism. However, the true mate to his *Mind of the Child* was his 1885 monograph *Spezielle Physiologie des Embryo* (Special Physiology of Embryos), a portion of which was translated into English (see Coghill & Legner, 1937). Its detailed procedures (he invented the ooscope to peer inside the egg) and observations on the earliest embryonic and fetal movement and sensitivity were undertaken to discover the primordial, physiological ontogeny of behavior. Many of Preyer's observations led to his doctrine of *motor primacy* of action. As George E. Coghill, himself a significant contributor to behavioral embryology, wrote, it was an "epochal work."

Preyer taught at the Universities of Berlin, Bonn, Heidelberg, Jena, and Vienna, where he inspired numerous students, of whom the most famous was Hans Spemann, the Nobel laureate in biology for 1935. Preyer died young, at age 56, but was early recognized for the significance of the work that he reported in a large number of publications. Preyer's research and thinking displayed methodological and technological virtuosity, curiosity, and sensitivity and exhaustive familiarity with research and theoretical literature. Darwin would have admired what he had inspired: a body of work that, leaping the barrier of a century, is still capable of being read with profit by researchers of development in humans and animals.

Bibliography

Boring, E. G. (1929). *A history of experimental psychology.* New York: Century.

Cairns, R. B. (1983). The emergence of developmental psychology. In P. H. Mussen (Series Ed.) & W. Kessen (Vol. Ed.), *Handbook of child psychology: Vol. 1. History, theory, and methods* (pp. 41–102). New York: Wiley.

Coghill, G. E., & Legner, W. K. (1937). Embryonic motility and sensitivity. *Monographs of the Society for Research in Child Development, 2*(6, Serial No. 13).

Gottlieb, G. (1973). Dedication to W. Preyer (1841–1897). In G. Gottlieb (Ed.), *Studies on the development of behavior and the nervous system: Vol. 1. Behavioral embryology* (pp. xv–xix). San Diego, CA: Academic Press.

Kessen, W. (1965). *The child.* New York: Wiley.

Preyer, W. T. (1973). *The mind of the child.* New York: Arno Press. (A reprint of the original English translation of *Die Seele des Kindes*; original work published 1882)

Preyer, W. T. (1893). *Mental development in the child* (H. W. Brown, Trans.). New York: Appleton.

Richard A. Littman

PRIMARY EDUCATION. *See* Elementary Education.

PRIMARY INTERVENTION. *See* Intervention.

PRINCE, MORTON (1854–1930), American physician and psychopathologist. Prince was born in Boston on 21 December 1854 into a prominent family of Democratic politicians. As a Harvard undergraduate in 1875 he came under the influence of William James, just then beginning his own career in psychology. In 1879, Prince won Harvard Medical School's Boylston Prize for an essay on the psychologically related topic "Mind and Body." Upon completing his M.D., he interned for a year at Boston City Hospital and studied briefly in Strasbourg and Vienna. After starting his medical career as a rhinologist, he began specializing in diseases of the nervous system and problems of abnormal psychology and psychopathology. This followed the successful treatment of his mother for nervous instabilities by the famous neurologist Jean Martin Charcot at the Salpêtrière in Paris. In 1885, Prince became physician for diseases of the nervous system at Boston City Hospital and published his first book, *Theory of Mind and Human Automatism*, a holistic defense of biological materialism.

During this period Prince worked with William James and James Jackson Putnam on the experimental committee on hypnotism for the American Society for Psychical Research, replicating the hypnotic experiments of British psychical researchers and the French psychopathologists, such as Pierre Janet. Using hypnosis on Harvard undergraduates, they artificially simulated various characteristics of trance mediumship as well as the symptoms of hysteria. These investigations provided scientific justification for the introduction of psychotherapeutic methods such as light trance, crystal gazing, and automatic writing into the treatment of ambulatory psychoneurosis at both the Massachusetts General Hospital under Putnam and the Boston City Hospital under Prince.

Between 1898 and 1899, Prince began to formulate his own biological theory of dynamic subconscious processes, based largely on a fusion of Pavlov, Janet, and Hughlings-Jackson. Following the lead of researchers such as William James and Boris Sidis, Prince also became an expert on hysteria and multiple personality. In 1902, he accepted a professorship in neurology at Tufts Medical School and became strategically placed there, and at Boston City Hospital, as the new field of psychotherapeutics burst upon the national scene. Between 1900 and 1910, the Boston School of Abnormal Psychology suddenly became an international focus of attention by aligning English, French, Swiss, and American researchers into a loose-knit consortium around the dissociation theory of multiple states of consciousness, a model that differed radically from the developing theories of Freud. Prince was a driving force behind this movement. He also became a member of the American Psychological Association in 1906.

Prince's best remembered book, *Dissociation of a Personality: A Biographical Study in Abnormal Psychology*, appeared in 1905. This case study of Miss Christine L. Beachamp clove to William James's idea that personality is, in reality, a plurality of selves, and argued that Miss Beachamp represented the extreme case of a condition which to a greater or lesser extent exists in all of us, and which, if not too marked, is entirely normal.

Prince is also remembered as the principal founder and editor of the *Journal of Abnormal Psychology* (later to become the *Journal of Abnormal and Social Psychology*). Intending the journal to be dedicated to the scientific discussion of psychotherapy, he invited Freud to contribute to the inaugural issue. However, because it was not to be exclusively a psychoanalytic journal, Freud declined. Instead, James Jackson Putnam reported on the first use of psychoanalysis at the Massachusetts General Hospital between 1903 and 1905, the first article to focus on psychoanalysis in the English language.

Prince followed these accomplishments with his only systematic treatise, *The Unconscious* (1914), which he first delivered as a series of lectures at the University of California at Berkeley in 1910. He edited two other books, *The Subconscious*, a symposium he had sponsored through Harvard University in 1906, and *Psychotherapeutics*, the English edition of papers delivered at a major conference on American psychotherapy held in New Haven in 1909.

In 1924, Prince traveled abroad as lecturer on abnormal psychology at the universities of London, Oxford, Cambridge, and Edinburgh, and returned to contribute to the Powell Lectures at Clark University. Then, in 1926, at the age of 72, in a major attempt to reshape the course of psychology at Harvard, he endowed the Harvard Psychological Clinic, deliberately founding it within the School of Arts and Sciences as an experimental research facility rather than a clinical area of the medical school. As associate professor of abnormal and dynamic psychology at Harvard College, he lectured to large classes of undergraduates on the older dynamic psychology. His first assistant was Henry A. Murray, who would later take the clinic in an entirely different direction, introducing psychoanalysis and Jungian psychology into the new field of personology. Only Murray's right-hand man, Robert White, continued to study hypnosis and dissociation in the tradition of Prince, Putnam, and James, at least while Prince was still alive.

Prince was honored by his colleagues in 1929 when Abraham A. Roback edited a volume of his collected papers entitled *Clinical and Experimental Studies in Personality*. He died at the age of 76 on 31 August 1930.

Bibliography

Casey, D. M. (1948). *La theorie du subconscient de Morton Prince*. Paris: Presses Universitaires de France.

Hale, N. G., Jr. (Ed). (1975). *Morton Prince, psychotherapy and multiple personality: Selected essays*. Cambridge, MA: Harvard University Press.

Marx, O. M. (1970) Morton Prince and the dissociation of a personality. *Journal of the History of the Behavioral Sciences* 6(2) 120–130.

Prince, M. H. (1885). *Theory of mind and human automatisms*. Philadelphia: Lippincott.

Prince, M. H. (1906). *Dissociaton of a personality: A biographical study in abnormal psychology*. New York: Longmans, Green.

Prince, M. H. (1910). *Psychotherapeutics: A symposium*. Boston: R. G. Badger.

Prince, M. H. (1914). *The unconscious: The fundamentals of human personality, normal and abnormal*. New York: Macmillan.

Roback, A. A. (Ed). (1929). *Clinical and experimental studies in personality*. Cambridge, MA: Sci-Art Pub.

Rosenzweig, S. (1987). Sally Beachamp's career: A psychoarcheological key to Morton Prince's classic case of multiple personality. *Genetic, Social, and General Psychology Monographs*, 113 (1) 5–60;

Taylor, W. S. (1928) *Morton Prince and abnormal psychology*. New York: Appleton.

White, R. W. (1992). Who was Morton Prince? *Journal of Abnormal Psychology* 101 (4) 604–606.

Prince burned most of his papers. Some case records and miscellaneous manuscripts have been preserved at Rare Books, Countway Library of Medicine, Harvard Medical School.

Eugene Taylor

PRISONERS OF WAR. During military conflicts prisoners are often taken by the opposing force and held until the war ends, sometimes for many years afterward. Each prisoner of war (POW) situation differs from every other, depending upon the time in history at which the incident occurred, the culture of the captor, the duration of captivity, its harshness, and the support received from others, both while in captivity as well as upon return. When attempting to delineate the long-term effects of a POW experience, in addition to the factors already mentioned, one must also consider individual differences in abilities to withstand isolation, pain, and coercive persuasion (Hunter, 1983, 1991).

Factors in Effective Coping

A few examples will illustrate how difficult the task is to generalize as to the residuals of wartime captivity. With regard to cultural differences, a Japanese soldier taken POW by the enemy during World War II might have chosen to commit suicide as he believed it was the "honorable" thing to do, whereas an American soldier would probably have made every effort to survive his ordeal in order to fight again. Duration of captivity is another factor that must be taken into account in trying to understand a particular POW situation. Prisoners held more than 3 years have been shown to exhibit greater residuals of captivity than those held for shorter periods of time. It seems reasonable that length of captivity would be related to later effects, primarily because the longer the captivity, the more severe the malnutrition and lack of medical attention the POWs would have suffered.

Support from others has also been found to be an important variable in coping with a POW experience. When prisoners are held in groups, they do better at managing their stresses than if they are isolated completely from others. Upon release, support from fellow countrymen and family members has also been found to correlate with later adjustment. When United States POWs returned from Germany and Japan at the end of World War II in the mid-1940s, they came back to a cheering nation. When the Vietnam conflict ended in the early 1970s, returning military men came back to antimilitary sentiments, both from the public and sometimes even from their own family members, especially teenagers. Attempting to understand what effects captivity has on any particular person, one must also look at individuals themselves. Older individuals appear to cope better with prolonged severe stress than those who are very young. Higher commitment to a professional military career also assists in coping, in contrast to the draftee soldier who is later taken captive. Individuals who characteristically feel they have control over what happens to them (an internal locus of control), rather than always assuming that chance solely determines their fate (an external locus of control), usually manage any difficult stressful trauma more adequately (Hunter, 1991).

Attempts to Improve the Treatment of POWs

In very early times, POWs were of no value whatsoever to their captors but were merely excess baggage for an advancing warring force. Thus, they were killed upon capture. More recently, POWs were sometimes held as "bargaining chips" for negotiations that occur when war terminates. The Geneva Conventions made an effort to prescribe proper treatment of wartime POWs. Unfortunately, the idealism of the Geneva Conventions subsequent to World War I and the "honorable treatment" of bona fide POWs under those conventions were short-lived, if recognized at all by some nations, or were recognized by a captor for some prisoners but not for others (Hunter, 1991).

Long-Term Captivity Effects

Studies carried out by many nations of the world suggest that the physical deprivations and psychological stresses endured while in captivity have lifelong effects on subsequent physical and emotional health, family adjustment, and occupational history (Cohen & Cooper, 1954; Eitinger, 1961; Hunter, 1980; Keehn, 1980; Nefzger, 1970; Page & Ostfeld, 1994; Segal, Hunter, & Segal, 1976). These later effects of captivity, which include persistent irrational irritability, acute startle reaction, repetitive nightmares, depression, and survivor guilt (that is, "Why did I survive, when others did not?"), have variously been referred to as "nostalgic psychoses," "reaction states of liberation," "mania of return," "post-incarceration late injury," "concentration camp syndrome," or "KZ syndrome," and "survivor syndrome," among others. With the development of the *Diagnostic and Statistical Manual III (DSM–III)* by the American Psychiatric Association in 1980, this cluster of symptomatology related to postcaptivity effects now comes under the category of posttraumatic stress disorder (PTSD). However, it should be noted that not all former prisoners of war will suffer PTSD following wartime captivity.

Research on the Effects of Wartime Captivity

Many studies have been carried out worldwide to determine precisely what the physiological and psychological residuals of long-term wartime captivity are, some investigators emphasizing the psychological effects, others the physiological effects. Few military women have become prisoners of war, and little research has been conducted to determine if female POWs' long-term effects differ from those of men (Skelton & Skelton, 1995).

For several decades mortality and morbidity data have been collected and analyzed on American World War II and Korean War POWs at the Medical Follow-up Agency of the National Academy of Sciences in Washington, D.C. (Beebe, 1975; Cohen & Cooper, 1954; Keehn, 1980; Nefzger, 1970; Page & Ostfeld, 1994). During and after the war in Southeast Asia, one of the longest, most carefully planned prospective studies, with carefully matched comparison subjects, was initiated and implemented at the San Diego Center for Prisoner of War Studies from 1971 until 1978. That study of Vietnam-era POWs (including family members) continues today at the Navy Aerospace Research Institute in Pensacola, Florida (Hunter, 1980, 1984, 1991; McCubbin, Dahl, Metres, Hunter, & Plag, 1974; Nice, Garland, Milton, Baggett, & Mitchell, 1996).

Conclusions

Despite military POWs' abilities to cope with prolonged extreme stress, it is the captors who ultimately determine whether a particular POW lives or dies. When military persons are captured and held for many months or years, families also must cope with their own form of "wartime captivity" (Hunter, 1984). Nonetheless, it has been found that prisoners of war (and family members) are able to manage much harsher and much longer captivities than they had ever imagined possible prior to the event. In their attempts to cope, former POWs discover that it is important to feel they retain some degree of control. With the *will to live* and the *mind*, POWs are able to cope with extreme, continuing stress, with minimal long-term effects. All POWs must discover the coping techniques that are best for them. However, although each experience may *differ* from all others, effective coping strategies that evolve during incarceration tend to be quite *similar*, regardless of culture, location, or time in history.

Bibliography

American Psychiatric Association. (1980). *Diagnostic and statistical manual of mental disorders* (3rd ed.). Washington, DC: Author.

Beebe, G. (1975). Follow-up studies of World War II and Korean war prisoners: II. Mortality, disability, and maladjustments. *American Journal of Epidemiology, 101*, 400–422.

Cohen, B. M., & Cooper, M. Z. (1954). *Veterans Administration Medical Monograph: A follow-up study of World War II prisoners of war*. Washington, DC: Government Printing Office.

Eitinger, L. (1961). Pathology of the concentration camp syndrome. *Archives of General Psychiatry, 5* (10), 371–379.

Hunter, E. J. (1980). Lessons learned from the Vietnam POW/MIA studies. In C. R. Figley (Ed.), *Stress disorders among Vietnam veterans: Theory, research, and treatment implications* (pp. 188–206). New York: Brunner/Mazel.

Hunter, E. J. (1983). Coercive persuasion: The myth of free will? *Air University Review, 34*(2), 100–111.

Hunter, E. J. (1984). Treating the military captive's family. In F. Kaslow & R. Ridenour (Eds.), *Treating the military family: Dynamics and treatment* (pp. 167–196). New York: Guilford Press.

Hunter, E. J. (1991). Prisoners of war: Readjustment and rehabilitation. In R. Gal & A. D. Mangelsdorff (Eds.), *Handbook of military psychology* (pp. 741–757). Chichester, England: Wiley.

Keehn, R. J. (1980). Follow-up studies of World War II and Korean war prisoners. III. Mortality to January 1, 1976. *American Journal of Epidemiology, 111*, 194–211.

McCubbin, H. I., Dahl, B. B., Metres, P. J., Jr., Hunter, E. J., & Plag, J. A. (Eds.). (1974). *Family separation and reunion: Families of prisoners of war and servicemen missing in action* (Cat. No. D-206.21: 74–70). Washington, DC: U.S. Government Printing Office.

Nefzger, M. D. (1970). Follow-up studies of World War II and Korean war prisoners. I. Study plan and mortality findings. *American Journal of Epidemiology, 91*, 123–139.

Nice, D. S., Garland, C. F., Milton, S. M., Baggett, J. D., & Mitchell, R. E. (1996). Long-term health outcomes and medical effects of torture among US Navy prisoners of war in Vietnam. *Journal of the American Medical Association, 276*(5), 375–381.

Page, W. F., & Ostfeld, A. M. (1994). Malnutrition and ischemic heart disease in former prisoners of war of World War II and the Korean conflict. *Journal of Clinical Epidemiology, 47*(12), 1437–1441.

Segal, J., Hunter, E. J., & Segal, Z. (1976). Universal consequences of captivity: Stress reactions among divergent populations of prisoners of war and their families. *International Social Sciences Journal, 38*, 593–609.

Skelton, W. P. III, & Skelton, N. K. (1995). Women as prisoners of war. *Military Medicine, 160*(11), 113–115.

Edna J. Hunter-King

PRISONS AND CORRECTIONAL INSTITUTIONS. The discipline of psychology addresses many substantive issues that relate to correctional institutions, criminal offenders, and the problems of crime, punishment, and rehabilitation. These include prevention of criminal behavior and its precursors, direct intervention through psychosocial treatments, prediction of future risk, and examination of the prison environment as a setting for potential change, both positive and harmful. Across this spectrum, psychologists have directed their attention to specific groups of offenders, such as the increasing number of incarcerated mentally ill, as well as toward the policies and systems designed to manage the nearly 2 million persons confined in jails and prisons in the United States. Of note, the U.S. incarceration rate exceeds all countries but Russia and is four to six times greater than that of most developed nations. In the last two decades of the twentieth century, prison growth has continuously accelerated. Psychologists are being employed in increasing numbers in correctional settings, but their contributions have been limited by the rapid expansion and sheer volume of offenders in confinement. Many correctional psychologists began their work with little or no prior experience or training with offenders.

Like other socially controversial issues, imprisonment policy is often guided by political considerations that reflect prevailing beliefs and attributions about criminal conduct. Yet psychological research and theory have been an undercurrent in influencing how the correctional system responds to law violators. For example, modern penology assumes that offenders differ widely in their need for secure incarceration and in their amenability to potentially life-changing interventions. Assessing these differences, prescribing and delivering behavioral change programs, evaluating the effectiveness of particular treatments for specific offenders, and measuring the impact of prison environments follow directly from this premise. These issues also have been examined in federal lawsuits challenging prison conditions, deficiencies, and excesses.

Risk Assessment

When felony offenders are sentenced to correctional institutions, the length of their confinement typically is based on certain formulas and guidelines. Other decisions, such as their actual prison placement and the type of housing and freedom of movement within a custodial setting, are less automatic, and they depend, in part, on psychological characteristics. Two overlapping concerns are primary: (a) the probability that a given offender will be a predator (or victim) or otherwise disruptive within a particular setting; and (b) the likelihood of adjustment as the degree of supervision and security is relaxed. These are not static determinations but can be revised as new information is accumulated. Rapid prison growth, however, has made such evaluations far from systematic. In assessing the level of custody and supervision required, independent reviewers often find that actual assignments are more restrictive (and typically more costly) than warranted by objective risk indicators.

Debate continues also about whether risk of violence (or similar undesirable outcomes) is better predicted by personality traits or by evocative or coercive environments or circumstances. Recent research reveals how these elements may be effectively combined. Studies also indicate that so-called clinical judgment approaches to prediction are usually inferior to more objective, mainly actuarial methods. Current research argues for combining traits, criminal history, needs, and context factors. Instruments and structured evaluations that address these elements have been successfully, though infrequently, used.

To reduce antagonism and conflict among confined offenders, some prison systems have adopted strategies for separating residents based on psychological characteristics. This approach goes beyond the fairly universal practice of designating entire institutions as maximum, or minimum, or other level of security. For example, assessment schemes that address inmate aggression, vulnerability, and adaptability provide a framework for forming compatible groupings within a given institution. As a management corollary, correctional staff may be assigned to specific housing units based on their preferred style of interaction and their success with particular offenders. These elements—staff characteristics, physical design, unit rules, and type of program involvement—all may converge around such management themes as structure and control or treatment and support. Several studies suggest that reduced disciplinary infractions and improved staff morale can be expected. Despite the general attractiveness of this model, few systems have adopted it on a wide scale.

Treatment Assignment

Ideally, psychologists prescribe treatment based on the assessed needs of the offender, particularly needs that are directly associated with criminal conduct. The scarcity of treatment resources makes careful allocation particularly important. As background, it should be noted that opinion about the value of offender rehabilitation programs has vacillated. The 1960s was an era of unbridled enthusiasm; however, this attitude shifted to a "nothing works" mentality that held for nearly two decades, although more recent research supports guarded optimism. One lesson learned is that generic, one-size-fits-all treatment efforts are likely to fail. Instead, based on increasing awareness of the diverse traits and highly varied profiles exhibited by offenders, treatment strategies must be specifically tailored.

Psychological treatment is often directed toward offenders with a history of sexual assault, substance abuse, or poor impulse control, as well as those with more clearly defined mental disorders. The proportion of prison inmates with serious mental disorders, variously estimated to be between 10 and 20% has increased partly as a result of restrictive civil commitment laws and the lack of community mental health alternatives. (This figure does not include those whose criminal history is more reflective of antisocial or other personality disorders.) Both state and federal correctional systems have special housing units for mentally ill offenders. The literature supports the use of behavioral and psychosocial treatments for these offenders, but many institutions have too few appropriately trained staff to implement comprehensive programs.

Prison environments often create their own kind of psychological maladjustment: In crowded, large institutions (many house more than 2,000 inmates), the prospects for positive, reformative experiences are limited. The presence of predatory, aggressive offenders and the additional stress associated with densely populated, close quarters may lead some less able offenders to seek protection. Others may resort to self-injurious, sometimes suicidal behavior. The practice of isolating and confining offenders for long periods also has been shown to produce symptoms of mental disorder. By contrast, the opportunity for meaningful work and training activities appears to reduce institutional stress, irrespective of its effect on future law violation. Crisis intervention for the severely mentally ill and for those who threaten or attempt suicide occupies a significant proportion of available mental health resources.

Some offenders may be unresponsive to psychological treatment. For example, within the group of offenders categorized as antisocial personality disorder (APD), a subgroup (designated as psychopaths) is particularly persistent. These extremely challenging individuals are estimated to comprise between 15 and 25% of incarcerated law violators. They have not only the characteristically impulsive lifestyle of the antisocial personality, but also an apparent lack of remorse, empathy, or emotional depth and an interpersonal style that is manipulative, superficial, deceitful, and self-inflating. This combination of traits greatly increases the probability of violent reoffending and of institutional misconduct. Such individuals appear less amenable to programs that promote positive behavior change, although superficially they may seem quite compliant and well motivated.

Drug-involved offenders have received considerable legal and psychological attention, and they now are the most rapidly growing segment of the prison population. Prison-based substance abuse treatment typically is patterned after a 12-step, self-help model. Such programs have increased dramatically in number, but their effectiveness has not been well researched. The target concern is justified since substance abuse, especially alcohol, is implicated as a major risk factor for a number of offenders. [*See* Twelve-Step Programs.]

Treatment Outcomes

Although some writers remain pessimistic, evidence for the effectiveness of well-matched offender treatment is growing, and the number of methodologically sound studies has increased. Meta-analysis (combining the results of available treatment studies) is now used to detect consistently effective (or ineffective) regimes and their degree of impact. Certain program characteristics and clinical procedures emerge as having an increased chance of reducing recidivism:

1. Behavioral-cognitive treatments emphasizing short-term positive consequences, designed to alter both skills deficits and attitudinal correlates of offending (social skills training, prosocial modeling, and anger management are examples).
2. Programs that address multiple problems.
3. Treatments that are intensive, of some reasonable duration, that provide transition to less secure, ultimately, community settings, and that provide follow-up support.

Community-based interventions generally produce even greater success than in-prison versions. Encouragingly, positive effects are found with offenders who have relatively high-risk profiles (i.e., whose past criminal conduct and associated characteristics predict higher rates of recidivism). Low-risk offenders may be harmed by certain interventions. As implied, interventions should be appropriately matched to the needs and characteristics of the individual offender. Practitioners and researchers also now recognize the critical need to deliver a given program with a high level of treatment integrity, that is, to rigorously follow an established protocol or set of guidelines.

The correctional system's ability to implement such programs does not appear nearly so promising. Providing resources for staff training, appropriate treatment assignments, and the requisite strategies of monitoring, follow-up, and relapse prevention is both expensive and, at present, politically unpopular. Also generally unavailable are correctional research and evaluation branches within each jurisdiction. As evidence of effective interventions becomes more widely known, the necessary resources may follow. The financial costs of incarceration alone may encourage renewed attention to the possibilities of rehabilitation.

Prison Design and Population Trends

Correctional institutions in the United States as well as those worldwide reveal a remarkable range of building designs and staffing patterns. This diversity reflects historical philosophical swings in the social purposes of imprisonment. Over time, beliefs also have vacillated regarding the prospects of changing human behavior, as have assumptions about how to promote such change. Virtually every imaginable physical design configuration has been attempted. Some modern facilities are technologically advanced and feature mechanized, remote means of controlling movement and interactions. Correctional officers may be stationed in protected "bubbles," and the corresponding management approach tends to be impersonal, providing only minimal human contact. Other facilities are more open, environmentally friendly settings that encourage interaction and "normalization." Such diverse designs reflect a valid need to provide for very different types of offenders. However, even for high-risk offenders, an interactive staffing model ultimately may promote a more secure environment and, consequently, both reduce disciplinary infractions and increase offenders' participation in programs. Such "dynamic" security, wherein staff circulate in the living units, relies on officer-inmate relationships and may avoid an artificial security-treatment separation. Instead, correctional staff may participate directly in the treatment regime and thereby extend the capability of sparsely available clinicians.

Though crime per se is generally a 15- to 30-year olds' phenomenon, as sentences lengthen and life-without-parole sentences increase, large numbers of offenders will eventually grow old in prison. Staffing and physical designs will have to address the accompanying health and psychological problems. "Prison nursing home" seems a contradiction in terms, but some are already in use. The prison gerontologist may soon become a viable occupation. At the other end of the spectrum, younger, persistent, antisocial, and gang-affiliated offenders, whose primary adaptation to prison life is one of violence and intimidation, appear to be increasing in numbers. Although environments themselves may promote aggression and rule violation, correctional administrators nevertheless are faced with a substantial management challenge. In response, some 30 "supermax" facilities have been built in the United States. These undertake an extreme combination of isolation and high-tech methods in controlling disruptive offenders. Although short-lived in the 1970s, a behavior modification approach to this dilemma was attempted in which hard-to-manage offenders earned privileges and progressed toward reduced isolation by their increased rule compliance. However, extreme deprivations, though not required by the underlying psychological theory, were a routine feature of such regimes, and human rights advocates justifiably prevailed in objecting to these programs. Ironically, some ultrahigh-security facilities currently deny prisoners access to all but basic needs, but few means are available to redress these extreme conditions and no effectiveness evaluations have been conducted.

Female offenders also are a fast-growing segment of the correctional enterprise. Still small on a percentage basis, their ranks have increased from approximately 4 to 6% of incarcerated offenders in the last decade. Nearly two thirds are parents of minor children. Although research on female offenders has been conducted piecemeal and has rarely been longitudinal, similar factors are implicated in their criminal conduct as have been noted for men: family, peer, school, and economic concerns. Behavioral adaptations, however, are likely to be more diverse and include depression and anxiety disorders, contributing to an even higher mental illness prevalence than has been observed in male offenders. Histories of sexual abuse also are proportionately higher. Incarcerated women evidence a substantial array of health problems including infectious and communicative disease, HIV infection (a major concern in America's prisons), substance abuse, reproductive health problems, as well as co-occurring psychiatric disorders. Intervention programs for women should embrace some of the features noted earlier, but also should focus on appropriate vocational skills as well as critical parenting issues. Treatment outcome studies have been notably absent.

Summary

Psychologists can play an important role in correctional institutions. To date, the promise for positive impact has been only partially fulfilled. As the number and diversity of offenders in prison grow, new problems will require creative solutions. The strength of psychological methods—for assessment, treatment, outcome evaluation, and comprehending the interaction between persons and environments—offers the promise of important new insights and application in the management and treatment of incarcerated offenders.

Bibliography

Acoca, L. (1998). Defusing the time bomb: Understanding and meeting the growing health care needs of incarcerated women in America. *Crime and Delinquency, 44*, 49–69.

Clements, C. B. (1996). Offender classification: Two decades of progress. *Criminal Justice and Behavior, 23*, 121–143. Reviews trends in assessing offender risk and needs, particularly as they relate to correctional management and treatment planning.

Gendreau, P., & Andrews, D. (1996). *Correctional Program Assessment Inventory (CAPI)* (6th ed.). Saint John, New Brunswick, Canada: University of New Brunswick. Provides a template for evaluating how closely correctional programs adhere to the known treatment literature and to principles derived from the last decade of research.

Haney, C., & Zimbardo, P. (1998). The past and future of U. S. prison policy: Twenty-five years after the Stanford prison experiment. *American Psychologist, 53*, 709–727. The authors who conducted the classic Stanford prison experiment trace, with considerable pessimism, the current failure to examine how powerful institutional environments create counterproductive behavior and harm. An excellent documentation of prison growth in the United States with particular reference to disproportionate minority representation and drug-involved offenders.

Hare, R. D. (1993). *Without conscience: The disturbing world of the psychopaths among us.* New York: Pocket Books. A highly readable account of the unique characteristics of, and problems presented by, individuals with psychopathic traits; Hare is the leading researcher on this topic.

Johnson, R. (1996). *Hard time: Understanding and reforming the prison* (2nd ed.). Belmont, CA: Wadsworth. A measured analysis of why current prisons are unnatural environments for offender reform; proposes sensible recommendations that encourage mature coping and the minimization of unnecessary pain.

Martinson, R. (1974). What works? Questions and answers about prison reform. *Public Interest, 35,* 22–54. This classic review launched, or at least gave credibility to, a reactive period of prison philosophy described as "nothing works." The shortcomings of Martinson's analysis have been well documented, but the surrounding controversy stimulated a new generation of more sophisticated, better controlled studies, many with positive outcomes. Researchers now use the phrase "what works" to suggest a more targeted approach to treatment.

Morris, N., & Rothman, D. J. (Eds.). (1995). *The Oxford history of the prison: The practice of punishment in western society.* New York: Oxford University Press. Edited by two well-known observers and critics of institutional history, this book traces both the physical and social dimensions of incarceration; extensive illustrations and bibliography.

Rice, M. E., & Harris, G. T. (1997). The treatment of mentally disordered offenders. *Psychology, Public Policy, and Law, 3,* 126–183. Underscores the wide diversity of offenders with mental disorders and reviews the treatment literature for specific symptom patterns; violence risk assessment is seen as a cornerstone of evaluation, and community treatment and relapse prevention are emphasized.

Rideau, W., & Wikberg, R. (1992). *Life sentences: Rage and survival behind bars.* New York: Time Books. Written by prisoners who worked on the staff of Louisiana's Angola State Prison newspaper (the *Angolite*), this book provides a vivid perspective of life behind bars. The failure of prison reform is uniquely interpreted and integrated with modern penal theory (uncensored).

Schlosser, E. (1998). The prison-industrial complex. *Atlantic Monthly, 282*(6), 51–77. Argues persuasively that prisons have become big business and that their growth will probably continue regardless of actual need.

Stoff, D. M., Breiling, J., & Maser, J. D. (Eds.). (1997). *Handbook of antisocial behavior.* New York: Wiley. Comprehensive reviews by nearly 100 researchers on topics ranging from early childhood risk factors to psychopharmacological treatment of offenders. Considerable emphasis on prevention, community alternatives, and demonstrably successful treatments of juveniles. Many of the same approaches, primarily behavioral and highly focused, are proving of value with adult offenders, although treatment resistance and institutional barriers may be more pronounced.

Teplin, L. A., Abram, K. M., & McClelland, G. M. (1997). Mentally disordered women in jail: Who receives services? *American Journal of Public Health, 87,* 604–609. Documents the prevalence of mental disorders and the shortage of appropriate services for female offenders.

Van Voorhis, P., Braswell, M., & Lester, D. (1997). *Correctional counseling and rehabilitation* (3rd ed.). Cincinnati, OH: Anderson. A basic introduction to issues of offender assessment, management, and treatment. Contributing authors review specific approaches to interventions for different offender groups; excellent summary of empirically supported treatment with an extensive reference list.

Webster, C. D., & Jackson, M. A. (Eds.). (1997). *Impulsivity: Theory, assessment, and treatment.* New York: Guilford Press. This volume is particularly helpful in connecting the common elements of impulsive behavior: risk assessment and treatment research topics are integrated by contributors from correctional and mental health backgrounds; specific risk assessment schemes such as suicide in correctional settings and sexual assault are provided.

Carl B. Clements

PRIVACY. The definition of privacy, or privacy regulation, is the selective control of access to the self or group (Altman, 1975). This rich and dynamic concept captures the complex ways in which people pace and regulate interactions with others, notably, how they open and close themselves to interaction. Privacy processes have been documented around the globe, and privacy regulation has been described as a "cultural universal" because every society has developed its own unique mechanisms for regulating privacy (Altman & Chemers, 1980). By encompassing both opening-up and closing-off processes, this definition differs from privacy analyses that focus exclusively on how people close themselves off or how individuals' preferences for solitude guide their perceptions and behaviors (Newell, 1995).

The idea of "selective control" means that people choose when, with whom, and how to interact in an open and accessible or closed and inaccessible way. "Access" refers to the nature of the contact: Individuals may desire to control *physical* access to themselves, such as whether they allow touching, prefer to keep others at a distance, or desire total isolation. People also control *psychological* access, that is, access to personal information about themselves such as their perceived weaknesses, anonymous benevolent acts, sexual preferences, and the like. Another facet of "access" involves control over both inputs and outputs. For example, people try to control whether they accept intimate disclosures from others (inputs) or reveal intimate information about themselves (outputs). Thus, "selective control of access" means that people may seek to be intimate or superficial, accessible or inaccessible, and monitor both inputs and outputs in physical and psychological domains.

The final component of the definition refers to the actor(s), "the self or group," indicating that individuals and groups of any size—including dyads—can regulate privacy. Members inside a group control their interactions as subgroups or individuals; the group as a whole controls interactions with other individuals or groups.

Thus, "privacy regulation is an *interpersonal boundary control process*, which paces and regulates interaction with others. Privacy regulation by persons and groups is somewhat like the shifting permeability of a cell membrane . . . [sometimes] receptive to outside inputs and sometimes closing off contact with the outside environment" (Altman, 1975, p. 10). Desires to seek or avoid contact vary from time to time and situation to situation. Preferences may be related to biological rhythms and energy levels, immediate and longer-term interaction experiences, specific social partners, and other factors. Thus, in dialectic fashion, the opposing processes of accessibility and inaccessibility are in constant dynamic tension and flow as people regulate self-other boundaries over time (Altman, Vinsel, & Brown, 1981).

Effective privacy regulation is fundamental to personal and social viability, so it is not surprising that humans have developed numerous mechanisms for controlling interactions with others. The primary privacy regulation mechanisms are (1) *verbal* and *paraverbal* cues of invitation or rejection; (2) *nonverbal* processes such as *personal space*, body movements and positions, gestures, facial expressions, and so on; and (3) physical and environmental cues, including *territoriality* and other regulation and use of the physical environment. Cross-cultural analyses suggest that different societies use different combinations of mechanisms to achieve levels of openness and closedness appropriate for their cultural values and physical settings. Mechanisms conducive to viability in one society are not necessarily those that enable effective functioning in other societies.

Research has examined how people succeed or fail to regulate privacy (Werner, Altman, & Brown, 1992). Altman's (1975) model of privacy regulation suggests that both *crowding* and *loneliness* result from inadequate control over interaction. Other outcomes and indicators of viability have also been studied. For example, a study of college dormitory residents found that those who effectively used opening up and closing off mechanisms were more likely to remain in college, that is, to be academically viable. Research in work settings suggests that people are more productive and more satisfied with their work spaces when they have more control over access. People in open office plans often complain about noise and visual inputs from others while expressing concerns that their own actions and private conversations are available to others. Employees also complain if their work group is not accessible to them, suggesting that office designs need to provide for both opening up and closing off processes.

Studies in unusual settings help to illuminate the role of privacy regulation in effective functioning. In prisons, residential group homes, and psychiatric hospitals, residents who can regulate interactions with others are less aggressive (regulating via partial walls around their beds; ownership of a spot in the television room). In a military setting, naval recruits who used effective regulation mechanisms (controlling personal disclosures and establishing clear physical territories) were more likely to complete a 10-day social isolation experience. Altman and Ginat's (1996) study of modern polygamous families revealed complex patterns of privacy regulation among husbands and sister-wives. Access to separate territories and respect for one another's places and belongings were essential to viability in these relationships.

Recent changes in technology have created new issues of privacy regulation. Sometimes computer-mediated communication is disrupted because people cannot accurately read each other's expressed or desired levels of intimacy. In other cases, such as the anonymity of chat rooms, openness is facilitated and participants take on pseudonyms and alternate personae as strategies for achieving intimacy. An ongoing concern is the large amount of personal information now available in computer data banks. The information needs to be accessible to legitimate users, but must be protected from unauthorized access. Legal and ethical concerns abound about stolen identities and financial records, control over psychiatric and medical background information, industrial espionage, and so on (see Burgoon, 1982). These and related concerns provide continuing evidence that privacy regulation is a complex construct that operates at many levels of functioning, exists in every society, and affects many aspects of social and business life.

Bibliography

Altman, I. (1975). *Environment and social behavior: Privacy, personal space, territory, and crowding.* Monterey, CA: Brooks /Cole (reprinted by Irvington Press, New York, 1981). Extensive literature review of privacy and privacy regulation mechanisms such as personal space and territoriality.

Altman, I., & Chemers, M. M. (1980). *Culture and environ-*

ment. Monterey, CA: Brooks/Cole. Dialectic processes that link people and settings in different cultures.

Altman, I., & Ginat, J. (1996). *Polygamous families in contemporary society*. New York: Cambridge University Press.

Altman, I., Vinsel, A., & Brown, B. B. (1981). Dialectic conceptions in social psychology: An application to social penetration and privacy regulation. In L. Berkowitz (Ed.), *Advances in experimental social psychology, Vol. 14* (pp. 107–160). New York: Academic Press. Examination of privacy regulation as a dynamic, dialectical process.

Brown, B. B., Werner, C. M., & Altman, I. (1998). Choicepoints for dialecticians: A dialectical/transactional perspective on close relationships. In B. Montgomery & L. Baxter (Eds.), *Dialectical approaches to studying personal relationships* (pp. 137–154). Mahwah, NJ: Erlbaum. Dialectic processes and transactional unities.

Burgoon, J. K. (1982). Privacy and communication. In M. Burgoon (Ed.), *Communication yearbook, Vol. 6* (pp. 206–249) Beverly Hills, CA: Sage. Legal and ethical aspects of privacy.

Newell, P. B. (1995). Perspectives on privacy. *Journal of Environmental Psychology, 15*, 87–104. Comprehensive review of definitions and research on the solitude side of privacy.

Werner, C. M., Altman, I., & Brown, B. B. (1992). *Journal of Social and Personal Relationships, 9*, 297–323. A transactional approach to interpersonal relations: Physical environment, social context, and temporal qualities.

Carol M. Werner, Irwin Altman, and Barbara B. Brown

PRIVATE PRACTICE. Psychologists have practiced in the private sector since 1945. As professions go, 54 years is relatively young. Establishing an independent profession that offered services to the public required setting standards for licensure; developing educational standards and accreditation for programs, creating a climate for private practice, and providing support structures.

What Private Practitioners Do

Most practitioners do some form of psychotherapy, such as psychoanalysis, cognitive behavioral therapy, marital therapy, family therapy, child (play) therapy, biofeedback therapy, and many other forms. They also do psychological assessments, which include intelligence testing, personality testing, neuropsychological assessment, and clinical interviews. Consultation is offered to industry, organizations, schools, government, individuals, and families. Private practices are conducted in offices, hospitals, clinics, schools, and even on talk shows on television and radio.

The Evolution of Practice

In the early days of clinical psychology, graduate programs did not encourage their students to enter private practice. Research and teaching were the hallmarks of psychology. In the 1950s and 1960s, as a result of the growing popularity of psychology as a major in universities, graduate program admissions were flooded with psychology applicants. Most of these potential students wanted clinical training and many had ambitions to enter private practice. Role models had become more available, particularly with the advent of professional schools in the 1970s. Private practitioners interested in the educational enterprise became adjunct professors at professional schools that were developing around the country and participated as supervisors of students in practicums and internships. As long as there were private practitioners visible to the students and supportive of them going into private practice, the students' dreams could become reality. By the 1990s the field seemed like a secure world. The profession thrived and was seen as prestigious. Many entered the field because they enjoyed the autonomy and wanted to be their own boss. They could be free to create the conditions of their work, provide the kind of therapy they decided was best for their patients including the frequency of contact, and set fees that met the client's needs as well as their own as psychologists.

How Does One Get Training in the Private Practice Modality?

Most graduate programs and professional schools offer very little in the nuts and bolts of (1) how to set up a practice; (2) how to choose a location (i.e., in your own home, in an office elsewhere, in a hospital); (3) how to market private practice—how to obtain referrals and become known in the community; (4) how to network; (5) what insurance is required; (6) what are the continuing education requirements in each particular state law; and (7) what organizations can be joined for contacts, support, and education (Cantor & Moldawsky, 1985). Most of this information is learned at workshops sponsored by state associations, Divisions of the American Psychological Association (APA) (e.g. Division of Independent Practice) and independent entrepreneurs. The literature on setting up a practice is sparse. However, there are some books listed in the Bibliography that can prove very useful, such as Morgenau (1990) and Heller (1997). Most psychologists, when first entering private practice, seek supervision for their cases, which not only helps them with the therapeutic process but provides guidance and modeling regarding the practical aspects of managing a practice.

Organizations and Structures That Support Private Practice

To support practice psychologists have needed licensure laws in every state. This required state psychological associations to learn how to get laws passed. With the help of the APA Committee on State Licensing, guidelines were written and state associations' legislative committees entered the world of the state legislature. Lobbying and developing support for licensure bills was one of the ways the profession established itself in the minds of the public. Freedom-of-choice laws followed licensure. These were laws that stated if an individual had insurance coverage for a mental condition, then licensed psychologists could be the practitioner of choice. Over the last 20 years, 45 states enacted such laws. It took 20 years of political action to be recognized under Medicare, the Federal Government's health support for the elderly. Throughout this period psychologists were becoming politically sophisticated and developing legislative committees in their state associations. These committees continue to function and remain vigilant in order to protect the gains achieved in law. No other part of psychology requires such vigilance as does private practice. A doctoral degree is the educational level required to practice psychology independently. Practicing psychologists have strong organizational support by the Practice Directorate of the American Psychological Association, The Association for the Advancement of Psychology (AAP), and Division 42 of the American Psychological Association. In return, private practitioners must support these efforts with dues, including a special assessment to the Practice Directorate of APA.

Private Practice in the "New Age" of Managed Care

Today, health-care insurance is primarily controlled by managed care subsidiaries. These large managed care companies determine the terms of reimbursing mental health treatment. Paperwork has increased for the practitioner. Typically, reimbursed sessions are limited to once a week for 6 to 10 visits. This has created a serious problem for those therapists who have been used to seeing their patients for multiple visits per week, as is customary in depth psychology. For the most part, these are psychologists who have been trained to use the therapeutic relationship (the relationship that develops between the therapist and the patient) as the matrix for healing.

As the cost containment pressure increased, the fees of practitioners have declined dramatically. In the past decade, mental health treatment has declined 54%. Autonomy has been dramatically curtailed and morale is very low. However, practitioners are free to determine whether they choose to depend on managed care referrals for all, part, or any of their practice. One can still set the conditions of one's work and charge a fee commensurate with one's experience and training. The marketplace has changed and specialty, "niche" practices have emerged. That is, psychologists have training in specific areas, such as eating disorders, alcoholism and substance abuse, or marital problems and the public is getting accustomed to seek services for specific problems.

Carleton (1998) recently reported that the impact of managed care has been felt in graduate programs, as they now emphasize short-term models of treatment. Many psychologists oppose the modification of training to suit the economic climate and believe that students should be trained in the full breadth of psychological modalities.

Recently, bills have been submitted to the U.S. Congress to provide greater patient protection legislation (such as the right to sue the HMO and hold them accountable for denial of treatment).

Developing an established practice takes about 5 years. Many referrals come from former clients so time is needed to create satisfied clients who will recommend you to others (Moldawsky, 1990).

Despite today's complexities, private practice is still an allure for many psychologists who have learned and can learn how to survive in the marketplace. The rewards are more than financial. They are the pleasures of doing the work as one has been trained in making clinical determinations about treatment, seeing patients improve, and contributing to society's welfare in a respected and worthwhile profession.

[*See also* Careers in Psychology.]

Bibliography

Cantor, D. W., & Moldawsky, S. (1985). Training for independent practice: A survey of graduate programs in clinical psychology. *Professional Psychology: Research and Practice, 16*(6), 768–772.

Carleton, E. K. (1998). An examination of doctoral level psychotherapy in light of the proliferation of managed care. *Professional Psychology: Research and Practice, 29* (3), 304–306.

Freudenberger, H. (1985). How to market ourselves in the future. *Psychotherapy in Private Practice* 3(3), 33–37.

Goldman, G. D. (1972). The establishment of a private practice. In G. D. Goldman & G. Stricker (Eds.). *Practical problems of a private psychotherapy practice* (pp. 3–27). Springfield, IL: Charles C. Thomas.

Heller, Kalman M. (1997). *Strategic marketing: How to achieve independence and prosperity in your mental health practice.* Sarasota, FL: Professional Resource Press.

Moldawsky, S. (1990). Is solo practice dead? *American Psychologist, 45*(4), 544–546.

Morgenau, E. A. (1990). *The encyclopedic handbook of private practice.* New York: Gardener Press.

Pressman, Robert H. (1979). *Private practice: A handbook on the independent mental health practitioner.* New York: Gardener Press.

Shinberg, E. (1997). *Handbook of private practice in psychology.* New York: Brunner/Mazel.

Stanley Moldawsky

PROACTIVE INHIBITION. *See* Forgetting.

PROBABILITY. *See* Statistical Significance.

PROBLEM SOLVING. *See* Thinking, *article on* Problem Solving.

PRODIGIES. The term *prodigy* usually refers to an individual who has made an unusually good start in life and displays exceptional capabilities while still a child. Apart from the fact that prodigies are intriguing in their own right, these young men and women are interesting because their unusual early progress can shed light on the circumstances in which people become capable of impressive achievements. In particular, the fact that many adult geniuses were prodigies as children prompts the question of whether precocious development is an essential forerunner of exceptional levels of expertise in maturity.

A complicating factor is that deciding whether or not a child is a prodigy is not as easy is it might appear to be. One problem is that is difficult to make comparisons across different domains of knowledge or skill. Hence, faced with a remarkable violinist aged 9 and an outstanding 10-year-old mathematician, there is no objective way of deciding which of them is more exceptional, or of knowing whether or not either or both of them should be described as a child prodigy.

A further barrier to objectively categorizing individuals as prodigies and nonprodigies arises from the fact that there is a less than perfect relationship between the extent to which a child's attainments are indeed exceptional and the likelihood of adults becoming aware of those attainments, and consequently deciding to call the child a prodigy. The main reason for this is simply that different kinds of capabilities vary greatly in the extent to which they are likely to be noticed and remarked upon. If the activity in which a child excels takes the form of performance at a musical instrument, a sport such as tennis, or chess, it is almost certain that, so long as the child's abilities are genuinely exceptional, that will come to the attention of teachers or other adults. But if the child's field of expertise is not one in which outstanding accomplishments are so readily displayed, the likelihood of the child's special attainments being noticed will be considerably smaller.

Consequently, while a substantial number of young people who excel as performers, such as musicians like Mozart, have been widely acknowledged to be child prodigies, the equally rare skills of a young scientist or a child whose precocity takes the form of superior philosophical understanding have often gone unnoticed. For instance, although Einstein already possessed a remarkably precocious understanding of science in childhood, he was not regarded at the time as being a prodigy. There is every reason to believe that many children who have not been regarded as prodigies have been just as exceptional as other children who were described as prodigies. Undoubtedly, then, the fact that a particular child has or has not been described as a prodigy is a very imprecise indication of the extent of the young person's actual exceptionality.

Is it necessary to have been a child prodigy (recognized as such or otherwise) in order to become an exceptionally able adult? The fact that many geniuses and exceptionally creative individuals had already been extraordinarily competent while they were still children suggests that it might be. Yet it only takes one exception to disprove the rule. Charles Darwin is such an exception. Darwin is one of the most universally acknowledged geniuses of all time, and his childhood progress has been traced in considerable detail, but he was definitely no child prodigy. He seems to have been a conscientious child, but despite the fact that he enjoyed a caring and supportive family background his early progress was in no respect other than average.

If being a child prodigy is not an indispensable precursor to excellence in maturity, is it nevertheless advantageous? In some fields of expertise it definitely is, for a variety of practical reasons. Making exceptionally good early progress does not guarantee that someone will make major achievements, but it can help to make that possible. This is especially likely in those fields of expertise in which reaching high levels of accomplishment necessitates undergoing the lengthy and concentrated training required for acquiring the knowledge and skills that an individual needs to draw upon. Thus, in many sports and in the performing arts, and also in mathematics and the sciences, it is unusual for someone to become an exceptionally successful adult without having been a prodigy or near-prodigy during childhood. However, in fields of expertise in which adult proficiency is less closely depended upon the possession of a particular body of knowledge or skills, it is less common for the most successful practitioners to have been child prodigies. Relatively few statesmen and politicians, for instance, have been prodigies during their childhoods.

The majority of child prodigies have come from stable and supportive home backgrounds, and in many instances a parent has taken considerable pains to provide the child with exceptional educational opportunities at an early age. That is true of Mozart and other famous prodigies, such as John Stuart Mill. Studies of the early lives of capable young musicians have shown that the vast majority have received considerable help and support from their parents. Cases of children who have been prodigies without having been given much help by parents or other adults are fairly rare. However, they are not entirely unknown, even if the "rags to riches" stories that are sometimes to be encountered in the autobiographical accounts of famous people are often inaccurate. The scientist Michael Faraday is an example of a person who fits reasonably comfortably into the prodigy category despite coming from a very poor family and leaving school early. In the past, demonstrating signs of excellence in childhood was a way of enabling a child from a poor background to be brought to the attention of wealthy individuals who were prepared to finance the child's education. John Stuart Mill's father, James Mill, is one example of a bright young man who benefited from that kind of sponsorship and was consequently able to enjoy a glittering adult career.

[*See also* Giftedness; *and* Talent.]

Bibliography

Csikszentmihalyi, M., Rathunde, K., & Whalen, S. (1993). *Talented teenagers: The roots of success and failure.* Cambridge, England: Cambridge University Press.

Feldman, D. H. (1986). *Nature's gambit: Child prodigies and the development of human potential.* New York: Basic Books.

Howe, M. J. A. (1990). *The origins of exceptional abilities.* Oxford, England: Blackwell.

Radford, J. (1990). *Child prodigies and exceptional early achievers.* London: Harvester Wheatsheaf.

Winner, E. (1996). *Gifted children: Myths and realities.* New York: Basic Books.

Michael J. A. Howe

PROFESSIONAL CONSULTATION. A psychologist observes the day-to-day activities at an elementary school and meets regularly with the principal to discuss the academic achievement of specific students. The psychologist tries to understand academic achievement from the perspective of the principal, teachers, parents, and students while also taking into account the culture and history of the school. The psychologist learns that parental involvement in the school has been declining over the last several years and that the school's curriculum is outdated. The psychologist works with the principal on mutually agreed goals to increase parental involvement and to obtain additional financial resources to acquire instructional materials. In addition, the consultant aids in the creation of social environmental resources, such as mentors and curriculum materials that would improve the school's issues. The psychologist does this work with the goal to improve the functioning of the entire school, including custodians, secretaries, students, teachers, and parents. This psychologist is carrying out mental health consultation.

Consultation has several different meanings. Consultation can refer to technical or professional advice offered about a specific person, situation, or organizational issue. Consultation can also be an intervention strategy to improve the quality of the work environment. Consultants can be psychologists, social workers, psychiatrists, or other specialists. The people for whom they consult are referred to as consultees. Consultants are directive and provide insights or information that can make a difference to consultees in how they think and what they can do to change a troublesome situation. Consultants do not usually focus on intrapsychic or personal issues, which are the focus of the therapist. In contrast to supervisors, consultants do not have direct responsibility over the consultee. Consultants usually attend to a specific topic about a particular situation at one point in time. Consultation may focus on the elements of a specific program, the administration of the program, or issues of individual consultees.

Recently, as the opening example states, consultation has emphasized not only the consultee but the larger setting in which the consultee works or resides. This type of consultation focuses on the relationship of the consultees with their co-workers and requires an assessment of the total organization and its multiple levels and subunits. This approach is anchored in a public health philosophy; the aim is to help the largest number of people through working with only a few people.

This public health approach to consultation was developed by Erich Lindemann and Gerald Caplan beginning in the late 1940s. Mental health consultation occurred originally with classroom teachers, public health and hospital nurses, pediatricians, and welfare workers. Unlike traditional mental health intervention strategies such as psychotherapy, mental health consultation focused on helping the consultee cope with issues in their work environment. The relationship of the consultant and the consultee was the means to achieve this aim. This earlier approach to consultation is referred to as a psychodynamic approach. The work conducted by early consultants demonstrated that changing how individuals respond to their work environment is a valid and important method or route to improve the mental health of individuals. In effect, consultation has helped to bridge clinical practice with organizational practice to create a supportive social environment.

During the past 50 years, consultation interventions have expanded. Consultees now include nonprofit organizations, child-care providers, police departments, nursing homes, public aid departments, juvenile correctional facilities, prisons, hospitals for the mentally ill, community mental health centers, and industrial settings.

Today, there are behavioral, cognitive-behavioral, organizational, and ecological approaches to consultation. Behavioral consultation relies on behavioral technology principles. For example, a consultant might help a teacher understand how children's behaviors are shaped and maintained in a classroom environment. The teacher may then be able to change the classroom environment so that the behavior of individual children is improved. One of the biggest contributions of behavioral consultation is that it provides a technology to evaluate the efficacy of consultation. A cognitive-behavioral approach is similar to that of a behavioral approach. It focuses on how people's thoughts or cognitions contribute to feelings and behavior.

Organizational consulting uses behavioral science concepts to help organizations study and improve themselves. This method follows a systems assessment of the consultee's organization. The goal of organizational consulting often includes improving the quality of life of the organization and thereby enhancing the functioning of all individuals. The organizational approach emphasizes the relationship between formal and informal social norms in the organization and how these standards of behavior help or hinder the functioning of the organization. This approach assumes that qualities of the organization create the basis for satisfaction and productivity for all its members.

An ecological approach is based on a similar idea that the consultant is aware of how the people in the consultee's setting create and use personal, organizational, and community resources. The aim of the ecological approach is similar to the organizational approach: to improve the capacity of the organization to become a satisfying, nurturing, and productive setting. The multiple facets and features of the specific consultee's setting are the foci of ecological consultation. The consultant creates recommendations that relate directly to all levels and parts of the organization. The ecological perspective aims to enhance the interdependence of individuals and the various organizational subunits. The premise of this approach is that a healthy environment depends upon a dynamic interplay between the personal and environmental resources in that environment.

The practice of consultation rarely follows any one of these methods. Consultants may rely on techniques or strategies from two or more approaches to consultation. For example, a consultant who is working with a principal of a school to improve classroom behavior may follow a behavioral consultation model. The same consultant, however, may rely on a psychodynamic approach when the principal discusses his own reactions to particular students or teachers or an ecological approach when working to improve the total school environment and its relationship to the larger school system or community.

Consulting requires unique skills and knowledge. The content of training programs tends to vary depending on the approach of consultation. There are three predominant models of training. First, consultee-centered approaches focus on gaining skills such as: (1) building and maintaining relationships with consultees, (2) understanding the clients of the consultee, (3) detecting emotional reactions that may be interfering with the consultee's working relationship with clients, (4) collaborating with the consultee, and (5) understanding the context in which the consultee works.

Second, training in behavioral approaches is based on the idea that behavior is learned and that it can be altered by changing different aspects of the environment that can reinforce positive behavior. Training in behavioral consultation is focused on teaching consultants to identify existing relationships between consultee behavior and the social environment and then develop interventions to address the persons' relationship to the environment. Trainees gain an understanding of learning theory and specific techniques of behavior change.

Third, training in organizational and ecological approaches both emphasize the ability to understand organizational functioning and then develop interventions that lead to systemic change. These interventions are aimed to improve both the total organization and the functioning of its various subparts and individuals. Trainees learn organizational theories and principles. They also learn social system assessment and intervention skills as well as evaluation and research skills to assess the effectiveness of their consultation efforts. All of the above training approaches help consultants develop the ability to translate social science concepts so that these concepts are useful and understandable to consultees.

The field of mental health consultation has grown and developed substantially. Consultation has become an important way of using knowledge from the mental health professions and organizational and community psychology to improve the qualities and functioning of schools, communities, and a variety of organizations. Consultation stands out among psychotherapy and many mental health interventions in that it involves fewer mental health professionals to facilitate positive changes. As the various consultation methods continue to evolve, greater attention is being given to topics like the effectiveness of consultation as a preventive strategy, the effects that consultants have on consultees, and the degree of satisfaction of clients who work, live, or are a part of the organization where consultation has been provided.

Bibliography

Bergan, J. R., & Kratochwill, T. R. (1990). *Behavioral consultation & therapy.* New York: Plenum Press.

Caplan, G. (1964). *Principles of preventive psychiatry.* London: Basic Books.

Cooper, S., & Hodges, W. F. (Eds.). (1983). *The mental health consultation field.* New York: Human Sciences Press.

Erchul, W. P. (Ed.). (1993). *Consultation in community, school, and organizational practice: Gerald Caplan's contribution to professional psychology.* Washington, DC: Taylor & Francis.

Kratochwill, T. R., & Bergan, J. R. (1990). *Behavioral consultation in applied settings: An individual guide.* New York: Plenum Press.

Kelly, J. G., & Hess, R. E. (1987). *The ecology of prevention: Illustrating mental health consultation.* New York: Haworth Press.

U.S. Department of Health and Human Services. (1986). *Handbook of mental health consultation.* (No. 86-1446). Rockville, Maryland: Author.

Wilson, C. D., & Lubin, B. (1997). *Research on professional consultation and consultation for organizational change.* Westport, CT: Greenwood Press.

Alison B. Miller and James G. Kelly

PROFESSIONAL EDUCATION. *See* Technical and Professional Education.

PROFESSIONAL ORGANIZATIONS. There are hundreds of psychological organizations, ranging from international associations that represent psychologists all over the world to groups that may represent psychologists in a single city, or small geographical area. In addition, there are national and international organizations devoted to specific areas of interest in research, practice, or social issues, credentialing and licensing organizations, psychology student groups and interdisciplinary organizations involving psychology. This article presents a taxonomy of professional psychological organizations.

International Congresses

Before there were international or even national psychology organizations, international congresses were held to bring together scholars with a common interest in the new discipline. The first such congress took place in Paris in 1889, and, except during the two world wars, congresses have been held every 3 to 5 years. Since 1951, the International Congress of Psychology (ICP) has been organized under the auspices of the International Union of Psychological Sciences (IUPsyS), and since 1972 they have been held every 4 years.

The International Association of Applied Psychology has organized the International Congress of Applied Psychology (ICAP) since 1920. ICAPs are currently held every 4 years, 2 years after the preceding ICP, so there is a congress every 2 years.

In addition to these major world congresses, a great many other international psychology meetings are held each year, some under the sponsorship of an international organization and others organized on an ad hoc basis.

International Organizations: General

Three associations broadly represent psychology throughout the world.

The International Union of Psychological Sciences (IUPsyS). Since its establishment in 1951, IUPsyS has been the major representative of scientific psychology. IUPsyS is one of 25 unions representing different scientific disciplines, each of which is an organization composed of national member organizations, not more than one national member organization per country. As of 1999, IUPsyS represented approximately 60 national members, which in turn represented most of the 500,000 or so psychologists around the world. In addition to sponsoring the International Congress of Psychology every 4 years, IUPsyS publishes *The International Journal of Psychology* and facilitates communication among its national members.

International Association of Applied Psychology (IAAP). IAAP, which has individual members in 70 countries, was established in 1920 to represent the interests of applied psychologists. IAAP has 13 membership divisions reflecting its members' diverse interests, ranging from organizational psychology to traffic psychology. In addition to sponsoring the International Congress of Applied Psychology every 4 years, IAAP publishes the *International Journal of Applied Psychology* and cooperates with other international groups to promote applied psychology.

International Council of Psychologists (ICP). ICP, the successor organization to the National Council of Women Psychologists, in 1999 had members in over 80 countries. ICP sponsors annual meetings, usually in the summer and usually geographically close to the annual meeting of the American Psychological Association. ICP publishes a newsletter and a journal, *World Psychology*, and has consulting status at the United Nations, where it is one of several organizations working on issues important to psychologists.

International Associations: Regional

The European Federation of Professional Psychology Associations and the Interamerican Society of Psychology are the two major regional psychological associations that hold regular conventions in years when neither IUPsyS nor IAAP are holding their congresses. In addition, IAAP and IUPsyS jointly sponsor regional congresses on a periodic basis, usually in developing areas of the world.

European Federation of Professional Psychology Associations (EFPPA). EFPPA was established in 1981 to represent professional psychological organizations in the European countries. EFPPA currently has 28 member organizations. EFPPA sponsors a periodic newsletter and has sponsored the European Congress of Psychology in alternate years since 1989.

Interamerican Society of Psychology (SIP). SIP is an association of approximately 1,000 individual members in North, South, and Central America. SIP has held meetings in alternate years since the early 1950s.

Other Regional Meetings. Since 1995, regional congresses of psychology have been held, primarily in developing areas of the world, under the cosponsorship of IUPsyS and IAAP. These congresses usually do not involve permanent regional organizations: rather, they are organized primarily by the host country, and most participants come from the surrounding region, although psychologists from other regions are welcome to register and attend. Regional congresses have been held in Ghuangzhou, China (1995) and Mexico City (1997).

International Associations: Specialized

There are a great many international organizations that represent psychologists who are interested in specific areas of research or practice. Ten international organizations are affiliated with IUPsyS. In addition, there are at least 65 others, and probably more. There are also at least 30 specialized organizations that primarily focus on members in a particular region, such as Europe or the Asian South Pacific.

National Associations: General

Several national associations were established around the turn of the century and by 1925 eight associations had been established in the United States, France, United Kingdom, Germany, Argentina, Italy, China, and India. By 1998, nearly 60 national associations had been recognized by IUPsyS, and there were national associations in at least 15 other countries.

The United States. The American Psychological Association (APA), established in 1892, was the first national association. It remains the largest and is arguably the most complex of the national associations. In 1998, APA had 155,000 members and affiliates, including 87,000 members, fellows, and associate members, and 68,000 affiliate members, including students, high school teachers, and international affiliates. Most psychologists in the United States are members of APA (75% of an estimated 106,000 doctoral-level psychologists). APA's structure includes 50 divisions ranging in size from 283 to 7,000 members. All APA members are eligible to be division members, and some belong to several. Divisions have their own officers, newsletters, and sometimes journals; some have offices and staff. Some are independently incorporated.

APA's affiliate organizations include 58 independent psychological associations in 50 states and 5 Canadian provinces plus the District of Columbia, Puerto Rico, and the Virgin Islands. These associations are separately incorporated and, like the divisions, have their own officers and administrative structure. They range in size from 25 to 6,000 members. The primary governing body of APA, the Council of Representatives, includes representatives from the divisions and from the state and provincial associations (SPPAs). Seven regional psychological associations, representing the geographical regions of the country, are also affiliated with APA. With 1,700 Canadian members, 1,000 members residing in other countries, and 3,500 international affiliates, APA functions as an international as well as a national psychological organization.

Other U.S. Associations. Most large cities in the United States have local associations. Also, there are associations that are primarily academic, applied, or public interest in membership as well as organizations set up to perform specific functions such as credentialing, licensing, or coordinating education and training.

Academic. The largest of the academically oriented associations is the American Psychological Society (APS) with approximately 16,000 members and student members. APS, which was established by some APA members who disagreed with a decision by the APA membership not to reorganize into a federation, maintains a substantial membership overlap with APA. APS holds an annual convention and publishes a newsletter and two journals. Other associations that primarily attract academic psychologists include the Psychonomic Society, the Psychometric Society, the Society of Experimental Psychologists, and the Society for Multivariate Experimental Psychology. Several national groups focus on education and training, including the Council of Graduate Departments of Psychology, the National Council of Schools of Professional Psychology, the Council of Undergraduate Psychology Programs, the Council of Training Directors, and the Association for Psychology and Postdoctoral Internship Centers.

The major honorary society for psychology students is Psi Chi, the National Honor Society in Psychology, founded in 1929 for the purposes of encouraging, stimulating, and maintaining excellence in scholarship, and advancing the science of psychology. Membership is open to graduate and undergraduate men and women who are making the study of psychology one of their major interests and who meet the minimum qualifications. Psi Chi is a member of the Association of College

Honor Societies and is an affiliate of the American Psychological Association (APA) and the American Psychological Society (APS). Psi Chi's sister honor society is Psi Beta, the national honor society in psychology for community and junior colleges.

The American Psychological Association of Graduate Students (APAGS) has seen a significant increase in its membership numbers. Graduate students who are APA student affiliates automatically become members of APAGS and undergraduate students are also eligible for membership. Begun in 1988 with 18,000 students, the group grew to over 41,000 student affiliate members by 1999.

APAGS was established to promote the highest standards in the research, teaching, and practice of psychology in order to further the education and development of all students involved in the study of psychology; to represent all graduate study specialties of psychology and facilitate exchange of information between these groups; to promote graduate student leadership development in order to communicate and advocate the concerns of graduate students; and to establish and maintain channels of communication between APAGS and schools, universities, training centers, institutions, and other members of the psychological community.

Applied. Associations that focus on the application or practice of psychology include the National Association of School Psychologists, Association of Applied Social Psychologists, American Association of Correctional Psychologists, American Academy of Forensic Psychologists, the National Organization of VA Psychologists (NOVA Psi), the Society for Psychologists in Management, and many others.

Public Interest. Associations that focus on social issues and public policy include Psychologists for Social Responsibility, Association of Women in Psychology, and Association of Lesbian and Gay Psychologists. In addition, there are several national ethnic minority psychological associations such as the Association of Black Psychologists, Asian American Psychological Association, the Society of Indian Psychologists, and the National Hispanic Psychological Association.

Credentialing and Licensing Organizations. The American Association of State and Provincial Licensing Boards, the American Board of Professional Psychology, and the National Register of Health Service Providers in Psychology assist psychologists by verifying their credentials.

Other National Associations. There were estimated to be over 500,000 psychologists worldwide in 1992 (using local definitions, usually nondoctoral for most countries other than the United States and Canada). These are unevenly distributed, with the majority in the industrialized nations. Some countries have several national associations. IUPsyS recognizes only one member organization in each country, although that may be a national academy of sciences that coordinates more than one organization. In 1999, approximately 60 countries were members of IUPsyS. Some national associations are well developed, with full-time staff, publications, and a full range of membership activities; others, primarily staffed by volunteers, have limited resources and activities.

Interdisciplinary Associations

Many psychologists participate in national and international organizations that are psychology related and include members of other disciplines. National associations include the American Orthopsychological Association, Cognitive Sciences Society, Society for Neurosciences, American Educational Research Association, American Association for the Advancement of Science, Association for Behavior Analysis, Acoustical Society of America, Society for the Exploration of Psychotherapy Integration, and Society for Psychotherapy Research. International groups include the World Federation for Mental Health, the International Society for Research on Aggression, the International Society for Research on Emotion, and the International Association for Clinical and Experimental Hypnosis.

[*Many associations, institutions, and organizations are the subjects of independent entries.*]

Raymond D. Fowler

PROJECTIVE TECHNIQUES. The term *projective techniques* designates several assessment procedures that usually consist of a fixed series of relatively ambiguous stimuli designed to elicit unique, sometimes highly idiosyncratic, responses. Individuals are presented with a standard set of ambiguous and evocative stimuli in a relatively unstructured context and are asked to respond to these stimuli. Responses are recorded verbatim and evaluated by a trained clinician or judge. Typical of this type of assessment procedure are the Rorschach inkblots, the social-interpersonal pictures of the Thematic Apperception Test (TAT), and various versions of the Sentence Completion and Word Association tests. These procedures have provoked a great deal of controversy; opinions range from the belief that personality assessment is incomplete without data from at least one or more of these projective procedures to the view that these techniques lack reliability and validity and that interpretations of personality organization and functioning derived from these procedures are no better than reading tea leaves. [*See* Rorschach Test; Thematic Aperception Test; *and the biography of Rorschach*].

The term projective techniques, derived from an imprecise use of the psychoanalytic concept of projection, was initially based on the assumption that individuals "project" aspects of their personalities into their responses to these ambiguous, sometimes provocative stimuli—that the content (themes) of the responses reflect an individual's basic concerns and preoccupations, and thus, directly reveal important aspects of personality organization and functioning. In more contemporary usage, projective techniques are viewed as procedures that evoke a reasonably consistent sample of an individual's cognitive processes, especially representational capacities (i.e., mental representations of self, others, and of their actual potential relationships), so that clinicians and investigators can observe the processes through which an individual constructs meaning in relatively unstructured and ambiguous circumstances (Blatt, 1990; Leichtman, 1996). The use of a well-defined series of ambiguous stimuli creates an experimental context for observing aspects of an individual's thought processes: the relative accuracy, content, organization, structure, affective tone, and the sequence of responses, as well as the individual's style of verbalization, and his attitudes toward his responses and the interpersonal relationship he establishes with the examiner. Thus, projective techniques provide a wide range of observations of how an individual responds to ambiguity, with the assumption that careful observations of these responses can provide valuable data for understanding the complexities of an individual's cognitive, perceptual, motivational, affective, and interpersonal functioning.

Projective techniques, in important respects, are very different from personality inventories, like the Minnesota Multiphasic Personality Inventory (MMPI), which usually present well-structured, focused questions to which individuals respond either true or false or, using a fixed (e.g., 5-point) scale, indicate the extent to which each item is like or unlike them. Although investigators can assess with relative ease the reliability and the validity of these more structured personality inventories, it is much more difficult to apply psychometric procedures to projective techniques because of the unique, multidimensional, and complex ways individuals respond to the ambiguous and provocative stimuli. Thus, projective techniques are not a test in the usual sense, but are instead more accurately viewed as quasi-experimental procedures in which responses to ambiguous, but standard, stimuli under relatively unstructured instructions enable us to evaluate, in considerable detail, aspects of the structural organization and thematic content of an individual's thought processes. Responses given to these ambiguous stimuli under unstructured circumstances are usually complex verbal statements that can range from the relatively conventional to the highly idiosyncratic. Thus, responses to projective techniques can provide the opportunity to study the content and organization of cognitive processes in ways that may not be available through many other procedures. Much of the value of these projective procedures resides, however, not in the procedures themselves but in the conceptual model(s) with which the clinician and investigator approaches the responses, as well as in his or her skill in understanding the implications of the complex interactions among the perceptual, cognitive, affective, and interpersonal processes that entered into the construction of the responses. Thus, one can not assess directly the reliability and validity of these assessment procedures; any assessment of projective techniques must include an appraisal of the clinician and investigator and the evaluation procedures and asumptions used to assess the complex, open-ended responses given to these evocative stimuli. It is inappropriate, therefore, to conclude that the Rorschach, the TAT, the Sentence Completion, or Word Association procedures, per se, are reliable or unreliable, valid or invalid. Reliability and validity depends on which projective assessment procedure is being used, by whom, with what scoring or conceptual system, and for what purpose.

Substantial changes have occurred over the years in the theoretical models used to assess responses to projective techniques. It is important to note that most of the assessment procedures considered as projective techniques were developed during the first half of the twentieth century. The inkblots were established by Hermann Rorschach in 1921, the TAT by Morgan and Murray in 1935, and a variety of sentence completion and other associational procedures have been developed, initially beginning with Galton in 1879 and 1883 and by Jung in 1910. Many of the methods for assessing responses to these various procedures were also developed early in this century on the basis primarily of a drive theory conception of personality organization or on psychological theories of sensation and perception that were dominant in psychology in the first half of the twentieth century. Much of the criticism of projective techniques has focused on the clinical research application of projective techniques that used these very early evaluation procedures. Even the procedure predominant today for scoring Rorschach responses, the Comprehensive System developed by John Exner, is essentially an amalgam of various scoring systems developed from 1920 to 1950.

During the early part of the twentieth century, the primary foci in psychological discourse and investigation was sensation, perception, and the careful observation of behavioral responses and their manifest stimulus antecedents. Cognitive processes and the mind were considered unavailable for scientific study; cognitive processes were viewed as unobservable subjective experiences that occurred in what was called at that time, the mysterious impenetrable "black box." The mental processes that linked stimulus input to behavioral response were considered beyond the realm of scientific inquiry. Psychology was predominantly a behavioral science and the basic unit of analysis was the unit of stimulus-response, with little attention given to the processes that mediated stimulus input and behavioral response. In addition, the primary motivational force in both learning theory and psychoanalysis was essentially hedonic—drive dominated—with little consideration given to the interpersonal field and concepts of self and of others. Thus, the theoretical models available in psychology for personality assessment with projective methods in those early years were either theories of perception, units of stimulus-response, the hedonic (drive or instinct) models of learning theory and early psychoanalysis, or the psychiatric view that psychological disturbances were biological diseases rather than disruptions of normal psychological development (Blatt, 1990).

In the mid-1950s, psychologists (e.g., Osgood, 1953) began to consider the processes within the "black box" that might be mediating the links between stimulus input and behavioral response. With the cognitive revolution (Gardner, 1985) beginning around 1960, psychologists became increasingly interested in cognitive processes and issues of mental representation—the processes that create organization and establish meaning for the basic information provided by perception. Psychologists began to investigate how cognitive structures are established as schemas (Bartlett, 1932; Neisser, 1967, 1976; Piaget, 1937/1954, 1945/1962, 1926/1963), plans (Miller, Galanter, & Pribram, 1960), prototypes or templates (Fiske & Taylor, 1984), scripts (Shank & Abelson, 1977), scenes (Tomkins, 1979), and expectancies (Feather, 1966), and how these cognitive structures guide and influence experience and behavior. Consistent with the emphasis on structuralism and semeiotics as a basic conceptual model in many other disciplines in the second half of the twentieth century, the emphasis on representational processes has extended psychology from a science of behavior to a cognitive science concerned with the construction of meaning. This emphasis on representation and the construction of meaning began to dominate many areas of psychology including developmental and social psychology, and led to the emergence of cognitive psychology as a major new area within the discipline. Psychological science also increasingly came to appreciate that basic cognitive structures often emerge, develop, and are expressed in the intimacy of interpersonal relationships.

The cognitive revolution—the emphasis of representational processes and the construction of meaning—has not only reshaped many areas of psychology (i.e., developmental, social, cognitive, and clinical), but has begun to have a major impact on personality assessment, especially on the use of projective techniques. The Rorschach, for example, is no longer considered just a "test of perception" (e.g., Beck, Exner, Rorschach) from which one can infer behavioral tendencies, but is viewed as an experimental procedure that presents an individual with ambiguity and allows for the systematic investigation of how an individual constructs meaning in well-specified but relatively ambiguous conditions. Thus, projective techniques have increasingly been viewed as procedures for assessing cognition as well as perception, for assessing the construction of meaning, and for understanding the relativism of individual cognitive constructions and how they relate to important individual differences (Blatt, 1990; Leichtman, 1996).

This representational approach to projective techniques requires a fuller understanding of personality development and psychopathology, an understanding beyond viewing human functioning as a learned behavioral response or a cluster of manifest symptoms. A constructivist approach to projective techniques requires a conception of psychopathology that is more than a series of descriptive taxonomies based on an atheoretical categorization of manifest symptoms, as in the diagnostic and statistical manuals (*DSM*) of the American Psychiatric Association. This new approach to personality development and disturbance, articulated primarily by psychologists with a psychoanalytic orientation, requires a conceptualization of psychological development throughout the life cycle and how severe and sustained disruptions of normal developmental processes can lead to various forms of psychopathology that involve differential impairments in basic cognitive structures and disruptions of interpersonal relationships (e.g., Blatt, 1991, 1995; Rapaport, Gill, & Schafer, 1945; Schafer, 1954).

Thus, it should come as little surprise that, since 1960, research and clinical use of projective techniques has been increasingly influenced by the cognitive revolution in psychology. Jane Loevinger (Loevinger, 1979), for example, used a theoretical model of ego development to develop a system for evaluating a sentence completion test and demonstrated the validity of this sentence completion procedure in a wide range of investigations of psychological development. Several research teams (e.g., Westen, Klepser, Ruffins, Silverman, Lifton, & Boekamp, 1991) used psychoanalytic object-relations theory to construct a new approach to the TAT. And several investigators independently approached the Rorschach as a method for evaluating cognitive-affective processes. Robert Holt (Holt, 1977) used fundamental psychoanalytic formulations of two basic types of mental activity to develop an extensive methodology for evaluating primary and secondary process thinking, and Blatt and Ritzler (1974) investigated various forms of thought disorder on the Rorschach, as disturbances of the capacity to establish and maintain cognitive-affective and interpersonal boundaries. Several groups of investigators developed methods for analyzing the Rorschach, as well as responses to other projective procedures, from a psychoanalytic object relations perspective. They studied the relationship of personality organization to an individual's concepts of self and other and their actual and potential interactions. Mayman and colleagues (e.g., Mayman, 1967; Urist, 1977), for example, investigated object representation from the perspective of psychoanalytic psychosexual theory and a theory of ego states, and Blatt and colleagues (e.g., Blatt, Brenneis, Schimek, & Glick, 1976) integrated the cognitive developmental theories of Piaget and Werner with aspects of developmental psychoanalytic theory to study the differentiation, articulation, and integration of the concept of the object on the Rorschach, as well as in spontaneous descriptions of significant (e.g., mother and father) others (e.g., Blatt, Chevron, Quinlan, Schaffer, & Wein, 1988) and of the self (Bers, Blatt, Sayward, & Johnson, 1993). Coonerty (1986) developed a method for evaluating Rorschach responses for themes of separation-individuation derived from the developmental theoretical model proposed by Margaret Mahler; Cooper and colleagues (e.g., Cooper, Perry, Hoke, & Richman, 1985) developed a procedure for evaluating Rorschach responses in terms of Winnicott's theories of transitional phenomena; Burke and colleagues (e.g., Burke, Friedman, & Gorlitz, 1988) applied a psychoanalytic theory of the development of object relations, from symbiosis to individuation, to the analysis of Rorschach responses; and several research groups have developed methods for assessing the type and quality of psychological defenses on the Rorschach (e.g., Cooper, Perry, & Arnow, 1988; Lerner & Lerner, 1982) and on the TAT (e.g., Cramer, 1991). Cramer (1996) and Leigh, Westen, Barends, and Mendel (1992) also demonstrated the value of interpreting responses to the TAT in terms of complex narrative structures.

These approaches to the interpretation of responses given to projective procedures are based on the articulation of sophisticated theoretical models of personality development and psychopathology that focus on the unfolding of various levels of psychological organization throughout the life cycle and view the various forms of psychopathology as disruptions of these normal developmental processes. These approaches place particular emphasis on the cognitive-affective structures that emerge from, and in turn, impact on interpersonal relationships throughout life, especially concepts of self and others. Thus the revolution that has occurred in psychology in the last half of the twentieth century, and has transformed psychology from a science of behavior to a science of cognitive and representational structures, has also created new and creative ways of approaching responses to projective techniques. This approach has had considerable impact on clinical research and clinical practice. A wide range of research has derived from this approach. Theoretically based differentiations of responses to projective procedures that are related to carefully specified and well-controlled criteria have resulted in considerable support for the reliability and validity of these approaches to projective procedures (Blatt, 1975; Blatt & Berman, 1984).

These developments in psychological science and these new approaches to the evaluation of responses to projective techniques have also enriched the role of projective techniques in clinical practice. But it is important to emphasize that the skill of the clinician plays a central role in the use of projective techniques in clinical assessment, especially if the purpose of the assessment is more than just a search for an appropriate diagnostic label. Projective techniques, in combination with other assessment procedures, especially the Weschler Intelligence Test, can be invaluable in the assessment of the relative strengths and weaknesses of adaptive and defensive capacities—the processes and mechanisms the individual uses to cope with psychological conflicts and demands (Allison, Blatt, & Zimet, 1968). Projective techniques can provide observations that can enable the skillful clinician to understand how an individual integrates various levels of drive, defense, conflict, and adaptive capacities—the nature and extent of psychological conflicts, the hierarchical organization of defenses and their relative effectiveness, the capacity for reality testing and the modulation of affect, and the capacity for and the quality of interpersonal relationships. These approaches to projective techniques have also enabled us to assess an individual's self-representations as well as representations of emotionally significant aspects of his interpersonal world—wishes and fears about significant others and the ways an individual negotiates interpersonal conflict. These new approaches to projective techniques have demonstrated the potential that projective procedures can have in psychological assessment, especially assessment designed to explore more fully the fascinating complexities of the human mind.

Bibliography

Allison, J., Blatt, S. J., & Zimet, C. N. (1968). *The interpretation of psychological tests.* New York: Harper & Row.

Bartlett, F. C. (1932). *Remembering.* Cambridge: Cambridge University Press.

Bers, S. A., Blatt, S. J., Sayward, H., & Johnston, R. (1993). Normal and pathological aspects of self descriptions and their change over long-term treatment. *Psychoanalytic Psychology, 10,* 17–37

Blatt, S. J. (1975). The validity of projective techniques and their clinical contributions. *Journal of Personality Assessment, 39,* 327–343.

Blatt, S. J. (1990). The Rorschach: A test of perception or an evaluation of representation. *Journal of Personality Assessment, 54,* 236–251.

Blatt, S. J. (1991). A cognitive morphology of psychopathology. *Journal of Nervous and Mental Disease, 179,* 449–458.

Blatt, S. J. (1995). Representational structures in psychopathology. In D. Cicchetti & S. Toth (Eds.). *Rochester Symposium on Developmental Psychopathology: Vol. 6. Emotion, Cognition, and Representation* (pp. 1–33). Rochester, NY: University of Rochester Press.

Blatt, S. J., & Berman, W. H. (1984). A methodology for the use of the Rorschach in clinical research. *Journal of Personality Assessment, 48,* 226–239.

Blatt, S. J., Brenneis, C. B., Schimek, J. G., & Glick, M. (1976). The normal development and psychopathological impairment of the concept of the object on Rorschach. *Journal of Abnormal Psychology, 85,* 364–373.

Blatt, S. J., Chevron, E. S., Quinlan, D. M., Schaffer, C. E., & Wein, S. (1988). *The assessment of qualitative and structural dimensions of object representations* (Rev. ed.). Unpublished manuscript, Yale University at New Haven, CT.

Blatt, S. J., & Ritzler, B. A. (1974). Thought disorder and boundary disturbances in psychosis. *Journal of Consulting and Clinical Psychology, 42,* 370–381.

Burke, W. F., Friedman, G., & Gorlitz, P. (1988). The psychoanalytic Rorschach Profile: An integration of drive, ego, and object relations perspectives. *Psychoanalytic Psychology, 5,* 193–212.

Coonerty, S. (1986). An exploration of separation-individuation themes in borderline personality disorder. *Journal of Personality Assessment, 50,* 501–511.

Cooper, S. H., Perry, J. C., & Arnow, D. (1988). An empirical approach to the study of defense mechanisms: I. Reliability and preliminary validity of the Rorschach Defense Scales. *Journal of Personality Assessment, 52,* 187–203.

Cooper, S. H., Perry, J. C., Hoke, L., & Richman, N. (1985). Transitional relatedness and borderline personality disorders. *Psychoanalytic Psychology 2,* 115–128.

Cramer, P. (1991). *The development of defense mechanism: Theory, research, and assessment.* New York: Springer-Verlag.

Cramer, P. (1996). *Storytelling, narrative and the Thematic Apperception Test.* New York: Guilford Press.

Feather, N. T. (1966). Effects of prior success and failure on expectations by success and subsequent performance. *Journal of Personality and Social Psychology, 3,* 278–298.

Fiske, S. T., & Taylor, S. E. (1984). *Social cognition.* New York: Random House.

Gardner, H. (1985). *The mind's new science: A history of the cognitive revolution.* New York: Basic Books.

Holt, R. R. (1977). A method for assessing primary process manifestations and their control in Rorschach responses. In M. Rickers-Ovsiankina (Ed.), *Rorschach psychology* (pp. 375–420). Huntington, NY: Kreiger.

Leichtman, M. (1996). *The Rorschach: A developmental perspective.* Hillsdale, NJ: Analytic Press.

Leigh, J., Westen, D., Barends, A., & Mendel, M. (1992). The assessment of complexity of representations of people using the TAT and interview data. *Journal of Personality, 60,* 809–837.

Lerner, H. D., & Lerner, P. M. (1982). A comparative study of defensive structure in neurotic, borderline, and schizophrenic patients. *Psychoanalysis and Contemporary Thought, 5,* 77–115.

Loevinger, J. (1979). Construct validity of the Sentence Completion Test of Ego Development. *Applied Psychological Measurement, 3,* 281–311.

Mayman, M. (1967). Object-representations and object-relationships in Rorschach responses. *Journal of Projective Techniques and Personality Assessment, 31,* 17–24.

Miller, G., Galanter, E., & Primbram, K. (1960). *Plans and the structure of behavior.* New York: Holt, Rinehart, & Winston.

Morgan, C., & Murray, H. A. (1935). A method for investigating fantasies: The Thematic Apperception Test. *Archives of Neurological Psychiatry, 34,* 289–306.

Neisser, U. (1967). *Cognitive psychology.* New York: Appleton-Century-Crofts.

Neisser, U. (1976). *Cognition and reality.* San Francisco: Freeman.

Osgood, C. E. (1953). *Method and theory in experimental psychology.* New York: Oxford University Press.

Piaget, J. (1954). *The construction of reality in the child* (M. Cook, Trans.). New York: Basic Books. (Original work published 1937)

Piaget, J. (1962). *Play, dreams and imitation in childhood.* New York: Norton. (Original work published 1945)

Piaget, J. (1963). *The language and thought of the child* (M. Warden, Trans.). New York: Harcourt Brace. (Original work published 1926)

Rapaport, D., Gill, M. M., & Schafer, R. (1945–1946). *Diagnostic psychological testing* (Vols. 1–2). Chicago: Year Book.

Schafer, R. (1954). *Psychoanalytic interpretation in Rorschach testing.* New York: Grune & Stratton.

Shank, R. C., & Abelson, R. (1977). *Scripts, plans, goals and understanding.* Hillsdale, NJ: Erlbaum.

Tomkins, S. S. (1979). Script theory: Differential magnification of effects. In H. F. Howe & R. A. Dienstbier (Eds.), *Nebraska symposium on motivation, 1978* (Vol. 26). Lincoln: University of Nebraska.

Urist, J. (1977). The Rorschach test and the assessment of object relations. *Journal of Personality Assessment, 41,* 3–9.

Westen, D., Klepser, J., Ruffin, S. A., Silverman, M., Lifton, N., & Boekamp, J. (1991). Object relations in childhood and adolescence: The development of working representations. *Journal of Consulting and Clinical Psychology, 59,* 400–409.

Sidney J. Blatt

PROPAGANDA. The original use of the term *propaganda* referred to the concerted effort of the Roman Catholic Church to disseminate the true faith to Christians who had gone astray and to non-Christians who had never known it. The term acquired a pejorative meaning in this century when it was used by all modern states to mold public opinion in support of their policies. An early definition of propaganda referred to techniques for influencing human action by manipulating spoken, written, pictorial, or musical representations. This definition is unsatisfactory because it applies to all forms of communication, including education, persuasion, and advertising, none of which share propaganda's seedy reputation. Jowett and O'Donnell (1992) resolved this problem by highlighting the motives of the communicator. They defined propaganda as the deliberate, systematic attempt to shape perceptions, manipulate cognitions, and direct behavior to achieve a response that furthers only the intent of the propagandist. By contrast, education seeks to promote mutual understanding of all parties to the interaction, and persuasion to promote mutual fulfillment of their needs.

The Ubiquity of Propaganda

Propaganda is used more than ever before due to the increase in the number and diversity of target audiences and to technological advances that have enhanced the capacity to reach these audiences. Electronic media have made propaganda cheaper and potentially more effective than other social control techniques. There are as many kinds of propaganda as there are conflicts—religious, national, ethnic, social, and economic. It may be used at any time (e.g., before, during, and after war) to define, redefine, or construct new social realities in the minds of target audiences. It may be used in any place (e.g., street corner, podium, cinema, theater, press, radio, television, internet, and battlefield) to instigate or to resolve conflicts in the direction favored by the propagandist.

Black and White Propaganda in International Conflicts

Propaganda is most effective when it is based, at least in part, on facts (so-called white propaganda). When the facts do not serve the interests of propagandists, they turn to disinformation based entirely on forgery, deception, lies, and/or staged events (so-called black propaganda). The KGB, the Soviet Secret Police, invented modern disinformation and used it extensively, albeit unsuccessfully, to influence public opinion and policy throughout the world by arranging for forged documents to surface and to reveal the "nefarious" plans and ignominious behavior of Western governments, chiefly the United States.

There have been numerous efforts to influence the course and outcome of armed conflict by the judicious use of psychological warfare, with propaganda being one of its major weapons. Propaganda designed to undermine ideological commitment had little success in inducing German soldiers to surrender in the closing years of World War II. By contrast, tactical propaganda, designed to promote highly specific behaviors in specific situations, was effective. For example, when battlefield loudspeakers described the hopelessness of the German position and the importance of saving one's own life, units already weakened by casualties and insufficient supplies listened to loudspeaker instructions on how to surrender safely by using "safe conduct passes" dropped by air, and either deserted their post or surrendered.

The United States invasion of Panama in 1989 is a testimonial to successful propaganda. Overwhelming public support for the invasion was achieved by publicizing some unattractive truths about the Noriega government (e.g., drug dealing by Noriega himself), concealing some unattractive truths about the behavior and motives of the United States government vis-à-vis Panama throughout this century, and minimizing the loss of life, limb, and property experienced by the civilian population as a consequence of the invasion.

Propaganda and Terrorism

Terrorism has become an effective weapon in the strategic arsenal of some nation-states and revolutionary groups to change the behavior of victims and of media spectators many miles from the actual events. The perpetrators and the victims of terror have become actors in a morality play presented in real time on a worldwide stage, produced and directed by imaginative propagandists. Violent malevolence is placed in the context of a morally justifiable cause, and the audience is both horrified and enthralled by the events and the interpretation provided by the actors for their actions. Soviet military policy in Afghanistan to terrorize the native population into submission was ultimately unsuccessful because it delegitimized the puppet Afghan government established by the Soviet invaders and created martyrs for local revolutionary armies. Islamic fundamentalists in Egypt killed Western tourists and local Egyptian Christians (Copts) in order to undermine the economy and topple the government. Their counterparts in Algeria slaughtered innocent villagers in order to terrorize the majority of Algerians into submission. In each case they hoped to further their cause.

The Science of Propaganda and the Moral Dilemmas of Scientists

Many social and political scientists were active in the field of propaganda analysis before, during, and immediately after World War II. Interest and activity in the field waned because techniques used to enhance the effectiveness of propaganda—the manipulation of sentiment rather than reason and the exclusion of pertinent information that would weaken the impact of the message—raised moral dilemmas in scientists who developed and fine-tuned these techniques. Social and political scientists today—much like nuclear scientists during and following World War II—are aware that their theoretical formulations, creative applications, and systematic follow-up of these applications may be abused by powerful people in their own society. The use of propaganda within a democracy is not necessarily antithetical to its traditions, if there is equal access by all parties to a conflict to the various media. Since equal access is the exception rather than the rule, even in democratic countries, the use of propaganda may threaten democratic traditions. This is why many social psychologists and political scientists prefer to train target audiences to recognize propaganda for what it is rather than to enhance its effectiveness on behalf of some group or cause. Nevertheless, a great deal of theoretical and applied research on propaganda takes place both in social and cognitive psychology, in other disciplines, and in interdisciplinary fields.

[*See also* Terrorism.]

Bibliography

Bloom, R. W. (1991). Propaganda and active measures. In R. Gal & A. D. Mangelsdorff (Eds.), *Military psychology* (pp. 693–709). New York: Wiley.

Jackall, R. (Ed.). (1995). *Propaganda.* New York: New York University Press.

Janowitz, M., & Hirsch, P. (Eds.). (1981). *Reader in public opinion and mass communication* (3rd ed.). New York: Free Press/Macmillan.

Jowett, G. S., & O'Donnell, V. (1992). *Propaganda and persuasion* (3rd ed.). London: Sage.

Katz, D., Cartwright, D., Eldersveld, S., & Lee A. M. (Eds.). (1954). *Public opinion and propaganda.* New York: Dryden Press.

Silverstein, B. (1987). Toward a science of propaganda. *Political Psychology, 8,* 49–59.

Noach Milgram

PROPRIOCEPTION. The English physiologist Charles Sherrington first used the word "proprioception" to refer to sensations produced by the body itself as opposed to exteroceptive sensations that arise from the external environment. The term "proprioception" is now often used interchangeably with kinesthesia, although the former is more encompassing in that it includes the vestibular system in addition to sensations of movement, position, and muscle force.

Perception of Limb Movement and Position

Sensory receptors in muscles provide the central nervous system with information about the length of muscles, the rate at which muscle length changes, and the forces muscles generate. These sensory signals enable people to detect limb movements, perceive changes in limb position, and estimate the weight of objects that they support. Receptors in the skin and joints also contribute to these perceptual processes, although the exact nature of their contributions and whether they are the same for all joints remain to be determined.

The ability to detect the movement of a joint depends on several factors including the particular joint moving, the velocity of the movement, and whether the muscles controlling the joint are relaxed or contracting. Proximal joints such as the shoulder or hip have a greater sensitivity to movement than more distal joints such as those found in the hand or foot. This superiority of proximal joints is not surprising as they move more slowly than distal joints and when they rotate there is a larger displacement of the endpoint of the movement (the hand or the foot) than with the same angular rotation at a more distal joint. The ability to detect a movement improves as the velocity of the movement increases up to some critical velocity, which for the distal finger joints is about 10°/second, and then remains stable. Movement thresholds also decrease (i.e., there is better detection) if a movement occurs while the muscles acting on the joint are actively contracting rather than relaxed, and at some velocities can be up to ten times smaller if the muscles are contracting.

In contrast to the perception of limb movement, the ability to detect a change in limb position is not influenced by the velocity of the movement. It is even possible to move a joint at velocities that are so slow (less than 2°/minute) that the movement is imperceptible, but once the movement has stopped subjects perceive that the limb is now in a different position from where it was previously. This shows that it is possible to make independent judgments of the position and movement of a limb and that the perception of limb position is not necessarily derived from perceiving movement amplitude.

Perception of Force

Information about the forces generated by muscles during the course of voluntary motor activities arises from at least two sources. First, within the muscle and tendon itself are Golgi tendon organ receptors that discharge in response to changes in intramuscular force. Second, it appears that force information can be derived from the motor command sent from the cerebral cortex to the muscles. Correlates or copies of this command are transmitted to the sensory areas of the brain and are assumed to reflect the magnitude of the descending motor signal. These centrally mediated sensations are often termed a sense of effort.

Results from a number of experiments indicate that whenever there is an increase in the motor command sent to the muscles, because of fatigue or weakness resulting from injury to the motor pathways, there is a corresponding increase in the perceived magnitude of the force produced, even when the force remains constant. With fatigue, for example, even though the weight of a heavy object being held remains constant, over time there is a very marked increase in its perceived heaviness. In this situation the neural input required to maintain the muscle force increases as the muscle fatigues, whereas the afferent signals arising from Golgi tendon organ receptors remain constant or possibly decrease over time. These findings have been interpreted as indicating that our perception of force is based on information that is derived centrally from the descending motor command and not from the activity of peripheral receptors in the muscle. This conclusion should not be interpreted as dismissing a contribution from peripheral receptors such as Golgi tendon organs, as it has been shown that under some conditions people can estimate muscle force when only these receptors could be providing the relevant signals.

Role of the Vestibular System

The vestibular system is considered part of the proprioceptive system because it is involved in the control of postural stability and spatial orientation, but at the same time is functionally related to the visual system because it detects linear and rotary motion of the head and is involved in oculomotor control. In order to have an accurate perception of the position of one's body in space, which is required to maintain postural stability, orientation information from the vestibular, somatosensory, and visual systems must be organized and combined. Each of these sensory systems measures orientation from a different perspective and uses a different frame of reference. The vestibular system uses an inertial-gravitational reference point, whereas the somatosensory system determines orientation from external support surfaces, and the visual system uses the orientation of objects in the person's field of view. In response to perceived changes in orientation, a person must be able to move the body in a coordinated manner.

Motion sickness, a common complaint of nausea, sweating, and drowsiness, during rough weather on a ship or plane, occurs when rotatory and linear accelerations combine to produce a stimulus that is unusual for the organism. The vestibular system appears to be essential to its genesis, in that people with loss of function of the vestibular organs do not experience motion sickness. Exposure to a microgravity environment during space flight also results in activity of the vestibular system that differs from that experienced on earth, and so can cause symptoms of motion sickness. People vary in their degree of susceptibility to motion sickness and the same individual may have different responses in different gravito-intertial force environments. Prolonged exposure to these environmental conditions usually results in adaptation with the associated decrease in motion sickness.

Bibliography

Clark, F. J., & Horch, K. W. (1986). Kinesthesia. In K. Boff, L. Kaufman, & J. P. Thomas (Eds.), *Handbook of perception and human performance, Vol. 1* (pp. 13:1–13:62). New York: Wiley. An excellent review chapter that covers many of the psychophysical experiments that have been conducted on the kinesthetic system in considerable detail.

Gandevia, S. C. (1996). Kinesthesia: Roles for afferent signals and motor commands. In L. B. Rowell & J. T. Shepherd (Eds.), *Handbook of physiology. Section 12: Exercise regulation and integration of multiple systems* (pp. 128–172). New York: Oxford University Press. A review chapter describing the properties of muscle, skin, and joint receptors and their role in kinesthesia.

Howard, I. P. (1986). The vestibular system. In K. Boff, L. Kaufman, & J. P. Thomas (Eds.), *Handbook of perception and human performance: Vol. 1* (pp. 11:1–11:30). New York: Wiley.

Jones, L. A. (1986). The perception of force and weight: Theory and research. *Psychological Bulletin, 100*, 29–42.

McCloskey, D. I. (1981). Corollary discharges: motor commands and perception. In V. B. Brooks (Ed.), *Handbook of physiology. The nervous system: Vol. 2. Motor control* (pp. 1415–1447). Bethesda, MD: American Physiological Society.

Lynette A. Jones

PROSOCIAL BEHAVIOR. Prosocial behavior represents a broad set of actions that are "defined by society as generally beneficial to other people and to the ongoing political system" (Piliavin, Dovidio, Gaertner, & Clark, 1981, p. 4). Two main categories of prosocial behavior are helping and altruism (see Batson, 1998; Schroeder, Penner, Dovidio, & Piliavin, 1995; for a related category, cooperation, see Komorita & Parks, 1994; for social support, see Wills, 1992). [*See* Altruism; *and* Social Support.]

Helping represents an intentional action that has the outcome of benefitting another person. Attempts to identify essential characteristics of helping have suggested several key dimensions, such as planned versus spontaneous, direct versus indirect, and emotional versus instrumental action.

Within psychology, altruism involves the motivation underlying helping. Classic definitions have included internal motivation as a critical feature of altruistic helping. Altruism has been defined as a special type of helping in which the benefactor provides aid to another person *without anticipation of rewards from external sources for providing assistance* while incurring some personal costs for taking this action. More recent perspectives have emphasized the importance of further distinguishing the different types of internal motivations involved in helping. For Batson (1991, 1998), "Altruism is a motivational state with the ultimate goal of increasing another's welfare" (Batson, 1991, p. 6). In contrast, egoistic helping is motivated by the ultimate goal of improving one's own welfare.

Three of the most central questions that have been addressed in the literature on helping and altruism are (1) When do people help? (2) Why do people help? and (3) Who helps?

When Do People Help?

Many of the earlier studies of when people help focused on nonemergency situations and thus considered helping to be guided by many of the same external factors (e.g., norms) and internal influences (e.g., personality) as other forms of socially valued behaviors. By the mid-1960s, stimulated by dramatic incidents in the news about failures of bystanders to intervene to save the lives of others, empirical attention turned to emergency situations and to the relatively unique nature of helping behavior. Much of this research was shaped by Latané and Darley's (1970) pioneering decision model of bystander intervention.

Decision Model of Intervention. Latané and Darley's (1970) decision model of bystander intervention proposed that whether or not a person helps depends upon the outcomes of a series of prior decisions. The bystander must: (1) notice that something is wrong, (2) define it as an emergency, (3) decide whether to take personal responsibility, (4) decide what kind of help to give, and (5) decide to implement the chosen course of action. A negative decision at *any* step means the bystander will not help. Extensive support for this model comes not only from studies of emergency situations but also from research on other circumstances, ranging from preventing someone from driving drunk or making a decision about whether to donate a kidney to a relative.

With respect to the first step of the model, bystanders are more likely to notice events that are more vivid. Other aspects of the physical environment, such as the overstimulation and crowding that occurs in an urban environment, can reduce the likelihood that people notice the event and thus can reduce helping. Environmental stressors can also have a negative impact on people's moods. Negative moods, such as depression, that focus people on their own needs inhibit helping. In contrast, pleasant environments can facilitate helping in part through positive mood.

One of the basic factors that can influence whether a situation, once noticed, is interpreted as a situation requiring assistance (Step 2 of the model) is the clarity of the event. Bystanders are much more likely to help victims who make their need clearer with overt distress cues (e.g., screams) that indicate that the situation is serious and rapidly deteriorating (Piliavin, Dovidio, Gaertner, & Clark, 1981). The social environment is also important. When other bystanders act calm, they define ambiguous situations as nonemergencies; when other bystanders act alarmed, they suggest that the situation is one requiring help.

Once the need for assistance is determined, bystanders must decide *who* is responsible for helping (Step 3 of the model). When a person is the only witness to an emergency, he or she bears all of the responsibility; in contrast, when a bystander believes that other people are also witnessing the event and that these other people can help, *diffusion of responsibility* may occur. The belief that others will take action can relieve bystanders from assuming personal responsibility for intervention, because it can be reasoned that *their* assistance is no longer necessary (Latané & Darley, 1970). Diffusion of responsibility is more likely to occur when personal danger is involved in helping, when other witnesses are perceived as better able to help, and when norms permit or support it; it is less likely to occur when the other witnesses are incapable of intervention (Dovidio, Piliavin, Gaertner, Schroeder, & Clark, 1991; Piliavin, Dovidio, Gaertner, & Clark, 1981).

Whereas the first three steps of the Latané and Darley model have received careful empirical scrutiny and support, the fourth and fifth steps, deciding what to do and implementing the chosen course of action, have not been the focus of substantial research. Nevertheless, the work that does exist is generally supportive. People with first-aid training, for instance, offer more medically effective help than do people without relevant training.

Whereas the Latané and Darley model offers a broad framework on when people will help, a *cost-reward* perspective allows a more detailed analysis of how the nature of the situation and characteristics of the victim influence helping.

Cost-Reward Framework. A cost-reward analysis of helping assumes an economic view of human behavior: People are motivated by self-interest to maximize their rewards and to minimize their costs in determining their actions in a potential helping situation (Piliavin, Dovidio, Gaertner, & Clark, 1981). There are two categories of costs and rewards: those for helping (e.g., time, danger) and those for *not* helping (e.g., guilt or shame). Examples of rewards for helping are money, fame, and self-praise. Current research is consistent with the central tenet of the cost-reward approach: Factors that decrease the net costs (costs minus rewards) for helping or increase the costs for not helping facilitate intervention (Dovidio, Piliavin, Gaertner, Schroeder, & Clark, 1991).

The cost-reward perspective also assumes that assessments of costs and rewards are subjective and thus may be influenced by characteristics of the person in need and of the potential benefactors. More positive attitudes toward a person in need (for example, based on attraction, similarity, or common group membership; see Dovidio, 1984) may increase rewards for helping (e.g., more value associated with the recipient's gratitude), decrease costs for helping (e.g., less anxiety about how the person will respond to help), or increase costs for not helping (e.g., stronger feelings of guilt), and thereby increase helping. Whereas positive attitudes promote helping, negative attitudes can decrease it. In addition, personal goals can shape perceptions of costs and rewards and produce different *motivations* for helping.

Why Do People Help?

Research on motivations for helping addresses the issue of why people help. Approaches have focused on three types of mechanisms: (1) learning, (2) arousal and affect, and (3) social and personal standards.

Learned Helpfulness. Two basic learning processes in helping are operant conditioning and social learning. Consistent with the principles of operant learning, people are more likely to help others when their previous helping responses have been positively reinforced (for example, by praise). Conversely, people may learn *not* to help others because helping has led to negative consequences (see Grusec, 1991; Staub, 1981). Whereas punishment *for* helping reduces subsequent helping, punishment for *not* helping does not increase prosocial behavior. Punishment arouses negative feelings (e.g., anger) that are incompatible with a prosocial orientation and, thus, may interfere with the socialization of concern for others and intrinsic motivations for helping (Grusec, 1991).

Social learning, either through modeling or direct instruction, can also facilitate helping (see Grusec, 1991). Consistent with general principles, the consequences to the model (e.g., positive, neutral, negative), characteristics of the model (e.g., status, attractiveness, similarity), states of the observer (e.g., mood), and relationship between the observer and the model (e.g., attachment between a child and parent) moderate the influence of prosocial models. Parental models have a strong and prolonged impact on helping.

The relationship between the nature of rewards and helpfulness, however, varies developmentally. Very young children are usually motivated by specific material rewards and punishments, older children are motivated by social approval, and adolescents are motivated by self-satisfaction and personal conviction. Prosocial moral reasoning also proceeds developmentally. Preschool children engage mainly in hedonistic and self-centered moral reasoning, whereas older children demonstrate more sophisticated and other-oriented kinds of reasoning—and, generally, more helpfulness.

Arousal and Affect. Arousal and affect play important roles in helping and altruism. People are aroused by the distress of others (Eisenberg & Fabes, 1991). This phenomenon is so strong and universal that some researchers have proposed that empathic arousal, arousal generated vicariously by another person's distress, has a biological and evolutionary basis. Indeed, studies of identical twins have suggested the heritability of empathy.

Although many researchers agree that empathic arousal is important and fundamental in helping (see Dovidio, 1984), there is much less agreement about how it feels to be empathic and how this emotion actually motivates people to help. Empathic arousal can produce a range of emotions: upset (Piliavin et al., 1981), sadness (Cialdini, Kenrick, & Baumann, 1982), tension, or concern for the victim (Batson, 1991). The emotion experienced is influenced by the attributions that people make about the causes of the other person's situation, with attribution of responsibility and controllability being particularly important dimensions. How arousal is interpreted can shape the nature of prosocial motivation.

According to the negative state relief model (Cialdini, Kenrick, & Baumann, 1982), harming another person or witnessing another person being harmed can produce negative feelings such as guilt or sadness. People who experience these negative states are then motivated to reduce them. People learn through socialization and experience that helping can make them feel good, which can relieve their negative mood.

Two fundamental assumptions of the negative state relief model have received considerable support. The first assumption is that, because people are motivated to improve their own mood and other events besides helping (e.g., praise) may just as effectively make the person feel better, exposure to these events can relieve the motivation to help caused by negative states. The second assumption of this model, which has also received support, is that negative moods motivate helping only if people believe that their moods can be improved by helping or have developmentally internalized the rewarding properties of helping.

Whereas the negative state relief model is based directly on principles of operant conditioning and on virtually the sole concern with one's own well-being, other affective models focus more on the reaction to another person's distress. Arousal is a central motivational concept in the Piliavin et al. (1981) *arousal: cost-*

reward model (see also Dovidio, Piliavin, Gaertner, Schroeder, & Clark, 1991). Specifically, this tension-reduction model proposes that when a bystander's empathic arousal is attributed to the other person's distress, it is emotionally experienced by the observer as unpleasant and the bystander is, therefore, motivated to reduce it. A cost-reward analysis shapes the direction that this action will take, but one normally efficient way of reducing this arousal is by helping to relieve the other's distress. Supportive of the model, facial, gestural, and vocal indications of empathy, physiological arousal, as well as self-reports of empathy are consistently positively related to helping (see Dovidio, Piliavin, Gaertner, Schroeder, & Clark, 1991).

In contrast to egoistic models of helping, Batson and his colleagues (see Batson, 1991) propose the *empathy-altruism hypothesis*. Although they acknowledge that egoistically motivated helping occurs, Batson and his colleagues argue that altruism—defined as helping with the primary goal of improving the other person's welfare—also exists. According to the empathy-altruism hypothesis, whereas sadness and personal distress produce egoistic motivations to help, empathic concern (e.g., sympathy, compassion) creates altruistic motivation. Supportive of the hypothesis, people who experience relatively high levels of empathic concern (and who presumably are altruistically motivated) show high levels of helpfulness even when it is easy to escape the situation and when helping is not perceived as instrumental in improving the benefactor's own mood.

Several researchers have proposed alternative, egoistic interpretations to Batson and his colleagues' conclusions about altruistic motivation (see Batson, 1998). These explanations include (1) empathy-specific punishments, which are additional costs for not helping (e.g., feelings of guilt or shame) that are generated by empathic concern and make people likely to help even when helping requires moderate effort; (2) empathy-specific rewards, which are special rewards for helping (e.g., joy at the other's relief) that are associated with feeling empathic concern; (3) empathy-aroused sadness, which is sadness that occurs with empathic concern and primarily underlies the response; and (4) self-other merging, which involves an extension of one's self and therefore one's self-interest. The data are controversial and inconsistent (e.g., Batson et al., 1997; Cialdini, Brown, Lewis, Luce, & Neuberg, 1997; see also Batson, 1998). On balance, however, the contention that altruistic motivation does exist remains a viable and influential interpretation of the findings.

Social and Personal Standards. Normative theories of helping emphasize that people help others because they perceive it to be the socially appropriate response. One involves the *norm of social responsibility*, which proscribes that people are expected to help others who are dependent on them (Berkowitz, 1972). Supportive of this position, people are more likely to help others in greater need (Piliavin, Dovidio, Gaertner, & Clark 1981), unless helping commits them to a long-term dependency relationship or the person in need is responsible for creating his or her own plight. Collectivistic cultures have stronger social responsibility norms than do individualistic cultures.

This norm can also become internalized within one's self-concept. Individuals who come to see themselves as helpful and socially responsible people subsequently show relatively high levels of helpful behavior (Grusec, 1991). Regular and public commitments to helping, such as donating blood, can lead to the development of a role-identity consistent with those behaviors. Helping may also be functional in fulfilling personal needs and motives, such as to express one's values and to provide new learning opportunities.

A second type of norm relates to feelings of fairness and involves perceptions of reciprocity, equity, and social justice (see Dovidio, 1984). Consistent with the reciprocity norm, people typically reciprocate assistance to others who have helped them. Reciprocity is strong for most casual relationships, but may be weaker in more intimate communal relationships for which people are primarily concerned about their partner's welfare. Reciprocity is such a fundamental, cross-cultural principle that some researchers have proposed that there may be biological and genetic bases (see Schroeder, Penner, Dovidio, & Piliavin, 1995). Concerns for fairness and balance can also motivate prosocial action to relieve inequity or injustice.

Who Helps?

Individual differences play an important role in helping as they do in other social behaviors. This section examines demographic and personality differences in helping.

Demographic Differences in Volunteering. People contribute a significant amount of their time and resources (e.g., over $123 billion annually in the United States) to help others. In general, people who have greater resources give more. Education, sex, and age are all systematically associated with donating and volunteering (see Schroeder, Penner, Dovidio, & Piliavin, 1995). Higher education levels, which are related to higher socioeconomic status, are also associated with greater giving. Traditionally, men give more money and women give more time to charity. Age relates to giving, but in a curvilinear way. Younger and older people donate less money and time formally to charitable organizations than do people between 35 and 55 years old. However, among the elderly a significant amount of helping also occurs in more informal ways. In addition, religiosity is positively related to donating.

Individual Differences in Helping. Individual differences in spontaneous, short-term helping typically relate to factors that are critical in determining when people help (e.g., perceptions of costs and rewards) and motivations for helping (e.g., empathic arousal).

Comprehensive reviews of helping research have found that in the majority of the studies, men were more likely to help than women in the United States (Eagly & Crowley, 1986) and cross-culturally. Moreover, due in part to different gender roles and socialization that can influence the amount of empathy experienced and the perceptions of costs and rewards, men and women also differ in when they help. As a consequence of greater empathy and consistent with gender-role expectations, women are much more likely than men to provide their friends with personal favors, social support, and informal counseling about personal or psychological problems. In contrast, men are more likely than women to help someone in instrumental or in "heroic" ways that involve physical danger.

Personality variables that have been found to relate to helping are also typically relevant to empathy and perceptions of costs and rewards. Higher levels of dispositional empathy are positively related to helping. People who have greater confidence in their abilities, who are less safety oriented, and who are more likely to accept personal responsibility (all of which may affect perceptions of costs and rewards) are more likely to help, particularly in instrumental ways (see Dovidio, Piliavin, Gaertner, Schroeder, & Clark, 1991). People who are relatively high on the constellation of traits of empathy, a sense of responsibility, and a concern for the welfare of others are particularly likely to engage in prosocial behavior, both spontaneous helping and long-term volunteering (Penner, Fritzsche, Craiger, & Freifeld, 1995).

Situational factors can moderate the impact of personality. The person X situation approach suggests that, with respect to helping, personality variables are more important as cues about the need of the victim and how the potential helper should behave become weaker (Penner, Fritzsche, Craiger, & Freifeld, 1995; Staub, 1981) and as the personality variables relate more directly to the most salient, critical aspects of the helping situation (e.g., arousal, costs; Schroeder, Penner, Dovidio, & Piliavin, 1995).

Summary and Conclusions

In summary, the processes involved in when people help, why people help, and who helps appear relatively systematic and interrelated. Prosocial behavior involves both affective and cognitive influences. Individual, developmental, and cultural differences moderate these effects. Affectively, the need or distress of others elicits empathic arousal. Depending on how it is interpreted, this arousal can inhibit prosocial action or produce altruistic or egoistic motivations. Cognitively, people consider their relationships to others and assess the costs and rewards for various courses of action. As many models emphasize, the affective and cognitive components are not independent. Previous learning and current assessment of costs and rewards can influence the experience of arousal; arousal can influence the assessment of costs and rewards or the salience of previously learned associations. Thus, although there are unique aspects of various prosocial actions, such as spontaneous helping, altruism, donating, and volunteering, they share many similar underlying processes and principles.

[*See also* Altruism; Antisocial Behavior; *and* Social Support.]

Bibliography

Batson, C. D. (1991). *The altruism question: Toward a social-psychological answer.* Hillsdale, NJ: Erlbaum.

Batson, C. D. (1998). Altruism and prosocial behavior. In D. T. Gilbert, S. T. Fiske, & G. Lindzey (Eds.), *The handbook of social psychology* (4th ed., Vol. 2, pp. 282–315). New York: McGraw-Hill.

Batson, C. D., Sager, K., Garst, E., Kang, M., Rubchinsky, K., & Dawson, K. (1997). Is empathy-induced helping due to self-other merging? *Journal of Personality and Social Psychology, 73,* 495–509.

Berkowitz, L. (1972). Social norms, feelings, and other factors affecting helping behavior and altruism. In L. Berkowitz (Ed.), *Advances in experimental social psychology* (Vol. 6, pp. 63–108). New York: Academic Press.

Cialdini, R. B., Kenrick, D. T., & Baumann, D. J. (1982). Effects of mood on prosocial behavior in children and adults. In N. Eisenberg (Ed.), *The development of prosocial behavior* (pp. 339–359). New York: Academic Press.

Cialdini, R. B., Brown, S. L., Lewis, B. P., Luce, C., & Neuberg, S. L. (1997). Reinterpreting the empathy-altruism relationship: When one into one equals oneness. *Journal of Personality and Social Psychology, 73,* 481–494.

Dovidio, J. F. (1984). Helping behavior and altruism: An empirical and conceptual overview. In L. Berkowitz (Ed.), *Advances in experimental social psychology* (Vol. 17, pp. 361–427). New York: Academic Press.

Dovidio, J. F., Piliavin, J. A., Gaertner, S. L., Schroeder, D. A., & Clark, R. D., III (1991). The Arousal: Cost-Reward Model and the process of intervention: A review of the evidence. In M. S. Clark (Ed.), *Review of personality and social psychology: Prosocial behavior* (Vol. 12, pp. 86–118). Newbury Park, CA: Sage.

Eagly, A. H., & Crowley, M. (1986). Gender and helping behavior: A meta-analytic review of the social psychological literature. *Psychological Bulletin, 100,* 283–308.

Eisenberg, N. A., & Fabes, R. A. (1991). Prosocial behavior and empathy: A multimethod developmental perspective. In M. S. Clark (Ed.), *Review of personality and social psychology: Prosocial behavior* (Vol. 12, pp. 34–61). Newbury Park, CA: Sage.

Grusec, J. E. (1991). The socialization of empathy. In M. S. Clark (Ed.), *Review of personality and social psychology: Prosocial behavior* (Vol. 12, pp. 9–33). Newbury Park, CA: Sage.

Komorita, S. S., & Parks, C. D. (1994). *Social dilemmas.* Madison, WI: WCB Brown & Benchmark.

Latané, B., & Darley, J. M. (1970). *The unresponsive bystander: Why doesn't he help?* New York: Appleton-Century-Crofts.

Penner, L. A., Fritzsche, B. A., Craiger, J. P., & Freifeld, T. S. (1995). Measuring the prosocial personality. In J. Butcher & C. Spielberger (Eds.), *Advances in personality assessment* (Vol. 10, pp. 147–163). Hillsdale, NJ: Erlbaum.

Piliavin, J. A., Dovidio, J. F., Gaertner, S. L., & Clark, R. D., III. (1981). *Emergency intervention.* New York: Academic Press.

Schroeder, D. A., Penner, L. A., Dovidio, J. F., & Piliavin, J. A. (1995). *The psychology of helping and altruism: Problems and puzzles.* New York: McGraw-Hill.

Staub, E. (1981). *Positive social behavior and morality: Vol. 1. Social and personal influences.* New York: Academic Press.

Wills, T. A. (1992). The helping process in the context of personal relationships. In S. Spacapan & S. Oskamp (Eds.), *Helping and being helped: Naturalistic studies* (pp. 17–48). Newbury Park CA: Sage.

John F. Dovidio

PROSOCIAL DEVELOPMENT IN CHILDHOOD AND ADOLESCENCE. Prosocial behavior frequently is defined as voluntary behavior intended to benefit another. One type of prosocial behavior is altruism, which is prosocial behavior that is sympathetically or morally, rather than egoistically, motivated. Although psychologists generally are more interested in altruism than in the larger domain of prosocial behavior, it is difficult to differentiate the two (and some claim that real altruism does not exist). Thus, in most of the research, children's motives for their prosocial actions are unclear, and the focus is on the broader domain of prosocial responding.

The Development of Prosocial Behavior

The ability to engage in prosocial behavior emerges early in life. By the age of ten months to fourteen months, infants frequently express agitation when viewing others in distress. Self-distressed reactions to the distress of others decrease in frequency during the second year of life, and between 1 and 2 years of age, infants sometimes make an effort to interact positively with or help distressed or sad individuals, especially parents. Initially, these efforts tend to consist of positive physical contact, such as patting the other person, but by 18 to 24 months of age, the child's interventions include more controlled acts of direct assistance. In addition, young children frequently try to assist with household chores.

At a young age, toddlers may not fully distinguish between their own and another person's inner states and may confuse the two. Consequently, their prosocial actions may be more appropriate for alleviating their own distress than that of the other person. With development, children's prosocial actions appear to become more situationally appropriate and sensitive.

Children's prosocial behavior continues to increase in frequency from infancy into adolescence. Age differences have been found for sharing, comforting, and instrumental helping, and they tend to be greater in studies with experimental/structured designs than in naturalistic or correlational studies. Moreover, when one controls for differences between studies on a variety of study characteristics, age differences are larger when prosocial behavior is measured with self- or other-reports than with observations.

The consistency of children's prosocial behavior across settings and time also seems to increase with age. In the first few years of life, such consistency is low. However, researchers sometimes have found moderate consistency in preschoolers', elementary-school children's, and adolescents' prosocial behavior across time and settings.

Younger and older children differ not only in the frequency of their prosocial behavior, but also in their reasons for their prosocial actions. In general, older children are more likely than younger children to assist for self-reported or apparently altruistic or other-oriented motives, whereas younger children are more likely to assist in order to obtain material or social rewards.

Moreover, when resolving hypothetical prosocial moral dilemmas, children's reasoning changes with age. In a prosocial moral dilemma, story protagonists must choose whether to assist another at a cost to the self in situations in which the role of laws, rules, authorities, and formal social obligations is minimal. In a longitudinal study, Eisenberg and her colleagues (1995) found that young children tend to use primarily hedonistic reasoning and some needs-oriented (primitive empathic) reasoning. In elementary school, needs-oriented reasoning increases, hedonistic reasoning decreases, and children begin to express concern with approval, enhancing interpersonal relationships, and behaving in stereotypically "good" ways. In late elementary school or thereafter, children start to verbalize reasoning reflecting abstract principles, internalized affective reactions (e.g., guilt or positive affect about the consequences of one's behavior for others or living up to internalized principles), self-reflective sympathy, and perspective-taking. Reasoning concerning role-taking, internalized norm/rule/values, generalized reciprocity across members of society, internalized affective reactions based on concern about the consequences of one's behavior for others, and positive affect related to internalized values and living up to those values increases with age into early adulthood. Given that prosocial behavior tends to be correlated with higher-level and more other-oriented moral reasoning (and with lower hedonistic reasoning), it is likely that age-related changes in prosocial moral reasoning reflect age-related differences in the goals and motives underlying children's prosocial behavior. However, it is clear that children at all ages sometimes act in a prosocial manner for primarily egoistic reasons.

Cultural Differences

Marked differences in people's prosocial behavior have been observed across societies. In some traditional cultures, such as the Ik in Africa, aggression, ridicule, and cruelty have been commonplace, whereas in other cultures social interchanges are characterized by caring, helping, and support. Children in traditional cultures tend to assist family members and neighbors more than children in industrial communities. Even in industrial societies, children in collectivist cultures with an emphasis on the group (e.g., Japan) appear to be more prosocial with peers than children from individualistic cultures (e.g., the United States). However, it is not clear whether the cross-cultural differences that have been observed hold when unfamiliar people are the targets of aid.

Children reared in traditional rural, semiagricultural communities also cooperate more than children raised in industrial, urban settings. Furthermore, children from traditional societies who are exposed to the dominant urban culture (e.g., in their schools) tend to be less cooperative than children from the same cultural group with less exposure to urban culture.

The reasons for the observed cross-cultural and subcultural differences in prosocial and cooperative behavior are unclear. Some existing research is consistent with the conclusion that cross-cultural differences in warm, supportive parenting may account for some of the variation. Socializers in different cultures also vary in the degree to which they teach and reinforce prosocial and cooperative values and behaviors. In traditional cultures, the survival of the group often depends on cooperation and helping among kin and neighbors. Consequently, in everyday life, children cooperate and help others, often as part of their chores (e.g., when caring for siblings). In fact, variations across cultures in the degree to which children are assigned chores that significantly contribute to the well-being of the family have been linked to cross-cultural differences in children's prosocial behavior. Similarly, in collectivist societies, even if they are industrialized, the well-being of others in the group is generally of central importance. For example, in collectivist societies, prosocial actions are seen as more obligatory than in individualistic societies, and privileges and social acknowledgement in the classroom are dependent on group rather than individual accomplishments (so children are reinforced for helping one another).

Socialization in the Family

Researchers conducting studies of twins have found that there is a genetic component to prosocial behavior, one that may be due to empathy having some genetic basis. [*See* Empathy.] Nonetheless, individual differences in prosocial behavior within a culture are likely due, in part, to the effects of socialization at home and in the larger community.

Researchers have found that prosocial children tend to have parents who model prosocial actions, value prosocial behavior, and apply ethical principles to a broad spectrum of humanity. Parents of prosocial children also tend to use reasoning (inductions) in disciplinary interactions, especially reasoning that appeals to the child's ability to empathize and sympathize, and infrequently resort to physical punishment or threats. In general, parents of prosocial children appear to be authoritative and democratic—they are supportive, use reasoning for discipline, but are also directive in terms of making their expectations for appropriate behavior clear. In addition, the provision of opportunities for children to engage in prosocial activities has been linked to children's prosocial proclivities.

Teachers and schools also influence children's prosocial development. For example, school-based programs that emphasize rational discipline, cooperation, and prosocial values, and that provide activities designed to enhance children's sympathy and understanding of others and their feelings, appear to foster elementary-school children's prosocial and cooperative behavior. The quality of the teacher-child relationship has also been related to children's consideration for others and empathy with unfamiliar peers. Moreover, there appears to be a modest relation between children's viewing of prosocial television programming and their prosocial behavior.

Children can also learn and practice prosocial behaviors through interactions with siblings. By eighteen months of age, siblings sometimes share, help, comfort, and cooperate with each other. There is initial evidence that the quality of the sibling relationship is related to the degree to which the siblings engage in prosocial actions with one another. Because older children, especially girls, often engage in the care giving and helping of younger siblings, they may have greater opportunity to develop prosocial competencies than other children.

Gender Differences in Prosocial Behavior

Consistent with gender stereotypes, girls in general are higher in measures of prosocial behavior than boys. When the effects of a variety of study characteristics are controlled, the sex difference for instrumental helping is smaller than those for other measures of prosocial behaviors (e.g., kindness, sharing, aggregated measures of prosocial behavior). This pattern of findings is interesting because in adulthood, men are higher than women in many types of instrumental helping (probably especially the helping of strangers and helping when doing so would be considered chivalrous). In addition, sex differences in children's prosocial behavior have been significantly larger when the target of the prosocial action has been an adult or an unspecified person than when the target has been another child. The gender difference favoring girls is also greater when prosocial behavior has been measured with self- or other-reports relative to observation of prosocial behavior. Thus, although girls appear to be more prosocial in general, this difference may be amplified when people report on their own or others' prosocial behavior, due to the general perception that girls are the more prosocial sex.

Girls and boys do not differ in their prosocial moral judgment in elementary school. By adolescence, however, girls tend to have higher-level moral reasoning and also use more of some other-oriented modes of moral judgment (e.g., reasoning discussing perspective taking) than do boys.

Personal Characteristics Associated with Children's Prosocial Behavior

Prosocial children differ from their peers on a variety of personal characteristics. Children who perform more prosocial behaviors than their peers, especially behaviors that appear to be altruistically motivated, tend to be relatively high in moral judgment and perspective-taking (i.e., the ability to understand others' internal mental states and feelings). Prosocial children also tend to verbalize other-oriented modes of prosocial moral reasoning and are relatively sympathetic and empathic toward others' negative emotions and states. [*See* Sympathy.] Recent data are consistent with the conclusion that the combination of sympathy and perspective taking is linked to prosocial behavior; children were more likely to donate to a needy peer if they not only evidenced relatively sophisticated perspective-taking skills, but were also sympathetic (and understood units and value of money). These findings are consistent with theoretical formulations in which prosocial behavior, especially altruism, often is motivated by perspective-taking, moral values, and sympathy. However, perspective taking and sympathy generally would not be expected to be related to prosocial behaviors that are enacted for egoistic reasons; nor is prosocial moral reasoning related to prosocial behaviors that are performed habitually without much thought and/or are low in cost.

In addition, sociable and assertive children seem especially likely to engage in some types of prosocial acts, including those that are performed outside of the home and require social initiative and spontaneity (e.g., behaviors performed without being requested). In contrast, nonassertive children help and share primarily when asked, and they may often comply with a request because they have difficulty asserting themselves. Moreover, prosocial children are viewed by adults as socially skilled, well regulated, and constructive copers. Prosocial children tend to be high in level of positive social interactions with peers and in the expression of positive emotion. Although prosocial behavior and aggression are sometimes positively correlated in the early years, they often are negatively related in older children. Thus, prosocial behavior tends to be related to a constellation of dispositional characteristics that involve positive social interactions—and that constellation is likely due to genetic and environmental factors.

Acknowledgments. Work on this entry was supported by a grant from the National Institutes of Mental Health (1 R01 HH55052) and Research Scientist Development and Research Scientist Awards from the National Institute of Mental Health (K05 M801321).

Bibliography

Cohen, A. (1990). *The brighter side of human nature: Altruism and empathy in everyday life.* New York: Basic Books.

Eisenberg, N. (1986). *Altruistic emotion, cognition, and behavior.* Hillsdale, NJ: Erlbaum.

Eisenberg, N. (1992). *The caring child.* Cambridge, MA: Harvard University Press.

Eisenberg, N., Carlo, G., & Van Court, P. (1995). Prosocial development in late adolescence. *Child Development, 66,* 911–936.

Eisenberg, N., & Fabes, R. A. (1991). Prosocial behavior and empathy: A multimethod, developmental perspective. In P. Clark (Ed.), *Review of personality and social psychology* (Vol. 12, pp. 34–61). Newbury Park, CA: Sage.

Eisenberg, N., & Fabes, R. A. (1998). Prosocial development. In W. Damon (Series Ed.) & N. Eisenberg (Vol. Ed), *Handbook of child psychology: Vol. 3. Social, emotional, and personality development* (5th ed., pp. 701–778). New York: Wiley.

Eisenberg, N., & Mussen, P. (1989). *The roots of prosocial behavior in children.* Cambridge, England: Cambridge University Press.

Hunt, M. (1990). *The compassionate beast*. New York: Morrow.

Oliner, S. P., & Oliner, P. M. (1988). *The altruistic personality: Rescuers of Jews in Nazi Europe*. New York: Free Press.

Olweus, D., Block, J., & Radke-Yarrow, M. (Eds.). (1986). *Development of antisocial and prosocial behavior: Research, theories, and issues*. Orlando, FL: Academic Press.

Radke-Yarrow, M. R., Zahn-Waxler, C., & Chapman, M. (1983). Children's prosocial dispositions and behavior. In P. H. Mussen (Ed.), *Carmichael's manual of child psychology* (E. M. Hetherington, Vol. Ed.), (Vol. 4, pp. 469–546). New York: Wiley.

Zahn-Waxler, C., Radke-Yarrow, M. R., Wagner, E., & Chapman, M. (1992). Development of concern for others. *Developmental Psychology, 28*, 126–136.

Nancy Eisenberg

PROSPECT THEORY. *See* Decision Making.

PROTOTYPE. *See* Schema.

PSEUDOMEMORY. *See* False Memory.

PSI. *See* Parapsychology.

PSI BETA. The national honor society in psychology for community and junior colleges, Psi Beta recognizes and promotes excellence in scholarship, leadership, research, and community service for outstanding psychology students. The society was chartered in Tennessee on 5 November 1981. Members of Psi Chi, the national honor society for 4-year colleges, who were teaching at 2-year colleges were the impetus for founding Psi Beta; they were eager to offer their students and colleagues the advantages of honor society membership that they had experienced as students. Psi Chi, as a member of the Association of College Honor Societies (ACHS), which regulates honor society standards, was not permitted at that time to charter chapters or induct members at 2-year colleges. Therefore, Ruth Cousins, Psi Chi executive director for 33 years, inspired the founding of Psi Beta by convincing her daughter, Carol Tracy, to create the honor society in psychology for community and junior colleges. In 1977, Tracy began the process. Eleven chapters formed the charter group with Jim Hail, of McLennan Community College in Waco, Texas, as national president. He, Tracy, and the other faculty sponsors from the charter chapters, formed the first national council. Within 5 years, Psi Beta had 42 chapters and a cumulative total of 1,400 members.

Psi Beta functions as a federation of chapters operated by faculty advisors, student members, and a national council. The council determines the direction and policies of the organization. The vice presidents are faculty sponsors elected to the council by chapters for 2-year terms to represent their respective regions: Eastern, Midwestern, Southeastern, Southwestern, and Western/Rocky Mountain. The president is a former regional vice president elected to the council by the chapters for a 3-year term as president-elect, president, and past president. Psi Beta's executive director serves as the council's secretary-treasurer and administers the national office.

In 1986, Psi Beta's president and executive director participated for the first time with Psi Chi at the American Psychological Association (APA) convention. Four Psi Beta members shared in Psi Chi's programs at the 1987 APA convention. The highlight was an invited address by B. F. Skinner, who autographed a copy of Psi Beta's first handbook, printed in 1986–1987. In 1988 APA approved Psi Beta's affiliation, and the council began holding annual business meetings in conjunction with the APA national convention. Psi Beta scheduled programs for the first time at the 1989 APA convention. Annual programs include a chapter information exchange, award presentations, a workshop on innovative teaching methods, now cosponsored with APA's Division Two, and the Ruth Hubbard Cousins Distinguished Lecture, honoring Psi Beta's first honorary member. Distinguished lecturers at APA have been Robert Sternberg, Philip Zimbardo, Neal E. Miller, Stephen F. Davis, Wilbert J. McKeachie, Charles Brewer, Carole Wade, and Jane Halonen. Psi Beta vice-presidents work with APA's Education Directorate and the Council for Teachers of Undergraduate Psychology to plan programs for regional psychology meetings.

The American Psychological Society (APS) affiliated Psi Beta in 1991, enabling Psi Beta to schedule a chapter information exchange at APS annual conventions and permitting Psi Beta students to join APS as student affiliates. Psi Beta was admitted to membership in ACHS on 19 February 1994, and has the distinction of being the first 2-year college honor society member of ACHS.

Numerous awards are presented annually to Psi Beta members and chapters. Included are three Allyn & Bacon research paper awards. A Harcourt Brace Outstanding Chapter Award, the Carol Tracy Community Service award, and the Virginia Staudt Sexton Faculty

Sponsor award, established in 1990 by Sexton, a former Psi Chi national president and the second Psi Beta honorary member.

In 15 years Psi Beta had chartered 130 chapters with a cumulative membership of 12,000. To celebrate Psi Beta's fifteenth anniversary, the national council arranged many "firsts" for Psi Beta. The council adopted a national Psi Beta song and selected a community service project, Heather's Teddy Bears, as Psi Beta's first national service project. A Hall of Fame was established to induct chapters celebrating 15 consecutive active years. The council held its first retreat to update Psi Beta's mission. A video about Psi Beta for chapters and applicants to view was produced, and a Web page (www.psibeta.org) was constructed. Faculty advisors and council members developed a psychology career curriculum for faculty and models for chapters to utilize for sponsoring psychology career days, leadership workshops, miniconventions, transfer orientation workshops, and feedback poster sessions.

Annually, Psi Beta publishes fall, winter, and spring newsletters, and a chapter handbook which includes a section on leadership for chapter officers. These publications are preserved in the Archives of the History of American Psychology at Akron, Ohio.

Psi Beta's most innovative project, Diversity Project 2000, was designed and directed by former Psi Beta President Sandra Ladd of West Valley College in Saratoga, California. The program, first supported by APA's Office of Ethnic Minority Affairs and the Center for Mental Health Services, was initiated in 1994. This leadership and mentoring program provides outstanding ethnic-minority students studying psychology at 2-year colleges with a 2-day summer institute followed by 2 days' attendance at the APA national convention with mentors who encourage the students to pursue careers in psychology. Up to 30 students have participated annually since 1994. The codirector, Robin J. Hailstorks, 1996–1997 Psi Beta president from Prince George's Community College in Largo, Maryland, is a member of the APA Commission on Ethnic Minority Recruitment, Retention, and Training in Psychology.

Carol Tracy, who served as the first executive director, has continued to be appointed by the Psi Beta National Council. The national office is located in Chattanooga, Tennessee. The Psi Beta logo was officially registered with the U.S. Patent and Trademark Office on 13 December 1994.

Bibliography

Cousins, R. H., Tracy, C., & Giodano, P. (1992). Psi Chi and Psi Beta: The two national honor societies in psychology. In A. E. Puente, J. R. Matthews, & C. L. Brewer (Eds.), *Teaching psychology in America: A history* (pp. 403–427). Washington, DC: American Psychological Association.

Carol Tracy

PSI CHI. Outstanding psychology students in 4-year colleges and universities are eligible for membership in Psi Chi, the national honor society in psychology. Each new inductee into Psi Chi learns the meaning of the words *psyche* and *cheires. Psyche* refers to the mind and those activities that enrich the mind. *Cheires* refers to the use of the hands in the conduct of research. Thus Psi Chi members are encouraged to become participants in the scientific base that girds their discipline. This philosophy has guided the society since its inception.

It is fitting that a student-centered honor society had its beginnings with students. In 1928 two University of Kansas psychology students, Frederick H. Lewis and Edwin B. Newman, sensed the need for such an organization and presented their idea to a group of contemporaries.

After a series of three organizational meetings, the official founding of Psi Chi took place on 4 September 1929 at Yale University as part of the Ninth International Congress of Psychology. Fourteen schools were present to sign the original document that created the society, and 22 institutions were afforded charter chapter status. Cofounders Edwin B. Newman and Frederick H. Lewis were elected president and historian, respectively. Although Psi Chi was the preferred name for the new organization, the name was already in use, and the group was called Sigma Pi Sigma for 1 year until the desired name was available. Despite the fact that Psi Chi dealt with rather pedestrian matters (e.g., provisions for regional vice presidents, election requirements, terms of office, rituals, etc.) during its first 2 years, the 1930 meeting saw the selection of Ruth B. Guilford as secretary-treasurer and the appearance of the mimeographed *Psi Chi Newsletter*.

The 1932 Psi Chi convention witnessed the incubation and development of one of Psi Chi's enduring strengths, the support and encouragement of student research. In 1934, the proposal that Psi Chi develop a new journal to publish such research was made and rejected because financial support was uncertain. This same proposal would reappear and meet with the same fate in the 1960s and 1970s. The establishment of the *Psi Chi Journal of Undergraduate Research* would have to wait until the 1990s. By the end of the 1930s, 34 Psi Chi chapters were chartered.

As the United States entered World War II, Psi Chi president Stuart Cook encouraged the society to concentrate its interests and energies on the war effort. The lull in chartering new chapters engendered by World War II was followed by a rapid increase in growth after the war. By the end of the 1940s, the society consisted of 69 chapters.

The growth seen during the late 1940s was a barometer of things to come; Psi Chi was to mature and establish its presence during the 1950s. For example, Psi Chi's award program to recognize student accomplishments was begun in 1950 with the Steuart Henderson Britt Award to support student research projects. The awards program, expanded and diversified in recent years, stands as a continued commitment to student professional development.

The continuing liaison between Psi Chi and the American Psychological Association (APA) also has its roots in the early 1950s when Psi Chi news began to be featured in the APA journal *American Psychologist* and the provision of facilities for Psi Chi sessions became part of the annual APA convention. Psi Chi and APA were officially affiliated in 1958.

Although Psi Chi seemed poised to make its national presence felt, the 1950s were not without obstacles to overcome. Due to unanticipated resignations by a succession of executive secretaries, it was not until 1956 that a national office was established at the APA building in Washington, D.C. The national office made filing, record keeping, and clerical matters infinitely more efficient; however, the cost of maintaining an office in Washington threatened the financial stability of the organization. In 1958, the tenth executive secretary, Ruth H. Cousins, was hired and charged with finding a resolution to the financial crisis. Perhaps no single individual is as closely associated with the growth and prosperity of Psi Chi as is Ruth Cousins. For example, her desire to have well-known psychologists deliver lectures at the annual Psi Chi convention was formalized in 1959 as the Psi Chi Distinguished Lecture. Likewise, Psi Chi took a significant step forward when Cousins's efforts to have the organization become a member of the Association of College Honor Societies reached fruition in 1965. Psi Chi was no longer a fraternal organization; it was the national honor society in psychology. In recognition of her service and importance to Psi Chi, Cousins's title was changed to executive director in 1969. She retained this title until her retirement on 1 October 1991, when Kay Wilson assumed the position of executive officer.

Psi Chi's history from the 1960s to the present is one of continued growth, expansion, and diversification. For example, the cumulative membership reached 100,000 in 1976; by October 1999 Psi Chi had 959 chapters and had inducted 365,000 members.

By the 1970s Psi Chi's dedication to promoting and rewarding student research resulted in the establishment of the annual J. P. Guilford Undergraduate Research Award and the Edwin B. Newman Graduate Research Award, cosponsored with APA. During the 1990s the awards program was expanded to include the Psi Chi/Allyn & Bacon Psychology Awards for empirical research papers, Psi Chi Regional Research Awards to support the presentation of outstanding research at the regional conventions, Psi Chi National Convention Research Awards to support the presentation of outstanding research at the APA and American Psychological Society conventions, and Psi Chi/Thelma Hunt Research Awards, which provide three annual awards to study questions related to Psi Chi. Additionally, a program of small undergraduate research grants was begun in 1997. Following 2 years of planning, 1996 witnessed the publication of the first issue of the *Psi Chi Journal of Undergraduate Student Research*. Published quarterly, this lively journal is served by a large staff of faculty reviewers and is dedicated to publishing quality student research.

As Psi Chi enters for the twenty-first century, the legacy of its nearly 75-year history is clear; it continues to seek effective ways to facilitate the professional growth of students. Clearly, *psyche* and *cheires* are more than words heard only at induction ceremonies.

Bibliography

Cousins, R. H., Tracy, C., & Giodano, P. (1992). Psi Chi and Psi Beta: The two national honor societies in psychology. In A. E. Puente, J. R. Matthews, & C. L. Brewer (Eds.), *Teaching psychology in America: A history* (pp. 403–427). Washington, DC: American Psychological Association. A readable and detailed chapter that delineates the development of psychology's national honor societies for 4-year colleges (Psi Chi) and 2-year colleges (Psi Beta). Cousins and Tracy were instrumental in the development of Psi Chi and Psi Beta, respectively.

Psi Chi: The National Honor Society in Psychology. *Eye on Psi Chi.* Chattanooga, TN: Author. Published three times a year, this lively newsletter features articles of interest to members and news of chapter activities. It provides excellent accounting of current national initiatives, national awards programs, and the composition of the Psi Chi national council.

Stephen F. Davis

PSYCHE AND SOUL. The idea of soul is among the most elusive, complicated concepts in western intellectual history, central to ancient physics, metaphysics, cosmology, anthropology, eschatology, epistemology, and ethics. Soul is translated from the variously nuanced Greek *psuchē*, Hebrew *nefesh*, Latin *anima*, French *âme*, and German *Seele*. It differs from but relates intimately to *pneuma*, *ruach spiritus/spirare*, *esprit*, and *Geist*. Soul dictates an anthropology that regards persons as embodied souls or ensouled bodies, and a psychology defined as the logos or speech of the *psuchē*.

Selected Ancient Theories of Soul

Homer (ninth century BCE) understood *psuchē* as the free soul, the vital force residing in breath or blood that differed from various forms of soul that perished with the body. At death, *psuchē* departed for the underworld. A free soul that leaves the body during sleep, trance, and death was common to many cultures, accounting for the earliest theories of dream interpretation, and leading to diverse shamanistic practices involving transmigration of the soul, a widespread belief in bilocation (the simultaneous existence of stuporous and astral bodies), experiences of the *Doppelgänger* and *déjà vu*, and various paranormal phenomena. James Hillman, in *The Dream and the Underworld* (New York, 1979), retains the ancient link between *psuchē* and underworld.

The Pythagoreans (sixth century BCE) regarded the body as a tomb for the immortal soul, the person's core that could through various reincarnations (metempsychoses) rise to the Divine. During the fourth century BCE body-soul dualism became firmly established in Hippocratic medicine. Plato (c. 427–347 BCE) postulated an essentially unitary soul with an immortal vital principle and the three functions of appetite, spirit, and reason residing in the liver, heart, and head. Through the reasonable function of reminiscence (anamnesis), the immortal soul was able to recover the Forms or Ideas (true reality) that it knew before its association with a body. Freud gave the psyche a Platonic structure by dividing it into id, ego, and superego. Jung adopted a Platonic cosmology in his doctrine of archetypes (Forms). In Aristotle (384–323 BCE), *anima* became the principle of motion unique to living things, thus firmly establishing the doctrine of vitalism. The soul was characterized by entelechy, or inherent purpose, movement towards a predestined end, a notion retained in Hillman's *The Soul's Code* (New York, 1996). Epicurus (341–270 BCE) and the Stoics were atomists for whom the soul was the finest form of matter that gave form, order, and life to the cosmos. Individual souls emanated from the world soul, and the soul's otherworldly home corresponded to the immanent but impalpable starry or planetary world. This approach forged the link with astrology that characterizes contemporary New Age psychology.

Origins and Destiny of the Soul

The soul's existence and its transmission to the body are explained by three origin theories that dominate religious and cosmological tradition: The soul is created out of nothing; it has a divine element begotten of God (or the demi-urge); or it emanates from God. Soul is transmitted in accordance with one of three theories accounting for the soul's current imperfect condition. Creationists have believed for millennia that a new soul is created for each human being at conception, or within a few weeks of conception (for example, Aristotle and Aquinas). This belief undergirds pro-life, antiabortion ethics. Traducianists believe that the soul is transmitted along with the body by the parents. Preexistentianists (reincarnationists) believe that the human soul's previous existence accounts for its current circumstances, as in the law of karma, thus linking origins to destiny.

One version of the soul's destiny is allegorized in the Cupid and Psyche myth, which portrays the soul's blessed preexistence, its troubled earthly sojourn, and its future immortal state. Religious and literary texts report a great variety of often contradictory perspectives on the soul's earthly pilgrimage and its fate after its death. The earthly soul may be possessed by demons or evil spirits and tempted by or sold to the Devil. It may be purified through the practices of gnostic mystery religions or by passing through purgatory. The dead soul may leave the body to dwell in the underworld (Hades or She'ol), from whence it can be summoned by conjurers or mediums; it may dwell in Elysium or the Isle of the Blessed; it may encounter eternal damnation in Hell or eternal bliss in Paradise; it may be annihilated; it may or may not be resurrected. The soul's destiny may involve reincarnation in other bodies during its evolution from immaturity to spiritual illumination, as taught in the doctrines of Hinduism, Sikhism, Jainism, and Qabbalistic Judaism. Or the dead soul may take on an imaginal body, as taught in Sufism. Then, the realm of soul is a kind of transitional, illusory space, as depicted in Roberts Avens's *Imaginal Body* (Washington, D.C., 1982).

The Soul/Spirit Relationship

In *Über die Seelenfrage* (1861), Gustav Theodor Fechner reviewed possible relationships between soul and spirit:

> In the first sense spirit and soul as a whole are opposed to the body as a whole. In the second sense the spirit is the active principle, masculine, creative, generative . . . while the soul is the desiring, the receptive, the feminine side. . . . In the third sense the spirit is the higher, the soul the lower—no longer a queen but a maidservant. (In Walter Lowrie, *Religion of a Scientist*, London, 1946, p. 89)

The simple distinction between spirit/soul and body constitutes the traditional Christian dichotomy, a mind–body dualism in which soul and spirit are combined or equated. The others are versions of trichotomy, differentiating soul from spirit. Lucretius (c. 98–55 BCE) distinguished between *anima* (spirit, soul, animating principle) and *animus* (intellect, mind, faculty of representation, directing principle): *animus* directs both body and *anima*. The Chinese *Book of Changes* distinguishes between Yin, the receptive, consolidating, female element, and Yang, the active, creative, expanding male element: their relationship is complementary, competitive, and dialectic. Jungian psychology incorporates both Lucretian and Chinese elements. In Christian trichotomy, *psuchē* is regarded either as mediating between body and *pneuma*, or as a secondary to and proceeding from *pneuma*. Many nineteenth-century biblical psychologists differentiated rational, immortal soul (*pneuma*) from animal, sensitive, and affectional spirit (*psuchē*). Nineteenth-century German Romantic philosophers understood soul (*Seele*) to be responsible for intellectual knowledge, whereas spirit (*Geist*) opened the person to the divine light. A distinction between soul and spirit was central to Otto Rank's will psychology and Roberto Assagioli's psychosynthesis; Hillman (1979), regards soul as "a world of imagination, passion, fantasy, reflection, that is neither physical nor material on the one hand, nor spiritual and abstract on the other, yet bound by them both" (p. 68). The psychiatrist Gregory Zilboorg, in *Psychoanalysis and Religion* (New York, 1962), and the logotherapist Viktor Frankl, in *The Unconscious God* (New York, 1975), used the soul versus spirit distinction to argue for a clear demarcation of the roles of the psychotherapist and the pastoral counselor or spiritual director.

Loss of Soul in Discipline and Person

In *Psychology and the Soul* (Philadelphia, 1950), Otto Rank develops the historical hypothesis that in "the animistic era, psychologizing was a *creating* of the soul; in the religious era, it was a *representing* of the soul to one's self; in our era of natural science it is a *knowing* of the individual soul" (p. 11). Rank noted that twentieth-century psychology had become "both a scientific 'psychology without a soul' and a kind of overburdening of the inner spiritual self" (p. 31). Early proponents of the "new" psychology—inspired by the 1845 antivitalism pact of Ernst Brücke and Emil du Bois-Reymond—rejected the soul as a vital principle. This rejection inspired William McDougall's apologetic for animism in *Body and Mind* (New York, 1911) and Hans Driesch's defense of vitalism in *The Problem of Individuality* (London, 1914) and *Mind and Body* (London, 1927). A similar rejection of the "higher" theological soul led William James to defend immortality in *Human Immortality* (New York, 1898) and Hubert Gruender, in *Psychology Without a Soul: A Criticism* (St. Louis, 1911), to defend the soul's substantiality, simplicity, and spirituality as bases for its immortality.

Naturally occurring maladies of the soul/spirit have been described throughout history and across cultures, with perhaps the best-known consisting of the inner anguish of spiritual purgation described by St. John of the Cross (1542–1591) in *Dark Night of the Soul* (New York, 1990) and the despair portrayed by Søren Kierkegaard (1813–1855) in *The Concept of Dread* (Princeton, 1957) and *The Sickness unto Death* (New York, 1989), and depicted in Frank Lake's *Clinical Theology* (London, 1966) as central to the schizoid condition. The existential reality of such afflictions led Driesch to assert in *The Crisis in Psychology* (Princeton, 1926) that psychology cannot ignore metaphysical assumptions without suicidal results. McDougall, in *Religion and the Sciences of Life* (London, 1934), argued for a return to the Dionysian perspective of the romantics that took seriously the soul's spiritual striving. W. H. Sheldon, in *Psychology and the Promethean Will* (New York, 1936), postulated an *animectomy complex*, a fear of soul loss or amputation, that resulted from modern, intellectualized psychology. A soul-sensitive psychology can also heal such forms of soul pathology as the depersonalized, disembodied self described in R. D. Laing's *The Divided Self* (London, 1959) and folk illnesses of soul loss such as susto and espanto. Buddhism "cures" such torment through philosophy, teaching that the ontological soul is nonsubstantial and illusory.

[*Many of the people mentioned in this entry are the subjects of independent biographical entries.*]

Bibliography

Burwick, F., & Douglass, P. (Eds.). (1992). *The crisis in modernism: Bergson and the vitalist controversy*. New York: Cambridge University Press.

Eliade, M. (Ed.). (1993). *The encyclopedia of religion* (Vols. 1, 3–16, in 7). New York: Macmillan. Reprint of 1987 edition. This may be the best single source for examining the soul from the perspective of comparative religion. The encyclopedia features a series of nine articles clarifying primitive, ancient near eastern, Greek and Hellenistic, Indian, Buddhist, Chinese, Jewish, Christian, and Islamic concepts of the soul. The soul's origins and destiny are covered in related articles.

Everson, S. (Ed.). (1991). *Companions to ancient thought: Vol. 2. Psychology*. New York: Cambridge University Press. This volume offers in-depth explorations of ancient thought regarding *psuchē* and covers a period of 800 or more years, focusing on the thought of Heraclitus, Plato, Aristotle, Epicurus, and Plotinus, and the schools of Stoicism, Pyrrhonism, and Greek medicine.

Freyhofer, H. H. (1982). *The vitalism of Hans Driesch: The success and decline of a scientific theory*. Frankfurt am Main: Peter Lang.

Friedrich, G. (Ed.). (1974). *Theological dictionary of the New Testament* (Vol. 9). Grand Rapids, MI: Wm. B. Eerdmans. A standard etymological source for students of the Judeo-Christian scriptures, with extensive use of Hebrew and Greek texts. It includes an extensive entry (pp. 608–660) on uses of *psuchē* and its cognates in classical Greek, the Old Testament, Judaism, the New Testament, and Gnostic literature. The abridged, one-volume edition (1985) contains a shorter entry (pp. 1342–1353) with transliterated terms.

Helminiak, D. (1996). *The human core of spirituality: Mind as psyche and spirit.* Albany: State University of New York Press. Helminiak offers a unique and scholarly argument, based on the philosophical theology of Bernard Lonergan, for the position that mind is double, comprising both psyche and spirit.

Hillman, J. (1992). *Re-visioning psychology.* New York: HarperPerennial. (Reprint of the 1975 edition.) This is a classic philosophical and historical foundation for the contemporary therapeutic emphasis on the soul. Hillman borrows from the Romantic poets Blake and Keats the notion of "soul-making," asserting that "the purpose of life is to make psyche of it, to find connections between life and soul." This is worked out through explorations of personifying (imagining things), pathologizing (falling apart), psychologizing (seeing through), and dehumanizing (soul making). Hillman builds on ideas first developed in *Suicide and the Soul* (New York, 1964).

Klein, D. B. (1970). *A history of scientific psychology: Its origins and philosophical background.* New York: Basic Books. In addition to furnishing extensive philosophical and theological background concerning the soul, Klein makes explicit the links between historical and contemporary psychological theories.

Lewis, C. S. (1956). *Till we have faces.* London: Geoffrey Bles; New York: Harcourt Brace Jovanovich, 1980. In a novel that has become a literary classic, the Cupid and Psyche myth as recorded in the *Metamorphses* of Lucius Apuleius Platonicus (c. 125 CE) is transformed into an allegory illustrating not only the purification of the soul but also the (Jungian) individuation and realization of the psyche.

Loder, J. E., & Neidhardt, W. J. (1992). *The knight's move: The relational logic of the spirit in theology and science.* Colorado Springs: Helmers & Howard. The authors defend a distinction between spirit and soul (and related biblical paradoxes and contradictions) using "the strange loop model" in which apparent polarities are in fact a unity.

Watson, R. I. (1963). *The great psychologists: From Aristotle to Freud.* Philadelphia: J. B. Lippincott. Watson includes extensive discussion of *psyche* and related terms and of the controversies around vitalism.

Winkler, G. (1992). *The soul of the matter: A Jewish-Kabbalistic perspective on the human soul before, during, and after "life."* New York: Judaica Press.

Hendrika Vande Kemp

PSYCHIATRY is a branch of medicine concerned with the study and treatment of persons suffering with personality, behavioral, and mental problems. Much like the field of psychology, psychiatry is both an ancient and a new field of study. It traces its roots to earliest times of the philosophers and medicine men. In ancient times, persons suffering from psychic and physical symptoms were not distinguished from one another, and those who attempted to relieve such suffering claimed to have religious or magical powers of healing. In some clans, this was the head, or one who had survived a catastrophe, or who had a "revelation" (sometimes following a convulsion or trance) that they were a healer. Those suffering from mental problems were often seen as being "possessed" by demons, which had to be exorcised by either opening the skull (trepanning) or frightening the demons away through the uttering of incantations or other elaborate techniques. In keeping with the law of effect, only the successful "treatments" were remembered and added to the healer's reputation as all-powerful. No doubt many of the medicine men had no idea as to why any particular treatment worked, but were encouraged by any success that occurred.

The contributions of the Greek philosophers were significant in medicine, as the field turned from superstitious and magical thinking (e.g., ills caused by demons or humors) to rational thought that investigated the origins of illness as deriving from the body itself. Although mental ills were more difficult to understand than physical ones, the role of the brain and learning were now more available for study. Then, during the Middle Ages, in Western civilization (not so in the Islamic and Asian cultures) such rational thought was suppressed by religious zealots, only to be revived with the Renaissance and the era of reason and observation.

Modern psychiatry had its foundations in the eighteenth century, with the separation of "mentally disturbed" persons from criminals, mentally retarded, and other persons considered outcasts in society. Philippe Pinel (1745–1826) is well known as one who removed forcible restraints in the management of the mentally ill. He also began a system of classification of mental diseases. At the time, two distinct trends in psychiatry emerged, which still prevail today. Pinel and others advocated a treatment of patients which emphasized encouraging positive attitudes and thinking. On the other hand, many physicians viewed the etiology of mental problems as stemming from the biological substrate or caused by insults to the physiological systems of the brain. The dominant treatments of such ills were the administration of medications, bloodletting, shock treatments, or surgery that would alter brain functioning. Whatever the treatment, the importance of providing separate institutions for the study and care of the mentally ill laid the foundation for the new medical field of psychiatry.

In America, the earliest facilities for the mentally disturbed were in Williamsburg, Virginia (now restored for visitors), and in Philadelphia, Pennsylvania, where Benjamin Rush (1745–1813), who was regarded as the father of American psychiatry, treated patients. Rush was a remarkable and scholarly man. He was a signer of the Declaration of Independence and in addition to the first book on psychiatry in America, wrote on a wide range of philosophical and political subjects. Although he attributed emotional problems to organic causes, he advocated humane treatment for mental patients. He experimented with many treatment approaches, including having the patient in a chair which was twirled around to force blood to the brain.

At the same time as these developments, two physicians, trained in Vienna and practicing in Paris, each made popular although controversial contributions to early psychiatry. Franz Joseph Gall (1758–1828) developed a system of diagnosing personality traits and disorders based on the shape of the skull. Phrenology soon fell into disrepute, but Gall's work in cerebral localization was a stimulant to much research in brain function and behavior. The other, Franz Mesmer (1734–1815), began an equally controversial approach to the understanding of behavior. His concept of animal magnetism was the precursor of hypnosis, which remains an important practice in psychiatry and was the object of scientific study by Jean Martin Charcot (1825–1893), progenitor of the next great development in the field of psychiatry.

The rapid developments in physiology, chemistry, and hygiene during the end of the nineteenth century ushered in the modern era of medicine. As the century came to a close, the career of one man in Vienna radically influenced the field of psychiatry. It was probably the publication of Sigmund Freud's *The Interpretation of Dreams* in 1900, in which he described the discovery of the unconscious, that marked the beginning of modern-day psychiatry. His works began a movement to understand mental and emotional problems that not only influenced psychiatry but spread to the fields of psychology and social work as well. For the next half-century, psychoanalysis and its evolving theories dominated the profession of psychiatry with neuropsychiatric approaches mainly focused on the most serious mentally ill population. Many of the concepts of psychoanalysts became enormously popular in Western culture and were influential in the upbringing of children, as well as in the arts and literature.

Sigmund Freud (1856–1939) was trained as a neurologist, but became interested in hypnotism and other "talking" treatments of emotional illness. He invented psychoanalysis, first by analyzing himself and then his patients in Vienna. The method requires the patient to lie on a couch and "free associate" (say whatever comes to mind). Each session lasts for about an hour and continues four or five times a week for 3 years or more. The analyst listens from behind or to one side of the patient and interprets the associations presented that may give insight into the problems. Freud's writings on the interpretation of dreams, causes of hysteria, and the symbolic expressions of the unconscious are classic in psychiatric and psychological literature. Among Freud's many followers, several, such as Alfred Adler (1870–1937), Otto Rank (1884–1939), and Carl Gustav Jung (1875–1961) dissented from the master and diverged into their own concepts of the etiology of personality disorders. They, too, were prolific writers and developed their own strident followers. The circle of psychiatrists influenced by Freud were physicians and the tradition of medical training for psychoanalysis remained strong until recently when nonmedically trained mental health professionals were allowed into the societies of psychoanalysts. Ironically, one of the leading disciples of Freud, his daughter, Anna, one of the leaders in the field of child psychiatry, never went to medical school.

The legacy of Sigmund Freud continued to influence the field of psychiatry for many decades, with strict followers of his views being called "Orthodox Freudians" and evolving theorists using the term *Neo-Freudians*. One of the latter, who emphasized the sociological, interpersonal, and current events in an individual's life as contributing to personality development, as opposed to infantile, historical, and biological events, was Harry Stack Sullivan (1892–1949). He believed that the therapist should not listen passively to the patient, but be a participant observer, who objectively offers suggestions and insights into the therapy. Although not as well known to the public as the method of psychoanalysis, other therapies which attempted to alleviate severe mental illness continued to develop in the late nineteenth century and into the twentieth century.

One of the important advances in the field was developing a format for identifying and classifying abnormal behaviors, which then could be studied in systematic ways. Emil Kraepelin (1856–1926), a German psychiatrist, wrote a nosology of mental illness which was first published in 1883. The system he developed was to dominate the field of psychiatry until the mid-twentieth century and was accepted as the framework for classifying abnormal behavior until the development of a new system in early 1950 under the auspices of the American Psychiatric Association. The *Diagnostic and Statistical Manual of Mental Disorders* (APA, 1994) is used worldwide as a basis for defining and classifying various forms of disorders and is revised and updated as new knowledge is obtained.

During the early part of the twentieth century, many of the physical treatments of the mentally disturbed were "hit and miss" remedies involving diets, sleep inducements, surgery, and abrupt shocks to the system. An important treatment for schizophrenia involved the administration of insulin, which produced a convulsion (due to the rapid decrease in blood sugar level) and then a coma state in the patient. Although the exact causes of the behavioral changes occurring following the coma have never been identified, the treatment became a popular intervention. Convulsive therapy was also produced with electroshock, which was first used in 1938 by an Italian psychiatrist, Ugo Cerletti (1877–1963). The treatment has undergone modifications to reduce the risk of physical injury during the convulsion, but is still used today in cases of severe depression.

Neurosurgical procedures with the mentally ill in the United States were developed principally under the leadership of Harvey Cushing (1869–1939) at Johns Hopkins University. In the late 1940s, a Portuguese neurologist, Egas Moniz (1874–1955) and an American neurologist, Walter Freeman (1895–1972) introduced prefrontal lobotomy surgery on psychotic patients who were resistant to shock treatments. The surgery destroyed the white matter of the frontal lobes of the brain and caused irreversible personality changes. Although the treatment was administered to over 50,000 persons, questions were raised as to the ethics of the procedure. However, with the introduction of psychotropic medication, the number of surgeries declined.

Psychopharmacology opened a whole new horizon in psychiatry and has put other physical intervention approaches far into the background. In the early 1950s, psychiatric patients began to be treated with serpasil, reserpine, and other drugs derived from a medicinal plant used by ancient Indian physicians. The drugs had a sedative or depressant effect. Later, chlorpromazine was found to tranquilize schizophrenic patients, without causing depression. One of the most successful drug therapies has been the use of lithium, which is particularly helpful for mania and for bipolar (manic-depressive) patients. The use of antipsychotic drugs dramatically changed the course of treatments for persons with chronic mental illness from long hospitalizations to shorter ones. Most treatment is now on an outpatient basis in community mental health facilities.

Drug therapy has also been used with persons suffering from more mildly disabling conditions, such as mild symptoms of depression or anxiety. The first widely popular drug was meprobamate (Miltown) which was introduced in 1950. Since then, drug therapies have tended to follow courses of popular use, with Librium following Miltown, then Valium, and then Prozac. Drug therapy has been particularly useful in helping patients take advantage of psychotherapy, which is best coordinated with psychotropic approaches. One of the principle areas of research interest of psychiatrists is in developing specific drugs for specific psychiatric conditions.

As a medical specialty, psychiatry is based on the premise that biological causes are at the root of mental and emotional problems. But there are psychiatrists who do not adhere to the "biological model" (see Szasz, 1974) and treat these problems as social and behavioral ills. Some have argued that by reducing poverty and its accompanying stresses, the number of psychiatric problems would be drastically reduced. Although a minority view, it has raised awareness that societal and cultural forces do have an impact on personal adjustment. The fields of social and community psychiatry provide an opportunity to study issues of social concern and to consult with community agencies, government, and other organizations working in the public domain.

The breadth of psychiatry can also be seen in the work with children's disorders. Psychiatrists working with children have learned that many approaches may be helpful, and a full understanding of family history and family interactions is essential in dealing with children with behavioral and emotional problems.

The model for interdisciplinary collaboration was initiated with the creation of child guidance clinics, founded by William Healy in Chicago, Illinois, in 1909. The model of the clinic staffed with psychiatrists, psychologists, and social workers spread to other clinics and to adult facilities as well. Traditionally, psychiatrists were the directors of such clinics, with each profession having well-defined roles. However, through the years, the roles of administrator, parent interviewer, child evaluator, and therapist are now shared by any of the core mental health professionals. In inpatient psychiatric facilities, psychiatric nurses often carry out much of the day-to-day therapy that is needed by the patients.

Although the mental health field consists of 4 core professions, psychiatry, clinical psychology, clinical social work, and psychiatric nursing, the professionals may have similar roles in clinical settings. However, the training paths differ for each field. In order to be a psychiatrist, one must complete medical school and a residency in the field. Following the residency in psychiatry, there may be special training in psychoanalysis, neurology, psychopharmacology, or other areas. Training in psychoanalysis requires that the students complete their own personal analysis, usually with a professional called a "training analyst." The training for a clinical psychologist differs in that the student must complete a doctorate degree (Ph.D. or PsyD.) in psychology, which includes a year of clinical internship in a mental-health setting. Following graduation, the student may continue supervised clinical training for a year (in order to qualify for the state licensing examination), or complete postdoctoral work in a clinical facility. Specialization in fields such as clinical child psychology, forensic psychology, and psychopharmacology require further course work and supervised work experience.

Psychiatrists may choose to be certified by the American Board of Psychiatry, but may practice without such certification. The professional organization for psychiatrists in the United States is the American Psychiatric Association which has about 40,000 members.

[*Many of the people mentioned in this article are the subjects of independent biographical entries.*]

Bibliography

American Psychiatric Association. (1994). *Diagnostic and statistical manual of mental Disorders (DSM–IV)*. Washington, DC: Author.

Arieti, S. (Ed.). (1974). *The foundations of psychiatry*. New York: Basic Books.

Cole, R. (1989). Psychiatry: Past and future. In H. I. Kaplan & B. J. Sadock (Eds.). *Comprehensive textbook of psychiatry* (5th ed, pp. 2132–2157). Baltimore, MD: Williams & Wilkins.

Hales, R. E., & Yudofsky, S. C. (1987). *Textbook of neuropsychiatry*. Washington, DC: American Psychiatric Press.

Kaplan, H. I., & Sadock, B. J. (1989). *Comprehensive textbook of psychiatry* (5th ed.) Baltimore, MD: Williams & Wilkins.

Kaplan, H. I., & Sadock, B. J. (1998). *Synopsis of psychiatry: Behavioral science clinical psychiatry*. Baltimore, MD: Lippincott, Williams & Wilkins.

Pardes, H. (1986). Neuroscience and Psychiatry: Marriage or coexistence? *American Journal of Psychiatry, 143*, 10.

Shorter, E. (1997). *A history of psychiatry: From the era of asylum to the age of Prozac*. New York: Wiley.

Szasz, T. (1974). *The myth of mental illness*. New York: Harper & Row.

Tasman, A., Kay, J., & Lieberman, J. A. (Eds.). (1997). *Psychiatry*. Philadelphia, PA: Saunders.

Donald K. Freedheim

PSYCHOANALYSIS. [*This entry comprises five articles*:

History of the Field
Theories
Methods of Study
Psychoanalysis and Philosophy
Psychoanalytic Psychotherapies

The first article provides an overview of the broad history of the field from its inception to the present. The second and third articles discuss the theories and methods of study of psychoanalysis. The last two articles examine the critiques and defenses of psychoanalysis and review the history and development of psychoanalytic treatment.]

History of the Field

Psychoanalysis, at least Freudian psychoanalysis, is (1) most broadly defined, a theory of mental functioning and human nature; (2) a theory of psychological development; (3) a theory of psychopathology, particularly of the neuroses; and (4) a method of treatment. The qualifier "Freudian psychoanalysis" is included because the above definition does not apply equally to other psychoanalytic theories that are not as comprehensive and all-embracing as Freudian theory. The latter can be referred to as *psychodynamic theories*.

Among the features that distinguish Freudian theory from other theories (both nonpsychoanalytic and non-Freudian psychodynamic theories) are the former's (1) emphasis on unconscious mental processes, particularly unconscious wishes, desires, and defenses; much of human behavior is understood in terms of the interplay and dynamic interaction between unconscious wishes, fantasies, and desires, on the one hand, and the anxiety and guilt they elicit and the defenses developed in order to cope with these dysphoric affects, on the other. The above description implies (2) a view of human behavior from the perspective of inner conflict. According to a Freudian point of view, virtually all behavior—dreams, slips of the tongue, and neurotic symptoms, as well as intentional adaptive action—reflects a compromise among different conflicting demands and motives within the individual's personality and (3) a central role particularly for sexual drives and wishes and, to some extent, for aggressive drives and wishes.

Clinical Foundations and Emergence as a Clinical Discipline

The prototypic pathology that early psychoanalysis, along with other approaches at the time, conceptualized and attempted to treat was hysteria, the pathology of the day. Freud's early exposure to patients suffering from hysteria came from the approximately four months he spent with Jean Martin Charcot in 1885–1886 at the Sâlpetrière and from the account of his own colleague, Joseph Breuer, of his treatment of a patient called Anna O. in November 1882. Freud credited Breuer with the psychoanalytic method of treatment, a "talking cure" method in which merely talking about memories, thoughts, events, feelings, and so on—a process that Anna O. referred to as "chimney sweeping"—appeared to alleviate hysterical symptoms.

A good deal of Breuer and Freud's early account of hysteria was essentially no different from that of Janet. In *Studies on Hysteria* (1893–1895), Breuer and Freud refer to Janet approvingly, indicate their general agreement with his view on hysteria, and employ descriptive and explanatory terms such as "splitting of consciousness," "condition seconde," and "formation of separate psychical groups" that are entirely in accord with Janet's views.

Like Janet, Breuer and Freud believed that hysterical symptoms were due to the consequences of "banishment of a thought from personal consciousness" (Janet, as quoted in Ellenberger, 1970, p. 361). Freud soon came, however, to disagree with Janet's belief that the hysterical patient's constitutional weakness or hereditary deficiency was the primary predisposing factor in the production of hysterical symptoms. Indeed, the conceptual birth of psychoanalysis occurred when, diverging from both Janet's and Breuer's views, Freud described a kind of hysteria—"defense hysteria"—that occurred when an "incompatible idea" (i.e., a desire or thought about which the person is ashamed or guilty) aroused such "distressing affect . . . that the subject . . . had no confidence in his power to resolve . . . [it] by means of thought activity" (Freud, 1894, p. 47). The person's only solution was to put the idea out of his or her mind, that is, to repress it. Thus, according to Freud's new view, the "splitting of consciousness" and the isolation of a mental content from the rest of consciousness was not due to the hysterical patient's hereditary deficiency in integrative capacity, as Janet maintained, but was the result of a motivated act. In short, the individual wished, desired, remembered, or thought something of which he or she was so deeply ashamed, anxious, or guilty that he or she needed to put the distress-arousing content out of consciousness.

Although banished from consciousness, the idea and its accompanying affect persist and press for representation in consciousness. However, the affect remains unexpressed or undischarged, and the incompatible idea that has been banished from consciousness remains isolated and "cut off from associative communication with the rest of consciousness" (Freud, 1894, p. 46) and therefore is not subjected to rectification by other ideas. That is, according to Freud, when a mental content is banished from consciousness, it cannot be modulated or put into perspective by "associative communication" with other ideas. Thus, hysterical symptoms are caused by both the person's failure to discharge affect adequately and the failure of associative correction. The first failure leads to "strangulated affect," which, through a process Freud acknowledged that he did not understand, becomes "converted" into the somatic symptoms (thus the term *conversion hysteria*). The second failure prevents the "wearing away" and associative correction to which a traumatic memory is normally subjected when it enters the "great complex of associations" that constitutes normal consciousness. The result is that the traumatic memory remains isolated from the rest of the personality and operates like a "parasite" that exerts pathological influences on consciousness, including splitting of consciousness and the formation of a "second psychical group" of which the isolated (i.e., repressed) idea is the nucleus.

Implicit in the concept of repression is a shift from an early emphasis on ideas and affects generated by external trauma to an emphasis on ideas and affects generated by inner wishes, desires, and fantasies, which, Freud believed, were primarily sexual in nature. Any "incompatible ideas," however, can also generate the "pathogens" of unexpressed affect (which can be converted into somatic symptoms) and isolated ideas (leading to splitting of consciousness). Thus, when effective, Breuer's cathartic method (i.e., the airing and bringing to consciousness of repressed ideas and affects) succeeded in helping the patient express repressed ideas and affects and thus reduced the likelihood that they would be converted to somatic symptoms. Initially, hypnosis was the means by which such catharsis was accomplished.

Freud soon became disillusioned with hypnosis for a number of reasons. Although some symptoms could be removed through hypnosis, other symptoms soon took their place, presumably because the underlying conflict between the ego (in this original context, understood as one's sense of oneself and the kind of person one is) and the incompatible idea remained unresolved. After a brief period of using a "pressure" technique (in which Freud placed his hand on the forehead of the patient and suggested the return of repressed ideas and memories), it soon became apparent that this method was as limited as hypnosis in resolving underlying conflicts and in succeeding in integrating repressed and isolated ideas into the rest of the personality.

Eventually, hypnosis and the pressure technique were replaced by free association (i.e., the patient lies down and says whatever comes to his or her mind, without concern for the logical sequence of those contents) and interpretation (i.e., the analyst interprets the patient's associations with regard to the wishes, anxieties, conflicts, and defenses they indirectly reveal). The aims of treatment were no longer limited to the catharsis or "abreaction" of affect and the uncovering of unconscious material, but included insight, working through (i.e., what Freud [1926] referred to as "the period of strenuous effort" [p. 159] needed to maintain one's awareness and insight), and the assimilation of hitherto sequestered and ego-alien thoughts, wishes, and ideas into the rest of the individual's personality.

Paralleling modifications in technique were changes in Freudian theory. At the risk of oversimplifying these theoretical developments, they contained the following central elements: early on, like Janet, Freud focused on external trauma, but unlike Janet, he emphasized sexual trauma as the precipitating cause of hysteria and other neuroses. Early trauma gave way to a conflict between an incompatible idea (e.g., a wish, desire, or fantasy) and the ego as the precipitating cause of hysterical and other neurotic symptoms. Although, in principle, any incompatible idea could trigger neurotic symptoms, Freud believed that sexual ideas played a primary role. Or, to put it more accurately, it was the repression of sexual ideas that played a primary role in generating neurotic symptoms.

In his *Three Essays on the Theory of Sexuality* (1905), Freud developed a formal and comprehensive theory of a universal sexual instinctual drive that included the elements of infantile sexuality, psychosexual stages, (i.e., oral, anal, phallic, and genital), and the Oedipus complex. In accounting for neurosis, the emphasis now was more fully on universal sexual wishes and fantasies that needed to be defended against by repression and other defenses.

One can identify a final phase in Freud's theorizing in which the structural model of the personality predominates over the so-called topographical model. That is, the emphasis is not simply on whether a mental content or process is conscious or unconscious, but also on the structure of the personality (id, ego, or superego) to which it belongs. What mainly prompted this shift was Freud's recognition that repression (as well as other defenses) could be both unconscious and an ego function. Hence, one could not equate ego with consciousness. This new way of thinking led to the idea that anxiety triggers repression (and other defenses) rather than being caused by repression. It also influenced clinical work in the direction of greater attention to analysis of the patient's defenses rather than an earlier nearly exclusive focus on uncovering the content of unconscious wishes.

Divisions and Modifications

Almost from the beginning and continuing to the present day, psychoanalytic history has been characterized by rifts, schisms, divisions, and modifications of existing theory. More than any other substantive issue, it was the rejection of Freud's insistence on the primary role of the sexual drive as the superordinate motive force in psychic life that constituted the point of divergence between Freudian psychoanalytic theory, on the one hand, and both non-Freudian "dissidents" and post-Freudian theoretical developments, on the other. Among the well-known early dissidents were Jung, Adler, Reich, and Horney.

The rejection of Freud's drive or instinct theory continues to characterize contemporary psychoanalytic schools. Thus, for Kohut (e.g., 1984) it is the need for self-cohesiveness that is the primary motive force in psychic life. For Fairbairn (1952), "libido is primarily object-seeking rather than pleasure-seeking" (p. 82). A position generally similar to Fairbairn's is taken by the contemporary "relational" school of psychoanalysis (e.g., Mitchell, 1988). One must note the figure of Sandor Ferenczi, who, although he never broke "politically" with the psychoanalytic establishment, nevertheless entertained and published ideas that were clearly at variance with classical Freudian theory.

One must also note the development of psychoanalytic ego psychology and its major theorist, Heinz Hartmann. In contrast to other revisionists and modifiers, ego psychologists viewed their formulations as constituting not a departure or divergence from Freudian theory, but as a logical extension of Freud's structural theory. One of the basic claims that ego psychologists made is that certain ego functions (e.g., thinking, memory, movement) are genetically programmed and unfold in a regular, predicable way in an "average expectable environment," relatively independent of sexual and aggressive drives and wishes (i.e., they have a "primary autonomy"). Another claim is that although certain ego defenses (e.g., intellectualization) may have originally developed in the context of conflict over unacceptable wishes and impulses, they may become relatively autonomous of that original context (i.e., they may achieve "secondary autonomy") and assume an adaptive value in their own right. (It should be recognized that Hartmann's concept of secondary autonomy is virtually identical to Floyd Allport's concept of "functional autonomy.")

Accompanying the above modifications in theory were modifications in conceptions and techniques of psychoanalytic treatment, which can only be referred to and selectively sampled here. The concept of the analyst as a "blank screen" (on whom the patient projects his or her wishes, fantasies, conflicts, etc.) has given way to a picture of the analyst as an active and interactive partner with the patient—a "participant-observer," to use Sullivan's term.

In line with this more contemporary conception of psychoanalytic treatment, the role of transference and countertransference has come to the fore. Freud conceptualized transference as the transferring of attitudes, feelings, wishes, conflicts, and so on originally directed toward parents to the analyst. If, as Freud's reasoning went, the analyst remained neutral, "impenetrable," and like a blank screen, the patient's experience of the analyst could be understood as projections revealing earlier reactions and feelings. Analysis of these transference reactions would then reveal to the patient the nature of these earlier reactions. Freud understood countertransference as the analyst's own transference reactions to the patient's transference—as Freud (1910) put it, the analyst's reactions that "arise . . . as a result of the patient's influence on his unconscious feelings" (p. 144). Freud believed that these countertransferences needed to be overcome—either by self-analysis or by returning to analysis—if treatment was to proceed successfully.

Today, many analysts believe that the most significant and effective aspect of psychoanalytic treatment consists of transference interpretations that are guided by the analyst's scrutiny of his or her own countertransference reactions. In the new conception of psychoanalytic treatment, the very meanings of the terms *transference* and *countertransference* have changed. Thus, transference is no longer understood simply as a process in which the patient distorts and projects onto a blank screen, the analyst, attitudes, wishes, needs, expectations, and so on that he or she experienced in relation to early parental figures. Rather, according to Gill (1982), the patient's transference reactions are always plausible ones that are based on cues emitted by the analyst. And countertransference is no longer understood in terms of blind spots produced by the analyst's unresolved conflicts, and so on, but rather as the total range of the analyst's emotional and cognitive reactions to the patient, particularly to the patient's transference.

In this contemporary conception of psychoanalytic treatment, the here-and-now therapeutic relationship, rather than a focus on the patient's past, takes on a primary curative role. This is true in at least two ways: (1) the patient's experience of the relationship (interpretation of the transference) becomes the primary object of examination; and (2) the "corrective emotional experience," consisting of the analyst's nonjudgmental understanding and accepting attitude, is a crucial therapeutic factor.

The emphasis on transference and countertransference—which some have viewed as the new "common ground" of psychoanalysis, despite theoretical differences among the different schools—means that the here-and-now relationship between patient and analyst, rather than, say, uncovering of early memories, is the focus of therapeutic interpretation and attention.

Relation of Psychoanalysis to Other Disciplines

As far as its theoretical substance or content is concerned, it is clear that Freud viewed psychoanalysis as part of psychology. Freud attempted to develop a theory of mental functioning that employed primarily psychological concepts and formulations. Over the years, a good deal of research on psychoanalytic hypotheses has been carried out by psychologists—ranging, for example, from Sears's (e.g., 1943) early research program at Stanford, which attempted to subject psychoanalytic concepts to experimental tests, to current research on "repressive style" (e.g., Weinberger, 1990); and infant-mother attachment (e.g., Fonagy, Steele, & Steele, 1991; Main, 1991). (For a summary of research on psychoanalytic hypotheses and concepts, see, for example, Baron, Eagle, and Wolitzky (1992), and Westen (1998). There has also been an upsurge of interest in linking psychoanalytic concepts and formulations to developments in cognitive psychology (e.g., Bucci, 1997; Eagle, 1987; and in neuroscience (e.g., Westen, 1998).

Professional and Training Issues

For a long time, training in psychoanalysis at psychoanalytic institutes in the United States was, with few exceptions, limited to and dominated by physicians. This situation changed dramatically after the Division of Psychoanalysis (Division 39) of the American Psychological Association launched a successful lawsuit against the American Psychoanalytic Association. Psychoanalytic institutes associated with the American Psychoanalytic Association have accepted psychologists (and social workers) for psychoanalytic training in increasingly large numbers. The loss of the lawsuit appears to have constituted a blessing for previously medically dominated psychoanalytic institutes insofar as during the last several years, fewer physicians have applied for training.

Training in psychoanalysis is carried out at psychoanalytic institutes, a limited number of which are affiliated with universities but most of which are unaffiliated and independent. Training includes the candidate's undergoing his or her own analysis, generally with a so-called training analyst, course work, and a minimum number of supervised psychoanalytic cases. The International Psychoanalytic Association is an umbrella organization that includes various national psychoanalytic associations (such as the American Psychoanalytic Association). Among the criteria for individual membership in the International Psychoanalytic Association is training in and graduation from a psychoanalytic training institute that meets the standards set by the International; and among these standards is a training analysis that includes a minimum frequency of four sessions per week. (Although this minimum frequency is an explicitly stated criterion, it apparently is modified when local conditions make it necessary.)

Quite apart from professional-political concerns, a number of commentators recently have questioned the meaningfulness of defining psychoanalytic treatment solely or mainly in terms of such "external" criteria as frequency of sessions (and use of the couch). An essential point made by Gill (e.g., 1982) and others is that a psychoanalytic stance is defined by certain intrinsic criteria, such as analysis of the transference and of defenses, rather than by extrinsic criteria, such as frequency of sessions. As Gill (1982) has pointed out, it is possible to take a psychoanalytic perspective in a once- or twice-a-week treatment and fail to take such a perspective in a four- or five-times-a-week treatment.

Future Directions of Psychoanalysis

In discussing the future of psychoanalysis, one should distinguish between psychoanalytic treatment and psychoanalytic theory. Various trends (e.g., managed health care) do not bode well for at least the immediate future viability of psychoanalytic treatment—or for any other mode of long-term psychotherapeutic treatment in the United States. However, this needs to be distinguished from psychoanalytically informed psychotherapy with a variety of different clinical populations. The latter would seem to have a somewhat rosier future.

As far as psychoanalytic theory is concerned, the picture is complex. During the last several years, a number of writers and critics have sharply critiqued the epistemological foundations (i.e., how one obtains reliable knowledge of someone's unconscious mind, including his or her wishes and defenses) of psychoanalytic theory. Some of these critiques have been thoughtful, tightly reasoned, and disciplined (e.g., Grünbaum, 1993). Others have consisted of a mixture of serious substantive criticisms, somewhat shrill personal attacks on Freud's character, and wholesale dismissal of all aspects of psychoanalytic theory. The last, wholesale dismissal, has had a strong and widespread impact on the public reception of and attitude toward psychoanalysis, to the point where an issue of a popular periodical, *Time*, paraded the headline "Is Freud Dead?" On the other hand, as described above, significant psychological research is being carried out on phenomena and concepts inspired by psychoanalytic theory (e.g., some work on attachment). Researchers are also carrying out significant work on the psychoanalytic process (e.g., Weiss, Sampson, & the Mount Zion Psychotherapy Research Group, 1986). Also, there is considerable evidence supporting certain basic psychoanalytic assumptions—for example, the ubiquitousness of unconscious mental processes (Westen, 1998). Finally, it must be noted that whatever its shortcomings, psychoanalytic theory appears to be one of the few psychological theories that at least attempts to do justice to the richness and complexity of mental life.

Bibliography

Barron, J., Eagle, M. N., & Wolitzky, D. L. (1992). *Interface of psychoanalysis and psychology.* Washington, DC: American Psychological Association.

Breuer, J., & Freud, S. (1893–1895). Studies on hysteria. *Standard edition* (Vol. 2). London: Hogarth Press.

Eagle, M. N. (1987). The psychoanalytic and the cognitive unconscious. In R. Stern (Ed.), *Theories of the unconscious and theories of the self* (pp. 155–189). Hillsdale, NJ: Erlbaum.

Fairbairn, W. R. D. (1952). *Psychoanalytic studies of the personality.* London: Tavistock.

Fonagy, P., Steele, H., & Steele, M. (1991). Maternal representations of attachment during pregnancy predict the organization of infant-mother attachment at one year of age. *Child Development, 62,* 891–905.

Freud, S. (1894). The neuro-psychoses of defense. *Standard edition* (Vol. 3). London: Hogarth Press.

Freud, S. (1910). The future prospects of psychoanalytic theory. *Standard edition* (Vol. 11). London: Hogarth Press.

Freud, S. (1926). Inhibitions, symptoms, and anxiety. *Standard edition* (Vol. 20). London: Hogarth Press.

Gill, M. M. (1982). *Analysis of transference, Vol. I: Theory and technique.* New York: International Universities Press.

Grünbaum, A. (1993). *Validation in the clinical theory of psychoanalysis.* Madison, CT: International Universities Press.

Kohut, H. (1984). *How does analysis cure?* Chicago: University of Chicago Press.

Main, M. (1991). Metacognitive knowledge, metacognitive monitoring, and singular (coherent) vs. multiple (incoherent) model of attachment: Findings and directions for future research. In P. Harris, J. Stevenson-Hinde, & C. M. Parkes (Eds.), *Attachment across the life cycle* (pp. 127–159). New York: Routledge.

Mitchell, S. (1988). *Relational concepts in psychoanalysis: An integration.* Cambridge, MA: Harvard University Press.

Sears, R. (1943). Survey of objective studies in psychoanalytic concepts. *Social Science Research Council Bulletin,* 52.

Weinberger, D. (1990). The construct validity of the repressive coping style. In J. Singer (Ed.), *Repression and dissociation* (pp. 339–386). Chicago: University of Chicago Press.

Weiss, J., Sampson, H., & the Mount Zion Psychotherapy Research Group. (1986). *The psychoanalytic process: Theory, clinical observation, and empirical research.* New York: Guilford Press.

Westen, D. (1998). Toward a psychodynamically informed psychological science. *Psychological Bulletin, 124,* 333–371.

Morris N. Eagle

Theories

Psychoanalysis is the approach to the mind, psychological disorders, and psychological treatment developed by Sigmund Freud at the beginning of the twentieth century. The theory emerged from clinical observation and from Freud's attempt to understand and treat psychological disorders that had previously seemed incomprehensible. The hallmark of psychoanalysis from the start was the assumption that much of mental life is unconscious and consequently that understanding people requires interpreting the unconscious meanings underlying their overt or manifest behavior. Equally important was the concept of "psychodynamics," analogous to physical dynamics, in which mental forces (such as wishes and fears) combine and conflict, often unconsciously, frequently producing "solutions" to psychological problems that do not, on the surface, look like "answers" to any of them. Thus, from a psychoanalytic perspective, a fundamentalist Christian who experiences a severe conflict between his sexual desires (which are inborn) and his conscience may become preoccupied with fighting pornography because doing so allows him to remain preoccupied with sex while simultaneously disavowing his titillation. Contrary to the rationalism of many philosophical theories before his time and many psychological theories since, Freud emphasized that consciousness is only the tip of the psychic iceberg and that humans are remarkable in their potential not only for self-knowledge but also for self-deception.

Freud proposed a series of models of the mind that he never fully integrated, although together they provide a systematic view of personality and psychological development. (For a more thorough account, see Westen & Gabbard, 1999.) A common fallacy is that psychoanalysis began and ended with Freud's work. In fact, theoretical and therapeutic developments have continued since Freud's death in 1939. We begin here with Freud's models and then explore the evolution of psychoanalytic models of the mind that were developed later. We conclude by addressing the empirical evidence for psychoanalytic theories.

Freud's Models of the Mind

Freud's (1900) first model, his "topographic model," used a spatial metaphor of the mind, dividing mental processes into three types: conscious, preconscious, and unconscious. Conscious processes are those of which we are immediately aware (such as these words). Preconscious processes are not currently conscious but can readily be brought to consciousness (such as the year Freud died, mentioned in the paragraph above). Unconscious processes are inaccessible to consciousness because they are "repressed"—that is, kept from conscious awareness because they are threatening. Freud (1910) likened repression to the actions of a repressive government trying to keep material from public view. In the mind, he argued, a similar process can occur with "taboo" thoughts, feelings, or wishes.

Freud did not invent the concept of unconscious processes. Indeed, he took the notion of "the unconscious" as a driving force behind human behavior from the German philosophy of his time. What he added, however, were (1) a systematic model of how unconscious processes work and influence behavior; (2) a theory of how they generate a range of mild to relatively severe psychological problems, from the kinds of "neurotic" problems most people experience in their lives (e.g., not working up to potential, troubles with authority figures, emotional constriction, irrational fears, trouble maintaining fulfilling relationships) to more classic symptoms such as bulimia or depression; and (3) an approach to treatment based on tracking down the unconscious determinants of people's behaviors and symptoms.

Freud's second model was his "drive" or "instinct model." Influenced by the work of Charles Darwin, Freud argued that humans are essentially hairless monkeys, whose most sublime and noble pursuits are essentially transformations of the same kinds of motives shared by other animals. According to Freud, the two basic drives or instincts in humans are sex (libido) and aggression. (By "libido," Freud actually meant something other than just purely sexual desire; he also meant pleasure seeking more generally, including pursuit of emotional, social, and aesthetic pleasures.) Because these motives often come into conflict with social norms and values and with rules and standards children internalize from their parents, sexual and aggressive desires frequently cannot be expressed directly. Because they are rooted in our biology, however, they do not simply go away; rather, they find indirect expressions in phenomena as varied as daydreaming about sex or romance, selecting a career likely to attract a potential spouse because of its status or income potential, competing on the sports field, and playing aggressive video games. Indeed, the rating boards in the United States that determine the appropriateness of movies for young audiences seem to be composed exclusively of Freudians, whose two criteria for rating movies are sex and aggression. Freud would not have been surprised that these are the themes that tend most to titillate people in movies (evident in their prevalence) and that people simultaneously find most conflictual and threatening and hence set up boards to censor them.

Freud's (1905) third model, his "development model," focused on the child's evolving quest for pleasure and recognition of the social limitations of pleasure seeking. Thus, he tied psychological development to the development of one of his two drives (sex) in his theory of "psychosexual development." To understand these stages, one must view them both concretely and metaphorically, in terms of both specific bodily experiences (zones of pleasure and conflict) and broader psychosocial conflicts and concerns (Erikson, 1963). When things go well, the child passes from one stage to the next without major problems; when they go less well, the child may develop fixations on issues from a particular stage or may regress later to issues from that stage.

The first stage is the oral stage, roughly the period of infancy, in which children explore the world using their mouths and find themselves in a dependent state. People with oral conflicts (fixation on, or regression to, oral issues) are often needy and dependent. The second stage is the anal stage and corresponds to the toddler years. In this stage, the child learns that the anal region can be a zone of pleasure but is also confronted with the demand for self-control. Thus, the child at this stage must confront what it means to be told what to do (on and off the potty). Problems at this stage can lead a person to become stingy, withholding, conflicted about authority, or obsessed with cleanliness and order (or the opposite, unconcerned with "messes"). In the phallic stage (early childhood), children discover the genitals as powerful zones of pleasure and have to deal with the conflict involved in loving and wanting an exclusive relationship with their opposite-sex parent while fearing that their same-sex parent would not appreciate this desire (the Oedipus complex). More broadly, the most important feature of this stage is the child's identification with his or her parents, that is, the attempt to become like them and to internalize their values, mannerisms, attitudes, and so forth. Problems at this stage can lead to competitiveness with members of the same sex, inhibition about "standing out" or competing, problems with sexual performance, or fixation on romantic partners who are inappropriate or unavailable (such as a woman who repeatedly gets involved in relationships with married men). In the latency stage (middle childhood), Oedipal wishes become submerged, the sexual wishes (oral, anal, and phallic) that Freud believed little children harbor become repressed, and the child learns the skills and competences necessary in his or her culture. Finally, in the genital stage (beginning in adolescence), the individual pursues mature sexual aims (intercourse, reproduction, and parenting) and attempts to become fully capable of adult love and fulfilling work.

Freud's (1993) final model, the "structural model," argued that personality consists of three structures (constellations of processes that serve particular functions) that interact and often conflict: the id (the wishful, instinctive, repressed part of the psyche), superego (internalized morality), and ego (the "executive" or decision-making part of the mind that somehow has to reconcile the demands of the id and superego while simultaneously attending to reality). Central to this model, and to all of Freud's models, is the notion of a mind in conflict, with different parts of the personality pulling us in different directions. According to Freud, psychic conflict is essentially built into human nature by virtue of two facts. The first is our dual nature as (1) biological organisms with natural desires (the wish for pleasure and the desire to hurt other people, especially when we are angry at them) and (2) creatures of culture, who have to learn to regulate our impulses in order to get along with others and maintain their affection. Second, conflict is built into the mind because the people we love the most are inevitably those who frustrate and disappoint us the most. Most people rarely talk to a stranger as rudely as they talk to a spouse or sibling. According to Freud, this conflict is inherent in the human condition.

This was the state of the art around 1939 when Freud died. To be sure, during his lifetime, many who had initially found his views compelling "defected" and started their own schools of dynamic psychology. These theorists included Alfred Adler, who focused more on conscious motives, social desires other than sexuality, and feelings of inadequacy and competition; Carl Jung, who offered a somewhat mystical approach to the mind that argued for the presence of various inborn symbols; and Erich Fromm, Karen Horney, and Harry Stack Sullivan, all of whom took exception to Freud's primary focus on "internal reality"—the world inside people's heads—to the exclusion of the cultural, historical, and social contexts. What united these various "neo-Freudian" theorists was rejection of Freud's instinct theory and his emphasis on psychosexual development. With the exception of Jung, whose thought included a mixture of sound clinical observation and idiosyncratic spiritual notions (and whose ideas have remained outside mainstream psychoanalysis), the ideas of many of these thinkers have, in recent years, crept into mainstream psychoanalysis in different guises, although often unacknowledged. Indeed, today, most psychoanalysts and psychodynamically oriented psychotherapists reject Freud's dual instinct theory and his argument that sexuality is the driving force in human relationships.

Developments Since Freud

In the 60 years since Freud's death, psychoanalytic models have changed substantially. Whereas Freud's theory focused most on the more primitive, wishful, and conflictual parts of human nature, the "ego psychology" that emerged in the 1940s out of Freud's structural model focused on the adaptive capacities of the mind, notably cognition, defense (protection against unpleasant feelings through mechanisms such as repression), and impulse control (see Blanck and Blanck, 1974; Vaillant, 1992). Of particular importance were developments in the theory of the mechanisms of defense that people use to regulate their emotions, such as intellectualization (thinking in abstract and intellectual ways about things that are really laden with emotion), denial (refusal to acknowledge realities or feelings that are obvious to others), and reaction formation (turning desires into their opposites, such as dealing with fantasies of exciting sexual acts by perceiving them as repulsive).

Many theorists remain more classically Freudian, continuing to focus on psychic conflicts, particularly those concerning sex and aggression (Brenner, 1982). Among the most important contributions of contemporary adherents to a more classical psychoanalytic approach is the concept of compromise formation. A "compromise formation" is a compromise among competing motives, many of which are unconscious, that attempts to optimize their satisfaction. For example, one patient, whose relationship with his wife had been unhappy for years, felt terribly guilty about leaving her. When he finally did, however, he moved into a shabby apartment in a seedy section of town, even though he could have afforded a much more pleasant abode. Exploration of his conflicts suggested that this was a compromise between his wish to leave his wife and to be with other women and a need to punish himself for his "selfishness" to avoid severe guilt. The compromise formation he selected was to live uncomfortably and to make himself unattractive to women by living in an apartment that belied his considerable wealth and status.

Perhaps the major development since Freud's time (although its roots lay in his own papers written around the time of World War I) is "object relations theories" (see Greenberg and Mitchell, 1983; Mitchell, 1988). "Object relations" refer to the mental representations or views people hold of themselves, others, and relationships and to the cognitive, emotional, and behavioral processes that underlie the capacity to form and maintain intimate relationships (Westen, 1991). According to object relations theorists, people seek relationships, not sexual objects. In this view, our primary needs are for intimate contact with others, not necessarily with their genitals. Thus, whereas Freud conceived of development in terms of a series of psychosexual stages, or stages in the development of pleasure seeking (especially sexual pleasure seeking), object relations theorists have offered models of the development of the capacity to form mature, intimate, interdependent relationships with others (e.g., Fairbairn, 1952; Kernberg, 1984). Perhaps the most important object relations theorist was John Bowlby (1969), who developed attachment theory, which attempted to explain the bonds that develop between children and their primary caregivers, and brought together psychoanalytic clinical observation with research on other primates. The most recent renditions of object relations theory are "relational theory" or "relational psychoanalysis" (Aron, 1996; Mitchell, 1988).

Another related development of the last 30 years is "self psychology," developed by Heinz Kohut (1971). According to self psychology, humans have fundamental needs for self-esteem and self-coherence (that is, a sense of "hanging together" rather than "falling apart"). According to Kohut, unempathic parenting in the early years of life can lead people to have chronic problems with self-esteem, such as low self-esteem or grandiose views of themselves that compensate consciously for an unconscious sense of worthlessness.

Freud was a brilliant thinker but not a tidy one; he never really announced, "I'm abandoning the topographic model now and am replacing it with the structural model" or "I have this new theory of anxiety that sort of replaces aspects of my old drive theory," so his followers continued to use different aspects of his various models for many years. The confusion is compounded by the development of post-Freudian models such as relational theory, since no one is entirely sure how compatible relational models are with more classically Freudian models of psychic conflict or whether all sexual conflicts or dysfunctions, once viewed as the kernel of neurosis, can really be understood as simply derivative of relational problems. (Sometimes a penis is just a penis.)

The major models of the mind advanced by Freud and his followers do, however, suggest a general model of personality defined by three questions (Westen, 1998a). The first question is about motivation: What do people wish for, fear, and value, and to what extent are these motives compatible or contradictory and conscious or unconscious? This is the question addressed by most of Freud's models of the mind, particularly his drive theory, as well as by contemporary classical psychoanalytic theories. Most contemporary psychoanalytic theorists and practitioners believe that people are motivated by many things (including sex and aggression, but also by needs for self-esteem, a sense of competence, relationships, etc.) and that emotions regulate much of human behavior. The second question pertains to adaptation and addresses the concerns of the ego psychologists: What psychological resources does the person have to cope with internal and external challenges, including ways of thinking, feeling, regulating emotions through conscious coping strategies and unconscious defense mechanisms, and regulating impulses? The third question addresses the issues raised by object relations theorists, relational theorists, and self psychologists: How does the person experience the self, others, and relationships, and to what degree, and in what ways, is the individual capable of forming relationships with others? For each of these questions, a hallmark of the psychoanalytic approach is the assumption that understanding them requires placing them in a developmental context. What is their developmental course, both normatively and in cases of less than optimal development? And how do specific experiences affect development in these areas?

The Scientific Status of Psychoanalytic Theories

From the start, the data for psychoanalytic theories have been primarily the data of clinical observation. Although clinical practice has provided an important window to the mind, psychoanalysts have been slow to recognize the importance of using more systematic, replicable, scientific procedures to test, refine, revise, and discard aspects of their theories, although this situation is changing. Today, experimental data support five central aspects of psychoanalytic theory (Westen, 1998b). First, much of mental life—including thoughts, feelings, motives, and defenses against unpleasant ideas, feelings, fears, or wishes—is unconscious. Second, individuals can have conflicting feelings toward the same person or situation that motivates them in opposing ways and often leads to compromise solutions. Third, stable personality patterns begin to form in childhood, and childhood experiences play an important role in personality development, particularly in shaping the ways people form later social relationships. Fourth, mental representations of the self, others, and relationships guide people's interactions with others and influence the ways in which they become psychologically symptomatic. Finally, personality development involves not only learning to regulate sexual and aggressive feelings but also moving from an immature, socially dependent state to a mature, interdependent one.

For example, attachment theory, rooted in psychoanalysis, suggests that the way children form attachments in their earliest years of life with their caregivers shapes the underlying patterns of thought, feeling, and motivation they bring to subsequent relationships (Main, 1995). Researchers studying adult attachment—that is, the attachment relationships people form as adults (e.g., with spouses)—find four attachment styles or patterns that resemble similar patterns seen in infants: (1) a secure pattern, in which the individual feels relatively safe and comfortable in the relationship; (2) an anxious-ambivalent or "preoccupied with attachment" pattern, in which the individual is chronically worried or conflicted about the relationship; (3) an avoidant or "dismissing of attachment" pattern, in which the individual deals with anxiety and discomfort in intimate relationships by shutting off interpersonal needs and denying unpleasant feelings in relationships; and (4) a disorganized pattern, typically seen in people who have not resolved childhood trauma or loss, in which the person has incoherent representations of attachment figures, cannot seem to predict or understand why attachment figures behave the way they do, and tends to be erratic and unpredictable with lovers, children, and others.

An illustration of research in this area that supports many of the five basic theoretical points outlined above is a study by Dozier and Kobak (1992), who produced physiological evidence of a discordance between what individuals with an avoidant attachment style know and feel consciously and unconsciously. The investigators monitored participants' physiological arousal while asking them to recall unpleasant memories of experiences with their parents from childhood. The more individuals showed avoidant strategies for dealing with attachment-related distress—by claiming that they had no such feelings—the more physiological reactivity they showed while answering emotionally evocative questions about separations, rejections, and parental threats. In other words, people who defend against attachment-related distress by avoiding consciousness of discomfort in their relationships with attachment figures may succeed in eliminating the feelings from consciousness, but this does not eliminate the feelings unconsciously.

[*See also* Attachment Theory; Countertransference; Drive; Motivation; *and* Transference.]

Bibliography

Aron, L. (1996). *A meeting of minds: Mutuality in psychoanalysis.* Hillside, NJ: Analytic Press.

Blanck, G., & Blanck, R. (1974). *Ego psychology: Theory and practice.* New York: Columbia University Press.

Bowlby, J. (1969). *Attachment and loss: Volume 1. Attachment.* New York: Basic Books.

Brenner, C. (1982). *The mind in conflict.* New York: International Universities Press.

Dozier, M.,& Kobak, R. (1992). Psychophysiology in attachment interviews: Converging evidence for deactivating strategies. *Child Development, 63,* 1473–1480.

Erikson, E. (1963). *Childhood and society* (2nd ed.). New York: Norton.

Fairbairn, W. R. D. (1952). *Psychoanalytic studies of the personality.* London: Routledge & Kegan Paul.

Freud, S. (1900/1953). The interpretation of dreams. In J. Strachey (Ed. and Trans.), *The standard edition of the complete psychological works of Sigmund Freud* (Vol. 4, pp. 1–338). London: Hogarth Press.

Freud, S. (1905/1953). Three essays on the theory of sexuality. In J. Strachey (Ed. and Trans.), *The standard edition of the complete psychological works of Sigmund Freud* (Vol. 7, p. 123–245). London: Hogarth Press.

Freud, S. (1910/1953). *Five lectures on psychoanalysis.* (pp. 1–48). New York: Norton.

Freud, S. (1933/1964). New introductory lectures on psychoanalysis. In J. Strachey (Ed. and Trans.), *The standard edition of the complete psychological works of Sigmund Freud* (Vol. 22, pp. 1–182). London: Hogarth Press.

Greenberg, J. R., & Mitchell, S. (1983). *Object relations in psychoanalytic theory.* Cambridge MA: Harvard University Press.

Kernberg, O. (1984). *Severe personality disorders.* New Haven, CT: Yale University Press.

Kohut, H. (1971). *The analysis of the self: A systematic approach to the treatment of narcissistic personality disorders.* Madison, CT: International Universities Press.

Main, M. (1995). Recent studies in attachment: Overview, with selected implications for clinical work. In S. Goldberg, R. Muir, & J. Kerr (Eds.), *Attachment theory: Social, developmental, and clinical perspectives* (pp. 407–474). Mahwah, NJ: Erlbaum.

Mitchell, S. (1988). *Relational concepts in psychoanalysis.* Cambridge, MA: Harvard University Press.

Vaillant, G. (Ed.). (1992). *Ego mechanisms of defense: A guide for clinicians and researchers.* Washington, DC: American Psychiatric Association Press.

Westen, D. (1991). Social cognition and object relations. *Psychological Bulletin, 109,* 429–455.

Westen, D. (1998a). The scientific legacy of Sigmund Freud. Toward a psychodynamically informed psychological science. *Psychological Bulletin, 124,* 333–371.

Westen, D. (1998b). Case formulation and personality diagnosis: Two processes or one? In J. Barron (Ed.), *Making diagnosis meaningful* (pp. 111–138). Washington, DC: American Psychological Association Press.

Westen, D., & Gabbard, G. (1999). Psychoanalytic approaches to personality. In L. Pervin & O. John (Eds.),

Handbook of personality: Theory and research (2nd ed., pp. 57–101). New York: Guilford Press.

Drew Westen

Methods of Study

During the course of Sigmund Freud's career, the term *psychoanalysis* came to have several meanings. It was described as a theory of personality and the mind, as well as a method of treatment for neurotic disorders. Another central definition portrayed psychoanalysis as a unique method for studying mental processes (including the unconscious) that would otherwise remain inaccessible. Freud's psychotherapy treatments became his method for producing evidence to support his conceptions of normal personality development and psychopathology. However, Freud's therapy itself was not static. It changed over time as he refined his goals and experienced obstacles to "making the unconscious conscious."

Perhaps the biggest shift in treatment approach was his backing away from directly trying to alleviate patients' discomforts in favor of emphasizing attempts to gain knowledge about the underlying cause of psychological symptoms and the dynamic forces that shape personality. This change in aim—from symptom amelioration to knowledge acquisition—led him to modify his treatment techniques. Freud initially followed the lead of his colleague Joseph Breuer in using hypnosis to aid patients in surmounting hysterical symptoms (those with no organic cause) by reexperiencing painful forgotten memories and feelings. He theorized that symptoms (often body discomforts) were translations of past traumas and conflicts that patients found too distressing to admit to awareness. He believed that increasing awareness would rob symptoms of their defensive purpose and lead to their dissipation. Finding that many patients could not be hypnotized, Freud altered his technique to forceful suggestions that obliged patients in the waking state to remember things that they were presumably trying to shut out. Because patients frequently resisted these suggestions and became unproductive, the technique was changed again. Freud proposed that resistance could be lowered by invoking what came to be known as the "fundamental technical rule of psychoanalysis": free association. Now patients were asked to become dispassionate self-observers reporting all thoughts, no matter how seemingly disconnected, which came into awareness. The analyst, by suspending preconceptions, could presumably help patients understand underlying meanings and symbolism in the stream of associations by piecing together themes revealed by the communications. This last change in technique was important because it led Freud to claim that patient productions—"free associations"—were unfettered by the analyst's suggestion or manipulation. Therefore, he argued, the case study could be used as an objective means for gathering data to substantiate (or refute) hypotheses about personality development and psychopathology.

Freud desperately wanted conclusions derived from observations during therapy hours to be accepted as untainted and objective. Acceptance of this idea was critical for establishing the scientific respectability of his case study method for developing personality theories. He struggled mightily to establish the idea that people could be altered therapeutically by simply learning the truth about warded-off ideas and conflicts and that this therapeutic gain could be achieved without the analyst's influencing the nature of the productions. He never came to terms with the inherent conflict involved in trying to learn about people while simultaneously trying to change them.

The validity of psychoanalytic propositions has, of course, been debated by a variety of scholars who note shortcomings in the case study method for validating theories that can be applied to all people. One problem is the restricted nature of the sample. Reviews of Freud's cases established that he wrote about relatively few people in any detail, raising questions about how representative his presentations were of his practice or of the population. Furthermore, analysis of the nature of all the cases Freud ever mentioned in writing revealed that they were a rather unrepresentative sample. Two thirds of his clients were women, almost all of them were between the ages of 20 and 44, and most came from the upper economic class. Although Freud asserted that his methods had special applicability to problems of neurosis, many of his major clients would likely be diagnosed as psychotic using today's standards. In addition, scrutiny of Freud's cases has shown that he was not particularly successful as a therapist and that what he advocated as technique did not match well with what he actually did. Thus, descriptions of cases drawn from his own writings, those of his patients, interviews, and letters show that he did not remain nondirective, preserve confidentiality, or refrain from revealing information about himself to the majority of his clients. This was not an atmosphere in which dispassionate objectivity could be assured.

The truth value of psychoanalytic observations obtained from case studies has been challenged by philosophers as well as mental health professionals. For example, philosopher Adolph Grunbaum, while defending the potential for psychoanalysis to produce scientifically defensible theories, questioned the suitability of the psychoanalytic treatment encounter as a source of unblemished data. He disputed what he calls Freud's "Tally Argument" as a standard for substantiating the validity of psychoanalytic hypotheses. The Tally Argument holds that an analyst's interpretations can be effective only if they "tally with what is real." According to this rationale, durable therapeutic success occurs only when the analyst's interpretations are historically accurate or close to the mark. Conversely, it is assumed that if there is therapeutic success, an analyst's interpretations must have been accurate. This speculation is rejected by many because of observations that the patient's response is often shaped by the power of the analyst's suggestions, by the need to comply with or resist the analyst, and by the possible unreliability of memories of earlier experiences produced during treatment sessions. Equating therapeutic success with the need for accurate interpretations of the patient's history also does not square with repeated findings that other psychotherapy approaches, not reliant on therapist interpretations, often produce substantial, durable rates of recovery.

Although many psychoanalysts continue to cling to the case study method as a rich source of data, some have backed away from the need to find out what "really happened" in the past. Scholars such as Donald Spence advocate making a distinction between historical truth and narrative truth. Psychoanalysis for this group is allied with the hermeneutic tradition and modeled on nonempirical disciplines like literary criticism or history. From this perspective, analysts' interpretations are not to be guided principally by concerns about "historical truth" but rather by the pragmatic desire to be helpful. In this regard, "artistic truths" built on weaving compelling, pleasing stories that serve as comforting explanations for patients' symptoms may prove most beneficial and hence most desirable.

In the wake of Freud's groundbreaking theories, a series of psychoanalytic revisionists and neo-Freudians (such as Adler, Jung, Erikson, Sullivan, Guntrip, Klein, Kohut, and Kernberg) developed contrasting and sometimes challenging alternatives to Freud's formulations. The term *psychoanalysis* lost precision in the midst of the many voices competing for theoretical acceptance. Challengers often suggested downgrading the centrality of sexual impulses and conflicts for human motivation while variously placing emphasis on factors like the importance of self-representations, social and cultural forces, and so forth. Such debates among schools of thought were frequently stimulating and rich in imagery. However, because of reliance on evidence drawn primarily from personal experience and case study, there was no satisfying way to arrive at objective decisions about which theories merited acceptance and which rejection.

The ideas propounded by Freud and other psychoanalytic thinkers have unquestionably exerted profound influence on historical and contemporary psychology. In fact, Friman, Allen, Kerwin, and Larzelere, writing in a 1993 issue of the *American Psychologist*, demonstrated that psychoanalytic journal references continue to be cited in social science publications at a substantial, relatively steady rate. Furthermore, an examination of literature in the arts and humanities shows that Freud continues to be cited more than all other sources in history except Lenin, Shakespeare, the Bible, and Plato. Yet, many psychologists have had a nagging discomfort about psychoanalysts' reluctance to subject their theories to scientific tests. Although intrigued by psychoanalytic creativity and the obvious impact of psychoanalytic thought on American and world culture, they have yearned for empirical evidence assessing the validity of the pronouncements.

Over time, a number of psychologists began devising experiments to test the soundness of psychoanalytic formulations. Early studies tended to be crude and oversimplified attempts to capture psychoanalytic hypotheses. However, they represented an initial bringing together of theories and accepted scientific method that was to grow. In 1942, a series of studies examining the concept of repression was analyzed by David Rapaport. This was followed, in 1943, by Robert Sears's *Survey of Objective Studies of Psychoanalytic Concepts*, which described about 150 studies of psychoanalytic ideas. Approximately 10 years later (1952), the respected psychologist Ernest Hilgard surveyed a variety of experiments bearing on psychoanalytic concepts. It is true that most early reviews were very critical, but they indicated, by their existence, the launching of attempts at serious scientific measurement of the elusive subjective psychoanalytic world.

Major reviews of the scientific evidence examining Freud's theories began appearing again in 1972 with Paul Kline's book *Fact and Fantasy in Freudian Theory*, an appraisal of about 700 studies. This was followed by two volumes (see the Bibliography) published by Seymour Fisher and Roger P. Greenberg in 1977 (reissued in 1985) and 1996. These works represent the most comprehensive reviews, respectively surveying about 1,800 and 3,000 empirical studies of Freudian concepts.

The existence of literally thousands of studies bearing on psychoanalytic speculations attests to the robustness of the enterprise and the possibility of supporting or challenging psychoanalytic notions with research data. The initial criticism that laboratory-driven tests of psychoanalytic thought are too simplistic is out of step with a burgeoning literature. Researchers have developed an array of creative and sometimes ingenious methods to try to capture the complexities revealed in the consulting room. They have pressed into service technological advances like audio and video recordings, as well as advances in research design and statistics that were unimaginable during Freud's lifetime. Clearly, individual studies do not fully encompass the breadth of clinical observation. Yet, networks of replicable research findings from the laboratory and the field are indispensable when trying to corroborate theory in a convincing fashion.

Waves of studies have now been marshaled to throw light on many areas of thought important to analytic concerns. For example, there is now evidence showing that considerable processing of information occurs outside of awareness (unconscious processes). Through the use of subliminal techniques, which rely on the delivery of visual or auditory stimuli below the awareness threshold, effects on thoughts, feelings, and behavior have been demonstrated. Findings have been broadly consistent with the "New Look" in perception, described in the 1940s, 1950s, and 1960s, which postulated that expectations, defenses, and motives impact the way in which things are viewed and interpreted. Refreshing reviews and debates about the scientific literature on unconscious functioning appeared in a series of papers devoted to this topic in a 1992 issue of the *American Psychologist*, as well as in books such as Kenneth Bowers and Donald Meichenbaum's *The Unconscious Reconsidered* (New York, 1984) and Robert Bornstein and Joseph Masling's *Empirical Perspectives on the Psychoanalytic Unconscious* (1998).

Another interesting area of empirical work involves attempts to test psychoanalytic ideas about transference. Do past experiences lead to distortions and recurrent handicapping patterns in present relationships with others, including therapists? Using theoretically driven statistical analyses of therapy session transcripts, researchers (such as Luborsky and Crits-Cristoph; Weiss and Sampson) have been able to substantiate that individuals display repetitive, meaningful relationship patterns and do attempt to test, in predictable ways, their distorted beliefs about others. Relatedly, investigators (like Ainsworth; Sroufe and Fleeson) report indications of continuity between relationship attachment styles in early childhood and subsequent adjustment and behavior during later years.

The cited examples offer but a tiny glimpse of the diverse efforts being employed to reconcile psychoanalysis with the scientific method. The quantity of research evidence amassed is now quite respectable and contradicts any belief that psychoanalytic concepts are untestable. Reviews also show that psychoanalysis does not stand or fall as a unitary theory. Increasing methods of study have shown that, like everyone else, Freud and analysts who followed him turned out to be right about some things but wrong about others.

Bibliography

Ainsworth, M. D. S. (1979). Infant-mother attachment. *American Psychologist, 34*, 932–937.

Fisher, S., & Greenberg, R. P. (1985). *The scientific credibility of Freud's theories and therapy*. New York: Columbia University Press.

Fisher, S., & Greenberg, R. P. (1996). *Freud scientifically reappraised: Testing the theories and therapy*. New York: Wiley.

Grunbaum, A. (1984). *The foundations of psychoanalysis: A philosophical critique*. Berkeley: University of California Press.

Grunbaum, A. (1993). *Validation in the clinical theory of psychoanalysis: A study in the philosophy of psychoanalysis*. Madison, CT: International Universities Press.

Hilgard, E. R. (1952). Experimental approaches to psychoanalysis. In E. Pumpian-Minlin (Ed.), *Psychoanalysis as science* (pp. 3–45). Stanford, CA: Stanford University Press.

Luborsky, L., & Crits-Cristoph, P. (1998). *Understanding transference: The core conflictual relationships theme method* (2nd ed.). Washington, DC: American Psychological Association.

Lynn, D. J., & Vaillant, G. E. (1998). Anonymity, neutrality, and confidentiality in the actual methods of Sigmund Freud: A review of 43 cases, 1907–1939. *American Journal of Psychiatry, 155*, 163–171.

Spence, D. P. (1982). *Narrative truth and historical truth: Meaning and interpretation in psychoanalysis*. New York: Norton.

Sroufe, L. A., & Fleeson, W. (1986). Attachment and the construction of relationships. In W. W. Hartup & Z. Rubin (Eds.), *Relationships and development* (pp. 51–71). Hillsdale, NJ: Erlbaum.

Weiss, J., Sampson, H., & the Mount Zion Psychotherapy Research Group (1986). *The psychoanalytic process: Theory, clinical observation and empirical research*. New York: Guilford Press.

Westen, D. (1990). Psychoanalytic approaches to personality. In L. Pervin (Ed.), *Handbook of personality theory and research* (pp. 21–65). New York: Guilford Press.

Roger P. Greenberg

Psychoanalysis and Philosophy

The discipline of Freudian psychoanalysis, from which most versions of psychodynamic psychology have developed, is usually understood to imply adherence to several central precepts or foci of interest, and each of these has evoked a history of philosophical debate. Examples of such precepts include: the idea that conscious thought and action are conflictually or contradictorily determined by unconscious fantasy processes; the idea that humans always resist or defend against conscious awareness of the influence of the unconscious motivations connected with these fantasy processes; and the idea that the dynamics of thinking and feeling originate in the erotic tendencies of the body, resulting in the special significance that childhood trauma has for the formation of adolescent and adult mental functioning.

Such ideas concerning the conditions of human experience have a profound philosophical impact, particularly in the areas of epistemology and ethics. Even the earliest pioneers of psychoanalytic thinking were embroiled in controversies concerning the philosophical implications of their discipline. For example, Sigmund Freud was criticized both by Carl Jung for being too concerned with the scientific status of psychoanalysis and by Alfred Adler for being insufficiently concerned with this issue. Subsequent reactions to psychoanalytic ideas, within Western philosophy, have been both appreciative and critical. These debates have sometimes been heated, and not infrequently founded on conceptual misunderstandings. For convenience, philosophical debate over psychoanalytic ideas may be divided into that based on "analytic" or "logical-empiricist" philosophies and that based on "continental" philosophies.

Logical-Empiricist Philosophies

Dialogue between psychoanalysts and logical-empiricist philosophers, who all accept some principle of empiricism with an attendant interest in the methodological procedures of the natural sciences, has been most active around questions of psychoanalytic epistemology, and especially around the controversial ideas of repressed unconscious motivations or meanings and the defensive character of self-conscious awareness. The debates on these questions have focused both on the validity of psychoanalytic concepts when subjected to scientific scrutiny outside the clinical situation, and on the procedures by which beliefs might be tested, or evidence for interpretations assessed, within the psychoanalytic treatment situation.

Over the course of the twentieth century, a large literature has evolved reporting empirical research on hypotheses derived from psychoanalytic theories, especially in the areas of general personality development and organization, cognitive processes, psychopathology, and treatment process or outcome. A general problem with the enterprise of empirically testing psychoanalytic hypotheses in an extrapsychoanalytic context has been the complexity of psychoanalytic conceptualizations, with the concomitant difficulty in achieving agreement as to the proper manner of operationalizing psychoanalytic ideas about human functioning. Nevertheless, ideas generated on the basis of clinical experience in psychoanalysis have had an enormously fertile impact on the field of empirical psychology as a whole. The contemporary state of this impact is indicated in the American Psychological Association's anthology, *Interface of Psychoanalysis and Psychology* (edited by James W. Barron, Morris N. Eagle, and David L. Wolitzky, Washington, D.C., 1992).

As discussed by several commentators, including Marshall Edelson, from within logical-empiricism, there have been three major philosophical attacks on the scientific status of psychoanalysis as a clinical discipline. First, logical positivists, such as Ernst Nagel in the 1950s, argued that psychoanalytic ideas are frequently presented in theoretical terms that are so vague as to be unamenable to adequate empirical support or verification. The force of this criticism has waned not only with the increasing specification of psychoanalytic conceptualizations, but also, as discussed by Frederick Suppes (*The Structure of Scientific Theories*, Urbana, Illinois, 1977) and others, with the general decline of logical positivism as a viable philosophy of science.

Second, Karl Popper (in *Conjectures and Refutations*, London, 1963) claimed that psychoanalytic propositions are presented in such a manner as to be incapable of falsification by empirical evidence, and hence that psychoanalysis fails to meet the standards that should define a science as argued by Popper himself in *The Logic of Scientific Discovery* (New York, 1959). The force of this criticism has waned not only because it has been suggested that Popper tended to "misdepict" the psychoanalytic conceptualizations that he attempted to critique, but also because serious problems have been demonstrated with his falsificationist view of the scientific method.

Third, Adolf Grünbaum, in a series of publications since the early 1980s, has attacked psychoanalysis as nonscientific on the basis of the criteria of eliminative inductivism. Grünbaum argued that psychoanalytic conceptualizations, although potentially falsifiable, are not scientifically credible because adequately uncontaminated data cannot be obtained from within the psychoanalytic treatment relationship. Currently, many commentators believe that Grünbaum's writings constitute the strongest critique of the scientific claims of psychoanalysis, and the debate following Grünbaum's attacks has been ongoing through the 1990s. Many proponents of psychoanalytic science have attempted to show that Grünbaum's depiction of the interpretive discipline of psychoanalysis has been excessively narrow or otherwise distorted, and several apologists have attempted to demonstrate that Grünbaum's criteria for scientific method can actually be met by improved specification of the procedures for testing psychoanalytic hypotheses within the clinical psychoanalytic setting.

Continental Philosophies

Whereas logical-empiricist philosophies are, in a certain sense, heirs to the tradition of Cartesian-Kantian metaphysics, a history of Western philosophical thinking, mostly of European origin, breaks with the foundational assumptions of this tradition. Throughout the twentieth century, psychoanalysis has profoundly influenced, and been influenced by, several of these post-Hegelian, post-Kierkegaardian, and post-Nietzschean currents. These include diverse philosophical movements such as hermeneutics, phenomenology, existentialism, surrealism, narratology and narratological constructivism, critical theory and "negative dialectics," linguistic structuralism, poststructuralism, and deconstruction.

An important feature shared by many of these philosophical currents is that considerations of ontology and *ethicality* (a term that is used rather differently from the common notion of *ethics*) are given priority over the deliberations of conventional epistemologies. This results from a refusal merely to endorse the dichotomy of knower and known (subject/object, mind/world) that is assumed by logical-empiricist metaphysics and the Cartesian-Kantian tradition. Preeminently, these continental philosophies consider those matters of being, time, and language by which the duality of knower and known becomes possible. For example, Edmund Husserl, in his 1901 *Logical Investigations* (translated by J. N. Findlay, London, 1970), and elsewhere, argued that the traditional philosophical ideal of establishing some absolute standpoint of knowledge, outside the vicissitudes of human experience, by which the mind and the world might be depicted, must be relinquished in favor of methodical investigation of the contingencies of experience itself, the "phenomena." Martin Heidegger, in his 1927 *Being and Time* (translated by J. Macquarrie and E. Robinson, New York, 1962), as well as in his subsequent writings, moved radically away from the Husserlian enterprise of phenomenology to attempt an articulation of the ontological, ethical, and even aesthetic conditions of human experience that precede the constitution of any epistemological effort. A central tenet of many of these continental philosophies is that the structure of an epistemological attitude depends on a prior *ethical* commitment that usually operates without investigation or articulation. This tenet is well illustrated in the writings of Emmanuel Levinas (e.g., see his *Collected Philosophical Papers*, translated by A. Lingis, Dordrecht, Netherlands, 1987), but it is also well exhibited in structuralist and poststructuralist philosophies.

All these philosophical currents have, in many different ways, profoundly and controversially influenced the understanding of psychoanalytic discourse. For example, psychoanalytic processes are now often viewed as less interesting in terms of their apparent production of objectivistic formulations about mental life, and more interesting in terms of their discursive mobilization of the subject that enunciates conscious awareness to become more responsive to what is its constitutive "other." The claim is that the latter is an ontological and ethical venture that opens the subject to new potentials of knowing and being, through relational refigurations of the language and the eroticism by which the subject of psychic reality has "being."

Such views have become especially influential since the psychoanalytic expositions of Jacques Lacan, in his *Écrits* (Paris, 1966) as well as his many *Séminaires*, and since the poststructuralist writings of Jacques Derrida along with those of feminist psychoanalysts, such as Julia Kristeva and Luce Irigaray, who have been influenced by Derrida's "deconstructive" work. The latter have advanced an important but philosophically controversial viewpoint that the very structure of knowledge assumed by logical-empiricist epistemologies has patriarchal commitments that must be deconstucted in order to free the human subject, ontologically and ethically, toward new ways of knowing and being. Unlike those philosophies that have evaluated psychoanalysis from within the suppositions of logical-empiricism, such arguments take very seriously Freud's notion that the dynamics of human cognition, affect, and behavior always originate and depend on the polyvalent experiences of bodily eroticism.

[*See also* Epistemology; Epistemology of Practice; Hermeneutics; *and* Philosophy, *article on* Philosophy of Science.]

Bibliography

Barratt, B. B. (1993). *Psychoanalysis and the postmodern impulse: Knowing and being since Freud's psychology.* Baltimore, MD: Johns Hopkins University Press. An extended argument in favor of psychoanalysis as a feminist and deconstructive mode of discourse.

Derrida, J. (1987). *The postcard* (A. Bass, Trans.). Chicago, IL: University of Chicago Press. (Original work published 1980.) Contains some of Derrida's deconstructive work that is most directly relevant to psychoanalysis.

Edelson, M. (1984). *Hypothesis and evidence in psychoanalysis.* Chicago, IL: University of Chicago Press. A careful and thorough response to Grünbaum's critique of the scientific status of psychoanalysis by demonstrating how hypothesis testing might operate clinically.

Efron, A. (1985). *The sexual body: An interdisciplinary perspective* [Special issue]. *Journal of Mind and Behavior, 6*(1 & 2). An examination of social scientific and philosophical resistances to Freud's ideas concerning the centrality of eroticism in the formation of the human mind.

Ellenberger, H. (1970). *The discovery of the unconscious.* New York: Basic Books. An influential study of the philosophical origins of Freud's ideas about the significance of unconscious mental life.

Grünbaum, A. (1984). *The foundations of psychoanalysis: A philosophical critique.* Berkeley: University of California Press. A critique of the scientific status of psychoanalysis from the standpoint of eliminative inductivism.

Habermas, J. (1982). *Knowledge and human interests.* (J. J. Shapiro, Trans.). London: Heinemann. (Original work published 1968.) An influential study of the way in which "interests" shape the constitution of knowledge systems, including a section on the "liberatory" interests of psychoanalysis.

Hook, S. (Ed.). (1959). *Psychoanalysis, scientific method and philosophy*. New York: New York University Press. A compilation of papers by philosophers and psychoanalysts written at the height of the controversies between Freudian psychology and logical-empiricism, including the influential essay by Ernest Nagel.

Irigaray, L. (1985). *Speculum of the other woman* (G. C. Gill, Trans.). Ithaca, NY: Cornell University Press. (Original work published 1974.) An exposition of the erotic structures of particular philosophical viewpoints as well as a critique, from within psychoanalysis, of patriarchal aspects of some psychoanalytic theorizing.

Kristeva, J. (1974). *La révolution due langage poétique*. Paris: Seuil. [Partially translated by M. Waller as *Revolution in Poetic Language*, New York, Columbia University Press, 1984.] Kristeva's first major work and probably still an important source for her semiotic/feminist approach to psychoanalysis.

Lingis, A. (1989). *Deathbound subjectivity*. Bloomington: Indiana University Press. An excellent discussion of the influence of death on the formation and experience of the human subject, as well as a useful introduction to continental philosophical approaches to ideas associated with the notion of the ego.

Wilden, A. (1968). *System and structure: Essays in communication and exchange*. London: Tavistock. An influential exposition of structuralist and semiotic theories as they apply to psychoanalysis and other topics.

Barnaby B. Barratt

Psychoanalytic Psychotherapies

This overview of psychoanalytic psychotherapies focuses on their history as treatments, their techniques, their theory of therapeutic change, and their supports by systematic empirical research.

History of Development of Psychoanalytic Therapy

Psychoanalytic therapy is the oldest form of psychotherapy based on systematic observation. It took its initial shape toward the end of the nineteenth century in the early observations of Breuer and Freud (1895/1955) as they examined patients to try to understand a disorder known as hysteria, characterized by psychological symptoms that appear to be physical, such as paralyses or anaesthesias. The therapy continued to be developed throughout Freud's career. Over this long time, psychoanalytic therapy evolved into two related but somewhat different treatment forms: (1) psychoanalysis (also sometimes called psychoanalytic therapy, to distinguish the multiple meaning of psychoanalysis from a particular form of treatment), and (2) a usually shorter form called psychodynamic, dynamic, or psychoanalytic psychotherapy.

The original group of practicing psychoanalysts were disciples of Freud who thought of themselves as part of what was often referred to then as "the psychoanalytic movement." Over the last century, psychoanalytic organizations became established in many countries. The International Psychoanalytical Association now has over 9,000 members in over 30 countries; the United States has about 3,000 members in the American Psychoanalytic Association, about 3,000 in the American Psychological Association's Division of Psychoanalysis, and several thousands more in many smaller groups. Psychoanalysts have typically included physicians, psychologists, social workers, and a few others from other disciplines. To be qualified they must go through a rigorous training that typically consists of 5 years of didactic courses, their own personal psychoanalysis, and the completion of the psychoanalytic therapy of three patients along with concurrent weekly supervision for each patient.

Psychoanalysis as a Therapy: Theory and Technique

In its usual form, psychoanalysis is an individual treatment with only the patient and the analyst present. The patient reclines on a couch with the analyst seated further back in order for the patient not to be distracted by seeing the analyst. The patient and analyst meet for 45- or 50-minute sessions, four to five times a week, although sometimes only three times a week. The treatment tends to last from 3 to 5 years in its traditional open-ended form, although some treatments last much longer. The patient is instructed at the outset to try to say what comes to mind as completely as possible. Inevitably, the patient's stream of spoken thoughts runs into resistances; at these points the analyst typically offers clarifications and interpretations.

The main techniques of psychoanalysis as a therapy have often been described in Freud's writings and in those of many others, including Brenner (1995). But there are many variations in the ways the treatment is conducted. These variations are greatest in the frequency of the sessions, the form of the instructions delivered to the patient about the necessity of communicating one's thoughts and feelings completely, and the frequency and accuracy of interpretations. Accurate interpretations are aimed at increasing the patient's insight into the patient's conflicts because in psychoanalytic theory, the acquisition of such insight is the primary vehicle for achieving the patient's goals. Each of the techniques is used but not necessarily to the same degree in all forms of psychoanalytic treatment. The four sections that follow discuss each of four classes of the main techniques of psychoanalytic therapies:

Facilitating Associative Freedom. Freud (1912/1958b) referred to free association as the "fundamental rule of psychoanalysis"—"the patient should communicate everything that occurs to him without criticism or selection" (p. 112). Several treatment practices were intended to facilitate associative freedom: (1) the instruction given at the start of the psychoanalysis for the patient to try to say what comes to mind as freely as possible; (2) the high frequency of sessions per week and length of treatment over several years; (3) the prone position, which is calculated to avoid the distraction of seeing the analyst; and (4) the analyst's interpretation of resistances that appear in the course of free association. These conditions—along with associations to dreams—may set up in the patient a distinctively changed, free-associative state of consciousness.

Allowing the Development of Rapport and Alliance. Freud (1913/1958) recommended that the analyst should do nothing to interfere with the development of rapport and of therapeutic alliance so that they will develop naturally: "It remains the first aim of the treatment to attach the patient to it and to the person of the doctor . . . It is certainly possible to forfeit this first success if from the start one takes any standpoint other than that of sympathetic understanding" (pp. 139–140).

Psychoanalytic patients will not usually require special provisions of supportive conditions. However, for some severely ill patients it is necessary to prevent the patient from getting sicker by actively strengthening defenses (Gill, 1951). For one school of psychoanalysis, "self psychology" (Kohut, 1977), it is even mandated for the analyst to remain supportive of the patient's self-esteem and need for acceptance—a task that requires particular empathy.

Responding to the Patient's Associations with Accurate Interpretations. A central technique of psychoanalysis is accurate interpretations. To achieve this, the analyst must first be able to make fitting formulations of transference patterns (that is, the pattern in relationships with others in the past that is also mirrored in the relationship with the analyst) because "in analysis transference emerges as the most powerful resistance to the treatment" (Freud, 1912/1958a, p. 101). To do this task, the analyst must infer from the patient's associations the pattern of relationships that characterize both the current pattern to the analyst and to other people (the "here and now" of Gill, 1985), as well as the pattern to the patient's parents and caregivers in the patient's early life. A typical formulation of the central relationship pattern (as in Luborsky & Crits-Christoph, 1998) begins with a wish and ends with its consequences in relation to others and in relation to the self; for example, "I [the patient] wish to be close, but the other person doesn't allow it; and so I get anxious." The consequences in this example are both from the other person as well as from the self.

Dealing With and Using Countertransference. Countertransference is defined as the analyst's personal reactions to the patient's transference. These reactions can distort the analyst's accuracy of understanding the patient's associations, and consequently, the analyst's responses to the patient. Such intrusions can be a subtle but major source of interference in the treatment. Various methods have been offered for avoiding countertransferential distortions (Luborsky, 1984) or for being able to use them constructively (Gill, 1985). Countertransference was once seen as "bad" and to be avoided, but now analysts attempt to learn what the patient tends to draw from people from these reactions.

Psychodynamic Therapies and Their Techniques

Psychodynamic psychotherapies exist in many formats. The treatment has broadened to adapt to the needs of more psychiatrically severe patients, such as in Kernberg's (1976) application to severe personality disorders and borderline patients. Psychodynamic psychotherapies have both short-term (usually 12 to 25 sessions) and long-term (2 to 3 or more years) forms. In contrast to psychoanalysis proper, the period of training for psychodynamic psychotherapy is much shorter. It is practiced by many psychiatrists, psychologists, and social workers, and is the most widely performed of all the types of psychotherapy.

Most psychodynamic therapies fall within the psychoanalytic tradition initiated by Freud. A much smaller number of treatments that resemble psychoanalysis reflect instead other offshoots of that tradition. Some long-term variants follow the precepts of Alfred Adler, with emphasis on the striving for power and the sense of inferiority, and are often called Adlerian analysis. Those that derive from Carl Jung with emphasis on the emergence of archetypal group symbols are often called Jungian analysis. In addition, influential psychoanalytic therapies of two other kinds have also been fashioned: interpersonal, derived from the work of Harry Stack Sullivan (Sullivan, 1953), and "object-relations" therapy, which focuses on relationships with others (Fairbairn, 1954), which reflects developments within the psychoanalytic tradition Freud initiated. There are also several group-format psychoanalytic treatments.

Certain treatments described below are relatively short-term variants. Mann's therapy (1973), a 12-session psychotherapy, provides a consistent focus on improving the patient's self-image and on the patient's "central complaint." Davanloo's therapy (1978) focuses on interpretations of resistances, especially those about the patient's passivity as a means of dealing with anger; the therapist is confrontational, especially in relation to the patient's defenses. Sifneos's (1979) short-term anxiety-provoking therapy (STAPT) is another treatment that focuses on anxiety-arousing interpretations of the patient's current situation, typically in terms of the parallels of the Oedipal triangle in the patient's early versus current situation (that is, the competition for love of a parent with the parent of the opposite sex). Another approach is supportive-expressive (SE) dynamic psychotherapy (Luborsky, 1984), which is guided by a manual for both short-term and for long-term psychoanalytic psychotherapies, with a focus on interpretations based on the Core Conflictual Relationship Theme (CCRT; Luborsky & Crits-Christoph, 1998). There is also the similar time-limited dynamic psychotherapy (TLDP) of Strupp and Binder (1984), which instead bases its interpretations on a related central relationship pattern measure, called "the cyclical maladaptive pattern." The short-term treatment by M. J. Horowitz (1991), "configurational analysis," follows a conceptual model for intrapsychic conflict about relationships.

Research Support for the Concepts and Efficacy of Psychoanalytic Therapy

Most research with psychoanalytic therapy fits the clinical-theoretical case study style that is usual in psychoanalytic writing, and most discoveries that added to knowledge about psychoanalytic therapy have come from such case studies. The successes of the early psychoanalytic observations, theories, and method have had the effect of confirming many psychoanalysts in their sole reliance on that research style, despite its limitations in independent confirmation by other observers and the neglect of the possibility of supplementing or of combining that style with a more controlled and quantitative research approach (Schachter & Luborsky, 1998). The American Psychoanalytic Association has operated, for approximately the last 25 years, the Fund for Psychoanalytic Research, which supports well-controlled studies (some of which combine clinical and systematic empirical methods), partly to try to balance the field's predominant and almost sole allegiance to the clinical-theoretical research style. In addition, the International Psychoanalytical Association has now set up a similar but much larger program for training in and support of both kinds of studies.

Researchers studying dynamic therapies have, like researchers studying other forms of treatment, primarily used a manual format for explaining, illustrating, and monitoring therapeutic techniques by carrying out randomized controlled trials. Among dynamic psychotherapy's varied techniques, two broad types of categories have been identified: supportive and expressive. Supportive techniques are aimed at allowing, maintaining, and encouraging the patient's level of functioning; expressive techniques are aimed at facilitating the patient's expressions about the problems and conflicts, leading to improved understanding of them. For providing supportiveness, the therapist needs to be alert to allowing and, if necessary, assisting the patient to experience a bond with the therapist and to collaborate in the treatment tasks. For increasing the patient's expressiveness, the therapist mainly focuses on interpreting the patient's conflicts. In the course of the treatment, the patient reexperiences some of his or her conflictual relationship problems; by the therapist's attention to the meaning of the relationship conflicts, a working through can occur in the form of a gradual mastery and resolution of the symptoms. The central techniques can be conveyed by a sample of the recommendations followed by therapists in dynamic psychotherapy, especially in the supportive-expressive version of dynamic psychotherapy (Luborsky & Mark, 1991):

1. *Be sensitive to allowing the patient to form a helping alliance.* This directive is the most basic supportive technique.
2. *Formulate and then interpret the central relationship patterns.* This directive advises the means of using the most important expressive techniques. Researchers have studied these patterns using the Core Conflictual Relationship Theme (CCRT) method, a reliable, clinically meaningful method for extracting the most frequent, transference-related themes across the narratives patients tell about their relationships with others, including with the therapist. Use of the CCRT method is illustrated in the example below.

Mr. Edward Howard's CCRT early in treatment:	An example of an interpretation based on the CCRT:
Wish 1: I want to be close to others.	"You wanted a positive response from me but felt I would not give it."
Wish 2: I want to receive affection.	
Wish 3: I want to be distant as (a way to be safer).	
Response from other: But the other person rejects my wishes.	
Response of self 1: I feel resentment.	
Response of self 2: I feel self-blame.	
Response of self 3: I feel anxiety.	

3. *Understand and interpret the symptoms in terms of where they fit into the central relationship pattern.* An example of the recommended technique was just given above: "Your anxiety comes when you feel rejected in your wish for closeness."
4. *Attend to and then interpret the patient's concerns about separating from the therapy and from the therapist when treatment nears completion.*

Studies of the Outcomes of Psychoanalytic Therapy. That there are considerable benefits from psychoanalytic treatment for most patients is given some support by many outcome studies done over the years, as summarized by Bachrach, Galatzer-Levy, Skolnikoff, & Waldron (1991). What is most lacking among the outcome studies are comparisons of psychoanalytic treatment with other long-term treatments. However, there are a few comparisons of long-term treatment (not psychoanalysis itself) with short-term treatment. Among the practical difficulties with doing proper comparisons are the length of psychoanalytic treatment and the need for the comparison treatment to be an equally long but different treatment.

In coping with these difficulties, the Menninger Foundation Psychotherapy Project (Wallerstein, 1986) is a special study of the treatment of the mostly severely ill patients who come to the Menninger Foundation. The project compared long-term treatment for 22 patients in psychoanalytic therapy with long-term treatment of 20 patients in psychoanalytically oriented supportive psychotherapy. Initial and outcome evaluations were tape-recorded but the treatment sessions themselves were not. Contrary to expectations, both groups showed significant benefits, although different kinds of patients responded in predictably different ways to the two forms of treatment (see below).

Predictors of the Outcomes of Psychoanalytic Therapy. Predictors for the outcomes of psychoanalysis as a therapy have not been studied directly but studies of *psychodynamic psychotherapy* have yielded predictors that are likely to be similar (Luborsky, Crits-Cristoph, Mintz, & Auerbach, 1988). These predictors included two prominent ones: initial psychiatric severity of the diagnosis (the higher the severity, the *less* the improvement), and the therapeutic alliance (the higher the early alliance, the greater the improvement). Tests of predictors by controlled studies of psychoanalysis itself are now in the beginning phases in the Penn Psychoanalytic Collection, a unique set of completely tape-recorded cases. Each of the treatments has been evaluated by two independent clinical judges, first for the level of functioning of the patient in the early stage and then for the level of functioning in the late stage of the treatment, with one measure of change as the difference between these two points.

Development of Reliable Measures of the Transference Pattern. Because of the central role of accurate interpretation of the transference in psychoanalysis, reliable measures of the transference pattern are vital. As noted earlier, the usual judgments of transference, even by experienced psychoanalysts, do not agree well with each other (DeWitt, Kaltreider, Weiss, & Horowitz, 1983). A clinician-observer judgment method for the content of the transference was constructed by Luborsky in which the judge rated evidence for three components within the narratives in psychoanalytic sessions: the wishes, responses from other, and the responses of self; the three together formed the Core Conflictual Relationship Theme (CCRT). Judgments of the CCRT show a good level of agreement between independent judges and support most of Freud's 23 major observations about transference (Luborsky & Crits-Cristoph, 1998). Supporting both the integrity of the method and the generality of transference patterns, recent research has shown that the CCRT in the session's narratives told before the therapist has been met is significantly similar to the CCRT from the session's narratives told after the therapist has been met (Barber, Luborsky, Crits-Cristoph & Diguer, 1998).

Reanalysis of Major Outcome Studies Using Blatt's Dimension of "Anaclitic" Versus "Introjective." A reanalysis of three major studies of the outcomes of psychoanalytic psychodynamic treatments showed the utility of the personality dimensions studied by Sidney Blatt. These studies included reanalyses of data from the Menninger Psychotherapy Project (Wallerstein, 1986) by Blatt (1992), the Austen Rigg's Center study by Blatt and Ford (1994), and the NIMH Treatment for Depression Collaborative Research Program (TDCRP) by Blatt, Zuroff, Bondi, Sanislow, & Pilkonis (1998). As Blatt proposes, some patients are more concerned with loss and separation, whereas others are more concerned with autonomy and meeting high standards for themselves. As described in Blatt and Ford (1994), the *anaclitic* dimension involves a preoccupation with the pressures of relationships and the use of the defenses of denial and repression. The *introjective* dimension involves a preoccupation with a sense of self as separate, autonomous, and independent, with much use of the defenses of intellectualization and rationalization. In each of these studies, both anaclitic and introjective patients made substantial treatment gains, but there were special changes in each dimension, and the two types of patients were also differentially responsive to different types of treatments.

In sum, over the past 100 years, much knowledge has been gained about psychodynamic psychotherapy, including the following: (1) Good reliability has been shown for making dynamic formulations from treatment sessions by the CCRT method (Luborsky & Diguer, 1998); (2) The benefits achieved by dynamic psychotherapy have been shown to be substantial (Crits-Christoph, 1992; Luborsky, Diguer, Luborsky, & Schmidt, 1999) ; (3) In comparative treatment studies, patients in various short-term psychotherapies compared tend not to differ from each other significantly in their amount of improvement. In fact, so far evidence from comparative treatment studies has shown that the amount of benefits are not significantly different among different brief psychotherapies but there is a deficiency of studies of long-term therapies (Luborsky, Diguer, Luborsky, & Schmidt, 1999).

[*See also* Psychotherapy.]

Acknowledgments. Research Scientist Award DA00168 and Paul Crits-Christoph's Penn Center for Psychotherapy Research are gratefully acknowledged.

Bibliography

Bachrach, H. M., Galatzer-Levy, R., Skolnikoff, A., Waldron, S. (1991). On the efficacy of psychoanalysis. *Journal of the American Psychoanalytic Association, 39*, 871–916.

Barber, J. P., & Crits-Christoph, P. (1995). *Psychodynamic psychotherapies for psychiatric disorders* (Axis I) (pp. 131–160). New York: Basic Books.

Barber, J. P., Luborsky, L., Crits-Christoph, P., & Diguer, L. (1998). Stability of the CCRT from before psychotherapy starts to the early sessions. In L. Luborsky and P. Crits-Christoph (Eds.), *Understanding transference: The core conflictual relationship theme method* (pp. 253–260). Washington, DC: American Psychological Association.

Blatt, S. J. (1992). The differential effect of psychotherapy and psychoanalysis on anaclitic and introjective patients: The Menninger Psychotherapy Research Project revisited. *Journal of the American Psychoanalytic Association, 40*, 691–724.

Blatt, S. J., & Ford, R. Q. (1994). *Therapeutic change: An object relations perspective.* New York: Plenum Press.

Blatt, S. J., Zuroff, D. C., Bondi, C. M., Sanislow, C. A., & Pilkonis, P. A. (1998). When and how perfectionism impedes the brief treatment of depression: Further analyses of The National Institute of Mental Health Treatment of Depression Collaborative Research Program. *Journal of Consulting and Clinical Psychology, 68*, 423–428.

Brenner, C. (1995). Some remarks on psychoanalytic technique. *Journal of Clinical Psychoanalysis, 4*, 413–428.

Breuer, J., & Freud, S. (1955). Studies on hysteria. In J. Strachey (Ed. and Trans.), *The standard edition of the complete psychological works of Sigmund Freud* (Vol. 2, pp. 255–305). London: Hogarth Press. (Original work published 1893–1895)

Crits-Christoph, P. (1992). The efficacy of brief dynamic psychotherapy: A meta-analysis. *The American Journal of Psychiatry, 149*, 151–158.

Davanloo, H. (1978). *Basic principles and techniques in short-term psychodynamic psychotherapy.* New York: Spectrum.

DeWitt, K. N., Kaltreider, N., Weiss, D. S., & Horowitz, M. J. (1983). Judging change in psychotherapy: Reliability of clinical formulations. *Archives of General Psychiatry, 40*, 1121–1128.

Fairbairn, W. R. (1954). *An object-relations theory of the personality.* New York: Basic Books.

Freud, S. (1953). The interpretation of dreams. In J. Strachey (Ed. & Trans.), *The standard edition of the complete psychological works of Sigmund Freud* (Vols. 4 & 5). London: Hogarth Press. (Original work published 1900)

Freud, S. (1958a). The dynamics of the transference. In J. Strachey (Ed. and Trans.), *The standard edition of the complete psychological works of Sigmund Freud* (Vol. 12, pp. 99–108). London: Hogarth Press. (Original work published 1912)

Freud, S. (1958b). Recommendations to physicians practicing psycho-analysis. In J. Strachey (Ed. and Trans.), *The standard edition of the complete psychological works of Sigmund Freud* (Vol. 12, pp. 111–120). London: Hogarth Press. (Original work published 1912)

Freud, S. (1958). On beginning the treatment (Further recommendations on the technique of psycho-analysis). In J. Strachey (Ed. and Trans.), *The standard edition of the complete psychological works of Sigmund Freud* (Vol. 12, pp. 121–144). London: Hogarth Press. (Original work published 1913)

Gill, M. (1951). Ego psychology and psychotherapy. *Psychoanalytic Quarterly 20*, 60–71.

Gill, M. M. (1985). The interactional aspect of transference: Range of application. In E. A. Schwaber (Ed.), *The transference in psychotherapy: Clinical management* (pp. 87–102). New York: International Universities Press.

Horowitz, M. J. (Ed.). (1991). *Persons, schemas and maladaptive interpersonal behavior.* Chicago: University of Chicago Press.

Kernberg, O. F. (1976). *Object relations and clinical psychoanalysis.* New York: Aronson.

Kernberg, O. F. (1984). *Supportive psychotherapy in severe personality disorders: Psychotherapeutic strategies.* New Haven: Yale University Press.

Kohut, H. (1977). *The restoration of the self.* New York: International Universities Press.

Luborsky, L. (1984). *Principles of psychoanalytic psychotherapy: A manual for supportive-expressive (SE) treatment* (pp. 1–270). New York: Basic Books.

Luborsky, L. (1996). *The symptom-context method: Symptoms as opportunities in psychotherapy.* Washington, DC: American Psychological Association.

Luborsky, L., & Crits-Christoph, P. (1998). *Understanding transference* (2nd ed.). Washington, DC: American Psychological Association.

Luborsky, L., Crits-Christoph, P., Mintz, & Auerbach, A. (1988). *Who will benefit from psychotherapy? Predicting therapeutic outcomes.* New York: Basic Books.

Luborsky, L., Diguer, L., Luborsky, E., & Schmidt, R. (1999). Is it true that everyone has won and all must have prizes? An update. In Ianowsky, D. (Ed.). *Psychotherapy in the 1990s—implications and outcomes* (pp. 3–22). Washington, DC: American Psychiatric Press.

Mann, J. (1973). *Time-limited psychotherapy.* Cambridge, MA: Harvard University Press.

Schachter, J., & Luborsky, L. (1998). Who's afraid of psychoanalytic research? Analysts' attitude toward reading clinical versus empirical research papers. *International Journal of Psychoanalysis, 79*, 965–970.

Shevrin, H., Bond, J. A., Brakle, L. A. W., Hertel, R. K., Williams, W. J. (1996). *Conscious and unconscious processes: Psychodynamic, cognitive and neurophysiological convergences.* New York: Guilford Press.

Sifneos, P. (1979). *Short-term dynamic psychotherapy: Evaluation and technique.* New York: Plenum Press.

Stone, L. (1961). *The psychoanalytic situation: An examina-*

tion of its development and essential nature. New York: International Universities Press.

Strupp, H., & Binder, J. (1984). Psychotherapy in a new key: A guide to time-limited dynamic psychotherapy. New York: Basic Books.

Sullivan, H. S. (1953). *The interpersonal theory of psychiatry.* New York: Norton.

Wallerstein, R. (1986). *Forty-two lives in treatment: A study of psychoanalysis and psychotherapy.* New York: Guilford Press.

Lester Luborsky

PSYCHOBIOGRAPHY may be defined as the explicit use of psychological theory or research in biography. Contrary to the opinion of many, it is not a quaint, marginal, slightly disreputable branch of the science of psychology, but rather it is closely linked with central goals of the discipline. The argument is not that psychology should be nothing but the study of individual lives, but that the psychological study of lives in contexts is at least one of the central objectives of the fields. Four objectives of personality psychology are: (a) developing integrative personality theories (such as psychoanalysis, humanistic, evolutionary theories); (b) studying individual and group differences in cognitive and personality dimensions (such as intelligence, achievement motivation, anxiety); (c) analyzing specific processes or classes of behavior (such as aggression, substance abuse, altruism); and (d) increasing understanding of individual persons and lives, whether of clients, research participants, historical figures, or ourselves. Psychobiography follows this fourth aim of pursuing the understandings of individual lives, an objective which remains important no matter how much progress is made in nomothetic cognitive science or neuroscience.

Psychobiography is traditionally identified as beginning with Freud's *Leonardo da Vinci and a Memory of His Childhood* (1910/1957) and an associated cluster of psychobiographical studies by members of the Vienna Psychoanalytic Society. Early psychoanalytic psychobiographies included analyses of Shakespeare through *Hamlet* by Ernest Jones, the artist Giovanni Segantini by Karl Abraham, and Socrates by Karpas. By the end of the 1930s, there were psychobiographical studies of writers including Tolstoy, Dostoevsky, Molière, Sand, Goethe, Coleridge, Nietzsche, Poe, and Rousseau, and of public figures ranging from Caesar and Alexander the Great to Lincoln and Darwin. Although the 1940s were a relatively slow period for psychobiography, the 1950s marked a major turning point in terms of more methodologically sophisticated studies, including Erik Erikson's *Young Man Luther: A Study in Psychoanalysis and History* (1958) and Alexander and Juliette George's *Woodrow Wilson and Colonel House: A Personality Study* (1956/1964), books that are still frequently assigned in college courses. To mention just a sample of the more prominent psychobiographies in recent years, there have been influential studies of Henry James by Leon Edel, Hitler by Robert Waite, Stalin by Robert Tucker, James and John Stuart Mill by Bruce Mazlish, Beethoven by Maynard Solomon, and Samuel Johnson by Walter J. Bate (see Gilmore, 1984, for more than 1,700 references in psychobiography and psychohistory).

Within academic psychology, the study of individual lives was pursued by a number of figures at Harvard University, including personality psychologists like Henry A. Murray, Gordon Allport, and Robert White. The single most influential figure in modern psychobiography was undoubtedly Erik Erikson (1902–1994), also at Harvard from 1960 to 1970, whose studies *Young Man Luther* (1958) and *Gandhi's Truth* (1969) had an enormous impact, drawing public attention to psychobiography and psychohistory not only within psychology and psychiatry, but in the culture at large.

Erikson (1958) argued that psychological concepts and assumptions are inevitably embedded in accounts and interpretations of lives and that even those opposed to a systematic psychology are forced to draw on an implicit psychology. From this perspective, there is no alternative to utilizing some forms of psychology, and the only argument is about whether commonsense psychology can be usefully supplemented with formal psychology.

What kind of psychology should be used? For the early psychoanalysts, psychobiography was conceived and practiced as applied psychoanalysis. In recent decades, however, many have argued that psychobiography and psychohistory should be defined more broadly to include the application of any systematic psychological theory or research to biography. Thus, psychoanalytic psychobiography is one prominent branch of psychobiography. Yet there may also be psychological biographies drawing from phenomenological theory, behavioral theory, or cognitive science, or from work in developmental, social, or abnormal psychology.

In an effort to establish more securely the study of individual lives and psychobiography in relation to academic psychology, *Life Histories and Psychobiography* (Runyan, 1982) provided a critical review of case-study, idiographic, and psychobiographical methods. The discussion of psychobiography analyzed issues such as the kinds of evidence needed for psychobiographical interpretation, and the critical evaluation of alternative psychobiographical interpretations. This was illustrated with an analysis of 13 different psychodynamic explanations proposed for why Vincent Van Gogh cut off the lower half of his left ear in December 1888 and took it to a prostitute named Rachel, asking her to keep it carefully. The book also discussed issues such as the dangers of psychological reductionism in psychobiography, the extent to which adult personality and behavior can or cannot be attributed to childhood experience, and the relative contributions of psychoanalytic and nonanalytic psychology to psychobiography.

Important contributions of psychologists to psychobiography may be illustrated with a number of more recent books. First, *Psychobiography and Life Narratives* (McAdams & Ochberg, 1988) includes a diverse array of theoretical perspectives to psychobiography, including the application of Silvan Tomkins's script theory to the lives of Nathaniel Hawthorne and Eleanor Marx by Rae Carlson, a quantitative analysis of Eriksonian themes of identity, intimacy, and generativity in the writings of Vera Brittain by Abigail Stewart, Carol Franz, and Lynn Layton, and a study of achievement affiliation and power motives in Richard Nixon by David Winter and Leslie Carlson.

Second, *Personology: Content and Method in Personality Assessment and Psychobiography* (Alexander, 1990) provides original psychobiographical interpretations of Freud, Jung, and Harry Stack Sullivan and suggests interpretive guidelines for archival or clinical material, useful in both clinical case studies and psychobiography.

Third, an important recent book in psychobiography is Alan Elms's *Uncovering Lives: The Uneasy Alliance of Biography and Psychology* (1994), which provides methodological advice for practicing psychobiography and a set of fascinating psychobiographical interpretations of psychologists, science fiction writers, and political figures. Several of Elms's interpretations illustrate the power of psychobiographical interpretation for illuminating the personal side of psychology, literature, and culture.

To start at the beginning of the field, Elms argued that in Freud's study of Leonardo da Vinci, Freud outlined sound methodologial guidelines for the field, such as avoiding arguments based on a single clue or avoiding pathographizing the subject yet ended up violating each of these guidelines in the work itself. Why? Freud completed his Leonardo study in 6 intense months of work, and Elms suggested that the adequacy of his study was compromised by personal issues such as Freud's self-identification with Leonardo, his sexual and emotional frustrations in his marriage, Freud's childhood erotic feelings toward his mother, possible homosexual attraction to Fliess and Jung, and Freud's ideas about sublimation of sexuality into creativity.

Elms also provided a psychobiographical perspective on B. F. Skinner, particularly on personal issues involved in writing his utopian novel *Walden Two* (1948). The book is partly a dialog between Burris, "a pedestrian college teacher," and Frazier, the founder of Walden Two, "a self-proclaimed genius who has deserted academic psychology for behavioral engineering" (Elms, 1994, p. 87). Skinner indicated that this novel was written "with an emotional intensity that I have never experienced at any other time," and described it as "pretty obviously a venture in self-therapy, in which I was struggling to reconcile two aspects of my own behavior represented by Burris and Frazier" (p. 87). After writing the book, Skinner wrote: "I'm now a thoroughgoing Frazieriain as a result and I'm no longer Burris" (p. 99). In other words, he is no longer the plodding college teacher but more the brilliant maverick applying behaviorial principles to the redesign of society. Elms effectively interpreted the writing of this book as a midlife identity crisis, which resonates back to an earlier identity crisis Skinner had in his "dark year" at age 22 when he initially became a behaviorist.

Significant contributions to psychobiography have also been made by those in disciplines other than psychology, including history, political science, and literature (see Runyan, 1988 and 1997, for a review of other disciplines contributing to psychohistory, and a quantitative analysis of books, articles, and dissertations in psychobiography from before 1920 to 1980).

[*See also* Literature; Music; *and* Political Leadership.]

Bibliography

Alexander, I. E. (1990). *Personology: Method and content in personality assessment and psychobiography*. Durham, NC: Duke University Press.

Elms, A. C. (1994). *Uncovering lives: The uneasy alliance of biography and psychology*. New York: Oxford University Press.

Erikson, E. H. (1958). *Young man Luther: A study in psychoanalysis and history*. New York: Norton.

Erikson, E. H. (1969). *Gandhi's truth*. New York: Norton.

Freud, S. (1957). *Leonardo da Vinci and a memory of his childhood*. In J. Strachey (Ed. & Trans.), *The standard edition of the complete psychological works of Sigmund Freud* (Vol. 12, pp. 3–82). London: Hogarth Press. (Original work published 1910)

George, A. L., & George, J. (1964). *Woodrow Wilson and Colonel House: A personality study*. New York: Dover. (Original work published 1956)

Gilmore, W. J. (1984). *Psychohistorical inquiry: A comprehensive research bibliography*. New York: Garland.

McAdams, D., & Ochberg, R. (Eds.). (1988). *Psychobiography and life narratives*. Durham, NC: Duke University Press.

Runyan, W. M. (1982). *Life histories and psychobiography: Explorations in theory and method*. New York: Oxford University Press.

Runyan, W. M. (Ed.). (1988). *Psychology and historical interpretation*. New York: Oxford University Press.

Runyan, W. M. (1997). Studying lives: Psychobiography and the conceptual structure of personality psychology. In R. Hogan, J. Johnson, & S. Briggs (Eds.), *Handbook of personality psychology* (pp. 41–69). San Diego, CA: Academic Press.

William McKinley Runyan

PSYCHODYNAMIC PSYCHOTHERAPY. *See* Psychoanalysis, *article on* Psychoanalytic Psychotherapies.

PSYKOKINESIS. *See* Parapsychology.

PSYCHOLINGUISTICS. [*This entry provides a broad survey of the field of psycholinguistics. It comprises five articles*: An Overview; Syntax and Grammar; Semantics; Discourse Comprehension; and Linguistic Determinism. *For independent entries related to psycholinguistics, see* Language; *and* Sociolinguistics.]

An Overview

Psycholinguistics is the study of human language processing, involving a range of abilities, from cognition to sensorimotor activity, that are recruited to the service of a complex set of communicative functions. It relates to the traditional academic disciplines of linguistics, psychology, education, anthropology, and philosophy, and particularly to the cross-disciplinary areas of speech science, cognitive science, artificial intelligence, neurolinguistics, and language learning, teaching, and rehabilitation. The field has roots that go back to the development of the modern disciplines of psychology and linguistics, in the debates between Wundt and Paul in the late nineteenth century. It was radically affected by the shift to the behaviorist paradigm culminating in Skinner's major treatment of language behavior and has been prominent as a research-active field in the recent period, since Chomsky's review of that work.

Language is a pretheoretical concept, which does not fall out neatly from categories used in the study of symbolic communication systems (semiotics). It is transmitted through the vocal-auditory communication channel (speech), but not all vocal-auditory activity represents language. The vocal-auditory channel is argued to be primary: historically older, more widely distributed, and acquired earlier by children. Processing considerations, from both normal and impaired language use, reinforce this conclusion. Language also uses the manual-visual channel, but not all manual-visual activity is language; and those manual-visual systems that represent a corresponding spoken language in some way (writing, by hand or keyboard), are distinct in many ways from those that do not (autonomous sign language systems such as American Sign Language). Against this diversity, the challenge is to characterize the sense that the same message may be perceived or produced in speech, writing, or sign, or even merely thought. There is a tendency to regard monolingual abilities as the norm although multilingual abilities are the norm in many if not most areas of the world.

Language processing may be understood in terms of three orders of time scale and three levels of representation. The time scale of ontogenesis captures acquisition-development, particularly of a first language; second and other languages, in childhood and adulthood, represent a rather different field of inquiry, but still within the broader sense of psycholinguistics. More centrally, microgenesis refers to moment-by-moment language use, which is not exclusive of ontogenesis but has been particularly studied in the mature language user. It may be broken down further into the two dimensions of macrochronic products of language (e.g., at what point in the time-course of a spoken word is it recognized? what on-line modifications are made to spoken or written text?); and microchronic control processes underlying the products (e.g., differential timing of motor events underlying speech production or perception, yielding overlapping or coarticulated signal elements, or perceptual integration; and speed pronoun interpretation, or ambiguity resolution). Finally, phylogenesis looks to the origins and development of language in the species, a field that has recently grown in importance, in which constraints may be sought from both ontogenetic and microgenetic considerations. In terms of representation, processing involves (using a computer analogy) the mechanisms which support any system of operating instructions; the programs which such systems of operating instructions constitute; and the operating environment, necessary for the running of programs. Passing "language" (e.g., linguistic competence, the ideal speaker-hearer's native knowledge of their language, which drives mainstream linguistic theory) through the microgenesis prism yields a spectrum of measurable language behaviors (linguistic performance), which define the testing ground of psycholinguistic theories. An early question was how far the linguists' characterization of linguistic competence could be taken at face value, given that it depends on a metalinguistic performance category of introspecting language intuitions supported by rule formulation and hypothesis testing.

Theoretical approaches to child and adult language processing have been quite distinct. In child language, the concept of acquisition implies something "out there" for the child to acquire, as opposed to development which emphasizes the internal growth of language abilities in the child. Acquisition theorists stress the inadequacy of learning processes operating on environmental stimuli, and posit innate mechanisms for which input data serve only as a trigger. Hard-wired modules serve the functions of language, defined as Universal Grammar, with parameterization of principles to account for the range of human languages to be acquired. The gradual curve of increasing language abilities over time in the child reflect either an innate schedule for these mechanisms to come on-stream (maturation theory), or interaction with other aspects of cognitive development (strict competence theory). Developmental theorists have argued the case for subtle and continuous interactions between the environment (especially forms of language addressed to children) and internal abilities, and between language and other aspects of cognition; each development forming the base for the next (constructionist theory). According to this approach, the notion "human language" falls out from the properties of the human brain and the mind it supports, though it is recognized that language plays a formative role in the development of the mind.

Theories of adult language processing have divided principally over the architecture of linguistic levels involved: thus, for speech input, is the speech signal exhaustively processed prior to the recognition of words? Alternatively, does the recognition of words contribute to signal perception (i.e., are there top-down as well as bottom-up flows of information), particularly in noisy environments? Does lexical access lead directly to interpretation of the message? Or is syntactic parsing required as part of message construction (i.e., exhaustive vs. partial processing), particularly where real-world constraints on interpretation are relatively weak? In relation to sequential input, maximally bottom-up models endorse serial processing: the first stage of operations is carried through for a given sequential domain prior to its being output to the next stage (e.g., signal processing before lexical access; lexical access before parsing/interpretation). By contrast, maximally interactive models search only as much of the sequential signal as is required to support parallel determination of which word is functioning in which role of which utterance type, and representing which message structure. Arguments from the highly specialized nature of aspects of language processing have supported the notion of modules which operate serially with respect to each other; arguments from the complexity of language operations have supported the concept of connectionist architectures, where any level can influence the operation of any other. Similar considerations apply to language processing resulting in speech output. Psycholinguistics thus focuses on the language abilities of the individual, in terms of the processes that mediate the various input and output modalities. This focus takes in the language signal, and the abstract language system, in an area defined between nonlinguistic cognition and the neurophysiological substrate.

The speech signal, processed under immediate time pressures, shows compatibility between what the vocal system is designed to produce and what the auditory system is specialized to perceive. The written language signal is much less constrained by the processing demands of the visual system, and orthographies of the written languages of the world are heterogeneous in their organizing characteristics. Traditional organization includes, for instance, logographic (representing word meanings, as in Chinese) and phonographic systems (representing the way words sound) with phonographic systems further breaking down into syllabaries (symbols representing a subword sound sequence of (consonant+vowel), alphabetic systems (representing the minimal segmental consonants and vowels), and the consonantal word-root systems of semiotic tradition. But this account obscures the hybrid mixtures encountered in particular orthographies; for example, logographic or specialized forms such as "%," in English and phonographic elements in Chinese characters.

A fundamental issue is to determine how far language reflects modality-specific aspects of processing. Vocal-auditory processing from the perspective of the listener involves the identification of relevant speech percepts against the background of irrelevant channel activity, and in the face of marked acoustic variability, both within and between speakers, and including auditory-visual integration and the role of contextual information; the identification of many words (stem and affixal morphemes) per second, from among tens of thousands of alternative candidates; the parsing of interword grammatical relationships such as subject-predicate and verb-object, from a rapidly fading auditory signal, amid further incoming information; the mapping of word and interword structural analyses onto meaning representations, and the integration of these into general cognition (understanding).

At this point we make contact with the relation between thought and language. There are categories of knowledge that are perceptually based and prelinguistic (e.g., focal colors which are available for differential linguistic encoding). There are linguistic meanings that are processed through the words and sentences of the abstract language system, and which may have relational properties (e.g., the boundaries between primary color terms, and locative expressions such as *to the left of*. There are inferential interpretative processes, in terms of which the speaker's intentions may be encoded and understood, and which may result in indirectness of thought-language (e.g., in polite requests such as "Can you open the window?") and in discoursal reference, where part-whole relations may be evident (e.g., previous mention of "a bicycle" permits the use of shared knowledge-definite reference to the "seat," even though this item has not been previously introduced). Shared knowledge between speaker and listener is not enough to guarantee communication: it is necessary to determine what is of immediate relevance in a given linguistic context and nonlinguistic situation.

For the speaker, the processes include (1) the formulation of message structure out of general cognition, according to constraints which will take the listener's needs into account; (2) selecting which aspects to configure into the message, and a particular linearization of them; (3) activation of appropriate word-sized and constructional schemata (and choosing between these, as "failure to comprehend" vs. "not understanding"); (4) mapping these schemata onto appropriate speech forms via utterance-frames specified with grammatical formatives such as "the____will____a____in the____") and slots for lexical forms to be copied into, and establishing articulatory goals for the local (segmental) and distal (intonational) implementation of the speech signal.

A further fundamental question is at what point(s) the processing pathways converge from perception of the spoken and visual forms of language. For the mature reader, fixations between ballistic eye movements up to about 5 per second account for 90% of reading time, and provide opportunities for character sequences to be processed in parallel, in a way that is highly complex even at the level of processing in the ganglion cells of the retina, transmitting information simultaneously about illumination, edge, orientation, etc. Stable fixation patterns mature in children only some years after they start reading, reflecting developments in central processing and refinement of ocular-motor control down to one quarter of one degree of visual angle. According to the indirect access view, the visual signal is recorded into the sound properties of words before lexical access takes place. The direct access view looks to words being stored as visual forms, with graphophonological interactions arising postlexically, for instance in the effect of regularly versus irregularly spelled words (actually a continuum rather than a dichotomy). Handwriting and keyboard output patterns exhibit spatiotemporal invariance, in terms of velocity in relation to letter curvature, pen-to-page frictional forces, and interstroke intervals depending on keyboard layout (same- vs. two-hand operation). Much more than in case of speech, overall inter- and intraindividual "hand" patterns seem to be a function of individual words in sentences (i.e., there is not so much of an "intonational" effect of words in sentential contexts).

In terms of methodology and the type of data studied, we may recognize differential degrees of emphasis in terms of comprehension versus production processing, comprehensive versus particular approaches, and on-line versus off-line data.

In child language, from the nineteenth century diarists on, there has been a relatively greater emphasis on more or less constrained production data, as a primary ground for developing hypotheses which may then be tested against comprehension evidence. In adult studies, comprehension has been relied on longer and more intensively, and there is a tendency on the part of some psycholinguists to regard comprehension as more of the essence of psycholinguistic inquiry. However, there has been a significant development of models of language production, to a large extent based on more naturalistic evidence, leading to a historical association between experimental-comprehension and naturalistic-production studies.

Comprehensiveness with respect to data collection varies greatly. Attempts have been made to characterize the child's language abilities in the round, at least for the early stages. The resulting "grammar-writing" approach has been criticized for its inability, in principle, to be anything more than corpus-bound, unless supported by comprehension evidence. In adult studies, however, naturalistic production data has focused on marked types of behavior. Thus, errors in word retrieval (e.g., tip-of-the-tongue phenomena, and substitutions, exchanges, etc., of sounds/letters and words), and patterns of pausing, repairs, or reformulations have been crucial to the determination of levels and processes in production models. By contrast, the data on fluent, on-target productions has been much less used.

Many studies have shown the sensitivity of language processing to task effects of various kinds, including the types of response measures used. Interpretation of ambiguous words or constructions, or of anaphoric devices can be tapped via quite natural but distal end-state measures of comprehension, but also by less natural but proximal means (e.g., measuring the outcome from competing stimuli to each ear, response latency, or monitoring eye-movements in reading or, more generally, physiological reactions during processing, including cerebral blood flow and evoked brain response potentials). In many cases, the on-line data provide different information from the end-state, suggesting that the latter reflects later organizational and storage processes.

Disorders of language processing have been traditionally divided into *developmental* and *acquired.* Apart from language processing impairment in aging, the latter is mainly accounted for by aphasia (language disorder arising from specific brain injury), a term which has been applied to developmental disorders in the past, but which is not generally accepted now. Aphasiology has been strongly influenced by the medical model since its origins in the late nineteenth century, and out of a spate of disputes there has emerged a mainstream tradition which recognizes a taxonomy of classical syndromes defined in terms of site of lesion, and the general language measures such as fluency, comprehension, repetition, and naming. Such classification is still found in contemporary test batteries, but increasingly, neuropsychological modeling approaches have taken psycholinguistic concepts—usually of specific aspects of language processing such as parsing or lexical access—and proposed new syndromes, for instance surface and deep dyslexia. Much current research shows a flight of syndromes to symptoms, across heterogeneous groups of aphasics, and increasing use of linguistic model-theoretic concepts such as trace and functional categories. An area of particular interest is aphasic disorders found in sign language users.

In developmental disorders, the search for a powerful taxonomy is still in progress; patterns of mismatch between chronological age, mental age, and language age yield the possibilities of language so-called in the context of general learning disability (e.g., Down syndrome), and specific language impairment (SLI), defined by exclusion of nonverbal impairment and any other affecting condition: hearing impairment or congenital blindness, where acquisition of symbolic-reference functions of language may be severely compromised, or neurological conditions as in Landau–Kleffner syndrome.

Considerable linguistic diversity is encountered within non-SLI conditions; within SLI, the search is for distinct patterns of manifestation, and the possible locus of processing deficits, for instance in "feature blindness" to those grammatical contrasts which are marked in the morphology of a language, or in underspecification of verbs in terms of the types of grammatical structures in which they may occur. Further patterns test the notion of the language-cognition interface, for instance semantic-pragmatic disorder, in which the child's language repertoire may be more or less impaired, but the functional implementation of it is observed to be continually inappropriate.

Psycholinguistics continues to be a diverse and active research field, involving computational modeling and the development of increasingly robust machine-based language generation, interpretation and translation systems, input to language policy in education, including bilingual situations, and language rehabilitation, the development of theories of language structure and function, and working toward an understanding of mind-brain relations. There are signs that, after a period of rather antithetical positions on the defining issues of the properties (e.g., modular vs. connectionist architectures), and the relation between orders of description (e.g., substrate, capacities, and executive control), that the field is preparing increasingly detailed evidence for more balanced interpretation in terms of a mix of hereditary, learned, language-specific, and language-neutral factors. The cross-linguistic perspective will be crucial to discovering the human-general properties of language processing.

Michael Garman

Syntax and Grammar

People have the remarkable ability to produce sentences that convey novel messages and to extract those messages from sentences they read or hear. The systematic knowledge of their language that permits them to do such things is called grammar. Grammar is traditionally taken to include syntax (roughly, the division of a sentence into its constituents and the description of the structural relations among these constituents), morphology (the form of words, including inflectional prefixes, suffixes, and infixes that signal relations among words and phrases), and phonology (the sound structure of the language, including prosody, the pattern of tones and rhythms in the language). Some linguists such as Noam Chomsky create "generative grammars," which are formal theories of our grammatical knowledge or competence. Psycholinguists, on the other hand, create theories of our linguistic performance. They try to understand how we use our implicit knowledge of grammar to comprehend surprising sentences like *The mouse ate the cat* and to make fine distinctions among sentence meanings like *John helped the child to first base* versus *John helped the child on first base.*

In the 1960s, at the beginning of the cognitive revolution in psychology, debate raged over whether people used grammar to produce and understand sentences. If they did use grammar, the argument went, they were engaging in cognitive operations that went far beyond the power of the behaviorist theories that were dominant at the time. The outcome of this debate now seems clear: People do use their knowledge of their language's grammar in producing and comprehending sentences. They do not simply chain words together, but instead represent the hierarchical structure of sentences. Thus, they implicitly know that *The beautiful girl likes x* is embedded within the subject of the sentence *The boy whom the beautiful girl likes just arrived.* They also seem able to process long-distance dependencies, such as the relationship between *the boy* and *likes* in the example just given. Relationships like this can extend across an arbitrarily long embedded phrase and exceed the explanatory power of any stimulus-response theory. Even if the debate over whether grammar is relevant to language use has stopped, the debate about how grammar is used in language comprehension and production is still very lively.

Empirical Phenomena of Comprehension and Production

When we hear or read a sentence, we understand it nearly word by word, with little delay. In a classic demonstration using the "fast-shadowing" technique (repeating out loud what one hears, trying to stay no more than a quarter second behind the input message), Marslen-Wilson (1973) showed that mispronunciations of a word's end (e.g., *cigareppe*) were often spontaneously corrected. This happened more often in normal than in scrambled sentences, indicating that in a supporting grammatical context words were being identified in the span of a quarter second or so. In reading, when one's eyes land on an implausible word or a word that clashes with one's understanding of the preceding part of a sentence (e.g., on *fell* in *While Mary was mending the sock fell off her lap*), they are likely to jump back immediately to an earlier part of the sentence or to fixate on the word *fell* for longer than the normal quarter second or so (Frazier & Rayner, 1982). It appears that readers quickly begin the process of changing their mind about the grammatical structure of the early part of the sentence when they read *fell*.

The quick response to the implications of the word *fell* illustrates an interesting phenomenon of language comprehension called garden-pathing. A great many sentences of any language are ambiguous, at least temporarily. Their words can be related to each other in different ways, as *the sock* could be taken to be the direct object of *mend* or the subject of the main clause in the previous paragraph's example. To understand how people understand sentences, psycholinguists study how they deal with ambiguity. Sometimes people seem to deal with ambiguity by committing to a single analysis and then being disrupted when that analysis turns out to be wrong. They are said to be "led down the garden path" in sentences like Bever's *The horse raced past the barn fell* (1970). People take *raced* to be the main verb with *the horse* as its subject, and have great difficulty reanalyzing *raced* as a passive participle, with *the horse* as its logical direct object (as in *The horse that was raced past the barn fell*). However, as various researchers have pointed out, some sentences with the same "reduced relative clause" structure as Bever's are comprehended without difficulty. Stevenson and Merlo, for example, note that the reduced relative clause sentence *The butter melted in the microwave was lumpy* is perfectly easy to understand (1997). Presumably, such differences reflect both grammatical factors such as differences between verbs like *melt* and verbs like *race* and extragrammatical factors such as plausibility.

Grammatical factors also play important roles in language production. One phenomenon that illustrates this comes from the analysis of "slips" of the tongue, speech errors like *sot holdering iron* and *Seymour sliced the knife with a salami* (Fromkin, 1971; Garrett, 1975). To take just one fact about such errors, sound exchange errors like the first example essentially always involve two words from the same syntactic phrase, while word exchange errors like the second example usually involve words from two different phrases. It appears that speech errors honor the hierarchical division of sentences into phrases, one aspect of syntactic structure.

Another phenomenon of speech production has been called priming (Bock, 1986). If a person has to describe a picture (e.g., of lightning hitting a church), how one chooses to phrase the description is affected by the grammatical structure of a previously said sentence. If an experimenter had just had the person repeat a passive sentence that had nothing to do with churches or lightning, he or she was likely to describe the picture as *A church is being hit by lightning*, but if the sentence the person just recited was in the active voice, he or she was likely to describe the picture as *Lightning is hitting a church*.

Architectures and Mechanisms of Linguistic Performance

In order to understand a sentence in a nearly word-by-word fashion and to deal with the impact of ambiguity as well as we do, we must efficiently integrate our knowledge of grammar and our knowledge of what is being talked about and who is doing the talking. We cannot, as the very first modern theories of sentence comprehension claimed, wait for the end of a clause and then apply "reverse transformations" to recover the deep structure of the sentence. We must have some cognitive ability to use our knowledge of grammar quickly and efficiently. How grammatical knowledge is structured, how different types of knowledge are compartmentalized or linked to each other, and how all this knowledge is used in real time are the main questions about the architectures and mechanisms of language processing.

Linguists generally assume that grammar is modular, divided into distinct and separate components. For example, syntax is viewed as a module, a component, of grammar, distinct from phonology or semantics. One can characterize our knowledge of syntax without ever mentioning phonology. But even if everyone agrees that our knowledge of grammar is modular, there is sharp disagreement over the extent to which our use of grammar in language comprehension or production is modular.

Modularity in cognitive processing is a notion developed by J. A. Fodor (1983) to refer to a cluster of properties that characterizes independently functioning cognitive systems. A modular system is supposed to be domain specific (specialized, presumably through evolutionary mechanisms), informationally encapsulated (sensitive to only a limited range of information), fast, and automatic. Some theorists argue in favor of the modularity of grammatical processing (e.g., Frazier, 1987). They observe that, in order to interpret a string of words, a grammatical structure has to be imposed on the string. Upon reading *John knew the answer . . .* one thinks about whether an answer is the kind of thing that can be known only if one takes *the answer* to be the grammatical direct object of *know*. Modularity theorists argue that the human sentence-processing mechanism creates a grammatical structure in the shortest possible time, and that it does so by being highly modular and using its grammatical knowledge in the quickest possible way. They make explicit claims about how grammatical knowledge is used to build grammatical structure, word by word. A common claim is that the simplest grammatical structure will be built most quickly, and therefore is preferred. For example, the grammatical structure in which *the answer* is the direct object of *know* is simpler than the structure in which it is the subject of a sentence complement, as it must be in *John knew the answer was wrong*. Modularity theorists have shown that a wide variety of temporarily ambiguous sentences disrupt comprehension when the ambiguity is resolved in a way that goes against the preferred structure, as happened with *was wrong*.

Other theorists (e.g., MacDonald, Pearlmutter, & Seidenberg, 1994; Marslen-Wilson & Tyler, 1987) are more impressed with how readers and listeners can use many different sorts of information, grammatical and extragrammatical, in arriving at an interpretation of a sentence. They claim that the human sentence-processing mechanism is not modular, but interactive. They note that meaning and experience make sentences like *The butter melted in the microwave was lumpy* much easier than syntactically similar garden-path sentences. They argue that various types of information, grammatical and extragrammatical, are used together to build the initial grammatical analysis of a sentence, and that the impact of grammatical information is tempered by what extragrammatical knowledge is available. These theorists advance a variety of types of experimental evidence in favor of their position. Their evidence includes demonstrations that extragrammatical knowledge is used very quickly in the process of sentence understanding and that strong manipulations of meaning or context can sometimes overcome and eliminate the garden-pathing effects emphasized by modularity theorists. Some recent interactive theorists emphasize the effects that the frequency of exposure to different grammatical constructions has on how difficult the constructions are, and cast their theories as connectionist, constraint-satisfaction models.

Emerging Questions About the Use of Grammar

Psycholinguists have not yet settled the question of whether grammatical knowledge is used in any special, modular way, or whether it is simply one of many important sources of information used in an interactive fashion. But their quest to answer this question has led them to pose new and equally interesting questions. One concerns the universality of the human sentence-processing mechanism. Do users of all languages comprehend and produce sentences in their languages in essentially the same way (apart from honoring the differences among their grammars)? Or do users of different languages employ fundamentally different processes to comprehend and produce sentences? In the past few years, this question has led psycholinguists to extend their research beyond English and study languages with superficially very different grammars. The initial explorations seem to indicate that the same sorts of principles (e.g., garden pathing when a sentence turns out to be more complex than it appeared to be) apply in all languages, but the question is far from answered.

An even deeper question concerns the acquisition of language. In the past 30 years, students of this topic have made great strides by assuming that children born to any language community share a common set of abstract principles (universal grammar) at birth. The task of learning language amounts to figuring out what choices one's language makes from among those offered by universal grammar. This position is clearly an intellectual cousin of the modularity claim about sentence processing. Both positions claim that humans have a distinct, specialized capacity for learning or using language. As one might expect, this nativist claim has been strongly challenged in recent years. Theorists influenced by empiricist approaches to learning developed in the modern connectionist tradition have argued that grammatical knowledge does not have to be built into the child via his or her genes. They suggest instead that it can emerge as a result of exposure to people using grammatical sentences.

Bibliography

Bever, T. G. (1970). The cognitive basis for linguistic structures. In J. R. Hayes (Ed.), *Cognition and the development of language* (pp. 279–352). New York: Wiley.

Bock, J. K. (1986). Syntactic persistence in language production. *Cognitive Psychology, 18*, 355–387.

Chomsky, N. (1986). *Knowledge of language: Its nature, origin, and use*. New York: Praeger. Noam Chomsky shaped the development of modern linguistics. This is one of the books in which he explores the implications of his work for broad questions.

Elman, J., Bates, E., Johnson, M. H., Karmiloff-Smith, A.,

Parisi, D., & Plunkett, K. (1996). *Rethinking innateness: A connectionist perspective on development.* Cambridge, MA: MIT Press. A recent, strongly stated defense of empiricist, nonnativist, approaches to language and cognition.

Fodor, J. A. (1983). *Modularity of mind.* Cambridge, MA: MIT Press.

Fodor, J. A., Bever, T. G., & Garrett, M. F. (1974). *The psychology of language: An introduction to psycholinguistics and generative grammar.* New York: McGraw-Hill. The classic textbook presenting the results of the first decade of modern psycholinguistics.

Frazier, L., & Rayner, K. (1982). Making and correcting errors during sentence comprehension: Eye movements in the analysis of structurally ambiguous sentences. *Cognitive Psychology, 14,* 178–210.

Frazier, L., & Rayner, K. (1987). Resolution of syntactic category ambiguities: Eye movements in parsing lexically ambiguous sentences. *Journal of Memory and Language, 26,* 505–526.

Frazier, L., & Clifton, C., Jr. (1996). *Construal.* Cambridge, MA: MIT Press. A recent statement of a mostly modular approach to sentence understanding, with reviews of earlier work.

Fromkin, V. A. (1971). The nonanomalous nature of anomalous utterances. *Language, 47,* 27–52.

Garrett, M. F. (1975). The analysis of sentence production. In G. Bower (Ed.), *Psychology of learning and motivation.* New York: Academic Press.

Gernsbacher, M. A. (Ed.). (1994). *Handbook of psycholinguistics.* San Diego, CA: Academic Press. Contains articles that cover much of psycholinguistics in great detail. The articles by Mitchell (sentence parsing), Bock and Levelt (sentence production), and Bloom (language acquisition) are of special relevance.

MacDonald, M. C., Pearlmutter, N. J., & Seidenberg, M. S. (1994). Lexical nature of syntactic ambiguity resolution. *Psychological Review, 101,* 676–703.

Marslen-Wilson, W. D. (1973). Linguistic structure and speech shadowing at very short latencies. *Nature, 244,* 522–523.

Marslen-Wilson, W. D., & Tyler, L. K. (1987). Against modularity. In J. Garfield (Ed.), *Modularity in knowledge representation and natural language understanding.* Cambridge, MA: MIT Press.

Miller, J., & Eimas, P. (Eds.), *Handbook of perception and cognition: Speech, language, and communication* (2nd ed., Vol. 11). San Diego: Academic Press. Contains articles by Frazier and by Tanenhaus and Trueswell exploring how grammatical knowledge might be represented and used.

Stevenson, S., & Merlo, P. (1997). Lexical structure and parsing complexity. *Language and Cognitive Processes, 12,* 349–399.

Charles Clifton, Jr.

Semantics

Semantics is the study of meaning in language. In psycholinguistics, semantics can refer to meaning at the lexical (or morphemic), sentence, and discourse levels. From a processing perspective, the questions include how the meanings of words and sentences are represented in the cognitive system, and how the meanings of sentences and words are arrived at or used during comprehension. In linguistics, a clear distinction is drawn between the meaning of a sentence and the meaning of an utterance. For example, the sentence *Some psychologists like math* logically means that *there is at least one psychologist who likes math* and that *perhaps all psychologists like math* (this is sentence semantics). However, if someone uttered such a sentence, a listener would assume that the speaker was asserting that, to his or her knowledge, *some but not all psychologists like Math.* This distinction corresponds to Grice's Maxim of Quantity (1975), in that we would assume that if the speaker knew that all psychologists like math, he or she would say so. The distinction is between speaker (or utterance) meaning, which includes pragmatic implicature, and sentence meaning, which is what the sentence alone means when it is stripped of pragmatic implicature, leaving just the semantics. The distinction is very important, in that speakers often use indirect speech acts and figurative language, both of which require a listener to recognize that the speaker does not expect the listener to give the utterance a literal sentence meaning. These problems for interpretation are discussed below.

The Mental Lexicon and Word Meaning

Without word meaning there can be no interpretation of language at all. The mental lexicon is a construct to enable people to recognize words. For any word that can be recognized, there is an entry in the mental lexicon. Since word recognition can be considered a stage in getting to the meaning of a word, an entry in the lexicon can be considered a pointer to the meaning of a word.

Various accounts of how the meanings of content words (or open-class words, including nouns, verbs and modifiers) are represented have been suggested. For example, words might be represented as a set of features which define that word. So *dog* might be entered: *is a pet, is a mammal, has four legs, is hairy, has a tail,* and so on. There have been investigations of how this kind of knowledge is stored in the mind, and one account claimed that features were represented only at the highest level to which they apply. For example, all mammals breathe air, so when storing this fact at the lexical entry for *mammal,* there is no need to represent it with examples of things known to be mammals (such as a fox, human, whale, etc.). This would predict that it takes longer to decide that a human breathes air than to decide that a mammal breathes air, and although early evidence supported this view (Collins & Quillian, 1969), it is now recognized that the claim is too general and that often properties are stored directly with exemplars, even if that leads to redundancy of fact storage.

An alternative view, still based on representing words as sets of features, is the Spreading Activation Model (Collins & Loftus, 1975), in which concepts and properties are assumed to be labeled nodes, connected to each other such that the most related nodes are nearest (or have the strongest connections). With this model, it is assumed that when a word is encountered, activity propagates from that node to adjacent nodes, with the nearest (most strongly connected) node receiving the earliest and most complete activation. This theoretical perspective matches well with the empirical observation of the laboratory effect of priming, which is most commonly understood in the spreading activation framework.

Semantic Classification

In semantic classification, the problem is to assign the correct category to a word. This is a fundamental process that has enjoyed considerable experimental study. In the earliest laboratory tasks, one might be asked to verify whether *a canary is a bird* or *a whale is a fish*. It is assumed that this process takes place by evaluating the properties (features) associated with the proposed instance and the class itself. Research into this process has shown that categories themselves are represented as prototypes: for instance, the concept "bird" is closer to something like a "robin" than to "ostrich." Furthermore, it takes longer to decide that a typical class member (robin or sparrow) is a bird than it does to decide about an atypical class member (goose or ostrich) (see, e.g., Rosch, 1973). This shows that features associated with member and category are compared, and the more features there are in common the faster a response can be made. By the same token, if there is a lot of overlap between a nonmember and a class, then a no response is slowed down (e.g., *A whale is a fish* is slower to be evaluated no than *A robin is a fish*).

The faster processing of a typical class member also applies to the reading of a text. For instance: *John saw a sparrow fly past the shed. The bird seemed to be injured.* Here the time to read the second sentence is shorter for *sparrow* than it would have been for *goose*, an atypical member of the class bird. Thus, classification phenomena occur during normal reading, and classification as an implicit process is part of normal reading (Garrod & Sanford, 1977).

Classification is an enormous technical problem, and it is not always possible to say what it is that defines something as a member of a category (e.g., Wittgenstein's well-known problem of how one defines what should be called a game). Important efforts to understand classification have been made by Minsky (1975), who solved some classification problems through his idea of frames, and Lakoff (1987), who noted that many category names appear to be used in a metaphorical sense.

Priming

When one word is related to another, priming can occur, and the effect can be used to investigate how meaning enters into processes of language comprehension. Meyer and Schvaneveldt (1971) showed that presenting a word will facilitate (or prime) the subsequent processing (and recognition) of a related word (e.g., *nurse* facilitates *doctor*, but *bread* does not). This robust effect, called associative priming, can occur through purely semantic relationships between the words (because they share a lot of common features) or because the words are simply associated with one another through usage.

The technique has proved useful in determining which meanings are activated during the processing of words in discourse. For example, using priming data, Swinney suggested that when an ambiguous word like *bank* (meaning either *riverbank* or *financial institution*) is encountered in contexts that clearly disambiguate the intended meaning, both meanings are initially activated (because associates of both meanings are primed). After a very short delay, however, context inhibits the "unwanted" meaning.

Meaning in Discourse Comprehension

During comprehension, it is assumed that the meanings of words are recruited as each word is fixed by the eye, or heard. This is the process of incremental interpretation. Empirically, it can be shown that some of the meaning of a word is automatically accessed in this way (Traxler & Pickering, 1996). However, there is also evidence that not all of the meaning of a word is accessed incrementally, if at all. The question *How many animals of each sort did Moses put on the Ark?* is an interesting one. People typically answer "two," but fail to notice that it was in fact Noah and not Moses who did the putting. This effect, the Moses Illusion (Ericksen & Mattson, 1981), shows that people may use only some of the meaning of a word during reading, especially if context means that the contribution that word is likely to make to a message is small.

Nonliteral Meaning: Idioms and Figurative Language

Much of the interpretation that a speaker requires of a listener may be nonliteral. For example, indirect speech acts require listeners to treat one kind of speech act as another. So a question (*Could you close the window?*) might need to be treated as a request (*Please close the window*). Other nonliteral utterances include idioms, such as *John kicked the bucket* or *Mary broke the ice at the party*. With idioms, some may be considered not analyzable into smaller components, but as having a fixed meaning that is learned as the meaning of the whole word string. However, it has been shown that with many idioms, it is possible to change the words and still get a good interpretation (e.g., *Shatter the ice*), so it is wrong to treat all idioms as unanalyzable units.

Possibly the largest class of nonliteral utterances in terms of variety is the metaphor, in which statements of class membership are literally false, as in *My surgeon is a butcher* or *Harry is an animal.* To understand these utterances, it is necessary to give them nonliteral interpretations. According to the literal truth hypothesis, people first evaluate sentences for literal truth, and if a literal interpretation turns out to be unintelligible or unreasonable, then they give the utterance a nonliteral interpretation. This model has enjoyed much favor (e.g., Clark & Lucy, 1975; Glucksberg & Keysar, 1990; Searle, 1983) but has been seriously challenged because it predicts comprehension of nonliteral meaning to be slower than comprehension of literal meaning. For instance, Gibbs (1979) showed that people take no longer to process indirect requests, such as *Must you open the window?* to mean *Do not open the window,* presented in story contexts, than to understand literal uses of the same expressions (meaning, *Need you open the window?*). These data suggest that people do not need to obtain a literal meaning first in order to comprehend an indirect speech act, which runs against the traditional model. In a similar way, Glucksberg, Gildea, and Bookin suggested that metaphorical meaning is computed automatically and that it can interfere with literal-meaning computation, so establishing literal meaning cannot be a prior, modular stage (1982).

Lakoff and his colleagues showed the full extent of metaphorical and metonymic language in normal usage, and Lakoff has suggested that many of our concepts are metaphorically structured. He suggested certain basic metaphorical systems that might be used to generate many of the ways we habitually use to speak of things. For instance, the expressions *on top of the world* or *down in the dumps* come from a "good is up, bad is down" metaphor; the expression *John's arithmetical skills are a bit rusty* come from a "mind is machine" metaphor. Indeed, the apparent ubiquity of nonliteral interpretation leads directly to the proposal that it is difficult to know when to compute literal meaning, and that perhaps the cognitive system is designed to avoid having to face this problem (see Recanati, 1995).

Bibliography

Clark, H., & Lucy, P. (1975). Understanding what is meant from what is said: A study in conversationally conveyed requests. *Journal of Verbal Learning and Verbal Behavior, 14,* 56–72.

Collins, A. M., & Loftus, E. F. (1975). A spreading activation theory of semantic processing. *Psychological Review, 82,* 407–428.

Collins, A. M., & Quillian, M. R. (1969). Retrieval time from semantic memory. *Journal of Verbal Learning and Verbal Behavior, 8,* 240–248.

Erickson, T. A., & Mattson, M. E. (1981). From words to meaning: A semantic illusion. *Journal of Verbal Learning and Verbal Behavior, 20,* 540–552.

Garrod, S. C., & Sanford, A. J. (1977). Interpreting anaphoric relations: The integration of semantic information while reading. *Journal of Verbal Learning and Verbal Behavior, 16,* 77–90.

Gibbs, R. (1979). Contextual effects in understanding indirect requests. *Discourse Processes, 2,* 1–10.

Glucksberg, S, Gildea, P., & Bookin, H. (1982). On understanding nonliteral speech: Can people ignore metaphors? *Journal of Verbal Learning and Verbal Behavior, 21,* 85–98.

Glucksberg, S., & Keysar, B. (1990). Understanding metaphorical comparisons: Beyond similarity. *Psychological Review, 97,* 3–18.

Grice, L. P. (1975). Logic and conversation. In P. Cole & J. L. Morgan (Eds.), *Syntax and semantics: Vol. 3. Speech acts.* New York: Academic Press.

Lakoff, G. (1987). *Women, fire, and dangerous things.* Chicago: University of Chicago Press.

Meyer, D. E., & Schvaneveldt, R. W. (1971). Facilitation in recognizing pairs of words: Evidence of a dependence of retrieval operations. *Journal of Experimental Psychology, 90,* 227–234.

Minsky, M. (1975). A framework for representing knowledge. In P. H. Winston (Ed.), *The psychology of computer vision.* New York: McGraw-Hill.

Recanati, F. (1995). The alleged priority of literal interpretation. *Cognitive Science, 19,* 207–232.

Rosch, E. (1973). On the internal structure of perceptual and semantic categories. In T. E. Moore (Ed.), *Cognitive development and the acquisition of language* (pp. 111–144). New York: Academic Press.

Searle, J. (1983). *Intentionality.* Cambridge, UK: Cambridge University Press.

Swinney, D. A. (1979). Lexical access during sentence comprehension: (Re)consideration of context effects. *Journal of Verbal Learning and Verbal Behavior, 18,* 545–567.

Traxler, M. J., & Pickering, M. J. (1996). Plausibility and the processing of unbounded dependencies: An eye-tracking study. *Journal of Memory and Language, 35,* 454.

A. J. Sanford

Discourse Comprehension

A king had an only son that he thought the world of. But this prince was always unhappy. He would spend days on end at his window staring into space.

The apparent simplicity of this folktale opening disguises numerous comprehension problems. The meaning of each word, such as *king,* must be retrieved from memory. Complex grammatical constructions must be unraveled. The pronouns *he* and *his* must be related to the correct male individual.

A sequence of coherent written or spoken sentences forms a discourse. During the past 40 years, cognitive psychologists have achieved many noteworthy advances concerning how understanders grasp ordinary discourse at a rapid pace, despite the numerous underlying tasks. These advances have addressed the representation of discourse meaning, the mental processes of comprehension, and the contributing comprehension subtasks.

Multiple Levels of Discourse Representation

For communication to succeed, understanders must be able to represent speakers' thoughts in their minds. Ideally, verbal messages take the form of grammatical strings of words, such as *The wrestler broke the lock.* However, the memorization of this sentence in no way establishes whether the understander has correctly interpreted *lock* as a hold or a mechanical device. A general solution to the problem of discourse representation is that several levels of representation result from comprehension: the surface form of the message, a network of the ideas expressed in the message, and a mental model of the situation described by the message.

Representation of Surface Form. The surface representation of discourse might capture the precise word strings, such as *A-king-had-an-only-son.* Research has scrutinized the general characteristics of this representation. There is evidence that people have measurable memory for the specific wording, grammatical constructions, and order of appearance of ideas in a message. For example, in a recognition test, readers of this entry would at least slightly favor *But this prince was always unhappy* over the synonymous alternative, *But this prince was forever sad.*

Idea Networks. Theorists have proposed that understanders organize the simple ideas conveyed by a message into a network, termed the text base. For example, *A king had an only son* conveys the ideas, *the king had a son*, and *the son was an only son.* The presence of the same concepts in two ideas, such as *son*, results in a connection between them. As the understander proceeds through a message, the successive ideas are linked together. Directly stated ideas may be augmented by a small number of inferred ideas needed to identify connections among the stated ones.

Consistent with this analysis, sentence reading time increases systematically with the number of ideas conveyed by a sentence and the number of different of concepts that the sentence addresses, holding sentence length constant. Furthermore, after reading, concepts mentioned in a discourse activate concepts that appeared in the same ideas more than they activate concepts from different discourse ideas.

Situation Models. Discourse can refer to situations ranging from familiar human motives to complex mathematical problems. As a result, situation models must take many different forms. In general, situation models integrate discourse ideas with the understander's world knowledge. The reader of *Sally enjoyed the clowns and the elephants* might integrate the text ideas with knowledge about circus situations. Similarly, readers of the earlier "King sequence" are likely to organize it according to their general knowledge of a story's typical form.

The situation-model representation is the level least directly linked to the discourse. Therefore, evidence for its existence is perhaps the most striking. In one study, people read that a girl either picked or smelled a flower. After an additional text sentence describing the movements of the girl, the readers recognized *flower* more quickly if it had been picked than if it had been smelled. This suggested that a spatial situation model was constructed in which objects associated with the protagonist remained highlighted. The situation models constructed by understanders are influenced by their reading goals (e.g., entertainment versus proofreading), by their beliefs about the genre of a text (e.g., a story versus a newspaper article), and by subtle differences in the style of a message.

Conversational Situations. Conversation analysis from a philosophical tradition has emphasized that the speaker and listener strive to grasp one another's goals and intentions. In doing so, they construct a conversational situation model. In this framework, most utterances can be classified as telling (e.g., announcing, warning, or hinting), requesting, promising, expressing states of mind, or making official declarations. However, determining the speaker's intention can pose serious difficulties for the listener. *It's hot in here* can function as telling, or as requesting that the room be made cooler. For conversation to succeed, the speaker and listener must embrace the "cooperative principle," according to which the speaker must convey the correct quantity and quality of truthful and relevant information, and the listener must assume that the speaker is being cooperative. Consider the following dialogue:

A: Are you coming skiing this weekend?
B: I have a bad cold.

If A assumes that B is being cooperative, then B's reply, superficially off the topic, may be interpreted to convey that B is not going skiing because of illness.

The Multiple-Levels Hypothesis. In recognition testing immediately after reading an excerpt like the King narrative, people accept identical sentences (*But this prince was always unhappy*) much more often than implied sentences (*The prince had few friends*). This indicates that recognition rate increases with the number of consistent levels. Implied sentences are consistent only with the situation model, whereas identical sentences are consistent with all three levels. After 2 days, however, recognition of implied sentences rises almost to the "identical" rate. This suggests that the surface representation, which supports identical sentences, fades quickly, whereas the situation model, with which implied sentences are consistent, is enduring. Results of this sort support the multiple-levels hypothesis.

Coherence and Comprehension

Comprehension is cyclic. One brief phrase at a time, such as *He would spend days on end*, is considered by the understander. Comprehension subtasks such as word retrieval, grammatical analysis, and pronoun resolution extract the idea units underlying the phrase. These ideas, in turn, are deposited in a memory repository of limited capacity, called working memory. They must be quickly integrated with the evolving discourse text base and situation model. When the understander proceeds to the next phrase, only a small number of important and/or recent ideas from the preceding cycle are retained in working memory. The choice of these ideas dictates how succeeding ideas are linked to the discourse representations.

Retrieving Referents. To be comprehensible, a discourse must be coherent. That is, there must be identifiable links among its parts. Central to people's ability to detect these links is the distinction between given and new information. For example, in *An ant ate the jelly*, the definite article *the* designates *jelly* as given information, whereas the indefinite article *a* signifies *ant* as new information. For sentence comprehension to proceed smoothly, the understander must distinguish given and new information, identify a concept in the existing discourse representation (a referent) that matches the given idea and then integrate the new information with the referent.

Critical to this "given-new analysis" is how the given information provides information about the appropriate referent. In *A drop of jelly spilled on the table, An ant ate the jelly*, the *jelly* of the second sentence obviously refers to the entity denoted by *jelly* in the first sentence. In other circumstances, the retrieval of the referent is more complicated.

Anaphoric Reference. An anaphor is a linguistic expression that refers back to a preceding part of a message. Prominent among such devices is the pronoun. Insofar as pronouns typically refer to a previous discourse entity, they designate given information. Thus, in the sequence *But this prince was always unhappy; he would spend days . . .*, the pronoun *he* refers to the prince.

To function effectively, pronouns must provide convenient cues to their referents. The syntactic properties of the pronoun, such as its gender, number, and person, are usually effective cues. For example, people need less time to read the pronoun region of *Sally told John that SHE was late* than of *Sally told Donna that SHE was late* because in the first case, the pronoun's gender provides an unambiguous cue to its referent. It is also easier to resolve pronouns with one candidate referent than multiple candidates, and those with referents recent rather than much earlier in the discourse.

The meaning of discourse augments syntax and sometimes supersedes it in regulating pronoun resolution. Thus, the meaning of *Mary beat Helen at cards because SHE was a skillful player* clearly specifies Mary as skillful, despite the facts that both participants are female and Helen was mentioned more recently. Most strikingly, successful pronoun resolution sometimes depends on the discourse situation model, as follows:

(a) "Is Hank planning to attend the TGIF?" Jane asked.
(b) "The band is supposed to be great."
(c) "He certainly is," Tom said.

Experiments revealed that resolving the pronoun *he* to *Hank* is surprisingly easy, despite the appearance of sentence (b) between (a) and (c). This outcome has been attributed to the contribution of the situation model of narrative dialogue, one element of which involves the expectation that questions (sentence a) will receive answers (sentence c).

Discourse Inference. Pronouns are by no means the only anaphoric expressions. In the sequence *A king had an only son that he thought the world of, But THIS PRINCE was always unhappy*, the definite noun phrase *this prince* refers back to the *king's son*. However, this sequence poses a problem more challenging than resolving a pronoun; the reader must use general knowledge to relate *this prince* to *the king's son*. More demanding still is *The burglar was arrested; the policeman handcuffed him. Policeman* constitutes given information, but the prior sentence provides no candidate referent at all. However, one's knowledge about criminal arrests permits the inference linking the policeman to the burglar.

Bridging Inferences. Inferences that relate the current clause to the prior discourse are called bridging inferences. There is extensive evidence that people draw bridging inferences during comprehension. The extra effort of bridging processes is diagnosed by the fact that it takes longer to read phrases that must be bridged to prior discourse than to read phrases that involve a direct link (like the "jelly" sequence). After reading, memory measures can barely discriminate between candidate bridging inferences and explicit text ideas, suggesting that bridging inferences form part of the discourse representation.

By integrating discourse ideas and general knowledge, bridging inferences contribute to the situation model. Causal bridging inferences, such as the one linking the sentences *The lightning struck* and *The hut collapsed* are especially important. Causal relations constitute a central feature of the situation model for numerous discourse genres. Therefore, causal bridging inferences have been carefully inspected. In this regard, even when the two sentences *Laurie left early for the birthday party* and *She spent an hour shopping at the mall* are separated by several coherent sentences, readers still infer that Laurie shopped in order to buy a present. Likewise, people can discern causal inconsistencies between nonadjacent discourse sentences. Other features of this problem are still controversial. Preliminary evidence suggests that surface similarities are required to ensure that the understander will detect distant causal links, and that the presence of a satisfactory cause just before an outcome sentence blocks the detection of a more distant satisfactory cause.

Elaborative Inferences. Messages routinely carry implications about innumerable related ideas. For example, *The lightning struck* might suggest the elaboration that thunder followed. Such "elaborative inferences" sensibly embellish a sentence but do not bridge it to another specific discourse idea. Unlike bridging inferences, research has revealed that understanders do not reliably compute most elaborative inferences during comprehension, most likely because there are simply too many elaborations—lightning can imply thunder, loud noise, bright light, fear, and resulting damage. However, those elaborative inferences that are highly constrained by the discourse context are inferred. From *Sally enjoyed the clowns and the trapeze artists*, readers infer the *circus* theme; and from *Ron squeezed the fruit for breakfast*, people infer *oranges*. Furthermore, there is evidence that *thunder* may be fleetingly inferred from *The lightning struck*, but the inference fades quickly. The resolution of the complexities of inference processing will influence theories of the construction of discourse representations.

Acknowledgments. This research was funded by research grant OGP9800 from the Natural Sciences and Engineering Research Council of Canada.

Bibliography

Clark, H. H. (1996). *Using language*. New York: Cambridge University Press. An analysis of conversational communication.

Clark, H. H., & Haviland, S. E. (1977). Comprehension and the given-new contract. In R. Freedle (Ed.), *Discourse production and comprehension*. Hillsdale, NJ: Erlbaum. The original formulation of the given-new analysis.

Gernsbacher, M. A. (Ed.). *Handbook of psycholinguistics*. San Diego, CA: Academic Press. A treatment of modern psycholinguistic topics, including those of discourse comprehension.

Glenberg, A. M., Meyer, M., & Lindem, K. (1987). Mental models contribute to foregrounding during text comprehension. *Journal of Memory and Language, 26*, 69–83. Original experiments documenting the coordination of spatial and narrative situation models.

Graesser, A. C., Millis, K. K., & Zwaan, R. A. (1997). Discourse comprehension. *Annual Review of Psychology, 48*, 163–189. An overview of discourse comprehension lengthier than the present entry.

Graesser, A. C., Singer, M., & Trabasso, T. (1994). Constructing inferences during narrative text comprehension. *Psychological Review, 101*, 371–395. A theoretical treatment emphasizing the routine construction of situation models in narrative comprehension.

Grice, H. P. (1975). William James Lectures, Harvard University, 1967. Published in part as "Logic and conversation," in P. Cole & J. L. Morgan (Eds.), *Syntax and semantics* (Vol. 3, pp. 41–58). New York: Seminar Press. A theory of conversational speech.

Just, M. A., & Carpenter, P. A. (1992). A capacity theory of comprehension: Individual differences in working memory. *Psychological Review, 99*, 122–149. A comprehension theory that emphasizes the impact of the limited capacity of working memory.

Kintsch, W. (1998). *Comprehension: A paradigm for cognition*. New York: Cambridge University Press.

Kintsch, W., & van Dijk, T. A. (1978). Toward a model of text comprehension and production. *Psychological Review, 85*, 363–394. An influential theory of the mental processes that extract the text-base level of discourse comprehension.

Malt, B. C. (1985). The role of discourse structure in understanding anaphora. *Journal of Memory and Language, 24*, 271–289. Experiments documenting the relationship of situation models to anaphoric resolution.

McKoon, G., & Ratcliff, R. (1980). Priming in item recognition: The organization of propositions in memory for text. *Journal of Verbal Learning and Verbal Behavior, 19*, 369–386. Classic experiments of the activation among the idea units underlying text.

Singer, M. (1990). *The psychology of language: An introduction to sentence and discourse processes*. Hillsdale, NJ: Erlbaum. An analysis of the discourse processes literature from 1970 to 1990.

Murray Singer

Linguistic Determinism

Linguistic determinism, the view that language determines thought, popularized by Edward Sapir (1912) and Benjamin Lee Whorf (1956) has had an enormous impact on cognitive psychology in this century. This view, sometimes called the Sapir–Whorf Linguistic Relativity Hypothesis, came about from the following two notions: the idea that language reflects thought—a belief that can be traced back to the ancient Greeks; and the observation that languages differ greatly in how they code experience. For Sapir and Whorf, linguistic diversity reflected differences among speakers of different languages in how they perceived and categorized the world. The Sapir–Whorf hypothesis is also a theory of cognitive development in which young children are viewed as flexible in how they may perceive and categorize the world. Language is hypothesized to play a critical role in the perception and categorization of such a world. The Sapir–Whorf Hypothesis can be tested in two ways: across different language groups, by determining whether people who speak different languages show consequent differences in knowledge, and developmentally within a language group, by determining whether a particular cognitive achievement is caused by a preceding linguistic achievement.

There are good reasons to doubt the most extreme version of linguistic determinism which claims that all of cognition is determined by language. One reason comes from empirical evidence on how people perceive and categorize color. Languages differ in the number of basic color terms they provide. Some languages (e.g., English) have over 10 basic color terms, while other languages (e.g., Dani) have as few as two. Heider (1972) compared the color perception of speakers of English and of Dani. She found no differences between the English and Dani speakers in the ways they recognized and remembered colors. Thus, a speaker of Dani does not "see" a rainbow differently from a speaker of English, as an extreme version of the Sapir–Whorf Hypothesis would predict. Moreover, it appears that 3-month-old infants (who do not know any color words) perceive color very similarly to adults (Bornstein, Kessen, & Weiskopf, 1976). So young children do not come into the world completely flexible in how they organize all experience. Some aspects of cognition, such as color perception, are so highly constrained early in development that they cannot be influenced by language.

More moderate versions of linguistic determinism, however, seem to be correct. One source of evidence in support of the Sapir–Whorf Hypothesis is Levinson's work on spatial terms (1996). Languages differ in how they code spatial relations. For example, English and Dutch commonly use relative frames of reference, such as "to the right" and "to the left" when coding the positions of objects. Other languages, such as Tzeltal, a Mayan language spoken in parts of Mexico, use more absolute terms that approximate the meanings of *north* and *south*. So when asking for one of two cups on a table, a speaker of English might ask for the one "on the right," whereas a speaker of Tzeltal might ask for the "northernmost" one. Levinson (1996) compared how speakers of Dutch and Tzeltal recalled spatial relations between pairs of objects that could be coded either in terms of a relative (right-left) or an absolute (north-south) frame of reference. He found that the speakers of Tzeltal used an absolute frame of reference, while speakers of Dutch used a relative frame of reference. These findings indicate that the spatial reference points that dominate a language are the most accessible reference points in a nonlinguistic task.

Another example of language's effect on cognition comes from studies that have examined the relation between grammatical gender and categorization (e.g., Ervin, 1962; Sera, Berge, & Castillo, 1994; Martinez & Shatz, 1997). Some languages classify nouns that refer to inanimate objects such as *book* and *table*, as masculine or feminine in the same way that nouns that refer to *man* and *woman* are classified in these languages. Martinez and Shatz (1997) found that speakers of Spanish, a language with a grammatical gender system, spontaneously use grammatical gender as a basis for sorting pictures of inanimate objects. However, grammatical gender systems differ among themselves, and not all studies that have examined the relationship between grammatical gender and classification have found grammatical gender effects (e.g., Clarke, Losoff, McCracken, & Rood, 1984). For example, grammatical gender effects have not been observed among speakers of German, a language with a grammatical gender system. Thus, the specific properties of gender systems that affect categorization remain to be identified.

Researchers who have investigated the relationship between mass-count syntax and the classification of solid objects and aggregates also report the effects of language on cognition. Mass-count syntax refers to how different nouns are pluralized and counted. Count nouns take a final *s* in their plural forms, unlike mass nouns (e.g., cup-cups and bean-beans vs. corn-corns and furniture-furnitures). One might assume that the syntactic distinction between count and mass nouns reflects an underlying conceptual distinction between solid objects with constant shapes versus aggregates. However, whether a specific noun is classified as mass or count depends on the language. *Furniture* is a mass noun in English but a count noun in Spanish. Lucy (1992) has found that speakers of Yucatec Mayan, a numerical classifier language that treats many nouns as mass nouns, rely less on an object's shape when classifying entities than do English speakers. However, these findings contrast sharply with those of Soja, Carey, and Spelke (1991), which show that young English-speaking children distinguish between solid objects and aggregates before they acquire count-mass syntax. If children possess the conceptual distinction before the onset of language, how can there be language-driven difference among adults in these concepts? Imai and Gentner (1997) suggest that a distinction between solids and aggregates is made early in development, and then language influences the members of each category and the boundary between the two kinds.

Language can also influence the timing of cognitive achievements. One example comes from a classic study by Carroll and Casagrande (1958), who studied children who spoke Navaho, a language in which verb stems depend on the shape of the objects being described. Navaho-speaking 3-year-olds prefer to classify objects according to their shape more often than do their English-speaking age mates. However, English-speaking children begin to prefer to classify objects according to their shape at 4 years of age. Studying the effects of grammatical gender on gender identity, Guiora, Beit-Halachmi, Fried, and Yoder (1983) have found that children who speak Hebrew, another language with a grammatical gender system, are more likely than are English-speaking children to accurately identify their own gender at 25 months. More recent studies also suggest that language can affect the age at which children pick out the important, defining, properties of objects. Children who speak Spanish, a language with two forms of the verb *to be* that are regularly used to describe temporary versus permanent properties, identify the more permanent properties of objects at earlier ages than do English-speaking children (Sera, Reittinger, & Castillo, 1991; Sera, Bales, & Castillo, 1997).

Evidence from studies that include only speakers of English also suggest the effects of language on cognition. For example, Gelman and Gallistel (1978) have shown that young children's ability to accurately judge quantities initially depends on their knowledge of number words. Researchers have also found that labeling objects with nouns facilitates the formation of conceptual hierarchies in young children (Waxman, 1990).

In sum, although complete linguistic determinism cannot be correct, and there remain a number of controversial findings on the topic, language has been shown to influence cognition and its development in important ways.

Bibliography

Bornstein, M., Kessen, W., & Weiskopf, S. (1976). Color vision and hue categorization in young human infants. *Journal of Experimental Psychology: Human Perception and Performance*, 2, 115–129.

Carroll, J. B., & Casagrande, J. B. (1958). The function of language classifications in behavior. In E. E. Maccoby, T. M. Newcomb, & E. L. Hartley, (Eds.), *Readings in social psychology* (pp. 18–31). New York: Holt.

Clark, M., Lossoff, A., MacCracken, M., & Rood, D. (1984). Linguistic relativity and sex/gender studies: Epistemological and methodological considerations. *Language Learning*, 34, 47–67.

Ervin, S. M. (1962). The connotations of gender. *Word*, 18, 249–261.

Gelman, R., & Gallistel, R. (1978). *The child's understanding of number*. Cambridge, MA: Harvard University Press.

Guiora, A., Beit-Halachmi, B., Fried, R., & Yoder, C. (1983). Language environment and gender identity attainment. *Language Learning*, 32, 289–304.

Heider, E. R. (1972). Universals in color naming and memory. *Journal of Experimental Psychology*, 93, 10–20.

Imai, M., & Gentner, D. (1997). A cross-linguistic study of early word meaning: Universal ontology and linguistic influence. *Cognition*, 62, 169–200.

Levinson, S. L. (1996). Frames of reference and Molyneux's question: Cross-linguistic evidence. In P. Bloom, M. Peterson, L. Nadel, & M. Garrett (Eds.), *Language and space*. Cambridge, MA: MIT Press.

Lucy, J. (1992). *Grammatical categories and cognition: A case study of the linguistic relativity hypothesis*. Cambridge, UK: Cambridge University Press.

Martinez, I., & Shatz, M. (1997). Linguistic influences on categorization in preschool children: A cross-linguistic study. *Journal of Child Language*, 23, 529–545.

Sapir, E. (1912). Language and environment. *American Anthropologist*, n.s., 226–242.

Sera, M. D., Bales, D., & Castillo, J. (1997). *Ser* helps speakers of Spanish identify real properties. *Child Development*, 68, 820–831.

Sera, M. D., Berge, C., & Castillo, J. (1994). Grammatical and conceptual forces in the attribution of gender by English and Spanish speakers. *Cognitive Development*, 9, 261–292.

Sera, M. D., Reittinger, E., & Castillo, J. (1991). Developing definitions of objects and events in English and Spanish speakers. *Congnitive Development*, 6, 119–142.

Soja, N., Carey, S., & Spelke, E. (1991). Ontological categories guide young children's inductions of word meaning: Object terms and substance terms. *Cognition*, 45, 101–107.

Waxman, S. (1990). Linguistic biases and the establishment of conceptual hierarchies: Evidence from preschool children. *Cognitive Development*, 5, 123–150.

Whorf, B. L. (1956). *Language, thought, and reality*. Cambridge, MA: MIT Press.

Maria D. Sera

PSYCHOLOGY. [*This entry provides a broad survey of the field of psychology. It comprises seven articles*:

Definition
Classical Antiquity
The Middle Ages
Renaissance Through the Enlightenment
Nineteenth Century Through Freud
Early Twentieth Century
Post–World War II

Numerous independent entries related to psychology are included in the encyclopedia: Aviation Psychology; Biological Psychology; Careers in Psychology; Christianity and Psychology; Clinical Geropsychology; Clinical Psychology; Cognitive Psychology; Community Psychology; Comparative Psychology; Consumer Psychology; Consumerism of Psychological Services; Counseling Psychology; Cross-Cultural Psychology; Cultural Psychology; Developmental Psychology; Differential Psychology; Doctor of Psychology Degree; Educational Psychology; Ego Psychology Theory; Environmental Psychology; Evolutionary Psychology; Experimental

Psychology; Family Psychology; Forensic Psychology; Gestalt Psychology; Health Psychology; Hellenistic Psychology; Hispanic Psychology; Human Factors Psychology; Humanistic Psychology; Industrial and Organizational Psychology; Islam and Psychology; Judaism and Psychology; Law and Psychology; Mathematical Psychology; Military Psychology; Minority Psychology; Narrative Psychology; Neuropsychology; Parapsychology; Pediatric Psychology; Personality Psychology; Phenomenological Psychology; Police Psychology; Postmodern Psychology; Psychology of Men; Rehabilitation Psychology; Religion and Psychology; School Psychology; Social Psychology; Sport Psychology; Theoretical and Philosophical Psychology; *and* Transpersonal Psychology.]

Definition

Can psychology be defined? Yes, according to the American Psychological Association Web site: "Psychology is the study of mind and behavior." No, others argue. Psychology embraces diverse subfields and applications; we can point to them individually, but we cannot define an essence shared by all. Psychology's definition has been debated throughout its history.

Philosophers had always pondered the nature of mind. In the 1800s, physiologists studying the senses were puzzled by, and theorized about human perception. Neurologists noticed brain injuries affecting mental processes. In 1879, Wilhelm Wundt saw in these trends the need for an independent science, a science of immediate experience, the systematic analysis of the conscious human subjective world.

In 1890, William James defined psychology as "the science of mental life . . . its phenomena and their conditions. The phenomena are . . . feelings, desires, cognitions, reasonings, decisions, and the like" (p. 1). Both Wundt and James established early laboratories to study the experience of adult human perception, cognition, and feeling. These topics have been part of experimental (laboratory) psychology ever since, though methods and concepts have changed radically. Biopsychology, which combines physiological study with the study of mental processes, is also an active contemporary subfield.

Englargements and Modifications

But is psychology simply the study of human consciousness? Not since Sigmund Freud. Based on case studies of patients, Freud insisted that unconscious processes were central to understanding human personality and its motivations. (The study of personality remains an important contemporary subfield.)

Animal behavior became part of psychology in 1897. Then Edward L. Thorndike, interested in the evolution of mind, brought various animals into his laboratory and studied their learning processes. Thus began comparative psychology, the subfield that compares the behavior of different species. And children became part of psychology's concern when G. Stanley Hall and others took on the study of the development of mind from infancy through maturity, the subarea of developmental psychology.

Originally psychology was concerned with universal qualities of experience. Quantitative study of human differences began soon after mathematicians invented statistics. Francis Galton in 1884 and Alfred Binet in 1905 used statistics in constructing tests to measure intelligence. Statistics are now used in many subfields, and assessment of human differences remains a lively subarea.

In 1913, John Watson called for a new definition of psychology's subject matter and method. The only way to make psychology into a true science was to base it on systematic behavioral observations. Psychology should abandon the study of mental life completely and become the science of behavior. Research psychologists heeded his call to base the field on systematic, repeatable, behavioral observations—a position many, but not all, hold today. Though some continued to study mental processes, often through inferences from behavior (Wolfgang Köhler, Jean Piaget), mainstream experimental psychology embraced the definition: Psychology is the science of behavior.

Several trends converged mid-century to restore mental processes to the mainstream of experimental psychology. Computers, machines that process information, inspired investigators to study how people process information as they perceive and think. Developments in linguistics inspired psychologists to explore mental processes underlying language, making psycholinguistics a major subarea. Piaget's works, many written earlier, became recognized as major contributions to cognitive development. George Miller's (1962) textbook announced the new emphasis in its title: *Psychology: The Science of Mental Life* (but even in 1997, Carlson called his text *Psychology: The Science of Behavior*).

Factors outside psychology also broadened psychology's subject matter. Events surrounding World War II gave impetus to social psychology (an area that borders on sociology) as many new investigators joined the small cadre who had been studying the impact of social life on psychological processes. Social psychologists now focused on such topics as interpersonal relations, social influence, attitudes and attitude change, prejudice, and conflict resolution—as they still do today.

Psychology's Applied Fields

Most definitions emphasize psychology as a domain of study. But if psychology is what psychologists do, applications as well as research areas are defining parts of the field, and have been almost from the beginning.

Freud constructed his psychoanalytic model of the mind in conjunction with developing psychotherapy. Himself a physician, he realized medical degrees were not necessary for doing psychotherapy. Today, a psychotherapist may be a psychiatrist (with an M.D.), a clinical or counseling psychologist (with a Ph.D. or a Psy.D.), or a social worker (with an M.S.W.). Some psychotherapists are psychoanalytic; some are behavioral; some are cognitive; still others draw from different traditions or create their own blends.

Other applied professions have emerged as well. Educational psychologists work with schools and curricula. Industrial, organizational, and human engineering psychologists work in organizational settings and deal with problems such as how to organize work, choose workers, or design machines that are easy for people to use. Experts in psychological testing have applied their expertise to the development of tests explicitly for applied settings, such as education, industry, and the military. Applied cognitive psychologists work in artificial intelligence using knowledge of human problem solving to make machines "smarter." Some applied social psychologists work in conflict resolution; others do survey research and polling. Health psychologists apply principles, such as how to reduce stress, in order to enhance physical well-being. Forensic psychologists apply principles to various activities in the legal system.

Recent Developments

Psychology's subject matter continues to enlarge. Recently, psychologists concerned about the environment developed environmental psychology. New sensitivity to variations in human experience spawned areas such as cultural psychology (which borders on anthropology), the psychology of women, African American psychology, and subfields within subfields (e.g, within developmental psychology, the study of aging). Some psychologists have returned to psychology's roots in philosophy, examining and reflecting on the assumptions and implications of various philosophical and psychological approaches (the subfields of theoretical and philosophical psychology).

Psychologists continue to debate psychology's methods. Advocates of a new subarea, narrative psychology, question whether psychology should define itself as a science at all and suggest methods typical of literary studies, such as searching for themes as people tell their stories. Many others disagree. They draw on increasingly sophisticated laboratory and statistical methodologies and see these as essential to psychology's scientific base.

Amid all this variety in subfield and application, amid all this disagreement on method and subject matter, is there any way to characterize what makes psychology psychology? Some say no. Others sense a common concern for all psychologists, be they in basic research—from biopsychology to cultural psychology—or in applications. One way to speak of this common concern is this: Psychologists study individuals' meaningful activities and their conditions: activities in the mind as mental processes or observable as behavior, perhaps conscious, perhaps not: human activities first of all, but also animal; activities particular to a person, a social context, or culture, or humanly universal: meanings revealed in the activities in a single episode or in the patterning of a lifetime.

Bibliography

Asch, S. (1987). *Social psychology*. New York: Oxford University Press. First written in 1953, it has been reprinted by popular demand; a fine example of a concerned psychologist trying to make sense of the impact of social processes on people.

Baars, B. J. (1986). *The cognitive revolution in psychology*. New York: Guilford Press. Describes the mid-century movement in experimental psychology from behaviorism to cognitive approaches.

Carlson, N. R. (1997). *Psychology: The science of behavior*. Needham Heights, MA: Allyn & Bacon. A contemporary text that defines psychology as the study of behavior.

Gleitman, H. (1996). *Psychology*. New York: Norton. A fine introduction to the wide range of psychology's subject matter.

James, W. (1890). *Principles of psychology*. New York: Henry Holt. A classic early textbook many psychologists still read today.

Koch, S., & Leary, D. E. (Eds.). (1985). *A century of psychology as a science*. New York: McGraw-Hill. Articles in this volume by Koch, Miller, and Giorgi discuss whether contemporary psychology is unified enough to be defined.

Leahey, T. H. (1993). *A history of modern psychology*. Englewood Cliffs, NJ: Prentice Hall. A good account of the field's development.

Miller, G. A. (1962). *Psychology: The science of mental life*. Reading, MA: Addison Wesley. Delightful essays on the development of various subfields.

Charlotte L. Doyle

Classical Antiquity

The period we know as classical antiquity begins with the Homeric period and concludes with Hellenic cultural diffusion.

Homeric Foundations

Ancient Greek thought, as expressed both in philosophy and the arts, is pervasively influenced by the Homeric epics the *Iliad* and the *Odyssey*. The psychological perspectives of the ancient world are comparably indebted, for these poems are at once studies of character ("personality") and of the conditions that impel action, distort perception, cause thoughts and feelings, and shape social life.

Any brief account of the Homeric perspective must be incomplete and even misleading. For present purposes it is sufficient to draw attention to two features of the works that appear repeatedly in the later philosophical periods of Greek thought. First, there is the objectification of the human condition, a relentless examination of what it is that distinguishes gods and mortals, one mortal from another, one psychological state from another. The famous maxim inscribed at Delphi, "Know thyself," has something of an echo of the *Iliad* and the *Odyssey*, whose major figures are presented as a kind of typology, each engaged in both external combat and inner struggle. The self-indulgent anger of Achilles is no less portentous than the "wolf's rage" of Diomedes, who would turn on the gods themselves. In addition to objectifying the moral and psychological dispositions, the epics also, surprisingly, tend toward utterly naturalistic modes of explanation. Thus the impelling motives are found in the chest or the heart, conditions of the body causally producing passions and convictions that lead to action. Homer's gravely wounded hero falls to the ground audibly, life leaving the body as it loses the blood and the very organs that are life sustaining. There is a literal and a figurative earthiness in the accounts, with only occasional intrusions by the occult and chimerical.

Of equal importance are the simultaneous tentativeness and the multiplicity of explanations presented in these works. There is no pretention to certainty or infallibility, no last word, nothing that a later age would be obliged to take as a received truth. In a word, Homer was scripture, but not *revelation*, for even the Olympians themselves are accorded no particular epistemological authority. As for the Olympians, they tend to be concerned with their own affairs, often indifferent to and even contemptuous of human lives and foibles. They cannot be ignored, but they also cannot be counted on for help with the eternal questions. In the matter of fundamental truths and their implications, human beings are left to their own resources.

Pre-Socratic Philosophy

Greek settlement of the Aegean islands and coastal cities of Asia Minor was prompted initially by scarcity on the mainland and by attractive trading prospects. The first written versions of Homer's epics would be composed in Ionia, whose Greek colonists were further inclined toward philosophy by daily contact with radically different cultures based on radically different concepts and traditions. The first to call himself a philosopher was Pythagoras, from the Ionian island of Samos. Thales, Anaximander, and Anaximenes were from Miletus; Heraclitus from Ephesus; Anaxagoras from Clazomenae; Xenophanes from Colophon. In the Italian colonies would appear Philolaus from Tarentum; Empedocles from Acragas; Zeno and Parmenides from Elea. North of the Ionian cities, in Thrace and in communities around the Black Sea, the names of Protagoras, Democritus, and Leucippus are added.

Knowledge of pre-Socratic thought is fragmentary. The greatest of the pre-Socratic philosophers, Pythagoras, may never have written anything and strictly forbade his disciples to publicize his teaching. The thought of other pre-Socratics often comes down by way of commentators who have agendas of their own. Nonetheless, the fragmentary record is complete enough to convey the scientific and metaphysical depth of thought prevailing in the late seventh and sixth centuries BCE. Though predominantly cosmocentric, the philosophical schools were not indifferent to social and psychological issues—to the problem of knowledge and the problem of conduct, and the question of the very essence of human life.

Pythagoras exemplifies the deepest and most original thought of the period. His studies in Egypt and other Middle Eastern cultures exposed him to the most developed mathematical and cosmological thinking of the age. But he was less interested in the practical purposes to which older cultures put these discoveries than in their deeper implications. He was intrigued and inspired by the marked relationship between mathematical abstractions and actually existent and observable events and things. The best known of these relationships is the Pythagorean theorem, which is at once an abstract axiom of plane geometry and, at the same time, a relationship obtaining among all actual rectilinear triangles. An even more subtle form of the relationship is found in the relationship between numbers and music. Pythagoras is credited with the theory of musical harmony, but he was clearly interested less in this than in the larger implications arising from it. If, in fact, the full range of musical perceptions experienced as harmonious is generated by notes that stand in strict numerical relationships, it follows that the processes of perception must be grounded in similarly abstract and numerical relationships. Indeed, all of nature might be understood in just such relational terms. Taking the first four integers (the tetractys), 1, 2, 3, and 4, as primal, Pythagoras concluded that the first corresponded to the point, the second to the line, the third to the plane, and the fourth to the solid. These four integers are generative of a world of solid objects through a process that cannot be physical, for the physical world itself is produced by such means. Only the realm of soul could absorb the tetractys and then produce the material world.

Similarly, souls temporarily embodied in living persons possess truths beyond the reach and range of matter. The transitory physical objects of nature conceal that ultimate truth on which all reality depends. In Pythagoras, then, is found the tension between the abstract and the objective, the ideal and the "real," the spiritual and the material, that is confronted time and again by succeeding generations of philosophical inquiry.

Of comparable influence was Parmenides of Elea (b. 515 BCE?), who presented his philosophy in a poem that may originally have been titled "On Nature." Here he explored the various paths to truth; his critical guide is a goddess who leads him by way of a dialectical method. The most important conclusion he reaches is that real being is and must be eternal and unchanging and, as such, can never be discovered by the senses.

Plato's Psychology

The dialogues of Plato allegedly do no more than report the teaching of Socrates, but much of what is found in these works is surely Plato's own invention. Their composition spans a period of years such that one must distinguish between the early, the middle, and the late works, with sometimes dramatic departures found across these periods. In the broadest terms, the dialogues address four core problems: the problem of the knowable (ontology and metaphysics); the problem of knowledge (epistemology and psychology); the problem of conduct (ethics); and the problem of governance (political and social science).

How can one ever be sure that one knows anything? Is complete skepticism the most philosophically defensible position?

In *Meno* the young challenger taunts Socrates, who claims to be searching for the truth. Such an inquiry is impossible since if one does not know what the truth is, there is no starting point and if one does know, there is no need for the search in the first place. Socrates' reply takes advantage of the fact that Meno's servant is a young, uneducated "barbarian." He questions the boy about geometric figures drawn in the sand. As the boy answers each yes or no, Socrates leads him to a version of the Pythagorean theorem. The exercise illustrates the central precept of Socrates' theory of knowledge: knowledge is a *reminiscence*. The knower possesses rather than learns the truth. Thus understood, knowledge of what is abidingly true cannot arise from sensory commerce with the world of changing things; it can arise only from an essentially intuitive and rational awareness that is possessed by the soul itself.

In Plato's *Republic* the state (*polis*) is taken to be the enlargement of the individual. To learn what it is that makes the person good it becomes useful to ask what constitutes the good state. By constructing the perfect state, the philosopher must comprehend the attributes that define the perfected human being. In Book 3 of *The Republic* citizens are categorized as being made of gold, silver, brass, or iron, the point being that they are framed so differently by the gods that of necessity some rule and others serve. This illustrates the strong hereditarian element in Platonic psychology but tends to mask the comparably great emphasis placed on early education and lifelong discipline; education is to be very carefully orchestrated. Those epic poems that present the gods as lacking virtue are among those to be forbidden, as are works of fiction and "panharmonic" music.

Plato's psychology is nativistic but leaves ample room for developmental influences. He explicitly endorses a multistage theory of cognitive development. In *Laws*, for example, the Athenian stranger asserts that virtue and vice are known to the young only as pleasure and pain and that, since children instinctively love what is pleasurable and hate what is painful, the principal task of the educator is to make sure that true virtue becomes the object of love. Moreover, there are critical periods of development when the lessons of virtue are most effectively conveyed by music, since virtue fundamentally is a harmonious relationship between body and mind. This aim is furthered by close contact between parent and infant, by the rhythmic rocking of the young. The same theme is sounded in *The Republic*, in which the young are depicted as being out of harmony: Reason and passion have yet to establish the unique accord that constitutes virtue. Music and dance and other gymnastics must be employed because the very young mind is not yet able to assimilate rational principles directly. Thus, early education uses metaphor, not literal lesson. Nonetheless, the success of such education finally depends on the "quality of the wax," and only under rare circumstances will the children of a lower class qualify for the life of a Guardian, that is, one chosen to be trained to protect the city-state and devote himself to its security. If harmony is the goal, the sources of dissonance must be removed. As some of these are genetic accidents of nature, they must be "exposed" (i.e., to the elements). In any case, eugenic breeding can reduce such mistakes to a minimum.

Plato's theory of pleasure, it should be noted, is not to be confused with asceticism. Rather, it distinguishes three different types of pleasurable and painful experience. Some feelings are entirely *bodily*: the itch that can be soothed by scratching. Both body and soul participate in other feelings, such as a painful hunger relieved by anticipation of food. Some feelings, such as longing and love, only arise within the soul. Where body and soul are jointly engaged, the emotions are rich in cognitive content, but there can be feelings of the body without such content.

In *The Republic* Socrates likens the soul to the state. As the state contains three classes (merchants, auxiliaries, and counselors), the soul is occupied by three principles: the rational, the appetitive, and the passionate. The virtuous person is one who has harmonized these three principles such that reason controls appetite, and passion, as an auxiliary to reason, strengthens resolve. The view of reason and appetite as opposing forces is as old as the Homeric epics and as current as psychoanalytic theory. Where the balance is incomplete, where the three composites are in discord, the soul is sick and dying. While men and states are born with the capacity for such harmony, the capacity is actualized only under the leadership and guidance of the philosophically enlightened. Without this guidance the pleasures and pains of the flesh, which are the only sources of control for the child, continue to dominate the life of the adult. Addiction to the world of appearances only furthers the body's hold on the soul; the body being the soul's prison (*desmoterion*). On this account, both madness and ignorance are diseases calling for a form of therapy. The mad and the unjust both have ruling appetites to which reason becomes subservient.

Hippocrates

Of the many creative undertakings of classical Greece, surely Greek medicine must rank as high as any, and the Hippocratic school takes the laurel. That biological cast of thought reflected in Aristotle's works certainly benefited from the background influences of the Hippocratic school and from Greek science in general.

Hippocrates is not easily dated, nor can the Hippocratic medical writings be traced to any such person. They were developed over the course of more than a century and vary greatly in quality and content. Hippocrates came from Cos and thus is said to have fathered the Coan school of medicine. Plato's dialogues make reference to Hippocrates' disciples, so the work ascribed to Hippocrates was earlier than the dialogues, and it is customary to assign his lifetime to about 400 BCE. His teachings are preserved in a number of works, especially in the treatises of Galen (c. CE 130–200). Consistent across the various accounts is the empiricistic method of inquiry. The followers of Hippocrates reasoned that the body itself, and especially the humors of the body, required a delicate and harmonious balance. It was not uncommon for delirium and fits to be treated through the combination of specific foods and music. Diet was especially integral to therapy. In the Hippocratic works on *Epidemics* there is frequent reference to fever and cold, to "fluxes," or storms, of the humors. Similarly, remedies focus on sleep and rest, quietude and temperance.

The Hippocratics established clinically that injuries to either side of the head resulted in spasms on the contralateral side. There are also Hippocratic treatises on the venous supply to the brain and a nearly modern respect for the role of the brain in perception, movement, and any number of psychological processes and functions. The Hippocratic humoral theory of psychological dispositions accorded an unchangeably phlegmatic nature to some people (and therefore to their children); a bilious one to others, a choleric one to others. The justification for such attributions was not rigorously empirical but was surely based on family resemblances in the matter of temperament. Indirectly, such a genetic-type theory of personality lent support to the eugenic theories of Plato's Academy. Still, in the main, Hippocrates and his followers come close to the modern spirit of experimental science and clinical observation. They specifically rejected that Platonic version of "hypothesis," according to which all discourse must begin with self-evident truths, regarding such hypotheses as antithetical to the good care of patients and an understanding of their diseases. In place of these the Hippocratics compiled a veritable handbook of symptoms, therapies, and results. In the process, and through the translations and the influence of Galen, they had an effect on the practice and theory of medicine for over two thousand years. More subtly but just as surely, they required of any psychological philosophy that it address itself to the biological facts of human life and to the relationship between those facts and any theory that might be advanced to explain a psychological process.

Aristotle (385–332 BCE)

Aristotle studied in Plato's Academy for 20 years, from its founding (c. 347 BCE) until Plato's death (c. 347 BCE). His father was personal physician to the Macedonian king Amyntas II, father of Philip II and grandfather of Alexander the Great, whose teacher Aristotle became.

Though a devoted admirer and friend of his great teacher, Aristotle departed from Platonic philosophy in the range and details of his inquiries and in the mode of inquiry. His classical formulation of psychic processes in *On the Soul* has often been relied on to the neglect of his other works. However, any attempt to comprehend his remarkably complete and systematic psychology requires a generous sampling from many of his treatises, including those devoted to logic, ethics, politics, and metaphysics.

What is found through such an examination is a commitment to a distinctly ethological approach to psychological processes and phenomena. Aristotle attempts to identify the essential or defining properties of a given class of animal, link these to their special tasks and the pressures faced, and then explain the given form of life in terms of its successful adaptations. In both his *History of Animals* and *Parts of Animals* the accounts offered are entirely naturalistic, and his descriptions are often exacting and comprehensive. The teleological character of the accounts is often quite similar to what one now routinely encounters in contemporary ethological texts (though Aristotle, unlike Empedocles, did not explicitly advance an evolutionary theory).

In the treatise *On the Soul* Aristotle sets out to offer an account that is to be, in his words, fully "compatible with experience," avoiding the famous Socratic dialectical method. The first chapter treats both emotion and sensation as conditions of the soul that can only exist through the medium of a body. All such affections of the soul are to be conceived as derived from the body. This essentially physiological character of his psychology appears throughout his works, including those not directly concerned with psychological matters. In his *Physics*, for example, he argues that the affairs of the soul are brought about by alterations of something in the body. His teaching on sleep and dreams (*De Somniis*) again accounts for the phenomena by appealing to sensory-biological processes. Memory, too, is treated in purely biological terms. In *On Memory and Reminiscence*, he takes the act of recollection as the "searching for an image in a corporeal substrate" and explains the memory deficiencies of children, the aged, and the diseased in terms of biological anomalies. It is doubtful that Aristotle was a thoroughgoing materialist, however, for in various places he specifically distinguishes soul from the rational mind, the latter dwelling somehow within the soul but, unlike the soul, being imperishable.

Aristotle's theory of psychic functions covers the range from nutritive and reproductive processes to abstract rationality. The various powers (*dunameis*) or faculties of the soul differ in different species. The dividing line between the animal kingdom and all else is marked off by the power of sensation, this function being, says Aristotle, part of the very definition of "animal." Indeed, Aristotle subsumes a number of psychological functions, some quite complex, under perception. As a result, although he reserves abstract rationality to adult human beings, he grants nonhuman animals wide-ranging cognitive, emotive, and motivational states and dispositions.

Rationality carries with it the unique capacity for deliberated choice (*prohairesis*) on which the moral virtues depend. Accordingly, only those in possession of such rational power can be authentically courageous, magnanimous, just, and so on. But the nonhuman animal community offers attenuated examples of these attributes, such that the division between human and nonhuman psychology becomes less sharp the more widely one reads in Aristotle's surviving works.

Aristotle's theory of perception also emphasizes sensory *integration*, a process that is itself not sensory. Consider a cup of coffee. It is a hot, lightly sweetened, dark brown liquid. The various specialized sensory organs respond respectively to each of these attributes: the temperature, taste, color, and consistency. But the *experience* is not of separate attributes. Rather, there is a whole, fully integrated experience such that coffee becomes distinguished from any number of other stimuli that also happen to be dark, hot, sweet liquids. In addition to the classical five senses, then, there is also a *common* sense (*koine aisthesis; sensus communis*) by which experiences are forged out of the separate contributions from the different sense organs.

After rejecting the Platonic theory of natively possessed "true forms" in Book 2 of *On the Soul*, Aristotle considers how the mind comes to comprehend universal propositions that could not be given in experience. His solution calls for a distinction between the actual and the potential: mind has the potential for such comprehension, but for this to be actualized, it must be acted upon by the world. What the mind thinks must be in the mind, he says, as characters can come to be on a wax tablet on which as yet nothing has been etched. As a composite of complex processes, mental life must be supplied with information, else there would be nothing for the perceptual-cognitive processes to work on. Thus, the external world must cause physical responses in the sensory organs, these responses coming to depict or represent or stand as codes for the objects that cause them. Sensations set up certain motions within the soul. These subside in time but, if they have been produced often enough, they can be re-created, or at least a likeness of them can be re-created under comparable conditions. Through repetition (by custom or habit), certain movements reliably follow or precede others. Attempts to recall past events are only attempts to initiate the right *internal* events. This is why, when attempting to recall a sequence of events or objects, one must find the beginning of the appropriate series. When successful, an entire train of previously established associations is set in motion.

Of course, Aristotle knew that comprehensive scientific knowledge is not possible through mere acts of perception. He underscored the particularity of every such act and contrasted it with "that which is commensurately universal and true in all cases," which cannot be thus perceived. An understanding of the latter calls for standards of truth of an essentially cognitive nature by which mere facts become integrated into systematic bodies of knowledge. It is only through what Aristotle called demonstration that such knowledge becomes possible. Scientific knowledge is *demonstrative* in the sense of rational or logical demonstration. Such demonstrations are grounded in the syllogistic modes of argumentation that he invented. The major premise in such an argument may be a law of nature, the minor premise a fact of nature, and the conclusion a necessary and demonstrated conclusion. There is a certain kinship between this feature of Aristotle's philosophy of science and the nomological-deductive model defended in modern times by Karl Hempel and others.

No figure from antiquity until the seventeenth century would be as important to the history of psychology as Aristotle. His most general contribution was to locate the intellectual and motive features of mind in the natural sciences, while reserving the moral and political dimensions of human life to a much enlarged conception of nature itself. At the level of basic processes his psychology was biological and ethological, grounded in considerations not unlike those that Charles Darwin would develop centuries later. If his own version of empiricism did not go so far as to submit scientific truths merely to confirmation by the senses, it did establish the validity and importance of the world of sense. In the process, he presented the senses themselves as objects of study. He also proposed the first laws of learning, loosely drawn around the principle of association and fortified by principles of reinforcement. Except for his retreat toward a somewhat fatalistic hereditarianism in the *Politics*, he consistently emphasized the part played by early experience, education, practice, habit, and life within the *polis* itself in the formation of the psychological dispositions. In this way, he presented human psychology as a developmental subject whose parent science was at once civics and moral philosophy.

Stoic and Epicurean Psychology

The major Stoic philosophers were Zeno of Citium (Cyprus), who lived between 336 and 265 BCE, Cleanthes (c. 331–232 BCE) and Chrysippus (c. 280–206 BCE), both from Asia Minor. Later Stoics of the Christian era include Seneca (c. 4 BCE–65 CE), Epictetus (c. 50–138 CE), and Emperor Marcus Aurelius (121–180 CE). Epicurus (341–270 BCE) was born on Samos, and although his parents were Athenians his early education was received in Asia Minor from teachers versed in the philosophies of Plato and Democritus. His most famous spiritual descendant was the poet Lucretius (99–55 BCE), whose *De Rerum Natura* set to verse the tenets of Epicurean thought.

Stoicism and Epicureanism are rival philosophies, but they shared several characteristics of note, especially in their early development. Both were responses to the influential schools of the Cynics and Skeptics, responses designed to restore philosophy to respectability. Although Stoicism never matched the radical materialism of the Epicureans, both systems adopted a naturalistic perspective. Both also were spare in their ontologies, committed to the view that the universe is ultimately reducible to a single agency, force, element, or kind of "stuff." For the Epicurean it was atomic; for the early Stoics, something akin to fire or ether. The Stoics often referred to this "creative fire" as *Logos* and thought of the divine in the same physicalistic terms.

Perhaps the chief contribution of Stoic psychology was in the stress laid on the importance of language. The later Stoics especially regarded human linguistic prowess as effectively establishing a unique place and family from which all nonlinguists were forever excluded. Thus did the Stoics begin the tradition of regarding human beings as specially endowed with rights otherwise unavailable outside the human family. Central to Stoic thought is an ethics of rationality made possible by language—an ethics pitting rationality against emotion. Even the word *pathos*, which might generally be taken to refer to a passion or emotion, was generally intended within Stoic contexts to be regarded as a kind of *disease* of the soul or something on the way toward psychopathology, the cure for which was *apatheia*, the utter elimination of passions and emotions that would oppose or resist the authority of reason. It is with Stoicism that the ageless tension between rationality and emotionality is eliminated with the renunciation of emotion itself.

Epicurean psychology was more materialistic, associationistic, and sense-based. Experience is recorded in memory and can be revived in the form of concepts. By association, these concepts come to stand for the items originally given in experience. Frequent pairings of an actual apple with the word *apple* results in the expectation (*prolepsis*) of an apple when the word is heard. Since the only mode of verification is experience itself, questions regarding the truth or validity of experience are meaningless. All experience is the outcome of interactions (collisions) between material entities, the matter of the world and the matter of the sense organs. Random collisions can produce random outcomes, as disease can produce pathological outcomes. Nevertheless, the properly functioning sense organ responds to what is there. The soul itself is a type of material organization made up of common elements, fire, wind, and air, and a fourth unnamed element that makes it possible for stimulation to be distributed over and within the body. This last element is the most subtle but is material nonetheless. As a result of its activity, however, there arises the capacity for pleasure and for pain. The business of life—the very preservation of life—centers on these facts and functions.

Hellenistic Diffusion

The conquest of the Greek-speaking world by Alexander the Great resulted in the first wave of diffusion of Greek thought and culture, a diffusion that continued during the subsequent hegemony of the Roman empire. In their thirst for culture, Roman aristocrats imported hundreds of Greek scholars to teach their children and refine their arts and letters. Juvenal would declare Rome "a Greek city." Cicero stamped Roman law with Stoic reasonableness (even as he criticized Stoic philosophy), as Nero would traduce the lessons of Epicurus into a grotesque caricature. But from the time of the death of Alexander (323 BCE) to the completion of Justinian's legal *Codex* nearly a millennium later, Western conceptions of human nature and the conditions judged to be essential to its realization were understood in terms first developed by the ancient Greek thinkers and taught by them to the successive generations of those who came to rule them.

Bibliography

Barnes, J. (Ed.). (1984). *The complete works of Aristotle* (Vols. 1–2). Princeton, NJ: Princeton University Press.

Jowett, B. (Ed.). (1943). *The dialogues of Plato* (Vols. 1–2). New York: Random House.

Robinson, D. N. (1989). *Aristotle's psychology*. New York: Columbia University Press.

Sorabji, R. (1993). *Animal minds and human reason*. Indianapolis: Hackett.

Daniel N. Robinson

The Middle Ages

The Middle Ages has had a poor reputation among twentieth-century psychologists. Edwin Boring, in *A History of Experimental Psychology* (New York, 1929), held that late medieval thinking was based largely on theology and hence tended to be opposed to science. Gregory Zilboorg, in his *History of Medical Psychology* (New York, 1941), claimed that medieval medical practitioners were afraid to look into either normal or abnormal psychology and that the mentally ill were frequently regarded either as possessed by a devil or as witches. Introductory texts have occasionally taken this argument several stages further, claiming that the mentally ill in the Middle Ages were liable to be tortured or burnt at the stake as a consequence of the belief that they were possessed by a devil.

Historians of psychology in the later twentieth century did not substantiate claims that the mentally ill were routinely treated with cruelty in the Middle Ages. Moreover, they generally took a more sympathetic view of the period, finding that medieval philosophers, physicians, and even theologians produced and debated interesting theories of human behavior, although they seem to have done little to test them experimentally.

The Middle Ages

The Middle Ages are reckoned to run from the fourth or fifth century CE to the middle or end of the fifteenth century CE. A period of nearly 1,000 years naturally saw a great deal of change, not only politically, but also intellectually. In western and central Europe at least, the first part of the Middle Ages (until the eleventh century), is known as the Dark Ages, when the relative political and economic backwardness of society, which followed the collapse of the Roman Empire in the west and the breakdown of the Mediterranean world, was reflected in an apparently impoverished intellectual culture. Few writings of any kind survived from this period, and ancient writers like Plato and Aristotle seem to have been little read.

From the eleventh century onward, there was a political and economic revival that extended to intellectual fields. The revival entailed the establishment of universities, increased availability and translation of texts from Arabic and Greek, and an increase in new writing. The works of Aristotle were mostly translated during the twelfth century, and subsequently, most fields of intellectual activity, including psychology, were heavily influenced by these translations.

By the beginning of the ninth century, Islam had established itself in the Middle East, North Africa, and Spain, and intellectual activity flourished in these lands, although it languished in most of Europe. Islamic scholars discovered Aristotle's works well before western Europeans, and quickly produced innovative thinking of their own. Many of the works of these scholars, such as Ibn Sina (980–1037 CE) and Ibn Rushd (1126–1198 CE), were translated into Latin and widely read by later Europeans.

Whereas Europe was politically fragmented throughout the Middle Ages, the Christian Church provided a unifying force, and Latin was the language of intellectual activity in Europe just as Arabic was throughout Islam. In the twentieth century the Church was often thought to have exercised a stultifying if not downright repressive effect on medieval thinking in Europe, but in fact, the various institutions of the medieval Church were largely staffed by intellectuals who tended to regard the activities of other intellectuals liberally. One instance of this attitude is the respect that Christians accorded to the writings of Islamic scholars like Avicenna and Averroës, as Ibn Sina and Ibn Rushd were known in the West, or the Jewish philosopher Maimonides (1135–1204 CE). Medieval thinking about psychology seems to have been truly international.

It is also worth noting that the medieval Church helped set up many of the new European universities, tried to ensure that people consented to their marriages, and campaigned vigorously on a variety of children's welfare issues. On the other hand, almost all the medieval scholars, whether Christian, Islamic, or Jewish, were adherents to their religion and often sought to relate their religious views with their views on other subjects.

Psychology in the Middle Ages

There was no formal discipline called psychology in the Middle Ages, but a number of medieval writers, particularly those from the thirteenth century, discussed concerns similar to those of present-day psychologists. More important, at least a few, for example, Avicenna and Albertus Magnus (1193–1280), seem to have been genuinely interested in psychological theory. It is possible to discern at least two important psychological traditions in the writing of this period: a medical and a philosophical one, both stemming from ancient predecessors.

The medical tradition stemmed from the works of ancient physicians such as Hippocrates of Cos (c. 460–377 BCE), Galen (c. 130–200 CE), and Caelus Aurelianus (c. 255–320 CE). This tradition was carried on by Islamic and Jewish physicians such as Haly Abbas (died c. 994 CE), Avicenna, Averroës, and Maimonides. Constantinus Africanus (c. 1015–1087 CE) translated a number of Arabic medical texts into Latin, and later Christian physicians (e.g., St. Hildegard of Bingen, 1098–1179 CE; Arnold of Villanova, c. 1234–1311 CE) added their own ideas. From the point of view of psychology, the medical tradition is probably most important for its views on mental illness, but the theory of the humors and the theory of the inner senses both arose from this tradition as well.

The philosophical tradition clearly originated with Plato (c. 427–347 BCE), and Aristotle (c. 384–322 BCE), with the latter predominant in the later Middle Ages. In Christian Europe, the thinking of St. Augustine (354–430 CE) was also of great importance, and ensured that the European philosophical tradition also had a strong religious element. A number of thirteenth-century philosophers who were also members of religious orders wrote about psychological issues, paying particular attention to perception, cognitive psychology, emotions, and the will. Such writers included Albertus Magnus, St. Thomas Aquinas (1225–1274 CE), Roger Bacon (1214–1292 CE), and William of Ockham (c. 1285–1349 CE). The philosophical tradition, especially Aristotle's account, also provided the framework for the medieval view of the human being as a whole.

It would be a mistake to see the medical and philosophical traditions as conflicting. Avicenna and Averroës were exponents of both traditions, and although medieval Christians were sometimes easier to assign to one or another tradition, educated people were often well versed in both. The career of Petrus Hispanus (c. 1215–1277 CE) serves as an example. He received medical training, wrote widely on medical, philosophical, and philosophical issues, and became personal physician to Pope Gregory X; after Gregory's death, he became pope himself (John XXI).

Medieval writers discussed a variety of psychological topics. For example, the theologian Aquinas gave a detailed theory of the emotions. Most ancient theorists had held to theories of vision in which some quality was emitted by the eyes. Islamic scholars such as Avicenna and Alhazen (c. 965–1039 CE) pointed out the weaknesses of such theories and produced coherent accounts of visual perception in which the eyes were recipients of information. The remainder of this article concentrates on medieval theories of cognitive psychology, an area scholars of the time saw as of central significance, and on ideas about mental illness, because these have so often been misrepresented in modern times.

Medieval Cognitive Psychology

Medieval ideas about cognitive psychology derive from two major sources, the writings of Aristotle and especially his work on the soul, the *De Anima*, and the theory of the inner senses, which was laid down in late antiquity. Aristotle's *De Anima* may be the most popular psychological text of all time: It was prescribed reading for bachelor of arts degrees throughout Europe until the end of the Middle Ages. The book is short and at times obscure, but it offers a systematic account of psychology that fit in with Aristotle's ideas about other disciplines. Because of its obscurity, a number of medieval scholars wrote books or commentaries in which they set out what they thought Aristotle meant. Those by Averroës and Aquinas are probably the best known.

In the *De Anima*, Aristotle defined the soul as what the body is *for*. He differentiated the types of soul possessed by plants, animals, and humans by the different faculties they possess. Plants are capable of nutrition and reproduction. Animals have the additional faculties of appetite (which includes motivation), sensation, and locomotion. Some animals are capable of three cognitive processes: common sense, which sums up and differentiates the outputs of the five senses; imagination, the power to summon up images of objects previously seen; and memory. In Aristotle's psychology these faculties are believed to operate in physical organs. Humans have all the animal faculties plus those of reason and will, which are not apparently housed in physical organs.

Both the Islamic and the later Christian scholars seem to have set themselves the task of fleshing out this theory. This task was helped by a medical account developed around the fourth century CE, sometimes known as the theory of the inner senses, which postulated that the cognitive processes of the common sense, imagination, and memory were performed in the ventricles of the brain.

In Avicenna's version of the theory, there are three ventricles arranged linearly in the head, all filled with a fluid or *spirit*. Sensory information is sent to the front ventricle, which has connections to the middle ventricle, which in turn, connects to the rear ventricle. (The assumed anatomy differs markedly from the present-day account.)

In perception, the *common sense*, located at the front of the front ventricle, receives images (or *forms*) of objects in the world from the individual senses. At the back of the front ventricle is an *image-store*, which was supposed to have a waxy consistency that could retain these images indefinitely. The process of imagination involved displaying this stored form once again to the common sense.

Two processes that Avicenna thought took place in the middle ventricle extracted meaning from the images: *cogitation* put together or subtracted components of the images that had been previously perceived (this is how one can imagine a golden mountain, to take a medieval example); *estimation* abstracted implications or meanings from the images either instinctively or as the result of past experience. So, to take two of Avicenna's examples, the sheep instinctively fears the wolf, and the dog cringes in terror from the stick it has been beaten with before. Finally, the rear ventricle contained the *memory*, which stored the associations and meanings obtained from estimation.

The cognitive processes of animals could be completely explained by these operations. However, Avicenna believed that humans also had an immortal, rational soul or *mind* that had no physical organ at all. Avicenna suggested that the inner senses processed information about individual objects or events, whereas the mind processed more abstract, universal information. Also, in the normal waking person, the inner senses were under the control of the mind.

There was some debate about the details of the inner senses theory, but the basic paradigm was unchallenged from the fourth to the sixteenth century, and it is referred to by medieval physicians, philosophers, theologians, and even poets. Debate about the activities of the mind, which were only described in brief outline by Aristotle, was more intense, partly because religious issues were often involved. Medieval scholars questioned, for example, whether universals (like the concept of "cat") existed only in the mind or had some external reality; whether minds were individual or whether there was one collective mind in which all humans participated; how intellectual concepts might be stored; and how necessary the processes of the inner senses were for thinking.

Splitting cognitive functions between the inner senses and the immortal mind gave rise to theological problems. For example, if your memory for your individual actions is in the inner senses and perishes when you die, how can you know after your death what good or bad things you did when alive, and which earned you heaven or hell? But this disadvantage was offset by the range of phenomena that could be explained by the combined processes.

Dreaming and hallucination, for example, were easy to deal with. In the normal, waking person, imagination and cogitation are under the control of the mind, but when people are asleep or deranged, the images in the image-store are spontaneously retrieved and perceived. The inner senses were thought to include two memory stores (the image-store and the memory), and often the mind itself was thought to have a store for intellectual concepts or intellectual procedures such as the rules for speaking a foreign language. This partitioning of memory could be used to explain a range of phenomena. For example, Avicenna suggested that memories could be reconstructed if information had been lost from, say, the memory, but not from the image-store. Aquinas thought that the tip-of-the-tongue phenomenon arose when there were references stored in the mind, but the particular information stored in the inner senses could not be immediately accessed.

Mental Illness in the Middle Ages

Medieval ideas about mental illness were almost as bewildering an assortment as our own, but a unifying theme was supplied by the cognitive theory outlined here. It was generally believed that the normal waking person's activities were under the control of the mind. In cases of insanity this control was disrupted or corrupted and behavior would then, like an animal's, be simply determined by the inner senses and the appetites. Consequently, in later medieval legal theory and practice, and in the writings of theologians, the insane were not held accountable for their actions.

At least in the later Middle Ages, the normal causes of disruption were believed to be physiological or environmental. Probably the most influential medical account of mental illness stemmed from the humors theory originally proposed by Hippocrates, and widely elaborated by ancient and Islamic physicians. Mental disorder was thought to result from either an imbalance, or more usually an abnormality, in one of the four humors believed to be important in determining individual differences: blood, phlegm, yellow bile (choler), and black bile (melancholy). Typically, phrenitis (or frenzy) was held to result from overheated yellow bile, melancholy from abnormal black bile, and epilepsy from the blockage of the passages of the brain with abnormal bile or phlegm. Different symptoms might arise from different kinds of humoral abnormality or from the abnormality manifesting itself in different parts of the body. Thus, for example, in Constantinus Africanus's account of melancholy, feelings of alienation might result from black bile affecting the heart, and fear of the future from fumes of black bile literally darkening the imagination. Unsurprisingly, the symptoms of melancholy in his account are quite diverse, easily extending to cover those of present-day schizophrenia and endogenous depression.

Another medical theory distinguished mental disorders by the ventricle affected. Mania affected the front, melancholy the middle, and lethargy the rear ventricle. This idea was not easily compatible with the humors theory, but did fit easily with medieval cognitive theory.

Both medical practitioners and laypeople recognized the role of environmental factors in precipitating mental disorder. Thus, for example, the medieval English Court of Chancery seems to have determined such causes of mental disorder as blows to the head and grief. Constantinus Africanus's writings on mental disorder include a treatise on lovesickness. Interactions among the various different causes was also widely acknowledged. So, for example, people who were naturally of a melancholic humor were at particular risk if they undertook occupations likely to induce melancholy. Students and monks were believed to be especially susceptible.

Western European accounts from the early part of the Middle Ages often blamed mental disorder, especially where the symptoms resembled those of epilepsy, on demons, an attribution that has precedents in the New Testament. In the Islamic tradition and in the later Middle Ages in Christian Europe, mental disorder was less widely attributed to demonic possession, but the diagnosis was still occasionally made, especially in religious writing. The diagnosis seems to have been reserved mainly for unusual cases, for example, if a person actually claimed to be a demon. Toward the end of the Middle Ages, cases of demonic possession, among a variety of other ailments, sometimes spurred a hunt for the witch responsible. However, in these cases the object of the witch hunt was someone who might have brought about the possession, not the afflicted individual himself or herself.

The demonological and medical theories were not mutually exclusive. Religious writers describing cases they ascribed to possession sometimes reveal a fair knowledge of medieval medical theory. Moreover, it was often held that demons took advantage of an existing constitutional weakness, such as a tendency toward melancholy, in selecting their victims. Finally, possession too was believed to feature the disruption of the mind's normal control over behavior and its usurpation by a demon.

Treatments for mental disorder were quite diverse. Some were theoretically based: bloodletting, baths, head surgery, or a diet change to rid oneself of noxious humors; sexual diversion to aid the lovesick; exorcism and Holy Communion to aid the possessed. Others were not: music, pleasant scenes, prayer, and religious relics were thought to be beneficial regardless of the diagnosis (which was often tentatively held in any case). Records of the illnesses of the painter Hugo van der Goes (c. 1435–1482 CE) and the French King Charles VI (1368–1422 CE) portray well-meaning onlookers suggesting a variety of diagnoses and remedies, none of them very successful. An instance of the solicitude shown Charles during his periods of illness was his court's procurement of a mistress, Odette de Champdivers, when the king refused to recognize his wife.

Some medieval treatments must have been painful, and head surgery was probably dangerous. Moreover, the long-term mentally ill, especially those without substantial means, seem to have been low on priority lists for institutional care. However, neither painful treatment nor frequent neglect seems to have been motivated by a desire to punish either the patient or any demon thought to possess him or her. The idea that people possessed by a demon could be cured by torturing them or burning them at the stake would have seemed to a medieval clergyman quite as bizarre as it does to us.

Bibliography

Medieval Works Available in English Translation

Aquinas, T. (1964). *Summa theologiae.* London: Blackfriars. The classic of Catholic theology contains a good deal of psychology; see, for example, Volumes 11 and 12 on cognition, Volume 17 on the will, and Volumes 19 to 21 on emotion.

Averroës. (1961). *Epitome of parva naturalia* (H. Blumberg, Trans.). Cambridge. MA: Medieval Academy of America. Summary of some of Averroës's ideas on cognition.

Avicenna. (1952). *Avicenna's psychology: An English translation of Kitab Al-Najat, Bk. II, Ch. VI with historico-philosophical notes and textual improvements on the Cairo edition* (F. Rahman, Trans.). London: Oxford University Press. Avicenna's summary of his psychological ideas.

Lennox, W. G. (1941). John of Gaddesden on epilepsy. *Annals of Medical History* (3rd series), *1*, 283–307. An example of medieval thinking about mental illness.

Modern Works

Carruthers, M. J. (1990). *The book of memory: A study of memory in medieval culture.* Cambridge, UK: Cambridge University Press.

Clarke, B. (1975). *Mental disorder in earlier Britain.* Cardiff: University of Wales Press.

Harvey, E. R. (1975). *The inward wits: Psychological theory in the Middle Ages and the Renaissance.* London: Warburg Institute.

Jackson, S. W. (1986). *Melancholia and depression: From Hippocratic times to modern times.* New Haven, CT: Yale University Press.

Kemp, S. (1990). *Medieval psychology.* Westport, CT: Greenwood.

Kemp, S. (1996). *Cognitive psychology in the Middle Ages.* Westport, CT: Greenwood.

Kroll, J. (1973). A reappraisal of psychiatry in the Middle Ages. *Archives of General Psychiatry, 29*, 276–283.

Lindberg, D. C. (1976). *Theories of vision from Al-Kindi to Kepler.* Chicago: University of Chicago Press.

Wack, M. F. (1990). *Lovesickness in the Middle Ages: The 'Viaticum' and its commentaries.* Philadelphia: University of Pennsylvania Press.

Simon Kemp

Renaissance Through the Enlightenment

The Renaissance revived interest in individual personality, setting the stage for the emergence of psychology in the seventeenth century. Subsequently, psychology became socially important in the eighteenth century, and became a science in the nineteenth century. The history of the word *psychology* reflected this development. Although its etymological roots are Greek, *psuchē* ("soul") + *logos* ("word") = *psychology*, it appeared fitfully beginning in the 1600s, and gained general currency only in the nineteenth century. Instead, people wrote about a "science of human nature," or "mental" or "moral" science. Moreover, psychology was one of several human sciences that appeared in the five centuries after 1400, but it took many years for them to assume their modern forms. For a long time, a student of human nature was equally psychologist, sociologist, anthropologist, economist, and political scientist.

The Renaissance

The Renaissance is rightly celebrated for its creativity in the arts. For the history of psychology it initiated the transition from medieval to modern times. The distinctive development of the Renaissance was the reappearance of humanism: placing importance on individual human beings and their lives in this world as opposed to medieval concern with feudal social status and religious concern with their future lives in heaven or hell. As psychology is the science of individual mind and behavior, it owes a debt to humanism.

Although the Renaissance helped give birth to modern secular life, it began (as in the works of Francesco Petrarch, 1304–1374), by looking backward rather than forward. Renaissance writers derided the Middle Ages as dark and irrational and praised the Classical Age as enlightened and full of wisdom. The Party of the Ancients believed that people could do no more than imitate the glories of Greece and Rome. Right through the eighteenth century (the Enlightenment and Age of Reason) the influence of the Ancients lingered, as artists, architects, and political leaders looked to the Classical past for models of taste, style, and sound government.

Renaissance humanism turned the focus of human inquiry away from God and heaven toward nature. Freed from medieval religious prohibitions on dissection of the human body, artists such as Leonardo da Vinci (1452–1519) and physicians such as Andreas Vesalius (1514–1564) undertook their detailed anatomical study, beginning to see the body as an intricate but understandable machine, a key to scientific psychology. Since the dawn of time, people had closely observed nature but had rarely interfered in its operations. In the Renaissance, however, a new relationship between humans and nature took shape. Led by Francis Bacon (1561–1626), scientists began to interrogate nature by means of experimentation and sought to use their knowledge to control nature; Bacon said "knowledge is power." Throughout the twentieth century, psychology has followed Bacon's maxim, aiming to be a means of advancing human welfare. Applied psychology began with the Italian political writer, Niccolò Machiavelli (1469–1527), who linked the study of human nature to the pursuit of political power. Although he did not discard religious notions of right and wrong, Machiavelli looked unsparingly at human nature in the new naturalistic spirit, seeing humans as made more for sin than salvation. He told princes how to exploit human nature for their own ends while avoiding tempting paths of selfishness that could harm their nations.

From the Renaissance interest in understanding nature came a point of view halfway between religion and modern science: Renaissance naturalism. Magnets are mysterious: How does a special lump of metal attract and repel others? Traditional explanations cited the supernatural: The magnet is inhabited by a demon or is under the spell of a sorcerer. Renaissance naturalism, however, attributed the magnet's power to "a secret virtue, inbred by nature, and not by any conjuration." The magnet's power lay in the inherent nature of magnets, not in a demon or spell imposed on nature from without. Rejecting supernatural explanation represented a step toward science, but without an explanation of how magnetism worked, secret virtues remained as mysterious as demons.

Greater mysteries than magnetism, however, are life and mind. Why do living things move, but not stones? How do we perceive and think? Religion said a soul dwelled in bodies, making them alive and giving them experience and the capacity for action. In Greek, *psuche* meant "breath of life" (soul). Renaissance naturalism suggested that perhaps life and mind, like magnetism, were outcomes of natural powers possessed by living bodies, not infusions into nature from the soul. With regard to the mind, Renaissance naturalism suffered two drawbacks. As in the case of magnetism, it lacked any explanation of how the body caused mental activity. More disquieting was naturalism's implication that humans have no souls, so that our personalities will perish with our bodies. To a large degree, scientific psychology was created as scientists, beginning with René Descartes, wrestled with these questions. Psychology seeks to give detailed explanations of mind and behavior without invoking a supernatural soul.

The Renaissance Party of the Ancients, which looked to the Classical past as the source of all wisdom, was challenged by the Party of the Moderns, who asserted that modern men and women were equal to the creative giants of the past. They proved they were right with the Scientific Revolution.

The Scientific Revolution

The story of scientific psychology begins with the Scientific Revolution. The scientific revolution did more than create the idea that psychology might be a science, it gave rise to new conceptions of mind and body fundamental to psychology's development. The Scientific Revolution created the concept of consciousness, around which the first psychologies were organized, and created the concept that the universe is a machine, suggesting that living bodies were organic machines.

The Transformation of Matter. Ancient people thought of the universe as a living organism or as a book. As a living organism, the universe was an interconnected whole developing in an orderly way. The Stoics especially taught this, and Christians picked up the idea, seeing the universe as God's handiwork and history as God's unfolding plan. As a book, the universe was set of symbols to be deciphered. Thus, people tried to interpret the meaning of a comet as a sign of some impending event.

Basic to the Scientific Revolution was the idea that the world was neither a living organism nor a book, but a machine—a giant clockwork—following regular mechanical principles expressible in mathematical laws. The triumphant epitome and capstone of the revolution was the *Principia Mathematica* (1687) by Isaac Newton (1642–1727). Newton showed that the motions of the stars and planets, and the motions of physical bodies anywhere in the universe could be accounted for by a few laws of motion and gravity. Moreover, the mechanical conception of the universe promised that science would fulfill Bacon's promise and give humans power over nature. On the other hand, in the Newtonian scheme, Halley's comet was a dirty snowball in solar orbit, possessing no cosmic meaning at all.

Psychology would be deeply concerned with questions raised by the new mechanical philosophy. If the universe is not a living being, but a machine, are animals—and human beings—machines, too? What place, if any, does the soul have in science and the physical world? If things and events have no meaning, why do they *seem* to? How much of our perceptual experience belongs to things in themselves, and how much belongs only to us?

The Transformation of Experience. Prior to the scientific revolution, philosophers taught that we perceive the world directly. Objects in the world around us possess features, such as size, shape, and color, which are picked up by our perceptual apparatus. Moreover, ancient and medieval philosophers believed that properties of objects, events, and actions, such as being beautiful or moral, were likewise objective facts about the world that we perceive directly. Thus, for example, people find Michelangelo's *David* beautiful because it is, in fact, beautiful, and people find heroism in battle morally worthy because it is, in fact, morally worthy.

However, beginning with Galileo Galilei (1564–1642), scientists distinguished between *primary* and *secondary* sense properties (the terms are Locke's). Primary sense properties are those that actually belong to the physical world machine: they are objective. Secondary properties are those added to experience by our sensory apparatus: they are subjective. Galileo wrote in his book *The Assayer:*

> Whenever I conceive any material or corporeal substance I immediately . . . think of it as bounded, and as having this or that shape; as being large or small [and] as being in motion or at rest. . . . From these conditions I cannot separate such a substance by any stretch of my imagination. But that it must be white or red, bitter or sweet, noisy or silent, and of sweet or foul odor, my mind does not feel compelled to bring in as necessary accompaniments. . . . Hence, I think that tastes, odors, colors, and so on . . . reside only in the consciousness [so that] if the living creature were removed all these qualities would be wiped away and annihilated. (Cited in Smith, 1990)

The key word is *consciousness*. For ancient philosophers there was only one world, the real physical world with which we are in direct touch. But the concept of secondary sense properties created a new world, the inner world of consciousness, populated by mental objects (*ideas*) possessing sensory properties not found in objects themselves. Some of these secondary properties correspond to physical features. For example, color corresponds to different wavelengths of light to which retinal receptors respond. That color is not a primary property, however, is demonstrated by the existence of color-blind individuals, whose color perception is limited or absent. Objects are not colored, only ideas are colored. Other secondary properties, such as being beautiful or good are more troublesome, because they seem to correspond to no physical facts, but reside only in consciousness. Our modern opinion that beauty and goodness are subjective judgments informed by cultural norms is one consequence of the transformation of experience wrought by the scientific revolution.

Creating Psychology: René Descartes. The currents set in motion by the Renaissance and the scientific revolution came together in the work of René Descartes (1596–1650), who created an influential framework for thinking about mind and body fundamental to the founding of psychology. A devout reforming Catholic and working scientist, Descartes tried to reconcile his religious belief in the existence of a soul with his commitment to a mechanical view of the material universe as a clockwork machine governed by rigid mathematical laws. Although many of Descartes's specific theses were soon rejected, his framework endured for centuries. Descartes said that humans were souls united to mechanical bodies; animals were soulless machines. The only mental function he assigned to the soul was thinking—Descartes's famous *cogito, ergo sum* ("I think, therefore I exist")—including self-awareness and language.

Descartes inherited a problem that, although rooted in Greek philosophy and medicine, had become more urgent during the scientific revolution. Humans and animals share much that is commonly called *mental*, for example, animals clearly perceive, learn, and remember. Therefore, because animals have no souls, perception, learning, and memory must be functions of the body, not of the soul or mind. This realization led some thinkers to formulate two heresies. One placed the human soul outside the body altogether, seeing it as a divine inner light flowing from God during life and returning to him at death. The other—adopted by Renaissance naturalism—dispensed with the soul altogether, seeing humans as sophisticated animals and mind as a function of the brain.

Because both theories were inconsistent with personal immortality, Descartes was placed in a quandary. As a scientist, he accepted that animals were machines, and that therefore much of mental functioning was really the mechanical functioning of the body. As a Christian, he believed in a human soul that was spirit, not matter. Descartes's quandary became a crisis in 1633, when the Inquisition condemned Galileo. Descartes suppressed publication of his physical work, *The World*, and abandoned his book on psychology, *L'Homme* (Man). In it, Descartes had treated human beings as machines only, investigating how far human behavior could be explained physiologically. In two philosophical works, *Discourse on Method*, and *Meditations on First Philosophy*, Descartes tried to create a philosophy that would justify his science and protect him from heresy, drawing the Cartesian picture of consciousness, mind, and brain.

Descartes's dualism of body and soul reflected the new scientific distinction of physical and mental worlds. Descartes assumed living bodies were complex machines no different from the world machine. Animals were machines only; human beings were machines wherein dwelled the soul, the self. Descartes's picture has been aptly termed the *Cartesian theater*: The soul sits inside the body and views the world as on a theater screen, a veil of ideas interposed between knowing self and known world. Within the Cartesian framework, one could adopt two attitudes toward experience. The first attitude was that of natural science. Scientists continued to think of ideas as partial reflections of the physical world. Primary properties corresponded to reality; secondary ones did not.

The notion of consciousness as populated by ideas created the second, distinctively Cartesian attitude to experience that gave rise to psychology. One could examine ideas as such, not as projections from the world outside, but as objects in the subjective world of consciousness. Descartes created the idea of stepping back from experience and reflecting on it. A good route to understanding the Cartesian theater is through modern art, which began in the nineteenth century at the same time as scientific psychology. Prior to the Impressionists, painters had mainly tried to depict persons and places as they really were. Thus, our interest in a portrait of Napoleon is discovering what he looked like. Realistic paintings embody the traditional attitude to experience; our interest lies chiefly in the object painted, not the painting. Beginning with the Impressionists, however, painters adopted a new psychological attitude, asking people to look *at* the canvas, not *through* it to the world. They tried to capture subjective experience, how things looked and felt to the painter at one moment in time. The first experimental psychologists did the same, asking observers to describe how things appeared in consciousness rather than as the observers thought them to be in reality.

Psychology was created by introspection, reflecting on the screen of consciousness. The natural scientist inspects the objective natural world of physical objects; the psychologist introspects the subjective mental world of ideas. To psychologists was given the problem of explaining whence secondary properties come. If color does not exist in the world, why and how do we see color? Descartes also made psychology important for philosophy and science. For them to pursue truth, it became vital to sort out what parts of experience were objective and what parts were subjective chimeras of consciousness.

Descartes also participated in another project central to the founding of scientific psychology, linking mind to brain. Prior to Descartes, living bodies had been seen as markedly different from nonliving things either by possession of a life-giving spirit (the Greek *psuche*) or by possession of special powers denied nonliving matter. Descartes rejected both views, separating the thinking soul radically from the mechanical body. He formulated the important concept of the nervous reflex, creating the image of the bodily machine as a device responding automatically to external stimuli. Conceiving of living bodies as clockwork machines was implicitly accepted by most psychologists throughout the nineteenth and early twentieth centuries, creating conceptual problems that would not begin to dissolve until recently.

The Rise of Psychology

Understanding the place of mind and body in nature gave rise to several schools of thought.

Examining Mind. Several intertwined questions arose from the new scientific, Cartesian, view of mind and its place in nature. Some are philosophical. If I am locked up in the subjective world of consciousness, how can I know anything about the world with any confidence? Asking this question created a degree of paranoia in subsequent philosophy. Descartes began his quest for a foundation upon which to erect science by suspecting the truth of every belief he had. Eventually he came upon the apparently unassailable assertion that "I think, therefore I am." But Descartes's method placed everything else in doubt, including the existence of God and the world. Related to the philosophical questions are psychological ones. How and why does consciousness work as it does? Why do we experience the world as we do, rather than some other way? Because the answers to the philosophical questions depend on the answers to the psychological ones, examining the mind—doing psychology—became the central preoccupation of philosophy. Several philosophical-psychological traditions ensued, the empiricist, realist, idealist, and historical-cultural traditions.

The Empiricist Tradition. The empiricist tradition is the most important for the history of psychology in Britain and America. Notwithstanding the subjectivity of consciousness, empiricism began with John Locke (1632–1794) by accepting consciousness at face value, trusting it as a good, if imperfect, reflection of the world. In many respects, Locke was similar to Descartes. He trained in medicine, worked in science (he was a friend of Newton's), and aimed for a new philosophy consistent with the new science. However, Locke was less entangled in metaphysical issues than Descartes, and his thought had a more practical, commonsense cast, perhaps because he was an educator and politician, writing for the general public, not philosophers.

Locke concisely summarized the central thrust of empiricism, "We should not judge of things by men's opinions, but of opinions by things," striving to know "the things themselves." Locke's picture of cognition is essentially that of Descartes. We are acquainted not with objects, but with *ideas* that represent them. Locke differed from Descartes in denying that any of the mind's ideas are innate. Descartes had said that some ideas (such as the idea of God) cannot be found in experience, but are inborn, awaiting activation by appropriate experiences. Locke said that the mind was empty of ideas at birth, being a *tabula rasa* (blank slate) upon which experience writes. However, Locke's view is not too different from Descartes's view because he held that the mind is furnished with numerous mental abilities, or faculties, which tend automatically to produce certain ideas (such as the idea of God) from the raw material of experience. Locke distinguished two sources of experience, sensation and reflection: sensation reveals the outside world, whereas reflection reveals the operations of our minds.

Later empiricists took the "way of ideas" further, creating deep and unresolved questions about human knowledge. The Irish Anglican bishop and philosopher George Berkeley (1685–1753) began to reveal startling implications of the way of ideas. Berkeley's work is an outstanding example of how the new Cartesian conception of consciousness invited psychological investigation of beliefs heretofore taken for granted. The way of ideas assumes with common sense that there is a world outside consciousness. However, through a penetrating analysis of visual perception, Berkeley challenged that assumption. The world of consciousness is three-dimensional, possessing height, width, and depth. However, Berkeley pointed out, visual perception begins with a flat, two-dimensional image on the retina, having only height and width. Thus, as someone leaves us, we *experience* him or her as getting farther away, while on the retina (the screen of the Cartesian theater) there is only an image getting smaller and smaller.

Berkeley argued that the third dimension of depth was a secondary sense property. We infer the distance of objects from information on the visual screen (such as linear perspective) and from bodily feedback about the operations of our eyes. Painters use the first kind of cues on canvases to create illusions of depth. So far, Berkeley acted as a psychologist proposing a theory about visual perception. However, he went on to develop a striking philosophical position termed *immaterialism*. Depth is not only an illusion when it's on canvas, it's an illusion on the retina, too. Visual experience is, in fact, two-dimensional, and the third dimension is a psychological construction out of bits and pieces of experience assembled by us into the familiar three-dimensional world of consciousness. Belief in an external world depends upon belief in three-dimensional space, and Berkeley reached the breathtaking conclusion that there is no world of physical objects at all, only the world of ideas. Breathtaking as Berkeley's conclusion may be, but it rested on hardheaded reasoning. Our belief that objects exist independently of our experience of them—that my car continues to exist when I'm indoors—is an act of faith. This act of faith is regularly confirmed, but, Berkeley said, we have no knock-down *proof* that the world exists outside the Cartesian theater. We see here the paranoid tendency of modern thought: the tendency to be skeptical about every belief, no matter how innocent (true) it may seem, and in Berkeley we see how this tendency depends upon psychological notions about the mind.

Skepticism was developed further by David Hume (1711–1776), one of the most important modern thinkers, and his skeptical philosophy began with psychology: "[A]ll the sciences have a relation . . . to human nature," and the only foundation "upon which they can stand" is the "science of human nature." Hume drew out the skeptical implications of the way of ideas by relentlessly applying empiricism to every commonsense belief. The world with which we are acquainted is the world of ideas, and ideas are held together by the mental force of association. In the world of ideas we may conceive of things that do not actually exist, but are combinations of simpler ideas that the mind combines on its own. Thus, the chimerical unicorn is only an idea, being a combination of two other ideas that do correspond to objects: the idea of a horse and the idea of a horn. Likewise, God is a chimerical idea, composed from ideas about omniscience, omnipotence, and paternal love. The self, too, dissolves in Hume's inquiry. He went looking for the self and could find in consciousness nothing that was not a sensation of the world or the body. A good empiricist, Hume thus concluded that because it cannot be observed, the self is a sort of psychological chimera, though he remained uncertain how it was constructed. Hume expunged the soul in the Cartesian theater, leaving its screen as the only psychological reality.

Humean psychology seemed to make scientific knowledge unjustifiable. Our idea of causality—a basic tenet of science—is chimerical. We do not see causes themselves, only regular sequences of events, to which we add a subjective feeling, the feeling of a necessary connection between an effect and its cause. More generally, any universal assertion, such as "All swans are white," cannot be proved, because they have only been confirmed by experience so far. We might one day find that some swans are black (they live in New Zealand). Hume appeared to reach the alarming conclusion that we can know nothing for certain beyond the immediate content of our conscious sensations. Science, religion, and morality were all thrown in doubt, because all assert theses or depend on assumptions going beyond experience, which may, therefore, some day prove erroneous. Hume was untroubled by this conclusion, anticipating the later post-evolutionary pragmatism of C. S. Peirce and William James. Beliefs formed by the human mind are not provable by rational argument, Hume said, but they are reasonable and useful, aiding us mightily in everyday life. Other thinkers, however, were convinced that philosophy had taken a wrong turn.

The Realist Tradition. Hume's fellow Scottish philosophers, led by Thomas Reid (1710–1796), offered one diagnosis and remedy. Berkeley and Hume challenged common sense, suggesting that external objects do not exist, or, if they do, we cannot know them or causal relationships among them with any certainty. Reid defended common sense against philosophy, arguing that the way of ideas had led philosophers into a sort of madness. Reid reasserted and reworked the older realist tradition. We see objects themselves, not inner representations of them. Because we perceive the world directly, we may dismiss Berkeley's immaterialism and Hume's skepticism as absurd consequences of a mistaken notion, the way of ideas. Reid also defended a form of nativism. God made us, endowing us with mental powers (faculties) upon which we can rely to deliver accurate information about the outside world and its operations.

Scottish realism contained a hidden challenge to the first scientific psychology. The psychology of consciousness was predicated upon the way of ideas. Natural scientists studied the physical objects of the world machine, and psychologists studied the mental objects of the world of consciousness. However, according to realism, the world of consciousness does not exist, because we perceive objects, not ideas. What appears to be introspection of an inner world of consciousness is, in fact, direct perception of the world itself. In the twentieth century, psychologists such as E. C. Tolman and B. F. Skinner used realist arguments to attack introspective psychology in support of behaviorism. Instead of studying mythical ideas, psychologists should study the relationship between the behavior of organisms and the world in which they act.

The Idealist Tradition. Another diagnosis and remedy was offered in Germany by Immanuel Kant (1724–1804), who, like Reid, found Hume's ideas intolerable because they made genuine knowledge unreachable. Reid located Hume's error in the way of ideas, abandoning it for a realist analysis of cognition. Kant, on the other hand, located Hume's error in empiricism and elaborated a new version of the way of ideas that located truth inside the mind. Empiricists taught that ideas reflect, in Locke's phrase, "things themselves," the mind conforming itself to objects that *impress* (Hume's term) themselves upon it. But for Kant, skepticism deconstructed empiricism. The assumption that mind reflects reality is but an assumption, and once this assumption is revealed—as Berkeley and Hume did—the ground of true knowledge disappears.

Kant upended the empiricist assumption that the mind conforms itself to objects, declaring that objects conform themselves to the mind, which imposes a universal, logically necessary structure upon experience. Things in themselves (noumena) are unknowable, but things as they appear in consciousness (phenomena) are organized by the mind in such a way that we can make absolutely true statements about them. Take, for example, the problem addressed by Berkeley, the perception of depth. Things in themselves may or may not be arranged in Euclidean three-dimensional space; indeed, modern physics says that space is non-Euclidean. However, the human mind imposes Euclidean three-dimensional space on its experience of the world, so we can say truly that phenomena are necessarily arrayed in three-dimensional space. Similarly, the mind imposes other categories of experience on noumena to construct the phenomenal world of human experience.

A science fiction example may clarify Kant's point.

Imagine the citizens of Oz, the Emerald City, in whose eyes are implanted at birth contact lenses making everything a shade of green. Ozzites will make the natural assumption that things *seem* green because things *are* green. However, Ozzites' phenomena are green because of the contact lenses, not because things in themselves are green. Nevertheless, the Ozzites can assert as an absolute and irrefutable truth that every phenomenon is green. Kant argued that the categories of experience are logically necessary preconditions of any experience whatsoever by all sentient beings. Therefore, because science is about the world of phenomena, we can have genuine, irrefutable, absolute knowledge of that world, and should give up inquires into Locke's "things themselves."

Kantian idealism produced a radically expansive view of the self. Instead of concluding with Hume that it is a construction out of bits and pieces of experience, Kant said that it exists prior to experience and imposes order on experience. Kant distinguished between the empirical ego (the fleeting contents of consciousness) and the transcendental ego. The transcendental ego is the same in all minds and imposes the categories of understanding on experience. The self is not a construction from experience, it is the active constructor of experience. In empiricism the self vanished; in idealism it became the only reality.

Idealism influenced early German psychology. Because the transcendental ego creates consciousness, it cannot enter into consciousness. Psychology, idealists held, did not deserve the name of science because the most important part of the mind, the self, could not be observed. As a young man psychology's founder, Wilhelm Wundt, sided with Locke saying that introspection could fathom thought. Later, he sided with Kant, restricting experimental psychology to the study of immediate experience, proposing to study the higher mental processes by other methods. One of psychology's early disputes—the imageless thought controversy—was created by arguments over the scope of introspection. The dispute helped pave the way for behaviorism by throwing doubt on the value of all introspection. The degree to which people know the causes of their behavior remains controversial.

The Historical-Cultural Tradition. Our final tradition opposed the tendencies of the scientific revolution by denying that the human sciences could or should be natural sciences. This dissenting viewpoint was articulated first in obscurity by the Italian philosopher Giambattista Vico (1668–1744), and more influentially by the German writer Johann Herder (1744–1803), who stated its motto: "We live in a world we ourselves create." Human beings are not solely natural objects (machines) because we live social lives in human cultures constructed by the process of history. Therefore, there can be no science encompassing all human beings. Humans live in different cultures, have lived in different ones in the past, and will construct new ones in the future. The spatiotemporal universality of natural science (gravity and matter are the same in all times and places) does not hold in the human world. Some of human nature has physical roots, but much, perhaps most, has social roots. Whereas part of psychology can emulate physics (studying the human mind as related to its brain), much should emulate history (studying the human mind as related to its culture). The historical-cultural tradition became important in the nineteenth-century German psychology.

Examining Mind and Body. So far we have discussed issues created by the Cartesian separation of consciousness from the world. Descartes also made problematical the nature of the connection between soul and body. It seems obvious that the soul gets information about the world through the body and controls its actions. Descartes taught that soul and body interact through the pineal gland, the screen of the Cartesian theater. By pushing it around, Descartes thought, the soul could control the operations of the nerves. However, Cartesian interactive dualism quickly came under attack. One of Descartes's correspondents, Princess Elisabeth of Bohemia (1615–1680), asked the key question: "How can body be pushed by something immaterial?" Descartes could give no good answer.

The problem persisted through the eighteenth century, although most early psychologists adopted a variation on dualism: the thesis of psychophysical parallelism proposed by Gottfried Wilhelm von Leibniz (1646–1716). He said that mind and body are separate, that every mental event has a physical event corresponding to it, but that the latter does not actually cause the former. Although this position was convenient, making psychology separate from physiology, it left its own mysteries such as why mind and body seem to interact, or if they do not, of what use is studying an impotent mind? Leibniz's parallelism gave rise to the first experimental research in psychology, Gustav Fechner's psychophysics, which tried to precisely measure the correlation of stimulus and sensation.

Idealism (including immaterialism) is a monist answer to the mind-body problem, claiming that only mind exists, matter being an illusion. Another radical—even socially dangerous—monistic answer to the mind-body problem was materialism: the claim that only matter exists, the mind being the illusion. The banner of materialism was first publicly hoisted in 1748 by a physician, Julien-Offray de la Mettrie (1709–1751) in his book *L'Homme machine* (The man-machine). La Mettrie took the step Descartes would not, could not, or feared to, take, and proposed that thought was a brain process. Discarding the soul was a bold and dangerous step. It threatened Christian belief in the reality and immortality of the soul; it suggested that if human beings are machines, then there is no free will, and moral responsibility is an illusion. For many people, materialism was and is a profound threat to their conception of themselves, society, and their eternal hopes.

Examining Other Minds. In severing the mind from the world and from the body, Descartes made the existence of other minds problematical. In the Cartesian view, mind is private consciousness. But how do I know if other beings have minds? Descartes answered that I know within myself that I think, and that I express my thoughts in language. Therefore, any creature possessing language also possesses a thinking soul. Since only humans have language, only humans have souls.

The problem of other minds did not become important until after the acceptance of evolution in the nineteenth century. Evolution suggested that contrary to Descartes, animals have minds, albeit simpler ones than ours. Modern controversies over other minds were foreshadowed in *L'Homme machine*, when La Mettrie tackled the problem of other minds from his materialist perspective. He proposed teaching language to apes, as if they were deaf children. If apes can learn language, Descartes would be refuted and the existence of the soul thrown in doubt. In the twentieth century, when Noam Chomsky revived Descartes's thesis that language is a species-specific human ability, some psychologists put La Mettrie's hypothesis to the test. In reaching a Cartesian conclusion, the computer scientist Alan Turing (1912–1954) said we would know computers were intelligent when they used language as well as humans do.

Human Nature, Morality, and Society

The following describes philosophical developments in the seventeenth and eighteenth centuries.

The Enlightenment Project. In the wake of scientific revolution, social thinkers of the eighteenth-century Enlightenment—the philosophes—began to rethink morals and government along scientific lines. Especially in France, where the most radical ideas abounded, they rejected tradition and religion. The key question was that of moral authority: Why should I do what society tells me to do? In the past, tradition and religion were the sources of moral authority. However, their claims were predicted on the assumption that goodness was a primary, objective property of actions and events. When goodness became thought of as a secondary property, the authority of tradition and religion became suspect. The philosophes turned to science as a superior fount of moral authority. Descartes and his successors subjected every common belief about the mind and the world to conscious, rational scrutiny, and the philosophes did the same for every received belief about morality and society. Again, the key to these new inquiries was human nature: Are people inherently good or evil? Given our nature, what is the just society? Such questions made the human sciences, especially psychology, socially important. It became imperative to settle scientifically the nature of human nature, and perhaps, to replace traditional religious means of social control with scientific ones. As psychological inquiry into the nature of the mind issued in a skeptical crisis, psychological inquiry into human social nature issued in a moral crisis.

Examining Human Nature. Modern inquiry into humans as social creatures began with the English thinker Thomas Hobbes (1583–1679). Hobbes was a devotee of the new mechanical-mathematical philosophy and functionally an atheist. He asked a question central to psychology: What would people be like as animals, living without society or culture? He thought he had an empirically confirmed answer. Having survived the horrors of the English Civil War, in which the governmental institutions ceased to function, Hobbes thought that without government there would be "war of every one against every one," making human lives "solitary, nasty, brutish, and short." Hobbes depicted human nature as violently dangerous, needing to be checked by strong, even authoritarian, governments. More disturbingly, Hobbes suggested that moral authority is a chimera; the only reality is force. Hobbes's unpleasant analysis of human motives, human society, and the illusion of morality has haunted social thought ever since. And it rests on psychological conclusions about human nature.

Numerous responses to Hobbes's challenge arose, each predicated upon a different understanding of human nature. For the history of psychology in America, the most important response came from the Scottish commonsense philosophers. They observed that human life is orderly even when unregulated by law, suggesting that human beings were, as Aristotle had taught, inherently social creatures, designed (for the Scots, by God) to live peaceably together. Scottish realism shaped their social philosophy. They said we have a *moral sense* through which we intuitively see that some actions are good and others evil. The Scottish system of psychology was widely taught in American colleges through the 1870s as part of religious character building. When experimental, physiologically oriented German psychology was brought to America, it found the "old psychology" already in place, resisting the idea that psychology become a natural science. Although the "new psychology" triumphed, the effects of the old linger in American psychologists' devotion to practical, applied psychology.

The Enlightenment project took a different, less moderate, turn in France. Lockean empiricism came to France carrying the imprimatur of Voltaire. Around the time of the French Revolution, a group of thinkers called the Ideologues (followers of the way of ideas), pushed empiricism to the limit, arguing that not only is the mind void of ideas at birth, it is equally void of faculties. Allied to materialism, French empiricism offered a vision of humanity that made some philosophes heady with possibilities. If there is no human nature, if human beings are mere clay to be shaped by society, then as John Watson and B. F. Skinner said later, we can make human beings to order. We are neither good nor evil by nature, but are made good or evil by society. Tradition and religion have made people ignorant and therefore bad, but rightly trained and educated, people can be made perfectly virtuous. This vision has inspired some and horrified others, and whether it is correct depends upon psychology.

The Counter-Enlightenment. Those who found the philosophes' vision horrifying saw their fears coming true as the French Revolution descended from veneration of reason to the Reign of Terror. A reaction against the Enlightenment arose, making important new claims about human nature and human life. The roots of Counter-Enlightenment reach back to the scientific revolution. A contemporary of Descartes, Blaise Pascal (1623–1662), was a mathematician and physicist who came to detest Cartesian reason. A religious man, he was filled with dread by the meaningless universe depicted by science. Reason alone, he concluded, was an insufficient guide to life, writing, "The heart has its reasons that reason does not understand." Pascal raised an important and enduring psychological and moral question: What role should emotion play in leading a good life? From the time of the Stoics through the Enlightenment, the party of reason urged that emotion should be ignored, suppressed, even expunged, because reason offered the best path to truth. For Pascal and the Counter-Enlightenment Romantics, reason had come to a dead end, offering a view of the universe empty of meaning, and a view of society empty of moral authority. They turned to emotion and other nonrational aspects of human nature to make up reason's shortcomings.

Romantic ideas cropped up in various places. Hume wrote that "reason is and ought only to be the slave of the passions." Passion gives us goals, reason calculates how to achieve them. The concept of causality has irrational roots in the human feeling that effects *must* follow upon causes. The Scots' moral sense was an intuitive, nonrational perception of right and wrong. Kant's transcendental ego lay beyond rational knowing, and later idealists said it posited the world into existence by a romantic act of will. The first widely influential Romantic was Jean-Jacques Rousseau (1712–1778). Hobbes's opposite, he said that humans were naturally virtuous and peaceable noble savages, being made wicked by society. The impulses of the heart, he said, were always right. Against the Enlightenment, he argued that science had made people worse, not better, off. People should flee the Enlightenment's breeding ground, the city, for the countryside, to dwell with unsophisticated country folk.

The historical-cultural tradition was also linked to the Counter-Enlightenment. Against Descartes, Johann Herder wrote, "I feel! I am!" His motto that we live in a world we create led to a more respectful attitude to culture and history than that of the philosophes. They famously promoted tolerance for cultural differences, because they saw them as irrational. But precisely because they saw them as irrational, they did not respect them. According to the Marquis de Condorcet, "The time will come when the sun will shine only on free men who have no master but their reason." As the claims of reason are universal, there is only one rational way of life, to be discovered and maintained by science. Against this, Herder asserted that humans are not fully human unless they participate in a living, developing, culture of their own in which they find meaning and inspiration. To abolish tradition (culture) was to abolish humanity.

By 1789, the year of the French Revolution, psychology was well established as a philosophical, if not yet scientific, discipline. It had also become clear that psychology—the science of human nature—would be critical to all future discussions of human values and human life.

[*Many of the people mentioned in this entry are the subjects of biographies.*]

Bibliography

Burtt, E. A. (1954). *The metaphysical foundations of modern science.* Garden City, NY: Doubleday. Although dated in historical detail, Burtt vividly captured the depth of the change between the ancient and modern worldviews.

Butterfield, H. (1965). *The origins of modern science 1300–1800.* New York: Free Press. A standard history of the scientific revolution.

Dennett, D. D. (1991). *Consciousness explained.* Boston: Little, Brown. Coined term *Cartesian theater*; tried to break grip of Cartesianism on modern psychology.

Farrell, J. (1996). *Freud's paranoid quest: Psychoanalysis and modern suspicion.* New York: New York University Press. Discusses the paranoid tendency in modern philosophy, seeing psychoanalysis as its final dead end.

Gaukroger, G. (1995). *Descartes: An intellectual biography.* Oxford, England: Clarendon Press. Fully rounded treatment of Descartes, not only as philosopher, but as scientist and man of religion.

Hampson, N. (1982). *The Enlightenment: An evaluation.* Harmondsworth, England: Penguin. Lively history of the Enlightenment and the ideas that shaped it.

Leahey, T. H. (2000). *A history of psychology: Main currents in psychological thought* (5th ed.) Upper Saddle River, NJ: Prentice Hall. Comprehensive text covering psychology from Greek to modern times.

Manent, P. (1998). *The city of man.* Princeton, NJ: Princeton University Press. Broad exploration of the social and political consequences of modern philosophical-psychological thought.

Outram, D. (1995). *The Enlightenment.* Cambridge, England: Cambridge University Press. Brief but historiographically thorough treatment of the Enlightenment.

Rorty, R. (1979). *Philosophy and the mirror of nature.* Princeton, NJ: Princeton University Press. Influential and ground-breaking work on the influence of the way of ideas on philosophy and psychology.

Searle, J. (1994). *The rediscovery of the mind.* Los Angeles: University of California Press. A useful counterpoint to Dennett; explores why science fears subjectivity.

Smith, A. M. (1990). Knowing things inside out: The Scientific Revolution from a medieval perspective. *American Historical Review,* 95, 726–744.

Smith, R. (1997). *The Norton history of the human sciences.* New York: Norton. Broad history of the human sciences from the sixteenth century on, with an emphasis on psychology.

Taylor, C. (1989). *The sources of the self: The making of modern identity.* Cambridge, MA: Harvard University Press. Philosophical exploration of modern concepts of the self.

Thomas H. Leahey

Nineteenth Century Through Freud

Psychology became a science in the nineteenth century. The roots of this new science were many. Philosophers provided psychology's conceptual framework; physiologists provided knowledge of the nervous system and experimental methods; and social reformers and psychiatrists provided motives for using science to improve the human condition. This article will describe the movements, ideas, and discoveries leading to and shaping scientific psychology, concentrating on developments in the United States, the home of twentieth century psychology.

Central Controversies

The new field of psychology was shaped by disputes over its definition and scientific nature.

Subject Matter. What does psychology study? The Cartesian paradigm gave one answer: Psychology is the study of consciousness, and the first psychologists defined psychology as the *science* of consciousness. They claimed a fixed subject matter, consciousness, and a unique method, introspection, for examining it. However, no science of human nature could completely avoid studying what people do. In Germany, Immanuel Kant proposed a science of behavior called *anthropology,* and in Britain, John Stuart Mill proposed a similar science called *ethology.* As the human sciences sorted themselves out in the nineteenth and twentieth centuries, psychology gradually extended its scope to include everything about human beings as individuals, adding the studies of individual behavior and individual differences to the study of consciousness. The other human sciences came to focus on human society (sociology), culture (anthropology), and history.

A Science and Its Methods. Interacting with considerations concerning psychology's subject matter was psychology's status as a science. Could psychology, especially defined as the study of consciousness, be a science at all? If so, what sort of science should it be and what methods should it use? These questions were debated throughout the nineteenth century. Some thinkers, especially the post-Kantian German idealists and the founder of positivism, Auguste Comte (1798–1857), expressed serious reservations about whether there could be a science of mind and consciousness at all.

Idealists doubted that conscious experience, the *empirical ego,* could be quantitatively measured. Experience might be qualitatively described, but without numerical measurement in more than one dimension, there could be no mental equivalent of Newton's mathematical laws, and thus no science of the mind. More important was the impossibility of studying the self, the transcendental ego. Because the self *had* experiences, the idealists held, it could not become an object *of* experience. Thus, the higher mental processes could not be observed. A psychology from which the study of thought, human's greatest possession, was excluded, would not deserve the name of science.

Comte proposed a hierarchy of sciences from which psychology was pointedly excluded. The most basic science was physics, upon which was founded chemistry, upon which was founded biology, upon which was founded the most recent and ultimate science, sociology. The soul *(psuche)* did not exist, Comte held, so there could be no science *(logos)* of it. He hoped that phrenology, a biological science of the brain, would provide the knowledge of human nature needed by sociologists. Comte's ideas were later refined by the logical positivists, whose philosophy of science provided arguments for redefining psychology as the science of publicly observable behavior.

In Great Britain, empiricist philosophers developed an alternative conception of the mind friendlier to its scientific treatment. Most significant for psychology was Mill (1806–1873), who answered Kant and Comte directly. Surely, he argued, we can observe consciousness, behavior, and some aspects of thought with varying degrees of rigor, and build up a discipline of the mind. Like meteorology, such a discipline might never achieve the precision of physics, but it would be worthy of the name of science and be practically useful. Mill's pragmatic approach to defining science and psychology continued in his friend and successor Alexander Bain (1818–1903), and through him, in early American psychology. Prior to the Civil War, however, American psychology was virtually synonymous with the morally oriented psychology of the eighteenth-century Scots.

A third, often vocally dissident, tradition arose in Germany, drawing inspiration from Giambattista Vico and Johann Herder. Idealists and empiricists differed over to what degree psychology could be a science, but they agreed that if psychology was going to be a science, it should aspire to discover the laws governing mind and behavior. The model for psychology (and the other human sciences) was physics. As Mill put it, "The backward state of the moral sciences can only be remedied by applying to them the methods of physical science, duly extended and generalized." Mill's scheme was put into action by the first psychology laboratories. Against Mill's idea (shared by the positivists) that all sciences should be modeled on physics, the historian Wilhelm Dilthey (1833–1911) said that there was not one kind of science, but two: *Naturwissenschft* ("natural science") for whom the model was physics, aiming at laws, prediction, and control; and *Geisteswissenschaft* (literally, "spiritual science," usually translated as "human science," a term used here to include all sciences that study human beings by whatever method) was modeled after history. Historians typically seek no universal laws, but attempt to explain particular chains of unique events by trying empathetically and sympathetically to enter into a past culture and its people, aiming not at prediction and control, but at what Dilthey called *Verstehen* ("understanding").

The concerns of Vico, Herder, and Dilthey are connected with one the most profound and difficult issues facing the scientific explanation of human mind and behavior. Philosopher Georg Friedrich Wilhelm Hegel (1770–1831) first stated the issue in its modern form: Natural science deals with the causes of events, but human action involves reasons and motives that are not physical causes. Suppose a woman shoots her husband one night. The killing is murder if she intended to kill him for an inheritance. However, it may have been a horrible accident: she may have thought that she was shooting an intruder. From the standpoint of natural science, the cause of the event is the same, a bullet entering a brain, but to understand what happened in human terms—and thus to decide between murder and accident—we must look into the wife's mind as she pulled the trigger. Motives and reasons are related to human moral (social) life, not to our physical lives, and therefore it was (and is) unclear how they should be treated by natural science.

Only in Germany were challenges to psychology as a natural science proposed, and psychologists ultimately rejected them. Elsewhere, psychologists followed the Newtonian path with little debate. Nevertheless, although Dilthey's has been a minority perspective, it has offered important critiques of mainstream natural science psychology. In the twentieth century, the hermeneutic movement has viewed psychology more like literary criticism than science, and the followers of Ludwig Wittgenstein (1889–1951) have wrestled with the place of reasons, motives, and social contexts in human behavior.

Empiricism and Idealism. In addition to quarreling over psychology's methods and aspirations, idealists and empiricists waged a battle over the nature of mind and reality. Empiricists subordinated the subjective to the objective, and idealists subordinated the objective to the subjective. Although this battle was over metaphysics, it nevertheless shaped the early definition and development of psychology. (This statement is a serious but unavoidable overgeneralization for a short article. There were empiricists, such as William James in his radical empiricism and some later positivists, who agreed with the idealists that the only knowable reality was the world of ideas. The key distinction here is the split between empiricists who viewed the mind as relatively passive and idealists who saw it as active.) Both groups accepted the general picture of the Cartesian theater, agreeing that consciousness is a screen of ideas, but disagreed about what lay beyond and underneath consciousness.

Empiricists identified mind with consciousness and depicted consciousness as a surface onto which ideas were directly projected by sensory processes in the brain. In this view, consciousness was a mirror of nature, the image on the mind's view screen directly reflecting the reality outside the person. Ideas containing more than one distinct sensation were thought of as compounds made up of many atomic sensory units bound together on the screen of consciousness by association, just as distinct objects in space are bound together by gravity. This picture of the mind was developed most fully by British philosophers from Locke to Mill, but also influenced French and German psychology, especially after the rise of positivism.

In empiricists' hands, psychology, defined as the science of consciousness, became a kind of mental chemistry. Its job was to identify the basic elements of conscious experience (as the periodic table lists the basic physical elements) and to describe the laws that regulate their combination (as chemistry describes the laws regulating how atoms combine to form molecules). To this introspective task was added the goal of linking sensory experience and association formation to underlying physiological processes. This kind of psychology was a tendency in all early psychology laboratories, but was most pronounced in English and American ones. Its purest expression was in Edward Bradford Titchener's (1867–1927) structural psychology.

Idealists followed Kant in refusing to identify mind with consciousness. Consciousness (the relatively trivial empirical ego) was a surface, but under this surface was the transcendental ego, the self. Moreover, consciousness was not a mirror of the world outside. The transcendental ego imposed necessary and universal categories of understanding on perceptions, constructing reality as we know it. Some idealists went further, saying the self posited the outside world into existence. Empiricists subordinated the subjective world of consciousness to the objective world it reflected, and the self disappeared. Idealists subordinated the objective world to the self, and physical reality disappeared. Unsurprisingly, idealism linked up with Romanticism. Romantic emphasis on feeling and creativity sat ill with empiricism's passive, mirror mind, but fit well with idealism's profound and powerful self that posited the world by its own will.

The philosophy of idealism had important implications for psychology as the study of consciousness. The most important concerned the scope of scientific psychology and the existence and nature of will. By setting the transcendental ego outside the possibility of experience, it implied that thought and other higher mental processes perforce eluded scientific study. The German founder of psychology, Wilhelm Wundt (1832–1920), originally held that introspection and physiology could study and explain thought as well as consciousness, giving his early writings more resonance with empiricism than his later ones, in which he accepted idealist strictures on the experimental study of thought. In these, Wundt made common cause with the Vico–Herder–Dilthey thesis in order to create a complete science of mind. He divided psychology into two parts. One, *physiological psychology*, was the experimental study of consciousness, linked increasingly weakly to the study of the nervous system. The other, *Völkerpsychologie* (literally, "folk psychology"; however, this and all other translations are misleading), was the nonexperimental study of thought and most other higher mental processes through their expression in language, myth, and culture.

Idealists and Romantics exalted the human will. Wundt reflected the idealist spirit, calling his psychology "voluntaristic." James so believed in will that he left psychology to develop his own form of idealism and his vision of a morally strenuous life. Nevertheless, idealism soon vanished from psychology. Outside Germany, empiricism, positivism, and materialism sharply limited its influence, and psychology proceeded as a comprehensive science on the model of physics. In Germany, similar ideas triumphed among Wundt's rivals, who emphasized experimentation and a thoroughgoing naturalism. His *Völkerpsychologie* went largely unread, and he was not invited to the first meeting of the German Society for Experimental Psychology in 1904. Still, idealist influences persist, for example, mildly in the cognitive psychology of perception and memory, and radically in the movements of contextualism and constructivism. Cognitive psychologists do not assert that the mind posits the world, but do say that the world as we experience and remember it is shaped by an active mind. Contextualists and constructivists deride the idea of objective truth (that mind can mirror nature), and insist that all knowledge is socially constructed.

Mind or Matter? In severing the mind from the world, René Descartes severed the mind from its body. As a consequence, the role and even existence of mind became problematical. How are mind and body related? Do minds exist? Are there other minds?

How Are Mind and Body Related? The first question asked was how mind and body could interact. Descartes assumed they did: the body provided the soul with a window on the world, and the soul exercised control of the body. However, he did not satisfactorily explain *how* they interacted. During the nineteenth century, most psychologists adopted Leibniz's psychophysical parallelism. Although this position conveniently gave psychologists their own realm, consciousness, to study, it left nagging problems, such as why mind and body seem to interact, and the value of studying an impotent mind. By the end of the century psychologists began to replace the seemingly pointless introspective study of an impotent mind with the more useful study of behavior.

Do Minds Exist? One apparent solution to the problem of mind-brain interaction was materialism, denying that minds exist. As the century unfolded, scientific advances made dualism less, and materialism more, plausible. The challenge of materialism was most acute for psychologists in the empiricist camp. Believing that mind was more fundamental than matter, idealists saw materialism as a pernicious error to be defeated, but for the scientific prospects of psychology, idealism had the drawback of setting the transcendental ego outside investigation. Empiricism had a different drawback. Empiricist psychology identified mind with consciousness, which had the virtue of making psychology a natural science. However, because it was a surface floating over the brain, not the self, consciousness might simply be a brain process, and psychology might someday vanish into physiology. Idealism suggested that psychology was not a science, whereas empiricism and materialism suggested that it was a temporary one.

The specter of materialism haunted psychology throughout the century. When Gall declared that the brain is the organ of the mind, the way the stomach is the organ of digestion, he and his followers were denounced as dangerous materialists. In the later nineteenth century, when scientific psychologists began to link consciousness and brain, they, too, were suspect in the eyes of many. In the United States, for example, the "old psychologists" (followers of the Scots) feared and denounced the "new psychologists" (the German-inspired experimental physiological psychologists) for neglecting the care of the soul, which for them was the proper mission of psychology.

Controversies over Darwinian evolution were linked to materialism. Descent of humans from animals suggested that we, too, are soulless machines. Darwin's bulldog, Thomas H. Huxley (1825–1895) famously (or notoriously) declared that consciousness is a useless by-product of the brain's activity. James rejected this automaton theory in his *Principles of Psychology* (New York, 1890), arguing that consciousness's adaptive function was choice. Ultimately, however, he abandoned psychology for philosophy, in part, because he could not reconcile his faith in free will with his conviction, expressed in *Principles*, that as a science, psychology must be "cerebralist," committed to tightly linking mind and brain. James later became heavily involved in psychical research, the paradoxical endeavor to use scientific means (empirical research) to prove a religious point: the existence of the soul.

Much of the seeming threat of materialism stemmed from the reigning conception of machines. If one accepts the Cartesian idea that animals are machines, and then concludes with Darwin that we are but animals, one seems forced to conclude that we are machines having no control over our behavior. Purpose (flexibly pursuing a goal when faced with obstacles) seemed, like David Hume's vanishing self, to be an illusion in need of explanation. This viewpoint was held by most behaviorists in the twentieth century.

However, the computer has destroyed Descartes's image of machines as clockwork mechanisms. A chess-playing computer program has a purpose (winning) and generates possible moves from among which it chooses the most promising. Seeing humans as machines—as cognitive science does today—is not inconsistent with seeing them as having goals and exercising choice. However, the computer model of the mind has not solved the problem of conscious experience. It remains unclear how matter generates consciousness. More radically some ask, as James did in 1905, "Does consciousness exist?"

Are There Other Minds Than Mine? In severing the mind from the world and from the body, Descartes made the existence of other minds problematical. In the Cartesian view, mind is private consciousness. But how do I know if other beings have minds? Descartes would answer: I know within myself that I think and that I express my thoughts in language. Therefore, any creature possessing language also possesses a thinking soul. Because only humans have language, only humans have souls.

In the nineteenth century, evolution erased Descartes's bright line between man and animal. Animal psychologists, led by George John Romanes (1848–1894), Conwy Lloyd Morgan (1852–1936) and Darwin himself, began looking for mind in animals, creating the field of comparative psychology. They soon had trouble reconciling what they found with Cartesian mechanism. Animals do not react to stimuli with unchangeable reflexes, but can learn new adaptive behaviors to attain their goals. The first comparative psychologists believed that animals as well as humans have consciousness (mind) and are therefore not machines. Some important early twentieth-century psychologists, such as Edward C. Tolman (1886–1959) agreed, although they referred vaguely to purposes and cognitions rather than to mind or consciousness. Nevertheless, most psychologists followed Edward L. Thorndike (1874–1949) and Clark L. Hull (1884–1952), who asserted that animals (and humans) are machines. They proposed stimulus-response reflex theories of behavior that explained purpose away.

Innovations

Innovations of the nineteenth century transformed philosophical psychology into scientific psychology.

Neuroscience. From ancient times thinkers had proposed speculative theories of how mental processes were linked to the brain and nervous system. However, not until the nineteenth century did physiology, including neurophysiology, make real progress. By the time scientific psychology began, a general, if limited, picture of neural and brain processes had emerged from two parallel tracks of research. One track was driven by disputes about whether mental functions were localized in different parts of the cerebral hemispheres, beginning with the work of Franz Joseph Gall (1758–1828). Although often reviled as a charlatan, Gall is now widely regarded as the first neuroscientist, possessing a sound orientation, fatally flawed by a mistaken method. Gall proposed that the brain, including the cerebral hemispheres, was a collection of distinct biological organs, each housing a different active mental ability such as language, or behavioral tendency such as lust.

Gall's system, which he never named, was both fresh and forward looking. Earlier reasoning about brain and mind had imposed philosophical theories on conjectures about the brain. Gall discarded philosophy for the direct examination of the brain. Even his critics conceded that Gall was a brilliant anatomist of both human and animal brains. Gall was the first behavioral psychologist, inspecting brain and behavior instead of introspecting consciousness. His biological orientation led him to look at mental faculties as adaptive brain functions, anticipating post-Darwinian psychology. Unlike philosophers, particularly the idealists who believed the self was identical in everyone, Gall studied individual differences, a major pursuit of modern psychology.

However, Gall's erroneous method and the pseudoscience of phrenology that his followers built around it tainted his thesis of localization. Lacking modern methods for studying the brains of living organisms, Gall tried to correlate differences in peoples' mental abilities with the sizes of different areas of the brain. He thought that large brain areas would create hills on peoples' skulls and small areas would leave valleys. Thus, he studied murderers and musicians, for example, looking for the cranial hills that housed murder and tune. Beginning with J. C. Spurzheim (1776–1832), phrenologists turned Gall's tentative science of brain and mind into the first popular psychology. They speculatively finished Gall's map, teaching their devotees how to know themselves and others by reading the bumps on their heads. Phrenology was especially popular in the United States, where its concerns for individual differences and use of psychology in the service of business and social reform foreshadowed the course of German psychology in pragmatic America. [*See* Phrenology.]

The manifest silliness of phrenology provoked rejection of the idea of localization of function by establishment thinkers. Alexander Bain, for example, systematically examined the claims of phrenologists and argued that associationism could account for the same facts without the hypothesis of separate cerebral organs. The prestigious French scientist Pierre Flourens (1794–1867) attacked the idea of localization of brain function. On the basis of rather crude experiments, he advanced the thesis of equipotentiality, arguing that the cerebral hemispheres act as a mass, having only one function, thought, or intelligence. Phrenology was pushed to the dim margins of scientific respectability, and the idea of localization of cerebral function was temporarily suppressed.

The other track in neuroscience concerned the nervous system. Luigi Galvani (1737–1798) demonstrated that nerves conduct impulses by electricity rather than by "animal spirits" as earlier believed. François Magendie (1783–1855) experimentally demonstrated that nerves transmit impulses only in a single direction: afferent (sensory) nerves carry impulses to the spinal cord and brain, and efferent (motor) nerves carry impulses from the brain and spinal cord to the muscles. British physician Charles Bell (1774–1842) may have independently proposed this hypothesis. Over the course of the century many scientists contributed to understanding the nervous system at the level of the cell, or individual neuron, and to formulating the concept of the synapse, the small gap across which neurons communicate.

Meanwhile, the thesis of localization of function gradually regained respectability. An important discovery was made in 1861 by the clinical neurophysiologist Pierre Paul Broca (1824–1880), who was able to show a connection between damage to a specific area of the left cortex (now called Broca's area) and loss of a specific mental ability, language. In 1870, Gustav Fritsch (1838–1927) and Eduard Hitzig (1838–1907) experimentally demonstrated localization in a dog's brain, and a "new phrenology" was born. However, the localized functions revealed by their experiments were not those of Gall. Instead of active brain organs such as theft, Fritsch and Hitzig discovered centers that controlled specific movements of the dog's limbs.

The two tracks merged into a general picture of the brain and nervous system influentially summarized in Sir David Ferrier's (1843–1928) *The Functions of the Brain* (London, 1876). Afferent neurons carry sensory information to the brain, whose specialized sensory areas represent the world. Neurons in the so-called association cortex connect the sensory centers to motor centers, which send out efferent signals controlling responses to stimuli. This conception of brain and nervous system was tailor-made for integration with associationism. As the brain was a reflex device linking stimulus and response, the mind was an associative device linking sensations together and linking sensations with actions. This integration was offered by many European writers, in Britain most notably by Alexander Bain. Psychology seemed to have a sound material basis on which to erect a natural science.

Ultimately, the reflex theory of the brain proved too simple. For example, it knew nothing of the rich neurochemistry by which the brain operates. More importantly for early psychology, it rejected Gall's notion that the brain was a collection of organs actively causing behavior, accepting, instead, the Cartesian understanding of machines as simple push-pull devices. The reflex theory saw the brain as like an old-fashioned telephone switchboard, passively connecting incoming stimulus with outgoing response. The causes of behavior lay in the environment containing the stimuli to which organisms react, not in the brain or its mind. The reflex theory of the brain added to the specter of materialism by seeming to make free will impossible.

The reflex theory, often allied to empiricism and associationism, constrained psychological theory for a century. An example is James's famous theory of emotion, first proposed in the 1880s, and adumbrated and defended in *Principles*. James said that the origins of emotion lie not in the brain, but in behavior: We do not run from a threat because we feel afraid, we are afraid because we find ourselves running from it. Through most of the twentieth century, psychologists proposed stimulus-response theories of behavior to match their conception of the brain. Not until the computer metaphor replaced the switchboard metaphor in the 1970s did the stimulus-response reflex model die.

Methods. Following the scientific revolution, being a natural scientist meant quantitatively measuring one's subject matter, and ideally, performing experiments. In the nineteenth century, experimental and psychometric methods came into existence.

The first experimental technique to appear was mental chronometry, measuring the speed of mental processes. On the brain side, the premier physiologist of the nineteenth century (with whom Wundt studied), Hermann von Helmholtz (1821–1894), measured the speed of neural transmission. On the mental side, astronomers developed mental chronometry to solve a disturbing problem. Before photography, astronomers mapped the stars by noting the exact time (registered by the ticks of a special clock) at which a star crossed their telescope's reticle. Unfortunately, two astronomers making the same observation at the same time often disagreed about the moment of transit, throwing doubt on the accuracy of star maps. The German astronomer Friedrich Bessel (1784–1846) studied these differences in judgment time, hoping to reconcile different astronomers' observations by means of "personal equations" comparing them. The Dutch physiologist F. C. Donders (1818–1889) then developed a "subtractive method" for measuring inner mental processes. A task such as responding differently to two lights could be analyzed as a compound of a simple reaction, the response to the light, and a preceding judgment, or discrimination, of which light had occurred. The judgment time could then be measured indirectly by subtracting the time for a simple response to one light from the (longer) time taken to respond to two. Chronoscopes, special clocks for finely measuring reaction times, were mainstays of early laboratories, and mental chronometry is still widely used in cognitive psychology.

Some historians date the inception of experimental psychology to 1860, when Gustav Theodor Fechner (1801–1887) published *Elements of Psychophysics*. Fechner was a somewhat eccentric physicist at Leipzig (where Wundt founded the first laboratory) who became concerned with mathematically demonstrating the correspondence between mind and body. He developed sophisticated methods for precisely measuring the conscious sensation resulting from a stimulus of known value. For example, subjects might discriminate among varying weights, and these judgments could then be mapped onto the objective differences in the values of the weights. Out of this work came something Kant said was impossible, the first psychological law, Fechner's law, that the strength of a sensation (S) is a logarithmic function of the strength of the stimulus (R, for *Reiz*), multiplied by a constant: $S = k \log R$.

Psychophysical scaling, like mental chronometry, was a staple of the early laboratories and remains in use today, for example, in measuring pain. But it had a more general importance for the founding of psychology. Following Descartes, philosophers had introspected their minds, but never settled such seemingly straightforward questions as how many ideas consciousness held at a single time. Led by Wundt, scientific psychologists saw that the failure of philosophical or armchair introspection lay in its lack of methodical control. Psychophysics provided a model for making introspection scientific: expose subjects (originally called *observers* of consciousness) to known stimuli that could be systematically varied and collect from them simple reports on what they found in consciousness. Thus, one might present subjects with simple arrays of letters under varying conditions (e.g., different exposure times, different number or physical arrangements of letters), and ask them to report how many they could see. Unlike results from philosophers' armchairs, results from laboratory experiments were quantitative and reliable. Scientific psychology was underway.

The companion to experimentation was *psychometrics*, measuring differences in mental attributes by means of a mental test, a term coined in 1890 by American psychologist James McKeen Cattell (1860–1944). Various nineteenth-century psychologists developed techniques of mental testing, but the most important—certainly in the English-speaking world—was Sir Francis Galton (1822–1911), with whom Cattell studied after taking his degree with Wundt. A cousin of Darwin's, Galton was interested in the evolution of mental abilities, chiefly intelligence. He sought ways to measure intelligence and pioneered statistical methods for treating psychometric data. For example, he invented the correlation coefficient to determine if schoolchildren who do well in one subject do well in others, and he established an anthropometric laboratory for testing people on a wide variety of capacities. Although Galton pioneered mental testing, his own tests proved to be of little value, and were replaced by sounder ones, such as Alfred Binet's (1857–1911) test of intelligence.

Galton also pioneered the application of psychometrics to social issues. He believed that intelligence and other mental traits were highly heritable and that the intelligence of Britons was declining. To remedy the situation, Galton proposed schemes of eugenics, selectively breeding people for high intelligence, the way horses are selectively bred for speed. Although ignored at first, eugenics was later practiced (in ways Galton would have rejected) in the twentieth century by countries as diverse as Nazi Germany, socialist Sweden, and individualistic America, causing human misery and scientific and social disputes.

Mental testing changed psychology. It broadened the scope of psychology to include topics such as intelligence and personality that lay outside introspective and experimental reach. Mental testing also pushed psychology in applied directions, away from the pure research of the German laboratories. The field of clinical psychology began in 1896 with the establishment of a "psychological clinic" at the University of Pennsylvania by Wundt's student, Lightner Witmer (1867–1956). The clinic tested the mental abilities of children referred by the Philadelphia school system. Similarly, psychology of business commenced with Walter Dill Scott's (1869–1955) use of mental tests for employee selection. Mental testing also began a profound alteration of psychology's subject matter. Although they recorded behavior—a keypress, a verbal report—experimentalists were really interested in getting at subjective states of consciousness. Mental testing, however, was a more thoroughly objective affair. An intelligence quotient was not an introspective report of a private conscious fact, but was a summary record of success and failure on a test, a fact in its own right. Mental testing thus represented a step toward defining psychology as a science of behavior, the study of what people do, rather than what they experience.

Institutions. Social institutions important for the new scientific psychology changed or were created in the nineteenth century. Because psychology began as an academic discipline, it was shaped by institutions of higher education that varied significantly from country to country. Germany led the world in scientific research and postgraduate education. Before Bismarck created the second German Empire in 1871, the German-speaking world was a collection of petty princedoms. Because each prince wanted his own university, Germany had more of them than any other nation. Moreover, Germany created the modern secular, government-supported, research-oriented university. In the United States, by contrast, small colleges run by religious denominations dominated higher education. Scottish commonsense psychology was an integral part of the curriculum, taught to polish the souls of the students. Thus, when Wundt created scientific psychology in Germany, he meant it to be a pure science, and early German psychologists resisted making psychology into psychotechnics. In America, the old Scottish psychology briefly opposed the new German scientific psychology. Although it nominally lost the struggle, its businesslike attitude remained, and American psychology turned to applications ranging from giving tests to building, as one psychologist said after World War II, a "science of values."

If the research university was the dominant influence on nineteenth-century German psychology, business was the dominant influence on American psychology, reinforcing the practical orientation of the old psychology. In Germany, universities were centrally controlled by elite scientists and philosophers devoted to the pursuit of knowledge for its own sake. In the United States, colleges (and universities when they began) were diversely controlled by pragmatic business people devoted to the pursuit of practical knowledge, pushing American psychology to be more applied. Eventually, applied psychology sprang up everywhere, including Germany, and is now the main occupation of psychologists everywhere.

Psychology's practical direction worldwide was reinforced by changes in the nature of government. During the nineteenth century, governments broadened their responsibilities from keeping peace and waging war to tending the general welfare of their subjects and citizens. Particularly in the United States, political and business leaders looked to science for new means of social control. After the Civil War, the nation moved from being a collection of isolated rural communities of relatives and neighbors to an urbanized, industrial, politically emancipated population of mobile strangers. Many opinion leaders, especially in the Progressive movement, thinking that tradition and religion were no longer suitable guides to life or effective means of social control, looked to the human sciences, including psychology, for new ways to manage society and business. In this environment friendly to expertise, learned professions and organizations arose in the late nineteenth century, including the American Psychological Association (APA) (1892). In his 1899 APA President's address, John Dewey (1859–1952)—the great Progressive philosopher of the twentieth century—linked the birth of psychology to the social changes wrought by urban industrialization. As long as tradition was a sufficient guide to life, said Dewey, people had few conscious decisions to make, and a science of consciousness had little value. In a rapidly changing world, however, people have to make many new conscious decisions—where to live, what work to do, for whom to vote—and a science of consciousness came into existence.

Founding Psychologies

Scientific psychology had three foundings. The first was the psychology of consciousness established by Wilhelm Wundt (1832–1920). The second was the psychology of adaptation, begun by popular writer Herbert Spencer (1820–1903), but given greatest voice by William James (1842–1910). The third was psychoanalysis, launched by Sigmund Freud (1856–1939).

Psychology of Consciousness. The guiding ideas of the psychology of consciousness have already been described. It defined psychology in the Cartesian way as the experimental science of consciousness as such, and experimental research on consciousness had been underway since 1860. Wundt's paramount achievement was institutional, creating at Leipzig in 1879 the first institute able to grant doctoral degrees in psychology.

The psychology of consciousness was, however, short-lived. It was cramped; Wundt's attempt to broaden it with his *Völkerpsychologie* went nowhere. It was rent by schisms that seemed more characteristic of philosophy than science. Wundt's theories were challenged by the Gestalt psychologists, who rejected the idea that consciousness is composed of associated ideas, and by the related act psychology of Franz Brentano

(1838–1917), which focused on mental activity rather than conscious content. Its emphasis on pure research could not resist societies' desires that psychology be useful. It ran into grave questions it seemed unable to answer. At Würzburg, Wundt's former student Oswald Külpe (1862–1915), tried, against Wundt's protests, to study thinking with experimental introspection. His findings could not be replicated consistently, leading many psychologists to conclude that introspection was unscientific; they replaced the psychology of consciousness with the more useful psychology of behavior, discarding consciousness as an object of scientific study.

Psychology of Adaptation. The psychology of adaptation began in 1855 when Spencer gave the psychology of consciousness an evolutionary twist in his *Principles of Psychology* (London). Before evolution, philosophers and psychologists took mind for granted, being concerned with *how* it works. Evolution, however, posed new questions, the most important being *why* we have minds (consciousness) at all. "If the doctrine of evolution is true," Spencer wrote, "the inevitable implication is that Mind can be understood only by observing how mind is evolved." Not an original thinker, Spencer espoused the standard empiricist view of consciousness as a mirror, simply adding that being able to internally represent the world was adaptive.

James, too, rethought philosophy and psychology in the light of evolution. He was the most influential of the pragmatists, who, inspired by evolution, rejected the traditional philosophical quest for eternal Truth. Just as species change to adapt to new environmental challenges, our beliefs change with experience. There is no fixed Truth, only currently useful—adaptive—truths. James carried pragmatism and evolution into psychology. For him, consciousness is useful not primarily because it represents the world, but because it is a "fighter for ends," giving its bearer interests and the power to choose adaptive courses of action.

James himself remained a psychologist of consciousness. However, after James, consciousness gradually disappeared from psychology. Functionalism slowly turned into behaviorism, concerned with action rather than thought. The psychology of adaptation has proved itself adaptive, remaining the broad orientation of the vast majority of working psychologists.

Psychotherapy and Psychoanalysis. Although people tend to think of psychologists as psychotherapists, and psychoanalysis as the premier form of psychotherapy, psychoanalysis is only one form of psychotherapy, and both arose in psychiatry.

Background: Psychiatry and Neurology. Like psychology, psychiatry was born in the nineteenth century. Johann Christian Reil (1759–1813) coined the term in 1808, although the older term *alienist* remained widely used. Psychiatry entered the German university a little earlier than psychology, in 1865, through the efforts of Wilhelm Griesinger (1817–1868). In August 1887, two Dutch psychiatrists first used the word "psychotherapy."

Asylums for the insane gave birth to psychiatry. Asylums had been around since the Middle Ages, but only in the late 1790s did they try to cure rather than merely isolate the insane. The administrators of a few asylums began to practice "moral [mental] therapy," freeing inmates from their chains and instituting regimes of attentive care. In 1801, an influential textbook by Phillipe Pinel (1745–1826) made moral therapy the gold standard for asylum psychiatry. Problems less severe than madness were treated by neurologists. Neurologists supervised rest cures at spas and consulted with patients in private offices. By the end of the century, however, the two fields had become effectively merged under the rubric of *psychiatry*.

A great problem facing psychiatrists was seeing through bizarre symptoms to underlying illnesses. The first to succeed was Emil Kraepelin (1856–1926), a psychiatrist who became fascinated by psychology and undertook study in Wundt's laboratory. Thus trained as a scientist, he sifted through case histories looking for patterns of symptoms and outcomes. From his research came the first scientifically informed psychiatric diagnosis, *dementia praecox*, now known as schizophrenia.

Two theories about the cause of mental illness contested the field of psychiatry. One viewed mental illnesses as physical ailments. Madness was caused by troubles in the brain; lesser syndromes such as hysteria or neurasthenia, by troubles in the nervous system. Whether attempted cures were psychological, as in moral therapy (including talking to patients), or physical (e.g., electrotherapy, passing electrical currents through the body), psychiatrists and neurologists mostly agreed that they were treating biological disorders. The rival view said the causes of mental illness lay in the patient's psychological history and life circumstances. This "Romantic psychiatry" focused on patients' religious and moral lives and was the forerunner of psychoanalysis.

Psychoanalysis. After doing scientific research of lasting importance on the structure of neurons, Sigmund Freud (1856–1939) turned to consulting-office neurology in order to afford marriage. Although Freud, like the other founders, wanted psychology to be a science, in psychoanalysis he created something of a cult, complete with secrecy (Freud destroyed his early letters and notes), a rite of laying on of hands (training analysis), and a heroic myth of origin (Freud's self-analysis).

Freud was initially attracted to the idea of making psychology scientific by tying it closely to neuroscience and wrote a manuscript, "Project for a scientific psychology," which he later tried to suppress. For reasons shrouded in mystery and controversy, he abandoned his "psychology for neurologists" for what became psychoanalysis. He came to believe that his patients were not biologically ill, but suffered from deliberately forgotten (repressed) traumas experienced in early childhood. At first he said the traumas were sexual seductions by older children, nurses, and tutors, but later came to conclude that the traumas were fantasies of sex with the opposite-sex parent (the Oedipus complex). Psychoanalytic therapy involved retrieving these supposed repressed fantasies, often under great pressure from Freud. Freud's search for repressed fantasies and hidden meanings connects him with the paranoid trend in modern philosophy, according to which every belief is assumed false until proven true. According to psychoanalysis, underneath consciousness is not the self or the brain but a deceptive, seething cauldron of repressed furies, the unconscious. [*See* Psychology, *article on* Renaissance through the Enlightenment.]

Freud did not abandon biology completely. He espoused a form of Lamarckian evolution, holding that the Oedipus complex was an individual reenactment of the murder of the first human father by his sons, an event seared into humanity's collective unconscious. He also held that his stages of psychosexual development recapitulated human evolution. Most famously, Freud traced his patient's troubles to sexuality, for him the key human motive, and indisputably biological.

Freud gathered disciples about him, but important ones abandoned or were expelled from psychoanalysis. Typically, dissidents rejected what they saw as Freud's excessive emphasis on sexuality. Alfred Adler (1870–1937), for example, stressed feelings of inferiority and a compensating "will to power." The most important of Freud's dissident followers was Carl Gustav Jung (1875–1961). Before studying with Freud, Jung had established himself as an internationally known psychiatrist. Freud had worried that because most of his followers were Jewish, the influence of psychoanalysis might be ghettoized, and he anointed the Gentile Jung his "crown prince." However, Jung's thinking departed markedly from Freud's, being more sympathetic to, and influenced by, religious and moral concerns. To Jung, Freud was excessively materialistic, seeing only the darker side of human nature and oblivious to spiritual yearnings. Inevitably, Freud and Jung fell out. Jung was forced from the leadership of the psychoanalytic movement, and in their last letters, Freud and Jung traded diagnoses as insults.

Psychoanalysis shared important tensions with experimental psychology. The most important was viewing psychoanalysis as *Naturwissenschaft* or *Geisteswissenschaft*. Freud insisted that psychoanalysis be a natural science, but his practice was more like literary interpretation than scientific investigation. For example, in what he regarded as his masterwork, *The Interpretation of Dreams* (New York, 1900) Freud offered a theory of dream production rooted in his "Project." However, when interpreting dreams, Freud deployed literary methods depending on word play, allegory, and symbolism. Jung's rival analytic psychology adopted this interpretive approach to the mind, as Jung looked for universal patterns of symbolism across history and cultures. This hermeneutic (though not always Jungian) form of psychoanalysis is now the major force in psychoanalysis, literary criticism, and cultural studies. The same tension arose in Freud's attempt to build his science on conversations with patients. Psychotherapists know their clients as individuals, with names, life stories, and personal problems, whereas scientific psychologists know their subjects as impersonal specimens of *Homo sapiens*. Freud thought he could move from particular, unique experiences to scientific generalizations about human nature everywhere and every time. For example, having fabricated an early memory of sexually desiring his mother and fearing his father, Freud concluded it was a universal experience, the Oedipus complex. Instead of concluding that some children sometimes have these feelings, Freud's dedication to scientific universality led him to formulate a universal law from a single case. Today, many therapists reject Freud's scientific preposession, seeing therapy as constructing a narrative of the client's life that resolves the past and enables the future.

Psychoanalysis powerfully shaped the twentieth century and Freudian ideas became commonplace. The idea of psychiatry as a "talking cure" for psychiatric disorders helped lead to the creation of clinical psychology in the 1940s, although psychologists rarely practiced psychoanalysis, developing their own methods, such as Carl Rogers's client-centered psychotherapy. To a growing number of critics however, Freudian psychoanalysis should be regarded as a relic of nineteenth-century psychology and psychiatry.

Toward the Twentieth Century

World War I brought the nineteenth century, and nineteenth-century psychology, to an end. The unspeakable horrors of the war shattered nineteenth-century faith in the inevitability of progress. To many, the war was the Freudian unconscious made manifest. Germany especially experienced a deep crisis in politics, culture, and philosophy, and psychologists offered worldviews to replace those that had failed. For example, Gestalt psychology and its philosophical ally, phenomenology, proposed a new holistic analysis of consciousness meant to support old humanistic values. Everywhere during the war, psychology turned in applied directions, as psychologists worked on varied military projects. This trend was most powerful in the United States, where applied psychology was already valued. After the war, the numbers of American applied psychologists grew exponentially, creating powerful tensions between academic scientists and working professionals. In 1913, just before the war broke out, John B. Watson launched the movement of behaviorism, which would dominate twentieth-century American psychology. Increasingly, psychological ideas affected how people understood themselves, others, and their societies. By 1918, what had begun as an obscure science pursued by small bands of men and women was emerging as the foundation of a new, psychological, society.

[*See also* Philosophy, *articles on* Philosophy of Mind *and* Philosophy of Science; *and* Psychoanalysis, *article on* History of the Field. *Also, many of the people mentioned in this entry are the subjects of biographies.*]

Bibliography

Boring, E. G. (1929). *A history of experimental psychology.* New York: Appleton-Century-Crofts. Out of print but widely available; an enlarged edition was published in 1950. Erudite, tightly focused history emphasizing the nineteenth century, by a second-generation psychologist. Although now regarded as historically naïve, it is invaluable for its wealth of detail; contains extensive bibliographies.

Bringmann, W. G., Lück, H. E., Miller, R., & Early, C. E. (Eds.). (1997). *A pictorial history of psychology.* Chicago: Quintessence. Topically organized and lavishly illustrated history of scientific psychology. It should not be relied on as a comprehensive history, however, because the articles are uneven in coverage and quality.

Brozek, J. (Ed.). (1984). *Explorations in the history of psychology in the United States.* Lewisburg, PA: Bucknell University Press.

Buxton, C. (Ed.). (1986). *Points of view in the history of psychology.* San Diego, CA: Academic Press.

Ellenberger, H. F. (1970). *The discovery of the unconscious.* New York: Basic Books. Massive history of ideas leading to the founding of psychoanalysis.

Finger, S. (1994). *Origins of neuroscience.* New York: Oxford University Press. Topically organized illustrated history of neuroscience from its earliest days to the present.

Kucklick, B. (1977). *The rise of American philosophy: Cambridge, Massachusetts 1860–1930.* New Haven, CT: Yale University Press. Harvard was the center of American philosophy in the nineteenth and early twentieth centuries. This book chronicles Harvard philosophy in detail, treating its impact on psychology when psychology was part of Harvard's philosophy department.

Leahey, T. H. (2000). *A history of psychology: Main currents in psychological thought* (5th ed.). Upper Saddle River, NJ: Prentice Hall. General survey of the history of psychology from Greek times to 1980; includes extensive critical bibliographies.

Leahey, T. H., & Leahey, G. E. (1983). *Psychology's occult doubles.* Chicago: Nelson-Hall. Account of allegedly pseudoscientific movements such as phrenology that affected psychology's development.

Piñero, J. M. L. (1983). *Historical origins of the concept of neurosis.* Cambridge, England: Cambridge University Press.

Rieber, R. W. (Ed.). (1980). *Wilhelm Wundt and the making of a scientific psychology.* New York: Plenum Press.

Scruton, R. (1995). *Modern philosophy: An introduction and survey.* New York: Allen Lane/Penguin. Topically organized and readable, if somewhat opinionated, survey of philosophy since Descartes.

Shorter, E. (1997). *A history of psychiatry.* New York: Wiley. Well-written, up-to-date history of the field by a leading social historian. By refusing to see the development of psychoanalysis as the culmination of the history of psychiatry, Shorter places psychoanalysis in its proper place against the modern background of biological psychiatry.

Smith, R. (1997). *The Norton history of the human sciences.* New York: Norton. General survey of all the human sciences, but focusing on psychology, from c. 1600 to the present.

Soffer, R. N. (1978). *Ethics and society in England: The revolution in the social sciences, 1870–1914.* Berkeley: University of California Press.

Webster, R. (1995). *Why Freud was wrong.* New York: Basic Books. Excellent revisionist treatment of psychoanalysis carefully linking it to mistaken nineteenth-century ideas about mental illness.

Woodward, W. W., & Ash, M. G. (Eds.). (1982). *The problematic science: Psychology in nineteenth-century thought.* New York: Praeger.

Young, D. (1970). *Mind, brain, and adaptation in the nineteenth century.* Oxford, England Clarendon Press. Authoritative history of nineteenth-century neuroscience.

Thomas H. Leahey

Early Twentieth Century

In the early 1900s American psychology was still a modestly sized enterprise, but it was in a propitious position to advance, for it had a rich and diverse cache of intellectual ideas about mental life from which to draw that had been developed in the previous century. In addition, the young profession had ample room to locate in the ongoing expansion of colleges and universities, and could make contact with an engaging public interested in things "psychological." Psychology did prosper within this climate. By the end of World War II the science had secured an influential place in American society and had created a host of subspecialties applicable to a myriad of intellectual and social problems. Thus, in less than half a century psychology had expanded rapidly in terms of scientific work, scope of subject matter, and practical utility. However, while increasing in number of practitioners and domains, the science drastically reduced the eclectic intellectual perspectives and methods that had been present at the century's beginning. The intervening years, then, comprised first a flourishing followed by a diminuation of the scientific possibilities for explaining and examining the human psyche and actions.

The simultaneous growth in volume of work produced and the constriction of theories and methods is not explicable in terms of crucial discoveries or the creation of an optimum theory of the human mind. Rather, psychology's bid to become a *bona fide* science and, hence, a legitimate and reliable instrument for assessing and regulating human life, required that the discipline attain a certain consensus among its practitioners over what counts as valid knowledge. Perhaps more important, the strong identification with scientific utility demanded that the discipline develop research techniques which could be used efficiently as well as effectively to calibrate and evaluate psychological phenomena. Consequently psychologists strove to generate knowledge that was useful to the administration of life, both private and public. Any account of the viable theories, schools, and systems of early-twentieth-century psychology must attend to the numerous forces (both internal and external to the science) that fostered the maturation of only a few credible perspectives and methodologies.

The rise of a scientific, academic psychology, however, is not all of the story of psychology in America. A professional psychology also emerged outside of academic settings and eventually situated itself within the academy under the banner of clinical psychology. Further, psychology during the early years of the century became more than a professional occupation: among the middle class it came to be an exciting pastime and ultimately an important guide for personal life.

Ideas Galore

If psychology at the turn of the century were to be depicted in terms of intellectual leadership, then several individuals would be needed to represent this pluralistic science. it would be accurately represented via the diverse works of Edward B. Titchener, William James, and G. Stanley Hall.

Although all three psychologists shared a dedication to creating a scientific psychology, they differed significantly in what each meant by the word *scientific* and what the intellectual foundation of this "psychology" would be. British-born Edward B. Titchener (1867–1927) trained in Germany with Wilhelm Wundt, and while working at Cornell University modeled much of his conception of scientific psychology after chemistry. All mental events, according to Titchener, consisted of some combination of a finite number of basic sensation-elements. These elementary sensations are connected to form complex ideas and perceptions. Titchener's psychology made no room for ideas about volunteerism (either free will or apperception); rather, mental processes were nothing more than combinations of elemental sensations. The scientific task of the psychologist was to use rigorous methods of introspection to record and catalogue these basic sensations, which ultimately could be explained reductionistically—by discovering the physiology of sensations. Titchener's vision of psychological science was that of a pure science, one unconcerned with application or relevance to everyday life.

American-born William James (1842–1910) studied chemistry and medicine at Harvard University, where he remained as a professor for most of his career. For much of his life James was committed to a natural science model of psychology. His conception of science, as well as his understanding of psychological life, was founded on pragmatism, a distinctly American philosophical position claiming that beliefs were never certain but were deemed veridical if they produced successful action. Influenced by Darwinism as well, James held that beliefs evolve and that it is the function, not the content, of mental events that constitute the proper subject matter of psychology. According to James, consciousness and the will had evolved and were central components of mental life. His *Principles of Psychology* (1890) outlined a discipline based on these premises as well as on the claim that psychology should be practical, encompassing studies of the self, consciousness, will, emotions, attention, and automatic functions. His psychology, then, was volunteeristic and rejected mechanistic and reductionist models of the mind. Accordingly, James encouraged the use of various research methods that ranged from a phenomenological approach to introspection to experimental and comparative techniques.

G. Stanley Hall (1844–1924), also an American, received the first Ph.D. degree in psychology in America. He was committed to establishing a scientific psychology that was diverse in theory and method and that would effectively illuminate and guide human activities. Among Hall's efforts to foster this psychology was the founding of the *American Journal of Psychology* in 1887 and the American Psychological Association (APA) in 1892. His conception of human nature was informed largely by evolutionary theory and, in particular, the notion that individual development recapitulated racial evolution. For Hall, scientific psychology encompassed all features of mental life, from intelligence and emotions to morality and religion. He addressed these and other subjects in popular as well as scientific articles. His own work along with that of his students displayed the use of diverse methods of inquiry, including experimentation, tests, questionnaires, case studies, and history. This intellectual magnanimity resulted too in his appreciation of the work of Sigmund Freud (1856–1939): Hall invited and hosted Freud's only visit to America (1909).

These three psychologists merely intimate the pluralism of psychology at the beginning of the century. To their projects could be added John Dewey's (1859–1952) efforts to extend psychology to the engineering of a progressive education, James McKeen Cattell's

(1860–1944) work to place psychology among the natural sciences, Edward L. Thorndike's (1874–1949) dedication to the psychology of learning, and Hugo Münsterberg's (1863–1916) projects to explain consciousness without will and to apply psychological knowledge to business and the courtroom. These are but a few of the innovative psychologists who committed their careers to the "new psychology" in America.

This eclectic spirit of growth was not to last long, and with U.S. entrance into World War I psychologists had cause to reconsider and reorient their researches. However, the war alone is not responsible for the ensuing constriction in scientific activities: An atmosphere of intellectual pluralism initiated controversies over perspectives and interpretations of experiments, and therefore the discipline's maturation as a legitimate science required a certain consolidation of practices. After the war, American psychologists had a new understanding of the science, particularly its place in society. These researchers resumed their scientific investigations with a heightened and critical self-consciousness about their intellectual differences.

Psychology in Society

The two decades between 1890 and 1910 constituted a crucial time for the professional foundation of psychology. Americans were coming to recognize the value of science, notably its apparent utility in enhancing commercial productivity and health. Science, including psychology, ultimately was portrayed as a practical pursuit, and American psychologists adopted this utilitarian attitude. The reformism of the progressive era held that experts were a necessary component in rectifying social injustices and aiding less fortunate members of society gain a healthier status. In terms of the management of these individuals, many social problems were deemed in need of psychological expertise. World War I provided a compelling case for psychologists' involvement in social policy and a unique opportunity to demonstrate psychology's scientific efficacy.

In the first decade of the century, psychology had yet to devise sophisticated techniques that could be applied to social reform agendas, but psychologists both benefited from and contributed to a discourse about expertise that was to set the stage for later applications of psychology to human welfare. Psychologists rehearsed the thesis that people needed expert guidance. As Robert Yerkes (1876–1956) put it, "Millions of human beings—unfortunate but all unconscious of what they are missing—go through life blind to the psychological world" (1911, p. 13). Yerkes's observation that humans needed psychological guidance found its test site in the entrance of the United States into World War I. In fact, Yerkes, although trained as a comparative psychologist, was a leader in mobilizing psychologists to contribute to the war effort. Twelve committees of the American Psychological Association were established for these ends, and psychologists quickly developed a rating scale for selecting suitable candidates for officer training and an intelligence test for detecting those individuals who were mentally unfit for service in the army. The actual efficacy of these tests is debatable, as are psychologists' overall effects on the war effort. However, psychologists' war involvement elevated the status of the science in general and mental testing in particular. Historians now generally concur that while psychology did not contribute significantly to the war, the science benefited tremendously from psychologists' involvement.

After the war, psychologists eagerly extended their skills to the resolution of human problems: they brought newly honed scales and fresh if technical language to the worlds of business, education, law, and social welfare. Professional organizations, like the Psychological Corporation, were established in the 1920s to foster commercial uses of psychology. This expansion of psychological expertise was not limited to formal institutions, as psychologists also disseminated their skills and knowledge directly to the public via popular articles and books. These writings enlightened readers about psychological thinking just as it proffered notions of expertise. Psychology could explain the stock market crash of 1929, as well as marital discord, racial prejudice, and the adolescent's misbehavior. It was used to argue for certain immigration laws just as it was employed to guide parents in toilet training their children.

Psychology extended its new theories and findings to an eager populace. Psychologists' engagement in applied ventures as well as their popular writings in magazines and newspapers fueled America's fascination with psychological interpretations of everyday life. Ordinary domestic routines, individual idiosyncrasies, and major life passages as well as national politics and economic conditions were analyzed in psychological terms. Concepts such as *personality, self,* and *motivation* became key to these interpretations. So phenomenal was this interest in psychology that historians have referred to the preoccupation as a "national mania," a "cult of the self," and the beginning of the "culture of the therapeutic" (Morawski, 1982). Psychology thus became a dominant interpretive tool, and perhaps the greatest influence of the discipline was its nurturance of emotional life in America (Pfister & Schnog, 1997).

By the end of the 1920s, psychology had made a place for itself in the academy, in commerce, and in the minds of many middle-class Americans. These applied and popular psychologies still reflected the pluralist spirit of the beginning of the century. However, psychology as it was being developed within universities was constricting, not expanding, its analytic scope, scientific methods, and theory. The first three decades of the century saw the ascendancy of experimental methods of inquiry and a small assortment of theories, with one perspective—behaviorism—dominating.

In this welcoming cultural environment psychology flourished, grew, and eventually became deeply involved in the management of social welfare. The American Psychological Association was founded in 1892 with only 31 members and by 1929 had 1,000 members and associates; after this period an exponential growth in members began, reaching almost 20,000 in 1950 and 50,000 in 1980. In 1900 approximately 40 psychological laboratories had been established in universities and colleges; 25 years later there were over 115 such research sites. During this time psychologists' duties and demographics shifted notably. One change was occupational: whereas in 1916 76% of the APA membership was classified as being employed as professors and only 8% as applied psychologists, by 1938 the percentage of teachers had dropped to 50% and applied psychologists had risen to 28% of the membership. Throughout this time psychology remained a primarily White profession. In its early years, however, it outranked all other sciences in the number of women who attained Ph.D. degrees, although few gained access to academic opportunities. As a group, women were overrepresented in applied work.

Methods of Inquiry

The laboratories being constructed in the early 1900s were critical to the science's self-definition as well as its legitimacy as a field of intellectual inquiry. Predominant in the new laboratories were the techniques of what was later critically termed brass instrument psychology. These were the methods of experimental introspection where subjects are presented with standard, controlled situations (stimuli) and instructed to give readily quantifiable or classifiable responses. Developed in Germany by Wilhelm Wundt and brought to America by the students who trained with him, introspection set the climate of exacting, controlled, and replicable experiments, ideals that would endure in psychology after the method of introspection itself was abandoned.

Wundt's version of introspection was intended to uncover the elements of consciousness by observing and recording the dependence of sensory experiences on stimulation varying in intensity, temporal duration, and location. Given the fact that introspection required exacting and immediate (unreflected) responses, subjects were trained to serve as the object of investigation. In fact, psychologists typically served as subjects (called "observers") in each others' experiments.

Techniques of introspection were designed to study abstract mental events, ultimately to reveal basic sensation-elements and the laws of their connection. Titchener was the foremost proponent of introspection in America, and during his long career at Cornell University he trained a large number of American students in introspective methods. Despite its strong and rigorous beginnings, introspection did not fare well in America. Not only was the method (and the underlying theory of mental events) inhospitable to practical application, but it did not suit the growing spirit of positivism, a philosophy of science that argued for the exclusive study of observable phenomena and not abstract entities.

At the beginning of the twentieth century, several other methods were being employed by American psychologists. Evolutionary theory had motivated some to develop comparative techniques with which to compare mental abilities of humans and other animals. Unsatisfied by the informal and uncontrolled observations of some evolutionary theorists, Americans such as E. L. Thorndike developed highly controlled laboratory experiments for assessing mental abilities. Thorndike designed experimental "puzzle boxes," which the animal had to solve in order to escape (and then be fed). The rise of functionalism, a metatheory emphasizing the centrality of mental processes (or functionings) over mental content, invited further developments in methods. With a new interest in functions being propagated via the theories of Dewey and James, psychologists became more interested in the objective observation of responses to stimuli rather than in the mental events associated with those responses. Comparative psychology and functionalism, then, shifted the focus to observable behavior in general and learning in particular. This shift had methodological implications. First, the roles of the experimenter and subject were clearly separated, a role distinction that was to enable distinct assumptions about the mental actions of the experimenters and subjects. In turn, distinct classes of subjects (children, people of color) could be studied. Second, the move toward studying observable behaviors made possible the refinement of objective measures. Finally, the focus on observable behaviors and learning afforded the opportunity to create laboratory analogs to everyday activities: experimenters could devise experimental situations, for instance, which simulated the classroom, labor tasks, or social interactions.

Soon American psychologists came to value an experimental method characterized by scrupulous control of stimulus variables and environmental conditions of the laboratory, precise measurements, and distinct roles of experimenter and subject. Experimentation became the hallmark of the science and the central feature in the training of new psychologists. Notable here is the fact that other methods were used in the early years of the century: survey techniques, observations in natural settings, self-report, case studies, and testing techniques. Although these techniques would continue to be employed, they routinely were perceived as falling short of the objectivity, control, and predictability afforded by laboratory experimentation.

Schools and Systems

As psychological methods contracted in number and experimentation became a dominant mode of inquiry, a number of systematic models of psychology were being produced. In addition to what was being termed the structural (content of mental events) and functional (mental processes) perspectives, psychologists counted among their intellectual schools Gestalt psychology, psychoanalysis, holistic psychology, dynamic psychology, and behaviorism. Some of the schools had few adherents and a short life. Freudian psychoanalysis, for instance, was quickly rejected as unscientific as well as being overly attentive to unconscious processes and sexuality. Gestalt psychology, with its emphasis on the metaphysics of immediate mental experience (and not behavior), lack of exact measurements, and roots in German psychology, never quite found a home in the United States.

Given this diversity of systematic models, historians often refer to the time between the two world wars as the period of "schools and systems." Whether or not certain schools were even viable candidates for acceptance, it appears that in the decade following World War I psychologists staged their last substantive disputes over the nature of their discipline. These disputes often consisted of arguments about subject matter, notably whether behavior or consciousness was the proper object of study. So loaded was the ultimate outcome that these debates spawned a frequently cited witticism that first psychology gave up soul, then mind, and now would surrender its consciousness (but at least it would have some behaviors). Through these debates psychologists moved toward a consensus about psychology's status as a science and its practical utility in society. However, they also displayed a crisis in confidence—an uneasiness about their accomplishments, promises, and potential. Some historians have viewed these internal self-doubts as side effects of the controversies over schools and systems. To many psychologists working in that period, however, such professional disequilibrium was symptomatic of a larger problem: the social and psychological infirmities of psychologists themselves. They suspected that the very stuff they observed and measured in their subjects—imperfect behaviors, irrational actions, and emotional expressions—also was manifested in conflicts and disunity among researchers, errors in research, and preoccupation with metaphysics. Such admissions of the cognitive shortcomings of the psychologist ultimately underscored the absolute necessity of the experimental method. The controlled and deductive method of experimentation would force rational and logical thinking and yield uncontaminated objective knowledge. Experimental research replaced the outmoded notion of human reason. Clark Hull's (1884–1952) articulation of the hypothetico-deductive method and a factorylike organization of research cemented faith in experimentation. In the end, this methods-based resolution of psychologists' postwar uncertainties eliminated many of the contesting theory schools. The tremendous faith in experimentation, combined with positivist beliefs in the study of observables and the commitment to a practical science, tilted the contest heavily in favor of behaviorism, a theory commitment that would dominate research until the 1970s.

Behaviorism

Although behaviorism has diverse intellectual roots going back into the nineteenth century, the name John B. Watson (1878–1958) has become eponymous with the idea of behaviorism. Trained as an animal psychologist at the University of Chicago, Watson gave a series of lectures in 1913, which in its published form was to become known as the behaviorist manifesto. The manifesto rejected the study of consciousness as unscientific; it claimed that to be a natural science, psychology must be dedicated to the study of observable behaviors that represent the human organisms' adjustments to their environment. Watson described a new psychology dependent upon the controlled conditions of the laboratory where responses could be predicted on the basis of the particular stimuli presented. Behaviorism, then, was grounded on the wholesale rejection of the idea that mental processes determine behavior along with affirmation of the notion that behavioral adaptations follow lawful patterns of acquisition and extinction. Habit and learning were the core foci of behaviorists' observations.

After a hiatus created by World War I, psychologists began to appreciate behaviorism's objectivity as well as its practical utility. Within a decade there emerged numerous variations; for instance, "methodological behaviorism" did not reject notions of consciousness but conceded that conscious experience did not lend itself to scientific scrutiny, while "strict behaviorism" denied that any such consciousness exists (Leahey, 1997). By the following decade, behaviorism dominated and psychologists had generated complex theories of learning that then were compared and empirically tested.

Behaviorism appeared to be the perfect solution to the diverse desiderata of American psychologists. The theory's insistence that only observable actions be studied fulfilled the desire for psychology to be a science in that it met the criteria of describing, predicting, and controlling observable phenomena. Behaviorism also manifested functionalists' interests in understanding the organism's adaptation to the environment. Third, it provided researchers with objects whose analysis could be standardized and shared among the rapidly expanding numbers of researchers; on this count it was far better than the apparently fuzzy and idiosyncratic experiences of consciousness. Finally, behaviorism promised to deliver a remarkably useful science. Its anticipation of revealing laws of habit formation and learning was exceptionally well suited to the reform ideologies of social control. In fact its mechanistic model of behavior adjustment combined with its implicit social hierarchy (of experts and the unknowing) has been found to buttress the emerging corporate culture of America (O'Donnell, 1985).

Behaviorism's distinctly American qualities extended even further than the mandates for social control: behaviorism also contained, perhaps paradoxically, a faith in human self-improvement. Behaviorists' popular writings conveyed a spirit of perfectibility. Watson even published an account of a utopia based on behaviorist principles that described the human betterment that could ensue in a behavioristically managed society. Watson described his utopia in an explicit treatise on ideals of perfection as well as the behavioral means to attain that end, yet his famous study of little Albert exemplifies faith in human improvement. The experimental conditioning of a young boy to fear certain stimulus objects not only illustrated the acquired nature of neurosis and irrational behaviors but also intimated the possibilities for cultivating more rational and socially productive beings.

Testing and Classifying

The establishment and proliferation of mental testing seems scientifically and culturally at odds with the development of a functionalist perspective in general and behaviorism in particular. While mental testing is founded on the assumptions of relatively fixed mental abilities that differ in degree and kind among individuals, the functionalist proviso, with its focus on performance or adaptive action, eschews individual differences and abstract mental abilities. In some senses, these two programs do champion distinct models of human psychology, one highlighting the organism in its environment and the other fixing on the native content of the organism. However, in their modern form, these models shared intellectual origins in Darwinian theory: functionalism represented the evolutionary theses of adaptation and selection, and individual differences assessment reflected the evolutionary notion of natural variation.

Interest in classifying and measuring individual differences has not always been linked with evolutionary theory. Nineteenth-century phrenologists and anatomists attempted to measure physical differences, assuming them to be correlates of psychological differences. In the same century, physicians concerned with mental competence devised tests to classify degrees and types of intelligence. However, it was the work of Darwin's cousin Francis Galton (1822–1911) that set the stage for modern studies of individual differences in psychological abilities. Following Darwinian theory, Galton's interest was in measuring various human physical and psychological faculties and demonstrating the heritability of these traits. His design of measuring instruments and statistical methods influenced American psychologists in their efforts to assess individual differences. Inspired by Galton, for instance, James McKeen Cattell developed what he called mental tests and employed them in several studies.

Meanwhile, in France Alfred Binet (1857–1911) and Théodore Simon's (1873–1961) work on individual differences resulted in the construction of a test of intelligence. Their test was designed in response to the French government's request for a means to assess schoolchildren whose mental ability was below average. The resultant 1908 Binet–Simon test was therefore practical (not linked to evolutionary theory) and involved calculation of a mental age that took chronological age into account. The scale assumed that mental age increases with chronological age and that these are norms or averages for intelligence at each chronological age.

Binet and Simon's work quickly made its way to the United States, and its early revisions by two American psychologists illustrate the discipline's (and culture's) multiple interests in measuring individual differences. The various projects for quantifying the mind and distinguishing differences between minds, especially in regard to what was believed to be intelligence, clearly if unfortunately demonstrates just how psychology was infused with cultural interests. Henry H. Goddard (1866–1957) studied with Hall at Clark University and undertook research in education and mental deficiency. He employed the early version of the Binet scale to assess and classify grades of the mentally deficient (using classificatory terms such as *idiot, imbecile,* and *moron*). Influenced also by evolutionary ideas about the inheritance of individual attributes, Goddard made provocative claims (including his 1913 book *The Kallikak Family*) about the tendency for feeblemindedness to run in families. A cultural preoccupation with genetic fitness fueled theory and observation alike. Another student of Hall, Lewis M. Terman (1877–1956), found the Binet–Simon test invaluable to his scientific attempts to measure degrees of intelligence. His revisions of their test resulted in a highly successful scale for measuring intelligence and enabled him to further his studies of exceptional or "gifted" children. Terman soon was involved in the preparation of tests for army recruits during World War I. These new tests, Army Alpha for men who could read English and Army Beta for those who could not, introduced a significant alteration in mental testing techniques. As a paper-and-pencil measure it was the first successful use of group testing that provided substantial time savings over individual testing.

In the United States, tests of individual differences met with acceptance and proliferated largely for practical purposes. Intelligence tests were used in education, and other mental tests, devised to assess specific abilities or skills, were developed to aid in personnel selection and vocational training. Yet, in addition to this practical impetus, mental testing served racist purposes; some psychologists wanted to develop theories of individual differences that were in accord with the Darwinian notion of the inheritance of characteristics. Numerous psychologists, for instance, utilized the newly devised intelligence tests and test data to examine supposed racial and ethnic differences in intelligence. Once again, these projects to quantify mental traits were undergirded by dominant cultural beliefs; in many cases, these were racist and sexist. Carl C. Bingham thus analyzed the army test data and concluded that intelligence varied according to nationality. Many psychologists used the tests to ascertain differences in intelligence between Whites and African Americans, most of them concluding that the latter were the inferior group. Yet another use of testing involved development of tests of personality or internal psychic states that could differentiate groups of individuals. For example, in 1936, Terman and Catherine Cox Miles created a test of masculinity and femininity that measured differences between normal men and women, which the intelligence tests purportedly failed to do. Such developments in tests and test usage indicate that the measurement of differences was intimately connected with theories of inheritance (and nature-nurture debates) as well as with the political dynamics of American culture.

Maturing side by side, behaviorism and mental testing both reflected and fostered a major debate about humankind that was to continue for the entire century. The data and theories from these scientific projects provided the framework for debating whether the central psychological characteristics of humans were determined by their biology (nature) or their experiences in the world (nurture). These research programs produced a discourse on nature versus nurture: was intelligence inherited, was educational success the result of learning, do early childhood experiences influence the formation of personality? At no point were these debates simply or only academic. Psychologists' involvement in eugenics campaigns and their lobbying for immigration laws, for instance, were linked with their deterministic belief in the biological basis of psychological attributes. Likewise, researchers' arguments for improving the social and educational environment of Negro youth and their appeals for child guidance clinics were guided by belief in the environmental determinants of behavior. The high stakes in nature-nurture controversy were set by such political as well as scientific implications, and the intractability of the debate was established by its historical origins in modern science's metaphysical distinction between culture and nature.

Disciplinary Expansion

Behaviorism and mental testing provide ample evidence that by the early twentieth century there existed a genuinely American psychology—one that was rigorously scientific, expanding, and practical. Even the theoretical rift between these two movements, one championing function and the environment and the other emphasizing traits and biological determinism, was American in spirit. Early twentieth-century America provided unique opportunities for certain individuals to advance economically and socially while it simultaneously maintained racist and class divisions in lifestyle. American psychology, despite the near-hegemony of its theories and methods, nevertheless was becoming a heterogeneous discipline, one that was "generous" (Rose, 1992) in that it could be appropriated and used by other professionals and organizations and used in whatever way suited their objective for human conduct.

In addition to the ideology of its scientific theories, psychology was becoming diversified in another sense by the creation of specialties or subdisciplines within the field. By the end of World War II, most psychologists identified themselves with one of these subdisciplines: social psychology, abnormal psychology, developmental psychology, educational psychology, personality, or sensation and perception. In 1945, the American Psychological Association formally recognized this professional pattern of 19 divisions representing the various specialties.

Another feature in the professional maturation of psychology was the development of clinical psychology, a subfield devoted to the diagnosis and treatment of mental illness. During the first two decades of the twentieth century, many psychologists who considered themselves experimentalists also engaged in the study and treatment of psychological problems. By the end of the nineteenth century, medically trained psychiatrists were abandoning organic theories of mental illness in favor of psychological-based theories, including those being proposed by Pierre Janet (1859–1947) and Sigmund Freud (1856–1939). This theory transition opened the way for the new experimental psychologists to conduct studies on the mentally ill as well as with delinquents and troubled children. With the creation of varied psychotherapeutic theories and techniques, psychologists also became involved in their development and evaluation. Despite the fact that much of this early involvement included noted experimentalists, including Yerkes and Watson, there existed an uneasy tension between psychologists committed to laboratory psychology and those devoted to applied psychology or psychotherapy. In 1937 the American Association of Applied Psychology was created to serve the professional needs of clinical psychologists and shortly thereafter the APA made organizational adjustments to accommodate these psychologists.

[*Many of the people mentioned in this article are the subjects of independent biographical entries.*]

Bibliography

Hilgard, E. R. (1987). *Psychology in America.* San Diego, CA: Harcourt Brace Jovanovich.

James, W. (1950). *Principles of psychology.* New York: Dover. (Original work published 1890)

Leahey, T. H. (1997). *A history of psychology: Currents in psychological thought* (4th ed.). Upper Saddle River, NJ: Prentice Hall.

Morawski, J. G. (1982). Assessing psychology's moral heritage through our neglected utopias. *American Psychologist, 37:* 1082–1095.

O'Donnell, J. M. (1985). *The origins of behaviorism: American psychology, 1870–1920.* New York: New York University Press.

Pfister, J., & Schnog, N. (Eds.). (1997). *Inventing the psychological: Toward a cultural history of emotional life in America.* New Haven, CT: Yale University Press.

Rose, N. (1992). Engineering the human soul: Analyzing psychological expertise. *Science in Context, 5:* 351–372.

Scarborough, E., & Furumoto, L. (1987). *Untold lives: The first generation of American women psychologists.* New York: Columbia University Press.

Sokal, M. M. (Ed.). (1987). *Psychological testing and American society, 1890–1930.* New Brunswick, NJ: Rutgers University Press.

Yerkes, R. M. (1911). *Introduction to psychology.* New York: Henry Holt.

Jill Morawski

Post–World War II

Psychology in the pre–World War II era was on the threshold of becoming both a major academic discipline and an applied profession. It had some unresolved problems, particularly involving mind-body issues, but in the main the academic wing of psychology had adopted British empiricism as its philosophy and was therefore behavioristic in orientation. The professional wing had been struggling to achieve its unique identity. We will survey the post–World War II era in terms of these academic and professional developments. Our focus is on the United States, which was actually the leader in psychological studies before the war.

Academic Developments

Although behaviorism had dominated academic circles since the 1920s, there were significant variations in outlook within this camp.

Behaviorism Versus Gestalt Psychology. John B. Watson (1878–1958), the father of behaviorism, was no longer active in academia, but there were three major figures vying for leadership: Clark L. Hull (1884–1952), E. C. Tolman (1886–1959), and B. F. Skinner (1904–1990). All of these men were committed to psychology as a science, which at that time meant Newtonian science. The philosophical outlook of Newtonianism was realism. A scientist was someone who not only sought to empirically validate his or her theory through a "control and prediction" logic of a hypothesis corresponding to "observed reality," but a restriction was placed on the kind of theory a "genuine" scientist might use to explain any observed findings. All causal analysis had to be done in terms of mechanistic or "efficient" causation—the sort of thing that takes place when one billiard ball bumps into another; the first ball thrusts the second along. The stimulus-response (S-R) sequence in Watsonian behaviorism is conceived in a similar antecedent-consequent fashion.

Problems among the behaviorists arose over the nature of the mechanistic process. Tolman had been influenced by the Gestalt psychologist, Kurt Koffka (1886–1941). Gestalt psychology had been founded by Max Wertheimer (1880–1943), who was supported in this effort by Koffka, Wolfgang Köhler (1887–1967), and to a lesser extent, Kurt Lewin (1890–1947). Gestalt theory draws on continental philosophy, which emphasizes organization, totality, and the essential quality of things. The British followed a Lockean, bottom-up strategy of explanation, while the gestaltists pursued a more Kantian, top-down phenomenological approach. British empiricism called for observing reality, which was presumably "there" to be concretely measured. Phenomenologists believed that the observer contributed to what was under observation, that there was no completely free-standing reality "there" to measure in the first place.

The 1920s was the period when Gestalt psychology reached its zenith at Berlin University, where Köhler and Wertheimer were located. But after being repressed and threatened by the Nazis, the gestaltists immigrated from Germany to America before war broke out. Unfortunately, their views never caught on in American universities. They had better luck among applied psychologists like Carl Rogers (1902–1987). Even so, Tolman borrowed enough from Koffka to generate a conflict with Hull. Tolman had modified Watson's simple S-R habit formulation to suggest that there was a "cognitive map" that animals (white rats) acquired while learning to do things like running a maze. He backed his argument with empirical research. The cognitive map was said to "mediate" between the S and the R. Tolman referred to his approach as *purposive behaviorism*. The cognitive map "pictured" the goal box for the animal, where food and water could be found at the end of the maze. Tolman believed that an animal's improvement in maze running from trial to trial was empirical proof of purpose.

Hull found a way of explaining purpose as a mechanistic response in its own right. He claimed that in repeatedly running to attain the reward (food, water) at the end of a maze, animals began making "eating-like" responses even before they got to the goal box. This gave the appearance of purpose, but it was actually nothing but an *anticipatory goal response*, a fraction of the complete sequence of "running to eat." In other words, the animals were already getting in position to eat in running faster as they came closer to the goal box, and made head rotations, salivated, and so forth even before the goal had been reached. Such actions appear to be purposive but are merely learned responses, as when a human being begins putting silverware in place, picking up the napkin, looking about in expectation that food will soon be served. Such actions are an aspect of the total behavior called dining and they are responses to stimuli, not purposes. The debate over whether behavior was purposive and what "purpose" could mean was never solved, and in fact, Skinner was to add a new dimension to the issue.

Skinner favored Hull's position that human behavior lacked true purpose, but he reached this conclusion from a totally different approach. Skinner frequently said that although he was a behaviorist he was *not* an S-R theorist. He did not accept the view that responses were "stimulated" by antecedent stimuli. This was the traditional understanding of a behavioral sequence dating back to work by the Russian physiologist, Ivan Pavlov (1849–1936), on elicitation of salivation in the dog. Skinner (1931) argued that behavioral responses were not brought on by such elicitation in the natural state. Rather, an animal's behavior consisted of "operant" responses which actually acted (operated) on the environment to bring about contingently reinforcing states of affairs or not! The fox must run to catch the hare if it is to eat. Looked at externally or extraspectively, it appeared that the animal was operantly responding for a purpose. But Skinner denied this, saying instead that operant responses were emitted and then contingently reinforced by the environment. When Skinner later extended his theory to the behavior of human beings he argued the same way, including the claim that language (verbal behavior) was also carried on without purpose. We emit or say things and believe things that have previously been reinforced by our environment. Our verbal usage is shaped, so that even though we may say "I intend to drink some water" just before doing so, this is not an intentional, purposive action. We are merely emitting what has been shaped into our behavior earlier when we were thirsty and learned how to express this need.

In the mid-1950s there was an extremely influential research project carried out which seemed to prove that people participating in experiments could be manipulated linguistically like this without being aware of what was taking place (Greenspoon, 1955). A host of reseachers followed up to show that, in point of fact, Pavlovian (classical) or Skinnerian (operant) conditioning seemed to require both an awareness and a willingness by participants to comply with what the experimental design suggested to them before a conditioning effect could be demonstrated (Brewer, 1974). Indeed, a subject who was aware of what was going on in the experiment could negate the expected sequence in what definitely appeared to be an intentional manner (Page, 1972). This issue of conditioning with or without awareness and cooperation is still being debated, but at the very least, the confident attitude once expressed by John Watson that he could shape people any way he wanted them to be is no longer voiced by behaviorists.

Actually, something of this same variety occurred in work with lower animals where it was found that behavioral conditioning is constrained by an animal's evolutionary history. Some rather intelligent animals (such as the pig) cannot be conditioned to go against what "comes naturally" (like rooting) in their behavior (see Breland & Breland, 1961). In the reverse direction, chimpanzees were found capable of linguistic communication with humans through use of hand signals (Griffin, 1981). But, gradually, the area known as comparative psychology began to wane as behavioral accounts shifted more to sociocultural explanations. There was a great cry for "ecologically correct" (lifelike) research. The traditional Darwinian reduction of behavior to biological structures that traced back in evolutionary history to lower animals gave way to new advances in genetics, DNA, and related hereditary considerations. Animal laboratories in academic centers declined noticeably in the 1960s. Even so, biological influences on behavior continue to be studied in what has become the burgeoning field of biopsychology. The older, Darwinian rationale for comparative psychology has given way to an even more assertive—and controversial—theory known as *sociobiology* (Wilson, 1975). In fact, this view holds that psychology will one day be explained away by biology. Biological perspectives in psychology have spawned different disciplines in psychology such as biological psychology, physiological psychology, psychobiology, and neuroscience. Neuroscience is an interdisciplinary approach to understanding the relationship between the mind and the brain (Urbach, 1997). All of these disciplines are concerned with the biological mechanisms underlying human thought and behavior in the form of sensing, synthesizing, integrating, and responding to the environment.

In the 1920s, Jean Piaget had initiated a series of

cognitive studies on the acquisition of knowledge in children. He relied on logical analysis rather than on behavioristic mechanisms in his cognitive theory. As a result, his work was generally ignored until the 1960s when, along with the questioning of behavioristic theory, there was a growing sympathy among psychologists for cognitive speculations. Piaget seemed to fit the bill, and his work has had a significant influence in the fields of educational and developmental psychology. Piaget had postulated a developmental sequence of four major stages through which he believed children sequentially matured. In recent years this stage theory has been brought into question, but the influence of Piaget's thought on psychology continues to be felt—especially in educational circles.

A Cognitive Revelation. Beginning in roughly 1960 the term *cognitive* changed from a Kantian (continental) to a Lockean (British) interpretation. This was to have an influence on the development of behaviorism, as reflected in the theorizing of Albert Bandura (1986). Trained in the Hullian tradition, Bandura added significantly to this style of S-R explanation by postulating a triadic form of causation—including a person's (1) internal cognitions, affects, and biology; (2) external, overt behaviors; and (3) environmental pressures to perform or believe in certain ways. Each of these sources of causation influenced the other in a reciprocal manner. An important cognitive influence on a person's performance in life's challenging circumstances is *self-efficacy*. This is the sense of conviction that a person has regarding whether he or she can execute the behavior required to produce some outcome—such as passing an examination, or hosting a party. As it is a learned behavior, achieved by accomplishing challenging tasks as well as modeling the behavior of others, Bandura's self-efficacy is seen by some as a further development of mediational theorizing. Bandura believes that agency (producing desired results) can be understood through triadic causation and the development of efficacy both in persons and social groups.

Returning to the matter of how cognition is to be understood, a Kantian (phenomenological) formulation is framed in the first-person or introspective terms, considering things from the perspective of "I, me, us, we" and so on. A Lockean (empiricistic) understanding of cognition is framed in a third-person or extraspective perspective, referring to "that, it, they, them" and so on. Purposive explanation is introspective for it assigns responsibility to an identity or identities whose actions can only be understood from their own point(s) of view. Mechanistic accounts are extraspective, understanding behavior as taking place according to impersonal forces "over there." This shift in meaning of cognition was the result of a "Cognitive Revolution" that descended upon psychology. The impetus for this revolution in psychological theorizing was the perfection of electronic computer technology. The term *artificial intelligence* (AI) was coined to typify this approach. The general consensus is that AI as a field of study was born at an institute sponsored by the Rockefeller Foundation, held at Dartmouth College in the summer of 1956 (Newell & Simon, 1972, pp. 873–889).

It would seem that a machine, by its very nature, cannot be explained introspectively. And yet, if we want to assign purpose to some behaving organism we must see things from this organism's (introspective) point of view. Mechanism has traditionally been understood as the very opposite of intentionality or purposeful action. But with the advent of computers a new line of argument arose, one which seemed to capture a truly cognizing, intending machine! To grasp this argument we must understand the concepts of input, output, and especially feedback. Feedback is the return of some of the machine's signaling output as input, so that a computer is continually monitoring its ongoing actions. Positive feedback signals what is taking place and negative feedback signals whether some preselected goal or target is "on" or "off" course. If a missile—a cybernetic machine—is for some reason off course, the negative feedback will automatically redirect its firing mechanisms to put it back on target. This self-correcting capacity of negative feedback has prompted many AI enthusiasts to believe that negative feedback is the same thing as purposive behavior, intentionality, or free will (Rosenblueth, Wiener, & Bigelow, 1943).

Alan Turing (1912–1954) further captured the imagination of psychologists when he introduced a strategy in which a computer expert could write machine programs that misled people into thinking that the machines which processed these programs were alive (1950). For example, a person might engage the computer in a "conversation," typing questions to be answered by the prearranged program (giving the illusion of talking to the machine). If the program could fool the person into believing that another person was answering these questions from another location, then the "Turing test" would have been passed. The program has *simulated* the cognitions of an actual, living person. If we combine this feat with the self-correcting nature of the cybernetic machine, it seems as though a completely mechanistic account of psychology is now possible. Some pretty optimistic predictions along this line have been made by those who would like to turn psychology into AI (Simon, 1985, p. 89).

The cognitive revolution was heavily underway by the 1980s but it was not without its detractors. First of all, the question has been raised by many as to whether there is anything truly revolutionary in the theoretical accounts underlying computing machinery. Clark Hull had built calculating machines to solve various problems, and many see little difference between Hullian S-R formulations and the input-output concept. Both are based on blind, efficient causation. Doubtless Hull could have found a way of explaining feedback through mediation. When framed as "information" being input and output, it is easy to think of meaningful messages taking place. Actually, the meaning of a computer is all in the program as written and logically arrayed by the programmer—a human being! The information under electronic signaling, the actual mechanism of a computer, has nothing to do with meaning (Shannon & Weaver, 1962, pp. 3, 99). Nor can the machine spontaneously negate the directions of its executive program. It cannot say no to its unquestionable assumptions in the impulsively illogical way that human beings can. The "it" here reminds us that computers are not understood introspectively. Psychologists favoring an introspective account of human behavior will doubtless continue to express dissatisfaction with the computer model.

Although the meaning of cognition has shifted to involve extraspective, mechanistic accounts, there have always been strong advocates for the original Kantian meaning. For example, from 1950 to 1960 a "New Look" in perceptual theory and research was advanced (Bruner et al., 1957). The emphasis here was on an active role for the perceiver, who contributed to what was actually "seen" based on personal motivation. Words that had a negative meaning took longer to be recognized when flashed on a screen than words with a positive meaning. Some psychologists took this to be a *perceptual defense*, an intentional effort to avoid the unpleasant. In time, such work led to studies on *subliminal perception*, as when the word *popcorn* is flashed on a movie screen too rapidly to be seen but nevertheless appears to suggest the purchase of popcorn to those watching the movie. Once again, there is disagreement over whether or not such subliminal perceiving is possible.

Humanistic Psychology. The rise of humanistic psychology was led by Carl Rogers, Abraham Maslow (1908–1970), and others, also in line with Kantian precepts. This was called a "Third Force" in academic circles, adding to the first force of behaviorism and the second of psychoanalysis. Psychoanalysis has been continually and roundly criticized for its lack of grounding in empirical research. No academic department in the United States adopted a lasting Freudian or Jungian outlook, although most of them offered some coursework in these theories. Psychoanalysis was tied to institutes established outside of academia.

By the 1970s there was much criticism of the traditional interpretation of psychology as a physical or natural science. Critics felt that psychologists were wrong in modeling their discipline after the physical sciences. Some critics even held that psychology was not a science at all. Those psychologists who wished to humanize psychology, or to make it more relevant to everyday living, promoted alternative approaches such as qualitative research, hermeneutics, dialogue, transcendental meditation, and transpersonal psychology to mention a few of the leading recommendations. Much debate was carried on in this context regarding the philosophy of science embraced by psychology, with special emphasis on loosening the rabid empiricism of the old in favor of a more diverse approach that would bring greater interest to the field. Critics charged that traditional laboratory research was resulting in miniscule, arcane findings read by few and adding up to very little of lasting worth. Others were dissatisfied with the mechanization of psychology that we have already noted. A strong trend to so-called *constructionist* (or constructivist), theoretical formulations in psychology began to be seen in the 1980s and 1990s, leading to what is sometimes called a "postmodern" form of explanation.

Postmodernism is not a strict or formal point of view, but rather a kind of ubiquitous criticism of any and all traditionally authoritative outlooks. If you state a fact, even a scientific fact based on empirical evidence, the postmodern analyst will show you how you are actually construing this fact drawing on assumptions that are always open to question and negation. This is not simply cultural relativism—as merely suggesting that your assumptions would be unacceptable in another culture. The binding tie of many if not all postmodernist views is a conviction that it is impossible to arrive at a truth that is certain, either between or within a common cultural context. Postmodernists are likely to suggest that not only are we humans locked into a language system that gives us our thoughts (reminiscent of Skinner!), but we are locked into an ultimately undecidable course of linguistic exchange or dialogue. We can discuss and debate endlessly, but we cannot arrive at even a relative, arbitrary, culture-bound truth. Any meaningful text encompassed by a written account or verbal argument can be shown to bear the roots of its own negation, so that we can *deconstruct* this meaning and turn it into its very opposite. Critics of postmodernism say that it is a nihilistic formulation which fails to say what is to be done to clarify and correct such meaning-exchanges. Even so, many psychologists are fascinated with this challenging analysis of the human condition.

Thus, at the beginning of the twenty-first century we find academia seemingly poised to effect some basic conceptual changes in its theoretical approach. We may be seeing what Kuhn (1970) called a scientific revolution about to take place, going beyond what the cognitive revolution involved. Only time will tell. We next turn to the major professional developments that have taken place following World War II.

Professional Developments

It should be evident at this point that psychology has had more than its share of challenging problems in trying to maintain a scientific posture in academia while facing the growing demands of a service profession in the larger society. Before World War II the American Psychological Association (APA) was slow to grant unqualified membership to applied disciplines like clinical psychology. In reaction to this, many of its members broke away in 1938 to form the American Association of Applied Psychology (AAAP). It was not until 1944 that a reconciliation was achieved and the applied psychologists returned to the fold.

At the end of World War II about 44,000 servicemen and women were hospitalized with service-connected problems. A large proportion of them suffered from psychological maladjustments of one sort or another. Other veterans who were not hospitalized also experienced chronic emotional disorders from their wartime experience. To meet the need for counseling and psychotherapy, in 1946 the U.S. Veterans Administration introduced a program to train clinical psychologists that was to have tremendous influence on the growth of this profession. The subsequent Korean and Vietnam wars also helped further the use and acceptance among the broader public of such psychological treatments.

The rapid growth of clinical psychology generated concern over the exact nature of this profession. In 1947 the APA appointed a committee chaired by David Shakow (1901–1981) which, in 1949, sponsored a conference at Boulder, Colorado. The aim of this conference was to establish guidelines for training in clinical psychology. Its official report concluded that clinical psychologists should be trained first and foremost as scientists, and second as practicing clinicians. The resultant "Boulder model" of clinical psychology, which called for research expertise leading to the doctoral degree, is known as the scientist-practitioner model (Raimy, 1950).

By the 1960s there were more openings in clinical psychology than doctoral graduates to fill these positions (Schofield, 1966). Other areas of psychological application including social, developmental, forensic, and industrial-organizational, grew at three times the rate of academic areas like experimental psychology (Tryon, 1963). With the advancing longevity of the citizenry, geriatric psychology was to become a major aspect of caregiving. The applied trend can be seen in the founding of various divisions in the APA, many of which seem unrelated to scientific pursuits, as, for example, Psychologists in Public Service, Rehabilitation Psychology, Community Psychology, Exercise and Sport Psychology, and Media Psychology. A growing number of psychologists with traditional scientific interests complained that the APA had become a guild, interested primarily in furthering the financial goals of its members rather than seeking the basic principles of psychology. Applied psychologists answered by pointing out how their so-called basic science colleagues were influenced by granting agencies, which used project funding to direct what would or would not be empirically investigated. Economic factors were apparently at play on both sides of the coin.

By the mid-1960s mounting evidence accrued that strongly suggested that few clinical psychologists opted for a career in basic science. Undoubtedly, the social upheavals of the 1960s involving struggles over civil rights, rising crime rates, increasing use of drugs, and mounting opposition to the Vietnam War contributed to the motivation among applied psychologists to put their energies into rectifying these social and personal problems in living. A huge majority of clinical psychologists chose to work in the private sector, many times opening their own practices of diagnosis and treatment (Shakow, 1965). In the face of such developments another conference was held in 1973 at Vail, Colorado. The resultant "Vail model" recognized the importance of professional clinical training per se. In effect, the "scientist" emphasis of the Boulder model was dropped. The Vail model called for training in professional graduate schools that awarded a Doctor of Psychology (Psy.D.) instead of the Ph.D. This meant that a graduate student in a Psy.D. program did not have to present a research dissertation in order to be granted the degree. Graduates from Psy.D. programs have since made great contributions to the professional aspects of psychology and have been duly recognized in winning awards and achieving the distinction of being elected president of the APA. However, the predominant aspiration among graduate clinical programs in the United States remains the Boulder model.

There was an unresolved problem for those research psychologists (now in the minority!) who felt they were not being properly represented by the increasingly applied orientation of APA. In the 1980s several attempts to satisfy such dissidents were made, but no reorganization of APA seemed to work. The final plan designed to correct things was put before the APA membership in 1988, but it was rejected by two thirds of those voting. That fall a separate organization called the American Psychological Society (APS) was founded by the dissidents. The APS promised to "give psychology away" rather than sell it—a phrase taken from George Miller's (1969) earlier presidential address to the APA in which he cautioned against the heavy trend toward applied psychology, with its attendant economic motives. History had therefore repeated itself, except now it was the basic scientists (APS) and not the applied professionals (AAAP) who walked out to found a separate organization from APA. Whether there will be another reconciliation only time will tell. Dynamic tensions within the APA have been an integral part of its history. Clinical and theoretical dialogue between divergent viewpoints will surely continue into the future. In 1977, the APA was composed of 50 divisions, and it celebrated the fiftieth anniversary of its divisional structure. APA division membership has grown by 17% over the last 10 years. Divisions within the APA continue to proliferate, and their relationship to APA continues to change and clarify over the years. With well over 110,000 members, the APA also recognizes the American Psychological Association for Graduate Students (APAGS) with over 40,000 members in 1997. The APA is the world's largest organization for psychologists.

Although there were clinicians who had a consistent theoretical outlook in their work, such as the nondirective therapists who followed Carl Rogers, the theoretical rationale employed by most applied psychologists is best typified as eclectic. That is, surveys consistently revealed that a psychologist working in the field adapted her or his theory to the problem at hand, rather than adjusting the problem to fit only one preconceived theory. In psychotherapy, for example, we might find the same clinician who uses a neo-Freudian insight approach when working with adults relying on Skinnerian operant conditioning in working with children. In fact, a therapist might proffer an analytical insight to the same client with whom he is using some kind of behavior modification technique to reduce symptoms.

Whereas in the 1930s one would not be likely to hear of something called "cognitive behaviorism," it became increasingly common to do so in the closing decades of the twentieth century. In all likelihood, this is just another manifestation of the effort we saw Bandura making to bring comprehensive explanations to psychology. Psychologists in the applied field were just as prone to introduce complexity into their views, or to combine theoretical formulations, as were psychologists in academia. The older schools of thought are gradually melding together. At the same time, however, there are new approaches to psychotherapy springing up almost monthly. Some of these, such as George A. Kelly's (1905–1967) constructive alternativism, are welcome additions. But most of the others seem to be mere variations on established themes.

Psychology's growth of popularity in American society has been phenomenal. It is consistently among the top selections as a major course of undergraduate study in colleges across the country. Businesses, church groups, the military complex—everywhere one looks in the post–World War II period there are signs of psychological involvement. Practicing clinicians have established certification and licensing requirements to further strengthen their professional identity. Due to rising costs, there has been a growing influence on the practice of psychology from third-party sources like insurance companies, who try to set standard fees, and the use of specific therapeutic techniques for the treatment of specific disorders. There are expectations that to keep costs down in the future, many clients will have therapy with practitioners holding a master's degree, under the supervision of a Ph.D. psychologist. Terminal master's degree programs in clinical psychology date back to the late 1940s and early 1950s. In the late 1990s there were over three hundred master's programs related to psychology, graduating over 8,000 psychologists each year. In 1983, it was estimated that 28,000 master's level professionals were working in the field of psychology. The Council of Applied Master's Programs in Psychology (CAMPP) and The North American Association of Master's in Psychology (NAMP) are relatively new organizations created to support master's programs in psychology and master's practitioners. There is an ongoing debate as to whether to admit master's psychologists to full membership in the APA. An interesting aspect of the growth of psychology as a discipline and profession is the fact that more women are selecting psychology for both undergraduate and graduate study. Indeed, it is common to hear that a "feminization" of psychology took place over the final third of the twentieth century.

A continuing debate in clinical work has to do with just how successful psychotherapy is, and whether or not we really can train people to be effective therapists. The evidence suggests that psychotherapy per se does help people to adjust (Lambert & Bergin, 1992). But there is little proof that having advanced training in clinical work makes a great difference. Therapists with master's degrees do as well as those with Ph.D. degrees (Dawes, 1994). Some Ph.D. clinicans seem therefore to want their clinical practice to be raised a notch. That is, they believe they should have the right to prescribe certain medications. Others think this should remain the responsibility of a physician. It was mentioned in the section on academic developments that biopsychology has been making great strides. Despite serious questions concerning the ultimate value of drug treatment (Fisher & Greenberg, 1997, pp. 115–172), emotional disorders such as depression are increasingly treated with pharmacological agents. But if psychology is being engulfed by biology ("socio-" or otherwise) in the academic realm and by medicine in the professional realm, what does that leave for it to do on its own?

Comment

It may appear, given our overview glance at psychology since World War II, that we have here a discipline in serious difficulty. It must confront other specialties like biology and computer science which threaten to explain it away. There is a seemingly unbridgeable split between its basic science and applied wings. Critics dismiss it as not being a legitimate science to begin with, and at the very least find that it has no business seeking to apply its "unsatisfactorily" established principles. Even some of psychology's advocates want its academic home shifted over from the sciences to the humanities. There are unsettled internal questions concerning its concepts, especially regarding whether human beings are purposive organisms or robots. Its therapies are under fire as supposedly ineffective. And its gender recruiting is increasingly one-sided, which can bias its developmental direction. Indeed, psychology's very popularity in the broader culture may dilute its potential to be a focused discipline.

How one interprets these issues will obviously influence any conclusion regarding the future of psychology. We can frame them with hopeful optimism or dour pessimism. There are surely challenges ahead for this discipline, but pessimism hardly seems warranted. It is probably more reasonable to view these challenges as reflecting the inevitable growing pains of a vibrant and much needed realm of knowledge in human affairs. Growing pains are rarely fatal and usually overcome. There is every indication that psychology will be successful in this regard and thereby continue to make a unique and important contribution to knowledge in the twenty-first century.

Bibliography

American Psychological Association. Available Web site: http://www.apa.org/psychnet/[1998, December 18].

Bandura, A. (1986). *Social foundations of thought and action: A social cognitive theory*. Englewood Cliffs, NJ: Prentice Hall.

Breland, K., & Breland, M. (1961). The misbehavior of organisms. *American Psychologist, 16*, 681–684.

Brewer, W. F. (1974). There is no convincing evidence for operant or classical conditioning in adult humans. In W. B. Weimer & D. S. Palermo (Eds.), *Cognition and the symbolic processes* (pp. 1–42). Hillsdale, NJ: Erlbaum.

Bruner, J. S., Brunswik, E., Festinger, L., Heider, F., Muenzinger, K. F., Osgood, C. E., & Rapaport, D. (1957). *Contemporary approaches to cognition*. Cambridge, U.K.: Cambridge University Press.

Dawes, R. M. (1994). *House of cards: Psychology and psychotherapy built on myth*. New York: Free Press.

Fisher, S., & Greenberg, R. (1997). *From placebo to panacea: Putting psychiatric drugs to the test* (pp. 115–172). New York: Wiley.

Greenspoon, J. (1955). The reinforcing effect of two spoken sounds on the frequency of two responses. *American Journal of Psychology, 68*, 409–416.

Griffin, D. R. (1981). *The question of animal awareness: Evolutionary continuity of mental experience* (Rev. ed.). New York: Rockefeller University Press.

Kuhn, T. S. (1970). *The structure of scientific revolutions* (2nd ed.). Chicago: University of Chicago Press.

Lambert, M. J., & Bergin, A. E. (1992). Achievements and limitations of psychotherapy research. In D. K. Freedheim (Ed.), *History of psychotherapy: A century of change* (pp. 360–390). Washington, DC: American Psychological Association.

Lowe, H. (Ed.) (1990). National Conference on Applied Master's Training in Psychology. *Proceedings*. Norman, OK: University of Oklahoma Press.

Miller, G. A. (1969). Psychology as a means of promoting human welfare. *American Psychologist, 24*, 1063–1075.

Newell, A., & Simon, H. A. (1972). *Human problem solving*. Englewood Cliffs, NJ: Prentice Hall.

Page, M. M. (1972). Demand characteristics and the verbal operant conditioning experiment. *Journal of Personality and Social Psychology, 23*, 372–378.

Raimy, V. (Ed.). (1950). *Training in clinical psychology*. New York: Prentice Hall.

Rosenblueth, A., Wiener, N., & Bigelow, J. (1943). Behavior, purpose and teleology. *Philosophy of Science, 10*, 18–24.

Schofield W. (1966). Clinical and counseling psychology: Some perspectives. *American Psychologist, 21*, 122–131.

Shakow, D. (1965). Seventeen years later: Clinical psychology in the light of the 1947 committee on training in clinical psychology report. *American Psychologist, 20*, 353–367.

Shannon, C. E., & Weaver, W. (Eds.). (1962). *The mathematical theory of communication*. Urbana, IL: University of Illinois Press.

Simon, H. A. (1985). *The science of the artificial* (2nd ed.). Cambridge, MA: MIT Press.

Skinner, B. F. (1931). The concept of the reflex in the description of behavior. *Journal of General Psychology, 5*, 427–458.

Tryon, R. C. (1963). Psychology in flux: The academic-professional bipolarity. *American Psychologist, 18*, 134–143.

Turing, A. (1950). Computing machinery and intelligence. *Mind, 59*, 433–460.

Urbach, T. (1997). From brain to mind: Event-related potential evidence for sentence comprehension processes. *American Behavioral Scientist, 40*, 754–781.

Wilson, E. O. (1975). *Sociobiology: The new synthesis*. Cambridge, MA: Harvard University Press.

Joseph F. Rychlak and Andrea Struckman

PSYCHOLOGY OF MEN. Those not familiar with this field sometimes ask: Isn't all psychology the psychology of men? The answer is yes: men have been the focal point of most psychological research, but this has been in studies that viewed men as representative of humanity as a whole. Feminist scholars have challenged this viewpoint by arguing for a gender-specific approach, and in the last quarter of the twentieth century have (re)written the psychology of women. In the same spirit, men's studies scholars have begun to examine masculinity not as a proxy for the species but rather as a complex and problematic construct in its own right. In so doing, they have provided a framework for a psychological approach to men and masculinity that questions traditional norms of the male role, such as the emphasis on competition, status, toughness, and emotional stoicism, and views certain male problems (such as violence, devaluation of women, fear and hatred of homosexuals, detached fathering, and neglect of health needs) as unfortunate but predictable results of the male role socialization process. They have also provided a framework for creating positive new definitions of masculinity that support the optimal development of men, women, and children.

The new psychology of men views gender roles not as biological or even social givens but rather as psychologically and socially constructed entities that bring certain advantages and disadvantages, and, most importantly, can change. This perspective acknowledges the biological differences between men and women but argues that "masculinity" and "femininity" are not based on biological sex. Rather these notions are socially constructed from biological, psychological, and social experience to serve particular purposes. Traditional constructions of gender serve patriarchal purposes; nontraditional constructions, such as Gilmore (1990) described among the Tahitians and the Semai, serve more egalitarian purposes.

Joseph Pleck demonstrated that the paradigm that had dominated the research on masculinity for 50 years (1930–1980), the gender role *identity* paradigm (which assumes that people have an inner psychological need to have a gender role identity, and that optimal personality development hinged on its formation), not only poorly accounts for the observed data but also promotes the bifurcation of society on the basis of stereotyped gender roles. In its place, Pleck proposed the gender role *strain* paradigm, which argues that appropriate gender roles are determined by the prevailing gender ideology and are imposed on the developing child by parents, teachers, and peers: the cultural transmitters who subscribe to the prevailing gender ideology.

The gender role strain paradigm has stimulated research on three varieties of male gender role strain: discrepancy strain, dysfunction strain, and trauma strain. *Discrepancy strain* results when one fails to live up to one's internalized manhood ideal. *Dysfunction strain* results even when one fulfills the requirements of the male code, because many of the characteristics viewed as desirable in men can have negative side effects on the men themselves and on those close to them. *Trauma strain* results from the ordeal of the male role socialization process, which is now recognized as inherently traumatic.

Bibliography

Brod, H. (1987). *The making of the masculinities: The new men's studies.* Boston: Unwin Hyman.

Gilmore, D. (1990). *Manhood in the making: Cultural concepts of masculinity.* New Haven, CT: Yale University Press.

Levant, R. F., & Pollack, W. S. (Eds.). (1995). *A new psychology of men.* New York: Basic Books.

Pleck, J. H. (1981). *The myth of masculinity.* Cambridge, MA: MIT Press.

Ronald F. Levant

PSYCHOMETRICS. The term *psychometrics* may be traced back to the Greek words *psyche*, meaning "breath," life, soul, or mind and *metron*, referring to measure. Current usage of the term focuses on psychometrics as the psychological theory and technique of mental measurement, or as the branch of psychology dealing with measurable factors. Modern psychometrics, therefore, concerns both the theory and application of principles of psychological measurement and testing.

Although the first applications of the practice of psychological measurement may be traced putatively back to 2200 BCE with the use of civil service examinations in ancient China, the origins of the modern practice of psychometrics are associated with Francis Galton. In 1884, at the International Health Exhibition in London, Galton initiated his laboratory, where measurements on a battery of physical and behavioral characteristics were undertaken. In addition to collecting data, Galton also sought to summarize the relationships among variables, and, in doing so, he developed the modern conceptualization of correlation.

Psychometrics focuses on four primary areas: reliability, validity, item analysis, and norming. Within each of these domains there are both theoretical explications as well as applied practices.

Reliability

Reliability refers to the consistency or reproduceability of measurement. Reliability is the degree to which individual differences in measurement are based either on "true" differences in the property being evaluated or on random error. Classical reliability theory holds that observed test scores may be partitioned into two independent components representing true score and error. This consistency of measurement is commonly operationalized as within test-item homogeneity or internal consistency reliability, alternate-form reliability, test-retest stability, or interrater reliability. Both internal consistency reliability and alternate-form reliability concern themselves with content sampling, that is, the degree to which items on a test represent the universe of content from which they are sampled. Internal consistency is computed from the single administration of a test and is based on the average correlation between test items. Statistics quantifying internal consistency reliability include split-half reliability, Kuder-Richardson 20, Kuder-Richardson 21, and coefficient alpha. Alternate-form reliability is based on the administration of two parallel forms of the same test and is calculated using a correlation coefficient. With immediate administration of the two forms, unreliability is attributable to content sampling; for time-lagged administration of the forms, both content sampling and time sampling contribute to the unreliability or error of measurement. Test-retest stability is calculated from two administrations, separated in time, of the same measure to the same objects or persons. A correlation between the two measurements is computed to represent this index of reliability, and unreliability is associated with time sampling. Interrater reliability is examined in situations where more than one rater or judge undertakes the measurement of objects or persons. Quantification of this form of reliability may include a correlation coefficient and Cohen's kappa statistic.

Validity

Whereas reliability centers on the consistency of measurement, the focus of validity is on what is being measured and how well. The three major types of validity are content validity, criterion validity, and construct validity. These overlap considerably and should not necessarily be regarded as distinct. Content validity refers to the degree to which test-item content is sampled representatively from the universe or domain of content implied by a theoretical definition of the characteristic being measured. The evaluation of content validity is usually undertaken by expert judges acquainted with the test domain of interest. Criterion validity refers to how well scores on a test relate to some particular criterion measure, that is, another index of the psychological attribute of interest. Criteria may be postdictive, concurrent, or predictive (i.e., in the past, present, or future, respectively) and validity is typically summarized through the use of a correlation coefficient. Construct validity refers to the degree to which a test measures an hypothesized characteristic. Rather than involving a single result, the establishment of construct validity considers a set of relationships with both other relevant and other irrelevant measures. That a measure is significantly related to other indices of the same psychological characteristic (i.e., has convergent validity) and not to other indices of unrelated attributes (i.e., has discriminant validity), assists in demonstrating the construct validity of that measure. Construct validity is a more general form of validity and is often viewed as incorporating both content and criterion validity.

Item Analysis

Item analysis represents a set of procedures used to evaluate the statistical merits of individual items comprising the psychological measure or test. These procedures may be used to select items for a test from a larger pool of initial items or to evaluate items on an established test. Analysis may consider the proportion of individuals who provide a particular response to an item. This may be used to ensure that each item has adequate variance and is therefore capable of contributing to the variance associated with test scores. The correlation between an item's responses and scores on the total test is frequently computed and used to select items that enhance test-internal consistency reliability. The analysis and selection of items based on correlations between an item's responses and scores on a criterion measure may foster test criterion validity. Examining whether an item's properties differ as a function of individuals' group membership may assist in determining and reducing the presence of test bias. In addition to these more commonly used procedures, more advanced factor analytic and item response methods may also be applied.

Norming

Because a particular object's or individual's score on a measure or test is not intrinsically meaningful, interpretation of the score requires its comparison to a distribution of scores associated with a comparison group. Norming involves the collection of a distribution of measures or test scores for some representative sample for which a particular measurement score may then be compared. Once normative data have been collected, an individual raw score may then be transformed into an interpretable scale that offers more meaning for the transformed score. Transformations may be linear or nonlinear, and resulting, commonly used scales include percentiles, standard scores, T scores, and stanines.

[*See also* Reliability; *and* Validity.]

Bibliography

American Educational Research Association, American Psychological Association, & National Council on Measurement in Education. (1985). *Standards for educational and psychological testing*. Washington, DC: Author. Includes detailed test standards endorsed by three professional organizations.

Anastasi, A. (1988). *Psychological testing* (6th ed.). New York: Macmillan.

DuBois, P. H. (1970). *A history of psychological testing*. Boston: Allyn & Bacon. A chronology of psychometrics.

Ghiselli, E. E., Campbell, J. P., & Zedeck, S. (1981). *Measurement theory for the behavioral sciences.* New York: Freeman.

Kline, P. (1986). *A handbook of test construction: Introduction to psychometric design.* New York: Methuen.

Nunnally, J. C., & Bernstein, I. H. (1994). *Psychometric theory* (3rd ed.). New York: McGraw-Hill.

Rust, J., & Golombok, S. (1989). *Modern psychometrics: The science of psychological assessment.* New York: Routledge.

Thorndike, R. L. (1971). *Educational measurement* (2nd ed.). Washington, DC: American Council on Education.

Ronald R. Holden

PSYCHOMETRIC SOCIETY. The Psychometric Society was founded in 1935, having its first organizational meeting in February and its first professional meeting in September in Hanover, New Hampshire. The first president of the society was L. L. Thurstone, and the first secretary, treasurer, and chairperson of the membership committee were Paul Horst, Jack Dunlap and John Stalnaker, respectively. The initial objective of the society was to establish and promote psychology as a quantitative rational science. Psychometric research was expanded to include military interests during and after World War II because of the U.S. military's extensive necessity to test draftees' abilities and to classify them.

In March 1936, the first issue of the society's quarterly journal, *Psychometrika,* was published, with Paul Horst and Albert K. Kurtz as coeditors. Since then, *Psychometrika* has enjoyed the status of the leading journal in this area. The initial objective has been printed at the beginning of each issue of *Psychometrika,* and it is still the purpose of the society.

The president of the Psychometric Society is elected by vote of the membership and assumes the leadership for one year. Since 1935, an annual meeting has been held in the United States or Canada, usually at the place where the current president resides. In June 1978, led by Karl Joreskog of Sweden, European meetings of the society started. Since then, the European meeting has been held usually in every other year.

Although the Psychometric Society started as a small group of American psychometricians, its size has grown and international membership has been promoted. By the late 1990s, it had approximately 550 regular and student members. Most regular members hold doctoral degrees in psychology, mathematics, or statistics. Approximately 30% of the members reside in more than 30 countries other than the United States or Canada, spanning six continents.

Although "encouraging mathematical psychology" was emphasized in the presidential address at the first meeting, theories and models based on stochastic processes have gradually become dominant among the papers published in *Psychometrika,* and nonstochastic mathematical modelers have tended to depart from the Psychometric Society. They eventually formed the Society of Mathematical Psychology, and the first issue of the *Journal of Mathematical Psychology* was published in 1964. In spite of these philosophical differences, the two societies have kept fairly close relationships with each other, and in 1978 they held a joint meeting in Hamilton, Ontario, Canada. Lawrence Hubert organized the first joint meeting of the Psychometric Society and the Classification Society of North America in 1984 in Santa Barbara, California. Joint meetings were later held in 1991 in New Brunswick, New Jersey, and in 1998 in Champaign, Illinois. Many members of the Psychometric Society have also joined and presented papers at the annual meetings of related organizations such as the National Council on Measurement in Education, the American Educational Research Association, the American Psychological Association, and the American Statistical Association. Cooperative relationships have also been extended to areas outside of psychology, education, and statistics, as exemplified by interdisciplinary exchanges of ideas and methodologies with chemometricians.

A broad range of topics has been presented at Psychometric Society meetings and published in *Psychometrika,* including factor analysis, covariance structure, cluster analysis, structural equation modeling, classical and modern mental test theories, various psychological scalings that include both unidimensional and multidimensional approaches, various multivariate analysis methods, and other statistical topics, to name a few. For the first 10 years, from 1936 through 1945, papers on factor analysis amounted approximately to one third of all papers published in *Psychometrika,* outnumbering those on any other topic. The dominance of factor analysis continued in the 1950s and 1960s but was gradually replaced by that of item response theory, also known as latent trait theory, latent trait models, and modern mental test theory. Publication of F. M. Lord and M. R. Novick's *Statistical Theories of Mental Test Scores* in 1968 and pioneer expansions of latent trait models to include polychotomous and continuous responses, in addition to dichotomous responses and the multidimensional latent space (F. Samejima, 1969, 1972, 1973, & 1974), were examples of stimuli that accelerated this tendency. In 1997, for example, the papers presented at the Society's North American and European meetings represented more than 20 major categories, and those on item response theory and its applications to computerized adaptive testing accounted for 40% of all the papers.

As the computational tools for psychometric research changed from hand calculators, to electric calculators, to mainframe computers, and finally to microcomputers and work stations, different types of computational methods have been developed. Today, Psychometric Society members contribute significantly to the research of general psychologists and other researchers by providing methodologies, computer algorithms, and software. A few examples of these programs are LISREL (K. G. Joreskog et al.), LOGIST (F. M. Lord et al.), BILOG (R. D. Bock et al.), MULTILOG (D. Thissen et al.), SIBTEST (W. Stout et al.), TORSCA (F. W. Young & W. S. Torgerson), MDSCAL (J. B. Kruskal), MULTISCALE (J. O. Ramsay), and MAPCLUS (P. Arabie & J. D. Carroll). In addition, research outcomes produced by members of the Psychometric Society have been used by many mental measurement and testing organizations, including the Educational Testing Service, American College Testing, and the Law School Admission Council, as well as by the military.

The Psychometric Society started giving doctoral dissertation awards at its annual meeting in 1993. A committee of three former presidents selects the prize winner(s) each year. The first winners were Carolyn Anderson of the University of Illinois in the United States and Eric Maris Katholieke of the University of Leuven in Belgium.

Many members of the society have been awarded grants for psychometric research from different federal and local agencies, including the National Science Foundation and the National Institute of Mental Health, as well as from the military and industry. Notably, the Office of Naval Research awarded sizable grant money to researchers developing item response theory and its applications to computerized adaptive testing from the second half of 1970s until the first half of 1990s.

[*See also* Psychometrics.]

Bibliography

Green, B. F. (Ed.). (1986). Fiftieth anniversary section. *Psychometrika, 51,* 1–68. The first 10 articles in this issue of *Psychometrika* review the history of psychometrics and the journal *Psychometrika.*

Van der Linden, W. J., & Hambleton, R. K. (Eds.). (1997). *Handbook of modern item-response theory.* Heidelberg, Germany: Springer-Verlag. The first chapter of this volume provides an excellent overview of modern psychometrics.

Fumiko Samejima

PSYCHONEUROENDOCRINOLOGY concerns the relationships among behavior, the nervous system, and the endocrine system. The nervous system and the endocrine system are intimately connected through their direct and indirect reciprocal influences. Moreover, behavior can be viewed as both a cause and an effect of neuroendocrinological adjustments. Whereas behavior can produce changes in our internal functions, alterations in neuroendocrinological function can also change our behavior. Thus, study of the interdependence of psychological, neurological, and hormonal mechanisms is the basis of psychoneuroendocrinology. One major focus of psychoneuroendocrinology today is the study of environmental stressors and their effect on the neuroendocrine system, its constituent target organs, and hence normal and abnormal bodily function. Another major focus is the study of how alterations in neuroendocrinological systems can affect behavior in normal circumstances and in psychopathological states.

History

The nineteenth-century French physiologist Claude Bernard noted that one of the most important requirements for life is to maintain stability of the internal body fluid environment in the face of a changing external environment. A critical function of the psychoneuroendocrinologic system is to mediate our internal adaptation to the changing external environment. The stability of the internal environment was subsequently termed *homeostasis* by the American physiologist Walter Cannon. In the 1920s, Cannon noted that various physical and emotional stressors evoked release of epinephrine and norepinephrine from the adrenal medullae and sympathetic nerves. The adaptive significance of these neuroendocrinological adjustments is now widely appreciated. For example, the classic stress response, sometimes referred to as the *defense reaction,* has been conceptualized as preparation for fight or flight. The anticipatory and concerted bodily adjustments accompanying intense stimulation facilitate our ability to mobilize energy stores, to perform better the fight or flight response, and hence, to be more likely to adapt successfully to environmental threats or demands. However, when environmental demands persist over a prolonged period of time, depletion of important neural and endocrine secretagogues may occur, potentially resulting in dysfunction at the behavioral and/or physiological level. In the 1930s, Canadian physician scientist Hans Selye described responses that were mediated by the pituitary-adrenocortical system that occur in conjunction with a wide variety of long-lasting stressors. He theorized that the adaptive response to stress was composed of three stages: alarm, resistance, and exhaustion. This response, labeled the *general adaptation syndrome,* helped bridge the fields of psychology and medicine by linking psychological stress to a neuroendocrine-mediated model of disease susceptibility.

Control of Endocrine Function by the Brain

The neurobiological basis of psychoneuroendocrinology centers around a small group of neurons and neurosecretory cells in the hypothalamus. The hypothalamus is a brain stem structure that is intimately involved in systemic regulation, through complex control loops, of body heat, water balance, food intake, and sexual drive, as well as visceral responses to emotionally significant events. When environmental events are interpreted as emotionally meaningful, activation occurs in a complex series of neural networks including, among others, the limbic system and brain stem. These networks provide excitatory and inhibitory input to various nuclei of the hypothalamus that, in turn, initiate a cascade of neural and endocrine events that ultimately affects major organ systems throughout the body. Some hypothalamic neurons directly release vasopressin and oxytocin from the posterior pituitary into the systemic circulation. Other specialized hypothalamic neurons secrete releasing or inhibiting peptide hormones into localized vascular beds of the hypophysial-portal system. This specialized vasculature carries these peptides to the anterior pituitary where they act directly on secretory endocrine cells. Important hormone release stimulating or inhibiting peptides of the hypothalamus include corticotropin releasing factor (CRF), thyrotropin releasing hormone (TRH), luteinizing hormone releasing hormone (LH-RH), growth hormone releasing hormone (GH-RH), prolactin releasing factor (PRF), and prolactin inhibitory factor (PIF). Thus, the concerted endocrine response to psychologically meaningful stimulation is mediated chiefly through specialized hypothalamic nuclei.

The Pituitary: The Master Endocrine Gland

Under control by the hypothalamus, endocrine cells of the anterior pituitary release several protein hormones into the systemic circulation. These hormones travel in the bloodstream to distant sites of action where they stimulate release of other hormones or act directly on target tissue. For example, thyroid-stimulating hormone (TSH) induces secretion of thyroid hormones from the thyroid gland, whereas adrenocorticotropic hormone (ACTH), sometimes referred to as corticotropin, stimulates release of cortisol from the adrenal cortex. The two gonadotropes, follicle-stimulating hormone (FSH) and luteinizing hormone (LH), promote secretion of the sex steroids, estrogen, progesterone, and testosterone, from the gonads. These two hormones also have direct effects on development of the sperm and ova cells. Some anterior pituitary hormones do not evoke release of other hormones as their primary function, but rather have systemic effects directly on nonendocrine target tissues. Prolactin directly controls breast development and lactation, whereas growth hormone produces metabolic effects on various organs and tissues. The opioid peptide endorphin is released (often concomitantly with ACTH) from the anterior pituitary and has a number of important systemic functions, many of which remain to be elucidated.

Modulation of the Pituitary by Feedback Inhibition

Negative feedback loops ultimately limit hormone secretion for many of these endocrine systems through inhibitory effects at the level of the hypothalamus and the pituitary. For example, cortisol released into systemic circulation from the adrenal cortex is capable of inhibiting hypothalamic neurons containing CRF and is also capable of directly inhibiting pituitary release of ACTH. Thyroid hormones can inhibit TSH from the pituitary and possibly also TRH from the hypothalamus. Gonadal hormones can suppress release of both LH and FSH. There is a considerable research focus on the integrity of these control loops in the etiology of various physio- and psychopathologies.

Neuroendocrinologic Effects of Psychological Stress

A cascade of physiological adjustments occurs upon exposure to psychological stress. The exact pattern of response depends on several factors, including the type and duration of stress. Some types of stress necessitate active behavioral coping responses, whereas other stressors must be passively endured. The behavioral response or nonresponse to a stressor will be one determinant of the pattern of physiological adjustment. For example, exposure to repeated pain stimuli can produce profoundly different systemic consequences, depending on the availability and acquisition of an effective behavioral coping response. Painful stimuli that are ultimately inescapable or unavoidable can evoke a persistent behavioral passivity sometimes referred to as *learned helplessness*. There are, however, concomitant neuroendocrine adjustments involving the opioid peptides that produce a stress-induced analgesia. This neuroendocrinologically mediated adjustment provides a physiological mechanism for coping with inescapable psychological stress. Stress-induced analgesia can be classically conditioned and is thought to have an important role in the psychophysiological adjustment to traumatic stress.

Despite the nuances of stimulus specificity, there is a generalized neuroendocrine reaction characteristic of the initial response to a wide variety of stressors. Exposure to a stimulus that is appraised by the organism as threatening activates a cascade in the two major effector branches of the classic defense reaction. One of the two major branches is the sympathoadrenomedullary system. Activity in parts of the brain associated with emotion stimulate midbrain nuclei in the locus coeruleus, raphe nucleus, and parabrachial nucleus as well as hypothalamic neurons containing CRF and other substances. Some of these hypothalamic neurons send axons to the lower brain stem and the spinal cord, influencing the activity of the sympathetic nervous system. Sympathetic fibers projecting to the adrenal medullae evoke release of epinephrine into systemic circulation. This circulating epinephrine causes a number of important systemic adjustments, including increased rate and force of contraction of the heart, thus increasing cardiac output and delivery of oxygenated blood. Meanwhile, activation of postganglionic sympathetic neurons evokes release of the primary sympathetic nervous system neurotransmitter, norepinephrine. The consequence of widespread sympathetic discharge is to produce selective constriction in vascular beds of the gut and skin as well as epinephrine-like responses in the heart. This sympathetic neuronal discharge, in conjunction with the action of adrenomedullary epinephrine, will facilitate an effective redistribution of blood flow from the gut and skin to the skeletal musculature.

The other primary effector division of the classic defense response is the hypothalamic-pituitary-adrenocortical (HPA) system. This system diverges from the sympathoadrenomedullary system in the hypothalamus, where stimulation of paraventricular neurons causes release of CRF peptides into portal blood. CRF is then transported to the anterior pituitary where it stimulates release of ACTH into systemic circulation. ACTH is then carried through the blood stream to the adrenal cortices, where it stimulates release of cortisol into systemic circulation. Cortisol facilitates adaptation to stressful stimuli by several effects on metabolism, including stimulation of protein catabolism, gluconeogenesis, and inhibition of both glucose uptake and oxidation in peripheral tissues.

The Role of Psychoneuroendocrinology in Disease

The relationship between psychoneuroendocrine function and both psycho- and physiopathology is of current interest from theoretical and clinical perspectives. Selective abnormalities of behavior and physiology have been associated with altered psychoneuroendocrinological function. However, the precise cause and effect relationships among these systems remains to be fully elucidated.

There is extensive current interest in the psychoneuroendocrinology of behavior disorders. For example, there is a large literature linking major depression to abnormalities of both the hypothalamic-pituitary-adrenocortical and the hypothalamic-pituitary-thyroid axes. There is emerging consensus that a large number of depressed individuals have hyperactivity of the HPA axis. Although thyroid hormones appear normal in depression, there are alterations in the TSH response to TRH. The role of HPA and thyroid axis abnormalities in depression is intriguing, and there appear to be similar endocrine abnormalities in other disorders, including Alzheimer's disease and anorexia nervosa. Psychoneuroendocrinological abnormalities may also be found in substance abuse disorders, anxiety disorders, and schizophrenia. The meaningfulness of these observations remains to be detailed, but the implications for understanding the causes and treatment for many forms of psychopathology are exciting.

There are also intimate links between psychoneuroendocrinological function and physiopathology. Chronic hyperreactivity of the defense response pathways can contribute to the development of disease or can precipitate or exacerbate an existing pathological process. Several diseases have been linked to possible abnormalities of the neuroendocrine response to psychological stress. Some theorists suggest that essential hypertension may represent the advanced stage of a developmental disorder of central control of the sympathoadrenomedullary system. Alterations in opioid inhibition of sympathoadrenal responses may leave the circulatory system disinhibited, functionally disordered, and thus vulnerable to end-organ consequences of periodic and repeated blood pressure elevations.

Psychological stress and its neuroendocrine consequences can also contribute to coronary heart disease, diabetes, cancer, and perhaps many other diseases. Chronic psychological stress exacerbates atherogenesis in animal models and may have similar effects in humans. In women, estrogen may provide some protection from heart disease, but its precise psychoneuroendocrinologic significance remains to be determined. Acute psychological stress and its effects on the sympathetic nervous system can trigger or exacerbate ischemia and myocardial infarction in individuals with coronary heart disease. For example, sympathoadrenal hormones can lower the threshold for ventricular fibrillation. Moreover, the increased myocardial oxygen demand associated with the circulatory response to stress may precipitate ischemia in heart muscle with a compromised blood supply. In diabetes mellitus, systemic release of epinephrine during psychological stress can inhibit insulin, thus exaggerating hyperglycemia. Neuroendocrinological effects of stress on the immune system may have significant consequences for bodily response to cancer and may also be significant in the development of hormone-sensitive tumors such as breast cancer. Interestingly, there is a rapidly growing literature on the effects of maternal stress hormones on the developing fetus. During acute maternal stress, fetal heart rate can increase as much as maternal heart rate, suggesting that there may be potentially harmful neuroendocrinological consequences of psychological stress during pregnancy. Theoretically, excessive exposure of the developing fetal nervous system to maternal stress hormones may permanently alter the subtle balance between excitatory and inhibitory neuroendocrine mechanisms, perhaps with life-long consequences.

[*See also* Endocrine Systems; *and* Neuropsychology.]

Bibliography

Cannon, W. B. (1929) *Bodily changes in pain, hunger, fear and rage*. New York: Brandford.

Cohen, I. B. (1957). Foreword to *An introduction to the study of experimental medicine* by Claude Bernard. New York: Dover.

McCubbin, J. A., Kaufmann, P. G. & Nemeroff, C. B. (1991). *Stress, neuropeptides, and systemic disease*. San Diego: Academic Press.

Nemeroff, C. B. (1989). Clinical significance of psychoneuroendocrinology in psychiatry: Focus on the thyroid and adrenal. *Journal of Clinical Psychiatry, 50* (Suppl.), 13–20.

Palkovits, M. (1987). Organization of the stress response at the anatomical level. In E. R. De Kloet, V. M. Wiegant, & D. De Wied (Eds.), *Neuropeptides and brain function* (pp. 47–55). Amsterdam: Elsevier.

Selye, H. (1976). *The stress of life*. New York: McGraw-Hill. (Original work published 1936)

Stratakis, C. A., & Chrousos, G. P. (1995). Neuroendocrinology and pathophysiology of the stress system. *Annals of the New York Academy of Science, 771*, 1–18.

Tsigos, C. & Chrousos, G. P., (1996). Stress, endocrine manifestations, and disease. In C. L. Cooper (Ed.), *Handbook of stress, medicine, and health* (pp. 61–85). Boca Raton, FL: CRC Press.

James A. McCubbin

PSYCHONEUROIMMUNOLOGY (PNI) embodies the study of behavioral, neural, endocrinc, and immune system interactions. For most of the twentieth century, the immune system was viewed as a powerful and autonomous functioning unit capable of both protecting the body from foreign antigens and mutated cells, as well as creating anaphylactic and autoimmune reactions that could kill or seriously cripple its host. Up until the mid-1970s, the idea that these processes might be influenced by psychosocial phenomena, such as environmental stimuli, perceptual processes, and affective response, no less by the central nervous system (CNS), was completely foreign in the mainstream biomedical research community. Robert Ader and colleagues led the initial work in PNI with experiments demonstrating that immunologic responses and immune suppression could be classically conditioned. The fact that immunosuppressive reactions could be classically conditioned to neutral stimuli (e.g., saccharine-sweetened water) following repeated pairings with established immunosuppressive agents supported the notion that neural–immune system interactions might be plausible. David Felten and colleagues established a "hardwired" anatomical basis for neural-immune interactions through their discoveries that sympathetic noradrenergic fibers terminate in the thymus, bone marrow, spleen, and lymph nodes where they appeared to synapse with lymphocytes and monocytes stored in those "lymphoid organs." Concurrently published evidence of adrenergic and cholinergic receptors on lymphocytes was also critical in establishing a physical basis through which both arms of the autonomic nervous system—sympathetic and parasympathetic—could signal cells of the immune system.

Animal research conducted in the 1980s established that immunologic activities are communicated back to the hypothalamus and hippocampus, instigating changes in neurotransmitters and endocrine substances that have immunoregulatory properties. It is now agreed that the paraventricular nucleus (PVN) of the hypothalamus is a chief juncture for immunoneural feedback control of the limbic–hypothalamic–pituitary–adrenocortical (LHPA) axis. It is believed that LHPA axis activation by cytokine production during immune responses is part of a governing system designed to regulate immune system activation (e.g., inflammation) following antigenic challenge. More recently, it has been shown that peripherally produced cytokines such as interleukin-1 (IL-1) can also feed back to the CNS by way of receptors on the vagus nerve. Whereas the LHPA axis provides an important immunoregulatory circuit during normal immune system activities, stress-related and depression-associated central noradrenergic depletion disinhibits corticotrophin releasing hormone (CRH) production with resulting increases in adrenocorticotropin hormone (ACTH) and cortisol. These changes may set the stage for less adaptive corticosteroid-induced inhibition of immune functioning, decreasing host defenses against pathogenic challenges and possibly increasing disease susceptibility.

Together this work shows that at least two stress-related pathways can influence the immune system: the LHPA axis by way of CRH, ACTH, and corticosteroids; and the sympathoadrenomedullary (SAM) system through the release of peripheral catecholamines. Adrenocortical hormones can impact several aspects of cellular immunity through intracytoplasmic glucocorticoid receptors on lymphocytes, whereas catecholamines work ostensibly by way of lymphocyte adrenergic receptors. Several other hormones, including but not limited to endorphins, enkephalins, substance P, growth hormone, thyroid hormones, androgens and estrogens, prolactin, arginine vasopressin, and neuropeptide-Y have also been shown to modulate immune functioning. It is significant that the magnitude and direction of their effects can vary widely with dosage and across donors.

Discoveries of anatomical and chemical media capable of orchestrating neural-endocrine-immune system interactions have gone a long way to legitimize the subdiscipline of PNI over the last two decades of the twentieth century. Since autonomic nervous system fibers and the LHPA axis are both known to change as individuals process environmental stimuli, they provide at least some of the rationale for how stress-related physiological changes could communicate with components of the immune system and work as part of a neural-endocrine–immune network designed to facilitate adaptation to external challenge. In so doing, these discoveries suggest mechanisms possibly explaining the long-held belief that psychosocial phenomena such as stressful experiences, personal losses, and emotional reactions, as well as interventions designed to modify the magnitude and chronicity of these experiences, could forecast the development or exacerbation of physical disease.

Psychosocial Phenomena Associated with Immune System Changes in Humans

Numerous psychosocial factors are associated with changes in the immune system. Some of these include depression and depressed mood, stressful experiences, and stress moderators such as appraisals of control, coping strategies, emotional expression, and social support.

Depression and Depressed Mood. One of the most widely investigated immune measures in studies of clinical depression is lymphocyte proliferative response (LPR) to mitogens. This test measures the ability of lymphocytes to expand clonally when stimulated with plant lectins, which act as harmless analogues of antigens, referred to as mitogens. A meta-analytic review of work relating depression and immunity found a reliable relationship between depression and decrements in a variety of immune measures, including LPR to mitogens, especially in older individuals and those with greater depression severity. Even in those not diagnosed with a depressive disorder, depressed mood was significantly correlated with the degree of impairment in several cell-mediated immune indices. Another review published at this time concluded that individuals with a depressive diagnosis show lower numbers of total lymphocytes, as well as lower natural killer cell cytotoxicity (NKCC) and neutrophil activity. Generally, these immune decrements appear to be limited to individuals with unipolar depression and those who are older. One intervention study demonstrated that treatment with a serotonin antagonist decreased depressive symptoms and restored neutrophil activity to levels similar to control participants over a 6-week trial, whereas another found that lymphocyte counts appeared to normalize during successful antidepressant pharmacotherapy.

Therefore, there is some evidence that depressive symptoms may covary with alterations in immune function in humans, although the mechanisms underlying these relations are yet to be worked out. Depressive symptoms include a constellation of affective (mood), interpersonal (social withdrawal), and biobehavioral (sleep disturbances) phenomena, any of which could influence certain aspects of the immune system. Whereas PNI investigations of depressive disorders and depressed mood have been extensive, far less is known about immunologic correlates of anxiety-related disorders such as panic and posttraumatic stress disorder, although this area is drawing increasing attention.

Stressful Experiences. The specific effects of different acute and chronic stressors, individual differences in intrapersonal and interpersonal stress moderator variables, and stress-associated health behavior changes (e.g., sleep) on the human immune system have been well-documented. These stressful experiences range from everyday events such as school examinations, sleep deprivation, and caregiving for sick or demented relatives, to more dramatic events such as death of a spouse, marital separation and divorce, nuclear reactor accidents, and natural disasters. The immune decrements most consistently associated with such stressors tend to be functional indices such as NKCC and increased antibody titers to herpes viruses.

One of these immune indices, NKCC, measures the ability of a type of lymphoid cell (NK) to kill tumor cell targets spontaneously when placed in culture, and represents an aspect of the immune system conferring protection against intracellular viral infections and novel tumors. Impairments in NKCC have been associated with bereavement, clinical depression and depressed affect, posttraumatic stress disorder symptoms following a natural disaster, and being a caregiver for a demented spouse or relative. Another immune functional measure frequently related to stressors is immunoglobulin-G (IgG) antibody titers to common and usually "latent" herpes virus infections such as Epstein-Barr virus (EBV) and herpes simplex virus (HSV). Elevations in these antibody titers are believed to reflect either reinfection with, or reactivation of, prior viral infections, and a rising titer is believed to result from inadequate cellular immune control of these reactivated infections. Elevated herpes virus titers have been related to marital separation and divorce, being a caregiver for a demented relative, and being a resident of Three Mile Island during the time of the nuclear reactor accident.

These associations are responsible for some of the highest stress-immune correlations documented in humans to date. In contrast, immune system indices reflecting lymphocyte cell counts and salivary immunoglobulin-A (IgA) have not been consistently related to stressors.

Stress Moderators. According to many PNI models, psychosocial factors relate to immune system changes by way of stress- or mood-induced changes in neurohormones. Clearly, several neuroendocrine responses are known to be altered as a function of an individual's appraisal (i.e., controllable vs. uncontrollable) of, and coping response (i.e., active vs. passive) to, stressful stimuli. Immunologic decrements and elevations in adrenocortical hormones have also been observed in those reporting higher levels of loneliness, suggesting that social support may contribute significantly to the degree of immune system decrements observed during stressful periods. Spousal social support, marital distress, and hostile interactions between marital partners have been related to decrements in several cellular immune function measures. We also know that perceptions of a loss of personal control, helplessness/hopelessness, and low self-efficacy, a use of passive coping strategies, and insufficient expression of negative emotions have all been associated with decreased LPR to mitogens and elevated antibody titers to EBV. Therefore, it can be reasoned that many PNI relationships might be mediated, in part, by neurohormonal changes that are linked to an individual's appraisals of, coping responses to, and resources available for dealing with environmental stimuli. Thus, efforts to characterize the mechanisms underlying stressor-immune interactions in humans must take into account these appraisal, coping, and interpersonal processes because they can moderate the nature, degree, and duration of neuroendocrine responses. Recent theoretical models proposing reversible and irreversible stress-associated neuroanatomical changes involving structures critical for LHPA and SAM hormonal regulation and efficient neuroimmune interactions have laid the groundwork for a new breed of investigations designed to identify the mechanisms underlying the negative health consequences of chronic and repeated stressor exposure.

Clinical Health Science Applications of Psychoneuroimmunology Research

Despite a large, though not always consistent literature relating a variety of stressors, stress moderators, and distress states to indices of human immunity, very little is known about the health relevance of these associations. One set of health-related studies focused on the role of stressors in the development of infectious disease by using cross-sectional and longitudinal natural history designs as well as some innovative experimental viral exposure and vaccination paradigms. These studies have been restricted to healthy populations. Another set of studies used natural history designs and randomized experimental interventions to examine the role of stressor exposure and stress management interventions in the course of life-threatening diseases such as human immunodeficiency virus (HIV) infection and certain cancers, both of which are believed to be affected by various components of the immune system.

Stressors and Disease Processes in Healthy Persons. Ronald Glaser and colleagues showed that students who were least stressed and anxious about impending medical shool examinations were the most likely to seroconvert (produce a primary antibody response) to hepatitis B virus (HBV) after the first vaccine inoculation. Those with the greatest social support had the strongest immune response to the vaccine by the time of the third inoculation. Stressors and stress moderators have also been related to HBV vaccination responses by other teams in the Netherlands and New Zealand. Among aging caregivers, chronic stress was associated with poorer primary antibody responses to influenza virus vaccination. Together, these studies suggest that among healthy persons, chronic stressors, coping responses, and social support may each influence immunologic components associated with primary antibody responses to novel pathogens.

Stressful life events and perceived stress have also been associated with the development of upper respiratory infections (URIs) in people exposed to live viruses in several studies conducted over the past two decades. Individuals experiencing elevated stressful events and greater perceived stress show a greater likelihood of developing cold symptoms and actual infections (indicated by either viral shedding or antibody titer elevations) after viral exposure. Thus, stressors may interfere with immune system defenses that are critical in conferring resistance to viral pathogens encountered. However, to date, no study has provided evidence for any stressor-induced immunologic mediator of subsequent infectious disease symptoms in humans exposed to viruses.

Another paradigm has been used to study the effects of stressors on another process that may have relevance for infectious disease: wound healing. Women serving as caregivers for relatives with dementia showed a slower rate of wound healing in the weeks following an experimental forearm punch biopsy as compared to age-matched women not acting as caregivers. Similar stress effects were documented on oral wound healing in healthy dental students. Such findings are important for understanding ways to optimize recovery from different forms of injury as well as surgery. Emotional distress levels preceding and persisting after surgery may influence the recovery process, possibly amplifying and protracting certain neuroendocrine responses caused by the surgical trauma itself. Stressor effects superimposed on surgery-associated changes in immune system functioning may not only slow wound healing, but may increase the likelihood of infectious complications following surgery. Conversely, stress reduction interventions during such periods may optimize recovery and reduce the risk of infectious complications. Despite the encouraging findings emerging from studies of infectious disease processes in healthy individuals, determining whether PNI processes are predictive of clinical health changes is perhaps most efficiently examined by studying people whose immune systems are already functioning abnormally (suppressed or overactivated) due to an extant disease process.

Stressors and Disease Processes in Diseased Populations. Amelioration of stress may slow the progression of disease processes in persons with immunologically mediated conditions.

HIV/AIDS. Since stressors, perceived loss of control, social isolation, and depression are prevalent in HIV-infected persons and have been related to decrements in immune indices known to be altered by HIV infection, it is reasonable that these psychosocial phenomena might influence disease course in HIV-infected individuals by way of PNI mechanisms. Stressful life events, depressive symptoms, fatalistic appraisals, denial coping, distraction coping, and social support have all been shown to predict the rate at which T-helper cells (CD4)—the primary target of the virus—decline over time in HIV-infected persons. However, other studies have failed to find any associations between CD4 declines and these variables, disparities that may be attributable, in part, to the use of heterogeneous populations, insensitive measures, or inadequate follow-up periods.

Some studies have examined how psychosocial factors relate to indices of immune functioning in HIV-infected persons. More frequent use of active coping and less use of passive coping and avoidance are related to the ability of HIV-infected persons to preserve functions such as NKCC and LPR to mitogens. Elevated stressful life events, low social support, concealing one's sexual orientation from others, denial coping, and excessive rumination predict faster disease progression, whereas active confrontation of stressors appears to predict slower disease progression in HIV-infected men. However, no study to date has shown that immune changes associated with these psychosocial phenomena mediate their associations with disease endpoints.

Stress-reducing interventions such as cognitive-behavioral stress management (CBSM) appear to reduce cortisol and norepinephrine output and to lower antibody titers to herpes viruses such as EBV and HSV in conjunction with anxiety and dysphoria reductions in HIV-infected men. Other work has observed that HIV-infected men receiving massage therapy show increases in cytotoxic T-lymphocytes, NK cell number, and NKCC in conjunction with decreased anxiety and 24-hour urinary cortisol output. Two studies revealed that greater distress reductions during psychosocial intervention predicted slower rates of immunologic decline up to 2 years later, although neither of these interventions was causally related to either immunologic or clinical health declines over this period. These studies support the efficacy of stress reduction interventions for increasing psychological adjustment and immune functioning, which in turn may or may not contribute to changes in health status in HIV-infected people at early and middle stages of the disease. Since interventions such as CBSM can decrease anxiety and tension levels as well as denial and depressed affect, they may facilitate adherence to medical treatment regimens providing a possible stress-health, behavioral-immune pathway. The improvements in immune function that have been associated with CBSM suggest the possibility that psychosocial interventions can help reconstitute the compromised immune system once pharmacologic agents have contained further replication of HIV.

Neoplastic Disease. The role of the immune system in controlling different types of carcinomas in humans remains controversial. Some cancers whose course appears to be associated with psychosocial factors on the one hand and immune system components on the other include malignant melanoma and cervical cancer. A greater use of active coping predicts longer survival time, whereas the use of repressive coping predicts shorter survival in individuals with malignant melanoma. Elevated negative life events, passive coping, emotional inhibition, and pessimistic appraisals have all been associated with greater promotion of cervical neoplasia. Some of these psychosocial variables have been associated with immune measures in cancer populations. For instance, greater pessimism was associated with lower NKCC in women at increased risk for cervical carcinoma. Although the largest collection of psychosocial factors has been associated with disease course in individuals with breast cancer, the role of the immune system as a mediator of these associations remains unclear at present.

As in the case of HIV infection, there is some evidence that psychosocial interventions can modulate certain aspects of immune functioning in some individuals with cancer. Rarely have these immune changes been shown to predict the course of cancer or survival. One series of studies came close to establishing these links. Individuals with malignant melanoma assigned to a 6-week stress reduction group showed improvements in coping and reductions in distress that were followed by increases in interferon-stimulated NKCC 6 months later. This team found that persons with malignant melanoma assigned to the intervention group enjoyed a greater disease-free interval and greater survival rate at 6-year follow-up as compared to those in the standard-care control. However, although baseline NKCC and intervention-related changes in active coping both predicted a more favorable disease course, intervention-related changes in NKCC did not predict either disease-free interval or survival over time.

A widely publicized study also demonstrated that individuals with metastatic breast cancer (a cancer not usually viewed as immunogenic) who were assigned to a long-term expressive supportive group therapy intervention lived twice as long as similar women assigned to standard care. It is possible that the opportunity for emotional expression, processing, and assimilation and the social support offered during this and similar interventions contributed to the greater longevity seen in group members. The extent to which these psychosocial changes offer survival benefits by way of immune system changes remains speculative. There is some evidence across psycho-oncology studies that psychosocial factors are more likely to be associated with disease course in younger persons and those at earlier stages of disease, suggesting that initial PNI work should focus on these cancer populations. Other cancers including prostate cancer, leukemias, and rare but immunogenic cancers such as Kaposi's sarcoma and Burkitt's lymphoma may also be fruitful areas for further PNI investigations. In addition, immune measures characterizing the repertoire of cytotoxic T-cells and macrophages in response to cancer-specific antigens should be incorporated into immunologic batteries being used to establish PNI relationships in different cancer populations. Finally, it is critical that future PNI research with individuals with cancer control for ongoing adjuvant therapies such as chemotherapy, radiation, hormonal therapy, and immunotherapy, as each of these can have a significant effect on immunologic measures.

Health Frontiers in Psychoneuroimmunology. PNI research paradigms are now being used to address questions concerning other diseases and syndromes that are likely mediated by the immune system. Briefly, some of these include: allergies and asthmatic conditions, tuberculosis, rheumatoid arthritis, multiple sclerosis, and systemic lupus erythematosus. In addition to these diseases, poorly understood conditions such as chronic fatigue syndrome (CFS) have been studied from a PNI perspective because CFS symptom exacerbations have been tied to both stressors and immune system abnormalities. Diseases previously thought to be independent of immune system activities, such as coronary artery disease, are now beginning to receive attention from PNI researchers. This may be a fruitful venture, given that myocardial infarction and the underlying stenotic process have been linked to stress, social isolation, depression, and negative affect on the one hand, and cytokine dysregulation on the other. It may be that these well-established psychosocial risk factors for myocardial infarction contribute to disease pathophysiology by way of alterations in infection-mediated inflammatory responses, and that both immunoregulatory cytokines and these psychosocial factors operate through a common neuroendocrine factor.

PNI mechanisms may play an important role in determining health outcomes for individuals who are more vulnerable to disease after undergoing treatments such as surgery, chemotherapy, radiation therapy, and tissue transplantation, and more work is likely to be emerging in these areas in coming years. Despite the encouraging results that have emerged in the PNI literature since 1970, it is important to note that inconsistent findings have emerged for most phenomena studied: At best, psychosocial factors account for less than 25% of the variance in immune measures, and stress-induced immunologic changes rarely fall out of the normal range among healthy persons. Moreover, although cognitive-affective-neuroendocrine mechanisms are often proposed as mediators of PNI associations, stress-induced changes in diet, sleep, physical exercise, medication adherence and side effects, and substance abuse may also serve as mediators, because each of these has been independently associated with immune system and physical health changes. What we have learned about PNI associations and underlying mechanisms from healthy individuals, as well as human and animal models of infectious, neoplastic, and autoimmune diseases, may allow researchers to address remaining questions and develop effective theory-based interventions for the large populations of vulnerable persons who might benefit from future advances in this field.

[*See also* Immune System; *and* Neuropsychology.]

Bibliography

Ader, R., Cohen, N., & Felten, D. (1995). Psychoneuroimmunology: Interactions between the nervous system and the immune system. *Lancet, 345*, 99–103.

Antoni, M. H., Cruess, D., Wagner, S., Lutgendorf, S., Kumar, M., Ironson, G., Klimas, N., Fletcher, M. A., & Schneiderman, N. (in press). Cognitive-behavioral stress management effects on anxiety, 24-hour urinary catecholamine output, and T-cytotoxic suppressor cells over time among symptomatic HIV-infected gay men. *Journal of Consulting and Clinical Psychology.*

Antoni, M. H., Schneiderman, N., Fletcher, M., Goldstein, D., Laperriere, A., & Ironson, G. (1990). Psychoneuroimmunology and HIV-1. *Journal of Consulting and Clinical Psychology, 58*(1), 38–49.

Bovjberg, D. (1991) Psychoneuroimmunology: Implications for oncology? *Cancer, 67*, 828–832.

Cohen, S., Tyrrell, D. A., & Smith, A. P. (1991). Psychological stress in humans and susceptibility to the common cold. *New England Journal of Medicine, 325*, 606–612.

Fawzy, F., Fawzy, N., Hyun, C., Elashoff, R., Guthrie, D., Fahey, J., & Morton, D. (1993). Malignant melanoma.

Effects of an early structured psychiatric intervention, coping, and affective state on recurrence and survival 6 years later. *Archives of General Psychiatry, 50*, 681–689.

Felten, D., Felten, S., Bellinger, D., Carlson, S., Ackerman, K., Madden, K., Olscowka, J., & Livnat, S. (1987). Noradrenergic sympathetic neural interactions with the immune system: Structure and function. *Immunological Review, 100*, 225–260.

Glaser, R., Kiecolt-Glaser, J. K., Bonneau, R., Malarkey, W., & Hughes, J. (1992). Stress-induced modulation of the immune response to recombinant hepatitis B vaccine. *Psychosomatic Medicine, 54*, 22–29.

Herbert, T., & Cohen, S. (1993). Stress and immunity in humans: A meta-analytic review. *Psychosomatic Medicine, 55*, 364–379.

Ironson, G., Wynings, C., Schneiderman, N., Baum, A., Rodriquez, M., Greenwood, D., Benight, C., Antoni, M. H., LaPerriere, A., Huang, H., Klimas, N., & Fletcher, M. A. (1997). Posttraumatic stress symptoms, intrusive thoughts, loss and immune function after Hurricane Andrew. *Psychosomatic Medicine, 59*, 128–141.

Irwin, M., Daniels, M., Smith, T., Bloom, E., & Weiner, H. (1987). Impaired natural killer cell activity during bereavement. *Brain Behavior and Immunity, 1*, 98–104.

Kiecolt-Glaser, J., & Glaser, R. (1995). Psychoneuroimmunology and health consequences: Data and shared mechanisms. *Psychosomatic Medicine, 57*, 269–274.

Kiecolt-Glaser, J., Marucha, P., Malarkey, W., Mercado, A., & Glaser, R. (1995). Slowing of wound healing by psychological stress. *Lancet, 346*, 1194–1196.

Lutgendorf, S., Antoni, M., Ironson, G., Klimas, N., Starr, K., Schneiderman, N., McCabe, P., Cleven, K., & Fletcher, M. A. (1997). Cognitive-behavioral stress management intervention decreases dysphoric mood and herpesvirus-type 2 antibody titers in HIV-seropositive gay men. *Journal of Consulting and Clinical Psychology, 65*, 31–43.

Maier, S., Watkins, L., & Fleshner, M. (1994). Psychoneuroimmunology: The interface between brain, behavior and immunity. *American Psychologist, 49*, 1004–1017.

McEwen, B. (1998). Protective and damaging effects of stress mediators. *New England Journal of Medicine, 338*, 171–179.

Spiegel, D., Bloom, G. C., Kramer J. S., Gottheil, E. (1989). Effect of psychosocial treatment on survival of patients with metastatic breast cancer. *Lancet, 2*, 888–891.

Michael H. Antoni

PSYCHONOMIC SOCIETY. Experimental psychologists formed the Psychonomic Society to facilitate the dissemination of information concerning the science of psychology through annual meetings and the publication of scientific journals.

The primary organization of American psychologists since 1892 has been the American Psychological Association (APA). Psychology, however, is a very diverse field, and during the twentieth century various groups on both the practice and experimental sides of psychology have organized alternative organizations at times when members felt that their interests were not being adequately represented in the APA. The Psychonomic Society is such an organization. Its roots can be traced to discussions at the December 1958 meetings of the American Association for the Advancement of Science in Washington, D.C. There was a feeling among experimental psychologists that the APA was becoming too strongly oriented toward the practice of psychology at the cost of representation of the interests of experimentalists. Discussion continued at a meeting of the Society of Experimental Psychologists that fall, and an organizing committee, composed of Wilfred J. Brogden, William K. Estes, Frank A. Geldard, Clarence H. Graham, Lloyd G. Humphreys, Clifford T. Morgan, William D. Neff, Kenneth W. Spence, S. Smith Stevens, and Benton J. Underwood, was formed in the summer of 1959. William S. Verplanck served as secretary-treasurer and did much of the spadework for the fledgling organization, and Morgan's efforts were especially notable.

The Organizing Committee first met on 29 and 30 December at the Hotel Morrison in Chicago: The official founding of the new society was dated 31 December 1959. The issue of selecting a name was controversial and not settled at that time. Eventually, the word *psychonomic*, which means, roughly, the science of the mind, was adopted by correspondence.

From the beginning, the issue of the Psychonomic Society membership has been inextricably tied to the organization of annual meetings. The organizers wanted to maintain tight quality control over the papers presented but to avoid the refereeing of abstracts or papers. They therefore set strict standards for membership and adopted the principle that once accepted as a member, the individual has the right to present a paper at the annual meeting unrefereed. To become a member, an individual had not only to have received a Ph.D. degree in psychology but also to have published significant research beyond the doctoral dissertation. In practice, this has often meant that the individual must have five articles stemming from postdoctoral research in refereed journals.

At the time of the first annual meeting of the Psychonomic Society at the University of Chicago in September 1960, there were 736 members; as of 1997, there were nearly 2,000. In addition, there were 550 Associates—Ph.D.-degree-holding experimental psychologists who had not yet met the criteria for full membership.

The founders of the Psychonomic Society wished to keep governance simple, avoiding an excessive administrative structure. The Psychonomic Society is run by a 12-person governing board, with each member serving a 6-year term. The terms are staggered so that the membership nominates and elects two new board members each year. The board elects its own chair yearly: The position is more administrative than honorary. Much of the society's business is handled through the publications office in conjunction with a secretary-treasurer, who is appointed by the board. The primary committees are a membership committee and a publications committee.

The first 37 annual meetings of the Psychonomic Society were held in 18 different cities: St. Louis was the most popular site. Most meetings have been held in the fall and have run 2 days. A meeting in the late 1990s had 1,681 registrants. There is no registration fee.

Consistent with the wishes of the founders, the meetings are rather spare, with a focus on the communication of scientific information. From the beginning, the emphasis has been on contributed papers from members. Poster sessions were added in 1988, thus opening the society to greater participation by associates. The 666 presentations at the 1995 meeting included 336 oral presentations of papers and 330 posters. Although there were no symposia in the early years, there are now two symposia per meeting.

The Psychonomic Society currently publishes six journals in experimental psychology. The journal publishing program was initiated outside of the administrative structure of the Psychonomic Society by Clifford T. Morgan, who had the personal resources needed to undertake such an endeavor. [*See the biography of Morgan.*] The founders viewed publications as a key component of improved communication among experimental psychologists and explored unsuccessfully various ways to bring existing journals within the Psychonomic Society imprimatur. In 1964 Morgan began publishing *Psychonomic Science*, a journal of brief research reports with a short publication lag. When this was a success, he added *Psychonomic Monograph Supplements*, now defunct. Morgan gave the journals to the Psychonomic Society in 1967. Nevertheless, Morgan continued to supervise the journals and to provide financial support. The society was able to weather the crisis of Morgan's death in 1976 and continued to develop the program.

The journal set has evolved over time with additions, subtractions, and name changes. *Behavior Research Methods, Instruments, and Computers* was added in 1968, and *Perception and Psychophysics* was begun in 1971 to cover sensory and perceptual psychology. In 1973 *Psychonomic Science* evolved into the *Bulletin of the Psychonomic Society* plus three new refereed journals: *Animal Learning and Behavior, Memory and Cognition*, and *Psychobiology*. The *Bulletin of the Psychonomic Society* was terminated in 1993. The journal had offered an outlet, generally unrefereed, for brief articles. By 1993 it was felt that such a vehicle was no longer needed, and the fully refereed *Psychonomic Bulletin and Review* replaced it in 1994.

The Psychonomic Society was founded to supplement other organizations of psychologists rather than to replace them. It has fulfilled its founders' intentions of facilitating communication among experimental psychologists through both annual meetings and its publications.

Bibliography

Dewsbury, D. A. (1997). History of the Psychonomic Society: II. The journal publishing program. *Psychonomic Bulletin and Review, 3*, 322–338.

Dewsbury, D. A. (1997). History of the Psychonomic Society: III. The meetings of the Psychonomic Society. *Psychonomic Bulletin and Review, 4*, 350–358.

Dewsbury, D. A. (1997). History of the Psychonomic Society: IV. The development of the Psychonomic Society. *Psychonomic Bulletin and Review, 4*, 492–500.

Dewsbury, D. A., & Bolles, R. C. (1995). The founding of the Psychonomic Society. *Psychonomic Bulletin and Review, 2*, 216–233.

Garner, W. R. (1976). Clifford Thomas Morgan: Psychonomic Society's first chairman. *Bulletin of the Psychonomic Society, 8*, 409–415.

Donald A. Dewsbury

PSYCHOPATH. *See* Antisocial Personality Disorder.

PSYCHOPATHOLOGY. Mental illness or abnormality is called psychopathology. Despite their differences in etiology (causation) and clinical characteristics, all forms of psychopathology can be viewed as conditions that adversely affect psychological functioning in some way. Nevertheless, the precise boundaries distinguishing psychopathology from normal psychological functioning have proven to be elusive.

The Concept of Mental Illness

What is mental abnormality, and how does it differ from normality? The answer to this question has yet to be conclusively resolved. For example, psychopathologists have expended a great deal of time and effort over the question of whether such conditions as homosexuality, premenstrual syndrome, alcohol dependence (alcoholism), and attention-deficit/hyperactivity disorder (childhood hyperactivity) should be classified as mental illnesses (incidentally, the first two of these conditions are not currently classified as formal mental illnesses, whereas the last two are). Such controversies underscore a crucial question: What criteria, if any, can be used to distinguish abnormality from normality?

Proponents of a statistical model, such as Sir Henry Cohen, contend that mental illness is best conceptualized in terms of statistical rarity: A condition is abnormal if it is found in only a small percentage of the population. This conceptualization squares with the fact that many mental illnesses are rare. For example, schizophrenia, a condition characterized by severe disturbances in thinking and emotion, is found in about 1% of the population worldwide.

Nevertheless, a statistical model is problematic for three reasons. First, it provides no guidance concerning the cutoff points for differentiating abnormality from normality. Should abnormality be defined as the uppermost 1% of the population, the uppermost 5%, or some other figure? In most cases, the answer is arbitrary. Second, because this model does not indicate which dimensions are relevant to psychopathology, it mistakenly classifies high scores on certain dimensions, such as intelligence and altruism, as pathological. Third, a statistical model erroneously assumes that common conditions are nonpathological. For example, it implies that widespread radiation sickness following an atomic explosion is normal.

Advocates of a subjective distress model posit that mental illnesses are conditions that cause psychological pain in affected individuals. It is undeniable that many mental illnesses, such as major depression and obsessive-compulsive disorder, produce considerable subjective distress. Nevertheless, other conditions, such as psychopathy (a condition marked by an absence of guilt, empathy, and close emotional attachments) and the manic phase of bipolar disorder (a condition marked by extreme levels of elation, energy, and grandiosity), are typically associated with little or no subjective discomfort.

Proponents of a biological model, such as Sir R. E. Kendell, maintain that mental illness can be defined in terms of a biological disadvantage, such as reduced life span or reduced fitness (i.e., the capacity of an individual to pass on its genes to future generations), to the individual. Some mental illnesses are associated with clear-cut biological disadvantages; approximately 15% of individuals with major depression eventually commit suicide, and approximately 10% of inpatients with anorexia nervosa (a condition marked by failure to maintain normal body weight and intense fears of gaining weight) eventually die of starvation. Nevertheless, a biological model falls prey to numerous counterexamples. Being an African American male in most U.S. inner cities reduces one's average life span relative to general population norms but is not a disorder; being a priest (who elects to have no children) reduces one's fitness but is similarly not a disorder.

Advocates of a sociological, or labeling, model, such as Thomas Szasz, argue that mental illness is a myth. According to Szasz, individuals labeled as mentally ill suffer not from a disorder of the mind or brain but from "problems in living." These individuals march to the beat of a different drummer and consequently experience difficulty adjusting to society. Sociological theorists contend that psychiatric labels are cross-culturally relative because societal norms for expected behavior differ across cultures. They further posit that psychiatric labels become self-fulfilling prophecies because they lead observers to interpret ambiguous behaviors as indicative of abnormality.

David Rosenhan conducted a study (1973) that is commonly cited in support of labeling theory. Rosenhan and seven other normal individuals posed as pseudopatients (fake patients) in 12 psychiatric hospitals. These pseudopatients informed the admitting physicians that they were hearing a voice saying "empty, hollow, thud." All were promptly admitted to the hospital and were retained there for an average of nearly 3 weeks. Interestingly, in 11 of 12 cases they were discharged with diagnoses of "schizophrenia in remission." Rosenhan also claimed that the hospital staff often interpreted the pseudopatients' normal behaviors (e.g., note taking) as indicative of abnormality. These results led Rosenhan to conclude that mental abnormality and normality cannot be meaningfully differentiated and that labels color observers' perceptions of ambiguous behaviors.

Nevertheless, the evidence for labeling theory is less impressive than it superficially appears. As Robert Spitzer (1975) pointed out, the fact that the pseudopatients were released with diagnoses of "in remission" (which means "showing no signs of pathology") indicates that the mental health professionals who observed them were able to distinguish normality from abnormality. Moreover, diagnostic labels may be less cross-culturally relative than labeling theorists have assumed. In a study of the Yorubas of Nigeria and the Eskimos of the Bering Strait, Jane Murphy (1976) found that these cultures possessed labels for disorders that were strikingly similar to schizophrenia and psychopathy. Murphy's findings run counter to the suppositions of most labeling theorists because they suggest that certain psychological conditions are recognized across wide cultural boundaries.

Jerome Wakefield (1992) pointed out that despite its shortcomings, the sociological model touches on an important truth: all mental illnesses are negatively valued. Specifically, Wakefield contends that mental illnesses are harmful dysfunctions. The "harm" component of Wakefield's analysis involves societal values concerning a condition's undesirability, and "dysfunction" involves the failure of a system to function in the fashion designed by natural selection. According to Wakefield, a specific phobia of cats is a mental illness because it is negatively valued by society and because the fear system was not evolutionarily designed to become activated by stimuli that are not objectively dangerous. Nevertheless, Wakefield's analysis may have its shortcomings. For example, it assumes that all mental illnesses involve failures of psychological or physiological systems. But some mental illnesses, such as anxiety disorders, probably represent adaptive defenses to subjectively perceived threats. Moreover, Wakefield's analysis presumes that there is a relatively unambiguous dividing line between dysfunction and adaptive function. But the functioning of many systems, such as the anxiety system, may be continuously distributed, with no clear-cut demarcation between normality and abnormality.

In response to the shortcomings of previous attempts to analyze the concept of mental illness, some authors, such as Ethan Gorenstein (1992), have concluded that this concept is intrinsically undefinable. Scott Lilienfeld and Lori Marino (1995), and Lawrence Kirmayer (1994) have further suggested that mental illness is a Roschian concept. Roschian concepts lack defining features (features that are individually necessary and jointly sufficient for category membership) and possess fuzzy boundaries. Consequently, the question of whether an individual or object belongs to the category is scientifically arbitrary. Moreover, Roschian concepts are organized around a prototype that comprises all of the features of the category. The category of "lake," for example, is a Roschian concept because there is no set of features that unambiguously define a lake. Moreover, although there are prototypical examples of lakes (e.g., one or more of the U.S. Great Lakes), the distinction between lakes and both ponds and seas is arbitrary from a scientific standpoint.

According to a Roschian view, mental illnesses cannot be explicitly defined because no scientific criteria can distinguish abnormality from normality. Even if this view is correct, however, it would not imply that specific mental disorders are not amenable to scientific inquiry. As Gorenstein (1992) observed, the concept of "drug" is probably undefinable, as there are no strict scientific criteria for distinguishing drugs from nondrugs. But this problem has not stopped pharmacologists from studying the biochemical properties and behavioral effects of specific drugs. Similarly, researchers can engage in the scientific examination of specific mental illnesses even if the broader concept of mental illness is not strictly scientifically definable.

Levels of Understanding in Psychopathology

As Alan Kazdin has noted, psychopathological conditions can be hierarchically differentiated in terms of our levels of understanding regarding their pathology (i.e., the physiological changes that accompany the condition) and etiology. At the lowest level of the hierarchy, syndromes can generally be thought of as constellations of signs (observable indicators) and symptoms (unobservable indicators that are known only because they are reported by the individual) that covary across individuals. For example, depression is a syndrome because the presence of one of its signs (e.g., crying) or symptoms (e.g., sadness) is associated with an increased likelihood of others.

Disorders, in turn, are syndromes that cannot be accounted for by other conditions. In the current diagnostic system, for example, obsessive-compulsive disorder can be diagnosed only if its symptoms (e.g., recurrent fears of contamination) and signs (e.g., recurrent washing) cannot be accounted for by a specific phobia (e.g., an irrational fear of dirt).

At the highest level of the hierarchy, diseases are disorders whose pathology and etiology are well understood. For example, sickle cell anemia is a disease because its pathology (e.g., crescent-shaped blood cells) and etiology (a recessive gene) are known. Few, if any, current psychopathological conditions can be considered genuine disease entities because the pathologies and etiologies of almost all mental illnesses have yet to be discovered. The only potential exception involves mental disorders of organic origin, such as Alzheimer's disease, whose pathology is well documented and whose etiology is partly understood.

Classification and Diagnosis

Whatever their theoretical and methodological differences, all psychopathology researchers agree that the domain of mental illness is enormously heterogeneous in its causes and characteristics. To increase our understanding of mental illnesses, it is necessary to reduce this heterogeneity by slicing up the pie of psychopathology into narrower and more homogeneous categories. Classification refers to the development of a systematic taxonomy for placing individuals into categories. Diagnosis is the process of placing individuals into the categories created by a classification system.

The concepts of reliability and validity are essential for evaluating the adequacy of diagnoses yielded by a classification system. Reliability refers to the consistency of a diagnosis; a reliable diagnosis can be measured in a repeatable fashion across time and situations. Reliability can be assessed in several ways, two of which are test-retest reliability and interrater reliability. Test-retest reliability refers to the extent to which diagnoses are consistent over relatively long time periods, such as 6 months. Although test-retest reliability is a useful indicator of reliability, it is relevant only for conditions that tend to be chronic (i.e., relatively stable over long time intervals), such as schizophrenia. Diagnoses that tend to be episodic (i.e., that come and go over relatively brief periods of time), such as major depression, would not generally be expected to exhibit high test-retest reliability.

Interrater reliability, which is typically indexed in psychopathology research by the Kappa coefficient, refers to the extent to which diagnosticians can agree on patients' diagnoses. This coefficient measures raters' agreement on diagnoses after correcting for chance, with "chance" operationalized as the base rate (prevalence) of the disorder being assessed. If two diagnosticians work in a setting in which the base rate of schizophrenia is 90%, the finding that they agree with each other on the diagnosis of schizophrenia in 90% of cases could plausibly be attributed to chance. The Kappa coefficient corrects for chance agreement and thereby provides a conservative estimate of interrater reliability.

Validity refers to "truth in advertising": a valid diagnosis measures what it purports to measure. Validity cannot exist without reliability. Just as a bathroom scale cannot validly measure weight if it yields dramatically different estimates of weight for the same person, a diagnosis cannot validly measure a mental illness if it yields dramatically different scores on measures of psychopathology across time and situations. Nevertheless, reliability can exist without validity. For example, a clinician who bases the diagnosis of schizophrenia entirely on individuals' height (e.g., "Schizophrenics are people who are over seven feet tall") would be making reliable but invalid diagnoses of schizophrenia. Reliability is necessary but not sufficient for validity.

How do psychopathology researchers determine the validity of a diagnosis? Eli Robins and Samuel Guze (1970) outlined a set of criteria for addressing this question. According to these authors, a valid diagnosis must do at least the following four things: (1) distinguish the disorder from superficially similar disorders; (2) predict the natural history (i.e., course and eventual outcome) of diagnosed individuals; (3) predict the family history of diagnosed individuals; (4) predict the laboratory, biological, and personality findings of diagnosed individuals. In addition, although not explicitly mentioned by Robins and Guze, a valid diagnosis should ideally be able to predict the treatment response of diagnosed individuals.

According to Robins and Guze (1970), a valid diagnosis does more than describe the individual's behavior: It provides us with new information. When the diagnosis of schizophrenia has been correctly made, for example, we have learned that the individual (1) exhibits disturbances of thought and emotion that are not entirely accounted for by conditions that are superficially similar to schizophrenia, such as mood disorders (e.g., bipolar disorder); (2) is likely to exhibit a chronic course with relatively poor outcome; (3) has a increased risk of schizophrenia among biological family members; (4) has a heightened probability of exhibiting certain biological and laboratory abnormalities, such as enlarged cerebral ventricles and poor smooth pursuit eye-movement tracking; and (5) is likely to exhibit a positive response to medications that block the activity of the neurotransmitter dopamine.

Systems of Classification in Psychopathology

The earliest system of psychiatric classification dates back at least to Hippocrates (c. 460–377 BCE), who identified three major mental disorders: melancholia (depression), mania (excitement), and phrenitis (brain fever). Hippocrates and his discipline Galen further contended that personality abnormalities were due to excesses of four bodily humors (chemicals). Melancholic (depressed) individuals have an excess of black bile, sanguine (cheerful) individuals an excess of blood, choleric (hot-tempered) individuals an excess of yellow bile, and phlegmatic (apathetic) individuals an excess of phlegm. A more recent categorization, which although influential is no longer included in the formal diagnostic nomenclature, is the distinction between neurosis and psychosis. Neurotics are individuals who are mildly affected, possess insight into the nature of their problem, and retain adequate reality testing (i.e., the ability to distinguish fantasy from reality), whereas psychotics are individuals who are severely affected, possess little or no insight into the nature of their problem, and have lost their capacity for reality testing. This distinction, although useful, has its shortcomings: Many conditions (e.g., borderline personality disorder) represent a mixture of both neurotic and psychotic features, and some conditions (e.g., major depression) are characterized by neurotic features in some individuals and psychotic features in others.

Prior to the 1950s, the state of psychiatric classification in the United States remained relatively disorganized. Because there was no standard system of classification, what one diagnostician meant by "schizophrenia," for example, often bore little correspondence to what other diagnosticians meant by this label. This situation changed in 1952, when the American Psychiatric Association released the first edition of the *Diagnostic and Statistical Manual of Mental Disorders* (*DSM–I*). *DSM–I* provided the first relatively clear descriptions of major psychiatric conditions, thereby facilitating agreement among diagnosticians in their use of labels. *DSM–II*, which appeared in 1968, was similar to *DSM–I* but provided slightly greater detail regarding the signs and symptoms of many diagnostic categories.

Despite their strengths, *DSM–I* and *DSM–II* were suboptimal for several reasons. First, the interrater reliabilities yielded by these manuals were often low. In part, this was because *DSM–I* and *DSM–II* contained global and relatively vague descriptions of mental illnesses and therefore required considerable subjective judgment on the part of diagnosticians. Second, *DSM–I* and *DSM–II* were influenced by psychoanalytic conceptions of mental illnesses and made extensive references to defense mechanisms and other concepts derived from Freudian theory. Consequently, diagnosticians whose orientation was not psychoanalytic (e.g., behaviorists) found themselves hard pressed to use these manuals for diagnostic purposes. Third, many critics argued that *DSM–I* and *DSM–II* conceptualized mental illnesses in a virtual vacuum, as they provided little information regarding contextual variables (e.g., coexisting medical conditions, life stressors) that often played important roles in the etiology and maintenance of psychopathology.

In response to these criticisms, the American Psychiatric Association, with Robert Spitzer at the helm, issued *DSM–III* in 1980. *DSM–III* was a major advance in psychiatric classification and diagnosis and represented a marked departure from its predecessors in three ways.

First, *DSM–III* provided standardized diagnostic criteria and algorithms for the diagnosis of mental illnesses. For each condition, *DSM–III* delineated both the specific signs and symptoms composing the diagnosis and the method by which these signs and symptoms are combined to reach a diagnosis. Although *DSM–III*'s use of diagnostic criteria and algorithms has sometimes been maligned as the "Chinese menu" approach to diagnosis ("choose two from Column A, three from Column B," and so on), this approach has markedly decreased the subjectivity of diagnostic decision making. Indeed, there is evidence that the interrater reliabilities of many diagnoses increased following *DSM–III*, although some authors, such as Stanley Kirk and Herb Kutchins (1992), contend that this increase has been exaggerated. Reliability has been further enhanced by the development of structured psychiatric interviews, such as the Diagnostic Interview Schedule (DIS), which provide diagnosticians with standardized questions and follow-up probes with which to assess diagnostic criteria.

Second, the developers of *DSM–III* elected to be theoretically agnostic and to omit concepts that were tied to a specific theoretical orientation, such as psychoanalysis. This alteration allowed diagnosticians of varying theoretical orientations to use the manual with equal ease and comfort.

Third, *DSM–III* adopted a multiaxial approach to diagnosis, in which each individual is described along a series of axes, or dimensions. This approach encourages diagnosticians to adopt a more holistic approach to diagnosis by considering contextual factors other than the individual's mental illness per se. In *DSM–III* and its revisions, the first two axes are restricted to mental illnesses; the last three axes assess other dimensions relevant to psychological functioning. On Axis I are found most of the major mental disorders, including substance-related disorders, schizophrenia and other psychotic disorders, mood disorders, anxiety disorders, and eating disorders. The distinction between Axis I and Axis II underscores the difference between conditions such as major depression that tend to be superimposed on the individual's preexisting functioning (Axis I) and conditions such as personality disorders that represent the individual's stable and long-standing patterns of relating to the world (Axis II). Most personality disorders are believed to represent extreme levels of personality traits (e.g., egocentricity, impulsivity) that interfere with functioning. The five axes of *DSM–IV*, which are similar to those of *DSM–III*, are displayed in Table 1.

PSYCHOPATHOLOGY. Table 1. The five axes of *DSM–IV*

Axis I:	Major clinical syndromes (e.g., schizophrenia, bipolar disorder)
Axis II:	Personality disorders (e.g., borderline personality disorder); mental retardation
Axis III:	Medical disorders
Axis IV:	Psychosocial stressors
Axis V:	Overall level of adaptive functioning

The revised edition of *DSM–III* (*DSM–III–R*), which appeared in 1987, and the fourth edition (*DSM–IV*), which appeared in 1994, retained all of the major innovations of *DSM–III*. Nevertheless, both represented a move away from a monothetic approach to diagnosis, which was emphasized in *DSM–III*, toward a polythetic approach. In a monothetic approach, signs and symptoms are individually necessary and jointly sufficient for a diagnosis. In *DSM–III–R* and *DSM–IV*, in contrast, the criteria for most diagnoses are neither necessary nor sufficient. The advantage of a polythetic approach is increased interrater reliability: two diagnosticians who disagree regarding the presence of a single criterion do not automatically disagree on the diagnosis.

Criticisms of *DSM–III*, *DSM–III–R*, and *DSM–IV*

Despite their strengths, *DSM–III* and its progeny have been the targets of several criticisms. Some critics, such as George Vaillant (1984) and David Faust and Richard Miner (1986), charged that these manuals emphasize reliability at the expense of validity. Specifically, they contended that many of the diagnostic criteria in *DSM–III*, *DSM–III–R*, and *DSM–IV*, although highly objective, have stripped the diagnostic system of much of its richness and complexity. For example, the *DSM–IV* diagnosis of antisocial personality disorder (ASPD) is intended to assess the core features of psychopathy. Nevertheless, because *DSM–IV*'s developers believed that the personality traits of psychopathy, such as callousness and self-centeredness, are difficult to assess reliably, they opted for a diagnosis emphasizing readily agreed-upon antisocial actions, such as vandalism and physical aggression. Although the *DSM–IV* diagnosis of ASPD may be more reliable than the classic trait-based definition of psychopathy, some authors, such as David Lykken (1995), argue that its neglect of personality features has attenuated its validity.

Another potential problem with DSM–III and its revisions is the extensive comorbidity among diagnostic categories. Comorbidity is typically defined as the co-occurrence of two or more diagnoses within an individual. Although comorbidity is common among Axis I conditions, it is especially rampant among Axis II conditions (see Table 1). It is not uncommon for patients to simultaneously meet criteria for three, four, or even five personality disorders. Many critics argue that the presence of comorbidity suggests serious problems with the validity of *DSM–III* and its successors, because an ideal classification system yields mutually exclusive categories with few overlapping cases. Nevertheless, defenders of the current diagnostic system note that extensive comorbidity is found in organic medicine and often reflects the fact that certain conditions (e.g., acquired immune deficiency syndrome) dramatically increase individuals' risk of developing other conditions (e.g., Kaposi's sarcoma, pneumonia).

Whatever their shortcomings, *DSM–III* and its heirs clearly represent important achievements in psychiatric classification. These manuals have rendered the diagnostic process more explicit and thus more open to corrective feedback. Moreover, by delineating standardized criteria and algorithms that can be used by diagnosticians of different theoretical persuasions, they have increased reliability and permitted research consumers to draw more confident generalizations across studies.

Dimensional Models of Psychopathology

Most classification systems, including *DSM–IV*, implicitly adopt a categorical model, in which mental conditions are conceptualized as either present or absent. According to *DSM–IV*, an individual either meets criteria for schizophrenia, for example, or does not. Some researchers argue, however, that this categorical model should be either replaced or supplemented by a dimensional model. Proponents of a dimensional system contend that most forms of abnormality differ from normality in degree rather than kind. As Paul Meehl (1986) noted, a major goal of the next generation of psychopathology researchers should be to determine which mental disorders are taxonic and which are dimensional. As defined by Meehl, a taxon is a scientifically nonarbitrary class, that is, a category that exists in nature rather than in the minds of diagnosticians.

Nevertheless, many diagnosticians have been reluctant to embrace a dimensional system. In part, this reluctance stems from a lack of consensus regarding which dimensions should be used to characterize psychopathology. Some researchers, such as Paul Costa, Robert McCrae (1992), and Thomas Widiger (1993), have suggested that the Big Five dimensions of Extraversion, Neuroticism, Conscientiousness, Agreeableness, and Openness to Experience provide a comprehensive framework for both normal and abnormal personality. Psychopathy, for example, might be conceptualized within this framework as a condition marked by high Extraversion, low Neuroticism, low Conscientiousness, low Agreeableness, and normal Openness to Experience. The Big Five have been found to underlie individuals' scores on omnibus personality tests (i.e., tests assessing a broad spectrum of personality traits) and appear to be cross-culturally generalizable.

Nevertheless, not all researchers accept the Big Five as a model for psychopathology. Hans Eysenck, for example, contended that three dimensions—Extraversion, Neuroticism, and Psychoticism—rather than five are sufficient to account for most mental disorders. According to Eysenck, individuals with elevated Neuroticism are susceptible to anxiety disorders, mood disorders, and related conditions, whereas individuals with elevated Psychoticism are susceptible to schizophrenia and related conditions. Moreover, certain forms of psychopathology are difficult to accommodate within the Big Five. Schizophrenia, for example, is characterized by disturbances in thinking and perception that may not be adequately represented by any of these five dimensions. Moreover, there is some evidence that schizophrenia and related conditions may be taxonic rather than dimensional.

Epidemiological Studies and Risk Factors for Psychopathology

How prevalent are mental illnesses in the population, and what risk factors are associated with their prevalences? These are the principal questions addressed by the field of epidemiology, which examines the distribution of illnesses in the population. There have been several large-scale epidemiological studies of psychopathology. Perhaps the best known is the Epidemiological Catchment Area (ECA) study sponsored by the National Institute of Mental Health in the early 1980s. The ECA study was designed to estimate the prevalence of Axis I conditions in the general population and to examine demographic differences in their prevalences. The ECA investigators randomly sampled households in several major U.S. cities and used a structured psychiatric interview (the DIS) to assess the presence of *DSM–III* diagnoses in the 6 months prior to the study. Data were obtained on more than 20,000 adults.

The ECA study revealed that the most common Axis I conditions were specific phobias, such as fears of blood or flying (4.5–11.8%), agoraphobia (a condition typically associated with panic attacks that involves avoidance of situations in which escape is difficult or help from others is unavailable) (2.7–5.8%), alcohol dependence and abuse (4.5–5.7%), major depression (2.2–3.5%), dysthymia (chronic but low-grade depression, (2.1–3.8%), and drug dependence and abuse (1.8–2.2%).

Between 29 and 38% of adults reported a history of at least one Axis I condition. In addition, the ECA study revealed that less than one third of mentally ill individuals have obtained treatment. Subsequent epidemiological studies have largely corroborated the ECA findings. A 1994 study by Ronald Kessler and colleagues indicated that approximately 30% of the U.S. population met criteria for one or more *DSM–III–R* Axis I conditions over a 1-year period. Moreover, 56% of respondents with one Axis I condition met criteria for other Axis I conditions.

The ECA study uncovered important differences in the risks of mental illnesses across different groups. Among women, the most common diagnoses were specific phobias, agoraphobia, and major depression, whereas among men the most common diagnoses were alcohol and drug abuse and dependence and specific phobias. The rates of most conditions decreased after age 45, and certain conditions, such as drug dependence and abuse and ASPD, were found to be predominantly illnesses of young adulthood. The ECA study also revealed ethnic differences in the prevalences of certain conditions. For example, the rates of depression were lower in African Americans and Hispanics than Whites, and the rates of alcohol and drug abuse and dependence were lower in young African Americans compared with young Whites.

Over the past several decades, researchers have become increasingly cognizant of cross-cultural differences in the distribution of psychopathology. The nature of these differences, however, remains controversial. Arthur Kleinman (1988), for example, has criticized the traditional pathogenetic/pathoplastic model, which posits that biological factors are essentially cross-culturally invariant and that cultural factors act only to influence their behavioral manifestations. According to Kleinman, this model underestimates the cultural specificity of psychopathology. Whether or not Kleinman is correct, it is clear that many forms of psychopathology exhibit striking differences across cultures. For example, a disorder known as koro, which is marked by intense anxiety regarding the possibility that the penis (or in women, the breasts or vulva) will retract and disappear, is reported almost exclusively in Malaysia, Singapore, and China. Anorexia nervosa, in contrast, seems largely confined to Western societies.

Approaches to the Causes of Psychopathology

Psychopathology researchers utilize a variety of approaches to the etiology of mental illnesses. As noted in the previous section, epidemiological studies can shed light on risk factors for psychopathology. Behavior genetic studies, such as twin and adoption designs, allow investigators to disentangle the roles of genetic and environmental factors in the causation of mental illnesses. For most major Axis I disorders, including schizophrenia, mood disorders, anxiety disorders, and alcohol dependence, genetic factors have been found to exert a moderate to large influence. Environmental factors also play a substantial role in these conditions, although the precise nature of these factors (e.g., parenting styles, prenatal viral exposure) often remains to be ascertained.

The findings of behavior genetic researchers suggest that a diathesis-stress model provides a useful framework for the etiology of many mental illnesses. According to this model, psychopathology results from the interaction between a biological (often genetic) predisposition and environmental precipitants. A diathesis-stress model posits that neither genetic nor environmental risk factors alone are sufficient to produce psychopathology; both are required.

Some psychopathology researchers focus most of their energies on the diathesis side of the diathesis-stress equation, others on the stress side. Some use brain imaging techniques and biochemical assays to examine biological markers (physiological correlates) of mental illnesses. These markers may in some cases be causes or indicators of underlying disease processes. Schizophrenia, for example, is associated with enlarged cerebral ventricles and degeneration of the cerebral cortex, both of which may provide clues to pathogenic processes. Other researchers examine environmental factors that increase risk for mental illness. For example, hospitalized schizophrenics who return to families with high levels of expressed emotion (EE)—a variable reflecting the extent to which family members are critical, hostile, and emotionally overinvolved—have higher rates of relapse than those who return to low-EE families. EE may thus play a critical role in the maintenance, and perhaps etiology, of schizophrenia. The ultimate hope of researchers is that the identification of causal factors will provide valuable leads to both the treatment and prevention of mental illnesses.

Although many psychopathology researchers examine the influence of risk factors at a single point in time, the discipline of developmental psychopathology explores the causes and manifestations of mental illnesses over time, often from childhood to adulthood. Developmental psychopathologists, such as Sir Michael Rutter, contend that the causes and behavioral expressions of many conditions change dramatically with age. For example, depression often manifests itself as irritability rather than sadness in young children; attention-deficit/hyperactivity disorder is typically marked by decreasing levels of impulsivity and overactivity but constant levels of inattention with age. A primary goal of developmental psychopathology is thus to identify and understand the sources of both continuity and change in mental illnesses throughout the life span.

Bibliography

American Psychiatric Association (1994). *Diagnostic and statistical manual of mental disorders* (4th ed.). Washington, DC: Author. Provides diagnostic criteria and detailed descriptions for all major mental disorders, as well as useful information regarding their epidemiological characteristics.

Costa, P. T., & McCrae, R. R. (1992). Four ways five factors are basic. *Personality and Individual Differences, 13*, 653–665.

Eysenck, H. J. (1991). Dimensions of personality: 16, 5, or 3?—Criteria for a taxonomic paradigm. *Personality and Individual Differences, 12*, 773–790.

Faust, D., & Miner, R. A. (1986). The empiricist in his new clothes: *DSM–III* in perspective. *American Journal of Psychiatry, 143*, 962–967.

Goodwin, D. W., & Guze, S. B. (1996). *Psychiatric diagnosis* (5th ed.). New York: Oxford University Press. A comprehensive overview of the clinical features, natural history, family history, and epidemiology of major mental disorders (e.g., schizophrenia, anxiety, and mood disorders).

Gorenstein, E. E. (1992). *The science of mental illness.* San Diego, CA: Academic Press. A first-rate discussion of the conceptual underpinnings of theory and research in psychopathology.

Kazdin, A. E. (1983). Psychiatric diagnosis, dimensions of dysfunction, and child behavior therapy. *Behavior Therapy, 14*, 73–99. Contains a discussion of different levels of understanding in psychiatric diagnosis.

Kessler, R. C., McGonagle, K. A., Zhao, S., Nelson, C. B., Hughes, M., Eshleman, S., Wittchen, H-U., & Kendler, K. S. Lifetime and 12-month prevalence of DSM-III-R psychiatric disorders in the United States: Results from the National Comorbidity Study. *Archives of General Psychiatry, 51*, 8–19.

Kirk, S. A., & Kutchins, H. (1992). *The selling of DSM–III: The rhetoric of science in psychiatry.* New York: Aldine de Gruyter.

Kirmayer, L. J. (1994). Rejoinder to Professor Wakefield. In S. A. Kirk & S. D. Einbinder (Eds.), *Controversial issues in psychiatric diagnosis* (pp. 41–71). New York: Raven Press.

Kleinman, A. (1988). *Rethinking psychiatry: From cultural category to personal experience.* New York: Free Press.

Lilienfeld, S. O., & Marine, L. (1995). Mental disorder as a Roschian concept: A critique of Wakefield's "harmful dysfunction" analysis. *Journal of Abnormal Psychology, 104*, 411–420.

Lykken, D. T. (1995). *The antisocial personalities.* Hillsdale, NJ: Erlbaum.

Matarazzo, J. D. (1983). The reliability of psychiatric and psychological diagnosis. *Clinical Psychology Review, 3*, 103–145. A detailed review of studies of the interrater reliability of major diagnostic categories.

Meehl, P. E. (1986). Diagnostic taxa as open concepts: Metatheoretical and statistical questions about reliability and construct validity in the grand strategy of nosological revision. In T. Millon & G. L. Klerman (Eds.), *Contemporary directions in psychopathology: Toward the DSM–IV* (pp. 215–231). New York: Guilford Press. A superb discussion of often-overlooked conceptual and methodological problems in psychiatric classification and diagnosis. For more advanced readers.

Murphy, J. M. (1976). Psychiatric labeling in cross-cultural perspective. *Science, 191*, 1019–1028.

Robins, E., & Guze, S. B. (1970). Establishment of diagnostic validity in psychiatric illness: Its application to schizophrenia. *American Journal of Psychiatry, 126*, 983–987. Outlines a comprehensive approach to the validation of psychiatric diagnoses.

Rosenhan, D. L. (1973). On being sane in insane places. *Science, 179*, 250–258.

Spitzer, R. L. (1975). On pseudoscience, logic in remission, and psychiatric diagnosis: A critique of Rosenhan's "On being sane in insane places." *Journal of Abnormal Psychology, 84*, 442–452.

Spitzer, R. L., Williams, J. B. W., & Skodol, A. E. (1980). *DSM–III*: The major achievements and an overview. *American Journal of Psychiatry, 137*, 151–164.

Vaillant, G. E. (1984). The disadvantages of *DSM–III* outweigh its advantages. *American Journal of Psychiatry, 141*, 542–545.

Wakefield, J. C. (1992). The concept of mental disorder: On the boundary between biological facts and social values. *American Psychologist, 47*, 373–388. A thoughtful summary and critique of the major attempts to delineate the boundaries between mental normality and abnormality.

Widiger, T. A. (1993). The *DSM–III–R* categorical personality disorder diagnoses: A critique and an alternative. *Psychological Inquiry, 4*, 75–90.

Widiger, T. A., & Frances, A. (1985). The *DSM–III* personality disorders: Perspectives from psychology. *Archives of General Psychiatry, 42*, 615–623. A readable overview of personality trait and interpersonal approaches to psychiatric diagnosis.

Scott O. Lilienfeld

PSYCHOPHARMACOLOGY. [*This entry comprises two articles*: Pharmacotherapy *and* Ethnopsychopharmacology. *The lead article describes and defines pharmacotherapy. The companion article discusses ethnopsychopharmacology* *and provides a history of the field's study of the ethnic and racial response to drugs. See also the following related entries*: Antianxiety Medication; Antidepressants; Antineurotic Medication; Antipsychotic Medication; Depressants, Sedatives, and Hypnotics; Drugs; Ethics, *article on* Ethics in Research; *and* Stimulants.]

Pharmacotherapy

Psychoactive drugs produce behavioral, emotional, or cognitive effects. Clinical psychopharmacology is the use of such drugs to treat mental and behavioral disorders. The drugs are prescribed by psychiatrists, pediatricians, neurologists, and family physicians as medications for mental illness, anxiety, depression, epilepsy, and substance abuse. Clinical psychologists are not ordinarily licensed to prescribe drugs because they do not hold medical degrees. (At the time of this report, the U.S. armed forces were evaluating the possibility of training clinical psychologists to prescribe psychoactive medicines in the military.) Instead, clinical psychologists provide psychological, behavioral, and cognitive therapies that patients often need in addition to (or instead of) medication. Research psychologists also play important roles in studying the effects of medication and in developing scientific knowledge of brain functioning.

Psychopharmacology is associated with the neuroscience model of mental disorders. Emphasis is given to understanding drug effects in terms of genetics, brain structure and biochemistry, and the functioning of the central nervous system. Most psychoactive medicines exert their clinical effects on one or more neurotransmitters, the substances responsible for the transmission of impulses from one nerve cell to another, or on the receptors for neurotransmitters. Future progress in understanding these substances, in identifying related substances and processes, and in understanding how the genetic code affects these substances all may lead to improved drugs.

Interaction and Adverse Effects

Any time a person is taking more than one medicine, attention must be paid to possible interactions between medications. In most cases, when a psychoactive drug enters the bloodstream, most of it binds to plasma proteins and has no clinical effects. Instead, clinical effects are caused by the relatively small amount of unbound drug (free fraction) in the bloodstream. If a second drug that binds to the same plasma proteins is given, competition for binding sites may cause a large increase in the free fraction of the first drug, resulting either in toxicity or in another significant effect.

Drug interaction also can occur as a consequence of changed rates of metabolism. If drug A induces or inhibits the enzymes that metabolize drug B, the peak amount of drug B available at a site of action may be increased or decreased, altering drug B's usual clinical effects. Other causes of interactions include additive or antagonistic effects, as when two drugs that each lower blood pressure produce an excessive decrease when given together, or absorption effects, as when the action of one medication increases or decreases the rate of absorption by the gastrointestinal tract of a second medication. Drug interactions can be minimized or controlled by proper planning of dosages, administration times, or routes and by the choice of medication preparation. However, careful monitoring of drug effects is always needed.

Adverse drug reactions are noxious unintended events associated with medications. Usually these reactions can be managed by monitoring the effects of drugs and adjusting their dosages or by using alternative agents. The probability of adverse side effects varies considerably, depending on the type of medication, the dosage, and the individual. Adverse reactions common to many psychoactive agents include anticholinergic effects (e.g., blurred vision, constipation, dry mouth, urinary hesitance), extrapyramidal symptoms (restlessness to the point of being unable to sit still, bizarre postures, lack of movement, spasms, tics, facial grimacing, to-and-fro rhythmic movements), and sedation (daytime drowsiness). Tardive dyskinesia (sucking and smacking of lips, lateral jaw movements, tongue thrusting, rolling movements of shoulders or limbs, excessive salivation) is a complex of adverse extrapyramidal symptoms that occurs after prolonged use of antipsychotic drugs. This condition may persist throughout life. Other possible adverse effects include blood abnormalities (aplastic anemia, agranulocytosis, leukocytosis, eosinophilia, thrombocytopenia), cardiovascular effects (e.g., dysrhythmias, hypotension, hypertension), cholestasis (slowing of bile passage through the liver), confusion, dermatological reactions, dizziness, falls, jitteriness, learning impairment, tics, tremors, urinary dysfunction (enuresis, incontinence, nephrogenic diabetes insipidus), seizures, and sleep disturbance. Death is rare but some cases have been documented, resulting from overdosage, toxic reactions, or interactions.

Major Drug Classes

There are six types of drugs. These will now be discussed.

Antipsychotics. The modern era of psychopharmacology is usually traced to 1952, when Delay, Deniker, and Harl reported that chlorpromazine (Thorazine) had antipsychotic effects distinct from the simple sedative effects of previously used drugs. Antipsychotic drugs, also called *neuroleptics* or *major tranquilizers*, are used for schizophrenia and other psychotic conditions.

They reduce the intensity of the core symptoms of psychosis, including thought disorder (loose associations, conceptual disorganization), hallucinations, delusions, and withdrawal. These symptoms are not cured, however, and the drugs may have to be used for years. Individual variations in response to these medications are considerable. Most persons who respond positively do so within the first 6 weeks of treatment (Kinon, 1993). Relapse rates within 1 to 2 years are significant, with some authorities citing rates as high as 50% even when the medicines are continued (Schatzberg, Cole, & Debattista, 1997).

The antipsychotics also are used in the treatment of aggression or irritability with psychotic features, as well as in various movement disorders such as the tics seen in Tourette syndrome and the stereotypes seen in autism. They are widely used for the treatment of self-injurious behavior in people with mental retardation or autism, although many authorities believe that they are overused for this purpose and recommend trials of antidepressants instead (Reiss & Aman, 1998).

The "typical" (or first-generation) antipsychotics are phenothiazines, butyrophenone, thioxanthene, and dihydroindolone. The "atypical" (or second-generation) antipsychotics include dibenzodiazepine, thienobenzodiazepine, benzisocazole (risperidone), and phenolindole (sertindole). The main advantage of most second-generation drugs is that they have fewer side effects. The most commonly prescribed antipsychotics are Haldol, Mellaril, Navane, and Thorazine—all typical agents—as well as Clozaril and Risperdal, which are atypical. All of the antipsychotic medications in use today are based on dopamine antagonism, which seems to be an important mechanism responsible for their antipsychotic effects.

Antipsychotics do not produce physical dependency. However, adverse side effects are a concern. The drugs cause sedation, which can interfere with everyday learning or functioning. They also cause a variety of movement disorders such as tardive dyskinesia. In rare instances, they trigger neuroleptic malignant syndrome, a condition in which body temperature can reach lethally high levels. Withdrawal of neuroleptics is sometimes associated with various motor symptoms, including tardive dyskenisia, weight loss, insomnia, and anticholinergic rebound (characterized by vomiting, diarrhea, and diaphoresis).

Antidepressants. Antidepressant medicines were introduced in 1957 (Crane, 1957; Kuhn, 1957). Today, antidepressants are used for the treatment of depressive episodes, obsessive-compulsive disorder, panic disorder, eating disorder, enuresis, attention-deficit hyperactivity disorder (ADHD), and, to a lesser extent, aggression. Authorities disagree about their effectiveness for severe depressive states such as melancholia. At least one-half of depressed patients respond to antidepressants, although it often takes about three weeks or longer for benefits to appear. Their efficacy in children is not yet well established but their use with this population is growing.

Antidepressants include the tricyclics and related compounds, monoamine oxidase inhibitors (MAOIs), selective serotonin reuptake inhibitors (SSRIs), and atypical agents. Early MAOIs interacted with tyramine, a substance found in certain foods and beverages (e.g., cheese, salami, fruits, beer), causing life-threatening hypertensive reactions. The newer reversible MAOIs (e.g., moclobemide, brofaromine) have fewer side effects and no dietary restrictions. The tricyclic and heterocyclic compounds (e.g., amitriptyline, clomipramine, imipramine), which are fairly effective against depression but can cause cardiovascular complications (particularly dysrhythmias), are being superseded by the SSRIs (e.g., fluoxetine, sertraline), which also are highly effective but do not cause anticholinergic or cardiovascular side effects and are significantly safer in overdose. The atypical antidepressants (e.g., trazodone, buproprion, venlafaxine, and nefazodone), so called because their chemical structures differ from those of other antidepressant drugs, act against depressive symptoms similarly to the tricyclics, but with fewer significant side effects.

All of these classes of agents have their uses, since individual patients may respond better to one than to another. The trade names of frequently prescribed antidepressants include Parnate (MAOI); Tofranil, Norpramin, Anafranil, Elavil, and Pamelor (tri- and heterocyclics); Prozac, Zoloft, and Paxil (SSRI's); and Desyrel, Wellbutrin, Effexor, and Serzone (atypicals).

The tricyclics and the SSRI antidepressants also are used to treat other conditions. Clomipramine (Anafranil) and fluvoxamine (Luvox) are indicated for the treatment of obsessive-compulsive disorder, although cognitive-behavior therapy offers the possibility of a cure.

Antidepressants affect dopamine, norepinephrine, and serotonin. Effects are mediated through blockade of presynaptic neurotransmitter reuptake, direct agonist or antagonist activity, or inhibition of neurotransmitter degradation.

Anxiolytics. These medications are commonly prescribed for the management of anxiety or anxiety disorders. At low doses these drugs have antianxiety properties; at higher doses they sedate and induce sleep. Many anxiolytics have anticonvulsant properties. The benzodiazepines (e.g., diazepam, lorazepam, and alprazolam), which were introduced in the early 1960s, are the most widely prescribed anxiolytics because they are effective and fairly safe in overdose. However, they cause physical dependency. Their most common side effect is daytime drowsiness. The trade names of commonly used benzodiazepines include Valium, Ativan, and Xanax.

In 1987 Buspirone became the first nonbenzodiazepine anxiolytic to be introduced in the United States in 25 years. Used in short-term treatment of generalized anxiety disorder, it offers clinical effectiveness comparable to that of the benzodiazepines and the advantage of fewer withdrawal symptoms when it is discontinued.

Beta blockers (e.g., propranolol) and alpha-2 agonists (clonidine) also are used as antianxiety agents on the theory that certain symptoms of anxiety suggest involvement of the beta-adrenergic arm of the sympathetic nervous system. These drugs may also calm anxiety-induced aggression. Inderal has been the most widely used beta blocker for this condition, but newer, more selective agents are beginning to replace it.

Sedatives and Hypnotics. These drugs are used to treat insomnia or to induce sleep quickly in extremely agitated patients. Phenobarbital was widely used for sedation prior to 1965, but it is now used mostly for the treatment of epilepsy. Trazodone, a serotonergic tricyclic, is gaining favor for bedtime sedation.

Stimulants. In 1937, amphetamines were reported to reduce disruptive behavior and hyperactivity and to improve academic performance in schoolchildren (Bradley, 1937; Molitch & Eccles, 1937). Today, these drugs are used by as many as 3% of schoolchildren in the treatment of ADHD. About 70% of the children treated show increased attention span, decreased disruptive behavior, and improved academic performance. Chronic use is required for several years, but the drugs are considered relatively safe. In clinical doses, these medicines do not cause physical dependency in children who take them for ADHD. Stimulants also are used in the treatment of ADHD and obesity in adults. The trade names of commonly prescribed stimulants include Dexedrine, Ritalin, and Cylert.

Mood Stabilizers. The use of lithium salts for the treatment of mania was introduced by Cade in 1949, but it was not until the 1970s that a technology for controlling their toxic effects became available to support their widespread clinical use. Lithium is the first-line treatment for most cases of mania (bipolar disorder), but anticonvulsant drugs, especially carbamazepine and valproic acid, are preferred in rapid cycling and in children. Carbamazepine or valproate also are used for patients who are impulsive or have episodic, uncontrolled outbursts of violent rage. Verapamil, a calcium channel-blocking agent, also has been found useful in the treatment of mania. The trade names of widely used mood stabilizers include Eskalith and Lithane, and those of popular anticonvulsants include Tegretol, Depakene, and Depakote.

Medications Used to Treat Substance Abuse. Psychoactive drugs are used in the treatment of substance abuse in several ways. They are used to treat comorbid psychological conditions such as anxiety and depression. They also are used to counteract the effects of intoxication, to manage withdrawal symptoms, and to help prevent reuse through sensitization. Success is heavily dependent on the patient's cooperation and motivation. Psychopharmacological treatments are best used as part of an overall psychological treatment program aimed at behavior modification and the resolution of associated psychological problems.

The benzodiazepines (which are anxiolytics) are used in the management of alcohol withdrawal symptoms and panic reactions induced by hallucinogens. Disulfiram (Antabuse) is used to sensitize the person to alcohol, so that consumption produces nausea and other reactions aimed at conditioning aversion to drinking during long-term treatment. This approach is often unsuccessful because of frequent lapses in patient compliance. Naltrexone and methadone are used to prevent euphoric reactions to heroin. Methadone produces cross-tolerance with heroin, but it is a safer, more manageable drug. Nicotine chewing gum and topical patches have been used in the treatment of smoking. (Nicotine also is used to treat adult ADHD and Tourette syndrome).

The psychoactive medicines that have the most potential for abuse are the anxiolytics, sedatives, and stimulants. Some school districts have had problems recently with children as young as age 10 selling or injecting methylphenidate (Ritalin), a stimulant drug.

Special Populations

Concerns have been raised about the misuse of psychoactive drugs with certain special populations, especially the elderly in nursing homes, persons with mental retardation or developmental disabilities, and children. Large quantities of drugs have been given to residents of nursing homes, allegedly at times to sedate them for the convenience of the staff rather than to meet the patients' needs. Government regulations now require that psychoactive drugs be used to treat specific psychological conditions and prohibit their use for undefined behavior control.

Individuals with mental retardation have been heavy consumers of these drugs. Surveys show that as many as 40% of mentally retarded persons residing in large institutions and 30% of those seen by community agencies take psychotropic medications on a daily basis. The drugs sometimes are prescribed indefinitely, with no endpoint for treatment identified. Many of the users are nonverbal and cannot easily alert caregivers about possible side or adverse effects. This situation has provoked a number of lawsuits, resulting in the promulgation of federal and state regulations.

Developmental researchers have special concerns about the use of psychoactive agents with children. Research on the effects of these medications on the developing brain is sparse; instead, their effects on children often need to be inferred from their effects on adults. Sometimes children cannot alert family members or physicians about adverse side effects. Daytime drowsiness and other effects of these agents may interfere with academic performance.

These considerations suggest the need for much more research on the safety and efficacy of psychoactive agents in special populations. Although psychoactive medicines offer many benefits for special populations, they also pose special risks that need to be evaluated carefully.

Need for Psychological Treatment

By themselves, psychoactive drugs do not cure mental illnesses. They lessen the symptoms of mental illness, but the symptoms often reappear after the medication is withdrawn. Some patients do not respond at all, and many still show significant (although reduced) symptomatology even while on medication. Psychoactive drugs do not solve the life problems that give rise to stress, anxiety, depression, and other signs of mental illness. Often they are best used to manage symptoms while patients undergo other forms of therapy, counseling, or training.

Although safer medications have become available in recent years, all of them are associated with a number of possible adverse side effects. Some of these effects—such as daytime drowsiness, movement disorder, or jitteriness—significantly impair the person's quality of life. It is extremely important that psychoactive medications not be viewed as panaceas and not be used as substitutes for addressing the psychological, family, and social problems in patients' lives.

Bibliography

Bradley, C. (1937). The behavior of children receiving benzedrine. *American Journal of Psychiatry, 94*, 577–585.

Delay, J., Deniker, P., & Harl, J. (1952). Utilization therapeutique psychiatrique d'une phenothiazine d'action centrale elective. *Ann. Med. Psychol. (Paris), 110*, 112–117.

Molitch, M., & Eccles, A. K. (1937). The effect of benzedrine sulfate on the intelligence scores of children. *American Journal of Psychiatry, 94*, 587–590.

Perry, P. J., Alexander, B., & Liskow, B. I. (1997). *Psychotropic drug handbook* (7th ed.). Washington, DC: American Psychiatric Press. Research-oriented overview of psychoactive medications.

Reiss, S., & Aman, M. G. (1998). *Psychotropic medication and developmental disabilities: The international consensus handbook*. Washington, DC: American Association on Mental Retardation. Comprehensive review of research and clinical experience concerning the effects of psychoactive medications on people with mental retardation and developmental disabilities.

Schatzberg, A. F., Cole, J. O., & DeBattista, C. (1997). *Manual of clinical psychopharmacology*. Washington, DC: American Psychiatric Press. Clinical-oriented overview of psychoactive medications.

Werry, J. S., & Aman, M. G. (1993). *Practitioner's guide to psychoactive drugs for children and adolescents*. New York: Plenum Press. Comprehensive review of research and clinical experience concerning the effects of psychoactive medications on children.

Steven Reiss

Ethnopsychopharmacology

Ethnopsychopharmacology is a new scientific field that deals with issues related to ethnic and cultural variations in the use of and response to psychoactive agents across divergent groups, as well as the mechanisms responsible for such differences. Ethnopsychopharmacology should not be equated with studies of the use of "folk medicine"in psychiatry. This distinction is particularly important in view of the long association of the term *ethnopharmacology* with folk medicine, ethnobotany, and pharmacognosy. As defined here, ethnopsychopharmacology is conceptually linked with the term *pharmacoanthropology*, defined as the interdisciplinary study of interethnic or population differences in response to exogenous chemicals. However, relatively speaking, pharmacoanthropology focuses more on theoretical issues related to variations in drug responses across populations, as well as how they relate to evolutionary events; in contrast, ethnopsychopharmacology focuses more on the clinical implications of the knowledge of such variations.

History

Reports of substantial cross-national differences in the dose range and side effect profiles of neuroleptics started to appear soon after these powerful therapeutic agents became available in the early 1950s. A series of later surveys suggested that similar cross-national contrasts existed for other classes of psychotropics. Generally speaking, it appeared that higher doses of psychotropics were used in industrialized Western countries than in less industrialized regions in the world. Later on, these observations were supported by findings of differences in responses to psychotropic drugs among patients with different ethnic backgrounds who were treated in the same clinical setting. Most of these reports involved comparisons between Asians and Caucasians, which showed that Asians often were effectively treated with substantially smaller doses of neuroleptics, tricyclic antidepressants (TCAs), benzodiazepines, and lithium. Much less information is available on other ethnic groups. However, several studies suggest that Hispanics may also be more sensitive than Caucasians to the effect of neuroleptics and TCAs. In contrast, drug prescription pattern studies have consistently documented the use of higher doses of neuroleptics, as well as the more frequent use of the long-acting depot injection form of these medications, in African Americans.

In the early 1980s, several research groups independently started to measure the concentrations of psychotropics and to determine their pharmacokinetic profiles (explained below) on patients and normal volunteers with different ethnic backgrounds. These studies showed that (1) when exposed to similar doses of neuroleptics and benzodiazepines, Asians were significantly more likely to have substantially higher serum concentrations of these drugs; the results were inconsistent with the findings concerning TCAs, with several studies showing higher TCA levels in Asians and others showing no significant difference; (2) one study comparing Mexican American and Caucasian normal volunteers showed no difference in their pharmacokinetic profiles of nortriptyline (a TCA); (3) there was no difference in the pharmacokinetics of two neuroleptics between Black and Caucasian Canadians; (4) there was no difference in the pharmacokinetics of lithium among Asian, African American, and Caucasian bipolar patients; however, Asian patients responded clinically to significantly lower therapeutic lithium concentrations than their Caucasian and African American counterparts; and (5) African Americans and African Blacks manifested a higher lithium ratio (intracellular vs. extracellular lithium concentrations) and more side effects related to lithium administration. In addition, studies using similar laboratory procedures have demonstrated that Asian volunteers often showed significantly greater neuroendocrine secretion than their Caucasian counterparts after a challenge dose of a neuroleptic was administered, suggesting the existence of ethnic differences in the brain's sensitivity to medications.

In the last decade, attempts have been made to examine the mechanisms that may explain some of the observed ethnic differences in the pharmacokinetics of psychotropics, as well as other biological responses to these drugs, which in turn may help to explain the existence of ethnic differences in dose ranges and side effect profiles observed in clinical settings. Two ongoing projects currently conducted by our research groups are (1) the delineation of the genetic control and expression of various drug-metabolizing enzymes involved in the biotransformation of psychotropics and (2) the concentration of lithium in the brain, as measured by magnetic resonance imaging spectroscopy, a noninvasive method for measuring chemicals *in vivo*. It is expected that research in these areas will lead to a better understanding of the extent of, as well as the underlying reasons for, ethnic variations in responses to psychotropic drugs observed in clinical settings.

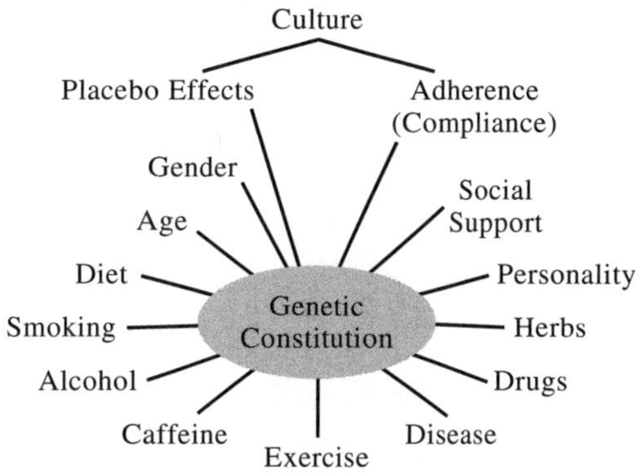

PSYCHOPHARMACOLOGY: Ethnopsychopharmacology. Figure 1. Factors affecting drug response.

Mechanisms

As shown in Figure 1, many factors converge to determine an individual's response to a particular medication. These factors often vary significantly across ethnic groups and thus are relevant for understanding ethnic variations in responses to psychotropic drugs. They are generally grouped into three major categories: pharmacokinetics, pharmacodynamics, and sociocultural considerations.

Pharmacokinetics is the study of the fate and disposition of xenobiotics ("foreign" bioactive substances) in the body. Simply put, it has to do with the question, What does the body do to the drug? It is usually divided into four components: absorption, distribution, metabolism, and excretion. Of these, metabolism varies most significantly across ethnic groups. Metabolism is mediated by many enzymes, which in turn are controlled by discrete genes. Mutations of these genes may inactivate, reduce, or enhance the activity of these enzymes, leading to differential rates of drug metabolism and hence to different dose range and side effect profiles. Of note is the fact that the majority of these drug-metabolizing enzymes are "polymorphic," meaning that multiple forms of these enzymes, resulting from different mutation patterns, exist in any given population. Equally important is that for many of these genes, the patterns of such mutations vary substantially across ethnic groups. Table 1 shows the percentage of various forms of mutation affecting the activity of CYP2D6, a cytochrome P-450 enzyme that mediates the biotransformation of the majority of neuroleptics and TCAs, as well as many of the novel neuroleptics and serotonin reuptake inhibitors.

PSYCHOPHOPHARMACOLOGY: Ethnopsychopharmacology. Table 1. Ethnicity and major CYP2D6 mutations

	Enzyme inactivation		Decreased activity		Increased activity
Ethnic Group	CYP2D6*5	CYP2D6*4	CYP2D6*10	CYP2D6*17	CYP2D6*2XN
African Blacks	4%	2%		40%	
Caucasians	5%	23%	5%		1%
East Asians	6%	1%	47%		
Amerindians	0%	17%			
Mexican Americans	2%	8%	13%		
Spaniards	1.6%	11.6%			7%

CYP2D6*5: gene deletion; CYP2D6*4: multiple point deletion leading to splicing defect; CYP2D6*10: point mutations; CYP2D6*17: point mutations; CYP2D6*2XN: gene amplifications

The activity of many of these drug-metabolizing enzymes is not only controlled genetically but is also sensitive to various environmental factors, many of which are shown in Figure 1. These factors modulate the activity of the enzymes through either inhibition or induction. The former action is best exemplified by the inhibiting effect of substances such as grapefruit juice and corn on the expression of CYP3A4, a cytochrome P-450 enzyme that mediates the metabolism of many benzodiazepines and some of the TCAs, novel neuroleptics, and newer antidepressants (such as nefazodone). Asian and Hispanic dietary practices have been linked to decreased CYP3A4 activity, which may be responsible for the slower metabolism of psychotropic drugs in some of the findings described above. By contrast, a protein-rich diet has been shown to induce the activity of some of these enzymes (e.g., CYP1A2), which may be partially responsible for the faster drug metabolism often observed in Caucasians compared to other ethnic groups, as well as in industrialized populations compared to more traditional societies.

In contrast to pharmacokinetics, much less is known about factors determining pharmacodynamics, which asks the question, What does the drug do to the body (target organ)? In the case of psychotropics, the target organ is the brain, and it is generally believed that the effects of psychotropics are mediated by their interactions with different receptor systems. Although our understanding of these receptor systems is rudimentary, the field is progressing rapidly, and many of these receptors have been cloned. Surprisingly, these receptors also have been found to be highly polymorphic (i.e., mutations exist in a portion of any population), and the frequencies of these mutations also show substantial ethnic variations. How these variations might translate into receptor responses and eventually into clinical responses is still unknown. However, it is highly plausible that ethnic variations in the structure or function of some of these receptors might have pharmacodynamic consequences, and research in this area should help to provide explanations for some of the clinical phenomena described earlier (e.g., ethnic differences in the therapeutic levels of lithium).

Lastly, it should be noted that various nonpharmacological factors, including compliance, placebo effect, the influence of stress, support styles, and personality styles, also exert significant influences on the response to psychotropic drugs. Beliefs and expectations about the effects of drugs in general, and psychotropics in particular, are deeply embedded in the patient's sociocultural milieu and determined by his or her cultural and personal antecedents. It is unclear to what extent these effects are mediated by "symbolic" mechanisms and in what ways they are mediated by biological means (the expectation of a larger drug effect leading to an enhanced pharmacodynamic response). These are exciting and challenging questions awaiting research in the future.

Acknowledgments. This work was supported in part by NIMH Research Center on the Psychobiology of Ethnicity MH47193.

Bibliography

Kalow, W. (1991). Interethnic variation of drug metabolism. *Trends in Pharmacological Science 12*, 102–107. A short overview article that concisely presents extant data and discusses their clinical and theoretical relevance.

Kalow, W. (1992). *Pharmacogenetics of drug metabolism.* New York: Pergamon Press. An exhaustive, authoritative, thorough review of the field of pharmacogenetics. Many chapters extensively discuss mechanisms responsible for individual and interethnic variations in drug responses. Highly technical; basic knowledge of pharmacology, biochemistry, and molecular biology required.

Lin, K. M., Poland, R. E., & Anderson, D. (1995). Psychopharmacology, ethnicity and culture. *Transcultural Psychiatric Research Review, 32*, 1–40. This condensed overview chapter updates information that was not included in the 1993 book edited by the same research group.

Lin, K., Poland, R., & Nakasaki, G. (1993). *Psychopharmacology and psychobiology of ethnicity*. Washington, DC: American Psychiatric Press. An extensive and fairly complete review of issues relevant to ethnopsychopharmacology. Chapters are divided according to classes of psychotropics (e.g., antidepressants, lithium) and include information relevant to all ethnic groups when applicable. There also is one chapter that discusses the effect of nonpharmacological factors on drug responses. Several chapters also address questions related to the extent and significance of biological diversity (i.e., ethnic variations of putative neurobiological correlates of psychiatric syndromes).

Lin, K. M., Poland, R. E., Wan, Y., Smith, M., & Lesser, I. M. (1996). The evolving science of pharmacogenetics: Clinical and ethnic perspectives. *Psychopharmacology Bulletin, 32*, 205–217. This review paper discusses the clinical theoretical significance of recent developments in pharmacogenetics and focuses on their application to ethnic minority populations.

Rudorfer, M. (1993). Pharmacokinetics of psychotropic drugs in special populations. *Journal of Clinical Psychiatry* 54 (Suppl.), 50–54. This paper provides an extensive review of the influence of factors including ethnicity, gender, and age on the pharmacokinetics of psychotropic drugs. It is scholarly and concise.

Smith, M., & Lin, K. M. (1996). A biological, environmental, and cultural basis for ethnic differences in treatment. In P. M. Kato & T. Mann (Eds.), *Health psychology of special populations: Issues of age, gender, and ethnicity*. New York: Plenum Press. This is an updated review of issues relevant to ethnopsychopharmacology presented in a user-friendly format.

Walker, S. R., Lumley, C. E., & McAuslane, N. (Eds). (1994). *The relevance of ethnic factors in the clinical evaluation of medicines*. Dordrecht, the Netherlands: Kluwer. This book evolved from an international conference that focused on "harmonizing" the process of drug development across countries. Researchers and pharmaceutical company representatives discussed issues including the extent and meaning of ethnic variations in drug metabolism, drug prescription patterns in different countries, and the practice of drug regulation in several developed countries.

Keh-Ming Lin

PSYCHOPHYSICS. Mental events are mostly the result of environmental events. We hear the sounds of a marching band. We see the redness of a perfect rose. But the transduction of these physical signals into neural impulses by the sensory organs does not fully capture the psychic quality of our experiences. In his *Elemente der Psychophysik* (The Elements of Psychophysics; Leipzig, 1860) Gustav T. Fechner declared that he had unraveled this relation between mind and body. He proposed a way to proceed logically from the magnitude of the physical stimulus to its psychic magnitude, and that, he asserted, was the crux of the mind-body problem.

Today, we remain unconvinced that Fechner, in fact, solved this foundational philosophical issue. However, his pioneering research program remains central not only to sensory psychology but also to the study of human perception, values, decisions, and a host of practical problems. These problems range from the design of noise abatement devices to tame jetliners, to the measurement of the effectiveness of the cockpit displays of those aircraft. Fechner's research program recognized that the physical stimuli that excite sense organs possess magnitudes measurable by physical variables (e.g., energy amplitude, frequency, or mass). But are there measurable energy levels that cannot be experienced? For example, can you taste a grain of salt dissolved in a glass of water? Can you see a dimming star at dawn? Such questions address the psychological concept of the absolute threshold or *absolute limen* (AL).

Measurements of the AL had already been made by Ernst H. Weber in 1834. He used an apparatus to stimulate the skin with two points that could be finely adjusted in their separation. He found that different places on the body varied in sensitivity. On the fingertips a very small separation was felt as two points, whereas on the lower back a separation of 1.5 centimeters was often reported as a single point. These findings support the conjecture that all sense receptors possess a limited sensitivity: an absolute threshold. Such measurements are used today to quantify sensory deficits in hearing or visual acuity. In other experiments on weight discrimination, Weber found that more weight had to be added to a heavier item than to a lighter one to notice a difference. From these data he postulated a second threshold based on differences in stimulation, *a difference limen* (DL). The DL is the amount of stimulation added to a given stimulus to perceive a difference. His two-point threshold studies led Weber to treat the AL as if it were a DL between no stimulation and some stimulation. We shall see this idea expanded in the theory of signal detection.

Weber's data suggested a mathematical relation between the present stimulus magnitude and the amount added to produce a change in sensation. This equation, later named by Fechner as Weber's law, is $\Delta I = kI$, where ΔI is the difference in intensity needed to perceive a difference (ΔI is the DL). The value of ΔI is calculated by multiplying the intensity I, at which it is measured by some constant k, estimated from experimental data. So if the stimulus level of intensity I equals 100, and the amount added to notice a difference is 5 units, then $\Delta I = 5$, and $k = 100/5 = .05$. So for $I = 200$, and k still .05, you predict that $\Delta I = 10$,

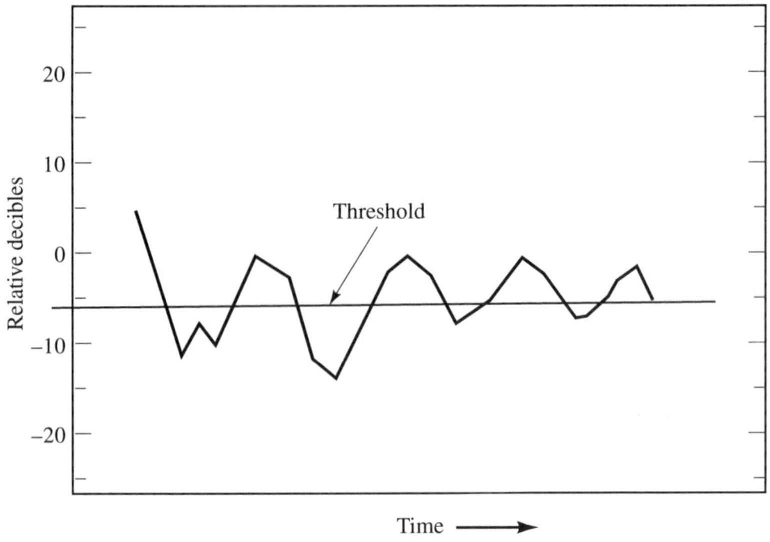

PSYCHOPHYSICS. Figure 1. A trace of the back-and-forth data tracking the judgments of an observer from a Békésy audiometer. These data are used to estimate the observer's AL.

and check your answer by the data. To determine the value of the DL (ΔI in Weber's law) at any intensity level, you need only to know the value of k. Fechner called that number the Weber fraction. Today, Weber's law would be called a mathematical model of the difference threshold. Much of psychophysics is concerned with the design and development of such models to capture the behavioral properties of environmental stimulation.

Starting in 1850, and for the next 10 years, Fechner designed and developed techniques to study human sensation and perception. His methods of measuring various psychophysical thresholds have become common diagnostics in many areas. Ophthalmologists, audiologists, and other medical disciplines rely on threshold determinations using Fechner's methods. These psychophysical methods can be either measurements of the AL or measurements of the DL. The way they are measured defines their behavioral properties.

Measuring the AL

One of Fechner's methods for determining the AL is that of ascending and descending limits. It starts with the stimulus well below the threshold, and slowly increases its intensity until the observer is aware of its presence. This value is recorded. Then the experimenter starts well above the threshold and slowly decreases the intensity until the stimulus is not reported. The values of the threshold going up and down are averaged over several trials. That average is the AL.

In 1945 George von Békésy invented a machine for measuring these thresholds for sound, the Békésy audiometer. This device plays a series of tones through a headset. The listener presses a button when a tone is heard, and that action reduces the intensity of the next tone. When the listener stops pressing the button, the machine reverses course and slowly begins to increase the sound intensity. This audiometric method is still used to measure hearing loss by assessing the AL at varying frequencies to plot out a loudness threshold function. Such a function shows that we are most sensitive to sounds whose frequencies are near speech levels, whereas sounds of lower and higher frequencies need more energy to make then audible. The tracing in Figure 1 shows data from a Békésy audiometer. The solid horizontal line is the average crossing point and represents the AL. Sometimes this methodology is called a staircase procedure, and can be used to measure the AL in many modalities.

Measuring the DL

Fechner named the observed value of the DL the *just noticeable difference* (jnd). So the three terms, ΔI, DL, and jnd all refer to the same concept, but the jnd represents the value of the concept in operational terms. To demonstrate how to measure the jnd, Fechner constructed a set of nine identical cylinders filled with different amounts of buckshot. They all weighed about 300 grams, varying by 2 grams each. He designated 300 grams as the standard weight. The nine weights were 292, 294, 296, 298, 300, 302, 304, 306, and 308 grams, respectively. This method of constant stimulus differences required the observer to lift the 300-gram standard weight and then one of the nine weights selected at random. The observer was asked to report whether the variable weight was lighter or heavier than the standard. This judgment was made for each weight several hundred times. From these data, one may then calculate the proportion of times each weight had been judged heavier or lighter. The two judgments are complementary: If a given weight was judged to be heavier 70% of the time, then it must have been judged lighter

30% of the time. The results of such an experiment are shown in Figure 2.

Fechner defined the jnd as half the stimulus difference on the abscissa (or x-axis) between the weight that gave a 25% heavier response and the weight that gave 75% heavier judgments. You may note that this makes the size of the jnd a conventional, and not an absolute, value. To find the jnd, draw horizontal lines from the 25% and 75% points on the ordinate to intercept a curve faired through the data points as shown in Figure 2. From those intercepts, vertical lines are drawn to the abscissa, and the difference between the stimulus values at these locations (divided by 2) is the jnd. For these data, the value is about 2.6 grams.

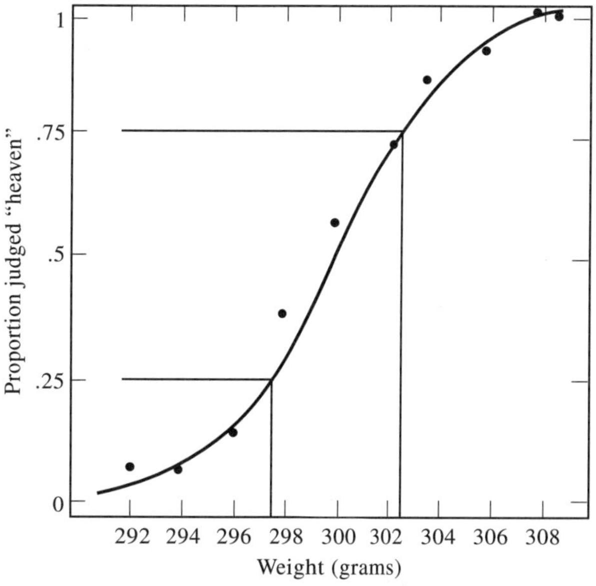

PSYCHOPHYSICS. Figure 2. Data and the fitted curve from a DL determination for hefted weights. The .75 intercept on the abscissa equals 302.8 grams; the .25 intercept equals 297.6 grams. The difference is 5.2 grams, which when divided by 2 yields a jnd of 2.6 grams.

Fechner's Law—Perceptual Scales

With these limenal methods of threshold determination in hand, Fechner then turned to the central problem: how to assign numbers to *physical* stimuli that represent their *psychological* magnitude. He had operationally defined the jnd, and chosen that *variability* as the unit of psychological measurement. Even though Weber had shown that the jnd varied in physical magnitude depending on where it was measured, Fechner postulated that the psychological magnitude of the jnd was always the same. This implies that units of equal psychological magnitude have unequal physical measures. But this inequality follows a law—Weber's law—and consequently, by mathematical reasoning, the psychological continuum can be represented as a function of the physical continuum. If we accept both Weber's law and the psychic equality of all jnds, as Fechner did, then the logarithm of the physical magnitude ϕ is equal to the psychological magnitude ψ: $\psi = k \log \phi + c$. In this equation k and c determine the slope and intercept of the function. Figure 3 shows the nature of this lawful relation, called Fechner's law (for a simple derivation of the law, see Galanter, 1994, pp. 113–114). The empirical curve in Figure 3 becomes a straight line if the abscissa is converted to the logarithm. Also notice that the curve cuts the abscissa slightly above the zero point. This intercept is the level of the absolute threshold.

The publication of Fechner's law forever changed the quantitative and experimental study of psychology. He introduced operationalism, behaviorism, and quantitative experimentation into the examination of mental life. His conception, that mental processes can be measured, led to a vast array of work in many practical arenas. The adoption of logarithmic translations of physical quantities became common in engineering and applied science, taking such forms as the decibel scale in physical acoustics, and logarithmic translations of other energy measures in optics. But perhaps most significant, he changed the way we look at *variability*. Variability became a quantity that represented a central metric in all of science, not merely a reflection of error.

An experimental method of measuring psychological experience provided a launching pad for interpreting the neurological and physiological substrate of the sense organs and their connections within the brain. The techniques of sensory psychophysics were used to map psychological processes to their anatomical loci. Details of the sensory pathways, and the synaptic junctions of these systems as they branch and converge in the brain, inform us of the way our neural structure underlies our experience. But the role of psychophysical understanding has extended beyond its obvious relevance to sensory experience. Indeed, a new role for this old discipline emerged from psychophysical studies conducted after World War II.

The Theory of Signal Detection

In these previous experiments, it was assumed that the observer's judgments faithfully represented his or her state of mind. Such an assumption seems plausible, and was rarely challenged. In fact, the data from these psychophysical experiments support this notion so overwhelmingly that one is hard-pressed to object to its veracity. Whenever this assumption was questioned, the remedy was to introduce a novel event to the experiment as a "catch trial." For example, if, in the absence of any stimulus, the observer reports the presence of the stimulus, then this is noted as a false alarm (FA). Such catch trials were rarely implemented, and were not treated as bearing on the data unless the observer

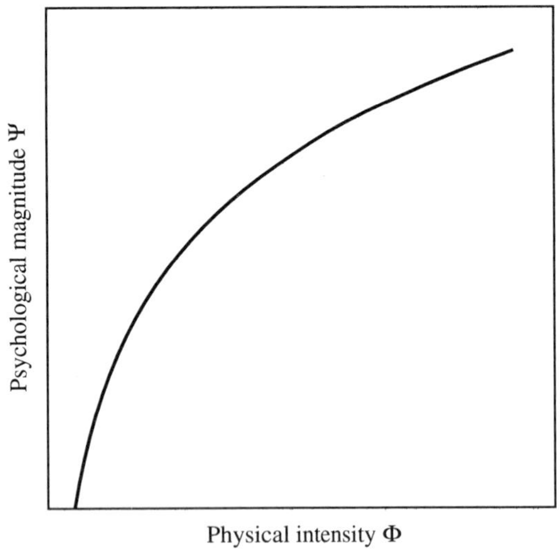

PSYCHOPHYSICS. Figure 3. A graph of Fechner's law showing the arithmetic relation between physics (Φ) and psyche (ψ). for Log Φ, the function is linear.

made too many errors. In contexts where the outcome of the experiment could have significant consequences (e.g., if the observer were being evaluated as an airplane pilot, or if a physician were examining an x-ray for a tumor), these consequences might be thought to influence, or bias, the response. There is always the possibility that correctly reported stimuli (hits) are actually just guesses. One solution for this problem is to use the FAs to correct for guessing. We can do this correction as follows:

> probability of true detection of the stimulus =
> (probability of hits − probability of FA) /
> (1 − probability of FA)

This formula is similar to various methods used to correct true–false tests for guessing, But like such test corrections, there appears to be no principled way to set the level of adjustment. A real theory is needed.

This issue was addressed, and a new theory with experimental consequences was proposed by Wilson P. Tanner, Jr., and John Swets in 1954. Their exposition, (and its later adoption and extensions by the entire psychophysics community) represents a revision of limenal psychophysics as profound as that of Fechner. This theory of signal detection (TSD) can be explained most easily by adjusting the classical AL experiment. Instead of varying the stimulus energy and estimating the point at which it is just detectable, consider an experiment that presents a stimulus of fixed energy emerging from a noise background, let's say 50% of the time. Call P(S) the (S)timulus present proportion and P(N) the (N)oise background alone proportion. In this case, P(S) = P(N) = .5. The observer can make one of two responses on each occasion or trial of the experiment: "yes" (y), meaning "I believe the stimulus is present," and "no" (n), meaning "I believe the stimulus is not present." This leads to a matrix as in Figure 4.

Note that the entries in this matrix will estimate the four (conditional) probabilities corresponding to the four states of the listener's behavior relative to the stimulus presentation: $p(y|S)$, a hit probability; $p(n|S)$, a miss probability; $p(y|N)$, a false alarm (FA), probability; and $p(n|N)$, a correct rejection probability. Even though there are four numbers in the matrix, only two are needed to capture all the information. Because $p(y|S) = 1 - p(n|S)$, and $p(y|N) = 1 - p(n|N)$, the proportion of hits and false alarms is sufficient to calculate the other two entries. This fact is used to display any datum in a graph on the unit square such as Figure 5.

Each point in Figure 5 represents the result of one experiment, in this case, measurement of the detectability of a weak tone signal embedded in a noise background on half the trials. The other half of the trials consist of presentations of the noise alone. The observer reports whether the tone is present or absent on each of several hundred trials. The FA proportions are plotted on the x-axis and the hits on the y-axis. To get the flavor of the data, consider the data points for observers A and B. Who hears better? Even though they both report the signal when it is present an equal proportion of times, A has fewer false alarms than B. What about A and C? Here, they both have made an equal number of false alarms, but A has more hits. So far neither of these comparisons raises any interesting

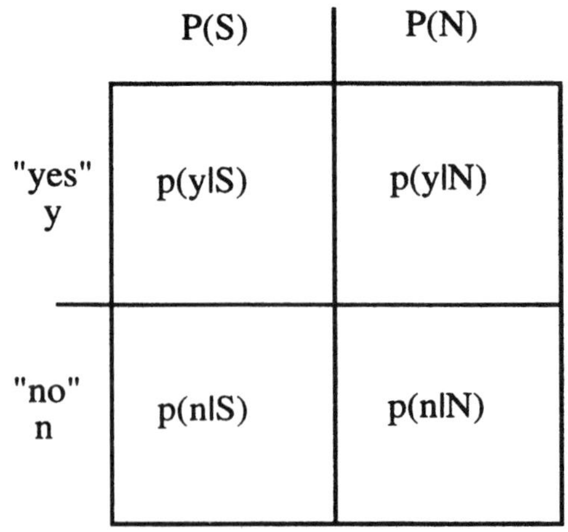

PSYCHOPHYSICS. Figure 4. The data matrix of a signal detection experiment. P(S) and P(N) are the proportion of times a signal or noise alone is presented. The observer responds "yes" or "no" and so generates an estimate the four probabilities shown.

questions, but now compare B and C. Observer B shows more hits and more FAs, C shows fewer hits but also fewer FAs. Clearly, without a theory we are hard-pressed to make the comparison. To complicate things even further, we now confess that B and C are the same person on two different days. Why the difference? You will recall that one problem with limenal experiments was not knowing whether the consequences of a certain judgment could influence that judgment. Now we reveal that on the first day our observer received a matrix of rewards and costs as shown in Figure 6. Notice that hits are strongly rewarded, and FAs are only lightly fined. Figure 7 shows the alternate payoff matrix used on the second day: high fines for FAs and only nominal rewards for hits. The results show that these payoffs strongly influence the experimental outcome. Clearly, more than the signal is influencing the response. The rewards and costs have an effect on the responses. Therefore, we need a theory that accommodates biases that payoffs may generate, without presuming that these biases change the state of the perceptual system. Bias by payoffs suggests that the desires and aversions of the observer (in this case winning and losing money) can influence the responses. But just as these payoff matrices have such an effect, so do the proportions of *S* and *N*. In Figure 5 observer D (who is really the same person as observer A and therefore possesses the same sensitivity) has changed responses as a result of changes in P(S) from .5 to .9 (meaning that P(N) = .1). With these odds, the observer comes to expect frequent

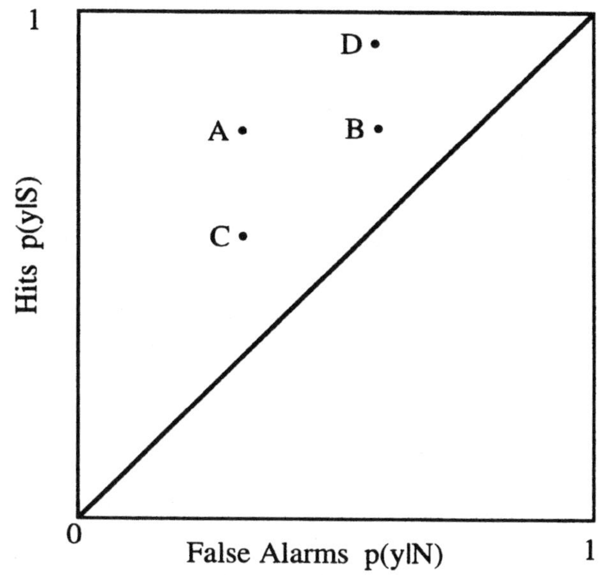

PSYCHOPHYSICS. Figure 5. The data from several observers in a signal detection experiment. It is difficult to compare such data without a theory.

	P(S)	P(N)
"yes" y	$1.00	$ – .05
"no" n	$ – .05	$ .05

PSYCHOPHYSICS. Figure 6. A payoff matrix that presses the observer to say "yes."

signals, especially when it is hard to decide. So we see that both expectations and motivations can influence behavior that we might easily have attributed to the sensory systems.

In Fechner's classic scenario, the stimulus is thought to provoke an internal representation that may or may not exceed an internal threshold value. The variability in sensory judgments may be attributed to either variations in the magnitude of the internal representation, or changes of the threshold level, or both. All of this variability is accommodated by taking the appropriate average. However, there is nothing in the classical scenario that accommodated the role of nonsensory effects on judgments.

The theory of signal detectability was adapted by psychophysicists from communication engineering to replace the classical theory of sensory thresholds. TSD proposes a more elaborate structure. Physically identical stimuli give rise to internal representations that are distributed on a hypothetical continuum. The distribution is assumed to be a normal distribution. The noise events are also represented by a similar normal distribution displaced to the left on the axis as shown in Figure 8. Because these events (S or N) have no numerical values, the underlying perceptual structure must ultimately depend on the response proportions. Therefore the theory scales this axis by taking each value of the ordinate of the S distribution at a point z, $f_s(z)$ and dividing it by the ordinate of the N distribution at z, $f_N(z)$. This defines the axis as a likelihood ratio $1(x) = f_s(z)/f_N(z)$. In Figure 8 standard deviations are used as the unit of measurement on the abscissa.

In addition to representing the stimuli, response bias produced by changes in payoffs or presentation probabilities may also be represented on this axis. The ver-

	P(S)	P(N)
"yes" y	$ .05	$ – 1.00
"no" n	$ – .05	$ .05

PSYCHOPHYSICS. Figure 7. A payoff matrix that presses the observer to say "no."

tical line in Figure 8 shows the position of a criterion, *C*, which the observer uses to decide whether to say yes or no. *C* is defined in likelihood ratio terms as $\beta = f_s(C)/f_N(C)$. Because we placed the criterion in Figure 8 at the point where the two distributions cross, the values of $f_s(C)$ and $f_N(C)$ are equal, so $\beta = 1$. But as the payoffs and the presentation probabilities change, the criterion may move and β will change. A stimulus event that strikes a point to the left of the criterion will elicit a no response; one to the right a yes. We can normalize the areas under each distribution to equal 1. So the area under the N distribution to the right of the criterion equals $p(y|N)$; the area under the S distribution to the right of the criterion represents $p(y|S)$. The average distance between the S and the N distributions depends solely on the strength of the stimulus. Because we measure this distance in standard deviation units, its theoretical value (d') is the difference between the mean of S and the mean of N, divided by the standard deviation (*SD*) of the distributions: $d' = (m_S - m_N /SD$.

TSD provides a model for detection of weak signals. If we vary the payoffs or the presentation probabilities while keeping signal strength constant, we generate a function that relates hits to false alarms. The curve labeled ROC in Figure 9 is an example of this function. Every point on the curve represents the same judgmental sensitivity. The curve itself shows how biases change judgments even when stimuli are identical. Such an iso-sensitivity curve is often called a response (or receiver) operating characteristic: an ROC curve. The experimental data allow us to calculate the theoretical value: $d' = z\ [p(ylN)] - z[(py|S)]$, where $z[p(y|S)]$ is the standard score associated with the hit proportion, which is then subtracted from the *z* score for false alarms (values of *z* can be found in Galanter, 1994, p. 166). If we vary signal strength instead of varying bias, we can generate an iso-bias curve, shown as the dashed line in Figure 9.

This theory of stimulus detection also implies that there is actually no stimulus threshold. If the two distributions, S and N, move closer together, there will always be some difference in hit proportions that will reveal the slightest separation. Only when the distributions overlap exactly will $d' = 0$. In fact, TSD and its associated experimental methods shift our attention from sensory processes to the question of uncertainty in decision making. This extends the scope of problems that psychophysical techniques can fruitfully explore. Memory can be tested by using these methods. For example, an observer is given a list of words to remember. Later he is given a new list that includes some words from the first list, and is asked to indicate whether a word is new or old. Then, d' will represent memorial discrimination, and β will measure bias toward report-

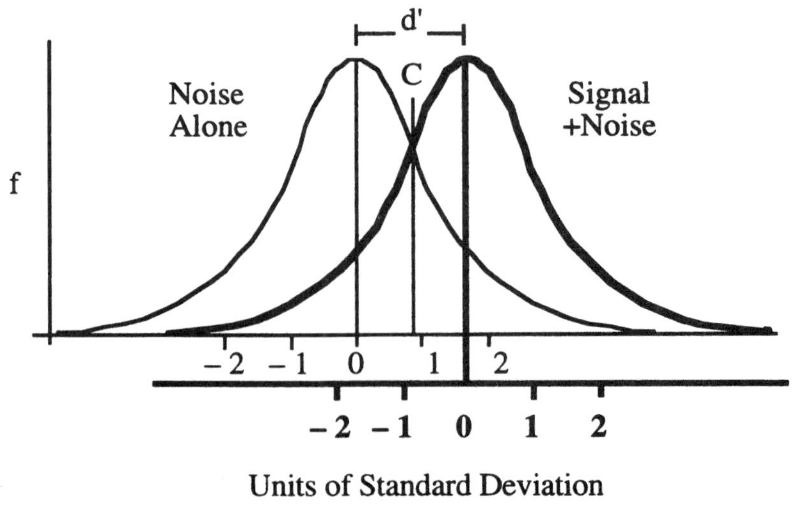

PSYCHOPHYSICS. Figure 8. The two distributions (signal plus noise, and noise alone) that form the abstract structure of the theory of signal detection.

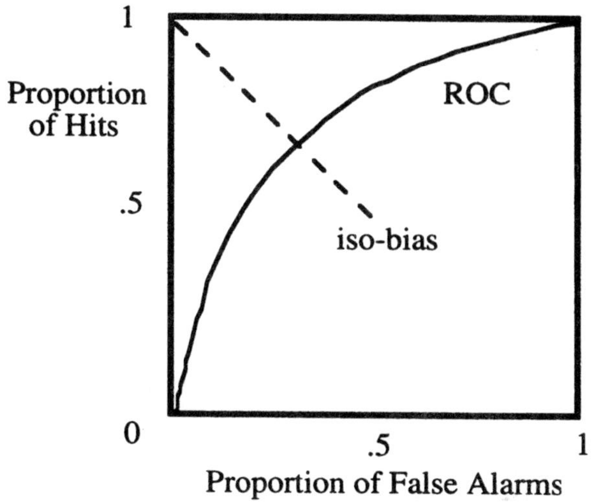

PSYCHOPHYSICS. Figure 9. An ROC or iso-sensitivity function that relates hits to false alarms when the signal strength is fixed, and an iso-bias function that shows how hits and false alarms change when payoffs or expectations change.

ing old versus new items. In a different context, TSD lets us determine whether taste sensitivity really changes after eating, as it might seem to. Actually d' remains the same before and after meals. However, β changes to bias responses so that taste sensitivity seems to decrease.

Back to Perceptual Scales

These new methods of limenal measurement paralleled new experiments on perceptual measurement. Is perceived loudness of a sound related to the limenal limits of the auditory system? Fechner would say yes, because his law construed perceptual magnitude to be the top of a pile of jnds, each stacked chip proportionately larger than the one beneath it. Early tests of this theory were conducted by having people sort different weights into categories. In one form of the experiment, judges sorted 50 weighted envelopes into 7 categories from 1 (*lightest*) to 7 (*heaviest*). When averaged, the logarithm of the weights in each category was linearly related to the category number. This *category scaling* procedure is used to assess magnitudes of everything from physical attractiveness (on a scale from 1 to 10), to attitudes toward ethnic groups, to candy preferences. When used in surveys, one person's judgments are combined with judgments from a larger sample to represent magnitudes of social and political attitudes.

In 1872 Belgian psychophysicist J. A. F. Plateau asked several artists to paint a gray halfway between a black and a white sample that he gave them. The artists worked in studios with varying amounts of light ranging from candlelight to midday sun; consequently, the energy reflected from the paint patches varied widely. When Plateau recovered his samples he found that the painted grays were essentially identical. The fact that the grays matched meant that brightness ratios were controlling the judgments. This makes the mathematical relation between the apparent brightness of the samples and their physical reflectance, a power function: $\psi = c\ (\phi^k)$. The exponent k is the slope, and c is the intercept. This empirical formula confounds Fechner's law by separating perceptual magnitudes from thresholds. Hundreds of studies of dozens of sensory systems empirically support this power function. The most common experimental method is *magnitude estimation*. For example, an observer is presented with a stimulus, and told that it represents a perceptual magnitude of 100 (both the stimulus and the number are often called a *modulus*). Then, additional stimuli of varying physical magnitude are presented. The observer is asked to assign numbers to each of these new stimuli. The numbers represent the apparent magnitude of the new stimulus as compared to the modulus. When the data are appropriately averaged, a graph of the magnitude estimations versus the actual physical magnitudes are often power functions with exponents that appear to depend on the modality. For example, the exponent for painfulness of an electric shock is about 3.5, whereas for the brightness of a disk of light it is near 0.33. Lifted weights (Fechner's favorite modality) yield an exponent of 1.45, whereas that of the judged length of lines is close to 1. Figure 10 shows the form of these functions in arithmetic coordinates. The mathematical form of the power function will convert

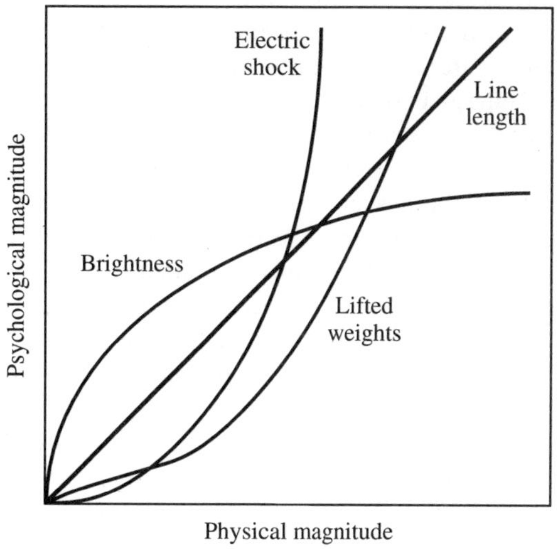

PSYCHOPHYSICS. Figure 10. Graphs of psychological magnitude as it depends on physical magnitude for different modalities.

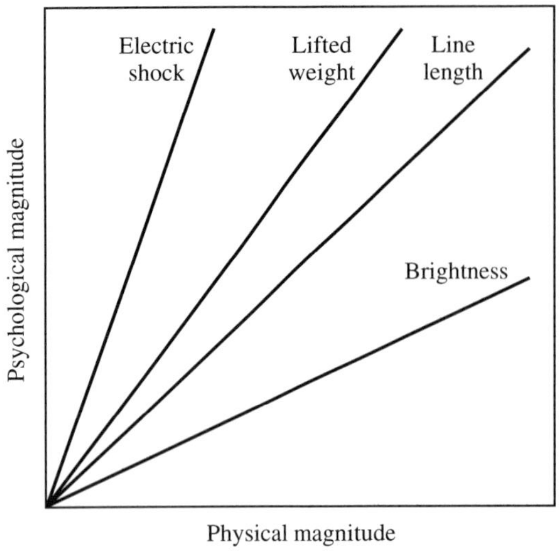

PSYCHOPHYSICS. Figure 11. Double logarithmic transformations of the functions in Figure 10 that show more clearly the differences in the psychophysical relations of the various sensory modalities.

the curves into straight lines if the logarithmic values of both the stimulus and the perceptual dimension are plotted against each other. The arithmetic is $\log \psi = k \log \phi + c$, a linear function when transformed by the logarithm (Figure 11 shows these functions).

But how do we reconcile this with category scales that appear to obey Fechner's law? When the logarithmic scales are compared to the power function scales, a nonlinear relation consistently arises for some sensory systems. Stevens and Galanter (1957) labeled sensory systems that gave rise to such nonlinear relations *prothetic*. Prothetic systems add stimulus energy to the same receptors. On systems that substitute one set of receptors for another, the relation often appears to be linear. These continua are called *metathetic*. Sound levels that add sound energy in order to change psychological loudness are prothetic. But variations in sound frequency that change perceived pitch depend on stimulation of different regions of the basilar membrane. Therefore pitch is a metathetic continuum. Magnitude and category functions for pitch are almost linearly related.

These psychophysical magnitude functions are used in many and varied contexts (e.g., using psychological measures of loudness to set legal limits on aircraft overflight noise). In social contexts they assign psychic measures to attitudes, interests, and even to monetary magnitudes. They are used to predict the outcomes of complex decisions in situations of high risk and sociopolitical practice.

[*See also the biographies of Fechner, Stevens, and Weber.*]

Acknowledgments. This project was supported, in part, by the National Science Foundation's Division of Undergraduate Education through grant DUE# 96-52839. Opinions expressed are those of the author and not necessarily those of the Foundation.

Bibliography

Galanter, E. (1962). Contemporary psychophysics. In T. Newcomb (Ed.), *New directions in psychology* (pp. 89–156). New York: Holt, Rinehart & Winston. First exposition of signal detection for undergraduate students.

Galanter, E. (1962). The direct measurement of utility and subjective probability. *American Journal of Psychology, 75*, 208–220. Applications of scaling methods to the psychological value of money, and the magnitude of subjective probabilities.

Galanter, E. (1984). Detection and discrimination of environmental change. In I. Darian-Smith (Ed.), *Handbook of physiology: A critical, comprehensive presentation of physiological knowledge and concepts. Section I: The nervous system. Vol. 3. Sensory processes. Part I* (pp. 103–121). Washington, DC: American Psychological Association.

Galanter, E. (1994). *Psych tech notes* (V 2.1). New York: Adams, Bannister, Cox. A handbook of techniques, including tables of *d′* and other useful data.

Geschieder, G. A. (1997). *Psychophysics, the fundamentals* (3rd ed.). Mahwah, NJ: Erlbaum. The textbook for advanced undergraduates.

Green, D. M., & Swets, J. A. (1966). *Signal detection theory and psychophysics*. New York: Wiley. A high-level mathematical resource for experimentalists and other researchers.

Linker, E., Moore, M. E., & Galanter, E. (1964). Taste thresholds, detection models and disparate results. *Journal of Experimental Psychology, 67*, 59–66. A classical case disconnecting perception and response bias.

Marks, L. (1974). *Sensory processes*. San Diego, CA: Academic Press.

Pollack, I., Norman, D. A., & Galanter, E. (1964). An efficient nonparametric analysis of recognition memory. *Psychological Science, 1*, 327–328. Uses of psychophysical techniques for more than sensory analysis.

Ross, H. E. (1997). On the possible relations between discriminability and apparent magnitude. *British Journal of Mathematical and Statistical Psychology, 50*, 187–203. An excellent exposition of the relation between Fechnerian limenal data and the scaling of perceptual domains.

Stevens, S. S. (1975). *Psychophysics: Introduction to its perceptual, neural and social prospects*. New York: Wiley.

Stevens, S. S., & Galanter, E. (1957). Ratio scales and category scales on a dozen perceptual continua. *Journal of Experimental Psychology, 54*, 377–412. The original discovery of a nonlinear relation between category and magnitude scales.

Swets, J. A., Tanner, W. J., Jr., & Birdsall, T. G. (1961). Decision processes in perception. *Psychological Review, 68*, 301–340. A tutorial on the theory of signal detection.

Eugene Galanter

PSYCHOPHYSIOLOGY. *See* Cognitive Electrophysiology.

PSYCHOSEXUAL STAGES. The Victorians were prudes. Human sexuality, which had cultural acceptance and recognition in the Middle Ages and the Renaissance, was driven underground by the Reformation and was deeply buried by the cultural mores of the second half of the nineteenth century. In the thousand years that followed the collapse of the Roman empire, the average family slept together. Children were exposed to the parents' lovemaking, as were grandparents and other members of the household. The age of consent was often as low as 8 years old for girls. The incongruence between biological reality and social norms was evident to Freud, as it must have been to all thoughtful, self-aware individuals. By making the inconsistency between average expectable experience and social constraint the cornerstone of his theory of psychopathology, Freud shocked the Victorian mind out of its complacent hypocrisy and radically altered Western civilization in the final years of its second millennium.

In his early theories (Freud, 1900, 1905), Freud proposed that sexual urges provide a motivation for psychic functioning, that an energizing process, which he called the libido, lay behind sexual behavior as well as the development of most features of mental life. Adult psychopathology, as well as ways of behaving characteristic of a particular individual (personality), were based on the vicissitudes of early childhood sexual development. Sexual feelings were presumed to create conflict with the environment but also within the child's mind, leading to their purposeful exclusion from conscious thinking—an exclusion that, because of the energy-based conception of mental function, the individual had to hold in place by the application of energic countermeasures (counter-cathexes). The term psychosexual may be a misnomer. "Psychosensual" may be a more appropriate designation since Freud's use of the term sexual referred to pleasures derived from any body area and libido referred to the hypothesized energy underlying all such pleasures. The instinctual drive is always unconscious. Its derivatives, the mental representations, are invested with psychic energy (cathected) and have the potential to achieve consciousness as wishes or fantasies.

Freud distinguished three erogenous zones that, when stimulated, had the potential to bring pleasure and gratification: the mouth, the anus, and the genitals. He reported a maturational sequence according to which each of these zones was prominent as a source of pleasure during early childhood. This lies at the heart of his theory of psychosexual development, with the oral, anal, and infantile genital phases (the latter of which also came to be known as phallic). Freud, as well as Abraham (1924) and Ferenczi (1913) linked adult personality as well as its neurotic symptomatology to libidinal development. They concluded that either excessive gratification or frustration could result in the hypercathexis of particular ideas, leading to so-called silent fixation points, which give no hint of their presence until the individual is confronted by particularly difficult life circumstances. He then resorts to regression. If the fixation is manifest, the person is thought to be arrested, at least partially, at a certain stage of development.

Five instinctual phases of development, each with its subphases, have been distinguished. The first year of life is characterized as the oral phase, with the first 6 months as generally passive-dependent, gratified by sucking. After this time there is increased aggression and even sadism where biting combines sexual and aggressive gratification. Arrest at this stage is indicated by passive behavior in individuals happy to assume positions of dependency or, in others, by continued pleasure from activities employing biting and chewing. Eating disorder or substance abuse (alcoholism) might be considered as associated with oral fixation.

The gratifications of the anal phase were considered to focus on withholding, expelling, messing, touching, smelling, and looking. The child in the second year often becomes curious about defecatory activities. In adult personality, arrest is often indicated by reactions against these wishes such as excessive tidiness and orderliness as well as continuity of tendencies rooted in this phase, such as excessive obedience (authoritarianism) or monetary withholding (parsimony). Regression to this phase is exemplified by obsessive-compulsive disorder.

The final point of infantile sexuality is the genital phase, when children of both sexes become preoccupied with genital interests and anatomical features, usually in the fourth year of life. In both genders a sense of envy of the mature sexual body of the parent is thought to develop with typical anxieties surrounding the wish to acquire this from the parent (e.g., castration anxiety in the boy). Sexual feelings toward the parent of the opposite sex (the Oedipus complex) lead to a fear of retaliation, intensifying these worries. Arrest at this stage may be indicated in a continued desire to demonstrate sexual adequacy either symbolically (e.g., through the possession of phallic equivalents such as sports cars) or unusual sexual behavior, such as inverted or negative Oedipus complex, thought to underpin homosexuality. Although infantile genital anxieties are involved in all neurotic problems, childhood phobias are often considered to be specifically linked to this phase.

From the sixth or seventh year of life until puberty, Freud believed that there was a diminution of sexual activity. He referred to this period as latency. There is no quiescence of sexual activity in this phase and masturbatory activity remains almost universal. Nevertheless, as the child's self-control becomes stronger, drive activity takes a lesser role until puberty. In preadolescence the child has to cope with dramatic bodily changes and regression in psychosexual development is a common consequence, at least in boys. Adolescence is marked by the menarche in girls and the first ejaculation in boys, invariably confusing for both genders, although boys tend to be particularly poorly prepared for these biological changes. Anxieties associated with these changes are thought to derive from the intensification of incestuous fantasies prompted by the maturing body, which is now experienced as capable of performing the forbidden acts. Some authors link the dramatic increase in psychiatric morbidity associated with adolescence to massive regressions brought about by the reemergence of Oedipal phase conflicts.

In evaluating psychosexual theory from the point of view of modern developmental theory, we should acknowledge Freud's contribution in bringing the awareness of psychologists to the formative nature of childhood sexuality. Freud's theoretical formulations were mechanistic and reductionist. They were based on the principles of contemporary physics using the principles of conservation, displacement, and discharge of energy as organizing constructs. George Klein (1976) was one of the first to point out that Freud's clinical observations were independent of the theoretical framework in which they were couched. Clinical data concerning psychosexual development is subject to empirical testing and growth. For example, we might observe that infantile genitality probably starts in the first year of life rather than in the third; that a constellation of character traits generally considered as the anal personality may exist but may be unrelated to experiences of toilet training, and so on. The notion of psychic energy, however, lacks neuropsychological reference and is, therefore, unlikely to develop or evolve.

More important from a clinical standpoint, is a change of emphasis in modern psychoanalysis away from the theory of instincts and toward a concern with the object of instincts: human relationships. Freud recognized this distinction when he contrasted the concern of the ancients with instinct and the concern of modern civilization with finding an excuse for instinct in the merits of the object (1905, p. 149). By now it is clear that children represent relationships independently of their psychosexual development. While instinctual aspects may color interpersonal relations, and the former may use the latter as a vehicle (representing instinctual wishes in terms of specific interpersonal relations), when seeking an understanding of individual differences in terms of personality or psychopathology, current psychoanalytic emphasis is on pathogenesis through maladaptive object relations rather than sexuality.

[*See also* Libido; *and* Psychoanalysis, *article on* Theories.]

Bibliography

Abraham, K. (1924). A short study of the development of the libido, viewed in the light of mental disorders. In D. Bryan & A. Strachey (Eds.), *Selected papers on psychoanalysis* (pp. 418–501). New York: Basic Books 1953.

Ferenczi, S. (1913). Stages in the development of the sense of reality. In E. Jones (Ed.), *First contributions to psychoanalysis* (pp. 213–239). London: H. Karnac, 1980.

Freud, S. (1900). The interpretation of dreams. In J. Strachey (Ed.), *The standard edition of the complete psychological works of Sigmund Freud* (Vols. 4, 5, pp. 1–715). London: Hogarth Press.

Freud, S. (1905). Three essays on the theory of sexuality. In J. Strachey (Ed.), *The standard edition of the complete psychological works of Sigmund Freud* (Vol. 7, pp. 123–230). London: Hogarth Press.

Klein, G. S. (1976). Freud's two theories of sexuality. *Psychological Issues, Monograph, 36*, 14–70.

Peter Fonagy

PSYCHOSIS has been traditionally defined as involving "gross distortion and disorganization of a person's mental capacity . . . and capacity to recognize reality" (Stedman, 1976). From the earliest descriptions of the most strange, bizarre, and dysfunctional clusters of behaviors, it has been consistently recognized and noted that the constellation of behavioral phenomena now referred to as *psychotic* entails serious impairments or abnormal disruptions in the most fundamental higher brain functions: perception, cognition and cognitive processing, and emotional affect accompanying affectively valenced perceptions and cognitions.

It is these human epistemological functions of the central nervous system (CNS) that constitute the core neurophysiological architecture through which neuropsychological representations of objects, space, relationships, and phenomena (i.e., objective sensory stimuli/"reality") are experienced and are retained. Similarly, these processes provide for coherently organized and pragmatically valid interpretations of external reality as perceived (i.e., individual personal cosmologies of ourselves and the world around us), including moods and affects consistent with the qualitative nature of the sensory-perceptual and/or internal cognitive experiences. When these higher order brain functions are seriously disrupted or impaired, the individual may experience intrabrain-generated sensations perceived as emerging from invalid, distorted, or even nonexistent stimulus sources. These kinds of organized sensory-perceptual experiences are known as hallucinations and commonly entail disturbed individuals "hearing" voices talking to them, calling them vile names, or commanding them to do or not do certain acts. Similarly, visual hallucinations involve the person "seeing" people, animals, phantasmagori monsters that are not, in fact, present or even existent. Somewhat less common are olfactory hallucinations ("smelling" nonpresent odors), and tactile and somatosensory hallucinations (e.g., "feeling" nonexistent insects, snakes, or other "stimuli" on or inside one's body).

With respect to cognition and information-processing disturbances, two basic types of dysfunctions can occur in psychoses. The normally organized, coherent, logical, sequential patterns of cognitive processing are significantly disrupted, impairing certain areas of reasoning and goal-oriented thinking. Although seldom totally pervasive, even the fractional percentage of normal cognitive processing disrupted can be debilitating or even devastating to the person. These disruptions commonly take the form of totally unrelated ideations suddenly intruding into a given train of thought, or certain ideations being oddly excluded or blocked suddenly and (to both client and therapist) usually inexplicably, or the train of thought being derailed: suddenly jumping to a very unrelated train of thought. Although most people occasionally experience such cognitive phenomena in milder forms, persons with certain forms of psychoses do so at higher frequencies in more severe and disruptive ways. Aside from a person self-reporting and describing these phenomena, traditionally referred to as *looseness of association*, they are also evidenced in the psychotic person's speech. It is difficult to mimic such symptomatic cognitive processes, but perhaps a bit of elementary school playground doggerel exemplifies these speech-reflected phenomena (at least in the extreme):

Thirty days hath September
April, June, and no wonder
All the rest eat peanut butter
Except Grandma and
She drives a Buick.

It can be understood then how someone with these kinds of cognitive dysfunctions and disorganization would experience substantial difficulties in a variety of natural environmental settings and tasks, even aside from his or her internal distress. Again, psychotic symptomatology does not constitute the majority of such an individual's behavior. The vast majority of people with psychotic disorders are not constantly hallucinating or unable to engage in logical, coherent, sequentially organized thinking. However, the fraction of time that they do suffer these dysfunctions is often severely impairing and usually frightening and disturbing to themselves and to people around them.

In addition to disrupted, dysfunctional cognitive information *processing*, the second basic form of cognitive symptomatology in psychoses entails cognitive *content* (e.g., ideations, conceptual interpretations, beliefs) that is not only factually false, but is so irrationally inconsistent with the specific "evidence" upon which that content may be allegedly derived, and furthermore, so disparate from common knowledge of general reality as to be categorized as delusional. From the clinical standpoint, a critical factor is not just that certain ideations or beliefs are delusional, but that they evoke intrinsic, aversive emotions in the individual and/or that they provoke or contribute to overtly maladaptive behaviors. The false belief that one's beloved spouse is trying to poison you, for example, would not only induce substantial emotional distress, but could very likely lead to dangerous retaliatory or even preemptive acts.

Finally, psychotic conditions frequently involve the particularly odd phenomena in which the subjective emotional state and its overt, affectual expression are grossly inconsistent in magnitude and/or quality from the affective properties usually associated with certain types of cognitive content. For example, in schizophrenic psychoses, an individual may appear emotionally dull, flat, or even devoid of feeling while discussing what would otherwise appear to be extremely delightful, exciting, or even humorous verbal-ideational content. Similarly, such an individual may smile and giggle while telling about his or her mother's death by cancer.

Of course, individuals suffering from one or another form of psychotic disorder display a variety of other symptomatic behaviors. However, these four basic human epistemic processes constitute the core brain-behavioral dysfunctions in psychoses: significantly distorted sensory-perceptual processes (hallucinations); disorganization in cognitive information processing (loose association, thought disorder); false, unrealistic, irrational beliefs inconsistent with evidence and not widely held or endorsed by a relevant culture or subculture (delusions); and emotional states and their affective expressions that are grossly inconsistent with the relevant present environmental setting or circumstances and/or grossly qualitatively inconsistent with accompanying cognitive content (inappropriate affect). It is because of these dysfunctions in the fundamental, epistemic biopsychological processes that psychoses have been usually described in both clinical and common language as conditions in which the individual loses contact with reality or can't distinguish important and salient features of reality from sui generis fantasy. [*See* Schizophrenia.]

Historical Perspectives

Considering the bizarre yet mysterious nature of the behavioral manifestations and symptoms of psychoses, it is no wonder that premodern scientific explanations of such strange behaviors were equally bizarre. Although ancient Greek physicians such as Alcmaeon (fifth century BCE) and subsequently the great Hippocrates (460–370 BCE) recognized the brain as the anatomical organ of "the mind," that is, of sensation-perception and thought, more superstitious, supernatural explanations for psychotic symptoms gained ascendancy. In fact, the idea that certain hallucinatory perceptions and bizarre delusional belief systems were the work of the devil or demons, although occasionally attributed to God or some saint, persisted literally well into the twentieth century. It followed, then, that treatments be designed to somehow break the spell or otherwise rid the body and/or soul of the demonic presence. Whereas religious rites of exorcism were often the initial remediations attempted, when those failed (as of course they usually did), more brutal forms of physical exorcism involving torture were employed. The notion was that if the body could be made to suffer excruciating pain, it would become so intolerably uncomfortable that the demon would flee. Unfortunately, many individuals died because, presumably, their own souls could not tolerate that degree of pain and suffering either. In many cases, particularly where the psychotic person was already disliked, feared, or otherwise highly suspect, he or she would be accused of being a witch or of having formed a pact with the devil. Under torture or as associated with their psychoses, they would often confess and subsequently be burned at the stake.

Subsequent to the Age of Enlightenment (late eighteenth century) and especially under the influence of the Romantic idealism in philosophy of such writers as the French philosopher Jean-Jacques Rousseau (1712–1778), treatment of the mentally ill, even those persons with the most bizarre, disorganized, dysfunctional behaviors, became more humane if not more efficacious. During this time the currently pejorative terms such as *insane, lunatic, moron,* and *maniac* came into common, as well as clinical, usage. Nomenclature aside, treatments became increasingly benign and usually entailed removal to quiet, pastoral settings, though occasionally some peculiar experimental treatments such as Rush's whirling chair would be endorsed. (This early nineteenth-century device spun people rapidly around their vertical axis!)

By the late nineteenth and early twentieth centuries, theories about the etiology of psychoses came under the influence of the emerging nature versus nurture debate. The questions raised a hundred years ago are essentially the same ones asked today regarding the etiology of symptomatic patterns of bizarre, abnormal, dysfunctional behavior: Where do these things come from? How can we best treat them or even prevent them from developing? Although psychoanalytic and later some Skinnerian behavioral theorists postulated a number of environmental, early life experience, or conditioning-learning explanations for psychoses as well as for other clinical syndromes, empirical research findings have not supported these hypotheses or theories with respect to psychoses. Instead, several lines of evidence have converged to indicate that psychoses are fundamentally abnormal perceptual-cognitive-affective behavioral manifestations of neuropathophysiology.

1. Classic psychotic behaviors most commonly occur as central, syptomatic components of disorders that are now known to be basically biological disorders, major affective disorders, and especially in schizophrenias (Nasrallah, 1993; Rush, Stewart, Garner, & Waller, 1998).

2. Psychotic symptoms that are quite similar and in many cases identical to those exhibited in schizophrenias and major affective disorders can be induced by certain neurotoxic compounds, particularly cocaine and amphetamine stimulants, but also by a variety of psychoactive chemicals.

3. Similar but often not identical psychotic symptoms appear as sequelae (a) of known neurological disorders such as certain brain tumors and in some cases of Alzheimer's disorder; (b) of some general medical conditions, for example, certain endocrine disorders; and (c) in the neurological condition of alcoholic delirium tremens (Rosenberg & Pleasure, 1998).

4. Pharmacologic compounds that share certain neurochemical properties (e.g., dopamine-2 and serotonin-2 antagonism) have been found efficacious in the treatment of similar forms of psychotic symptoms regardless of the disorder or dysfunctional condition with which they are associated. For example, haloperidol is usually effective in reducing auditory hallucinations and paranoid delusional cognitions in both schizophrenia, paranoid type, and amphetamine abuse–induced psychoses (Alford & Bishop, 1991).

5. After a century of psychoanalytic and a half century of behavioristic theorizing, there is no credible empirical evidence that any form of psychosis, much less psychotic disorder, results from any environmental, childrearing, or other life-experience factor alone. Indeed, it is almost impossible to socially induce a full-blown psychosis in an otherwise previously normal person through social environmental experience, even in concentration or prisoner-of-war camps. Contrary to popular misconceptions, it is extremely rare for a previously normal individual to develop a clear, unequivocal pattern of psychotic symptoms due to social isolation, brainwashing, or even torture, except where environmental independent variables induce abnormal *biological* states (e.g., starvation, extreme temperatures, electrolyte or hormonal imbalance, etc.).

6. Similarly, no form of verbal, stimulus conditioning, or other social or experiential therapy alone has been found efficacious when targeting the central, core

symptomatology of psychoses as would be expected if these were primarily learned behaviors. In marked contrast, pharmacotherapy has been repeatedly demonstrated effective in the majority of cases, frequently modifying not only hallucinatory and cognitive *processing* dysfunction, but even the cognitive content (e.g., paranoid delusional beliefs). Indeed, patients diagnosed with psychotic disorders that are chronic in nature exhibit a very high relapse rate with return of floridly psychotic symptoms subsequent and consequent to their discontinuation of their antipsychotic medication. Such clinical findings are consistent with psychoses being a biological disruption of normal brain-behavioral function, which function tends to return toward its premorbid level when the biochemical/physiological pathology is relieved or at least shifted toward normal biological processes.

Treatment

As psychotic disorders are fundamentally disorders of brain pathophysiology, it is not surprising that the principle mode of efficacious treatment is biological, specifically psychopharmacological. There are two general classes of pharmacologic agents that have been found effective in treating various psychotic symptoms. The first and older of these are compounds that partially block the transmission of signals from one nerve cell to the next in those CNS neural networks that use the chemical dopamine as the transmitter substance. These are, therefore, referred to as dopamine antagonists and include a wide range of drugs ranging from the early chlorpromazine to the more recent haloperidol. A related group of compounds exerts a somewhat more selectively antagonism of subtypes of dopamine receptors and also somewhat selectively blocks a receptor subtype of the neurochemical transmitter serotonin (5-hydroxytryptamine or 5-HT). These are currently termed atypical antipsychotics and have been found to have a greater specificity of action yet broader range of therapeutic effect, but usually with fewer side effects. In addition, some chemically unrelated compounds under certain conditions contribute to the relief of psychotic behavior. Lithium carbonate may relieve manic psychotic symptoms in bipolar disorder, whereas benzodiazepines such as diazepam usually contribute to the relief of the more floridly psychotic behavior in individuals suffering alcoholic delirium tremens. In such cases, it is likely that the reduction of some psychotic symptoms results indirectly from these compounds' therapeutic action in more general CNS neurophysiological stabilization. What is clear is that both the traditional (multidopamine receptor antagonists) and the newer atypical (more selective dopamine-2 and serotonin) antagonists are usually effective in substantially reducing psychotic sensory-perceptual and cognitive symptoms. The effects are seen across a variety of psychotic disorders or conditions, including schizophrenias, bipolar disorders, drug-induced psychoses, and even some psychotic symptoms (e.g., hallucinations) in some cases of Alzheimer's disorder and other CNS organic psychoses. The clinical pharmacologic finding that these two related classes of compounds (in contrast to other classes of psychopharmacologic agents) do usually exert a therapeutic action on such a variety of clinical disorders and conditions entailing psychotic symptoms further suggests that most psychotic conditions *share* some fundamental biopathological physiology.

Drug-induced toxic psychoses usually reverse relatively quickly when treated with antipsychotic medications and usually do not require ongoing medication management. Similarly, psychoses that result from acute medical disorders affecting the CNS (e.g., hyperthyroidism) usually fully reverse when the medical condition is successfully treated. Psychoses that are the consequence of irreversible CNS damage associated with such conditions as Alzheimer's disease, alcoholic encephalopathy, and neurosyphilis often exhibit at least a partial remission of such psychiatric symptoms as hallucinations when treated with even relatively low dosages of antipsychotic medications but otherwise demonstrate limited improvement. Psychoses occurring as part of the syndrome of psychological-behavioral disturbances in bipolar and schizophrenic disorders show varying degrees of symptom remission ranging from minimal effect to essential clinical remission. In most such cases, substantial symptom remission occurs but typically does so gradually over several weeks. Long-term maintenance is required utilizing antipsychotic medications in the case of schizophrenias or mood stabilizers (e.g., lithium carbonate, carbamazepine) in the case of bipolar disorder.

In addition to pharmacotherapy, various psychotherapeutic, milieu, and learning and social influence therapies have been traditionally used in treatment of major psychotic disorders. In spite of early, overly optimistic claims of some of these, none has been shown effective for most individuals with one or another chronic psychotic disorder unless it is combined with appropriate pharmacotherapy. Persons suffering from a major psychotic disorder exhibit behavioral excesses, deficits, and dysfunctions that may reflect brain-behavior performance problems, or may reflect deficits in their basic behavioral repertoires. Although medications can ameliorate most performance problems that result from basic brain physiological dysfunction, drugs, of course, cannot directly modify the learning history and, therefore, the basic behavioral repertoire. Fortunately, from the standpoint of efficiency and practicality of treatment availability, most of the dysfunctional symptoms in most persons with chronic psychotic disorders are, in fact, performance dysfunctions arising from brain pathophysiology. Therefore, appropriate antipsychotic medications can reduce, if not entirely alleviate, most of the more behaviorally disruptive symptoms in most individuals. In fact, many behavioral problems that may initially appear to be repertorial deficits will be found to have been performance problems that medication alone can substantially improve.

Individuals with major psychotic disorders, however, can have serious and disruptive behavioral deficits that resulted from impaired learning, that is, deficits in behavioral repertoire per se. In such cases, reeducative psychotherapeutic procedures can substantially contribute to the overall improvement in such individuals, particularly with respect to social-interpersonal skills and to academic and job tasks. These are major factors in the successful long-term adjustment of these individuals within their natural environments, thus contributing to lower relapse rates as well.

In general, individuals who exhibit severely debilitating clusters of psychotic symptoms such that they cannot successfully perform basic self-management skills, or who are a significant danger to themselves or others, are hospitalized and medicated. During their hospitalization, psychological evaluations begin to identify dysfunctional behaviors that are responsive to pharmacotherapy and those that require learning principle–based reeducative procedures. Where indicated, these therapeutic procedures are begun during hospitalization and followed up in outpatient treatment. In addition, basic occupational, self-care, and social living capacities are assessed. Where necessary, employment and/or living arrangements are modified in order to better match the individual's global level of functioning and thus his or her long-term adjustment. In many less severe cases, these therapeutic procedures and goals can be accomplished in a partial hospitalization or even an outpatient setting. However, almost all individuals with some form of chronic psychotic disorder require at least intermittent outpatient visits with the primary focus on assessing mental status, environmental behavioral functioning, and medication management.

In conclusion, psychotic behaviors remain among the more bizarre and frightening of psychological symptoms, though much less so today than when demons, spirits, and devils were believed to be their cause. Similarly, effective treatment has reduced their debilitating impact, and the recognition that they are of a biological etiology has contributed to less guilt among patients, parents, and relatives and to less shame and fear. Because so similar psychotic symptoms can and do appear in such a variety of neuropsychiatric conditions (e.g., from drug intoxication to schizophrenia to Alzheimer's disease), it is likely that these biobehavioral symptoms share many common neurophysiological components within the context of their broader but diverse diagnostic conditions or disorders.

Further advances in neuroscience are likely to provide a more comprehensive identification of the specific neurochemistry and particular receptor physiology that underlie such psychotic symptoms as hallucinations, delusions, and disrupted cognitive processing. This will allow pharmacologic compounds with even greater specificity of action to be formulated, both to increase the efficacy of drug treatment and to decrease the variety and severity of side effects.

[*See also* Delusions; *and* Hallucinations.]

Bibliography

Alford, G. S., & Bishop, A. (1991). Psychopharmacology. In M. Hersen, A. E. Kazdin, & A. S. Bellack (Eds.), *The clinical psychology handbook* (2nd ed., pp. 667–694). Elmsford, NY: Pergamon Press.

Nasrallah, H. A. (1993). Neurodevelopmental pathogenesis of schizophrenia. *Psychiatric Clinics of North America, 16*, 269–280.

Rosenberg, R. N., & Pleasure, D. E. (Eds.). (1998). *Comprehensive neurology* (2nd ed.). New York: Wiley.

Rush, A. J., Stewart, R. S., Garner, D. L., & Waller, D. A. (1998). Neurobiological bases for psychiatric disorders. In R. N. Rosenberg & D. E. Pleasure (Eds.), *Comprehensive neurology* (2nd ed.). New York: Wiley.

Stedman, T. L. (1976). *Stedman's medical dictionary* (23rd ed.). Baltimore, MD: Williams & Wilkins.

Geary S. Alford and Leslie Karns

PSYCHOSOMATIC ILLNESS. The relationship between the mind (*psyche*) and body (*soma*) in health and illness has a long history of theory and research in medicine and a recent history of theory and research in psychology. The term "psychosomatic medicine" was officially used in the 1930s with the creation of the journal *Psychosomatic Medicine*. The sister basic science, psychophysiology, was formally established in the 1950s with the creation of the journal *Psychophysiology*. New terms such as "behavioral medicine," "health psychology," and "mind-body health" were formalized in the 1980s with the creation of journals such as the *Journal of Behavioral Medicine, Health Psychology*, and *ADVANCES: The Journal of Mind-Body Health*.

According to *Webster's Dictionary* (1977), the term "psychosomatic" has two related meanings: "(1) designating or of a physical disorder of the body originating in or aggravated by the psychic or emotional processes of the individual, and (2) designating the branch of medicine using a psychological approach to the study of causes and treatment of physical disorders." Webster's definition of psychosomatic is very close to the definition used by the founding editors of the journal *Psychosomatic Medicine*.

> The aim of *Psychosomatic Medicine* . . . is to encourage and bring together studies which make a contribution to the understanding of the organism as a whole, in somatic and psychic aspects . . . Pertinent examples are: investigations of experimental neuroses, of frustration, of physiological changes accompanying emotion, of vegetative and hormonal disturbances, and of psychiatric aspects of general and specific medical problems (1939, p. 1).

Though this description is somewhat dated (for example, the word "psychic" was used by the editors to refer to psychological—not parapsychological—processes), it clearly conveys the origin of the field.

In their introductory statement to the journal, the editors emphasized that "psychosomatic medicine is not equivalent with what is understood by the term psychiatry." They explained that "the principal interest of psychiatry is the diseased mind" whereas psychosomatic medicine covers a "different and broader field. Its object is to study in the interrelation the psychological and physiological aspects of all normal and abnormal bodily functions and thus to integrate somatic therapy and psychotherapy." In a word, "psychosomatic medicine concerns itself with the psychological approach into general medicine" (p. 3).

Psychosomatic illnesses are disorders where psychological factors are believed to play an important role in the etiology and/or pathogenesis of physical diseases. In the 1930s, the prevailing psychological theories were psychoanalytic theory (from psychiatry) and learning theory (from psychology). In the first article published in the journal *Psychosomatic Medicine*, "Psychological Aspects of Medicine," Franz Alexander (1939) shared his dream that psychosomatic medicine should be truly interdisciplinary and integrative, and that "the need for more knowledge here is excruciatingly obvious." He quoted Alan Gregg as saying:

> Psychiatry is astir, neurophysiology is crescent, neurosurgery flourishes, and a star still hands over the cradle of endocrinology . . . Contributions from other fields are to seek from psychology, cultural anthropology, sociology and philosophy as well as from chemistry and physics and internal medicine to resolve the dichotomy of mind and body left by Descartes. (1936, p. 9).

Biophysical and psychosocial theory and research have evolved substantially over the past 50 years. As indicated by the creation of such new fields as psychoneuroimmunology, the hypothesis that the mind plays a role in all diseases (including cardiovascular, immunological, and neurological diseases) to various degrees is becoming ever more established. From this perspective, all diseases can be said to be "psychosomatic" (the classic term) or "biopsychosocial spiritual" (the evolving term).

Bibliography

Alexander, F. (1939). Psychological aspects of medicine. *Psychosomatic Medicine, 1* (1), 7–18.

Gregg, A. (1936). The future of medicine. *Harvard Medical Alumni Bulletin.*

Introductory statement. (1939). *Psychosomatic Medicine, 1* (1), 3–5.

Webster's New Twentieth Century Dictionary of the English Language. (1977). (Unabridged, 2nd ed.), New York: Collins World.

Gary E. Schwartz

PSYCHOSURGERY. The unfortunate term *psychosurgery* (surgery of the psyche evokes a puzzling image) refers to attempts to reverse the ravages of mental disorder by various forms of surgical intervention on parts of the brain. The era of its maximum employment, roughly from 1935 to 1960, was one in which several forms of relatively radical biological treatments for serious mental disorders were developed, flourished briefly, and then receded as their limitations and/or hazards became apparent. The single exception is that of electroconvulsive therapy (ECT), which continues in widespread use today as a reasonably safe and effective treatment for serious mood disorders. The advent of psychosurgery was thus very much a product of its time, and was to become without doubt the most controversial of all psychiatric treatments ever introduced.

The possible surgical treatment of psychiatric disorders was first proposed by Portuguese neurologist Antonio de Egas Moniz in 1933. Noting the behavioral effects (seeming passivity, calmness) in primates following the experimental ablation of the frontal lobes of the brain, Moniz reasoned that the same effects might be achieved in mentally disturbed humans by surgical interruption of neural connections between the frontal brain areas and deeper centers such as the thalamus. In light of then available surgical technology, any such operation would produce quite extensive and permanent destruction of brain tissue. If, from a contemporary perspective, this proposal therefore seems unduly rash, or worse, it must be recalled that it was made in an era desperately lacking in any satisfactory remedies for the more severe mental disorders. Nor were there satisfactory means available to contain the wild, uncontrolled, and dangerous behavior to which many hospitalized mental patients were then subject. As testimony to the importance attached to his work, Moniz was to receive the 1949 Nobel Prize in medicine.

With his surgeon colleague Almeida Lima, Moniz developed a technique of making "core" cuts in frontal brain tissue by introducing through a burr hole in the top of the skull, and at various angles and depths, a leucotome, a thin hollow instrument containing a flexible steel band. When judged to be at the prescribed location within the brain, the band was pushed out of an opening in the shaft of the instrument into the brain substance, forming a loop. The entire instrument was then rotated such that the steel loop severed a roughly spherical mass, about 1 centimeter in diameter, from its surrounding brain tissue. This "coring" was performed bilaterally. Reporting on the first twenty patients receiving this procedure, Moniz (*Tentatives opératoires dans le traitement de certaines psychoses*, Paris, 1936) declared one third recovered, one third improved, and one third unimproved. Considering the dismal prognoses then attending serious mental disorders, these figures were greeted by many as indicating striking success for the operation.

An extremely rapid proliferation of varying surgical techniques ensued for "disconnecting" the anterior frontal lobes from deeper brain structures, particularly in the United States, where the leading figures were neurologist Walter Freeman and neurosurgeon James Watts (Freeman & Watts, *Psychosurgery*, Springfield, MA, 1950). Included among these procedures were *bilateral topectomy* (symmetrical bilateral excision of parts of the frontal cortex), *bilateral cortical undercutting* (undercutting of the frontal lobes in the subcingulate or suborbital regions), *bilateral thalamotomy* (electrocoagulation of the dorsomedial thalamic nuclei), *bimedial lobotomy* (cutting of the medial portion of the white matter of the frontal lobes in the frontal plane), and *bilateral cingulectomy* (surgical excision or isolation of the anterior cingulate gyrus).

The best known and probably most widely used of these operations were the "standard" *prefrontal lobotomy* (PFL) and the *transorbital lobotomy* (TOL), both popularized in particular by Freeman and Watts. In the PFL procedure the skull is trephined bilaterally three centimeters behind and slightly above the outer juncture of the eyelids, through which opening a blunt knife is inserted some 4 to 5 centimeters into the brain tissue. Its handle is manipulated in an upward and downward motion parallel to the coronal suture—of course severing everything in the path of the blade.

In the TOL procedure, one that was to become widely used by psychiatrists because it was thought not to require operating room facilities or neurosurgical expertise, the approach to the prefrontal brain was made through the orbital plate, the thin bony wall of the eye socket. The patient was first given two to four consecutive electroconvulsive treatments to achieve anesthesia, following which a pointed instrument was inserted into the vault above the eyeball and driven with a mallet through the orbital plate to a depth (from the eyelid) of up to 7 centimeters. With the instrument in place, its handle was then maneuvered through a prescribed range of angles to sever as much as possible of the thalamofrontal interconnection. This operation, too, was always done on both sides.

As the above list of procedures demonstrates, temerity or squeamishness were not characteristics strongly represented among the earliest group of psychosurgeons. In fact, thousands of mental hospital patients in the United States alone underwent one or another of these operations in the era immediately preceding the introduction and widespread use of neuroleptic medication in the late 1950s. Some of them, estimated at 1 to 4%, died as an immediate consequence of the surgery. Freeman himself (In S. Arieti (Ed.), *American Handbook of Psychiatry*, Vol. 2, New York, 1959) reports 21 deaths among the astounding 744 TOLs he performed on state hospital patients in West Virginia.

Many surviving patients, as gradually became clear, permanently lost abilities essential to independent functioning in the world at large. One of the sisters of President John F. Kennedy, Rosemary, suffered such a fate in receiving psychosurgical treatment for oppositional and erratic behavior (Goodwin, 1987). Some surviving patients, in contrast, appeared genuinely to have been helped by these procedures, in the sense of some tradeoff of benefits received relative to losses sustained.

Although the effects of brain injury, surgically or otherwise produced, are never wholly predictable, the adverse "personality" changes often deriving from these operations generally conformed to what is known as a "frontal lobe syndrome." As described, the latter has two main attributes: (1) apathy, indifference, and loss of initiative, and/or (2) loss of inhibitory control, the person seeming to indulge every appetite, whim, or impulse without restraint or forethought of consequences. Freeman (1959), with an élan that appears to have been characteristic, refers to the latter as "all the Boy Scout virtues in reverse" (p. 1523). Postoperative obesity, sometimes extreme, was a troublesome side effect. Epileptic seizures were also a common sequel to prefrontal lobotomy, possibly because a substantial amount of presumably necrotic tissue was left in the brain postoperatively. Unfortunately, a frequent consequence was that the lobotomized patient now had no hope whatever of eventually living outside an institution.

Granted the unavailability of effective alternatives for controlling patient violence, etc., it remains somewhat puzzling how such an obviously hazardous and crude type of intervention, still in widespread use only a half-century ago, became as popular as it did. Two reasons appear prominent:

1. Prior to about 1960, mental hospitals, especially the public ones where most patients went, had deteriorated into dreadful, overcrowded places of limited resources, poorly trained staff, and extremely discourag-

ing outcome statistics for the chronic patients "warehoused" within their walls (Deutsch 1948). The advent of psychosurgery, accompanied by much ballyhoo and poorly examined claims of recovery or marked improvement, opened an avenue promising to relieve long-standing malaise, demoralization, and a relentless sense of futility among the staffs of these institutions.

2. The professional discipline of psychiatry, partly because of its strong embrace of Freudian psychoanalytic doctrine (which is widely regarded as irrelevant to the severe, chronic mental disorders and to biomedical science) during the first two thirds of the twentieth century, was in danger of losing contact with its mother discipline of medicine. The advent of psychosurgery became an opportunity to prove that psychiatry was still a specialty within medicine, and that psychiatrists were still physicians. It was a need that was eventually fulfilled with the soon to follow advent of the major psychotropic drugs. The TOL procedure, in particular, enabled venturesome psychiatrists to become, as it were, brain surgeons.

Walter Freeman was a tireless advocate of this development. He traveled far and wide, sometimes at his own expense, to teach the technique to groups of hospital psychiatrists. His boundless confidence is evident in his own words:

> About 10 per cent of patients should be re-operated upon. Good results may be anticipated in about a third of such patients, but with a greater risk of undesirable personality changes. However, since the neurotic or psychotic disturbance is apt to progress unless appropriate measures are undertaken, there is little to lose. Some patients respond finally to a third or even a fourth lobotomy who otherwise would have been classified as failures. (Freeman, 1959, p. 1523)

Despite an enthusiasm that was to a large extent (as we now know) unwarranted, PFL and related procedures did on occasion result in clearly improved functioning for some patients, as already noted. That fact was underscored when, in the mid-1970s, the U.S. Congress enjoined the National Commission for the Protection of Human Subjects of Biomedical and Behavioral Research to examine in detail the outcomes of psychosurgical procedures (Culliton, *Science*, 1976, *194*, 299–301). Acknowledging past excesses and abuses, the Commission concluded that with more modern and circumscribed surgical approaches employing stereotactic targeting, some psychiatric disorders—notably chronic severe depression—could often be significantly relieved. It singled out for particularly favorable attention the *cingulotomy* procedure, wherein communication between the frontal lobes and the limbic system is precisely severed. The commission also warned, however, that such benefits were sometimes accompanied by detectable losses in cognitive and other higher-level functions. It recommended continued cautious exploration of the psychosurgical domain within the context of strict regulations and safeguards to protect patient interests.

That continuing exploration remains in effect, although its public acknowledgement is relatively subdued. It was rarely mentioned, for example, in the professional literature of the 1980s and 1990s. Nevertheless, it is estimated that in the late twentieth century some 200 to 300 "psychosurgeries" per year were performed worldwide, although it must be emphasized that these modern operations, almost without exception, are far more precisely targeted and confined in extent than the early "meat cleaver" lobotomies described above. Contemporary approaches make full use of high-tech imaging apparatus and stereotactic triangulation of the relatively tiny brain areas thought to be primarily implicated in the patient's problems. They also employ a variety of more highly controllable methods of producing minute lesions, such as radioactive implants, cryoprobes, electrical coagulation, proton beams, ultrasonic waves, and the "gamma knife."

Meanwhile, substantial progress has also been made in more carefully differentiating the types of disorder most likely to be responsive to psychosurgical therapy. Chronic, intractable depressions have already been mentioned as among the candidates, and some treatment-resistant bipolar (manic-depressive) disorder patients have benefited from lesioning in the subcaudate nucleus of the brain (called a tractotomy). In addition, severe, treatment-refractory obsessive-compulsive disorder has a record of responding well to this approach (Reid, Balis, & Sutton, *The Treatment of Psychiatric Disorders*, Bristol, PA, 1997). This greater care in patient selection is buttressed by a far greater sensitivity to the patient's welfare and rights. These procedures are normally carried out only as a last resort, and then with exquisite finesse, caution, full disclosure of risks, and informed consent.

In fact, probably most such operations today are not intended, strictly speaking, to alter "psychic" functions at all. While the distinction is often less than clear, various *neurological* anomalies that impair behavioral functioning are the more usual basis for considering brain surgery as a potential corrective. For example, some cases of Parkinsonism (characterized in part by muscle rigidity and marked tremor) can now be alleviated by punctate destruction with heated needle electrodes of portions of structures deep within the brain. So can the uncontrolled violence associated with some forms of epileptic seizure. Severe and chronic pain, as in many terminal cancer patients, may also be relieved by similar methods. It is unfortunate that these highly refined types of surgical intervention are sometimes confused with the unrestrained cutting of an earlier era, arousing unmerited reactions of rejection and fear.

Bibliography

Rodgers, J. E. (1992). Psychosurgery: Damaging the brain to save the mind. *Psychology Today, 26,* 35–86 (nonconsecutive). Provides an informative account of modern psychosurgery, featuring a full case history of "Matthew," whose surgery for dangerous epileptic rages was successful.

Valenstein, E. S. (Ed.). (1980). *The psychosurgery debate: Scientific, legal, and ethical perspectives.* San Francisco: Freeman.

Valenstein, E. S. (1986). *Great and desperate cures.* New York: Basic Books. Focusing on the career of Walter Freeman, this scholarly book addresses the question of how such a destructive procedure as prefrontal lobotomy came to be accepted as standard psychiatric practice.

Robert C. Carson

PSYCHOTHERAPY. [*This entry provides a broad survey of the field of psychotherapy. It comprises three articles:*

Research
Clinical Practice
Approaches

Numerous independent entries related to psychotherapy are included in the encyclopedia: Child and Adolescent Psychotherapy; Computerized Psychotherapy; Constructivist Psychotherapy; Eclectic Psychotherapy; Ethnocultural Psychotherapy; Experiential Psychotherapy; Integrative Psychotherapy; Interpersonal Psychotherapy; Psychoanalysis, *article on* Psychoanalytic Psychotherapies; Rational Emotive Psychotherapy; *and* Religion and Psychotherapy.]

Research

Psychotherapy research is the use of appropriate scientific methods to describe, explain, and evaluate psychotherapeutic procedures. It complements clinical expertise and direct practical experience as a source of valid, generalizable knowledge about psychotherapy.

Psychotherapeutic procedures refer to a range of professional activities that lead to the enhancement of personal well-being, the relief of emotional distress, and the improvement of life functioning—primarily through specific forms of communication and interaction. This definition excludes treatments that are primarily biological, chemical, or physical in nature, and also excludes spontaneously occurring events that may enhance well-being, relieve distress, or enhance effectiveness (e.g., a promotion at work or falling in love). Exclusion of biological, chemical, or physical interventions is not meant to imply their ineffectiveness. By the same token, exclusion of influential events that occur normally as part of the life cycle does not deny that such events may instigate profound and positive transformations in one's life. Currently recognized psychotherapeutic procedures include methods from various theoretical orientations such as humanistic, psychodynamic, behavioral, and systemic approaches.

The use of appropriate scientific methods refers to strategies and techniques for conducting explicit, controlled, systematic, and increasingly precise observations and analyses of human behavior and experience. By this criterion, traditional case histories have limited scientific value because they consist of impressionistically reported observations made in an uncontrolled and unsystematic fashion. Nevertheless, traditional case histories may be didactically valuable as clinical narratives bearing witness to the successes and the problems met in applying various treatment methods. Examples of currently utilized research methods—developed primarily in the disciplines of psychology, sociology, anthropology, medicine, and public health—include controlled experiments, naturalistic or quasi-experimental research, surveys, and systematic single-case studies.

Psychotherapy research concentrates primarily on two areas and their interrelations: process research, which seeks to identify specific change processes; and outcome research, which compares the relative efficacy or effectiveness of psychotherapeutic interventions.

Process Research

The descriptive efforts of psychotherapy researchers have focused mainly on events that can be observed to occur during treatment sessions. Such events can include interactions between patient and therapist and experiences during sessions subsequently reported by patients and therapists. Process research took form when therapists' consulting rooms were opened to audio (and, subsequently, to video) recording, so that actual practices could be scrutinized repeatedly, in detail, by multiple observers (Orlinsky & Russell, 1994). In addition to recordings, postsession questionnaires and structured interviews have also been used in process research to collect systematic reports from patients and therapists about what they experienced during sessions.

In analyses of process variables, a distinction is often made between technique and relationship variables. Technique and relationship variables are sometimes also referred to as specific and common, respectively, on the presumption that technical factors differentiate (i.e., are specific to) particular treatment approaches, whereas relationships between patients and therapists are present in all treatment approaches (i.e., are common, or "nonspecific").

A more important though typically implicit distinction reflects the contrasting conceptions of process held by researchers. Some define *process* simply to include whatever occurs in and between patients and therapists in their reciprocal roles. These researchers generally seek to determine what patients and therapists actually do, feel, think, and want in varying circumstances and treatment conditions. However, other researchers define *process* primarily in terms of events within patients that lead to psychological improvement. Their research focuses on whether, and how much, particular therapeutic conditions or interventions contribute to the patient's progress. The variables and measurement procedures used in studies guided by these two conceptions often overlap, leading to some confusion that could be minimized by referring to one as treatment process research and the other as change process research (Orlinsky, Grawe, & Parks, 1994).

The dominant research design in treatment process research has been the naturalistic study (quasi-experiment), which involves systematic observations of selected process variables under normal conditions of clinical practice, that is, observations are made of specific cases at different points in time, applying the same measures in the same way for all cases. One or more treatment cases may be involved, and statistical procedures are used to extract consistent information from the multiplicity of observations. Analyses may examine the relation among two or more variables, for example, the relation between therapists' use of interpretive techniques and the extent to which patients experience insight during sessions, given varying qualities of therapeutic alliance between patients and therapists. Analyses may also focus on patterns or configurations of variables, for example, patterns of emotion experienced during therapy sessions.

Change process research, by contrast, tends to favor a more experimental approach. Investigators who hold hypotheses about the consequences of certain technical interventions may test them by actively varying their presence or absence, or their relative strength, on different occasions during sessions. The attempt to test various aspects of treatment under controlled conditions may extend even further to include the construction of comprehensive treatment manuals and the training of therapists to act competently in accordance with the essential procedures specified by a manual.

Treatment process studies tend to give a macroscopic view of therapeutic events, tracing the broad outlines of actual practice, whereas change process studies tend to provide detailed, microscopic views of the events that may make therapy effective. A taxonomy and review of therapy process variables that have been studied can be found in "Process and Outcome in Psychotherapy" (1994), by Orlinsky, Grawe, and Parks.

Outcome Research

The evaluative efforts of psychotherapy researchers have focused mainly on comparing the psychological symptoms, degree of behavioral effectiveness, and level of emotional well-being of patients before and after treatment. They also focus on the relative ability of different treatments to produce beneficial changes for specified types of patients. The early work of outcome researchers was driven by a critical challenge to the general value of psychotherapeutic treatments posed by Hans Eysenck (1952). The outcome studies that accumulated during the subsequent 25 years in response to Eysenck's challenge clearly established the efficacy of psychotherapy (Smith, Glass, & Miller, 1980; Lipsey & Wilson, 1993, Bergin & Garfield, 1994).

The pressure to justify the use of specific types of treatment for specific types of patients has been fueled during the 1980s and 1990s by the rapid economic expansion and intense competitive pressures experienced in health-care delivery. This recent outcome research has also been formulated along two distinct lines of inquiry concerning, respectively, the efficacy and effectiveness of treatments. Some researchers (e.g., Howard, Moras, Brill, Martnovich, & Lutz, 1996) have phrased the efficacy question as "Can [a treatment] work under special, experimental conditions?" and the effectiveness question as "Does [a treatment] work in practice?" (p. 1059).

The research design of choice for assessments of treatment efficacy has been the controlled clinical trial or double-blind experiment. In both of these, patients are recruited to meet specified research criteria. They are then randomly assigned to one or more treatment and control conditions, where feasible, in such a way that neither patients nor therapists are informed about which group the patient is in. However, the practical and ethical restrictions involved in studying human subjects limit the researcher's control (e.g., with respect to patient dropout or therapist withdrawal of patients showing adverse effects), and thus make it impossible to fulfill the exact requirements of this experimental design. The lapses and compromises that occur in each study always limit the confidence with which conclusions can be drawn from it, yet the combination of findings from a great many such studies can often sufficiently offset the limitations of individual studies to demonstrate effects of genuine importance.

By contrast, treatment effectiveness studies seek to determine the actual benefit of therapies in the uncontrolled, often highly variable conditions of applied clinical practice. Some treatments may be more difficult to implement or may have more limited relevance in circumstances where therapists have varying degrees of training and patients typically have treatment preferences and multiple problems. Many research designs are possible in assessing treatment effectiveness, including the addition of outcome measures to systematic naturalistic process studies or even to single-case studies. Researchers have also freed themselves from the traditional pre/post design of outcome research to include evaluations of patient functioning at various points during treatment. Making multiple assessments during treatment has permitted researchers to study the process of outcome, for example, by fitting mathematical functions such as growth curves to the evaluation data, in effect, charting the course of treatment for individual patients in a clinically relevant way (e.g., Sperry, Brill, Howard, & Grissom, 1996).

Determinants of Process and Outcome

The explanatory efforts of researchers have focused primarily on determining the linkages between therapeutic processes and outcomes, and the separate and joint influences of patients' and therapists' characteristics on both process and outcome. The former is called process-outcome research; the latter, matching or aptitude-treatment interaction research. (Summaries of major findings in these areas can be found in Bergin & Garfield, 1994. An introduction to matching or aptitude-treatment interaction research can also be found in Shoham-Salomon, 1991.)

Studies of patients and therapists that are not directly related to traditional process or outcome variables also add information valuable for an overall understanding of the mental health field. Studies of patients explore topics such as the epidemiology of psychiatric disorders and the utilization of mental health services (e.g., Howard et al., 1996; Taube, Mechanic, & Hohmann, 1989). Studies of psychotherapists have examined the impacts on them of providing treatments for varied numbers and types of patients, both positive (e.g., continued professional development) and negative (e.g., burnout).

Limitations and Problems

One significant limitation of psychotherapy research derives from the fact that data analysis in most studies follows a traditional model of statistical group comparisons that has tended to obscure the range of impacts that treatments have on individual patients (Howard, Krause, & Vessey, 1994; Lyons & Howard, 1991). This has been offset to some extent by a growing commitment to systematic quantitative analyses of single cases (e.g., Hill, 1989), but such studies in turn face problems of limited generalizability and of how to combine results across patients.

A problem whose complexity has been recognized but not yet fully resolved may also be noted in regard to the assessment of therapeutic outcomes. Judgments of outcome involve both a descriptive determination of change in a patient's condition and an evaluation of that change as desirable or undesirable by some value criterion, that is, as improvement or deterioration (e.g., Strupp, Hadley, & Gomes-Schwartz, 1977). Outcome assessments are inherently related to the observational and value perspectives of the raters (Krause & Howard, 1976). This means that outcome assessment cannot be fully objective.

Psychotherapy research reflects an evolving set of investigative methods and a body of knowledge whose frontiers are marked by unresolved problems. Researchers understand, as consumers of research also need to, that knowledge claims must always be tempered by an awareness of potential biases and limitations inherent in any empirical inquiry. Nevertheless, well-replicated research results generally represent the best available knowledge and should be valued in that light.

Research Knowledge and Clinical Practice

A group that should be prominent among consumers of psychotherapy research but evidently is not consists of clinical practitioners (Morrow-Bradley & Elliott, 1986). The reasons for this curious failure of communication have been discussed by both researchers and clinicians (e.g., Talley, Strupp, & Butler, 1994). One is that, although obviously relevant to each other, psychotherapy research and psychotherapy practice are very different tasks with very different knowledge requirements. Researchers need theories as guides to design studies involving many cases and as aids in interpreting their results. Clinicians need theories as schemas to understand the problems presented by individuals who consult them, and as guides to respond in ways that are helpful. In addition, the disparity between practice and research is evident in the attitude of mind that each fosters. Research breeds an orientation that may be called cognitive modesty, an orientation that says, "Assume nothing." Practice, on the other hand, demands an attitude of mind that may be called cognitive confidence. To act effectively, therapists surely must act. These differences need to be recognized and respected in order that knowledge acquired through psychotherapy research can be translated into forms that are useful to clinicians.

Bibliography

Bergin, A. E., & Garfield, S. L. (Eds.). (1994). *Handbook of psychotherapy and behavior change* (4th ed). New York: Wiley.

Eysenck, H. J. (1952). The effects of psychotherapy: An evaluation. *Journal of Consulting Psychology, 16*, 319–324.

Hill, C. E. (1989). *Therapist techniques and client outcomes: Eight cases of brief psychotherapy*. Newbury Park, CA: Sage.

Howard, K. I., Cornille, T. A., Lyons, J. S., Vessey, J. T., Lueger, R. J., & Saunders, S. M. (1996). Patterns of mental health service utilization. *Archives of General Psychiatry, 53*, 696–703.

Howard, K. I., Krause, M. S., & Vessey, J. T. (1994). Analysis of clinical trial data: The problem of outcome overlap. *Psychotherapy, 31*, 302–307.

Howard, K. I., Moras, K., Brill, P. L., Martinovich, Z., & Lutz, W. (1996). Evaluation of psychotherapy: Efficacy, effectiveness, and patient progress. *American Psychologist, 51*, 1059–1064.

Krause, M. S., & Howard, K. I. (1976). Program evaluation in the public interest. *Community Mental Health Journal, 12*, 291–300.

Lipsey, M. W., & Wilson, D. B. (1993). The efficacy of psychological, educational, and behavioral treatment: Confirmations from meta-analysis. *American Psychologist, 48*, 1181–1209.

Lyons, J. S., & Howard, K. I. (1991). Main effects analysis in clinical research: Statistical guidelines for disaggregating treatment groups. *Journal of Consulting and Clinical Psychology, 59*, 745–748.

Morrow-Bradley, C., & Elliott, R. (1986). The utilization of psychotherapy research by practicing psychotherapists. *American Psychologist, 41*, 188–197.

Orlinsky, D. E., Grawe, K., & Parks, B. (1994). Process and outcome in psychotherapy—noch einmal. In A. E. Bergin & S. L. Garfield (Eds.), *Handbook of psychotherapy and behavior change* (4th ed.). New York: Wiley.

Orlinsky, D. E., & Russell, R. L. (1994). Tradition and change in psychotherapy research: Notes on the fourth generation. In R. L. Russell (Ed.), *Reassessing psychotherapy research*. New York: Guilford Press.

Shoham-Salomon, V. (Ed.). (1991). Special section: Client-therapy interaction research. *Journal of Consulting and Clinical Psychology, 59*, 203–244.

Smith, M. L., Glass, G. V., & Miller, T. I. (1980). *The benefit of psychotherapy*. Baltimore, MD: Johns Hopkins Press.

Sperry, L., Brill, P. L., Howard, K. I., & Grissom, G. R. (1996). *Treatment outcomes in psychotherapy and psychiatric interventions*. New York: Brunner/Mazel.

Strupp, H. H., Hadley, S. W., & Gomes-Schwartz, B. (1977). *Psychotherapy for better or worse: The problem of negative effects*. New York: Aronson.

Talley, P. F., Strupp, H. H., & Butler, S. F. (Eds.). (1994). *Psychotherapy research and practice: Bridging the gap*. New York: Basic Books.

Taube, C. A., Mechanic, D., & Hohmann, A. A. (Eds.). (1989). *The future of mental health services research*. Washington, DC: U.S. Government Printing Office.

David E. Orlinsky and Kenneth I. Howard

Clinical Practice

Clinical practice in psychology has experienced a veritable explosion in numbers, activities, and knowledge over the past 40 years. Once confined to a few hundred psychologists in hospitals performing psychological testing and diagnostic evaluations, clinical practice now encompasses more than 80,000 licensed psychologists engaged in multiple professional activities in a myriad of private and public settings. Indeed, two thirds of the American Psychological Association membership provides some health services.

The term *clinical practice* frequently evokes a narrow view of a psychologist conducting psychotherapy with one distressed client in a private practice or a hospital. In fact, the practice of psychology is far wider and inclusive. First, psychological practice has a broader concern than treatment; we are also dedicated to assessment, research, and prevention. Second, most practitioners routinely treat couples and families, not solely individuals. Third, psychologists recognize the need to promote healthy behavior and adaptive functioning; they do not simply treat mental disorders. Fourth, the application of psychology takes us far beyond the reaches of clinics and offices to the daily reality of human behavior, be it in schools, workplaces, homes, neighborhoods, or organizations.

Professional Activities

Psychologists are routinely involved in a multitude of professional activities. Psychotherapy and assessment occupy the lion's share of their time: 37% and 15%, respectively. One half or more of clinical psychologists also regularly teach (averaging 9% of their time), supervise the clinical work of other professionals (7% of their time), consult with organizations or agencies (7% of their time), manage or administer (11% of their time), and research or write (10% of their time). The overarching impression is that psychologists are involved in a myriad of stimulating ventures on a regular basis.

Over 90% of clinical and counseling psychologists routinely conduct psychotherapy. The amount they do tends to vary as a function of their principal place of employment: psychologists in full-time private practice devote about 80% of their day to direct care, whereas psychologists located in hospitals devote an average of 61% to direct-care provision and 24% to academic and administrative responsibilities. Two thirds of psychologists employed as full-time university professors conduct psychotherapy and clinical supervision.

Individual psychotherapy is the mainstay of clinical practice. Practically all psychologists in practice conduct some individual psychotherapy and, on average, devote approximately 65 to 70% of their therapy time to it. More than one half regularly perform marital/couples therapy and family therapy, but these formats accounted for only 10% and 9% of treatment time, respectively. Fewer psychologists (30–40%) conduct group therapy.

In terms of psychological assessment, the clinical interview is the most widely used assessment method in practice, occupying about 40% of assessment time on average. However, about one half of licensed psychologists also conduct intellectual testing and objective personality testing. Both the amount of time devoted to, and the percentage of psychologists involved in, projective personality testing continue to decline over time, while neuropsychological testing has risen sharply in the past decade.

Research Commitment

A core commitment and distinctive characteristic of psychological practice is that of research. Indeed, psychologists are known as the researchers among the clinicians as well as the clinicians among the researchers. This commitment is manifested in their doctoral training, professional activities, and publication experiences.

In training, psychologists are required to complete multiple courses in statistics and research methods and are educated in psychological science, in addition to their clinical pursuits. The doctoral degree ordinarily requires completion of a formal dissertation or major research paper. Some doctoral programs in psychology train research producers and some do not; however, all are designed to train psychologists who will consume research and apply it to clinical practice.

Reflecting this training, approximately 80% of clinical and counseling psychologists have published one or more scholarly articles. Many psychologists employed in full-time clinical work continue to write and conduct research. Perhaps most importantly, the best of psychological science can be applied to the clinical case at hand.

Practice Settings

The primary employment site of clinical and counseling psychologists is independent practice, where 40% are employed. Of those psychologists not employed full-time in private practice, most engage in some part-time private practice. The next most frequent employment site is a college or university, which accounts for about 20% (15% in psychology departments and 5% in other departments). Institutional clinical settings, such as hospitals and clinics, account for most of the remaining positions (approximately 19%). Many psychologists find employment in other settings, such as professional schools, correctional facilities, managed care organizations, nursing homes, child and family services, rehabilitation centers, school systems, psychoanalytic institutes, and health maintenance organizations, to name a few. The reach of psychological practice is certainly expanding. Employment sites range from the corporate world and military settings to school systems and general health care.

Theoretical Orientations

The traditional manner of practicing psychology was from a particular theoretical orientation, or therapy "school." However, over the past 20 years the modal theoretical orientation of practicing psychologists has been eclecticism or integration. Thirty to forty percent of psychologists self-identify themselves as eclectics, that is, attempting to blend therapy methods from several different orientations and tailoring them to the needs of the particular patient and disorder. The next most popular theories are cognitive (24% of clinical psychologists, 11% of counseling psychologists), psychodynamic/psychoanalytic (18% and 12%, respectively), behavioral (13% and 8%), interpersonal (5%), existential/humanistic (4% and 14%, including person-centered), and systems (4% and 5%). A small percentage of psychologists embrace a smattering of other theories, traversing the alphabet from Adlerian, bioenergetics, and constructivism to Zen Buddhism.

A psychotherapy theory describes the clinical phenomena, delimits and prioritizes the relevant information, and integrates it all into a coherent body of knowledge that guides conceptualization and treatment. Without a guiding theory, psychologists would be bombarded with literally hundreds of pieces of information in a single session. In the first interview, is it more important to ask about color preferences, early memories, parent relationships, life's meaning, disturbing emotions, environmental reinforcers, thought processes, sexual conflicts, or something else? At any given time, should a psychologist empathize, confront, teach, model, support, question, restructure, interpret, or remain silent in a therapy session? The model of humanity embedded within a psychotherapy theory impacts which human capacities will be studied and cultivated, and which will be ignored and underdeveloped.

Psychologist Characteristics

Psychological practitioners are a heterogeneous but highly educated lot. Approximately one third of licensed psychologists are women, but with two thirds of current doctoral students in psychology being women, this percentage will steadily grow. Only 7 to 8% of contemporary clinical and counseling psychologists hail from a racial or ethnic minority; this figure, too, is steadily growing as organized psychology responds to the urgent need for minority and culture-sensitive clinicians. Forty-eight of the 50 states (and full membership in the American Psychological Association) require the doctoral degree for licensure as an independent psychologist; as a result, the vast majority of health-service providing psychologists possess a doctorate. This degree has historically been the Ph.D. and occasionally the Ed.D., but it is being complemented with the newer designation of Psy.D. (doctor of psychology). The doctorate takes an average of 6 or 7 years (including the internship) of graduate school following receipt of a baccalaureate degree.

Patient Characteristics

Psychologists assist people of differing disorders and ages. For example, in one large study (Knesper, Pagnucco, & Wheeler, 1985), a psychologist's typical caseload was composed of 48% of patients suffering from an anxiety disorder or neurotic condition, 28% with a primary relationship problem, 6% with a major affective disorder, 5% with schizophrenia, 4% with substance abuse, and 3% from sexual disorder. Practically all psychologists treat adults, and most treat children and older adults. A rising percentage of psychologists choose to specialize in one disorder, age, or activity, for example, seeing only children or patients with physical health problems, or only offering neuropsychological evaluations.

Professional Fees

Professional fees largely depend on the setting in which the service is conducted. In public clinics, patients frequently receive psychotherapy for free or for a modest fee based on their income, say, $15 for a session. In private practice, psychologists' usual and customary fee for a 50-minute psychotherapy session averaged $100 in 1995. The vast majority of insurance companies pay part of this amount. The median fee for patients with managed care insurance was $75 and $90 for third-party patients. Most psychologists report that their customary fees have either remained the same (thus actually decreasing when adjusted for inflation) or eroded by an average of $5 due to the impact of managed care.

Industrialization of Clinical Practice

Over the past 40 years, psychological practice has grown from a cottage industry of autonomous and largely independent practitioners to part of an industrialized health-care system in which the payers (typically insurance companies) determine the type and reimbursement for services rendered. Managed care comes in many guises, but shares several common mechanisms for managing psychotherapy costs. These include restricting access to treatment (e.g., only "medically necessary" services for major disorders); limiting the amount of psychotherapy (e.g., 4 to 10 sessions); using lowest cost providers (e.g., master's and baccalaureate-level clinicians); implementing utilization review (e.g., after three or four sessions); approving primarily short-term, symptom-focused psychotherapies; shifting to outpatient care (e.g., only hospitalize if suicide attempt); allowing referrals only through primary care physicians acting as "gatekeepers"; and restricting patient's freedom of choice in providers and treatments.

The advent of managed care has profoundly influenced psychologists and their patients. First, managed care patients occupy an escalating proportion of psychologists' caseloads; in one study the median percent of managed care patients increased from 5% in 1993 to 20% in 1995 and to 50% in 1997 (Norcross, Karg, & Prochaska, 1997). Some form of managed care now covers 75% of Americans who attain their health benefits through their jobs. Second, practitioners' incomes are decreasing because industrialization requires cheaper labor. Psychologists now face increased competition from nondoctoral mental health professionals, such as counselors and social workers. Recent income surveys demonstrate that, as a group, practicing psychologists are losing income when adjusted for inflation. Depending on the survey and methodology, in the last two years psychologists averaged 2% less net income, or adjusting for inflation, lost 6 to 18% of their income. Third, the producer in any industrial revolution—in this case, the psychologist—is losing control over services as control shifts to business interests. Managed care has forced 65% of psychologists to adopt time-limited therapy techniques, 48% to reduce their patient load, 49% to change their therapy approach, 64% to shorten the length of therapy, and 63% to experience a reduction in income (*Psychotherapy Finances*, 1995).

How have psychologists taken to these changes? In a word, negatively. In response to a survey conducted by the APA Practice Directorate, 15,918 psychologists were asked to evaluate the impact of managed care. Fully 80% replied that it was having a negative impact. Precisely how the industrialization of health care will shape psychological practice in the future remains to be seen.

Into the Future

In the meantime, the clinical practice of psychology continues to expand in terms of personnel, application, and specialization. Psychologists are engaged in a variety of activities and employed in a myriad of settings—a valued diversity that probably contributes to their high and enduring career satisfaction (90% report some degree of satisfaction with their chosen career) and to the sustained influx of new psychologists (over 2,500 new doctorates in clinical and counseling psychology each year). Psychologists' research commitment and their multiple proficiencies (psychotherapy, assessment, consultation, supervision, administration, etc.) should enable them to not only adapt but also to prosper in an uncertain future characterized by the industrialization of health care and the largely unmet behavioral health needs of the population.

Bibliography

Bergin, A. E., & Garfield, S. L. (Eds.). (1994). *Handbook of psychotherapy and behavior change* (4th ed.). New York: Wiley.

Howard, A., Pion, G. M., Gottfredson, G. D., Flattau, P. E., Oskamp, S., Pfafflin, S. M., Bray, D. W., & Burstein, A. G. (1986). The changing face of American psychology. *American Psychologist, 41*, 1311–1327.

Knesper, D. J., Pagnucco, D. J., & Wheeler, J. R. C. (1985). Similarities and differences across mental health service providers and practice settings in the United States. *American Psychologist, 40*, 1352–1369.

Koocher, G. P., Norcross, J. C., & Hill, S. (Eds.). (1998). *Psychologists' desk reference.* New York: Oxford University Press.

Norcross, J. C., Karg, R., & Prochaska, J. O. (1997). Clinical psychologists and managed care: Some data from the Division 12 membership. *Clinical Psychologist, 50*(1), 4–8.

Norcross, J. C., Karg, R., & Prochaska, J. O. (1997). Clinical psychologists in the 1990s. *Clinical Psychologist, 50*(3), 4–11.

Prochaska, J. O., & Norcross, J. C. (1998). *Systems of psychotherapy: A transtheoretical analysis* (4th ed.). Pacific Grove, CA: Brooks/Cole.

Ridgewood Financial Institute. (1995). Survey report. (Entire issue 249). *Psychotherapy Finances, 21*(1). Jupiter, FL: Author.

Watkins, C. E., Lopez, F. G., Campbell, V. L., & Himmell, C. D. (1986). Contemporary counseling psychology: Results of a national survey. *Journal of Counseling Psychology, 33*, 301–309.

John C. Norcross and Mireika Kobayashi

Approaches

An approach to, or theory of, psychotherapy provides practitioners with a road map, a means by which they can understand patients, patient pathologies and problems, and how they might be remedied (Ford & Urban, 1998). Such an approach "is an attempt to organize and integrate knowledge and to answer the question 'Why?'" (Patterson & Watkins, 1996, p. 1), providing practitioners with a meaningful conceptual framework that anchors their clinical work (Karasu, 1992).

The field of psychotherapy has a long, rich history, which can be traced back to early efforts at psychological healing carried out by the magician, medicine man, and later the philosopher-priest. Those early efforts gave way to the current practice of the scientific psychotherapist. Many important figures paved the way for that emergence, including Franz Mesmer, who developed Mesmerism (a treatment referred to as the beginning of American psychotherapy), Bernheim, Jean-Martin Charcot, Pierre Janet, and Joseph Breuer, all of whom contributed to our understanding of hypnosis and the power of suggestion. While the work of Mesmer began in the latter part of the eighteenth century, the work of most others mentioned took place in the latter part of the nineteenth century.

Within those years Sigmund Freud began working with Breuer, studying hypnosis and a disorder referred to as hysteria. From those studies and his extrapolations from them, Freud went on to establish psychoanalysis. His approach was the most detailed, well thought out, comprehensive theory that had thus far been put forth. His approach addressed development, pathology, personality, and treatment. Current approaches to psychotherapy owe a debt to Freud; many are revisions or extensions of his original thinking or reactions against it. Freud, an ardent observer, believed in testing out ideas by means of experimentation. He vigorously applied the scientific method to the practice of psychotherapy, facilitating moves from the magician, medicine man, and philosopher-priest to the current grounding of "scientific psychotherapist."

Approaches to psychotherapy largely can be clustered into five broad-based categories: psychoanalytic/psychodynamic, behavioral, cognitive, humanistic, and integrative/eclectic.

Psychoanalytic/Psychodynamic Therapies

The analytic/dynamic approach, according to Gordon Allport, views people as "reactive beings in depth"—reacting to the unconscious forces that influence and affect their lives. Theoretically, unconscious conflict is given key emphasis; therapy is oriented to understanding and making meaning out of what is unconscious.

Freud's work as an analyst and scholar can be broken down into four periods: (1) 1895 to 1900, when he began to theorize about unconscious motivation, transference, resistance, repression, and neurotic etiology; (2) 1900 to 1910, when libido theory was put forth; (3) 1910 to the early 1920s, when the role of aggression was more forcefully incorporated into his theory; and (4) the mid-1920s to 1939, when methods of therapy and societal applications were given greater emphasis. His monumental body of work includes such books as *The Interpretation of Dreams, Three Contributions to the Theory of Sex, The Ego and the Id,* and *Civilization and Its Discontents.* His case studies provide good examples of how he conceptualized and made meaning of his patients' pathologies.

Since Freud, other forms of psychoanalysis or psychodynamic therapy have been put forth. Some of the more prominent would include analytical psychotherapy, proposed by the Swiss psychiatrist Carl Jung, psychoanalytic ego psychology, object relations theory, Sullivan's interpersonal psychoanalysis, and Kohut's self-psychological approach. Some of the differences between those approaches have been described by Eagle and Wolitzky (1992). However, most of the approaches share several features in common: emphasis on dealing with the unconscious in treatment (e.g., to make the unconscious conscious); emphasis on the role of unconscious conflict in causing patient pathology; emphasis on the role of analyzing the transference in treatment; using dream analysis in treatment; and using interpretations in treatment.

Behavior Therapy

Behavior therapies emphasize the importance of learning in the development of normal and abnormal behaviors. For example, abnormality could be the product of having learned maladaptive behaviors or having failed to learn adaptive behaviors. Behavior therapies have always emphasized the significance of being scientific, objective, and putting therapy to the test.

Some of the most prominent contributors to the development of behavior therapy include Ivan Pavlov, who discovered a form of learning referred to as classical conditioning, and E. L. Thorndike, who discovered a form of learning referred to as instrumental or operant conditioning. Classical conditioning, learning by association, and operant conditioning, learning by means of rewards and punishments, laid the foundation for major developments in behavioristic learning theory for decades to come. Other notables who contributed to behavior therapy's development included B. F. Skinner, H. J. Eysenck, and Joseph Wolpe.

Behavior therapy began to emerge in the 1950s. Spurred by a dissatisfaction with psychoanalytic formulations, a desire for more experimental, scientifically grounded procedures, and animal studies of neurotic behavior, behavior therapy based on classical and operant conditioning principles took form.

Wolpe has been a major force in using a classical-conditioning approach to therapy, for example, helping patients with anxiety problems overcome them by means of relaxation or "desensitizing" them to the stimuli that cause anxiety. Operant conditioning has been used to help patients modify such maladaptive behaviors as nonassertiveness, nail biting, and overeating, by, for example, having a reward follow the performance of a desired behavior.

Behavior therapy is a continually evolving form of treatment, and in the 1970s it began to separate itself into distinct theoretical submovements: applied behavior analysis (consistent with Skinner's work), the neo-behavioristic, mediational S-R model (consistent with Wolpe's work), social learning theory (consistent with Bandura's work), paradigmatic behaviorism, and cognitive behavior therapy. Those submovements continue in force today.

Cognitive Therapy

Meichenbaum pointed out that the cognitive approach "emerged, in part, out of an increasing dissatisfaction with both the theoretical and empirical bases of a strictly behavior therapy approach" (1995, pp. 142–143). In cognitive therapy, primary theoretical and treatment attention is given to cognition—what we think. Dysfunctional emotions and behaviors are seen as resulting from or being significantly affected by dysfunctional cognitions. By modifying those cognitions, making them functional and adaptive, dysfunctional emotions and behaviors can be modified.

Albert Ellis and Aaron Beck are two primary figures associated with the rise of cognitive therapy. Ellis first called his form of treatment rational therapy, later referred to it as rational emotive therapy, and more recently changed it to rational emotive behavior therapy. The most recent change was made to reflect the comprehensiveness of the approach, in that it deals with cognition, affect, and behavior. Ellis gives credit to a variety of individuals who influenced his thinking, including the philosopher Epictetus, who said, "Men are disturbed not by events, but by the views they take of them."

Aaron Beck has termed his therapy approach, simply enough, cognitive therapy. Like Ellis, Beck's work reflects the preeminence of using cognitions in understanding and treating patients. He has detailed the mechanics and theory of his approach with a number of psychological disorders, including depression, anxiety disorders, phobias, and personality disorders.

Humanistic Therapy

Four major themes are of primary importance in humanistic approaches to psychotherapy (Rice & Greenberg, 1992, pp. 198–199):

1. "Commitment to a phenomenological approach . . . grounded in the belief in the uniquely human capacity for reflective consciousness, and in the belief that it is this capacity that can lead to self-determination and freedom"
2. Belief that an actualizing tendency of some sort exists within us
3. Belief that humankind is capable of self-determination
4. Belief in the importance of having concern and respect for others.

Allport referred to the humanistic view as proactive, not reactive.

Words such as *freedom, responsibility, self-actualization, self-determination, awareness,* and *self-discovery* have come to be associated with the humanistic tradition. As Rice and Greenberg (1992) have rightly pointed out, those responsible for pioneering humanistic therapy were all directly or indirectly influenced by humanistic philosophers such as Martin Buber, Jean-Paul Sartre, and Søren Kierkegaard.

The three foundational, most influential forms of humanistic psychotherapy have been identified as client-centered, Gestalt, and existential. Client-centered therapy was developed by Carl Rogers. He believed that certain conditions, for example, therapist empathy, were necessary and sufficient for patient personality change to occur. His approach to therapy has been termed revolutionary, rejecting the view that therapists were the authorities on their patients' inner experience, rejecting the emphasis on "techniques" and questioning the value of traditional diagnosis and assessment in psychotherapy. He emphasized the preeminence of the therapeutic relationship as characterized by care, concern, empathy for, and interest in the patient to facilitate change.

Perls was instrumental in developing Gestalt therapy. Some of his more prominent publications include *Ego, Hunger, and Aggression, Gestalt Therapy Verbatim, In and Out of the Garbage Pail, The Gestalt Approach and Eyewitness to Therapy*, and *Gestalt Therapy: Excitement and Growth in Personality*. He emphasized organismic holism and organismic balance, the importance of here-and-now awareness, and accepting responsibility for oneself. While his approach is categorized as humanistic, Perls himself was seen by some as being confrontational, abrasive, and frustrating in his encounters with patients. In the last 20 years, Gestalt therapy has softened and placed more emphasis on the "I-Thou" of the therapist-patient encounter. According to Patterson and Watkins, "This seems to be the most prominent modification in Gestalt therapy in recent years" (1996, p. 381).

Existential approaches began to take form in the 1940s and 1950s throughout different countries in Europe. In some cases, such approaches were termed existential psychoanalysis, but even then there was typically a rejection of Freud's more biologized theory, with emphasis instead being given to free will, self-determinism, responsibility, and finding meaning in life. Some of the major figures representing this viewpoint include Binswanger, Boss, Bugental, Rollo May, and Yalom.

Integrative/Eclectic Therapy

Integrative/eclectic therapy, according to Arkowitz,

> includes various attempts to look beyond the confines of single-school approaches [e.g., psychoanalysis, behavior therapy] in order to see what can be learned from other perspectives. It is characterized by an openness to various ways of integrating diverse theories and techniques . . . the integrative approaches of today all attempt to build some coherent framework for understanding or predicting change and for determining the choice of therapy procedures. (1992, pp. 262–263)

The integrative/eclectic therapist feels free to draw upon any of the approaches already described here but would do so within a grounded theoretical view.

Three forms of integrative/electic psychotherapy have been identified: technical eclecticism, theoretical integration, and common factors. Technical eclecticism, the least theory-bound of the three, is grounded in psychological science, empiricism, and is actuarial in nature. This perspectice, best represented by Lazarus's multimodal therapy and Beutler's systematic eclectic therapy, strives to predict what treatment works best for whom. Any such predictive efforts are guided by data on what has worked before for other patients with similar problems and characteristics. With theoretical integration, conceptual efforts are made to integrate two or more theoretical systems. Dollard's and Miller's efforts, as well as Wachtel's, to synthesize psychoanalytic and behavioral approaches serve as good examples. Theoretical integration entails a synthesis of both theory and technique, the hope being that results of combined therapies would be superior to those achieved by any single therapy alone. With common factors, the focus is on identifying those key elements, shared across therapeutic systems, that effect patient change. Proponents of this view include Frank and Goldfried; they believe that (a) core ingredients to effective therapy, whatever the brand, exist and can be identified, and (b) by identifying those ingredients, more effective and parsimonious treatments will result.

In the 1930s, the first rumblings about theory integration and eclecticism emerged (French, 1933; Rosenzweig, 1936). From that point up until about 1980, those rumblings continued and grew somewhat louder. In the 1980s an explosion occurred; an increasing number of integrative/eclectic therapy books were written, integrative/eclectic therapy journals were established (e.g., the *Journal of Psychotherapy Integration*), and the Society for the Exploration of Psychotherapy Integration was formed. In the 1990s activity and interest in integrative/eclectic therapy has continued.

[*Many of the people mentioned in this article are the subjects of independent biographical entries.*]

Bibliography

Arkowitz, H. (1992). Integrative theories of therapy. In D. K. Freedheim (Ed.), *History of psychotherapy: A century of change* (pp. 261–303). Washington, DC: American Psychological Association.

Eagle, M. N., & Wolitzky, D. L. (1992). Psychoanalytic theories of psychotherapy. In D. K. Freedheim (Ed.), *History of psychotherapy: A century of change* (pp. 109–158). Washington, DC: American Psychological Association.

Ford, D. H., & Urban, H. B. (1998). *Contempory models of psychotherapy: A comparative analysis*. New York: Wiley.

French, T. M. (1933). Interrelations between psychoanalysis and the experimental work of Pavlov. *American Journal of Psychiatry, 89*, 1165–1203.

Karasu, T. B. (1992). *Wisdom in the practice of psychotherapy*. New York: Basic Books.

Meichenbaum, D. H. (1995). Cognitive-behavioral therapy in historical perspective. In B. Bongar & L. E. Beutler (Eds.), *Comprehensive textbook of psychotherapy: Theory and practice* (pp. 140–158). New York: Oxford University Press.

Patterson, C. H., & Watkins, C. E., Jr. (1996). *Theories of psychotherapy* (5th ed.). New York: HarperCollins.

Rosenzweig, S. (1936). Some implicit common factors in diverse methods in psychotherapy. *American Journal of Orthopsychiatry, 6*, 412–415.

C. Edward Watkins, Jr.

PSYCHOTICISM. Biological relatives of psychotic patients often also show signs of abnormality (e.g., bizarre ideas). This observation intrigued the founders of modern psychiatry (e.g., Emil Kraepelin, 1856–1926, and Eugen Blueler, 1857–1939) and suggested that there may be an underlying susceptibility ("diathesis") to psychosis that is present in the general population in mild form but is fully expressed in psychotic disorder (i.e., schizophrenia, unipolar depression, and manic-depression).

Hans Eysenck (1916–1997), working at the Institute of Psychiatry (University of London), proposed in the *The Scientific Study of Personality* (1952) that this susceptibility to psychosis represented an important dimension of personality (i.e., psychoticism, in addition to extraversion and neuroticism, which was earlier proposed by Eysenck in *Dimensions of Personality*, 1947). In later years, Hans and Sybil Eysenck developed questionnaire measures of psychoticism, using statistical procedures (e.g., factor analysis), with the first questionnaire being published in 1975 (Eysenck Personality Questionnaire). This psychoticism dimension is found cross-culturally and in the statistical studies of other personality psychologists (although they often prefer different labels, for example, emotional detachment, independence, nonconformity, impulsivity, agreeableness, conscientiousness, constraint).

The Eysencks' conception of psychoticism is not restricted to psychosis but also encompasses antisocial and criminal behavior (including psychopathy or sociopathy). The linking of psychosis and psychopathy has proved controversial; however, empirical studies support such a link, for example, as indicated by (1) a common genetic basis to psychosis and psychopathy; (2) a higher incidence of psychosis and psychopathy among children separated shortly after birth from schizophrenic mothers (e.g., Heston, 1966); (3) similarities in the performance of those diagnosed as having psychotic and psychopathic disorders (e.g., hemisphere asymmetries); and (4) the effectiveness of antipsychotic medication in the treatment of psychopathic symptoms.

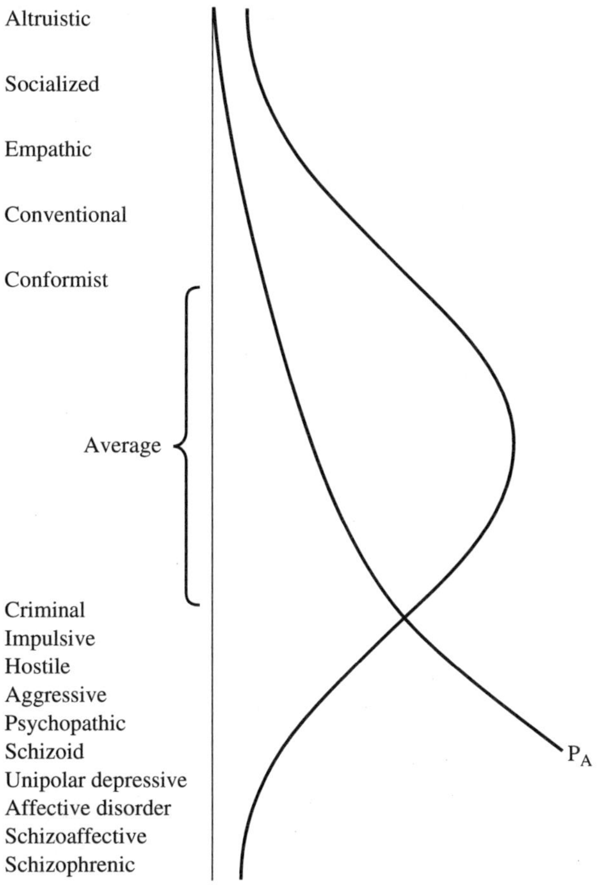

PSYCHOTICISM. Figure 1. A diagrammatic representation of the continuum view of psychoticism.

Hans Eysenck's view that susceptibility to psychotic and neurotic disorders is distributed in the general population—reflecting a continuum view of normality-abnormality—challenges the medical model of psychiatry, which asserts that abnormal behaviors are qualitatively different from normal ones. But it is now known that the symptom boundaries between different psychotic conditions are less distinct than the categorical view assumes and that familial studies point to a spectrum of psychotic disorder rather than discrete disorders (e.g., a schizophrenic parent may have a manic-depressive child). Eysenck's continuum view of psychoticism is illustrated in Figure 1, where higher levels of psychoticism are hypothesized to be associated with an increased probability (P_A) of antisocial/psychotic behaviors. The expression of these disorders depends on environmental stressors (Claridge, 1997, provides a critical valuation of psychoticism and Eysenck's contribution to psychopathology).

The questionnaire measure of psychoticism asks questions about everyday habitual behaviors (e.g., giving money to charity; liking practical jokes that harm others; indifference to animal and child suffering). Low-psychoticism individuals are characterized as being cooperative, empathic, conventional, and tender-minded; high-psychoticism individuals as impulsive, aloof, nonconforming, aggressive, inhumane, lacking in responsibility; having disregard for the law, danger, and the feelings of others; and a preference for the unusual and bizarre. They also tend to hold dogmatic and extreme (left and right) political attitudes. Consistent with these generalizations, research confirms that, compared with low-psychoticism people, high-psychoticism individuals have unsatisfactory marriages, poor work records, low levels of job satisfaction, a higher incidence of infidelity, a greater willingness to engage in risky and varied sexual behavior; more favorable attitudes, as well as physiological arousal, to sexual scenes depicting aggression, and more favorable attitudes toward conflict resolution through the use of violence. Consistent with their higher incidence of antisocial acts, males have significantly higher average psychoticism scores.

The susceptibility to psychosis and psychopathy is evident from an early age. Children who score high on the child version of the psychoticism scale are more prone to learning and behavioral difficulties and antisocial behavior; they also tend to be disliked by teachers and peers, who see their behavior as spiteful and disruptive (in contrast to extraverted children, who misbehave out of high spirits and are perceived as "lovable rogues").

High-psychoticism does, however, have positive aspects. It may serve as a coping mechanism in individuals who are also high in neuroticism: anger and suspicion may be preferable to the fear, depression, and hopelessness associated with neurotic disorder. Under certain circumstances (e.g., in times of war) society, too, may value the expression of psychoticism traits. Psychoticism is also associated with creativity, at least in nonpsychotic individuals (Eysenck, 1995).

Experimental research shows that high-psychoticism individuals have a deficit in stimulus processing, as seen in their inability to inhibit unimportant and irrelevant stimuli as measured by such behavioral paradigms as latent inhibition. This lack of appropriate cognitive inhibition of irrelevant stimuli may help to explain the co-occurrence of such disparate behaviors as psychosis, psychopathy, and creativity. A loosening of associations and overinclusive thinking may produce either a thought disorder in psychosis (schizophrenics often report being overwhelmed by extraneous stimuli, e.g., auditory hallucinations) or creativity in high-psychoticism (and intelligent but not psychotic) individuals (i.e., combining associations in novel ways or producing creative solutions). Defective stimulus processing, resulting in impaired conditioning or learning of social rules, may also account for the poor socialization associated with high psychoticism. Psychoticism effects seem to be mediated in large part by the action in the brain of dopamine, a neurotransmitter that is also implicated in impaired cognitive inhibition and schizophrenia.

Technical deficiencies with the measurement of psychoticism (e.g., skewed distribution) have been noted, and some psychologists (e.g., Zuckerman, 1991) have argued that psychoticism should be more accurately described as a measure of psychopathy, not psychosis proneness (the fact that schizophrenics do not have particularly high psychoticism scores seems to support this argument). However, convincing answers to these apparent problems have been given by Eysenck (1992; for a neuropsychological model of schizophrenia that demonstrates the relevance of psychoticism, see Gray et al., 1991). A more substantive issue is whether symptom-based measures of psychosis proneness in the normal population (i.e., "schizotypy scales" that measure magical thinking, perception aberration, etc.) are better suited to the study of psychosis than the broad measure of psychoticism, which measures many disparate, albeit related, constructs (Claridge, 1997).

Bibliography

Claridge, G. (1997). Eysenck's contribution to understanding psychopathology. In H. Nyborg (Ed.), *The scientific study of human nature: Tribute to Hans J. Eysenck at eighty* (pp. 364–387). Oxford, UK: Elsevier Science.

Eysenck, H. J. (1947). *Dimensions of personality*. London: Kegan Paul.

Eysenck, H. J. (1992). The definition and measurement of psychoticism. *Personality and Individual Differences, 13*, 757–785.

Eysenck, H. J. (1995). *Genius: The natural history of creativity*. Cambridge, UK: Cambridge University Press.

Eysenck, H. J., & Eysenck, S. B. G. (1975). *Manual of the Eysenck Personality Questionniare (Adults)*. London: Hodder and Stoughton.

Eysenck, H. J., & Eysenck, S. B. G. (1976). *Psychoticism as a dimension of personality*. New York: Crane, Russak.

Gray, J. A., Feldon, J., Rawlins, J. N. P., Hemsley, D. R., & Smith, A. D. (1991). The neuropsychology of schizophrenia. *Behavioural and Brain Sciences, 14*, 1–84.

Heston, L. l. (1966). Psychiatric disorders in foster home-reared children of schizophrenic mothers. *British Journal of Psychiatry, 112*, 819–825.

Zuckerman, M. (1991). *Psychobiology of personality*. Cambridge, UK: Cambridge University Press.

Philip J. Corr

PSY.D. *See* Doctor of Psychology Degree.

PUBERTY. *See* Adolescence.

PUBLICATION. *See* Ethics, *article on* Ethics in Publication; *and* Research Dissemination.

PUBLIC HEALTH. Psychological science and practice are associated with public health in many ways. Public health can be defined generally as efforts designed to enhance health in human populations through organized community effort. Health, according to the World Health Organization, includes physical, mental, social, and economic well-being. Thus, psychology is considered to be a vital aspect of public health, and many of the issues studied by psychologists are also relevant. Public health includes five broad domains: social and behavioral sciences, epidemiology, health services administration, environmental health sciences, and biostatistics. International health, maternal and child health, dental public health, nutrition, toxicology, and gerontology are other topical areas that are typically subsumed under one or more of the five central public health domains. While public health can be distinguished in this way, these areas often overlap.

The field of psychology plays a role in each of the five areas of public health. Psychological theories are relevant for health behavior change, organizational functioning, and ecological assessment. Psychological research methods are often applied to health issues such as measurement, social experimentation, questionnaire design, data collection procedures, and data analytic approaches. Psychological practice is also applied in health-related contexts, including counseling, organizational consultation, and community intervention. Psychologists can often be found working in schools of public health and in preventive-medicine contexts. The subdisciplines of psychology most relevant to public health are community, applied social, applied developmental, clinical, and health psychology. Other related areas include quantitative psychology, personality, and organizational psychology.

Social and Behavioral Sciences

Psychology is directly related to the social and behavioral science domain of public health. This is the area of public health most connected to social and behavioral interventions (i.e., health education) and the study of health behavior. Health education is a process designed to enable people, organizations, and communities to voluntarily make decisions, modify actions, and change social conditions for the improvement and maintenance of health. Health behavior refers to the actions of individuals that may either promote or compromise health. The behavior may be individual (e.g., smoking cigarettes) or social (e.g., support to a homebound friend). Psychologists may play a role in the health education process by developing and evaluating interventions or studying health behavior and its antecedents and consequences. They have, for example, implemented and evaluated smoking cessation programs, examined the role of parenting on adolescent problem behavior, and studied the association of social support and coping.

Health education interventions focus on promoting health, preventing disease, and managing illness. They range from individually focused behavior change to community-level change. Psychological theories—stages of change theory, theory of reasoned action, the health belief model, self-efficacy, and self-regulation theory—are often applied to health behavior change. Relevant health behaviors include wellness behavior, preventive health behavior, risk behavior, and illness behavior. Wellness and preventive health behavior refer to individuals who are not yet sick but engage in behavior to improve health (wellness behavior) or prevent the onset of a disease (preventive health behavior). Psychologists often study ways of motivating people to engage in healthy behavior through interventions to change normative beliefs, enhance self-efficacy, and reinforce healthy behaviors. Peer education and experiential learning strategies are often used to help people engage in health-promoting behaviors.

Risk behavior refers to engaging in activity that increases the likelihood of a health-compromising outcome, such as drinking and driving, injection drug use, and ignoring medical regimes. Illness behavior refers to the actions that sick individuals take to get well, such as taking medication or rehabilitation. Psychologists' efforts to address risk behavior include strategies to help people develop alternative behaviors, strengthen protective factors (e.g., social skills to avoid peer pressure), and eliminate risk factors from the environment. Illness behavior may be addressed by psychologists who help people improve stress management, develop strategies to encourage compliance with medical regimens, and enhance social support.

Organizational change is also a focus of health education. Public health professionals may work with organizations to help them adopt new ways of doing their work (i.e., diffusion of innovation) or integrate new programs into existing structures. Development and implementation of a work-site wellness program is one example of organizational change that may involve a public health educator. This effort may include educating workers about health-promoting behaviors, developing a fitness facility with health education programs (e.g., smoking cessation, weight reduction, or exercise), and improving cafeteria offerings for more healthful eating options. Psychologists have played a role in these kinds of organizational efforts.

Community-level strategies for change include community organizing, employing community health workers, using the media, and influencing local policy change. Community organizing involves efforts to mobilize residents to work together to address a common problem. Residents may mobilize their neighbors to improve access to health care, enhance environmental conditions (e.g., reduce noise and increase lighting), or develop a mutual help group. Community health outreach worker (CHOW) strategies typically employ local residents to conduct door-to-door canvasing to provide health education information and to help organize residents. Media interventions consist of public service announcements placed in local media outlets promoting healthy behavior and advocacy for health-promoting public policy. Public health interventions designed to change local policy may use several strategies (e.g., media advocacy and community organizing), but the goal is to influence policy rather than any one individual's health behavior. Policies that have been targeted in public health include efforts to reduce tobacco sales to minors, the use of leaded paint and gasoline, and handgun violence.

Psychologists have helped organize communities to oppose toxic waste dumping, prevent school violence, and promote neighboring. They have also worked with mutual help groups, assisted with community-wide campaigns to educate residents about HIV/AIDS, and worked with low-income residents to improve housing conditions. Psychologists also help conduct consumer assessments to identify effective and relevant community interventions. They may help develop message content as well as the method by which it is distributed.

Regardless of the level of analysis, public health interventions typically focus on promoting health or preventing disease. Health promotion refers to efforts designed to encourage healthy behaviors. Disease prevention emphasizes efforts to thwart the onset of a disease (primary prevention), detect a disease early and treat it to minimize its effects (secondary prevention), or reduce the long-term consequences of a disease (tertiary prevention). Primary prevention examples include immunization efforts, social-skills training for children, and condom distribution programs. Secondary prevention examples include health screening programs for cancer or heart disease and efforts to help HIV-infected individuals prevent the onset of AIDS. Tertiary prevention typically involves rehabilitation and avoidance of worsening disease effects. Examples include helping people to walk again after an orthopedic injury and assisting people to return to the community after an inpatient stay for alcohol dependence.

Relapse prevention is another area of public health education in which psychologists play a role. It refers to interventions designed to help individuals who engaged in an addictive behavior to maintain healthy behavior or avoid unhealthy behavior. For example, individuals who have successfully quit smoking cigarettes often need help to avoid a relapse. Psychological methods are consistent with, and have been applied to, all four types of prevention.

Epidemiology

Epidemiology refers to the study of social and environmental factors that influence health problems. This may include the analysis of the distribution and determinants of disease and injury in the human population. Social epidemiology is the subspecialty most closely linked to psychology. It involves the study of the effects of demographic factors such as age, socioeconomic status, race, and ethnicity, and social factors such as interpersonal relationships, family influences, and community participation on health and disease. Psychologists, like epidemiologists, often search for those factors found to predict or cause either a healthy or deleterious outcome. They develop risk models and identify the etiology of disease. The study of stress and its effect on health and mental health is one area where psychologists and epidemiologists overlap considerably. Stress is a risk factor for both infectious and noninfectious disease. Psychologists have studied stress as both a cause and consequence of maladaptive adjustment and have examined how various other factors such as social support may reduce the effects of stress on adverse health outcomes. In addition, psychologists have been involved in developing valid and reliable measures of stress (e.g., daily hassles and life events).

Epidemiology also includes describing the prevalence and incidence of a disease in a population. Prevalence is the proportion of a population identified as having a disease (e.g., anorexia, drug addiction, or hepatitis) within a specified time period. Incidence is the number of new cases detected within a specified time period. This might be the number of new cases of asthma, gonorrhea, or attention deficit disorder. Psychologists often conduct studies that examine the prevalence and incidence of health-related knowledge, attitudes, behaviors, and disorders.

Health Services Administration

Health service administration involves the set of arrangements that exist in a society designed to organize and finance the provision of personal health services. This includes both policy formation and analysis and issues of administration. The health care system is constantly undergoing change, ranging from new technologies and procedures to new financing arrangements. The current health-care system is experiencing an immense transformation as the provision of health care services becomes more team oriented and less hierarchical, and more integrated and less segregated. This has required redesigning work, reformulating both provider and consumer roles and responsibilities, and reengineering organizations to respond to different financial and service delivery approaches. Organizational psychologists often assist health care professionals to address these issues. They help develop health care teams, train staff to adapt to new roles and work expectations, and create more horizontally organized structures.

Organizational psychologists are also involved in assisting health organizations (e.g., hospitals, clinics, and health maintenance organization) to provide more consumer-friendly and efficient service. Consumer satisfaction surveys, the evaluation of medical protocols (e.g., the effects of a new surgical procedure on rehabilitation time, quality of life, and costs), and the assessment of service utilization are issues in which psychologists may play a role. These efforts may also involve issues connected to hospital management, executive training, and linking with health education efforts.

Environmental Health Sciences

Environmental health ranges from issues regarding the effects of toxins on mental and physical functioning to issues of social justice. Toxicologists may examine the neurological damage caused by various substances (e.g., pesticides, lead, or radiation). Neuropsychologists can play a role in this research by offering their expertise about neurological function and testing. Occupational health issues such as safety procedures, human factors, and worker training are also considered part of this domain of public health. Over 100 million workers in the United States are exposed to a variety of occupational hazards that pose significant health risks. These include hazardous materials and fumes, traumatic injury, noise, and stress. Psychologists may play a role in developing and evaluating procedures for handling dangerous chemicals, training workers, or designing displays for control panels (i.e., human factors).

Biostatistics

Biostatistics is the development and application of statistical methods for the analysis of health data. Psychological quantitative methods and biostatistics overlap to a great extent. Health research more often uses category-dependent variables such as the presence or absence of a disease or behavior. Thus, log linear modeling and odds ratios are typical analytic methods used. In addition, biostatisticians develop and apply methods for analyzing longitudinal data. Public health researchers also examine change in risk, behavior, or disease over time. Most public health interventions include multiple data-collection points. Survival analysis is also used by biostatisticians, allowing researchers to examine time to event (i.e., length of time to the occurrence of an outcome). Thus, they may examine those factors postponing or initiating an event, such as sexual initiation, birth, illness, or death. Psychological methods that are particularly helpful for public health researchers include multivariate techniques such as factor analysis, multiple analysis of variance (MANOVA), and discriminant analysis.

[*See also* Prevention.]

Bibliography

Becker, M. H. (1986). The tyranny of health promotion. *Public Health Review, 14*, 15–25.

Glanz, K., Lewis, F. M., & Rimer, B. K. (1996). *Health behavior and health education: Theory, research, and practice* (2nd ed.). San Francisco, CA: Jossey-Bass.

Minkler, M. (1997). *Community organizing and community building for health*. New Brunswick, NJ: Rutgers University Press.

Runyan, C. W., DeVellis, R. F., DeVellis, B. E., & Hochbaum, G. M. (1982). Health psychology and the public health perspective: In search of the pump handle. *Health Psychology, 1*, 169–180.

Shumaker, S., Schron, E. B., & Ocene, J. K. (1990). *The handbook of health behavior change*. New York: Springer.

Syme, S. L. (1986). Strategies for health promotion. *Preventive Medicine, 15*, 492–507.

Winett, R. A., King, A. C., & Altman, D. A. (1990). *Health psychology and public health*. New York: Pergamon Press.

Marc A. Zimmerman

PUBLIC OPINION. *See* Political Behavior; *and* Political Decision Making.

PUBLIC POLICY. Public policy refers generally to the formulation, implementation, and evaluation of the distribution of public resources. As scientists, scholars, citizens, and professionals, psychologists participate (with other disciplines) in public policy through the application of psychological findings and methods of research to understanding and prioritizing public needs, selecting among alternative responses to those needs, and evaluating the effectiveness of those responses. Some psychologists conduct applied research to determine society's needs and evaluate distinctions among alternative solutions. Other psychologists advocate on behalf of specific human needs (e.g., prenatal care) or of specific solutions to needs (e.g., preschool services for low-income youth). Some psychologists serve as members of the legislative staffs and committees that formulate decisions about the allocation of public funds, the nature of public services, and the definition of individual and public responsibility. Psychologists have even been elected to Congress (e.g., Representative Strickland of Ohio) and, in that capacity, directly influence policy formation (Strickland, 1996).

Psychology's widespread involvements in efforts

with implications for public policy makes evident the discipline's appreciation of the seriousness of its responsibility and the potential importance of its contributions. Its efforts have served society's struggles with setting educational mandates and curricula; structuring access to and the nature of social and health services; influencing attitudes toward and the control of health-compromising behaviors (such as diet, exercise, sexuality, substance use, and abuse, etc.); and promoting some values (e.g., positive parenting, family values, optimal child development) while opposing others (e.g., the use of corporal punishment). On these and countless other matters, the discipline has made substantive impacts (Lorion, Iscoe, DeLeon, & VandenBos, 1996).

Methods of Policy Involvement

Psychologists influence relevant legislation through formal or informal briefing sessions with individual legislators (or their staff) and the preparation and submission of written summaries of scientific and clinical findings that describe the nature, extent, consequences, and alternatives for responding to issues related to public health and welfare. Psychologists, for example, have appeared as witnesses before Congressional committees considering legislation relating to health and mental health care benefits within managed care settings; continued and expanded Head Start programs; funded innovative services for educationally handicapped children; and the regulated sale of tobacco and alcohol to minors. Congressional committees have learned from psychologists of the emotional and behavioral consequences of elective abortions; the developmental benefits of day-care programs; the cost-benefits of preventive and health promotive interventions compared to treatment of mental disorders; and the emotional and behavioral implications of proposed health and welfare system reforms.

In most of these instances, psychologists with scientific and clinical expertise in the relevant subject matter present brief verbal statements and answer questions from legislators. Typically, a written copy of the psychologist's statement along with an extended analysis of the issue is provided to the committee and its staff. As noted, psychologists involved in policy matters also engage in formal and informal discussions with those responsible for crafting the enabling legislation or translating legislation into the regulatory structures that ultimately determine a program's implementation and day-to-day operation.

Psychologists have also served the public welfare by providing *amicus curiae* ("friend of the court") briefs on judicial matters of significant social concern. Such briefs summarize the salient scientific literature and explain the behavioral and emotional aspects of the issue before the court. A groundbreaking example of this approach is psychology's contributions to the historic 1954 Supreme Court decision on desegregating the nation's schools, that is, *Brown v. Board of Education*. In their brief, psychologists detailed the negative emotional effects of segregation for all children, white and black. For the first time, the Supreme Court determined that the results of social science research met its rules of evidence. Ultimately, the Court ruled that segregation was harmful; its decision led to the desegregation of the nation's schools.

As explained by Sarason (1996), that precedent contributed substantially to legislative support for the early development of Head Start (as a means of overcoming the segregating consequences of poverty) and other civil rights legislation. It also contributed to passage of Public Law 94–142 ("The Education of All Handicapped Children's Act of 1975"), which required that handicapped children be educated in "the least restrictive environment." This legislation allowed the integration of children with intellectual deficits or other handicapping conditions (e.g., motor impairments) into mainstream classrooms. It enabled nonhandicapped children to have direct contact with and, ideally, greater understanding of, handicapped children. In this instance, psychological findings sensitized policy makers and the public to the negative emotional consequences of segregation (whatever its basis). The 1954 decision illustrates the rippling effects of psychological information on public services as well as on public attitudes and behaviors toward those experiencing emotional, behavioral, or developmental need.

Psychologists do not, however, influence public policy solely through their contributions to judicial proceedings and deliberations about pending legislation. Through their research and public debates about their findings, psychologists bring to public attention matters related to the acceptance and support of variations in lifestyle, behavior, and attitudes. Examples of such topics include consideration of the differential effects and effectiveness of parenting strategies; of variations in household composition (e.g., single-parent families; blended families; multigenerational families), of support services for pregnant adolescents, the elderly, those with chronic mental illnesses, and AIDS victims as well as their loved ones. Such debates have provided to the public, to service providers, and to public officials insights into the emotional and behavioral experiences of individuals so effected. In turn, public examination of the needs of these individuals may bring into awareness how people think about and behave and may shape public opinion about what should be changed and the form such changes should take.

As noted, psychologists are also directly involved in the formation, implementation, and evaluation of public policies at many levels (DeLeon, 1988). Public service represents not only a means to an end but a highly respected professional option. Psychologists bring to policy development their distinctive preparation in methods of scientific inquiry along the continuum from descriptive and qualitative studies through rigorously controlled laboratory experiments. As service providers, they can apply that investigatory perspective to formulating hypotheses about how social problems evolve, are sustained, and can be altered. Psychologists bring to public service a unique approach to asking questions about human thought, emotion, development, change, and motivation.

Discipline-Focused Involvements

At this point, readers might infer that the discipline's policy-related contributions are altruistic and solely concerned with the welfare of the general public and some of its underserved members. Many of the discipline's efforts to shape public policy, however, have admittedly targeted "guild issues," that is, legislation, regulations, and funding patterns that define or influence the limits of professional education, the delivery of mental health services, and the conduct of social and behavioral science. The American Psychological Association and its state counterparts, through their staff and lobbyists, for example, advocated strongly for states to regulate who can be called a "psychologist" and to limit the use of psychological methods (e.g., psychodiagnostic assessment, psychotherapy) to appropriately qualified individuals. Because of these efforts, licensing and certification of psychologists occurs in all 50 states.

These same political forces have influenced federal and state support for "freedom of choice," that is, individuals' right to decide for themselves whether to obtain, and have reimbursed from public or private sources, mental health services from a psychologist, psychiatrist, or other mental health service provider. Such legislation requires health insurance carriers and, increasingly, public funding sources to reimburse mental health services regardless of the provider's disciplinary background. Passage of freedom-of-choice legislation contributed substantially to the economic viability of the independent practice of professional psychologists. Relative to the public welfare, it also substantially expanded the number and diversity of mental health providers available to the population.

In light of the increasing use of psychopharmacological agents to treat emotional disorders ranging from psychoses (e.g., schizophrenia), cyclothymic conditions (e.g., manic-depressive disorder), affective disorders (e.g., depression, panic attacks) to attentional and behavioral problems in children (e.g., ADHD), recent efforts have focused on the question of whether psychologists, with appropriate additional training, should be authorized to prescribe relevant medications. This issue is hotly contested within the discipline, between advocates within the discipline and other health-care providers (especially physicians) and with those responsible for funding and regulating health care services (e.g., DeLeon, Fox, & Graham, 1991). By raising the issue to national attention and publicly debating its pros and cons, psychologists will also provide an opportunity for the consumers of health-care services to reflect on factors that determine access to services, the costs of those services, and the expertise and oversight necessary to ensure the quality of those services. Whatever the outcome of this series of debates, it is certain to substantively shape the nation's future health care.

Responding to Albee's (1959) analysis that critical shortages of mental health personnel would compromise full implementation of the community mental health movement, psychologists advocated to Congress for the continuation and expansion of federal support for doctoral training in clinical psychology begun in response to the large number of mental health casualties following World War II and the Korean conflict (Phares & Trull, 1997). Support from the Veteran's Administration for such training clearly increased the number of psychologists and other mental health professionals available to meet the nation's needs. As shortages of personnel decreased, that support extended to the National Institute of Mental Health and became increasingly targeted to expanding the pool of mental health providers who were members of minority groups and/or specializing in services for underserved populations such as the elderly, children, and residents of inner-city and rural areas. The advantages for the discipline of such lobbying and policy-shaping efforts are obvious. By expanding the number and diversity of mental health professionals and shaping their expertise to respond to identified national needs, the discipline can argue that its efforts also served the public welfare by increasing its awareness of, access to, and use of mental health services.

Advocating for Social Health and Welfare

To the extent that the findings of psychological science benefit the public, the discipline's efforts to influence federal funding for social and behavioral science research and to inform policy makers and the public of the benefits of such research for the nation's health and welfare (e.g., Coon & Sprenger, 1998) represents a reasonable bridge between advocacy efforts for what might be called "guild issues" and seemingly less self-interested public welfare issues. The two largest organizations of psychologists, the American Psychological Association and the American Psychological Society, invest much of their time and resources in advocating for parity in public expenditures for understanding the biological and biochemical aspects of illness and impairment and for understanding the social, emotional, and behavioral factors related to the etiology, evolution, treatment, and prevention of morbidity and mortality. The public significance of such parity is substantial.

Since Surgeon General Richmond's seminal report, *Healthy People* (1979), public health officials have focused on the significant contribution of individual attitudes and behaviors to the nation's health. Richmond (1979) noted: "Perhaps as much as half of U.S. mortality in 1976 was due to unhealthy behavior or lifestyle; 20% to environmental factors; 20% to human biological factors; and only 10% to inadequacies in health care" (p. 9). Morbidity and mortality associated with violence, substance abuse, and AIDS make evident the currency of Richmond's alert.

Throughout the past decade, psychology has increased its efforts to convince policy makers and the public that the salience of behaviors and attitudes for the nation's health must be reflected in their fiscal support for research on social and behavioral factors. A recent report by the National Academy of Science's Institute of Medicine (Mrazek & Haggerty, 1994) underscores this point even further. In their analysis, the nation's capacity to reduce death, disability, and emotional distress resulting, for example, from addictive behaviors, unprotected sexual intercourse, violence in families and in communities, and parenting limitations, depends on the findings of social and behavioral scientists focused on disease prevention and health promotion.

In arguing for increased support for such studies, psychology can point to increasing evidence of its potential for reducing individual and social threats to the public's health and welfare. A few examples illustrate the promise of sustained work on issues of significance to public health and welfare. A 25-year follow-up of Head Start (begun under the direction of psychologist Dr. Edward Zigler as a "Great Society" program) documents its cost-effective developmental, academic, and life-span benefits (Barnett, 1993). Two decades of research on the design, implementation, and evaluation of home visitation for high-risk mothers and infants documents its contributions to reductions in infant mortality and morbidity, child abuse, maternal depression, family dependence on public welfare, and increases in the educational and occupational achievements of both mothers and infants (Olds, O'Brien, Racine, Glazner, & Kitzman, 1998). Echoing the Head Start findings, this approach to home visitation achieved its results both consistently and cost-effectively.

More than two decades of work by Jason and his colleagues (Jason, 1998) make evident how the systematic application of behavioral principles can reduce risks to public health and safety. In a succession of creative and ingenious programs to alter risky behaviors (ranging from the collection of dog wastes, the use of infant safety seats, smoking reduction, weight control, to HIV/AIDS prevention), Jason has demonstrated how carefully designed but easily implemented interventions can alter in health-enhancing ways individuals' attitudes and behaviors. In explaining his work, Jason clearly articulates the mix of persuasion, public information, accountability, and perseverance necessary to achieve desired changes in public laws and practices. It is evident from his work that extensive political preparation is necessary to obtain the fiscal support, attention, and participation of policy makers and the public necessary to carry out field-based studies on important health-related practices. It is also clear from all three of the examples reviewed (i.e., Zigler's work on Head Start; Old's work on home visitation; and Jason's work on public health safety) that the resulting scientific findings alone will not produce lasting changes unless they are made available to relevant audiences (i.e., policy makers and effected members of the public) through understandable and accessible reports, media presentations, and communication to lay audiences.

Bearing Unpopular News

Involvement in public policy matters and in efforts to change individual attitudes and behaviors in ways that are health promotive rather than health compromising frequently requires being the bearer of unwanted or unpopular information. In some cases, one must challenge the assumptions of those responsible for making decisions about public policy and allocation of public funds. MacCoun's (1998) analysis of the implications of harm reduction, for example, illustrates this point. In examining national policies regarding funding for the treatment and prevention of alcohol and other drug involvement, MacCoun questioned established and firmly held political commitments to the goals of supply reduction (e.g., using military and police resources to limit the availability of cocaine, marijuana, or heroin) and demand reduction (e.g., treatment of users to terminate their use or the dissemination of preventive interventions with the intent of continued abstinence among nonusers). MacCoun argues that significant reductions in the social and health problems associated with substance involvement can be achieved by controlling how much and under what circumstances use occurs. His position argues for an objective review of a number of widely held assumptions concerning the legalization of use and established age barriers to alcohol, tobacco, and other drug use.

In an equally controversial report, Bickman (1996) challenged the assumption that more mental health services were necessarily related to better outcomes. This assumption is widely held by many of his colleagues and by those who have argued against the limitations on services associated with managed care. Bickman's findings raise questions about the criteria by which one determines the quantity of services necessary to effect change, the degree of change defining "improvement," and, most critically, the factors by which service quality and appropriateness are to be determined. Beyond their implications for the delivery of mental health services to children, Bickman's findings raise a series of very important questions whose answers can impact on how policy makers understand the results of social science investigations, the confidence they place in those results, and generalizing from the study to the real world.

A Commitment to the Public Welfare

Thus, psychologists involved in public policy or in research on issues relevant to the public's health, safety, and welfare will not speak in one voice nor are they likely to always report what those responsible for deciding which needs to serve, with what funds, and in what ways want to hear. Consequently, those who pursue this professional course should expect to be controversial at times and confronted with demands from many directions to justify their conclusions. Uncomfortable though that role and position may be, however, the discipline must invest a portion of its resources and its expertise in that endeavor. Bevan (1982) noted in his 1982 APA presidential address: "The days when we could hermetically seal ourselves off from the untidiness of the real world are long since gone. If our potential is going to be realized, not only will guild issues and issues of intellectual substance have to be faced, but so also will the question of the public's interest . . ." (p. 1320). Bevan challenged the discipline to recognize and meet its responsibilities to the public. Those included designing its science in the service of the nation's purposes, recognizing its obligation to be accountable for the interpretation and the applications of its findings and the reality that public funding of social and behavioral research represents not an entitlement for the researcher but an investment by the public. In return for that investment, the public has the right to expect precision in the design of scientific studies, objectivity in the interpretation and application of its findings, and candor in the examination of society's needs and available resources and approaches for their resolution. Inherent in the methods and foci of psychology specifically and the social and behavioral sciences generally, appears to be an obligation for public involvement. Rather than implicitly accepting the Hippocratic dictum "do no harm," Bevan's words suggest that the discipline commit itself to the principle "Beyond all else, contribute to the public good!"

Bibliography

Albee, G. W. (1959). *Mental health manpower trends.* New York Basic Books.

Barnett, W. S. (1993). Benefit-cost analysis of preschool education: Findings from a 25-year follow-up. *American Journal of Orthopsychiatry, 63,* 500–508.

Bevan, W. (1982). A sermon of sorts in three plus parts. *American Psychologist, 37,* 1303–1322.

Bickman, L. (1996). A continuum of care: More is not always better. *American Psychologist, 51,* 689–701.

Coon, D. J., & Sprenger, H. A. (1988). Psychologists in service to science: The American Psychological Association and the American Association for the Advancement of Science. *American Psychologist, 53,* 1253–1269.

DeLeon, P. H. (1988). Public policy and public service. *American Psychologist, 43,* 309–315.

DeLeon, P. H., Fox, R. E., & Graham, S. R. (1991). Prescription privileges: Psychology's next frontier? *American Psychologist, 46,* 384–393.

Jason, L. A. (1998). Tobacco, drug and HIV prevention media interventions. *American Journal of Community Psychology, 26,* 151–188.

Lorion, R. P., Iscoe, I., DeLeon, P. H., & VandenBos, G. R. (Eds.). (1996). *Psychology and public policy: Balancing public service and professional need* (pp. 1–20). Washington, DC: American Psychological Association.

MacCoun, R. J. (1998). Toward a psychology of harm reduction. *American Psychologist, 53,* 1199–1208.

Mrazek, P. J., & Haggerty, R. J. (Eds.). (1994). *Reducing risks for mental disorders: Frontiers for preventive intervention research.* Washington, DC: National Academy Press.

Olds, D., O'Brien, R. A., Racine, D., Glazner, J., & Kitzman, H. (1998). Increasing the policy and program relevance of results from randomized trials of home visitation. *Journal of Community Psychology, 26,* 85–100.

Phares, E. J., & Trull, T. J. (1997). *Clinical psychology: Concepts, methods and profession.* Pacific Grove, CA: Brooks/Cole.

Richmond, J. B. (1979). *Healthy people: The surgeon general's report on health promotion and disease prevention.* Washington, DC: U.S. Department of Health, Education, and Welfare/Public Health Service.

Sarason, S. B. (1996). *Revisiting "The culture of the school and the problem of change."* New York: Columbia University Press.

Strickland, T. (1996). Moving psychology toward (self) recognition as a public resource: The views of a congressman psychologist. In R. P. Lorion, I. Iscoe, P. H. DeLeon, & G. R. VandenBos (Eds.), *Psychology and public policy: Balancing public service and professional need* (pp. 369–390). Washington, DC: American Psychological Association.

Raymond P. Lorion

PUBLIC SERVICE. In psychology, public service activities encompass the totality of services required to improve the human condition in an incredibly complex society. Psychology is unique among the social sciences inasmuch as it embraces not only a clear scientific perspective but also a strong public service emphasis, reflected in the American Psychological Association's (APA) creation of public interest as one of its four primary directorates. The twin goals of the APA are to advance psychology as a science and a profession and to promote human welfare. In practice, public service ranges from activities that target a single individual to those that target an entire nation, from developing effective research and clinical procedures to translating these procedures into public policies that could significantly alleviate national—even global—social problems.

History of Public Service

The founders of American psychology viewed the role of psychologists as extending well beyond the therapy office. For example, Lightner Witmer started the first child-guidance clinic in 1896, paving the way for school as well as clinical psychology. G. Stanley Hall, perhaps the first public service psychologist, trained the psychiatrist Adolph Meyer and psychologists Shephard Ivory Franz, Henry Herbert Goddard, Turner, and Gisell. The early 1890s saw psychologists employed in public hospitals, and in 1906 the Vineland Training School was established to train the mentally retarded. Other child guidance clinics soon followed. Two other early twentieth-century examples of public service in psychology include Munsterberg's pioneering work on industrial psychology and Margaret Otis's work with delinquent girls at the Trenton State Home.

World War I psychologists were involved in testing nearly 2 million men, and after the war public service flourished, with psychologists entering state prisons and other institutions. Around 1920, Thorndale, Yerkes, Watson, and Thurstone worked with the Civil Service Commission to develop aptitude and intelligence tests and new methods of job analyses. The 1920s and 1930s were a time of rapid growth for psychologists with a public service orientation. Hospitals, clinics, schools, homes for the retarded, and industrial plants became sites for psychology's applied mission.

After World War II the demand for mental-health services and psychotherapy for military personnel increased dramatically and unexpectedly, fundamentally altering roles for clinical psychologists. In response to this demand, the Veterans Administration (VA) became the largest employer of psychologists and emphasized psychotherapy in unprecedented ways. Such psychotherapy, while effective, reaches only a small portion of those in need. The profession's continued overemphasis on individual-level treatment and individual psychology, and underemphasis on preventive interventions and sociocommunity-level conceptualizations of human behavior, have led policymakers and the public to view psychologists as having little to add to discussions of social policy. Seymour Sarason has long encouraged psychology to expand its realm by asking, "If we could not do psychotherapy, what would we do?"

In response, many of psychology's leaders have argued for psychology to use its knowledge and personnel to benefit the surrounding society. In his 1969 presidential address, George Miller stated, "There is every evidence of external opportunity and internal motivation for giving psychology away." In 1979, the opportunities for psychology's public service mission were also echoed by past president Charles Kiesler, who said:

> I dream of psychological knowledge playing an integral role in all national policies affecting human beings. . . . There should be . . . a psychologist on the advisory board of every mental health center . . . , on every board of every state health planning agency, on every governor's science advisory council, and on local advisory units of every member of Congress. . . . I see psychology, then, as a national force for the future.

This passion for a psychology in the public interest continues today and is reaffirmed in the words of its past president, Martin Seligman: "We believe that America today is entering a world-historical moment. . . . Our vision is that psychology in the twenty-first century will move from being solely a remedial profession to being a positive social force."

Managed care has created changes in the American health-care system that present an opportunity to reenvision how psychology can best contribute to human welfare. Making long-term commitments to improving social policy and social institutions could create a profession that is more diverse and more effective.

Psychologists in Public Service

The career paths presented below illustrate some of the primary settings where psychologists fulfill a public service mission.

Psychologists in Public Service (Division 18 of the APA). Public service psychologists are involved in clinical, rehabilitation, and consultation programs for persons with emotional and behavioral problems. Aspects of their public service include research and evaluation, training, and public policy formulation. Division members work with a broad socioeconomic client population in America's major public sector settings: community mental-health centers, state hospitals, VA medical centers, criminal justice systems, and police and public safety settings. Members of Division 18 match and implement mental-health treatment programs for millions of patients treated in inpatient and outpatient programs and develop programs for the homeless mentally ill and for persons who suffer from severe and persistent mental illness. VA psychologists serve the nation's veterans in medical centers and outpatient clinics through patient care, research, and training. Through their internship programs, VA medical centers have played a major role in training doctoral-level psychologists. Psychologists in the police and public safety section work for local, state, and federal law enforcement agencies, fire departments, and nuclear regulatory agencies, developing effective mental-health programs for law enforcement and public safety personnel. Their public service activities include protecting client confidentiality and client privileges and carrying out the duties to warn and protect. Psychologists in the evaluation section are concerned with treatment effectiveness, mental-health services research, and systems analysis. They promote evaluation, psychological service delivery, and public policy development.

Public Service in Academia. Psychologists in an academic setting have opportunities to use the unique resources of a university to realize a public service mission. They serve on advisory boards and councils at the community, state, and national levels, assist agencies and communities in preparing grants, serve on human rights committees at state mental hospitals, and organize student volunteers. Historically, academic institutions have three purposes—education, research, and public service—that are not necessarily distinct. Teaching and scholarship can also have a strong public service element. For example, modern educators offer courses with a service-learning component; both communities and students benefit. Students gain course credit for working in supervised service settings that allow them to apply concepts in the real world. Such work often influences career choices by contributing to students' awareness of the rewards of public service. Courses themselves are often socially relevant; for example, a course on human development can teach child rearing and discipline as well as how to select day care and improve Head Start. Professors also add a public service dimension by teaching nontraditional students such as parents, businesspeople, and legislators.

Academics are often called upon to do applied scholarship that directly seeks to improve human understanding and the human condition through community needs assessments, program evaluations, curricula development, human-service demonstration projects, and policy studies. Applied scholarship advances a public service mission by generating information that is both scholarly and useful for nonacademic as well as academic audiences. For example, psychologists working as data partners for a state Kids Count project develop and disseminate information on the health status of children to a wide audience of child advocates. Doing more public service and applied research makes sense because Congress and the public are increasingly demanding that universities do more to serve the public good.

School Psychologists. Today's school psychologist's role extends beyond the child and includes classroom structure, teachers, the family, the neighborhood, and the community. This expanded role reflects the current movement away from testing to accessing and linking the many settings in which learners reside. School psychologists are frequently members of a team of school professionals concerned with school norms, violence, parent involvement, crisis intervention, and the prevention of problems. They are becoming more involved in health issues such as smoking, substance abuse, and teen pregnancy, and in prevention efforts such as programs to decrease bullying and violence and programs to reduce the early onset of risky behaviors. An advantage of their role is their ability to reach learners of all ages, cultures, and social circumstances in a setting with little stigma. In the twenty-first century we may see school psychologists spend more time establishing parenting groups and consulting with parents, accessing social supports for families, and collaborating with agencies and other school professionals to solve school-wide problems. Their major focus may shift away from individual children to the prevention of problems for the school and community at large.

Applied Psychological Science. Applied psychologists have long emphasized the importance of bringing their shared knowledge and skills to bear on significant social problems. As the science of psychology has matured and established a substantive knowledge base, many of its subspecialities have developed a public service or applied mission. Many of APA's 52 divisions, from Mental Retardation and Developmental Disabilities to Psychology of Women and Peace Psychology, have become more applied, and others like Developmental and Social psychology have developed graduate programs designed to train applied scientists. The goal of applied developmental science is not just to understand, but to intervene in social problems.

Applied psychologists shape interventions such as programs to minimize risk-taking in adolescents, programs to increase compliance with medical regimes, and high quality early intervention and preschool programs for disadvantaged children. They evaluate social programs like Head Start and the effectiveness of public policies such as Education for All Handicapped Children Act (PL 94–142). Applied psychologists also use their knowledge and research to develop effective public policy. The discovery of the "battered child syndrome" contributed to child-abuse reporting legislation in all 50 states and grants to combat child abuse, while documenting increases in maternal employment and its psychological significance for families helped bring about the passage of the Family and Medical Leave Act in 1993.

Public Service in the Community. Many psychologists, including members of APA's Division 27 (Society for Community Research and Action) and applied social or environmental psychologists realize that the best way to fulfill their public service mission is to work in and with the community. Community psychologists share the conviction that psychology should be used to promote public welfare and that psychologists should reach out to everyone in their own communities. To do this, community psychologists have given up the mental-health office and decided to work in naturally occurring settings that most influence people's lives.

A starting point for understanding community psychology is the Community Mental Health Centers Act of 1963, which attempted to treat people in their own communities rather than isolate the mentally ill. Despite the problems associated with deinstitutionalization, lessons were learned that have educated psychologists to work in the community more effectively. Contemporary community psychologists continue to have a strong public service mission, but today their service is less likely to be a curative helper with individuals and more likely to involve consultation, program development, or program evaluation working with schools, the workplace, the legal system, and other organizations. Moreover, involving the community meaningfully and transferring program ownership helps make initiatives a permanent part of a community's infrastructure.

Community psychologists have created some of the most acclaimed community-based prevention and health promotion programs in the country. These address issues of critical social importance, such as adolescent pregnancy, substance abuse, and violence prevention. Some are aimed at middle school children to minimize the negative effects of their parents' divorce. Others—like JOBS intervention, developed for adults coping with job loss—resulted in less depression and higher paying jobs. The San Francisco Depression Prevention Research Project, targeted at adults at risk because of poverty and minority status, significantly reduced the incidence of depression.

Community psychologists also develop programs to promote psychological strengths and competencies. One of many social competency interventions, I Can Problem Solve, helps children develop self-control, communication skills, and problem-solving techniques while resisting negative social influences. The program, which has been disseminated nationally, results in more positive social adjustment and reduced aggressive and socially inappropriate behaviors. Other community psychologists attempt to change the conditions that give rise to problems rather than change individuals. In confronting a problem like substance abuse, they develop multilevel interventions that seek to reduce risks in the child, the peer group, the family, the school, and the community simultaneously. To realize their public service mission, community psychologists develop accessible and culturally sensitive services to underserved populations, such as minorities, gays, lesbians, the poor, people with AIDS, and the homeless. They also work to eradicate some of the root causes of mental illness and problems in living—racism, sexism, and ageism.

Additional Public Service Career Paths. Public service opportunities can be found in a wide range of settings. These include such federal agencies as the Substance Abuse and Mental Health Services Administration, Environmental Protection Agency, departments of Labor, Education, Justice, Energy, and Defense, Centers for Disease Control and Prevention, and the National Institute of Mental Health and the National Institute on Drug Abuse (both part of the National Institutes of Health) as well as quasi-governmental and private entities like the National Academy of Science and the National Mental Health Association. In addition, state and local mental health authorities and, increasingly, nongovernmental and private sector venues such as foundations, think tanks, and research institutes, offer psychologists the opportunity to serve the public. With the downsizing of the federal government and the increased flexibility afforded by block grants, state and local governments may need the expertise of public service–oriented psychologists. At the same time, foundations like Annie E. Casey, Carnegie, William T. Grant, and Rockefeller, and think tanks like the Search Institute, Families and Work Institute, and Manpower Demonstration Research Corporation are at the forefront of the public service mission in America. They disseminate research findings to national leaders, propose projects for governmental bodies like the National Governors Association, and evaluate social programs. They also anticipate and fund major policy initiatives like different approaches to helping families move from welfare to work.

Public Service Activities

Psychologists have opportunities to perform public service through two activities—research and public policy—that cut across all of psychology's subspecialties.

Research. By conducting basic and applied research, psychologists have the opportunity to make important public service contributions. In 1992, the American Psychological Society identified six broad national concerns: productivity in the workplace, school and literacy, the aging society, drug and alcohol abuse, health, and violence in America. A report issued that same year by the National Behavioral Science Research Agenda Committee on the Human Capital Initiative argued persuasively for psychologists to assume leadership roles in tackling these issues. The report explained that social problems cost taxpayers hundreds of billions of dollars. Psychological research is relatively inexpensive, but the cost of not knowing is enormous. The report recognized that all too often we simply do not know the best way to deal with these challenges and concluded that discovering solutions will require mounting serious research programs. Applied researchers have already developed interventions and programs that can help with some of our most pressing social problems. To illustrate, a recent meta-analysis of substance abuse curricula in the schools identified a number of effective, empirically validated interventions. Unfortunately, those are not the interventions in place in most schools. Additionally, because so much research is done in isolation there is often a lengthy delay between completing effective research projects and delivering the technology to front-line community service providers. Psychologists must both conduct applied research and make sure effective programs get used by efficiently translating research into practice.

Public Policy. Public policy refers to the totality of all laws, regulations, court rulings, and administrative procedures that guide the nation in solving socially agreed-on problems. The APA's Public Policy Office (PPO), established in 1987, is the most visible national presence advocating for psychology in the public interest. It is important to have an advocacy program at the federal level because federal legislation affects every citizen. Congressional leaders and federal agency representatives need to know about successful prevention theory and research aimed at curbing such social and health problems as youth violence, HIV transmission, and other sexually transmitted diseases, adolescent pregnancy, and child abuse. The PPO disseminates information about research findings in these areas to policy makers through Congressional briefings, testimony before Congressional committees, presentations before federal agency advisory panels, and other means. The PPO has also worked with Vice President Al Gore and a coalition of child and mental-health advocates to persuade the cable and network television industry to adopt a uniform set of symbols to inform parents of the specific content of television programs (i.e., sex, violence, or mature language). This decision was based on the extensive research of psychologists who have demonstrated the potentially harmful effects of violent programming on children, and the need for greater parental involvement and control over what their children watch.

Historically, psychology has not recognized the need for training programs to get psychologists involved in public policy. The APA Congressional Science Fellowship Program is rectifying this problem, thereby bringing psychology's expertise to a wide range of national priorities.

Other public service opportunities afforded psychologists are organized under the APA's Public Interest Directorate. Examples include specific projects on AIDS, violence, and women's health, publications and programs targeted at racism, and an educational campaign, Talk to Someone Who Can Help, which helps citizens know when to seek treatment.

Future Trends

According to the 1995 Occupational Outlook Handbook, public service growth areas that can be filled by psychologists correspond to social issues and concerns such as addictions, environment, health, marital strife, violence, and crime. Movement toward prevention and education in addition to diagnosis and assessment presents opportunities to apply existing psychological knowledge and develop research in these areas. A 1995 APA report, Forecast for Employment, by Kohout and Gaddy, concluded that career opportunities are impressive but require that psychologists go beyond traditional roles.

The year 1980 was a turning point for the first time since World War II, as many new psychologists took positions outside academia as within it. At the same time, graduate training programs began to redirect students toward applied research in preparation for nonacademic careers. If these developments continue, a significant expansion may take place in applied psychology, as well as a dramatic enlargement in the discipline's public service role and a chance to address broader global issues—war, racism, violence—that affect all of humankind.

[*See also* Careers in Psychology; Public Policy; *and* United States Department of Veterans Affairs.]

Bibliography

APA Public Policy Office. (1995). *Psychology in the public interest*. Washington, DC: American Psychological Association. Describes how psychologists can participate in the public policy process. Discusses the legislative process, how to communicate with legislators, and how to use the resources of the APA Public Policy Office to carry out advocacy efforts.

Levine, M. L., & Perkins, D. V. (1997). *Principles of community psychology: Perspectives and applications*. New York: Oxford University Press. Provides extended discussion of social problems, the conceptual foundations of community psychology, and the application of community-psychology principles to promote effective change.

Lorion, R. P., Iscoe, I., Deleon, P. H., & Vanden Bos, G. R. (Eds.). (1996). *Psychology and public policy: Balancing public service and professional need*. Washington, DC: American Psychological Association. Presents the coevolution of psychology and public policy, as well as the opportunity for psychology to inform policy decisions. Documents the discipline's relevance to a broad array of social issues that influence public welfare and concludes with advice on how psychology can best help to shape the public agenda.

Meissen, G., Colgate, J., Slavich, S., & Petersan, P. (1995). A survey of graduate education in community psychology. *Community Psychologist, 28*(4), 6–27. Surveys masters and doctoral programs in community and clinical-community psychology. Summarizes curricula, program characteristics, training sites, dissertations, and special features.

Perry, M. J., Albee, G. W., Bloom, M., & Gullotta, T. P.

(1996). *Training and career paths in primary prevention.* Thousand Oaks, CA: Sage.

Sternberg, R. J. (Ed.). (1997). *Career paths in psychology.* Washington, DC: American Psychological Association. Includes detailed descriptions of career paths in psychology, including careers in: academic organizations; clinical, counseling, and community psychology; and other diverse settings such as government, schools, the workplace, and health settings.

Wicherski, M., & Kohout, J. (1997). *1995 doctorate employment survey.* Washington, DC: American Psychological Association. Presents data on employment all of 1995 doctorates in psychology and compares trends since 1975. Includes information on employment status and settings, job perceptions and satisfaction, postdoctoral training, and salaries.

Joseph Galano and Beverly Peterson

PUNISHMENT. [*This entry comprises two articles:* Research *and* Developmental Perspectives. *The first article provides a broad overview of the psychological research on punishment. The second article examines punishment from the perspective of developmental psychology.*]

Research

Punishment is a behavioral process wherein the consequences of a behavior make that behavior less likely in the future. Consequences that make subsequent occurrences of an activity less likely are called *punishers* or *punishing stimuli,* and they are defined as such by their effectiveness. Consequences that do not result in subsequent reduction in the targeted behavior are not punishers, even if they are intended to be so and even if there is reason to believe that the consequences are painful or otherwise aversive. If presentation of a stimulus (e.g., an electric shock) or a situation as a consequence of responding reduces the subsequent frequency of that activity, the process is defined as *positive punishment.* If removal of a stimulus or situation as a consequence of the activity reduces its subsequent likelihood, the process is called *negative punishment.* Negative punishment procedures are sometimes called *omission* procedures. A common form of negative punishment is arranging a "time-out" from the possibility of positive reinforcement as a consequence of behavior. [*See* Operant Conditioning.]

Historically it was suggested that punishment was not effective in producing substantial or permanent effects on behavior (Thorndike, 1927). This conclusion was based on experiments with low-intensity punishers or with stimuli that were not punishers at all. Subsequent research, however, revealed that punishment can have profound and lasting effects on performance (Azrin & Holz, 1966; Masserman, 1946).

Punishment is best conceptualized as the opposite of reinforcement rather than as a procedure whose effects are mediated by negative reinforcement of behavior that competes with the punished activity. That is, punishment is effective directly, not because the individual learns to avoid the punisher by engaging in some other activity. Several lines of evidence support this view. First, direct measurement of the most likely alternative activity that could emerge via negative reinforcement to compete with the response that produces the punisher has not revealed any necessary increase in that behavior (e.g., Rachlin & Herrstein, 1969). Second, psychoactive drugs like chlorpromazine that decrease negatively reinforced behavior do not alter the effects of punishment, and drugs like diazepam that decrease the effectiveness of punishment do not alter behavior maintained by negative reinforcement (Carlton, 1971). Third, addition of punishment to both alternatives in a two-alternative choice situation results in increased preference for the more favorable alternative, an outcome consistent with the notion that punishment directly reduces the frequency of the behavior punished (deVilliers, 1980).

A second commonality between reinforcement and punishment is that a contingent relation between an activity and its consequence is necessary for the process to occur. A contingency between an activity and the punisher results in greater suppression of behavior than behavior-independent presentation of the punisher alone (e.g., Camp, Raymond, & Church, 1967). That is, punishment effects are not due simply to generalized suppression.

Even if a contingent relation exists between an activity and a punishing stimulus, several factors determine the effectiveness of the relation in decreasing the frequency of behavior. As might be assumed, the intensity, or magnitude, of the punishing consequence can be important. Generally, more intense punishment (e.g., louder or more prolonged noise) yields greater reduction in the frequency of the punished activity than does less intense punishment. This general result, however, depends on previous experience with the punishing stimulus. Prior experience with an intense punisher can render a less intense punisher more effective, whereas previous exposure to a less intense punisher can weaken the effect of a more intense one (Raymond, 1969). Relatively weak punishers may become less effective over time, perhaps demonstrating adaptation, whereas intense punishers tend to retain their effectiveness (Azrin, 1960).

A second important factor is how quickly punishment follows the act to be punished. Longer delays between the activity and the punisher result in less effective punishment (Azrin, 1956).

A third factor of significance is whether punishment occurs following every instance of the targeted activity or only some of them. Intermittent punishment is arranged by "schedules of punishment," consisting of rules that describe which instances of the activity will be punished. Punishment is most effective if every instance is punished (Cipani, Brendlinger, McDowell, & Usher, 1991). Schedules of punishment that correspond to schedules of reinforcement tend to produce results that are the opposite of those produced by schedules of reinforcement. For example, a fixed-interval schedule of punishment that specifies delivering punishment for the first response after a fixed period of time has elapsed produces fast responding early in the interval and slow responding as the end of the interval nears (Azrin & Holz, 1966). Exactly the opposite pattern results from fixed-interval schedules of reinforcement.

The experimental study of punishment not only indicates that the factors just listed modulate the effectiveness of punishment but also point to a source of complication that exists when punishment is implemented, either in the laboratory or in nonlaboratory situations. The complications originate in the fact that punishment is applied to behavior that is occurring at some (undesirable in the real world) frequency. This means that the factors responsible for the occurrence of the behavior have to be taken into account. In the laboratory, the behavior to be punished usually is established through operant conditioning. Factors important in the development and maintenance of operant behavior interact with the effects of punishment. For instance, establishment of operant behavior usually requires implementation of establishing operations (or "motivation"). Effectiveness of punishment (i.e., the degree by which responding is reduced by punishment) is inversely related to the level of the motivation to respond. For example, key pecking by pigeons, established and maintained by occasional food presentation, is more easily reduced by punishment when the pigeons are mildly food deprived than when they are more severely food deprived (Azrin, Holz, & Hake, 1963). Also important are conditions of intermittent reinforcement in maintaining the behavior to be punished. As an illustration, even though not much research has been devoted to this important issue, punishment is generally more effective in reducing behavior maintained by interval schedules of reinforcement than behavior maintained by ratio schedules of reinforcement.

Interestingly, although very little research has been conducted on this issue, it appears that whether behavior is maintained by positive or negative reinforcement has little impact on the effectiveness of punishment or its sensitivity to factors like punishment frequency or delay (Baron, Kaufman, & Fazzini, 1969).

In some cases, it is not known what factors are responsible for the behavior that is targeted for punishment. For example, nocturnal bruxism (grinding of teeth while asleep) has been treated successfully with punishment (Heller & Strang, 1973), despite the fact that the origins of the bruxism were unknown.

Because punishment is applied to behavior that is occurring for known or unknown reasons, the possibility exists that punishment may interact in unintended ways with the factors responsible for the behavior to be punished. Such interactions can undermine the intended effects of punishment. For example, the delivery of a punisher can serve a discriminative function (i.e., in everyday parlance, it can serve as a cue that something good might happen). Consider a "guilty parent" syndrome in which the following occurs. A child misbehaves in some way, and a parent administers some form of punishment (e.g., takes away a favorite toy). The child expresses her dismay by crying loudly. To calm or distract her, the parent decides to give the child a rare treat such as ice cream. Repeated experiences of this scenario may result in increased misbehavior because punishment leads to access to ice cream. Similar effects have been shown in the laboratory. Holz and Azrin (1961) trained pigeons to peck a key under an intermittent schedule of food presentation. Two test sessions were conducted each day. In the first session, intermittent reinforcement occurred, as did punishment (a 0.1-second electric shock) after each peck. In the second session, conducted with the same apparatus, pecks had no consequences. Parameters were adjusted so that pecking occurred in the first session at about 50% of the rate observed without punishment. In the second session, few pecks occurred. As a test, one day in the second session, pecks produced brief shocks (but still no food). Pecking increased dramatically, indicating that the presence of electric shocks served a discriminative function (i.e., served as a cue that food might be available).

Punishment frequently has effects in addition to or separate from its direct effect of decreasing the likelihood of the targeted activity. Sometimes these are referred to as *side effects* of punishment. Chief among these is that punishment may elicit or evoke reactions, either emotional or behavioral, or both, that may either compete with or augment the targeted response. For example, presentation of an electric shock through the floor may elicit jumping. If jumping were the activity targeted for reduction through punishment, reduction might be difficult to produce. Conversely, the actions elicited by the punishment may be incompatible with the targeted activity and may thereby enhance the effects of punishment.

Another possible side effect is that the situation in which punishment is delivered may become aversive so that it promotes escape, an instance of negative reinforcement. Ironically, despite the fact that punishment itself does not appear to depend on negative reinforcement for its effects, it nevertheless can produce situations in which negative reinforcement of behavior becomes likely (Azrin, Hake, Holz, & Hutchinson, 1965). Escape from a situation in which punishment is present can occur even when the magnitude of the punishment effect is relatively small. Even though punishers may be minimally effective in reducing the frequency of the targeted behavior, their presence can make the situation itself aversive and therefore set the stage for powerful negative reinforcement effects. This last point is important for any plans to use punishment in practical settings because it implies that aspects of the situation itself (e.g., a classroom), including a person (or persons) who delivers punishment if it is socially mediated (e.g., a teacher), may become aversive stimuli and therefore avoided. A potential result, therefore, would be that punishment, instead of reducing the frequency of the targeted behavior, causes the situation to be avoided altogether, so that not only is the targeted activity eliminated but so also is all behavior appropriate to the situation (e.g., academic activity).

Bibliography

Azrin, N. H. (1956). Some effects of two intermittent schedules of immediate and nonimmediate punishment. *Journal of Psychology, 42*, 3–21.

Azrin, N. H. (1960). Effects of punishment intensity during variable-interval reinforcement. *Journal of the Experimental Analysis of Behavior, 3*, 123–142.

Azrin, N. H., Hake, D. F., Holz, W. C., & Hutchinson, R. R. (1965). Motivational aspects of escape from punishment. *Journal of the Experimental Analysis of Behavior, 8*, 31–44.

Azrin, N. H., & Holz, W. C. (1966). Punishment. In W. K. Honig (Ed.), *Operant behavior: Areas of research and application* (pp. 380–447). New York: Appleton-Century-Crofts.

Azrin, N. H., Holz, W. C., & Hake, D. F. (1963). Fixed-ratio punishment. *Journal of the Experimental Analysis of Behavior, 6*, 141–148.

Baron, A., Kaufman, A., & Fazzini, D. (1969). Density and delay of punishment of free-operant avoidance. *Journal of the Experimental Analysis of Behavior, 12*, 1029–1037.

Camp, D. S., Raymond, G. A., & Church, R. M. (1967). Temporal relationship between response and punishment. *Journal of Experimental Psychology, 74*, 114–123.

Carlton, P. L. (1971). *A primer of behavioral pharmacology*. New York: Freeman.

Cipani, E., Brendlinger, J., McDowell, L., & Usher, S. (1991). Continuous vs. intermittent punishment: A case study. *Journal of Behavior Therapy and Experimental Psychiatry, 20*, 147–156.

deVilliers, P. A. (1980). Toward a quantitative theory of punishment. *Journal of the Experimental Analysis of Behavior, 33*, 15–25.

Heller, R. F., & Strang, H. R. (1973). Controlling bruxism through automated aversive conditioning. *Behavior Research and Therapy, 11*, 327–329.

Holz, W. C., & Azrin, N. H. (1961). Discriminative properties of punishment. *Journal of the Experimental Analysis of Behavior, 4*, 225–232.

Masserman, J. H. (1946). *Principles of dynamic psychiatry*. Philadelphia: Saunders.

Rachlin, H., & Herrstein, R. J. (1969). Hedonism revisited: On the negative law of effect. In B. A. Campbell & R. A. Church (Eds.), *Punishment and aversive behavior* (pp. 83–109). New York: Appleton-Century-Crofts.

Raymond, G. A. (1969). *Accentuation and attenuation of punishment by prior exposure to aversive stimulation*. Unpublished doctoral dissertation, Brown University. *Dissertation Abstracts International, 30*(1-B), 416–417.

Thorndike, E. L (1927). The law of effect. *American Journal of Psychology, 39*, 212–222.

Marc N. Branch

Developmental Perspectives

In psychology, punishment refers to anything that reduces, or is intended to reduce, the likelihood of a behavior's being repeated. (Punishment is the opposite of reward, which refers to something that increases, or is intended to increase, the likelihood of a behavior's being repeated.) A punishment can be something that is applied or added (as in a spanking or the expression of disappointment), or it can be something that is taken away or removed (as in the withholding of a child's allowance or a parent's affection). In either case, the purpose of the punishment is to weaken or reduce the frequency of the behavior that is being punished. In the field of developmental psychology, punishment is usually discussed under the broader heading of "socialization" or, as it is more commonly known, "discipline"—the process through which parents attempt to shape the child's behavior.

Types of Punishment

Generally speaking, punishment within the context of the parent-child relationship takes one of two forms: power assertion or love withdrawal. When parents punish their child through the assertion of power, they take advantage of the differences that exist between themselves and the child with respect to physical size or access to resources. Spanking, hitting, yelling, depriving children of something they want, sending children to their rooms, or placing children on time-out are all examples of power assertion because they all take advantage of the parent's relatively greater power over the child.

Punishment through power assertion may be contrasted with love withdrawal, which is a form of punishment that relies on the child's emotional relationship to the parent. Parents use love withdrawal when they punish a child by making him or her feel guilty or ashamed, by emphasizing their disappointment with the child's behavior, or by making the child feel that he or she is less loved because of the offending behavior. It is also possible to punish a child in a way that relies simultaneously on power assertion and love withdrawal (e.g., when a parent screams at a child that the youngster has been a disappointment).

Developmental psychologists have devoted considerable effort to research on punishment and its effects on the child. Indeed, the study of discipline, of which the study of punishment is an important part, is one of the oldest topics in developmental psychology. In general, whereas early research asked relatively straightforward questions about the utility of different types of punishment in gaining the child's compliance, recent research has asked more subtle questions about the conditions under which punishment is made more or less effective. In addition, contemporary studies have examined both the intended effects and the unintended, or unanticipated, consequences of different forms of punishment. In general, this research has led to two main conclusions: first, that the effectiveness of any punishment depends strongly on the context in which it is applied, and second, that different types of punishment may have similar effects on compliance but very different, unintended consequences for the child's development.

When Is Punishment Effective?

The effectiveness of any punishment depends less on the type of punishment employed than on the context in which it is applied. Numerous factors have been found to influence punishment effectiveness, the most important of which is probably the nature of the child's relationship with the parent. Power assertion, for example, is effective only to the extent that the parent actually has power over the child. Screaming at a 3-year-old, who is likely to fear angering the parent, may well gain the child's compliance; in contrast, screaming at a 13-year-old, who is probably less fearful, is unlikely to be very effective. Similarly, withholding a 7-year-old's allowance as a form of punishment may well work because the child is dependent on the parent for money, but withholding the allowance of a 16-year-old who has a part-time job is less likely to be successful. The effectiveness of love withdrawal as a means of punishment depends on the strength of the emotional connection between the parent and child. A child who loves and admires a parent is much more susceptible to feeling guilty or ashamed when the parent expresses disappointment than is a child whose feelings toward the parent are less positive. In general, therefore, punishment is more effective when it is administered in the context of a meaningful relationship.

A second factor that influences the effectiveness of punishment is its timing. Generally speaking, any punishment—whether power assertion or love withdrawal—is far more effective in shaping the child's behavior when it is administered immediately after the offending action rather than at a later time. When a child receives a spanking right after he or she has run out into the street, for example, the punishment is much more likely to prevent similar actions in the future than if a parent delays spanking the child until later in the day. Similarly, a parent who catches a child stealing something and expresses disappointment at that moment is more likely to make an impression on the child than is a parent who temporarily ignores the misdeed and waits for a while before reacting.

Third, the effectiveness of any punishment is influenced by the regularity with which it is applied. Children are far more likely to desist from a particular behavior when it is punished consistently than when parents attend to the behavior only occasionally. Consider, for example, a parent who wishes to stop a child from using foul language. Administering punishment each time the youngster swears (e.g., by deducting a portion of the child's weekly allowance for each offensive word) will diminish the behavior faster than a more intermittent, less vigilant approach. Many psychologists who work with parents to improve their child-rearing practices work specifically on helping parents to be more consistent in their discipline.

Finally, the effectiveness of punishment is affected by the temperament and personality characteristics of the child. Children differ in the extent to which they are fearful, for example, and it is likely that power-assertive techniques designed to gain compliance by inducing fear in the child (e.g., when a parent threatens a spanking) are more likely to be effective with children whose fear is more easily aroused than with children who are relatively more fearless. Similarly, children who tend to feel guilty or anxious are more susceptible to love withdrawal as a form of punishment than are children who are less prone toward these emotions. Because children in the same family can have very different temperaments, parents often find that brothers and sisters in the same household respond differently to the same punishment.

Unintended Consequences of Physical Punishment and Love Withdrawal

Although both power assertion and love withdrawal are potentially effective in shaping the child's behavior, research on each type of punishment indicates that their use may also affect the child in ways that are not intended. It is important, therefore, that parents understand that a particular type of punishment may have multiple effects on the child—some of which are desired but others of which are problematic. Most of the research on the unanticipated consequences of punishment has focused on physical, or corporal, punishment. Less work has examined the unintended consequences of love withdrawal, although recent research suggests that this form of punishment may have ill effects on the child as well. Little is known about the unintended consequences of other types of power assertion (such as deprivation of privileges, "time-out," etc.), although most developmental psychologists believe that these can be safe and appropriate strategies for disciplining children, especially when coupled with nonpunitive forms of discipline.

Physical punishment—inflicting physical pain on the child by spanking, hitting, or some other method—is one of the oldest, most widely used, and most controversial forms of discipline. Developmental psychologists and child-rearing experts have varied tremendously over the years in their views of physical punishment; at certain times, it was considered an essential part of effective discipline, whereas at others it was denounced as little more than child abuse. Cultures also vary greatly in their acceptance of the practice because attitudes toward various approaches to discipline are closely linked to societal beliefs about the nature of childhood and the purpose of socialization.

Most contemporary psychologists believe that physical punishment probably does more harm than good, and few child-rearing experts today recommend it. Although physical punishment has been shown to be effective in gaining the child's compliance, it has also been shown to have adverse effects on the child's development. Three drawbacks of physical punishment have been identified. First, many studies have shown that children who have been spanked or hit by their parents are more likely to act aggressively toward other children, presumably because they have learned from their parents that physical aggression is an acceptable response to frustration. Ironically, then, parents who use spanking to discipline their child for misbehavior may inadvertently promote more misbehavior when the child is out of the home environment. Children who are temperamentally predisposed toward aggression are most likely to be affected in this way, which only exacerbates their aggressiveness.

Second, physical punishment is thought to be far more effective in the short term than in the long run. Thus, although a spanking may make an immediate impression on a child, it is less likely to have a lasting impact on the child's behavior or to discipline the child in a way that will generalize beyond the context in which the punishment is administered. As a consequence, parents who rely on physical punishment may find that their child continues to misbehave, even after being punished numerous times. This, in turn, may lead the parent to perceive the child as difficult or hard to manage.

Finally, physical punishment can easily spiral out of control, to the point where the child's safety is seriously threatened. Many instances of child abuse begin as disciplinary confrontations in which the parent uses physical punishment simply as a means of gaining the child's compliance. Without intending to injure the child, a parent who habitually turns to physical punishment runs the risk of seriously hurting the youngster.

Although less is known about the adverse impact of love withdrawal on the child's development, several writers have theorized that the excessive use of this form of punishment may increase children's risk of developing anxiety and depression. Although it is normal, and even beneficial, for children to feel guilty when they misbehave, youngsters who come to believe that their relationship with their parent is on shaky ground, or is highly dependent on pleasing the parent, may develop feelings of insecurity and uneasiness. Youngsters who are timid or anxious may be especially susceptible to the ill effects of love withdrawal.

Punishment and Discipline

Punishment, of course, is not the only way to discipline children. The child's behavior can also be shaped by reward, induction (a form of discipline in which the parent attempts to influence the child's behavior through reasoning or explanation), and modeling (where the parent provides discipline by demonstrating how the child is expected to behave). Generally speaking, punishment and reinforcement are more effective when used for short-term purposes (i.e., to change a child's immediate behavior), whereas induction and modeling are more effective when used for long-term purposes (i.e., to influence the child's future development).

There is no truth to the widely held belief that it is better for the child's development to use reward than punishment or that punishment is inherently bad for the child. Indeed, most good parents use a combination of punishment, reinforcement, induction, and modeling in rearing their children because different situations call for different disciplinary strategies. All of these strategies can be highly effective means of discipline as long as they are used in a developmentally appropriate and consistent fashion. Although physical punishment and love withdrawal may have unintended and even deleterious consequences, other forms of punishment, such as deprivation of privileges, can be employed safely and effectively. Overall, punishment is likely to be most effective when it is balanced by, and administered in conjunction with, other forms of discipline and in the context of a warm parent-child relationship.

[*See also* Discipline.]

Bibliography

Bornstein, M. (Ed.). (1995). *Handbook of parenting.* Mahwah, NJ: Erlbaum.

Bugental, D., & Goodnow, J. (1998). Socialization processes.

In W. Damon (Series Ed.) & N. Eisenberg (Vol. Ed.), *Handbook of child psychology* (5th ed., pp. 389–462). New York: Wiley.

Kutner, L. (1991). *Between parent and child*. New York: Morrow.

Maccoby, E., & Martin, J. (1983). Socialization in the context of the family: Parent-child interaction. In E. M. Hetherington (Ed.), *Handbook of child psychology: Vol. 4. Socialization, personality, and social development* (pp. 1–101). New York: Wiley.

Steinberg, L., & Levine, A. (1997). *You and your adolescent: A parent's guide for ages 10 to 20* (Rev. ed.). New York: HarperCollins.

Laurence Steinberg

PURKINJE, JOHANNES (1787–1869), Czech physiologist. Purkinje was born in Libochovice, a small community in Northern Bohemia. His father died when the boy was only 6 years old, and the family was left with few resources. At the age of 11 Jan left home to continue his elementary education for 3 years in the city of Mikulov, in Moravia, as a choirboy at a school managed by the the Piarist religious teaching order. From 1801 to 1804 he attended the Piarist high school ("gymnasium") and joined the order in 1804. He left the order to begin studies at the University of Prague (1807–1809). After interrupting his studies to serve as a private tutor, in Prague and elsewhere, he studied medicine from 1814 to 1818, the culmination of his studies being an outstanding dissertation, written in German and entitled *Contributions to the Knowledge of Vision from a Subjective Viewpoint*. It was published in 1819 in Prague and reprinted in 1823. Its companion volume, *The New Contributions*, was published in Berlin in 1825.

Purkinje spent the years 1823 to 1850 as professor of physiology and pathology in Silesia, at the University of Vratislavia (Breslau in German, Wrocław in Polish), returning to Prague as professor of physiology. He died in 1869.

Psychology was Purkinje's lifelong love, even though there were long interruptions in his involvement in this field. His first serious encounter with psychological literature took place when he was 19 years old. He was 32 and 36 when his two volumes on vision appeared in print, gave lectures on empirical and physiological psychology between the ages of 40 and 55, and in his late 60s he wrote, in Czech, a historically oriented essay on contemporary psychology. These are brief examples rather than a full account of his activities relevant to psychology.

Robert Watson's *Eminent Contributors to Psychology* (New York, 1974, 1976) lists Purkinje's primary psychological works, as well as secondary references about him. E. G. Boring's classic history (1942) also devotes substantial attention to Purkinje's work, including his observations on such phenomena as the sensations induced by pressure on the eyeball and by electrical currents; afterimages that follow exposure to dazzling light; and color sensitivity in indirect vision.

Purkinje's best known psychological contribution, sometimes called the *Purkinje shift* or the *Purkinje phenomenon* and pertaining to the perceived brightness of differing colors under differing illumination levels, was introduced by him in 1825 in the following words: "The intensity of illumination has a marked effect on the brightness of the perceived colors. . . . Let us place before us [spectral] colors at daybreak, when it just begins to dawn. At the beginning we see only dark and gray. Just the colors that [in daylight] are most vivid, the reds and the greens, appear darkest. . . . I could first perceive blue. The shades of red that in daylight are the brightest . . . appear for a very long time dark."

Bibliography

Boring, E. G. (1942). *Sensation and perception in the history of experimental psychology*. New York: Appleton-Century-Croft.

Brožek, J. (1989). Purkinje phenomenon: The original and a later account. *Perceptual and Motor Skills, 68*, 566. Contains a translation of Purkinje's paragraph which describes the "Purkinje phenomenon."

Brožek, J., & Hoskovec, J. (1997). Jan Evangelista Purkyně (Purkinje). In W. G. Bringmann, H. E. Lueck, R. Miller, & C. E. Early (Eds.), *A pictorial history of psychology* (pp. 90–96). Chicago: Quintesence. Documents, in both text and pictures, Purkinje's work relevant to psychology. Includes refences to publications that appeared at two anniversaries: 100 years after Purkinje's death (1969) and 200 years after Purkinje's birth (1987).

Purkinje, J. (1819). *Beitraege zur Kenntniss des Sehens in subjectiver Hinsicht* [Contributions to the knowledge of vision from a subjective viewpoint]. Prague: Fr. Vetterl. Contains the text of Purkinje's doctoral dissertation of 1818 presenting his early studies on vision.

Purkinje, J. (1825). *Neue Beitraege zur Kenntniss des Sehens in subjectiver Hinsicht* [New contributions to the knowledge of vision from a subjective viewpoint]. Berlin: G. Reimer. Reports Purkinje's subsequent studies on vision.

Watson, R. I. (1974, 1976). *Eminent contributors to psychology*. New York: Springer. Lists primary and secondary references.

Josef Brožek and Jiří Hoskovec

Q

QUADRAPLEGIA. *See* Rehabilitation Psychology.

QUALITATIVE RESEARCH refers, in the broadest sense, to research that produces descriptive data: people's own written or spoken words and observable behavior. Qualitative methods are rooted, and have a long history, in the social and behavioral sciences. Franz Boas and Jacob Malinowski can be credited with establishing fieldwork as a legitimate anthropological endeavor, beginning just after the turn of the twentieth century. In sociology, qualitative methods first became popular in the studies of the Chicago school from approximately 1910 to 1940. During this period, researchers associated with the University of Chicago produced detailed participant observation studies of urban life; rich life histories of juvenile delinquents and criminals, and a classic study by W. I. Thomas and Florian Znaniecki (*The Polish Peasant in Europe and America*, New York, 1927) of the life of immigrants and their families in Poland and America based on personal documents. Qualitative methods have been used in psychology as well, although to a much more limited extent, for example, Gordon W. Allport's *Use of Personal Documents in Psychological Sciences* (New York, 1942) and Robert Coles's *Children of Crisis* (Boston, 1964). [*See the biography of Boas.*]

Interest in qualitative methodology waned toward the end of the 1940s and beginning of the 1950s with the evolution of *grand theories* and quantitative methods. With the exception of William Foote Whyte's *Street Corner Society* (Boston, 1943), few qualitative studies were taught and read in social science departments during this era.

Since the 1960s there has been a reemergence in the use of qualitative methods. So many powerful, insightful, and influential studies have been published based on these methods that they have been impossible to discount. What was once an oral tradition of qualitative research has been recorded in monographs and articles. In addition, books have been published that examine the philosophical underpinnings of qualitative research, relate qualitative methods to theory development, describe writing strategies for reporting qualitative research, and contain personal accounts of researchers' experiences in the field. In sociology alone, there are journals devoted to qualitative studies and to qualitative inquiry generally.

The growing interest in qualitative research in the social and behavioral sciences has paralleled an increased acceptance of these methods in applied fields. Qualitative methods are increasingly used for program evaluation and policy research. Journals and texts on qualitative research can be found in such diverse applied areas of inquiry as health research, education, disability studies, social work, and special education.

In addition, there is a long tradition of action research linked to qualitative studies in the social sciences. Chicago school researchers sought to change conditions in urban slums through their incisive field reports and studies. On the basis of research at state institutions for the so-called mentally retarded, in-depth descriptive reports of institutional abuse and neglect have been prepared for federal courts, the popular media, policy makers, and organizations composed of people with disabilities and their families. Research is never free of values. When we get close to people, especially those society considers deviant, we develop a deep empathy with them. We learn that official views of morality present only one side of the picture. Howard Becker (*Social Problems*, 1966–1967, *14*, 239–247) took the position that we should side with society's underdogs, those who do not have a forum for their views. [*See* Action Research.]

Qualitative research is rooted in the phenomenological tradition. The phenomemologist, or interpretivist, is committed to understanding social phenomena from the actor's own perspective and examining how the world is experienced. A number of theoretical perspectives are associated with phenomenology, including symbolic interactionism, ethnomethodology, feminist research, and postmodernism. [*See* Feminist Psychology; Postmodern Psychology; *and* Symbolic Interaction Theory.]

The phenomenologist seeks understanding through qualitative methods, such as participant observation (sometimes referred to as *fieldwork* or *ethnography*), in-depth, open-ended interviewing, and analysis of personal documents, among others. *Participant observation* refers to research in natural settings involving social interaction between the researcher and the informants, during which data are systematically and unobtrusively collected. Participant observers enter the field with the hope of establishing open relationships with informants. They conduct themselves in such a way that they become an unobtrusive part of the scene, people the participants take for granted. Ideally, informants forget that the observer is there to do research. Many of the techniques used in participant observation correspond to everyday rules about inoffensive social interaction. In-depth interviewing involves capturing informants' perspectives on their lives, experiences, or situations, as expressed in their own words, through repeated face-to-face encounters between the researcher and informants. In stark contrast to structured interviewing, qualitative interviewing is flexible and dynamic. Qualitative interviewing has been referred to as nondirective, unstructured, nonstandardized, and open-ended interviewing. The in-depth interview is modeled after a conversation between equals, rather than a formal question-and-answer exchange. [*See* Phenomenology.]

Participant observation and in-depth interviewing can be used alone or in conjunction with each other. The primary difference between participant observation and in-depth interviewing lies in the settings and situations in which the research takes place. Whereas participant observers conduct their studies in natural field situations, interviewers conduct theirs in situations specifically arranged for the purposes of the research. The participant observer gains first-hand knowledge of what people say and do in their everyday lives. The interviewer relies extensively on verbal accounts of how people act and what they feel. Analysis of personal documents, such as diaries, photo albums, scrapbooks, and letters, can be a valuable source of information about people's experiences and perspectives, particularly if used in conjunction with participant observation and in-depth interviewing. [*See* Archival Research.]

Qualitative methodology is more than a set of data-gathering techniques, it is a way of approaching the empirical world. Aspects of this approach include the following:

1. Qualitative research in inductive. Barney Glaser and Anselm Strauss (*The Discovery of Grounded Theory: Strategies for Qualitative Research*, Chicago, 1967) coined the phrase "grounded theory" to refer to the inductive theorizing process involved in qualitative research. Researchers follow a flexible research design. As they learn about a setting and how participants view their experiences, they make decisions regarding additional data to collect on the basis of what has already been learned. Qualitative researchers develop concepts, insights, and understandings from patterns in the data, rather than collecting data to assess preconceived models, hypotheses, or theories. At the same time, pure induction is impossible; all researchers operate with various assumptions about the world. Thus, qualitative researchers use broad theoretical frameworks; however, the objective is to make sure that the theory fits the data and not vice versa.

2. Qualitative researchers are concerned with the meanings people attach to things in their lives. Central to the phenomenological perspective and hence qualitative research is understanding people from their own frames of references and experiencing reality as they experience it. Qualitative researchers empathize and identify with the people they study in order to understand how those people see things. They attempt to suspend, or set aside, their own perspectives and taken-for-granted views of the world.

3. Qualitative researchers are concerned with how people think and act in their everyday lives. Qualitative research has been described as naturalistic. This means that researchers adopt strategies that parallel how people act in the course of daily life, typically interacting with informants in a natural and unobtrusive manner. In participant observation, most researchers try to "blend into the woodwork," at least until they have grasped an understanding of a setting. In qualitative interviewing, researchers model their interviews after a normal conversation, rather than a formal question-and-answer exchange. Although qualitative researchers cannot eliminate their effects on the people they study, they attempt to minimize or control those effects or at least understand them when interpreting data.

4. In qualitative methodology, the researcher looks at settings and people holistically; people, settings, or groups are not reduced to variables, but are viewed as a whole. The qualitative researcher studies people in the context of their pasts and the situations in which they find themselves. When we reduce people's words and acts to statistical equations, we can lose sight of the human side of social life. When we study people qualitatively, we get to know them personally and experience what they experience in their daily struggles in society. We learn about concepts such as beauty, pain,

faith, suffering, frustration, and love, whose essence is lost through other research approaches.

5. Qualitative researchers emphasize the meaningfulness of their research. Qualitative methods allow us to stay close to the empirical world. They are designed to ensure a close fit between the data and what people actually say and do. By observing people in their everyday lives, listening to them talk about what is on their minds, and looking at the documents they produce, the qualitative researcher obtains first-hand knowledge of social life. Whereas qualitative researchers emphasize the meaningfulness of their studies—or what some people term *validity*—quantitative researchers emphasize reliability and replicability in research. This is not to say that qualitative researchers are unconcerned about the accuracy of their data. A qualitative study is not an impressionistic, off-the-cuff analysis based on a superficial look at a setting or people. It is systematic research conducted with demanding, although not necessarily standardized, procedures. [*See* Reliability; *and* Replication in Research.]

6. For the qualitative researcher, all perspectives are worthy of study. The goal of qualitative research is to examine how things look from different vantage points. The student's perspective is just as important as the teacher's; the juvenile delinquent's as important as the judge's; the paranoid's as important as the psychiatrist's; the homemaker's as important as the wage earner's; the minority member's as important as the majority member's; that of the researched as important as the researcher's. In qualitative studies, those whom society ignores—the poor and the deviant—often receive a forum for their views.

7. Qualitative research is a craft. Qualitative methods have not been as refined and standardized as other research approaches. This is in part an historical artifact that is changing with the establishment of conventions for collecting and analyzing data, and in part a reflection of the nature of the methods themselves. Qualitative researchers are flexible in how they go about conducting their studies. The researcher is a craftsperson. The qualitative behavioral scientist is encouraged to be his or her own methodologist. There are guidelines to be followed, but never rules. The methods serve the researcher: never is the researcher a slave to procedure and technique.

[*See also* Case Study; Data Collection; *and* Single-Case Experimental Design.]

Bibliography

Bogdan, R. C., & Biklen, S. K. (1998). *Qualitative research in education: An introduction to theory and methods* (3rd ed.). Boston: Allyn & Bacon. Describes qualitative research in education, including history, theory, and research techniques.

Denzin, N. K., & Lincoln, Y. S. (Eds.). (1994). *Handbook of qualitative research*. Thousand Oaks, CA: Sage. Examines the various paradigms for doing qualitative research, the strategies developed for studying people in their natural setting, and a variety of techniques for collecting, analyzing, interpreting, and reporting findings.

Lincoln, Y. S., & Guba, E. G. (1985). *Naturalistic inquiry*. Thousand Oaks, CA: Sage. Discusses theoretical aspects of naturalistic inquiry as well as practical aspects of conducting naturalistic research.

Schwandt, T. A. (1997). *Qualitative inquiry: A dictionary of terms*. Thousand Oaks, CA: Sage. Considers the key concepts and issues in qualitative inquiry, with a focus on philosophical and methodological concepts.

Taylor, S. J., & Bogdan, R. (1998). *Introduction to qualitative research methods: A guidebook and resource* (3rd ed.). New York: Wiley. Provides detailed description of qualitative data collection, including participant observation and in-depth interviewing, as well as information related to writing and publication of qualitative studies.

Steven J. Taylor, Robert C. Bogdan, and Pamela Walker

QUALITY OF LIFE (QOL) is a frequently used term that has implicit meaning to almost everyone. Less frequently, it is defined in a way that allows for clear understanding and measurement. In an early definition, Campbell, Converse, and Rogers (1976) stated that quality of life is "a vague and ethereal entity, something that many people talk about, but which nobody very clearly knows what to do about." Nevertheless, they discussed quality of life as being comprised of broad concepts that can affect global life satisfaction, including housing, employment opportunities, personal safety, family, educational systems, leisure pursuits, and good health. More recently, the term quality of life has been coopted by the medical care arena and used to apply specifically to those areas of life that are most affected by health or illness. This has led to the more recent term "health-related quality of life" (Bergner, 1989).

The importance of QOL has to be viewed in the context of the more general field of the investigation of outcomes of diseases and their treatment. The three most commonly measured outcomes include quantity of life, quality of life, and economic cost. Quantity of life refers to length of survival time with a certain disease. Economic costs are the direct and indirect economic impact of disease and its treatment. Historically, length of survival was the only outcome measure considered to be important. However, with the advances made in the treatment of life-threatening illnesses, and the transformation of such illnesses as cancer and acquired immunodeficiency syndrome (AIDS) into chronic conditions, quality of life has increasingly been recognized as an equally important outcome. For example, improvement of quality of life is one of two potential benefits set forth by the United States Food and Drug Administration when considering approval of new anticancer drugs (Johnson & Temple, 1985).

Quality of life has been defined as "the extent to which one's usual or expected physical, emotional and social well-being are affected by a medical condition or its treatment" (Cella, 1995). This definition encompasses the two widely accepted aspects of quality of life: subjectivity and multidimensionality (Aaronson, 1988). Subjectivity refers to the necessity of measuring quality of life from the individual's viewpoint. Traditional medicine frequently focused either on objective measurements such as decreases in tumor size or on outside observer (e.g., physician, nurse) reports of patients' health status, such as the Karnofsky Performance Status rating (Karnofsky, Abelmann, Craver, & Burchenal, 1948). However, quality of life is an individual's subjective appraisal of illness or treatment effects. While subjectivity is an inherent part of psychological measurement, it is only with the growth of the field of quality of life that traditional medicine has accepted the value of subjective patient reports. Observations that two people with the very same objective health status can report very different QOL, due to differences in expectations and coping abilities, have bolstered the acceptance of patient-reported measures (Testa & Simonson, 1996).

Multidimensionality is the other crucial aspect of QOL. Although such wide ranging single variables as weight loss and depression have been considered to be quality of life indicators, there is a growing consensus that QOL is multidimensional. Seven dimensions of QOL are commonly agreed to be important (Kornblith & Holland, 1994). These are: (a) physical well-being, or the experience of physical symptoms such as pain and nausea; (b) functional well-being, or the ability to participate in normal daily activities such as work and leisure pursuits; (c) emotional well-being, comprised of both positive affective states (e.g., happiness, peace of mind) and negative affective states (e.g., sadness, anxiety); (d) family well-being, or the ability to maintain family relationships and communication; (e) social functioning, which is the ability to participate and enjoy social roles and activities; (f) treatment satisfaction, including financial concerns; and (g) sexuality/intimacy, including body image concerns. Two other dimensions of QOL that are considered important are a global evaluation of QOL (i.e., a single item that taps patients' perceptions of their overall QOL) and total QOL, which is a sum of all of the dimensions into a total score. Other dimensions, including cognitive functioning (Aaronson, Cull, Kaasa, & Sprangers, 1995), social stigma (Peterman, Cella, Mo, & McCain, 1997), and spirituality (Brady, Peterman, Fitchett, Mo, & Cella, in press) have been identified by some as important to consider in certain settings.

A large number of valid and reliable questionnaires are available for the assessment of QOL. These can be divided into generic health status instruments, generic illness instruments and disease-specific instruments. Generic health status questionnaires can be completed by anyone, including those who do and who do not have a medical illness: they are applicable across all populations; and provide benchmarks for comparisons across diverse groups. Examples of general health status questionnaires are the Nottingham Health Profile (NHP: Hunt, McEwan, & McKenna, 1985) and the Short Form-36 from the Medical Outcomes Study (SF-36; Ware & Sherbourne, 1992).

Generic illness instruments are applicable for populations with any medical diagnosis or condition, and can be used for comparisons of different illnesses, different levels of disease severity, or different types of interventions. In addition to measuring general health status, generic illness instruments typically provide an assessment of perceptions of the impact of illness/disability. Examples of generic illness instruments include the Sickness Impact Profile (SIP; Bergner, Bobbitt, Carter, & Gilson, 1981) and the Functional Assessment of Chronic Illness Therapy (FACIT; Cella, 1997).

Finally, disease-specific measures are designed to assess the QOL of people with specific illnesses (e.g., cancer, asthma), specific types of treatment (e.g., chemotherapy, lung transplant), or specific symptoms (e.g., nausea, incontinence). The Diabetes Quality of Life instrument (DQOL; DCCT Research Group, 1988) and the Functional Living Index–Cancer (FLIC: Schipper, Clinch, McMurray, & Levitt, 1984) are two examples of disease-specific instruments.

Each type of instrument has particular advantages. Generic health status measures allow for comparisons across healthy and ill populations. For example, comparisons of the health status of different age groups might be made. Generic illness instruments allow an investigator to make comparisons across diseases. For example, Patrick and Deyo (1989) demonstrated, using scores on the SIP (Bergner, Bobbitt, Carter, & Gilson, 1981), that the impact of amyotrophic lateral sclerosis (ALS) was significantly greater than that of chronic obstructive pulmonary disease and chronic pain, which in turn had a greater impact than arthritis and angina. Such cross-disease comparisons are increasingly important in the determination of allocation of limited health-care resources (Patrick & Deyo, 1989). Disease-specific instruments provide more detailed assessments for specific diseases, and as such, are often more acceptable to medical personnel and patients. They are also likely to be more sensitive to specific treatment-related changes in QOL. The growing trend in QOL research is to combine a generic instrument with a disease-specific one, in order to provide the fullest coverage of important QOL areas. For example, Hawker, Melfi, Paul, Green, and Bombardier (1995) found that both generic and disease-specific QOL measures were of value in assessing the well-being of patients receiving knee replacement surgery. The generic measure was more sensitive to general health status and the presence of comorbid physical conditions, while the disease-specific measure was more sensitive to degree of knee disability.

There are at least four common uses of quality of life data. The most typical use is the evaluation of two (or more) treatments that are being compared in a clinical trial. For example, looking at QOL and survival data can determine if people on a particular treatment: (a) have both a clear survival advantage and report better QOL; (b) have similar survival times as people on the other treatment, but report better QOL; (c) live a shorter time than people on another treatment, but report better QOL; or (d) have shorter survival and poorer QOL than those on the other treatment. This information can then be used to inform clinical practice.

A second use of QOL information is as a planning tool for rehabilitation efforts or palliative care. Quality of life can provide a detailed assessment of disease and treatment effects, as well as the global impact of those effects on the person's daily life. For example, a patient's completed QOL measure might reveal anxious or depressive symptoms for which psychological help can be obtained, or a complaint of pain might be noted on the QOL measure despite the patient not mentioning it during the physical exam: this can provide a starting point for patient-physician communication about medical, psychological, or social interventions that might improve the patient's well-being.

Third, quality of life data might be used to predict patients' responses to future treatment. For example, Cella, Fairclough, Bonomi, Kim, and Johnson (1997) demonstrated that baseline QOL predicted treatment response and survival in patients with metastatic lung cancer. In addition, change in QOL from baseline to six weeks of treatment also predicted survival for these patients. This type of information might be used, subsequently, as a prognostic indicator or for the stratification of patients during random assignment to treatments (Gotay, 1996).

Fourth, QOL data is important for treatment decision-making, particularly in palliative care. There is a growing recognition that simply prolonging life, regardless of the quality of that life, is not a universally desired goal. Research on people's preferences for aggressive, life-prolonging treatments and for end-of-life decisions have demonstrated the importance of QOL judgments in the decision-making process. For example, Yellen and Cella (1995) demonstrated that people are willing to consider undergoing very aggressive and toxic treatments despite slim chances of survival if they report good social well-being and if they have children. Cicirelli (1997) found that a majority of elderly people would opt to continue living despite very poor quality of life characterized by pain, immobility, and extreme dependence on others. These findings demonstrate the absolute necessity of considering each person's individual assessment of what makes life worth living.

The first challenge for the field of QOL, establishing psychometrically valid measurements, has been largely met, particularly in oncology. The evaluation of QOL in other diseases is in varying stages of development (Spilker, 1995). Significant challenges remain for the field as a whole, however. Two of these challenges are the identification of clinically significant, or meaningful, changes in QOL and the development and testing of conceptual models linking medical and psychological variables to QOL.

Addressing the first challenge, identifying clinically significant QOL changes, is necessary to be able to answer the question of whether a change observed in response to an intervention is really meaningful and important, or whether it is simply statistically significant. Approaches to this question include examining the association between QOL change scores and patient global ratings of change in different life dimensions (e.g., Jaeschke, Singer, & Guyatt, 1989) and changes in life stress units (Testa & Simonson, 1996). This information can then be used to evaluate the effectiveness of a particular treatment, or to determine the need for a change in treatment strategy when a clinically significant decline in QOL is noted.

A second challenge is to develop and test models of factors that might affect QOL. The majority of literature to date has focused on the impact of medical treatments and diseases on QOL. However, there are a vast number of psychological, social, cultural, and economic factors that might affect a person's report of QOL in response to a particular level of impairment. One model for understanding the interrelationships of these variables has been proposed by Gotay (1996). She suggests that cancer diagnosis and treatment can result in symptoms and functional limitations. The amount of distress and life satisfaction experienced by the patient, in light of these symptoms, will be filtered by individual factors, sociocultural factors, and resources. Distress and satisfaction might, therefore, be combined together in unique ways as determined by patient preferences. Wilson & Cleary (1995) have proposed another model that relates physiological variables, symptom reports, and physical functioning to QOL. Certainly, evaluation of these types of models is crucial to an understanding of the predictors of QOL and the potential for modifying it through interventions.

In summary, the field of QOL is a dynamic, exciting, and rapidly growing one. Perhaps because of the relative recency of the explosion of QOL research, however, its value appears not to have been widely understood or recognized by the field of psychology. In fact, a search of PsychInfo for several of the top psychology journals revealed that only 27 articles with the subject term QOL had been published from 1984 to 1997 in *Health Psychology, Journal of Consulting and Clinical Psychology, Annals of Behavioral Medicine,* and *Journal of Personality and Social Psychology*. Certainly, the focus on QOL as an outcome of medical treatments and illnesses has necessitated that significant attention be focused on publishing in medical journals, with the goal of making QOL acceptable to the medical personnel who need to use it and on disseminating QOL research findings to those actively involved in medical settings.

However, the field of psychology has made extremely valuable contributions to the field of QOL research. First, the ability to convince medical practitioners that it is possible to obtain a valid and reliable measure of the patients' perspective of their illness and treatment was grounded in demonstration of the psychometric properties of QOL measures. Instrument development and measurement expertise of psychologists has been crucial in this regard. Second, psychologists working in the QOL field frequently have clinical experience with medical patients that informs their ability to design and conduct QOL research with great clinical relevance. Third, there is an increasing emphasis on the evaluation of QOL among populations with mental illness (e.g., Atkinson, Zibin, & Chuang, 1997). In conclusion, it appears likely that the next decade will witness a growing recognition of quality of life research by psychology, as the past decade has shown its growth within medicine and health care.

Bibliography

Aaronson, N. K. (1988). Quality of life: What is it? How should it be measured? *Oncology, 2(5)*, 69–74.

Aaronson, N. K., Cull, A., Kaasa, S., & Sprangers, M. (1995). The European Organization for Research and Treatment of Cancer (EORTC) modular approach to quality of life assessment in oncology: An update. In B. Spilker (Ed.), *Quality of life and pharmacoeconomics in clinical trials* (pp. 179–189). New York: Raven Press.

Atkinson, M., Zibin, S., & Chuang, H. (1997). Characterizing quality of life among patients with chronic mental illness: A critical examination of the self-report methodology. *American Journal of Psychiatry, 154(1)*, 99–105.

Bergner, M. (1989). Quality of life, health status, and clinical research. *Medical Care, 27*, S148–S156.

Bergner, M., Bobbitt, R. A., Carter, W. B., & Gilson, B. S. (1981). The Sickness Impact Profile: Development and final revision of a health status measure. *Medical Care, 19*, 787–805.

Brady, M., Peterman, A. H., Fitchett, G., Mo, M., & Cella, D. (in press). A case for including spirituality in quality of life measurement in oncology. *Psycho-Oncology.* [*Spirituality and quality of life in oncology.* Paper presented at the meeting of the American Psychological Association, Chicago, IL, August 1977.]

Campbell, A., Converse, P. E., & Rogers, W. L. (1976). *The quality of American life.* New York: Russel Sage Foundation.

Cella, D. (1997). *Manual of the Functional Assessment of Chronic Illness Therapy (FACIT) Scales.* Evanston, IL: Evanston Northwestern Healthcare.

Cella, D. F. (1995). Measuring quality of life in palliative care. *Seminars in Oncology, 22(2 Suppl 3)*, 73–81.

Cella, D. F., Fairclough, D. L., Bonomi, P. B., Kim, K., & Johnson, D. (1997). Quality of life in advanced non-small cell lung cancer: Results from eastern cooperative oncology group study E5592. *Proceedings of the American Society of Clinical Oncology, 16*, 2a.

Cicirelli, V. G. (1997). Relationship of psychosocial and background variables to older adults' end-of-life decisions. *Psychology and Aging, 12(1)*, 72–83.

DCCT Research Group. (1988). Reliability and validity of a diabetes quality of life measure for the Diabetes Control and Complications trial (DCCT). *Diabetes Care, 11*, 725–733.

Gotay, C. C. (1996). Trial-related quality of life: Using quality of life assessment to distinguish among cancer therapies. *Journal of the National Cancer Institute Monographs, 20*, 1–6.

Hawker, G., Melfi, C., Paul, J., Green, R., & Bombardier, C. (1995). Comparison of a generic (SF-36) and a disease specific (WOMAC) instrument in the measurement of outcomes after knee replacement surgery. *Journal of Rheumatology, 22*, 1193–1196.

Hunt, S. M., McEwan, J., & McKenna, S. P. (1985). Measuring health status: A new tool for clinicians and epidemiologists. *Journal of the Royal College of General Practitioners, 35(273)*, 185–188.

Jaeschke, R., Singer, J., & Guyatt, G. H. (1989). Measurement of health status: Ascertaining the minimal clinically important difference. *Controlled Clinical Trials, 10*, 407–415.

Johnson, J. R., & Temple, R. (1985). Food and Drug Administration requirements for approval of new anticancer drugs. *Cancer Treatment Reports, 69*, 1155–1159.

Karnofsky, D. A., Abelmann, W. H., Craver, L. F., & Burchenal, J. H. (1948). The use of the nitrogen mustards in the palliative treatment of carcinoma. *Cancer, 1*, 634–656.

Kornblith, A. B., & Holland, J. C. (1994). *Handbook of measures for psychological, social, and physical function in cancer. Volume 1: Quality of life.* New York: Memorial Sloan-Kettering Cancer Center.

Patrick, D. L., & Deyo, R. A. (1989). Generic and disease-specific measures in assessing health status and quality of life. *Medical Care, 27(3 Suppl)*, S217–S232.

Peterman, A. H., Cella, D., Mo, M., & McCain, N. (1997). Psychometric validation of the revised Functional Assessment of Human Immunodeficiency Virus Infection (FAHI) quality of life instrument. *Quality of Life Research, 6*, 572–584.

Schipper, H., Clinch, J. J., McMurray, A., & Levitt, M.

(1984). Measuring the quality of life of cancer patients: The Functional Living Index-Cancer: Development and validation. *Journal of Clinical Oncology, 2,* 472–483.

Spilker, B. (1995). *Quality of life and pharmacoeconomics in clinical trials.* New York: Raven Press.

Testa, M. A., & Simonson, D. C. (1996). Assessment of quality-of-life outcomes. *New England Journal of Medicine, 334(13),* 835–840.

Ware, J., & Sherbourne, C. D. (1992). The MOS 36-item Short Form Health Survey (SF-36)-I: Conceptual framework and item selection. *Medical Care, 30,* 473–483.

Wilson, I. B., & Cleary, P. D. (1995). Linking clinical variables with health-related quality of life. *Journal of the American Medical Association, 273(1),* 59–65.

Yellen, S., & Cella, D. (1995). Someone to live for: Social well-being, parenthood status, and decision-making in oncology. *Journal of Clinical Oncology, 13(5),* 1255–1264.

Amy H. Peterman and David Cella

QUASI-EXPERIMENTS. *See* Nonrandomized Designs.

QUETELET, LAMBERT ADOLPHE JACQUES (1796–1874), Belgian statistician and sociologist. Adolphe Quetelet was born in Ghent, the son of a municipal officer who died when Quetelet was 7. By the age of 17 he was teaching mathematics in a private school and at 19 was an instructor at the Royal College in Ghent. In 1817 the University of Ghent was founded and Quetelet, now both instructor and student, received its first doctor of science degree in 1819. He then spent 9 years at the Athenaeum in Brussels, first as professor of elementary mathematics and then as chair of higher mathematics. In his youth he showed literary and artistic skills, writing the libretto for an opera and publishing poetry. Quetelet maintained that it was the influence of J. G. Garnier, professor of astronomy and mathematics, a friend of Fourier and one of Poisson's instructors, who turned him toward mathematics and away from his preference for letters.

His election to the *Académie royale des sciences et belles-lettres de Bruxelles* revitalized the society and fired his lifelong enthusiasm for academic and intellectual organizations. It is said that at the time of his death he was a member of over 100 such bodies.

A visit to Paris at the end of 1824 led Quetelet to meet Poisson, von Humboldt, Fresnel, and, most significantly, Laplace, who instructed him on probability theory. This experience almost certainly planted the seed that led to his "social physics" and his application of statistics to social and moral problems. He was appointed to head the new Royal Observatory of Brussels, and he was to extend one of astronomy's most useful tools, the law of frequency of error, now commonly referred to as the *normal distribution,* to the examination of human characteristics.

The frequency distribution of the chest measurements of almost 6,000 Scottish soldiers followed the distribution. However, the distribution of the heights of French conscripts showed a difference between the observed and expected frequencies around the value of the minimum height for military service. Now the "normal" curve was used for inference, for Quetelet suggested that the excess below the height and the deficiency above it meant that a large number of men had been fraudulently rejected.

It was Quetelet's view that the average value of mental and moral, as well as physical, characteristics represented the ideal type, *l'homme moyen* (the average man) for which nature was constantly striving. This view aroused much criticism. It was suggested that a being who was a composite of all average values would be a monstrosity! Quetelet's own pronouncements were somewhat inconsistent in that he sometimes promoted the view of the "average being" as a universal biological type and at other times suggested that the average differed across groups and circumstances. Nevertheless, his methods were the forerunners of work that attempts to establish norms in biology, anthropology, and the psychology of individual differences. He suffered a stroke in 1855, and afterward, though he continued to write, he never fully regained his intellectual power. He died in 1874 after a short illness.

Bibliography

Cowles, M. (1989). *Statistics in psychology: An historical perspective.* Hillsdale, NJ: Erlbaum.

Hankins, F. H. (1908). *Adolphe Quetelet as statistician.* New York: Columbia University Press.

Lottin, J. (1912). *Quetelet: Statisticien et sociologue* [Quetelet: Statistian and sociologist]. New York: Burt Franklin.

Quetelet, L. A. (1975). *Letters addressed to H. R. H. the Grand Duke of Saxe-Coburg and Gotha on the theory of probabilities as applied to the moral and political sciences* (O. G. Downes, Trans.). Ann Arbor, MI: Xerox University Microfilms. (Original work published in 1835)

Michael Cowles

R

RACIAL IDENTITY. *See* Ethnic and Racial Identity.

RACISM is a term whose popularity stems from its use in the *Report of the National Advisory Commission on Civil Disorders* (1968). Racism is related to concepts such as discrimination, prejudice, and stereotypes (see Dovidio, Brigham, Johnson, & Gaertner, 1996), but it is a more encompassing term than any of these. Discrimination, prejudice, and stereotypes refer, respectively, to unfair social behavior, attitude, and beliefs. *Discrimination* is defined as a selectively unjustified negative *behavior* toward members of the target group that involves denying "individuals or groups of people equality of treatment which they may wish" (Allport, 1954, p. 51). *Prejudice* is commonly defined as an unfair negative *attitude* toward a social group or a person perceived to be a member of that group. A *stereotype* is a generalization of *beliefs* about a group or its members that is unjustified because it reflects faulty thought processes or overgeneralization, factual incorrectness, inordinate rigidity, an inappropriate pattern of attribution, or a rationalization for a prejudiced attitude or discriminatory behavior.

Racism represents the coordinated interaction of particular types of stereotypes, prejudice, and discrimination. According to Jones (1997), racism has three fundamental components. First, racism is rooted in beliefs about group differences (stereotypes) that are assumed to reflect fundamental biological differences. Second, racism also involves well-differentiated negative evaluations and feelings about the other group (prejudice) relative to one's own. Whether or not the other group is described explicitly as inferior, one's own group is believed to be superior. Third, racism reflects the disparate treatment of groups (discrimination) by individuals and institutions in ways that are justified by and tend to perpetuate negative beliefs, attitudes, and outcomes. At its very essence, racism involves not only negative attitudes and beliefs but also the social power that enables these to translate into disparate outcomes that disadvantage other races or offer unique advantages to one's own race at the expense of others. As Feagin and Vera (1995) explain, "Racism is more than a matter of individual prejudice and scattered episodes of discrimination" (p. ix); it involves a widely accepted racist ideology and the power to deny other racial groups the "dignity, opportunities, freedoms, and rewards" that are available to one's own group through "a socially organized set of ideas, attitudes, and practices" (p. 7).

Whereas psychologists have typically studied stereotypes, prejudice, and discrimination in terms of intrapsychic (e.g., cognitive, motivational, or psychodynamic) processes and interactions between individuals (Tajfel & Turner, 1979), racism operates significantly at broader social levels, as well. [*See* Social Identity.] Jones (1997) has identified three applications of the term racism. The first is *individual racism*, which relates to the joint operation of personal stereotypes, prejudice, and discrimination to create and support disparities between members of different groups. The second is *institutional racism*, which refers to the intentional or unintentional manipulation or toleration of institutional policies (e.g., poll taxes, admissions criteria) that unfairly restrict the opportunities of particular groups of people. The third is *cultural racism*. Cultural racism involves beliefs about the superiority of one's racial cultural heritage over that of other races and the expression of this belief in individual actions or institutional policies. Thus, cultural racism includes elements of individual and institutional racism. Because of its broader scope and emphasis on institutions as well as individuals, racism is a common focus of research in political science (see Klinker & Smith, 1999) and sociology (see Feagin & Vera, 1995), as well as in psychology.

Individual Racism

Individual racism is closely affiliated with racial prejudice. Although prejudice has generally been conceptualized as an attitude, prejudice scales often include items concerning the defining elements of racism—specifically, endorsement of statements about innate group differences, the relative inferiority of the other group, and policies that reinforce or exacerbate group differences in fundamental resources (e.g., education, wealth; see Brigham, 1993).

Approaches to individual racism have emphasized both overt and covert influences. Some of these focus on the open expression of individual racism to fulfill personal needs and desires. Much of the traditional work on personality and prejudice was based on a Freudian psychoanalytic model that assumes that prejudice is an indicator of an underlying intrapsychic conflict. The consequences of this conflict are projection, displacement, and the development of an authoritarian personality (Adorno, Frenkel-Brunswik, Levinson, & Sanford, 1950; see also Altemeyer, 1998)—and, ultimately, the expression of individual racism. Alternatively, nonpsychodynamic models have proposed that prejudice and racism are the result of motivations to restore feelings of self-esteem, achieve a sense of superior status, or support a social hierarchy that favors one's group. Social dominance orientation represents an individual difference in "one's general support for group-based systems of social stratification" (Sidanius, Levin, & Pratto, 1998, p. 138). When groups are defined by race, racism is the consequence. Other approaches, which have focused on commonalities across people rather than on individual differences, have viewed prejudice and individual racism as attitudes, like other attitudes, that are acquired through socialization and are functional.

Many contemporary approaches to individual racism acknowledge the persistence of overt, intentional forms of racism but also consider the role of automatic or unconscious processes and indirect expressions of bias. Devine and her colleagues (e.g., Devine & Monteith, 1993), for example, proposed that through common socialization experiences White Americans in general develop a knowledge of cultural stereotypes of Blacks. Because of the repeated exposure, these stereotypes become automatically activated by the actual or symbolic presence of Blacks. Although both high- and low-prejudice people (identified by self-reports) are equally aware of cultural stereotypes and show similar levels of automatic activation, only low-prejudice people make a conscious attempt to prevent those negative stereotypes from influencing their behavior. Moreover, lower prejudice people are more likely to have personal standards prescribing that they behave in a nonprejudiced way toward Blacks, internalize these standards more strongly, and experience more compunction and guilt when they deviate from these standards-which, in turn, motivates efforts to behave in a less biased way in the future.

As the work of Devine and her colleagues illustrates, automatic associations, which may be activated unconsciously, do not necessarily correspond to conscious and deliberative attitudinal expressions. Thus, implicit (automatic and unconscious) and explicit (conscious and deliberative) attitudes and beliefs may be largely unrelated (see Greenwald & Banaji, 1995). A dissociation between automatic responses and self-reported prejudice is also consistent with other conceptions of the current nature of individual racism among whites. Two of these are the aversive racism framework and symbolic (or modern) racism theory. These perspectives suggest that whereas traditional forms of individual racism are direct and overt, contemporary forms are indirect and subtle.

In contrast to "old-fashioned" racism, which is blatant, aversive racism (Dovidio & Gaertner, 1998) represents a subtle, often unintentional, form of bias that characterizes many White Americans who possess strong egalitarian values and who believe that they are nonprejudiced. Aversive racists also possess negative racial feelings and beliefs (which develop through normal cognitive biases and socialization) of which they are unaware or which they try to dissociate from their nonprejudiced self-images. Because aversive racists consciously endorse egalitarian values, they will not discriminate directly and openly in ways that can be attributed to racism; however, because of their negative feelings they will discriminate, often unintentionally, when their behavior can be justified on the basis of some factor other than race (e.g., questionable qualifications for a position). Thus, aversive racists may regularly engage in discrimination while they maintain a nonprejudiced self-image.

According to symbolic racism theory (Sears, 1988) and its related variant modern racism theory (McConahay, 1986), negative feelings toward Blacks that Whites acquire early in life persist into adulthood but are expressed indirectly and symbolically, in terms of opposition to busing or resistance to preferential treatment, rather than directly or overtly, as in support for segregation. McConahay (1986) further proposed that because modern racism involves the rejection of traditional racist beliefs and the displacement of anti-Black feelings onto more abstract social and political issues, modern racists, like aversive racists, are relatively unaware of their racist feelings. However, whereas symbolic and modern racism are subtle forms of contemporary racism that seem to exist among political conservatives, aversive racism seems to be more strongly associated with liberals. Nevertheless, like aversive racism, the negative effects of modern and symbolic racism are observed primarily when discrimination can be justified on the basis of factors other than race.

Both traditional, overt forms of individual racism and contemporary, subtle forms can contribute to social policies that form the basis of institutional racism. In particular, blatant racial prejudice relates to support for policies that unconditionally restrict the rights and opportunities of minority groups, whereas subtle racism is associated with support for the *status quo* or for restrictions when other justifications (e.g., lack of credentials) are available.

Institutional Racism

Institutional racism involves the differential impact of policies, practices, and laws on members of racial groups and on the groups as a whole. Institutional racism can develop from intentional racism (e.g., limiting immigration on the basis of assumptions about the inferiority of other groups), motivations to provide resources to one's own group (e.g., attempts to limit another group's voting power), or as a by-product of policies with one explicit goal but with unintended systematic race-based effects (e.g., differential mandatory penalties for trafficking crack and powder cocaine). Explicitly race-based policies are typically associated with the development of ideologies that justify them. Historically, for example, White Americans developed racial ideologies that helped to justify the laws that enabled them to achieve two important types of economic exploitation: slavery and the seizure of lands from native tribes (Klinker & Smith, 1999). Thus, although the belief that race is a biological construct is fundamental to racism, race is actually a social construction that permits the exploitation of one group over another with the development of the ideology that justifies it (Fields, 1990). What particular groups become racialized (e.g., Blacks, Italians, Jews) depends on the function it serves for the dominant group. For instance, during the period of significant immigration from southern Europe to the United States during the early 1900s that generated social and economic threats to many Americans, Italians were characterized as racially intellectually inferior. In Nazi Germany, Jews were racialized for economic and political gain.

Moreover, although individual racism may produce actions, such as political support for laws and policies, that lead to institutional racism, institutional racism operates at a level independent of individual racism. Institutional racism does not require the active support of individuals, intention to discriminate, or even the awareness of discrimination. Racism becomes "ritualized" in ways that minimize the effort and energy individuals and groups must expend to support it (see Feagin & Vera, 1995). Once laws and policies are established, individual or collective action, intention, and awareness of unfair consequences are important mainly for efforts to oppose them.

Institutional racism is typically not widely recognized as being racially unfair because it is embedded in laws (that are normally assumed to be right and moral), is ritualized, and is accompanied by racial ideologies that justify it. However, what is seen as fair and just can vary with the perspective that one takes. One perspective is microjustice. It includes perceptions of justice that are relevant to specific individuals and focuses on whether transactions between individuals are fair (e.g., procedural justice). Another perspective is macrojustice, which refers to perceptions of fairness that encompass the broader social, historical, legal, and moral contexts and considers whether outcomes over time are fair (distributive justice). Policies and laws that appear to be fair at the micro level may be unfair at a more macro level.

Because institutional racism is not necessarily intentional or explicitly race based, its operation is often inferred from systematically disparate outcomes between racial groups that can logically be traced back to differential and unfair impact of policies, even those that might appear to be non-race-related. These effects may appear economically (e.g., in loan policies), educationally (e.g., in admission and financial aid policies), in the media (e.g., the overrepresentation of groups associated with violence or poverty), in the criminal justice system (e.g., racial differences in the death penalty), and in mental and physical health (e.g., social stress; see Jones, 1997). Racial ideologies and values often also become deeply embedded in the fiber of one's culture and thus define what is normal and appropriate for the society in general, a phenomenon known as cultural racism.

Cultural Racism

When one group exerts the power to define cultural values for the society, cultural racism occurs. It involves not only the preference for one's groups's culture, heritage, and values (ethnocentrism) but also the imposition of this culture on other groups. As a consequence, the essence of racism is communicated to and by members of all racial groups in everyday activities and is passed on across generations.

Jones (1997), for example, has identified five fundamental domains of human experience on which cultures differ: time, rhythm, improvisation, oral expression, and spirituality (the TRIOS model). Dominant U.S. culture has valued a future time orientation, stable and predictable rhythms of activity, planning ahead rather than improvising, written over oral expression, and a belief in personal control instead of an emphasis on spirituality. Beyond this model, cultures differ systematically in their emphasis on individual outcomes or collective outcomes. The United States reflects an individualistic culture. To the extent that adherence to these cultural standards is valued, rewarded, and defined as normal at the expense of racial groups who express other cultural values, cultural racism may be operating.

Summary and Conclusions

Racism represents a particular constellation of racial stereotypes, prejudice, and discrimination. Stereotypic differences are assumed to reflect racial differences; prejudicial attitudes may be in the form of negative attitudes toward other racial groups or reflect positive beliefs in the racial superiority of one's own group; discrimination may occur intentionally or unintentionally, or personally or impersonally. Whereas individual racism is closely affiliated with prejudice, institutional racism involves the operation of social and institutional policies that unfairly benefit the dominant group and/or unfairly adversely affect other racial groups. Cultural racism, which includes elements of both individual and institutional racism, represents the imposition of the dominant group's cultural standards on other racial groups in the society. Although racism may involve overt antipathy and bigoted intent, it also can operate unconsciously but pervasively at the individual, institutional, or cultural level. Because it can become ritualized in custom and policy and rationalized by racial ideologies, racism can often go unrecognized or unacknowledged.

Changes in legislation that have made discrimination immoral and illegal have helped to address overt, traditional forms of racism. Contemporary forms of racism, however, continue to exist and affect the lives of people in subtle but significant ways by influencing access to important resources. Racism that is institutionalized and becomes embedded in the culture can also affect the personal identities of majority and minority group members in fundamental ways. In particular, racial identities develop and diverge as a function of one's group's experiences and how one interprets, internalizes, and adjusts to those experiences. The racial identity and culture of Black Americans, for example, have been hypothesized to reflect an evolutionary component, which developed from the cultural foundation of an African past, and a reactionary component, which is an adaptation to the historical and contemporary challenges of minority status in the United States. Helms (1995) proposes that Black racial identities may involve different stages (or statuses), such as conformity to the standards of the dominant group and the devaluing of one's own racial group, immersion-emersion that reflects the idealization of one's own group and the rejection of the dominant group, and integrative awareness that represents the valuing of one's own group with the capacity to collaborate constructively with other groups. In addition, because of the pervasiveness of racism, Black Americans may internalize racial stereotypes that, when activated, even without endorsement, can adversely influence their performance in significant ways (e.g., on achievement tests; Steele, 1998). Thus, the unique power of racism resides in how it can shape members of different groups to think, interpret, behave, and react in ways that contribute to the perpetuation of racial disparities and reinforce racism, without necessarily involving their intention, awareness, or active support.

[*See also* Discrimination; *and* Prejudice.]

Bibliography

Adorno, T. W., Frenkel-Brunswik, E., Levinson, D. J., & Sanford, R. N. (1950). *The authoritarian personality.* New York: Harper.

Allport, G. W. (1954). *The nature of prejudice.* Reading, MA: Addison-Wesley.

Altemeyer, B. (1998). The other "authoritarian personality." In M. P. Zanna (Ed.), *Advances in experimental social psychology* (Vol. 30, pp. 47–92). San Diego, CA: Academic Press.

Brigham, J. C. (1993). College students' racial attitudes. *Journal of Applied Social Psychology, 23,* 1933–1967.

Devine, P. G., & Monteith, M. J. (1993). The role of discrepancy-associated affect in prejudice reduction. In D. M. Mackie & D. L. Hamilton (Eds.), *Affect, cognition, and stereotyping: Interactive processes in intergroup perception* (pp. 317–344). Orlando, FL: Academic Press.

Dovidio, J. F., Brigham, J. C., Johnson, B. T., & Gaertner, S. L. (1996). Stereotyping, prejudice, and discrimination: Another look. In N. Macrae, M. Hewstone, & C. Stangor (Eds.), *Foundations of stereotypes and stereotyping* (pp. 276–319). New York: Guilford Press.

Dovidio, J. F., & Gaertner, S. L. (1998). On the nature of contemporary prejudice: The causes, consequences, and challenges of aversive racism. In J. Eberhardt & S. T. Fiske (Eds.), *Confronting racism: The problem and the response* (pp. 3–32). Newbury Park, CA: Sage.

Feagin, J. R., & Vera, H. (1995). *White racism.* New York: Routledge.

Fields, B. J. (1990, May/June). Slavery, race, and ideology in the United States of America. *New Left Review, 181* 95–118.

Greenwald, A. G., & Banaji, M. R. (1995). Implicit social cognition: Attitudes, self-esteem, and stereotypes. *Psychological Review, 102,* 4–27.

Helms, J. E. (1995). An update of Helms' white and people of color racial identity models. In J. G. Ponterotto, J. M. Casas, L. A. Suzuki, & C. M. Alexander (Eds.), *Handbook of multicultural counseling* (pp. 181–198). Thousand Oaks, CA: Sage.

Jones, J. M. (1997). *Prejudice and racism* (2nd ed.). New York: McGraw-Hill.

Klinker, P. A., & Smith, R. M. (1999). *The unsteady march: The rise and decline of American commitments to racial equality*. New York: Free Press.

McConahay, J. B. (1986). Modern racism, ambivalence, and the modern racism scale. In J. F. Dovidio & S. L. Gaertner (Eds.), *Prejudice, discrimination, and racism* (pp. 91–125). Orlando, FL: Academic Press.

Report of the National Advisory Commission on Civil Disorders (1968). New York: Bantam Books.

Sears, D. O. (1988). Symbolic racism. In P. A. Katz & D. A. Taylor (Eds.), *Eliminating racism: Profiles in controversy* (pp. 53–84). New York: Plenum Press.

Sidanius, J., Levin, S., & Pratto, F. (1998). Hierarchical group relations, institutional terror, and the dynamics of the criminal justice system. In J. Eberhardt & S. T. Fiske (Eds.), *Confronting racism: The problem and the response* (pp. 136–165). Newbury Park, CA: Sage.

Steele, C. M. (1998). A threat in the air: How stereotypes shape intellectual identity and performance. In J. Eberhardt & S. T. Fiske (Eds.), *Confronting racism: The problem and the response* (pp. 202–233). Newbury Park, CA: Sage.

Tajfel, H., & Turner, J. C. (1979). An integrative theory of intergroup conflict. In W. G. Austin & S. Worchel (Eds.), *The social psychology of intergroup relations* (pp. 33–48). Monterey, CA: Brooks/Cole.

John Dovidio

RAMÓN Y CAJAL, SANTIAGO (1852–1934), Spanish neuroanatomist. As described in his autobiography (1901, 1917/1937), Ramón y Cajal, also known as Cajal, was born in Petilla de Aragon. He was rebellious and difficult in his youth. Not one for school, he loved to sketch and wished to become an artist. His father, a surgeon, opposed the artist idea and managed to interest his son in neuroanatomy. Cajal then settled down and worked toward his medical degree.

After he received his diploma in 1873, he enlisted in the army and just barely survived malaria during service in Cuba. Once discharged, his health improved, and he received a temporary appointment at his alma mater, the medical school in Zaragoza.

Anxious to find a more secure position, Cajal traveled to Madrid to take an examination for a professorship. There he "discovered" the microscope and immediately bought one for himself. After he was appointed director of the anatomical museum in Zaragoza, he married and fathered the first of his six children.

In 1884, Cajal accepted the chair of anatomy in Valencia. Three years later, while in Madrid to administer anatomical examinations, he visited Luis Simarro, who introduced him to Camillo Golgi's silver stain. Cajal became enamored with the potential of the stain but first had to overcome its uncertain character. Thus, he set out to improve his slides in a number of ways, including cutting thicker sections and using birds and young mammals, because they have little myelin.

Cajal could find no evidence for neurons physically fusing into the sorts of nets envisioned by Joseph von Gerlach or Golgi. He therefore rejected "reticular" theory and began to promote the idea that neurons are independent units, just like other body cells. At the time, he did not know that anatomists William His and August Forel had also suggested that neurons may communicate by simple contact or by sparks jumping across tiny gaps (called "synapses" by Charles Scott Sherrington in 1893).

Cajal then financed his own journal to publish his findings. Although he sent copies of his *Revista Trimestral* to major research centers in northern Europe, he soon realized that his target audience did not read Spanish. Hence, he decided to show his slides at a meeting of the German Anatomical Society in Berlin. There, in 1889, he presented his material and argued convincingly that neurons do not fuse with each other (an idea that would become known as the "neuron doctrine"). Albrecht von Kölliker, who previously had been a reticularist, became his strongest supporter at this time.

Upon his return to Spain, Cajal continued his neuroanatomical research. In 1890, he described how a developing neuron sends forth an axon with a clublike head, which pushes other cells aside as it grows toward its target. He called the battering ram a "growth cone." The idea that the nervous system is dynamic soon led to speculation that closure and separation at the synapse could account for learning and forgetting, wakefulness and sleep, and other phenomena.

Cajal also began to write that the nervous impulse must travel from the dendrites to the cell body and then to the axon. He based the notion of a physiological one-way street strictly on his anatomy. In 1891, he called this idea the "law of dynamic polarization."

After he moved to the University of Madrid in 1892, Cajal continued to be his era's leading neuroanatomist. For his sustained efforts to describe and understand the structural organization of the nervous system—from the retina and olfactory bulb to the cerebral cortex—he was awarded the 1906 Nobel Prize. The honor was shared with Camillo Golgi who, to Cajal's surprise, still supported the reticular theory.

Cajal wrote more than a hundred articles and more than a dozen books on neuroanatomy after he returned from Stockholm as a national hero. A complete listing of his works can be found at the back of recent reprintings of his autobiography. His most important neuroanatomy books have been translated into English and French and include *Histologie du système nerveux de l'homme et des vertébrés, Degeneration and Regeneration of the Nervous System, Neuron Theory or Reticular Theory?, Studies on the Cerebral Cortex,* and *New Ideas on the Structure of the Nervous System in Man and Vertebrates.*

Santiago Ramón y Cajal received almost every honor that could be bestowed upon a scientist. Working for years by himself on previously neglected Spanish soil, he set neuroanatomy on its modern course and established a standard of excellence for brain researchers around the world.

Bibliography

Works by Ramón y Cajal

Cajal, S. Ramón y. (1909, 1911). *Histologie du système nerveux de l'homme et des vertébrés* (2 vols., L. Azoulay, Trans.). Paris: Maloine.

Cajal, S. Ramón y. (1928). *Degeneration and regeneration of the nervous system* (R. M. May, Ed. and Trans.). London: Oxford University Press.

Cajal, S. Ramón y. (1937). *Recollections of my life* (E. H. Craigie, Trans.). Philadelphia: American Philosophical Society. (Original work published 1901, 1917, 2 vols.)

Cajal, S. Ramón y. (1954). *Neuron theory or reticular theory?* (M. U. Purkiss and C. A. Fox, Trans). Madrid: Instituto Ramón y Cajal. (Original work published 1935)

Cajal, S. Ramón y. (1955). *Studies on the cerebral cortex* (L. M. Kraft, Trans.). London: Lloyd-Luke.

Cajal, S. Ramón y. (1988). *Cajal on the cerebral cortex: An annotated translation of the complete writings* (J. DeFelipe and E. G. Jones, Trans.). New York: Oxford University Press.

Cajal, S. Ramón y. (1990). *New ideas on the structure of the nervous system in man and vertebrates* (N. Swanson and L. W. Swanson, Trans.). Cambridge, MA: MIT Press.

Works about Ramón y Cajal

Cannon, D. F. (1949). *Explorer of the human brain: The life of Santiago Ramón y Cajal.* New York: Henry Schuman.

Shepherd, G. (1991). *Foundations of the neuron doctrine.* New York: Oxford University Press.

Sherrington, C. S. (1949). Santiago Ramón y Cajal, 1852–1934. *Obituary Notices of the Royal Society, 4,* 425–441.

Stanley Finger

RANDOMIZED EXPERIMENTS are used to answer questions about the real world. The design of a randomized experiment can take many different forms. The simplest experimental design is the randomization and analysis plan used with a t test for independent samples. Consider a randomized experiment to determine whether behavioral therapy or hypnosis is more effective in helping smokers break the habit. The independent variable, called treatment A, is the two types of therapy. Let the dependent variable be a self-report rating of desire for a cigarette 3 months after therapy. The two levels of treatment A are denoted by a lower case letter a and a subscript: a_1 denotes behavioral therapy and a_2 denotes hypnosis. Suppose that 30 smokers who want to stop smoking are available to participate in the experiment. We want to randomly assign $n = 15$ smokers to each of the $p = 2$ therapies so that the $(np)!/(n!)^p = 155{,}117{,}520$ possible assignments have the same probability. This can be done by numbering the smokers from 1 to 30 and drawing numbers from a table of random numbers. The smokers who were assigned the first 15 numbers drawn between 1 and 30 are assigned to treatment level a_1; the remaining smokers are assigned to a_2. The layout for this randomized experiment is shown in Figure 1.

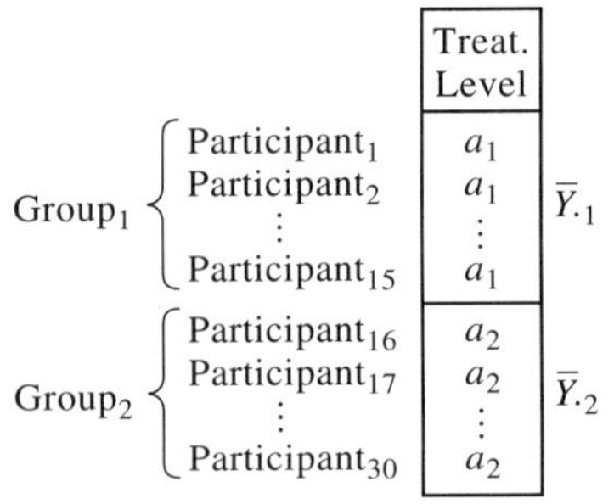

RANDOMIZED EXPERIMENTS. Figure 1. A layout for a t test for an independent-samples design in which 30 participants have been randomly assigned to two levels of treatment A. The mean cigarette consumption for participants in treatment levels a_1 and a_2 is denoted by $\overline{Y}_{\cdot 1}$ and $\overline{Y}_{\cdot 2}$, respectively.

This example illustrates an essential feature of randomized experiments: the random assignment of participants to treatment levels. Random assignment has two purposes. First, it helps distribute the idiosyncratic characteristics of participants over the treatment levels so that they do not selectively bias the outcome of the experiment. Second, random assignment permits the computation of an unbiased estimate of experimental error effects and helps to ensure that the error effects are statistically independent. The use of random assignment gradually gained acceptance in the 1920s and 1930s as a result of Ronald A. Fisher's pioneering research and writing in *The Design of Experiments* (1934) and *Statistical Methods for Research Workers* (1925). Prior to Fisher's work, most researchers used systematic schemes not subject to the laws of chance to assign participants to treatment levels.

Fisher is best known for developing the analysis of variance, ANOVA, which is a procedure for testing the omnibus null hypothesis that $p \geq 2$ population means are equal. The t test for the independent-samples design described earlier involves randomly assigning participants to two treatment levels. A completely randomized ANOVA design, also called a one-way or one-factor design, extends this procedure to two or more treatment levels. For example, if 45 smokers are available to participate in the smoking experiment, they can be randomly assigned to three therapies, say, behavioral modification, hypnosis, and cognitive therapy. The layout for this randomized experiment is the same as that shown in Figure 1, except that there are three treatment levels, a_1, a_2, and a_3, and three groups of participants.

Fisher popularized two other principles of good experimentation: replication and local control, or blocking. Replication in this context refers to the observation of two or more participants under identical experimental conditions. [*See* Replication in Research.] Fisher observed that replication enables a researcher to estimate experimental error effects and obtain a more precise estimate of treatment effects. Blocking, on the other hand, is an experimental procedure for isolating variation attributable to a nuisance variable. As the name suggests, nuisance variables are undesired sources of variation that can affect the dependent variable. There are many sources of nuisance variation. Differences among individuals is one. Other sources include variation in the presentation of instructions to participants, changes in environmental conditions, and errors in recording participants' responses. Three experimental approaches are used to deal with nuisance variables:

1. Hold the variable constant.
2. Assign participants to the treatment levels randomly so that known and unsuspected sources of variation among the participants are distributed over the entire experiment and do not affect just one or a limited number of treatment levels.
3. Include the nuisance variable as one of the factors in the experiment.

The last approach uses local control or blocking to isolate variation attributable to the nuisance variable so that it does not appear in estimates of treatment and error effects.

Let's reconsider the cigarette smoking experiment. It is reasonable to assume that difficulty in breaking the smoking habit is related to the number of cigarettes that a person smokes per day. The design of our experiment can be improved by isolating this nuisance variable. This can be accomplished by using the experimental design for a dependent-samples *t* test. Instead of randomly assigning 30 participants to the treatment levels, we can form pairs of participants who are matched with respect to number of cigarettes smoked per day. A simple way to match the participants is to rank them in terms of the number of cigarettes they smoke. The participants ranked 1 and 2 are assigned to block one, those ranked 3 and 4 are assigned to block two, and so on. In this example, 15 blocks of matched

	Treat. Level	Treat. Level
Block_1	a_1	a_2
Block_2	a_1	a_2
Block_3	a_1	a_2
⋮	⋮	⋮
Block_{15}	a_1	a_2
	$\bar{Y}_{\cdot 1}$	$\bar{Y}_{\cdot 2}$

RANDOMIZED EXPERIMENTS. Figure 2. A layout for a *t* test for dependent-samples design in which each block contains two participants whose cigarette consumption prior to the experiment was similar. The two participants in each block are randomly assigned to the treatment levels.

participants can be formed. The participants in each block are then randomly assigned to the two types of therapy. The layout for this experiment is shown in Figure 2. If our hunch is correct, that difficulty in breaking the smoking habit is related to the number of cigarettes smoked per day, the *t* test for dependent-samples design should result in a more powerful test of a false null hypothesis than the *t* test for independent-samples design. The increased power results from isolating the nuisance variable of number of cigarettes smoked per day and thereby obtaining a more precise estimate of treatment effects and a reduction in the size of the error effects.

A randomized block ANOVA design extends the blocking procedure used with a *t* test for dependent-samples design to two or more treatment levels. For example, if 45 smokers are available to participate in the smoking experiment, they can be assigned to blocks of size three so that those within a block are more similar with respect to the number of cigarettes smoked per day than those in different blocks. The three matched participants in each block are then randomly assigned to the three treatment levels. The layout for this randomized experiment is the same as that shown in Figure 2, except that there are three treatment levels, a_1, a_2, and a_3.

Any variable that is correlated with the dependent variable other than the independent variable can be used to form blocks. In the smoking example, a block consisted of participants who were matched on a relevant variable. A block can consist of identical twins or litter mates who are matched with respect to genetic characteristics. Matching may result from a process of mutual selection, as in the case of a husband and wife, who are often similar in socioeconomic background, educational level, interests, and values. Alternatively, a block can consist of one participant who is observed under each of the treatment levels. If repeated mea-

	c_1	c_2	c_3
b_1	a_1	a_2	a_3
b_2	a_2	a_3	a_1
b_3	a_3	a_1	a_2

RANDOMIZED EXPERIMENTS. Figure 3. A three-by-three Latin square; a_1, a_2, and a_3 denote the levels of treatment A; b_1, b_2, and b_3 denote the levels of nuisance variable B; and c_1, c_2, and c_3 denote the levels of nuisance variable C.

sures are obtained, the order of presentation of the treatment levels should be randomized independently for each participant if the nature of the treatment permits it.

The randomized block design enables a researcher to isolate one nuisance variable. A Latin square design uses a similar blocking procedure to isolate two nuisance variables. The design derives its name from an ancient puzzle that was concerned with the number of different ways that Latin letters can be arranged in a square matrix so that each letter appears once in each row and once in each column. An example of a 3×3 Latin square is shown in Figure 3. An ANOVA design based on this Latin square enables a researcher to test the hypothesis that the three population means for treatment A are equal while isolating the effects of two nuisance variables, one assigned to the rows of the square and one assigned to the columns. The randomization procedures for a Latin square design are more complicated than those described earlier. (See the experimental design books in the bibliography.)

The three simple ANOVA designs—completely randomized, randomized block, and Latin square designs—are called building block designs by this author because they can be combined to form more complex factorial and hierarchical designs. Factorial and hierarchical designs are used to test null hypotheses for two or more

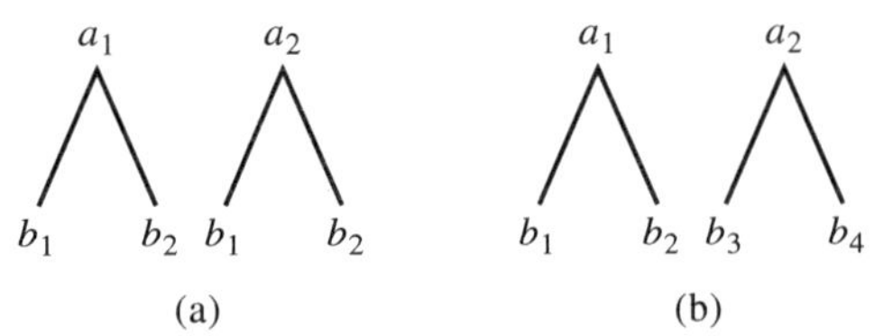

RANDOMIZED EXPERIMENTS. Figure 4. In (a), treatments A and B are crossed because each level of treatment B appears once and only once with each level of treatment A, and vice versa. In (b), treatment B is nested in treatment A because b_1 and b_2 appear only with a_1, while b_3 and b_4 appear only with a_2.

		Treat. Comb.	
Group_1	Participant_1	a_1b_1	$\bar{Y}_{\cdot 11}$
	⋮	⋮	
	Participant_n	a_1b_1	
Group_2	Participant_{n+1}	a_1b_2	$\bar{Y}_{\cdot 12}$
	⋮	⋮	
	Participant_{2n}	a_1b_2	
Group_3	$\text{Participant}_{2n+1}$	a_2b_1	$\bar{Y}_{\cdot 21}$
	⋮	⋮	
	Participant_{3n}	a_2b_1	
Group_4	$\text{Participant}_{3n+1}$	a_2b_2	$\bar{Y}_{\cdot 22}$
	⋮	⋮	
	Participant_{4n}	a_2b_2	

RANDOMIZED EXPERIMENTS. Figure 5. A layout for a two-treatment completely randomized factorial design in which $4n$ participants are randomly assigned to the $pq = (2)(2) = 4$ combinations of treatments A and B.

treatments. The distinguishing feature of a factorial design is that the levels of all treatments are crossed. Two treatments are completely crossed if each level of one treatment appears once with each level of the other treatment, and vice versa. In a hierarchical design, the levels of at least one treatment are nested in those of another, and the levels of the remaining treatments are completely crossed. For example, In a two-treatment completely randomized hierarchical design, treatment B is nested in treatment A so that each level of B appears with only one level of A. The distinction between crossed and nested treatments is illustrated in Figure 4.

From the standpoint of randomization and analysis, the simplest factorial design is the two-treatment completely randomized factorial design, with p levels of treatment A and q levels of treatment B. The treatment combinations of the design are obtained by completely crossing the levels of two treatments, as illustrated in Figure 4(a). Participants are randomly assigned to the pq treatment combinations. The layout for the design is shown in Figure 5. This design is sometimes called a two-way classification design or a two-factor design. These designations are not precise because they could refer to any of ten different factorial designs.

A two-treatment completely randomized factorial design enables a researcher to test null hypotheses for treatment A, treatment B, and the $A \times B$ interaction. The interaction test is unique to factorial designs. Two treatments are said to interact if differences in the dependent variable for the levels of one treatment are different at two or more levels of the other treatment. When two treatments interact, a graph in which treatment-combination means are connected by lines will always reveal at least two nonparallel lines for one or more segments of the lines. The presence of a signifi-

		Treat. Comb.	Treat. Comb.	
Group$_1$ a_1	Block$_1$	a_1b_1	a_1b_2	
	⋮	⋮	⋮	$\bar{Y}_{.1.}$
	Block$_n$	a_1b_1	a_1b_2	
Group$_2$ a_2	Block$_{n+1}$	a_2b_1	a_2b_2	
	⋮	⋮	⋮	$\bar{Y}_{.2.}$
	Block$_{2n}$	a_2b_1	a_2b_2	
		$\bar{Y}_{..1}$	$\bar{Y}_{..2}$	

RANDOMIZED EXPERIMENTS. Figure 6. A layout for a two-treatment split-plot factorial design in which $2n$ blocks, each containing $q = 2$ matched participants, are randomly assigned to the $p = 2$ levels of treatment A. The matched participants in each block are randomly assigned to the q levels of treatment B.

cant interaction indicates that tests of the respective treatments must be interpreted with caution.

Factorial and hierarchical designs also can be constructed from two or more randomized block designs by crossing or nesting, respectively, the treatment levels of the designs. For example, a two-treatment randomized block factorial design can be constructed by crossing the p and q treatment levels of two randomized block designs in each of n blocks. Then n sets of pq-matched participants are randomly assigned to the pq treatment combinations in the n blocks. Alternatively, a block can consist of one participant who is observed pq times. The randomization procedures described earlier for a randomized block design should be used. If either p or q is moderately large, the number of treatment combinations in each block may be prohibitively large. R. A. Fisher and Frank Yates addressed this problem in the late 1920s by developing confounding schemes in which only a portion of the treatment combinations in the experiment are assigned to each block. Their work was extended in the 1940s by David J. Finney and Oscar Kempthorne. The benefit of confounding, reducing the number of treatment combinations in a block or an experiment, comes at a price. The effects of the sources of variation that are confounded are indistinguishable. The two-treatment split-plot factorial design, the most popular design in the behavioral and social sciences, confounds treatment A with groups of participants to reduce the number of treatment combinations in each block from pq to q. The design is constructed by combining a completely randomized design having p treatment levels with a randomized block design having q treatment levels. The layout for the design is shown in Figure 6.

The block size of randomized experiments also can be reduced by confounding one or more interactions with groups of participants. This form of confounding produces randomized block and Latin square confounded factorial designs. A third form of confounding, treatment-interaction confounding, reduces the number of treatment combinations that must be included in a randomized experiment to some fraction—½, ⅓, ¼, ⅛, ⅑, and so on—of the total number of treatment combinations. These designs, which are called fractional factorial designs, are often used as pilot studies to identify the most promising independent variables.

[*See also* Experimental Psychology.]

Bibliography

Cochran, W. G., & Cox, G. M. (1950). *Experimental designs.* New York: Wiley. This classic textbook was one of the first to contain detailed plans for confounded and fractional factorial designs and incomplete block designs.

Edwards, L. K. (Ed.). (1993). *Applied analysis of variance in behavioral science.* New York: Marcel Dekker. Advanced topics in randomized experiments are critically examined by leading methodologists.

Federer, W. T. (1955). *Experimental design: Theory and application.* New York: Macmillan. This classic textbook reflects the impact of agricultural research on the design of experiments.

Fisher, R. A. (1990). *Statistical methods, experimental design, and scientific inference.* New York: Oxford University Press. This is a reissue in a single volume of three of Fisher's more influential textbooks.

Keppel, G. (1991). *Design and analysis: A researcher's handbook* (3rd ed.). Englewood Cliffs, NJ: Prentice Hall. This textbook provides a readable introduction to experimental design for researchers in the social sciences.

Kirk, R. E. (1995). *Experimental design: Procedures for the behavioral sciences* (3rd ed.). Pacific Grove, CA: Brooks/Cole. This textbook provides comprehensive coverage of all of the experimental designs used in behavioral and educational research.

Maxwell, S. E., & Delaney, H. D. (1990). *Designing experiments and analyzing data.* Belmont, CA: Wadsworth. This textbook examines experimental designs from a model-comparison perspective.

Rosnow, R. L., & Rosenthal, R. (1997). *People studying people: Artifacts and ethics in behavioral research.* New York: Freeman. This textbook provides a readable introduction to issues surrounding the use of human participants in randomized experiments.

Winer, B. J., Brown, D. R., & Michels, K. M. (1991). *Statistical principles in experimental design* (3rd ed.). New York: McGraw-Hill. This book has been a standard reference on experimental design for behavioral scientists since 1961.

Roger E. Kirk

RANK, OTTO (1884–1939), Austrian psychoanalyst. Along with Sandor Ferenczi, Rank pioneered short-term dynamic psychotherapy and anticipated many trends in contemporary analytic theory, notably self-psychology and object-relations theory (Menaker, 1982). Born Otto Rosenfeld, in Vienna, Rank had an alchoholic, occasionally abusive, and deeply indifferent father whose name he renounced in his late teens (Roazen, 1974). He came from humble origins and exerted an extraordinary effort to educate himself while working at various menial jobs—machinist and glass-blower, among others. In 1904, he read Freud's *Interpretation of Dreams* and began work on a monograph, *Der Kunstler* (The Artist), which he presented to Sigmund Freud in 1905, and which was published in 1907. Freud read it and appointed Rank as secretary of the Viennese Psychoanalytic Society in 1906, educating him at his own expense. In 1912, Rank defended his doctoral dissertation on the Lohengrin Saga at the University of Vienna. Being well versed in literature, history, and comparative mythology, Rank—along with Hanns Sachs—became coeditor of Freud's journal for culture and social psychology, *Imago*, when Jung vacated that post. In response to Jung's "defection," he was also appointed to Freud's "Secret Committee," which included Sachs, Ernst Jones, Karl Abraham, Max Eitington, and Sandor Ferenczi, who later became a close personal friend.

In 1914, Rank published *The Myth of the Birth of the Hero* (Rank, 1964), the most Freudian of all his books. The following year Rank was conscripted. In 1924, he coauthored with Sandor Ferenczi *The Development of Psychoanalysis*, which advocated abandoning the passive, neutral stance favored by Freud in favor of a more active technique. It also raised the prospect of collaborative efforts with other therapeutic approaches (Ferenczi & Rank, 1956). This alarmed other committee members and elicited admonitions from Freud about excessive therapeutic optimism (Grosskurth, 1991).

Rank's book *The Trauma of Birth*, also published in 1924, won a more positive response from Freud but elicited howls of indignation from committee members. Here Rank treated separation from the mother as the deepest source of unconscious anxiety, rather than (Oedipal) castration anxiety, which by his account was really a symbolic reenactment of the earlier separation from the mother (Rank, 1973)—an idea Ferenczi defended that same year (in slightly modified form) in *Thalassa: A Theory of Genitality* (Ferenczi, 1989). For all its faults, *The Trauma of Birth* was a probing, thoughtful book, which forced Freud to reconsider his own views on anxiety, issuing in a fruitful reformulation in 1926 in *Inhibitions, Symptoms, and Anxiety* (Freud, 1989).

In *The Trauma of Birth*, Rank attempted to carve out a place for himself as an independent thinker. Jones and Abraham would not tolerate this while Freud was alive, so Rank moved to Paris and, ultimately, to New York in 1934. Initially, Rank tried to sustain a certain loyalty in opposition, hoping Freud would see through the self-interested machinations of Jones and Abraham. He even tried to enlist Ferenczi's support. When Ferenczi abandoned him in 1926, Rank became bitterly disillusioned with Freud. The first published evidence of this is in *Art and Artist*, published in 1932 (Rank, 1968). Subsequent efforts, like *Truth and Reality* in 1936 (Rank, 1978) and *Beyond Psychology* in 1941 (Rank, 1958) also contained scathing dismissals of Freud, along with lengthy reflections on the urge to self-creation, the centrality of will in personality formation, the longing for surrogate immortality, and the perils of conformity.

Professionally speaking, Rank flourished in America, where his impact on the artistic community was electric and was amply attested to in the writings of Anais Nin and Henry Miller, among others. In the therapeutic arena, he had a profound influence on clinical social work, especially in Philadelphia, and on humanistic psychologists Carl Rogers and Ernest Becker. But like many European émigrés, he never became very fond of America, and he died in exile and in anguish. In 1903, before meeting Freud, Rank had contracted rheumatic fever, which left his heart permanently damaged. His conflicts with Freud and his followers, the loss of Ferenczi and eventually of his wife Beata (who was secretly loyal to Freud and whom he divorced in 1938) left him acutely vulnerable and depleted (Roazen, 1974). He died of a heart attack on 31 October 1939.

[*Many of the people mentioned in this article are the subjects of independent biographical entries.*]

Bibliography

Works by Rank

Rank, O. (1958). *Beyond psychology*. New York: Dover.

Rank, O. (1964). *The myth of the birth of the hero*. New York: Vintage Books.

Rank, O. (1968). *Art and artist: Creative urge and personality development*. New York: Norton.

Rank, O. (1973). *The trauma of birth*. New York: Harper & Row.

Rank, O. (1978). *Truth and reality*. New York: Norton.

Roazen, P. (1974). *Freud and his followers*. New York: New American Library.

Works about Rank

Ferenczi, S. (Repr. 1989). *Thalassa: A theory of genitality*. Maresfield: Karnac.

Ferenczi, S., & Rank, O. (1956). *The development of psychoanalysis*. New York: Dover.

Freud, S. (1989). *Inhibitions, symptoms, and anxiety*. New York: Norton.

Grosskurth, P. (1991). *The secret ring: Freud's inner circle*

and the politics of psychoanalysis. New York: Addison-Wesley.
Menaker, E. (1982). *Otto Rank: A rediscovered legacy*. New York: Columbia University Press.

Daniel Burston

RANSCHBURG, PAL (1870–1945). Hungarian psychiatrist and experimental psychologist. Born in Györ, Hungary, Ranschburg graduated from the Medical Faculty of Budapest University in 1894 and worked at the university's Psychiatric and Neuropathological Clinic until 1902. Supported by the donation of a grateful recovered patient, he founded the first Hungarian psychological laboratory at the Teacher's College of Mental Hygiene in 1902, directing it until 1928. This laboratory later developed into the Psychological Institute of the Hungarian Academy of Sciences and remains one of the leading psychological institutes in the country. After resigning from the clinic, Ranschburg supported himself with his private practice in neurology and psychiatry, never receiving any fee for his psychological and research activities.

In addition to his role as the founder of experimental psychology in Hungary, Ranschburg worked to get psychology established and recognized as an independent profession by his countrymen. Consequently, he was honored in 1928 by being elected as the first president of the Hungarian Psychological Association.

Ranschburg's scientific research was linked to his empirical work on medical, clinical, and mental hygienic issues. Like many of his era's scientists, he was greatly concerned with the problem of how learned material is recalled and what factors play a role in forgetting. Research on memory and its underlying mechanisms engaged many psychologists of the late nineteenth century, from Hermann Ebbinghaus to William James's student Mary Calkins. Several colleagues of Georg Elias Müller, working in the psychological laboratory at Göttingen, Germany, were among them. Under Müller's direction they explored retroactive inhibition as the main cause of forgetting. In this phenomenon, later-learned material inhibits the recall of similar material learned earlier.

Ranschburg's research followed the path of Müller. In 1901, he conducted memory experiments comparing psychiatric patients with normal controls. The following year, on the basis of the results, he formulated and published his statements on homogeneous inhibition, or what became known as the Ranschburg effect. In this phenomenon, similarity of elements has an impeding effect on memory performance. A series of elements seen or heard for a short time is retained in memory with more difficulty when two or more of the to-be-remembered elements are the same or similar. Inaccuracies appear at the time the similar elements are reproduced, as when a subject recalls the number 141993 as 141903. Difficulty arises, according to Ranschburg (1902), because the similar elements strive to merge into a single one.

In the following decades, Ranschburg's inhibition had many supporters and opponents in the scientific literature. Karl Stumpf at the University of Berlin, Hugo Münsterberg at Harvard University, and many others worked on the phenomenon of homogeneous inhibition and tried to explain its occurrence. For example, Münsterberg, the first theoretician of psychotechnics and the psychology of work, repeated Ranschburg's experiments and related the phenomenon of homogeneous inhibition to the problem of montony in the workplace (Münsterberg, 1912).

The *Prägnanz* principle of form perception, drawn from Gestalt psychology, has been used to explain the phenomenon of homogeneous inhibition, on the assumption that the similar elements easily form a single whole in perception. Other research (Wolf and Jahnke, 1968) has shown that the Ranschburg effect decreases when the subject is informed about the phenomenon in advance.

[*Many of the people mentioned in this article are the subjects of independent biographical entries.*]

Bibliography

Jahnke, J. C. (1969). The Ranschburg effect. *Psychological Review, 76*, 592–605.
Münsterberg, H. (1913). *Psychology and industrial efficiency*. Boston: Houghton Mifflin. (Original work published 1912)
Ranschburg, P. (1902). Über Hemmung gleichzeitiger Reizwirkungen: Experimenteller Beitrag zur Lehre von Bedingungen der Aufmerksamkeit. *Zeitschrift für Psychologie und Physiologie der Sinnesorgane, 30*, 39–86.
Ranschburg, P. (1905). Über die Bedeutung der Ahnlichkeit beim Erlernen, Behalten, und bei der Reproduktion. *Journal für Psychologie und Neurologie, 5*, 93–127.
Wolf, T. M., & Jahnke, J. C. (1968). The effects of intraserial repetition on short-term recognition and recall. *Journal of Experimental Psychology, 77*, 572–580.

György Kiss

RAPAPORT, DAVID (1911–1960). Hungarian American psychologist. Rapaport was born in Budapest in 1911, studied mathematics and physics at the University of Budapest, and received his doctorate in psychology from the Royal Hungarian University. His doctoral thesis was on the history of the concept of association from Bacon to Kant. He came to the United States in 1938 and after working briefly at Mount Sinai Hospital in New York and Osawatomie State Hospital in Kansas, he moved to the Menninger Clinic in Topeka, Kansas, in 1940. After a period of time, he became chief psychologist and head of research at Menninger. In 1948, he moved to the Austen Riggs Center in Stockbridge, Massachusetts, where he remained until his death in 1960.

As Holt (1967) points out, Rapaport's career was divided into three phases: his work on psychological assessment; his systematization of psychoanalytic theory, particularly psychoanalytic ego psychology; and his empirical work on a psychoanalytic attention-cathexis theory of learning, which he took up during the last years of his life.

With regard to the first phase, Rapaport, Gill, and Schafer's *Diagnostic Psychological Testing* (Chicago, 1945–1946, rev. ed. 1968) was virtually a bible among students and practitioners engaged in psychodynamically oriented psychological assessment. This book helped establish clinical psychology as a profession during a period in its history when psychological assessment was one of the distinctive clinical activities that psychologists could offer.

The second phase is characterized by the work for which Rapaport is best known, namely, his systematization of and contributions to psychoanalytic theory. As Gill (1967) notes, "Rapaport's central goal was to make of psychoanalysis a general psychology" (p. 6)—a goal he shared with Heinz Hartmann. His main specific interest, what he referred to as the "red thread" (Gill, 1967, p. 4) of his work, was his interest in the thought processes (Rapaport, 1951). Insofar as thinking is viewed in psychoanalytic theory as a basic ego function, Rapaport's interest in thought processes naturally led him to an abiding concern with psychoanalytic ego psychology. Rapaport's writings (along with those of Hartmann) represent the most articulate and systematic expression of an ego psychology perspective in the psychoanalytic literature.

Taking as his starting point Hartmann's writings on ego autonomy, one of the questions with which Rapaport was concerned was how ego functions can achieve relative autonomy from both instinctual drive and the external environment. As he put it, "Man can interpose delay and thought not only between instinctual promptings and action . . . he can likewise modify and postpone his reaction to external stimulation" (1967, p. 723).

In developing his ideas on ego autonomy, Rapaport attempted to take account of and integrate empirical findings from psychology, for example, the then new work on sensory deprivation, which suggested to Rapaport that "when . . . stimulus nutriment is not available, the effectiveness of . . . [ego] structures . . . may be impaired" (1967, p. 728). Rapaport's hypothesis was investigated by Leo Goldberger (1961; 1966) and Goldberger and Robert Holt (1958), who studied both the general effects of perceptual isolation and individual differences in adequacy of coping with it.

Rapaport's attempt at systemizing psychoanalytic theory, as well as his later efforts to carry out empirical work on a psychoanalytic theory of learning, do not appear to have had much lasting impact. Indeed, contemporary psychoanalytic theories reject concepts such as id and drive and have little or no interest in notions of ego autonomy as well as in other ideas with which Rapaport was concerned. Rapaport, however, stands as a model of a psychoanalytic theorist who viewed psychoanalysis as part of psychology, who was aware of and constantly tried to relate findings from psychology to psychoanalytic formulations, who was interested in and capable of rigor and clarity of thought, and who was vitally concerned with empirical and theoretical accountability.

Bibliography

Gill, M. M. (1967). In Memoriam: David Rapaport, 1911–1960. In M. M. Gill (Ed.) *The collected papers of David Rapaport*, pp. 3–7. New York: Basic Books.

Goldberger, L. (1961). Reactions to perceptual isolation and Rorschach manifestations of the primary process. *Journal of Projective Techniques, 25*, 287–302.

Goldberger, L. (1966). Experimental isolation: An overview. *American Journal of Psychiatry, 122*, 774–782.

Goldberger, L., & Holt, R. R. (1958). Experimental interferences with reality contact (perceptual isolation). *Journal of Nervous and Mental Disease, 127*, 99–112.

Hartmann, H. (1939/1958). *Ego psychology and the problem of adaptation.* New York: International Universities Press.

Holt, R. R. (1967). David Rapaport: A memoir. In R. R. Holt (Ed.), Motives and thought: Psychoanalytic essays in honor of David Rapaport. *Psychological Issues Monograph, 18/19* (Vol. 5, pp. 7–17). New York: International Universities Press.

Rapaport, D. (1951). *Organization and pathology of thought.* New York: Columbia University Press.

Rapaport, D. (1967). *Collected papers* (M. M. Gill, Ed.). New York: Basic Books.

Morris N. Eagle